INTELLECTUAL PROPERTY

CASES AND MATERIALS

Fourth Edition

∎ ∎ ∎

By

Margreth Barrett

Professor of Law,
University of California,
Hastings College of Law

AMERICAN CASEBOOK SERIES®

WEST®

A Thomson Reuters business

Mat #40889748

American Casebook Series is a trademark registered in the U.S. Patent and Trademark Office.

COPYRIGHT © 1995 WEST PUBLISHING CO.
West, a Thomson business, 2001, 2007
© 2011 Thomson Reuters
    610 Opperman Drive
    St. Paul, MN 55123
    1–800–313–9378
Printed in the United States of America

ISBN: 978–0–314–20821–7

For Ken, Andrew and Robin

PREFACE TO THE FIRST EDITION

This book is designed for use in a three or four-hour law school survey course in intellectual property. It can easily be adapted to a two-hour course dedicated to selected intellectual property doctrines. The book should be used with a statutory supplement containing the federal Patent, Copyright and Trademark Acts, such as Roger Schechter's SELECTED INTELLECTUAL PROPERTY AND UNFAIR COMPETITION STATUTES, REGULATIONS AND TREATIES, which is published by West Publishing Company.

While the book places greatest emphasis on the federal law of patents, copyrights, trademarks, and unfair competition, it also provides substantial coverage of state trade secret, unfair competition and right of publicity doctrines. I have chosen what I consider to be the most logical, straightforward organization. However, recognizing that reasonable minds may differ on the issue of organization, I have designed the book to have self-contained chapters, sections, and subsections that can readily be reorganized in a syllabus to suit the tastes of the instructor.

The book begins with an introductory chapter that explores the basic themes, concepts and policies underlying the whole of intellectual property law. This sets the stage for the subsequent chapters, which demonstrate how these themes, concepts and policies have influenced the development of the individual substantive intellectual property doctrines.

The book then addresses the three intellectual property doctrines that provide rights in ideas and information. Chapter Two reviews the state law of trade secrets. Chapter Three provides a thorough overview of federal patent law. The cases in the patents chapter are specifically selected to be accessible to students of all educational backgrounds, featuring inventions whose technical aspects do not obscure the courts' discussions of the relevant legal concepts. Chapter Four concludes this portion of the book with a short discussion of how familiar common-law doctrines addressing contracts, unjust enrichment, and confidential relationships may be used to provide legal rights in ideas and information when trade secret and patent doctrines do not apply.

Chapter Five reviews federal copyright law, which provides rights in original forms of expression. The chapter first examines copyright eligibility limitations, then explores the difficulties courts have encountered in applying these limitations to particular categories of copyrightable subject matter, such as factual compilations, computer programs, and the designs of useful articles. The chapter then turns to the rights conveyed by copyright law, and issues of copyright ownership and duration. The chapter discusses copyright formalities, including notice of copyright, but recognizes their shrinking importance under recent amendments to the Copyright Act.

The next three chapters examine legal protection of business good will and related trade values. Chapter Six addresses trademark law, focusing primarily on federal statutory law, but noting points at which statutory rights depart from the underlying common-law trademark cause of action. Chapter Seven examines the unfair competition doctrines preventing passing off, false advertising, product disparagement, misappropriation, and trademark dilution. In the case of the first three of these doctrines, it compares the federal cause of action under Lanham Act § 43(a) with the traditional common-law claim. This portion of the book winds up, in Chapter Eight, with a discussion of state rights of publicity, which protect an individual's interest in the publicity value in his or her identity.

The final chapter addresses the relationship of all the various state and federal intellectual property doctrines under the supremacy clause of the United States Constitution, and the effect of Copyright Act section 301 on state intellectual property causes of action.

In recognition of the increasingly international nature of intellectual property protection, the book integrates discussion of international issues throughout. Several of the chapters describe relevant multinational intellectual property treaties, and analyze their influence on domestic intellectual property law. They also discuss key differences between United States intellectual property practices and those of other countries, both as a vehicle for evaluating existing domestic doctrines and for anticipating future amendments, as nations continue their attempts to harmonize international intellectual property rules.

The book incorporates most, if not all, of the seminal Supreme Court and federal appellate decisions that are generally recognized as the bedrock of intellectual property doctrine. Otherwise, the reported case opinions are very recent, selected to reflect the most current views and trends. In the patents chapter, most of the reported opinions emanate from the United States Court of Appeals for the Federal Circuit, which, since 1982, has exercised exclusive jurisdiction over all intermediate appeals in patent cases. I have made every attempt to select cases with interesting, accessible facts. Text and notes between the reported case opinions provide background information, freeing the class and instructor to move beyond the basics during class. Recognizing that a survey course case book can only go so far on any topic, I have provided references to more in-depth treatments of a wide array of issues.

I have edited the cases and other reported materials. Three asterisks (* * *) indicate that text has been omitted. Inserted material is enclosed in brackets. I have deleted citations and footnotes without indication. Footnotes retained in the case opinions reflect their original numbers.

I would like to thank the Hastings College for its support in this project, and Linda Weir, Hastings librarian extraordinaire. Thanks also to Eric Ethington, Kimberley Davis–Marks, Sunil Kulkarni, and David Rapallo for their invaluable research assistance. I am very grateful to the numerous authors and copyright owners who graciously permitted me to reprint their materials. They are identified in footnotes associated with the materials they contributed. Finally, I would like to thank my colleagues, and my husband, Ken Louden, for their tolerance and support.

M.B.

San Francisco, 1995

PREFACE TO THE SECOND EDITION

The law of intellectual property is developing at a breath-taking pace: This second edition of the case book captures and incorporates a large range of new developments.

First, it provides an overview and analysis of a number of important new Acts of Congress, including: (1) the Digital Millennium Copyright Act, which arms copyright owners with causes of action to prevent the circumvention of encryption, watermarking, and similar technological rights protection measures, and provides safe harbors against infringement liability for Internet service providers; (2) the Intellectual Property and Communications Omnibus Reform Act of 1999, which provides a new, express cause of action against cybersquatting, and revises U.S. patent law significantly to harmonize U.S. patent practices with those of other countries; (3) The Digital Performance Rights in Sound Recordings Act, which augments the rights of sound recording copyright owners; (4) the Federal Trademark Dilution Act of 1995, which provides extensive and controversial new federal rights to owners of "famous" trademarks; and (5) the Sonny Bono Copyright Term Extension Act of 1998, which further extends the copyright term.

The second edition also incorporates a stream of new decisions from the U.S. Supreme Court (particularly in the areas of patent and trademark law) and a host of important new case developments from the Circuit Courts of Appeals.

I have added a number of notes discussing and analyzing intellectual property issues that have arisen with the advent of the Internet and other "high tech" developments. These include the policy questions arising from application of traditional copyright principles in the Internet context; the copyright and trademark implications of hyperlinking and framing on the Internet; the proliferation of "business method" patents; the proper balance of interests in cybersquatting cases, and more.

I have also added problems for class discussion throughout the case book to facilitate class discussion, and stimulate further thought about the implications of the issues covered in the main cases.

Finally, I have substantially reorganized parts of the book—most particularly the chapter on trademarks. In the latter case, I have incorporated discussion of "passing off" and trademark dilution (which formerly appeared in the chapter on unfair competition) into the trademarks chapter, and have adopted a new organization of the trademark materials, which I believe will make the materials more accessible to students.

I would like to thank Matt Narensky, Chia Fischer, Jason Angell, Victoria Crawford and Lisa Lambert for their invaluable research assistance with this edition. My thanks, also, to the Hastings College of Law for its support.

MARGRETH BARRETT

San Francisco, 2001

PREFACE TO THE THIRD EDITION

The third edition incorporates a host of new developments in intellectual property law, updating the book through the summer of 2006. It reproduces or discusses all of the numerous Supreme Court decisions that have come down since 2001, as well as Congress' important enactments in the field. The book also incorporates a wide range of new developments arising from the Federal and Regional Circuit Courts of Appeals, and provides a number of intriguing new problems for class discussion. Key new features include:

With regard to trademarks and unfair competition—
–A new section on trademarks on the Internet. (This section examines how courts are interpreting and construing the "trademark use" and "likelihood of confusion" requirements in a range of Internet contexts, such as the incorporation of marks into "forum" web site domain names and the use of marks to key banner advertisements or trigger pop-up ads);
–A new section exploring the First Amendment implications of infringement and dilution claims against unauthorized uses of marks in non-commercial speech (particularly in the Internet context);
–An improved and expanded section on the Anticybersquatting Consumer Protection Act;
–New discussion of the "well-known marks" doctrine;
–A new section on "trademark use" as a prerequisite to infringement and dilution liability;
–A reworked section on geographically deceptively misdescriptive marks;
–A reworked and enhanced section on trade dress functionality;
–A reworked section on trademark dilution;
–Expanded discussion of the Madrid Protocol;
–Updated and enhanced discussion of trademark fair use;
–Reworked and updated materials on the scope of Lanham Act § 43(a);

With regard to patents—
–Updated discussion of business method patents;
–Enlarged and improved discussion of the non-obviousness requirement;
–A reorganized and enhanced section on patent claim interpretation;
–Discussion of recently proposed legislative changes to the Patent Act;
–Updated discussion of the scope of the § 102(b) statutory bar;
–Reworked and updated discussion of the law governing parallel imports;
–Updated discussion of the patent reexamination process;
–An expanded and improved section on patent infringement remedies;

With regard to copyrights—

–An expanded section on digital rights management;

–An updated discussion of "conceptual separability";

–Enhanced discussion of the range of standards courts apply to evaluate copyright infringement;

–Updates on moral rights;

–New developments in the interpretation of Copyright Act § 117;

–An enhanced section on indirect copyright infringement;

–An enhanced section on copyright duration;

–Reworked materials on copyright ownership;

With regard to state publicity rights—

–Reworked and enhanced materials regarding First Amendment limitations on state publicity rights.

As in prior editions, I have edited the cases and other reported materials. Three asterisks (* * *) indicate that text has been omitted. Inserted material is enclosed in brackets. I have deleted citations and footnotes without indication. Footnotes retained in the case opinions reflect their original numbers.

I would again like to thank the Hastings College for its support for this project, and Stephen Lothrop and Linda Weir for their invaluable assistance. I am grateful to the authors and copyright owners who graciously permitted me to reprint their materials. They are identified in footnotes associated with the materials they contributed. Finally, I would like to thank Kenneth, Andrew and Robin Louden for being there when I needed them.

M.B.

San Francisco, 2006

PREFACE TO THE FOURTH EDITION

This fourth edition updates the case book through the summer of 2010. As always, things have been lively since the prior edition, particularly in the field of patent law. This edition reproduces three new Supreme Court decisions, and eleven important Circuit-level opinions. It also incorporates a host of salient and intriguing new case decisions into the note materials and as new problems for class discussion. Given this influx of significant new matter, I have also made a concerted effort to identify and trim away more expendable materials from earlier editions, to keep the casebook streamlined and teachable.

This edition drops the separate chapter on state protection of undeveloped ideas, and incorporates discussion of this issue into the chapter on trade secret protection. It also cuts back somewhat on its coverage of the non-trademark unfair competition causes of action—false advertising, product disparagement and misappropriation—and the materials on federal law preemption of state claims. I re-edited case decisions in all of the chapters to tighten their focus.

The newly revised patents chapter provides the Supreme Court's recent decisions in *Bilski v. Kappos* (regarding patentable subject matter); *KSR International Co. v. Teleflex, Inc.* (regarding the non-obviousness standard); and *Quanta Computer, Inc. v. LG Electronics, Inc.* (clarifying application of the doctrine of exhaustion); as well as the Federal Circuit's opinion in *Net MoneyIn, Inc. v. Verisign, Inc.* (anticipation) and its en banc opinion in *DSU Medical Corp. v. JMS Co., Ltd.* (indirect infringement). I completely reworked the materials on design patents to feature the Federal Circuit's en banc decision in *Egyptian Goddess, Inc. v. Swisa, Inc.* and its subsequent opinion, *Richardson v. Stanley Works.* Expanded and updated note materials consider the Federal Circuit's en banc decision in *Ariad Pharmaceuticals, Inc. v. Eli Lilly & Co.* (written description requirement); *In re Seagate Technology LLC* (enhanced damages); *NTP, Inc. v. Research in Motion, Ltd.* (extraterritorial application of U.S. patent law); and a range of other issues.

The revised copyright chapter provides the Seventh Circuit's decision in *Schrock v. Learning Curve International, Inc.* (clarifying the standard of originality in derivative works); the Eleventh Circuit's decision in *Oravec v. Sunny Isles Luxury Ventures, L.C.* (rights in architectural works); and the Ninth Circuit's decision in *Perfect 10, Inc. v. Amazon.com, Inc.* (hyperlinks as public display or distribution). Updated note materials address a number of additional cases, including *Intervest Construction, Inc. v. Canterbury Estate Homes, Inc.* (scope of protection for architectural works); *Cartoon Network, LP v. CSC Holdings, Inc.* (the implications of RAM copying and the scope of the public performance right); and *Asset Marketing Systems, Inc. v. Gagnon* (implied licenses). I have expanded and updated case book discussions of online "distributions to the public;" the range of standards for evaluating substantial similarity; deletion of copyright management information under the Digital Millennium Copyright Act; and the proper standard for injunctive relief.

Finally, the revised trademarks chapter provides the Second Circuit's opinion in *Rescuecom Corp. v. Google, Inc.* (regarding the "trademark use" prerequisite to infringement liability) and a completely reworked section on Trademark Dilution. This new section features a trio of Circuit-level decisions that explore the bounds of the Trademark Dilution Revision Act of 2006: *Starbucks Corp. v. Wolfe's Borough Coffee, Inc.* (Second Circuit); *Louis Vuittan Malleteir SA v. Haute Diggity Dog, LLC* (Fourth Circuit); and *V Secret Catalogue, Inc. v. Moseley* (Sixth Circuit). I also added a new overview of the historical development of the law of trademarks and unfair competition, to help students understand the underlying purposes of the law and the Lanham Act's relationship to common law. There is a new freestanding note on the extraterritorial reach of U.S. trademark law. The Notes and Questions sections discuss a number of new decisions, such as *Toyota Motor Sales, USA, Inc. v. Tabari* (incorporation of marks into domain names as nominative fair use); and *In re Spirits International, N.V.* (the "materiality" standard under Lanham Act § 2), and I used a rich cross-section of other new decisions as the basis for new problems for class discussion.

As in the past, I have included three asterisks (* * *) to indicated deleted text, and brackets to indicate material added by the editor. I have deleted citations and footnotes without express indication, to facilitate easy reading.

I would like to thank the University of California's Hastings College of Law for its support in this project, Linda Weir for her outstanding library support, and Bahareh Samsami for her excellent research assistance.

MARGRETH BARRETT

San Francisco, California
September 2010

Summary of Contents

TABLE OF CONTENTS

PART THREE. RIGHTS IN ORIGINAL FORMS OF EXPRESSION

Page

TABLE OF CASES

The principal cases are in bold type. Cases cited or discussed in the text
are in roman type. References are to pages. Cases cited in principal
cases and within other quoted materials are not included.

TABLE OF STATUTES

INTELLECTUAL
PROPERTY
CASES AND MATERIALS
Fourth Edition

PART ONE

INTRODUCTION

■ ■ ■

CHAPTER ONE

INTRODUCTION TO INTELLECTUAL PROPERTY LAW

■ ■ ■

I. THE NATURE OF UNITED STATES INTELLECTUAL PROPERTY LAW

"Intellectual property law" encompasses a number of distinct legal doctrines: patent law, copyright, trademarks and unfair competition, trade secrets, the right of publicity, and common-law protection for ideas. Federal law governs patents, copyrights, trademarks and some unfair competition causes of action. Other unfair competition causes of action, trade secret law, the right of publicity and idea law are provided by state common law and statutes.

While each of the intellectual property doctrines is distinct, they all have characteristics in common. Each provides limited rights in intangible products of investment, intellect and/or labor, whether they be inventive ideas, accumulations of information, original means of expression, business good will, or the "persona" of a celebrity. Moreover, as discussed below, each doctrine has been shaped by much the same set of critical public policy concerns.

The primary purpose of intellectual property law is to ensure a rich, diverse and competitive marketplace. To achieve this purpose, intellectual property doctrines all provide property rights as incentives to individuals who create new products, services or works of art or literature. Property rights in the fruits of creativity increase the chances that the creator can recoup his investment in the creation process and make a profit from his work. By making creative endeavors financially feasible and potentially rewarding to large numbers of people, intellectual property laws facilitate provision of a variety of creative products and services to the public.

In addition to economic incentives, however, a competitive marketplace requires free access to innovation: Competitors need the freest possible use of others' intellectual creations in order to copy and improve on them. Requiring competitors to "re-invent the wheel" is highly inefficient. The ability to copy results in still greater variety and lower prices in

2

the marketplace. Moreover, since the general public is meant to be the ultimate beneficiary of this bounty of products and services, it is important that the general public have as much access to the products of creativity as possible.

Obviously, the goals of giving creators rights in their works and ensuring that competitors and the public have free use of those works can conflict. Each intellectual property doctrine seeks to achieve the optimal balance between provision of private property rights and retention of public access to the products of creativity, in order to enhance the competitive marketplace to the fullest possible extent. Each intellectual property doctrine grants property rights to provide an incentive to create, but limits those rights, seeking to provide the greatest public access possible without undermining that incentive.

INTERNATIONAL NEWS SERVICE
v. ASSOCIATED PRESS

Supreme Court of the United States, 1918.
248 U.S. 215, 39 S.Ct. 68, 63 L.Ed. 211.

MR. JUSTICE PITNEY delivered the opinion of the Court.

The parties are competitors in the gathering and distribution of news and its publication for profit in newspapers throughout the United States. The Associated Press, which was complainant in the District Court, is a cooperative organization, incorporated under the Membership Corporations Law of the state of New York, its members being individuals who are either proprietors or representatives of about 950 daily newspapers published in all parts of the United States. * * * Complainant gathers in all parts of the world, by means of various instrumentalities of its own, by exchange with its members, and by other appropriate means, news and intelligence of current and recent events of interest to newspaper readers and distributes it daily to its members for publication in their newspapers. The cost of the service, amounting approximately to $3,500,000 per annum, is assessed upon the members and becomes a part of their costs of operation, to be recouped, presumably with profit, through the publication of their several newspapers. Under complainant's by-laws each member agrees upon assuming membership that news received through complainant's service is received exclusively for publication in a particular newspaper, language, and place specified in the certificate of membership, that no other use of it shall be permitted, and that no member shall furnish or permit anyone in his employ or connected with his newspaper to furnish any of complainant's news in advance of publication to any person not a member. And each member is required to gather the local news of his district and supply it to the Associated Press and to no one else.

Defendant is a corporation organized under the laws of the state of New Jersey, whose business is the gathering and selling of news to its customers and clients, consisting of newspapers published throughout the United States, under contracts by which they pay certain amounts at stated times for defendant's service. It has widespread news-gathering agencies; the cost of its operations amounts, it is said, to more than $2,000,000 per annum; and it serves about 400 newspapers located in the various cities of the United States and abroad, a few of which are represented, also, in the membership of the Associated Press. The parties are in the keenest competition between themselves in the distribution of news throughout the United States; and so, as a rule, are the newspapers that they serve, in their several districts.

Complainant in its bill, defendant in its answer, have set forth in almost identical terms the rather obvious circumstances and conditions under which their business is conducted. The value of the service, and of the news furnished, depends upon the promptness of transmission, as well as upon the accuracy and impartiality of the news; it being essential that the news be transmitted to members or subscribers as early or earlier than similar information can be furnished to competing newspapers by other news services, and that the news furnished by each agency shall not be furnished to newspapers which do not contribute to the expense of gathering it. * * *

The bill was filed to restrain the pirating of complainant's news by defendant * * * by copying news from bulletin boards and from early editions of complainant's newspapers and selling this, either bodily or after rewriting it, to defendant's customers.

The District Court, upon consideration of the bill and answer, with voluminous affidavits on both sides * * * refused at that stage to restrain the systematic practice admittedly pursued by defendant, of taking news bodily from the bulletin boards and early editions of complainant's newspapers and selling it as its own. The court expressed itself as satisfied that this practice amounted to unfair trade, but as the legal question was one of first impression it considered that the allowance of an injunction should await the outcome of an appeal. Both parties having appealed, the Circuit Court of Appeals * * * remanded the cause, with directions to issue an injunction against any bodily taking of the words or substance of complainant's news until its commercial value as news had passed away. The present writ of certiorari was then allowed.

The only matter that has been argued before us is whether defendant may lawfully be restrained from appropriating news taken from bulletins issued by complainant or any of its members, or from newspapers published by them, for the purpose of selling it to defendant's clients. Complainant asserts that defendant's admitted course of conduct in this regard both violates complainant's property right in the news and constitutes unfair competition in business. And notwithstanding the case has proceeded only to the stage of a preliminary injunction, we have deemed it proper to consider the underlying questions, since they go to the very merits of the action and are presented upon facts that are not in dispute. As presented in argument, these questions are: (1) Whether there is any property in news; (2) Whether, if there be property in news collected for the purpose of being published, it survives the instant of its publication in the first newspaper to which it is communicated by the news-gatherer; and (3) whether defendant's admitted course of conduct in appropriating for commercial use matter taken from bulletins or early editions of Associated Press publications constitutes unfair competition in trade.

The federal jurisdiction was invoked because of diversity of citizenship, not upon the ground that the suit arose under the copyright or other laws of the United States. Complainant's news matter is not copyrighted. It is said that it could not, in practice, be copyrighted, because of the large number of dispatches that are sent daily; and, according to complainant's contention, news is not within the operation of the copyright act. Defendant, while apparently conceding this, nevertheless invokes the analogies of the law of literary property and copyright, insisting as its principal contention that, assuming complainant has a right of property in its news, it can be maintained (unless the copyright act be complied with) only by being kept secret and confidential, and that upon the publication with complainant's consent of uncopyrighted news of any of complainant's members in a newspaper or upon a bulletin board, the right of property is lost, and the subsequent use of the news by the public or by defendant for any purpose whatever becomes lawful.

* * *

In considering the general question of property in news matter, it is necessary to recognize its dual character, distinguishing between the substance of the information and the particular form or collocation of words in which the writer has communicated it.

No doubt news articles often possess a literary quality, and are the subject of literary property at the common law; nor do we question that such an article, as a literary production, is the subject of copyright by the terms of the act as it now stands. * * *

But the news element—the information respecting current events contained in the literary production—is not the creation of the writer, but is a report of matters that ordinarily are *publici juris*; it is the history of the day. It is not to be supposed that the framers of the Constitution, when they empowered Congress "to promote the progress of science and useful arts, by securing for limited times to authors and inventors the exclusive right to their respective writings and discoveries," (Const. art. 1, § 8, par. 8), intended to confer upon one who might happen to be the first to report a historic event the exclusive right for any period to spread the knowledge of it.

We need spend no time, however, upon the general question of property in news matter at common law, or the application of the copyright act, since it seems to us the case must turn upon the question of unfair competition in business. And, in our opinion, this does not depend upon any general right of property analogous to the common-law right of the proprietor of an unpublished work to prevent its publication without his consent; nor is it foreclosed by showing that the benefits of the copyright act have been waived. We are dealing here not with restrictions upon publication but with the very facilities and processes of publication. The peculiar value of news is in the spreading of it while it is fresh; and it is evident that a valuable property interest in the news, as news, cannot be maintained by keeping it secret. Besides, except for matters improperly disclosed, or published in breach of trust or confidence, or in violation of law, none of which is involved in this branch of the case, the news of current events may be regarded as common property. What we are concerned with is the business of making it known to the world, in which both parties to the present suit are engaged. That business consists in maintaining a prompt, sure, steady, and reliable service designed to place the daily events of the world at the breakfast table of the millions at a price that, while of trifling moment to each reader, is sufficient in the aggregate to afford compensation for the cost of gathering and distributing it, with the added profit so necessary as an incentive to effective action in the commercial world. The service thus performed for newspaper readers is not only innocent but extremely useful in itself, and indubitably constitutes a legitimate business. The parties are competitors in this field; and, on fundamental principles, applicable here as elsewhere, when the rights or privileges of the one are liable to conflict with those of the other, each party is under a duty so to conduct its own business as not unnecessarily or unfairly to injure that of the other.

Obviously, the question of what is unfair competition in business must be determined with particular reference to the character and circumstances of the business. The question here is not so much the rights of either party as against the public but their rights as between themselves. And, although we may and do assume that neither party has any remaining property interest as against the public in uncopyrighted news matter after the moment of its first publication, it by no means follows that there is no remaining property interest in it as between themselves. For, to both of them alike, news matter, however little susceptible of ownership or dominion in the absolute sense, is stock in trade, to be gathered at the cost of enterprise, organization, skill, labor, and money, and to be distributed and sold to those who will pay money for it, as for any other merchandise. Regarding the news, therefore, as but the material out of which both parties are seeking to make profits at the same time and in the same field, we hardly can fail to recognize that for this purpose, and as between them, it must be regarded as quasi property, irrespective of the rights of either as against the public.

In order to sustain the jurisdiction of equity over the controversy, we need not affirm any general and absolute property in the news as such. The rule that a court of equity concerns itself only in the protection of property rights treats any civil right of a pecuniary nature as a property right; and the right to acquire property by honest labor or the conduct of a lawful business is as much entitled to protection as the right to guard property already acquired. It is this right that furnishes the basis of the jurisdiction in the ordinary case of unfair competition.

* * *

Not only do the acquisition and transmission of news require elaborate organization and a large expenditure of money, skill, and effort; not only has it an exchange value to the gatherer, dependent chiefly upon its novelty and freshness, the regularity of the service, its reputed reliability and thoroughness, and its adaptability to the public needs; but also, as is evident, the news has an exchange value to one who can misappropriate it.

The peculiar features of the case arise from the fact that, while novelty and freshness form so important an element in the success of the business, the very processes of distribution and publication necessarily occupy a good deal of time. Complainant's service, as well as defendant's, is a daily service to daily newspapers; most of the foreign news reaches this country at the Atlantic seaboard, principally at the city of New York, and because of this, and of time differentials due to the earth's rotation, the distribution of news matter throughout the country is principally from east to west; and, since in speed the telegraph and telephone easily outstrip the rotation of the earth, it is a simple matter for defendant to take complainant's news from bulletins or early editions of complainant's members in the eastern cities and at the mere cost of telegraphic transmission cause it to be published in western papers issued at least as early as those served by complainant. Besides this, and irrespective of time differentials, irregularities in telegraphic transmission on different lines, and the normal consumption of time in printing and distributing the newspaper, result in permitting pirated news to be placed in the hands of defendant's readers sometimes simultaneously with the service of competing Associated Press papers, occasionally even earlier.

Defendant insists that when, with the sanction and approval of complainant, and as the result of the use of its news for the very purpose for which it is distributed, a portion of complainant's members communicate it to the general public by posting it upon bulletin boards so that all may read, or by issuing it to newspapers and distributing it indiscriminately, complainant no longer has the right to control the use to be made of it; that when it thus reaches the light of day it becomes the common possession of all to whom it is accessible; and that any purchaser of a newspaper has the right to communicate the intelligence which it contains to anybody and for any purpose, even for the purpose of selling it for profit to newspapers published for profit in competition with complainant's members.

The fault in the reasoning lies in applying as a test the right of the complainant as against the public, instead of considering the rights of complainant and defendant, competitors in business, as between themselves. The right of the purchaser of a single newspaper to spread knowledge of its contents gratuitously, for any legitimate purpose not unreasonably interfering with complainant's right to make merchandise of it, may be admitted; but to transmit that news for commercial use, in competition with complainant—which is what defendant has done and seeks to justify—is a very different matter. In doing this defendant, by its very act, admits that it is taking material that has been acquired by complainant as the result of organization and the expenditure of labor, skill, and money, and which is salable by complainant for money, and that defendant in appropriating it and selling it as its own is endeavoring to reap where it has not sown, and by disposing of it to newspapers that are competitors of complainant's members is appropriating to itself the harvest of those who have sown. Stripped of all disguises, the process amounts to an unauthorized interference with the normal operation of complainant's legitimate business precisely at the point where the profit is to be reaped, in order to divert a material portion of the profit from those who have earned it to those who have not; with special advantage to defendant in the competition because of the fact that it is not burdened with any part of the expense of gathering the news. The transaction speaks for itself and a court of equity ought not to hesitate long in characterizing it as unfair competition in business.

The underlying principle is much the same as that which lies at the base of the equitable theory of consideration in the law of trusts—that he who has fairly paid the price should have the beneficial use of the property. It is no answer to say that complainant spends its money for that which is too fugitive or evanescent to be the subject of property. That might, and for the purposes of the discussion we are assuming that it would furnish an answer in a common-law controversy. But in a court of equity, where the question is one of unfair competition, if that which complainant has acquired fairly at substantial cost may be sold fairly at substantial profit, a competitor who is misappropriating it for the purpose of disposing of it to his own profit and to the disadvantage of complainant cannot be heard to say that it is too fugitive or evanescent to be regarded as property. It has all the attributes of property necessary for determining that a misappropriation of it by a competitor is unfair competition because contrary to good conscience.

The contention that the news is abandoned to the public for all purposes when published in the first newspaper is untenable. Abandonment is a question of intent, and the entire organization of the Associated Press negatives such a purpose. The cost of the service would be prohibitive if the reward were to be so limited. No single newspaper, no small group of newspapers, could sustain the expenditure. Indeed, it is one of the most obvious results of defendant's theory that, by permitting indiscriminate publication by anybody and everybody for purposes of profit in competition with the news-gatherer, it would render publication profitless, or so little profitable as in effect to cut off the service by rendering the cost prohibitive in comparison with the return. The practical needs and requirements of the business are reflected in complainant's by-laws which have been referred to. Their effect is that publication by each member must be deemed not by any means an abandonment of the news to the world for any and all purposes, but a publication for limited purposes; for the benefit of the readers of the bulletin or the newspaper as such; not for the purpose of making merchandise of it as news, with the result of depriving complainant's other members of their reasonable opportunity to obtain just returns for their expenditures.

It is to be observed that the view we adopt does not result in giving to complainant the right to monopolize either the gathering or the distribution of the news, or, without complying with the copyright act, to prevent the reproduction of its news articles, but only postpones participation by complainant's competitor in the processes of distribution and reproduction of news that it has not gathered, and only to the extent necessary to prevent that competitor from reaping the fruits of complainant's efforts and expenditure, to the partial exclusion of complainant. * * *

It is said that the elements of unfair competition are lacking because there is no attempt by defendant to palm off its goods as those of the complainant, characteristic of the most familiar, if not the most typical, cases of unfair competition. But we cannot concede that the right to equitable relief is confined to that class of cases. In the present case the fraud upon complainant's rights is more direct and obvious. Regarding news matter as the mere material from which these two competing parties are endeavoring to make money, and treating it, therefore, as *quasi* property for the purposes of their business because they are both selling it as such, defendant's conduct differs from the ordinary case of unfair competition in its trade principally in this that, instead of selling its own goods as those of complainant, it substitutes misappropriation in the place of misrepresentation, and sells complainant's goods as its own.

Besides the misappropriation, there are elements of limitation, of false pretense, in defendant's practices. The device of rewriting complainant's news articles, frequently resorted to, carries its own comment. The habitual failure to give credit to complainant for that which is taken is significant. Indeed, the entire system of appropriating complainant's news and transmitting it as a commercial product to defendant's clients and patrons amounts to a false representation to them and to their newspaper readers that the news transmitted is the result of defendant's own investigation in the field. But these elements, although accentuating the wrong, are not the essence of it. It is something more than the advantage of celebrity of which complainant is being deprived.

    * * *

The decree of the Circuit Court of Appeals will be Affirmed.

MR. JUSTICE HOLMES, dissenting.

When an uncopyrighted combination of words is published there is no general right to forbid other people repeating them—in other words there is no property in the combination or in the thoughts or facts that the words express. Property, a creation of law, does not arise from value, although exchangeable—a matter of fact. Many exchangeable values may be destroyed intentionally without compensation. Property depends upon exclusion by law from interference, and a person is not excluded from using any combination of words merely because some one has used it before, even if it took labor and genius to make it. If a given person is to be prohibited from making the use of words that his neighbors are free to make some other ground must be found. One such ground is vaguely expressed in the phrase unfair trade. This means that the words are repeated by a competitor in business in such a way as to convey a misrepresentation that materially injures the person who first used them, by appropriating credit of some kind which the first user has earned. The ordinary case is a representation by device, appearance, or other indirection that the defendant's goods come from the plaintiff. But the only reason why it is actionable to make such a representation is that it tends to give the defendant an advantage in his competition with the plaintiff and that it is thought undesirable that an advantage should be gained in that way. Apart from that the defendant may use such unpatented devices and uncopyrighted combinations of words as he likes. The ordinary case, I say, is palming off the defendant's product as the plaintiff's but the same evil may follow from the opposite falsehood—from saying whether in words or by implication that the plaintiff's product is the defendant's, and that, it seems to me, is what has happened here.

Fresh news is got only by enterprise and expense. To produce such news as it is produced by the defendant represents by implication that it has been acquired by the defendant's enterprise and at its expense. When it comes from one of the great news collecting agencies like the Associated Press, the source generally is indicated, plainly importing that credit; and that such a representation is implied may be inferred with some confidence from the unwillingness of the defendant to give the credit and tell the truth. If the plaintiff produces the news at the same time that the defendant does, the defendant's presentation impliedly denies to the plaintiff the credit of collecting the facts and assumes that credit to the defendant. If the plaintiff is later in Western cities it naturally will be supposed to have obtained its information from the defendant. The falsehood is a little more subtle, the injury, a little more indirect, than in ordinary cases of unfair trade, but I think that the principle that condemns the one condemns the other. It is a question of how strong an infusion of fraud is necessary to turn a flavor into a poison. The dose seems to me strong enough here to need a remedy from the law. But as, in my view, the only ground of complaint that can be recognized without legislation is the implied misstatement, it can be corrected by stating the truth; and a suitable acknowledgment of the source is all that the plaintiff can require. * * *

MR. JUSTICE BRANDEIS, dissenting.

* * *

No question of statutory copyright is involved. The sole question for our consideration is this: Was the International News Service properly enjoined from using, or causing to be used gainfully, news of which it acquired knowledge by lawful means (namely, by reading publicly posted bulletins or papers purchased by it in the open market) merely because the news had been originally gathered by the Associated Press and continued to be of value to some of its members, or because it did not reveal the source from which it was acquired?

* * *

News is a report of recent occurrences. The business of the news agency is to gather systematically knowledge of such occurrences of interest and to distribute reports thereof. The Associated Press contended that knowledge so acquired is property, because it costs money and labor to produce and because it has value for which those who have it not are ready to pay; that it remains property and is entitled to protection as long as it has commercial value as news; and that to protect it effectively, the defendant must be enjoined from making, or causing to be made, any gainful use of it while it retains such value. An essential element of individual property is the legal right to exclude others from enjoying it. If the property is private, the right of exclusion may be absolute; if the property is affected with a public interest, the right of exclusion is qualified. But the fact that a product of the mind has cost its producer money and labor, and has a value for which others are willing to pay, is not sufficient to ensure to it this legal attribute of property. The general rule of law is, that the noblest of human productions—knowledge, truths ascertained, conceptions, and ideas—became, after voluntary communication to others, free as the air to common use. Upon these incorporeal productions the attribute of property is continued after such communication only in certain classes of cases where public policy has seemed to demand it. These exceptions are confined to productions which, in some degree, involve creation, invention, or discovery. But by no means all such are endowed with this attribute of property. The creations which are recognized as property by the common law are literary, dramatic, musical, and other artistic creations; and these have also protection under the copyright statutes. The inventions and discoveries upon which this attribute of property is conferred only by statute, are the few comprised within the patent law. There are also many other cases in which courts interfere to prevent curtailment of plaintiff's enjoyment of incorporeal productions; and in which the right to relief is often called a property right, but is such only in a special sense. In those cases, the plaintiff has no absolute right to the protection of his production; he has merely the qualified right to be protected as against the defendant's acts, because of the special relation in which the latter stands or the wrongful method or means employed in acquiring the knowledge or the manner in which it is used. Protection of this character is afforded where the suit is based upon breach of contract or of trust or upon unfair competition.

The knowledge for which protection is sought in the case at bar is not of a kind upon which the law has heretofore conferred the attributes of property; nor is the manner of its acquisition or use nor the purpose to which it is applied, such as has heretofore been recognized as entitling a plaintiff to relief.

* * *

Plaintiff * * * contended that defendant's practice constitutes unfair competition, because there is "appropriation without cost to itself of values created by" the plaintiff; and it is upon this ground that the decision of this court appears to be based. To appropriate and use for profit, knowledge and ideas produced by other men, without making compensation or even acknowledgment, may be inconsistent with a finer sense of propriety; but, with the exceptions indicated above, the law has heretofore sanctioned the practice. Thus it was held that one may ordinarily make and sell anything in any form, may copy with exactness that which another has produced, or may otherwise use his ideas without his consent and without the payment of compensation, and yet not inflict a legal injury; and that ordinarily one is at perfect liberty to find out, if he can by lawful means, trade secrets of another, however valuable, and then use the knowledge so acquired gainfully, although it cost the original owner much in effort and in money to collect or produce.

Such taking and gainful use of a product of another which, for reasons of public policy, the law has refused to endow with the attributes of property, does not become unlawful because the product happens to have been taken from a rival and is used in competition with him. The unfairness in competition which hitherto has been recognized by the law as a basis for relief, lay in the manner or means of conducting the business; and the manner or means held legally unfair, involves either fraud or force or the doing of acts otherwise prohibited by law. * * *

* * * He who follows the pioneer into a new market, or who engages in the manufacture of an article newly introduced by another, seeks profits due largely to the labor and expense of the first adventurer; but the law sanctions, indeed encourages the pursuit. He who makes a city known through his product, must submit to sharing the resultant trade with others who, perhaps for that reason, locate there later. * * *

The means by which the International News Service obtains news gathered by the Associated Press is also clearly unobjectionable. It is taken from papers bought in the open market or from bulletins publicly posted. No breach of contract such as the court considered to exist in *Hitchman Coal & Coke Co. v. Mitchell*, 245 U.S. 229, 254, 38 Sup. Ct. 65, 62 L.Ed. 260, L. R. A. 1918C, 497, Ann.Cas. 1918B,461; or of trust such as was present in *Morrison v. Moat*, 9 Hare, 241; and neither fraud nor force is involved. The manner of use is likewise unobjectionable. No reference is made by word or by act to the Associated Press, either in transmitting the news to subscribers or by them in publishing it in their papers. Neither the International News Service nor its subscribers is gaining or seeking to gain in its business a benefit from the reputation of the Associated Press. They are merely using its product without making compensation. That they have a legal right to do, because the product is not property, and they do not stand in any relation to the Associated Press, either of contract or of trust, which otherwise precludes such use. * * *

STANLEY v. COLUMBIA BROADCASTING SYSTEM, INC.

Supreme Court of California, *en banc*, 1950.
35 Cal.2d 653, 221 P.2d 73.

* * *

Traynor, Justice (dissenting).

Abstract ideas are common property freely available to all. What men forge out of these ideas with skill, industry, and imagination, into concrete forms uniquely their own, the law protects as private property. It gives the special form the stamp of recognition; it does so to stimulate creative activity. It does something more to stimulate creative activity: it assures all men free utilization of abstract ideas in the process of crystallizing them in fresh forms. For creativeness thrives on freedom; men find new implication in old ideas when they range with open minds though open fields. They would indeed be stifled in their efforts to create forms worth protecting, if in the common through which they ranged they were diverted from their course by one enclosure after another. "We must take care to guard against two extremes equally prejudicial: The one that men of ability, who have employed their time for the service of the community, may not be deprived of their just merits and the reward of their ingenuity and labor; the other, that the world may not be deprived of improvements, nor the progress of the arts be retarded. The act that secures copyrights to authors guards against the piracy of the words and sentiments, but does not prohibit writing on the same subject." (Lord Mansfield, in *Sayre v. Moore*, 1 East 361, 101 Eng.Rep. 140.)

It would be ironic if copyright law, designed to encourage creative activity, became the instrument of its destruction. The very function of creative activity is to keep the common field in continuous germination; it is not for copyright law to render it barren by a succession of enclosures denying access to those who would cultivate it. "The object of copyright is to promote science and the useful arts. If an author, by originating a new arrangement and form of expression of certain ideas or conceptions, could withdraw these ideas or conceptions from the stock of materials to be used by other authors, each copyright would narrow the field of thought open for development and exploitation, and science, poetry, narrative, and dramatic fiction and other branches of literature would be hindered by copyright, instead of being promoted. A poem consists of words, expressing conceptions of words or lines of thoughts; but copyright in the poem gives no monopoly in the separate words, or in the ideas, conception, or facts expressed or described by the words. A copyright extends only to the arrangement of the words. A copyright does not give a monopoly in any incident in a play. Other authors have a right to exploit the facts, experiences, field of thought, and general ideas, provided they do not substantially copy a concrete form, in which the circumstances and ideas have been developed, arranged, and put into shape." To insure free trade in ideas, therefore, the monopoly created by copyright is limited to "the arrangement and combination of the ideas * * * the form, sequence, and manner in which the composition expresses the ideas."

* * *

SEARS, ROEBUCK & CO. v. STIFFEL CO.

Supreme Court of the United States, 1964.
376 U.S. 225, 84 S.Ct. 784, 11 L.Ed.2d 661.

MR. JUSTICE BLACK delivered the opinion of the Court.

* * *

The grant of a patent is the grant of a statutory monopoly. * * * Patents are not given as favors, as was the case of monopolies given by the Tudor monarchs, but are meant to encourage invention by rewarding the inventor with the right, limited to a term of years fixed by the patent, to exclude others from the use of his invention. During that period of time no one may make use, or sell the patented product without the patentee's authority. 35 U.S.C. § 271. But in rewarding useful invention, the "rights and welfare of the community must be fairly dealt with and effectually guarded." *Kendall v. Winsor*, 21 How. 322, 329 (1859). To that end the prerequisites to obtaining a patent are strictly observed, and when the patent has issued the limitations on its exercise are equally strictly enforced. To begin with, a genuine "invention," or "discovery" must be demonstrated "lest in the constant demand for new appliances the heavy hand of tribute be laid on each slight technological advance in an art." Once the patent issues, it is strictly construed, it cannot be used to secure any monopoly beyond that contained in the patent, the patentee's control over the product when it leaves his hands is sharply limited, and the patent monopoly may not be used in disregard of the antitrust laws. Finally, and especially relevant here, when the patent expires the monopoly created by it expires, too, and the right to make the article—including the right to make it in precisely the shape it carried when patented—passes to the public.

Thus the patent system is one in which uniform federal standards are carefully used to promote invention while at the same time preserving free competition. Obviously a State could not, consistently with the Supremacy Clause of the Constitution,[8] extend the life of a patent beyond its expiration date or give a patent on an article which lacked the level of invention required for federal patents. To do either would run counter to the policy of Congress of granting patents only to true inventions, and then only for a limited time. * * *

In the present case the "pole lamp" sold by Stiffel has been held not to be entitled to the protection of either a mechanical or a design patent. An unpatentable article, like an article on which the patent has expired, is

---

8. U.S. Const., Art. VI.

in the public domain and may be made and sold by whoever chooses to do so. What Sears did was to copy Stiffel's design and to sell lamps almost identical to those sold by Stiffel. This it had every right to do under the federal patent laws. That Stiffel originated the pole lamp and made it popular is immaterial. "Sharing in the goodwill of an article unprotected by patent or trade-mark is the exercise of a right possessed by all—and in the free exercise of which the consuming public is deeply interested." *Kellogg Co. v. National Biscuit Co.*, 305 U.S., at 122. To allow a State by use of its law of unfair competition to prevent the copying of an article which represents too slight an advance to be patented would be to permit the State to block off from the public something which federal law has said belongs to the public. * * *

     * * *

Nᴏᴛᴇs ᴀɴᴅ Qᴜᴇsᴛɪᴏɴs

1. *What is "property?"* The key issue in International News Service v. Associated Press ("*I.N.S.*") was whether the news gathered by Associated Press constituted "property," in which Associated Press could assert rights. What is "property?" Does the Court say? As one court has put it, "property rights" are "rights which are recognized and protected by the courts by excluding others therefrom. The designation is therefore more in the nature of a legal conclusion than a description." Metropolitan Opera Association, Inc. v. Wagner–Nichols Recorder Corp., 199 Misc. 786, 101 N.Y.S.2d 483 (1950), *aff'd*, 279 App.Div. 632, 107 N.Y.S.2d 795 (1951). Was the *Metropolitan Opera* court saying, essentially, that "property" exists whenever a legislative body or court, acting in its proper capacity, says that a person has enforceable rights against others in something (regardless of whether that something is tangible or intangible)? Does that appear to be the *I.N.S.* Court's understanding of the "property" designation?

To what do legislative bodies and courts look in deciding whether to recognize rights (and thus designate "property")? Public policy, or the law-maker's perception of the public good, is often the guiding principle. What public policy led the majority in *I.N.S.* to find that Associated Press had property rights in the news it gathered, at least vis-a-vis I.N.S.? Did the majority merely base its finding of property rights on its determination that the news had value to Associated Press, as Justice Holmes suggests, or was there more involved? Was it merely that the defendant, I.N.S., got a free ride?

Is "reaping where one has not sown," or "taking a free ride" inherently immoral? Should it be discouraged in all cases? In any case? Why does Justice Brandeis believe that the existence of free riding should not give rise to a property right in the "ridee?" Consider the following:

> [T]he potential free riders—the users, copyists, and adapters—are not mere parasites. Many are creators themselves. They may reach markets different than those reached by the original creators, or they may bring new perspective, reduced cost, special expertise, deeper insights, or innovative technology to the exploitation and adaptation of established works. It is true that very often such putative defendants would be able to obtain

licenses to utilize the valuable work and that, in those cases, giving the creator protection would not inhibit the flowering of derivative works and new uses. But, at other times complications, such as transaction costs, strategic maneuvering, and income effects—or the perceived inappropriateness of using a market to mediate certain qualitative judgments—will leave us less than satisfied that the grant of a property right to an initial creator will lead to optimal economic development or to optimal opportunities for cultural and individual expression.

* * *

* * * A culture could not exist if all free riding were prohibited within it. Every person's education involves a form of free riding on his predecessors' efforts, as does every form of scholarship and scientific progress. Further, a bedrock proposition of the common law is that persons ordinarily should not be required to pay for the benefit of others' labor unless they have agreed in advance to do so, by contract. Although exceptions to this proposition exist, it has yet to be repudiated in the wholesale way that the adoption of an unlimited reap/sow principle would require.

Gordon, *On Owning Information: Intellectual Property and the Restitutionary Impulse,* 78 Va. L. Rev. 149, 157–58, 167–68 (1992).[1] As you will see, the "free rider" issue arises often in the field of intellectual property. Notwithstanding the considerable influence of the *I.N.S.* majority opinion (*I.N.S.* was decided as "federal common law" prior to the decision in Erie Railroad Co. v. Tompkins, 304 U.S. 64, 58 S.Ct. 817, 82 L.Ed. 1188 (1938), and thus is not binding on the states), the existence of free riding on the part of the defendant does not always lead to a finding for the plaintiff. What was the Supreme Court's attitude toward free riding in *Sears*?

What public policy concerns lead the Supreme Court to deny protection for the lamp design in the *Sears* opinion excerpt? What public policy concern motivated Justice Traynor in arguing that there should be no property in the idea at issue in the *Stanley* case?

In *Sears,* the Court notes that Congress deliberately limited the availability, duration and scope of patent protection for inventions. It did so in order to balance the conflicting public interests in granting an incentive to invent and making inventive concepts available to competitors, to stimulate competition. Likewise, in his dissent in *Stanley,* Justice Traynor notes that copyright protection for works of authorship is limited to an author's particular means of expressing an idea, and never gives rights in the underlying idea itself. This limitation, he indicates, is meant to balance the competing interests in giving an incentive to authors and leaving as much in the public domain for other authors' use as possible. Is the majority in *I.N.S.* also concerned with this balance? If so, how does the majority accommodate the conflicting interests? In your opinion, does it reach the appropriate accommodation?

2. *The balance.* As noted above, each of the intellectual property doctrines seeks to obtain a proper balance between the provision of enforceable

---

1. © 1992 by Wendy J. Gordon. Reprinted by permission of the copyright owner.

rights to creators and the retention of a vigorous public domain. Thus, the property rights granted in intellectual property are limited and conditional.

Patent law grants inventors of new and useful processes, machines, articles of manufacture or compositions of matter the right to prevent others from making, using, selling, offering to sell, or importing their invention (and in the case of a process, the product of their invention) in the United States—a strong property right. But utility patents are available only for those inventions that are worth the inconvenience of a strong property right from the public's standpoint—those that meet the standards of novelty, non-obviousness, and usefulness. Moreover, the law conditions granting a patent on the inventor's fully disclosing the invention to the public, so that the public will have use of the knowledge underlying the invention. The patent monopoly is limited in duration. After it ends, the invention enters the public domain, and all are free to exploit it. They are assisted in doing so by the inventor's earlier mandatory disclosure.

Trade secret law provides property rights in a business' invention or other proprietary information if the invention or information gives the business a competitive advantage and is kept secret. These property rights, however, fall far short of those afforded by a patent. The trade secret owner may only prevent others from taking or using the secret when the others have obtained it through a breach of confidence, industrial espionage, or some other improper conduct. Competitors obtaining the secret through proper means, such as independent discovery or reverse engineering, are free to use it. Moreover, the business loses its trade secret rights once the invention or information becomes public.

The common-law idea doctrines recognize enforceable property rights in ideas, but in most cases only enable the idea "owner" to enforce her rights against parties who are in a direct contractual or quasi-contractual relationship with her, so that the general public's ability to use the idea is unaffected. In many cases, even this modest protection is limited to ideas that meet standards of novelty and concreteness.

Copyright law grants "authors" (including artists, architects, choreographers, cinematographers, etc.) a number of exclusive rights in their works of authorship: the right to reproduce, adapt, publicly distribute, publicly display and publicly perform the work, or authorize others to do each of these things. As Justice Traynor noted in his *Stanley* dissent, however, these rights only extend to the author's particular mode of expressing his or her ideas. The author obtains no rights in the underlying ideas or facts being expressed. Moreover, the Copyright Act imposes a number of exceptions to the author's rights, permitting a wide variety of public uses deemed harmless to the copyright owner or in the public interest. Again, like patents, copyrights are limited in duration, usually lasting only seventy years after the author's death.

Trademark and unfair competition laws recognize limited property rights in trademarks, service marks, trade names, and trade dress (words, devices or symbols indicating a product or service's *origin*) in order to facilitate marketplace competition. These indicia of origin play an important role in a competitive marketplace because of the information they convey about the products and services they identify. This information enables consumers to exercise their preferences among competing brands, which in turn encourages businesses to invest in the development of high quality goods and services. But the law imposes limits on the types of words, symbols or devices that can be claimed as protectible indications of origin, in order to ensure that competitors are not deprived of essential means of expression. In addition, the property rights granted in indicia of origin are limited: In most cases, owners may only enjoin others' use of similar indicia when that use causes a likelihood of consumer confusion about the source or sponsorship of goods or services, or about the affiliation of their producers.

Finally, the right of publicity encourages persons such as actors, sports figures, and singers to develop their talents and make them available to the public by giving them the exclusive right to commercially exploit their identities. Publicity law only enables such persons to control *commercial* uses of their identities, however. And the First Amendment limits publicity rights to ensure that others may use identities for purposes of political, educational, and artistic expression. Again, the exclusive rights of commercial exploitation are generally limited in duration.

    3.   *The pragmatic approach vs. natural rights.* As the case opinions and Note 1 suggest, United States legislative bodies and courts traditionally have taken a pragmatic approach to the definition, application and justification of intellectual property rights. They generally have not viewed authors, inventors and other creators as possessing an inherent, natural property right in their intangible creations. In those instances in which the law grants them property rights, it does so for pragmatic reasons, to obtain an overall social benefit, such as greater creative output. This pragmatic view is reflected in the language of the Constitution itself: Article 1, section 8, clause 8 of the U.S. Constitution, known as the Copyrights and Patents Clause, gives Congress the power to grant copyrights and patents in order "[t]o promote the Progress of Science and Useful Arts."

An alternative view is that authors, inventors and other creators have "natural," inherent rights in the products of their labor and intellect, for such products are extensions of the creators' own personalities and selves. This view, influenced by John Locke and Georg Wilhelm Friedrich Hegel, has occasionally influenced the development of United States intellectual property law, but has been much more influential in civil law nations, such as France and Germany, particularly with regard to works of authorship. Some important differences between the United States' intellectual property laws and those of other nations today arise as the result of this basic difference in philosophy. Does the majority opinion in *I.N.S.* implicitly embrace the notion that one has a natural right in the product of his labor and creativity?

For discussion of philosophical and historic approaches to intellectual property rights, see Gordon, *A Property Right in Self–Expression: Equality and Individualism in the Natural Law of Intellectual Property*, 102 Yale L.J. 1533 (1993); Jane C. Ginsburg, *A Tale of Two Copyrights: Literary Property in Revolutionary France and America*, 64 Tul. L. Rev. 991 (1990); Symposium on Law and Philosophy, 13 Harv. J. L. & Pub. Pol'y 757–947 (1990); Symposium, Property: The Founding, the Welfare State, and Beyond, 13 Harv. J. L. &

Pub. Pol'y, 97–124 (1990); Hughes, *The Philosophy of Intellectual Property*, 77 Geo. L. J. 287 (1988).

4. *Why have a separate law for intellectual property?* Why is it necessary to have a separate body of law to protect intangible intellectual creations? Is the long-established common law of personal property inadequate to protect the interests at stake? Assume that after many years of research and effort an engineer develops a better mousetrap. First, she conceives of the principle on which the mousetrap will operate and the proper method of construction. Then she actually builds a prototype of wood, metal, cheese and other tangible materials. Before she can market the mousetrap, a thief steals the prototype. The laws of personal property should apply. The engineer may seek a court decree requiring the thief to return the prototype and pay the value of the engineer's lost use. (Amounts paid to Acme Rent-a-Cat for interim protection?) Is the engineer made whole?

What if, having had brief possession of the prototype, the thief was able to discover the concept underlying the mousetrap? That inventive concept is probably much more valuable to the engineer than the physical manifestation of it. Most likely the concept took more time, effort and resources to develop than the prototype, and offers greater commercial opportunities. Could a court order the thief to return the concept to the engineer? Indeed, has the thief "stolen" the concept if the engineer still has it herself? Information, unlike physical objects, is not diminished when shared. The laws of replevin and conversion were designed with physical objects in mind, and may be difficult to adapt to the theft of a concept.

Suppose that the engineer mass produces copies of the mousetrap and puts them on the market. X buys one, takes it home, and figures out how it works. He then uses that knowledge to make his own copies of the mousetrap and sell them in competition with the engineer. Since X has no research and development investment to recoup, he can sell cheaper than the engineer, and ultimately drive her out of the market. Would the laws of conversion and replevin as we know them offer the engineer any relief against X? Should the engineer be able to obtain relief against X? If so, why?

5. *The need for an incentive and the lack of exactitude.* Judicial, legislative and academic authorities routinely justify granting inventors, authors, and business people property rights in their intangible creations on the ground that they need an incentive to engage in the creative process. The theory is that without the assurance of an exclusive right to exploit the creation commercially (enhancing their chance of recouping their investment and making a profit), creators might not consider it worth their while to invest their talents and resources in creating new inventions or new works of art and literature and making them available to the public. In your opinion, is this assumption warranted? In all cases? In some cases? (And if only in some cases, which ones?) If the assumption is warranted, how extensive must the property rights be in order to give the needed stimulus? In fact, there is little hard data to prove or disprove the assumption that property rights are needed as an incentive or that the amount of creative output in the United States would significantly decrease if property rights were reduced or denied. Nor is there any certain means of determining the point at which rights will exceed

what is necessary to provide an incentive and interfere unnecessarily with the public domain. The shaping of intellectual property laws is, at best, an inexact science. For an interesting and lively argument about the necessity for copyright protection for authors and publishers, see Breyer, *The Uneasy Case for Copyright: A Study of Copyright in Books, Photocopies, and Computer Programs,* 84 Harv. L. Rev. 281 (1970); Tyerman, *The Economic Rationale for Published Books: A Reply to Professor Breyer,* 18 U.C.L.A. L. Rev. 1100 (1971); Breyer, *Copyright: A Rejoinder,* 20 U.C.L.A. L. Rev. 75 (1972).

6. *Jurisdiction.* The United States Constitution expressly authorizes Congress to provide for patents and copyrights in Article 1, Section 8, Clause 8, which provides:

> The Congress shall have power * * *
>
> (8) To promote the Progress of Science and useful Arts, by securing for limited Times to Authors and Inventors the exclusive Right to their respective Writings and Discoveries * * *.

Congress draws its power to regulate trademarks and unfair competition from the Commerce Clause, Article I, Section 8, Clause 3:

> The Congress shall have power * * *
>
> (3) To regulate Commerce with foreign Nations, and among the several States, and with the Indian Tribes * * *.

The states retain the power to regulate intellectual property under the Tenth Amendment. However, the U.S. Constitution's Supremacy Clause (Article VI) imposes some limitations. The states may not act if Congress has acted in the field and intended to preempt the field, or if the state law stands "as an obstacle to the accomplishment and execution of the full purposes and objectives of Congress" in enacting the federal law. Hines v. Davidowitz, 312 U.S. 52, 67, 61 S.Ct. 399, 404, 85 L.Ed. 581, 586 (1941).

As one might expect, a number of defendants in state intellectual property causes of action have challenged the state intellectual property doctrines as preempted by federal patent and copyright laws under the Supremacy Clause. The Supreme Court's standards for evaluating such claims have tended to shift over the years and have created some confusion about the extent to which the states may create or enforce intellectual property rights. The tensions between state and federal laws are addressed at length in the final chapter of this book.

II.   INTERNATIONAL CONSIDERATIONS

Given today's global economy, American intellectual property lawyers are likely to become involved in international transactions. Each year large numbers of foreign inventors, authors and businesses apply for United States patents[2] and seek United States registration of trademarks

---

2. According to U.S. Patent and Trademark Office statistics, approximately 52% of U.S. utility patents granted in 2008 were issued to foreign applicants. Twenty-one percent of the U.S. patents issued in 2008 went to Japanese applicants alone. German inventors received the next largest number of U.S. patent grants—approximately 6% of the total. U.S. Patent and Trademark Office,

and copyrights. They require the assistance of American lawyers in this process, in exploiting their intellectual property rights in the United States, and in litigating disputes in United States courts. American businesses, in turn, are exporting large quantities of goods and services that are protected by United States intellectual property laws. These United States businesses turn to their domestic attorneys for advice about ways to obtain equivalent intellectual property protection in the foreign nations for which the products and services are bound.

Of course, a nation's patent, copyright and trademark laws apply only within the boundaries of that nation. A United States patent owner seeking to market its product world-wide and to assert intellectual property rights in the product in each foreign nation it enters must obtain a separate patent or trademark registration in each nation. While the U.S. company will rely on local lawyers to assist in the application process in each nation, and to appear in that nation's courts, the company's United States lawyers may be called upon to coordinate its application and enforcement strategies abroad. Accordingly, it is useful not only to understand United States intellectual property laws but also to be familiar with the United States' international intellectual property relations.

The United States is a party to numerous bilateral treaties regarding intellectual property protection, and to a number of multinational intellectual property conventions. Two multinational conventions which are particularly relevant are the Berne Convention for the Protection of Literary and Artistic Works ("Berne Convention"), regarding copyright protection, and the Paris Convention for the Protection of Industrial Property ("Paris Convention"), regarding patent, trademark and unfair competition protection. Each is administered by the World Intellectual Property Organization ("WIPO"), which is an agency of the United Nations, and each has well over 160 members. Both the Berne and the Paris Convention are founded on the notion of national treatment. This means that each Convention member must give as great protection to nationals of other member nations as it gives to its own nationals. So, for example, if countries X and Y are both members of the Paris Convention, a national of X may apply for a patent in Y, and Y must treat his application and resulting patent as favorably as it would the application and patent of a national of Y.

While the Berne and Paris Conventions specify some minimum standards of intellectual property protection, as well as national treatment, member nations retain significant discretion in determining the nature and scope of protection they will afford, particularly in the case of patent and trademark protection. Thus, even among Convention members, the availability and scope of patents, trademark registrations, copyrights and other forms of intellectual property protection may vary considerably. Another problem is that even when nations enact comprehensive intellec-

Office for Electronic Information Products, *Patents By Country, State, and Year–Utility Patents* (December 2008), http://www.uspto.gov.

tual property protection, some are lax in enforcing their laws. These and other problems led the United States and other developed countries to seek a new multinational agreement that would both strengthen and harmonize international intellectual property protection.

This quest came to fruition in the mid–1990's, through the Uruguay Round of multilateral trade negotiations under the auspices of the General Agreement on Tariffs and Trade ("GATT"), which produced the Agreement on Trade–Related Aspects of Intellectual Property Rights, Including Trade in Counterfeited Goods ("TRIPs"). The comprehensive TRIPs provisions incorporate existing international standards for intellectual property protection, including those set forth in the Berne and Paris Conventions, and impose a number of new substantive standards for copyrights, trademarks, geographical indications, industrial designs, patents, semiconductor chip designs, and trade secrets. Nations accepting TRIPs must bring their intellectual property laws into compliance with these substantive standards, and must satisfy specific TRIPs standards for *enforcing* intellectual property rights, both internally and at international borders. The new World Trade Organization, which administers TRIPs and the other Uruguay Round agreements, provides dispute resolution mechanisms to resolve disputes among member nations over compliance with TRIPs intellectual property protection standards. When member nations are determined to be in violation of their TRIPs obligations, failure to bring themselves into compliance may be penalized through imposition of trade sanctions.

As we proceed through this book, we will consider some of the substantive standards for patent, copyright, and trademark protection that the WIPO treaties and TRIPs impose on member nations, and how those standards have influenced U.S. law. The following article provides a more in-depth description of WIPO and the WTO TRIPs Council, and discusses the relative roles of these institutions in promoting international intellectual property protection.

CHALLENGES FOR THE WORLD INTELLECTUAL PROPERTY ORGANIZATION AND THE TRADE–RELATED ASPECTS OF INTELLECTUAL PROPERTY RIGHTS COUNCIL IN REGULATING PROPERTY RIGHTS IN THE INFORMATION AGE

Pamela Samuelson
[1999] European Intellectual Property Review 578[3]

* * *

An Overview of WIPO and the Treaties It Administers

The World Intellectual Property Organization is a subdivision of the United Nations, which has responsibility for, among other things, admin-

---

3. © Pamela Samuelson, 1999. Reprinted by permission of the copyright owner.

istering the Berne Convention for the Protection of Literary and Artistic Works and the Paris Convention for the Protection of Industrial Property. It also oversees a number of more specialized treaties, such as those that protect semiconductor chip designs and sound recordings. In this capacity, WIPO hosts meetings at which national delegations discuss possible revisions of, or supplementation to, existing treaties as well as proposals for new treaties. Once consultations have produced a relative consensus on the desirability of new or revised norms, WIPO will convene a diplomatic conference to consider draft treaties embodying those norms. The most recent example was the December 1996 diplomatic conference that considered three draft treaties: one to supplement the Berne Convention mainly dealing with digital copyright issues, one to supplement the Rome Convention to extend rights it confers on performers and producers of sound recordings, and one to create a new treaty to protect the contents of databases. Treaties supplementing the Berne and Rome Conventions were concluded at this conference.[9]

One reason that international agreements on intellectual property norms have historically been difficult to achieve arises from substantial differences in national intellectual property norms and traditions. A major focus of international treaty-making on intellectual property matters has, as a consequence, been on promoting the norm of "national treatment." This requires nations to accord to the intellectual creations of foreign nationals at least as much protection as the nation accords to similar works created by its own nationals. It thus outlaws one form of blatant national protectionism, such as the nineteenth-century practice of the United States that protected the literary works of American authors but not those of foreign authors.

Although international intellectual property treaties typically aspire to harmonize national intellectual property rules, they have generally left many issues to the discretion of individual nations, including whether to protect certain kinds of works and the scope or duration of protection certain works should enjoy. The Berne Convention, for example, leaves to national decision-making whether copyright protection should be available to aesthetically designed useful articles (such as teapots or furniture), requiring only that, if a nation offers copyright protection to such designs created by its own nationals, it must also protect the designs of foreign creators.

Even a cursory reading of the treaties administered by WIPO reveals that they aim to standardize at least some components of the major intellectual property regimes. The Paris Convention, for example, sets forth basic principles of patent, utility model, industrial design, and trade mark protection systems. Harmonization goals of past treaties have been

---

9. WIPO Copyright Treaty, adopted by the Diplomatic Conference. WIPO Doc. CRNR/DC/89 (December 20, 1996) ("WIPO Copyright Treaty"); Agreed Statements Concerning the WIPO Copyright Treaty, adopted by the Diplomatic Conference on December 20, 1996, WIPO Performances and Phonograms Treaty, adopted by the Diplomatic Conference, WIPO Doc. CRNR/DC/90 (December 20, 1996).

undermined to some degree by the long-standing practice of allowing countries to accede to WIPO-administered treaties while reserving a right not to implement certain norms in the treaty. The United States, for example, is a member of the Paris Convention but does not have either a utility model law or an industrial design law as such. Nations have also been given considerable leeway in implementing treaty norms to conform to their traditions. Established state practices have historically been given considerable deference.

A distinguishing feature of the Berne Convention was its insistence that a nation's copyright law needed to meet certain minimum standards before the nation could join the Berne Union and enjoy the benefits of the Treaty. These minima include granting authors of literary works the right to control reproductions of their works in copies for the life of the author plus 50 years. Another minimum standard is making such protection arise automatically and not imposing any formalities, such as requiring registration of a claim of copyright as a precondition of protection. The Berne Union has been somewhat loose about what constitutes compliance with Berne minima, seemingly on the philosophy that it will be easier to goad a repenting sinner along the road to redemption once it becomes a member of the fold.

The resistance to adherence to international norms can be illustrated by U.S. examples. The United States did not join the Berne Union until 1989, in larger part because it did not wish to comply with certain Berne minima. The United States had, for example, a long tradition of requiring copyright notices on all published copies of a work. Omission of such notices generally led to the work being dedicated to the public domain under U.S. law. Berne Union members, however, frown on such formalities, regarding them as undermining the rights of authors to reap the benefits of their creations. Although the United States dropped its mandatory copyright notice provisions in the Berne implementation legislation, it retained a rule requiring U.S. nationals to register claims of copyright with the U.S. Copyright Office before they can bring a lawsuit to complain of copyright infringement. Although the Berne Convention regards registration requirements as another kind of improper formality, it accepts the United States imposing formalities on its own nationals, forbidding only imposition of formality requirements on authors from other Berne Union nations. In this respect at least, foreign authors are treated better under U.S. law than are U.S. authors.

Another Berne Convention minimum standard that the United States has resisted is Berne's requirement to protect the "moral rights" of authors. Under the convention, nations must recognize the right of authors both to be identified as the creators of their works and to safeguard their works from destruction or mutilation. The United States relied principally on certain state moral rights laws and on a federal law regulating false designations of origin to say it was in compliance with the attribution right requirement. Far less plausible was the U.S. argument that it was in compliance with the integrity component of the Berne moral rights norm. U.S. publishers do not care for the idea of giving authors the right to enjoin them from editing out a segment of a book. Even less do motion picture studios wish to provide cinematographers or movie directors with a legal right to stop the colourisation of movies or editing that the studio regards as necessary to enhance the commercial appeal of a film. Although the United States eventually amended its copyright law to grant attribution and integrity rights to authors of certain works of visual art, the issue of U.S. compliance with Berne moral rights requirements remains a sore subject both internationally and in Hollywood, where directors, cinematographers, and actors remain intent on attaining recognition of their moral rights under the Berne Convention.

The principal reason that the United States finally joined the Berne Convention in 1989 was not because it had been converted to the high protectionist norms that the Convention lays down but because it needed to be a member of the Berne Union in order to have a stronger influence on international copyright policy. This was obviously in the U.S. national interest, given the dramatic increase in exports of U.S. copyright products in the second half of the twentieth century and the vulnerability of those products to the large-scale unauthorized copying that undermined U.S. export markets. The United States needed international co-operation to control such piracy, and the Berne Union was at [the] time the only forum where this kind of co-operation could feasibly be obtained.

Once the United States became a member of the Berne Union, it lost no time in exercising leadership there. Shortly after U.S. accession to the Berne Convention, the U.S. delegation to WIPO-sponsored meetings about a possible supplementary agreement to the Berne Convention insisted that any such agreement include a provision calling on nations to protect computer programs and databases as literary works within the meaning of the Convention. Because WIPO had previously proposed a *sui generis* form of legal protection for computer programs and because a number of countries had adopted or were considering other legal regimes for computer program protection, the U.S. proposal was far from a sure thing at the time. The United States lobbied hard for its proposal, no doubt in part because it hoped that this would preserve U.S. dominance in the world market for those classes of intellectual products.

In succeeding years, as discussions on a supplementary agreement to Berne continued, the United States proposed other treaty provisions that would benefit U.S. copyright industries. Working with WIPO officials, with the committee of experts responsible for drafting treaties to consider emerging norms, and with European allies, the United States was largely successful in promoting its digital agenda in the most recent round of WIPO copyright and neighboring rights negotiations. The treaties included U.S.-initiated norms calling for protection of computer programs and databases as literary works and the protection of copyright management information attached to digital versions of protected works. WIPO itself had a big stake in the successful conclusion of these new treaties, as several other recent treaty-making activities it had initiated had been unsuccessful.

The TRIPs Agreement and the TRIPs Council

Even as the United States was beginning to exercise leadership in Berne Union meetings on digital copyright and other issues, it was vigorously pursuing an alternative strategy to enhance international protection of intellectual property rights. The United States played a central role in the negotiations that led to the successful conclusion of the agreement on Trade–Related Aspects of Intellectual Property Rights as an annex to the agreement establishing the World Trade Organization.

U.S. support for TRIPs grew in substantial part out of dissatisfaction with WIPO, the treaties WIPO processes yielded, and the lack of effective enforcement mechanisms to deal with national deviations from WIPO treaty norms. WIPO-sponsored negotiations tended to take a painfully long time and to result in treaties with weaker norms than the United States perceived to be in its national interest. Even worse was the fact that, once a norm became part of a WIPO-administered treaty, there was no effective international mechanism to enforce it. Although the Berne Convention contemplates that one nation can challenge another nation's compliance with Berne norms before the International Court of Justice ("ICJ"), the Treaty also permits countries to declare that they will not be bound by an ICJ ruling on Berne compliance matters. In practice, this rendered the Berne enforcement system toothless. Before TRIPs, countries with grievances about another nation's non-compliance with intellectual property norms had little recourse other than bilateral negotiations to resolve disputes over these rights.

The United States hoped that TRIPs would remedy the perceived deficiencies of the WIPO-centered regime for the international protection of intellectual property rights. Following Berne's example, TRIPs establishes minimum protection standards not just for copyright but also for several other classes of intellectual property rights, including rights in sound recordings and broadcasts, trade marks, industrial designs, patents, semiconductor chip designs, and trade secrets. For the most part, TRIPs establishes its norms by incorporating provisions of the Berne and Paris Conventions, but it does so selectively. The moral rights provision of the Berne Convention, for example, is explicitly omitted from the TRIPs Agreement. In addition, the unfair competition provision of the Paris Convention is incorporated into TRIPs only in so far as it provides a framework for protection of undisclosed information (*i.e.* trade secrets). TRIPs also establishes some norms not found in the major conventions, such as requiring WTO members to regulate the rental of sound recordings, computer programs and motion pictures. In addition, TRIPs, like most WIPO-administered treaties, obliges countries to respect national treatment principles.

The most heralded accomplishment of TRIPs is, however, its dispute settlement process. At long last, there is an international mechanism with which to resolve complaints about inadequacies of intellectual property protection. A state that believes its nationals have been harmed by another state's failure to protect intellectual property rights can file a complaint with the WTO alleging a violation of TRIPs. If efforts at conciliation and mediation prove unsuccessful, the TRIPs Council will convene a panel of experts to rule on the validity of the complaint. If the panel and the appellate body that has authority to review the panel's ruling uphold the complaint, the offending nation will have to choose between adjusting its law or enforcement practices and facing trade sanctions by the victor. Trade sanctions may even be levied against products unrelated to the violation of TRIPs norms (*e.g.* inadequate protection of sound recordings may, for example, eventually lead to trade sanctions against exports of textiles.) The goal of these sanctions is not to punish the offending nation but to give it more urgent reasons to meet its obligations under TRIPs.

Lawyers understandably emphasize the formal dispute settlement process as the main accomplishment of TRIPs. However, informal dispute resolution before the TRIPs Council will generally precede the formal complaint process and, in general, will be preferable to formal resolutions. Notwithstanding the sabre-rattling of copyright industry representatives from the United States and elsewhere, it is a serious matter for countries to bring a formal action against other nations before an international tribunal. Threatening a formal complaint may, however, help induce voluntary compliance in some cases.

Two other roles of the TRIPs Council are worthy of mention. The TRIPs Council has responsibility for oversight of national intellectual property policy making and judicial enforcement. TRIPs requires nations to report to the TRIPs Council on developments in their intellectual property laws and policies. The purpose of these reports is to enable the TRIPs Council to have advance knowledge of such developments. Should the TRIPs Council regard a particular policy or practice as undermining TRIPs norms, it may discourage adoption of this policy at the national level. TRIPs Council oversight may also serve a prophylactic function, obviating the need for disputes over intellectual property rights to be brought to the WTO. The TRIPs Council also has responsibility for determining whether new norms ought to be folded into TRIPs. If an international consensus exists in support of modified or additional norms, the TRIPs Council can recommend to the WTO Ministerial Conference that the conference amend TRIPs to incorporate these new norms.

The Complex Relationship of TRIPs and WIPO–Administered Treaties

TRIPs has a complex interrelationship with WIPO-administered treaties. The complexity arises both as to long-standing treaties, such as the Berne Convention, whose norms TRIPs incorporates by reference, and as to later concluded treaties, such as the WIPO Copyright Treaty adopted in Geneva in December 1996. This section explores some of these interrelationship issues. Although it focuses principally on the interrelationship of TRIPs and the Berne Convention, the same interrelationship issues arise in relation to other WIPO-administered treaties as well.

Professor Neal Netanel was among the first to explore in detail how Berne *qua* Berne (that is, the treaty in and of itself) might differ from Berne in TRIPs (that is, Berne Treaty norms incorporated by reference into TRIPs).[42] The most obvious difference lies in the exclusion from TRIPs of the moral rights provision of the Berne Convention. But Netanel points out that more subtle differences may manifest themselves as provisions incorporated by reference into TRIPs. Berne in TRIPs may, for example, have a somewhat different meaning from Berne *qua* Berne owing to differences in the purpose of each agreement. The main purpose of TRIPs, after all, is "to reduce distortions and impediments to international trade," whereas the main purpose of the Berne Convention is "to protect, in as effective and uniform manner as possible, the rights of authors in their literary and artistic works." Because TRIPs is largely indifferent to the rights of authors and the Berne Convention is largely indifferent to trade principles, some variance in meanings could arise. As Professors Dreyfuss and Lowenfeld have pointed out, the vocabularies of free trade and of intellectual property, as well as the core values of each field, are substantially different. This too may contribute to variances in shades of meaning when interpreting the same norm in different contexts.

As yet unclear is the relative tolerance of the TRIPs Council and WTO dispute panels, on the one hand, and the Berne Union, on the other, concerning national interpretations of Berne norms. As noted above, the Berne tradition has deferred heavily to established state practice, permitted some minor (and some not-so-minor) reservations to Berne norms, and left much to the discretion of national legislatures. Berne has concentrated on establishing norms, rather than enforcing them. Will the TRIPs Council and WTO panels be as accepting of national deviations as Berne has been? If not, this would widen the gap between Berne *qua* Berne and Berne in TRIPs.

* * *

Subsequent Agreements and TRIPs

TRIPs establishes most of its substantive norms by incorporating reference-specific provisions of existing intellectual property treaties. Interesting questions arise about the obligations of WTO members when treaty provisions incorporated into TRIPs are subsequently amended or revised, when an incorporated-by-reference treaty is more generally amended or supplemented by a later treaty, and when wholly new international treaties on intellectual property matters are concluded. * * *

* * *

---

42. Neil Netanel, "The Next Round: The Impact of the WIPO Copyright Treaty on TRIPs Dispute Settlement" (1997) 37 *Virginia Journal of International Law* 441. See also Paul Edward Geller, "Can the GATT Incorporate Berne Whole?" [1990] E.I.P.R. 423.

The good news for U.S. industries is that there is now in place an international consensus in support of far-reaching minimum standards for protection of intellectual property rights, an international mechanism aimed at ensuring that nations effectively enforce these standards, and a system for building consensus to adopt new intellectual property norms as they are needed. WTO membership is sufficiently attractive to induce nations to conform their intellectual property laws and enforcement practices to TRIPs norms in order to be granted, or to retain, this status. China's desire to become a member of WTO may, for instance, be the strongest lever the United States could have to induce enforcement of intellectual property rights that will benefit U.S. industries. Even the prospect of U.S. complaints to WTO against countries that fail to protect intellectual property rights may have an enforcement-inducing effect beneficial to U.S. industries, without complaints needing to be made.

* * *

NOTES AND QUESTIONS

1. *Foreign infringement.* U.S. businesses have long complained of rampant "piracy" of their intellectual property abroad, and particularly in developing countries, where intellectual property laws traditionally have not been as strong as in the United States, and enforcement of existing laws has been lax. Assume that X Company is an American manufacturer of pharmaceutical products and has a United States patent for a new drug. It sells the new drug under the trademark "Xana," which it has registered in the United States. X Co. sells the drug under its trademark throughout the world, and has obtained a patent and registered its trademark in every country that would allow it to do so. The term "piracy" might be applied loosely to any of the following situations:

    (a) Y Co. manufactures the same drug and sells it under the name Xana without X Co.'s permission in countries in which X Co. has both a patent and registered trademark protection.

    (b) Y Co. manufactures a different drug and sells it without X Co.'s permission under the name Xana in countries in which X Co. has a trademark registration.

    (c) Y Co. manufactures the same drug without X Co.'s permission in countries in which X Co. has a patent, but sells the drug under another trademark.

    (d) Y Co. manufactures the same drug without X Co.'s permission and sells it under the name Xana in countries in which X Co. has neither a patent (because the countries afford no patent protection for drugs) nor a valid trademark registration.

    (e) Y Co. manufactures the same drug without X Co.'s permission and sells it under another name in countries in which X Co. has no patent (because the countries afford no patent protection for drugs).

Are the social ramifications of Y's activity the same in each case? In your opinion, should the term "piracy" be applied to situations (d) and (e)?

2. *Developed vs. developing nations.* What are the respective costs and benefits of maintaining a strong system of intellectual property protection? Assuming that the benefits outweigh the costs in the United States, would the same necessarily be true in developing countries? On what, if any, basis might the governments of developing nations conclude that a strong intellectual property system would not be beneficial?

PART TWO

RIGHTS IN IDEAS AND INFORMATION

■ ■ ■

To assist in learning intellectual property law, it is useful conceptually to divide the various intellectual property doctrines into three groups: 1) those doctrines that provide property rights in ideas and information; 2) those doctrines that protect original means of expressing ideas and information; and 3) those doctrines that are designed to protect consumer interests, good will and related intangible trade values.

Part Two, consisting of Chapters Two and Three, will focus on the doctrines that fall within the first group, providing property rights in ideas and information. Chapter Two will address the state law of trade secrets and a small collection of state common-law doctrines sometimes referred to collectively as "idea law," or the "law of undeveloped ideas." Chapter Three will examine the federal law of patents.

Part Three, consisting of Chapter Four, will examine federal copyright law. Copyright provides rights in original ways of expressing ideas and information.

Part Four, consisting of Chapters Five, Six and Seven, will focus on the state and federal trademark and unfair competition laws, and the state right of publicity. All of these doctrines recognize limited "property-like" rights as a means of protecting consumer interests, promoting competition, and protecting business' economic interests in consumer good will and related intangible trade values.

The final Part, consisting of Chapter Eight, will examine the status of *state* intellectual property doctrines in light of the United States Constitution's Supremacy Clause and Copyright Act § 301, 17 U.S.C. § 301, which preempts state causes of action that duplicate federal copyright infringement claims.

CHAPTER TWO

<hr>

TRADE SECRET LAW AND RELATED
STATE DOCTRINES

■ ■ ■

I. THE THEORY OF TRADE SECRET PROTECTION

CYBERTEK COMPUTER PRODUCTS, INC. v. WHITFIELD

California Superior Court, 1977.
203 U.S.P.Q. 1020, 1977 WL 22730.

TITLE, JUDGE.

* * *

I.

In this action for injunctive relief and damages arising out of alleged misappropriation by defendants of confidential information and trade secrets in connection with plaintiff's computer software system, the Court has bifurcated the issue of liability from that of damages pursuant to stipulation of the parties, and has now concluded the trial of the liability issue. * * *

[T]he dispute essentially arises out of the prior employment of defendant Whitfield by plaintiff, and his subsequent employment by defendant Tracor in the same field of endeavor. Plaintiff was formed in 1969 for the purpose of engaging in the business of furnishing computer related services to the life insurance industry. Defendant Whitfield was one of the founding officers of plaintiff, and had a substantial background and expertise in computer software, as specifically related to its use in the life insurance business. He purchased shares in plaintiff, and in his capacity as an employee of plaintiff, directly participated in the design and development of plaintiff's on-line new business computer system known as the Auto/Issue System, his responsibilities including the specific design of some major portions of the system. For a time he had management responsibility for this system, and subsequently was a senior analyst involved in its design, programming and testing.

In connection with his employment, defendant Whitfield executed an Employee Nondisclosure Agreement, dated December 2, 1970, which provided among other things that the techniques and methods relating to plaintiff's products were trade secrets and confidential, and that he would not at any time disclose to anyone outside of plaintiff any information about plaintiff's products which related to the design, use or development of such products. The agreement specifically made reference to the Auto/Issue System. He voluntarily terminated his employment and relationship with plaintiff on March 31, 1971, at which time he acknowledged in writing that he understood his agreement with plaintiff not to disclose confidential information, and that he had returned all confidential material to plaintiff. He thereafter did some consulting work for defendant Tracor between July and October, 1971, commenced full-time employment with said defendant on November 15, 1971, and ever since that time has remained in said defendant's employ. His duties with defendant Tracor have included responsibility for the development of an insurance on-line new business system, which would provide substantially the same capabilities as plaintiff's Auto/Issue System, and which was to be marketed in direct competition to plaintiff's Auto/Issue System.

Plaintiff developed its Auto/Issue System over a period of approximately two years, from November, 1969 through approximately November, 1971. Since that time it has been marketing the system. Defendant's similar system, which it has named Trac/70, has been substantially though not completely developed, but is nevertheless being marketed at the present time in competition with plaintiff's Auto/Issue System. It was stipulated by the parties that plaintiff and defendant Tracor have each expended in excess of $500,000 in the development of their respective systems.

II.

Plaintiff has at all times maintained and enforced a corporate policy which requires its employees to execute Employee Nondisclosure Agreements such as that executed by defendant Whitfield, and which further requires its potential and actual licensees to execute nondisclosure agreements prior to receiving Auto/Issue documentation other than marketing material. Plaintiff also at all times material herein maintained additional reasonable measures of security which clearly demonstrate plaintiff's intention to keep information concerning its products, including the Auto/Issue System, confidential, such as the marking of documentation relating to its products as confidential, the use of registration numbers in connection with copies of its documentation, and permitting only authorized personnel to have access to its Auto/Issue documentation other than marketing materials. Defendant Tracor has likewise taken similar steps relating to security in order to protect the confidentiality of its on-line new business system known as Trac/70.

III.

It is plaintiff's contention that during defendant Whitfield's consultations and employment with defendant Tracor, he has been substantially and directly involved in the design of said defendant's Trac/70 System, in connection with which he has utilized and disclosed plaintiff's trade secrets and confidential information in violation of his duty to plaintiff, and in breach of his specific Nondisclosure Agreement with plaintiff. Both defendants deny any responsibility to plaintiff, and contend that the alleged trade secrets and confidential matter claimed by plaintiff are in fact not trade secrets or confidential, but rather are well known concepts in the computer industry, that they are, therefore, not confidential, and that defendant Whitfield has merely utilized his substantial degree of skill and experience in his employment by defendant Tracor which he had developed prior to his employment with plaintiff and which he has the right to so utilize.

IV.

There are a number of basic threshold issues to be determined by the Court, which appear to involve mixed questions of law and fact. Among these are the following: Do any or all of the 12 items set forth in plaintiff's Exh. 1A (said exhibit purports to enumerate the areas of design and development of the Auto/Issue System which constitute the confidential information and trade secrets concerning which plaintiff is entitled to protection), or any combination thereof, constitute confidential information or trade secrets? * * * What was the intention of the parties under said nondisclosure agreement? Was any of said alleged confidential matter or trade secrets disclosed by defendant Whitfield to defendant Tracor in connection with the development of the Trac/70 System?

V.

While there may have been a question in the past as to whether or not computer software is susceptible of protection under the trade secret doctrine, it is clear that such protection is available today in practically all jurisdictions. See 38 George Washington Law Review 909, and cases cited by both plaintiff and defendants in their respective trial briefs, all of which make it amply clear that computer software is protectible under the trade secret doctrine, given appropriate facts and circumstances.

[In the next several sections of the opinion, the court finds, among other things, that the confidentiality agreement Whitfield signed is valid, and that the existence of such a contractual agreement, while not essential to a finding of trade secret misappropriation, is an important factor for consideration.]

X.

Simply stated, plaintiff's position is that some 12 areas of development and design in its Auto/Issue System set forth in extremely technical language in Exh. 1A constitute trade secrets, or at least highly confidential matter which should be protected either on the theory that defendant Whitfield breached his confidential duty to plaintiff or breached his express covenant of nondisclosure. To determine this issue, it is necessary to attempt to glean a definition of a trade secret from the authorities and case law, and that examination of the authorities and cases makes it immediately obvious that while the simplistic definitions found therein are easily understood, the application thereof to a highly technical area such as computer software programs is extremely difficult. Section 757 of the Restatement of Torts, Comment b, generally defines a trade secret as any formula, pattern, device or compilation of information which is used in one's business, and which gives him an opportunity to obtain an advantage over competitors who do not know or use it. In spite of this simple definition, it further states that an exact definition of a trade secret is not possible, and lists some factors to be considered in determining the existence or nonexistence of a trade secret. Briefly stated, these include the extent to which the information is known by others outside of the business or employees of the business, the extent of measures taken to guard the secrecy of the information, the value of the information, the effort and expense involved in developing it, and lastly the ease or difficulty with which the information could be properly acquired or duplicated by others. As to some of the latter factors, plaintiff clearly comes within their ambit, as the evidence is virtually uncontradicted that reasonably strict security measures were taken to guard the secrecy of the Auto/Issue System, in excess of $500,000 was expended by plaintiff to develop it, license fees of somewhere between $100,000 and $200,000 are charged plaintiff's customers for the right to use the system, and a formidable and expensive task is faced by any competitor who might desire to properly acquire or duplicate it. The serious conflict in the evidence arises, however, in connection with the factor dealing with the issue as to the extent to which the information is known to others outside of plaintiff's business. Defendants essentially contend that we are not dealing with trade secrets, nor for that matter even confidential matter to any degree, because all the alleged items set forth in Exh. 1A are not secret or confidential information but rather consist of well known concepts in the computer and data processing industry, and consequently cannot by any stretch of the imagination be considered confidential or secret. This issue was joined in the traditional battle of the experts, with Dr. Gilbert and others testifying on behalf of plaintiff to the effect that Exh. 1A indeed did include unique and confidential approaches not known to the computer industry in general, and Mr. Shafto and others testifying on behalf of defendants to the contrary. The technical nature of their testimony would be mind-boggling to the average lay person, as it was to the court, and this is amply demonstrated by the fact that Mr. Shafto, an obviously well qualified expert in the computer field, testified that he had great difficulty in even understanding the meaning of the descriptive language of the alleged trade secrets found in Exh. 1A. The Court has carefully considered all of the testimony, and has concluded that at least to some degree, defendants' position is correct in that some of the approaches utilized in the Auto/Issue System, standing separately, are general concepts known to experts in the computer industry. The cases indicate, and plaintiff concedes that general concepts are not protectible, per se, as trade secrets. However, the cases further indicate that while general concepts are not protectible, the specific implementation involving a particular combination of general concepts may well amount to a trade secret. See Winston Res. Co. v. Minnesota Mining & Mfg. Co., supra, involving the manufacture of a tape recording device, supporting this theory. That court pointed out that the same general concepts had been used in developing defendants' machine as had been used in plaintiff's machine, that such development involved the use of general concepts and approaches which were known in the industry, and were, therefore, not in and of themselves susceptible of trade secret protection. However, the court further pointed out that while the general approach and the basic mechanical elements thereof were not trade secrets, that the specifications of these basic mechanical elements and their relationship to each other embodied in plaintiff's machine were not publicly known, were arrived at only after painstaking research and extensive trial and error, and therefore, constituted a trade secret entitled to protection. In other words, the court found that the specific embodiment of the general concepts and approach into a combination of parts was protectible, even though all or some of them might well be known to the industry. The Court believes that the principle annunciated in these cases applies to our case, and that while some of the concepts set forth in Exh. 1A are general concepts not susceptible of protection, that the entire bundle or combination of these concepts as developed and utilized by plaintiff in its Auto/Issue System do constitute trade secrets which are protectible under the circumstances. As pointed out in the above mentioned Restatement of Torts, as well as in 80 Harvard Law Review 1432, at page 1452, any information which provides a competitive advantage over competitors may well constitute a trade secret, and in the Court's view it is obvious that the combination of factors involved in the Auto/Issue System must give the plaintiff its protection under this doctrine.

XI.

Having concluded that the confidential matter in question should not have been disclosed by defendant Whitfield, the next issue which must be determined is whether in fact there was such a disclosure by him in connection with his work on the development of Tracor's Trac/70 System. Defendant Whitfield contends that since he took away no actual documentation or physical material relating to the Auto/Issue System, it must follow that he did not disclose or use any confidential information relating thereto, but rather merely made use of his expertise and general know-how in the development of Trac/70. Putting it in another way, defendants contend that Trac/70 was independently developed, and was not copied from plaintiff's Auto/Issue System. This presents an extremely close question of fact for the Court to determine, and the Court is not unmindful of the classic confrontation in the law of the policy which strives to extend some protection to an employer from the breach of confidence of a former employee in taking away and utilizing trade secrets with the policy of the law which protects an employee in his right to carry on his trade or profession after he leaves his employer. The Court also has considered the well recognized principle that where a defendant in a trade secret case claims independent development, that the burden then shifts to the defendant and places upon the defendant a heavy burden of persuasion to show that the production was a result of independent development and not from the use of information confidentially secured during the prior employment. * * *

Looking to the evidence, it is not seriously controverted, and the Court finds that there are in fact substantial similarities in the Auto/Issue System and the Trac/70 System. Such similarity, while not determinative of the issue, is of obvious importance, and must be given weight. Granted that the systems are not identical, many cases indicate that such identity is not required, and that trade secrets need not be exactly copied in order to impose liability. Likewise, the conceded difference in terminology utilized in the systems is not significant.

Defendants have also argued that many of the similarities are purely coincidental, since there were relatively few options which every expert in the field would consider in arriving at methods of approach for a new business on-line system. However, plaintiff presented evidence to the effect that there were in fact significant design choices, and that similar choices utilized by defendants would, therefore, indicate copying rather than independent development. This again is a question of fact, and the Court accepts Dr. Gilbert's testimony to the effect that there were significant design choices, and not as indicated by defendants, choices only as to insignificant details. Furthermore, even if the Court resolves the conflict in the evidence regarding whether or not defendant Whitfield took away with him documentation concerning the Auto/Issue System in favor of defendant Whitfield, the cases are clear that documentation need not be taken in order to establish liability, since appropriation by memory alone is proscribed. As pointed out in 38 George Washington Law Review, page 909 at pages 938 and 939, the weight of authority indicates that appropriation by memory will be proscribed under the same circumstances as an appropriation via more tangible means.

When the Court considers all of the above factors, and adds thereto the ingredient sustained by the evidence that defendant Whitfield had complete knowledge and understanding of plaintiff's system, and in addition supervised and oversaw the development of defendants' system, the Court concludes and finds that defendant Whitfield did disclose and utilize substantial aspects of plaintiff's Auto/Issue System in the development of the Trac/70 System.

XII.

Defendant Whitfield's liability having been established, the Court must finally determine whether defendant Tracor also has liability under the circumstances. The cases indicate, as does Section 757 of the Restatement of Torts, that a new employer may also be liable for misappropriation of trade secrets, provided that he utilizes the information with notice of the secret nature thereof and with notice that the employee has disclosed it in breach of his duty to the former employer. The evidence indicates that before any substantial development of the Trac/70 System was begun, defendant Whitfield had been placed on notice by plaintiff by letter concerning a possible trade secret violation, and defendant Tracor was apprised of said demand by defendant Whitfield. In addition, it is conceded by defendants that the instant lawsuit was actually filed before any substantial development of the Trac/70 system. Under these circumstances, the Court finds that defendant Tracor was on notice of the potential liability in this matter, and consequently the Court finds that defendant Tracor has liability herein along with defendant Whitfield.

NOTES AND QUESTIONS

1. *Key influences on the law of trade secrets.* Trade secret doctrine developed in the common law and, since 1939, has been greatly influenced by the first Restatement of Torts, §§ 757 and 758. Restatement of Torts § 757 provides:

> One who discloses or uses another's trade secret, without a privilege to do so, is liable to the other if
>
> (a) he discovered the secret by improper means, or
>
> (b) his disclosure or use constitutes a breach of confidence reposed in him by the other in disclosing the secret to him, or
>
> (c) he learned the secret from a third person with notice of the facts that it was a secret and that the third person discovered it by improper means or that the third person's disclosure of it was otherwise a breach of his duty to the other, or
>
> (d) he learned the secret with notice of the facts that it was a secret and that its disclosure was made to him by mistake.[1]

Restatement of Torts § 758 provides:

> One who learns another's trade secret from a third person without notice that it is a secret and that the third person's disclosure is a breach of his duty to the other, or who learns the secret through a mistake without notice of the secrecy and the mistake,
>
> (a) is not liable to the other for a disclosure or use of the secret prior to receipt of such notice, and
>
> (b) is liable to the other for a disclosure or use of the secret after the receipt of such notice, unless prior thereto he has in good faith paid value for the secret or has so changed his position that to subject him to liability would be inequitable.[2]

---

1. © 1939 by The American Law Institute. Reprinted with the permission of The American Law Institute.

2. © 1939 by The American Law Institute. Reprinted with the permission of The American Law Institute.

Courts' frequent reliance on these Restatement provisions (as exemplified in *Cybertek* and in the *duPont* opinion, *supra*) led to greater uniformity among the states than might otherwise have occurred. When the American Law Institute undertook to draft the Restatement (Second) of Torts in 1977, it omitted provisions regarding trade secret protection on the ground that trade secret doctrine is "no more dependent upon Tort law than it is on many other general fields of the law * * *." Restatement (Second) of Torts, vol. 4 at 1 (1977). Nonetheless, the first Restatement provisions continued to be quite influential. In the late 1980's and early 1990's, the American Law Institute drafted a new Restatement (Third) of Unfair Competition, which includes provisions on trade secret law which are similar, for the most part, to those of the First Restatement of Torts. These provisions can be found in Restatement (Third) of Unfair Competition §§ 39–45 (1995).

Another important development in trade secret law occurred in 1979, when the National Conference of Commissioners on Uniform State Laws published the Uniform Trade Secrets Act. The Uniform Act was designed to be enacted by individual state legislatures, and over 45 states have now adopted it or its 1985 revised version.[3] Key provisions of the Uniform Act are quoted in the notes below. As its title suggests, the Uniform Act was intended to codify and further unify state trade secret laws. In many respects the Uniform Act codified common-law rules that had already been established by the courts, with the influence of Restatement of Torts §§ 757 and 758. Thus, the Uniform Act and the Restatement of Torts are similar in most respects and the Restatement provisions continue to be influential in interpreting the law, even in jurisdictions that have adopted the Uniform Act. For a detailed discussion of the Uniform Act and a comparison with Restatement of Torts §§ 757 and 758, see Klitzke, *The Uniform Trade Secrets Act*, 64 Marq. L. Rev. 277 (1980).

Under either the Restatement or the Uniform Act, analysis of most trade secret claims breaks down into two basic inquiries: 1) does the information or idea at issue qualify as a trade secret; and 2) if it does, is the defendant's acquisition, disclosure or use of it prohibited under one of the theories set forth in Restatement of Torts §§ 757 and 758 or their counterpart, § 1 of the Uniform Trade Secrets Act?

2. *The definition of "trade secret."* The court in *Cybertek* refers to the Restatement of Torts definition of trade secret information, which is set forth in § 757, comment b:

> A trade secret may consist of any formula, pattern, device or compila-tion of information which is used in one's business, and which gives him an opportunity to obtain an advantage over competitors who do not know or use it. It may be a formula for a chemical compound, a process of manufacturing, treating or preserving materials, a pattern for a machine or other device, or a list of customers. It differs from other secret information in a business * * * in that it is not simply information as to single or ephemeral events in the conduct of the business, as, for example, the amount or other terms of a secret bid for a contract or the salary of

---

3. California adopted the Uniform Trade Secrets Act in 1985, eight years after the decision in *Cybertek*.

certain employees, or the security investments made or contemplated, or the date fixed for the announcement of a new policy or for bringing out a new model or the like. A trade secret is a process or device for continuous use in the operation of the business.

Section 757, comment b, provides six factors which should be considered in determining whether given information constitutes a trade secret:

> (1) the extent to which the information is known outside of [plaintiff's] business; (2) the extent to which it is known by employees and others involved in his business; (3) the extent of measures taken by him to guard the secrecy of the information; (4) the value of the information to him and to his competitors; (5) the amount of effort or money expended by him in developing the information; (6) the ease or difficulty with which the information could be properly acquired or duplicated by others.[4]

See also Restatement (Third) of Unfair Competition § 39, cmt. d (1995). The Uniform Trade Secrets Act, § 1(4), provides:

> "Trade secret" means information, including a formula, pattern, compilation, program, device, method, technique, or process, that
>
>> (i) derives independent economic value, actual or potential, from not being generally known to, and not being readily ascertainable by proper means by, other persons who can obtain economic value from its disclosure or use, and
>>
>> (ii) is the subject of efforts that are reasonable under the circumstances to maintain its secrecy.[5]

Why should Restatement of Torts § 757 comment (b) require that the plaintiff use the secret continuously in his business? This is one of the points at which the Uniform Trade Secrets Act differs from Restatement § 757. The drafters of the Uniform Act deliberately deleted the requirement. Likewise, the Restatement (Third) of Unfair Competition deletes the requirement. Restatement (Third) of Unfair Competition § 39 cmt. d (1995). In your opinion, which approach makes more sense? See Uniform Trade Secrets Act § 1, Commissioners' Comment (1979).

3. *The secrecy requirement.* Why should protection be limited to information that is secret? What factors did the *Cybertek* court find relevant in determining that the secrecy requirement was satisfied in that case?

(a) The extent to which the information is known outside of the plaintiff's business. Information that is widely known by the public or by others in the plaintiff's field of business will not qualify as a trade secret. However, the secrecy need not be absolute. Restatement of Torts § 757, comment b, provides that "[o]thers may also know of the information independently, as, for example, when they have discovered the process or formula by independent invention and are keeping it secret. Nevertheless, a substantial element

---

4. © 1939 by The American Law Institute. Excerpts from Restatement of Torts § 757 cmt. b are reprinted with the permission of The American Law Institute.

5. These portions of the Act have been reprinted with the permission of the National Conference of Commissioners on Uniform State Laws. Copies of the Act may be ordered from the National Conference at a nominal cost at 676 North St. Clair Street, Suite 1700, Chicago, Illinois 60611.

of secrecy must exist, so that, except by the use of improper means, there would be difficulty in acquiring the information." See also Restatement (Third) of Unfair Competition § 39, cmt. f (1995).

(b) The ease or difficulty with which the information could be acquired properly by others. If the information is available in trade journals or other published sources, it is not likely to qualify. Likewise, if the information can be ascertained by simply examining the claimant's finished product, trade secrecy status will be destroyed as soon as the product is publicly distributed. The fact that the information can be learned through complex "reverse engineering" of the product, however, generally will not negate trade secrecy status, as long as the defendant learned the information through improper means. See Uniform Trade Secrets Act, § 1, Commissioners' Comment.

(c) The extent to which the trade secret is known by employees and others connected with the plaintiff's business. Clearly, the owner of a trade secret must be able to use it, and to use it effectively, she must be able to disclose it to some of her employees. Likewise, she may need to share the trade secret with certain of her distributors, licensees, joint venturers and others with whom she works closely. This is permissible, as long as the owner limits the information to those who actually need to know it, and takes reasonable precautions to ensure that they keep the information confidential. See Restatement of Torts, § 757, cmt. b (1939); Restatement (Third) of Unfair Competition § 39, cmt. f (1995).

(d) The measures the plaintiff takes to guard the secrecy of the information. A plaintiff must anticipate ways that competitors might obtain her trade secret and take reasonable steps to prevent them from doing so. Her duty, however, is limited to what is reasonable under the circumstances. See E. I. duPont deNemours & Co., Inc. v. Christopher, 431 F.2d 1012 (5th Cir.1970), *cert. denied*, 400 U.S. 1024, 91 S.Ct. 581, 27 L.Ed.2d 637 (1971). Some courts have suggested that a cost-benefit analysis should be used to evaluate the reasonableness of requiring the plaintiff to take a particular precaution. Will the benefit of added security outweigh the cost of the precaution? If not, the plaintiff will not be required to take the precaution. This approach recognizes that absolute security may not be economically efficient. The court's reasoning in In the Matter of Innovative Construction Systems, Inc., 793 F.2d 875 (7th Cir.1986), is instructive. In that case the U.S. Court of Appeals for the Seventh Circuit, applying Wisconsin law, found that there was sufficient evidence to uphold (against a motion for judgement n. o. v.) a jury verdict for Innovative, granting it trade secret protection in its formulas for producing simulated brick paneling:

> Innovative did not require its employees to sign nondisclosure agreements. Employee guidelines posted within the production area did not mention the confidential nature of the formulas. Furthermore, employees were not given exit interviews concerning the confidential nature of the formulas. Bowen Supply contends that this establishes "as a matter of law that [Innovative] did not take the steps necessary to impress upon its employees the need to keep its formulas secret." We disagree.

> * * * [T]he relevant question is whether, under the circumstances, the measures adopted were reasonable.

For us to require written non-disclosure statements or exit interviews as a matter of law would overlook the nature of the special verdict interrogatory. In asking whether particular efforts were reasonably adequate under the circumstances, the jury is called upon in part to exercise their common-sense judgment in determining whether additional measures were necessary to guard the secrecy of the formulas. In essence, this requires an assessment of the size and nature of Innovative's business, the cost to it of additional measures, and the degree to which such measures would decrease the risk of disclosure. What may be reasonable measures in one context may not necessarily be so in another. Under the facts of this case, it is sufficient that the employees were apprised of the secret nature of the formulas, and were told, and agreed, to keep that information confidential.

Innovative also did not employ security personnel, and the plant was not locked during working hours. Suppliers, job applicants, and personal friends of employees were not denied entry into the manufacturing area. Bowen Supply argues that this establishes as a matter of law that Innovative failed to take reasonably adequate steps to guard the secrecy of its formulas. We disagree.

Innovative introduced testimony that, because of the wet cement generated in the production of Panel Brick, nonemployees would not enter the manufacturing area to an extent sufficient to closely observe the process. We must be mindful also that on appeal Innovative is not claiming trade secret status for the entire production process, but for the formulas only. These formulas, aside from that for the slurry coat, were kept in a notebook in the plant manager's office, and hence out of view. There is no indication in the record that the amount of time such nonemployees were allowed in the plant was substantial, and there is certainly no reason to think that they were in a position to glean the information contained in the formulas from the causal observation of the manufacturing process.

As to the slurry formula, which was posted in the dye shed, the jury was shown a diagram of the plant area, and one of Innovative's witnesses marked on the diagram the area that visitors entered. Hence, the jury was given sufficient evidence from which it could determine the probability whether someone other than an employee could have seen the slurry formula, and whether additional security measures were necessary under the circumstances. We find that there is sufficient evidence to support the inference that the measures adopted by Innovative to guard the secrecy of its formulas from non-employees were reasonably adequate.

Finally, Bowen Supply argues that Innovative took inadequate steps to guard the secrecy of its formulas when discussing the possible sale of its business to others. Several companies, including Bowen Supply, had expressed an interest in acquiring Innovative. Representatives from some of these companies would inspect the manufacturing plant. Innovative did not require either the companies or their representatives to sign non-disclosure agreements.

Innovative introduced evidence, however, that written non-disclosure agreements were not normally used in the industry, at least during the preliminary stages of acquisition relevant here. Innovative also introduced testimony that it either obtained oral pledges of confidentiality from interested parties or did not divulge confidential information to them. In regard to representatives of Bowen Supply who occasionally visited the production facility, Innovative introduced testimony that it would hide some of the raw materials used in the process and bring out others in their stead to prevent these representatives from learning the formulas. One such representative testified that, although he was allowed to observe the production line, he was unable to determine how the final product was made. Another representative of Bowen Supply stated that the plant was not in operation at the time he visited it. Yet another Bowen Supply official testified that he learned very little about the production process during his visits, and did not indicate that he had either learned or had access to the formulas.

A representative of another company expressing an interest in acquiring Innovative prepared a report that contained a general description of Panel Brick, including a list of the gross proportions of raw materials used to produce it. Innovative subsequently sent a copy of this report to Bowen Supply. Innovative offered testimony that the representative who compiled the report was pledged to secrecy. The report did not disclose the exact proportions of raw materials used to produce Panel Brick, nor did it indicate the proportions of these materials relative to the three layers in which they were applied. After a thorough examination of this document and of the Panel Brick formulas, we hold that a reasonable jury could find that Innovative did not compromise the secrecy of those formulas by sending the report to Bowen Supply. Furthermore, we find that the evidence as a whole, together with all reasonable inferences drawn therefrom, supports the jury's finding that Innovative took reasonably adequate steps to ensure the secrecy of its formulas.

Id., 793 F.2d at 884–86.

What precautions would you advise your clients to take as a routine matter in order to maintain the secrecy of their "know-how" and proprietary information?

Some clients go to much greater lengths to protect their valuable trade secrets than the plaintiff in *Innovative Construction*. According to report, only two executives of the Coca–Cola Company know the formula for Coke, and they are not allowed to fly together on the same airplane. There is only one written version of the formula, and it is kept in the vault of an Atlanta bank. It can be removed only by resolution of the Coca–Cola Board of Directors. In 1985, during the course of litigation between the Coca–Cola Company and some of its bottlers, a Federal District Judge ordered Coca–Cola to disclose its formulas for old Coke, new Coke, diet Coke and caffeine-free Coke in discovery. The court provided that the disclosure would be made pursuant to a protective order which would prevent the formulas being made available to anyone outside of the litigation. The Coca–Cola Company flatly refused to comply with the order, risking contempt-of-court charges and a possible default judgement in the litigation. See *Coca-Cola Is Told to Disclose Secret of Coke Formula*, Wall St. J., Aug. 21, 1985, at 8, col. 2. In a letter to the Court, Coca–Cola stated: "The Company has concluded that disclosure of its secret formulae, regardless of the terms of any protective order, could well lead ultimately to public disclosure. In that event, the gravity of the harm to the Company and its bottling system would be incalculable and irreparable." 32 Pat. Trademark & Copyright J. (BNA) No. 783 at 123 (June 5, 1986). Fortunately for Coca–Cola, the judge decided merely to enter a preclusion order in the litigation, giving the bottlers "the advantage of every possible inference that fairly could be drawn from the formulae evidence sought," and ordered Coca–Cola to pay the bottlers' expenses and fees attributable to the Company's failure to obey the court's discovery order. Coca–Cola Bottling Co. of Shreveport, Inc. v. The Coca–Cola Co., 110 F.R.D. 363, 369 (D.Del.1986).

4. *The competitive value requirement.* Information must have "competitive value" in order to qualify as a trade secret. That is, it must derive value from the fact that the owner has it and his competitors do not. Why impose this requirement? What evidence did the *Cybertek* court rely on to find that the plaintiff's computer program had the requisite value?

Most courts have understood the "competitive value" requirement to mandate that the alleged trade secret provide economic, or commercial benefits to its owner. In Religious Technology Center v. Wollersheim, 796 F.2d 1076 (9th Cir.1986), *cert. denied*, 479 U.S. 1103, 107 S.Ct. 1336, 94 L.Ed.2d 187 (1987), a religious group developed materials to be used in the course of its religious practices, and maintained them in secrecy. Another religious group obtained a copy of the materials and threatened to publish it. The first group brought an action for trade secret infringement. The U.S. Court of Appeals for the Ninth Circuit, applying California law, held that the plaintiffs' materials did not constitute trade secrets:

> To be protectible as a trade secret under either Restatement section 757 or the new California statute [the Uniform Trade Secrets Act], the confidential material must convey an actual or potential *commercial* advantage, presumably measurable in dollar terms. We do not accept that a trade secret can be based on the *spiritual advantage* the Church believes its adherents acquire over non-adherents by using the materials in the prescribed manner.

Id. at 1090. In a later opinion in the same case, the Court of Appeals clarified that its opinion in *Wollersheim* did not preclude recovery if the plaintiff alleged and proved that its materials had economic, as well as spiritual value. The plaintiffs, returning to District Court after the *Wollersheim* opinion, alleged that "Defendant will obtain an economic advantage that they would not otherwise possess which will be used to divert parishioners, the value and goodwill of which cannot be monetarily measured." Religious Technology Center v. Scott, 869 F.2d 1306, 1310 (9th Cir.1989).

5. *The trade secret cause of action.* Assuming that the plaintiff has a valid trade secret, his property rights are by no means absolute. Trade secret law only enables the owner to prevent others' acquisition, disclosure or use of the secret if their actions involve a breach of confidential duty or other improper behavior. Restatement of Torts § 757, set forth above, prohibits

disclosure or use of trade secrets under four scenarios, each involving a breach of confidence or other improper behavior either on the part of the defendant himself or on the part of the person who supplied the trade secret to the defendant.[6] The Uniform Trade Secrets Act, § 1 (1) and (2), provides as follows:

(1) "Improper means" includes theft, bribery, misrepresentation, breach or inducement of a breach of a duty to maintain secrecy, or espionage through electronic or other means;

(2) "Misappropriation" means:

(i) acquisition of a trade secret of another by a person who knows or has reason to know that the trade secret was acquired by improper means; or

(ii) disclosure or use of a trade secret of another without express or implied consent by a person who

(A) used improper means to acquire knowledge of the trade secret; or

(B) at the time of disclosure or use, knew or had reason to know that his knowledge of the trade secret was

(I) derived from or through a person who had utilized improper means to acquire it;

(II) acquired under circumstances giving rise to a duty to maintain its secrecy or limit its use; or

(III) derived from or through a person who owed a duty to the person seeking relief to maintain its secrecy or limit its use; or

(C) before a material change of his position, knew or had reason to know that it was a trade secret and that knowledge of it had been acquired by accident or mistake.[7]

Compare the language of Restatement § 757 with Uniform Act § 1, above. Is there any material difference in coverage? On what basis does the *Cybertek* court justify granting relief to the plaintiff? Can you pinpoint the precise subdivision of Restatement of Torts § 757 and Uniform Act § 1 under which the *Cybertek* fact situation would fall?

The meaning of "improper means" other than breach of confidence will be considered in a later section. Breaches of confidence are considered in Note 6, below.

6. *Breaches of Confidence.* There are several different approaches to finding a duty of confidentiality, or duty to maintain secrecy, on the part of defendants in trade secret cases.

---

6. With regard to Restatement § 757(d), using a trade secret with notice that it was obtained by mistake can be viewed as "improper" behavior because it is unethical. The corresponding provisions of the Restatement (Third) of Unfair Competition can be found in §§ 40–43.

7. Reprinted with the permission of the National Conference of Commissioners on Uniform State Laws.

First, the defendant may have a duty by virtue of her relationship to the plaintiff. For example, an agent owes a duty of loyalty to her principal which includes a duty to refrain from disclosing the principal's confidential information which she learned within the scope of the agency relationship. See Restatement (Second) of Agency § 395 (1958). When an employer gives an employee a trade secret to use in the course of her duties, for example, and the employee has notice that it is a secret, her duty of loyalty to the employer dictates that she refrain from using or disclosing the trade secret without the employer's permission. This is true even if there is no express contractual agreement to this effect between them. Other relationships in which a duty of confidentiality exists include the traditional "fiduciary" relationships such as partnership and joint venture relationships, and attorney-client relationships.

Second, courts sometimes imply a duty of confidentiality through "contract implied in fact" and "contract implied in law" ("quasi-contract") theories. A contract implied in fact is simply a contractual agreement between the parties whose existence is proven through the parties' actions (which manifest a meeting of minds) rather than through their express words. Did the parties, through their actions, indicate agreement that if the plaintiff revealed the trade secret to the defendant, the defendant would refrain from disclosing or using it without the plaintiff's permission? A contract implied in law, or quasi-contract, in contrast, is not based on evidence of the parties' intent. Rather, courts imply a contractual duty of confidence in order to avoid an injustice. Would permitting the defendant to make free use of the trade secret under the circumstances result in unjust enrichment? If so, the court may impose a duty on the defendant to maintain the trade secret in confidence and refrain from exploiting it.

A court might rely on either of the implied contract theories to find a duty of confidentiality in a given case. For example, assume that X Company approaches Y, a wealthy person, about investing a large sum of money in the business. In the course of his pitch, the president of X Company tells Y that the investment will be a good one because X Company has a special "top secret" manufacturing process. Y asks what it is, and the president tells her. Note that under these circumstances, Y had notice that the process was confidential and asked to hear it. In doing so, she could be characterized as impliedly acknowledging the secrecy and agreeing to retain it as a condition of disclosure, regardless of whether she ultimately invests in X Company. She might also be characterized as agreeing that her use of the secret will be limited to the purpose for which it was disclosed: making an investment decision. This characterization would result in a contract implied in fact. A court unwilling to find agreement on Y's part might still justify imposing a duty of confidentiality on the grounds that Y would be unjustly enriched, under the circumstances, if permitted to use the X Company's trade secret. This would result in a contract implied in law.

What if the president, in the course of making his pitch, specifically asked Y if she wanted to hear the process, and she said yes? Same result? What if the president simply revealed the process (without any express discussion about whether Y wanted to hear it) and Y listened without protest? Should Y still owe a duty of confidentiality? What if Y protested, but the president told her anyway? See Restatement of Torts, § 757, cmt. j (1939); Restatement

(Third) of Unfair Competition § 41, cmt. b (1995); I R. Milgrim, Milgrim on Trade Secrets, §§ 3.02–3.03 (1999).

Finally, a duty of confidentiality may arise from an express contractual provision. Express employee nondisclosure agreements, such as the one in *Cybertek*, are widely used in the United States. In addition to employees, trade secret owners frequently ask suppliers, distributors, purchasers, licensees and others associated with the business who might have access to confidential information to sign express nondisclosure agreements. Why should businesses resort to such express contractual agreements to maintain information in confidence when their employees and business associates are likely already to be subject to a duty of confidentiality under the common law, as described above? Should it matter which of the above bases the court relies on to find a duty?

7. *Licenses.* A license is a contract in which the owner of a trade secret or other intellectual property authorizes another party (the "licensee") to use the intellectual property without liability, generally in return for payment. Licensing a trade secret gives an owner flexibility and the opportunity to capitalize more fully on the trade secret.[8] As a general matter, persons who retain title to property and merely license others to use it have greater leeway under the law to control the recipients' use than do persons who convey title to the property outright. Software manufacturers and distributors, in particular, have seized upon the license mechanism in an attempt to retain trade secrecy in the computer programs they market. In the case of custom-made programs or programs disseminated to a limited number of users, software companies may license their customers to use the program, rather than sell the program outright. In the license agreement, the software company requires the customer to retain the program in confidence and act in a manner that will preserve secrecy. (For example, the customer may be required to promise not to reverse engineer the program's object code to learn how the program works.)

It is not feasible for software companies to negotiate individual licenses in the case of mass-marketed programs. Accordingly, they have devised the "shrink-wrap license." Here is an example: On the outside of the package of its mass-marketed word processing program, in prominent print directly under the cellophane wrapping, X Company instructs persons buying the program to read the accompanying "legal agreement." The "agreement" states that the act of using the software will indicate the buyer's consent to the terms and conditions of the agreement, and will bind him. If he doesn't agree, he should return the unused program for a refund. The agreement then goes on, among other things, to say that while payment of the price of the software transfers full title to the disk in which the software is embodied, it merely creates a license to use the computer program itself, title to the program remaining in the manufacturer. The agreement then provides that

---

8. Of course, licensing also exposes the owner to greater risk. The more people who know and use the trade secret, the more risk there is that the information will reach competitors or the general public, compromising its status as a trade secret. While the licensing process may give rise to an implied duty of confidentiality under the common law, licensors generally include express confidentiality provisions in the license agreement, and require the licensee to undertake specific precautions to protect the secret.

the program is the manufacturer's trade secret and that the purchaser may not reverse engineer, decompile, disassemble or translate the object code. Doing these things will terminate the license and subject the buyer to liability. Should shrink-wrap agreements of this sort be enforceable? If you were challenging the validity of such an agreement in court, what arguments would you raise?

In sales of computer programs over the Internet, distributors may employ "click-wrap" licenses, which serve the same purpose as shrink-wraps. Here, the distributor provides access to the restrictions on the purchaser's computer screen and requires the purchaser to "click" his consent to them before he can complete the purchase transaction and receive the program via electronic transmission. Would the same arguments that might be raised against enforcement of shrink-wraps be applicable in the case of click-wraps?

There has been tremendous uncertainty regarding the enforceability of such "mass-market" license restrictions. Recently, the American Law Institute (ALI) undertook to draft a set of guidelines for enforcement of "standard form transfers of generally available software." See American Law Institute, Principles of the Law of Software Contracts (Proposed Final Draft, 2009). The Principles essentially suggest that such forms be deemed enforceable contracts as long as the terms are reasonably accessible and reasonably comprehensible. *Id.*, at § 2.02. However, the Principles recommend that courts be especially sensitive to several potential defenses: 1) that enforcement will conflict with (and therefore be preempted by) federal patent and copyright laws; 2) unconscionability; and 3) voidness for reasons of public policy. *Id.*, §§ 1.09–1.11.

8. *Use of the trade secret.* Is it relevant to a trade secret misappropriation claim that the defendant altered the trade secret, adapting it to his own needs, or perhaps greatly improving it? In such a case, can the defendant be deemed to be "using" the plaintiff's trade secret? Should there be a point at which the defendant's alterations are so great that he escapes liability altogether?

9. *Liability of persons receiving the trade secret from someone other than the plaintiff.* The *Cybertek* court held both Whitfield and his new employer, Tracor, liable for trade secret misappropriation. Under which of the Restatement of Torts §§ 757 or 758 theories can Tracor's liability be justified? Under which of the subsections of Uniform Trade Secrets Act § 1? To be liable under either the Restatement or the Uniform Act, persons obtaining a trade secret through an intermediate source, rather than directly from the plaintiff, must have notice, or reason to know, that the information is a trade secret and was obtained or is being disclosed through improper conduct or a breach of confidence. Under what circumstances should recipients be deemed to have notice of these facts? See Restatement of Torts, § 757, cmts. l, m (1939); Restatement (Third) of Unfair Competition § 40, cmt. d (1995). What is the earliest point at which Tracor may have had the requisite notice?

10. *Treatises.* For comprehensive treatment of trade secret issues, see R. Milgrim, Milgrim on Trade Secrets (2009); M. Jager, Trade Secrets Law (2005); and M. Epstein, Epstein on Intellectual Property (5th ed. 2006 & Supp.). For a thought-provoking exploration of the history and policy justifica-

tions underlying trade secret law, see Bone, *A New Look at Trade Secret Law: Doctrine in Search of Justification*, 86 Cal. L. Rev. 241 (1998).

PROBLEMS

1. Federated Metal Products, Inc., is a medium-sized business with a research and development department consisting of five engineers. Federated has informal hiring practices: It does not require its workers to sign formal employment or confidentiality agreements. However, it does periodically notify employees with access to confidential information that they are working with company trade secrets, and that the secrets should be retained in confidence. Federated restricts outsiders' access to areas of the plant that might reveal trade secret information about its manufacturing processes, and restricts the ability of outsiders to gain access to its internal computer network. However, it has never adopted security measures to limit employees' ability to reproduce or transmit sensitive documents over the company's internal computer network.

At the company's direction, Federated's research and development staff collaborated in a series of experiments to improve on a standard, commercially available chemical solution the company used to coat metal tool molds in its manufacturing process. They devised and tested thirteen variations on the chemical formula. As a result of their experiments, they learned that eight of the variations made no appreciable difference, four actually decreased manufacturing efficiency as compared with the standard formula, and one variation resulted in a material improvement in efficiency. They described their results in a memorandum, which was lodged in an intra-departmental database. The information contained in the memorandum was not generally known in the industry, though a small handful of other companies had conducted their own somewhat similar tests, retaining the results in secrecy. A heading at the top of the memorandum cautioned that the information was confidential in nature.

Edwards joined the Federated research and development department several months after the memorandum was drafted. He came across it in the database and made a copy for himself. When he left Federated's employ a year later to join the research and development staff of a competitor, he took his copy with him. Subsequently he relied on it in advising his new employer not to proceed with tests of five variations of the chemical solution it used to coat its metal molds. He explained that he had "had experience" with the proposed experimental variations, and that they would either fail to improve, or actually impair, the efficiency of the manufacturing process. The competitor took Edwards at his word and did not proceed with its plans to test the five variations.

Does Federated have a viable cause of action for trade secret misappropriation against Edwards or his new employer?

2. Martinez is a professional "finder" of targets for corporate acquisition (that is, a professional "matchmaker" for corporate takeovers and mergers). One day Martinez took Lee, the president of Megacorp, Inc., to lunch. Martinez hoped to convince Lee that Megacorp should contract with

him for acquisition finder services. To impress Lee, he told her about some of his recent "finds." He described how he had found the perfect acquisition target for his client, Bigfish Corp. "It's fat with cash," he said, "and ripe for the picking." Martinez leaned forward and lowered his voice: "I'll tell you in confidence," he whispered, and paused dramatically. "Bigfish has high standards for corporate acquisitions, and this little company, Fishstix, Inc., is right on the money." Martinez went on to explain that he had discovered Fishstix and deduced its desirability as a take-over target after a month of laborious research in specialized business and financial news and Security Exchange Commission databases.

Lee had never heard of Fishstix, Inc. After lunch, she returned to her office and instructed her staff members to do some quick research on Fishstix, and to advise her on the potential advantages of a takeover. Within three days Megacorp had launched a take-over bid, and ultimately acquired Fishstix. Business page reporters nationwide lauded the acquisition as a highly profitable one for all concerned.

All, that is, except for Martinez, who will not collect a finder's fee from Bigfish. Has he got a viable cause of action against Lee and Megacorp for trade secret misappropriation?

3. Computer programs are originally written in "source code," a language comprised of words and mathematical notations that trained persons can read. When a program is completed, it is translated into "object code," which directs the electrical impulses that operate the computer. Most object code is impossible for humans to read. It is the object code that is encoded on the disk, chip or other medium distributed to program users. Assume that a software company mass-produces and distributes disks containing its program to the public, but keeps its source code in confidence, locked away in the company safe. Should proprietary information contained in the program's structure be deemed sufficiently "secret" to merit trade secret protection, if the information is taken for use in a manner that constitutes a breach of confidence or improper conduct?

4. Assume that A Company manufactures carbonated drinks. A Company and B Company enter into negotiations for B to become a bottler and distributor of A's carbonated drinks. During negotiations, A's representative tells the B Company representative that A will want B to use its (A's) trade secret bottling method, because it preserves the "fizz" better than other methods. B Company agrees to use the method and also to keep it in confidence. After the agreement is finalized, A reveals the bottling method to B. B uses the method in bottling and distributing A's carbonated drink for three years. Then B Company goes out of business. A finds another bottler/distributor to replace B.

The following year, C Company, which makes and distributes its own carbonated drinks, buys the assets of the now defunct B Company. When it takes an inventory, it finds a set of written instructions for bottling which, while not labeled as such, is A Company's secret method. C finds the method useful and implements it in its bottling plant.

Two years later, A Company learns that C is using the secret method and demands that C cease all further use. C refuses and continues to use the method. Six months later, A files a lawsuit against C Company for trade secret misappropriation. Assuming that the method is in fact A Company's trade secret, should A prevail?

5.   D Company and E Company are competitors. One day an executive of D prepares a letter to the president of E, and instructs her secretary to attach some documents to it and put it in the mail. While the secretary is assembling the attachments, a copy of D Company's trade secret customer list, which is also on the secretary's desk, accidentally gets mixed in and is sent along with the letter to the president of E Company. The list is marked "confidential." Is E Company free to use the list under the Uniform Trade Secrets Act? Under Restatement § 757?

6.   Owners of copyright in motion pictures are hesitant to make digital copies of their motion pictures available on digital versatile discs (DVDs) due to their fear that purchasers will copy and distribute them over the Internet, undercutting their market. Accordingly, they create a protection scheme that will prevent digital copies from being made. This system, known as "Content Scrambling System" (CSS), is an encryption system. It encrypts the movies on DVDs, so that they cannot be played in DVD players lacking a set of master keys and a decryption algorithm. DVD players equipped with the keys and algorithm can play the movie, but cannot be used to copy it. The copyright owners license various manufacturers of DVD players to incorporate the master keys and algorithm into their DVD players, but bind the licensees to maintain the CSS technology in confidence.

The encryption software is subject to a license restriction that expressly prohibits users from reverse engineering it. Johansen, a European, nonetheless reverse engineers it and obtains the underlying proprietary information about how to "unlock" the CSS encryption. He then writes his own software (called DeCSS) that decrypts movies stored on DVDs and enables users to copy and distribute those movies. Johansen posts his DeCSS program on his web site. Subsequently, U.S. web site operators copy Johansen's program and post it on their own web sites. They allege, among other things, that the DeCss program will enable Linux users to use and enjoy DVDs, and make Linux more attractive and viable to consumers.

The motion picture copyright owners sue the U.S. web site operators for trade secret infringement. Assuming that the CSS technology was a trade secret at the time Johansen reverse engineered it, how would you evaluate the claim? Would enjoining the U.S. web site operators violate the First Amendment?

A. THE SPECIAL PROBLEMS OF CUSTOMER INFORMATION, GENERAL EMPLOYEE KNOWLEDGE AND SKILL

FLEMING SALES CO., INC. v. BAILEY

United States District Court, Northern District of Illinois, 1985.
611 F.Supp. 507.

SHADUR, DISTRICT JUDGE.

[Fleming Sales Company, Inc. ("Fleming") charges Joseph Bailey ("Bailey") and his company, Unlimited Sales of America, Inc. ("Unlimited") with trade secret misappropriation. Defendants have moved for summary judgment.]

FACTS[1]

Fleming, a family-owned manufacturers' representative business, has an original equipment manufacturers ("OEM") division headquartered in Elkhart, Indiana. Through its OEM division, Fleming is engaged by recreational vehicle ("RV") component manufacturers ("Fleming's principals") to market their products to RV manufacturers ("Fleming's customers"). Bailey was hired as a salesman in the OEM division in March 1977. In July 1980 Bailey was made General Manager of the OEM division, and in August 1983 he was placed on the Fleming Board of Directors. In the meantime he had turned the OEM division into a substantially better business operation for Fleming.

Despite Bailey's relatively rapid rise at Fleming, he had for some time been dissatisfied over what he perceived as his limited freedom to run the OEM division without oversight by Fleming management (he had been promised a "free hand" in that respect) and his limited future prospects in its family-owned structure. On April 27, 1984 Bailey wrote to Fleming Board Chairman Jack Grady ("Grady") explaining his dissatisfactions and announcing his decision to resign from Fleming and the Board of Directors effective May 1, 1984. In fact Bailey continued as OEM division head until May 18 and continued to receive his salary and benefits until the end of May. Bailey had entered into no written employment contract with Fleming, nor had he signed a restrictive covenant of any kind in Fleming's favor.

In late 1983, several months before his resignation from Fleming, Bailey joined with James Clipp ("Clipp") to form Unlimited for the manufacture of a rigid blind product to be sold as an accessory for RVs. Though formed in January 1984, Unlimited did not begin substantial

---

1. Rule 56 principles impose on the party moving for summary judgment the burden of establishing the lack of a genuine issue of material fact. For that purpose the court must, in viewing the evidence, draw all reasonable inferences in the light most favorable to the nonmovant. * * *

operations before June 1984. It has yet to begin manufacture of the rigid blind product.

In late June Bailey and Clipp formed a second company, Unified Sales of America, Inc. ("Unified"), to compete with Fleming's OEM division in the representation of RV component manufacturers. Bailey hired several Fleming salesmen to work with him at Unified and began to develop Unified's business with Fleming's principals and customers. Soon thereafter (in August 1984) Fleming initiated this lawsuit.

TRADE SECRETS CLAIM

Fleming contends Bailey has misappropriated several kinds of information, learned in the course of his employment and protectible as trade secrets, that he is now using to compete with the OEM division:

(1) the names and addresses of Fleming's customers;

(2) other information about customers, including the names of contact people and the customers' prior purchasing and payment histories, projected needs and buying procedures; and

(3) information as to Fleming's principals and other sources of supply, including the terms of principals' contracts with Fleming.

* * *

In 1982 Indiana adopted the Uniform Trade Secrets Act, Ind. Code §§ 24–2–3–1 to 24–2–3–8 (the "Act"), which authorizes injunctive relief, damages and recovery for unjust enrichment in trade secret misappropriation cases. Where the misappropriation was willful and malicious, the Act also allows an award of exemplary damages. * * *

What the parties' dispute really boils down to is whether or not the items of information defendants allegedly misappropriated qualify as "trade secrets" under the Act. If they do not, Fleming has no action against defendants for their use of the information, for Fleming did not elect to bind Bailey by a restrictive covenant of any kind.

After extensive discovery defendants assert there is no reasonable predicate for inferring the information (1) derives independent economic value by virtue of its confidentiality or (2) was the subject of efforts reasonably calculated to maintain its secrecy. Defendants contend each item of information was rather (1) general business knowledge bred of experience (and consequently lacking "independent economic value") or (2) information "readily ascertainable by proper means" or (3) both. In addition defendants say Fleming did not make reasonable efforts to maintain the secrecy of the information. Fleming retorts genuine fact issues exist as to each of those contentions.

This opinion will consider the parties' arguments as to each item of information in turn, but it is first worth taking a step backward to gain a perspective that might otherwise get lost in the welter of citations to cases, affidavits and depositions the parties have set out against one another. Trade secrets law in general and the Act in particular were never intended "to act as a blanket *post facto* restraint on trade." *Steenhoven v. College Life Ins. Co. of America*, 460 N.E.2d 973, 975 n. 7 (Ind.App.1984). Thus the identity of a business' customers is no doubt a legitimate business interest protectible by a restrictive covenant, and the same may perhaps be true of other knowledge a company has amassed simply by virtue of having been in a particular line of business for a long period of time. But that right to impose contractual restraints does *not* render the same knowledge "trade secrets" in the absence of such restraints. Knowledge derived from experience does not automatically carry with it the ability to forestall others who have shared that experience (and thus that knowledge).

In other words, a court called on to define boundaries in this area must take care to strike a balance between (1) the underlying purposes of trade secrets law (to maintain standards of commercial ethics and to encourage research and innovation) and (2) the equally strong policy against inhibiting competition in the marketplace.[4] Analysis of Fleming's claims discloses it has sought to stifle legitimate competition rather than to resist unwarranted encroachment on its property rights.

1. Customer Lists

Fleming says Bailey, through his employment as general manager of its OEM division, had access to a comprehensive list of Fleming's customers. While there is no allegation—and no evidence—Bailey took a copy of the list with him when he left his employment,[5] Fleming does assert he took with him knowledge of the customers' names—knowledge he later used to compete (unfairly) against Fleming. Defendants do not deny Bailey came away from Fleming with a knowledge of who its customers were, but defendants argue (1) Fleming did not exert reasonable efforts to maintain the secrecy of that information and (2) the information was readily ascertainable by other means.

Fleming has offered affidavit and deposition evidence indicating a policy of maintaining the confidentiality of the customer list and virtually all other business information. Grady Aff. p. 11 says he "has given directions and established the policy that as much information as possible of Fleming is to remain confidential." Each Fleming employee received a "Rules and Regulations" letter specifying as one basis for termination "[c]ommunication or action detrimental to Fleming Sales Company, including but not limited to, exposing confidential information." As for customers' identity in particular, Fleming has tendered a showing its complete list of customers was available to only a few top Fleming

---

4. Fleming Surreply Mem. 6 is simply wrong in contending the distinction between "confidential information" and "trade secrets" is purely "semantic."

5. In fact Bailey swears:

In connection with my resignation and leaving Fleming I did not take with me any Fleming business records.

Fleming offers no affirmative evidence to the contrary, with one exception discussed later in this opinion.

employees, though OEM division salesmen and office personnel had access to lists identifying all of Fleming's Elkhart customers and some, but not all of, its customers outside Indiana. Fleming claims no other employee had access to the list.

Defendants acknowledge there is at least a fact issue as to how widely the customer lists were distributed within Fleming. Defendants point out, however (1) account lists were provided to Fleming's *principals* from time to time and (2) Fleming has no written policy and no clearly articulated procedures to ensure the confidentiality of the customer lists. For example the lists are not kept under lock and key or marked "confidential," and salesmen routinely keep copies in their offices. Moreover customer list information necessarily appeared on shipping documents stored in Fleming's warehouses.

Of course the absence of specific confidentiality procedures (whether written or unwritten) does not itself negate the existence of "reasonable" efforts to maintain secrecy—all the Act requires. Fleming's OEM division was, after all, a *sales* organization. Constant dealings with its customers—whether by phone, letter or in person—was the essence of the business. Naturally Fleming employees whose business it was to maintain that contact needed ready access to customer information. By the same token, distribution of account list information to principals or on occasion to other customers may well have been necessary to the pursuit of Fleming's business. Fleming was plainly not required to shoot itself in the foot to meet the "reasonable efforts" requirement of the Act. So long as Fleming scrupulously limited distribution of customer list information to employees and outsiders whose access was necessary to Fleming's successful pursuit of its business, it must be deemed to have satisfied the "reasonable efforts" requirement, particularly if those given access to the information were also advised to preserve its confidentiality, as Fleming indicates they were.[6] Were that the critical issue, the factual dispute as to Fleming's efforts in that regard (a dispute defendants acknowledge) would compel denial of defendants' motion.

But there is more to the story. All the efforts in the world to preserve confidentiality of information will not suffice if the information is not secret in the first place—if it is "readily ascertainable" by other proper means. Defendants point to several pieces of evidence demonstrating the customer list information could be procured by such other means:

> 1. Grady stated that as a rule Fleming's principals know "the customers purchasing its products, the amount of product purchased, and the prices paid for those products."
>
> 2. Many of Fleming's customers are listed either in telephone directory Yellow Pages or in the trade publication *RV Business*.

---

6. No matter how scrupulous Fleming may have been in handling the customer lists, they might nevertheless not qualify as trade secrets if the demands of Fleming's business required so broad a distribution (either inside or outside the company) as to make it impossible as a practical matter to maintain confidentiality. That question need not be resolved in light of the text analysis.

3. Others in the business testified (a) competing sales companies generally know who each other's customers are and (b) it is generally easy for a principal's competitor to find out who that principal's customers are.

Fleming counters only by arguing defendants are unlikely to be able to reproduce Fleming's customer list from those sources. Not all principals will necessarily be willing to identify their existing customers to new sales companies. Similarly *RV Business* and the Yellow Pages list only a relatively small proportion of the customers on Fleming's list. So, too, a general knowledge of a competitor's customers is something significantly less than access to the customer list itself.

Those assertions may perhaps create a factual issue as to defendants' ability to reproduce the entire customer list precisely from other sources. But what Rule 56 requires is a "material" (that is, outcome-determinative) factual issue. Here it is undisputed that substantial information as to the identity of Fleming's customers is available from other sources. And Fleming has come forward with no evidence at all showing defendants have sought to pursue customers they would not have discovered even without Bailey's exposure to the Fleming list.[7] Especially in a market where customers did business with more than one sales company or were open to the possibility of shifting business from one company to another, it is simply unreasonable to construe the Act's "readily ascertainable" standard as requiring exact duplication of the information on the customer list.

One other aspect of the problem bears mentioning—an aspect that bears not only on the customer-list issue but on each of the other claimed "trade secrets" categories. Fleming Mem. 5 (emphasis in original) urges "Bailey alone could not have taken Fleming's principals from it; he had to have the help of *Fleming's* salesmen."[8] But absent some independent tort (such as actionable interference with advantageous relationships) or extraordinary circumstances * * *, it is perfectly permissible to build an organization by hiring a competitor's personnel. And if the consequence is that the individual employees' knowledge of pieces of the competitor's business is aggregated to provide a more comprehensive view of the total picture, that too can legitimately serve as the source of "readily ascertainable" information in the sense of the Act. Even the proverbial six blind men, if they pooled their information, might well produce a reasonably good description of the elephant.

7. Eli Magee, an individual with wide experience in the RV business, testified that even customer companies new to the business become generally known in the industry within six months to a year via advertising and exhibitions at trade shows.

8. Fleming Mem. 15–16 says in a pejorative tone:

In fact, Defendant Bailey has assigned Fleming's former salesmen to exactly the same territories they had previously covered for Fleming. In Indiana, this means the exact same customers as they previously have visited as Fleming salesmen. In particular, they are now soliciting Fleming's customers for Fleming's former principal Vernco.

Thus no genuine issue of *material* fact exists as to the availability of the substance of Fleming's customer list from other legitimate sources. Defendants are part way home on their motion.

2. *Other Information As to Customers*

Fleming also claims trade secret protection for other types of customer information including:

> knowledge of the individual persons at these customers to contact in order to effectuate sales; the prior purchasing history of the customers; the product and service requirements; their present and future projected needs; the packages that Fleming must put together in order to sell particular products; their payment histories; and their buying procedures.

Fleming does not assert any of that information was systematically recorded or compiled in any way, though it says much of the information was supplied to Fleming salesmen in the course of their training. Again Fleming claims to have exerted reasonable efforts to maintain its confidentiality.

Once more that represents only part of the story, and a skewed version at that. Fleming seeks to make the "trade secrets" label carry too much baggage. All the information it tries to wrap in the Act's mantle is nothing more than the kind of knowledge any successful salesman necessarily acquires through experience. In the Act's terms, it is information "readily ascertainable by proper means" over the course of time without efforts beyond those ordinarily exerted by salesmen in developing customers.

That is not to say Bailey may not have derived some benefit from his access to the collective experience of Fleming's OEM division (experience to which Bailey himself doubtless contributed significantly during the course of his employment). It is rather to say such information comprises general skills and knowledge acquired in the course of employment. Those are things an employee is free to take and to use in later pursuits, especially if they do not take the form of written records, compilations or analyses.

Any other rule would force a departing employee to perform a prefrontal lobotomy on himself or herself. It would disserve the free market goal of maximizing available resources to foster competition. Or to frame the issue in the way discussed earlier in this opinion, it would not strike a proper balance between the purposes of trade secrets law and the strong policy in favor of fair and vigorous business competition.

All this does not render helpless an employer worried that the skills and knowledge an employee acquires during the course of employment will give him or her an undue competitive advantage. Nothing prevents such an employer from guarding its interests by a restrictive covenant.[10]

---

10. Of course the concern about inhibiting fair competition also informs the law of restrictive covenants. In Indiana, as in most jurisdictions, *Licocci v. Cardinal Associates, Inc.*, 445 N.E.2d 556, 561 (Ind.1983):

But it would really be unfair competition to allow the employer *without* such a covenant to obtain trade secret status for the fruits of ordinary experience in the business, thus compelling former employees to reinvent the wheel as the price for entering the competitive market. Once again defendants must prevail.

3. *Information As to Principals*

Fleming Mem. 16 concedes the identity of its principals is widely known and therefore not a trade secret, but it says other principal-related information is: the identity of the contact people, the sales volumes for particular products, the existence of "minor" items provided by principals or other suppliers for use with a principal's products or necessary to permit use of the products, and the terms of Fleming's contracts with principals. No elaboration is required here: All the earlier analysis as to customer-related information applies with equal force. Once more the information is part and parcel of a salesman's experience in the RV business. Bailey naturally carried away from his years at Fleming a familiarity with the contracts, products and personnel of the principals he did business with, not to mention an awareness of what products sold best. For reasons already surveyed the Act's "trade secret" definition simply does not embrace that kind of information.

Fleming tries to bolster its claim by pointing to defendants' possession of some papers containing information about Fleming's relationship with its principals and other suppliers. Bailey discovered those documents, all from the 1981–83 period, in his garage well after this litigation began, and he produced them in response to a Fleming document request. Bailey has explained he periodically carried papers home during the course of his employment and at one point, well before his resignation, stored them all in a box in his garage. Fleming has offered nothing to contradict that explanation. What really controls, however, is that the specific documents Fleming points to do not—even with all inferences in Fleming's favor as Rule 56 requires—create a *material* fact issue. One of them compiles basic information about a number of Fleming principals, including the commissions each pays to Fleming. But because that information is of the sort Bailey was likely to know anyway, and because there is no evidence to indicate defendants made use of the document, Bailey's mere possession is insufficient to raise a genuine issue of fact.

Also among the papers in the box Bailey found in his garage were invoices with the names of two suppliers who provide Fleming with products for resale. Fleming argues the identity of those suppliers is secret, yet Bailey approached one of them—Runglin International ("Runglin")—in an effort to obtain goods for his new sales company. Fleming

---

All such covenants as this are in restraint of trade and are not favored by the law. They will be enforced only if they are reasonable with respect to the covenantee, the covenantor, and the public interest.

But if an express covenant were nonenforceable because of overbreadth, the employer could scarcely expect protection from the common law (or the codified common law) of trade secrets.

says that shows Bailey was making use of information gleaned from the documents he had retained. Defendants, however, point to Grady's own deposition testimony that he and Bailey traveled to the Orient in 1984 with a Runglin representative to explore foreign supplier sources. Bailey thus knew of Runglin independently of the documents. Again there is nothing to suggest Bailey's retention of the documents was anything but the oversight he claims it was.

4. Conclusion

There is a telling passage at Fleming Mem. 17:

> [T]he RV Business Directory reveals a most important fact concerning Defendants' actions relative to Fleming. The directory lists several hundred manufacturers of equipment utilized by the RV industry. Bailey could easily have undertaken to represent these other manufacturers. Furthermore, Bailey could have solicited the many thousands of manufacturers of equipment not currently involved with the RV business to bring them into that industry as did Ken Lail. However, Bailey chose not to follow this course of action; rather, he went after those principals whom he had personal contact with because of his position with Fleming, that is, Fleming's principals.

Fleming unconsciously reveals something of itself: Its desire to attach a "trade secrets" label to its own generalized business skills, and to the skills acquired by Bailey while in its employ, simply to prevent competition by its former employee.

But as the Indiana Court of Appeals stated in *Steenhoven*, 460 N.E.2d at 975 n. 7:

> Insofar as College Life attempts to merely restrain Steenhoven's competition, we believe the Uniform Trade Secrets Act to be an improper vehicle therefor. The fact that Steenhoven possesses certain knowledge acquired within the course of his employment does not mandate that, upon his departure, Steenhoven must wipe clean the slate of his memory.

So here Fleming may not look to the Act to restrain competition from Bailey, especially given the nature of the information in issue here. Fleming has come forward with nothing to indicate that the allegedly misappropriated information rose to the "trade secrets" level. Business experience and knowhow as reflected in that information, however valuable, are not something the law protects from the rigors of the marketplace. Defendants' motion is granted as to Count I and its trade secrets claims.

[The court granted summary judgement to the defendants.]

Notes and Questions

1. *Customer lists as trade secrets.* What leads the *Fleming* court to find that the customer list fails to qualify as a trade secret?

Compare Webcraft Technologies, Inc. v. McCaw, 674 F.Supp. 1039 (S.D.N.Y.1987). In that case, Webcraft, a custom printer engaging in "in-line finishing," sought relief against McCaw, its former sales representative. McCaw had signed a Webcraft employment agreement which, among other things, barred disclosure of Webcraft's "trade secrets," which the agreement defined as including the names and needs of Webcraft customers and pricing information and "any other confidential information or data relating to the business of Webcraft which is not publicly known." *Id.*, at 1043. The agreement also required McCaw to return any documents regarding Webcraft's business upon termination of her employment. After approximately three years of employment with Webcraft, McCaw decided to move to Tech Web, a competitor of Webcraft's which also engaged in in-line finishing. While discussing prospective employment with Tech Web, McCaw gave a Tech Web representative a list of her fifteen or twenty best known customers and customer prospects at Webcraft. After agreeing to take the position at Tech Web, but before notifying Webcraft of her resignation, McCaw passed other confidential Webcraft information to Tech Web, including job specifications on accounts sought by Webcraft, pricing information, and a sketch of a proposed Webcraft product. Upon leaving Webcraft, McCaw took her rolodex, which contained customer names and contacts, eight pages of Webcraft quotes and pricing sheets relating to three jobs she had pursued while at Webcraft. Notwithstanding an exit interview and subsequent letter from Webcraft reminding her of her obligations under the employment contract, upon arriving at Tech Web, McCaw contacted most of her former Webcraft customers and viable prospects to solicit their business. She also gave her Webcraft customer and prospective customer information to her new employer, which entered it into its computer data base.

In considering the merits of Webcraft's claims against McCaw, the court found that the Webcraft customer list was likely to be found a trade secret under both New Jersey and New York law, but that the list of prospective customers probably was not:

> The list of prospects is put together from easily available sources. Although considerable work goes into compilation of the list, which includes some 10,000 names, McCaw may be correct that it would not be considered a trade secret.

> The list of Webcraft's customers is a completely different matter. Although it may be self-evident that Company A is a prospective customer for any seller of printing services, Webcraft sells the unusual in-line finishing process. The evidence shows it is a long, difficult process to educate and convert a prospective customer to the benefits of the process. Thus the confidential value of Webcraft's customer list lies not only in its identification of *someone's* customers for printing, but more importantly, especially for competitors in the in-line process like Tech Web, in that it identifies customers who have learned and have bought the benefits of in-line finishing.

> McCaw testified that developing a customer is an "arduous" process, that took between two months and two years to accomplish. The sales representative would first attempt, generally through a series of tele-

phone calls, to identify the proper contact at the prospect. Then, the telephone contact would be followed-up by letters, the sending of samples, attendance at meetings, development of presentations, and attempts to learn customer preferences and demands, and pricing information. As McCaw testified, "[i]t would take follow-up calls monthly or bi-weekly to keep in touch and develop a rapport with a customer." Ultimately, Webcraft might be asked to quote a job, which might or might not result in the placement of an order.

The long time needed to develop a customer was largely because "[t]he specialized nature of Webcraft's business was not useful to many people, many kinds of advertising or direct mail customers," and because "[t]o utilize Webcraft's technology, a lot of development takes place on the creative side, on the marketing side." "[E]ducating those people as to what in-line finishing is, is a very difficult, tedious and long process. Most people are intimidated by technology, not understanding it."

* * *

The evidence shows that Webcraft's customer lists took enormous time and effort to develop, including the development of a specialized knowledge of the customer's operations and needs; that the identity of customers for in-line finishing was by no means available to a stranger, but was confidential and a valuable trade secret. It was of particular value to Tech Web, whose own list coincided with McCaw's Webcraft list as to only two names.

In addition, * * * McCaw physically removed the portion of her customer and prospect list represented in her rolodex. Although she maintains that she could have remembered the names and contacts of her few customers and only took the rolodex for convenience, the fact remains that she took the list and no doubt it helped her remember far more than she could have remembered without it.

Finally, * * * McCaw signed an agreement including a non-solicitation provision and a trade secrets provision which expressly included customer lists within its protection.

I find that Webcraft is likely to succeed on the merits in demonstrating that the customer lists qualify as a trade secret, and that it is entitled to a preliminary injunction by reason of McCaw's misappropriation of it.

Id., at 1045–46.

How might one reconcile the result in *Fleming* with the result in *Webcraft*?

2. *Other "customer-related" and business information.* In *Fleming*, the plaintiff also alleged trade secret rights in such information as the contact person at each customer's office, the prior purchasing history of customers and projections of their future purchases, customer service requirements, customer payment histories and purchasing procedures. Why does the court reject the claim? Could such information ever qualify as a trade secret? Again, consider Judge Leval's opinion in *Webcraft* with regard to the plaintiff's claim that the contacts at each of its customers and the pricing information McCaw took were trade secrets:

McCaw acknowledged that it could easily take several telephone calls over a period of time, and perhaps a meeting, to identify the proper contact. Babiuk testified that it takes "extensive work to identify" the proper contact.

In support of her contention that the identity of such contacts is not subject to trade secrets protection, McCaw relies on *Great Lakes Carbon Corp. v. Koch Industries, Inc.,* 497 F.Supp. 462, 471 (S.D.N.Y.1980). But she reads too much into that case. Although the friends and acquaintances acquired in the course of a history of business dealings in an industry are not generally considered a trade secret, different considerations apply where a list of useful and influential contacts among customers and prospects is accumulated with considerable effort for the benefit of the employer.

Although some of McCaw's contacts are apparently friends, and in one case a relative, in general the list represents the names which she discovered through substantial research for sales purposes at the expense of her employer. Many of these names were recorded in the rolodex which McCaw brought with her to Tech Web.

This is data collected on behalf of and at the expense of Webcraft. It is not generally available information; it is maintained in confidence and is valuable to a competitor. Webcraft is likely to succeed on the merits in showing that the contacts list qualifies as a trade secret.

* * *

There is little doubt that information which McCaw learned while employed at Webcraft concerning customer preferences and Webcraft's pricing is protectible.

Webcraft Technologies, Inc. v. McCaw, 674 F.Supp. at 1046. Again, how might one reconcile *Fleming* and *Webcraft*?

3. *Striking a balance.* The *Fleming* court justifies limiting the reach of trade secret protection in that case on policy grounds, stating, "a court called on to define boundaries in this area must take care to strike a balance between (1) the underlying purposes of trade secrets law (to maintain standards of commercial ethics and to encourage research and innovation * * *) and (2) the equally strong policy against inhibiting competition in the marketplace." 611 F.Supp. at 511–12. In your opinion, how would extending trade secret protection to the customer names and information in the *Fleming* case affect that balance? Did the court, in deciding that trade secret protection should not be afforded, strike the right balance?

We have considered the general policy "balance" that exists throughout intellectual property law: providing property rights as an incentive to create vs. assuring free access to information and ideas to enhance competition. Note that the *Fleming* court identifies a second policy goal for the right-hand side of that contest in trade secret law: In addition to providing an incentive to create, trade secret law undertakes to maintain standards of commercial ethics. How does the existence of that second goal affect the mix? How might its existence influence the outcome of a given case? Can you discern any influence in the outcomes in *Fleming* and *Webcraft*, discussed above?

4. *Simple memory of documents or information vs. the physical taking of documents.* *Cybertek* and *Fleming* both discussed whether the defendant had physically taken documents from his prior employer or had merely relied on his memory of the employer's trade secrets. In *Webcraft*, discussed above, the court made a point of mentioning that the defendant had in fact taken documents from her prior employer. Why should it matter whether or not the former employee took documents containing the alleged trade secret, as long as he used the trade secret without permission after leaving the plaintiff's employ? See Ed Nowogroski Insurance, Inc. v. Rucker, 137 Wash.2d 427, 971 P.2d 936 (Sup.Ct.1999).

NOTE: PROTECTION FOR INFORMATION THAT DOES NOT QUALIFY AS TRADE SECRET: COVENANTS NOT TO COMPETE AND NONDISCLOSURE AGREEMENTS

The *Fleming* court observed that its denial of trade secret protection would not render an employer helpless to protect itself against the competition of former employees using the skills and knowledge they acquired in its employ. According to the court, the employer could protect itself through use of a restrictive covenant. In footnote 10, however, the court acknowledged that "the concern about inhibiting fair competition also informs the law of restrictive covenants," and observed that all such covenants "are in restraint of trade and are not favored by the law. They will be enforced only if they are reasonable with respect to the covenantee, the covenantor, and the public interest." In *Cybertek*, the court suggested that nondisclosure agreements may protect information that does not constitute a trade secret, but ultimately did not rely on that principle in finding for the plaintiff. As a practical matter, what additional rights do contractual provisions give an employer beyond what it would obtain under the common law of trade secrets or the Uniform Trade Secrets Act?

For our present purposes, two types of covenants are relevant: the nondisclosure agreement (in which the employee agrees not to disclose trade secret or other confidential information of the employer during and after her employment) and the covenant not to compete (in which the employee agrees not to compete with the employer after leaving its employ). Many employment agreements contain both a nondisclosure covenant and a covenant not to compete.

a. Covenants not to compete. Employers often rely on covenants not to compete to prevent employees from using information obtained on the job to compete with them, as occurred in *Fleming*. They often are unsuccessful in enforcing them, however. While state laws vary, consider Illinois case law as an example. The Appellate Court of Illinois described that state's general rule regarding covenants not to compete in Morrison Metalweld Process Corporation v. Valent, 97 Ill.App.3d 373, 52 Ill.Dec. 825, 422 N.E.2d 1034 (1981):

> Because agreements not to compete are, to at least some extent, restraints of trade, courts scrutinize such agreements carefully to ensure that they do not injure the public by impeding competition. Courts also consider the promisor's right to pursue his livelihood without undue

constraints. Where the limitation as to time and territory is not unreasonable, however, injunctive relief is customary and proper. Therefore, when a party to an employment contract agrees, in exchange for certain benefits, to refrain from competing with his or her employer, that agreement should be enforced where equitable. The basic test for enforcing such a covenant is whether it is "reasonably necessary to protect the employer from improper or unfair competition." (*Iroquois Industries Corp. v. Popik* (1980), 91 Ill.App.3d 505, 507, 47 Ill.Dec. 279, 281, 415 N.E.2d 4, 6.) Implicit in this standard are two separate inquiries: (1) Does the employer have a legitimate business interest needing protection? (2) Is the restrictive covenant reasonable in scope?

Not every alleged business interest will be deemed protectible through a covenant not to compete. (*Nationwide Advertising Service, Inc. v. Kolar* (1975), 28 Ill.App.3d 671, 329 N.E.2d 300.) In *Nationwide* we recognized two general situations in which an employer's interest in its customers is "proprietary," that is, legally protectible. First, we noted that "[a] covenant not to compete will be enforced if the employee acquired confidential information through his employment and subsequently attempted to use it for his own benefit." Second, we stated that "[a]n employer's interest in its customers also is deemed proprietary if, by the nature of the business, the customer relationship is near-permanent and but for his association with plaintiff, defendant would never have had contact with the clients in question." (*Id.*)

Id. 97 Ill.App.3d at 375–76.

In Iroquois Industries Corp. v. Popik, 91 Ill.App.3d 505, 47 Ill.Dec. 279, 415 N.E.2d 4 (1980), the plaintiff, Iroquois, was a distributor of paper products and packaging materials. Defendant Popik was hired as a regular salesman and required to sign an employment agreement containing a nondisclosure covenant and a covenant not to compete. The agreement explicitly stated that the company's customer information was confidential and that for two years following his employment, Popik could not compete with Iroquois with respect to "actual or prospective accounts, clients or customers of [Iroquois] upon whom [Popik] called during the time he was employed." The business was a competitive one, which required that salesmen get to know their clients well. Popik was to sell the company's products to any account in the metropolitan Chicago area. The number of potential customers amounted to "tens of thousands." Popik generated 90% to 95% of the 209 customers he called upon while employed by Iroquois. He did this by "cold calling" businesses whose names he acquired from the telephone book or industrial directories available to all salesmen in the industry. Iroquois gave Popik about a dozen accounts, which were customers who had either not made recent purchases or had made small purchases. After about five years, Popik left Iroquois and went to work for a competitor. He disclosed the names of customers he had called upon while employed by Iroquois to his new employer and made calls upon some of those accounts, soliciting their business and making sales. Iroquois sought a preliminary injunction.

The court noted that the injunction was dependent upon the enforceability of the restrictive covenant, which in turn depended upon whether the covenant was reasonably necessary to protect a legitimate business interest on Iroquois' part. The court added that the "prevention of competition per se * * * is an unreasonable purpose which renders the covenant unenforceable." *Id.*, 91 Ill.App.3d at 507. The court pointed out that notwithstanding the assertion in the employment agreement, the customer names were not confidential information. The names of the customers were readily ascertainable from publicly available sources. Moreover, it could not be said that Popik learned of the customers from the plaintiff, since he developed 90% to 95% of them himself. Thus, Iroquois lacked a protectible business interest. "Absent evidence of a protectible business interest in the 209 customers, enforcement of the restrictive covenant would be an effort to prevent competition per se." *Id.*, 91 Ill.App.3d at 509. The court denied relief.

Of course, covenants not to compete are used to protect more than just customer information. See Modern Controls, Inc. v. Andreadakis, 578 F.2d 1264 (8th Cir.1978). In that case the Eighth Circuit noted that under Minnesota law,

> confidential business information which does not rise to the level of a trade secret can be protected by a properly drawn covenant not to compete. * * * An employer need only show that an employee had access to confidential information and a court will then determine the overall reasonableness of the covenant in light of the interest sought to be protected.

Id., at 1268. The court then found that the defendant/employee's access to the following "confidential business information" justified a preliminary injunction to enforce his covenant not to compete, even though the information had not been proved to be trade secret: a method of laying a thin glass layer over conductors, the manner of making electrical connections to the conductors, the methods followed in creating channels in a glass cover plate that fit over the conductors, the manner of bonding the cover plate and the processes used in exhausting the air within the bonded plate.

Enforcement of a covenant not to compete will only be granted if the covenant's restrictions are "reasonable." Virginia's three-part test for reasonableness is typical. Under that test, the court must inquire:

> (1) Is the restraint, from the standpoint of the employer, reasonable in the sense that it is no greater than is necessary to protect the employer in some legitimate business interest?

> (2) From the standpoint of the employee, is the restraint reasonable in the sense that it is not unduly harsh and oppressive in curtailing his legitimate efforts to earn a livelihood?

> (3) Is the restraint reasonable from the standpoint of sound public policy?

Blue Ridge Anesthesia & Critical Care, Inc. v. Gidick, 239 Va. 369, 389 S.E.2d 467, 469 (Va. 1990). Courts strictly construe covenants not to compete against the employer, and the employer bears the burden of demonstrating that the restraint is reasonable.

A number of states have enacted statutes addressing the validity of noncompetition agreements. See, e.g., Cal. Bus. & Prof. Code § 16600 (West

2008); La. Rev. Stat. Ann. § 23:921 (West Supp. 2009); Mich. Comp. Laws Ann. § 445.774a (West 2002); Tex. Bus. & Com. Code Ann. § 15.50 (West Supp. 2002). For example, California Business & Professional Code § 16600 provides: "Except as provided in this chapter, every contract by which anyone is restrained from engaging in a lawful profession, trade, or business of any kind is to that extent void." The chapter excepts noncompetition agreements in the sale or dissolution of corporations (§ 16601), partnerships (§ 16602), and limited liability corporations (§ 16602.5).

In a recent opinion, the California Supreme Court rejected arguments that this statutory language only applied to contracts *totally prohibiting* an employee from engaging in a profession, trade, or business, and stressed that even reasonable, narrow *limitations* were unenforceable. Edwards v. Arthur Andersen, LLP, 44 Cal.4th 937, 81 Cal.Rptr.3d 282, 189 P.3d 285 (2008). In *Andersen,* the noncompetition agreement prohibited Edwards, for an 18–month period, from performing professional services of the type he had provided while at Andersen, for any client on whose account he had worked during 18 months prior to his termination. It also prohibited Edwards from "soliciting" for a year after termination. The agreement defined "soliciting" as "providing professional services to any client of Andersen's Los Angeles office." The California Supreme Court held the agreement invalid because it restrained Edwards' ability to practice his profession. There was no need to consider whether the restrictions were "reasonable" under the circumstances.

b. Nondisclosure agreements. The courts in *Cybertek* and *Fleming* both indicated that a nondisclosure agreement may protect information that does not qualify as a trade secret. Contract law exists separately from the law of trade secrets. One might argue that parties should be able to contract for nondisclosure of information regardless of the nature of the information. Courts have indicated, however, that nondisclosure agreements that unreasonably restrain competition or unduly hinder an individual from pursuing his chosen livelihood will be unenforceable. Courts are unlikely to permit parties to do by nondisclosure agreement what they are prohibited from doing by covenant not to compete. See, e.g., Gary Van Zeeland Talent, Inc. v. Sandas, 84 Wis.2d 202, 267 N.W.2d 242 (1978). In *Van Zeeland Talent*, the employee signed an employment agreement providing, among other things, that he agreed that the employer's customer list was a valuable, special, and unique asset of the employer's business and that he would not disclose it during or after his employment. The employee later left his employment, taking a copy of the customer list with him and using it to compete with his former employer. The customer list consisted of names only, without accompanying information about customer needs, preferences, etc. Upon suit, the court found that the list could be recreated from other publicly available sources and that it did not constitute a trade secret. The court rejected the suggestion that the agreement created enforceable rights in the customer list even so, stating:

> [I]t is contrary to public policy to afford special protection to a restraint-of-trade mechanism where to do so does not give a special incentive for creativity that will inure to the benefit of the public at large. Accordingly, it is contrary to public policy to afford protection to material which is generated in the ordinary course of a business. * * *

[I]t is the public's right to have reasonable competition, irrespective of what self-serving declarations the employer may insist upon.

Id., 84 Wis.2d at 217.

Given the constraints on enforcement of covenants not to compete and nondisclosure agreements described above, what are the advantages of having them? Are there any disadvantages in having a written agreement?

For an historical perspective on the development of the law of trade secrets and restrictive covenants in the United States, see Fisk, *Working Knowledge: Trade Secrets, Restrictive Covenants in Employment, and the Rise of Corporate Intellectual Property, 1800–1920*, 52 Hastings L.J. 441 (2001).

PROBLEM

1. Chemical Co. sells industrial cleaning equipment and supplies. Lee, an employee of Chemical Co., signed an employment agreement containing a "Covenant Not to Divulge Trade Secrets," which provided:

> Lee agrees not to divulge any trade secrets of the Company. Trade secrets means any knowledge or information concerning any process, product, or customer of the Company and more generally any knowledge or information concerning any aspect of the business of the Company which could, if divulged to a direct or indirect competitor, adversely affect the business of Company, its prospects or competitive position. Lee shall not use for his own benefit any trade secret of Company in any manner whatsoever.

After many years of employment, Lee left Chemical Co. He refrained from selling cleaning equipment and supplies for a year and a half. Then he went to work for Cleaning Co., a direct competitor of Chemical Co., selling industrial cleaning equipment and supplies. Chemical Co. sues, seeking to enforce the agreement. Should it be enforced?

PEPSICO, INC. v. REDMOND

United States Court of Appeals, Seventh Circuit, 1995.
54 F.3d 1262.

FLAUM, CIRCUIT JUDGE.

Plaintiff PepsiCo, Inc., sought a preliminary injunction against defendants William Redmond and the Quaker Oats Company to prevent Redmond, a former PepsiCo employee, from divulging PepsiCo trade secrets and confidential information in his new job with Quaker and from assuming any duties with Quaker relating to beverage pricing, marketing, and distribution. The district court agreed with PepsiCo and granted the injunction. We now affirm that decision.

I.

The facts of this case lay against a backdrop of fierce beverage-industry competition between Quaker and PepsiCo, especially in "sports drinks" and "new age drinks."[2] Quaker's sports drink, "Gatorade," is the dominant brand in its market niche. PepsiCo introduced its Gatorade rival, "All Sport," in March and April of 1994, but sales of All Sport lag far behind those of Gatorade. Quaker also has the lead in the new-age-drink category. Although PepsiCo has entered the market through joint ventures with the Thomas J. Lipton Company and Ocean Spray Cranberries, Inc., Quaker purchased Snapple Beverage Corp., a large new-age-drink maker, in late 1994. PepsiCo's products have about half of Snapple's market share. Both companies see 1995 as an important year for their products: PepsiCo has developed extensive plans to increase its market presence, while Quaker is trying to solidify its lead by integrating Gatorade and Snapple distribution. Meanwhile, PepsiCo and Quaker each face strong competition from Coca Cola Co., which has its own sports drink, "PowerAde," and which introduced its own Snapple-rival, "Fruitopia," in 1994, as well as from independent beverage producers.

William Redmond, Jr., worked for PepsiCo in its Pepsi–Cola North America division ("PCNA") from 1984 to 1994. Redmond became the General Manager of the Northern California Business Unit in June, 1993, and was promoted one year later to General Manager of the business unit covering all of California, a unit having annual revenues of more than 500 million dollars and representing twenty percent of PCNA's profit for all of the United States.

Redmond's relatively high-level position at PCNA gave him access to inside information and trade secrets. Redmond, like other PepsiCo management employees, had signed a confidentiality agreement with PepsiCo. That agreement stated in relevant part that he

> w[ould] not disclose at any time, to anyone other than officers or employees of [PepsiCo], or make use of, confidential information relating to the business of [PepsiCo] ... obtained while in the employ of [PepsiCo], which shall not be generally known or available to the public or recognized as standard practices.

Donald Uzzi, who had left PepsiCo in the beginning of 1994 to become the head of Quaker's Gatorade division, began courting Redmond for Quaker in May, 1994. Redmond met in Chicago with Quaker officers in August, 1994, and on October 20, 1994, Quaker, through Uzzi, offered Redmond the position of Vice President—On Premise Sales for Gatorade. Redmond did not then accept the offer but continued to negotiate for more money. Throughout this time, Redmond kept his dealings with Quaker secret from his employers at PCNA.

On November 8, 1994, Uzzi extended Redmond a written offer for the position of Vice President–Field Operations for Gatorade and Redmond accepted. Later that same day, Redmond called William Bensyl, the Senior Vice President of Human Resources for PCNA, and told him that he had

---

2. "New age drink" is a catch-all category for non-carbonated soft drinks and includes such beverages as ready-to-drink tea products and fruit drinks. Sports drinks may also fall under the new-age-drink heading.

an offer from Quaker to become the Chief Operating Officer of the combined Gatorade and Snapple company but had not yet accepted it. Redmond also asked whether he should, in light of the offer, carry out his plans to make calls upon certain PCNA customers. Bensyl told Redmond to make the visits.

Redmond also misstated his situation to a number of his PCNA colleagues, including Craig Weatherup, PCNA's President and Chief Executive Officer, and Brenda Barnes, PCNA's Chief Operating Officer and Redmond's immediate superior. As with Bensyl, Redmond told them that he had been offered the position of Chief Operating Officer at Gatorade and that he was leaning "60/40" in favor of accepting the new position.

On November 10, 1994, Redmond met with Barnes and told her that he had decided to accept the Quaker offer and was resigning from PCNA. Barnes immediately took Redmond to Bensyl, who told Redmond that PepsiCo was considering legal action against him.

True to its word, PepsiCo filed this diversity suit on November 16, 1994, seeking a temporary restraining order to enjoin Redmond from assuming his duties at Quaker and to prevent him from disclosing trade secrets or confidential information to his new employer. The district court granted PepsiCo's request that same day but dissolved the order sua sponte two days later, after determining that PepsiCo had failed to meet its burden of establishing that it would suffer irreparable harm. The court found that PepsiCo's fears about Redmond were based upon a mistaken understanding of his new position at Quaker and that the likelihood that Redmond would improperly reveal any confidential information did not "rise above mere speculation."

From November 23, 1994, to December 1, 1994, the district court conducted a preliminary injunction hearing on the same matter. At the hearing, PepsiCo offered evidence of a number of trade secrets and confidential information it desired protected and to which Redmond was privy. First, it identified PCNA's "Strategic Plan," an annually revised document that contains PCNA's plans to compete, its financial goals, and its strategies for manufacturing, production, marketing, packaging, and distribution for the coming three years. Strategic Plans are developed by Weatherup and his staff with input from PCNA's general managers, including Redmond, and are considered highly confidential. The Strategic Plan derives much of its value from the fact that it is secret and competitors cannot anticipate PCNA's next moves. PCNA managers received the most recent Strategic Plan at a meeting in July, 1994, a meeting Redmond attended. PCNA also presented information at the meeting regarding its plans for Lipton ready-to-drink teas and for All Sport for 1995 and beyond, including new flavors and package sizes.

Second, PepsiCo pointed to PCNA's Annual Operating Plan ("AOP") as a trade secret. The AOP is a national plan for a given year and guides PCNA's financial goals, marketing plans, promotional event calendars, growth expectations, and operational changes in that year. The AOP, which is implemented by PCNA unit General Managers, including Redmond, contains specific information regarding all PCNA initiatives for the forthcoming year. The AOP bears a label that reads "Private and Confidential—Do Not Reproduce" and is considered highly confidential by PCNA managers.

In particular, the AOP contains important and sensitive information about "pricing architecture"—how PCNA prices its products in the marketplace. Pricing architecture covers both a national pricing approach and specific price points for given areas. Pricing architecture also encompasses PCNA's objectives for All Sport and its new age drinks with reference to trade channels, package sizes and other characteristics of both the products and the customers at which the products are aimed. Additionally, PCNA's pricing architecture outlines PCNA's customer development agreements. These agreements between PCNA and retailers provide for the retailer's participation in certain merchandising activities for PCNA products. As with other information contained in the AOP, pricing architecture is highly confidential and would be extremely valuable to a competitor. Knowing PCNA's pricing architecture would allow a competitor to anticipate PCNA's pricing moves and underbid PCNA strategically whenever and wherever the competitor so desired. PepsiCo introduced evidence that Redmond had detailed knowledge of PCNA's pricing architecture and that he was aware of and had been involved in preparing PCNA's customer development agreements with PCNA's California and California-based national customers. Indeed, PepsiCo showed that Redmond, as the General Manager for California, would have been responsible for implementing the pricing architecture guidelines for his business unit.

PepsiCo also showed that Redmond had intimate knowledge of PCNA "attack plans" for specific markets. Pursuant to these plans, PCNA dedicates extra funds to supporting its brands against other brands in selected markets. To use a hypothetical example, PCNA might budget an additional $500,000 to spend in Chicago at a particular time to help All Sport close its market gap with Gatorade. Testimony and documents demonstrated Redmond's awareness of these plans and his participation in drafting some of them.

Finally, PepsiCo offered evidence of PCNA trade secrets regarding innovations in its selling and delivery systems. Under this plan, PCNA is testing a new delivery system that could give PCNA an advantage over its competitors in negotiations with retailers over shelf space and merchandising. Redmond has knowledge of this secret because PCNA, which has invested over a million dollars in developing the system during the past two years, is testing the pilot program in California.

Having shown Redmond's intimate knowledge of PCNA's plans for 1995, PepsiCo argued that Redmond would inevitably disclose that information to Quaker in his new position, at which he would have substantial input as to Gatorade and Snapple pricing, costs, margins, distribution systems, products, packaging and marketing, and could give Quaker an unfair advantage in its upcoming skirmishes with PepsiCo. Redmond and Quaker countered that Redmond's primary initial duties at Quaker as Vice President—Field Operations would be to integrate Gatorade and Snapple distribution and then to manage that distribution as well as the promotion, marketing and sales of these products. Redmond asserted that the integration would be conducted according to a pre-existing plan and that his special knowledge of PCNA strategies would be irrelevant. This irrelevance would derive not only from the fact that Redmond would be implementing pre-existing plans but also from the fact that PCNA and Quaker distribute their products in entirely different ways: PCNA's distribution system is vertically integrated (i.e., PCNA owns the system) and delivers its product directly to retailers, while Quaker ships its product to wholesalers and customer warehouses and relies on independent distributors. The defendants also pointed out that Redmond had signed a confidentiality agreement with Quaker preventing him from disclosing "any confidential information belonging to others," as well as the Quaker Code of Ethics, which prohibits employees from engaging in "illegal or improper acts to acquire a competitor's trade secrets." Redmond additionally promised at the hearing that should he be faced with a situation at Quaker that might involve the use or disclosure of PCNA information, he would seek advice from Quaker's in-house counsel and would refrain from making the decision.

PepsiCo responded to the defendants' representations by pointing out that the evidence did not show that Redmond would simply be implementing a business plan already in place. On the contrary, as of November, 1994, the plan to integrate Gatorade and Snapple distribution consisted of a single distributorship agreement and a two-page "contract terms summary." Such a basic plan would not lend itself to widespread application among the over 300 independent Snapple distributors. Since the integration process would likely face resistance from Snapple distributors and Quaker had no scheme to deal with this probability, Redmond, as the person in charge of the integration, would likely have a great deal of influence on the process. PepsiCo further argued that Snapple's 1995 marketing and promotion plans had not necessarily been completed prior to Redmond's joining Quaker, that Uzzi disagreed with portions of the Snapple plans, and that the plans were open to re-evaluation. Uzzi testified that the plan for integrating Gatorade and Snapple distribution is something that would happen in the future. Redmond would therefore likely have input in remaking these plans, and if he did, he would inevitably be making decisions with PCNA's strategic plans and 1995 AOP in mind. Moreover, PepsiCo continued, diverging testimony made it difficult to know exactly what Redmond would be doing at Quaker. Redmond described his job as "managing the entire sales effort of Gatorade at the field level, possibly including strategic planning," and at least at one point considered his job to be equivalent to that of a Chief Operating Officer. Uzzi, on the other hand, characterized Redmond's position as "primarily and initially to restructure and integrate our—the distribution systems for

Snapple and for Gatorade, as per our distribution plan" and then to "execute marketing, promotion and sales plans in the marketplace." Uzzi also denied having given Redmond detailed information about any business plans, while Redmond described such a plan in depth in an affidavit and said that he received the information from Uzzi. Thus, PepsiCo asserted, Redmond would have a high position in the Gatorade hierarchy, and PCNA trade secrets and confidential information would necessarily influence his decisions. Even if Redmond could somehow refrain from relying on this information, as he promised he would, his actions in leaving PCNA, Uzzi's actions in hiring Redmond, and the varying testimony regarding Redmond's new responsibilities, made Redmond's assurances to PepsiCo less than comforting.

On December 15, 1994, the district court issued an order enjoining Redmond from assuming his position at Quaker through May, 1995, and permanently from using or disclosing any PCNA trade secrets or confidential information. * * *. The court, which completely adopted Pepsi-Co's position, found that Redmond's new job posed a clear threat of misappropriation of trade secrets and confidential information that could be enjoined under Illinois statutory and common law. The court also emphasized Redmond's lack of forthrightness both in his activities before accepting his job with Quaker and in his testimony as factors leading the court to believe the threat of misappropriation was real. This appeal followed.

II.

Both parties agree that the primary issue on appeal is whether the district court correctly concluded that PepsiCo had a reasonable likelihood of success on its various claims for trade secret misappropriation and breach of a confidentiality agreement.[3] We review the district court's legal conclusions in issuing a preliminary injunction de novo and its factual determinations and balancing of the equities for abuse of discretion.

A.

The Illinois Trade Secrets Act ("ITSA"), which governs the trade secret issues in this case, provides that a court may enjoin the "actual or threatened misappropriation" of a trade secret. 765 ILCS 1065/3(a). A party seeking an injunction must therefore prove both the existence of a trade secret and the misappropriation. The defendants' appeal focuses solely on misappropriation; although the defendants only reluctantly refer to PepsiCo's marketing and distribution plans as trade secrets, they do not seriously contest that this information falls under the ITSA.

---

3. The district court concluded that PepsiCo satisfied the other requirements for a preliminary injunction: whether PepsiCo has an adequate remedy at law or will be irreparably harmed if the injunction does not issue; whether the threatened injury to PepsiCo outweighs the threatened harm the injunction may inflict on Quaker and Redmond; and whether the granting of the preliminary injunction will disserve the public interest. * * *

The question of threatened or inevitable misappropriation in this case lies at the heart of a basic tension in trade secret law. Trade secret law serves to protect "standards of commercial morality" and "encourage [ ] invention and innovation" while maintaining "the public interest in having free and open competition in the manufacture and sale of unpatented goods." 2 Melvin F. Jager, Trade Secrets Law § IL.03 at IL–12 (1994). Yet that same law should not prevent workers from pursuing their livelihoods when they leave their current positions. It has been said that federal age discrimination law does not guarantee tenure for older employees. Similarly, trade secret law does not provide a reserve clause for solicitous employers.

This tension is particularly exacerbated when a plaintiff sues to prevent not the actual misappropriation of trade secrets but the mere threat that it will occur. While the ITSA plainly permits a court to enjoin the threat of misappropriation of trade secrets, there is little law in Illinois or in this circuit establishing what constitutes threatened or inevitable misappropriation. Indeed, there are only two cases in this circuit that address the issue: *Teradyne, Inc. v. Clear Communications Corp.*, 707 F.Supp. 353 (N.D.Ill.1989), and *AMP Inc. v. Fleischhacker*, 823 F.2d 1199 (7th Cir.1987).

In *Teradyne*, Teradyne alleged that a competitor, Clear Communications, had lured employees away from Teradyne and intended to employ them in the same field. In an insightful opinion, Judge Zagel observed that "[t]hreatened misappropriation can be enjoined under Illinois law" where there is a "high degree of probability of inevitable and immediate ... use of ... trade secrets." Judge Zagel held, however, that Teradyne's complaint failed to state a claim because Teradyne did not allege "that defendants have in fact threatened to use Teradyne's secrets or that they will inevitably do so." Teradyne's claims would have passed Rule 12(b)(6) muster had they properly alleged inevitable disclosure, including a statement that Clear intended to use Teradyne's trade secrets or that the former Teradyne employees had disavowed their confidentiality agreements with Teradyne, or an allegation that Clear could not operate without Teradyne's secrets. However,

> [t]he defendants' claimed acts, working for Teradyne, knowing its business, leaving its business, hiring employees from Teradyne and entering the same field (though in a market not yet serviced by Teradyne) do not state a claim of threatened misappropriation. All that is alleged, at bottom, is that defendants could misuse plaintiff's secrets, and plaintiffs fear they will. This is not enough. It may be that little more is needed, but falling a little short is still falling short.

Id. at 357.

In *AMP*, we affirmed the denial of a preliminary injunction on the grounds that the plaintiff AMP had failed to show either the existence of any trade secrets or the likelihood that defendant Fleischhacker, a former AMP employee, would compromise those secrets or any other confidential business information. AMP, which produced electrical and electronic connection devices, argued that Fleischhacker's new position at AMP's competitor would inevitably lead him to compromise AMP's trade secrets regarding the manufacture of connectors. In rejecting that argument, we emphasized that the mere fact that a person assumed a similar position at a competitor does not, without more, make it "inevitable that he will use or disclose . . . trade secret information" so as to "demonstrate irreparable injury."

It should be noted that *AMP*, which we decided in 1987, predates the ITSA, which took effect in 1988. The ITSA abolishes any common law remedies or authority contrary to its own terms. The ITSA does not, however, represent a major deviation from the Illinois common law of unfair trade practices. The ITSA mostly codifies rather than modifies the common law doctrine that preceded it. Thus, we believe that *AMP* continues to reflect the proper standard under Illinois's current statutory scheme.

The ITSA, *Teradyne,* and *AMP* lead to the same conclusion: a plaintiff may prove a claim of trade secret misappropriation by demonstrating that defendant's new employment will inevitably lead him to rely on the plaintiff's trade secrets. * * *. The defendants are incorrect that Illinois law does not allow a court to enjoin the "inevitable" disclosure of trade secrets. Questions remain, however, as to what constitutes inevitable misappropriation and whether PepsiCo's submissions rise above those of the *Teradyne* and *AMP* plaintiffs and meet that standard. We hold that they do.

PepsiCo presented substantial evidence at the preliminary injunction hearing that Redmond possessed extensive and intimate knowledge about PCNA's strategic goals for 1995 in sports drinks and new age drinks. The district court concluded on the basis of that presentation that unless Redmond possessed an uncanny ability to compartmentalize information, he would necessarily be making decisions about Gatorade and Snapple by relying on his knowledge of PCNA trade secrets. It is not the "general skills and knowledge acquired during his tenure with" PepsiCo that PepsiCo seeks to keep from falling into Quaker's hands, but rather "the particularized plans or processes developed by [PCNA] and disclosed to him while the employer-employee relationship existed, which are unknown to others in the industry and which give the employer an advantage over his competitors." *AMP*, 823 F.2d at 1202. The *Teradyne* and *AMP* plaintiffs could do nothing more than assert that skilled employees were taking their skills elsewhere; PepsiCo has done much more.

Admittedly, PepsiCo has not brought a traditional trade secret case, in which a former employee has knowledge of a special manufacturing process or customer list and can give a competitor an unfair advantage by transferring the technology or customers to that competitor. * * * PepsiCo has not contended that Quaker has stolen the All Sport formula or its list of distributors. Rather PepsiCo has asserted that Redmond cannot help but rely on PCNA trade secrets as he helps plot Gatorade and Snapple's new course, and that these secrets will enable Quaker to achieve a substantial advantage by knowing exactly how PCNA will price, distribute, and market its sports drinks and new age drinks and being able to respond strategically. * * * This type of trade secret problem may arise less often, but it nevertheless falls within the realm of trade secret protection under the present circumstances.

Quaker and Redmond assert that they have not and do not intend to use whatever confidential information Redmond has by virtue of his former employment. They point out that Redmond has already signed an agreement with Quaker not to disclose any trade secrets or confidential information gleaned from his earlier employment. They also note with regard to distribution systems that even if Quaker wanted to steal information about PCNA's distribution plans, they would be completely useless in attempting to integrate the Gatorade and Snapple beverage lines.

The defendants' arguments fall somewhat short of the mark. Again, the danger of misappropriation in the present case is not that Quaker threatens to use PCNA's secrets to create distribution systems or co-opt PCNA's advertising and marketing ideas. Rather, PepsiCo believes that Quaker, unfairly armed with knowledge of PCNA's plans, will be able to anticipate its distribution, packaging, pricing, and marketing moves. Redmond and Quaker even concede that Redmond might be faced with a decision that could be influenced by certain confidential information that he obtained while at PepsiCo. In other words, PepsiCo finds itself in the position of a coach, one of whose players has left, playbook in hand, to join the opposing team before the big game. Quaker and Redmond's protestations that their distribution systems and plans are entirely different from PCNA's are thus not really responsive.

The district court also concluded from the evidence that Uzzi's actions in hiring Redmond and Redmond's actions in pursuing and accepting his new job demonstrated a lack of candor on their part and proof of their willingness to misuse PCNA trade secrets, findings Quaker and Redmond vigorously challenge. The court expressly found that:

> Redmond's lack of forthrightness on some occasions, and out and out lies on others, in the period between the time he accepted the position with defendant Quaker and when he informed plaintiff that he had accepted that position leads the court to conclude that defendant Redmond could not be trusted to act with the necessary sensitivity and good faith under the circumstances in which the only practical verification that he was not using plaintiff's secrets would be defendant Redmond's word to that effect.

The facts of the case do not ineluctably dictate the district court's conclusion. Redmond's ambiguous behavior toward his PepsiCo superiors might have been nothing more than an attempt to gain leverage in employment negotiations. The discrepancy between Redmond's and Uzzi's comprehension of what Redmond's job would entail may well have been a simple misunderstanding. The court also pointed out that Quaker, through Uzzi, seemed to express an unnatural interest in hiring PCNA employees: all three of the people interviewed for the position Redmond ultimately accepted worked at PCNA. Uzzi may well have focused on recruiting PCNA employees because he knew they were good and not because of their confidential knowledge. Nonetheless, the district court, after listening to the witnesses, determined otherwise. That conclusion was not an abuse of discretion.

* * *

Thus, when we couple the demonstrated inevitability that Redmond would rely on PCNA trade secrets in his new job at Quaker with the district court's reluctance to believe that Redmond would refrain from disclosing these secrets in his new position (or that Quaker would ensure Redmond did not disclose them), we conclude that the district court correctly decided that PepsiCo demonstrated a likelihood of success on its statutory claim of trade secret misappropriation.

* * *

C.

For the same reasons we concluded that the district court did not abuse its discretion in granting the preliminary injunction on the issue of trade secret misappropriation, we also agree with its decision on the likelihood of Redmond's breach of his confidentiality agreement should he begin working at Quaker. Because Redmond's position at Quaker would initially cause him to disclose trade secrets, it would necessarily force him to breach his agreement not to disclose confidential information acquired while employed in PCNA. * * *

* * *

III.

Finally, Redmond and Quaker have contended in the alternative that the injunction issued against them is overbroad. They disagree in particular with the injunction's prohibition against Redmond's participation in the integration of the Snapple and Gatorade distribution systems. The defendants claim that whatever trade secret and confidential information Redmond has, that information is completely irrelevant to Quaker's integration task. They further argue that, because Redmond would only be implementing a plan already in place, the injunction is especially inappropriate. A district court ordinarily has wide latitude in fashioning injunctive relief, and we will restrict the breadth of an injunction only where the district court has abused its discretion. Nonetheless, a court abuses its discretion where the scope of injunctive relief "exceed[s] the extent of the plaintiff's protectible rights."

While the defendants' arguments are not without some merit, the district court determined that the proposed integration would require

Redmond to do more than execute a plan someone else had drafted. It also found that Redmond's knowledge of PCNA's trade secrets and confidential information would inevitably shape that integration and that Redmond could not be trusted to avoid that conflict of interest. If the injunction permanently enjoined Redmond from assuming these duties at Quaker, the defendants' argument would be stronger. However, the injunction against Redmond's immediate employment at Quaker extends no further than necessary and was well within the district court's discretion.

For the foregoing reasons, we affirm the district court's order enjoining Redmond from assuming his responsibilities at Quaker through May, 1995, and preventing him forever from disclosing PCNA trade secrets and confidential information.

NOTES AND QUESTIONS

1. *Employee freedom to move.* The *PepsiCo* decision makes it clear that courts' sensitivity to employees' interest in moving freely from one job to another will not always carry the day. Based on the *PepsiCo* decision, when will the "inevitable disclosure" doctrine apply? Should the doctrine be applied liberally? Should it have been applied in the *Cybertek* case, *supra*? Should it be applied in the absence of a covenant not to compete, signed by the defendant employee? The *PepsiCo* court based its use of the doctrine on the Uniform Trade Secrets Act prohibition of "threatened" misappropriation of trade secrets. Did such a threat exist? Should the plaintiff be required to show that the defendant employee has an intent to misappropriate the plaintiff employer's trade secret?

In Whyte v. Schlage Lock Co., 101 Cal.App.4th 1443, 125 Cal.Rptr.2d 277 (2002), a case that was factually similar to *Pepsico*, the California Court of Appeals flatly refused to adopt the doctrine of inevitable disclosure. The court reasoned:

> [T]he doctrine of inevitable disclosure creates a de facto covenant not to compete and runs counter to the strong public policy in California favoring employee mobility. * * *
>
>   * * *
>
> The chief ill in the covenant not to compete imposed by the inevitable disclosure doctrine is its after-the-fact nature: The covenant is imposed *after* the employment contract is made and therefore alters the employment relationship without the employee's consent. When, as here, a confidentiality agreement is in place, the inevitable disclosure doctrine in effect converts the confidentiality agreement into * * * a covenant not to compete. * * *
>
> The doctrine of inevitable disclosure thus rewrites the employment agreement and such retroactive alterations distort the terms of the employment relationship and upset the balance which courts have attempted to achieve in construing non-compete agreements. The result * * * is the imperceptible shift in bargaining power that necessarily occurs upon the commencement of an employment relationship marked

by the execution of a confidentiality agreement. When the relationship eventually ends, the parties' confidentiality agreement may be wielded as a restrictive covenant, depending on how the employer views the new job its former employee has accepted. This can be a powerful weapon in the hands of an employer; the risk of litigation alone may have a chilling effect on the employee. As a result of the inevitable disclosure doctrine, the employer obtains the benefit of a contractual provision it did not pay for, while the employee is bound by a court-imposed contract provision with no opportunity to negotiate terms or consideration.

Id., 101 Cal.App.4th at 1462–63, 125 Cal.Rptr.2d at 292–94 (quotation marks and citations omitted).

2. *Effect of the inevitable disclosure doctrine in "high velocity" labor markets.* Some sectors of industry—particularly high technology—are noted for the rapid speed in which skilled employees move from one firm to another. It has been suggested in some cases that this high employee mobility, which leads to considerable informal information sharing among firms, may significantly benefit the industry as a whole, leading to more rapid overall progress in the field. What, if any, effect would wide-scale adoption of the inevitable disclosure doctrine be likely to have in such situations? See Gilson, *The Legal Infrastructure of High Technology Industrial Districts: Silicon Valley, Route 128, and Covenants Not To Compete*, 74 N.Y.U.L. Rev. 575 (1999).

B. IMPROPER CONDUCT BEYOND BREACH OF CONFIDENCE

E.I. DuPONT DeNEMOURS & CO. v. CHRISTOPHER

United States Court of Appeals, Fifth Circuit, 1970.
431 F.2d 1012, *cert. denied* 400 U.S. 1024, 91 S.Ct. 581, 27 L.Ed.2d 637 (1971).

GOLDBERG, CIRCUIT JUDGE:

This is a case of industrial espionage in which an airplane is the cloak and a camera the dagger. The defendants-appellants, Rolfe and Gary Christopher, are photographers in Beaumont, Texas. The Christophers were hired by an unknown third party to take aerial photographs of new construction at the Beaumont plant of E. I. DuPont DeNemours & Company, Inc. Sixteen photographs of the DuPont facility were taken from the air on March 19, 1969, and these photographs were later developed and delivered to the third party.

DuPont employees apparently noticed the airplane on March 19 and immediately began an investigation to determine why the craft was circling over the plant. By that afternoon the investigation had disclosed that the craft was involved in a photographic expedition and that the Christophers were the photographers. DuPont contacted the Christophers that same afternoon and asked them to reveal the name of the person or corporation requesting the photographs. The Christophers refused to disclose this information, giving as their reason the client's desire to remain anonymous.

Having reached a dead end in the investigation, DuPont subsequently filed suit against the Christophers, alleging that the Christophers had wrongfully obtained photographs revealing DuPont's trade secrets which they then sold to the undisclosed third party. DuPont contended that it had developed a highly secret but unpatented process for producing methanol, a process which gave DuPont a competitive advantage over other producers. This process, DuPont alleged, was a trade secret developed after much expensive and time-consuming research, and a secret which the company had taken special precautions to safeguard. The area photographed by the Christophers was the plant designed to produce methanol by this secret process, and because the plant was still under construction parts of the process were exposed to view from directly above the construction area. Photographs of that area, DuPont alleged, would enable a skilled person to deduce the secret process for making methanol. DuPont thus contended that the Christophers had wrongfully appropriated DuPont trade secrets by taking the photographs and delivering them to the undisclosed third party. In its suit DuPont asked for damages to cover the loss it had already sustained as a result of the wrongful disclosure of the trade secret and sought temporary and permanent injunctions prohibiting any further circulation of the photographs already taken and prohibiting any additional photographing of the methanol plant.

The Christophers answered with motions to dismiss for lack of jurisdiction and failure to state a claim upon which relief could be granted. Depositions were taken during which the Christophers again refused to disclose the name of the person to whom they had delivered the photographs. DuPont then filed a motion to compel an answer to this question and all related questions.

On June 5, 1969, the trial court held a hearing on all pending motions and an additional motion by the Christophers for summary judgment. The court denied the Christophers' motions to dismiss for want of jurisdiction and failure to state a claim and also denied their motion for summary judgment. The court granted DuPont's motion to compel the Christophers to divulge the name of their client. Having made these rulings, the court then granted the Christophers' motion for an interlocutory appeal under 28 U.S.C.A. 1292(b) to allow the Christophers to obtain immediate appellate review of the court's finding that DuPont had stated a claim upon which relief could be granted. Agreeing with the trial court's determination that DuPont had stated a valid claim, we affirm the decision of that court.

This is a case of first impression, for the Texas courts have not faced this precise factual issue, and sitting as a diversity court we must sensitize our *Erie* antennae to divine what the Texas courts would do if such a situation were presented to them. The only question involved in this interlocutory appeal is whether DuPont has asserted a claim upon which relief can be granted. The Christophers argued both at trial and before this court that they committed no "actionable wrong" in photographing the DuPont facility and passing these photographs on to their client because they conducted all of their activities in public airspace, violated no government aviation standard, did not breach any confidential relation, and did not engage in any fraudulent or illegal conduct. In short, the Christophers argue that for an appropriation of trade secrets to be wrongful there must be a trespass, other illegal conduct, or breach of a confidential relationship. We disagree.

It is true, as the Christophers assert, that the previous trade secret cases have contained one or more of these elements. However, we do not think that the Texas courts would limit the trade secret protection exclusively to these elements. On the contrary, in Hyde Corporation v. Huffines, 1958, 158 Tex. 566, 314 S.W.2d 763, the Texas Supreme Court specifically adopted the rule found in the Restatement of Torts which provides:

> "One who discloses or uses another's trade secret, without a privilege to do so, is liable to the other if (a) he discovered the secret by improper means, or (b) his disclosure or use constitutes a breach of confidence reposed in him by the other in disclosing the secret to him
> * * *."

Restatement of Torts 757 (1939).

Thus, although the previous cases have dealt with a breach of a confidential relationship, a trespass, or other illegal conduct, the rule is much broader than the cases heretofore encountered. Not limiting itself to specific wrongs, Texas adopted subsection (a) of the Restatement which recognizes a cause of action for the discovery of a trade secret by any "improper" means.

* * *

The question remaining, therefore, is whether aerial photography of plant construction is an improper means of obtaining another's trade secret. We conclude that it is and that the Texas courts would so hold. The Supreme Court of that state has declared that "the undoubted tendency of the law has been to recognize and enforce higher standards of commercial morality in the business world." Hyde Corporation v. Huffines, *supra* 314 S.W.2d at 773. That court has quoted with approval articles indicating that the *proper* means of gaining possession of a competitor's secret process is "through inspection and analysis" of the product in order to create a duplicate. Later another Texas court explained:

> "The means by which the discovery is made may be obvious, and the experimentation leading from known factors to presently unknown results may be simple and lying in the public domain. But these facts do not destroy the value of the discovery and will not advantage a competitor who by unfair means obtains the knowledge *without paying the price expended by the discoverer*." Brown v. Fowler, Tex. Civ.App.1958, 316 S.W.2d 111, 114, writ ref'd n.r.e. (emphasis added).

We think, therefore, that the Texas rule is clear. One may use his competitor's secret process if he discovers the process by reverse engineering applied to the finished product; one may use a competitor's process if he discovers it by his own independent research; but one may not avoid these labors by taking the process from the discoverer without his permission at a time when he is taking reasonable precautions to maintain its secrecy. To obtain knowledge of a process without spending the time and money to discover it independently is *improper* unless the holder voluntarily discloses it or fails to take reasonable precautions to ensure its secrecy.

In the instant case the Christophers deliberately flew over the DuPont plant to get pictures of a process which DuPont had attempted to keep secret. The Christophers delivered their pictures to a third party who was certainly aware of the means by which they had been acquired and who may be planning to use the information contained therein to manufacture methanol by the DuPont process. The third party has a right to use this process only if he obtains this knowledge through his own research efforts, but thus far all information indicates that the third party has gained this knowledge solely by taking it from DuPont at a time when DuPont was making reasonable efforts to preserve its secrecy. In such a situation DuPont has a valid cause of action to prohibit the Christophers from improperly discovering its trade secret and to prohibit the undisclosed third party from using the improperly obtained information.

We note that this view is in perfect accord with the position taken by the authors of the Restatement. In commenting on improper means of discovery the savants of the Restatement said:

> "f. *Improper means of discovery.* The discovery of another's trade secret by improper means subjects the actor to liability independently of the harm to the interest in the secret. Thus, if one uses physical force to take a secret formula from another's pocket, or breaks into another's office to steal the formula, his conduct is wrongful and subjects him to liability apart from the rule stated in this Section. Such conduct is also an improper means of procuring the secret under this rule. But means may be improper under this rule even though they do not cause any other harm than that to the interest in the trade secret. Examples of such means are fraudulent misrepresentations to induce disclosure, tapping of telephone wires, eavesdropping or other espionage. A complete catalogue of improper means is not possible. In general they are means which fall below the generally accepted standards of commercial morality and reasonable conduct."
> Restatement of Torts 757, comment f at 10 (1939).

In taking this position we realize that industrial espionage of the sort here perpetrated has become a popular sport in some segments of our industrial community. However, our devotion to free wheeling industrial competition must not force us into accepting the law of the jungle as the standard of morality expected in our commercial relations. Our tolerance of the espionage game must cease when the protections required to prevent another's spying cost so much that the spirit of inventiveness is dampened. Commercial privacy must be protected from espionage which could not have been reasonably anticipated or prevented. We do not mean to imply, however, that everything not in plain view is within the protected vale, nor that all information obtained through every extra optical extension is forbidden. Indeed, for our industrial competition to remain healthy there must be breathing room for observing a competing industrialist. A competitor can and must shop his competition for pricing and examine his products for quality, components, and methods of manufacture. Perhaps ordinary fences and roofs must be built to shut out incursive eyes, but we need not require the discoverer of a trade secret to guard against the unanticipated, the undetectable, or the unpreventable methods of espionage now available.

In the instant case DuPont was in the midst of constructing a plant. Although after construction the finished plant would have protected much of the process from view, during the period of construction the trade secret was exposed to view from the air. To require DuPont to put a roof over the unfinished plant to guard its secret would impose an enormous expense to prevent nothing more than a school boy's trick. We introduce here no new or radical ethic since our ethos has never given moral sanction to piracy. The market place must not deviate far from our mores. We should not require a person or corporation to take unreasonable precautions to prevent another from doing that which he ought not do in the first place. Reasonable precautions against predatory eyes we may require, but an impenetrable fortress is an unreasonable requirement, and we are not disposed to burden industrial inventors with such a duty in order to protect the fruits of their efforts. "Improper" will always be a word of many nuances, determined by time, place, and circumstances. We therefore need not proclaim a catalogue of commercial improprieties. Clearly, however, one of its commandments does say "thou shall not appropriate a trade secret through deviousness under circumstances in which countervailing defenses are not reasonably available."

Having concluded that aerial photography, from whatever altitude, is an improper method of discovering the trade secrets exposed during construction of the DuPont plant, we need not worry about whether the flight pattern chosen by the Christophers violated any federal aviation regulations. Regardless of whether the flight was legal or illegal in that sense, the espionage was an improper means of discovering DuPont's trade secret. The decision of the trial court is affirmed and the case remanded to that court for proceedings on the merits.

NOTES AND QUESTIONS

1. *Improper means.* What standard does the *DuPont* court provide to determine whether a defendant's conduct was "improper?" What sorts of factors are courts likely to deem relevant in applying that standard? Why did the court find the defendants' conduct improper in the *DuPont* case? Does the concept of "reaping where one has not sown," or "taking a free ride," discussed in Chapter 1, figure into the court's analysis?

The Uniform Trade Secrets Act defines "improper means" as follows: " 'Improper means' includes theft, bribery, misrepresentation, breach or inducement of a breach of a duty to maintain secrecy, or espionage through electronic or other means." Uniform Trade Secrets Act § 1(1) (1985). Note that the Uniform Act categorizes breaches of confidential duty as one form of improper conduct, while Restatement of Torts § 757 categorizes improper conduct and breaches of confidential duty separately. Restatement of Torts § 757(a) & (b) (1939). Compare the Uniform Act provision with comment f of the Restatement, set forth in the *DuPont* court's opinion. Is the determination of a claim likely to differ depending on whether the Court applies the Uniform Act or the Restatement § 757 standard for improper conduct? See Restatement (Third) of Unfair Competition §§ 40, 43 (1995).

2. *Proper means*. If the defendant's (or its source's) means of obtaining the trade secret are "proper," and there is no duty of confidentiality, the defendant is free to use or disclose the trade secret with impunity. The *DuPont* court observes that proper means include independent discovery and reverse engineering. Why should discovery through reverse engineering be deemed proper? Could the defendants in *DuPont* argue that their activities only constituted reverse engineering? How might their activities be distinguished from the type of reverse engineering the court had in mind? What if the defendants had waited and taken aerial photographs of the fully completed DuPont plant and tried to learn the plaintiff's secret process from those photographs? Would their conduct still be improper?

CORPORATE SPYING, THE RIGHT WAY

Kathleen Pender. San Francisco Chronicle.[9]
May 30, 1985, at 27.

Companies that want to snoop on the competition don't have to rifle through trash bins, ply competitors with drinks and run phony help-wanted adds just to interview competitor's employees.

There are plenty of "legally and ethically acceptable ways" to spy on competitors, said Leila Kight, president of a Washington-based research firm that is conducting a seminar in San Francisco this week on corporate intelligence gathering.

Kight's firm, Washington Researchers Ltd., once had a client who wanted to know the plant production of a gelatin capsule manufacturer.

"We had two days to do it. We placed two strategic phone calls. The first was to the plant's union representative. We asked about the number and length of shifts, down-time and who supplied the equipment. Then we called the equipment supplier and asked him about the number of machines (he had sold to the plant) and machine capacity," Kight said.

With that information, estimating the plant's production was a simple calculation. Kight simply took shift length, subtracted down-time and multiplied by the number of shifts per day, the number of machines and the machine capacity per hour.

---

9. © San Francisco Chronicle, 1985. Reprinted by permission.

"If we had asked the union representative directly, 'How much of this do you manufacture?' I am not sure we would have gotten the answer," she said.

Kight believes such tactics are ethical as long as the researchers identify themselves, their companies and their general areas of interest. Many corporate information-seekers go beyond Kight's ethical bounds.

For three years, Kight polled seminar participants about seven hypothetical research strategies, all of which assumed varying degrees of misrepresentation or manipulation. The results imply that business ethics are taking a beating.

While only 30 percent said they would pose as a student job seeker to gain information about a competitor, 70 percent said they would buy drinks for competitors at an industry meeting to solicit sensitive information.

The respondents attributed far more ruthless behavior to their competitors—62 percent said other companies would send in undercover job seekers and 87 percent believed others would take advantage of tipsy competitors.

Corporate intelligence gatherers "are under a great deal of pressure," Kight said, "and the longer somebody is involved in intelligence gathering, the more adventuresome he may become."

Not all intelligence experts have abandoned ethics. "At the other end of the spectrum, I have had two people who wouldn't give their company information they found that had been over-disclosed (by a competitor) in a federal document," she said.

Some companies are so afraid of Securities and Exchange Commission regulations that they disclose more information than is required. Kight took advantage of over-disclosure to sleuth out information about Airsignal, a small division of MCI Telecommunications Corp.

"We knew MCI had bought Airsignal from Xerox, which had bought it from Western Union International. We went back to the Western Union documents and found out a lot of information about Airsignal. It was two years old, but it was a base," she said.

The best source of leaks is not published sources, but people. "Often, by being very direct and very bold, you can get people to cough up things you wouldn't believe," Kight said.

Ignorance and intrigue lead many people to let corporate secrets out of the bag. "Some just aren't thinking that the information may be damaging, especially if you ask for it innocuously. A lot of people will talk to you because they are interested in the topic of the conversation. Most people are more personally loyal to their own product, their own advancement, than they are to the company."

Kight's firm was founded in 1973 as an independent information service, which currently researches information for $85 an hour. Most of its clients are Fortune 500 companies who call when their own research staffs get overloaded or when they want to keep their identity confidential.

* * *

In 1978, Kight's firm was the only one offering corporate intelligence seminars. Today, she has several competitors, including McGraw–Hill. "In the last few years there has been a huge rush of companies trying to pin down information about the competitors," she said.

Most companies have been slow to develop defenses against this build-up in intelligence forces. Kight said she once offered a seminar on how to prevent prying, "but it bombed."

Companies "have a right to protect themselves. A company that does it well is admirable," Kight said. "But I look at this as a sporting event. The cleverest players come out ahead."

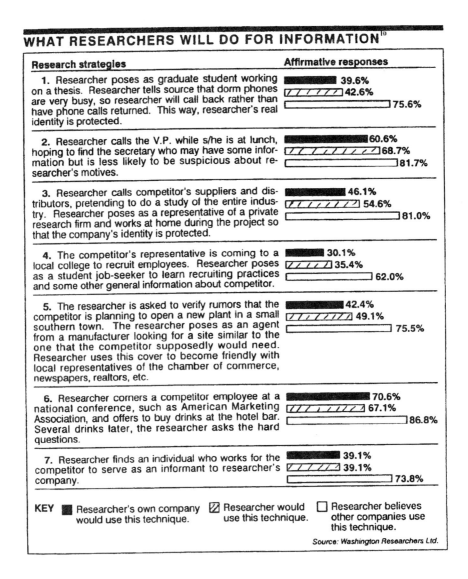

NOTES AND QUESTIONS

1. *Misappropriation of trade secrets?* Assume that the researcher was successful in eliciting trade secrets in each of the seven scenarios described in the chart, and apply the standards set forth in the *DuPont* opinion. In your opinion, might the researcher be liable for trade secret misappropriation? Did Ms. Kight's firm's efforts to learn the plant production of the gelatin capsule manufacturer exceeded the bounds?

10. © Washington Researchers, 1985. Graph reprinted by permission of Washington Researchers, Washington, D.C.

2. *Protecting trade secrets in litigation.* A business suspecting that a competitor has misappropriated its trade secret faces a dilemma: In order to litigate, the business will probably have to disclose the trade secret in its court filings or through discovery. While the court may grant protective orders to seal the record, bind parties obtaining access to the information to secrecy, or agree to hear sensitive information *in camera*, the risks involved may nonetheless convince the trade secret owner that it stands to lose more than it may gain in the litigation.

3. *Remedies for trade secret misappropriation.* Both injunctive relief and damages are available to trade secret plaintiffs. As in other contexts, the plaintiff must demonstrate irreparable injury and an inadequate remedy at law in order to obtain an injunction. This is relatively easy in many trade secret cases because a defendant's disclosure or use of a trade secret may significantly reduce its value or utterly destroy it, and the monetary loss to a trade secret owner may be difficult to measure.

Assuming that an injunction is warranted, how long should it last? Should it be perpetual, prohibiting the defendant from ever disclosing or using the plaintiff's information, or should it be shorter? If the latter, how should its duration be measured? Compare Valco Cincinnati, Inc. v. N & D Machining Serv., 24 Ohio St.3d 41, 492 N.E.2d 814 (1986) (court uses perpetual injunction as a means of penalizing particularly reprehensible conduct), with K-2 Ski Co. v. Head Ski Co., 506 F.2d 471 (9th Cir.1974) (injunction should be granted for the period of time it would have taken the defendant to reverse engineer the trade secret or obtain it through independent development). The Uniform Trade Secrets Act provides that "[u]pon application to the court, an injunction shall be terminated when the trade secret has ceased to exist, but the injunction may be continued for an additional reasonable period of time in order to eliminate commercial advantage that otherwise would be derived from the misappropriation." *Id,* at § 2(a) (1985). With regard to the scope, or breadth, of injunctions against use of trade secrets, see Restatement (Third) of Unfair Competition § 44 (1995).

Courts have employed several different means of measuring damages in trade secret cases. The Uniform Trade Secrets Act, as revised in 1985, provides that damages may include "both the actual loss caused by misappropriation and the unjust enrichment caused by misappropriation that is not taken into account in computing actual loss." *Id.,* § 3(a). Thus, to the extent that the defendant's wrongfully gained profit exceeds the plaintiff's actual loss, that excess is added to the amount of plaintiff's loss. Under what kinds of circumstances might the defendant's gain exceed the plaintiff's loss?

In lieu of damages measured by actual loss and unjust enrichment, the Uniform Act permits a plaintiff to recover the equivalent of a reasonable royalty payment for the defendant's use of the trade secret. See *id.* In that case, the court seeks to determine what a reasonable licensee would have been willing to pay and a reasonable licensor would have been willing to accept in arm's length negotiations for a license to use the trade secret.

The Uniform Act also authorizes an award of exemplary damages of up to twice the amount of compensatory damages in cases of "willful and malicious misappropriation." Uniform Trade Secrets Act, § 3(b) (1985). Moreover, in a distinct departure from the common law, the Uniform Act provides for an award of attorney's fees in cases of willful and malicious misappropriation and in certain cases of bad faith. See *id.*, § 4.

A number of states have enacted criminal penalties for theft of trade secrets. *See, e.g.,* Minn. Stat. Ann. § 609.52 (West Supp. 2000); N.Y. Penal Law § 165.07 (McKinney 1999). The Economic Espionage Act of 1996, Pub. L. No. 104–294, 110 Stat. 3488 (1996), makes theft of a trade secret a federal crime under a number of circumstances. Codified at 18 U.S.C. §§ 1831, *et. seq.*, the Act prohibits the knowing, unauthorized taking or communication of trade secrets when the actor intends or knows that the acts: (1) will benefit a foreign government, or (2) will injure the owner of the trade secret to the benefit of another. The Act extends criminal penalties to persons who attempt or conspire to do the prohibited acts, but provides no private civil cause of action.

4. *Protecting trade secrets abroad.* Assume that your client wishes to engage in international business transactions in which it will use its trade secrets in foreign countries or will license others to do so. How will you advise the client with regard to the risks and proper precautions to protect the secrets? While most nations have well-established patent, copyright and trademark laws, trade secret provisions have not traditionally been so common. However, the Agreement on Trade–Related Aspects of Intellectual Property Rights ("TRIPs") addresses trade secret protection. TRIPs Article 39 requires member nations to protect natural and legal persons' "undisclosed information" against unauthorized acquisition or use in a manner contrary to honest commercial practices as long as the information in question:

    (a) is secret in the sense that it is not, as a body or in the precise configuration and assembly of its components, generally known among or readily accessible to persons within the circles that normally deal with the kind of information in question;

    (b) has commercial value because it is secret; and

    (c) has been subject to reasonable steps under the circumstances, by the person lawfully in control of the information, to keep it secret.

II. OWNERSHIP OF TRADE SECRETS

STRUCTURAL DYNAMICS RESEARCH CORP. v. ENGINEERING MECHANICS RESEARCH CORP.

United States District Court, E.D. Michigan, 1975.
401 F.Supp. 1102.

FEIKENS, DISTRICT JUDGE.

I.

Structural Dynamics Research Corporation (SDRC) brought this action against three former employees, Kant Kothawala, Karan Surana and

Robert Hildebrand, for unfair competition, misappropriation and misuse of confidential and trade secret material, breach of confidential disclosure agreements and interference with SDRC's customer relations, and against Engineering Mechanics Research Corporation (EMRC) for conspiring with the individual defendants to accomplish the above purposes. It seeks both damages and a permanent injunction.

* * *

* * * This case was tried before the court sitting without a jury.

Both SDRC and EMRC are engaged in the business of structural analysis and testing. They are also engaged in the development of computer programs for such purposes for use in their business and for lease to other users.

Kothawala, Surana and Hildebrand were all formerly employed by SDRC in various technical capacities. Kothawala was employed by SDRC between August 3, 1972 and December 31, 1972 as a member of its Technical Staff.[2] Surana worked for SDRC from February of 1970 to January of 1973, initially as a project leader in the computer operations department and later as a member of the Technical Staff. Hildebrand was employed by SDRC as a project manager between August of 1972 and December 31, 1972. Each signed an Employee Patent and Confidential Information Agreement while so employed and, in addition, Kothawala executed an Employment Agreement.

These three individuals are now employed by EMRC. Kothawala is the President and sole shareholder. Surana is Vice–President of Engineering. Hildebrand is Manager of Applications.

Structural analysis involves, generally speaking, the prediction of how a physical structure will react when forces are applied to it. One of the methods used to solve structural analysis problems is a finite element computer program. The technical part of this dispute concerns two such programs. These computer programs are used to obtain an approximation of the reaction of a physical structure when forces are applied to it. This approximation is termed a mathematical model. It simulates actual conditions.

[In 1971, after attending a conference in which isoparametric elements were discussed, Surana began to investigate isoparametric technology. He concluded that an isoparametric program would be useful to SDRC in measuring stress on curved surfaces, and notified SDRC management of his conclusion. The management encouraged Surana to continue his efforts, though it required him to continue devoting time to other projects.]

In April, 1972 SDRC gave formal recognition to Surana's isoparametric research by the establishment of a time charge account. By that time

---

2. The Technical Staff is comprised of employees having significant technical expertise in the various areas of interest to SDRC. These employees provide technical assistance to project engineers and engage in research and development.

Surana had reduced to writing certain preliminary equations, computations and sketches necessary to the development of a program. He continued preliminary development work as time permitted until August.

[In August, 1972, Kothawala and Hildebrand came to work at SDRC. Shortly thereafter, Surana met with the technical staff and explained what he had been doing with regard to the isoparametric program. The group gave Surana authority to devote all his time to developing the program, and assigned Surana and Kothawala responsibility for drafting a formal written proposal. Kothawala was eventually assigned supervisory responsibility for the project.]

On August 23, 1972 Kothawala and Surana submitted a formal proposal. It stressed the importance of the proposed program to SDRC, the advantages and superiority of isoparametric elements, the significance of Surana's technical work to date and the uniqueness of the program. It also contained cost estimates and a timetable for completion. SDRC relied on these representations since no one employed by SDRC at this time other than Surana had any significant knowledge of isoparametric element theory or application.

On October 25, 1972 Kothawala and Surana issued a technical status report. Surana had developed the program to the point of running test problems. Kothawala stated that the program would "revolutionize" SDRC's problem solving ability. SDRC management felt this report established the feasibility of the program. Surana continued his work on the program throughout the rest of the year. He named the program "NIE-SA", an acronym for "Numerically Integrated Elements for System Analysis".

[In December 1972, Kothawala, who was dissatisfied with his opportunities at SDRC, requested to be released from his contract. SDRC released him from the contract except for the provisions pertaining to post-termination activities. Kothawala went to Detroit and established EMRC. Hildebrand also gave SDRC notice and went to Detroit to work for EMRC as Manager of Applications. Shortly thereafter, Surana gave his notice, staying only long enough to prepare a handwritten description of the program's status and explain the program to other SDRC employees. In March, 1973, Surana began to work for EMRC as Vice President of Engineering.]

Shortly after Kothawala arrived back in Detroit, he called upon American Motors Corporation (AMC). He had learned of its interest in acquiring structural analysis programs while employed by SDRC. On January 10, 1973 he proposed to develop for AMC a conventional, non-isoparametric, finite element program.

Then, on February 27, 1973, before AMC had acted on this proposal, Kothawala and Surana, who had now joined EMRC, submitted a new proposal for an isoparametric program substantially the same as NIESA in design, element library, solver and basic capabilities. Their proposal repeated the representations made to SDRC as to the uniqueness, superiority and value of an isoparametric element program. The written materials contained a number of paragraphs and a drawing taken from Kothawala's and Surana's August 23, 1972 formal proposal to SDRC.

In order to prepare a recommendation to its management, AMC personnel asked questions regarding specifics of the proposal. Kothawala responded by an undated letter. It is apparent from a comparison of the undated letter with the recommendation of Joseph Balnave, manager of AMC's computer center, written in mid-March, that the undated letter was written between February 27 and mid-March, since Balnave's recommendation of mid-March contains many of the specifics set out in the undated letter. In the undated letter Kothawala stated that the program being offered to AMC was partially finished, 1200 hours having been spent on it already and only 500 hours remaining for completion. Since defendants had not commenced working on the program at that time, it is clear that Kothawala offered American Motors the benefit of the time spent by him and Surana at SDRC. The partially finished program thus is SDRC's NIESA.

In March of 1973 EMRC commenced program development under an informal arrangement. In June formal approval for the funding of the program was obtained from AMC management. The program was completed about November 1, 1973. At that time Kothawala furnished AMC with certain program documentation which he stated was confidential and the property of EMRC. He instructed AMC to keep all aspects of the program in confidence in order to prevent any copying of the documents or program. He also refused AMC's request for a copy of the program code on grounds of confidentiality.

EMRC continued development of the program and added additional capabilities. In February of 1974 EMRC began marketing its program under the name "NISA", an acronym for "Numerically Integrated Elements for System Analysis".

SDRC, previously unaware of defendants' development activity, speeded up its own development work on NIESA. NIESA, renamed SUPERB, was placed on the market in April of 1974.

NISA and NIESA–SUPERB are very similar programs. The basic difference between them is that NISA is more fully developed, having the additional capacity to perform dynamic and heat conduction analysis. These additional capacities were included in Kothawala's and Surana's plan for the development of NIESA at SDRC. Thus, NISA is in a sense the implementation of the plan for development of NIESA.

* * *

II.

Plaintiff SDRC makes three basic arguments.

(a) Breach of trust on the part of the individual defendants (formerly employees of plaintiff) who used for their own advantage trade secrets owned by plaintiff and acquired by the individual defendants in a confidential relationship with plaintiff;

(b) Breach of contractual duty not to use or disclose confidential information;

(c) Unfair competition.

* * *

In this case Surana and Kothawala did not obtain the claimed trade secrets through improper means. In substantial measure they were the developers and innovators of a general purpose isoparametric computer program. They were hired by SDRC for research and development activity in this very field, and the manner of their acquisition of knowledge of this technology can in no sense be said to have been obtained improperly.

Does their subsequent use or disclosure of this technology, assuming it to be a trade secret, breach a duty of trust owed by these individual defendants to plaintiff? The *Restatement [of the Law of Torts]*, at 4, suggests this question by its comment: "apart from breach of contract, abuse of confidence or impropriety in the means of procurement, trade secrets may be copied as freely as devices which are not secret".

The relationship giving rise to a duty is not necessarily dependent upon contract; it may be based on agency principles or on specific dealings between parties in which a situation of trust arises and out of which sought-to-be-protected knowledge is acquired. Vital to a consideration of the creation of duty in such situations is the key question as to how the person acquiring such trade secret knowledge obtained it. If the subject matter of the trade secret is in being and an employee learns about it in the course of his employment in a relationship of confidence, the duty not to use or disclose trade secret knowledge adversely to his employer arises. On the other hand, if the subject matter of the trade secret is brought into being because of the initiative of the employee in its creation, innovation or development even though the relationship is one of confidence, no duty arises since the employee may then have an interest in the subject matter at least equal to that of his employer or in any event, such knowledge is a part of the employee's skill and experience. In such a case, absent an express contractual obligation by the employee not to use or disclose such confidential information acquired during his employment adverse to his employer's interest, he is free to use or disclose it in subsequent employment activity.

In *Wexler v. Greenberg*, 399 Pa. 569, 160 A.2d 430 (1960), the Pennsylvania Supreme Court held that in the absence of a contractual obligation not to use or disclose, no duty arose from the employment relationship itself that would prevent a chemist from using and disclosing secret chemical formulae developed by him in the course of his former employment. The court distinguished the cases in which an employer discloses to his employee a preexisting trade secret from those in which the employee himself develops the trade secret sought to be protected. A further distinction was then drawn within the category of employee-developed secrets. Where the employer assigns the employee to a specific development task and commits considerable resources and supervision to the project, a confidential relationship arises that prevents the employee from using or disclosing the fruits of his research. When, on the other hand, the developments are the product of the application of the employee's own skill, "without any appreciable assistance by way of information or great expense or supervision [from the employer], outside of the normal expenses of his job," 160 A.2d at 436, he has "an unqualified privilege" to use and disclose the trade secrets so developed. 160 A.2d at 437. *Accord, New Method Die & Cut–Out Co. v. Milton Bradley Co.*, 289 Mass. 277, 194 N.E. 80, 82 (1935) (defendant employee not required to maintain secrecy where he "took part to a substantial extent in developing the process," but "was not employed specifically for this purpose.")

While the question is concededly a close one, the court holds that the isoparametric program developed on the initial encouragement—and under the supervision—of Surana and Kothawala falls within the latter category.

Surana and Kothawala do not owe SDRC a duty not to use or disclose its trade secrets by reason of a relationship of confidence in employment. As the substantial developers and innovators of this technology they have an interest in it and unless they expressly contracted with SDRC not to use or disclose such knowledge or information in future employment activity, there is no duty imposed upon them by reason of their employment relationship with SDRC. Nor is such a duty created by any equitable doctrine of quasi-contract; i. e., a contract implied in law.

Accordingly, the court turns to the remaining question. Are there obligations imposed on the individual defendants not to use or disclose confidential information acquired in and during the course of their employment at SDRC because of express contractual agreements into which they entered?

III.

Here, all three individual defendants entered into an Employee Patent and Confidential Information Agreement. In it they agree:

> "(d) At no time either during his employment, on either a part or full-time basis with the Company or subsequent to termination of such employment will Employee divulge to any person, firm or corporation, or use (other than as required by the Company in the course of his employment) any privileged or confidential information, trade secret or other proprietary information including but not limited to information relating to the experimental and research work of the Corporation, its methods, processes, tools, machinery, formulae, drawings, or appliances imparted or divulged to, gained or developed by or otherwise discovered by Employee during his employment with the Company." * * *

Kothawala also executed a separate employment contract. He himself drafted some of its terms. SDRC had submitted a proposed contract to him. He found it unacceptable, insisted on modifications and then submitted his draft which was executed. It contains the following provisions:

* * *

"4. Neither during the period of employment nor at any time thereafter will Kothawala disclose to anyone any confidential information or trade secrets concerning the business affairs of SDRC, including but not limited to information relating to the experimental and research work of SDRC, their methods, processes, tools, machinery, formulae, drawings, or appliances imparted or divulged to, gained or developed by or otherwise discovered by Kothawala during his employment with SDRC. Upon termination of his employment, Kothawala will return to SDRC all objects, materials, devices or substances including notes, records, drawings, sketches, recordings, descriptions, samples, specimens, prototypes, models, blueprints, analyses, programs, or the like, and including any facsimile, replica, photograph or reproduction thereof, belonging to SDRC or relating to their respective business."

* * *

The agreements not to disclose confidential information impose obligations by their clear terms since these undertakings do not exclude information, technology or knowledge which the employee himself discovers, develops or contributes. Thus, if the contracts are valid and enforceable, defendants are under obligations not to use or disclose confidential information gained while employed at SDRC.

Some courts have held that such express contracts create a confidential relationship between employer and employee, breach of which results in liability. They use the doctrine of trade secrets in the decisional process. This court finds such an approach too restrictive, especially in an area of knowledge and rapid technological change such as the computer field.

The express contracts in issue apply not only to trade secrets but also to privileged, proprietary and confidential information. In this they are analogous to the breadth of coverage recognized under agency principles. In *Shwayder Chemical Metallurgy Corp. v. Baum*, 45 Mich. App. 220, 206 N.W.2d 484 (1973), it was held that while the process plaintiff sought to protect was not a trade secret, defendant stood in a fiduciary and confidential relationship to plaintiff, that he breached the duties and obligations arising from that relationship and was therefore liable for damages. *See Restatement (Second) of Agency* §§ 395 and 396.

These considerations apply to the express contracts in issue. Defendants are liable for breach of their contracts and are answerable in damages if they used or disclosed confidential information, knowledge or technology gained while employed at SDRC. This is so even though such information, knowledge or technology is not itself a trade secret.

[The court determines that Ohio law applies in the interpretation and enforcement of the contractual provisions.]

This brings the court to the issue of breach.

It is true that initial recognition of the importance of isoparametric elements in a new program, and the feasibility of development of such a program, must be credited to Surana and, to a lesser extent, to Kothawala. However, this information was acquired in the course of their employment and a fulfillment of their specific assigned responsibilities. This information had business value and SDRC had the sole right because of the express contracts to exploit the advantage. SDRC's possession of this information gave it an opportunity to gain an advantage over its competitors who did not have the information. The August 23, 1972 proposal by Kothawala is a significant compilation of marketing and technical planning for the program and this document was therefore proprietary and confidential. The court finds that SDRC relied on the representations of Kothawala and Surana including those contained in the August 23, 1972 document in its decision to devote its resources to the program. SDRC reasonably anticipated that part of its business advantage would flow from its early entry in the market—an advantage recognized by both sides. SDRC did not anticipate that the very employees who extolled the merits of the program and caused SDRC to undertake its development would use the same information to develop a competitive product and achieve the advantage of being first in the market. These actions by defendants breached their contractual obligations not to use or disclose confidential information.

The technical planning and development of NIESA to its stage of development in January, 1973, including the selection of elements, solver routine, organization of sub-routines, coding, and other factors contributing to the efficiency and effectiveness of the program, constituted important and confidential information, particularly prior to public release of the program. The technical accomplishments of Surana and Kothawala reflected in their work on NIESA amounted to a compilation of information which gave SDRC a competitive advantage. The existence or availability of abstract technical data does not detract from the confidentiality of the combination of such parts and data into a program of the type under consideration. This was conceded by Kothawala and confirmed by defendants' actions in dealing with the trade when great emphasis was placed by the defendants on the confidential nature of the NISA program and the competitive importance to EMRC in protecting such confidentiality.

The status report prepared for SDRC by Kothawala and Surana in October includes such information and it is likewise confidential and proprietary. This information had value and was confidential to SDRC. Surana's use of this information for defendants' benefit was a breach of his contract. This also holds true with respect to Kothawala, who hired Surana and participated in the unlawful use of information obtained at

SDRC, and who, as sole shareholder of EMRC, is presently the primary beneficiary of the illicit information.

Confidentiality of information can be determined from the manner in which defendants themselves treated the information prior to the litigation. Here the record is replete with statements by the defendants both to SDRC and to AMC as to the value, uniqueness and confidentiality of the program.

A quantity of documents belonging to SDRC were also found in possession of defendants when this action was commenced. These included:

* * *

Internal SDRC documents pertaining to the NIESA program including the August 23 and October 25 documents, customer information and prospective research and development activities.

Surana's notes prepared as part of his development work on NIESA. The court finds these notes to have significant value both in the case of NIESA and NISA.

The court does not credit defendant's explanation that these documents were permitted to be taken from SDRC's office. The court finds that they were taken without permission.

At a pretrial conference the court directed defendants to make a copy of the static portion of the NISA code available to plaintiff's counsel and experts pursuant to a protective order. The code which was furnished was dated December, 1974, and reflected many revisions made subsequent to defendants' initial code. Defendants have represented that no prior version of the NISA code remained. Portions of the NISA code were compared to the NIESA code as it existed in January, 1973. On the basis of this comparison, plaintiff's experts, Dr. Anderson of the Department of Aerospace Engineering at the University of Michigan, and Michael Coble, a computer programmer also affiliated with the University, concluded that defendants must have copied from the NIESA code. They made a careful analysis of the two programs and found not only similarity in the overall structure and organization (some of which might be explainable on functional grounds) but they found identical segments of code which were solely arbitrary and, most significantly, deviations or quasi-mistakes which, in their judgment, could only be explained by copying. Victor Nicholas, who completed the development of NIESA–SUPERB at SDRC, testified that the input data cards prepared by Surana for NIESA were taken verbatim into NISA. Except for cross-examination, defendants did not address these specifics relied on by the experts, but attributed such similarities as existed to Surana's memory. The court does not accept this explanation. Memory alone cannot explain the specifics which according to the experts do not make sense but are explainable only by copying. The court finds that defendants copied from the physical NIESA code.

The technical and business information which the court has found to have been misappropriated by defendants was treated by SDRC in a manner consistent with the preservation of its confidentiality. Although SDRC did not use the ultimate in policing measures, the professional caliber of its employees, and the nature of its development work made heavy-handed measures unnecessary. Moreover, the confidential nature of development work was specifically called to each employee's attention in his individual confidential disclosure agreement. The court finds that defendants Kothawala and Surana knew that information pertaining to NIESA was confidential and proprietary to SDRC.

SDRC did not disclose confidential information to outside parties in a manner inconsistent with preservation of confidentiality. To the extent that limited disclosure may have been made to representatives of United States Steel Corporation, that company's relationship to SDRC as its largest shareholder and a business partner was not inconsistent with the preservation of confidentiality.

* * *

The court has held that the NISA program of EMRC was developed through the use of the plaintiff's confidential information regarding the NIESA–SUPERB projects. The fact that the NISA program is at a later stage of completion that the status of NIESA at the time that Surana left SDRC or the fact that EMRC may have modified and added additional capabilities than those existing at the time that Surana left is not a defense to this action. There is no requirement that the defendants use the information in exactly the form in which they received it. Furthermore, the court finds that the later state of development of NISA is directly attributable to the head start that the use of SDRC's confidential information gave to EMRC in its pursuit of the NISA project.

* * *

Finally, the court finds that EMRC, the corporation of which defendant Kothawala is sole shareholder, is the entity through which this confidential information is being purveyed in the marketplace; it is liable with the individual defendants for agreeing with them to carry out this improper purpose. In view of these findings, it is unnecessary to consider plaintiff's contention as to unfair competition.

* * *

NOTES AND QUESTIONS

1. *Ownership of trade secrets created by employees.* The *Structural Dynamics* court set forth the common-law rule about ownership of trade secrets created by employees:

Where the employer assigns the employee to a specific development task and commits considerable resources and supervision to the project, a confidential relationship arises that prevents the employee from using or disclosing the fruits of his research. When, on the other hand, the developments are the product of the application of the employee's own skill, "without any appreciable assistance by way of information or great expense or supervision [from the employer], outside of the normal expenses of his job," he has "an unqualified privilege" to use and disclose the trade secrets so developed.

Structural Dynamics, 401 F.Supp. at 1112 (quoting Wexler v. Greenberg, 399 Pa. 569, 582–83, 160 A.2d 430, 436–37 (1960)).

One practitioner-scholar has approached the issue of ownership by dividing employee inventors into three groups: "specific inventive," "general inventive," and "non-inventive."

"Specific inventive" employment applies to an employee who is either (1) hired to invent a specific invention or (2) is assigned the task of making a specific invention or improvement to existing technology. In both cases, a specific invention or end result is contemplated. Specific inventive employment applies to the class of employees who are hired or employed to "invent," including research scientists, design engineers, and other employees whose "work" involves specific inventive activity. * * *

"General inventive" employment applies to the same class of employees who are subject to specific inventive employment, except that no specific invention or end result is contemplated. General research or design work usually is involved and, in many instances, the employee volunteers, or is encouraged by the employer, to pursue his or her creative instincts, even though they may diverge from assigned work. * * *

"Non-inventive" employment, as the term implies, does not involve any expectation of inventive activity. Shop or manufacturing employees, as well as non-technical employees, fall into this category.

Gullette, *State Legislation Governing Ownership Rights in Inventions Under Employee Invention Agreements*, 62 J. Pat. Off. Soc. 732, 733 (1980).[10]

The employer is generally found to own inventions of specific inventive employees. Courts have reasoned that specific inventive employees impliedly assign their inventions to their employer. The Supreme Court explained the rationale behind the rule in Solomons v. United States, 137 U.S. 342, 346, 11 S.Ct. 88, 89, 34 L.Ed. 667, 669 (1890):

If one is employed to devise or perfect an instrument, or a means for accomplishing a prescribed result, he cannot, after successfully accomplishing the work for which he was employed, plead title thereto as against his employer. That which he has been employed and paid to accomplish becomes, when accomplished, the property of his employer. Whatever rights as an individual he may have had in and to his inventive powers, and that which they are able to accomplish, he has sold in advance to his employer.

By contrast, noninventive employees generally will be found to retain ownership of their creations, even though they made them at work, with the

---

10. © R.L. Gullette, 1980. Reprinted by permission of the copyright owner.

employer's materials, or during work hours (though the invention may be subject to a shop right in the employer, as described in Note 2 below).

General inventive employees pose the difficult problems, and the results of employers' claims of an implied assignment by such employees are mixed. The court's finding may be influenced by any of a number of factors, including the nature and scope of the employment relationship, the amount of money or other resources the employer devoted to the inventive activity, how closely the employee's invention is related to the employer's business, whether the employee has assigned inventions to the employer in the past, and any other evidence of an implicit understanding between the parties about ownership of inventions. Compare Cahill v. Regan, 5 N.Y.2d 292, 184 N.Y.S.2d 348, 157 N.E.2d 505 (1959) (Court found defendant employee owned the re-usable can he developed during his employment. The court reasoned that employment to design or construct or devise methods of manufacture is not the same as specific employment to invent products. Moreover, while the defendant was told to develop the idea of the reusable can, which he had already conceived, he had not initially been directed to conceive of the idea.), with White's Electronics, Inc. v. Teknetics, Inc., 67 Or.App. 63, 677 P.2d 68 (1984) (Plaintiff, a manufacturer of metal detectors, hired defendant, an electrical engineer, "to invent and develop improvements in [plaintiff's] product line." Defendant conceived of an idea that would enable a metal detector automatically to provide the user with target identifying information. The court found that if the defendant made the invention while employed, he was obliged to assign it to the plaintiff, especially since he had assigned inventions to plaintiff in the past.)

In the *Structural Dynamics* case, who does the court find to be the owner of the computer program under the common-law rule—the plaintiff, or the defendants? Why? What was the impact of the nondisclosure agreement the defendants signed?

Note that the same common-law rule for determining ownership of employee-made inventions applies, regardless of whether the owner decides to rely on trade secret law or apply for a patent. While an application for patent must be made in the name of the inventor, an assignment of ownership implied by state law will vest title to the resulting patent in the employer. For a provocative critique of the development of the law regarding ownership of employee inventions, see Fisk, *Removing the "Fuel of Interest" from the "Fire of Genius": Law and the Employee–Inventor, 1830–1930*, 65 U. Chi. L. Rev. 1127 (1998). For an economic analysis of the rules of invention ownership, see Merges, *The Law and Economics of Employee Inventions*, 13 Harv. J. L. & Tech. 1 (1999).

2. *Shop rights*. When an employee/inventor is found to own the trade secret she developed during her employment, the employer may obtain a shop right in the trade secret if it is related to the employer's business and the employee, in developing it, used her employer's time, facilities, personnel, materials, money or other resources. Some courts have also required that the employee have initially allowed the employer to use the trade secret without paying special compensation for the right. See, e.g., Aetna–Standard Engineering Co. v. Rowland, 343 Pa.Super. 64, 70, 493 A.2d 1375, 1378 (1985). A

shop right is an irrevocable, non-exclusive, non-assignable right to use the trade secret, without an obligation to pay royalties. As one court described it: "This is an application of equitable principles. Since the servant uses his master's time, facilities and materials to attain a concrete result, the latter is in equity entitled to use that which embodies his own property" in his business. Cahill v. Regan, 5 N.Y.2d 292, 298, 184 N.Y.S.2d 348, 353, 157 N.E.2d 505, 509 (1959). The shop right rule applies to inventions in which the inventor/employee maintains trade secret protection as well as to inventions that the employee/inventor patents.

3. *Express assignment provisions.* In order to avoid the uncertainties of the common-law rule of invention ownership (and perhaps to obtain more rights in employee-made inventions than the common law would provide) many employers require employees to sign advance assignment agreements expressly assigning to the employer rights in any inventions they make during their employment. These provisions are generally enforced by the courts, as long as the inventions have some reasonable relationship to the employer's business and do not extend unduly beyond the period of the employee's employment. See, e.g., Ingersoll–Rand v. Ciavatta, 110 N.J. 609, 627, 542 A.2d 879, 888 (1988) (Court finds employee assignment of inventions made after termination of employment enforceable if reasonable. Such an assignment is not reasonable, and thus is unenforceable if it "(1) extends beyond any apparent protection that the employer reasonably requires; (2) prevents the inventor from seeking other employment; or (3) adversely impacts on the public."). Is widespread use of broad advance assignment agreements likely to have an impact on employees' incentive to invent?

In an effort to avoid employer abuses, some states have enacted statutes to regulate employee invention assignment agreements. See, e.g., Cal. Lab. Code §§ 2870–2872 (West Supp. 2000) (contractual provision requiring employee to assign rights to inventions is unenforceable with regard to inventions made entirely on employee's own time and with employee's own resources unless the invention relates to employer's business or results from work performed by employee for employer).

4. *Reliance on contract.* In *Structural Dynamics*, the court says it is not relying on trade secret law to determine the respective rights of the parties, but on the express contractual provisions signed by the defendants. Within the context of that case, what are the implications of that decision?

Consider the following criticism of the *Structural Dynamics* opinion:

We do not accept the analysis in *Structural Dynamics Research Corp. v. Engineering Mechanics Research Corp.*, 401 F.Supp. 1102, 1112, 1118–1119 (E.D.Mich.1975), cited by the plaintiff, in which the court held that two defendants "do not owe [the plaintiff] a duty not to use or disclose its trade secrets by reason of a relationship of confidence in employment" but were nevertheless bound by a general non-disclosure agreement. It is out of harmony with our cases and could turn a non-disclosure agreement into a non-competition agreement open ended and unenforceable as against public policy.

Dynamics Research Corp. v. Analytic Sciences Corp., 9 Mass.App.Ct. 254, 278 n. 32, 400 N.E.2d 1274, 1288 n. 32 (1980). What does the court mean? In your opinion, is its criticism valid?

PROBLEM

1. Widget, Inc. is a small company that manufactures and sells widgets. It has a total of thirty employees. One employee, an engineer named Walters, works in a small laboratory in the plant. His job is to keep the machines used in making the widgets in good repair, to trouble-shoot manufacturing problems, and to develop improvements in the manufacturing process and the finished product. Chang, a graduate student in mechanical engineering at a nearby university, works half-time at Widget as Walters' assistant. Chang spends much of her time on the job inspecting and maintaining the assembly-line machinery. She also assists Walters with various projects in the laboratory.

In the course of working with Walters, Chang became interested in a particular problem that the assembly-line workers were encountering. Walters made several experiments in an effort to solve the problem, and ultimately made an adjustment to one of the assembly-line machines (the "wiring machine"). Chang was critical of Walters' approach to the problem, and felt that his solution was inadequate. She devoted some thought to the problem while performing her more routine duties, and thought about it some more while at home. One day when Walters was on vacation, Chang finished her assigned work early and decided to work on her own solution to the problem. She consulted some of the literature that Walters kept in the lab, and this assisted her to further refine her ideas. She took graph paper from the shelf and did some sketches of a new component to be added to the wiring machine. This, she felt, would provide a much more efficient and reliable solution to the problem than Walters' adjustment.

Chang bypassed Walters and submitted her suggested improvement directly to the Company President in a memorandum. In the memorandum, which she marked "confidential," she described her improvement and explained why she thought it would work better than the measures Walters had taken. She concluded her memorandum with the statement: "I'm just a part-time worker, and I don't get paid very much. If the Company wants to implement my improvement, it will have to pay me extra for it." The President immediately sent a memo to Walters directing him to implement the idea. He sent a copy to Chang, thanking her for her contribution, but stating that her salary was her compensation. The Company had compensated employees for valuable suggestions on several occasions in the past, although it did not always do so.

Assuming that the improvement otherwise qualifies as a trade secret, what are Widget, Inc. and Chang's respective rights in it?

III.   RELATED STATE RIGHTS—"IDEA LAW"

The patent and trade secret laws sometimes fail to extend rights to ideas[11] such as marketing schemes, new product suggestions, or underlying themes for radio or television programs. The question of legal rights in such ideas frequently arises when a person discloses her idea to someone in a position to implement it, and the disclosee proceeds to use it without the discloser's permission and without paying her for it. For example, an employee discloses an idea for a time-saving cargo-loading device to her employer, who builds and uses the device but refuses to compensate the employee for the idea; or an applicant for an insurance sales position discloses a system for selling insurance in the course of an interview, and the insurance company implements the system, but refuses to hire the applicant-discloser.

Members of the public inundate the entertainment industry and manufacturers with unsolicited suggestions for new programs or products. While some of the suggestions may prove useful, many of them are old and redundant. Most recipients treat unsolicited suggestions with caution. An example illustrates the potential problem. In 1954 the National Broadcasting Corporation (NBC), which received thirty to forty thousand program suggestions each year, began broadcasting "Home," a "service-type" program like a magazine-of-the-air. On the basis of advance publicity, before the first program was aired, six different individuals made claims for compensation, alleging that the program would be based on an idea they had submitted to NBC. Following the first broadcast, three more persons made similar claims. None of these nine claimants' submissions dated back to 1929, the time at which, according to NBC's records, it had first begun to receive unsolicited suggestions for such a program. When the program went off the air in 1957, two lawsuits were still pending, and one claimant was still trying to enjoin the series. Olsson, *Dreams for Sale*, 23 L. & Contemp. Probs. 34, 55 (1958).

Assuming that a plaintiff can prove that the defendant did use her idea without permission, should she have a property right in the idea that entitles her to compensation? What are the policy implications? As in other areas of intellectual property, courts must consider not only the need for incentives to create, but also the danger that provision of property rights may retard the overall progress of the arts and marketplace competition. As Justice Traynor noted:

> [C]reativeness thrives on freedom; men find new implications in old ideas when they range with open minds through open fields. They would indeed be stifled in their efforts to create forms worth protect-

---

11. The term "undeveloped idea" is often used in this context, but the term may be misleading. As will be discussed *infra*, the doctrines developed to accommodate plaintiffs in this setting often restrict protection to "concrete" ideas. "Concrete" in this context may have a similar meaning to "developed."

ing, if in the common through which they ranged they were diverted from their course by one enclosure after another.

Stanley v. Columbia Broadcasting System, Inc., 35 Cal.2d 653, 673, 221 P.2d 73, 84–85 (1950) (Traynor, J., dissenting). Assuming that property rights are to be recognized, the timing may be an important consideration, too. If rights are given too early in the development of an idea, there may be less incentive for the originator to turn the idea into a finished work. On the other hand, the person who conceives of the idea may not be in a position to execute it. What rule of law will best facilitate cooperation between creators and executors, who may not be members of the same company?

Though traditional intellectual property doctrines failed to provide a remedy for the idea submitter in circumstances such as those described above, shortly after the turn of the century courts began to compile, somewhat haphazardly, a loose body of state common law to address such claims. Over time, courts and commentators began to categorize the accumulated "idea law" case opinions into several "theories" through which a plaintiff/idea submitter could recover the value of his idea or of his service in providing the idea to the defendant.

First, if the plaintiff can prove that the defendant made an explicit promise to pay for the idea, or can demonstrate an implied agreement to pay under the particular facts of the case, the courts may invoke traditional doctrines of contract law to enforce the promise as either an express or implied-in-fact contract. Due to the kinds of concerns expressed by Justice Traynor, however, many jurisdictions have manipulated traditional contract law to add a requirement that the idea be "novel" (and sometimes "concrete") before the express or implied contract to pay will be enforced.

Courts have also relied on a quasi-contract (or unjust enrichment) theory, which permits recovery when denial of payment will result in an injustice. Another theory finds a right to payment for an idea if the parties were in a confidential relationship in which the plaintiff reposed trust and confidence in the defendant's good faith. Again, in many quasi-contract and confidential relationship contexts the courts have superimposed a requirement that the idea at issue be novel and concrete. Finally, courts and commentators have occasionally paid lip service to a "property theory" for recovery for ideas, which appears to recognize property rights in an idea that is novel and concrete, even in the absence of a contract, unjust enrichment or a confidential relationship.

As you read the following case and notes, consider whether the courts have reached the proper accommodation of the conflicting public and private interests.

REEVES v. ALYESKA PIPELINE SERVICE CO.

Supreme Court of Alaska, 1996.
926 P.2d 1130.

PER CURIAM.

I. INTRODUCTION

This case raises issues concerning the protection of ideas. It arises out of John Reeves' claims that in 1991 Alyeska Pipeline Service Company (Alyeska) appropriated his idea for a visitor center at a popular turnout overlooking the Trans–Alaska Pipeline. The superior court granted summary judgment to Alyeska. We reverse in part and remand for further proceedings.

II. FACTS AND PROCEEDINGS

In 1985 Alyeska created a visitor turnout at Mile 9 of the Steese Highway between Fox and Fairbanks. The turnout had informational signs and provided visitors a view of the Trans–Alaska Pipeline. Before Alyeska constructed the turnout, visitors gained access to the pipeline by a nearby road and trespassed on the Trans–Alaska Pipeline right-of-way.

John Reeves, owner of Gold Dredge No. 8, a tourist attraction outside Fairbanks and near the turnout, contacted Alyeska in January 1991 to discuss a tourism idea he had. He spoke with Keith Burke, Alyeska's Fairbanks Manager. After receiving Burke's assurance that the tourism idea was "between us," Reeves orally disclosed his idea to build a visitor center at the turnout. He proposed that Alyeska lease him the land and he build the center, sell Alyeska merchandise, and display a "pig"[2] and a cross-section of pipe.

Burke told him the idea "look[ed] good" and asked Reeves to submit a written proposal, which Reeves did two days later. The proposal explained Reeves' idea of operating a visitor center on land leased to him by Alyeska. The proposal included plans to provide small tours, display a "pig," pipe valve, and section of pipe, sell refreshments and pipeline memorabilia, and plant corn and cabbage.

After submitting the proposal, Reeves met with Burke once again. At this meeting Burke told Reeves the proposal looked good and was exactly what he wanted. In Reeves' words, Burke told him, "We're going to do this deal, and I'm going to have my Anchorage lawyers draw it." Reeves claimed he and Burke envisioned that the visitor center would be operating by the 1991 summer tourist season.

Reeves alleges that Alyeska agreed during this meeting (1) to grant access to the turnout for twenty years; (2) to allow Reeves to construct and operate an information center; and (3) to allow Reeves to sell

---

2. A "pig" is a device which passes through the pipeline to clean interior pipe walls, survey interior pipe shape and detect corrosion.

merchandise and charge a $2.00 admission fee. Reeves stated that, in exchange, he agreed to pay Alyeska ten percent of gross receipts.

Over the next several months, Burke allegedly told Reeves that the deal was "looking good" and not to worry because it takes time for a large corporation to move. However, in spring 1991, Burke told Reeves that the visitor center was such a good idea that Alyeska was going to implement it without Reeves. By August 1991 Alyeska had installed a portable building at the turnout to serve as a visitor center; it built a permanent log cabin structure in 1992.

The members of the Alyeska Pipeline Club North (APCN) operated the visitor center and sold T-shirts, hats, and other items.[3] APCN does not charge admission. A section of pipeline and a "pig" are on display. APCN employees provide information and answer visitors' questions. Members of APCN had suggested in 1987 that Alyeska create a visitor center at the turnout. However, Alyeska had rejected the idea at that time. Before meeting with Reeves, Burke did not know that APCN's visitor center idea had been raised and rejected by Alyeska in 1987.

Approximately 100,000 people visited the visitor center each summer in 1992 and 1993. It grossed over $50,000 in sales each year. The net profit for 1993 was calculated to be $5,000–$15,000. APCN received all the profit.

Reeves filed suit in May 1993. By amended complaint, he alleged a variety of tort and contract claims. Judge Charles R. Pengilly granted Alyeska's motion for summary judgment on all claims; Reeves appeals. * * *

III. DISCUSSION

We will review a grant of summary judgment *de novo* and will adopt the rule of law that is most persuasive in light of precedent, reason, and policy. We are not bound by the trial court's reasoning and may affirm a grant of summary judgment on any alternative ground appearing in the record. To succeed on summary judgment a movant must show that there are no genuine issues of material fact and that it is entitled to judgment as a matter of law. * * *

Reeves sued Alyeska on claims of breach of oral contract, promissory estoppel, breach of implied contract, quasi-contract (unjust enrichment and quantum meruit), breach of the covenant of good faith and fair dealing, breach of license and/or lease agreement, and various torts related to the contractual relationships alleged.

This case presents several questions of first impression concerning the protection of business ideas. * * * Before reaching the merits of Reeves' claims we must first briefly discuss the law relating to the protection of ideas and the roles of novelty and originality.

---

3. Alyeska Pipeline Club North is a non-profit corporation run by Alyeska employees. It raises money to fund activities such as picnics and Christmas parties for Alyeska employees.

A. *Protection of Ideas*

The law pertaining to the protection of ideas must reconcile the public's interest in access to new ideas with the perceived injustice of permitting some to exploit commercially the ideas of others. Federal law addresses the protection of new inventions and the expression of ideas. Federal patent law protects inventors of novel, nonobvious, and useful inventions by excluding others from "making, using, or selling the invention" for a period of seventeen years. Federal copyright law protects an individual's tangible expression of an idea, but not the intangible idea itself. Copyright law creates a monopoly for the author that allows him or her to benefit economically from the author's creative efforts. It does not create a monopoly on the idea from which the expression originates; the idea remains available for all to use. Reeves' claims do not fall under these federal protections because his idea is not a new invention, nor is it expressed in a copyrighted work. Nevertheless, federal law is not the only protection available to individuals and their ideas.

Creating a middle ground between no protection and the legal monopolies created by patent and copyright law, courts have protected ideas under a variety of contract and contract-like theories. * * * These theories protect individuals who spend their time and energy developing ideas that may benefit others. It would be inequitable to prevent these individuals from obtaining legally enforceable compensation from those who voluntarily choose to benefit from the services of the "idea-person." The California Supreme Court expressed this concept in the following manner:

> Generally speaking, ideas are as free as the air and as speech and the senses, and as potent or weak, interesting or drab, as the experiences, philosophies, vocabularies, and other variables the speaker and listener may combine to produce, to portray, or to comprehend. But there can be circumstances when neither air nor ideas may be acquired without cost. The diver who goes deep in the sea, even as the pilot who ascends high in the troposphere, knows full well that for life itself he, or someone on his behalf, must arrange for air (or its respiration-essential element, oxygen) to be specifically provided at the time and place of need. The theatrical producer likewise may be dependent for his business life on the procurement of ideas from other persons as well as the dressing up and portrayal of his self-conceptions; he may not find his own sufficient for survival.

Desny v. Wilder, 46 Cal.2d 715, 299 P.2d 257, 265 (Cal.1956). The scope of idea protection, although primarily raised in the entertainment field, is not limited to that industry; it may also apply to business and scientific ideas.

We have not had occasion to address these theories in the context of the protection of ideas. In addressing each of Reeves' claims we must determine whether the special nature of ideas affects the application of traditional contract and contract-like claims. In making these determinations we are mindful of the competing policies of retaining the free exchange of ideas and compensating those who develop and market their ideas. On the one hand, protecting ideas by providing compensation to the author for their use or appropriation rewards the idea person and encourages the development of creative and intellectual ideas which will benefit humankind. On the other hand, protecting ideas also inevitably restricts their free use, potentially delaying or restricting the benefit any given idea might confer on society.

Reeves argues that requiring novelty and originality, as did the trial court, erroneously imports property theories into contract-based claims. He contends that so long as the parties bargained for the disclosure of the idea, the disclosure serves as consideration and the idea itself need not have the qualities of property. Alyeska argues that novelty and originality should be employed as limiting factors in idea cases because these cases are based on a theory of idea as intellectual property. Alyeska contends that in order to be protected, an idea must have "not been suggested to or known by the public at any prior time."

We find that the manner in which requirements such as novelty or originality are applied depends largely on which theory of recovery is pursued. Thus, we will address the parties' arguments concerning novelty as they apply to each of Reeves' theories of recovery.

B. Express Contract Claims

Reeves argues that he and Alyeska entered into three different oral contracts: (1) a confidentiality or disclosure agreement by which Alyeska promised not to use Reeves' idea without his participation, if Reeves disclosed the idea;[5] (2) a lease agreement by which Alyeska promised to lease the turnout to Reeves in exchange for a percentage of the center's profits; and (3) a memorialization agreement by which Alyeska promised to commit the agreement to writing.

* * *

* * * We consider each of the three alleged agreements in turn.[7]
* * *

Reeves argues that novelty and originality should not be required in express contract cases. He argues that California has rejected those requirements in contract cases. *See Desny*, 299 P.2d at 266 ("Even though the idea disclosed may be 'widely known and generally understood,' . . . it

---

5. Reeves refers to this agreement as a "confidentiality agreement." However, Reeves argues that Alyeska not only promised to keep his idea confidential, but promised not to use the idea without Reeves' participation. To label this alleged agreement a "confidentiality agreement" tends to overlook the participation portion of Alyeska's promise. We will refer to the first alleged contract as the "disclosure" agreement.

7. Alyeska does not argue explicitly that Reeves' idea must be novel and original to be the subject of an express contract. However, some of the cases it cites indicate that an idea that is not novel may not be protected by an express contract. *See Downey v. General Foods Corp.*, 31 N.Y.2d 56, 334 N.Y.S.2d 874, 877, 286 N.E.2d 257, 259 (1972) ("[W]hen one submits an idea to another . . . no asserted agreement [may be] enforced, if the elements of novelty and originality are absent. . . ."); *Garrido v. Burger King Corp.*, 558 So.2d 79, 84 (Fla.App.1990) ("The novelty requirement prevents a person from being able 'by contract [to] monopolize an idea that is common and general to the whole world.' ").

may be protected by an express contract providing that it will be paid for regardless of its lack of novelty.''). Reeves also notes that New York has recently moved away from requiring novelty in some express contract cases. *See Apfel v. Prudential–Bache Securities, Inc.*, 81 N.Y.2d 470, 600 N.Y.S.2d 433, 436, 616 N.E.2d 1095, 1098 (1993) (holding that novelty and originality were not required in cases involving disclosure of ideas in which there was a post-disclosure contract for the idea).

Because Reeves claims that the consideration he provided consisted of his services, not the idea itself, we need not determine whether a non-novel idea by itself may serve as consideration in an express contract.

1. *The Disclosure Agreement*

Reeves alleges that in exchange for the disclosure of his idea, Alyeska promised to keep the idea confidential and not to use the idea without entering into a contract with Reeves to implement the idea. Reeves' deposition testimony, when all inferences are taken in his favor, supports the existence of a disclosure agreement. Reeves testified that in his early conversations with Burke, he told Burke that he was in the tourism industry and had an idea that would help Alyeska. Reeves stated that Burke told him the idea ''was between us.'' Reeves testified that he ''didn't offer anything to Keith Burke until [Reeves] was told by [Burke] that we had a deal. This was between me and him, and this was going no place else.'' Reeves also testified that Burke had promised confidentiality and that Reeves believed that he and Burke had a ''done deal.''

Alyeska does not respond separately to Reeves' disclosure agreement claim. It instead argues that, notwithstanding Reeves' assertion there were three agreements, Reeves actually alleged only one contract, which included a purported twenty-year lease agreement. It argues that the statute of frauds applies because the alleged agreement concerns a lease for a period longer than one year and because performance would not be completed within one year.

We conclude that the statute of frauds does not apply to the alleged disclosure agreement. That alleged agreement was to be completed within one year. If Alyeska chose to implement the idea, it was to enter into a lease agreement with Reeves by the summer tourist season. Moreover, Reeves' disclosure to Alyeska constituted full performance of his side of the contract for disclosure. The statute of frauds consequently does not apply.

[The court goes on to hold, however, that the alleged agreement to lease the turnout for twenty years and the alleged agreement to memorialize the contract are barred by the statute of frauds.]

C. *Implied-in-Fact Contract*

The trial court's opinion did not address whether Reeves established a contract implied-in-fact. Reeves argues that he ''submitted uncontroverted evidence sufficient to find as a matter of law that Alyeska's actions established a contract implied in fact." We conclude that Alyeska failed to carry its burden of showing that it is entitled to judgment as a matter of law on this claim.

Reeves has made out a *prima facie* case for an implied contract. We have held that an implied-in-fact contract, like an express contract, is based on the intentions of the parties. "It arises where the court finds from the surrounding facts and circumstances that the parties intended to make a contract but failed to articulate their promises and the court merely implies what it feels the parties really intended."

In *Aliotti v. R. Dakin & Co.*, 831 F.2d 898, 902 (9th Cir.1987), the court listed the requirements for demonstrating an implied-in-fact contract under California law:

> [O]ne must show: that he or she prepared the work; that he or she disclosed the work to the offeree for sale; under all circumstances attending disclosure it can be concluded that the offeree voluntarily accepted the disclosure knowing the conditions on which it was tendered (i.e., the offeree must have the opportunity to reject the attempted disclosure if the conditions were unacceptable); and the reasonable value of the work.

There are three primary factual scenarios under which ideas may be submitted to another. The first involves an unsolicited submission that is involuntarily received. The idea is submitted without warning; it is transmitted before the recipient has taken any action which would indicate a promise to pay for the submission. Under this scenario, a contract will not be implied.

The second involves an unsolicited submission that is voluntarily received. In this situation, the idea person typically gives the recipient advance warning that an idea is to be disclosed; the recipient has an opportunity to stop the disclosure, but through inaction allows the idea to be disclosed. Under California law, if the recipient at the time of disclosure understands that the idea person expects to be paid for the disclosure of the idea, and does not attempt to stop the disclosure, inaction may be seen as consent to a contract. *Desny*, 299 P.2d at 267.

This view has been criticized as unfairly placing a duty on the recipient to take active measures to stop the submission. See 3 David Nimmer, Nimmer on Copyright § 16.05[C], at 16–38 (1994). The critics argue that inaction generally should not be considered an expression of consent to a contract.

We believe that a contract should not be implied under this scenario. An implied-in-fact contract is based on circumstances that demonstrate that the parties intended to form a contract but failed to articulate their promises. Only under exceptional circumstances would inaction demonstrate an intent to enter a contract.[14]

---

14. We recognize the possibility of a rare case in which inaction could express intent to form a contract. For example, a contract would be implied if the parties' history of dealings demonstrat-

The third scenario involves a solicited submission. Here, a request by the recipient for disclosure of the idea usually implies a promise to pay for the idea if the recipient uses it. Nimmer states,

> The element of solicitation of plaintiff's idea by defendant is therefore of great importance in establishing an implied contract. If defendant makes such a request, even if he attempts to frame the request in ambiguous or exculpatory language, most courts will nevertheless imply a promise to pay if the idea is used.

Id. at 16–40 to 16–41.

Reeves argues that Alyeska solicited his idea. He alleges that Burke asked him what the idea was, and later requested a written proposal. He contends that the request and Alyeska's later use of the idea created an implied contract for payment. These allegations are sufficient to survive summary judgment. A reasonable fact-finder could determine that Burke's actions implied a promise to pay for the disclosure of Reeves' idea. A fact-finder could also determine that Reeves volunteered the idea before Burke took any affirmative action that would indicate an agreement to pay for the disclosure. These possible conclusions present genuine issues of material fact.

Relying largely on cases from New York, Alyeska argues that novelty and originality should be required in an implied-in-fact claim. Reeves responds that we should follow California's example and not require novelty as an essential element of this sort of claim.

Idea-based claims arise most frequently in the entertainment centers of New York and California, but New York requires novelty, whereas California does not.[15]

We prefer the California approach. An idea may be valuable to the recipient merely because of its timing or the manner in which it is presented. In *Chandler v. Roach*, 156 Cal.App.2d 435, 319 P.2d 776 (1957), the court stated that "the fact that the [recipient of the idea] may later determine, with a little thinking, that he could have had the same ideas and could thereby have saved considerable money for himself, is no defense against the claim of the [idea person]. This is so even though the material to be purchased is abstract and unprotected material."

Implied-in-fact contracts are closely related to express contracts. Each requires the parties to form an intent to enter into a contract. It is ordinarily not the court's role to evaluate the adequacy of the consider-

---

ed that they had entered into similar contracts in the past, or if it were proven in a particular field or industry that a recipient's silence constitutes agreement to pay for an idea upon use.

15. Reeves argues that *Apfel v. Prudential–Bache*, 81 N.Y.2d 470, 600 N.Y.S.2d 433, 436, 616 N.E.2d 1095, 1098 (1993), a recent New York case, has abandoned the requirements of novelty and originality. In *Apfel*, the court held that parties may enter a contract, after disclosure of the idea, without a requirement of novelty or originality. However, *Apfel* does not necessarily eliminate a novelty requirement in idea cases. The court distinguished cases in which "the buyer and seller contract for disclosure of the idea with payment based on use, but no separate post-disclosure contract for use of the ideas has been made." New York law would appear to require an express post-disclosure contract in order to succeed on a contract claim for a non-novel idea.

ation agreed upon by the parties. The bargain should be left in the hands of the parties. If parties voluntarily choose to bargain for an individual's services in disclosing or developing a non-novel or unoriginal idea, they have the power to do so. The *Desny* court analogized the services of a writer to the services of a doctor or lawyer and determined there was little difference; each may provide a product that is not novel or original. It held that it would not impose an additional requirement of novelty on the work. Although Reeves is not a writer, his ideas are entitled to no less protection than those of writers, doctors, or lawyers. Therefore, Reeves should be given the opportunity to prove the existence of an implied-in-fact contract for disclosure of his idea.

* * *

E. Quasi–Contract Claim

Reeves argues that Alyeska was unjustly enriched because it solicited and received Reeves' services, ideas, and opinions without compensating Reeves. He argues that the trial court erred in granting summary judgment to Alyeska on his quasi-contract cause of action.

We have required the following three elements for a quasi-contract claim:

1) a benefit conferred upon the defendant by the plaintiff;

2) appreciation by the defendant of such benefit; and

3) acceptance and retention by the defendant of such benefit under such circumstances that it would be inequitable for him to retain it without paying the value thereof.

Quasi-contracts are "judicially-created obligations to do justice." "Consequently, the obligation to make restitution that arises in quasi-contract is not based upon any agreement between the parties, objective or subjective."

The trial court understood Reeves to be arguing that his idea was a property right that was stolen by Alyeska. Reeves, however, argues that "Alyeska took Reeves' concept, proposal *and services* without any payment to Reeves." (Emphasis added.) Reeves' quasi-contract claims must be divided into two categories. His claim that Alyeska appropriated his idea for a visitor center is necessarily a property-based claim that seeks recovery for the value of the idea itself; Reeves seeks a recovery based on "his" idea. His claims that Alyeska benefitted from his proposal and services, however, do not necessarily rely on the visitor center idea being property; these claims are based on his services of disclosing and drafting the proposal. The property and non-property claims are treated differently.

An idea is usually not regarded as property because our concept of property implies something that can be owned and possessed to the exclusion of others. To protect an idea under a property theory requires that the idea possess property-like traits. Courts consider the elements of novelty or originality necessary for a claim of "ownership" in an idea or concept. These elements distinguish protectible ideas from ordinary ideas that are freely available for others to use. It is the element of originality or novelty that lends value to the idea itself.

If the idea is not distinguished in this manner, its use cannot satisfy the requirements of a quasi-contract claim. The idea, even if beneficial to the defendant, cannot be conferred if the plaintiff has no right of possession. With no right of possession, the idea cannot be said to have been conferred by the plaintiff.[18] Despite Reeves' protestations, the idea of establishing a visitor center near the pipeline is neither original nor novel.[19]

Nevertheless, not all of Reeves' quasi-contract claims require that his idea be considered property and consequently novel or original. Reeves argues that Alyeska was unjustly enriched "by Reeves' efforts on its behalf, not merely on the 'concept that [Reeves'] idea was intellectual property.'" Therefore, we must analyze whether the parties' transactions give rise to a quasi-contract.

The facts alleged by Reeves demonstrate that Burke specifically asked Reeves to draw up a proposal and that Alyeska was going to "do this deal." There is also evidence Reeves was familiar with the Fairbanks summer tourist industry and had special expertise in that area. These facts present a genuine issue of fact as to whether Alyeska benefited from Reeves' experience or his written plan. Thus, there is a question of fact whether Reeves' idea had value to Alyeska in its timing or in how it was presented, rather than in its novelty or originality. Reeves' endorsement of the idea, in combination with his experience in the Fairbanks tourism industry, may have also been valuable to Alyeska. The fact that Alyeska rejected a similar idea in 1987 may indicate that some feature of Reeves' plan or presentation caused Alyeska to go forward with a visitor center. If Reeves' services unjustly enriched Alyeska, he should be compensated for the value of those services.

* * *

NOTES AND QUESTIONS

1. *Novelty.* As the *Alyeska* court observes, a number of jurisdictions have imposed a requirement that ideas be "novel" before they can be protected under express or implied contract, quasi-contract or property theories of recovery. What reasoning justifies such a requirement? Courts have differed in their definition of "novelty" in this context. Some have suggested that an

---

18. The court correctly granted summary judgment on Reeves' conversion claim for the same reason. If an idea is not considered property, it cannot be converted.

19. There may be some question about whether the idea was novel to Burke because he had not heard that in 1987 Alyeska Pipeline Club North had suggested the same idea. Reeves argues that the idea was novel as to Alyeska because Burke did not know of the rejected 1987 proposal until after he contracted with Reeves. The visitor center idea was not novel to Alyeska. It was aware of the 1987 visitor center proposal, and it already operated a visitor center in Valdez. Burke's ignorance of the specific 1987 proposal does not make the visitor center idea novel.

idea will be novel if it is original to the plaintiff, see, e.g., Stevens v. Continental Can Co., 308 F.2d 100, 104 (6th Cir.1962), *cert. denied,* 374 U.S. 810, 83 S.Ct. 1702, 10 L.Ed.2d 1034 (1963), while others have stated that the idea must be innovative in character. See, e.g., Lueddecke v. Chevrolet Motor Co., 70 F.2d 345, 348 (8th Cir.1934) (novelty requirement means that idea must be "nonobvious"). Others have suggested that the idea must be both original to the plaintiff *and* innovative in character. See, e.g., Downey v. General Foods Corp., 31 N.Y.2d 56, 286 N.E.2d 257, 334 N.Y.S.2d 874 (1972). How does the *Alyeska* court appear to define novelty? Which of the alternative approaches most effectively fulfills the purposes of imposing a novelty require-ment? See Barrett, *The "Law of Ideas" Reconsidered,* 71 J. Pat. & Trademark Off. Soc. 691, 710–12 (1989).

2. *Concreteness.* Some jurisdictions have also imposed a "concreteness" requirement, in addition to a novelty requirement. Why impose this require-ment? As in the case of the novelty requirement, the courts have differed somewhat in their definition of concreteness. Essentially, the cases can be divided into two general approaches. In the first approach, courts appear to require that the idea be reduced to some tangible form. Some opinions have stated that the idea must be in writing. See. e.g., Bailey v. Haberle Congress Brewing Co., 193 Misc. 723, 85 N.Y.S.2d 51 (1948). Other opinions have suggested that the idea must be incorporated into a tangible product. See, e.g., Tutelman v. Stokowski, 44 U.S.P.Q. 47, 48 (Pa.C.P. 1939).

The second approach to "concreteness" suggests that the idea must be fully developed—completed, fleshed-out in detail and ready for immediate implementation. See, e.g., Hamilton National Bank v. Belt, 210 F.2d 706, 708–9 (D.C.Cir.1953). This view has been particularly prevalent in connection with claims involving television and radio program ideas. When the idea has been developed into a detailed format, a plan for an entire series with descriptions of the characters' personalities, methods of portrayals, sample plots, and such, courts have found the ideas sufficiently concrete to merit protection. In *Hamilton Bank, supra,* the Court of Appeals for the District of Columbia found the plaintiff's plan for a weekly radio program featuring talent from local high schools sufficiently concrete to justify relief:

> We think * * * that in the field of radio broadcasting concreteness may lie between the boundaries of mere generality on the one hand and, on the other, a full script containing the words to be uttered and delineating the action to be portrayed. Where the plan is for a series of broadcasts the contents of which depend upon selection of talent at different times, a detailed program cannot be presented at the preliminary stages of negoti-ation. This should not in and of itself deprive the originator of a property right in his plan. * * * As we have seen, in addition to the utilization of student talent selected for each broadcast from a different high school, the show was to be presented and recorded as a student assembly, retaining the atmosphere of a school by referring to the show as a class, to the acts as assignments and to the action as recitations. There was to be a rendition of several pieces by the school glee club, a minimum of conversation and introductions, a brief acknowledgment of sponsorship at the beginning and end of the broadcast, and no provision for commercial "spots." And a very important element in the plan was the cooperation

and participation of the school authorities through the use of school buildings and facilities and the assistance of faculty members. These details, when added to the basic general idea which, alone, would be too abstract, give sufficient concreteness.

Id., 210 F.2d at 709.

3. *The express contract theory of recovery.* As the *Alyeska* court notes, some jurisdictions refuse to enforce an express agreement to pay for an idea that lacks novelty. The Connecticut Supreme Court established this rule in Masline v. New York, New Haven & Hartford Railroad Co., 95 Conn. 702, 112 A. 639 (1921). In *Masline,* the plaintiff, a brakeman and baggage master for the defendant's railroad, told the defendant that he had "information of value" that, if used by the defendant, would enable it to earn at least $100,000 a year without any expense. Plaintiff said he would furnish this information if the defendant would agree to give him five percent of the receipts gained from use. The defendant, through one of its vice presidents and another officer, agreed. Plaintiff then disclosed his idea, which was to sell advertising space in or on the railroad's stations, depots, rights of way, cars and fences. The defendant had not sold advertising before but immediately began to do so, earning a large amount of money. It refused to pay anything to plaintiff. When plaintiff sued to enforce the agreement, the court denied relief, stating:

> An idea may undoubtedly be protected by contract * * *. But it must be the plaintiff's idea. Upon communication to the defendant it at once did appear that the idea was not original with the plaintiff, but was a matter of common knowledge, well known to the world at large. He had thought of nothing new, and had therefore no property right to protect which would make his idea a basis of consideration for anything.

Id., 95 Conn. at 710–11. An appreciable number of other jurisdictions have followed the *Masline* court's lead, and have also imposed a concreteness requirement on express contracts to pay for ideas. Is the *Masline* reasoning consistent with the traditional rules of contract law regarding consideration?

Another approach which leads to the same result as *Masline* implies a condition into the express contract to pay that the idea must be novel and concrete. See, e.g., Soule v. Bon Ami Co., 201 App.Div. 794, 796, 195 N.Y.S. 574, 576 (1922), *affirmed,* 235 N.Y. 609, 139 N.E. 754 (1923). Why should the law *assume* that this was the parties' intent, when neither expressly so provided?

Is there a policy justification for refusing to enforce contractual agreements to pay for non-novel, non-concrete ideas? See Justice Traynor's famous dissent in Stanley v. Columbia Broadcasting System, Inc., 35 Cal.2d 653, 674, 221 P.2d 73, 84 (1950). As the *Alyeska* decision notes, California has declined to apply the novelty and concreteness restrictions when express agreements to pay are proven. See, e.g., Donahue v. Ziv Television Programs, Inc. 245 Cal.App.2d 593, 54 Cal.Rptr. 130 (1966). How does the *Alyeska* court deal with this issue? Can the facts in *Alyeska* be readily distinguished from the express contract cases in which the novelty requirement was imposed?

The Alaska court notes Apfel v. Prudential–Bache Securities, Inc., 81 N.Y.2d 470, 616 N.E.2d 1095, 600 N.Y.S.2d 433 (1993), in which the New York Court of Appeals clarified its rule regarding the novelty requirement in express contract claims. In *Apfel*, the plaintiffs, a lawyer and an investment banker, approached the defendant investment bank with a proposal for issuing municipal securities through a system that eliminated paper certificates and allowed bonds to be sold, traded, and held exclusively by means of computerized "book entries." Initially, the parties signed a confidentiality agreement that allowed defendant to review the techniques as detailed in a 99–page summary. Then, after nearly a month of negotiations, the parties entered into a sale agreement under which plaintiffs conveyed their rights to the techniques and defendant agreed to pay a stipulated rate based on its use of the techniques. This obligation to pay was to remain in effect even if the techniques became public knowledge or standard practice in the industry and applications for patents were denied. During the next couple of years, the parties carried out the terms of the contract. Then the defendant refused to make any further payments. It argued that the contract was unenforceable because it lacked consideration: New York case law provided that an idea could not serve as legally sufficient consideration unless it was novel, and the plaintiffs' idea lacked novelty. The court rejected the argument:

> Under the traditional principles of contract law, the parties to a contract are free to make their bargain, even if the consideration exchanged is grossly unequal or of dubious value. Absent fraud or unconscionability, the adequacy of consideration is not a proper subject for judicial scrutiny. It is enough that something of "real value in the eye of the law" was exchanged. The fact that the sellers may not have had a property right in what they sold does not, by itself, render the contract void for lack of consideration (see Wahl v. Barnum, 116 N.Y. 87, 95 [relinquishment of disputed claim is valid consideration even though claim is in fact invalid]).

> Manifestly, defendant received something of value here; its own conduct establishes that. After signing the confidentiality agreement, defendant thoroughly reviewed plaintiffs' system before buying it. Having done so, it was in the best position to know whether the idea had value. It decided to enter into the sale agreement and aggressively market the system to potential bond issuers. For at least a year, it was the only underwriter to use plaintiffs' "book entry" system for municipal bonds, and it handled millions of such bond transactions during that time. Having obtained full disclosure of the system, used it in advance of competitors, and received the associated benefits of precluding its disclosure to others, defendant can hardly claim now the idea had no value to its municipal securities business. * * *

> Thus, defendant has failed to demonstrate on this record that the contract was void or to raise a triable issue of fact on lack of consideration.

> Defendant's position rests on Downey v. General Foods Corp. (31 N.Y.2d 56) and Soule v. Bon Ami Co. (235 N.Y. 609) and similar decisions. It contends those cases establish an exception to traditional principles of

contract law and require that the idea must be novel before it can constitute valid consideration for a contract. While our cases have discussed novelty as an element of an idea seller's claim, it is not a discrete supplemental requirement, but simply part of plaintiff's proof of either a proprietary interest in a claim based on a property theory or the validity of the consideration in a claim based on a contract theory.

* * *

* * * *Downey, Soule* and cases in that line of decisions involve a distinct factual pattern: the buyer and seller contract for disclosure of the idea with payment based on use, but no separate postdisclosure contract for use of the idea has been made. Thus, they present the issue of whether the idea the buyer was using was, in fact, the seller's.

Such transactions pose two problems for the courts. On the one hand, how can sellers prove that the buyer obtained the idea from them, and nowhere else, and that the buyer's use of it thus constitutes misappropriation of property? Unlike tangible property, an idea lacks title and boundaries and cannot be rendered exclusive by the acts of the one who first thinks it. On the other hand, there is no equity in enforcing a seemingly valid contract when, in fact, it turns out upon disclosure that the buyer already possessed the idea. In such instances, the disclosure, though freely bargained for, is manifestly without value. A showing of novelty, at least novelty as to the buyer, addresses these two concerns. Novelty can then serve to establish both the attributes of ownership necessary for a property-based claim and the value of the consideration— the disclosure—necessary for contract-based claims.

There are no such concerns in a transaction such as the one before us. Defendant does not claim that it was aware of the idea before plaintiffs disclosed it but, rather, concedes that the idea came from them. When a seller's claim arises from a contract to use an idea entered into after the disclosure of the idea, the question is not whether the buyer misappropriated property from the seller, but whether the idea had value to the buyer and thus constitutes valid consideration. In such a case, the buyer knows what he or she is buying and has agreed that the idea has value, and the Court will not ordinarily go behind that determination. The lack of novelty, in and of itself, does not demonstrate a lack of value. To the contrary, the buyer may reap benefits from such a contract in a number of ways—for instance, by not having to expend resources pursuing the idea through other channels or by having a profit-making idea implemented sooner rather than later. The law of contracts would have to be substantially rewritten were we to allow buyers of fully disclosed ideas to disregard their obligation to pay simply because an idea could have been obtained from some other source or in some other way.

Id., 81 N.Y.2d at 475–78.

4. *The implied contract theory.* Companies receiving numerous unsolicited idea submissions have implemented practices, on the advice of their lawyers, that make it very difficult for submitters to demonstrate either an express or an implied contract to pay. Some companies simply return such submissions unopened. Another approach is to designate an employee to open

all mail and send a standard release form to unsolicited idea submitters, notifying them that their ideas will not be forwarded to the appropriate department for consideration unless the sender signs and returns the release. The release, of course, expressly disclaims or limits contractual obligation on the company's part. A third approach is to review the idea, but require a signed release from the submitter before proceeding with it. Submitters often have little choice but to sign the releases, since it is very much a buyer's market.

5. *The quasi-contract theory.* Quasi-contracts, or "contracts implied at law," are not based on the apparent intentions of the parties. They are obligations created by law for reasons of justice and equity. Did the defendant receive a benefit from the plaintiff under circumstances that as a matter of fairness obligate the defendant to pay? If so, the court may find an obligation, implied by law, to pay.

A classic example of a court's use of the quasi-contract theory can be found in Matarese v. Moore–McCormack Lines, 158 F.2d 631 (2d Cir.1946). In that case the plaintiff, an immigrant of little education who worked as a part-time stevedore on the defendant's pier, informed defendant's agent in charge of the pier that he had something which would facilitate cargo loading, save the defendant money and prevent accidents. The agent agreed to visit plain-tiff's home, where plaintiff demonstrated models of the devices he had invented. The agent promised the plaintiff one-third of what the defendant would save by use of the devices and offered plaintiff the job of supervising construction of the devices for the defendant, which plaintiff accepted. Defen-dant built and used a number of the devices, but refused to pay the plaintiff as promised and ultimately fired him. The plaintiff later obtained two patents on his devices. Plaintiff's claim of an express contract to pay for use of the devices failed because the agent lacked authority to bind the defendant company. The court nonetheless granted the plaintiff's prayer for recovery upon the theory of unjust enrichment:

> Courts have justly been assiduous in defeating attempts to delve into the pockets of business firms through spurious claims attempts made by telephoning or writing vague general ideas to business corporations and then seizing upon some later general similarity between their products and the notions propounded as a basis for damages. * * * Such schemes are quite different from the situation * * * at bar. Here the relationship between the parties before and after the disclosure, the seeking of disclosure by [the agent], [the agent's] promise of compensation, the specific character, novelty, and patentability of plaintiff's invention, the subsequent use made of it by defendants, and the lack of compensation given the plaintiff—all indicate that the application of the principle of unjust enrichment is required.

Id., 158 F.2d at 634.

In the quasi-contract context, courts generally require that the plaintiff's idea be novel and concrete before permitting recovery. They have reasoned that abstract or non-novel ideas cannot be the property of any individual, that they may be freely borrowed. When a defendant takes such an idea he is not unjustly enriched, because what he took was common property. The plaintiff had no right of exclusive ownership in it. See, e.g., Stanley v. Columbia Broadcasting System, Inc., 35 Cal.2d 653, 675, 221 P.2d 73, 86 (1950) (Traynor, J., dissenting). How does the Alaska Supreme Court approach the issue in the *Alyeska* case?

6. *The confidential relationship theory.* Cases under this heading are often treated as contract cases, since confidential relationships often are founded on express or implied agreements to retain information in confidence. Subsequent unauthorized disclosure or use can be viewed as a breach of contract. Confidential relationships are also found, however, when the parties have a preexisting relationship, one placing trust in the other to act in good faith. Thus, for example, family relationships, agency relationships, lawyer and client relationships may all give rise to a duty of confidentiality, without the need to find a specific implied agreement. For this reason, some authorities recognize breach of confidential relationship as a separate theory of recovery based in tort. If the person placing trust in the other reveals an idea to the other in the course of the confidential relationship, then the other has a duty to refrain from using or disclosing it without permission, and may be liable if he does so. Again, however, courts may require that the idea be novel and concrete before they will grant relief. Note that the tort or contractual character of an idea claim may affect the applicable statute of limitations, as well as the available remedies.

7. *The property theory.* Though courts and commentators often list a "property theory" as one of the accepted theories of recovery for ideas, there have been few, if any, attempts to fully define or explore its perimeters or its implications. The property theory appears to provide that a person with a novel, concrete idea has rights in it that are enforceable against the world. Anyone who copies the idea without the owner's authorization will be liable, as in an action for conversion. The idea owner's property rights in the idea might last until death or after, passing to successors in interest. What are the implications of this? Is such a property theory compatible with federal intellectual property law policy? Strong arguments can be made that such claims would be preempted by federal law. See Chapter Eight, *infra*. While courts frequently refer to a "property theory" of recovery, it is not clear that a court has actually relied on this theory to provide relief to a claimant. See Barrett, *The "Law of Ideas" Reconsidered, supra,* at 698–709.

8. *The relationship of idea law and trade secret law.* Is the body of "idea law" identified in this Chapter needed? Why isn't trade secret law sufficient to redress idea submission claims? Could the claim in the *Alyeska* case have been resolved adequately under trade secret law?

PROBLEMS

1. Jones, a keno writer with a Los Vegas hotel owned by Ace Corp., conceived the idea that the hotel should build and operate an adjacent recreational vehicle park. He developed a brochure that somewhat detailed the idea, and arranged for a meeting with the hotel's General Manager. After presenting the idea to the General Manager, Jones indicated that he desired to be compensated through a money payment or through participation in the

venture in an executive capacity. The General Manager told Jones he wasn't interested in the plan, and though he tried, Jones was unable to discuss it further with the General Manager. Two years later, the hotel opened a recreational vehicle park.

How would you evaluate Jones' legal rights against Ace Corp.?

2.   Cohen, a unit manager and financial analyst in United States Broadcast Co.'s ("USBC") Sports Division, contacted a USBC official outside of the Sports Division about some ideas he had for television programs. The official instructed him to submit his proposals in writing, which he did. One of the proposals was for a situation comedy featuring a non-stereotypical African–American family entitled "Father's Day." He informed USBC at that time that if it was interested in any of the proposals, he expected to be named executive producer and to receive appropriate credit and compensation as the creator of the eventual program. He also told USBC that the proposals were being submitted in confidence.

The official who requested the writing encouraged Cohen to "flesh out" his proposals and submit them to the USBC Vice President in charge of network television programming. In response, Cohen submitted a two-page memorandum for "Father's Day," which he described as a program combining humor with serious situations in a manner "similar to that of the old *Dick Van Dyke Show* but with a Black perspective." He explained that the show would attempt to depict life in a closely knit, non-stereotypical African–American family, with the addition of a contemporary urban setting. The proposal suggested that Bill Cosby play the part of the father, and made casting suggestions for a working spouse and five children. USBC decided not to pursue the proposal and returned it to Cohen the same month that he submitted it.

Four years later, USBC came out with *The Cosby Show*, a sit-com series about everyday life in an upper middle-class African–American family in New York, starring Bill Cosby. The depiction was non-stereotypical, and included a working wife and five children.

How would you evaluate Cohen's legal rights against USBC?

CHAPTER THREE

PATENTS

■ ■ ■

I. UTILITY PATENTS

A. INTRODUCTION

GRAHAM v. JOHN DEERE CO.

Supreme Court of the United States, 1966.
383 U.S. 1, 86 S.Ct. 684, 15 L.Ed.2d 545.

MR. JUSTICE CLARK delivered the opinion of the Court.

* * *

[I]t must be remembered that the federal patent power stems from a specific constitutional provision which authorizes the Congress "To promote the Progress of * * * useful Arts, by securing for limited Times to * * * Inventors the exclusive Right to their * * * Discoveries." Art. I, § 8, cl. 8. The clause is both a grant of power and a limitation. This qualified authority, unlike the power often exercised in the sixteenth and seventeenth centuries by the English Crown, is limited to the promotion of advances in the "useful arts." It was written against the backdrop of the practices—eventually curtailed by the Statute of Monopolies—of the Crown in granting monopolies to court favorites in goods or businesses which had long before been enjoyed by the public. The Congress in the exercise of the patent power may not overreach the restraints imposed by the stated constitutional purpose. Nor may it enlarge the patent monopoly without regard to the innovation, advancement or social benefit gained thereby. Moreover, Congress may not authorize the issuance of patents whose effects are to remove existent knowledge from the public domain, or to restrict free access to materials already available. Innovation, advancement, and things which add to the sum of useful knowledge are inherent requisites in a patent system which by constitutional command must "promote the Progress of * * * useful Arts." This is the *standard* expressed in the Constitution and it may not be ignored. And it is in this light that patent validity "requires reference to a standard written into the Constitution." *Great A. & P. Tea Co. v. Supermarket Equipment Corp.*, *supra*, 340 U.S. at 154, 71 S.Ct. at 131 (concurring opinion).

Within the limits of the constitutional grant, the Congress may, of course, implement the stated purpose of the Framers by selecting the policy which in its judgment best effectuates the constitutional aim. This is but a corollary to the grant to Congress of any Article I power. Within the scope established by the Constitution, Congress may set out conditions and tests for patentability. It is the duty of the Commissioner of Patents and of the courts in the administration of the patent system to give effect to the constitutional standard by appropriate application, in each case, of the statutory scheme of the Congress.

Congress quickly responded to the bidding of the Constitution by enacting the Patent Act of 1790 during the second session of the First Congress. It created an agency in the Department of State headed by the Secretary of State, the Secretary of the Department of War and the Attorney General, any two of whom could issue a patent for a period not exceeding 14 years to any petitioner that "hath * * * invented or discovered any useful art, manufacture, * * * or device, or any improvement therein not before known or used" if the board found that "the invention or discovery (was) sufficiently useful and important * * *." 1 Stat. 110. This group, whose members administered the patent system along with their other public duties, was known by its own designation as "Commissioners for the Promotion of Useful Arts."

Thomas Jefferson, who as Secretary of State was a member of the group, was its moving spirit and might well be called the "first administrator of our patent system." He was not only an administrator of the patent system under the 1790 Act, but was also the author of the 1793 Patent Act. In addition, Jefferson was himself an inventor of great note. His unpatented improvements on plows, to mention but one line of his inventions, won acclaim and recognition on both sides of the Atlantic. Because of his active interest and influence in the early development of the patent system, Jefferson's views on the general nature of the limited patent monopoly under the Constitution, as well as his conclusions as to conditions for patentability under the statutory scheme, are worthy of note.

Jefferson, like other Americans, had an instinctive aversion to monopolies. It was a monopoly on tea that sparked the Revolution and Jefferson certainly did not favor an equivalent form of monopoly under the new government. His abhorrence of monopoly extended initially to patents as well. From France, he wrote to Madison (July 1788) urging a Bill of Rights provision restricting monopoly, and as against the argument that limited monopoly might serve to incite "ingenuity," he argued forcefully that "the benefit even of limited monopolies is too doubtful to be opposed to that of their general suppression." V Writings of Thomas Jefferson, at 47 (Ford ed., 1895).

His views ripened, however, and in another letter to Madison (Aug. 1789) after the drafting of the Bill of Rights, Jefferson stated that he would have been pleased by an express provision in this form:

"Art. 9. Monopolies may be allowed to persons for their own productions in literature, & their own inventions in the arts, for a term not exceeding ___ years, but for no longer term & no other purpose." *Id.,* at 113.

And he later wrote:

"Certainly an inventor ought to be allowed a right to the benefit of his invention for some certain time. * * * Nobody wishes more than I do that ingenuity should receive a liberal encouragement." Letter to Oliver Evans (May 1807), V Writings of Thomas Jefferson, at 75–76 (Washington ed.).

Jefferson's philosophy on the nature and purpose of the patent monopoly is expressed in a letter to Isaac McPherson (Aug. 1813), a portion of which we set out in the margin.[2] He rejected a natural-rights theory in intellectual property rights and clearly recognized the social and economic rationale of the patent system. The patent monopoly was not designed to secure to the inventor his natural right in his discoveries. Rather, it was a reward, an inducement, to bring forth new knowledge. The grant of an exclusive right to an invention was the creation of society—at odds with the inherent free nature of disclosed ideas—and was not to be freely given. Only inventions and discoveries which furthered human knowledge, and were new and useful, justified the special inducement of a limited private monopoly. Jefferson did not believe in granting patents for small details, obvious improvements, or frivolous devices. His writings evidence his insistence upon a high level of patentability.

As a member of the patent board for several years, Jefferson saw clearly the difficulty in "drawing a line between the things which are worth to the public the embarrassment of an exclusive patent, and those which are not." The board on which he served sought to draw such a line and formulated several rules which are preserved in Jefferson's correspondence.[3] Despite the board's efforts, Jefferson saw "with what slow prog-

---

2. "Stable ownership is the gift of social law, and is given late in the progress of society. It would be curious then, if an idea, the fugitive fermentation of an individual brain, could, of natural right, be claimed in exclusive and stable property. If nature has made any one thing less susceptible than all others of exclusive property, it is the action of the thinking power called an idea, which an individual may exclusively possess as long as he keeps it to himself; but the moment it is divulged, it forces itself into the possession of every one, and the receiver cannot dispossess himself of it. Its peculiar character, too, is that no one possesses the less, because every other possesses the whole of it. He who receives an idea from me, receives instruction himself without lessening mine; as he who lights his taper at mine, receives light without darkening me. That ideas should freely spread from one to another over the globe, for the moral and mutual instruction of man, and improvement of his condition, seems to have been peculiarly and benevolently designed by nature, when she made them, like fire, expansible over all space, without lessening their density in any point, and like the air in which we breathe, move, and have our physical being, incapable of confinement or exclusive appropriation. Inventions then cannot, in nature, be a subject of property. Society may give an exclusive right to the profits arising from them, as an encouragement to men to pursue ideas which may produce utility, but this may or may not be done, according to the will and convenience of the society, without claim or complaint from anybody." VI Writings of Thomas Jefferson, at 180–181 (Washington ed.).

3. "[A] machine of which we are possessed, might be applied by every man to any use of which it is susceptible." Letter to Isaac McPherson, *supra,* at 181.

ress a system of general rules could be matured." Because of the "abundance" of cases and the fact that the investigations occupied "more time of the members of the board than they could spare from higher duties, the whole was turned over to the judiciary, to be matured into a system, under which every one might know when his actions were safe and lawful." Letter to McPherson, *supra*, at 181, 182. Apparently Congress agreed with Jefferson and the board that the courts should develop additional conditions for patentability. Although the Patent Act was amended, revised or codified some 50 times between 1790 and 1950, Congress steered clear of a statutory set of requirements other than the bare novelty and utility tests reformulated in Jefferson's draft of the 1793 Patent Act.

* * *

The difficulty of formulating conditions for patentability was heightened by the generality of the constitutional grant and the statutes implementing it, together with the underlying policy of the patent system that "the things which are worth to the public the embarrassment of an exclusive patent," as Jefferson put it, must outweigh the restrictive effect of the limited patent monopoly. The inherent problem was to develop some means of weeding out those inventions which would not be disclosed or devised but for the inducement of a patent.

* * *

NOTES AND QUESTIONS

1. *Patentability and the public benefit.* Thomas Jefferson's desire to provide an incentive to invent, but draw "a line between the things which are worth to the public the embarrassment of an exclusive patent, and those which are not," is reflected in our present Patent Act, 35 U.S.C.A. §§ 1–376, and in the extensive case law that construes and applies it. The present Patent Act provides that in order to qualify for a utility patent, an invention must be "novel" (§ 102), "non-obvious" (§ 103), and "useful" (§§ 101, 112).

The United States Patent and Trademark Office ("PTO") initially determines whether claimed inventions merit a patent. Inventors seeking a patent must submit a detailed application, containing specific claims which describe the innovative qualities of the invention. A patent examiner with technical training in the field of the invention then conducts a search of the prior art, or existing knowledge in the field, and determines whether the invention meets the novelty, non-obviousness, usefulness and other Patent Act requirements. A disappointed applicant may appeal a rejection to the Board of Patent Appeals and Interferences, 35 U.S.C.A. § 134, and from there he may either

"[A] change of material should not give title to a patent. As the making a ploughshare of cast rather than of wrought iron; a comb of iron instead of horn or of ivory * * *." *Ibid.*

"[A] mere change of form should give no right to a patent, as a high-quartered shoe instead of a low one; a round hat instead of a three-square; or a square bucket instead of a round one." *Id.*, at 181–182.

"[A combined use of old implements.] A man has a right to use a saw, an axe, a plane separately; may he not combine their uses on the same piece of wood?" Letter to Oliver Evans (Jan. 1814), VI Writings of Thomas Jefferson, at 298 (Washington ed.).

appeal directly to the United States Court of Appeals for the Federal Circuit, *id.*, §§ 141, 144; or obtain judicial review of patentability in the U.S. District Court for the District of Columbia. *Id.*, § 145.

If the PTO determines that patentability requirements are satisfied, it will issue a patent. The PTO's issuance of a patent, however, only provides a presumption that the invention is patentable. *Id.*, § 282. If the patentee attempts to enforce her patent in an infringement action, the defendant may challenge the validity of the patent, leading the court to undertake its own review. If the court determines that the invention fails to satisfy the provisions of the Patent Act, it will declare the patent invalid and refuse to enforce it.

To further ensure that the public benefits from the patent monopoly grant, the Patent Act requires the inventor to fully disclose his invention (and the best mode of practicing it) in the patent application, in a manner sufficient to enable a person of ordinary skill in the pertinent art to make or practice it. The PTO publishes this information—usually eighteen months after the application is filed and when the patent is granted. *Id.*, §§ 112–113, 122. The publication enables the public to learn from the invention, and apply what it learns by analogy to other endeavors. Moreover, as expressly required in the Constitution's Patent and Copyright Clause, U.S. Const. art. I, § 8, cl. 8, the duration of the patent monopoly is limited. Utility patents have traditionally lasted only seventeen years. In 1994, Congress amended the Patent Act to provide a term that endures for twenty years measured from the date the patent application was filed. *Id.*, § 154. Once the patent term expires, the inventor has no further exclusive rights: The public is free to exploit the invention as it wishes, and it is assisted in doing so by the inventor's earlier disclosures.

While a patent is the most difficult form of intellectual property protection to obtain, it also provides the strongest rights. The patent owner obtains the right to exclude others from making, using, selling, offering to sell, or importing the patented invention within the United States (or, if the invention is a process, from using, selling, offering to sell or importing products made by that process). *Id.*, § 154. It is not necessary for the patent owner to demonstrate that an alleged infringer of these rights copied her invention, for unlike trade secret law, patent law does not permit others to create the invention independently.

2. *Three kinds of patents.* The Patent Act provides for three kinds of patents: utility patents, design patents and plant patents. Utility patents were the original form of patents, and remain the most prevalent and economically significant form of U.S. patents today. For example, in 2008, the U.S. PTO granted 157,772 utility patents, but only 25,565 design patents, and 1,240 plant patents. Most of this chapter will focus on utility patents. Design and plant patents, which were added more recently to the Patent Act, will be examined briefly in Sections II and III of this chapter.

3. *The patent claims and specification.* Utility patent #5,425,497 (the " '497 patent"), which was issued on June 20, 1995 for a new form of cup holder, is reproduced in the Appendix. You should review the patent. Note that a major part of the patent document is comprised of technical drawings

and description. This is known as the patent specification. Its purpose is to describe and disclose the invention in a manner sufficient to enable a person with ordinary skill in the art to make or practice the invention, and to disclose the best embodiment of the invention that the inventor contemplates at the time of the patent application, as required in Patent Act § 112.

At the end of the specification you will see the words "We claim," followed by a series of numbered paragraphs. This last portion of the patent document constitutes the patent claims, which officially define the scope of the patented invention. The claims are often compared to the description of real property in a deed to land, as they set forth the "metes and bounds" of the invention, and notify others of what the inventor claims as his exclusive property.

In reviewing the language of a claim, you will see that it can be readily parsed into a list of specific elements. To prove that a defendant has infringed a claim, the patentee must demonstrate that the defendant's alleged infringing product or process includes each of the listed elements, or its equivalent. If the defendant's product or process lacks even one of the claim elements or its equivalent, it will not be found to infringe. For this reason, the claim elements are sometimes called "limitations." Each element/limitation limits the scope of the patent. Thus, in the '497 patent, claim number 1 is broader in scope than claims 2 and 3. What strategy explains the drafting practice, demonstrated in the '497 patent, of including a broad claim, followed by narrower versions of that claim?

THE ROLE OF PATENT LAW IN KNOWLEDGE CODIFICATION

Dan L. Burk.[1]
28 Berkeley Tech. L. J. 1009, 1009–1011 (2008).

Patents are problematic. The justification for patenting is less than clear. The grant of exclusive rights in a given technology clearly confers a potential benefit on the rights holder, but equally clearly creates an impediment to others who might wish to employ that technology. In the United States, the constitution authorizes Congress to implement a patent system in order to "promote the Progress of . . . useful Arts." But whether patents in fact promote progress, whether such progress is worth the cost, and under what circumstances, remains the subject of extended, ongoing debate.

The rationale for patenting long favored in judicial opinion is the "quid pro quo" theory: that patents are a bargain of sorts, between the inventor and the public, exchanging public disclosure of the claimed invention in return for the grant of a period of exclusive rights. But this explanation has never been entirely satisfactory. As a practical matter, patents are not production documents, and a good deal of the information that the technical community might like to divine from them is either accidentally or purposefully left out of the published patent. Additionally,

---

1. © 2008 Dan L. Burk. Reprinted by permission of the copyright owner.

it is unclear why an innovator would opt to trade disclosure of an invention for less than twenty years of exclusivity, when the alternative of keeping the invention as a trade secret is available in perpetuity. Of course, some inventions cannot be kept confidential enough to be maintained as trade secrets, but in those cases the patent bargain exchanges exclusivity for the disclosure of something that was bound to become public anyway.

Given the difficulties in the disclosure rationale, the dominant justification for the patent system has shifted toward an economic rationale based upon incentives. Under this prevalent view, the grant of exclusive rights deters quick imitation of the claimed invention and allows a period of supernormal profits that help to recoup the investment made in developing the invention. The incentive rationale reasons that innovators will be more likely to make an investment in new technologies if they know beforehand that a legal regime is in place that will afford them the opportunity to recover their investment.

But the most straightforward—or perhaps simplistic—explanation of patents as an innovation incentive fails to account for several characteristics of patents as found in practice. First, given the wide range of innovation profiles across various industries, it is not immediately clear how the same statute can prompt the necessary investment under so many varied circumstances. Recent commentary has attempted to offer some perspective as to how the patent system can in fact match incentives to the needs of different industries, but this requires a fairly intricate picture of how different industries experience the patent system and of the institutions that administer the patent system. Additionally, recent scholarship has also noted that the vast majority of patents appear never to be enforced, or even licensed, as one would expect if they are being used to recoup investments in innovation. Commentators have suggested that these apparently unused patents are being procured for other business purposes, such as financing, marketing, or strategic advantage. Extending this insight, other commentators have suggested that patents may play a more complex role in the economics of innovation, lowering transaction costs so as to facilitate more innovative organizational and market structures, rather than simply providing monopoly rents to the holders of exclusive rights.

This emerging body of literature suggests that, as a general matter, the nature and function of the patent system is far more complex, and far more dynamic, than might be predicted by the economics of a neoconservative incentive rationale. This in turn suggests that a reconsideration of the "disclosure" rationale might also be in order: just as a closer examination of the incentive rationale reveals a more complex and nuanced picture than might initially appear, so too a similar reexamination of the disclosure rationale might reveal nuances of the patent system that have gone previously unconsidered. Properly considered, aspects of disclosure or recordation of knowledge might play a more significant role, or at least a more interesting role, in the patent system than the familiar quid pro quo account of patenting might entail.

* * *

THE PATENT SYSTEM AND COMPETITIVE POLICY

Donald F. Turner.[2]
44 N.Y.U. L. Rev. 450, 452–58 (1969).

* * *

No one knows what the magnitude of underinvestment in the production of knowledge would be in the absence of special rewards, because it is fairly certain that a large amount of invention and innovation would take place in any event. Much research, as in universities and similar institutions, is relatively unaffected by the profit motive. Moreover, both economic analysis and empirical study indicate that a good deal of the research and other inventive and innovative activities of business enterprises would go on without special rewards of any kind. In many situations, this is a matter of competitive necessity; he who lags in invention and innovation will find himself driven from the market. Even without benefit of statutory protection, the inventor and innovator will often, if not usually, benefit from a headstart, full imitation lagging well behind. And in many of our imperfectly competitive markets, price competition may simply not be vigorous enough to prevent the inventor or innovator from recovering his developmental costs.

* * *

There is no doubt that the patent system, by giving a monopoly to the holder of a patentable invention and thus increasing the realizable reward for successful inventive activity, produces a substantial amount of invention and innovation that would not otherwise take place. There is also little doubt that the patent system evokes disclosure of some new knowledge that would otherwise remain secret, or at least remain secret for a longer period of time. * * *

Offsetting these benefits, however, are several significant costs. The first is the cost of having a patent system: the cost of administering it, the cost of patent litigation, and the cost of trying to figure out whether one has a patentable invention and whether one's activity infringes the patents of others. The second cost, and a substantial one, is underutilization of all the new patentable knowledge that would have been produced without a patent system. Generally speaking, the marginal cost of using new knowledge, once produced, is zero. Ideally, therefore, it should be freely available without cost to anyone for whom it has any positive value at all. By its very nature, of course, the patent monopoly restricts the use of new knowledge well below the social ideal, because even if its use is made generally available by licensing, it comes only at a price. Third, the patent system has contributed to the creation and perpetuation of monop-

---

2. © New York University Law Review, 1969. Reprinted by permission of the copyright owner.

oly power of dimensions and duration well beyond that intrinsic to the patents themselves. Fourth, the patent system often leads competitors of patent holders to invest resources in duplicating research, *i.e.*, to find noninfringing ways of obtaining the same or nearly the same result. * * * Fifth, the patent system has at times induced the use of research resources solely for the purpose of producing blocking patents. Sixth, the patent system has adverse effects on inventive activity in two respects. It tends to inhibit research in areas heavily hedged in by existing patents; the existence of large numbers of patents in a particular field reduces the likelihood of coming up with noninfringing results that can be profited from—in short, it reduces the probable rewards from inventive activity in that area. In addition, existing patents tend to increase the cost of solving any given research problem by shutting off those avenues of solution that would entail infringement.

Finally, the patent system would appear to worsen, rather than improve, the allocation of research resources as between applied research on the one hand and basic research on the other. As we have noted, unless there are special inducements, underinvestment in basic research is likely to be much more substantial than underinvestment in the production of new knowledge generally. Given the standards of invention incorporated in typical patent statutes, basic research would appear to be much less likely than applied research to produce what the law will call "invention." Thus, the patent system will tend to divert research resources away from basic research. This effect would not be a clear loss if the patent system so increased the total resources devoted to research that the resources spent on basic research, though relatively less, were absolutely greater. But even if this were so, the patent system obviously is not the ideal system for incentives in that it does not allocate research resources in the most beneficial way.

Can these adverse effects of the patent system, as we have known it, be reduced or eliminated by appropriate statutory revisions? I see no way of eliminating the loss caused by underutilization of new patentable knowledge that would have been produced without patent protection, for there is simply no feasible way of determining precisely or even crudely what those cases are. The underutilization cost could be reduced by requiring compulsory licensing at reasonable royalties, but could by no means be eliminated, for any positive royalty excludes uses of less value than the royalty price.

Compulsory licensing would also reduce, though not eliminate, the contribution of the patent system to monopoly power, to wasteful duplicating research, to the devotion of resources to obtaining blocking patents, and to the inhibitions on research imposed by patents in being. But compulsory licensing of course raises problems of its own. Arguably, it might so reduce the potential rewards of patents as to materially affect the patent incentive to inventive activity. Related to that problem, but involving more, compulsory licensing requires a determination of what is a "reasonable" royalty, a question for which there is simply no happy answer.

* * *

Finally, I see no practical way within the patent system itself for eliminating the probable bias against basic research. The solution would have to lie in some revision of the definition of patentable invention. But surely it would be intolerable to give a patent on most of the fundamental ideas that arise from basic research.

I believe this last consideration also demonstrates how unpersuasive the moral defense of the patent system is. Even if we assume that in an ideal world society should pay each creator of a new idea its full economic value, the impossibility of devising any workable scheme for doing so leaves no moral ground for paying some but not others—particularly when it is the fundamental discovery * * * that typically must go substantially underrewarded.

But a moment's reflection leads us to question the proposition that were it possible, society should feel a moral obligation to compel all who use an idea to pay monetary tribute to its creator. On this point, I can do no better than to quote Professor Rahl:

> In most of the important fields of human activity it is not usually considered wrong to imitate valuable things, ideas and methods. The more acceptable to society the thing is, the more others are encouraged to imitate it. Education is founded upon this premise, as is progress in science, art, literature, music, and government.
>
> * * *
>
> We have but to look around us to see that our "dynamic" economy is one which thrives upon and requires rapid imitation of innovated trade values.
>
> * * *
>
> * * * [W]e cannot have a general rule against copying of published trade values and at the same time have an effective system of competition. Although competition has many definitions and descriptions, it is clear to all that it cannot exist without the availability of reasonably close alternatives for the satisfaction of economic wants.
>
> * * *
>
> It is not freedom of competition which requires apology. It is interference with freedom which must always be explained.[5]

Therefore, the case for the patent system, if a case there be, must be an economic one, and, as we have seen, a clear case cannot be made. But neither can one make a convincing case against it. * * *

---

5. Rahl, The Right to "Appropriate" Trade Values, 23 Ohio St. L.J. 56, 70–72 (1962). * * *

NOTES AND QUESTIONS

1. *The case for patents.* Economists have suggested that in some, or even many cases, a patent may not be needed to ensure that the inventor is able to recoup her investment in research and development and turn a profit. The inventor has the advantage of lead time, which permits her to enter the market in advance of competitors and recoup much of her investment during the time that competitors are gearing up to enter. Moreover, by being the first in the market, she may be able to establish long-lasting commercial relationships that will continue to give her an advantage after her competitors have produced rival products. What is your opinion of this "head start" theory? Is the head start likely to provide the inventor with enough opportunity in enough cases to make patents unnecessary? Would your evaluation of the lead time argument vary, depending upon the subject area of the invention?

If, as Professor Turner suggests, our patent system has a detrimental effect on the allocation of research resources between applied and basic research, should we amend the patent laws to provide more patents for the results of basic research? On balance, does the patent system tend to increase or decrease the risk of investing in research and development?

For further discussion of the issues raised above, see Fritz Machlup, An Economic Review of the Patent System, Study No. 15, Subcomm. On Patents, Trademarks and Copyrights of the Comm. on the Judiciary, U.S. Senate, 85th Cong., 2d Sess. (1958). For more recent evaluations, see Kitch, *The Nature and Function of the Patent System*, 20 J. L. & Econ. 265 (1977); Merges & Nelson, *On the Complex Economics of Patent Scope*, 90 Colum. L. Rev. 839 (1990); Oddi, *Un-Unified Economic Theory of Patents—The Not–Quite–Holy Grail*, 71 Notre Dame L. Rev. 267 (1996). For an interesting evaluation of the effect of patents on the traditions of open communication and free flow of information and on the traditional reward structure in the scientific community, see Eisenberg, *Proprietary Rights and the Norms of Science in Biotechnology Research*, 97 Yale L. J. 177 (1987).

2. *The Court of Appeals for the Federal Circuit.* Creation of the United States Court of Appeals for the Federal Circuit, in 1982, was a landmark in the development and administration of U.S. patent law. The U.S. District Courts have exclusive jurisdiction of cases arising under the Patent Act.[3] 28 U.S.C. § 1338. Prior to 1982, appeals from district court decisions in patent cases were taken to the regional U.S. Circuit Courts of Appeals. Appeals from PTO decisions went to the U.S. Court of Customs and Patent Appeals. Over time, the various courts of appeals reached differing interpretations of the Patent Act, which led to considerable uncertainty and chronic forum shopping. See S. Rep. No. 275, 97th Cong., 1st Sess. 3–6 (1981).

The Federal Courts Improvement Act of 1982, Pub. L. No. 97–164, 96 Stat. 25, merged the Court of Customs and Patent Appeals and the U.S. Court

---

3. Section 337 of the Tariff Act of 1930, as amended, 19 U.S.C. § 1337, provides an administrative alternative to an infringement suit in district court when a U.S. patentee alleges that imported products infringe its patent. (A similar administrative procedure is available for claims that imported products infringe U.S. copyrights or registered trademarks.) The infringement claim is brought to the International Trade Commission (ITC) before an administrative law judge. This proceeding will generally provide a faster resolution than district court litigation, although the available remedies are more limited. Appeals from patent decisions in ITC proceedings can be appealed to the Court of Appeals for the Federal Circuit.

of Claims to form the U.S. Court of Appeals for the Federal Circuit. It provided that in addition to the jurisdiction exercised by the two constituent courts,[4] the new Court of Appeals for the Federal Circuit would have exclusive jurisdiction of appeals from patent infringement cases. 28 U.S.C. § 1295.[5] By consolidating patent matters in one court of appeals, the Act alleviated the disparities between circuits and the resulting forum shopping. In addition, concentrating patent matters in one appellate court has provided greater expertise in the resolution of patent issues. In the ensuing years, the Court of Appeals for the Federal Circuit has tended to ease the standards for obtaining patents and strengthen their protection. Indeed, commentators have credited this new court with dramatically increasing the value of patents.

In Holmes Group, Inc. v. Vornado Air Circulation Systems, Inc., 535 U.S. 826, 122 S.Ct. 1889, 153 L.Ed.2d 13 (2002), the plaintiff brought suit in the Kansas District Court seeking a declaratory judgment that its product did not infringe the defendant's product trade dress. The defendant asserted a compulsory counterclaim for patent infringement in its answer to the complaint. The Supreme Court held that the Court of Appeals for the Federal Circuit did not have appellate jurisdiction over the case. Rather, the appeal should go to the Court of Appeals for the Tenth Circuit.

The Supreme Court reasoned that, under the "well-pleaded-complaint" rule, a case will only fall under a district court's patent jurisdiction, and thus under the Federal Circuit's appellate jurisdiction, if the plaintiff's well-pleaded complaint establishes "either that the federal patent law creates the cause of action or that the plaintiff's right to relief necessarily depends on resolution of a substantial question of federal patent law." *Id.* at 830. In *Vornado*, it was clear that the plaintiff's complaint asserted no claim arising under federal patent law. The defendant's counterclaim, which appeared as part of the defendant's answer, could not provide the Federal Circuit with the necessary jurisdiction to hear the appeal.

3. *Additional resources.* There are several treatises that provide a comprehensive discussion and analysis of United States patent law and practice. Perhaps the foremost is Donald Chisum's multi-volume treatise, entitled Patents: A Treatise on the Law of Patentability, Validity, and Infringement, which is updated regularly with loose-leaf supplements. Another useful resource is J. Dratler, Intellectual Property Law: Commercial, Creative and Industrial Property (1991), which is also regularly updated.

B. THE SUBJECT MATTER OF UTILITY PATENTS

DIAMOND v. CHAKRABARTY

United States Supreme Court, 1980.
447 U.S. 303, 100 S.Ct. 2204, 65 L.Ed.2d 144.

MR. CHIEF JUSTICE BURGER delivered the opinion of the Court.

---

4. In addition to assuming the jurisdiction of these courts, the new Court of Appeals for the Federal Circuit adopted their precedents as its own. See South Corp. v. United States, 690 F.2d 1368, 1370 (Fed. Cir. 1982).

5. The Court of Appeals for the Federal Circuit's jurisdiction also includes appeals in Plant Variety Protection Act cases, and appeals from decisions of the International Trade Commission under § 337 of the Tariff Act of 1930, as well as appeals from PTO trademark registration decisions. 28 U.S.C. § 1295.

We granted certiorari to determine whether a live, human-made micro-organism is patentable subject matter under 35 U.S.C. § 101.

I

In 1972, respondent Chakrabarty, a microbiologist, filed a patent application, assigned to the General Electric Co. The application asserted 36 claims related to Chakrabarty's invention of "a bacterium from the genus *Pseudomonas* containing therein at least two stable energy-generating plasmids, each of said plasmids providing a separate hydrocarbon degradative pathway."[1] This human-made, genetically engineered bacterium is capable of breaking down multiple components of crude oil. Because of this property, which is possessed by no naturally occurring bacteria, Chakrabarty's invention is believed to have significant value for the treatment of oil spills.

Chakrabarty's patent claims were of three types: first, process claims for the method of producing the bacteria; second, claims for an inoculum comprised of a carrier material floating on water, such as straw, and the new bacteria; and third, claims to the bacteria themselves. The patent examiner allowed the claims falling into the first two categories, but rejected claims for the bacteria. His decision rested on two grounds: (1) that micro-organisms are "products of nature," and (2) that as living things they are not patentable subject matter under 35 U.S.C. § 101.

Chakrabarty appealed the rejection of these claims to the Patent Office Board of Appeals, and the Board affirmed the Examiner on the second ground. Relying on the legislative history of the 1930 Plant Patent Act, in which Congress extended patent protection to certain asexually reproduced plants, the Board concluded that § 101 was not intended to cover living things such as these laboratory created micro-organisms.

[The Court of Customs and Patent Appeals reversed.]

II

The Constitution grants Congress broad power to legislate to "promote the Progress of Science and useful Arts, by securing for limited Times to Authors and Inventors the exclusive Right to their respective Writings and Discoveries." Art. I, § 8, cl. 8. The patent laws promote this progress by offering inventors exclusive rights for a limited period as an incentive for their inventiveness and research efforts. The authority of Congress is exercised in the hope that "[t]he productive effort thereby

---

1. Plasmids are hereditary units physically separate from the chromosomes of the cell. In prior research, Chakrabarty and an associate discovered that plasmids control the oil degradation abilities of certain bacteria. In particular, the two researchers discovered plasmids capable of degrading camphor and octane, two components of crude oil. In the work represented by the patent application at issue here, Chakrabarty discovered a process by which four different plasmids, capable of degrading four different oil components, could be transferred to and maintained stably in a single *Pseudomonas* bacterium, which itself has no capacity for degrading oil.

fostered will have a positive effect on society through the introduction of new products and processes of manufacture into the economy, and the emanations by way of increased employment and better lives for our citizens."

The question before us in this case is a narrow one of statutory interpretation requiring us to construe 35 U.S.C. § 101, which provides:

> "Whoever invents or discovers any new and useful process, machine, manufacture, or composition of matter, or any new and useful improvement thereof, may obtain a patent therefor, subject to the conditions and requirements of this title."

Specifically, we must determine whether respondent's micro-organism constitutes a "manufacture" or "composition of matter" within the meaning of the statute.

III

In cases of statutory construction we begin, of course, with the language of the statute. And "unless otherwise defined, words will be interpreted as taking their ordinary, contemporary common meaning." We have also cautioned that courts "should not read into the patent laws limitations and conditions which the legislature has not expressed."

Guided by these canons of construction, this Court has read the term "manufacture" in § 101 in accordance with its dictionary definition to mean "the production of articles for use from raw or prepared materials by giving to these materials new forms, qualities, properties, or combinations, whether by hand-labor or by machinery." *American Fruit Growers, Inc. v. Brogdex Co.*, 283 U.S. 1, 11, 51 S.Ct. 328, 330, 75 L.Ed. 801 (1931). Similarly, "composition of matter" has been construed consistent with its common usage to include "all compositions of two or more substances and . . . all composite articles, whether they be the results of chemical union, or of mechanical mixture, or whether they be gases, fluids, powders or solids." *Shell Development Co. v. Watson*, 149 F.Supp. 279, 280 (D.C. 1957). In choosing such expansive terms as "manufacture" and "composition of matter," modified by the comprehensive "any," Congress plainly contemplated that the patent laws would be given wide scope.

The relevant legislative history also supports a broad construction. The Patent Act of 1793, authored by Thomas Jefferson, defined statutory subject matter as "any new and useful art, machine, manufacture, or composition of matter, or any new or useful improvement [thereof]." Act of Feb. 21, 1793, § 1, 1 Stat. 319. The Act embodied Jefferson's philosophy that "ingenuity should receive a liberal encouragement." 5 Writings of Thomas Jefferson 75–76 (Washington ed. 1871). Subsequent patent statutes in 1836, 1870, and 1874 employed this same broad language. In 1952, when the patent laws were recodified, Congress replaced the word "art" with "process," but otherwise left Jefferson's language intact. The Committee Reports accompanying the 1952 Act inform us that Congress intended statutory subject matter to "include anything under the sun that is made by man." S.Rep.No.1979, 82d Cong., 2d Sess., 5 (1952); H.R.Rep. No.1923, 82d Cong., 2d Sess., 6 (1952).

This is not to suggest that § 101 has no limits or that it embraces every discovery. The laws of nature, physical phenomena, and abstract ideas have been held not patentable. Thus, a new mineral discovered in the earth or a new plant found in the wild is not patentable subject matter. Likewise, Einstein could not patent his celebrated law that $E=mc^2$; nor could Newton have patented the law of gravity. Such discoveries are "manifestations of . . . nature, free to all men and reserved exclusively to none." *Funk Bros. Seed Co. v. Kalo Inoculant Co.*, 333 U.S. 127, 130, 68 S.Ct. 440, 441, 92 L.Ed. 588 (1948).

Judged in this light, respondent's micro-organism plainly qualifies as patentable subject matter. His claim is not to a hitherto unknown natural phenomenon, but to a nonnaturally occurring manufacture or composition of matter—a product of human ingenuity "having a distinctive name, character [and] use." The point is underscored dramatically by comparison of the invention here with that in *Funk*. There, the patentee had discovered that there existed in nature certain species of root-nodule bacteria which did not exert a mutually inhibitive effect on each other. He used that discovery to produce a mixed culture capable of inoculating the seeds of leguminous plants. Concluding that the patentee had discovered "only some of the handiwork of nature," the Court ruled the product nonpatentable:

> "Each of the species of root-nodule bacteria contained in the package infects the same group of leguminous plants which it always infected. No species acquires a different use. The combination of species produces no new bacteria, no change in the six species of bacteria, and no enlargement of the range of their utility. Each species has the same effect it always had. The bacteria perform in their natural way. Their use in combination does not improve in any way their natural functioning. They serve the ends nature originally provided and act quite independently of any effort of the patentee." 333 U.S., at 131, 68 S.Ct., at 442.

Here, by contrast, the patentee has produced a new bacterium with markedly different characteristics from any found in nature and one having the potential for significant utility. His discovery is not nature's handiwork, but his own; accordingly it is patentable subject matter under § 101.

IV

Two contrary arguments are advanced, neither of which we find persuasive.

(A)

The petitioner's first argument rests on the enactment of the 1930 Plant Patent Act, which afforded patent protection to certain asexually reproduced plants, and the 1970 Plant Variety Protection Act, which authorized protection for certain sexually reproduced plants but excluded bacteria from its protection. In the petitioner's view, the passage of these Acts evidences congressional understanding that the terms "manufacture" or "composition of matter" do not include living things; if they did, the petitioner argues, neither Act would have been necessary.

We reject this argument. Prior to 1930, two factors were thought to remove plants from patent protection. The first was the belief that plants, even those artificially bred, were products of nature for purposes of the patent law. This position appears to have derived from the decision of the Patent Office in *Ex parte Latimer*, 1889 Dec.Com.Pat. 123, in which a patent claim for fiber found in the needle of the *Pinus Australis* was rejected. The Commissioner reasoned that a contrary result would permit "patents [to] be obtained upon the trees of the forest and the plants of the earth, which of course would be unreasonable and impossible." The *Latimer* case, it seems, came to "se[t] forth the general stand taken in these matters" that plants were natural products not subject to patent protection. The second obstacle to patent protection for plants was the fact that plants were thought not amenable to the "written description" requirement of the patent law. See 35 U.S.C. § 112. Because new plants may differ from old only in color or perfume, differentiation by written description was often impossible.

In enacting the Plant Patent Act, Congress addressed both of these concerns. It explained at length its belief that the work of the plant breeder "in aid of nature" was patentable invention. S.Rep.No.315, 71st Cong., 2d Sess., 6–8 (1930); H.R.Rep.No.1129, 71st Cong., 2d Sess., 7–9 (1930). And it relaxed the written description requirement in favor of "a description ... as complete as is reasonably possible." 35 U.S.C. § 162. No Committee or Member of Congress, however, expressed the broader view, now urged by the petitioner, that the terms "manufacture" or "composition of matter" exclude living things. * * * The Reports observe:

> "There is a clear and logical distinction between the discovery of a new variety of plant and of certain inanimate things, such, for example, as a new and useful natural mineral. The mineral is created wholly by nature unassisted by man.... On the other hand, a plant discovery resulting from cultivation is unique, isolated, and is not repeated by nature, nor can it be reproduced by nature unaided by man...." S.Rep.No.315, *supra*, at 6; H.R.Rep.No.1129, *supra*, at 7 (emphasis added).

Congress thus recognized that the relevant distinction was not between living and inanimate things, but between products of nature, whether living or not, and human-made inventions. Here, respondent's microorganism is the result of human ingenuity and research. Hence, the passage of the Plant Patent Act affords the Government no support.

Nor does the passage of the 1970 Plant Variety Protection Act support the Government's position. As the Government acknowledges, sexually reproduced plants were not included under the 1930 Act because new varieties could not be reproduced true-to-type through seedlings. By 1970, however, it was generally recognized that true-to-type reproduction was possible and that plant patent protection was therefore appropriate. The 1970 Act extended that protection. There is nothing in its language or history to suggest that it was enacted because § 101 did not include living things.

In particular, we find nothing in the exclusion of bacteria from plant variety protection to support the petitioner's position. The legislative history gives no reason for this exclusion. As the Court of Customs and Patent Appeals suggested, it may simply reflect Congressional agreement with the result reached by that court in deciding *In re Arzberger*, 27 C.C.P.A. (Pat.) 1315, 112 F.2d 834 (1940), which held that bacteria were not plants for the purposes of the 1930 Act. Or it may reflect the fact that prior to 1970 the Patent Office had issued patents for bacteria under § 101.[9] In any event, absent some clear indication that Congress "focused on [the] issues ... directly related to the one presently before the Court," there is no basis for reading into its actions an intent to modify the plain meaning of the words found in § 101.

(B)

The petitioner's second argument is that micro-organisms cannot qualify as patentable subject matter until Congress expressly authorizes such protection. His position rests on the fact that genetic technology was unforeseen when Congress enacted § 101. From this it is argued that resolution of the patentability of inventions such as respondent's should be left to Congress. The legislative process, the petitioner argues, is best equipped to weigh the competing economic, social, and scientific considerations involved, and to determine whether living organisms produced by genetic engineering should receive patent protection. In support of this position, the petitioner relies on our recent holding in *Parker v. Flook*, 437 U.S. 584, 98 S.Ct. 2522, 57 L.Ed.2d 451 (1978), and the statement that the judiciary "must proceed cautiously when ... asked to extend patent rights into areas wholly unforeseen by Congress." *Id.*, at 596, 98 S.Ct. at 2529.

It is, of course, correct that Congress, not the courts, must define the limits of patentability; but it is equally true that once Congress has spoken it is "the province and duty of the judicial department to say what the law is." *Marbury v. Madison*, 1 Cranch 137, 177, 2 L.Ed. 60 (1803). Congress has performed its constitutional role in defining patentable subject matter in § 101; we perform ours in construing the language Congress has employed. In so doing, our obligation is to take statutes as we find them, guided, if ambiguity appears, by the legislative history and statutory purpose. Here, we perceive no ambiguity. The subject-matter

---

9. In 1873, the Patent Office granted Louis Pasteur a patent on "yeast, free from organic germs of disease, as an article of manufacture." And in 1967 and 1968, immediately prior to the passage of the Plant Variety Protection Act, that Office granted two patents which, as the petitioner concedes, state claims for living micro-organisms.

provisions of the patent law have been cast in broad terms to fulfill the constitutional and statutory goal of promoting "the Progress of Science and the useful Arts" with all that means for the social and economic benefits envisioned by Jefferson. Broad general language is not necessarily ambiguous when congressional objectives require broad terms.

     * * *

* * * This Court frequently has observed that a statute is not to be confined to the "particular application[s] . . . contemplated by the legislators." This is especially true in the field of patent law. A rule that unanticipated inventions are without protection would conflict with the core concept of the patent law that anticipation undermines patentability. Mr. Justice Douglas reminded that the inventions most benefiting mankind are those that "push back the frontiers of chemistry, physics, and the like." Congress employed broad general language in drafting § 101 precisely because such inventions are often unforeseeable.

To buttress his argument, the petitioner, with the support of *amicus*, points to grave risks that may be generated by research endeavors such as respondent's. The briefs present a gruesome parade of horribles. Scientists, among them Nobel laureates, are quoted suggesting that genetic research may pose a serious threat to the human race, or, at the very least, that the dangers are far too substantial to permit such research to proceed apace at this time. We are told that genetic research and related technological developments may spread pollution and disease, that it may result in a loss of genetic diversity, and that its practice may tend to depreciate the value of human life. These arguments are forcefully, even passionately, presented; they remind us that, at times, human ingenuity seems unable to control fully the forces it creates—that with Hamlet, it is sometimes better "to bear those ills we have than fly to others that we know not of."

It is argued that this Court should weigh these potential hazards in considering whether respondent's invention is patentable subject matter under § 101. We disagree. The grant or denial of patents on microorganisms is not likely to put an end to genetic research or to its attendant risks. The large amount of research that has already occurred when no researcher had sure knowledge that patent protection would be available suggests that legislative or judicial fiat as to patentability will not deter the scientific mind from probing into the unknown any more than Canute could command the tides. Whether respondent's claims are patentable may determine whether research efforts are accelerated by the hope of reward or slowed by want of incentives, but that is all.

What is more important is that we are without competence to entertain these arguments—either to brush them aside as fantasies generated by fear of the unknown, or to act on them. The choice we are urged to make is a matter of high policy for resolution within the legislative process after the kind of investigation, examination, and study that legislative bodies can provide and courts cannot. That process involves the balancing of competing values and interests, which in our democratic system is the business of elected representatives. Whatever their validity, the contentions now pressed on us should be addressed to the political branches of the Government, the Congress and the Executive, and not to the courts.

We have emphasized in the recent past that "[o]ur individual appraisal of the wisdom or unwisdom of a particular [legislative] course ... is to be put aside in the process of interpreting a statute." Our task, rather, is the narrow one of determining what Congress meant by the words it used in the statute; once that is done our powers are exhausted. Congress is free to amend § 101 so as to exclude from patent protection organisms produced by genetic engineering. Cf. 42 U.S.C. § 2181(a), exempting from patent protection inventions "useful solely in the utilization of special nuclear material or atomic energy in an atomic weapon." Or it may choose to craft a statute specifically designed for such living things. But, until Congress takes such action, this Court must construe the language of § 101 as it is. The language of that section fairly embraces respondent's invention.

* * *

MR. JUSTICE BRENNAN, with whom MR. JUSTICE WHITE, MR. JUSTICE MARSHALL, and MR. JUSTICE POWELL join, dissenting.

* * *

The patent laws attempt to reconcile this Nation's deep seated antipathy to monopolies with the need to encourage progress. Given the complexity and legislative nature of this delicate task, we must be careful to extend patent protection no further than Congress has provided. In particular, where there is an absence of legislative direction, the courts should leave to Congress the decisions whether and how far to extend the patent privilege into areas where the common understanding has been that patents are not available.[1]

In this case, however, we do not confront a complete legislative vacuum. The sweeping language of the Patent Act of 1793, as re-enacted in 1952, is not the last pronouncement Congress has made in this area. In 1930 Congress enacted the Plant Patent Act affording patent protection to developers of certain asexually reproduced plants. In 1970 Congress enacted the Plant Variety Protection Act to extend protection to certain new plant varieties capable of sexual reproduction. Thus, we are not dealing— as the Court would have it—with the routine problem of "unanticipated inventions." In these two Acts Congress has addressed the general problem of patenting animate inventions and has chosen carefully limited language granting protection to some kinds of discoveries, but specifically excluding others. These Acts strongly evidence a Congressional limitation that excludes bacteria from patentability.

---

1. I read the Court to admit that the popular conception, even among advocates of agricultural patents, was that living organisms were unpatentable.

First, the Acts evidence Congress' understanding, at least since 1930, that § 101 does not include living organisms. If newly developed living organisms not naturally occurring had been patentable under § 101, the plants included in the scope of the 1930 and 1970 Acts could have been patented without new legislation. Those plants, like the bacteria involved in this case, were new varieties not naturally occurring. Although the Court rejects this line of argument, it does not explain why the Acts were necessary unless to correct a pre-existing situation.[4] I cannot share the Court's implicit assumption that Congress was engaged in either idle exercises or mere correction of the public record when it enacted the 1930 and 1970 Acts. And Congress certainly thought it was doing something significant. The Committee Reports contain expansive prose about the previously unavailable benefits to be derived from extending patent protection to plants. Because Congress thought it had to legislate in order to make agricultural "human-made inventions" patentable and because the legislation Congress enacted is limited, it follows that Congress never meant to make items outside the scope of the legislation patentable.

Second, the 1970 Act clearly indicates that Congress has included bacteria within the focus of its legislative concern, but not within the scope of patent protection. Congress specifically excluded bacteria from the coverage of the 1970 Act. The Court's attempts to supply explanations for this explicit exclusion ring hollow. It is true that there is no mention in the legislative history of the exclusion, but that does not give us license to invent reasons. The fact is that Congress, assuming that animate objects as to which it had not specifically legislated could not be patented, excluded bacteria from the set of patentable organisms.

    * * *

NOTES AND QUESTIONS

1. *Plant patents, certificates of plant variety protection, and utility patents for plants.* The Plant Patent Act and the Plant Variety Protection Act, which provide patents or patent-like protection for certain plants, will be discussed further in Section II, *infra.* In 1985, following the reasoning in *Chakrabarty*, the Board of Patent Appeals and Interferences held that a corn plant, seed, and tissue culture with increased free tryptophan levels were proper utility patent subject matter. The Board found it irrelevant that the plant and seed might also qualify for protection under the Plant Patent Act or the Plant Variety Protection Act. See *Ex parte* Hibberd, 227 U.S.P.Q. 443 (PTO Bd. Pat. App. 1985). More recently, the Supreme Court has specified that sexually reproduced plants may be the subject of a utility patent, even though they may also be protected through a certificate of plant variety protection. J.E.M. Ag Supply, Inc. v. Pioneer Hi–Bred International, Inc., 534 U.S. 124, 122 S.Ct. 593, 151 L.Ed.2d 508 (2001). The Supreme Court found

---

4. If the 1930 Act's only purpose were to solve the technical problem of description referred to by the Court, most of the Act, and in particular its limitation to asexually reproduced plants, would have been totally unnecessary.

that neither the Plant Patent Act nor the Plant Variety Protection Act limits the scope of § 101's coverage.

2. *The aftermath of Chakrabarty.* Since the Supreme Court's decision in *Chakrabarty*, the PTO has issued a number of patents for genetically engineered microbes. In 1987, the PTO Board of Patent Appeals and Interferences, citing *Chakrabarty*, held that polyploid oysters manipulated and rendered sterile (and thus suitable for year-round consumption) were non-naturally occurring manufactures or compositions of matter within the meaning of Patent Act § 101. *Ex parte* Allen, 2 U.S.P.Q.2d 1425 (PTO Bd. Pat. App. 1987), *affirmed on other grounds,* 846 F.2d 77 (Fed.Cir.1988). Shortly thereafter, Donald Quigg, then Commissioner of Patents and Trademarks, published an interpretative rule announcing that the PTO considered "nonnaturally occurring non-human multicellular living organisms, including animals, to be patentable subject matter within the scope of 35 U.S.C. 101." 1077 Pat. & Trademark Off. Gazette 24 (1987). The Commissioner elaborated:

> A claim directed to or including within its scope a human being will not be considered to be patentable subject matter under 35 U.S.C. 101. The grant of a limited, but exclusive property right in a human being is prohibited by the Constitution. Accordingly, it is suggested that any claim directed to a non-plant multicellular organism which would include a human being within its scope include the limitation "non-human" to avoid this ground of rejection.

Id. Does the Constitution prohibit the granting of patents for genetically engineered people? If so, on what basis? See Note, *Patents on People and the U.S. Constitution: Creating Slaves or Enslaving Science?*, 16 Hastings Const. L.Q. 221 (1989).

The following year, the PTO granted the first patent for a genetically engineered warm-blooded animal—a mouse developed at Harvard University which had been genetically altered to carry cancer genes in its cells and thus develop tumors quickly if exposed to even small amounts of cancer-causing chemicals. The mouse was designed to be used in testing to determine the cancer-causing potential of chemicals and was expected to be especially useful in breast cancer research. U.S. Patent #4,736,866 (1988). Subsequently the PTO has issued a number of patents for genetically engineered farm animals. See, e.g., U.S. Patent #6,013,857 (2000) (transgenic bovines); U.S. Patent #5,942,435 (1999) (transgenic swine).

The *Chakrabarty* decision generated raging debates about the ethical, economic, environmental and political implications of patenting life forms, both in the media and in Congress. Farmers expressed grave concerns about the economic impact of having to pay royalties whenever patented livestock were reproduced. Some scientists argued that granting patents for biotechnological inventions would drive up research costs, leading researchers to channel their efforts into immediately profitable pursuits at the cost of long-term gains, and would encourage counter-productive secrecy among researchers. Environmentalists expressed concerns about the environmental impact of genetically engineered agricultural and medical microorganisms, which might be freely released into the atmosphere. There were also worries that genetic engineering would endanger the diversity of the natural gene pool. Numerous people posed ethical questions about the new relationship between humans and animals, and about the physical suffering that might be imposed on animals due to the incentive of patent monopolies. See, e.g., *Patents and the Constitution: Transgenic Animals, Hearings before the Subcomm. on Courts, Civil Liberties and the Administration of Justice of the House Comm. on the Judiciary*, 100th Cong., 1st Sess. (1987); Merges, *Intellectual Property in Higher Life Forms: The Patent System and Controversial Technologies*, 47 Md. L. Rev. 1051 (1988); Dresser, *Ethical and Legal Issues in Patenting New Animal Life*, 28 Jurimetrics J. 399 (1988); Gore, *Planning a New Biotechnology Policy*, 5 Harv. J. L. & Pub. Pol'y. 19 (1991). While numerous bills were introduced to restrict or regulate animal patents, Congress passed no significant legislation.

After *Chakrabarty*, would it be possible to patent new breeds of animals derived from classic methods of cross-breeding? The PTO has now granted numerous patents on genes and individual gene sequences, reasoning that the applicant's isolation and purification of DNA found naturally in living matter renders it patentable subject matter, as opposed to a natural phenomena or law of nature. Is this consistent with the Supreme Court's discussion in *Chakrabarty*?

3. *Statutory exclusions from patentability.* Notwithstanding the broad coverage of § 101, 42 U.S.C.A. § 2181(a) prohibits the patenting of "any invention or discovery which is useful solely in the utilization of special nuclear material or atomic energy in an atomic weapon." Also, see Patent Act §§ 181 *et. seq.*, which limit the issuance of patents in certain cases when issuance would be "detrimental to the national security."

BILSKI v. KAPPOS

United States Supreme Court, 2010.
561 U.S. ___, 130 S.Ct. 3218, 177 L.Ed.2d 792.

JUSTICE KENNEDY delivered the opinion of the Court, except as to Parts II–B–2 and II–C–2.* [Ed.: Justice Kennedy's opinion is edited so that only those portions that commanded five or more votes (and thus constitute the opinion of the Court) are set forth. Portions of Justice Stevens' concurrence (with which 4 justices joined) and Justice Breyer's concurrence follow the majority opinion.]

The question in this case turns on whether a patent can be issued for a claimed invention designed for the business world. The patent application claims a procedure for instructing buyers and sellers how to protect against the risk of price fluctuations in a discrete section of the economy. Three arguments are advanced for the proposition that the claimed invention is outside the scope of patent law: (1) it is not tied to a machine and does not transform an article; (2) it involves a method of conducting business; and (3) it is merely an abstract idea. The Court of Appeals ruled that the first mentioned of these, the so-called machine-or-transformation

---

* JUSTICE SCALIA does not join Parts II–B–2 and II–C–2.

test, was the sole test to be used for determining the patentability of a "process" under the Patent Act, 35 U.S.C. § 101.

I

Petitioners' application seeks patent protection for a claimed invention that explains how buyers and sellers of commodities in the energy market can protect, or hedge, against the risk of price changes. The key claims are claims 1 and 4. Claim 1 describes a series of steps instructing how to hedge risk. Claim 4 puts the concept articulated in claim 1 into a simple mathematical formula. Claim 1 consists of the following steps:

> "(a) initiating a series of transactions between said commodity provider and consumers of said commodity wherein said consumers purchase said commodity at a fixed rate based upon historical averages, said fixed rate corresponding to a risk position of said consumers;
>
> "(b) identifying market participants for said commodity having a counter-risk position to said consumers; and
>
> "(c) initiating a series of transactions between said commodity provider and said market participants at a second fixed rate such that said series of market participant transactions balances the risk position of said series of consumer transactions."

The remaining claims explain how claims 1 and 4 can be applied to allow energy suppliers and consumers to minimize the risks resulting from fluctuations in market demand for energy. For example, claim 2 claims "[t]he method of claim 1 wherein said commodity is energy and said market participants are transmission distributors." Some of these claims also suggest familiar statistical approaches to determine the inputs to use in claim 4's equation. For example, claim 7 advises using well-known random analysis techniques to determine how much a seller will gain "from each transaction under each historical weather pattern."

The patent examiner rejected petitioners' application, explaining that it " 'is not implemented on a specific apparatus and merely manipulates [an] abstract idea and solves a purely mathematical problem without any limitation to a practical application, therefore, the invention is not directed to the technological arts.' " The Board of Patent Appeals and Interferences affirmed, concluding that the application involved only mental steps that do not transform physical matter and was directed to an abstract idea.

The United States Court of Appeals for the Federal Circuit heard the case en banc and affirmed. The case produced five different opinions. Students of patent law would be well advised to study these scholarly opinions.

Chief Judge Michel wrote the opinion of the court. The court rejected its prior test for determining whether a claimed invention was a patentable "process" under § 101—whether it produces a " 'useful, concrete, and tangible result' "—as articulated in *State Street Bank & Trust Co. v. Signature Financial Group, Inc.*, 149 F.3d 1368, 1373 (1998). The court held that "[a] claimed process is surely patent-eligible under § 101 if: (1) it is tied to a particular machine or apparatus, or (2) it transforms a particular article into a different state or thing." The court concluded this "machine-or-transformation test" is "the sole test governing § 101 analyses," and thus the "test for determining patent eligibility of a process under § 101." Applying the machine-or-transformation test, the court held that petitioners' application was not patent eligible. Judge Dyk wrote a separate concurring opinion, providing historical support for the court's approach.

Three judges wrote dissenting opinions. Judge Mayer argued that petitioners' application was "not eligible for patent protection because it is directed to a method of conducting business." He urged the adoption of a "technological standard for patentability." Judge Rader would have found petitioners' claims were an unpatentable abstract idea. Only Judge Newman disagreed with the court's conclusion that petitioners' application was outside of the reach of § 101. She did not say that the application should have been granted but only that the issue should be remanded for further proceedings to determine whether the application qualified as patentable under other provisions.

* * *

II

A

Section 101 defines the subject matter that may be patented under the Patent Act:

> "Whoever invents or discovers any new and useful process, machine, manufacture, or composition of matter, or any new and useful improvement thereof, may obtain a patent therefor, subject to the conditions and requirements of this title."

Section 101 thus specifies four independent categories of inventions or discoveries that are eligible for protection: processes, machines, manufactures, and compositions of matter. "In choosing such expansive terms ... modified by the comprehensive 'any,' Congress plainly contemplated that the patent laws would be given wide scope." *Diamond v. Chakrabarty*, 447 U.S. 303, 308, 100 S.Ct. 2204, 65 L.Ed.2d 144 (1980). Congress took this permissive approach to patent eligibility to ensure that " 'ingenuity should receive a liberal encouragement.' "

The Court's precedents provide three specific exceptions to § 101's broad patent-eligibility principles: "laws of nature, physical phenomena, and abstract ideas." *Chakrabarty, supra*, at 309, 100 S.Ct. 2204. While these exceptions are not required by the statutory text, they are consistent with the notion that a patentable process must be "new and useful." And, in any case, these exceptions have defined the reach of the statute as a matter of statutory *stare decisis* going back 150 years. The concepts covered by these exceptions are "part of the storehouse of knowledge of all men ... free to all men and reserved exclusively to none." *Funk Brothers Seed Co. v. Kalo Inoculant Co.,* 333 U.S. 127, 130, 68 S.Ct. 440, 92 L.Ed. 588 (1948).

The § 101 patent-eligibility inquiry is only a threshold test. Even if an invention qualifies as a process, machine, manufacture, or composition of matter, in order to receive the Patent Act's protection the claimed invention must also satisfy "the conditions and requirements of this title." § 101. Those requirements include that the invention be novel, see § 102, nonobvious, see § 103, and fully and particularly described, see § 112.

The present case involves an invention that is claimed to be a "process" under § 101. Section 100(b) defines "process" as:

"process, art or method, and includes a new use of a known process, machine, manufacture, composition of matter, or material."

The Court first considers two proposed categorical limitations on "process" patents under § 101 that would, if adopted, bar petitioners' application in the present case: the machine-or-transformation test and the categorical exclusion of business method patents.

B

1

Under the Court of Appeals' formulation, an invention is a "process" only if: "(1) it is tied to a particular machine or apparatus, or (2) it transforms a particular article into a different state or thing." This Court has "more than once cautioned that courts 'should not read into the patent laws limitations and conditions which the legislature has not expressed.'" *Diamond v. Diehr,* 450 U.S. 175, 182, 101 S.Ct. 1048, 67 L.Ed.2d 155 (1981). In patent law, as in all statutory construction, "[u]nless otherwise defined, 'words will be interpreted as taking their ordinary, contemporary, common meaning.'" The Court has read the § 101 term "manufacture" in accordance with dictionary definitions, and approved a construction of the term "composition of matter" consistent with common usage.

Any suggestion in this Court's case law that the Patent Act's terms deviate from their ordinary meaning has only been an explanation for the exceptions for laws of nature, physical phenomena, and abstract ideas. See *Parker v. Flook,* 437 U.S. 584, 588–589, 98 S.Ct. 2522, 57 L.Ed.2d 451 (1978). This Court has not indicated that the existence of these well-established exceptions gives the Judiciary *carte blanche* to impose other limitations that are inconsistent with the text and the statute's purpose and design. Concerns about attempts to call any form of human activity a "process" can be met by making sure the claim meets the requirements of § 101.

Adopting the machine-or-transformation test as the sole test for what constitutes a "process" (as opposed to just an important and useful clue) violates these statutory interpretation principles. Section 100(b) provides that "[t]he term 'process' means process, art or method, and includes a new use of a known process, machine, manufacture, composition of matter, or material." The Court is unaware of any " 'ordinary, contemporary, common meaning' " of the definitional terms "process, art or method" that would require these terms to be tied to a machine or to transform an article. Respondent urges the Court to look to the other patentable categories in § 101—machines, manufactures, and compositions of matter—to confine the meaning of "process" to a machine or transformation, under the doctrine of *noscitur a sociis*. Under this canon, "an ambiguous term may be given more precise content by the neighboring words with which it is associated." This canon is inapplicable here, for § 100(b) already explicitly defines the term "process." See *Burgess v. United States,* 553 U.S. 124, 130, 128 S.Ct. 1572, 170 L.Ed.2d 478 (2008) ("When a statute includes an explicit definition, we must follow that definition.")

The Court of Appeals incorrectly concluded that this Court has endorsed the machine-or-transformation test as the exclusive test. It is true that *Cochrane v. Deener,* 94 U.S. 780, 788, 24 L.Ed. 139 (1877), explained that a "process" is "an act, or a series of acts, performed upon the subject-matter to be transformed and reduced to a different state or thing." More recent cases, however, have rejected the broad implications of this dictum; and, in all events, later authority shows that it was not intended to be an exhaustive or exclusive test. *Gottschalk v. Benson,* 409 U.S. 63, 70, 93 S.Ct. 253, 34 L.Ed.2d 273 (1972), noted that "[t]ransformation and reduction of an article 'to a different state or thing' is the clue to the patentability of a process claim that does not include particular machines." At the same time, it explicitly declined to "hold that no process patent could ever qualify if it did not meet [machine or transformation] requirements." *Flook* took a similar approach, "assum[ing] that a valid process patent may issue even if it does not meet [the machine-or-transformation test]."

This Court's precedents establish that the machine-or-transformation test is a useful and important clue, an investigative tool, for determining whether some claimed inventions are processes under § 101. The machine-or-transformation test is not the sole test for deciding whether an invention is a patent-eligible "process."

2

[In a deleted section that failed to secure a majority, Justice Kennedy stresses that, while the machine-or-transformation test "may provide a sufficient basis for evaluating processes similar to those in the Industrial Age—for example, inventions grounded in a physical or other tangible form"—there "are reasons to doubt whether the test should be the sole criterion for determining the patentability of inventions in the Information Age." The machine-or-transformation test "would create uncertainty as to the patentability of software, advanced diagnostic medicine techniques, and inventions based on linear programming, data compression, and the manipulation of digital signals."]

C

1

Section 101 similarly precludes the broad contention that the term "process" categorically excludes business methods. The term "method," which is within § 100(b)'s definition of "process," at least as a textual matter and before consulting other limitations in the Patent Act and this Court's precedents, may include at least some methods of doing business. See, *e.g.,* Webster's New International Dictionary 1548 (2d ed.1954) (defining "method" as "[a]n orderly procedure or process . . . regular way or manner of doing anything; hence, a set form of procedure adopted in investigation or instruction"). The Court is unaware of any argument that the " 'ordinary, contemporary, common meaning,' " of "method" excludes business methods. Nor is it clear how far a prohibition on business method patents would reach, and whether it would exclude technologies for conducting a business more efficiently. * * *

The argument that business methods are categorically outside of § 101's scope is further undermined by the fact that federal law explicitly contemplates the existence of at least some business method patents. Under 35 U.S.C. § 273(b)(1), if a patent-holder claims infringement based on "a method in [a] patent," the alleged infringer can assert a defense of prior use. For purposes of this defense alone, "method" is defined as "a method of doing or conducting business." § 273(a)(3). In other words, by allowing this defense the statute itself acknowledges that there may be business method patents. Section 273's definition of "method," to be sure, cannot change the meaning of a prior-enacted statute. But what § 273 does is clarify the understanding that a business method is simply one kind of "method" that is, at least in some circumstances, eligible for patenting under § 101.

A conclusion that business methods are not patentable in any circumstances would render § 273 meaningless. This would violate the canon against interpreting any statutory provision in a manner that would render another provision superfluous. This principle, of course, applies to interpreting any two provisions in the U.S. Code, even when Congress enacted the provisions at different times. This established rule of statutory interpretation cannot be overcome by judicial speculation as to the subjective intent of various legislators in enacting the subsequent provision. Finally, while § 273 appears to leave open the possibility of some business method patents, it does not suggest broad patentability of such claimed inventions.

2

[In this deleted section, which failed to win a majority, Justice Kennedy rejects arguments that, historically, patentable subject matter has been understood to exclude business methods. He acknowledges, however, that "some business method patents raise special problems in terms of vagueness and suspect validity," and notes that if "a high enough bar is not set when considering patent applications of this sort, patent examiners and courts could be flooded with claims that would put a chill on creative endeavor and dynamic change." He suggests that the Court's "precedents on the unpatentability of abstract ideas provide useful tools."]

III

Even though petitioners' application is not categorically outside of § 101 under the two broad and atextual approaches the Court rejects today, that does not mean it is a "process" under § 101. Petitioners seek to patent both the concept of hedging risk and the application of that concept to energy markets. Rather than adopting categorical rules that might have wide-ranging and unforeseen impacts, the Court resolves this case narrowly on the basis of this Court's decisions in *Benson, Flook,* and *Diehr,* which show that petitioners' claims are not patentable processes because they are attempts to patent abstract ideas. Indeed, all members of the Court agree that the patent application at issue here falls outside of § 101 because it claims an abstract idea.

In *Benson,* the Court considered whether a patent application for an algorithm to convert binary-coded decimal numerals into pure binary code was a "process" under § 101. The Court first explained that " '[a] principle, in the abstract, is a fundamental truth; an original cause; a motive; these cannot be patented, as no one can claim in either of them an exclusive right.' " The Court then held the application at issue was not a "process," but an unpatentable abstract idea. "It is conceded that one may not patent an idea. But in practical effect that would be the result if the formula for converting ... numerals to pure binary numerals were patented in this case." A contrary holding "would wholly pre-empt the mathematical formula and in practical effect would be a patent on the algorithm itself."

In *Flook,* the Court considered the next logical step after *Benson.* The applicant there attempted to patent a procedure for monitoring the conditions during the catalytic conversion process in the petrochemical and oil-refining industries. The application's only innovation was reliance on a mathematical algorithm. *Flook* held the invention was not a patentable "process." The Court conceded the invention at issue, unlike the algorithm in *Benson,* had been limited so that it could still be freely used outside the petrochemical and oil-refining industries.* Nevertheless, *Flook*

---

* [Ed.: The *Flook,* claims were drawn to a method for computing an "alarm limit"—a number. The claims extended to all uses of the formula in processes "comprising the catalytic chemical conversion of hydrocarbons." Since there are numerous such processes in the petrochemical and

rejected "[t]he notion that post-solution activity, no matter how conventional or obvious in itself, can transform an unpatentable principle into a patentable process." The Court concluded that the process at issue there was "unpatentable under § 101, not because it contain[ed] a mathematical algorithm as one component, but because once that algorithm [wa]s assumed to be within the prior art, the application, considered as a whole, contain[ed] no patentable invention." As the Court later explained, *Flook* stands for the proposition that the prohibition against patenting abstract ideas "cannot be circumvented by attempting to limit the use of the formula to a particular technological environment" or adding "insignificant postsolution activity."

Finally, in *Diehr,* the Court established a limitation on the principles articulated in *Benson* and *Flook.* The application in *Diehr* claimed a previously unknown method for "molding raw, uncured synthetic rubber into cured precision products," using a mathematical formula to complete some of its several steps by way of a computer. *Diehr* explained that while an abstract idea, law of nature, or mathematical formula could not be patented, "an *application* of a law of nature or mathematical formula to a known structure or process may well be deserving of patent protection." *Diehr* emphasized the need to consider the invention as a whole, rather than "dissect[ing] the claims into old and new elements and then ... ignor[ing] the presence of the old elements in the analysis." Finally, the Court concluded that because the claim was not "an attempt to patent a mathematical formula, but rather [was] an industrial process for the molding of rubber products," it fell within § 101's patentable subject matter.

In light of these precedents, it is clear that petitioners' application is not a patentable "process." Claims 1 and 4 in petitioners' application explain the basic concept of hedging, or protecting against risk: "Hedging is a fundamental economic practice long prevalent in our system of commerce and taught in any introductory finance class." 545 F.3d, at 1013 (Rader, J., dissenting). The concept of hedging, described in claim 1 and reduced to a mathematical formula in claim 4, is an unpatentable abstract idea, just like the algorithms at issue in *Benson* and *Flook.* Allowing petitioners to patent risk hedging would pre-empt use of this approach in all fields, and would effectively grant a monopoly over an abstract idea.

Petitioners' remaining claims are broad examples of how hedging can be used in commodities and energy markets. *Flook* established that limiting an abstract idea to one field of use or adding token postsolution components did not make the concept patentable. That is exactly what the remaining claims in petitioners' application do. These claims attempt to patent the use of the abstract idea of hedging risk in the energy market and then instruct the use of well-known random analysis techniques to

---

oil refinery industries, the claims covered a broad range of potential uses. They did not, however, cover *every* conceivable application of the formula.]

help establish some of the inputs into the equation. Indeed, these claims add even less to the underlying abstract principle than the invention in *Flook* did, for the *Flook* invention was at least directed to the narrower domain of signaling dangers in operating a catalytic converter.

* * *

Today, the Court once again declines to impose limitations on the Patent Act that are inconsistent with the Act's text. The patent application here can be rejected under our precedents on the unpatentability of abstract ideas. The Court, therefore, need not define further what constitutes a patentable "process," beyond pointing to the definition of that term provided in § 100(b) and looking to the guideposts in *Benson, Flook,* and *Diehr.*

And nothing in today's opinion should be read as endorsing interpretations of § 101 that the Court of Appeals for the Federal Circuit has used in the past. See, *e.g., State Street Bank & Trust Co. v. Signature Financial Group, Inc.,* 149 F.3d 1368, 1373 (Fed. Cir. 1998); *AT & T Corp. v. Excel Communications, Inc.,* 172 F.3d 1352, 1357 (Fed. Cir. 1999). It may be that the Court of Appeals thought it needed to make the machine-or-transformation test exclusive precisely because its case law had not adequately identified less extreme means of restricting business method patents, including (but not limited to) application of our opinions in *Benson, Flook,* and *Diehr.* In disapproving an exclusive machine-or-transformation test, we by no means foreclose the Federal Circuit's development of other limiting criteria that further the purposes of the Patent Act and are not inconsistent with its text.

* * *

JUSTICE STEVENS, with whom JUSTICE GINSBURG, JUSTICE BREYER, and JUSTICE SOTOMAYOR join, concurring in the judgment.

In the area of patents, it is especially important that the law remain stable and clear. The only question presented in this case is whether the so-called machine-or-transformation test is the exclusive test for what constitutes a patentable "process" under 35 U.S.C. § 101. It would be possible to answer that question simply by holding, as the entire Court agrees, that although the machine-or-transformation test is reliable in most cases, it is not the *exclusive* test.

I agree with the Court that, in light of the uncertainty that currently pervades this field, it is prudent to provide further guidance. But I would take a different approach. Rather than making any broad statements about how to define the term "process" in § 101 or tinkering with the bounds of the category of unpatentable, abstract ideas, I would restore patent law to its historical and constitutional moorings.

For centuries, it was considered well established that a series of steps for conducting business was not, in itself, patentable. In the late 1990's, the Federal Circuit and others called this proposition into question. Congress quickly responded to a Federal Circuit decision with a stopgap measure designed to limit a potentially significant new problem for the business community. It passed the First Inventors Defense Act of 1999 (1999 Act) (codified at 35 U.S.C. § 273), which provides a limited defense to claims of patent infringement, see § 273(b), for "method[s] of doing or conducting business," § 273(a)(3). Following several more years of confusion, the Federal Circuit changed course, overruling recent decisions and holding that a series of steps may constitute a patentable process only if it is tied to a machine or transforms an article into a different state or thing. This "machine-or-transformation test" excluded general methods of doing business as well as, potentially, a variety of other subjects that could be called processes.

The Court correctly holds that the machine-or-transformation test is not the sole test for what constitutes a patentable process; rather, it is a critical clue. But the Court is quite wrong, in my view, to suggest that any series of steps that is not itself an abstract idea or law of nature may constitute a "process" within the meaning of § 101. The language in the Court's opinion to this effect can only cause mischief. The wiser course would have been to hold that petitioners' method is not a "process" because it describes only a general method of engaging in business transactions—and business methods are not patentable. More precisely, although a process is not patent-ineligible simply because it is useful for conducting business, a claim that merely describes a method of doing business does not qualify as a "process" under § 101.

* * *

The [majority's] opinion is less than pellucid in more than one respect, and, if misunderstood, could result in confusion or upset settled areas of the law. Three preliminary observations may be clarifying.

First, the Court suggests that the terms in the Patent Act must be read as lay speakers use those terms, and not as they have traditionally been understood in the context of patent law. * * * [I]f this portion of the Court's opinion were taken literally, the results would be absurd: Anything that constitutes a series of steps would be patentable so long as it is novel, nonobvious, and described with specificity. But the opinion cannot be taken literally on this point. The Court makes this clear when it accepts that the "atextual" machine-or-transformation test is "useful and important," even though it "violates" the stated "statutory interpretation principles," and when the Court excludes processes that tend to pre-empt commonly used ideas.

Second, in the process of addressing the sole issue presented to us, the opinion uses some language that seems inconsistent with our centuries-old reliance on the machine-or-transformation criteria as clues to patentability. Most notably, the opinion for a plurality suggests that these criteria may operate differently when addressing technologies of a recent vintage (machine-or-transformation test is useful "for evaluating processes similar to those in the Industrial Age," but is less useful "for determining the patentability of inventions in the Information Age"). In moments of caution, however, the opinion for the Court explains—correctly—that the Court is merely restoring the law to its historical state of rest. ("This Court's precedents establish that the machine-or-transformation test is a useful and important clue, an investigative tool, for determining whether some claimed inventions are processes under § 101"). Notwithstanding this internal tension, I understand the Court's opinion to hold only that the machine-or-transformation test remains an important test for patentability. Few, if any, processes cannot effectively be evaluated using these criteria.

Third, in its discussion of an issue not contained in the questions presented—whether the particular series of steps in petitioners' application is an abstract idea—the Court uses language that could suggest a shift in our approach to that issue. Although I happen to agree that petitioners seek to patent an abstract idea, the Court does not show how this conclusion follows "clear[ly]" from our case law. The patent now before us is not for "[a] principle, in the abstract," or a "fundamental truth." Nor does it claim the sort of phenomenon of nature or abstract idea that was embodied by the mathematical formula at issue in *Gottschalk v. Benson* and in *Flook*.

The Court construes petitioners' claims on processes for pricing as claims on "the basic concept of hedging, or protecting against risk," and thus discounts the application's discussion of what sorts of data to use, and how to analyze those data, as mere "token postsolution components." In other words, the Court artificially limits petitioners' claims to hedging, and then concludes that hedging is an abstract idea rather than a term that describes a category of processes including petitioners' claims. Why the Court does this is never made clear. One might think that the Court's analysis means that any process that utilizes an abstract idea is *itself* an unpatentable, abstract idea. But we have never suggested any such rule, which would undermine a host of patentable processes. It is true, as the Court observes, that petitioners' application is phrased broadly. But claim specification is covered by § 112, not § 101; and if a series of steps constituted an unpatentable idea merely because it was described without sufficient specificity, the Court could be calling into question some of our own prior decisions.[2] At points, the opinion suggests that novelty is the clue. But the fact that hedging is " 'long prevalent in our system of commerce,' "cannot justify the Court's conclusion, as "the proper construction of § 101 ... does not involve the familiar issu[e] of novelty" that arises under § 102. At other points, the opinion for a plurality suggests that the analysis turns on the category of patent involved (courts should use the abstract-idea rule as a "too[l]" to set "a high enough bar" "when

2. For example, a rule that broadly-phrased claims cannot constitute patentable processes could call into question our approval of Alexander Graham Bell's famous fifth claim on " '[t]he method of, and apparatus for, transmitting vocal or other sounds telegraphically, as herein described, by causing electrical undulations, similar in form to the vibrations of the air accompanying the said vocal or other sounds, substantially as set forth,' " *The Telephone Cases,* 126 U.S. 1, 531, 8 S.Ct. 778, 31 L.Ed. 863 (1888).

considering patent applications of this sort"). But we have never in the past suggested that the inquiry varies by subject matter.

The Court, in sum, never provides a satisfying account of what constitutes an unpatentable abstract idea. Indeed, the Court does not even explain if it is using the machine-or-transformation criteria. The Court essentially asserts its conclusion that petitioners' application claims an abstract idea. This mode of analysis (or lack thereof) may have led to the correct outcome in this case, but it also means that the Court's musings on this issue stand for very little.

[Justice Stevens goes on to argue that the statutory definition of "process" relied on by the majority is not helpful because it defines a "process" as "a process, method, or art," and thus is "circular." He asserts that the term "process" should not be construed "in the ordinary sense of the word" (even if "manufacture" and "composition of matter" are) because it has "long accumulated a distinctive meaning in patent law" and is a term of art. When Congress enacted the current Patent Act in 1952, it intended to codify that long-established meaning. Justice Stevens then undertakes a lengthy historical analysis to conclude that: "Since at least the days of Assyrian merchants, people have devised better and better ways to conduct business. Yet it appears that neither the Patent Clause, nor early patent law, nor the current § 101 contemplated or was publicly understood to mean that such innovations are patentable. Although it may be difficult to define with precision what is a patentable 'process' under § 101, the historical clues converge on one conclusion: A business method is not a 'process.' "]

JUSTICE BREYER, with whom JUSTICE SCALIA joins as to Part II, concurring in the judgment.

I

I agree with JUSTICE STEVENS that a "general method of engaging in business transactions" is not a patentable "process" within the meaning of 35 U.S.C. § 101. * * *

I write separately, however, in order to highlight the substantial *agreement* among many Members of the Court on many of the fundamental issues of patent law raised by this case. * * *

II

In addition to the Court's unanimous agreement that the claims at issue here are unpatentable abstract ideas, it is my view that the following four points are consistent with both the opinion of the Court and JUSTICE STEVENS' opinion concurring in the judgment:

First, although the text of § 101 is broad, it is not without limit. "[T]he underlying policy of the patent system [is] that 'the things which are worth to the public the embarrassment of an exclusive patent,' ... must outweigh the restrictive effect of the limited patent monopoly." *Graham v. John Deere Co. of Kansas City,* 383 U.S. 1, 10–11, 86 S.Ct. 684,

15 L.Ed.2d 545 (1966). The Court has thus been careful in interpreting the Patent Act to "determine not only what is protected, but also what is free for all to use." *Bonito Boats, Inc. v. Thunder Craft Boats, Inc.,* 489 U.S. 141, 151, 109 S.Ct. 971, 103 L.Ed.2d 118 (1989). In particular, the Court has long held that "[p]henomena of nature, though just discovered, mental processes, and abstract intellectual concepts are not patentable" under § 101, since allowing individuals to patent these fundamental principles would "wholly pre-empt" the public's access to the "basic tools of scientific and technological work." *Gottschalk v. Benson,* 409 U.S. 63, 67, 72 (1972).

Second, in a series of cases that extend back over a century, the Court has stated that "[t]ransformation and reduction of an article to a different state or thing is *the clue* to the patentability of a process claim that does not include particular machines." *Diehr, supra,* at 184, 101 S.Ct. 1048 (emphasis added). Application of this test, the so-called "machine-or-transformation test," has thus repeatedly helped the Court to determine what is "a patentable 'process.'"

Third, while the machine-or-transformation test has always been a "useful and important clue," it has never been the "sole test" for determining patentability. * * * Rather, the Court has emphasized that a process claim meets the requirements of § 101 when, "considered as a whole," it "is performing a function which the patent laws were designed to protect (*e.g.,* transforming or reducing an article to a different state or thing)." *Diehr, supra,* at 192, 101 S.Ct. 1048. The machine-or-transformation test is thus an *important example* of how a court can determine patentability under § 101, but the Federal Circuit erred in this case by treating it as the *exclusive test.*

Fourth, although the machine-or-transformation test is not the only test for patentability, this by no means indicates that anything which produces a " 'useful, concrete, and tangible result,' " *State Street Bank & Trust Co. v. Signature Financial Group, Inc.,* 149 F.3d 1368, 1373 (C.A.Fed.1998), is patentable. "[T]his Court has never made such a statement and, if taken literally, the statement would cover instances where this Court has held the contrary." *Laboratory Corp. of America Holdings v. Metabolite Laboratories, Inc.,* 548 U.S. 124, 136, 126 S.Ct. 2921, 165 L.Ed.2d 399 (2006) (BREYER, J., dissenting from dismissal of certiorari as improvidently granted). Indeed, the introduction of the "useful, concrete, and tangible result" approach to patentability, associated with the Federal Circuit's *State Street* decision, preceded the granting of patents that "ranged from the somewhat ridiculous to the truly absurd." *In re Bilski,* 545 F.3d 943, 1004 (C.A.Fed.2008) (MAYER, J., dissenting) (citing patents on, *inter alia,* a "method of training janitors to dust and vacuum using video displays," a "system for toilet reservations," and a "method of using color-coded bracelets to designate dating status in order to limit 'the embarrassment of rejection' "). To the extent that the Federal Circuit's decision in this case rejected that approach, nothing in today's decision should be taken as disapproving of that determination.

In sum, it is my view that, in reemphasizing that the "machine-or-transformation" test is not necessarily the *sole* test of patentability, the Court intends neither to de-emphasize the test's usefulness nor to suggest that many patentable processes lie beyond its reach.

* * *

NOTES AND QUESTIONS

1. *Laws of nature, natural phenomena and abstract ideas.* As the *Bilski* opinion indicates, laws of nature, natural phenomena and abstract ideas are not patentable. Only *specific applications* of laws of nature, natural phenomena and abstract ideas can be patented. Thus, while Sir Isaac Newton could not obtain a patent for the law of gravity (which is a law of nature, natural phenomenon or abstract idea), one could obtain a patent for a new machine or process that applies or incorporates the law of gravity in its operation. What is the justification for the rule that laws of nature, natural phenomena and abstract ideas are not themselves patentable? Why is a "field of use" restriction insufficient to avoid a finding that a claim states an abstract idea? Is there a principled way to determine whether elements encompassed in claim language merely constitute "insignificant post-solution activity"? How would you define an "abstract idea"?

2. *The machine-or-transformation standard.* How does the machine-or-transformation test (inquiring whether a claimed process is tied to a particular machine or apparatus or transforms a particular article into a different state or thing) help to ensure that a claimed process is more than an abstract idea? In *Bilski*, how did the majority determine that the claimed risk-hedging process merely constituted an abstract idea? Did it engage in the machine-or-transformation inquiry, or did it consider other factors? If the latter, what factors?

How would the machine-or-transformation standard apply in the case of patents for biotechnological processes? For example, how would you evaluate the patentability of the process described in Problem 1, *infra*? What if the claimed invention was a method of determining the proper dosage of a drug for treatment of a medical disorder, consisting of: 1) administering a certain man-made drug to a subject; 2) observing the level of two specific drug metabolites in the subject; and 3) concluding whether the level falls within a predetermined range (and thus whether an adjustment in the dosage is required)?

3. *Business methods as patentable "processes."* In State Street Bank & Trust Co. v. Signature Financial Group, Inc., 149 F.3d 1368 (Fed. Cir. 1998), *cert. denied*, 525 U.S. 1093, 119 S.Ct. 851, 142 L.Ed.2d 704 (1999), the patent applicant claimed a data processing system to implement a particular type of mutual fund investment structure in which two or more mutual funds pool their investment funds into a single portfolio, to consolidate administration costs and gain various tax advantages. The system enabled the investment structure administrator, among other things, to monitor and record financial information; allocate expenses, gains and losses on a daily basis among the participating mutual funds; and determine the value of each participating

mutual fund's investment on any given day so that the value of publicly traded shares in the mutual fund could then be calculated. The claims for the system included elements of computer hardware. The Court of Appeals for the Federal Circuit found that the claims stated statutory subject matter—a machine.

The Federal Circuit rejected arguments that the data processing system at issue was an unpatentable "business method." While acknowledging that some authority existed for a "business method" exception to patentable subject matter, the court availed itself of the opportunity to "put this ill-conceived exception to rest." It explained that since the 1952 Patent Act, "business methods have been, and should have been, subject to the same legal requirements for patentability as applied to any other process or method." *State Street,* 149 F.3d at 1375.

Banks, Internet enterprises and other businesses affected by this ruling had not been accustomed to dealing with patents, but the *State Street* decision triggered a surge of patent applications, first for business method-related software, and later for business methods by themselves. Indeed, enterprising lawyers began to patent methods of arbitrating contract disputes and tax avoidance strategies. See, e.g., U.S. Patent No. 6567790 (issued May 20, 2003). Since "business methods" were rarely, if ever, patented in the past, and many business treated their innovative business methods as trade secrets, concern arose that the PTO's search of the prior art (which focuses primarily on prior patents and technical publications) in evaluating business method applications would fail to uncover information relevant to their novelty and obviousness. This, in turn, would lead the PTO to grant overly broad, unwarranted patents, with anticompetitive effect.

Many commentators and courts construed the Federal Circuit's decision in *Bilski* as an attempt to cut back significantly on patents for business methods. See, e.g., CyberSource Corp. v. Retail Decisions, Inc., 620 F.Supp.2d 1068, 1080 (N.D. Cal. 2009) ("In analyzing *Bilski,* one is led to ponder whether the end has arrived for business method patents * * *. Without expressly overruling *State Street,* the *Bilski* majority struck down its under-pinnings. * * * The closing bell may be ringing for business method patents, and their patentees may find they have become bagholders."). What is the likely impact of the *Supreme Court's* decision on the availability of patents for business methods?

Is a limited construction of "process," as advocated by Justice Stevens, consistent with the Court's opinion in *Chakrabarty*? How might one define "business methods?" Is Justice Steven's distinction between a "process that is useful for conducting business and a claim that merely describes a method of doing business" helpful? As a matter of policy, should business methods be considered patentable subject matter? Will doing so "promote the progress of useful arts," as required under the Patents and Copyrights Clause? Why or why not? Other countries have hesitated to follow the United States' lead in granting patents for business methods.

The Supreme Court suggests that the Federal Circuit might find ways, consistently with its opinion, to limit the availability of business method patents. Would it be possible to define "abstract ideas" in a manner that would encompass most business methods?

4. *Computer programs and mathematical algorithms.* In determining that the *Bilski* method constituted an unpatentable abstract idea, the Supreme Court relied heavily on *Gottschalk v. Benson, Parker v. Flook,* and *Diamond v. Diehr*, all of which involved claims to software, or mathematical algorithms. (These cases are sometimes called the Court's "software trilogy.") *Benson* held that mathematical algorithms (of which computer programs are comprised) are unpatentable abstract ideas. *Flook* took "the next logical step," and held that the prohibition against patenting abstract ideas could not be circumvented by attempting to limit the use of the algorithm to a particular technological environment or adding insignificant post-solution activity. *Diehr* limited the principles stated in *Benson* and *Flook* by holding that "an application of a law of nature or mathematical formula to a known structure or process may well be deserving of patent protection." Thus, claiming a mathematical algorithm as one element of a process, machine or article of manufacture does not necessarily preclude a patent. In *Diehr,* the Supreme Court found a that a claimed process for curing synthetic rubber, which combined well-known rubber-curing steps with use of a programmed computer (which repeatedly recalculated the necessary cure time given variables in mold temperature) constituted patentable subject matter. The Court explained that granting a patent on the process would not give a monopoly in the mathematical algorithm with which the computer was programmed—it would only give rights in the use of the algorithm in combination with the other claimed process steps. Thus the patentee claimed a specific application of the abstract idea, not the abstract idea itself.

In In re Alappat, 33 F.3d 1526 (Fed.Cir.1994), the claimed invention improved the ability of a finite pixel cathode-ray tube (a visual screen like that of a television) to show a smooth diagonal line. Because the visual screen has only a fixed number of pixels, or illumination points, which are all the same size, its display of strongly sloped lines may appear jagged. Alappat's invention alleviated the problem by varying the illumination intensity of each pixel according to an anti-aliasing algorithm (a mathematical formula). Essentially, Alappat's invention operated on one set of numbers (vector list data) and produced another set of numbers (pixel illumination intensity data). Alappat disclosed "hard-wired" logic circuitry to perform the algorithm, but drafted his claims in a manner that would encompass any general purpose computer programmed to perform the algorithm. The PTO denied a patent under Patent Act § 101, on the ground that the application merely claimed a mathematical algorithm. In a controversial *en banc* decision that produced seven separate opinions, the Court of Appeals for the Federal Circuit found that the application stated patentable subject matter.

The majority reasoned that because the claims encompassed structural elements (computer hardware), the claimed invention constituted a "machine," which is statutory subject matter. The Federal Circuit characterized the "mathematical algorithm" exception to patentability as a very narrow exception which applies only in cases in which the claim, as a whole, is to a disembodied mathematical concept, representing nothing more than a law of nature, natural phenomenon, or abstract idea. If, as in *Alappat,* the claim makes a practical application of the mathematical concept, then the exception should not apply. The majority dismissed the objection that the claims in that case were so broad that they would extend to any general purpose computer programmed to carry out the same algorithm. The majority noted that the programming "creates a new machine, because a general purpose computer in effect becomes a special purpose computer once it is programmed to perform particular functions pursuant to instructions from program software." Thus, a claim for a known, general-purpose computer in combination with a new mathematical algorithm constitutes a claim for a new machine, and patentable subject matter.

The dissent characterized the applicant's claim as having "no substance apart from the calculations involved," and argued that the majority's reasoning elevated form over substance: All that Alappat really claimed to have discovered was a mathematical algorithm, which is unpatentable subject matter. Drafting his claim to include computer hardware was a subterfuge that did not change the essence of the claim. The practical effect of the majority's reading of the claim was to grant a patent in an abstract idea or law of nature. The dissent also rejected the notion that a computer constitutes a new machine each time a new program is loaded into it, questioning the logic of basing a finding of "newness" for purposes of patentability on a difference that is strictly unpatentable in itself.

Patents have also been granted for claims to software elements stored in a memory device, such as a disk or chip. See In re Lowry, 32 F.3d 1579 (Fed.Cir.1994); U.S. Patent & Trademark Office, *Examination Guidelines for Computer–Related Inventions*, 61 Fed. Reg. 7478 (1996). In such cases, the claims are deemed to fall into the "article of manufacture" category of patentable subject matter, because when software is recorded on a computer-readable medium it becomes "structurally and functionally interrelated to the medium," which permits the computer program's functionality to be realized. *Id.* at 7481.

5. *In re Nuijten.* In In Re Nuijten, 500 F.3d 1346 (Fed. Cir. 2007), the applicant developed a method of reducing the distortion that watermarking created in transitory signals. The applicant was able to patent his process for encoding signals to reduce distortion, a device to perform the process, and a storage medium to hold the encoded signals. However, the Federal Circuit rejected his claims to the encoded signals themselves.[6] The court reasoned that the signals, as claimed, failed to fall into any of the section 101 categories of patentable subject matter.

The claims anticipated that the data would be embedded in some physical carrier, such as modulated electromagnetic waves, electrical signals, or pulses in fiber optic cables, though they did not limit the signals to any particular

---

6. The independent claim at issue stated:

A signal with embedded supplemental data, the signal being encoded in accordance with a given encoding process and selected samples of the signal representing the supplemental data, and at least one of the samples preceding the selected samples is different from the sample corresponding to the given encoding process.

The ensuing dependent claims added requirements that the embedded data be a watermark, that the signal be a video signal, and that the signal be an audio signal. *In re Nuijten*, 500 F.3d at 1351.

physical form. The court thus characterized the claims as describing "physical but transitory forms of signal transmission such as radio broadcasts, electrical signals through a wire, and light pulses through a fiber-optic cable, as long as those transmissions convey information encoded in the manner disclosed and claimed." *Id.*, at 1353.

The court held that the signals did not constitute a "process," because a process entails an act or series of acts. The signal claims did not call for any action, but merely claimed the product of action. *Id.*, at 1355. Nor were the signals "machines" within the meaning of section 101. The court defined a machine as "a concrete thing, consisting of parts, or of certain devices," a "mechanical device or combination of mechanical powers and devices to perform some function and produce a certain effect or result." *Id.*, at 1355. However, a "transitory signal made of electrical or electromagnetic variances is not made of 'parts' or 'devices' in any mechanical sense. While such a signal is physical and real, it does not possess concrete structure in the sense implied by these definitions." *Id.*

The court found the question of whether the signals constituted "manufactures" (or "articles of manufacture") more difficult, because they were man-made. However, it found that artificiality was insufficient by itself to render something an article of manufacture. Rather, Supreme Court precedent defined a section 101 "manufacture" as a tangible article or commodity.

> A transient electric or electromagnetic transmission does not fit within that definition. While such a transmission is man-made and physical—it exists in the real world and has tangible causes and effects—it is a change in electric potential that, to be perceived must be measured at a certain point in space and time by equipment capable of detecting and interpreting the signal. In essence, energy embodying the claimed signal is fleeting and is devoid of any semblance of permanence during transmission. Moreover, any tangibility arguably attributed to a signal is embodied in the principle that it is perceptible—e.g., changes in electrical potential can be measured. All signals within the scope of the claim do not themselves comprise some tangible article or commodity. This is particularly true when the signal is encoded on an electromagnetic carrier and transmitted through a vacuum—a medium that, by definition, is devoid of matter. Thus, we hold that Nuijten's signals, standing alone, are not "manufacture[s]" within the meaning of that term in § 101.

Id., at 1356–57.

Finally, the court held that since the signals were not "composed of matter," they could not be deemed "compositions of matter" for purposes of § 101. Accordingly, the signals did not fall into any of the section 101 categories of patentable subject matter, and the claims must be rejected.

Do you find the court's reasoning compelling? In this modern age, why should "manufactures" be limited to tangible things? Shouldn't statutory subject matter be construed broadly, to cover the full scope of technological ingenuity? Could the signals be deemed laws of nature, natural phenomena, or abstract ideas?

6. *Patents for new uses of old products.* Patent Act § 100 provides that the term "process" "includes a new use of a known process, machine, manufacture, composition of matter or material." Thus, for example, a person who discovers that a known chemical compound has previously unknown medicinal qualities may obtain a patent on the process of treating patients with the compound, assuming that the other requirements of the Patent Act are satisfied. As the Supreme Court has explained, this type of "process" patent is particularly important to inventors in chemical research:

> The number of chemicals either known to scientists or disclosed by existing research is vast. It grows constantly, as those engaging in "pure" research publish their discoveries. The number of these chemicals that have known uses of commercial or social value, in contrast, is small. Development of new uses for existing chemicals is thus a major component of practical chemical research. It may take years of unsuccessful testing before a chemical having a desired property is identified, and it may take several years of further testing before a proper and safe method for using that chemical is developed.

Dawson Chemical Co. v. Rohm & Haas Co., 448 U.S. 176, 221–22, 100 S.Ct. 2601, 2626, 65 L.Ed.2d 696, 718 (1980).

7. *Medical procedure patents.* Many countries limit the availability of patents for medical or surgical procedures on ethical or social policy grounds. It has been argued that issuance of medical procedure patents may chill doctors' free use of the best and latest available techniques in treating patients. Moreover, the availability of patents may inhibit the customary sharing of information in the field and add to the expense of health care. It has also been asserted that medical procedure patents are not needed because most discoveries are made in the course of doctors' practice, do not depend on capital investment, and are not needed as an incentive to invent. See generally *Medical Procedures Innovation and Affordability Act & Inventor Protection Act of 1995: Hearings on H.R. 1127 and H.R. 2419 Before the Subcomm. on Courts and Intellectual Property of the House Comm. on the Judiciary,* 104th Cong., 1st Sess. (1995).

Unlike other countries, the United States has not excepted any category of medical or surgical procedures from patentable subject matter. Most U.S.-patented medical process claims are directed to methods of using medical devices and pharmaceuticals, which may also be patented. These claims can be contrasted with claims for medical or diagnostic procedures, such as the Heimlich maneuver or CPR, that do not center on the use of chemical compounds or innovative medical devices. Although the PTO has issued patents for medical procedure inventions in the latter category, most of these have never been enforced. Rather, doctors traditionally have obtained them primarily as a means of claiming credit for their discoveries, with no expectation of a direct financial reward.

These patents became controversial in the 1990's when a doctor undertook to enforce a patent that he had obtained for a method of stitchless cataract surgery, which uses the internal pressure of the eye to seal a tunnel-like incision. The patentee brought an infringement suit against the Dartmouth–Hitchcock Clinic and a Vermont doctor who had been using and teaching the technique. He sought to enjoin unauthorized use and impose a royalty of $5 per use. The patentee's lawyers estimated that approximately one-third of the 10,000 U.S. ophthalmic surgeons used the technique. See 52 Pat. Trademark & Copyright J. 44 (BNA)(1996). At around the same time, a California obstetrician decided to enforce his patent on a method for determining the sex of a fetus through ultrasound, and Yale University stated its intention to enforce a patent on a method of detecting breast cancer tumors by examining tissue for Tamoxifen metabolites. 49 Pat. Trademark & Copyright J. 530–31 (BNA)(1995). The American Medical Association's and others' objections to these developments led to the introduction of bills in Congress to prevent the issuance of patents for such medical or diagnostic procedures, or to limit their enforcement.

Congress' solution ultimately was not to exclude any medical procedures from the subject matter of patents. To exclude them would have been inconsistent with the position the U.S. had taken in international patent negotiations, advocating that patents should be available for all fields of technology. Rather, Congress amended Patent Act § 287 to prohibit infringement remedies against certain persons—medical practitioners and related health care entities—who directly infringe or induce infringement of a patent through performance of a "medical activity." The term, "medical activity," is defined as "the performance of a medical or surgical procedure on a body." 35 U.S.C. § 287(c)(2)(A). There are, however, several very important exceptions: Infringement remedies remain available if the medical practitioner (1) makes unauthorized use of a patented machine, article of manufacture, or composition of matter; (2) practices a patented method of administering a composition of matter without authorization; or (3) practices a patented biotechnology process without authorization. Thus, the § 287(c) limitation is a rather narrow one, which applies primarily when the infringed patent claims a surgical or medical procedure that does not involve drugs as an important component, or patented devices. Even then, remedies for indirect infringement may be available to the patentee under certain circumstances.

Was Congress' response adequate? What arguments can be made in support of fully enforceable patents for all medical and diagnostic procedures?

PROBLEM

1. Cobalamin (vitamin B–12) and folate are B vitamins that are required by the body. Deficiencies in these vitamins can result in serious illnesses. X researches means of detecting such deficiencies and discovers that an elevated level of total homocysteine (an amino acid) in a patient's body fluids indicates a deficiency of these B vitamins. He then formulates a method of detecting vitamin B deficiency that consists of 1) measuring the level of the relevant amino acids in the patient's body, using any available means, and 2) noticing whether the amino acid level is elevated and, if so, concluding that a vitamin B deficiency exists.

X then obtains a patent. The relevant claim recites:

> A method for detecting a deficiency of cobalamin or folate in warm-blooded animals comprising the steps of:

assaying a body fluid for an elevated level of total homocysteine; and

correlating an elevated level of total homocysteine in said body fluid with a deficiency of cobalamin or folate.

X subsequently brings an infringement suit alleging that physicians have directly infringed by ordering assays from Lab and correlating the results as described in the patent claim. It seeks to hold Lab indirectly liable for that infringement under an inducement theory. Assume that under the claim any means used to assay a body fluid for an elevated level of total homocystein falls within the first step of the claim. Lab defends, arguing that the patent claim is invalid because it does not constitute patentable subject matter under Patent Act § 101. How would you evaluate this claim in light of *Chakrabarty*, *Bilsky*, and the other case decisions discussed in this Section?

C. STANDARDS OF PATENTABILITY

1. Section 101: Utility

BRENNER v. MANSON

United States Supreme Court, 1966.
383 U.S. 519, 86 S.Ct. 1033, 16 L.Ed.2d 69.

Mr. Justice Fortas delivered the opinion of the Court.

[Manson filed an application to patent a process for making certain known steroids. The PTO rejected the application on the ground that the application failed to disclose any utility for the steroid produced by the process. The Court of Customs and Patent appeals reversed, holding that "where a claimed process produces a known product it is not necessary to show utility for the product," so long as the product "is not alleged to be detrimental to the public interest."]

II.

Our starting point is the proposition, neither disputed nor disputable, that one may patent only that which is "useful." [T]he concept of utility has maintained a central place in all of our patent legislation, beginning with the first patent law in 1790 and culminating in the present law's provision that

"Whoever invents or discovers any new and useful process, machine, manufacture, or composition of matter, or any new and useful improvement thereof, may obtain a patent therefor, subject to the conditions and requirements of this title."

As is so often the case, however, a simple, everyday word can be pregnant with ambiguity when applied to the facts of life. That this is so is demonstrated by the present conflict between the Patent Office and the CCPA over how the test is to be applied to a chemical process which yields an already known product whose utility—other than as a possible object of scientific inquiry—has not yet been evidenced. It was not long ago that agency and court seemed of one mind on the question. In *Application of Bremner*, 182 F.2d 216, 217, 37 C.C.P.A. (Pat.) 1032, 1034, the court affirmed rejection by the Patent Office of both process and product claims. It noted that "no use for the products claimed to be developed by the processes had been shown in the specification." It held that "It was never intended that a patent be granted upon a product, or a process producing a product, unless such product be useful." Nor was this new doctrine in the court.

The Patent Office has remained stead-fast in this view. The CCPA, however, has moved sharply away from *Bremner*. The trend began in *Application of Nelson*, 280 F.2d 172, 47 C.C.P.A. (Pat.) 1031. There, the court reversed the Patent Office's rejection of a claim on a process yielding chemical intermediates "useful to chemists doing research on steroids," despite the absence of evidence that any of the steroids thus ultimately produced were themselves "useful." The trend has accelerated, culminating in the present case where the court held it sufficient that a process produces the result intended and is not "detrimental to the public interest."

It is not remarkable that differences arise as to how the test of usefulness is to be applied to chemical processes. Even if we knew precisely what Congress meant in 1790 when it devised the "new and useful" phraseology and in subsequent re-enactments of the test, we should have difficulty in applying it in the context of contemporary chemistry where research is as comprehensive as man's grasp and where little or nothing is wholly beyond the pale of "utility"—if that word is given its broadest reach.

Respondent does not—at least in the first instance—rest upon the extreme proposition, advanced by the court below, that a novel chemical process is patentable so long as it yields the intended product and so long as the product is not itself "detrimental." Nor does he commit the outcome of his claim to the slightly more conventional proposition that any process is "useful" within the meaning of § 101 if it produces a compound whose potential usefulness is under investigation by serious scientific researchers, although he urges this position, too, as an alternative basis for affirming the decision of the CCPA. Rather, he begins with the much more orthodox argument that his process has a specific utility which would entitle him to a declaration of interference even under the Patent Office's reading of § 101. The claim is that the supporting affidavits filed pursuant to Rule 204(b), by reference to Ringold's 1956 article, reveal that an adjacent homologue of the steroid yielded by his process has been demonstrated to have tumor-inhibiting effects in mice, and that this discloses the requisite utility. We do not accept any of these theories as an adequate basis for overriding the determination of the Patent Office that the "utility" requirement has not been met.

Even on the assumption that the process would be patentable were respondent to show that the steroid produced had a tumor-inhibiting effect in mice, we would not overrule the Patent Office finding that respondent has not made such a showing. The Patent Office held that, despite the reference to the adjacent homologue, respondent's papers did not disclose a sufficient likelihood that the steroid yielded by his process would have similar tumor-inhibiting characteristics. Indeed, respondent himself recognized that the presumption that adjacent homologues have the same utility has been challenged in the steroid field because of "a greater known unpredictability of compounds in that field." In these circumstances and in this technical area, we would not overturn the finding of the Primary Examiner, affirmed by the Board of Appeals and not challenged by the CCPA.

The second and third points of respondent's argument present issues of much importance. Is a chemical process "useful" within the meaning of § 101 either (1) because it works—*i.e.*, produces the intended product? or (2) because the compound yielded belongs to a class of compounds now the subject of serious scientific investigation? These contentions present the basic problem for our adjudication. Since we find no specific assistance in the legislative materials underlying § 101, we are remitted to an analysis of the problem in light of the general intent of Congress, the purposes of the patent system, and the implications of a decision one way or the other.

In support of his plea that we attenuate the requirement of "utility," respondent relies upon Justice Story's well-known statement that a "useful" invention is one "which may be applied to a beneficial use in society, in contradistinction to an invention injurious to the morals, health, or good order of society, or frivolous and insignificant"—and upon the assertion that to do so would encourage inventors of new processes to publicize the event for the benefit of the entire scientific community, thus widening the search for uses and increasing the fund of scientific knowledge. Justice Story's language sheds little light on our subject. Narrowly read, it does no more than compel us to decide whether the invention in question is "frivolous and insignificant"—a query no easier of application than the one built into the statute. Read more broadly, so as to allow the patenting of any invention not positively harmful to society, it places such a special meaning on the word "useful" that we cannot accept it in the absence of evidence that Congress so intended. There are, after all, many things in this world which may not be considered "useful" but which, nevertheless are totally without a capacity for harm.

It is true, of course, that one of the purposes of the patent system is to encourage dissemination of information concerning discoveries and inventions. And it may be that inability to patent a process to some extent discourages disclosure and leads to greater secrecy than would otherwise be the case. The inventor of the process, or the corporate organization by which he is employed, has some incentive to keep the invention secret while uses for the product are searched out. However, in light of the highly developed art of drafting patent claims so that they disclose as little useful information as possible—while broadening the scope of the claim as widely as possible—the argument based upon the virtue of disclosure must be warily evaluated. Moreover, the pressure for secrecy is easily exaggerated, for if the inventor of a process cannot himself ascertain a "use" for that which his process yields, he has every incentive to make his invention known to those able to do so. Finally, how likely is disclosure of a patented process to spur research by others into the uses to which the product may be put? To the extent that the patentee has power to enforce his patent, there is little incentive for others to undertake a search for uses.

Whatever weight is attached to the value of encouraging disclosure and of inhibiting secrecy, we believe a more compelling consideration is that a process patent in the chemical field, which has not been developed and pointed to the degree of specific utility, creates a monopoly of knowledge which should be granted only if clearly commanded by the statute. Until the process claim has been reduced to production of a product shown to be useful, the metes and bounds of that monopoly are not capable of precise delineation. It may engross a vast, unknown, and perhaps unknowable area. Such a patent may confer power to block off whole areas of scientific development, without compensating benefit to the public. The basic *quid pro quo* contemplated by the Constitution and the Congress for granting a patent monopoly is the benefit derived by the public from an invention with substantial utility. Unless and until a process is refined and developed to this point—where specific benefit exists in currently available form—there is insufficient justification for permitting an applicant to engross what may prove to be a broad field.

These arguments for and against the patentability of a process which either has no known use or is useful only in the sense that it may be an object of scientific research would apply equally to the patenting of the product produced by the process. Respondent appears to concede that with respect to a product, as opposed to a process, Congress has struck the balance on the side of nonpatentability unless "utility" is shown. Indeed, the decisions of the CCPA are in accord with the view that a product may not be patented absent a showing of utility greater than any adduced in the present case. We find absolutely no warrant for the proposition that although Congress intended that no patent be granted on a chemical compound whose sole "utility" consists of its potential role as an object of use-testing, a different set of rules was meant to apply to the process which yielded the unpatentable product. That proposition seems to us little more than an attempt to evade the impact of the rules which concededly govern patentability of the product itself.

This is not to say that we mean to disparage the importance of contributions to the fund of scientific information short of the invention of something "useful," or that we are blind to the prospect that what now seems without "use" may tomorrow command the grateful attention of the public. But a patent is not a hunting license. It is not a reward for the search, but compensation for its successful conclusion. "[A] patent system must be related to the world of commerce rather than to the realm of philosophy...."

* * *

MR. JUSTICE DOUGLAS dissents on the merits of the controversy for substantially the reasons stated by MR. JUSTICE HARLAN.

MR. JUSTICE HARLAN, concurring in part and dissenting in part.

* * *

Respondent has contended that a workable chemical process, which is both new and sufficiently nonobvious to satisfy the patent statute, is by its existence alone a contribution to chemistry and "useful" as the statute employs that term. Certainly this reading of "useful" in the statute is within the scope of the constitutional grant, which states only that "[t]o promote the Progress of Science and useful Arts," the exclusive right to "Writings and Discoveries" may be secured for limited times to those who produce them. Art. I, § 8. Yet the patent statute is somewhat differently worded and is on its face open both to respondent's construction and to the contrary reading given it by the Court. In the absence of legislative history on this issue, we are thrown back on policy and practice. Because I believe that the Court's policy arguments are not convincing and that past practice favors the respondent, I would reject the narrow definition of "useful" and uphold the judgment of the Court of Customs and Patent Appeals (hereafter CCPA).

The Court's opinion sets out about half a dozen reasons in support of its interpretation. Several of these arguments seem to me to have almost no force. For instance, it is suggested that "[u]ntil the process claim has been reduced to production of a product shown to be useful, the metes and bounds of that monopoly are not capable of precise delineation" and "[i]t may engross a vast, unknown, and perhaps unknowable area." I fail to see the relevance of these assertions; process claims are not disallowed because the products they produce may be of "vast" importance nor, in any event, does advance knowledge of a specific product use provide much safeguard on this score or fix "metes and bounds" precisely since a hundred more uses may be found after a patent is granted and greatly enhance its value.

The further argument that an established product use is part of "[t]he basic *quid pro quo*" for the patent or is the requisite "successful conclusion" of the inventor's search appears to beg the very question whether the process is "useful" simply because it facilitates further research into possible product uses. The same infirmity seems to inhere in the Court's argument that chemical products lacking immediate utility cannot be distinguished for present purposes from the processes which create them, that respondent appears to concede and the CCPA holds that the products are nonpatentable, and that therefore the processes are nonpatentable. Assuming that the two classes cannot be distinguished, a point not adequately considered in the briefs, and assuming further that the CCPA has firmly held such products nonpatentable, this permits us to conclude only that the CCPA is wrong either as to the products or as to the processes and affords no basis for deciding whether both or neither should be patentable absent a specific product use.

More to the point, I think, are the Court's remaining, prudential arguments against patentability: namely, that disclosure induced by allowing a patent is partly undercut by patent-application drafting techniques, that disclosure may occur without granting a patent, and that a patent will discourage others from inventing uses for the product. How far opaque drafting may lessen the public benefits resulting from the issuance of a patent is not shown by any evidence in this case but, more important, the argument operates against all patents and gives no reason for singling out the class involved here. The thought that these inventions may be more likely than most to be disclosed even if patents are not allowed may have more force; but while empirical study of the industry might reveal that chemical researchers would behave in this fashion, the abstractly logical choice for them seems to me to maintain secrecy until a product use can be discovered. As to discouraging the search by others for product uses, there is no doubt this risk exists but the price paid for any patent is that research on other uses or improvements may be hampered because the original patentee will reap much of the reward. From the standpoint of the public interest the Constitution seems to have resolved that choice in favor of patentability.

What I find most troubling about the result reached by the Court is the impact it may have on chemical research. Chemistry is a highly interrelated field and a tangible benefit for society may be the outcome of a number of different discoveries, one discovery building upon the next. To encourage one chemist or research facility to invent and disseminate new processes and products may be vital to progress, although the product or process be without "utility" as the Court defines the term, because that discovery permits someone else to take a further but perhaps less difficult step leading to a commercially useful item. In my view, our awareness in this age of the importance of achieving and publicizing basic research should lead this Court to resolve uncertainties in its favor and uphold the respondent's position in this case.

* * *

NOTES AND QUESTIONS

1. *The policy considerations.* If the purpose of patent law is to provide the optimal balance between promoting invention and preserving free competition, how stringent should the usefulness requirement be? Did the Court reach the right balance? Should possible future usefulness of a chemical compound in scientific research suffice to demonstrate usefulness? What if it can presently be shown that a chemical compound has a tumor-inhibiting effect on laboratory animals, but as yet, no tests demonstrate whether the compound will inhibit tumors in humans? See Nelson v. Bowler, 626 F.2d 853 (C.C.P.A.1980) (patent application for a chemical compound can satisfy the utility requirement by demonstrating a therapeutic use with animals—for example, inhibiting tumors in laboratory animals). Would granting a patent in situations such as *Brenner* serve as a roadblock to further research in the

field? In your opinion, what is the likely impact of the Court's decision on public disclosure of newly discovered chemical compounds and processes for making them?

While earlier case decisions suggested that "immoral" inventions lack utility, the trend is away from this approach to making the usefulness determination. In Juicy Whip, Inc. v. Orange Bang, Inc., 185 F.3d 1364 (Fed.Cir.1999), the Court of Appeals for the Federal Circuit considered the "usefulness" of a beverage dispenser that was designed to deceive consumers into thinking the dispensed beverage they were purchasing was "pre-mixed" when in fact it was being mixed as dispensed. The lower court had found that the dispenser invention lacked utility because its purpose was to increase sales by deception. The Court of Appeals rejected this reasoning. First, the court noted that many inventions, such as the cubic zirconium, imitation gold leaf, and synthetic fabrics, were designed to appear to be something else: "The fact that one product can be altered to make it look like another is in itself a specific benefit sufficient to satisfy the statutory requirement of utility." *Id.* at 1367. Besides, the court noted, "the principle that inventions are invalid if they are principally designed to serve immoral or illegal purposes has not been applied broadly in recent years."

> The requirement of "utility" in patent law is not a directive to the Patent and Trademark Office or the courts to serve as arbiters of deceptive trade practices. Other agencies, such as the Federal Trade Commission and the Food and Drug Administration are assigned the task of protecting consumers from fraud and deception in the sale of food products. * * *
>
> Of course, Congress is free to declare particular types of inventions unpatentable for a variety of reasons, including deceptiveness. * * * Until such time as Congress does so, however, we find no basis in section 101 to hold that inventions can be ruled unpatentable for lack of utility simply because they have the capacity to fool some members of the public.

Id. at 1366, 1368.

2. *Genes, partial gene sequences and the usefulness requirement.* Scientists seeking patents for genes and partial gene sequences have purified and isolated the genetic material at issue, separating it from other molecules naturally associated with it. Because this genetic material differs from the form found in nature, it can be deemed a "man-made" chemical compound, and thus patentable subject matter. The resulting patent covers the isolated and purified gene or partial gene sequence, but does not cover the genetic material as it occurs in nature. See Utility Examination Guidelines, 66 Fed. Reg. 1092, 1093 (2001).

However, Patent Act § 101 requires that the applicant seeking to patent a gene or partial gene sequence demonstrate a specific, substantial use for it. This requirement is likely to be met if the material can be used to produce a useful protein or if it hybridizes near and thus serves as a marker for a disease gene. It is not so clear that the requirement can be met if the biological functions of the particular genetic material are unknown, as is presently the case for many partial gene sequences. In such cases, alleged uses may be speculative or tenuous.

Critics have expressed a number of practical and policy concerns regarding the patenting of genes and partial gene sequences. (What possible objections might there be?) One very specific expressed concern has been that the PTO may grant patents for genes and partial gene sequences for which an insufficient demonstration of utility has been made. See *id.*, at 1093–97. In response to this criticism, the PTO undertook to draft new guidelines to assist examiners in evaluating the utility of applicants' inventions. Utility Examination Guidelines, 66 Fed. Reg. 1092 (2002). While the guidelines are applicable to all areas of technology, they were drafted with the issue of gene and partial gene sequence patents primarily in mind.

Under the guidelines, the examiner must review the claims and the supporting written description to determine if the claimed invention has a "well-established utility." An invention will have a well-established utility "(1) if a person of ordinary skill in the art would immediately appreciate why the invention is useful based on the characteristics of the invention * * *, and (2) the utility is specific, substantial, and credible." If the examiner fails to find a "well-established utility," then she must review the claims and supporting written description to determine whether the applicant has asserted any specific and substantial utility that is credible. Credibility must be assessed "from the perspective of one of ordinary skill in the art in view of the disclosure and any other evidence of record (*e.g.* test data, affidavits or declarations from experts in the art, patents or printed publications) that is probative of the applicant's assertions." An applicant only needs to provide one credible assertion of specific and substantial utility for the invention. If no assertion of specific and substantial utility made by the applicant is credible, and the claimed invention lacks a readily apparent well-established utility, the examiner must reject the claims under § 101 for lack of utility, and under § 112 ¶ 1 for failure to teach how to use the invention. *Id.,* at 1097–98.

Assume that an applicant claims purified nucleic acid sequences (known as "expressed sequence tags" or "ESTs") corresponding to genes expressed from corn leaf tissue. The precise structure or function of those genes and of the proteins they encode is not yet known. The ESTs can be used to help identify the unknown genes and to map their positions within a genome. This in turn will help scientists learn more about the underlying genes and their function. Under *Brenner*, can the applicant demonstrate the requisite utility? Can the ESTs be analogized to a microscope, for purposes of analyzing utility?

3. *Inoperability as lack of utility.* A patent may be denied for lack of utility if the invention fails to operate as claimed. For example, in Newman v. Quigg, 877 F.2d 1575 (Fed.Cir.), *modified*, 886 F.2d 329 (Fed.Cir.1989), *cert. denied*, 495 U.S. 932, 110 S.Ct. 2173, 109 L.Ed.2d 502 (1990), the applicant claimed to have invented a device that generated more usable energy than it consumed (a "perpetual motion" machine). The PTO found that such a device would violate "either the first or second law of thermodynamics," and rejected the application. In the course of district court review of the rejection, the applicant was ordered to submit a working model of the invention to the National Bureau of Standards for testing. When the National Bureau of Standards reported that tests failed to support the applicant's claims of more energy output than input, the district court held the claimed invention

unpatentable for lack of usefulness. The Court of Appeals for the Federal Circuit affirmed.

See also Fregeau v. Mossinghoff, 776 F.2d 1034 (Fed.Cir.1985). In that case the applicant claimed a method for enhancing the flavor of beverages by passing them through a magnetic field. A highly skeptical patent examiner rejected the claims for lack of utility due to inoperativeness. The applicant then submitted declarations from a Professor of Food Science who had conducted taste tests, averring that the test results demonstrated that the invention worked. The examiner remained unconvinced, finding that the declaration was not "evidence of the type convincing to the scientific community." The Board of Patent Appeals and Interferences and the district court agreed with the examiner. The Federal Circuit affirmed, noting that a *prima facie* case of inoperability had been established simply by the nature of the invention, thus shifting the burden to the applicant to rebut the presumption.

4. *Usefulness and pharmaceutical inventions.* If a patent applicant asserts that a chemical compound has therapeutic or pharmacological uses in humans, he must demonstrate that the compound is safe and effective for that purpose. The showing need not rise to the level required by the Food and Drug Administration, however. See Application of Anthony, 414 F.2d 1383 (C.C.P.A.1969).

Of course, the granting of a patent for a chemical compound does not in itself authorize the patentee to sell it commercially, if sale is prohibited by health and safety laws. The new patentee may still face lengthy regulatory proceedings in agencies such as the Food and Drug Administration in order to obtain permission to market its new compound. This regulatory review may take a number of years, so that by the time the patentee obtains the necessary permission to enter the market, much of its patent term has expired. To compensate for delays caused by the pre-market regulatory process, Congress has provided a procedure by which patents in certain kinds of regulated inventions can be extended. See Patent Act, §§ 155–56. In addition, from time to time, Congress enacts private relief bills to extend patent terms upon a showing of "extraordinary circumstances."

2. Section 102: Novelty

Most nations grant patents to the first inventor to file an application, which leads to a race to the patent office when two or more sets of inventors are working on similar projects. The United States, in contrast, has always favored granting a patent to the first person to make the invention. The novelty provisions in § 102(a), (e), and (g) work together to make it very difficult for a "subsequent inventor" to obtain a patent.

Section 102(a) provides that an applicant will be denied a patent if, prior to the applicant's invention date: 1) the invention was "known" in the United States; 2) the invention was "used" in the United States; 3) the invention was the subject of a patent anywhere in the world; or 4) the invention was revealed in a "printed publication" anywhere in the world.

Section 102(e) provides that even if the earlier invention was not disclosed to the public in any of the ways enumerated in subsection (a), its existence will preclude the subsequent inventor from obtaining a patent if it was disclosed in a U.S. patent application that was pending on the subsequent inventor's invention date and was later published under § 122(b) or granted. Note that the PTO retains pending patent applications in confidence for the first eighteen months after they are filed, and in some cases, until they are granted. 35 U.S.C.A. § 122. Thus, our subsequent-inventor applicant may have had no way of knowing of the earlier invention's existence at the time he invented and applied for a patent.

Section 102(g) places a final obstacle in the subsequent inventor's path to the Patent Office. Under subsection (g), the applicant will be denied a patent if: (1) prior to the applicant's invention date, another person made the invention in the U.S. and had not abandoned, suppressed or concealed it; or (2) another person has established in an interference action that he made the invention abroad prior to the applicant's invention date and had not abandoned, suppressed or concealed it.[7]

Net MoneyIN, Inc. v. VeriSign, Inc. explains when a prior publication will "anticipate" an applicant's invention, rendering it non-novel under § 102. The following notes explore how § 102(a), (e) and (g) work. But first, given § 102's emphasis on priority of invention, it is useful to discuss how the first inventor is identified.

The act of invention consists of two parts: the conception and the reduction to practice. An inventor conceives of the invention when he formulates a definite, complete idea of the operative invention, so that all that remains is the physical realization of it. The mental concept must be complete to the point that a person with ordinary skill in the art could then produce it without further invention.[8] The inventor may reduce the concept to practice in either of two ways. He may perform an *actual reduction to practice* by building a physical prototype of the invention (or in the case of a process, by actually carrying out the steps of the process) and ascertaining that it works for the intended purpose. The inventor may *constructively reduce the invention to practice* by filing a patent application which fully discloses the invention.

It is presumed that the first person to reduce the invention to practice is the first to invent. However, a person making a later reduction to practice may rebut that presumption by showing that he was the *first to*

---

7. A patent interference is a proceeding in the PTO to determine which claimant is the earlier inventor when there are conflicting claims. The PTO may declare an interference between pending applications or between an issued patent and an application, when each claims substantially the same invention. Patent Act § 104 limits the circumstances in which foreign inventors may rely on their foreign invention date in a patent interference proceeding.

8. The inventor must not only conceive of the invention, but also understand his creation to have the features comprising the inventive subject matter. An accidental invention, in which the prior inventor does not recognize or appreciate the invention's innovative qualities, does not anticipate a later one. See Invitrogen Corp. v. Clontech Laboratories, Inc., 429 F.3d 1052, 1063–66 (Fed. Cir. 2005).

conceive of the invention and was *reasonably diligent in reducing it to practice* from a date prior to the conception date of the first to reduce to practice.

The requirement that the first inventor to conceive exercise reasonable diligence in reducing the invention to practice balances the interest in rewarding and encouraging invention with the public's interest in the earliest possible disclosure of innovation, and is strictly construed. For example, in Griffith v. Kanamaru, 816 F.2d 624 (Fed. Cir. 1987), Griffith, a Cornell University researcher, conceived of his invention by June 30, 1981, and reduced it to practice on January 11, 1984. Kanamaru filed for a U.S. patent for the same invention on November 17, 1982. (In that particular case, Kanamaru's filing date was deemed both his conception date and his reduction to practice date.) Because he was the first to reduce to practice (by filing), Kanamaru was presumed to be the first to invent. To overcome that presumption, Griffith was required to demonstrate reasonable diligence from a date immediately before Kanamaru's filing date until the date that Griffith himself reduced the invention to practice.

Griffith experienced difficulty in justifying his inactivity in reducing to practice during a three-month period from June 15, 1983 to September 13, 1983. During that time he was waiting for a particular graduate student to be come available to assist with the project (he had promised her the opportunity because she needed it to qualify for her degree) and was following the Cornell policy of pursuing outside funding for the project. The Court of Appeals for the Federal Circuit found these justifications insufficient to establish diligence during this period. With regard to the graduate student, Griffith had not demonstrated a lack of other, equally qualified assistants. The court could not find "precedent to suggest that the convenience of the timing of the semester schedule justifies a three-month delay for the purpose of reasonable diligence." The court equated Griffith's outside funding justification to cases finding a lack of diligence when the delay was attributable to attempts to capitalize on the invention—refining the invention to the most marketable form, organizing corporations, or attracting investors for commercial manufacture and sale of the invention—prior to completing the reduction to practice.

Courts have found that short periods of inactivity were justified when attributable to personal hardships (such as the death of a relative) or practical, everyday problems (such as the need to work for a livelihood, or the need to develop means of testing the invention). Because the timing of an inventor's conception and subsequent efforts to reduce his invention to practice can be crucial, well-advised researchers keep elaborate laboratory notebooks in which they record their daily efforts, and have the notebooks notarized or witnessed on a regular basis. Such corroborating evidence may be essential in a priority contest.

NET MONEYIN, INC. v. VERISIGN, INC.

United States Court of Appeals, Federal Circuit, 2008.
545 F.3d 1359.

LINN, CIRCUIT JUDGE.

Net MoneyIN, Inc. ("NMI") appeals from a final judgment of the United States District Court for the District of Arizona, which held the asserted claims of U.S. Patents No. 5,822,737 ("the '737 patent") and No. 5,963,917 ("the '917 patent") invalid. * * * Because the district court applied an incorrect standard of law in finding claim 23 of the '737 patent invalid as anticipated under 35 U.S.C. § 102(a), * * * we reverse the grant of summary judgment of anticipation. * * *

I. BACKGROUND

This case involves systems for processing credit card transactions over the Internet and for addressing security concerns not present in direct retail transactions. In the early days of Internet commerce, merchants recognized that one key to the success of Internet sales would be the ability to provide customers with assurances of security in the processing of financial transactions over the Internet using credit cards, bank accounts, and other means of electronic payment. Responding to that need, the industry investigated encryption techniques and architectures to protect sensitive data. One such effort is reflected in a 1995 working document entitled "Internet Keyed Payments Protocol" ("the iKP reference"), published by the Internet Engineering Task Force and IBM. That document sets forth standards on "how payments may be accomplished efficiently, reliably[,] and securely." The iKP reference explains that its goal was "to enable Internet-based secure electronic payments while utilizing the existing financial infrastructure for payment authorization and clearance. The intent is to avoid completely, or at least minimize, changes to the existing financial infrastructure outside the Internet." To that end, the iKP reference suggests two standard models, or protocols.

In the first protocol, (1) the customer selects one or more items to purchase from the merchant's website; (2) the customer sends credit card information to the merchant; (3) the merchant sends the credit card information and amount of the purchase to the merchant's bank; (4) the merchant's bank seeks authorization for the purchase from the issuing bank over the existing banking network; and (5) the merchant's bank notifies the merchant (but not the customer) of transaction approval.

In the second protocol, (1) the customer selects one or more items to purchase on the merchant's website; (2) the customer sends an authorization request, along with its credit card information and the amount of the purchase, to the merchant's bank; (3) the merchant's bank seeks authorization from the issuing bank over the existing banking network; (4) the merchant's bank notifies the customer of transaction approval; and (5) the customer sends the authorization response to the merchant.

Unsatisfied with the early approaches taken by others, Mark Ogram, an inventor and patent attorney, set out to create a new payment model to remedy what he perceived as two deficiencies in the prior art protocols: "the fact that the customer had to send confidential information over the Internet to an unknown merchant; and the fact that credit card issuers imposed onerous financial requirements on merchants." Ogram's idea was to add a fifth entity, a "payment processing" or "financial processing" entity, to supplement the conventional model with four entities: the customer, merchant, merchant's bank, and issuing bank. According to Ogram, the new financial processing entity would: "(1) receive credit card account information and an amount to be charged from the customer when the customer placed the order; (2) seek authorization from the card issuer over the existing banking network; and (3) notify both the customer and the merchant of authorization."

On February 5, 1996, Ogram filed a patent application directed to a payment model utilizing a financial processing entity. He formed NMI shortly thereafter to implement the model as a business for processing credit card transactions over the Internet. Ogram's patent application resulted in the '737 and '917 patents, both of which are assigned to NMI. Claim 1 of the '737 patent is illustrative of the invention claimed:

1.   A financial transaction system comprising:

a) a first bank computer containing financial data therein, said financial data including customer account numbers and available credit data, said first bank computer including means for generating an authorization indicia in response to queries containing a customer account number and amount;

b) a merchant computer containing promotional data;

c) a customer computer being linked with said merchant computer and receiving said promotional data; and,

d) a financial processing computer remote from said merchant computer and having means for:

   1) receiving customer account data and amount data from said customer computer,

   2) querying said first bank computer with said customer account data and said amount data,

   3) receiving an authorization indicia from said first bank computer,

   4) communicating a self-generated transaction indicia to said customer computer, and,

   5) communicating the self-generated transaction indicia to said merchant computer.

According to their abstracts, the '737 and '917 patents relate to "[a]n automated payment system particularly suited for purchases over a distributed computer network such as the Internet."

In 2001, NMI filed suit for infringement of the '737 and '917 patents against a number of parties alleged to compete in the Internet credit card processing field, including VeriSign, Inc. and eProcessing Network (collectively, "VeriSign"). * * *

* * * VeriSign moved for summary judgment of invalidity, arguing that the iKP reference anticipated claim 23 of the '737 patent under 35 U.S.C. § 102(a). The district court granted VeriSign's motion. * * *

II. DISCUSSION

* * *

2. Anticipation

Claim 23 of the '737 patent recites an Internet payment system comprising five "links":

[1] a first link between a customer computer and a vending computer for communicating promotional information from said vending computer to said customer computer;

[2] a second link, initiated by said customer computer, between said customer computer and a payment processing computer, remote from said vending computer, for communicating credit card information and amount from said customer computer to said payment processing computer;

[3] a third link, initiated by said payment processing computer with a credit card server computer for communicating said credit card information and said amount from said payment processing computer to said credit card server computer, and for communicating, in response, an authorization indicia from said credit card server computer to said payment processing computer; [ ]

[4] a fourth link between said payment processing computer and said customer computer for communicating a transactional indicia[;]

[5] a fifth link between the payment processing computer and said vending computer for communicating said transactional indicia.

The district court, after finding all five of these links in the iKP reference, albeit in two separate disclosed examples, concluded that claim 23 was anticipated under 35 U.S.C. § 102(a) and therefore invalid. Specifically, the district court concluded:

All of the limitations of claim 23 can be found within the iKP reference. A simple combination would produce the system described in claim 23 of the '737 patent. That no specific example within iKP contains all five links does not preclude a finding of anticipation.

NMI contends that the district court's combination of two disclosed examples in order to find all elements of the claim was erroneous. VeriSign responds that the district court did not improperly rearrange the links in the iKP reference, but rather "merely relied on various express teachings from a single document that together completely disclose the five claimed links." Under VeriSign's theory, this was sufficient to establish anticipation, because all that is required is "that the four corners of a single, prior art document describe every element of the claimed invention." We disagree with VeriSign, and take this opportunity to clarify what a reference must show in order to anticipate a claimed invention.

Section 102(a) provides that an issued patent is invalid if "the invention [therein] was ... described in a printed publication ... before the invention thereof by the applicant." Section 102 embodies the concept of novelty—if a device or process has been previously invented (and disclosed to the public), then it is not new, and therefore the claimed invention is "anticipated" by the prior invention. As we have stated numerous times (language on which VeriSign relies), in order to demonstrate anticipation, the proponent must show "that the four corners of a single, prior art document describe every element of the claimed invention." This statement embodies the requirement in section 102 that the anticipating invention be "described in a printed publication," and is, of course, unimpeachable. But it does not tell the whole story. Because the hallmark of anticipation is prior invention, the prior art reference—in order to anticipate under 35 U.S.C. § 102—must not only disclose all elements of the claim within the four corners of the document, but must also disclose those elements "arranged as in the claim." *Connell v. Sears, Roebuck & Co.*, 722 F.2d 1542, 1548 (Fed.Cir.1983).

The meaning of the expression "arranged as in the claim" is readily understood in relation to claims drawn to things such as ingredients mixed in some claimed order. In such instances, a reference that discloses all of the claimed ingredients, but not in the order claimed, would not anticipate, because the reference would be missing any disclosure of the limitations of the claimed invention "arranged as in the claim." But the "arranged as in the claim" requirement is not limited to such a narrow set of "order of limitations" claims. Rather, our precedent informs that the "arranged as in the claim" requirement applies to all claims and refers to the need for an anticipatory reference to show all of the limitations of the claims arranged or combined in the same way as recited in the claims, not merely in a particular order. The test is thus more accurately understood to mean "arranged or combined in the same way as in the claim."

For example, in *Lindemann Maschinenfabrik GMBH v. American Hoist & Derrick Co.*, 730 F.2d 1452 (Fed.Cir.1984), we reviewed a district court's determination that a patent directed to a hydraulic scrap shearing machine was anticipated by a prior patent directed to a method for shearing spent nuclear fuel bundles. Because the district court had "treated the claims as mere catalogs of separate parts, in disregard of the part-to-part relationships set forth in the claims and that give the claims their meaning," we reversed. Although the prior art reference could be said to contain all of the elements of the claimed invention, it did not anticipate under 35 U.S.C. § 102 because it "disclose[d] an entirely different device, composed of parts distinct from those of the claimed invention, and operating in a different way to process different material differently." *Id.* at 1458. The reference thus was deficient because it did not disclose the elements of the claimed invention "arranged as in the claim" as required by 35 U.S.C. § 102.

* * *

* * * We thus hold that unless a reference discloses within the four corners of the document not only all of the limitations claimed but also all of the limitations arranged or combined in the same way as recited in the claim, it cannot be said to prove prior invention of the thing claimed and, thus, cannot anticipate under 35 U.S.C. § 102.

Here, the iKP reference discloses two separate protocols for processing an Internet credit card transaction. Neither of these protocols contains all five links arranged or combined in the same way as claimed in the '737 patent. Thus, although the iKP reference might anticipate a claim directed to either of the two protocols disclosed, it cannot anticipate the system of claim 23. The district court was wrong to conclude otherwise.

The district court was also wrong to combine parts of the separate protocols shown in the iKP reference in concluding that claim 23 was anticipated. Granted, there may be only slight differences between the protocols disclosed in the iKP reference and the system of claim 23. But differences between the prior art reference and a claimed invention, however slight, invoke the question of obviousness, not anticipation. *See* 35 U.S.C. § 103(a) ("A patent may not be obtained though the invention is not *identically* disclosed or described as set forth in section 102 of this title, if the differences between the subject matter sought to be patented and the prior art are such that the subject matter as a whole would have been obvious at the time the invention was made to a person having ordinary skill in the art to which said subject matter pertains." (emphasis added)) * * * . Thus, it is not enough that the prior art reference discloses part of the claimed invention, which an ordinary artisan might supplement to make the whole, or that it includes multiple, distinct teachings that the artisan might somehow combine to achieve the claimed invention. *See In re Arkley,* 455 F.2d 586, 587 (C.C.P.A. 1972) ("[T]he [prior art] reference must clearly and unequivocally disclose the claimed [invention] or direct those skilled in the art to the [invention] without *any* need for picking, choosing, and combining various disclosures not directly related to each other by the teachings of the cited reference.").

Because the parties do not contend that the iKP reference discloses all of the limitations recited in claim [23] arranged or combined in the same way as in the claim, and because it was error for the district court to find anticipation by combining different parts of the separate protocols in the iKP reference simply because they were found within the four corners of the document, we reverse the district court's grant of summary judgment of invalidity.

* * *

NOTES AND QUESTIONS

1. *Identity of invention.* As demonstrated in the *VeriSign* case, lack of novelty ("anticipation") under Patent Act § 102 entails "the presence in a single prior art disclosure of all elements of a claimed invention arranged as in that claim." Generally, an anticipating reference—for example, an earlier patent or publication—will expressly disclose all the elements (or "limitations") of the later-claimed invention. However, the courts have recognized "inherent anticipation," in which the reference does not expressly disclose all the elements of the later invention, but the non-express elements are nonetheless necessarily present in the thing described or disclosed in the reference.[9]

The novelty, statutory bar, and obviousness determinations are all made with reference to the prior art—earlier inventions, patents, and publications as described in § 102. However, while the obviousness determination may be made by combining two or more prior art references, § 102 anticipation requires that the invention be revealed (expressly or inherently) in a single reference—a single earlier invention, patent or publication. Essentially, the test for anticipation is the same as that for literal infringement. If something disclosed in a single reference would have literally infringed the patent if it arose after the patent became effective, then it will anticipate if it arose before the applicant's invention.

2. *Section 102(a).* Section 102(a) sets forth four different types of disclosure (or "prior art") that will anticipate a later invention and thus render it unpatentable.

a) The invention was known by others in this country prior to the applicant's invention. In Application of Borst, 345 F.2d 851 (C.C.P.A.1965), *cert. denied,* 382 U.S. 973, 86 S.Ct. 537, 15 L.Ed.2d 465 (1966), the Court of Customs and Patent Appeals set forth two requirements that must be satisfied in order to demonstrate that an invention was "known" prior to the applicant's invention, within the meaning of § 102(a). First, the invention must have been fully disclosed. Second, the invention must have been accessible to the public. *Id.,* 345 F.2d at 854.

With regard to the "fully disclosed" requirement, prior case law had held that in order to anticipate, an earlier invention must have been either actually or constructively reduced to practice. As noted *supra,* actual reduction to practice entails making a physical embodiment of the invention (or in the case of a process, carrying out the steps of the process) and ascertaining that the invention works for the intended purpose. Constructive reduction to practice entails filing a patent application for the invention. The *Borst* court reasoned that "the criterion should be whether the disclosure [was] sufficient to enable one skilled in the art to reduce the disclosed invention to practice. In other words, the disclosure must [have been such as would] give possession of the invention to the person of ordinary skill." While actual or constructive

---

9. For a useful discussion of the circumstances in which courts will find that an element (or "limitation") is "inherent" in a disclosure, even though not expressly described, see Dan L. Burk and Mark A. Lemley, *Inherency,* 47 Wm. & Mary L. Rev. 371 (2005).

reduction to practice would sufficiently disclose the invention, some other form of disclosure [in that case, an unpublished document] containing "a description of the invention fully commensurate with" a patent application could, too. Thus, as long as the disclosure was enabling, it "need not be of an invention reduced to practice, either actually or constructively." *Id.*, 345 F.2d at 855.

The *Borst* decision did not provide much guidance with regard to the second requirement—that the invention have been accessible to the public. Since "publications" constitute a separate category of prior art, presumably public disclosures that fall short of "publication" can qualify to make an invention "known" within the meaning of subsection (a). In Oak Industries, Inc. v. Zenith Electronics Corp., 726 F.Supp. 1525 (N.D.Ill.1989), the earlier inventor had demonstrated the invention to some visiting engineers from out of town. The court reasoned that by demonstrating or describing the invention to the visitors (who were skilled in the relevant art, and for purposes of the summary judgement motion, were presumed to have owed no duty of confidentiality), the first inventor made the invention available to the public. This was because the recipients of the disclosure, who were skilled in the art, were in a position to further disseminate the information, or use it to the public's benefit in their own work.

b) The invention was used by others in this country prior to the applicant's invention. Prior use of an invention, by its nature, requires that the invention have been actually reduced to practice. In addition, the prior use of the invention must have been accessible to the public. Connecticut Valley Enterprises, Inc. v. United States, 348 F.2d 949, 952 (Ct.Cl.1965). However, in this context, the "accessibility" requirement entails little more than an absence of affirmative steps to conceal. If the prior invention was used in the manner for which it was intended, the prior user need not have taken any affirmative steps to make the invention known widely to the public or to those skilled in the art. Moreover, the prior use need not have led to public understanding of the invention. Gillman v. Stern, 114 F.2d 28 (2d Cir.1940), *cert. denied*, 311 U.S. 718, 61 S.Ct. 441, 85 L.Ed. 468 (1941).

c) The invention was patented in this or a foreign country before the applicant's invention. Patents generally become part of the prior art for purposes of anticipation on the date they become effective, provided that their contents are at least minimally accessible to the public. In order to anticipate, the patent must fully describe the later invention. Why is it necessary to provide that patents will anticipate a U.S. invention—won't patents also constitute "printed publications?" Note that while U.S. patents are published and constitute "printed publications" at the time they are issued (and may have been published prior to being granted), that may not be true in the case of foreign patents.

d) The invention was described in a printed publication in this or a foreign country before the applicant's invention. A "printed publication" must describe the invention sufficiently to enable a person having ordinary skill in the art to make or practice the invention without undue experimentation.

The statutory phrase "printed publication" has been interpreted to give effect to ongoing advances in the technologies of data storage, retrieval, and dissemination. Because there are many ways in which a reference may be disseminated to the interested public, "public accessibility" has been called the touchstone in determining whether a reference constitutes a "printed publication" * * *. [It must appear that] the reference was sufficiently accessible, at least to the public interested in the art, so that such a one by examining the reference could make the claimed invention without further research or experimentation.

In re Hall, 781 F.2d 897, 898–99 (Fed.Cir.1986).

The range of references that may constitute a printed publication is quite wide: microfilm, photographs, and slides have all been found sufficient. It seems clear, however, that the information must be "fixed" or made tangible. Presumably, if a sales person at a trade show orally described a new invention to customers, this would not create a printed publication for purposes of § 102, no matter how detailed and precise the description.

When will a tangible reference be sufficiently accessible to the public to constitute a printed publication? In *In re* Wyer, 655 F.2d 221 (C.C.P.A. 1981), microfilm copies of a patent application were made available upon request in the Australian Patent Office and in its five sub-offices, and means were available in these locations for visitors to make their own copies. The Court of Customs and Patent Appeals found this sufficient to constitute a printed publication. In *Hall, supra,* the Federal Circuit found that a single graduate thesis in one German university library was sufficiently accessible, since it was indexed in a special dissertations catalog which was part of the general users' catalog, and was freely available to students, faculty and the general public. By contrast, in *In re* Cronyn, 890 F.2d 1158 (Fed.Cir.1989), the Federal Circuit found that a student thesis at an American college did not constitute a printed publication. In that case, undergraduate theses were described on individual index cards, which were filed alphabetically under the authors' names and kept in a shoe box in the chemistry department library. The court noted that these theses were not sufficiently accessible to the public since they were not cataloged or indexed in a meaningful way.

In Massachusetts Institute of Technology v. AB Fortia, 774 F.2d 1104 (Fed.Cir.1985), a paper was presented orally at a conference attended by 50 to 500 persons skilled in the subject matter. A copy of the paper was provided to the head of the conference and copies were distributed on request, without any restrictions, to as many as six persons. The court found that the paper constituted a printed publication. Compare Northern Telecom, Inc. v. Datapoint Corp., 908 F.2d 931 (Fed.Cir.), *cert. denied,* 498 U.S. 920, 111 S.Ct. 296, 112 L.Ed.2d 250 (1990), in which the Federal Circuit declined to find a printed publication. In that case, four reports were distributed to approximately fifty persons or organizations involved in a complex military project. While the reports were not under security classification, some or all of the reports contained the legend "Reproduction or further dissemination is not authorized ... not for public release." The reports were also housed in the library of a private corporation, with library access restricted to authorized persons. The court reasoned that there was no clear and convincing evidence that an interested person could have had access to the documents through the exercise of reasonable diligence.

In *In re* Klopfenstein, 380 F.3d 1345 (Fed. Cir. 2004), the inventors of a method of preparing foods containing extruded soy cotyledon fiber prepared a slide presentation that fully disclosed their invention. They printed the fourteen slides and pasted them on to poster boards and displayed the boards continuously for two and a half days at a meeting of the American Association of Cereal Chemists. Shortly thereafter they put the same slide presentation on display for part of a day at an Agriculture Experiment Station at a university. The inventors did not provide a disclaimer or notice to the intended audience prohibiting note-taking or copying of the presentation. However, they did not disseminate any copies of the presentation.

The Court of Appeals for the Federal Circuit found that the display constituted a printed publication, rejecting arguments that a disclosure must be either disseminated, indexed at a library, or cataloged in a database to qualify. The court reiterated that public accessibility is the key to finding a printed publication. It reasoned that in the absence of distribution or indexing, several factors should be considered to determine whether the reference was sufficiently publicly accessible: 1) the length of time the display was exhibited; 2) the expertise of the target audience; 3) the existence (or lack thereof) of reasonable expectations that the displayed material would not be copied; and 4) the simplicity or ease with which the displayed material could have been copied. *Id.*, 380 F.3d at 1350. Here, the poster boards had been displayed for three days to a audience comprised of persons with ordinary skill in the art of cereal chemistry. There were no facts to suggest that the inventors could expect the audience not to copy the information. Moreover, it would be relatively simple to copy the information from the boards, since the key information was concentrated on only a few of the boards, and each of these boards consisted of only three bulleted items of two concise sentences or less. Given this liberal opportunity for the audience of persons skilled in the art to copy, the court reasoned that it was appropriate to consider the display a printed publication.

   3. *Section 102(e).* In Alexander Milburn Co. v. Davis–Bournonville Co., 270 U.S. 390, 46 S.Ct. 324, 70 L.Ed. 651 (1926), the plaintiff obtained a patent for an improvement in a welding and cutting apparatus, and later sued the defendant for infringement. The defendant challenged the validity of the plaintiff's patent, alleging that plaintiff's inventor, Whitford, was not the first inventor. Whitford's alleged invention date was March 4, 1911—the date he filed his patent application. Plaintiff's patent issued on June 4, 1912. Evidence indicated that Clifford applied for a patent on January 31, 1911, which issued on February 6, 1912. Clifford's application gave a complete and adequate description of the improvement patented to Whitford, but did not claim it. The Supreme Court found that the disclosure in Clifford's application (which was retained in confidence by the PTO while the Clifford application pended) invalidated plaintiff's patent:

> We understand the Circuit Court of Appeals to admit that if Whitford had not applied for his patent until after the issue to Clifford, the disclosure by the latter would have had the same effect as the publication of the same words in a periodical, although not made the basis of a claim. The invention is made public property as much in the one case as in the other. But if this be true, as we think that it is, it seems to us that a sound

distinction cannot be taken between that case and a patent applied for before but not granted until after a second patent is sought. The delays of the Patent Office ought not to cut down the effect of what has been done. The description shows that Whitford was not the first inventor. Clifford had done all that he could do to make his description public. He had taken steps that would make it public as soon as the Patent Office did its work, although, of course, amendments might be required of him before the end could be reached. We see no reason in the words or policy of the law for allowing Whitford to profit by the delay and make himself out to be the first inventor when he was not so in fact, when Clifford had shown knowledge inconsistent with the allowance of Whitford's claim, and when otherwise the publication of his patent would abandon the thing described to the public unless it already was old.

Id., 270 U.S. at 401–402. In its subsequent revision of the patent laws, Congress codified the holding in *Milburn* by adopting 35 U.S.C. § 102(e), which currently provides that a person shall be entitled to a patent unless the invention was described in "a patent granted on an application for patent by another filed in the United States before the invention by the applicant * * * ". Note that if the earlier-filed application is granted, the disclosures contained in the patent become a part of the prior art *as of the time the application was filed*, rather than at the time the patent issues and is published. See Hazeltine Research, Inc. v. Brenner, 382 U.S. 252, 86 S.Ct. 335, 15 L.Ed.2d 304 (1965).

At the time the *Milburn* case was decided, and for many years thereafter, the PTO kept patent applications in confidence until the patent issued, at which point the patent, with its claims and enabling disclosure, was published. In the Intellectual Property and Communications Omnibus Reform Act of 1999, Congress amended Patent Act § 122 to provide that the PTO should publish most patent applications 18 months after their filing date. It simultaneously amended § 102(e) to provide that a person will not be entitled to a patent if the invention was described in "an application for patent, published under section 122(b), by another filed in the United States before the invention by the applicant for patent * * *." Pub. L. No. 106–113, § 4505, 113 Stat. at 1537–557.[10] An accompanying section-by-section analysis explained:

> Section 4505 amends section 102(e) of the Patent Act to treat an application published by the USPTO in the same fashion as a patent granted by the USPTO. Accordingly, a published application is given prior art effect as of its earliest effective U.S. filing date against any subsequently filed U.S. applications.

145 Cong. Rec. S14719 (daily ed. Nov. 17, 1999)(included in the record at the request of Sen. Lott). Disclosures in pending patent applications that are later granted or published are sometimes referred to as "secret prior art," because

---

10. Section 102(e) also provides that international patent applications filed pursuant to the Patent Cooperation Treaty ("PCT") should be treated as applications filed in the U.S., but only if they designate the U.S. and are published under PCT Art. 21(2) in English. For more information about the PCT, see pages 244–46, *infra*.

at the time that the later inventor invented, it might have been impossible for her to learn of the disclosures.

4. *Section 102(g).* Section 102(g) denies a patent for an invention if, before the applicant's invention date, "the invention was made in this country by another inventor who had not abandoned, suppressed or concealed it." 35 U.S.C. § 102(g).[11] What is the policy behind permitting a later inventor to obtain a patent if the earlier inventor has abandoned, suppressed or concealed the invention? When will an abandonment, suppression or concealment be found? The Court of Appeals for the Federal Circuit addressed this issue in Checkpoint Systems, Inc. v. U.S. International Trade Commission, 54 F.3d 756 (Fed. Cir. 1995):

> * * * A principal purpose of § 102(g) is to ensure that a patent is awarded to a first inventor. However, it also encourages prompt public disclosure of an invention by penalizing the unexcused delay or failure of a first inventor to share the "benefit of the knowledge of [the] invention" with the public after the invention has been completed.
>
> When determining whether an inventor has abandoned, suppressed, or concealed an invention, a period of delay between completion of the invention and subsequent public disclosure may or may not be of legal consequence. The delay may be inconsequential if, for example, it is reasonable in length or excused by activities of the inventor. Furthermore, there is no particular length of delay that is per se unreasonable. Rather, a determination of abandonment, suppression, or concealment has "consistently been based on equitable principles and public policy as applied to the facts of each case." A court must determine whether, under the facts before it, any delay was reasonable or excused as a matter of law.
>
> One way a prior inventor may avoid the disqualifying effect of § 102(g) is by promptly filing a patent application claiming the invention. In the usual context of an interference proceeding, each inventor involved in the proceeding will have filed a patent application, one of which may have matured into a patent. However, § 102(g) is applicable in other contexts as well, such as when it is asserted as a basis for invalidating a patent in defense to an infringement suit. In such a case, a first inventor may seek to avoid a determination of abandonment by showing that he or she marketed or sold a commercial embodiment of the invention or described the invention in a publicly disseminated document. See *Palmer v. Dudzik*, 481 F.2d 1377, 1387(CCPA 1973) (to negate a finding of suppression or concealment, the public must have gained knowledge of the invention which will insure its preservation in the public domain). If the prior inventor's activities following completion of the invention do not evidence abandonment, suppression, or concealment, § 102(g) will bar a later inventor from obtaining a patent. In cases in which an invention is disclosed to the public by commercialization, courts have excused delay

---

11. An earlier invention abroad can also serve as a basis for rejecting an application, if the earlier foreign inventor establishes, "during the course of an interference conducted under section 135 or section 291," her earlier invention date and a lack of abandonment, suppression or concealment. 35 U.S.C. § 102(g)(1).

upon proof that the first inventor engaged in reasonable efforts to bring the invention to market. See, e.g., *Engelhard Corp. v. M.C. Canfield Sons*, 13 USPQ2d 1561, 1564–65 (D.N.J.1989) ("[T]he company's delay was within the realm of 'reasonable business practices.' "); *Refac Elecs. Corp. v. R.H. Macy & Co.*, 9 USPQ2d 1497, 1506 (D.N.J.1988) ("The pivotal issue ... is whether the 'nature and tempo' of [the] activities between the initial invention/reduction-to-practice and ultimate market distribution are in accord with reasonable business practices...."), aff'd mem., 871 F.2d 1097 (Fed.Cir.1989). * * *

Id. 54 F.3d at 761–62. Assuming that the earlier inventor is engaging in "reasonable business practices" while gearing up to commercialize the invention, should it matter if she keeps it secret prior to its market release?

Suppose that the first inventor abandons, suppresses or conceals his invention, but later resumes activity and files a patent application. Will § 102(g) deprive him of a patent if no second inventor has appeared on the scene and filed an application? What if a second inventor files an application, but only after the first inventor has resumed? Consider Paulik v. Rizkalla, 760 F.2d 1270 (Fed.Cir.1985).

In *Paulik*, Paulik, an employee of the Monsanto Company, reduced his invention to practice in November, 1970, and again in April, 1971. Paulik immediately sent information about the invention to the Patent Department of his assignee, the Monsanto Company. While the Patent Department kept the project on active status, it assigned it a lower priority than other pending projects. Despite prodding from Paulik, the Patent Department only began work toward filing a patent application in January or February of 1975. On March 10, 1975, Rizkalla filed an application for patent for the same invention. On June 30, 1975, Monsanto's Patent Department filed its application for the Paulik invention. In the subsequent interference proceeding, Rizkalla relied on his filing date as his date of invention. The PTO Board of Patent Interferences held that Paulik's four-year delay from reduction to practice to filing was *prima facie* suppression or concealment, and awarded priority to Rizkalla. The Federal Circuit vacated and remanded.

The court held that Paulik was entitled to demonstrate that he (through his assignee) had renewed activity on the invention and had proceeded diligently to file his patent application from a date prior to Rizkalla's invention date. Upon making this proof, he could rely on his date of renewed activity as his date of invention for purposes of the priority determination. While Paulik's four years of inactivity would deprive him of the benefit of his original date of invention, his date of renewed activity, which predated Rizkalla's invention, would entitle him to priority and a patent. The court reasoned:

> The reason for the patent system is to encourage innovation and its fruits: new jobs and new industries, new consumer goods and trade benefits. We must keep this purpose in plain view as we consider the consequences of interpretations of the patent law such as in the Board's decision.
>
> A foreseeable consequence of the Board's ruling is to discourage inventors and their supporters from working on projects that had been

"too long" set aside, because of the impossibility of relying, in a priority contest, on either their original work or their renewed work. This curious result is neither fair nor in the public interest. We do not see that the public interest is served by placing so severe a sanction on failure to file premature patent applications on immature inventions of unknown value. In reversing the Board's decision we do not hold that such inventions are necessarily entitled to the benefits of their earliest dates in a priority contest; we hold only that they are not barred from entitlement to their dates of renewed activity.

Id., 760 F.2d at 1276.

5. *The "first-to-invent" system vs. the "first-to-file" system.* The United States has always subscribed to the belief that patents should be reserved for the first, or "true," inventor. The U.S., however, stands alone in awarding priority to the first to invent. Virtually all other nations award patents to the first inventor to file an application. See The Advisory Commission on Patent Law Reform, A Report to the Secretary of Commerce 43, 67 n.2 (1992). There has been considerable debate about whether the U.S. should change to a first-to-file system. What are the advantages and disadvantages of each approach?

Proponents of a change have argued that as markets become increasingly global, a uniform, world-wide system of determining priority is essential. Complying with two systems in the course of seeking world-wide patent protection is burdensome, and the burden outweighs any advantage that the first-to-invent system might offer over a first-to-file system. Moreover, proponents have argued that the first-to-file system is more efficient: It dispenses with lengthy, costly interference procedures and provides greater predictability. A first-to-file system may also lead to earlier disclosure of inventions, which can only benefit the public. Some have observed that the United States already has a *de facto* first-to-file system, since only a small percentage of applications entail interferences, and when they do, the first applicant to file usually wins. They further note that adopting a first-to-file system will not appreciably change the practice of U.S. inventors, since many U.S. companies, which file both for domestic and foreign patents on new inventions, already plan their patent-filing strategies with the foreign first-to-file requirements in mind.

Opponents to change counter that the first-to-invent system is fairer: The first person to invent is more deserving of a patent than the first inventor to file, and the public more readily accepts a system that rewards the first inventor. Moreover, a first-to-file system gives an undue advantage to large companies over small, back-yard inventors, who may lack the financial resources to file applications early in the inventive process and win a race to the Patent Office. Opponents also argue that a first-to-file system leads to a decrease in the quality of disclosure in patent applications. The inventor may be rushed to file an application before he has perfected the invention, fully tested it, and ascertained the best mode of practicing it. He is also rushed to file before having an opportunity to explore the commercial value of the invention. The resulting decrease in quality and increase in number of applications will overburden the PTO and affect the quality of its examination process.

What do you think? For a fuller discussion of these issues, see Report to the Secretary of Commerce, *supra*, at 43–46 (recommending that the United States change to a first-to-file system); Banner & McDonnell, *First-to-File, Mandatory Reexamination, and Mandatory "Exceptional Circumstance": Ideas for Better? Or Worse?*, 69 J. Pat. & Trademark Off. Soc. 595 (1987) (arguing against changing to a first-to-file system).

PROBLEMS

1. Baker has applied for a patent for a method of eliminating static in television signal reception. Her invention date is November 4, 2009. The facts show that Able created a device that executed each step of the method, as described in Baker's patent claims, in July, 2009. Between July and November 4, Able engaged in the following activities in connection with his device:

—He worked with representatives of Crowe Electric Supply to further develop and perfect the device, he contacted an engineer to discuss and arrange for refinements that would make the device more marketable, and contacted Davis about manufacturing the device commercially.

—He used one of the devices in 30 or 40 homes, in the course of his television repair service, to alleviate static in television reception. However, at these times Able never gave the device to the television owners to use or keep, or left it at their homes overnight.

—He met with an attorney in August to consult about patenting the device. However, he decided not to file an application for patent.

—In September, Able demonstrated the device to five visiting engineers from another city. These engineers were not affiliated with Able's business, though they, like Able, worked with television signal reception problems.

Assuming that these are all the relevant facts, should Baker's method be deemed novel for purposes of § 102?

2. Allen and Brown, U.S. university research professors, conceived of a new kind of widget and reduced it to actual practice in November, 2006. They made no attempt to license, manufacture or sell the widget, or to put their prototype to use. They also decided not to apply for a patent. They did not tell others about the invention, but went to work right away to write a paper that described it, and the scientific principles underlying it, working diligently on the paper until it was completed in February, 2008. They then submitted the paper to a scientific journal for publication, and the journal published it in September, 2008.

In December, 2006, Chen, a U.S. manufacturer of widgets, invented a widget that had all the same elements as Allen and Brown's. At that time, Chen decided not to file for a patent, and she also decided not to manufacture the widget for sale right away. She decided to postpone manufacture because she already had plans to renovate her factory in 2010, and she felt that it would be more cost efficient to undertake the manufacture after the renovations were complete. Meanwhile, Chen kept the widget secret, but engaged in no further work in connection with it.

In July, 2007, Davis invented a widget that had all the same elements as Allen and Brown's. He made his invention in South Africa, and during the next year, manufactured and sold 200 of the widgets in that country. Davis did not apply for a patent.

In January, 2008, Effinger invented a widget with the same elements as Allen and Brown's. In February, 2008, Chen changed her mind about patenting her widget, and applied for a patent. In March, 2008, Effinger filed a patent application, too.

Assume that the widget is "useful" and that in 2006, it was both novel and non-obvious. Evaluate Chen's and Effinger's right to a patent under Patent Act § 102.

3. Section 102: The Statutory Bar

MOLECULON RESEARCH CORP. v. CBS, INC.

United States Court of Appeals, Federal Circuit, 1986.
793 F.2d 1261, *cert. denied*, 479 U.S. 1030, 107 S.Ct. 875, 93 L.Ed.2d 829 (1987).

BALDWIN, CIRCUIT JUDGE.

* * *

A puzzle enthusiast since childhood, Nichols, in the summer of 1957, conceived of a three-dimensional puzzle capable of rotational movement. He envisioned an assembly of eight cubes attached in a 2 x 2 x 2 arrangement, with each of the six faces of the composite cube distinguished by a different color and the individual cubes being capable of rotation in sets of four around one of three mutually perpendicular axes.

During the period 1957–1962, while doing graduate work in organic chemistry, Nichols constructed several paper models of his puzzle, making cubes of heavy file-card type paper and affixing small magnets to the inside of the cubes. Although these models confirmed the feasibility of Nichols' conception, they lacked durability. A few close friends, including two roommates and a colleague in the chemistry department, had occasion to see one of these paper models in Nichols' room and Nichols explained its operation to at least one of them.

In 1962, Nichols accepted employment as a research scientist at Moleculon. In 1968, Nichols constructed a working wood block prototype of his puzzle which he usually kept at home but on occasion brought into his office. In January 1969, Dr. Obermayer, the president of Moleculon, entered Nichols' office and happened to see the model sitting on his desk. Obermayer expressed immediate interest in the puzzle and Nichols explained its workings. Obermayer asked whether Nichols intended to commercialize the puzzle. When Nichols said no, Obermayer suggested that Moleculon try to do so. In March 1969, Nichols assigned all his rights in the puzzle invention to Moleculon in return for a share of any proceeds of commercialization. On March 7, 1969, Moleculon sent Parker Brothers an actual model and a description of the cube puzzle. In the next three years, Moleculon contacted between fifty and sixty toy and game manufacturers, including Ideal. Ideal responded to the effect that it did not currently have an interest in marketing the puzzle. Moleculon itself did not succeed in marketing the Nichols cube.

On March 3, 1970, Nichols filed on behalf of Moleculon a patent application covering his invention. The '201 patent issued on April 11, 1972.

[In this suit, Moleculon alleges that the well-known Rubik's Cube puzzle infringes the '201 patent.]

1. § 102(b) on sale and public use bars

CBS argues that the subject matter of the '201 patent was in "public use" and "on sale" by Nichols, prior to the March 3, 1969 critical date (i.e., one year prior to filing of the patent application), thus rendering the patent invalid under section 102(b).

(a) Public Use

CBS labels as public use Nichols' displaying of the models to other persons (such as his colleagues at school) without any mention of secrecy. CBS ascribes only commercial purpose and intent to Obermayer's use of the wood model and argues that a conclusion of barring public use under § 102(b) is compelled. We disagree.

This is what the district court had to say:

The essence of "public use" is the free and unrestricted giving over of an invention to a member of the public or the public in general. What I see here, by contrast, is the inventor's private use of his own invention for his own enjoyment. "Private use of one's own invention is permissible."

While it is true that Nichols explained his puzzle to a few close colleagues who inquired about it and allowed Obermayer to in fact use it, the personal relationships and other surrounding circumstances were such that Nichols at all times retained control over its use as well as over the distribution of information concerning it. He never used the puzzle or permitted it used in a place or at a time when he did not have a legitimate expectation of privacy and of confidentiality. In these respects, I consider the exposure to Obermayer in Nichols' office no different than the exposure of Nichols' close friends in his home.

Here also the relationship between the participants in the alleged uses evidences a retention of control by Nichols. None of those participants had any basis for inferring that the puzzle was being given over by Nichols for their free and unrestricted use. Holding the public use bar inapplicable in these circumstances will not remove anything from the public domain. Moreover, there is absolutely no evidence in this case of commercially motivated activity by Nichols during the relevant period. Accordingly, the underlying policy against extending the effective term of exclusivity is not offended by a finding that the Nichols invention was not in public use.

CBS correctly recognizes that the district court's conclusion on public use under § 102(b) is subject to review as a question of law while the facts underlying the conclusion on public use are subject to the clearly erroneous standard of review.

CBS urges that the decision in *Egbert v. Lippmann*, 104 U.S. 333, 26 L.Ed. 755 (1881), compels a conclusion of public use in the present case. In *Egbert*, the claimed invention was drawn to improved corset-springs, also called corset-steels. In 1855, the inventor made and presented to his lady friend a pair of corset-steels which embodied the invention. She wore the steels for a long time. The inventor made and gave her another pair three years later which she also wore a long time. On several occasions, when the corset itself wore out, the steels were removed and placed into a new corset. In 1866, an application for patent was filed. It was on those facts that the Court observed that: "If an inventor, having made his device, gives or sells it to another, to be used by the donee or vendee, without limitation or restriction, or injunction of secrecy, and it is so used, such use is public, even though the use and knowledge of the use may be confined to one person."

The district court distinguished *Egbert* because here Nichols had not given over the invention for free and unrestricted use by another person. Based on the personal relationships and surrounding circumstances, the court found that Nichols at all times retained control over the puzzle's use and the distribution of information concerning it. The court characterized Nichols' use as private and for his own enjoyment. We see neither legal error in the analysis nor clear error in the findings.

As for Obermayer's brief use of the puzzle, the court found that Nichols retained control even though he and Obermayer had not entered into any express confidentiality agreement. The court held, and we agree, that the presence or absence of such an agreement is not determinative of the public use issue. It is one factor to be considered in assessing all the evidence. There can be no question that the court looked at the totality of evidence, and evaluated that evidence in view of time, place, and circumstances.

With regard to the question of control, CBS complains that "[t]he record is devoid of any testimony from the friends, associates and fellow workers who saw Nichols' cube and to whom its operation was explained." The simple answer is that CBS had the burden at trial to prove public use with facts supported by clear and convincing evidence. We think the district court's characterization of the evidence of record is entirely apt and we see no ground for reversal. Moreover, we agree with the district court that its conclusion on public use is consistent with the policies underlying the bar.

CBS further argues in connection with public use that the district court erred when it found no evidence of commercially motivated activity by Nichols prior to the critical date.[3] Although CBS attempts to paint a picture of commercialization from the discussions between Obermayer and Nichols, we see only the brush strokes of speculation. The record lacks hard evidence. Discussion between employer and employee does not by itself convert an employee's private pursuit into commercial enterprise with the employer. CBS also makes much of a February 6, 1969 phone call by Obermayer to Parker Brothers to see if the latter was interested in receiving a submission of a puzzle idea from an outside inventor. Nothing concerning the nature or workings of Nichols' puzzle was disclosed. Obermayer simply inquired whether and how an outsider could submit a puzzle for Parker Brothers' consideration. We agree with the district court that those facts do not show commercialization. Thus this case differs from other cases where commercial activity was said to violate the policies of section 102(b).

(b) On Sale

CBS argues that the claimed invention was on sale within the meaning of 35 U.S.C. § 102(b) because Nichols orally agreed prior to the critical date (e.g., during a January 1969 conversation between Nichols and Obermayer) to assign "all his rights in the puzzle invention" to Moleculon. According to CBS, Nichols not only assigned the right to apply for a patent on the invention but also conveyed title in his single wooden model.

Although the formal written assignment occurred after the critical date, the district court held that even if there were an earlier oral agreement, an assignment or sale of the rights in the invention and potential patent rights is not a sale of "the invention" within the meaning of section 102(b). We agree. The few cases we have found on this issue have uniformly held that such a sale of patent rights does not come within the section 102(b) bar. Such a result comports with the policies underlying the on sale bar, and with the business realities ordinarily surrounding a corporation's prosecution of patent applications for inventors.

As for CBS' contention that Nichols sold or agreed to sell the wood model of the puzzle, we quote the district court's relevant findings:

> There is no indication in the subsequent written instrument that the parties contemplated the sale or transfer to Moleculon of the single physical embodiment of the puzzle then in existence. Nor is there any other evidence in the record to that effect.

CBS has shown nothing approaching clear error concerning those findings.

Accordingly, we sustain the district court's determination that the claims are not invalid under section 102(b).

* * *

---

3. In some instances, commercially motivated activities may implicate both the public use and the on sale bars.

PFAFF v. WELLS ELECTRONICS, INC.

United States Supreme Court, 1998.
525 U.S. 55, 119 S.Ct. 304, 142 L.Ed.2d 261.

JUSTICE STEVENS delivered the opinion of the [unanimous] Court.

Section 102(b) of the Patent Act of 1952 provides that no person is entitled to patent an "invention" that has been "on sale" more than one year before filing a patent application.[1] We granted certiorari to determine whether the commercial marketing of a newly invented product may mark the beginning of the 1–year period even though the invention has not yet been reduced to practice.[2]

I

On April 19, 1982, petitioner, Wayne Pfaff, filed an application for a patent on a computer chip socket. Therefore, April 19, 1981, constitutes the critical date for purposes of the on-sale bar of 35 U.S.C. § 102(b); if the 1–year period began to run before that date, Pfaff lost his right to patent his invention.

Pfaff commenced work on the socket in November 1980, when representatives of Texas Instruments asked him to develop a new device for mounting and removing semiconductor chip carriers. In response to this request, he prepared detailed engineering drawings that described the design, the dimensions, and the materials to be used in making the socket. Pfaff sent those drawings to a manufacturer in February or March 1981.

Prior to March 17, 1981, Pfaff showed a sketch of his concept to representatives of Texas Instruments. On April 8, 1981, they provided Pfaff with a written confirmation of a previously placed oral purchase order for 30,100 of his new sockets for a total price of $91,155. In accord with his normal practice, Pfaff did not make and test a prototype of the new device before offering to sell it in commercial quantities.

The manufacturer took several months to develop the customized tooling necessary to produce the device, and Pfaff did not fill the order until July 1981. The evidence therefore indicates that Pfaff first reduced his invention to practice in the summer of 1981. The socket achieved substantial commercial success before Patent No. 4,491,377 (the '377 patent) issued to Pfaff on January 1, 1985.

---

1. "A person shall be entitled to a patent unless—

. . . .

"(b) the invention was patented or described in a printed publication in this or a foreign country or in public use or on sale in this country, more than one year prior to the date of the application for patent in the United States, or . . . ."

35 U.S.C. § 102.

2. "A process is reduced to practice when it is successfully performed. A machine is reduced to practice when it is assembled adjusted and used. A manufacture is reduced to practice when it is completely manufactured. A composition of matter is reduced to practice when it is completely composed." *Corona Cord Tire Co. v. Dovan Chemical Corp.*, 276 U.S. 358, 383, 48 S.Ct. 380, 72 L.Ed. 610 (1928).

After the patent issued, petitioner brought an infringement action against respondent, Wells Electronics, Inc., the manufacturer of a competing socket. [The district court found some of the claims valid and infringed. It rejected Wells' § 102(b) defense, finding that the one-year statutory period did not begin to run until petitioner reduced his invention to practice.]

* * *

The Court of Appeals reversed, finding all six claims invalid. Four of the claims (1, 6, 7, and 10) described the socket that Pfaff had sold to Texas Instruments prior to April 8, 1981. Because that device had been offered for sale on a commercial basis more than one year before the patent application was filed on April 19, 1982, the court concluded that those claims were invalid under § 102(b). That conclusion rested on the court's view that as long as the invention was "substantially complete at the time of sale," the 1–year period began to run, even though the invention had not yet been reduced to practice. * * *

Because other courts have held or assumed that an invention cannot be "on sale" within the meaning of § 102(b) unless and until it has been reduced to practice, and because the text of § 102(b) makes no reference to "substantial completion" of an invention, we granted certiorari.

II

The primary meaning of the word "invention" in the Patent Act unquestionably refers to the inventor's conception rather than to a physical embodiment of that idea. The statute does not contain any express requirement that an invention must be reduced to practice before it can be patented. Neither the statutory definition of the term in § 100[8] nor the basic conditions for obtaining a patent set forth in § 101[9] make any mention of "reduction to practice." The statute's only specific reference to that term is found in § 102(g), which sets forth the standard for resolving priority contests between two competing claimants to a patent. That subsection provides:

> "In determining priority of invention there shall be considered not only the respective dates of conception and reduction to practice of the invention, but also the reasonable diligence of one who was first to conceive and last to reduce to practice, from a time prior to conception by the other."

Thus, assuming diligence on the part of the applicant, it is normally the first inventor to conceive, rather than the first to reduce to practice, who establishes the right to the patent.

---

8. Title 35 § 100, "Definitions," states,

"When used in this title unless the context otherwise indicates—

"(a) The term 'invention' means invention or discovery...."

9. Section 101, "Inventions patentable," provides,

"Whoever invents or discovers any new and useful process, machine, manufacture, or composition of matter, or any new and useful improvement thereof, may obtain a patent therefor, subject to the conditions and requirements of this title."

It is well settled that an invention may be patented before it is reduced to practice. In 1888, this Court upheld a patent issued to Alexander Graham Bell even though he had filed his application before constructing a working telephone. Chief Justice Waite's reasoning in that case merits quoting at length:

"It is quite true that when Bell applied for his patent he had never actually transmitted telegraphically spoken words so that they could be distinctly heard and understood at the receiving end of his line, but in his specification he did describe accurately and with admirable clearness his process, that is to say, the exact electrical condition that must be created to accomplish his purpose, and he also described, with sufficient precision to enable one of ordinary skill in such matters to make it, a form of apparatus which, if used in the way pointed out, would produce the required effect, receive the words, and carry them to and deliver them at the appointed place. The particular instrument which he had, and which he used in his experiments, did not, under the circumstances in which it was tried, reproduce the words spoken, so that they could be clearly understood, but the proof is abundant and of the most convincing character, that other instruments, carefully constructed and made exactly in accordance with the specification, without any additions whatever, have operated and will operate successfully. A good mechanic of proper skill in matters of the kind can take the patent and, by following the specification strictly, can, without more, construct an apparatus which, when used in the way pointed out, will do all that it is claimed the method or process will do. . . .

"The law does not require that a discoverer or inventor, in order to get a patent for a process, must have succeeded in bringing his art to the highest degree of perfection. It is enough if he describes his method with sufficient clearness and precision to enable those skilled in the matter to understand what the process is, and if he points out some practicable way of putting it into operation."

The Telephone Cases, 126 U.S. 1, 536, 8 S.Ct. 778, 31 L.Ed. 863 (1888).[10]

When we apply the reasoning of The Telephone Cases to the facts of the case before us today, it is evident that Pfaff could have obtained a patent on his novel socket when he accepted the purchase order from Texas Instruments for 30,100 units. At that time he provided the manufacturer with a description and drawings that had "sufficient clearness and precision to enable those skilled in the matter" to produce the device. The parties agree that the sockets manufactured to fill that order embody Pfaff's conception as set forth in claims 1, 6, 7, and 10 of the '377 patent. We can find no basis in the text of § 102(b) or in the facts of this case for

10. This Court has also held a patent invalid because the invention had previously been disclosed in a prior patent application, although that application did not claim the invention and the first invention apparently had not been reduced to practice. *Alexander Milburn Co. v. Davis–Bournonville Co.*, 270 U.S. 390, 401–402, 46 S.Ct. 324, 70 L.Ed. 651 (1926).

concluding that Pfaff's invention was not "on sale" within the meaning of the statute until after it had been reduced to practice.

III

Pfaff nevertheless argues that longstanding precedent, buttressed by the strong interest in providing inventors with a clear standard identifying the onset of the 1–year period, justifies a special interpretation of the word "invention" as used in § 102(b). We are persuaded that this nontextual argument should be rejected.

As we have often explained, most recently in *Bonito Boats, Inc. v. Thunder Craft Boats, Inc.*, 489 U.S. 141, 151, 109 S.Ct. 971, 103 L.Ed.2d 118 (1989), the patent system represents a carefully crafted bargain that encourages both the creation and the public disclosure of new and useful advances in technology, in return for an exclusive monopoly for a limited period of time. The balance between the interest in motivating innovation and enlightenment by rewarding invention with patent protection on the one hand, and the interest in avoiding monopolies that unnecessarily stifle competition on the other, has been a feature of the federal patent laws since their inception. As this Court explained in 1871:

> "Letters patent are not to be regarded as monopolies ... but as public franchises granted to the inventors of new and useful improvements for the purpose of securing to them, as such inventors, for the limited term therein mentioned, the exclusive right and liberty to make and use and vend to others to be used their own inventions, as tending to promote the progress of science and the useful arts, and as a matter of compensation to the inventors for their labor, toil, and expense in making the inventions, and reducing the same to practice for the public benefit, as contemplated by the Constitution and sanctioned by the laws of Congress."

Seymour v. Osborne, 11 Wall. 516, 533–534.

Consistent with these ends, § 102 of the Patent Act serves as a limiting provision, both excluding ideas that are in the public domain from patent protection and confining the duration of the monopoly to the statutory term.

We originally held that an inventor loses his right to a patent if he puts his invention into public use before filing a patent application. "His voluntary act or acquiescence in the public sale and use is an abandonment of his right" *Pennock v. Dialogue*, 2 Pet. 1, 24, 7 L.Ed. 327 (1829) (Story, J.). A similar reluctance to allow an inventor to remove existing knowledge from public use undergirds the on-sale bar.

Nevertheless, an inventor who seeks to perfect his discovery may conduct extensive testing without losing his right to obtain a patent for his invention—even if such testing occurs in the public eye. The law has long recognized the distinction between inventions put to experimental use and products sold commercially. In 1878, we explained why patentability may turn on an inventor's use of his product.

"It is sometimes said that an inventor acquires an undue advantage over the public by delaying to take out a patent, inasmuch as he thereby preserves the monopoly to himself for a longer period than is allowed by the policy of the law; but this cannot be said with justice when the delay is occasioned by a bona fide effort to bring his invention to perfection, or to ascertain whether it will answer the purpose intended. His monopoly only continues for the allotted period, in any event; and it is the interest of the public, as well as himself, that the invention should be perfect and properly tested, before a patent is granted for it. Any attempt to use it for a profit, and not by way of experiment, for a longer period than two years before the application, would deprive the inventor of his right to a patent."

Elizabeth v. American Nicholson Pavement Co., 97 U.S. 126, 137, 24 L.Ed. 1000 (1877).

The patent laws therefore seek both to protect the public's right to retain knowledge already in the public domain and the inventor's right to control whether and when he may patent his invention. The Patent Act of 1836, 5 Stat. 117, was the first statute that expressly included an on-sale bar to the issuance of a patent. Like the earlier holding in Pennock, that provision precluded patentability if the invention had been placed on sale at any time before the patent application was filed. In 1839, Congress ameliorated that requirement by enacting a 2–year grace period in which the inventor could file an application. 5 Stat. 353.

In *Andrews v. Hovey*, 123 U.S. 267, 274, 8 S.Ct. 101, 31 L.Ed. 160 (1887), we noted that the purpose of that amendment was "to fix a period of limitation which should be certain"; it required the inventor to make sure that a patent application was filed "within two years from the completion of his invention," *ibid*. In 1939, Congress reduced the grace period from two years to one year. 53 Stat. 1212.

Petitioner correctly argues that these provisions identify an interest in providing inventors with a definite standard for determining when a patent application must be filed. A rule that makes the timeliness of an application depend on the date when an invention is "substantially complete" seriously undermines the interest in certainty.[11] More-over, such a rule finds no support in the text of the statute. Thus, petitioner's argument calls into question the standard applied by the Court of Appeals, but it does not persuade us that it is necessary to engraft a reduction to practice element into the meaning of the term "invention" as used in § 102(b).

---

11. The Federal Circuit has developed a multifactor, "totality of the circumstances" test to determine the trigger for the on-sale bar. See, e.g., *Micro Chemical, Inc. v. Great Plains Chemical Co.*, 103 F.3d 1538, 1544 (C.A.Fed.1997) (stating that, in determining whether an invention is on sale for purposes of 102(b), " 'all of the circumstances surrounding the sale or offer to sell, including the stage of development of the invention and the nature of the invention, must be considered and weighed against the policies underlying section 102(b)' "); *see also UMC Electronics Co. v. United States,* 816 F.2d 647, 656 (1987) (stating the on-sale bar "does not lend itself to formulation into a set of precise requirements"). As the Federal Circuit itself has noted, this test "has been criticized as unnecessarily vague."

The word "invention" must refer to a concept that is complete, rather than merely one that is "substantially complete." It is true that reduction to practice ordinarily provides the best evidence that an invention is complete. But just because reduction to practice is sufficient evidence of completion, it does not follow that proof of reduction to practice is necessary in every case. Indeed, both the facts of the *Telephone Cases* and the facts of this case demonstrate that one can prove that an invention is complete and ready for patenting before it has actually been reduced to practice.

We conclude, therefore, that the on-sale bar applies when two conditions are satisfied before the critical date. First, the product must be the subject of a commercial offer for sale. An inventor can both understand and control the timing of the first commercial marketing of his invention. The experimental use doctrine, for example, has not generated concerns about indefiniteness, and we perceive no reason why unmanageable uncertainty should attend a rule that measures the application of the on-sale bar of § 102(b) against the date when an invention that is ready for patenting is first marketed commercially. In this case the acceptance of the purchase order prior to April 8, 1981, makes it clear that such an offer had been made, and there is no question that the sale was commercial rather than experimental in character.

Second, the invention must be ready for patenting. That condition may be satisfied in at least two ways: by proof of reduction to practice before the critical date; or by proof that prior to the critical date the inventor had prepared drawings or other descriptions of the invention that were sufficiently specific to enable a person skilled in the art to practice the invention. In this case the second condition of the on-sale bar is satisfied because the drawings Pfaff sent to the manufacturer before the critical date fully disclosed the invention.

The evidence in this case thus fulfills the two essential conditions of the on-sale bar. As succinctly stated by Learned Hand:

> "[I]t is a condition upon an inventor's right to a patent that he shall not exploit his discovery competitively after it is ready for patenting; he must content himself with either secrecy, or legal monopoly."

Metallizing Engineering Co. v. Kenyon Bearing & Auto Parts Co., 153 F.2d 516, 520 (C.A.2 1946).

The judgment of the Court of Appeals finds support not only in the text of the statute but also in the basic policies underlying the statutory scheme, including § 102(b). When Pfaff accepted the purchase order for his new sockets prior to April 8, 1981, his invention was ready for patenting. The fact that the manufacturer was able to produce the socket using his detailed drawings and specifications demonstrates this fact. Furthermore, those sockets contained all the elements of the invention claimed in the '377 patent. Therefore, Pfaff's '377 patent is invalid because the invention had been on sale for more than one year in this country before he filed his patent application. Accordingly, the judgment of the Court of Appeals is affirmed.

NOTES AND QUESTIONS

1. *"In public use or on sale."* Are you satisfied that the *Egbert* and the *Moleculon* situations can be distinguished?

Suppose that Nichols had hosted a party for 20–30 guests, during which he demonstrated the puzzle to some of the guests for the purpose of getting feedback about it. Some of the guests picked the puzzle up and inspected it, and Nichols never explicitly asked the guests to maintain the puzzle in secrecy. Same result? See Beachcombers International, Inc. v. WildeWood Creative Products, Inc., 31 F.3d 1154 (Fed.Cir.1994).

Suppose that the applicant/inventor of a new process for making widgets secretly used the process to produce widgets for commercial sale more than a year prior to applying for a patent. The widgets placed on the market did not reveal the process used to make them. Should that use be deemed a "public use" that triggered the § 102(b) one-year statutory bar against the applicant/inventor? The Federal Circuit has held that it should. Kinzenbaw v. Deere and Co., 741 F.2d 383, 390 (Fed.Cir.1984), *cert. denied*, 470 U.S. 1004, 105 S.Ct. 1357, 84 L.Ed.2d 379 (1985). On the other hand, the Federal Circuit has held that a similar secret use by a person unrelated to the applicant does not constitute a public use for purposes of § 102(b) against the applicant. See W.L. Gore & Associates, Inc. v. Garlock, Inc., 721 F.2d 1540, 1550 (Fed.Cir. 1983), *cert. denied*, 469 U.S. 851, 105 S.Ct. 172, 83 L.Ed.2d 107 (1984). Normally, either the applicant's or a third party's public use or sale will trigger the § 102(b) statute of limitations against the applicant. Why should a distinction be made in this case?

If an invention does not yet exist in physical form, how can it be deemed on sale? Why should it be? Is the *Pfaff* "ready to patent" standard likely to provide greater certainty than the Federal Circuit's "substantially complete" standard? How is the "ready to patent" standard likely to affect application filing practices–will inventors generally need to file earlier in the process than under the old "substantially complete" standard?

Under the *Pfaff* decision, what will constitute a "commercial offer for sale"? Must the formal rules of contract law governing "offers" be met, or will more general advertising or promotion suffice? Which approach would make more sense from a policy standpoint? The Federal Circuit has subsequently ruled that actions will only constitute a "commercial offer" for purposes of § 102(b) if they satisfy the formal standards of an offer under the Uniform Commercial Code, allowing another party to create a binding contract for sale with a simple acceptance and consideration. The court reasoned:

> Though the [*Pfaff*] Court did not elaborate on what was meant by "a *commercial* offer for sale"—the issue not being directly presented–the language used strongly suggests that the offer must meet the level of an offer for sale in the contract sense, one that would be understood as such in the commercial community. Such a reading leaves no room for "activi-

ty which does not rise to the level of a formal 'offer' under contract law principles."

Applying established concepts of contract law, rather than some more amorphous test, implements the broad goal of *Pfaff*, which, in replacing this court's "totality of the circumstances" test with more precise requirements, was to bring greater certainty to the analysis of the on-sale bar. Courts are quite accustomed to and comfortable with determining whether a particular communication or series of communications amounts to an offer in the contract sense, and that type of determination is well established in law.

Group One, Ltd. v. Hallmark Cards, Inc., 254 F.3d 1041, 1046–47 (Fed. Cir. 2001), *cert. denied*, 534 U.S. 1127, 122 S.Ct. 1063, 151 L.Ed.2d 967 (2002).

Aside from technical drawings like the ones at issue in *Pfaff*, what sorts of descriptions might establish that an invention is ready to patent? An inventor's private journal entries? Descriptions of inventive concepts in bids for contracts? An oral description of the invention to a third party? In Robotic Vision Systems, Inc. v. View Engineering, Inc., 249 F.3d 1307 (Fed. Cir.), *cert. denied*, 534 U.S. 1018, 122 S.Ct. 542, 151 L.Ed.2d 420 (2001), an inventor orally explained his inventive method to a colleague with sufficient specificity that the colleague understood the invention and was able to write the software needed to implement it. The court found that this was sufficient to satisfy the *Pfaff* decision's "ready for patenting" requirement. The Federal Circuit added that it was not necessary that the inventor have complete confidence that his invention would work for its intended purpose: "It will be a rare case indeed in which an inventor has no uncertainty concerning the workability of his invention before he has reduced it to practice. No such requirement will be applied here." *Id.* at 1312.

What would it take to demonstrate that a patented *process* was on sale, for purposes of § 102(b)? See *In re* Kollar, 286 F.3d 1326 (Fed. Cir. 2002)(noting that a process is not sold in the same sense as a tangible item, and thus that sale of know-how describing the process and how to carry it out would not itself trigger the § 102(b) statute of limitations. However, sale of a tangible product made by the patented process would constitute a § 102(b) sale.)

2. *Experimental use or sale.* An *experimental* use or sale will not trigger the § 102(b) statute of limitations, even though it may otherwise be "public" in nature. The Supreme Court made this distinction in City of Elizabeth v. American Nicholson Pavement Co., 97 U.S. (7 Otto) 126, 24 L.Ed. 1000 (1877). In that case, the inventor had tested a 75–foot stretch of his new pavement on a well-traveled toll road for six years before applying for a patent. He inspected the pavement regularly and questioned the toll-collector about the public's reaction to it. In upholding the patent, the Court noted:

> The use of an invention by the inventor himself, or by any other person under his direction, by way of experiment, and in order to bring the invention to perfection, has never been regarded as [a public] use. * * *

Now, the nature of a street pavement is such that it cannot be experimented upon satisfactorily except on a highway, which is always public.

[S]uch use is not a public use, within the meaning of the statute, so long as the inventor is engaged, in good faith, in testing its operation. He may see cause to alter it and improve it, or not. His experiments will reveal the fact whether any and what alterations may be necessary. If durability is one of the qualities to be attained, a long period, perhaps years, may be necessary to enable the inventor to discover whether his purpose is accomplished. * * * So long as he does not voluntarily allow others to make it and use it, and so long as it is not on sale for general use, he keeps the invention under his own control, and does not lose his title to a patent.

Id., 97 U.S. (7 Otto) at 134–35. The Court stressed that it made no difference whether, during the period of experimental use, the public incidentally derived a benefit. Nor did it matter that the experimental use revealed how the invention was constructed. The inventor was entitled to take the necessary measures to perfect his invention, and it was in the public's interest that his invention be properly tested before a patent was granted. Since the inventor was engaging in a *bona fide* effort to perfect his invention, and was not using it for profit, the delay in filing did not unfairly prolong his monopoly beyond the period intended by the law.

Following *Elizabeth*, the Court of Appeals for the Federal Circuit found that an orthodontist/inventor did not lose the right to patent his dental appliance by using it on three patients over a period of six years prior to applying for a patent. TP Laboratories, Inc. v. Professional Positioners, Inc., 724 F.2d 965 (Fed.Cir.), *cert. denied*, 469 U.S. 826, 105 S.Ct. 108, 83 L.Ed.2d 51 (1984). The court noted that disclosure of the appliance to the patients was unavoidable in order to test it, and that while the inventor had failed to obtain pledges of confidentiality from the patients, it was unlikely under the circumstances that the patients would show the appliance to others who would understand its function or want to duplicate it. "In any event, a pledge of confidentiality is indicative of the inventor's continued control which here is established inherently by the dentist-patient relationship of the parties." *Id.*, 724 F.2d at 972. The court concluded:

A factor in favor of the patentee is that during this critical time the inventor had readily available all of the facilities of TP to commercially exploit the device. Yet, [the devices were not offered for sale to] competing orthodontists despite the fact this was one facet of the inventor's total business activity. Further, the inventor made no extra charge for fitting the three patients with the improved positioners although that in itself is not critical. The facts here indicate the inventor was testing the device, not the market. No commercial exploitation having been made to even a small degree prior to filing the patent application, the underlying policy of prohibiting an extension of the term is clearly not offended in this respect.

Indeed, none of the policies which underlie the public use bar and which, in effect, define it have been shown to be violated.

Id., 724 F.2d at 972–73.

Contrast *In re* Smith, 714 F.2d 1127 (Fed.Cir.1983). In *Smith*, Airwick conducted a test of the invention (a powder carpet deodorizer) with 76 homemakers more than a year prior to its application for patent. In the first phase of the test, Airwick showed homemakers a video presentation of the product concept, and obtained their reaction to the new product. In the second stage of the test, 40 of the homemakers were given a granular version of the composition and 36 were given a powder version. The homemakers were allowed to use the products in their own homes for about two weeks and were instructed to return any unused portion. Airwick imposed no confidentiality or other restrictions upon them, and made no attempt to control or observe the homemakers' use of the samples. After two weeks, Airwick interviewed 68 of the homemakers, asking, among other things, how the product vacuumed up, whether it deodorized, whether the homemakers had experienced any mechanical problems with their vacuum cleaners, which version the homemakers would buy, and what they would be willing to pay. As Airwick had predicted, the homemakers seemed to favor the powder version over the granular version. There had been some problems with regard to the fragrance. After the test, Airwick continued to work on the product scent and experiment with different product formulations.

The Federal Circuit rejected arguments that Airwick's use was experimental, noting that the experimental use exception to § 102(b) "does not include market testing where the inventor is attempting to gauge consumer demand for his claimed invention. The purpose of such activities is commercial exploitation and not experimentation." *Id.*, 714 F.2d at 1135. The court observed that Airwick could have performed experiments to obtain scientific data on its invention's operation and usefulness in its own laboratories. Its use of "typical housewives" to test the product, without restriction or supervision, indicated that it was seeking information that would assist it to gear its product to maximize potential sales before placing it on the market. The use of two versions of the product was only meant to determine which version the typical consumer would prefer, not to determine which version was technically superior. The use of the homemaker/consumers to evaluate the fragrance of the product was irrelevant because fragrance strength was not a claimed element of the invention. "It is settled law that the experimental use exception is not applicable to experiments performed with respect to unclaimed features of an invention." *Id.*, 714 F.2d at 1136. As to the continued experimentation with product formulations, the court noted that Airwick already knew that the powdery product would have better antistatic and antisoil properties than the granular type. Since it already knew the technical efficacy of these properties, further tests were not necessary and must have been planned for marketing purposes.

3. *Section 102(c).* Although § 102(c) refers to abandonment of the invention, the case law makes it clear that the provision actually deals with abandonment of the right to a patent. Such abandonment occurs when the inventor expressly or implicitly manifests an intention to relinquish the right to a patent. Courts in early cases used a finding of abandonment to prevent inventors from waiting too long to apply for a patent. For example, in Macbeth–Evans Glass Co. v. General Electric Co., 246 F. 695 (6th Cir.1917),

cert. denied, 246 U.S. 659, 38 S.Ct. 316, 62 L.Ed. 926 (1918), the inventor of a process for making glass opted to use the process as a trade secret and did so for nearly ten years. At that point he applied for and got a patent. Upon suit to enforce the patent, the court held the patent invalid as abandoned, reasoning that the plaintiff's election of trade secrecy implied a decision to forego a patent, and thus an abandonment. In law, a finding of "abandonment" generally turns on an evaluation of the relevant party's intent. In the § 102(c) context, one must consider whether the evidence indicates that the applicant intended to relinquish a patent. In *Macbeth*, the court acknowledged that the plaintiff might *in fact* have intended to retain the option of a patent as a backup in the event that secrecy later was lost. However, such an intent contemplated "an indefinite delay in disclosure of the invention and a practical and substantial enlargement of any period of monopoly recognized by statute," contrary to a "declared and subsisting public policy." *Id.,* 246 F. at 700. That being the case, the court deemed it appropriate to hold that as a matter of law, the plaintiff was put to an election between a patent and trade secrecy, and that his choice to pursue trade secrecy would be treated as a decision to forego a patent.

Today, § 102(b) would provide a means of invalidating the patent in *Macbeth*, and in many other instances in which an abandonment might be found within the meaning of § 102(c). As a result, § 102(c) is rarely invoked. Can you think of an instance in which a § 102(c) abandonment might not fall under the § 102(b) statutory bar?

Note that the question of "abandonment" for purposes of § 102(g) differs from the question of "abandonment" for purposes of § 102(c). In the § 102(g) context, the issue is whether the earlier inventor abandoned *the invention*, as opposed to the right to a patent.

4. *Section 102(d).* Section 102(d) requires inventors who have filed for a patent or inventor's certificate abroad to apply promptly for a United States patent. Study the language of subsection (d) closely. When, exactly, does it apply? For an explanation of the scope of subsection (d), see *In re* Kathawala, 9 F.3d 942 (Fed.Cir.1993).

PROBLEM

1. In August, 1998, Jones invented a new and innovative can opener. The following October, he made ten prototypes of the can opener and distributed them to ten neighboring households in the suburban neighborhood in which he lived, along with a detailed questionnaire asking the recipients to use the can opener in their homes, then fill out the questionnaire and return it to Jones. Among other things, the questionnaire stated that users should retain the can opener in confidence.

The questionnaire asked users about the conditions under which they used the can opener, the types and sizes of cans opened, the frequency of use, whether they had experienced any difficulties in using the can opener and the specific circumstances in which this had occurred. It also asked them whether they found the size and shape of the opener convenient, and how the can opener compared with other can openers that the recipients had owned or used. Jones collected the questionnaires and, finding that the can opener had worked consistently well for the users under a variety of conditions, decided to market it. He decided to have the can opener manufactured by a Hong Kong manufacturer, import the finished can openers, and distribute them himself to United States purchasers. He began to make inquiries about a Hong Kong manufacturer in January, 1999.

Meanwhile, in February, 1999, Jones attended a two-day kitchen wares exposition in New York. He set up a booth with a videotape player and monitor, and repeatedly played a five-minute videotape in which he described his new can opener and explained how it worked and why it worked better than existing can openers. A number of other kitchen wares producers and retailers saw the videotape. However, while Jones showed a prototype of the can opener on the videotape, he did not bring any of the prototypes with him to the exposition, and did not request or take orders for sales of the can opener. He told retailers visiting his booth that his purpose was merely to notify them that the can opener would be available for sale in the near future, and to give them his business card and collect their business cards.

In January, 2000, Jones received his first shipment of can openers from his Hong Kong manufacturer, and began a sales campaign to kitchen wares retailers and wholesalers. In March, 2000, he filed an application for a U.S. patent. How should his application be treated under Patent Act § 102(b)?

4. Section 103: Non–Obviousness

GRAHAM v. JOHN DEERE CO.

United States Supreme Court, 1966.
383 U.S. 1, 86 S.Ct. 684, 15 L.Ed.2d 545.

MR. JUSTICE CLARK delivered the opinion of the Court.

After a lapse of 15 years, the Court again focuses its attention on the patentability of inventions under the standard of Art. I, § 8, cl. 8, of the Constitution and under the conditions prescribed by the laws of the United States. Since our last expression on patent validity, the Congress has for the first time expressly added a third statutory dimension to the two requirements of novelty and utility that had been the sole statutory test since the Patent Act of 1793. This is the test of obviousness * * *.

The questions, involved in each of the companion cases before us, are what effect the 1952 Act had upon traditional statutory and judicial tests of patentability and what definitive tests are now required. We have concluded that the 1952 Act was intended to codify judicial precedents embracing the principle long ago announced by this Court in *Hotchkiss v. Greenwood*, 11 How. 248, 13 L.Ed. 683 (1851), and that, while the clear language of § 103 places emphasis on an inquiry into obviousness, the general level of innovation necessary to sustain patentability remains the same.

* * *

III.

The difficulty of formulating conditions for patentability was heightened by the generality of the constitutional grant and the statutes implementing it, together with the underlying policy of the patent system that "the things which are worth to the public the embarrassment of an exclusive patent," as Jefferson put it, must outweigh the restrictive effect of the limited patent monopoly. The inherent problem was to develop some means of weeding out those inventions which would not be disclosed or devised but for the inducement of a patent.

This Court formulated a general condition of patentability in 1851 in *Hotchkiss v. Greenwood*, 11 How. 248, 13 L.Ed. 683. The patent involved a mere substitution of materials—porcelain or clay for wood or metal in doorknobs—and the Court condemned it, holding:

> "[U]nless more ingenuity and skill * * * were required * * * than were possessed by an ordinary mechanic acquainted with the business, there was an absence of that degree of skill and ingenuity which constitute essential elements of every invention. In other words, the improvement is the work of the skilful mechanic, not that of the inventor." At p. 267.

Hotchkiss, by positing the condition that a patentable invention evidence more ingenuity and skill than that possessed by an ordinary mechanic acquainted with the business, merely distinguished between new and useful innovations that were capable of sustaining a patent and those that were not. The *Hotchkiss* test laid the cornerstone of the judicial evolution suggested by Jefferson and left to the courts by Congress. The language in the case, and in those which followed, gave birth to "invention" as a word of legal art signifying patentable inventions. Yet, as this Court has observed, "[t]he truth is, the word ['invention'] cannot be defined in such manner as to afford any substantial aid in determining whether a particular device involves an exercise of the inventive faculty or not." Its use as a label brought about a large variety of opinions as to its meaning both in the Patent Office, in the courts, and at the bar. The *Hotchkiss* formulation, however, lies not in any label, but in its functional approach to questions of patentability. In practice, *Hotchkiss* has required a comparison between the subject matter of the patent, or patent application, and the background skill of the calling. It has been from this comparison that patentability was in each case determined.

IV.

The 1952 Patent Act.

The Act sets out the conditions of patentability in three sections. An analysis of the structure of these three sections indicates that patentability is dependent upon three explicit conditions: novelty and utility as articulated and defined in § 101 and § 102, and nonobviousness, the new statutory formulation, as set out in § 103. The first two sections, which trace closely the 1874 codification, express the "new and useful" tests which have always existed in the statutory scheme and, for our purposes here, need no clarification. The pivotal section around which the present controversy centers is § 103. It provides:

"A patent may not be obtained though the invention is not identically disclosed or described as set forth in section 102 of this title, if the differences between the subject matter sought to be patented and the prior art are such that the subject matter as a whole would have been obvious at the time the invention was made to a person having ordinary skill in the art to which said subject matter pertains. Patentability shall not be negatived by the manner in which the invention was made."

The section is cast in relatively unambiguous terms. Patentability is to depend, in addition to novelty and utility, upon the "non-obvious" nature of the "subject matter sought to be patented" to a person having ordinary skill in the pertinent art. The first sentence of this section is strongly reminiscent of the language in *Hotchkiss*. Both formulations place emphasis on the pertinent art existing at the time the invention was made and both are implicitly tied to advances in that art. The major distinction is that Congress has emphasized "nonobviousness" as the operative test of the section, rather than the less definite "invention" language of *Hotchkiss* that Congress thought had led to "a large variety" of expressions in decisions and writings. * * *

* * *

We believe that [the] legislative history, as well as other sources, shows that the revision was not intended by Congress to change the general level of patentable invention. We conclude that the section was intended merely as a codification of judicial precedents embracing the *Hotchkiss* condition, with congressional directions that inquiries into the obviousness of the subject matter sought to be patented are a prerequisite to patentability.

V.

Approached in this light, the § 103 additional condition, when followed realistically, will permit a more practical test of patentability. The emphasis on non-obviousness is one of inquiry, not quality, and, as such, comports with the constitutional strictures.

While the ultimate question of patent validity is one of law, the § 103 condition, which is but one of three conditions, each of which must be satisfied, lends itself to several basic factual inquiries. Under § 103, the scope and content of the prior art are to be determined; differences between the prior art and the claims at issue are to be ascertained; and the level of ordinary skill in the pertinent art resolved. Against this background, the obviousness or nonobviousness of the subject matter is determined. Such secondary considerations as commercial success, long felt but unsolved needs, failure of others, etc., might be utilized to give light to the circumstances surrounding the origin of the subject matter sought to be patented. As indicia of obviousness or nonobviousness, these inquiries may have relevancy.

This is not to say, however, that there will not be difficulties in applying the nonobviousness test. What is obvious is not a question upon which there is likely to be uniformity of thought in every given factual context. The difficulties, however, are comparable to those encountered daily by the courts in such frames of reference as negligence and scienter, and should be amenable to a case-by-case development. We believe that strict observance of the requirements laid down here will result in that uniformity and definiteness which Congress called for in the 1952 Act.

While we have focused attention on the appropriate standard to be applied by the courts, it must be remembered that the primary responsibility for sifting out unpatentable material lies in the Patent Office. To await litigation is—for all practical purposes—to debilitate the patent system. We have observed a notorious difference between the standards applied by the Patent Office and by the courts. While many reasons can be adduced to explain the discrepancy, one may well be the free rein often exercised by Examiners in their use of the concept of "invention." In this connection we note that the Patent Office is confronted with a most difficult task. Almost 100,000 applications for patents are filed each year. Of these, about 50,000 are granted and the backlog now runs well over 200,000. This is itself a compelling reason for the Commissioner to strictly adhere to the 1952 Act as interpreted here. This would, we believe, not only expedite disposition but bring about a closer concurrence between administrative and judicial precedent.

Although we conclude here that the inquiry which the Patent Office and the courts must make as to patentability must be beamed with greater intensity on the requirements of § 103, it bears repeating that we find no change in the general strictness with which the overall test is to be applied. We have been urged to find in § 103 a relaxed standard, supposedly a congressional reaction to the "increased standard" applied by this Court in its decisions over the last 20 or 30 years. The standard has remained invariable in this Court. Technology, however, has advanced—and with remarkable rapidity in the last 50 years. Moreover, the ambit of applicable art in given fields of science has widened by disciplines unheard of a half century ago. It is but an evenhanded application to require that those persons granted the benefit of a patent monopoly be charged with an awareness of these changed conditions. The same is true of the less technical, but still useful arts. He who seeks to build a better mousetrap today has a long path to tread before reaching the Patent Office.

* * *

KSR INTERNATIONAL CO. v. TELEFLEX, INC.

United States Supreme Court, 2007.
550 U.S. 398, 127 S.Ct. 1727, 167 L.Ed.2d 705.

KENNEDY, J., delivered the opinion for a unanimous Court.

Teleflex Incorporated and its subsidiary Technology Holding Company—both referred to here as Teleflex—sued KSR International Company for patent infringement. The patent at issue, United States Patent No. 6,237,565 B1, is entitled "Adjustable Pedal Assembly With Electronic Throttle Control." The patentee is Steven J. Engelgau, and the patent is referred to as "the Engelgau patent." Teleflex holds the exclusive license to the patent.

Claim 4 of the Engelgau patent describes a mechanism for combining an electronic sensor with an adjustable automobile pedal so the pedal's position can be transmitted to a computer that controls the throttle in the vehicle's engine. When Teleflex accused KSR of infringing the Engelgau patent by adding an electronic sensor to one of KSR's previously designed pedals, KSR countered that claim 4 was invalid under the Patent Act, 35 U.S.C. § 103, because its subject matter was obvious.

[The Court describes the statutory non-obviousness standard and the objective method of analysis that it prescribed in *Graham v. John Deere, supra.*]

Seeking to resolve the question of obviousness with more uniformity and consistency, the Court of Appeals for the Federal Circuit has employed an approach referred to by the parties as the "teaching, suggestion, or motivation" test (TSM test), under which a patent claim is only proved obvious if "some motivation or suggestion to combine the prior art teachings" can be found in the prior art, the nature of the problem, or the knowledge of a person having ordinary skill in the art. See, *e.g., Al–Site Corp. v. VSI Int'l, Inc.,* 174 F.3d 1308, 1323–1324 (C.A.Fed.1999). KSR challenges that test, or at least its application in this case. Because the Court of Appeals addressed the question of obviousness in a manner contrary to § 103 and our precedents, we granted certiorari. We now reverse.

I

A

In car engines without computer-controlled throttles, the accelerator pedal interacts with the throttle via cable or other mechanical link. The pedal arm acts as a lever rotating around a pivot point. In a cable-actuated throttle control the rotation caused by pushing down the pedal pulls a cable, which in turn pulls open valves in the carburetor or fuel injection unit. The wider the valves open, the more fuel and air are released, causing combustion to increase and the car to accelerate. When the driver takes his foot off the pedal, the opposite occurs as the cable is released and the valves slide closed.

In the 1990's it became more common to install computers in cars to control engine operation. Computer-controlled throttles open and close valves in response to electronic signals, not through force transferred from the pedal by a mechanical link. Constant, delicate adjustments of air and fuel mixture are possible. The computer's rapid processing of factors beyond the pedal's position improves fuel efficiency and engine performance.

For a computer-controlled throttle to respond to a driver's operation of the car, the computer must know what is happening with the pedal. A cable or mechanical link does not suffice for this purpose; at some point, an electronic sensor is necessary to translate the mechanical operation into digital data the computer can understand.

Before discussing sensors further we turn to the mechanical design of the pedal itself. In the traditional design a pedal can be pushed down or released but cannot have its position in the footwell adjusted by sliding the pedal forward or back. As a result, a driver who wishes to be closer or farther from the pedal must either reposition himself in the driver's seat or move the seat in some way. In cars with deep footwells these are imperfect solutions for drivers of smaller stature. To solve the problem, inventors, beginning in the 1970's, designed pedals that could be adjusted to change their location in the footwell. Important for this case are two adjustable pedals disclosed in U.S. Patent Nos. 5,010,782 (filed July 28, 1989) (Asano) and 5,460,061 (filed Sept. 17, 1993) (Redding). The Asano patent reveals a support structure that houses the pedal so that even when the pedal location is adjusted relative to the driver, one of the pedal's pivot points stays fixed. The pedal is also designed so that the force necessary to push the pedal down is the same regardless of adjustments to its location. The Redding patent reveals a different, sliding mechanism where both the pedal and the pivot point are adjusted.

We return to sensors. Well before Engelgau applied for his challenged patent, some inventors had obtained patents involving electronic pedal sensors for computer-controlled throttles. These inventions, such as the device disclosed in U.S. Patent No. 5,241,936 (filed Sept. 9, 1991) ('936), taught that it was preferable to detect the pedal's position in the pedal assembly, not in the engine. The '936 patent disclosed a pedal with an electronic sensor on a pivot point in the pedal assembly. U.S. Patent No. 5,063,811 (filed July 9, 1990) (Smith) taught that to prevent the wires connecting the sensor to the computer from chafing and wearing out, and to avoid grime and damage from the driver's foot, the sensor should be put on a fixed part of the pedal assembly rather than in or on the pedal's footpad.

In addition to patents for pedals with integrated sensors inventors obtained patents for self-contained modular sensors. A modular sensor is designed independently of a given pedal so that it can be taken off the shelf and attached to mechanical pedals of various sorts, enabling the pedals to be used in automobiles with computer-controlled throttles. One such sensor was disclosed in U.S. Patent No. 5,385,068 (filed Dec. 18, 1992) ('068). In 1994, Chevrolet manufactured a line of trucks using modular sensors "attached to the pedal support bracket, adjacent to the pedal and engaged with the pivot shaft about which the pedal rotates in operation."

The prior art contained patents involving the placement of sensors on adjustable pedals as well. For example, U.S. Patent No. 5,819,593 (filed Aug. 17, 1995) (Rixon) discloses an adjustable pedal assembly with an electronic sensor for detecting the pedal's position. In the Rixon pedal the sensor is located in the pedal footpad. The Rixon pedal was known to suffer from wire chafing when the pedal was depressed and released.

This short account of pedal and sensor technology leads to the instant case.

B

KSR, a Canadian company, manufactures and supplies auto parts, including pedal systems. Ford Motor Company hired KSR in 1998 to supply an adjustable pedal system for various lines of automobiles with cable-actuated throttle controls. KSR developed an adjustable mechanical pedal for Ford and obtained U.S. Patent No. 6,151,976 (filed July 16, 1999) ('976) for the design. In 2000, KSR was chosen by General Motors Corporation (GMC or GM) to supply adjustable pedal systems for Chevrolet and GMC light trucks that used engines with computer-controlled throttles. To make the '976 pedal compatible with the trucks, KSR merely took that design and added a modular sensor.

Teleflex is a rival to KSR in the design and manufacture of adjustable pedals. As noted, it is the exclusive licensee of the Engelgau patent. Engelgau * * * has sworn he invented the patent's subject matter on February 14, 1998. The Engelgau patent discloses an adjustable electronic pedal described in the specification as a "simplified vehicle control pedal assembly that is less expensive, and which uses fewer parts and is easier to package within the vehicle." Claim 4 of the patent, at issue here, describes:

> "A vehicle control pedal apparatus comprising:
>
> a support adapted to be mounted to a vehicle structure;
>
> an adjustable pedal assembly having a pedal arm moveable in for[e] and aft directions with respect to said support;
>
> a pivot for pivotally supporting said adjustable pedal assembly with respect to said support and defining a pivot axis; and
>
> an electronic control attached to said support for controlling a vehicle system;
>
> said apparatus characterized by said electronic control being responsive to said pivot for providing a signal that corresponds to pedal arm position as said pedal arm pivots about said pivot axis between rest and applied positions wherein the position of said pivot remains constant while said pedal arm moves in fore and aft directions with respect to said pivot."

We agree with the District Court that the claim discloses "a position-adjustable pedal assembly with an electronic pedal position sensor attached to the support member of the pedal assembly. Attaching the sensor to the support member allows the sensor to remain in a fixed position while the driver adjusts the pedal."

Before issuing the Engelgau patent the U.S. Patent and Trademark Office (PTO) rejected one of the patent claims that was similar to, but broader than, the present claim 4. The claim did not include the requirement that the sensor be placed on a fixed pivot point. The PTO concluded the claim was an obvious combination of the prior art disclosed in Redding and Smith, explaining:

> " 'Since the prior ar[t] references are from the field of endeavor, the purpose disclosed . . . would have been recognized in the pertinent art of Redding. Therefore it would have been obvious . . . to provide the device of Redding with the . . . means attached to a support member as taught by Smith.' "

In other words Redding provided an example of an adjustable pedal and Smith explained how to mount a sensor on a pedal's support structure, and the rejected patent claim merely put these two teachings together.

Although the broader claim was rejected, claim 4 was later allowed because it included the limitation of a fixed pivot point, which distinguished the design from Redding's. Engelgau had not included Asano among the prior art references, and Asano was not mentioned in the patent's prosecution. Thus, the PTO did not have before it an adjustable pedal with a fixed pivot point. The patent issued on May 29, 2001 and was assigned to Teleflex.

Upon learning of KSR's design for GM, Teleflex sent a warning letter informing KSR that its proposal would violate the Engelgau patent. " 'Teleflex believes that any supplier of a product that combines an adjustable pedal with an electronic throttle control necessarily employs technology covered by one or more' "of Teleflex's patents. KSR refused to enter a royalty arrangement with Teleflex; so Teleflex sued for infringement, asserting KSR's pedal infringed the Engelgau patent and two other patents. Teleflex later abandoned its claims regarding the other patents and dedicated the patents to the public. The remaining contention was that KSR's pedal system for GM infringed claim 4 of the Engelgau patent. Teleflex has not argued that the other three claims of the patent are infringed by KSR's pedal, nor has Teleflex argued that the mechanical adjustable pedal designed by KSR for Ford infringed any of its patents.

C

The District Court granted summary judgment in KSR's favor. After reviewing the pertinent history of pedal design, the scope of the Engelgau patent, and the relevant prior art, the court considered the validity of the contested claim. By direction of 35 U.S.C. § 282, an issued patent is presumed valid. The District Court applied *Graham's* framework to determine whether under summary-judgment standards KSR had overcome the presumption and demonstrated that claim 4 was obvious in light of the prior art in existence when the claimed subject matter was invented. See § 102(a).

The District Court determined, in light of the expert testimony and the parties' stipulations, that the level of ordinary skill in pedal design was " 'an undergraduate degree in mechanical engineering (or an equivalent amount of industry experience) [and] familiarity with pedal control systems for vehicles.' " The court then set forth the relevant prior art, including the patents and pedal designs described above.

Following *Graham's* direction, the court compared the teachings of the prior art to the claims of Engelgau. It found "little difference." Asano taught everything contained in claim 4 except the use of a sensor to detect the pedal's position and transmit it to the computer controlling the throttle. That additional aspect was revealed in sources such as the '068 patent and the sensors used by Chevrolet.

Under the controlling cases from the Court of Appeals for the Federal Circuit, however, the District Court was not permitted to stop there. The court was required also to apply the TSM test. The District Court held KSR had satisfied the test. It reasoned (1) the state of the industry would lead inevitably to combinations of electronic sensors and adjustable pedals, (2) Rixon provided the basis for these developments, and (3) Smith taught a solution to the wire chafing problems in Rixon, namely locating the sensor on the fixed structure of the pedal. This could lead to the combination of Asano, or a pedal like it, with a pedal position sensor.

The conclusion that the Engelgau design was obvious was supported, in the District Court's view, by the PTO's rejection of the broader version of claim 4. Had Engelgau included Asano in his patent application, it reasoned, the PTO would have found claim 4 to be an obvious combination of Asano and Smith, as it had found the broader version an obvious combination of Redding and Smith. As a final matter, the District Court held that the secondary factor of Teleflex's commercial success with pedals based on Engelgau's design did not alter its conclusion. The District Court granted summary judgment for KSR.

With principal reliance on the TSM test, the Court of Appeals reversed. It ruled the District Court had not been strict enough in applying the test, having failed to make " 'finding[s] as to the specific understanding or principle within the knowledge of a skilled artisan that would have motivated one with no knowledge of [the] invention' . . . to attach an electronic control to the support bracket of the Asano assembly." The Court of Appeals held that the District Court was incorrect that the nature of the problem to be solved satisfied this requirement because unless the "prior art references address[ed] the precise problem that the patentee was trying to solve," the problem would not motivate an inventor to look at those references.

Here, the Court of Appeals found, the Asano pedal was designed to solve the " 'constant ratio problem' "—that is, to ensure that the force required to depress the pedal is the same no matter how the pedal is adjusted—whereas Engelgau sought to provide a simpler, smaller, cheaper adjustable electronic pedal. As for Rixon, the court explained, that pedal suffered from the problem of wire chafing but was not designed to solve it. In the court's view Rixon did not teach anything helpful to Engelgau's purpose. Smith, in turn, did not relate to adjustable pedals and did not "necessarily go to the issue of motivation to attach the electronic control on the support bracket of the pedal assembly." When the patents were interpreted in this way, the Court of Appeals held, they would not have led a person of ordinary skill to put a sensor on the sort of pedal described in Asano.

That it might have been obvious to try the combination of Asano and a sensor was likewise irrelevant, in the court's view, because " '[o]bvious to try' has long been held not to constitute obviousness."

The Court of Appeals also faulted the District Court's consideration of the PTO's rejection of the broader version of claim 4. The District Court's role, the Court of Appeals explained, was not to speculate regarding what the PTO might have done had the Engelgau patent mentioned Asano. Rather, the court held, the District Court was obliged first to presume that the issued patent was valid and then to render its own independent judgment of obviousness based on a review of the prior art. The fact that the PTO had rejected the broader version of claim 4, the Court of Appeals said, had no place in that analysis.

The Court of Appeals further held that genuine issues of material fact precluded summary judgment. Teleflex had proffered statements from one expert that claim 4 " 'was a simple, elegant, and novel combination of features,' " compared to Rixon, and from another expert that claim 4 was nonobvious because, unlike in Rixon, the sensor was mounted on the support bracket rather than the pedal itself. This evidence, the court concluded, sufficed to require a trial.

II

A

We begin by rejecting the rigid approach of the Court of Appeals. Throughout this Court's engagement with the question of obviousness, our cases have set forth an expansive and flexible approach inconsistent with the way the Court of Appeals applied its TSM test here. * * *

Neither the enactment of § 103 nor the analysis in *Graham* disturbed this Court's earlier instructions concerning the need for caution in granting a patent based on the combination of elements found in the prior art. For over a half century, the Court has held that a "patent for a combination which only unites old elements with no change in their respective functions . . . obviously withdraws what is already known into the field of its monopoly and diminishes the resources available to skillful men." *Great Atlantic & Pacific Tea Co. v. Supermarket Equipment Corp.,* 340 U.S. 147 (1950). This is a principal reason for declining to allow patents for what is obvious. The combination of familiar elements according to known methods is likely to be obvious when it does no more than yield predictable results. Three cases decided after *Graham* illustrate the application of this doctrine.

In *United States v. Adams,* 383 U.S. 39 (1966), a companion case to *Graham,* the Court considered the obviousness of a "wet battery" that varied from prior designs in two ways: It contained water, rather than the acids conventionally employed in storage batteries; and its electrodes were magnesium and cuprous chloride, rather than zinc and silver chloride. The Court recognized that when a patent claims a structure already known in the prior art that is altered by the mere substitution of one element for another known in the field, the combination must do more than yield a predictable result. It nevertheless rejected the Government's claim that Adams's battery was obvious. The Court relied upon the corollary principle that when the prior art teaches away from combining certain known elements, discovery of a successful means of combining them is more likely to be nonobvious. When Adams designed his battery, the prior art warned that risks were involved in using the types of electrodes he employed. The fact that the elements worked together in an unexpected and fruitful manner supported the conclusion that Adams's design was not obvious to those skilled in the art.

In *Anderson's-Black Rock, Inc. v. Pavement Salvage Co.,* 396 U.S. 57 (1969), the Court elaborated on this approach. The subject matter of the patent before the Court was a device combining two pre-existing elements: a radiant-heat burner and a paving machine. The device, the Court concluded, did not create some new synergy: The radiant-heat burner functioned just as a burner was expected to function; and the paving machine did the same. The two in combination did no more than they would in separate, sequential operation. In those circumstances, "while the combination of old elements performed a useful function, it added nothing to the nature and quality of the radiant-heat burner already patented," and the patent failed under § 103.

Finally, in *Sakraida v. Ag Pro, Inc.,* 425 U.S. 273 (1976), the Court derived from the precedents the conclusion that when a patent "simply arranges old elements with each performing the same function it had been known to perform" and yields no more than one would expect from such an arrangement, the combination is obvious.

The principles underlying these cases are instructive when the question is whether a patent claiming the combination of elements of prior art is obvious. When a work is available in one field of endeavor, design incentives and other market forces can prompt variations of it, either in the same field or a different one. If a person of ordinary skill can implement a predictable variation, § 103 likely bars its patentability. For the same reason, if a technique has been used to improve one device, and a person of ordinary skill in the art would recognize that it would improve similar devices in the same way, using the technique is obvious unless its actual application is beyond his or her skill. *Sakraida* and *Anderson's-*

Black Rock are illustrative—a court must ask whether the improvement is more than the predictable use of prior art elements according to their established functions.

Following these principles may be more difficult in other cases than it is here because the claimed subject matter may involve more than the simple substitution of one known element for another or the mere application of a known technique to a piece of prior art ready for the improvement. Often, it will be necessary for a court to look to interrelated teachings of multiple patents; the effects of demands known to the design community or present in the marketplace; and the background knowledge possessed by a person having ordinary skill in the art, all in order to determine whether there was an apparent reason to combine the known elements in the fashion claimed by the patent at issue. To facilitate review, this analysis should be made explicit. See *In re Kahn,* 441 F.3d 977, 988 (C.A.Fed.2006) ("[R]ejections on obviousness grounds cannot be sustained by mere conclusory statements; instead, there must be some articulated reasoning with some rational underpinning to support the legal conclusion of obviousness"). As our precedents make clear, however, the analysis need not seek out precise teachings directed to the specific subject matter of the challenged claim, for a court can take account of the inferences and creative steps that a person of ordinary skill in the art would employ.

B

When it first established the requirement of demonstrating a teaching, suggestion, or motivation to combine known elements in order to show that the combination is obvious, the Court of Customs and Patent Appeals captured a helpful insight. As is clear from cases such as *Adams,* a patent composed of several elements is not proved obvious merely by demonstrating that each of its elements was, independently, known in the prior art. Although common sense directs one to look with care at a patent application that claims as innovation the combination of two known devices according to their established functions, it can be important to identify a reason that would have prompted a person of ordinary skill in the relevant field to combine the elements in the way the claimed new invention does. This is so because inventions in most, if not all, instances rely upon building blocks long since uncovered, and claimed discoveries almost of necessity will be combinations of what, in some sense, is already known.

Helpful insights, however, need not become rigid and mandatory formulas; and when it is so applied, the TSM test is incompatible with our precedents. The obviousness analysis cannot be confined by a formalistic conception of the words teaching, suggestion, and motivation, or by overemphasis on the importance of published articles and the explicit content of issued patents. The diversity of inventive pursuits and of modern technology counsels against limiting the analysis in this way. In many fields it may be that there is little discussion of obvious techniques or combinations, and it often may be the case that market demand, rather than scientific literature, will drive design trends. Granting patent protection to advances that would occur in the ordinary course without real innovation retards progress and may, in the case of patents combining previously known elements, deprive prior inventions of their value or utility.

In the years since the Court of Customs and Patent Appeals set forth the essence of the TSM test, the Court of Appeals no doubt has applied the test in accord with these principles in many cases. There is no necessary inconsistency between the idea underlying the TSM test and the *Graham* analysis. But when a court transforms the general principle into a rigid rule that limits the obviousness inquiry, as the Court of Appeals did here, it errs.

C

The flaws in the analysis of the Court of Appeals relate for the most part to the court's narrow conception of the obviousness inquiry reflected in its application of the TSM test. In determining whether the subject matter of a patent claim is obvious, neither the particular motivation nor the avowed purpose of the patentee controls. What matters is the objective reach of the claim. If the claim extends to what is obvious, it is invalid under § 103. One of the ways in which a patent's subject matter can be proved obvious is by noting that there existed at the time of invention a known problem for which there was an obvious solution encompassed by the patent's claims.

The first error of the Court of Appeals in this case was to foreclose this reasoning by holding that courts and patent examiners should look only to the problem the patentee was trying to solve. The Court of Appeals failed to recognize that the problem motivating the patentee may be only one of many addressed by the patent's subject matter. The question is not whether the combination was obvious to the patentee but whether the combination was obvious to a person with ordinary skill in the art. Under the correct analysis, any need or problem known in the field of endeavor at the time of invention and addressed by the patent can provide a reason for combining the elements in the manner claimed.

The second error of the Court of Appeals lay in its assumption that a person of ordinary skill attempting to solve a problem will be led only to those elements of prior art designed to solve the same problem. The primary purpose of Asano was solving the constant ratio problem; so, the court concluded, an inventor considering how to put a sensor on an adjustable pedal would have no reason to consider putting it on the Asano pedal. Common sense teaches, however, that familiar items may have obvious uses beyond their primary purposes, and in many cases a person of ordinary skill will be able to fit the teachings of multiple patents together like pieces of a puzzle. Regardless of Asano's primary purpose, the design provided an obvious example of an adjustable pedal with a fixed pivot point; and the prior art was replete with patents indicating that a fixed pivot point was an ideal mount for a sensor. The idea that a designer hoping to make an adjustable electronic pedal would ignore Asano because Asano was designed to solve the constant ratio problem makes little sense. A person of ordinary skill is also a person of ordinary creativity, not an automaton.

The same constricted analysis led the Court of Appeals to conclude, in error, that a patent claim cannot be proved obvious merely by showing that the combination of elements was "obvious to try." When there is a design need or market pressure to solve a problem and there are a finite number of identified, predictable solutions, a person of ordinary skill has good reason to pursue the known options within his or her technical grasp. If this leads to the anticipated success, it is likely the product not of innovation but of ordinary skill and common sense. In that instance the fact that a combination was obvious to try might show that it was obvious under § 103.

The Court of Appeals, finally, drew the wrong conclusion from the risk of courts and patent examiners falling prey to hindsight bias. A factfinder should be aware, of course, of the distortion caused by hindsight bias and must be cautious of arguments reliant upon *ex post* reasoning. * * * Rigid preventative rules that deny factfinders recourse to common sense, however, are neither necessary under our case law nor consistent with it.

* * *

III

When we apply the standards we have explained to the instant facts, claim 4 must be found obvious. We agree with and adopt the District Court's recitation of the relevant prior art and its determination of the level of ordinary skill in the field. As did the District Court, we see little difference between the teachings of Asano and Smith and the adjustable electronic pedal disclosed in claim 4 of the Engelgau patent. A person having ordinary skill in the art could have combined Asano with a pedal position sensor in a fashion encompassed by claim 4, and would have seen the benefits of doing so.

* * *

B

The District Court was correct to conclude that, as of the time Engelgau designed the subject matter in claim 4, it was obvious to a person of ordinary skill to combine Asano with a pivot-mounted pedal position sensor. There then existed a marketplace that created a strong incentive to convert mechanical pedals to electronic pedals, and the prior art taught a number of methods for achieving this advance. The Court of Appeals considered the issue too narrowly by, in effect, asking whether a pedal designer writing on a blank slate would have chosen both Asano and a modular sensor similar to the ones used in the Chevrolet truck line and disclosed in the '068 patent. The District Court employed this narrow inquiry as well, though it reached the correct result nevertheless. The proper question to have asked was whether a pedal designer of ordinary skill, facing the wide range of needs created by developments in the field of endeavor, would have seen a benefit to upgrading Asano with a sensor.

In automotive design, as in many other fields, the interaction of multiple components means that changing one component often requires the others to be modified as well. Technological developments made it clear that engines using computer-controlled throttles would become standard. As a result, designers might have decided to design new pedals from scratch; but they also would have had reason to make pre-existing pedals work with the new engines. Indeed, upgrading its own pre-existing model led KSR to design the pedal now accused of infringing the Engelgau patent.

For a designer starting with Asano, the question was where to attach the sensor. The consequent legal question, then, is whether a pedal designer of ordinary skill starting with Asano would have found it obvious to put the sensor on a fixed pivot point. The prior art discussed above leads us to the conclusion that attaching the sensor where both KSR and Engelgau put it would have been obvious to a person of ordinary skill.

The '936 patent taught the utility of putting the sensor on the pedal device, not in the engine. Smith, in turn, explained to put the sensor not on the pedal's footpad but instead on its support structure. And from the known wire-chafing problems of Rixon, and Smith's teaching that "the pedal assemblies must not precipitate any motion in the connecting wires," the designer would know to place the sensor on a nonmoving part of the pedal structure. The most obvious nonmoving point on the structure from which a sensor can easily detect the pedal's position is a pivot point. The designer, accordingly, would follow Smith in mounting the sensor on a pivot, thereby designing an adjustable electronic pedal covered by claim 4.

Just as it was possible to begin with the objective to upgrade Asano to work with a computer-controlled throttle, so too was it possible to take an adjustable electronic pedal like Rixon and seek an improvement that would avoid the wire-chafing problem. Following similar steps to those just explained, a designer would learn from Smith to avoid sensor movement and would come, thereby, to Asano because Asano disclosed an adjustable pedal with a fixed pivot.

* * *

Like the District Court, finally, we conclude Teleflex has shown no secondary factors to dislodge the determination that claim 4 is obvious. Proper application of *Graham* and our other precedents to these facts therefore leads to the conclusion that claim 4 encompassed obvious subject matter. As a result, the claim fails to meet the requirement of § 103.

We need not reach the question whether the failure to disclose Asano during the prosecution of Engelgau voids the presumption of validity given to issued patents, for claim 4 is obvious despite the presumption. We nevertheless think it appropriate to note that the rationale underlying the presumption—that the PTO, in its expertise, has approved the claim—seems much diminished here.

IV

A separate ground the Court of Appeals gave for reversing the order for summary judgment was the existence of a dispute over an issue of material fact. We disagree with the Court of Appeals on this point as well. To the extent the court understood the *Graham* approach to exclude the possibility of summary judgment when an expert provides a conclusory affidavit addressing the question of obviousness, it misunderstood the role expert testimony plays in the analysis. In considering summary judgment on that question the district court can and should take into account expert testimony, which may resolve or keep open certain questions of fact. That is not the end of the issue, however. The ultimate judgment of obviousness is a legal determination. Where, as here, the content of the prior art, the scope of the patent claim, and the level of ordinary skill in the art are not in material dispute, and the obviousness of the claim is apparent in light of these factors, summary judgment is appropriate. Nothing in the declarations proffered by Teleflex prevented the District Court from reaching the careful conclusions underlying its order for summary judgment in this case.

* * *

We build and create by bringing to the tangible and palpable reality around us new works based on instinct, simple logic, ordinary inferences, extraordinary ideas, and sometimes even genius. These advances, once part of our shared knowledge, define a new threshold from which innovation starts once more. And as progress beginning from higher levels of achievement is expected in the normal course, the results of ordinary innovation are not the subject of exclusive rights under the patent laws. Were it otherwise patents might stifle, rather than promote, the progress of useful arts. See U.S. Const., Art. I, § 8, cl. 8. These premises led to the bar on patents claiming obvious subject matter established in *Hotchkiss* and codified in § 103. Application of the bar must not be confined within a test or formulation too constrained to serve its purpose.

KSR provided convincing evidence that mounting a modular sensor on a fixed pivot point of the Asano pedal was a design step well within the grasp of a person of ordinary skill in the relevant art. Its arguments, and the record, demonstrate that claim 4 of the Engelgau patent is obvious. In rejecting the District Court's rulings, the Court of Appeals analyzed the issue in a narrow, rigid manner inconsistent with § 103 and our precedents. The judgment of the Court of Appeals is reversed, and the case remanded for further proceedings consistent with this opinion.

NOTES AND QUESTIONS

1. *The obviousness standard.* The obviousness determination distinguishes those inventions that merit the "public embarrassment" of a patent monopoly from those that do not. It is the most difficult standard to satisfy. The *John Deere* Court states that in order to assess the obviousness of an invention under § 103, three basic factual findings must be made: 1) the scope and content of the prior art; 2) the differences between the prior art and the claims at issue; and 3) the level of ordinary skill in the pertinent art. Once these facts are ascertained, then the question of law can be determined: Would the subject matter of the patent application have been obvious at the time the invention was made to a person having ordinary skill in the art and knowledge of the pertinent prior art?

    a. *The scope and content of the prior art.* Patent Act § 102 identifies prior art for purposes of the § 103 obviousness determination. Pursuant to § 102(a), the prior art includes printed publications and patents anywhere in the world, as well as earlier inventions known or used in the United States, before the applicant's invention. Pursuant to § 102(e), the prior art encompasses inventions revealed in a U.S. patent application that was pending at the time of the invention at issue and was later published or granted. In addition, pursuant to § 102(g), the prior art includes inventions made in the United States prior to the applicant's and not abandoned, suppressed or concealed, and inventions established in an interference to have been made abroad prior to the applicant's and not abandoned, suppressed or concealed. Finally, the Court of Appeals for the Federal Circuit has held that information the applicant derived from another under the terms of § 102(f) may constitute prior art for purposes of determining the obviousness of the applicant's invention. OddzOn Products, Inc. v. Just Toys, Inc., 122 F.3d 1396 (Fed.Cir. 1997). So, for example, if the inventor had information about a prior invention and was influenced by it in making his own invention, that information will be deemed prior art for purposes of evaluating the obviousness of his invention, even though it was not disclosed to the public and would not be prior art against an inventor who had not actually received it. Recall that two or more pieces of prior art, or "references," may be combined to demonstrate that an invention is obvious.

    Section 103(c) limits the use of "secret prior art" against inventors who are working in a collaborative situation. Subsection (c)(1) provides:

> Subject matter developed by another person, which qualifies as prior art only under one or more of subsections (e), (f), and (g) of section 102 of this title, shall not preclude patentability under this section where the subject matter and the claimed invention were, at the time the claimed invention was made, owned by the same person or subject to an obligation of assignment to the same person.

35 U.S.C. § 103(c)(1). This provision was deemed necessary in light of today's large corporate and university research operations, where a range of different researchers may be working on similar or related projects for the same business or academic entity. As long as the invention has not reached the

public (under § 102(a)), the work of one researcher within the organization will not be used as prior art to render the work of another obvious and unpatentable. In 2004, Congress expanded § 103(c) to include secret prior art generated pursuant to a written "joint research agreement," as long as the patent application discloses the names of the parties to the agreement. Thus, the secret prior art generated by researchers pursuant to a joint venture among two or more separate research entities will not constitute prior art for purposes of an obviousness determination, as long as the conditions set forth in § 103(2) and (3) are met. This facilitates useful research partnerships among industry, academia and government agencies by allowing participants to share confidential information about their work.

Of course, for purposes of the obviousness determination, only the "pertinent" or "analogous" prior art is considered. Prior art is considered analogous if it is "from the same field of endeavor, regardless of the problem addressed," or if not in the same field as the inventor's endeavor, if it "is reasonably pertinent to the particular problem with which the inventor is involved." *In re* Clay, 966 F.2d 656, 659 (Fed.Cir.1992). The *Clay* case is illustrative. The applicant's invention was a process for storing refined liquid hydrocarbon product in a storage tank having a dead volume between the tank bottom and its outlet port. The process involved preparing a gelatin solution which gelled after it was placed in the tank's dead volume. A prior patent (the Hetherington patent) disclosed an apparatus for displacing dead space liquid using impervious bladders, or large bags, formed with flexible membranes. A second prior patent (the Sydansk patent) disclosed a process for reducing the permeability of hydrocarbon-bearing formations and thus improving oil production, using a gel similar to that used by Clay. The PTO had rejected the Clay application on the finding that while neither prior patent alone rendered the Clay patent obvious, the two in combination did. On appeal, the applicant argued that the Sydansk patent should not have been considered, because it was not analogous.

The Federal Circuit reasoned that the Sydansk patent could not be considered to be within Clay's field of endeavor simply because both related to the petroleum industry: Sydansk taught "the use of a gel in unconfined and irregular volumes within generally underground natural oil-bearing formations to channel flow in a desired direction," while the Clay application taught "the introduction of gel to the confined dead volume of a man-made storage tank." Clay's field of endeavor was "the storage of refined liquid hydrocarbons." The field of endeavor for the Sydansk patent was "the extraction of crude petroleum." *Id.* Nor did the court find the Sydansk patent reasonably pertinent to the problem Clay was trying to solve, so that he might have been motivated to consider it in resolving his own problem:

> Sydansk's gel treatment of underground formations functions to fill anomalies so as to improve flow profiles and sweep efficiencies of injection and production fluids through a formation, while Clay's gel functions to displace liquid product from the dead volume of a storage tank. Sydansk is concerned with plugging formation anomalies so that fluid is subsequently diverted by the gel into the formation matrix, thereby forcing bypassed oil contained in the matrix toward a production well. Sydansk is faced with the problem of recovering oil from rock, *i.e.*, from a matrix

which is porous, permeable sedimentary rock of a subterranean formation where water has channeled through formation anomalies and bypassed oil present in the matrix. Such a problem is not reasonably pertinent to the particular problem with which Clay was involved—preventing loss of stored product to tank dead volume while preventing contamination of such product. Moreover, the subterranean formation of Sydansk is not structurally similar to, does not operate under the same temperature and pressure as, and does not function like Clay's storage tanks.

* * *

A person having ordinary skill in the art would not reasonably have expected to solve the problem of dead volume in tanks for storing refined petroleum by considering a reference dealing with plugging underground formation anomalies.

Id., 966 F.2d at 659–60. Compare *In re* Icon Health and Fitness, Inc., 496 F.3d 1374 (Fed. Cir. 2007). In *Icon* the patent claimed a treadmill with a folding base that allowed the base to swivel into an upright storage position. Among other things, the claim called for a gas spring "to assist in stably retaining" the tread base in the upright position. The issue was whether it was appropriate to consider the Teague patent, which disclosed use of a dual-action spring in a bed that folded up into a cabinet, in evaluating the obviousness of the treadmill. While the Federal Circuit acknowledged that the folding bed fell outside the "treadmill art," it held the Teague patent analogous because it was reasonably pertinent to the problem addressed by the treadmill inventor: the need to stably retain a folding mechanism. The court explained:

> "A reference is reasonably pertinent if, even though it may be in a different field from that of the inventor's endeavor, it is one which, because of the matter with which it deals, logically would have commended itself to an inventor's attention in considering his problem." *In re Clay,* 966 F.2d 656, 659 (Fed. Cir. 1992). * * * We therefore have concluded, for example, that an inventor considering a hinge and latch mechanism for portable computers would naturally look to references employing other "housings, hinges, latches, springs, etc.," which in that case came from areas such as "a desktop telephone directory, a piano lid, a kitchen cabinet, a washing machine cabinet, a wooden furniture cabinet, or a two-part housing for storing audio cassettes." *In re Paulsen,* 30 F.3d 1475, 1481–82 (Fed. Cir. 1994).

> Icon's invention provides a treadmill with a folding mechanism and a means for retaining that mechanism in the folded position. The application specifically discusses the gas spring as part of a "lift assistance assembly . . . to apply a force or torque urging the tread base" towards the closed position. Nothing about Icon's folding mechanism requires any particular focus on treadmills; it generally addresses problems of supporting the weight of such a mechanism and providing a stable resting position. Analogous art to Icon's application, when considering the folding mechanism and gas spring limitation, may come from any area describing hinges, springs, latches, counterweights, or other similar mechanisms— such as the folding bed in Teague.

Id., 496 F.3d at 1379–80.

   b.   The differences between the prior art and the claims at issue. To evaluate obviousness, the claimed invention must be evaluated as a whole, taking the total mix of elements into account.

   c.   The level of ordinary skill in the pertinent art. The obviousness determination is made from the perspective of the person having ordinary skill in the art (sometimes called the "PHOSITA"), a fictitious person who is somewhat reminiscent of the ubiquitous "reasonable person" of torts law. In order to make the obviousness evaluation from this person's perspective, one must first determine his or her level of sophistication, skill and knowledge. According to the Court of Appeals for the Federal Circuit:

> Factors that may be considered in determining level of ordinary skill in the art include: (1) the educational level of the inventor; (2) type of problems encountered in the art; (3) prior art solutions to those problems; (4) rapidity with which innovations are made; (5) sophistication of the technology; and (6) educational level of active workers in the field. Not all such factors may be present in every case, and one or more of these or other factors may predominate in a particular case. The important consideration lies in the need to adhere to the statute, i.e., to hold that an invention would or would not have been obvious, as a whole, when it was made, to a person of "ordinary skill in the art"—not to the judge, or to a layman, or to those skilled in remote arts, or to geniuses in the art at hand.

Environmental Designs, Ltd. v. Union Oil Co. of California, 713 F.2d 693, 696–97 (Fed.Cir.1983). While the person from whose perspective the obviousness determination is made has only ordinary skill, that person is deemed to have knowledge of *all* the pertinent prior art.

   A good illustration of the "level of ordinary skill in the art" determination can be found in Daiichi Sankyo Co., Ltd. v. Apotex, Inc., 501 F.3d 1254 (Fed. Cir. 2007), *cert. denied,* 552 U.S. 1185, 128 S.Ct. 1259, 170 L.Ed.2d 68 (2008). The invention at issue was a method for treating otopathy (ear infections) with a topical antibiotic without damaging the ear. In evaluating the obviousness of this invention, the district court had concluded that the ordinary person skilled in the art "would have a medical degree, experience treating patients with ear infections, and knowledge of the pharmacology and use of antibiotics. This person would be … a pediatrician or general practitioner—those doctors who are often the 'first line of defense' in treating ear infections and who, by virtue of their medical training, possess basic pharmacological knowledge." *Id.* at 1257. The district court went on to find that the claimed invention would not be obvious to such a person, in light of the prior art.

   The Court of Appeals for the Federal Circuit reversed, holding that the PHOSITA would have a higher level of skill:

> * * * The inventors of the '741 patent were specialists in drug and ear treatments—not general practitioners or pediatricians. At the time of the invention, Inventor Sato was a university professor specializing in otorhinolaryngology; Inventor Handa was a clinical development department

manager at Daiichi, where he was involved with new drug development and clinical trials; and Inventor Kitahara was a research scientist at Daiichi engaged in the research and development of antibiotics. Additionally, others working in the same field as the inventors of the '741 patent were of the same skill level. * * *.

Further, the problem the invention of the '741 patent was trying to solve was to create a topical antibiotic compound to treat ear infections (otopathy) that did not have damage to the ear as a side effect. Indeed, most of the written description details the inventors' testing ofloxacin on guinea pigs and their findings that ototoxicity did not result from the use of their compound. Such animal testing is traditionally outside the realm of a general practitioner or pediatrician. Finally, while a general practitioner or pediatrician could (and would) prescribe the invention of the '741 patent to treat ear infections, he would not have the training or knowledge to develop the claimed compound absent some specialty training such as that possessed by the '741 patent's inventors. Accordingly, the level of ordinary skill in the art of the '741 patent is that of a person engaged in developing pharmaceutical formulations and treatment methods for the ear or a specialist in ear treatments such as an otologist, otolaryngologist, or otorhinolaryngologist who also has training in pharmaceutical formulations. * * *

Id., at 1257.

d. The legal determination of obviousness based on the findings of fact. The obviousness determination must be made as of the time the invention was made, without the benefit of hindsight. As one practitioner/scholar has pointed out:

[O]ne must * * * be quite vigilant, lest one commit the insidious sin of "hindsight": one may not use the teachings of the present invention as a guide to interpretation of the prior art, and of what the prior art would suggest to the hypothetical person of ordinary skill in the art, who knows the prior art but not the present invention. * * * [O]f course, the determination of what the prior art would suggest to this hypothetical person is to be made by one who *does* know the present invention, but who is expected to, in a sense, put that knowledge momentarily aside while viewing the prior art through the eyes of the person of ordinary skill, while at the same time keeping that knowledge well in mind, since he must recall clearly just *what it is* that the prior art must suggest, in order to render the invention obvious.

Harris, *Prospects for Supreme Court Review of the Federal Circuit Standards for Obviousness of Inventions Combining Old Elements*, 68 J. Pat. & Trademark Off. Soc. 66, 75 (1986).[12]

Most inventions consist of combinations of known elements. Combining two or more prior art references may reveal most or all of the elements the patentee has claimed. Obviousness will turn on whether the PHOSITA would know to combine them in the manner that the patent applicant/holder did. As the Supreme Court explains in *KSR*, the Federal Circuit had gravitated to a

---

12. © Robert W. Harris, 1986. Reprinted by permission of the copyright owner.

standard requiring that the prior art "teach, motivate or suggest" that the combination be made. The Supreme Court finds this approach too narrow and rigid as applied by the Federal Circuit, preferring to ask whether there was an apparent reason for the applicant to combine the constituent elements in the claimed manner. Based on the Court's discussion in *KSR*, what factors should the PTO and courts apply to make this determination? What is the potential impact of the shift in focus? As a matter of public policy, does a "rigid" standard such as the "teach, motivate or suggest" test, or a "flexible" standard, as advocated in *KSR*, make more sense?

In response to the *KSR* opinion, the PTO updated its own examination guidelines. The new guidelines outline seven "Rationales" under which an examiner might reject an applicant's patent claims as obvious:

(A) Combining prior art elements according to known methods to yield predictable results;

(B) Simple substitution of one known element for another to obtain predictable results;

(C) Use of a known technique to improve similar devices (methods, or products) in the same way;

(D) Applying a known technique to a known device (method, or product) ready for improvement to yield predictable results;

(E) "Obvious to try"—choosing from a finite number of identified, predictable solutions, with a reasonable expectation of success;

(F) Known work in one field of endeavor may prompt variations of it for use in either the same field or a different one based on design incentives or other market forces, if the variations would have been predictable to one of ordinary skill in the art;

(G) Some teaching, suggestion, or motivation in the prior art that would have led one of ordinary skill to modify the prior art reference or to combine prior art reference teachings to arrive at the claimed invention.

U.S.P.T.O., Examination Guidelines for Determining Obviousness Under 35 U.S.C. 103 in View of the Supreme Court Decision in KSR International Co. v. Teleflex Inc., 72 F.R. 57526 (Oct. 10, 2007).

2. *The secondary considerations.* In *John Deere*, the Supreme Court provided for "secondary considerations" in the obviousness determination:

Such secondary considerations as commercial success, long felt but unsolved needs, failure of others, etc., might be utilized to give light to the circumstances surrounding the origin of the subject matter sought to be patented. As indicia of obviousness or nonobviousness, these inquiries may have relevancy.

383 U.S. at 17–18. Why should evidence of commercial success, long felt but unsolved needs, or the failure of others be relevant to the determination of obviousness?

While the Court's reference to these considerations as "secondary" suggests that they may not be essential, the Court of Appeals for the Federal Circuit has emphasized their importance. The Federal Circuit has held that evidence relating to the "secondary considerations" (or "objective factors," as the Federal Circuit prefers to call them) must *always* be considered when present, regardless of whether the case is otherwise a close one or not. According to the Federal Circuit, this evidence "may often be the most probative and cogent evidence in the record. It may often establish that an invention appearing to have been obvious in light of the prior art was not." Stratoflex, Inc. v. Aeroquip Corp., 713 F.2d 1530, 1538–39 (Fed.Cir.1983). Moreover, the objective factors may serve "as insurance against the insidious attraction of the siren hindsight when confronted with a difficult task of evaluating the prior art" and may "reassure the decision maker." W.L. Gore & Assoc. v. Garlock, Inc., 721 F.2d 1540, 1553 (Fed.Cir.1983).

Under the Federal Circuit's guidance, the Supreme Court's short list of "secondary considerations" has grown considerably to include such factors as:

(1) movement of the persons skilled in the art in a different direction from that taken by the inventor;

(2) skepticism on the part of experts regarding the approach taken by the inventor;

(3) recognition and acceptance of the patent by competitors who take licenses under it to avail themselves of the merits of the invention; and

(4) the fact that the defendant copied the invention at issue, rather than alternatives in the public domain.

At the same time, the court has stressed that absence of such factors must not be taken as an indication that the invention is obvious. The Federal Circuit has ruled that such absence is a neutral factor.

Of course, a nexus must be demonstrated between objective factor evidence and the issue of obviousness before the evidence can carry any weight. For example, evidence of commercial success may be relevant to prove nonobviousness because marketplace competitors can be expected to take advantage of obvious opportunities for profit. If the commercially successful invention were obvious, persons seeking profit would have made the invention earlier. Before evidence of commercial success can be deemed reliable, however, it must appear that the commercial success was due to the alleged innovative aspects of the invention, and not to such factors as heavy advertisement and sales promotions or to features of the finished product that are not a part of the patented invention.

3. *The mental state of the inventor.* Suppose that an applicant made an invention by mistake (for example, she mistakenly added the wrong ingredient to a composition), or out of ignorance (she expected one result and got a different but useful one). Should the mental state of the inventor make a difference for purposes of determining whether to grant a patent? Should it matter whether the applicant made the invention in a "flash of creative genius" or through long years of methodical trial and error? When it enacted § 103, Congress made it clear that the inventor's mental state is not relevant: "Patentability shall not be negatived by the manner in which the invention was made." 35 U.S.C. § 103(a).

4. *Statutory Invention Registrations.* Patent Act § 157 authorizes the PTO to publish, without examination, a "statutory invention registration" if,

among other things, the registration application satisfies the invention disclosure requirements of § 112 and waives the right to receive a patent on the invention. Statutory invention registrations are defensive in nature. They provide a means for inventors who do not seek a patent on their inventions to ensure that others cannot later patent the same invention. Though the statutory invention registration gives no exclusive rights in the disclosed invention, it has the defensive attributes of a patent: the registration is effective as prior art for purposes of §§ 102 and 103.

A question has arisen about whether the registration will be treated as a patent pursuant to § 102(e), so that the registration will relate back to its filing date and serve as prior art from that time forward. The legislative history of the provision suggests that it will. See 130 Cong. Rec. H10,525 (Oct. 1, 1984).

PROBLEMS

1.   In 2008, Mary conceived and reduced to practice a novel, non-obvious machine for weaving fine fabric. She then began to work on developing a loom and a mechanical arm device, which would be used in connection with the machine, and sold with the machine as a package. It took Mary two years to perfect the loom and mechanical arm, and another six months to make the necessary preparations to begin mass producing the three components and put them on the market. Mary introduced the machine, loom and mechanical arm device, as a package, to the market in October, 2011. The loom and mechanical arm device are not patentable, but the machine is not usable without them. Mary has not sought to patent the machine.

In 2010, Jane invented a weaving machine which, while not exactly the same as Mary's, was obvious in light of Mary's machine. Will Jane be able to obtain a patent under Patent Act § 103?

2.   Jim invented a new type of widget in Australia in 2008, but did not take any steps to market or patent it, or publish any description of it. A year later, Jim demonstrated the new widget to Mark, a U.S. widget producer, who was visiting Jim's Australian laboratory. Mark later returned to the U.S. and commenced work on a new type of widget. In making his invention, Mark was influenced by Jim's widget. Mark later applied for a patent for the new widget he developed. Should Jim's earlier Australian widget be considered as prior art in evaluating the obviousness of Mark's widget?

3.   In the year 2005, in Paris, Pierre invented a new composition of matter that was especially effective in removing grease stains. He applied for a French patent in May, 2006, and a U.S. patent in August, 2006. The U.S. PTO published Pierre's application in November, 2007, but Pierre subsequently abandoned his application, so that a U.S. patent was never granted. Pierre was granted a French Patent in June, 2008. Jennifer invented a composition of matter that was obvious in light of Pierre's in the U.S. in September, 2006. Can Pierre's invention be considered as prior art in evaluating the patentability of Jennifer's?

4.   X and Y are both employees of ABC Corporation and both have a legal obligation to assign inventions they make while on the job to ABC Corp.

In 2008, X makes an invention, in which Y is not involved. In 2009, Y makes his own invention which is obvious in light of X's earlier work. Assuming that X's invention has not been abandoned, suppressed or concealed, should it be considered part of the prior art for purposes of evaluating the obviousness of Y's invention?

5.   Sections 102(b) and 103: The Interface

APPLICATION OF FOSTER

United States Court of Customs and Patent Appeals, 1965.
343 F.2d 980, *cert. denied*, 383 U.S. 966, 86 S.Ct. 1270, 16 L.Ed.2d 307 (1966).

ALMOND, JUDGE.

[The patent applicant appealed from a decision of the PTO Board of Appeals affirming the rejection of his application. At issue was the impact of an article, written by Binder and published in the magazine "Industrial and Engineering Chemistry," on the patentability of the applicant's invention. The article had appeared more than a year before the applicant had filed his application for patent. However, the applicant had introduced an affidavit demonstrating that he had made his invention before the article was published. (This is known as "swearing back"—making a sworn statement that the applicant completed the invention before the date of the prior art reference that the PTO examiner considers relevant in determining the patentability of the applicant's invention.) The court found that the Binder "reference" did not anticipate the applicant's claims—that is, the article did not fully disclose the applicant's invention. The court then turned to the remaining arguments.]

* * * Appellant argues that the affidavit establishes a date of invention prior to the publication date of the Binder reference, and that this * * * compels a finding that Binder cannot be considered in establishing obviousness of the claimed invention under 35 U.S.C. 103.

* * *

It is assumed by both parties—and it is unquestionably true—that when a reference fully discloses in every detail the subject matter of a claim, the statutory basis of a rejection on that reference is 35 U.S.C. 102(a) if the reference date is before the applicant's *date of invention*, thereby establishing want of novelty, and section 102(b) if the reference date is more than one year prior to the actual United States *filing date*, thereby establishing a so-called "statutory bar," more accurately, a one-year time-bar which results in loss of right to a patent, regardless of when the invention was made. In either of these situations, it is often said that the invention is "anticipated" by the reference and the reference is termed an "anticipation."

Proofs submitted in this case under Patent Office Rule 131 with respect to a reference not before us (because it was overcome thereby) have established that the applicant's invention date was prior to December 26, 1952. The Binder reference is the August 1954 issue of a periodical. It is seen, therefore, that it is subsequent to the date of invention but more than one year prior to the filing date, which was August 21, 1956. * * * Since the date of invention is earlier than the reference date, section 102(a) is necessarily inapplicable because the printed publication was not "before the invention thereof by the applicant" and there is statutory novelty. This leaves paragraph (b) of section 102 as the only paragraph of that section having possible relevancy.

It is appellant's position, as stated in his Reply Brief, that

"The *only* issue on this appeal is whether the claims define subject matter which is obvious in view of the reference and hence unpatentable under 35 U.S.C. 103. * * * "

Deeming that to be the sole issue, appellant further contends that the assumed rejection under section 103 is not before the court because * * * the Binder reference has been disposed of by the proof of an invention date prior to the date of Binder * * *.

* * *

Because of the importance of the question to the law of patents, we have deemed it desirable to reconsider * * * the result again urged on us here, as allegedly authorized by section 103, that a reference having a date more than a year prior to the filing date may be disposed of by showing an invention date prior to the reference date, contrary to the express provision in Patent Office Rule 131.[8]

Sections 101, 102 and 103, generally speaking, deal with two different matters: (1) the factors to be considered in determining whether a patentable invention has been *made*, i.e., novelty, utility, unobviousness, and the categories of patentable subject matter; and (2) "loss of right to patent" as stated in the heading of section 102, even though an otherwise patentable invention has been made. On the subject of loss of right, appellant's brief contains a helpful review of the development of the statutory law since 1793. It says:

* * *

"Manifestly, Section 102(b) from its earliest beginnings has been and was intended to be directed toward the encouragement of *diligence* in the filing of patent applications and the protection of the public from monopolies on subject matter which had already been fully disclosed to it."

8. "131. *Affidavit of prior invention to overcome cited patent or publication.*

(a) When any claim of an application is rejected on reference to a domestic patent which substantially shows or describes but does not claim the rejected invention, or on reference to a foreign patent or to a printed publication, and the applicant shall make oath to facts showing a completion of the invention in this country before the filing date of the application on which the domestic patent issued, or before the date of the foreign patent, or before the date of the printed publication, then the patent or publication cited shall not bar the grant of a patent to the applicant, *unless the date of such patent or printed publication be more than one year prior to the date on which the application was filed in this country.*" [Emphasis ours.] * * *

These statements are in accord with our understanding of the history and purposes of section 102(b). It presents a sort of statute of limitations, formerly two years, now one year, within which an inventor, even though he has made a patentable invention, must act on penalty of loss of his right to patent. What starts the period running is clearly the availability of the invention *to the public* through the categories of disclosure enumerated in 102(b), which include "a printed publication" anywhere describing the invention. There appears to be no dispute about the operation of this statute in "complete anticipation" situations but *the contention seems to be that 102(b) has no applicability where the invention is not completely disclosed in a single patent or publication*, that is to say where the rejection involves the addition to the disclosure of the reference of the ordinary skill of the art or the disclosure of another reference which indicates what those of ordinary skill in the art are presumed to know, *and to have known for more than a year before the application was filed*. Upon a complete reexamination of this matter, we are convinced that the contention is contrary to the policy consideration which motivated the enactment by Congress of a statutory bar. On logic and principle we think this contention is unsound, and we also believe it is contrary to the patent law as it has actually existed since at least 1898.

First, as to principle, since the purpose of the statute has always been to require filing of the application within the prescribed period after the time the public came into possession of the invention, we cannot see that it makes any difference *how* it came into such possession, whether by a public use, a sale, a single patent or publication, or by combinations of one or more of the foregoing. In considering this principle *we assume*, of course, that by these means *the invention has become obvious* to that segment of the "public" having ordinary skill in the art. Once this has happened, the purpose of the law is to give the inventor only a year within which to file and this would seem to be liberal treatment. Whenever an applicant undertakes, under Rule 131, to swear back of a reference having an effective date more than a year before his filing date, he is automatically conceding that he made his invention more than a year before he filed. If the reference contains enough disclosure to make his invention obvious, the principle of the statute would seem to require denial of a patent to him. The same is true where a combination of two publications or patents makes the invention obvious and they both have dates more than a year before the filing date.

As to dealing with the express language of 102(b), for example, "described in a printed publication," technically, we see no reason to so read the words of the statute as to preclude the use of more than one reference; nor do we find in the context anything to show that "a printed publication" cannot include two or more printed publications. * * *

  * * *

  * * * It follows that where the time-bar is involved, *the actual date of invention becomes irrelevant* and that it is not in accordance with either

the letter or the principle of the law, or its past interpretation over a very long period, to permit an applicant to dispose of a reference having a date more than one year prior to his filing date by proving his actual date of invention.

* * *

We wish to make it clear that this ruling is predicated on our construction of section 102(b) and has no effect on the * * * determination of obviousness under section 103 when a statutory time-bar is not involved. The existence of unobviousness under that section, as a necessary prerequisite to patentability, we reiterate, must be determined as of "the time the invention was made" without utilizing after-acquired knowledge.

The determination of unobviousness, however, relates to the determination of whether a patentable invention has been *made*. Whether there has been a *loss of right to a patent* on such invention is a distinct and separate issue, with which section 103 per se has nothing whatever to do. Its legislative history, which is well known and uncomplicated, shows that section 103 had but a single purpose which was to add to the statute a provision to take the place of the judge-made "requirement for invention." In doing that, the history also shows, the words "at the time the invention was made" were included for the sole purpose of precluding the use of hindsight in deciding whether an invention is obvious. We are sure Congress had no intent thereby to modify the law respecting *loss of right* based on the existence of a time-bar. * * *

Since we must reject Foster's contention that he can dispose entirely of Binder by showing an earlier invention date, it becomes necessary for us to consider whether there was a loss of right to a patent, i.e., whether the invention became obvious to the public at the time of the Binder publication.

* * *

NOTES AND QUESTIONS

1. *Section 102(b) vs. § 103.* In his dissent to the *Foster* opinion, Judge Smith wrote:

[T]he majority decision amounts to an interpretation of section 102(b) as though it contained the following italicized words:

"A person shall be entitled to a patent unless—* * * (b) the invention was patented or described in a printed publication in this or a foreign country or in public use or on sale in this country *or unless the invention became obvious* more than one year prior to the date of the application for patent in the United States * * *."

Thus, within the rationale of the majority opinion and its construction of section 102, it is no longer necessary for a patent or a publication to "describe" the invention to lay the basis for the loss of right to a patent under section 102(b). It is sufficient that a patent or a publication be found, or that some combination of the same can be put together after the applicant's date of invention and with the accuracy characteristic of perfect hindsight which make the invention "obvious" more than one year prior to the date of filing the patent application. Thus, in addition to changing the wording of section 102(b) as above suggested, the majority must also intend to rewrite section 103 so that the phrase "at the time the invention was made" now is to be limited by a proviso which reduces this time to a period of one year prior to the filing of the application.

343 F.2d at 996–97. Do you agree with Judge Smith's characterization of the majority's result? Does the *Foster* opinion change the meaning of § 103 so that obviousness is tested as of one year prior to the filing date of the application, rather than as of the date the invention was made?

PROBLEM

1. In September, 2009, Professor Smart conceived and reduced to practice a novel, non-obvious method of purifying a human enzyme for use in medical treatment. He did not immediately file a patent application, but continued work on related projects in his laboratory. In October, 2009, Professor Gupta published a paper regarding the purification of human enzymes in an Indian scientific journal which, while not describing Professor Smart's method, nonetheless rendered it obvious when considered in combination with an earlier method of purifying enzymes that was widely practiced in the United States. Professor Smart filed an application for U.S. patent in November, 2010. Should the application be granted? What if Professor Gupta had published his paper in February, 2010? In February, 2009?

6. Section 112: Disclosure

SPECTRA-PHYSICS, INC. v. COHERENT, INC.

United States Court of Appeals for the Federal Circuit, 1987.
827 F.2d 1524, *cert. denied,* 484 U.S. 954, 108 S.Ct. 346, 98 L.Ed.2d 372 (1987).

RICH, CIRCUIT JUDGE.

[Coherent owns both the Hobart and the Mefferd patents. The Hobart patent is directed to an ion laser structure and the Mefferd patent is directed to a method of fabricating the Hobart ion laser structure. The Hobart laser includes a series of copper cups attached to the inside of a ceramic tube.]

[Both the Hobart and Mefferd patents stress the importance of the bond between the copper cups and the tube. Dr. Hobart initially approached the problem of how to make the critical copper to ceramic bond by experimenting with soldering. These attempts were unsuccessful. Mefferd was then brought in to solve the attachment problem. His solution was brazing. While the patent specifications disclose pulse soldering as one method of bonding, brazing is clearly the preferred method of bonding. The patents disclose "TiCuSil" as the preferred brazing material. The titanium in this compound invades and wets the ceramic so that the copper-silver braze material can hold the copper to the ceramic. In the absence of an active metal alloy component such as titanium, the ceramic must be premetalized with, for example, moly-manganese, to provide a metallic surface to which the copper-silver braze material will adhere. The TiCuSil active metal process is preferred because it requires only one step and avoids the need for premetalization.]

[Through experimentation, Mefferd developed a six-stage braze cycle for using TiCuSil to attach the copper cups to the ceramic tube. "Braze cycle" is a term of art which refers to a process defined by specific parameters of temperature, length of times at given temperatures, atmosphere, and pressure. Mefferd's six-stage cycle produced a reliable braze joint between the copper cups and the ceramic tube. Because this approach worked, Coherent continued to use TiCuSil and never investigated the moly-manganese process or further experimented with soldering. Neither the Hobart nor the Mefferd patent, however, discloses the braze cycle or any additional information on brazing copper to ceramic using TiCuSil.]

[Spectra–Physics brought a declaratory judgment action against Coherent seeking a declaration that both the Hobart and the Mefferd patents were invalid. The lower court held both patents invalid for failure to disclose the six-stage braze cycle used by Coherent to manufacture the laser, which the court deemed a lack of enabling disclosure under the first paragraph of Patent Act section 112. The court found that section 112's best mode requirement was satisfied, however, because neither Hobart nor Mefferd deliberately or accidentally concealed brazing as the best mode of attaching the copper cups to the ceramic tube.]

To constitute adequate disclosure under the first paragraph of 35 U.S.C. § 112, a patent specification must set forth both the manner and process of making and using the invention (the enablement requirement) and the best mode contemplated by the inventor of carrying out the invention (the best mode requirement). The difference between these two is explained in *In re Gay*, 309 F.2d 769, 135 USPQ 311 (CCPA 1962):

> The essence of [the enablement requirement] is that a specification shall disclose an invention in such a manner as will enable one skilled in the art to make and utilize it. *Separate and distinct* from [enablement] is [the best mode requirement], the essence of which requires the inventor to disclose the best mode *contemplated by him*, as of the time he executes the application, of carrying out his invention. Manifestly, the sole purpose of this latter requirement is to restrain inventors from applying for patents while at the same time concealing from the public preferred embodiments of their inventions which they have in fact conceived.
>
> ... The question of whether an inventor has or has not disclosed what he feels is his best mode is, however, a question separate and

distinct from the question of the *sufficiency* of his disclosure to satisfy the requirements of [enablement].

Id. at 772, 135 USPQ at 315 (emphasis in original).

Thus, compliance with the best mode requirement focuses on a different matter than does compliance with the enablement requirement. Enablement looks to placing the subject matter of the claims generally in the possession of the public. If, however, the applicant develops specific instrumentalities or techniques which are recognized at the time of filing as the best way of carrying out the invention, then the best mode requirement imposes an obligation to disclose that information to the public as well.

The situation before us is one in which the patent specifications disclose more than one means for making the claimed invention, but do not adequately disclose the best means actually known to the inventors. The district court recognized that the specifications were inadequate under § 112, but incorrectly based its decision on a lack of enablement. As we explain, the problem is really one of best mode, and thus, while we disagree with the district court's views on these issues, the judgment that the patents are both invalid was correct and must be sustained.

2. ENABLEMENT

* * *

To be enabling under § 112, a patent specification must disclose sufficient information to enable those skilled in the art to make and use the claimed invention. The district court held both of the patents in suit invalid for lack of enablement based on their failure to disclose Coherent's six-stage braze cycle for brazing TiCuSil. The court found that the braze cycle was "necessary to the enjoyment of the invention [sic]."

Coherent's braze cycle, however, is applicable only to TiCuSil brazing, which is just one of the ways to make and use the claimed inventions. The Hobart patent calls for "means for attaching" the copper cups to the inside of the ceramic tube and Mefferd has essentially the same step of "permanently securing" the cups to the tube. The specifications identify as suitable attachment techniques the alternatives of TiCuSil brazing, moly-manganese brazing, and low-temperature pulse-soldering.

If an invention pertains to an art where the results are predictable, e.g., mechanical as opposed to chemical arts, a broad claim can be enabled by disclosure of a single embodiment, and is not invalid for lack of enablement simply because it reads on another embodiment of the invention which is inadequately disclosed.[5] Thus, it is sufficient here with respect to enablement that the patents disclose at least one attachment means which would enable a person of ordinary skill in the art to make and use the claimed inventions. Because the patents disclose the alterna-

---

5. This is also the logical implication of having a separate best mode requirement under § 112 which contemplates that the specification can enable one to make and use the invention and still not disclose a single preferred embodiment.

tives of moly-manganese brazing and pulse-soldering, their failure to also disclose Coherent's TiCuSil braze cycle is not fatal to enablement under § 112.

Spectra argues that the patents' references to the "moly-manganese process" is only in regard to low-temperature pulse-soldering, not brazing. We disagree. A fair reading of that paragraph as part of the general discussion of brazing, given that moly-manganese brazing was the most common method of bonding metal to ceramic, is that one skilled in the art would recognize that moly-manganese brazing was an alternative means of attachment. Spectra's Dave Wright, among others, testified that moly-manganese brazing was common in the industry and was well-known for brazing copper to ceramic.

The district court ignored the moly-manganese process, however, for the erroneous reason that it was "neither described nor advocated in the patents in suit." A patent need not teach, and preferably omits, what is well known in the art. While there is no elaboration of moly-manganese brazing in the patent specifications, the district court found that brazing was an old and well-known technique when the applications were filed.

* * *

As for the court's statement that moly-manganese was not "advocated" in the patents, this is another matter entirely. We can only surmise that the court somehow confused the enablement requirement with the best mode. Nonenablement is the failure to disclose *any* mode, and does not depend on the applicant advocating a particular embodiment or method for making the invention. In practical terms, where only an alternative embodiment is enabled, the disclosure of the best mode may be inadequate. But that is a question separate and distinct from the question whether the specification enabled one to make the invention at all.

* * *

3. BEST MODE

* * *

Because the best mode provision of § 112 speaks in terms of the best mode "contemplated by the inventor," there is no objective standard by which to judge the adequacy of a best mode disclosure. Instead, only evidence of "concealment," whether accidental or intentional, is considered. The specificity of disclosure required to comply with the best mode requirement must be determined by the knowledge of facts within the possession of the inventor at the time of filing the application.

Compliance with the best mode requirement, because it depends on the applicant's state of mind, is a question of fact subject to the clearly erroneous standard of review. This assumes, however, a proper legal understanding of the best mode requirement, which we find missing from the district court's analysis. In general, we do not disagree with the facts as found by the district court. It is only the court's ultimate conclusion that the best mode requirement was satisfied that we reject.

In analyzing compliance with the best mode requirement, the district court focused only on the generic rather than the specific information known to the inventors and found that neither Mefferd nor Hobart intentionally, deliberately, or accidentally "concealed the braze technique as the best mode of attaching the heat web to the alumina tube." The patent specifications make clear, however, that the best mode contemplated by the inventors, as least as far as the critical "means for attaching" the copper cups to the ceramic tube is concerned, was more than just brazing in general—it was TiCuSil active metal brazing. Coherent acknowledges as much by its references to TiCuSil as the "preferred" brazing material and by the fact that Coherent never used anything else.

The appropriate question then is not whether the inventors disclosed TiCuSil brazing *at all*—they did—but whether TiCuSil brazing was *adequately* disclosed. Even though there may be a general reference to the best mode, the quality of the disclosure may be so poor as to effectively result in concealment.

The facts found by the district court, when placed in the proper framework, plainly demonstrate that the TiCuSil brazing technique used by Coherent was not adequately disclosed. The court stated in findings of fact under the heading "ENABLEMENT":

> 2. The use to which Coherent put the TiCuSil braze material was, and was known to be by Coherent at the time, contrary to criteria for the use of TiCuSil as contained in the literature.

and again,

> 9. The references to brazing as used in the patents and the extraneous texts (Kohl, Wesgo Brochure) relied upon by Coherent, do not describe for the benefit of one skilled in the art of laser construction the manner in which the Mefferd method is usable for the construction of the Hobart apparatus by means of [TiCuSil] brazing.

The district court also found that the inventors were aware of the problems associated with TiCuSil:

> 4. The known difficulty recognized by Hobart and Mefferd in working with TiCuSil as a braze material for the purpose to which they put it is reflected in Hobart's disclosure dated March 1, 1979 ... that the titanium-copper-silver process is "not in high favor in the ceramic industry" and "not preferred as compared with what is called the moly-manganese technique which produces stronger and also less leak-prone seals" and essentially the same language in the May, 1979 patent disclosure signed by all of Hobart, Mefferd and Johnston.

Coherent admits that its braze cycle is not disclosed in either patent nor is it contained in the prior art. Instead, it maintains that its braze cycle is unique to its ovens, and because the performance of industrial ovens varies considerably, the actual parameters would be meaningless to someone who used a different oven. In support of its position, Coherent cites *In re Gay*, 309 F.2d at 769, 135 USPQ at 316, which states that "[n]ot every last detail is to be described, else patent specifications would turn into production specifications, which they were never meant to be." In doing so, however, Coherent was not discussing whether it had complied with the best mode requirement because the court had held in its favor on that issue; it was discussing whether it had complied with the enablement requirement on which the court had held against it.

First, it is not up to the courts to decide *how* an inventor should disclose the best mode, but *whether* he has done so adequately under the statute. Second, far from being a "production specification," Coherent did not disclose *any* details about its brazing process. It is this complete lack of detail which effectively resulted in its concealment.

Where the district court went wrong on the law while reaching the right result is starkly revealed in its conclusions of law. Under the heading of "BEST MODE" is this conclusion:

> 4.   There was no concealment deliberate or otherwise by Hobart or Mefferd of the brazing process as the best mode of bonding the heating web to the alumina tube.

As we have pointed out, however, this refers to brazing in general, not the actual brazing cycle with TiCuSil and all of the parameters which Coherent found to be its best mode, admittedly not disclosed. In contrast, but under the heading "ENABLEMENT," is the key conclusion of law which supports our conclusion and the judgment, reading as follows:

> 3.   The six stage braze cycle employed by Coherent, and developed by it, are [sic, is] necessary to the enjoyment of the invention taught by the patents in suit by a person skilled in the art of laser construction, and are [sic] not *sufficiently disclosed* by the patents in suit. [Original emphasis.]

For reasons above explained, Coherent's failure to disclose its "six stage braze cycle" fully supports the defense of non-compliance with the best mode requirement of the first paragraph of § 112 although the inventions as broadly claimed could be practiced without knowledge of it, which means that the patent specifications are enabling. The trial court evidently had a grasp on the essential facts but somehow got them into the wrong legal pigeonholes. With the aid of lawyers, this is not difficult to do.

Spectra's claim in this declaratory judgment complaint that the two patents in suit are invalid must therefore be sustained on the ground that they fail to disclose the best mode contemplated by the inventors for practicing their respective inventions.

* * *

NOTES AND QUESTIONS

1. *The quid pro quo.* Section 112 sets forth terms of the bargain struck between the inventor and the public when a patent is granted. In return for the privilege of a monopoly in the invention, the inventor must fully disclose the invention and the method of making and using it, so that the public may benefit from the new knowledge it represents during the patent term, and others can readily make, use, sell and import the invention when the patent expires. Full disclosure is the consideration the inventor pays for the patent. Failure to make that payment renders the patent invalid.

Section 112 imposes several separate requirements with regard to disclosure. First, the applicant must include one or more claims that clearly and distinctly describe the subject matter that the applicant regards to be his invention and give the public adequate notice of what is to be protected. Second, the specification must fully, clearly, and concisely describe how to make or practice the invention, sufficient to enable a person with ordinary skill in the art to make and use the invention without undue experimentation. This is sometimes called the "enablement requirement." Third, the disclosure must set forth the "best mode" that the inventor knows for carrying out the invention at the time he files the application. (The "best mode" requirement.) Finally, the specification must contain a "written description of the invention." (the "written description" requirement.)

The claims constitute the official definition of the invention to be patented. A claim is sometimes equated to the "metes and bounds" description of land in a deed to real estate. Like the metes and bounds description, the claim specifies the scope, or perimeter of the private property that is the subject of the patent grant. Novelty and nonobviousness are judged by the claims, and when a patent is granted, infringement is determined by reference to the claims.

The enabling, best mode and written description disclosures take place in the specification, which precedes the claims. As one authority has put it, "[t]he specification describes; the claims define." J.T. McCarthy, McCarthy's Desk Encyclopedia of Intellectual Property, 409 (2d ed. 1995). Nonetheless, when there is doubt about the meaning of a claim, the specification may be used to interpret it.

2. *Enablement.* Section 112 requires the patent applicant to describe how to make and use the invention sufficiently to enable a person skilled in the art to which it pertains to do so without undue experimentation. The Federal Circuit has provided a number of factors that courts should consider in determining whether a patent specification satisfies the enablement requirement, including:

1) the quantity of experimentation necessary; 2) the amount of direction or guidance provided; 3) the presence or absence of working examples; 4) the nature of the invention; 5) the state of the prior art; 6) the relative skill of those in the art; 7) the predictability or unpredictability of the art; and 8) the breadth of the claims.

In re Wands, 858 F.2d 731 (Fed. Cir. 1988). Why should the predictability or unpredictability of the art be relevant? Why should the breadth of the claims be relevant?

What are the implications of designating persons skilled in the art as the applicant's audience, as opposed to persons generally? In *Spectra-Physics*, the Hobart patent claim recited "means for attaching" the copper cups to the inside of the ceramic tube as an element of the invention. What are the implications of this language for a person seeking to determine the scope of the patent monopoly? What, if any, implications did the applicant's use of this language have with regard to the enablement requirement?

The enablement requirement does not require the applicant to enable a person with ordinary skill to mass-produce the invention. Should it? See Christianson v. Colt Industries Operating Corp., 822 F.2d 1544, 1562–63 (Fed.Cir.1987), *vacated on jurisdictional gds. and remanded for transfer to 7th Cir.,* 486 U.S. 800, 108 S.Ct. 2166, 100 L.Ed.2d 811 (1988).

In the case of inventions involving living materials it may be impossible to enable persons skilled in the art to make or use the invention with just a written description. In such cases, an applicant may be required to deposit a sample of the living materials with a recognized depository that complies with the United States' treaty obligations under the Budapest Treaty on the International Recognition of the Deposit of Microorganisms for the Purposes of Patent Procedure.[13] The depository will then make samples of the material available to those wishing to learn more about the invention.

3. *The best mode.* What purpose does the "best mode" requirement serve? How does the purpose differ from that of the "enablement" requirement? In *Spectra-Physics*, the patentees disclosed TiCuSil brazing in their application, but the court found that they did not do so adequately. What more was required? Why?

The Federal Circuit provided further elaboration on the best mode requirement in Chemcast Corp. v. Arco Industries Corp., 913 F.2d 923, 926–28 (Fed.Cir.1990):

> The best mode inquiry focuses on the inventor's state of mind as of the time he filed his application—a subjective, factual question. But this focus is not exclusive. Our statements that "there is no objective standard by which to judge the adequacy of a best mode disclosure," and that "only evidence of concealment (accidental or intentional) is to be considered," * * * assumed that both the level of skill in the art and the scope of the claimed invention were additional, objective metes and bounds of a best mode disclosure.

> Of necessity, the disclosure required by section 112 is directed to those skilled in the art. * * * Therefore, one must consider the level of skill in the relevant art in determining whether a specification discloses the best mode. We have consistently recognized that whether a best mode disclosure is adequate, that is, whether the inventor concealed a better mode of practicing his invention than he disclosed, is a function of not

---

13. Budapest Treaty on the International Recognition of the Deposit of Microorganisms for the Purposes of Patent Procedure, April 28, 1977, 32 U.S.T. 1241, T.I.A.S. 9768.

only what the inventor knew but also how one skilled in the art would have understood his disclosure. *See, e.g.,* * * * *W.L. Gore,* 721 F.2d [at] 1556, 220 USPQ [at] 315 (no best mode violation where inventor did not disclose the only mode of calculating stretch rate that he used, because that "mode would have been employed by those of ordinary skill in the art at the time the application was filed. As indicated, Dr. Gore's disclosure must be examined for § 112 compliance in light of knowledge extant in the art on his application filing date.") * * *. Thus, the level of skill in the art is a relevant and necessary consideration in assessing the adequacy of a best mode disclosure.

The other objective limitation on the extent of the disclosure required to comply with the best mode requirement is, of course, the scope of the claimed invention. "It is concealment of the best mode of practicing the *claimed invention* that section 112 ¶ 1 is designed to prohibit." *Randomex,* 849 F.2d at 588, 7 USPQ2d at 1053. Thus, in *Randomex,* the inventor's deliberate concealment of his cleaning fluid formula did not violate the best mode requirement because his "invention neither added nor claimed to add anything to the prior art respecting cleaning fluid." * * * Finally, in *DeGeorge* we reversed a finding that an inventor's nondisclosure of unclaimed circuitry with which his claimed circuitry interfaced violated the best mode requirement: "Because the properly construed claim does not include a word processor, failure to meet the best mode requirement here should not arise from an absence of information on the word processor." 768 F.2d at 1325, 226 USPQ at 763.

In short, a proper best mode analysis has two components. The first is whether, at the time the inventor filed his patent application, he knew of a mode of practicing his claimed invention that considered to be better than any other. This part of the inquiry is wholly subjective, and resolves whether the inventor must disclose any facts in addition to those sufficient for enablement. If the inventor in fact contemplated such a preferred mode, the second part of the analysis compares what he knew with what he disclosed—is the disclosure adequate to enable one skilled in the art to practice the best mode or, in other words, has the inventor "concealed" his preferred mode from the "public"? Assessing the *adequacy* of the disclosure, as opposed to its *necessity,* is largely an objective inquiry that depends upon the scope of the claimed invention and the level of skill in the art.

4. *The written description requirement.* Section 112 requires that the specification "contain a written description of the invention." This "written description" requirement is distinct from the enablement requirement: For example, one could teach (enable) a person of ordinary skill to move from point A to point B, but this would not necessarily "describe" point B. According to the Federal Circuit, the written description requirement is meant to assist the PTO to examine the application effectively; to assist courts to understand the invention and construe the claim; and to assist the public to understand and improve upon the invention and avoid the claimed boundaries of the patentee's exclusive right. Ariad Pharmaceuticals, Inc. v. Eli Lilly & Co., 598 F.3d 1336, 1345 (Fed. Cir. 2010) (en banc). The written

description requirement also performs a somewhat different function than the claim requirement:

> Claims define the subject matter that, after examination, has been found to meet the statutory requirements for a patent. Their principal function, therefore, is to provide notice of the boundaries of the right to exclude and to define limits; it is not to describe the invention, although their original language contributes to the description and in certain cases satisfies it. Claims define and circumscribe, the written description discloses and teaches.

Id., at 1347. The specification's written description must demonstrate that the inventor "had possession" of the claimed subject matter as of the application filing date. This test requires an "objective inquiry into the four corners of the specification from the perspective of a person of ordinary skill in the art." *Id.,* at 1351.

While written description problems have not been common in the past, they particularly tend to arise in the case of chemical and biological inventions, where a basic discovery may open the door to an entire category of further inventions that the inventor has not yet described. For example, in biotechnology, the discovery of a gene may enable the discovery of structurally related genes from the same or different species, even though the inventor does not yet know the structure of those related genes. Or the discovery of a new biological pathway may suggest methods of treating diseases by manipulating that pathway, even thought the inventor has not yet discovered the means to do so. In *Ariad*, the inventors were the first to identify a gene called NF-kB, which mediates several intracellular signaling pathways in cells of the immune system. The inventors recognized that inhibiting the activity of NF-kB could be the key to treating many diseases involving an overactive immune response. However, at the time the inventors filed their patent application, they had not actually identified any methods to inhibit the activity of NF-kB. Their claimed method consisted of a single step—reducing NF-kB activity in cells—which would encompass the use of all substances that would achieve the desired result. The specification did not disclose any specific substances that would fall into this category, but hypothesized three possibilities: decoy, dominantly interfering, and specific inhibitor molecules.

The *Ariad* court found this disclosure insufficient to satisfy the written description requirement. It explained that when a claim defines the boundaries of a whole category or genus of chemical compounds, the specification must demonstrate that the applicant has invented enough of the members of the category or genus to support a claim to all possible things that could exist within the group. Absent disclosure of specific chemical compounds that have been experimentally shown to accomplish the claimed result,

> the claims merely recite a description of the problem to be solved while claiming all solutions to it, and * * * cover any compound later actually invented and determined to fall within the claim's functional boundaries—leaving it to the pharmaceutical industry to complete an unfinished invention.

Ariad, 598 F.3d at 1353. The *Ariad* court found it unnecessary to decide whether the inventors had *enabled* methods of inhibiting NF-kB activity, because they had not adequately *described* such methods. Does this suggest a distinct role for the written description requirement in patent litigation?

The *Ariad* court recognized that the written description doctrine may disadvantage universities by denying patents for basic research, and reduce the incentive to invest in such research, but noted that "the patent law has always been directed to the 'useful Arts,' meaning inventions with a practical use."

> Much university research relates to basic research, including research into scientific principles and mechanisms of action, and universities may not have the resources or inclination to work out the practical implications of all such research, i.e., finding and identifying compounds able to affect the mechanism discovered. [However,] patents are not awarded for academic theories, no matter how groundbreaking or necessary to the later patentable invention of others. * * * Requiring a written description of the invention limits patent protection to those who actually perform the difficult work of "invention"—that is, conceive of the complete and final invention with all its claimed limitations—and disclose the fruits of that effort to the public. * * * [C]aims to research plans * * * impose costs on downstream research, discouraging later invention. The goal is to get the right balance, and the written description doctrine does so by giving the incentive to actual invention and not "attempt[s] to preempt the future before it has arrived." As this court has repeatedly stated, the purpose of the written description requirement is to "ensure that the scope of the right to exclude, as set forth in the claims, does not overreach the scope of the inventor's contribution to the field of art as described in the patent specification."

Id., 598 F.3d at 1353–54. In your opinion, does the written description requirement, as described in *Ariad,* reach the correct balance?

5. *The duty of candor.* While the Patent and Trademark Office has a large patent and technical library that PTO examiners use to identify prior art relevant to the novelty and obviousness of an invention, the library cannot supply examiners with all the information relevant to patentability. For example, it may be difficult or impossible for a patent examiner to learn of such things as public use or sale of an applicant's patented invention more than a year prior to the application, or lesser-known printed publications in foreign nations. To ensure that as much relevant information reaches the patent examiner as possible, the PTO's Rule 56 provides as follows:

> (a) * * * Each individual associated with the filing and prosecution of a patent application has a duty of candor and good faith in dealing with the Office, which includes a duty to disclose to the Office all information known to that individual to be material to patentability as defined in this section. The duty to disclose information exists with respect to each pending claim until the claim is cancelled or withdrawn from consideration, or the application becomes abandoned. [N]o patent will be granted on an application in connection with which fraud on the Office was practiced or attempted or the duty of disclosure was violated through bad faith or intentional misconduct. * * *

> * * *

(b) Under this section, information is material to patentability when it is not cumulative to information already of record or being made of record in the application, and

(1) It establishes, by itself or in combination with other information, a *prima facie* case of unpatentability of a claim; or

(2) It refutes, or is inconsistent with, a position the applicant takes in:

(i) Opposing an argument of unpatentability relied on by the Office, or

(ii) Asserting an argument of patentability.

A *prima facie* case of unpatentability is established when the information compels a conclusion that a claim is unpatentable under the preponderance of evidence burden-of-proof standard, giving each term in the claim its broadest reasonable construction consistent with the specification, and before any consideration is given to evidence which may be submitted in an attempt to establish a contrary conclusion of patentability.

* * *

37 C.F.R. § 1.56 (2009).

7. Inventorship

The Patent Act makes it clear that it is the *inventor* who is entitled to apply for a patent. See, *e.g.*, § 101 ("whoever invents or discovers any new and useful process, machine, manufacture, or composition of matter ... may obtain a patent"); § 102(f) ("A person shall be entitled to a patent unless ... he did not himself invent the subject matter sought to be patented"); § 111 ("Application for patent shall be made, or authorized to be made, by the inventor"); § 115 ("The applicant shall make oath that he believes himself to be the original and first inventor...."). The application must be pursued in the inventor's name even when she has assigned all rights in the invention to another, such as her employer.[14]

When an invention is made by two or more persons jointly, they must apply for a patent jointly. 35 U.S.C. § 116. When will persons qualify as joint inventors? First, each person claiming to be a joint inventor must have contributed to the final concept of the invention. Nartron Corp. v. Schukra U.S.A., Inc., 558 F.3d 1352 (Fed. Cir. 2009). One does not become a joint inventor merely by explaining well-known principles or concepts, or the state of the art to the inventor. Moreover, the joint inventor must "make a contribution to the claimed invention that is not insignificant in

---

14. The general rules regarding the ownership of an invention made by an employee during the course of employment are discussed in Chapter Two, *supra*. For example, if the employee/inventor was hired to do the research that lead to the invention, the common law may imply an assignment of ownership by the employee to the employer. Even if the common law would designate the employee as the owner of the invention, the employee may have signed an express agreement assigning to the employer in advance the rights in any inventions he makes while employed. When the employee has assigned ownership of the invention to the employer, the patent application nonetheless must be made in the name of the employee/inventor, even though the employer handles the application and the patent is issued to the employer as the assignee of the inventor of record. 35 U.S.C. § 152.

quality, when that contribution is measured against the dimension of the full invention." *Id.*, at 1356–57.

In addition, the purported joint inventors must have collaborated with one another. Kimberly–Clark Corp. v. Procter & Gamble Distributing Co., Inc., 973 F.2d 911 (Fed.Cir.1992), is illustrative. In 1979 and 1982, Buell, a Procter & Gamble employee, made a disposable diaper with inner flaps to control leakage. In 1982, Enloe, a Kimberly–Clark employee, conceived of a disposable diaper with inner flaps. Enloe's work lead to the issuance of a patent to Kimberly–Clark. In 1985, Lawson, a Proctor & Gamble employee, conceived of a disposable diaper that used inner flaps. Lawson worked alone on the invention, unaware of Buell's earlier work. (At the time, Buell was likewise unaware of Lawson.) Procter & Gamble, as Lawson's assignee, filed a patent application naming Lawson as the sole inventor and later obtained a patent.

The issue of priority arose in subsequent litigation between Procter & Gamble and Kimberly–Clark. Procter & Gamble asserted that the Lawson patent had priority over the Kimberly–Clark patent, on the grounds that Buell and Lawson were joint inventors, and Buell's work marked the actual date of conception for the Procter & Gamble diaper. Pursuant to 35 U.S.C. § 256, Procter & Gamble asked the court to order that the omission of Buell as an inventor in the Lawson patent be corrected. The district court found that Buell and Lawson were not joint inventors, and the Court of Appeals for the Federal Circuit affirmed.

The Federal Circuit found that Congress, in amending Patent Act § 116 in 1984, intended to codify the principles set forth in Monsanto Co. v. Kamp, 269 F.Supp. 818, 824 (D.D.C.1967). The *Monsanto* opinion had stated:

A joint invention is the product of *collaboration* of the inventive endeavors of two or more persons *working toward the same end* and producing an invention by their *aggregate* efforts. To constitute a joint invention, it is necessary that each of the inventors work on the same subject matter and make some contribution to the inventive thought and to the final result. Each needs to perform but a part of the task if an invention emerges from all of the steps taken together. It is not necessary that the entire inventive concept should occur to each of the joint inventors, or that the two should physically work on the project together. One may take a step at one time, the other an approach at different times. One may do more of the experimental work while the other makes suggestions from time to time. The fact that each of the inventors plays a different role and that the contribution of one may not be as great as that of another does not detract from the fact that the invention is joint if each makes some original contribution, though partial, to the final solution of the problem.

Monsanto, 269 F.Supp. at 824.

In finding that the Procter & Gamble employees, Buell and Lawson, were not joint inventors, the Federal Circuit explained:

What is clear is that the statutory word "jointly" is not mere surplusage. For persons to be joint inventors under Section 116, there must be some element of joint behavior, such as collaboration or working under common direction, one inventor seeing a relevant report and building upon it or hearing another's suggestion at a meeting. Here there was nothing of that nature. Individuals cannot be joint inventors if they are completely ignorant of what each other has done until years after their individual independent efforts. They cannot be totally independent of each other and be joint inventors.

Kimberly-Clark, 973 F.2d at 916–17.

In the absence of an assignment or an agreement to the contrary, each joint inventor is a joint owner of the patent, and each joint owner may exploit the patented invention freely without the consent of the other joint owners, and without accounting to them. 35 U.S.C. § 262

Especially in large research and development departments, where a number of persons may be involved in the inventive process, it may be difficult to determine exactly who qualifies as a joint inventor and include all such persons in the patent application. While failure to name the inventor or inventors correctly may result in invalidation of the patent, errors can be corrected if they were made without deceptive intent.

8. International Considerations

Comparative Considerations

Many similarities exist among the patent laws of the various nations. For example, foreign patent laws generally require that inventions be novel, non-obvious and useful in order to qualify for a patent, though each of these requirements may differ somewhat in nomenclature, scope and detail from its counterpart in United States law. Perhaps the most important *difference* between the U.S. and other nations' patent laws is the United States' emphasis on granting a patent to the first person to invent, rather than the first inventor to file an application. Another important difference is that most other nations lack a "grace period" comparable to that in Patent Act § 102(b): In many countries, virtually any introduction of the invention to the public via commercial activity or publication, either domestically or abroad, prior to the filing date will disqualify the invention. This poses a trap for unwary United States inventors—while taking advantage of the U.S. grace period, they may disqualify themselves for patents in much of the rest of the world. In addition, many countries do not require an applicant to disclose the "best mode" of carrying out her invention, as the U.S. does in Patent Act § 112. In these countries, the applicant need only adequately disclose one mode of carrying out the invention.

Traditionally, the duration of patent protection has differed from one country to the next. Countries have also differed significantly in the scope of subject matter deemed eligible for patent protection. While the United States has tended to offer patent protection for a very wide range of inventions ("anything under the sun that is made by man"), many developing nations, in particular, have denied patents for agricultural chemicals and pharmaceutical inventions, deeming a monopoly (and the ability to charge monopoly prices) to be contrary to the national interest. This refusal has led to considerable dissatisfaction on the part of U.S. drug and chemical industries, who have had to compete with replicas of their own innovative inventions abroad.

Multinational Filings

Needless to say, this variation in national patent laws is not conducive to obtaining global patent protection for a new invention. A company wishing to launch a global marketing campaign for an invention must apply for a patent in each country in which it plans to do business. Understanding and satisfying the substantive and procedural variations in each nation's patent laws can be difficult and expensive. A number of attempts have been made to ease this process.

1. The Paris Convention. The Paris Convention for the Protection of Industrial Property[15] was a first step. A multinational treaty with over 170 members (including the U.S.), the Paris Convention is founded on national treatment: it obligates each member to provide as great patent protection to the nationals of other member nations as it provides to its own nationals. While this gets the foreign applicant's foot in the door, it does not guarantee a high level of substantive patent protection: The Paris Convention prohibits discrimination, but imposes relatively few standards regarding the scope or extent of substantive protection that member nations must provide. Nor does the Paris Convention attempt to standardize member nations' patent application procedures.

Even though it does relatively little to harmonize national patent laws, the Paris Convention makes multinational filings easier through its foreign filing priority provision. Article 4 of the Paris Convention provides that a person who files an application for patent in any member country can claim his filing date in that country in subsequent filings in other member countries during the next twelve months. So, for example, if X Company files a patent application in member country #1 on January 1, 2006, all of the patent applications that it files in other member countries during the next twelve months will have an effective filing date of January 1, 2006.

The usefulness of this provision is made clear in art. 4(B):

> [A]ny subsequent filing in any of the other countries of the Union before the expiration of the [twelve-month] period * * * shall not be invalidated by reason of any acts accomplished in the interval, in particular, another filing, the publication or exploitation of the invention * * *.

---

15. Paris Convention for the Protection of Industrial Property, July 14, 1967, 21 U.S.T. 1629, 982 U.N.T.S. 369.

Recall that most foreign countries grant patents to the first inventor to file, rather than to the first person to invent, and lack the one-year "grace period" afforded to inventors under U.S. Patent Act § 102(b). Assume that X files in country #1 on January 1, 2009. Y makes the same invention and files for a patent in country #2 in August, 2009. Z publishes a paper disclosing the invention in October, 2009. X then files for a patent in country #2 in December, 2009. In the absence of Paris Convention art. 4, both Y and Z's actions are likely to disqualify X from obtaining a patent in country #2, because they occurred prior to his filing date. However, because of art. 4, country #2 will treat X's application as though it were filed on January 1, his filing date in country #1. X will be saved from the consequences of the intervening actions of Y and Z.

Article 4 thus gives an inventor some flexibility. As long as he files an application in one member country (which may be his own country), the inventor can take up to twelve months to test the marketability of the invention, and make the necessary preparations for foreign filings, without fear of losing his patent opportunities abroad in the interim. The substance of art. 4 is implemented in § 119 of the United States Patent Act.[16]

2. The Patent Cooperation Treaty. The Patent Cooperation Treaty ("PCT")[17] was an important second step in aiding the procurement of international patent protection. The PCT simplifies international patent filings by providing a centralized means of filing patent applications for a number of countries simultaneously. Administered by the International Bureau of the World Intellectual Property Organization ("WIPO"),[18] the PCT now has over 140 members, including the U.S. and most other developed nations.

The PCT entitles nationals or residents of member nations to file "international applications" for patents. They may do this by simply filing

---

16. The United States does not treat an art. 4 foreign filing date as the U.S. filing date in all circumstances. Suppose, for example, that a printed publication discloses X's invention (or renders it obvious) in May, 2010. X files for a patent in member country #1 in July, 2010. X then files for a patent in the U.S. in June, 2010. Will his foreign priority date of July, 2010 protect him against the running of § 102(b) in the United States? Consider the explicit wording of Patent Act § 119:

> [N]o patent shall be granted on any application for patent for an invention which had been patented or described in a printed publication in any country more than one year before the date of the *actual filing of the application in this country,* or which had been in public use or on sale in this country more than one year prior to such filing.

(emphasis added).

The Court of Customs and Patent Appeals has construed § 119 to preclude use of an applicant's foreign filing date to determine anticipation under Patent Act § 102(e). *In re* Hilmer, 359 F.2d 859, 862 (C.C.P.A. 1966) ("Section 119 only deals with 'right of priority.' The section does not provide for the use of a U.S. patent as an anticipatory reference as of its foreign filing date."). Note, by contrast, that a U.S. provisional application can serve as an anticipatory reference. *In re* Giacomini, 612 F.3d 1380 (Fed. Cir. 2010).

17. Patent Cooperation Treaty, June 19, 1970, 28 U.S.T. 7645, 1037 U.N.T.S. 213.

18. The World Intellectual Property Organization is a specialized agency of the United Nations, whose objective is to promote the protection of intellectual property throughout the world. It administers the Paris Convention and the PCT, as well as a number of other multinational intellectual property treaties.

a standardized international application with their home patent office, which designates all the other PCT member nations in which the applicant wishes to file. The applicant generally files in his own language and pays a fee in his own nation's currency. The receiving office checks to see that the application is in proper form and, if it is, assigns an international filing date, which will be either the date of a qualifying earlier filing under the Paris Convention or the date of the international filing itself. The effect of this is essentially the same as if a patent application had been filed with the national patent office of each designated member nation on that date. The application is then forwarded (if necessary) to an international searching authority, which conducts an international search of the relevant prior art. The United States' PTO is one of the international searching authorities. The search authority examines published patent documents and technical literature, and produces an international search report.

This search report gives the applicant a good sense of how likely he is to obtain a patent. The applicant then has the opportunity to amend his claims in order to avoid the prior art that has been found, or withdraw his application altogether, if he finds proceeding impractical in light of the search results. If the application is not withdrawn, it is published 18 months after the international filing date. By the end of the twentieth month, the application must be sent to the patent office of each of the designated nations in which a patent is sought. This begins the "national stage" of the process.

At this point, the applicant must send national fees to each national office and supply a translation of the application whenever required. He may need to hire local counsel to prosecute the patent in each national patent office. Each nation proceeds to apply its own law to determine whether a patent will be granted.

If the applicant chooses, directly after the international search and before the application is sent to the national patent offices, he can request an international preliminary examination. The purpose of this examination is to produce a nonbinding opinion about the novelty, inventiveness and industrial applicability of the invention.[19] While the preliminary examination is not binding on the national offices, it is generally highly regarded and thus is persuasive. When the preliminary examination is requested, this adds an additional ten months before the application must be sent to the designated national patent offices, initiating the "national stage."

Even though the PCT procedure does not avoid the cost and difficulty of prosecuting the application before each of the individual national patent offices, it nonetheless has proved popular, and is widely perceived as offering important advantages to international patent applicants. One of

---

19. Novelty, inventiveness and industrial applicability are the international criteria for patentability. They are conceptually similar to the U.S. requirements of novelty, nonobviousness and usefulness.

the most important perceived advantages is the period of time that it provides between the initial application and the point at which national fees and translations are due and appearances must be made before the individual national offices. This permits applicants to reserve their patent priority in a potentially large number of countries, while testing the commercial viability of their inventions. If the commercial prospects are not promising, they may discontinue prosecution prior to the national stage, avoiding the considerable cost and effort that the national stage entails.

Another advantage, of course, is that the applications can all be prepared in the same format. Applications meeting the form and content requirements of the PCT must be accepted in all member nations, though the nations may impose different requirements for direct applications. There may also be a savings of attorney time, as amendments to the claims can be made during the centralized international phase, avoiding duplicative actions in the various national offices.

The PCT is implemented in §§ 351–76 of the United States' Patent Act.[20]

    3. Other Efforts: the Patent Law Treaty and TRIPs. As international marketing of goods and services has become increasingly common, many nations have sought additional ways to harmonize the patent laws of the world. In the late 1980's and early 1990's a number of interested nations met, under the auspices of the World Intellectual Property Organization ("WIPO"), to attempt to draft a treaty establishing global *substantive* patent standards, including a uniform rule regarding patent priority, a uniform grace period, and disclosure requirements. See Moy, *The History of the Patent Harmonization Treaty: Economic Self–Interest as an Influence*, 26 J. Marshall L. Rev. 457 (1993); Fiorito, *The "Basic Proposal" for Harmonization of U.S. and Worldwide Patent Laws Submitted by WIPO*, 73 J. Pat. & Trademark Off. Soc. 83 (1991). While these efforts ultimately failed, negotiators were able to conclude a treaty (the Patent Law Treaty)[21] further harmonizing procedural filing requirements. Nations ratifying the new WIPO Patent Law Treaty accept standardized patent application forms (in the case of applications filed outside of the PCT process, which is already standardized), eliminate some unduly complex and expensive formalities that have been imposed in the past, provide relief and reinstatement of rights when applicants and patentees miss certain deadlines, and take other steps to conform their patent application process to international norms. The Patent Law Treaty thus further reduces the complexity and cost of obtaining international patent protection.

On another front, efforts were made in the late 1980's and early 1990's to bring minimum substantive standards of patent protection into

---

20. Another international patent agreement to which the U.S. adheres, the Strasbourg Agreement Concerning the International Patent Classification, March 24, 1971, 26 U.S.T. 1793, T.I.A.S. 8140, eases the international prior art search by providing an international classification system for patented subject matter.

21. Patent Law Treaty, Adopted at Geneva, June 1, 2000, 39 I.L.M. 1047.

the General Agreement on Tariffs and Trade ("GATT"), the leading world agreement regulating international trade. These efforts met with significant success. Among other things, the resulting Agreement on Trade Related Aspects of Intellectual Property Rights, Including Trade in Counterfeited Goods ("TRIPs" Agreement) harmonizes national laws regarding the term of patent protection, the scope of patentable subject matter, and the substantive rights and remedies to be provided to patentees.[22]

—The TRIPs Agreement provides that the term of patent protection must not end "before the expiration of a period of twenty years counted from the filing date." TRIPs, Art. 33.[23]

—TRIPs art. 28 specifies minimum rights that member countries must afford patentees: patentees must enjoy rights against the unauthorized "making, using, offering for sale, selling or importing" of their patented products. Process patents must convey the right to prevent unauthorized use of the process and the use, offer for sale, sale or importation of products obtained directly through the process.[24] The TRIPs agreement also places important limitations on members' ability to impose compulsory licenses and patent forfeiture.

—TRIPs article 27 provides for a broad range of patentable subject matter, that requires many nations to extend protection to categories of inventions they had previously excluded: "patents shall be available for any inventions, whether products or processes, in all fields of technology, provided that they are new, involve an inventive step and are capable of industrial application." There are some limitations on this broad provision, however: member nations may exclude from patentability

> (1) inventions whose commercial exploitation threatens "*ordre public* or morality, including to protect human, animal or plant life or health or to avoid serious prejudice to the environment;"

> (2) "diagnostic, therapeutic and surgical methods for the treatment of humans or animals;" and

---

22. For further discussion of the TRIPs Agreement, see Chapter One, *supra.*

23. In accepting the Uruguay Round, the United States was required to implement this term, in place of a patent term of 17 years counted from the date the patent issues, which it traditionally had provided. As amended, Patent Act § 154(a)(2) specifies that United States patent protection begins on the date the patent is issued and ends 20 years from the date on which the application for patent was filed *in the United States.* The term is not to be measured by reference to an earlier Paris Convention foreign filing priority date. Should the foreign filing of a PCT application that designates the United States trigger the 20–year term? See 35 U.S.C.A. § 363.

As will be discussed in the next Section, the U.S. has subsequently amended its Patent Act to provide for publication of many patent applications 18 months after their filing date. It has added a complimentary provision providing limited rights to patentees during the interim between the date their application is published and the date their patent issues. 35 U.S.C. § 154(d).

24. This provision also necessitated amendments to the United States Patent Act. Uruguay Round Agreements Act. See 35 U.S.C. §§ 154(a), 271 (a). Prior to the amendment, the U.S. had not recognized a patentee's right to prevent an offer for sale or the importation of its patented invention, or of products of its patented process.

(3) "plants and animals other than microorganisms, and essentially biological processes for the production of plants or animals other than nonbiological and microbiological processes." *Id.*

TRIPs art. 27 provides that "patent rights shall be available and patent rights enjoyable without discrimination as to the place of invention." This provision required amendment of § 104 of the United States Patent Act—a very important change. To better envision the issue, suppose that A invents and files an application for patent in Paris Convention member country #1 on January 1, 2006. B makes the same invention in the U.S. in July, 2006 and files for a U.S. patent in September, 2006. A then files for a U.S. patent in November, 2006. A has priority because he is treated as having filed in the U.S. on January 1 (prior to B's invention and filing) pursuant to Patent Act § 119.

Suppose, in contrast, the following facts: A conceives and reduces to practice in member country #1 in January, 2006. B conceives and reduces to practice the same invention in the U.S. in March, 2006. A files for a patent in member country #1 in June, 2006. B files for a patent in the U.S. in July. A then files for a patent in the U.S. in August, 2006. Who has priority? A has the earlier filing date (June) by virtue of Patent Act § 119. However, B can "swear back" to show that his actual date of invention was March, prior to A's filing date. Can A then swear back to show an invention date in member country #1 that precedes B's? Prior to amendments of Patent Act § 104 necessitated by U.S. adherence to the North American Free Trade Agreement ("NAFTA") and TRIPs, A could only rely on her effective date of application, or the date on which she "introduced" the invention into the United States, as her date of invention. Section 104 provided that "[i]n proceedings in the Patent and Trademark Office and in the courts, an applicant for a patent, or a patentee, may not establish a date of invention by reference to knowledge or use thereof, or other activity with respect thereto, in a foreign country, except as provided [in § 119]." This discrimination against foreign inventors had long rankled the United States' trading partners.

Review the amended version of § 104. When the United States joined the NAFTA, it was required to amend § 104 to except evidence of earlier invention in other NAFTA member countries. Pub. L. No. 103–182, § 331, 107 Stat. 2057, 2113–14 (1994). Adherence to the TRIPs required an amendment to add another, larger exception, permitting evidence of earlier invention in any other World Trade Organization member country. Uruguay Round Agreements Act, Pub. L. No. 103–465 § 531, 108 Stat. 4809, 4982–83 (1994).[25]

---

25. The Uruguay Round Agreements Act amendment of § 104 is effective for patent applications filed on or after January 1, 1996. Applicants and patentees may not establish a date of invention that is earlier than January 1, 1996 by reference to knowledge, use or other activity in another World Trade Organization member country. Uruguay Round Agreements Act, Pub. L. No. 103–465 § 531, 108 Stat. 4809, 4982–83 (1994).

What, if any, effect is the amendment of § 104 likely to have on the United States' continued adherence to a first-to-invent system?

D. THE PATENTING PROCESS

Patent applications are "one of the most difficult legal instruments to draw with accuracy." Sperry v. Florida, 373 U.S. 379, 383, 83 S.Ct. 1322, 1325, 10 L.Ed.2d 428, 431 (1963). The drafter must understand the technology underlying the invention, be able to describe the invention accurately, in a manner that satisfies the requirements of Patent Act § 112, and draft the patent claims in a manner that obtains for her client the broadest possible scope of patent protection in light of the prior art. The patent attorney must also master the procedural rules that govern representation of clients before the PTO. The process of filing a patent application and pursuing it to its conclusion is called "patent prosecution."

Examples of patent claims were provided in some of the prior case opinions. A copy of a complete patent for a simple invention is available in the Appendix. The following excerpt from Prof. Janicke's article provides an overview of the art of claim drafting. Following that excerpt is a very general overview of patent prosecution and related procedures. For more detailed information, see the Patent Act, the applicable regulations, 37 C.F.R. § 1.1, *et. seq.*, and D.S. Chisum, Patents: A Treatise on the Law of Patentability, Validity, and Infringement (2009).

1. Claim Drafting

WHEN PATENTS ARE BROADENED MIDSTREAM: A COMPROMISE SOLUTION TO PROTECT COMPETITORS AND EXISTING USERS

Paul M. Janicke.[26]
66 University of Cincinnati Law Review 7, 10–16 (1997).

* * *

The basic rules of claiming are, without too much oversimplification, fairly simple to state. First, the family of designs covered by the language of a valid claim must not include any design disclosed in the prior literature. This rule sets limits on claim breadth. An inventor who has discovered a new and nonobvious vehicle—for example, the first automobile—would like to claim simply "a vehicle." This would not be permissible because other members of the "vehicle" family were described in the prior literature—locomotives, wagons, steamships. Such a claim is invalid totally, not just the portion of its scope that embraces old things.

Second, the family of designs covered by the claim must include at least one member that is disclosed in the detailed part of the patent

---

26. © Paul M. Janicke, 1997. Reprinted by permission of the copyright owner.

application. This is typically the design developed by the inventor, which she had thought of as her "invention."[20] Last, someone else who, after the grant of the claim and without the permission of the patent owner, makes, sells, uses, or offers to sell in the United States, any design covered by the claim language, is normally liable for patent infringement.

What is patented, therefore, is not just the configuration the inventor brought to her lawyer, but nearly all other configurations that fit the claim language. For example, the first person to design a car may present her patent lawyer with drawings and a written description of a vehicle with a chassis, a body mounted on the chassis, an eight-cylinder engine, four wheels, headlights and tail lights, and a manual three-speed transmission to alter the torque on the wheels and allow driving at various speeds. It has two doors and crude brakes on the rear wheels. She tells her lawyer: "Here is my invention." There has been nothing like it before. It is new. The nearest thing in the prior literature is a horse-drawn wagon, also with chassis, wheels, headlights and tail lights.

The lawyer must first think about how to claim this development, perhaps like the following:

    1. A vehicle, comprising:

        (a) a chassis;

        (b) a body mounted on the chassis;

        (c) a plurality of wheels attached to the chassis; and

        (d) an engine for driving at least one of the wheels.

This claim is broad and omits recitation of the transmission, lights, doors, and brakes because future companies may try to market vehicles that lack one or more of those features. The lawyer has written a claim that encompasses vehicles with no transmission, no lights, no doors, and no brakes, even though they may be inferior to the design of his client. The claim also omits a recitation of the number of wheels because other inventors could develop vehicles with two, three, six, or eighteen wheels. The claim drafter wants to cover all such arrangements.

The drafter of the patent application also knows that during the term of the patent that will contain this claim, others will develop better cars than the one his client has disclosed—vehicles with automatic transmissions, four-barrel carburetors, disk brakes, heating, air-conditioning, or hundreds of other improvements, none of which his client has conceived.

---

20. 35 U.S.C. § 112 provides in part:

    The specification shall contain a written description of the invention, and of the manner and process of making and using it, in such full, clear, concise, and exact terms as to enable any person skilled in the art to which it pertains, or with which it is most nearly connected, to make and use the same, and shall set forth the best mode contemplated by the inventor of carrying out his invention.

35 U.S.C. § 112 (1994). The statute thus requires that the design thought by the inventor to be best at the time of filing the application must be disclosed therein. This could be the first-developed version within the claim, but there may have been a later-developed version pre-filing which the inventor thinks is better. If this is the case, the later version must be disclosed in the specification of the application.

The claim given above covers nearly all of those designs too, through the use of the word "comprising." The legal meaning of "comprising" is "including at least." It is open-ended, so that it will encompass many of the better designs of the future, as well as cruder designs without any lights and brakes.

Notice how misleading it would be to state that the inventor who gets a patent on this claim is being given a patent "on her device" or "for her device." Of course, the claim covers the design that the inventor originally developed but, more importantly, it also covers a host of other designs. This style of broad, generic claiming makes the patent grant more commercially significant and, therefore, more attractive as an incentive for capital formation to support the original development. It is uncertain whether this large breadth of coverage is required to facilitate the original innovation, or whether it places an undue burden on future research and development by blocking off too much ground. Nevertheless, this is the claim style presently in place in most technologies today.

Although he may have drafted the most commercially desirable claim, the lawyer knows that its weakness is that there can never be total assurance that a claim does not cover, in addition to the client's specific item, something old.[26] The prior literature and other possibly invalidating prior events cannot be fully known, and if the prior literature contains a disclosure of any structure within the claim, the claim will be invalid in toto. To mitigate this eventuality, drafters of patent claims usually include a number of claims of lesser scope for insurance purposes. As stated above, each claim is judged on its own merits for both validity and infringement purposes; only one valid claim need be infringed to give rise to a cause of action for infringement. Accordingly, in our example, the next narrower claim might read as follows:

2. The vehicle of claim 1, further comprising a brake attached to one of said wheels.[28]

In this example, the lawyer is hedging his bets. If the first claim is valid, he will not need the second claim, the scope of which lies wholly within the scope of the first. An infringer could not violate the second claim without infringing the first claim as well. While prosecuting the application before the PTO, however, it is impossible to know whether the first claim may, inadvertently, cover a vehicle design that appears in prior

---

26. We are using the term "literature" in the loose sense of all things mentioned in 35 U.S.C. § 102, *viz*, things offered for sale in the United States, things in public use in the United States, things described in prior patents and printed publications, and things built by others in the United States before the applicant-client's invention date.

28. This is a dependent claim. It depends, or hangs, from claim one. It is deemed by statute to have all the limitations (features) recited in claim one, plus the brake. See 35 U.S.C. § 112 (1994), which provides that "[a] claim in dependent form shall be construed to incorporate by reference all the limitations of the claim to which it refers." *Id.* § 112 (1994). This claim could just as well be written in independent form, writing out all the language of claim one plus the brake. Thus, dependent claims merely provide a shorthand notation form, with no substantive difference over writing the claim limitations out longhand.

literature about which the inventor is presently ignorant. Searches are, in many instances, not reliable to ferret out the most pertinent prior art.

Further, the lawyer does not want his client to be without any patent protection if the first claim is later invalidated in a court proceeding. For instance, if the unknown prior vehicle didn't have any brakes, the "brake" limitation of claim two could serve to distinguish that claim from the vehicle described in the prior literature. Claim two thus may be patentable even if the first claim is not. Commercially, once the client's car with brakes comes on the market, it is unlikely that a competitor could successfully market a car without brakes. Therefore, the competitor would be within the valid second claim and could be sued for infringement of that claim.

In the same vein, a third claim will be added, which might read as follows:

3. The vehicle of claim 2, further comprising:

   (a) a transmission connected between said engine and said wheel;

   (b) a pair of lights on the front of said body and a pair of lights on the rear of said body;

   (c) a plurality of doors in said body; and

   (d) a second brake, attached to another of said wheels;

   (e) and wherein said engine is an eight-cylinder engine.

The third claim is very narrow in scope, just short of what would reduce the patent coverage to a trivial level. The more technologically sophisticated the claim becomes, with many features recited, the narrower its scope and the easier the claim becomes to design around. However, a claim with all these limitations is more likely to be held valid, even when a court finds claims one and two to be invalid over the fully developed prior literature. If there is no such literature, the patent owner will never need this narrower claim. Additionally, the lawyer did not include an automatic transmission in the third claim. Although this would have made the claim still narrower, and hence even safer from attack, he is not allowed to recite in the claim any feature that is not disclosed in the disclosure portion of the patent application.

* * *

The rules about claim scope work readily enough in mechanical and electrical cases. For inventions in those fields, it is said that a single embodiment or design disclosed in a client's patent application will support a claim of any breadth. The only limit on scope is what the prior literature will allow. A claim is not allowed to have such breadth that it covers a configuration appearing in the prior literature. If it does include such a design, the entire claim is invalid and the patent owner will have to rely on her narrower claims for protection.

For broad claims involving the unpredictable arts such as chemistry or biochemistry, case law has traditionally held that more disclosure is needed, typically in the form of representative examples within the broad generic claim, or some form of direction on how to make other operable species within the claim. Although variations in the structure of a mechanical or electrical device, once imagined, are thought to lead to predictable performance characteristics, the same cannot be said of chemical or biochemical reactions. These are thought to be unpredictable in their performance or in the techniques needed for making them and, for that reason, the enablement provision of the statute is not satisfied by a single example within the genus claimed. However, in all other respects the availability of broad, generic claim language exists for all types of technologies.

In modern patent law, it is only *claims* that are allowed or rejected by examiners of the PTO, are later held valid or invalid by courts, and are capable of being infringed. Therefore, the entirety of patent law centers around these carefully crafted sets of words.

* * *

2. Patent Prosecution and Related Procedures

An application for patent consists of 1) a written specification, which describes the invention and sets forth claims at the end, as required under Patent Act § 112; 2) an oath or declaration stating (among other things) that the applicant believes herself to be the original and first inventor of the subject matter; 3) drawings, where required; and 4) the filing fee. The applicant's filing date is the date on which the PTO receives the specification and any required drawing. 35 U.S.C. § 111(a).

Inventors who wish to obtain an early filing date, but are unable or do not wish to make a full filing, may file a "provisional application." To make a provisional application, the inventor must file a written description of the invention, and drawings, but need not submit claims or an oath. The provisional application is not examined on its merits, and the filing fee is significantly lower than the fee for non-provisional applications. Once the applicant has filed a provisional application, she has up to twelve months to file a non-provisional application, complete with claims. Once it is filed, the non-provisional application receives the benefit of the earlier, provisional application filing date,[27] and proceeds to examination. 35 U.S.C. § 111(b).

The application is assigned for examination to the PTO examining group that works with the area of technology most nearly related to the claimed invention. The assigned examiner searches U.S. and foreign

---

27. A patent endures for a term of 20 years measured from the filing date. The filing date used for purposes of measuring the term is the non-provisional application filing date, not the provisional filing date. This gives strictly domestic applicants an advantage similar to the advantage that foreign applicants get under the Paris Convention when they rely on their earlier foreign filing date as their official U.S. filing date. (In that case, the foreign applicant's U.S. patent term is measured from the actual U.S. filing date, not from the claimed foreign filing date.)

patent documents and other available published literature to determine whether the claimed invention is novel and non-obvious, and studies the application for compliance with all of the legal requirements set forth in the Patent Act and the PTO rules of practice. The examiner notifies the applicant in writing of his initial decision. (This notification is called the first "office action," and generally will occur within 14 months.) If the initial decision is adverse, the notice states the reasons, and provides information or references to assist the applicant in evaluating whether to continue prosecuting the application. It is not uncommon for some or all of an applicant's claims to be rejected in the first office action. Relatively few applications are allowed as initially claimed. U.S. Patent and Trademark Office, General Information Concerning Patents (2005).[28]

As a result of amendments to Patent Act § 122, which became effective in 2000, a non-provisional utility patent application generally will be published during the course of the examination process—eighteen months after its earliest filing date.[29] However, the applicant may request that the application not be published if the applicant certifies that she has not and will not file an application to patent the invention in another country (or pursuant to an international agreement) that requires publication. Most other countries do publish applications 18 months after they are filed. Thus, § 122(b) essentially provides that if the applicant is not subjecting herself to publication by filing abroad, she can avoid having her domestic application published, and retain the trade secrecy status of the invention up to the point that the patent is issued (or if the application ultimately is rejected, indefinitely). What are the advantages of publishing applications 18 months after their filing date?

After being rejected in the first office action, the applicant may request reconsideration in writing, pointing out any alleged errors in the examiner's action, and responding to the examiner's objections. She may also amend the application, pointing out why she thinks the amended claims are patentable in view of the prior art the examiner cited in his initial rejection. After the applicant's reply, the examiner will reconsider the application and notify her of his determination, as in the first office action. This second office action usually will be made final. PTO, General Information, *supra*. If the patent application is found allowable, the PTO notifies the applicant. The applicant must then pay an issue fee. The patent is issued either to the applicant or her assignee, and the patent file is opened to the public. The patentee must pay periodic maintenance fees to maintain the patent in force. *Id.*

An applicant may appeal rejection to the Board of Patent Appeals and Interferences. The Board of Patent Appeals and Interferences consists of the Under Secretary of Commerce for Intellectual Property and Director of the United States Patent and Trademark Office, the Deputy Under

---

28.   This publication can be found on the PTO's web site: http://www.uspto.gov.

29.   The publication provisions took effect on November 29, 2000, and apply to all patent applications filed thereafter. Applications pending on the effective date could be published if the applicant so requested.

Secretary of Commerce for Intellectual Property and Deputy Director of the United States Patent and Trademark Office, the Commissioner for Patents, and a number of administrative patent judges. (Normally an appeal is heard by only three members.) As an alternative to appeal, when an applicant desires consideration of different claims or further evidence, she may file a continuation application. A continuation application is essentially a new application. However, if it is filed before expiration of the period for appeal, makes specific reference to the earlier application, and complies with other requirements, the continuation application will be entitled to the earlier application's filing date. *Id.*

If the Board of Patent Appeals and Interferences decides the applicant's appeal adversely to the applicant, she may appeal the decision directly, on the record generated in the PTO, to the Court of Appeals for the Federal Circuit.[30] 35 U.S.C. § 141. Alternatively, she may file a civil action against the Commissioner of Patents in the United States District Court for the District of Columbia, and obtain *de novo* review of the PTO's decision.[31] 35 U.S.C. § 145.

Interferences

Sometimes two or more applications are filed claiming substantially the same patentable invention. Since only one applicant/inventor may obtain a patent for the invention, the PTO will institute a proceeding, called an "interference," to determine which of the inventors was the first and thus is entitled to the patent. Interference proceedings may also arise between an application and a patent already issued, if the application was filed within a year of the issued patent's issuance and/or publication, and the conflicting application is not barred for some other reason. 35 U.S.C. § 135. The PTO estimates that about one percent of patent applications become involved in an interference proceeding. U.S. Patent and Trademark Office, General Information Concerning Patents, *supra.*

The question of priority will be determined by the Board of Patent Appeals and Interferences, based on evidence submitted by the parties. Interference proceedings are notoriously complex and expensive. The losing party may appeal to the Court of Appeals for the Federal Circuit or file a civil action against the winning party in the district court.

Reissuance

When an issued patent is defective in its specification or drawing, or because the patentee claimed more or less than he had a right to claim,

---

30. In Dickinson v. Zurko, 527 U.S. 150, 119 S.Ct. 1816, 144 L.Ed.2d 143 (1999), the United States Supreme Court addressed the standard of review that the court of appeals for the Federal Circuit should use in reviewing the PTO's findings of fact in denying an application. The Supreme Court held that when the patent applicant appeals directly to the court of appeals on the record, the court of appeals must apply the standard set forth in the Administrative Procedure Act. Under this standard, the court of appeals may only set aside PTO fact findings if they are arbitrary, capricious, or an abuse of discretion, or if they are unsupported by substantial evidence.

31. If the applicant opts to obtain *de novo* review of the PTO rejection in the U.S. District Court for the District of Columbia, any appeal from that review will go to the Court of Appeals for the Federal Circuit. However, in this case, the court of appeals will apply the "clearly erroneous" standard in reviewing the district court's fact findings.

and the defect is attributable to unintentional error, the patentee may request a reissue of the patent in corrected form. (No reissued patent can be granted enlarging the scope of the original claims unless applied for within two years after the original patent grant.) The reissued patent will be good for the remaining unexpired portion of the original patent's term. 35 U.S.C. § 251. Other means of correcting mistakes in the original patent are described at 35 U.S.C. §§ 254–256.

Assignments and Licenses

A patent is a form of personal property and may be assigned, bequeathed by will, or pass to the owner's heirs through intestate succession. Applications for patent, issued patents, and interests in patents can be assigned through a written instrument. The PTO records assignments sent to it for recording, and the recording serves as notice. An assignment will be void against a subsequent purchaser for valuable consideration without notice, unless it is recorded in the PTO within three months of its date or prior to the date of the subsequent purchase. 35 U.S.C. § 261.

NOTES AND QUESTIONS

1. *The Patent Bar.* Any lawyer who is qualified to practice in the federal courts may represent clients in patent litigation. However, the PTO regulates who may represent clients in patent prosecutions. Both lawyers and non-lawyers may be eligible. To qualify, one must pass a rigorous written examination administered by the PTO, which tests knowledge of the substance and procedure of patent practice. To sit for this exam, one must generally demonstrate a substantial number of college course credits in engineering, a range of physical sciences, or computer science. Persons registered to practice before the PTO who are not lawyers are known as patent agents. Those who are lawyers are called patent attorneys. The specific requirements for PTO registration as a patent attorney are set forth at 37 C.F.R. §§ 11.5–11.8.

2. *Reexamination.* There is little opportunity for interested third parties who oppose the granting of a patent to influence the PTO's initial patentability decision. Generally such persons must wait and challenge the validity of the patent once it is issued. This may be done as a defense against a patent infringement claim or in a declaratory judgment action, if standing requirements are satisfied. For those wishing to avoid the burden of litigation, an administrative alternative is available pursuant to the reexamination provisions in Patent Act §§ 302–18.

Section 302 provides that any person may request that the validity of an issued patent claim be reexamined in light of prior art patents or printed publications. If the Commissioner of Patents determines that the request raises a substantial question of patentability that was not considered in the course of the patent application process, he must issue an order for reexamination to resolve the question.

At this point the patent owner may file a statement addressing the issues raised. She may propose amendments or new claims to distinguish her invention from the prior art (though she may not thus enlarge the scope of a disputed claim). The person requesting the reexamination may reply. Upon termination of the reexamination and any appeals by the patentee, the Commissioner will issue and publish a certificate canceling any claims determined to be unpatentable, confirming any claims determined to be patentable, and incorporating in the patent any proposed amended or new claims that have been determined to be patentable.

The Commissioner may commence a reexamination at his own initiative. Note also that the patentee may herself request a reexamination. Why might a patentee wish to do so?

How useful an alternative to litigation does the reexamination procedure described above provide to third parties wishing to challenge an issued patent? It has been suggested that the *ex parte* nature of the reexamination procedure, which limits the third party's opportunity to argue his position, discourages use of reexamination requests as an alternative to court challenges. See, e.g., Advisory Commission on Patent Law Reform, A Report to the Secretary of Commerce, 117–123 (1992).

In response to this criticism, in 1999, Congress enacted an alternative, or optional *inter partes* reexamination procedure, which is codified at Patent Act §§ 311–18. Under these provisions, as later amended, a third party requesting *inter partes* reexamination is entitled to receive a copy of all documents filed by the patentee and all communications from the PTO to the patentee during the course of the reexamination. Each time that the patentee files a response to an action on the merits from the PTO, the third-party requestor has the right to file written comments addressing the issues raised by the Office or the patentee's response. The requestor also may appeal a decision favorable to the patentee to the Board of Patent Appeals and Interferences, and subsequently to the Court of Appeals for the Federal Circuit. However, once the patentability issues raised by the third-party requestor have been resolved against the requestor under this procedure, he is estopped from raising them (or other issues that might have been raised in the reexamination) in a subsequent civil action.

This new procedure has not proven to be as popular as was hoped. As the PTO has explained:

> Patentees insisted upon, and Congress legislated via the 1999 statute, that a challenger in an *inter partes* proceeding would be bound by its result by way of estoppel, including in subsequent litigation. However, the lack of such procedural mechanisms as discovery and cross-examination that would be available in litigation has apparently resulted in challengers being unwilling to invoke *inter partes* reexamination and risk its estoppel effect.

United States Patent and Trademark Office, *Report to Congress on Inter Partes Reexamination*, Executive Summary, *reprinted in* 69 Pat. Trademark & Copyright J. (B.N.A.) 204 (2004). In addition,

> The filing of an *inter partes* reexamination request is only applicable to patents that were issued from patent applications which were filed on or after enactment of the *inter partes* reexamination on November 29, 1999. All issued patents and all patent applications that were pending prior to

enactment (and subsequently issued as a patent) are excluded from eligibility for *inter partes* reexamination.

Id. The PTO has advocated creation of a new, more flexible and comprehensive post-grant administrative review process, somewhat similar to the post-grant opposition proceedings presently provided by the European Patent Office and the Japanese Patent Office. Under such an opposition system, for a limited time after a patent is granted, third parties could challenge the patent's validity on a wide range of substantive grounds in a proceeding before administrative judges, with closely controlled discovery and cross-examination. United States Patent and Trademark Office, *21st Century Strategic Plan* (2002). There has been considerable support for such a post-grant opposition procedure, although supporters have differed considerably over the details.

3. *The Patent Term.* Review the language of Patent Act § 154. The United States had for many years granted a term of 17 years for utility patents, measured from the date the patent issued. In 1994, Congress amended § 154 to substitute a term of 20 years, measured from the earliest U.S. patent application filing date. The United States' acceptance of the TRIPs Agreement necessitated the change. There was significant resistance to measuring the patent term from the application date due to fear that this would decrease the term whenever the application process took over 3 years. To ensure equitable treatment, the amendment provided for restoration of time lost from delays attributable to national security concerns, interference proceedings, or successful appeals of PTO decisions. The new term became effective for patents granted on applications filed after June 8, 1995. Under a transition provision, patents in existence on June 8, 1995 or granted on applications filed prior to that date endure for the longer of 17 years from issuance or 20 years from application date. See 35 U.S.C.A. § 154(c).

Even though the TRIPs amendments *measure* the patent term from the patent application date, patent protection *commences* upon patent issuance, as was the case prior to the amendments. In 1999, Congress further amended the Patent Act to provide that most patent applications will be published 18 months after their earliest filing date, and that patentees will enjoy limited, "provisional" rights against infringement during the period between publication and issuance. See 35 U.S.C. § 154(d). These provisional rights will be discussed more fully *infra*.

In the same 1999 amendments, Congress undertook to guarantee that patentees will enjoy *at least* 17 years of protection under the 20–years–from–filing term measure implemented in 1994. Congress provided (subject to certain exceptions and limitations) that the PTO *must* grant a patent within three years of the patent's U.S. filing date. For each day the PTO delays beyond the three-year period, a day will be added to the end of the patentee's term. However, the additional period will be reduced by any period of time in which the patentee failed to engage in reasonable efforts to conclude prosecution. This is to prevent patent applicants from using the term guarantee provisions strategically. See 35 U.S.C.A. § 154(b).

E. THE PATENTEE'S RIGHTS

1. The Right to Exclude Others From Directly Infringing the Patent

DEEPSOUTH PACKING CO., INC. v. LAITRAM CORP.

Supreme Court of the United States, 1972.
406 U.S. 518, 92 S.Ct. 1700, 32 L.Ed.2d 273.

MR. JUSTICE WHITE delivered the opinion of the Court.

* * * Petitioner and respondent both hold patents on machines that devein shrimp more cheaply and efficiently than competing machinery or hand labor can do the job. Extensive litigation below has established that respondent, the Laitram Corp., has the superior claim and that the distribution and use of petitioner Deepsouth's machinery in this country should be enjoined to prevent infringement of Laitram's patents. We granted certiorari to consider a related question: Is Deepsouth, barred from the American market by Laitram's patents, also foreclosed by the patent laws from exporting its deveiners, in less than fully assembled form, for use abroad?

I

A rudimentary understanding of the patents in dispute is a prerequisite to comprehending the legal issue presented. The District Court determined that the Laitram Corp. held two valid patents for machinery used in the process of deveining shrimp. One, granted in 1954, accorded Laitram rights over a "slitter" which exposed the veins of shrimp by using water pressure and gravity to force the shrimp down an inclined trough studded with razor blades. As the shrimp descend through the trough their backs are slit by the blades or other knife-like objects arranged in a zig-zag pattern. The second patent, granted in 1958, covers a "tumbler," "a device to mechanically remove substantially all veins from shrimp whose backs have previously been slit," by the machines described in the 1954 patent. This invention uses streams of water to carry slit shrimp into and then out of a revolving drum fabricated from commercial sheet metal. As shrimp pass through the drum the hooked "lips" of the punched metal, "projecting at an acute angle from the supporting member and having a smooth rounded free edge for engaging beneath the vein of a shrimp and for wedging the vein between the lip and the supporting member," engage the veins and remove them.

Both the slitter and the tumbler are combination patents; that is,

> [n]one of the parts referred to are new, and none are claimed as new; nor is any portion of the combination less than the whole claimed as new, or stated to produce any given result. The end in view is proposed to be accomplished by the union of all, arranged and combined together in the manner described. And this combination,

composed of all the parts mentioned in the specification, and arranged with reference to each other, and to other parts of the (machine) in the manner therein described, is stated to be the improvement and is the thing patented. *Prouty v. Ruggles*, 16 Pet. 336, 341, 10 L.Ed. 985 (1842).

The slitter's elements as recited in Laitram's patent claim were: an inclined trough, a "knife" (actually, knives) positioned in the trough, and a means (water sprayed from jets) to move the shrimp down the trough. The tumbler's elements include a "lip," a "support member," and a "means" (water thrust from jets). As is usual in combination patents, none of the elements in either of these patents were themselves patentable at the time of the patent, nor are they now. The means in both inventions, moving water, was and is, of course, commonplace. (It is not suggested that Deepsouth infringed Laitram's patents by its use of water jets.) The cutting instruments and inclined troughs used in slitters were and are commodities available for general use. The structure of the lip and support member in the tumbler were hardly novel: Laitram concedes that the inventors merely adapted punched metal sheets ordered from a commercial catalog in order to perfect their invention. The patents were warranted not by the novelty of their elements but by the novelty of the combination they represented. Invention was recognized because Laitram's assignors combined ordinary elements in an extraordinary way—a novel union of old means was designed to achieve new ends. * * *

II

The lower court's decision that Laitram held valid combination patents entitled the corporation to the privileges bestowed by 35 U.S.C. § 154, the keystone provision of the patent code. "[F]or the term of seventeen years" from the date of the patent, Laitram had "the right to exclude others from making, using, or selling the invention throughout the United States...." The § 154 right in turn provides the basis for affording the patentee an injunction against direct, induced, and contributory infringement, 35 U.S.C. § 283, or an award of damages when such infringement has already occurred, 35 U.S.C. § 284. Infringement is defined by 35 U.S.C. § 271 in terms that follow those of § 154:

> "(a) Except as otherwise provided in this title, whoever without authority makes, uses or sells any patented invention, within the United States during the term of the patent therefor, [directly] infringes the patent.

> "(b) Whoever actively induces infringement of a patent shall be liable as an infringer.

> "(c) Whoever sells a component of a patented machine, manufacture, combination or composition, or a material or apparatus for use in practicing a patented process, constituting a material part of the invention, knowing the same to be especially made or especially adapted for use in an infringement of such patent, and not a staple

article or commodity of commerce suitable for substantial noninfringing use, shall be liable as a contributory infringer.''

As a result of these provisions the judgment of Laitram's patent superiority forecloses Deepsouth and its customers from any future use (other than a use approved by Laitram or occurring after the Laitram patent has expired) of its deveiners "throughout the United States." The patent provisions taken in conjunction with the judgment below also entitle Laitram to the injunction it has received prohibiting Deepsouth from continuing to "make" or, once made, to "sell" deveiners "throughout the United States." Further, Laitram may recover damages for any past unauthorized use, sale, or making "throughout the United States." This much is not disputed.

But Deepsouth argues that it is not liable for every type of past sale and that a portion of its future business is salvageable. Section 154 and related provisions obviously are intended to grant a patentee a monopoly only over the United States market; they are not intended to grant a patentee the bonus of a favored position as a flagship company free of American competition in international commerce. Deepsouth, itself barred from using its deveining machines, or from inducing others to use them "throughout the United States," barred also from making and selling the machines in the United States, seeks to make the parts of deveining machines, to sell them to foreign buyers, and to have the buyers assemble the parts and use the machines abroad.[5] Accordingly, Deepsouth seeks judicial approval, expressed through a modification or interpretation of the injunction against it, for continuing its practice of shipping deveining equipment to foreign customers in three separate boxes, each containing only parts of the $1\frac{3}{4}$–ton machines, yet the whole assemblable in less than one hour. The company contends that by this means both the "making" and the "use" of the machines occur abroad and Laitram's lawful monopoly over the making and use of the machines throughout the United States is not infringed.

Laitram counters that this course of conduct is based upon a hypertechnical reading of the patent code that, if tolerated, will deprive it of its right to the fruits of the inventive genius of its assignors. * * * Deepsouth in all respects save final assembly of the parts "makes" the invention. It does so with the intent of having the foreign user effect the combination without Laitram's permission. Deepsouth sells these components as though they were the machines themselves; the act of assembly is regarded, indeed advertised, as of no importance.

* * * The District Court held that its injunction should not be read as prohibiting export of the elements of a combination patent even when

5. Deepsouth is entirely straightforward in indicating that its course of conduct is motivated by a desire to avoid patent infringement. Its president wrote a Brazilian customer: "We are handicapped by a decision against us in the United States. This was a very technical decision and we can manufacture the entire machine without any complication in the United States, with the exception that there are two parts that must not be assembled in the United States, but assembled after the machine arrives in Brazil."

those elements could and predictably would be combined to form the whole.

> "It may be urged that ... [this] result is not logical ... But it is founded on twin notions that underlie the patent laws. One is that a combination patent protects only the combination. The other is that monopolies—even those conferred by patents—are not viewed with favor. These are logic enough."

The Court of Appeals for the Fifth Circuit reversed, thus departing from the established rules of the Second, Third, and Seventh Circuits. In the Fifth Circuit panel's opinion, those courts that previously considered the question "worked themselves into ... a conceptual box" by adopting "an artificial, technical construction" of the patent laws, a construction, moreover, which in the opinion of the panel, "[subverted] the Constitutional scheme of promoting 'the Progress of Science and useful Arts' by allowing an intrusion on a patentee's rights."

III

We disagree with the Court of Appeals for the Fifth Circuit. Under the common law the inventor had no right to exclude others from making and using his invention. If Laitram has a right to suppress Deepsouth's export trade it must be derived from its patent grant, and thus from the patent statute. We find that 35 U.S.C. § 271, the provision of the patent laws on which Laitram relies, does not support its claim.

Certainly if Deepsouth's conduct were intended to lead to use of patented deveiners inside the United States its production and sales activity would be subject to injunction as an induced or contributory infringement. But it is established that there can be no contributory infringement without the fact or intention of a direct infringement. "In a word, if there is no [direct] infringement of a patent there can be no contributory infringer." * * *

The statute makes it clear that it is not an infringement to make or use a patented product outside of the United States. 35 U.S.C. § 271. Thus, in order to secure the injunction it seeks, Laitram must show a § 271(a) direct infringement by Deepsouth in the United States, that is, that Deepsouth "makes," "uses," or "sells" the patented product within the bounds of this country.

Laitram does not suggest that Deepsouth "uses" the machines. Its argument that Deepsouth sells the machines—based primarily on Deepsouth's sales rhetoric and related indicia such as price[9]—cannot carry the day unless it can be shown that Deepsouth is selling the "patented invention." The sales question thus resolves itself into the question of manufacture: did Deepsouth "make" (and then sell) something cognizable

---

9. Deepsouth sold the less than completely assembled machine for the same price as it had sold fully assembled machines. Its advertisements, correspondence, and invoices frequently referred to a "machine," rather than to a kit or unassembled parts.

under the patent law as the patented invention, or did it "make" (and then sell) something that fell short of infringement?

The Court of Appeals, believing that the word "makes" should be accorded "a construction in keeping with the ordinary meaning of that term," held against Deepsouth on the theory that "makes" "means what it ordinarily connotes—the substantial manufacture of the constituent parts of the machine." Passing the question of whether this definition more closely corresponds to the ordinary meaning of the term than that offered by Judge Swan in *Andrea* 35 years earlier (something is made when it reaches the state of final "operable" assembly), we find the Fifth Circuit's definition unacceptable because it collides head on with a line of decisions so firmly embedded in our patent law as to be unassailable absent a congressional recasting of the statute.

We cannot endorse the view that the "substantial manufacture of the constituent parts of [a] machine" constitutes direct infringement when we have so often held that a combination patent protects only against the operable assembly of the whole and not the manufacture of its parts. "For as we pointed out in *Mercoid v. Mid–Continent Investment Co.*, 320 U.S. 661, 676, 64 S.Ct. 268, 276, a patent on a combination is a patent on the assembled or functioning whole, not on the separate parts." *Mercoid Corp. v. Minneapolis–Honeywell Regulator Co.*, 320 U.S. 680, 684, 64 S.Ct. 278, 280 (1944). See also *Leeds & Catlin Co. v. Victor Talking Machine Co.*, 213 U.S. 301, 29 S.Ct. 495, 53 L.Ed. 805:

> "A combination is a union of elements, which may be partly old and partly new, or wholly old or wholly new. But whether new or old, the combination is a means—an invention—distinct from them." *Id.*, at 318, 29 S.Ct., at 500.

* * * In sum,

> "[i]f anything is settled in the patent law, it is that the combination patent covers only the totality of the elements in the claim and that no element, separately viewed, is within the grant." *Aro Mfg. Co. v. Convertible Top Replacement Co.*, 365 U.S. 336, 344, 81 S.Ct. 599, 604, 5 L.Ed.2d 592 (1961).

It was this basic tenet of the patent system that led Judge Swan to hold in the leading case, *Radio Corp. of America v. Andrea*, 79 F.2d 626 (C.A.2 1935), that unassembled export of the elements of an invention did not infringe the patent.

> "[The] relationship is the essence of the patent.
>
> " . . . No wrong is done the patentee until the combination is formed. His monopoly does not cover the manufacture or sale of separate elements capable of being, but never actually, associated to form the invention. Only when such association is made is there a direct infringement of his monopoly, and not even then if it is done

outside the territory for which the monopoly was granted." *Id.*, at 628.

* * *

We reaffirm this conclusion today.

IV

It is said that this conclusion is derived from too narrow and technical an interpretation of the statute, and that this Court should focus on the constitutional mandate

> "[t]o promote the Progress of Science and useful Arts, by securing for limited Times to Authors and Inventors the exclusive Right to their respective Writings and Discoveries . . . ," Art. I, § 8,

and construe the statute in a manner that would, allegedly, better reflect the policy of the Framers.

We cannot accept this argument. The direction of Art. I is that *Congress* shall have the power to promote the progress of science and the useful arts. When, as here, the Constitution is permissive, the sign of how far Congress has chosen to go can come only from Congress. We are here construing the provisions of a statute passed in 1952. The prevailing law in this and other courts as to what is necessary to show a patentable invention when a combination of old elements is claimed was clearly evident from the cases when the Act was passed; and at that time *Andrea*, representing a specific application of the law of infringement with respect to the export of elements of a combination patent, was 17 years old. When Congress drafted § 271, it gave no indication that it desired to change either the law of combination patents as relevant here or the ruling of *Andrea*. Nor has it on any more recent occasion indicated that it wanted the patent privilege to run farther than it was understood to run for 35 years prior to the action of the Court of Appeals for the Fifth Circuit.

Moreover, we must consider petitioner's claim in light of this Nation's historical antipathy to monopoly and of repeated congressional efforts to preserve and foster competition. As this Court recently said without dissent:

> "[I]n rewarding useful invention, the 'rights and welfare of the community must be fairly dealt with and effectually guarded.' *Kendall v. Winsor*, 21 How. 322, 329, 16 L.Ed. 165 (1859). To that end the prerequisites to obtaining a patent are strictly observed, and when the patent has issued the limitations on its exercise are equally strictly enforced." *Sears, Roebuck & Co. v. Stiffel Co.*, 376 U.S. 225, 230, 84 S.Ct. 784, 788, 11 L.Ed.2d 661 (1964).

It follows that we should not expand patent rights by overruling or modifying our prior cases construing the patent statutes, unless the argument for expansion of privilege is based on more than mere inference from ambiguous statutory language. We would require a clear and certain signal from Congress before approving the position of a litigant who, as respondent here, argues that the beachhead of privilege is wider, and the area of public use narrower, than courts had previously thought. No such signal legitimizes respondent's position in this litigation.

In conclusion, we note that what is at stake here is the right of American companies to compete with an American patent holder in foreign markets. Our patent system makes no claim to extraterritorial effect; "these acts of Congress do not, and were not intended to, operate beyond the limits of the United States," *Brown v. Duchesne*, 19 How., at 195, 15 L.Ed. 595 (1856), and we correspondingly reject the claims of others to such control over our markets. To the degree that the inventor needs protection in markets other than those of this country, the wording of 35 U.S.C. §§ 154 and 271 reveals a congressional intent to have him seek it abroad through patents secured in countries where his goods are being used. Respondent holds foreign patents; it does not adequately explain why it does not avail itself of them.

V

In sum: the case and statutory law resolves this case against the respondent. When so many courts have so often held what appears so evident—a combination patent can be infringed only by combination—we are not prepared to break the mold and begin anew. And were the matter not so resolved, we would still insist on a clear congressional indication of intent to extend the patent privilege before we could recognize the monopoly here claimed. Such an indication is lacking. * * *

MR. JUSTICE BLACKMUN, with whom THE CHIEF JUSTICE, MR. JUSTICE POWELL, and MR. JUSTICE REHNQUIST join, dissenting.

* * *

* * * I do not see how one can escape the conclusion that the Deepsouth machine was *made* in the United States, within the meaning of the protective language of §§ 154 and 271(a). The situation, perhaps, would be different were parts, or even only one vital part, manufactured abroad. Here everything was accomplished in this country except putting the pieces together as directed (an operation that, as Deepsouth represented to its Brazilian prospect, would take "less than one hour"), all much as the fond father does with his little daughter's doll house on Christmas Eve. To say that such assembly, accomplished abroad, is not the prohibited combination and that it avoids the restrictions of our patent law, is a bit too much for me. The Court has opened the way to deny the holder of the United States combination patent the benefits of his invention with respect to sales to foreign purchasers.

* * *

By a process of only the most rigid construction, the Court, by its decision today, fulfills what Judge Clark, in his able opinion for the Fifth Circuit, distressingly forecast:

"To hold otherwise [as the Court does today] would subvert the Constitutional scheme of promoting 'the Progress of Science and useful Arts, by securing for limited Times to Authors and Inventors the exclusive Right to their respective Writings and Discoveries.' U.S. Const., art. I § 8 Cl. 8. It would allow an infringer to set up shop next door to a patent-protected inventor whose product enjoys a substantial foreign market and deprive him of this valuable business. If this Constitutional protection is to be fully effectuated, it must extend to an infringer who manufactures in the United States and then captures the foreign markets from the patentee. The Constitutional mandate cannot be limited to just manufacturing and selling within the United States. The infringer would then be allowed to reap the fruits of the American economy—technology, labor, materials, etc.— but would not be subject to the responsibilities of the American patent laws. We cannot permit an infringer to enjoy these benefits and then be allowed to strip away a portion of the patentee's protection."

I share the Fifth Circuit's concern and I therefore dissent.

PAPER CONVERTING MACHINE CO.
v. MAGNA–GRAPHICS CORP.

United States Court of Appeals, Federal Circuit, 1984.
745 F.2d 11.

Nichols, Senior Circuit Judge.

[This appeal is from a judgment of the United States District Court awarding plaintiff Paper Converting damages for patent infringement.]

I

Although the technology involved here is complex, the end product is one familiar to most Americans. The patented invention relates to a machine used to manufacture rolls of densely wound ("hard-wound") industrial toilet tissue and paper toweling. The machine, commonly known as an automatic rewinder, unwinds a paper web continuously under high tension at speeds up to 2,000 feet per minute from a large-diameter paper roll—known as the parent roll or bedroll—and simultaneously rewinds it onto paperboard cores to form individual consumer products.

Before the advent of automatic rewinders, toilet tissue and paper towel producers used "stop-start" rewinders. With these machines, the entire rewinding operation had to cease after a retail-sized "log" was finished so that a worker could place a new mandrel (the shaft for carrying the paperboard core) in the path of the paper web. In an effort to increase production, automatic rewinders were introduced in the early 1950's. These machines automatically moved a new mandrel into the path of the paper web while the machine was still winding the paper web onto another mandrel, and could operate at a steady pace at speeds up to about 1,200 feet per minute.

In 1962, Nystrand, Bradley, and Spencer invented the first successful "sequential" automatic rewinder, a machine which not only overcame previous speed limitations, but also could handle two-ply tissue. This rewinder simultaneously cut the paper web and impaled it on pins against the parent roll. Then, after a new mandrel was automatically moved into place, a "pusher" would move the paper web away from the parent roll and against a glue-covered paperboard core to begin winding a new paper log.

On April 20, 1965, United States Patent No. 3,179,348 (the '348 patent) issued, giving to Paper Converting (to whom rights in the invention had been assigned) patent protection for machines incorporating the sequential rewinding approach. On September 1, 1972, Paper Converting applied to have the claims of the '348 patent narrowed by reissue, and on March 4, 1975, United States Patent No. Re. 28,353 (the '353 patent) issued on this application. The '353 patent, like the original '348 patent on which it is based, received an expiration date of April 20, 1982. Claim 1 of the '353 patent defines the improvement in the web-winding apparatus as an improvement comprising:

> (C) means for transversely severing said web to provide a free leading edge on said web for approaching a mandrel on which said web is to be wound in said path, and

> (D) pin means extensibly mounted on said roll for maintaining a web portion spaced from said edge in contact with said roll, and pusher means extensibly mounted on said roll to urge said maintained web portion against an adjacent mandrel.

Paper Converting achieved widespread commercial success with its patented automatic rewinder. Although there are not many domestic producers of toilet tissue and paper toweling, Paper Converting has sold more than 500 machines embodying the invention.

In 1979, Paper Converting brought the present action against Magna–Graphics for infringement of the '353 patent. After a trial concerning only issues of liability, the district court held the '353 patent valid and found it willfully infringed. * * *

[The district court found that Magna–Graphics had made two sales of infringing rewinders and associated equipment: one to the Fort Howard Paper Company (Fort Howard) under circumstances to be described, and one to the Scott Paper Company (Scott).]

III

A.

Magna–Graphics * * * argues that it should bear no liability whatsoever for its manufacture, sale, or delivery of the Fort Howard rewinder because that machine was never *completed* during the life of the '353 patent. We disagree.

In early 1980 Fort Howard became interested in purchasing a new high-speed rewinder line. Both Paper Converting and Magna–Graphics offered bids. Because Magna–Graphics offered to provide an entire rewinder line for about 10 percent less than did Paper Converting, it won the contract. Delivery would have been before the '353 patent expired. Magna–Graphics began to build the contracted for machinery, but before it completed the rewinder, on February 26, 1981, the federal district court in Wisconsin determined that a similar Magna–Graphics' rewinder built for and sold to Scott infringed the '353 patent. The court enjoined Magna–Graphics from any future infringing activity.

Because at the time of the federal injunction the rewinder intended for Fort Howard was only 80 percent complete, Magna–Graphics sought a legal way to fulfill its contract with Fort Howard rather than abandon its machine. First, Magna–Graphics tried to change the construction of the rewinder so as to avoid infringement. It submitted to Paper Converting's counsel three drawings illustrating three proposed changes, and asked for an opinion as to whether the changes would avoid infringement. Paper Converting's counsel replied, however, that until a fully built and operating machine could be viewed, no opinion could be given. Magna–Graphics, believing such a course of action unfeasible because of the large risks in designing, engineering, and building a machine without knowing whether it would be considered an infringement, instead negotiated with Fort Howard to delay the final assembly and delivery of an otherwise infringing rewinder until after the '353 patent expired in April 1982.

Magna–Graphics thereafter continued to construct the Fort Howard machine, all the while staying in close consultation with its counsel. After finishing substantially all of the machine, Magna–Graphics tested it to ensure that its moving parts would function as intended at a rate of 1,600 feet of paper per minute. Although Magna–Graphics normally *fully* tested machines at its plant before shipment, to avoid infringement in this instance, Magna–Graphics ran its tests in two stages over a period of several weeks in July and August of 1981.

To understand Magna–Graphics' testing procedure, it is necessary to understand the automatic transfer operation of the patented machine. First, from within a 72–inch long "cutoff" roll, a 72–inch blade ejects to sever the continuous web of paper which is wound around the bedroll. Then, pins attached to the bedroll hold the severed edge of the web while pushers, also attached to the bedroll, transfer the edge of the web towards the mandrel (the roll on which the paperboard core is mounted).

In the first stage of its test, Magna–Graphics checked the bedroll to determine whether the pushers actuated properly. It installed on the bedroll two pusher pads instead of the thirty pads normally used in an operating machine. It greased the pads and operated the bedroll to determine whether the pads, when unlatched, would contact the core on the mandrel. (Magna–Graphics greased the pads so as to provide a visual indication that they had touched the core.) During this stage of tests, no cutoff blades or pins were installed.

In the second stage of the test, Magna–Graphics checked the cutoff roll to determine whether the cutting blade actuated as intended. It tested the knife actuating mechanism by installing into the cutoff roll a short 4–inch section of cutter blade rather than the 72–inch blade normally used. After taping a 4–inch wide piece of paper to the outer surface of the cutoff roll, Magna–Graphics operated the cutoff roll to determine whether the latch mechanism would eject the blade to cut the paper. During *this* phase of the testing, no pins or pusher pads were installed. At no time during the tests were the pins, pushers, and blade installed and operated together.

To further its scheme to avoid patent infringement, Magna–Graphics negotiated special shipment and assembly details with Fort Howard. Under the advice of counsel, Fort Howard and Magna–Graphics agreed that the rewinder's cutoff and transfer mechanism would not be finally assembled until April 22, 1982, two days after the expiration of the '353 patent. With this agreement in hand, Magna–Graphics shipped the basic rewinder machine to Fort Howard on September 17, 1981, and separately shipped the cutoff roll and bedroll on October 23, 1981. The rewinder machine was not assembled or installed at the Fort Howard plant until April 26, 1982.

B

With this case we are once again confronted with a situation which tests the temporal limits of the American patent grant. We must decide here the extent to which a competitor of a patentee can *manufacture* and test during the life of a patent a machine intended solely for post-patent use. Magna–Graphics asserts that no law prohibits it from soliciting orders for, *substantially* manufacturing, testing, or even delivering machinery which, if *completely* assembled during the patent term, would infringe. We notice, but Magna–Graphics adds that it is totally irrelevant, that Paper Converting has lost, during the term of its patent, a contract for the patented machine which it would have received but for the competitor's acts.

Clearly, any federal right which Paper Converting has to suppress Magna–Graphics' patent-term activities, or to receive damages for those activities, must be derived from its patent grant, and thus from the patent statutes. "Care should be taken not to extend by judicial construction the rights and privileges which it was the purpose of Congress to bestow." * * *

The disjunctive language of the patent grant gives a patentee the "right to exclude others from making, using or selling" a patented invention during the 17 years of the patent's existence. 35 U.S.C. § 154. *See also* 35 U.S.C. § 271. Congress has never deemed it necessary to define any of this triad of excludable activities, however, leaving instead the meaning of "make," "use," and "sell" for judicial interpretation. Nevertheless, by the terms of the patent grant, *no* activity other than the unauthorized making, using, or selling of the claimed invention can constitute direct infringement of a patent, *no matter* how great the adverse impact of that activity on the economic value of a patent. * * *

Here, the dispositive issue is whether Magna–Graphics engaged in the making, use, or sale of something which the law recognizes as embodying an invention protected by a patent. Magna–Graphics relies on *Deepsouth Packing Co. v. Laitram Corp.*, 406 U.S. 518, 92 S.Ct. 1700, 32 L.Ed.2d 273, 173 USPQ 769 (1972). That case dealt with a "combination patent" covering machinery for shrimp deveining. The only active issue was whether certain export sales were properly prohibited in the district court's injunction and whether damages should include compensation for past infringement by these exports. The infringer had put in effect a practice of selling the machines disassembled for export, but with the subassemblies so far advanced, and with such instructions, that the foreign consignee could put them together on receipt in operable condition with an hour's work. The Supreme Court's five to four holding that these exports did not infringe was interwoven of three strands of thought: (1) that the patent laws must be construed strictly because they create a "monopoly" in the patentee; (2) that a "combination patent" is not infringed until its elements are brought together into an "operable assembly;" and (3) that an attempt to enforce the patent against a machine assembled abroad was an attempt to give it extraterritorial application and to invade improperly the sovereignty of the country where the final assembly and the intended use occurred.

Magna–Graphics' effort to apply *Deepsouth* as precedential runs into the obvious difficulty that the element of extraterritoriality is absent here, yet it obviously was of paramount importance to the *Deepsouth* Court. We must be cautious in extending five to four decisions by analogy. The analysis of *where* infringement occurs is applicable, Magna–Graphics says, to determining *when* an infringement occurs, whether before or after a patent expires. We have not found any case that has so held, and are not cited to any. It does not at all necessarily follow, for the *Deepsouth* analysis is made to avert a result, extraterritoriality, that would not occur whatever analysis was made in the instant case.

Although in *Deepsouth* the Court at times used broad language in reaching its decision, it is clear that *Deepsouth* was intended to be narrowly construed as applicable only to the issue of the extraterritorial effect of the American patent law. The Court so implied not only in *Deepsouth* ("[A]t stake here is the right of American companies to compete with an American patent holder *in foreign markets. Our patent system makes no claim to extraterritorial effect,* * * * " 406 U.S. at 531, 92 S.Ct. at 1708, 173 USPQ at 774 (emphasis added)), but in a subsequent decision as well ("The question under consideration [in *Deepsouth*] was whether a patent is infringed when unpatented elements are assembled into the combination *outside the United States." Dawson Chemical Co. v. Rohm & Haas Co.*, 448 U.S. 176, 216, 100 S.Ct. 2601, 2623, 65 L.Ed.2d 696, 206 USPQ 385, 405 (1980) (emphasis added)). * * *

While there is thus a horror of giving extraterritorial effect to United States patent protection, there is no corresponding horror of a valid United States patent giving economic benefits not cut off entirely on patent expiration. Thus, we hold that the expansive language used in *Deepsouth* is not controlling in the present case. The facts in *Deepsouth* are *not* the facts here. Because no other precedent controls our decision here, however, we nevertheless look to *Deepsouth* and elsewhere for guidance on the issue of whether what Magna–Graphics did is an infringement of the '353 patent.

    * * *

* * * It does seem as if the concept of an "operable assembly" put forward by Justice White in his majority opinion is probably something short of a full and complete assembly; thus, if the infringer makes an "operable assembly" of the components of the patented invention, sufficient for testing, it need not be the same thing as the complete and entire invention. The other thing is, if the infringer has tested his embodiment of the invention sufficiently to satisfy him, this may be a "use," because as held in *Roche Products, Inc.*, "use" includes use for the purpose of testing. * * *

    * * *

It is undisputed that Magna–Graphics intended to finesse Paper Converting out of the sale of a machine on which Paper Converting held a valid patent during the life of that patent. Given the amount of testing performed here, coupled with the sale and delivery during the patent-term of a "completed" machine (completed by being ready for assembly and with no useful noninfringing purpose), we are not persuaded that the district court committed clear error in finding that the Magna–Graphics' machine infringed the '353 patent.

To reach a contrary result would emasculate the congressional intent to prevent the making of a patented item during the patent's full term of 17 years. If without fear of liability a competitor can assemble a patented item past the point of testing, the last year of the patent becomes worthless whenever it deals with a long lead-time article. Nothing would prohibit the unscrupulous competitor from aggressively marketing its own product and constructing it to all but the final screws and bolts, as Magna–Graphics did here. We rejected any reduction to the patent-term in *Roche*; we cannot allow the inconsistency in the patent law which would exist if we permitted it here. Magna–Graphics built and tested a patented machine, albeit in a less than preferred fashion. Because an "operable assembly" of components was tested, this case is distinguishable from *Interdent Corp. v. United States*, 531 F.2d 547, 552 (Ct.Cl.1976) (omission of a claimed element from the patented combination avoids infringement). Where, as here, significant, unpatented assemblies of elements are tested during the patent term, enabling the infringer to deliver the patented combination in parts to the buyer, without testing the entire combination together as was the infringer's usual practice, testing the assemblies can be held to be in essence testing the patented combination and, hence, infringement.

That the machine was not operated in its optimum mode is inconsequential: imperfect practice of an invention does not avoid infringement. We affirm the district court's finding that "[d]uring the testing of the Fort Howard machine in July and August 1981, Magna–Graphics completed an operable assembly of the infringing rewinder."

* * *

NIES, CIRCUIT JUDGE, dissenting-in-part.

I dissent from the majority's holding that Magna–Graphics' activities in connection with the Fort Howard machine constitute direct infringement of any claim of Paper Converting's patent. The majority's conclusion necessitates giving a meaning to "patented invention" contrary to the definition set forth by the Supreme Court in *Deepsouth Packing Co. v. Laitram Corp.*

* * *

The majority holds that *incomplete assembly* of the patented invention is making, *testing of subassemblies* is using, and a *sale of an unassembled* machine is selling the *patented invention* within the meaning of the above section. The majority reasons that a contrary result would emasculate the congressional intent to prevent the making of a patented item during the patent's full term of 17 years. It could be said with equal validity that, given the lead time necessary to make the invention here, the majority effectively extends the patentee's right of exclusivity beyond the statutory 17 years.

I do not see in *Deepsouth* that the Supreme Court's only concern was the extraterritorial operation of our patent laws. The activities of Deepsouth under attack were all performed in the United States and were found not to result in direct or contributory infringement of the patent. That the activities of final assembly occurred abroad merely precluded a holding that Deepsouth's activities constituted contributory infringement. Contributory infringement cannot arise without a direct infringement. The situation in *Deepsouth* is exactly comparable to the one at hand. That the activities of final assembly occurred after the patent expired precludes holding Magna–Graphics to be a contributory infringer, there being no direct infringement by another to which the charge can be appended.

Thus, we are back to the dispositive direct infringement issue in *Deepsouth*, which is the same as the issue here. What is the meaning of "patented invention" in 35 U.S.C. § 271(a)? The alleged infringer, in each case, made and sold something, but was it the "patented invention"?

* * *

Nothing in Justice White's opinion in *Deepsouth* indicates that the concept of an operable assembly is "probably something short of a full and complete assembly," as the majority states. The Court had before it the Fifth Circuit opinion which had analyzed just such less-than-full-assembly situations. Repeatedly, the Court emphasized that the "patented invention" means that *all* of its claimed elements must be united.

Thus, if the *claimed* invention comprises the elements A, B, C and D, it is only the *combination* in its entirety that is protected. The making of the lesser combination A, B and D falls short of direct infringement, even though the missing element C is also supplied by the alleged infringer.

* * *

It is not surprising that Magna–Graphics' counsel read *Deepsouth* as permitting the course of conduct condemned here. The majority opinion is no less than a reversal of *Deepsouth*. Regardless of the reasonableness of the alternative interpretation of § 271(a) given by the majority, we are bound by the Supreme Court's decision. No greater prerogative to modify it accrues to us from a 5–4 vote than from a unanimous decision. Change must be left to Congress, or the Court itself. In *Deepsouth* the extension of patent protection which had been urged was viewed as a matter for a legislative directive * * *.

* * * We cannot assume that the present Court would find reason to depart from Deepsouth in the face of congressional inaction over the twelve years since the decision was handed down.[3]

Indeed, the *Deepsouth* decision is not without redeeming virtue. This is one of the few areas of patent law where a bright line can be, and has been, drawn. That consideration in itself has merit. A competitor should be able to look to the patent claims and know whether his activity infringes or not. Here, the majority provides no guidance to industry or the district courts. One cannot tell from the opinion whether testing and sales activity must also accompany substantial assembly, as it appears to hold, or whether simply substantially making the device preparatory to selling after the patent expires would be sufficient. Given the disjunctive language of the statute, no basis appears for "summing up" partial making with the testing of partial assemblies and with sales made by the alleged infringer. Those activities do not, in some nebulous way, supply the missing physical elements of the "patented invention."

* * *

---

3. Legislative efforts to overrule *Deepsouth* have been extensive. However, the thrust of proposed legislation has not been directed to changing the meaning of "patented invention." For example, pending H.R. 4526, 98th Congress, 1st Session, provides in relevant part:

(f) Whoever without authority supplies or causes to be supplied in the United States the material components of a patented invention, where such components are uncombined in whole or in part, intending that such components will be combined outside of the United States, and knowing that if such components were combined within the United States the combination would be an infringement of the patent, shall be liable as an infringer.

NOTES AND QUESTIONS

1. *The right to exclude.* Patent Act § 154, as amended, enumerates the patentee's rights in the negative: The patentee has the right to *"exclude others* from making, using, offering for sale or selling the invention throughout the United States or importing the invention into the United States." If the invention is a process, the patentee has the right to *"exclude others* from using, offering for sale or selling throughout the United States, or importing into the United States, products made by that process." (Emphasis added.) Note that a patent does not convey any affirmative rights to the patentee to make, use, sell, offer to sell or import the invention herself. Why not? Under what sorts of circumstances might a patentee be precluded from exploiting her own patented invention?

Likewise, the grant of a patent does not compel the patentee to make, use, sell, offer to sell or import the invention, or to license others to do so. Some nations have subjected patentees who fail to "work" their patents (exploit their inventions) domestically to compulsory licenses, or have provided that the "non-working" patentee forfeits the patent. Should the United States enact such provisions?

2. *Direct Infringement (§ 271(a)).* Patent Act § 271(a), as amended, provides that "whoever without authority makes, uses, offers to sell, or sells any patented invention within the United States, or imports into the United States any patented invention during the term of the patent therefor, infringes the patent." Note that any one of the enumerated acts will infringe. So, for example, a person who uses the invention without authority will be liable, even though she neither made nor sold it. Note, too, that direct infringement is a form of strict liability. The plaintiff need make no showing of intent, knowledge, or neglect on the defendant's part.

How does the Court in *Deepsouth* define "making?" How does it define "selling?" What constitutes "use?" Would a sales demonstration qualify as a "use"? How about a simple testing of an infringing article, to ensure that it works? Would display of an infringing article for sale suffice?

Do you agree with the majority in *Magna-Graphics* that the Supreme Court intended its *Deepsouth* definitions of "making" and "selling" to be "narrowly construed as applicable only to the issue of the extraterritorial effect of the American patent law?" If you are not so sure, can you find a way to distinguish the two cases on their facts, so that the *Magna-Graphics* result is still justified? Under the *Magna-Graphics* decision, what exactly does it take to "make" a patented apparatus?

The Uruguay Round Agreements Act endowed United States patentees with two additional rights that they did not have when *Deepsouth* and *Magna-Graphics* were decided: the right to exclude others from (1) offering to sell and (2) importing the patented invention. These rights became effective January 1, 1996. As a practical matter, how much do they add to the U.S. patentee's rights? If the *Deepsouth* patentee's rights had included the right to exclude offers to sell, would the Supreme Court have reached a different result? How might a right to exclude offers to sell have figured into the Federal Circuit's legal analysis in *Magna-Graphics*? See the definition of "offer to sell" in 35 U.S.C.A. § 271(i).

3. *The geographic and temporal scope of a patent.* As *Deepsouth* points out, a U.S. patent is only effective to prevent infringing acts *in* the United States, *during* the prescribed patent term. With regard to the geographic limitation, note that with today's international trade and communications systems, it is possible that some elements of an alleged infringing apparatus or method may be located or carried out in the United States, while others are located or carried out abroad. Given the language of § 271(a), should the U.S. patentee be able to recover? In NTP, Inc. v. Research in Motion, Ltd., 418 F.3d 1282 (Fed. Cir. 2005), the patentee held both method and apparatus patents in a system for enabling mobile telephone users to receive e-mail over a wireless network. It alleged that NTP's BlackBerry system infringed. The Blackberry system incorporated all of the claimed elements, but it maintained one of them—the system interface or "relay"—in Canada. The question thus was whether infringement occurred "within the United States," as required for direct infringement liability. The Federal Circuit held that a jury could find infringement of the *apparatus* claims. Even though the system included components located outside of the U.S., BlackBerry users "used" the system in the United States: They availed themselves of all the components collectively, and both controlled and benefited from the system in the United States. In contrast, there could be no infringement of the *method/process* claims. Infringing "use" of a process entails practice of each individual claimed step, and each step must be performed within the United States. *Id.,* 418 F.3d at 1318.

With regard to the temporal limitation, the *Magna-Graphics* majority expressed concern that a ruling in favor of the defendant would effectively deprive the patentee of the benefit of the last year of its patent term. What lead the majority to that conclusion? In her dissent, Judge Nies argued that the majority might effectively extend the patentee's right of exclusivity beyond the statutory patent term. What led her to that conclusion? Do you agree?

As we saw in connection with the § 102(b) statutory bar, the law generally looks unfavorably on a patentee's attempts to extend her effective monopoly beyond the intended patent term. Licenses to exploit a patented invention that impose royalty obligations beyond the expiration of the patent are deemed unenforceable as a matter of public policy. Brulotte v. Thys Co., 379 U.S. 29, 85 S.Ct. 176, 13 L.Ed.2d 99 (1964).

Until recently, U.S. patent protection has commenced only when the patent issues. There could be no infringement liability for acts occurring before that date. However, in 1999, Congress amended the Patent Act to provide that most U.S. patent applications must be published 18 months after their earliest claimed U.S. or foreign filing date.[32] See 35 U.S.C.A. § 122. It further amended § 154 to provide that applicants whose applications are

---

32. Exceptions to the publication requirement include: applications that are no longer pending at the eighteenth month; applications that are the subject of a secrecy order; and provisional applications. Moreover, as noted *supra*, any applicant who is not filing for a patent in another country that publishes applications may request that her application not be published in the United States. (Most applicants who will fall under this exception are those who are only seeking patent protection in the U.S.) 35 U.S.C.A. § 122.

Applicants may elect to have their applications published earlier than 18 months after filing. This will accelerate the time at which they begin to enjoy provisional rights, as described above.

published will enjoy "provisional rights" during the period between publication and actual issuance of a patent.[33] The rights are deemed "provisional" because they mature only on the issuance of the patent. The section-by-section analysis of the amendments, read into the Congressional Record by Senator Lott, explains:

> Generally, this provision establishes the right of the applicant to obtain a reasonable royalty from any person who, during the period beginning on the date that his or her application is published and ending on the date a patent is issued—
>
> (1) makes, uses, offers for sale, or sells the invention in the United States, or imports such an invention into the United States; or
>
> (2) If the invention claimed is a process, makes, uses, offers for sale, sells, or imports a product made by that process in the United States; and
>
> (3) had actual notice of the published application and, in the case of an application filed under the PCT designating the United States that is published in a language other than English, a translation of the application into English.
>
> The requirement of actual notice is critical. The mere fact that the published application is included in a commercial database where it might be found is insufficient. The published applicant must give actual notice of the published application to the accused infringer and explain what acts are regarded as giving rise to provisional rights.
>
> Another important limitation on the availability of provisional royalties is that the claims in the published application that are alleged to give rise to provisional rights must also appear in the patent in substantially identical form. To allow anything less than substantial identity would impose an unacceptable burden on the public. If provisional rights were available in the situation where the only valid claim infringed first appeared in substantially that form in the granted patent, the public would have no guidance as to the specific behavior to avoid between publication and grant. Every person or company that might be operating within the scope of the disclosure of the published application would have to conduct her own private examination to determine whether a published application contained patentable subject matter that she should avoid. The burden should be on the applicant to initially draft a schedule of claims that gives adequate notice to the public of what she is seeking to patent.
>
> * * *
>
> Amended section 154(d)(4) sets forth some additional rules qualifying when an international application under the PCT will give rise to provisional rights. The date that will give rise to provisional rights for international applications will be the date on which the USPTO receives a copy of the application published under the PCT in the English language; if the application is published under the PCT in a language other than

---

33. The amendments accord provisional rights to obtain a "reasonable royalty" to those applicants whose applications have been published under amended § 122(b), or pursuant to a PCT (Patent Cooperation Treaty) application designating the United States.

English, then the date on which provisional rights will arise will be the date on which the USPTO receives a translation of the international application in the English language.

145 Cong. Rec. S14708, 14719 (daily ed. Nov. 17, 1999)(included in the record at the request of Sen. Lott).

The new publication and provisional rights provisions bring the United States closer to the patent practices of Japan, the European Union, and other important world trading partners. When will application claims be "substantially identical" to the claims in the patent?

4. *Combination patents.* The Supreme Court, in *Deepsouth*, stresses that the plaintiff's patent is a "combination patent." Does the Court suggest how broad the category of "combination patents" is? The Court of Appeals for the Federal Circuit has expressed skepticism about any "combination patent" categorization and has tended to avoid it. Stratoflex, Inc. v. Aeroquip Corp., 713 F.2d 1530, 1541 (Fed.Cir.1983).

5. *Section 271(f).* The result in the *Deepsouth* case was unpopular with many U.S. industries, and lead to lobbying for Congress to eliminate the perceived loophole *Deepsouth* created in U.S. patent protection. After several attempts, in 1984, Congress amended the Patent Act to add the provisions set forth in § 271(f).

Subsection (f)(1) makes it an infringement to supply all or a substantial portion of the components of a patented invention from the U.S. in a manner that actively induces combination of the components outside the U.S., if the extraterritorial combination would infringe if it occurred domestically. Under subsection (f)(2), it is an infringement to supply even a single component of a patented invention from the U.S. if (1) the component is especially made or adapted for use in the patented invention and is not a staple article or commercial commodity that is suitable for substantial noninfringing uses, (2) the supplier knows that the component is so made or adapted, and (3) the supplier intends that the component be combined abroad in the patented invention in a manner that would infringe if it occurred in the U.S.

This clearly puts a stop to the practice at issue in *Deepsouth*, and addresses the dissent's concern that the *Deepsouth* decision allowed the infringer to reap the fruits of the American economy—its technology, labor, materials, etc.—but avoid responsibility for the American patent laws. However, concern about extraterritorial application of U.S. patent law has lead courts to construe subsection (f) conservatively and generally to decline to extend it beyond settings similar to that in *Deepsouth*. See, e.g., Microsoft Corp. v. AT & T Corp., 550 U.S. 437, 454–56, 127 S.Ct. 1746, 1758, 167 L.Ed.2d 737 (2007) (doubt about whether defendant's conduct infringed § 271(f) should be resolved by the presumption against extraterritoriality. " 'The presumption is not defeated just because [a statute] specifically addresses [an] issue of extraterritorial application;' it remains instructive in determining the extent of statutory exception."); Cardiac Pacemakers, Inc. v. St. Jude Medical, Inc., 576 F.3d 1348, 1365 (Fed. Cir. 2009)(en banc)(construing § 271(f) not to encompass process patents: "any ambiguity as to Congress' intent in enacting Section 271(f) is * * * resolved by the presumption against territoriality.").

What, if any, impact does subsection (f) have on the precedential value of the *Deepsouth* opinion? On the reasoning in *Magna-Graphics*? See Rotec Industries, Inc. v. Mitsubishi Corp., 215 F.3d 1246, 1252 n.2 (Fed.Cir.2000) ("§ 217(f) does not * * * change the nature of § 271(a) liability, as it provides a separate cause of action." Hence, as to claims brought under § 271(a), *Deepsouth* remains good law: one may not be held liable under § 271(a) for "making" or "selling" less than a complete invention.). But see *id.*, at 1260 (Newman, J. concurring)("the purpose of § 271(f) was to overrule *Deepsouth*").

6. *Section 271(g)*. Congress addressed another perceived loophole in the Omnibus Trade and Competitiveness Act of 1988, Pub.L. No. 100–418, §§ 9001–9007, 102 Stat. 1563. In this case, businesses were using U.S. patented processes abroad (where use would not infringe) to manufacture products which they then imported into the United States to sell in competition with the U.S. process patent holder. The products themselves were not patented, so the U.S. process patentee had little redress.[34] This practice deprived the U.S. process patent holder of much of the economic benefit of its patent monopoly.

The Omnibus Trade and Competitiveness Act provisions added subsection (g) to Patent Act § 271. Subsection (g), as later amended by the Uruguay Round Agreements Act, makes it an infringement for an unauthorized person to import into the U.S. or to sell, offer to sell or use within the U.S. a product made by a U.S. patented process. To avoid infringement claims regarding products that are only remotely derived from a patented process, subsection (g) provides that a "product which is made by a patented process will * * * not be considered to be so made after—(1) it is materially changed by subsequent processes; or (2) it becomes a trivial and nonessential component of another product."

During the legislative process, some parties expressed concern about the potential difficulty of avoiding liability under the new § 271(g), due to the difficulty of discovering that products were made by patented processes. To address this concern and avoid inequitable results, the Act channels infringement claims toward persons practicing the patented process and those controlling them, and persons having prior knowledge of infringement. It limits remedies against unknowing, innocent infringers, permitting such persons to sell or use inventory that they accumulated prior to notice that the inventory infringes. See 35 U.S.C.A. § 287(b). The Act also provides that a remedy against noncommercial users or retail sellers of products made by patented processes will only be available if no adequate remedy is available against importers or other users or sellers. *Id.*, § 271(g).

Patentees may face considerable difficulty proving that their process was used to create the accused product, especially when the manufacturer is not subject to discovery under the Federal Rules of Civil Procedure. In recognition of this difficulty, the Act provides for a presumption. If the court finds that a "substantial likelihood exists that the product was made by the patented

---

34. The Tariff Act, section 337, provided the opportunity to petition the International Trade Commission to bar such products from entering the country, in some circumstances. 19 U.S.C.A. § 1337.

process" and that "the plaintiff has made a reasonable effort to determine the process actually used," the product will be presumed to have been made with the patented process. The burden will shift to the defendant to prove that it was not. 35 U.S.C.A. § 295.

Assume that X Company has patented genetically altered cells that produce a human hormone, but not the process of using the altered cell to produce the hormone, or the hormone itself. A foreign company uses the claimed altered cells to produce the hormone abroad, and imports the hormone into the U.S. to sell in competition with the U.S. patentee. Will § 271(g) provide relief to the patentee? See Amgen Inc. v. U.S. International Trade Commission, 902 F.2d 1532 (Fed.Cir.1990).

7. *Section 271(e)*. Assume that X has a patent for a drug. Y, a generic drug manufacturer, wishes to enter the market with a generic version of the drug as soon as X's patent expires. A drug cannot be marketed without F.D.A. approval, and in order to obtain the necessary F.D.A. approval, Y must perform tests and submit data to demonstrate the drugs's safety and efficacy.

Y would like to perform the necessary tests during the final months of X's patent so that it can file for F.D.A. approval as soon as X's patent expires. Is Y free to make and use the patented drug to perform its tests during the final months of X's patent, or must it wait until the patent expires?

In Roche Products, Inc. v. Bolar Pharmaceutical Co., 733 F.2d 858 (Fed.Cir.1984), *cert. denied*, 469 U.S. 856, 105 S.Ct. 183, 83 L.Ed.2d 117 (1984), the Court of Appeals for the Federal Circuit held that performing the tests during the patent term would infringe X's patent. Given the significant time necessary to perform the tests, and the fact that no competitor could compete with X until it had performed the tests and obtained the necessary agency approval, the practical effect of this finding was to give X a considerable *de facto* extension of its patent term.

Congress enacted § 271(e) in response to the *Roche* decision. Subsection (e)(1), as amended, provides that it shall not be an act of infringement to make, use, offer to sell, sell, or import a patented invention[35] "solely for uses reasonably related to the development and submission of information under a Federal law which regulates the manufacture, use, or sale of drugs or veterinary biological products."

The Supreme Court has tended to construe this drug research and development safe harbor broadly. In Eli Lilly & Co. v. Medtronic, Inc., 496 U.S. 661, 110 S.Ct. 2683, 110 L.Ed.2d 605 (1990), the Court held that the subsection (e) exemption encompasses use of patented medical devices, as well as chemical compounds. More recently, in Merck KGAA v. Integra Lifesciences I, Ltd., 545 U.S. 193, 125 S.Ct. 2372, 162 L.Ed.2d 160 (2005), the Supreme Court clarified that the safe harbor exempts "all uses of patented inventions that are reasonably related to the development and submission of *any* information" under the Federal Food, Drug and Cosmetics Act, regardless of whether the use is made at the preclinical or clinical stage of the researcher's work, and regardless of whether the research concerns the potential

---

35. Section 271(e)(1) excepts "new animal drug or veterinary biological products" that are "primarily manufactured using recombinant RNA, hybridoma technology, or other processes involving site specific genetic manipulation techniques."

drug's safety, or its efficacy or other characteristics. Moreover, it is not necessary that the allegedly infringing experiment ultimately be included in a submission of information to the FDA. 545 U.S. at 201, 125 S.Ct. at 2380.

PROBLEMS

1. Consider the rights of the patentee in the following fact patterns.

a) X Company purchased one of Y's patented machines (which was in the final year of its patent), analyzed its constituent parts, and began to manufacture the parts. It then placed the parts into boxes, so that each box contained all the parts necessary to build one of the machines, along with instructions for assembly. It did not assemble or test any of the parts, and held the boxes until the day Y's patent expired. The day after the patent expired, X Co. immediately began advertising and selling the boxes of parts in the U.S. as "kits" for building the machine. Is X Co. liable to Y for infringement? Should it be?

b) In addition to the facts above, assume that while Y's patent was still in effect, X Co. advertised that the kit would be available for purchase commencing the day after the patent expired. Same analysis? What if X Co. offered the kit for sale to U.S. buyers prior to the patent expiration, but got no takers? What if it did succeed in making several sales in the U.S. prior to the expiration of the patent? What if, while Y's patent was still in effect, X Co. shipped some of the "kits" to purchasers in Canada, with strict instructions only to assemble the machine in Canada?

c) What if, instead of the facts above, X Co. manufactured the parts of Y's patented machine abroad and sold them to foreign purchasers during the patent term, but sent the foreign purchasers instructions for assembling the parts from its corporate headquarters in the United States?

d) What if Acme Co. exports a catalyst that is used in a U.S. patented process abroad? Should Acme be liable under § 271(f)?

e) Macrosoft, Inc., whose business facilities are in the United States, distributes its "Doors" software internationally by sending a master version of the software via electronic transmission to foreign computer manufacturers and authorized foreign "replicators." Pursuant to their licensing agreements with Macrosoft, the foreign recipients replicate the master versions they receive, generating multiple copies of Doors for installation on foreign-assembled computers that are then sold to foreign customers.

The master versions of Doors thus exported incorporate certain elements that, when installed on a computer, infringe TT&A's patent. TT&A sues Macrosoft for infringement, alleging, among other things, infringement under Patent Act § 271(f). How would you evaluate the claim?

2. Assume that X Co. contacts a company in China from X Co.'s New York City headquarters. It offers to sell the Chinese company products which will be manufactured in their entirety at a factory in Argentina. The products fall within the claims of Y Co.'s U.S. patent. Will Y Co. have a cause of action against X Co. for infringement of its U.S. patent?

3. Widgets were invented in the 1940's, and have been on the market in the U.S. and in other parts of the world ever since. They are not presently the subject of patent rights in any country in the world. In 1995, Alford discovered a new and more efficient process for manufacturing widgets. She obtained a U.S. patent for the new process in 1997. While Alford obtained a patent for her manufacturing process in some other countries, she did not obtain a Canadian patent for the process.

Bell Co. manufactures widgets in Canada, and uses Alford's manufacturing process. Bell Co. sells the widgets it manufactures to wholesale distributors, who then resell the widgets. In 2001, Clark, a New York business woman, bought a large lot of widgets manufactured by Bell Co. in Canada from a Canadian wholesale distributor. Clark shipped the widgets to New York and then resold them, in two separate transactions, to Dilan and Edwards.

At the time that Dilan purchased the widgets, he was aware of Alford's patent and that the widgets he was buying were made via Alford's patented process in Canada. He was pleased to have purchased the widgets at a much lower price than he would have obtained if he had bought directly from Alford's U.S. licensee. Dilan resold the widgets to the public through his chain of retail stores.

Edwards, on the other hand, was not aware of Alford's patent or of the origin of the widgets he purchased from Clark. Edwards ultimately resold the widgets to Fernandez, who then sold them, on a retail basis, to end users.

Is Alford likely to have a cause of action for infringement against Bell Co., Clark, Dilan, Edwards, Fernandez or Fernandez' end purchasers?

4. Foreign Pharmaceutical Co. uses a U.S. patented process abroad to identify an effective drug for treating particular medical symptoms. Assuming that Foreign Pharmaceutical brings information about the identity of the drug into the U.S., is it liable to the U.S. patent owner under Patent Act § 271(g)? What if it manufactures the drug that it identified through use of the patented process abroad and imports the drug into the U.S.?

QUANTA COMPUTER, INC. v. LG ELECTRONICS, INC.

United States Supreme Court, 2008.
533 U.S. 617, 128 S.Ct. 2109, 170 L.Ed.2d 996.

JUSTICE THOMAS delivered the opinion of the Court.

For over 150 years this Court has applied the doctrine of patent exhaustion to limit the patent rights that survive the initial authorized sale of a patented item. In this case, we decide whether patent exhaustion applies to the sale of components of a patented system that must be combined with additional components in order to practice the patented methods. The Court of Appeals for the Federal Circuit held that the doctrine does not apply to method patents at all and, in the alternative, that it does not apply here because the sales were not authorized by the license agreement. We disagree on both scores. Because the exhaustion doctrine applies to method patents, and because the license authorizes the sale of components that substantially embody the patents in suit, the sale exhausted the patents.

I

Respondent LG Electronics, Inc. (LGE), purchased a portfolio of computer technology patents in 1999, including the three patents at issue here: U.S. Patent Nos. 4,939,641 ('641); 5,379,379 ('379); and 5,077,733 ('733) (collectively LGE Patents). The main functions of a computer system are carried out on a microprocessor, or central processing unit, which interprets program instructions, processes data, and controls other devices in the system. A set of wires, or bus, connects the microprocessor to a chipset, which transfers data between the microprocessor and other devices, including the keyboard, mouse, monitor, hard drive, memory, and disk drives.

The data processed by the computer are stored principally in random access memory, also called main memory. Frequently accessed data are generally stored in cache memory, which permits faster access than main memory and is often located on the microprocessor itself. When copies of data are stored in both the cache and main memory, problems may arise when one copy is changed but the other still contains the original "stale" version of the data. The '641 patent addresses this problem. It discloses a system for ensuring that the most current data are retrieved from main memory by monitoring data requests and updating main memory from the cache when stale data are requested.

The '379 patent relates to the coordination of requests to read from, and write to, main memory. Processing these requests in chronological order can slow down a system because read requests are faster to execute than write requests. Processing all read requests first ensures speedy access, but may result in the retrieval of outdated data if a read request for a certain piece of data is processed before an outstanding write request for the same data. The '379 patent discloses an efficient method of organizing read and write requests while maintaining accuracy by allowing the computer to execute only read requests until it needs data for which there is an outstanding write request. Upon receiving such a read request, the computer executes pending write requests first and only then returns to the read requests so that the most up-to-date data are retrieved.

The '733 patent addresses the problem of managing the data traffic on a bus connecting two computer components, so that no one device monopolizes the bus. It allows multiple devices to share the bus, giving heavy users greater access. This patent describes methods that establish a rotating priority system under which each device alternately has priority access to the bus for a preset number of cycles and heavier users can maintain priority for more cycles without "hogging" the device indefinitely.

LGE licensed a patent portfolio, including the LGE Patents, to Intel Corporation (Intel). The cross-licensing agreement (License Agreement) permits Intel to manufacture and sell microprocessors and chipsets that use the LGE Patents (the Intel Products). The License Agreement authorizes Intel to " 'make, use, sell (directly or indirectly), offer to sell, import or otherwise dispose of' " its own products practicing the LGE Patents. Notwithstanding this broad language, the License Agreement contains some limitations. Relevant here, it stipulates that no license

> " 'is granted by either party hereto . . . to any third party for the combination by a third party of Licensed Products of either party with items, components, or the like acquired . . . from sources other than a party hereto, or for the use, import, offer for sale or sale of such combination.' "

The License Agreement purports not to alter the usual rules of patent exhaustion, however, providing that, " '[n]otwithstanding anything to the contrary contained in this Agreement, the parties agree that nothing herein shall in any way limit or alter the effect of patent exhaustion that would otherwise apply when a party hereto sells any of its Licensed Products.' "

In a separate agreement (Master Agreement), Intel agreed to give written notice to its own customers informing them that, while it had obtained a broad license " 'ensur[ing] that any Intel product that you purchase is licensed by LGE and thus does not infringe any patent held by LGE,' " the license " 'does not extend, expressly or by implication, to any product that you make by combining an Intel product with any non-Intel product.' " The Master Agreement also provides that " 'a breach of this Agreement shall have no effect on and shall not be grounds for termination of the Patent License.' "

Petitioners, including Quanta Computer (collectively Quanta), are a group of computer manufacturers. Quanta purchased microprocessors and chipsets from Intel and received the notice required by the Master Agreement. Nonetheless, Quanta manufactured computers using Intel parts in combination with non-Intel memory and buses in ways that practice the LGE Patents. Quanta does not modify the Intel components and follows Intel's specifications to incorporate the parts into its own systems.

LGE filed a complaint against Quanta, asserting that the combination of the Intel Products with non-Intel memory and buses infringed the LGE Patents. The District Court granted summary judgment to Quanta, holding that, for purposes of the patent exhaustion doctrine, the license LGE granted to Intel resulted in forfeiture of any potential infringement actions against legitimate purchasers of the Intel Products. The court found that, although the Intel Products do not fully practice any of the patents at issue, they have no reasonable noninfringing use and therefore their authorized sale exhausted patent rights in the completed computers under *United States v. Univis Lens Co.*, 316 U.S. 241 (1942). In a subsequent order limiting its summary judgment ruling, the court held that patent exhaustion applies only to apparatus or composition-of-matter claims that describe a physical object, and does not apply to process, or method, claims that describe operations to make or use a product. Because each of the LGE Patents includes method claims, exhaustion did not apply.

The Court of Appeals for the Federal Circuit affirmed in part and reversed in part. It agreed that the doctrine of patent exhaustion does not apply to method claims. In the alternative, it concluded that exhaustion did not apply because LGE did not license Intel to sell the Intel Products to Quanta for use in combination with non-Intel products.

* * *

II

The longstanding doctrine of patent exhaustion provides that the initial authorized sale of a patented item terminates all patent rights to that item. This Court first applied the doctrine in 19th-century cases addressing patent extensions on the Woodworth planing machine. Purchasers of licenses to sell and use the machine for the duration of the original patent term sought to continue using the licenses through the extended term. The Court held that the extension of the patent term did not affect the rights already secured by purchasers who bought the item for use "in the ordinary pursuits of life." *Bloomer v. McQuewan,* 14 How. 539, 549 (1853); see also *ibid.* ("[W]hen the machine passes to the hands of the purchaser, it is no longer within the limits of the monopoly"). In *Adams v. Burke,* 17 Wall. 453 (1873), the Court affirmed the dismissal of a patent holder's suit alleging that a licensee had violated postsale restrictions on where patented coffin-lids could be used. "[W]here a person ha[s] purchased a patented machine of the patentee or his assignee," the Court held, "this purchase carrie[s] with it the right to the use of that machine so long as it [is] capable of use."

Although the Court permitted postsale restrictions on the use of a patented article in *Henry v. A.B. Dick Co.,* 224 U.S. 1 (1912),[2] that decision was short lived. In 1913, the Court refused to apply *A.B. Dick* to uphold price-fixing provisions in a patent license. See *Bauer & Cie v. O'Donnell,* 229 U.S. 1, 14–17 (1913). Shortly thereafter, in *Motion Picture Patents Co. v. Universal Film Mfg. Co.,* 243 U.S. 502, 518 (1917), the Court explicitly overruled *A.B. Dick.* In that case, a patent holder attempted to limit purchasers' use of its film projectors to show only film made under a patent held by the same company. The Court noted the "increas-

---

2. The A.B. Dick Company sold mimeograph machines with an attached license stipulating that the machine could be used only with ink, paper, and other supplies made by the A.B. Dick Company. The Court rejected the notion that a patent holder "can only keep the article within the control of the patent by retaining the title," *A.B. Dick,* 224 U.S., at 18, and held that "any . . . reasonable stipulation, not inherently violative of some substantive law" was "valid and enforceable," *id.,* at 31. The only requirement, the Court held, was that "the purchaser must have notice that he buys with only a qualified right of use," so that a sale made without conditions resulted in "an unconditional title to the machine, with no limitations upon the use." *Id.,* at 26.

ing frequency" with which patent holders were using *A.B. Dick*-style licenses to limit the use of their products and thereby using the patents to secure market control of related, unpatented items. Observing that "the primary purpose of our patent laws is not the creation of private fortunes for the owners of patents but is 'to promote the progress of science and useful arts,'" the Court held that "the scope of the grant which may be made to an inventor in a patent, pursuant to the [patent] statute, must be limited to the invention described in the claims of his patent." Accordingly, it reiterated the rule that "the right to vend is exhausted by a single, unconditional sale, the article sold being thereby carried outside the monopoly of the patent law and rendered free of every restriction which the vendor may attempt to put upon it."

This Court most recently discussed patent exhaustion in *Univis*, 316 U.S. 241, on which the District Court relied. Univis Lens Company, the holder of patents on eyeglass lenses, licensed a purchaser to manufacture lens blanks[3] by fusing together different lens segments to create bi-and tri-focal lenses and to sell them to other Univis licensees at agreed-upon rates. Wholesalers were licensed to grind the blanks into the patented finished lenses, which they would then sell to Univis-licensed prescription retailers for resale at a fixed rate. Finishing retailers, after grinding the blanks into patented lenses, would sell the finished lenses to consumers at the same fixed rate. The United States sued Univis under the Sherman Act, 15 U.S.C. §§ 1, 3, 15, alleging unlawful restraints on trade. Univis asserted its patent monopoly rights as a defense to the antitrust suit. The Court granted certiorari to determine whether Univis' patent monopoly survived the sale of the lens blanks by the licensed manufacturer and therefore shielded Univis' pricing scheme from the Sherman Act.

The Court assumed that the Univis patents containing claims for finished lenses were practiced in part by the wholesalers and finishing retailers who ground the blanks into lenses, and held that the sale of the lens blanks exhausted the patents on the finished lenses. *Univis*, 316 U.S., at 248–249. The Court explained that the lens blanks "embodi[ed] essential features of the patented device and [were] without utility until ... ground and polished as the finished lens of the patent." The Court noted that:

> "where one has sold an uncompleted article which, because it embodies essential features of his patented invention, is within the protection of his patent, and has destined the article to be finished by the purchaser in conformity to the patent, he has sold his invention so far as it is or may be embodied in that particular article." *Id.*, at 250–251.

In sum, the Court concluded that the traditional bar on patent restrictions following the sale of an item applies when the item sufficiently embodies the patent—even if it does not completely practice the patent—such that its only and intended use is to be finished under the terms of the patent.

---

3. Lens blanks are "rough opaque pieces of glass of suitable size, design and composition for use, when ground and polished, as multifocal lenses in eyeglasses." *Univis*, 316 U.S., at 244.

With this history of the patent exhaustion doctrine in mind, we turn to the parties' arguments.

III

A

LGE argues that the exhaustion doctrine is inapplicable here because it does not apply to method claims, which are contained in each of the LGE Patents. LGE reasons that, because method patents are linked not to a tangible article but to a process, they can never be exhausted through a sale. Rather, practicing the patent—which occurs upon each use of an article embodying a method patent—is permissible only to the extent rights are transferred in an assignment contract. Quanta, in turn, argues that there is no reason to preclude exhaustion of method claims, and points out that both this Court and the Federal Circuit have applied exhaustion to method claims. It argues that any other rule would allow patent holders to avoid exhaustion entirely by inserting method claims in their patent specifications.

Quanta has the better of this argument. Nothing in this Court's approach to patent exhaustion supports LGE's argument that method patents cannot be exhausted. It is true that a patented method may not be sold in the same way as an article or device, but methods nonetheless may be "embodied" in a product, the sale of which exhausts patent rights. Our precedents do not differentiate transactions involving embodiments of patented methods or processes from those involving patented apparatuses or materials. To the contrary, this Court has repeatedly held that method patents were exhausted by the sale of an item that embodied the method. In *Ethyl Gasoline Corp. v. United States,* 309 U.S. 436, 446, 457 (1940), for example, the Court held that the sale of a motor fuel produced under one patent also exhausted the patent for a method of using the fuel in combustion motors.[4] Similarly, as previously described, *Univis* held that the sale of optical lens blanks that partially practiced a patent exhausted the method patents that were not completely practiced until the blanks were ground into lenses.

These cases rest on solid footing. Eliminating exhaustion for method patents would seriously undermine the exhaustion doctrine. Patentees seeking to avoid patent exhaustion could simply draft their patent claims to describe a method rather than an apparatus. Apparatus and method claims "may approach each other so nearly that it will be difficult to distinguish the process from the function of the apparatus." *United States ex rel. Steinmetz v. Allen,* 192 U.S. 543, 559 (1904). By characterizing their claims as method instead of apparatus claims, or including a method claim

---

4. The patentee held patents for (1) a fluid additive increasing gasoline efficiency, (2) motor fuel produced by mixing gasoline with the patented fluid, and (3) a method of using fuel containing the patented fluid in combustion motors. The patentee sold only the fluid, but attempted to control sales of the treated fuel. The Court held that the sale of the fluid to refiners relinquished the patentee's exclusive rights to sell the treated fuel.

for the machine's patented method of performing its task, a patent drafter could shield practically any patented item from exhaustion.

This case illustrates the danger of allowing such an end-run around exhaustion. On LGE's theory, although Intel is authorized to sell a completed computer system that practices the LGE Patents, any downstream purchasers of the system could nonetheless be liable for patent infringement. Such a result would violate the longstanding principle that, when a patented item is "once lawfully made and sold, there is no restriction on [its] *use* to be implied for the benefit of the patentee." *Adams,* 17 Wall., at 457. We therefore reject LGE's argument that method claims, as a category, are never exhaustible.

B

We next consider the extent to which a product must embody a patent in order to trigger exhaustion. Quanta argues that, although sales of an incomplete article do not necessarily exhaust the patent in that article, the sale of the microprocessors and chipsets exhausted LGE's patents in the same way the sale of the lens blanks exhausted the patents in *Univis.* Just as the lens blanks in *Univis* did not fully practice the patents at issue because they had not been ground into finished lenses, Quanta observes, the Intel Products cannot practice the LGE Patents—or indeed, function at all—until they are combined with memory and buses in a computer system. If, as in *Univis,* patent rights are exhausted by the sale of the incomplete item, then LGE has no postsale right to require that the patents be practiced using only Intel parts. Quanta also argues that the exhaustion doctrine will be a dead letter unless it is triggered by the sale of components that essentially, even if not completely, embody an invention. Otherwise, patent holders could authorize the sale of computers that are complete with the exception of one minor step—say, inserting the microprocessor into a socket—and extend their rights through each downstream purchaser all the way to the end user.

LGE, for its part, argues that *Univis* is inapplicable here for three reasons. First, it maintains that *Univis* should be limited to products that contain all the physical aspects needed to practice the patent. On that theory, the Intel Products cannot embody the patents because additional physical components are required before the patents can be practiced. Second, LGE asserts that in *Univis* there was no "patentable distinction" between the lens blanks and the patented finished lenses since they were both subject to the same patent. In contrast, it describes the Intel Products as "independent and distinct products" from the systems using the LGE Patents and subject to "independent patents." Finally, LGE argues that *Univis* does not apply because the Intel Products are analogous to individual elements of a combination patent, and allowing sale of those components to exhaust the patent would impermissibly "ascrib[e] to one element of the patented combination the status of the patented invention in itself." *Aro Mfg. Co. v. Convertible Top Replacement Co.,* 365 U.S. 336, 344–345 (1961).

We agree with Quanta that *Univis* governs this case. As the Court there explained, exhaustion was triggered by the sale of the lens blanks because their only reasonable and intended use was to practice the patent and because they "embodie[d] essential features of [the] patented invention." Each of those attributes is shared by the microprocessors and chipsets Intel sold to Quanta under the License Agreement.

First, *Univis* held that "the authorized sale of an article which is capable of use only in practicing the patent is a relinquishment of the patent monopoly with respect to the article sold." *Id.*, at 249. The lens blanks in *Univis* met this standard because they were "without utility until [they were] ground and polished as the finished lens of the patent." Accordingly, "the only object of the sale [was] to enable the [finishing retailer] to grind and polish it for use as a lens by the prospective wearer." Here, LGE has suggested no reasonable use for the Intel Products other than incorporating them into computer systems that practice the LGE Patents. Nor can we can discern one: A microprocessor or chipset cannot function until it is connected to buses and memory. And here, as in *Univis,* the only apparent object of Intel's sales to Quanta was to permit Quanta to incorporate the Intel Products into computers that would practice the patents.

Second, the lens blanks in *Univis* "embodie[d] essential features of [the] patented invention." The essential, or inventive, feature of the Univis lens patents was the fusing together of different lens segments to create bi-and tri-focal lenses. The finishing process performed by the finishing and prescription retailers after the fusing was not unique. As the United States explained:

> "The finishing licensees finish Univis lens blanks in precisely the same manner as they finish all other bifocal lens blanks. Indeed, appellees have never contended that their licensing system is supported by patents covering methods or processes relating to the finishing of lens blanks. Consequently, it appears that appellees perform all of the operations which contribute any claimed element of novelty to Univis lenses." Brief for United States in *United States v. Univis Lens Co.,* O.T.1941, No. 855 et al., p. 10.

While the Court assumed that the finishing process was covered by the patents, and the District Court found that it was necessary to make a working lens, the grinding process was not central to the patents. That standard process was not included in detail in any of the patents and was not referred to at all in two of the patents. Those that did mention the finishing process treated it as incidental to the invention, noting, for example, that "[t]he blank is then ground in the usual manner," U.S. Patent No. 1,876,497, p. 2, or simply that the blank is "then ground and polished," U.S. Patent No. 1,632,208, p. 1.

Like the Univis lens blanks, the Intel Products constitute a material part of the patented invention and all but completely practice the patent. Here, as in *Univis,* the incomplete article substantially embodies the patent because the only step necessary to practice the patent is the application of common processes or the addition of standard parts. Everything inventive about each patent is embodied in the Intel Products. They control access to main and cache memory, practicing the '641 and '379 patents by checking cache memory against main memory and comparing read and write requests. They also control priority of bus access by various other computer components under the '733 patent. Naturally, the Intel Products cannot carry out these functions unless they are attached to memory and buses, but those additions are standard components in the system, providing the material that enables the microprocessors and chipsets to function. The Intel Products were specifically designed to function only when memory or buses are attached; Quanta was not required to make any creative or inventive decision when it added those parts. Indeed, Quanta had no alternative but to follow Intel's specifications in incorporating the Intel Products into its computers because it did not know their internal structure, which Intel guards as a trade secret. Intel all but practiced the patent itself by designing its products to practice the patents, lacking only the addition of standard parts.

* * *

Finally, LGE's reliance on *Aro* is misplaced because that case dealt only with the question whether replacement of one part of a patented combination infringes the patent. First, the replacement question is not at issue here. Second, and more importantly, *Aro* is not squarely applicable to the exhaustion of patents like the LGE Patents that do not disclose a new combination of existing parts. *Aro* described combination patents as "cover [ing] only the totality of the elements in the claim [so] that no element, separately viewed, is within the grant." 365 U.S., at 344 * * *. *Aro's warning that no element can be viewed as central to or equivalent to the invention is specific to the context in which the combination itself is the only inventive aspect of the patent. In this case, the inventive part of the patent is not the fact that memory and buses are combined with a microprocessor or chipset; rather, it is included in the design of the Intel Products themselves and the way these products access the memory or bus.*

C

Having concluded that the Intel Products embodied the patents, we next consider whether their sale to Quanta exhausted LGE's patent rights. Exhaustion is triggered only by a sale authorized by the patent holder.

LGE argues that there was no authorized sale here because the License Agreement does not permit Intel to sell its products for use in combination with non-Intel products to practice the LGE Patents. It cites *General Talking Pictures Corp. v. Western Elec. Co.,* 304 U.S. 175 (1938), and *General Talking Pictures Corp. v. Western Elec. Co.,* 305 U.S. 124 (1938), in which the manufacturer sold patented amplifiers for commercial use, thereby breaching a license that limited the buyer to selling the amplifiers for private and home use. The Court held that exhaustion did not apply because the manufacturer had no authority to sell the amplifiers for commercial use, and the manufacturer "could not convey to petitioner what both knew it was not authorized to sell." *General Talking Pictures, supra,* at 181. LGE argues that the same principle applies here: Intel could not convey to Quanta what both knew it was not authorized to sell, *i.e.,* the right to practice the patents with non-Intel parts.

LGE overlooks important aspects of the structure of the Intel–LGE transaction. Nothing in the License Agreement restricts Intel's right to sell its microprocessors and chipsets to purchasers who intend to combine them with non-Intel parts. It broadly permits Intel to " 'make, use, [or] sell' " products free of LGE's patent claims. To be sure, LGE did require Intel to give notice to its customers, including Quanta, that LGE had not licensed those customers to practice its patents. But neither party contends that Intel breached the agreement in that respect. In any event, the provision requiring notice to Quanta appeared only in the Master Agreement, and LGE does not suggest that a breach of that agreement would constitute a breach of the License Agreement. Hence, Intel's authority to sell its products embodying the LGE Patents was not conditioned on the notice or on Quanta's decision to abide by LGE's directions in that notice.

LGE points out that the License Agreement specifically disclaimed any license to third parties to practice the patents by combining licensed products with other components. But the question whether third parties received implied licenses is irrelevant because Quanta asserts its right to practice the patents based not on implied license but on exhaustion. And exhaustion turns only on Intel's own license to sell products practicing the LGE Patents.

* * *

The License Agreement authorized Intel to sell products that practiced the LGE Patents. No conditions limited Intel's authority to sell products substantially embodying the patents. Because Intel was authorized to sell its products to Quanta, the doctrine of patent exhaustion prevents LGE from further asserting its patent rights with respect to the patents substantially embodied by those products.[7]

IV

The authorized sale of an article that substantially embodies a patent exhausts the patent holder's rights and prevents the patent holder from invoking patent law to control postsale use of the article. Here, LGE licensed Intel to practice any of its patents and to sell products practicing those patents. Intel's microprocessors and chipsets substantially embodied

---

7. We note that the authorized nature of the sale to Quanta does not necessarily limit LGE's other contract rights. LGE's complaint does not include a breach-of-contract claim, and we express no opinion on whether contract damages might be available even though exhaustion operates to eliminate patent damages. See *Keeler v. Standard Folding Bed Co.,* 157 U.S. 659, 666 (1895) ("Whether a patentee may protect himself and his assignees by special contracts brought home to the purchasers is not a question before us, and upon which we express no opinion. It is, however, obvious that such a question would arise as a question of contract, and not as one under the inherent meaning and effect of the patent laws").

the LGE Patents because they had no reasonable noninfringing use and included all the inventive aspects of the patented methods. Nothing in the License Agreement limited Intel's ability to sell its products practicing the LGE Patents. Intel's authorized sale to Quanta thus took its products outside the scope of the patent monopoly, and as a result, LGE can no longer assert its patent rights against Quanta. Accordingly, the judgment of the Court of Appeals is reversed.

NOTES AND QUESTIONS

1. *The doctrine of exhaustion.* Notwithstanding the patentee's § 154 right to exclude others from selling the patented invention, the doctrine of exhaustion (a.k.a. the doctrine of first sale) imposes an important restriction: Once the patentee releases a patented product into the stream of commerce by selling or authorizing it to be sold to another, he exhausts his legal right to control that product. The first purchaser, and those deriving title from her, may use and resell the product at will. See, e.g., Aro Manufacturing Co. v. Convertible Top Replacement Co., 377 U.S. 476, 84 S.Ct. 1526, 12 L.Ed.2d 457 (1964). Why impose this limitation on the patentee's power?

The United States' Patent Act does not codify the doctrine of exhaustion, but the doctrine is well established in the case law as a limitation on patentees' rights. Over the years, judicial decisions have explained its underlying purpose and justification. They note that the purpose of the patent law is to secure the benefit of an invention (and the investment in research and development underlying it) to the patentee, in order to provide an incentive to invent and as a means of rewarding the inventor for his act of disclosure to the public through the patent application process. However, they have stressed that this purpose is accomplished once the patentee has received the sales price or (in the case of sales by authorized licensees) royalty payment arising from the initial sale of the patented article. "[O]nce that purpose is realized the patent law affords no basis for restraining the use and enjoyment of the thing sold." United States v. Univis Lens Co., 316 U.S. 241, 250–52, 62 S.Ct. 1088, 86 L.Ed. 1408 (1942).

If the purpose of the Patent Act is to benefit inventors in order to incite greater creative endeavors, why shouldn't inventors be able to control subsequent dispositions of the patented article, as well as the initial one? The courts have stressed that the purpose of the patent law is not to ensure the greatest possible financial return to the patentee. Rather, the ultimate purpose of the patent law is to benefit the public. On balance, granting patentees control over the initial sale of patented articles will benefit the public by providing a financial incentive to invent and disclose inventions to the public. However, extending the patentee's rights beyond the initial sale would exceed what is strictly necessary to provide an incentive to invent, and interfere unduly with the free and efficient movement of goods in the marketplace. The Supreme Court has explained that in determining the extent of the patentee's rights in articles embodying the patented invention,

regard must be had for the dominant concern of the patent system. * * * "[T]he promotion of the progress of science and the useful arts is the 'main object;' reward of inventors is secondary and merely a means to that end." * * * "Whilst the remuneration of genius and useful ingenuity is a duty incumbent upon the public, the rights and welfare of the community must be fairly dealt with and effectually guarded. Considerations of individual emolument can never be permitted to operate to the injury of these."

United States v. Masonite Corp., 316 U.S. 265, 278–80, 62 S.Ct. 1070, 86 L.Ed. 1461 (1942)(*quoting* Pennock v. Dialogue, 27 U.S. (2 Pet.) 1, 19, 7 L.Ed. 327 (1829), and Kendall v. Winsor, 62 U.S. (21 How.) 322, 329, 16 L.Ed. 165 (1858)).

In the *Quanta* case, the patented inventions were methods, or processes. How can there be a "first sale" of a method? The *Quanta* Court equated the first sale of products equipped to practice the patented method with the first sale of patented products. But the products that the patent licensee sold could not actually practice the patented method until the purchaser combined them with other hardware elements. Can the rule set forth in *Quanta* be reconciled with the rule in *Deepsouth*, stating that the "invention" in a combination patent lies only in the combination of parts, so that uncombined parts cannot constitute the patented invention?

2. *Contracting around the doctrine of exhaustion.* Given the considerations discussed above, should patentees be able to contract around the doctrine of exhaustion? The Court of Appeals for the Federal Circuit has held that patentees can counteract the effect of the doctrine through express contractual provisions restricting purchasers' subsequent use or resale of the patented article. In Mallinckrodt, Inc. v. Medipart, Inc., 976 F.2d 700 (Fed. Cir.1992), the Federal Circuit found that the patentee could restrict purchasers of its patented medical device to a single use, and hold those who reused the device in violation of the restriction liable not only for breach of contract, but also for patent infringement. The court reasoned that the enforceability of restrictions on the use of patented goods derives from the patent grant itself, which is framed as "the right to exclude:" "This right to exclude may be waived in whole or in part. * * * As in other areas of commerce, private parties may contract as they choose, provided that no law is violated thereby * * *." 976 F.2d at 703.[36] Thus, conditional sales of goods embodying patented inventions do not trigger the doctrine of exhaustion. The doctrine of exhaustion is merely the default rule that applies in the absence of binding restrictions. In a subsequent decision, the Federal Circuit elaborated on its reasoning:

> As a general matter, * * * an unconditional sale of a patented device exhausts the patentee's right to control the purchaser's use of the device thereafter. The theory behind this rule is that in such a transaction, the patentee has bargained for, and received, an amount equal to the full value of the goods. This exhaustion doctrine, however, does not apply to

36. A contractual restriction might be unlawful under the patent misuse doctrine or antitrust law. The *Mallinckrodt* court noted that under the patent misuse doctrine or antitrust law, the appropriate criterion for determining whether a restriction (other than a price-fixing or tying restriction) is unenforceable is to inquire whether the restriction is "reasonably within the patent grant, or whether the patentee has ventured beyond the patent grant and into behavior having an anticompetitive effect not justifiable under the rule of reason." 976 F.2d at 708.

an expressly conditioned sale or license. In such a transaction, it is more reasonable to infer that the parties negotiated a price that reflects only the value of the "use" rights conferred by the patentee. As a result, express conditions accompanying the sale or license of a patented product are generally upheld. Such express conditions, however, are contractual in nature and are subject to antitrust, patent, contract, and any other applicable law, as well as equitable considerations such as patent misuse. Accordingly, conditions that violate some law or equitable consideration are unenforceable. On the other hand, violation of valid conditions entitles the patentee to a remedy for either patent infringement or breach of contract.

B. Braun Medical, Inc. v. Abbott Laboratories, 124 F.3d 1419, 1426 (Fed.Cir. 1997). The *Mallinckrodt* court acknowledged that contract law dictates whether a license restriction is binding on the purchaser, but explained that "the remedy for breach of a binding license provision is not exclusively in contract, for a license is simply a promise not to sue for what would otherwise be patent infringement." 976 F.2d at 708 n.7.

It is useful to note that the "licensing restriction" at issue in *Mallinckrodt* was not an individually negotiated agreement but rather took the form of an inscription stating "Single Use Only" on the device itself, and reiterated in a packaging insert. While the court did not find it necessary to determine whether this was sufficient to condition the sale, it noted that "[i]n accordance with the Uniform Commercial Code a license may become a term of sale, even if not part of the original transaction, if not objected to within a reasonable time." 976 F.2d at 708. The court made it clear that purchasers must have adequate notice of restrictions before they can be deemed binding.

The *Mallinckrodt* line of cases has made it possible for patentees to exert considerable post-sale control over their products: use restrictions, restrictions against enhancement, restrictions on resale. What is the likely impact of the *Quanta* decision on the *Mallinckrodt* line of reasoning?

Note that the first sale must have been authorized by the patentee before the doctrine of first sale applies. If the first sale was not authorized, each subsequent use and resale of the patented article will constitute a separate infringement of the patent.

3. *Repair vs. reconstruction.* The right to use and resell a patented article, which a purchaser and his successors obtain by virtue of the doctrine of exhaustion, encompasses the right to repair. Only when "repair" amounts to "reconstruction" is there an unauthorized "making," or second creation of the patented invention, which constitutes infringement. At what point does permissible repair become impermissible reconstruction?

In Dana Corp. v. American Precision Co., 618 F.Supp. 288 (N.D.Ill.), *aff'd*, 827 F.2d 755 (Fed.Cir.1987), defendant Century purchased old, worn patented clutches, disassembled them, and cleaned and sorted the parts. It salvaged those parts that could be reused, placing them in bins. Then, using a production line set-up, it reassembled a number of rebuilt clutches. In rebuilding, Century used old, salvaged parts as much as possible, but to the extent that there were insufficient used parts, it used replacement parts supplied by other defendants. Due to this process, the parts from a number of old clutches were mixed. Century made no attempt to ensure that when old clutch "A" was disassembled, the parts were kept together to constitute rebuilt clutch "A." A rebuilt clutch might be comprised of parts from a number of worn clutches, as well as replacement parts. The plaintiff patentee sold "key" replacement parts itself. It sued Century and its parts suppliers, alleging that Century's actions constituted direct infringement—an unauthorized "making" of the patented invention—under Patent Act § 271(a).

The patentee first argued that replacing "key parts" of the patented clutch constituted infringement, at least when the key parts were purchased from dealers other than the patentee. "Key parts," according to the patentee, were parts that are intimately connected with the "essential gist" of the patented invention. The court rejected this argument on the ground that none of the individual components of the clutches was itself the subject of patent rights. The patent in the clutch only extended to the invention's unique combination of known components. To prevent replacement of "key" components would essentially extend the patentee's rights to them, even though they were not individually patented or patentable. Nor did it make any difference, the court found, that several key parts were replaced—even if all were replaced—as long as the invention, viewed as a whole, was not completely spent.

How does one tell when the article, viewed as a whole, has become "spent?" In its appeal to the Court of Appeals for the Federal Circuit, the *Dana* patentee argued that whether the patented product is spent should turn on the owner's economic evaluation of the product: "a patented product should be deemed 'spent' when a user, making an objective economic decision, would replace the product rather than repair it, because it has no value to the owner except as scrap." 827 F.2d 755, 760 (Fed.Cir.1987). While finding this approach "interesting," the Federal Circuit rejected it, finding it too uncertain: "In the present case, for example, truck owners desiring to keep their trucks on the road would desire a quick replacement of their inoperative clutch with an existing rebuilt clutch. That decision rests little, if at all, on the owner's objective view of the defective clutch's condition." *Id.* How, then, should the "spentness" determination be made? See FMC Corp. v. Up-Right Inc., 21 F.3d 1073 (Fed.Cir.1994) (Court rejects argument that successive repairs to one machine may, over time, cumulatively amount to an infringing reconstruction).

In a subsequent decision, the Federal Circuit provided four factors to assist in the determination of whether the original product was "spent," so that purported "repairs" in fact constituted infringing "reconstruction":

1) The nature of the actions taken by the defendant;

2) The nature of the device and how it is designed (namely, whether one of the components of the patented combination has a shorter useful life than the whole);

3) whether a market has developed to manufacture or service the part at issue; and

4) objective evidence of the intent of the patentee.

Sandvik Aktiebolag v. E.J. Co., 121 F.3d 669 (Fed. Cir. 1997), *cert. denied*, 523 U.S. 1040, 118 S.Ct. 1337, 140 L.Ed.2d 499 (1998). What do these factors contribute to the question of "spentness"?

The patentee in *Dana* also argued that Century's production-line method of rebuilding the patented clutches made the rebuilding an infringing reconstruction, because by taking the clutches apart, and separating all the reusable parts into bins to be mixed with parts from other clutches, Century destroyed the identity of the original clutch. There was no continuity or identity between the original clutch and the rebuilt one that replaced it. The court rejected this argument, noting that to accept it would elevate form over substance. The patentee admitted that it would not constitute infringement to disassemble and rebuild each clutch individually. Use of a more efficient assembly-line approach to accomplish the same result should not change the legal outcome.

What if Century's records showed that the number of rebuilt clutches it produced exceeded the number of used clutches it purchased?

4. *Experimental use.* Notwithstanding the all-encompassing language of §§ 154 and 271(a), a minor exception to infringement liability has been recognized for purely experimental uses. The exception had its origin in Justice Story's opinion in Whittemore v. Cutter, 29 F.Cas. 1120, 1121 (C.C.D.Mass.1813), in which Justice Story noted: "[I]t could never have been the intention of the legislature to punish a man, who constructed [a patented] machine merely for philosophical experiments, or for the purpose of ascertaining the sufficiency of the machine to produce its described effects." Justice Story elaborated on this exception to liability in Sawin v. Guild, 21 Fed.Cas. 554, 555 (C.C.D.Mass.1813):

> "[T]he making of a patented machine to be an offense * * * must be the making with an intent to use for profit, and not for the mere purpose of philosophical experiments, or to ascertain the verity and exactness of the specification * * *." By 1861, the law was "well-settled that an experiment with a patented article for the sole purpose of gratifying a philosophical taste, or curiosity, or for mere amusement is not an infringement of the rights of the patentee." Poppenhusen v. Falke, 19 Fed.Cas. 1048, 1049 (C.C.S.D.N.Y.1861).

This "experimental use" exception has rarely been applied, and remains very narrow. For example, in *Roche Products, Inc. v. Bolar Pharmaceutical Co., Inc.*, discussed at p. 279, *supra*, the defendant generic drug company argued that the experimental use doctrine sheltered its use of plaintiff's patented drug in tests to demonstrate safety and efficacy and thus obtain F.D.A. approval to market a generic equivalent. The Court of Appeals for the Federal Circuit disagreed:

> Despite Bolar's argument that its tests are "true scientific inquiries" to which a literal interpretation of the experimental use exception logically should extend, we hold the experimental use exception to be truly narrow, and we will not expand it under the present circumstances. * * *

     * * *

Bolar's intended "experimental" use is solely for business reasons and not for amusement, to satisfy idle curiosity, or for strictly philosophical inquiry. * * * Bolar may intend to perform "experiments," but unlicensed experiments conducted with a view to the adaption of the patented invention to the experimenter's business is a violation of the rights of the patentee to exclude others from using his patented invention. It is obvious here that it is a misnomer to call the intended use *de minimis*. It is no trifle in its economic effect on the parties even if the quantity used is small. It is no dilettante affair such as Justice Story envisioned. We cannot construe the experimental use rule so broadly as to allow a violation of the patent laws in the guise of "scientific inquiry," when that inquiry has definite, cognizable, and not insubstantial commercial purposes.

Id., 733 F.2d at 863.

Several commentators have advocated reevaluating the experimental use exception, and enlarging its role to better balance the incentive function of patents against researchers' legitimate need for access to others' inventions. See, e.g., Eisenberg, *Patents and the Progress of Science: Exclusive Rights and Experimental Use*, 56 U. Chi. L. Rev. 1017 (1989).

PROBLEMS

1. X Co. sells its patented drill, consisting of a shank portion and a unique carbide tip geometry that has specially configured cutting edges. The drill tip is not separately patented. Over time and use, the drill tip dulls and may require resharpening. X Co. expects the drill tip to be resharpened, and issues guidelines explaining how to resharpen it. However, it does not manufacture or sell replacement drill tips.

Y offers a resharpening service, and also retips X Co.'s drills for customers when the drill can no longer be sharpened because it has chipped, cracked or simply worn down too far. Y's retipping process includes removing the worn or damaged tip by heating the tip to 1300 degrees Fahrenheit using an acetylene torch. Y then brazes a rectangular piece of new carbide onto the drill shank. After the piece of carbide has cooled, Y recreates the patented geometry of the cutting edges by machining the carbide. It does this by following X Co.'s instructions for tip resharpening.

Does Y's retipping service constitute repair or infringing reconstruction of the patented drills?

2. A Company patents and sells disposable computer printer cartridges. The cartridges can print approximately 200–2000 pages, depending on the cartridge used and the nature of the printing being done. Once the ink runs out, A Co. expects the cartridge to be discarded and replaced with a new one. Instructions accompanying the cartridges warn users that refilling the ink cartridges may reduce print quality, disclaim liability for printer damage caused by refilling, and advise the user to "discard old print cartridge immediately." B Co. buys large quantities of new, unused A Co. cartridges and modifies them so that they can be refilled and reused. B Co. then resells

the modified cartridges in a package with replacement ink. Should A Co. have a cause of action for patent infringement?

NOTE: PARALLEL IMPORT OF PATENTED GOODS

Another perplexing problem that arises in connection with the doctrine of exhaustion is its application to parallel imports. Parallel imports are goods that are sold or authorized for sale abroad by the U.S. intellectual property owner, but are subsequently imported into the U.S. without the U.S. intellectual property owner's authorization.[37] Assuming that a U.S. patentee (or an affiliated business entity) made the first sale of a U.S.-patented article abroad, or authorized a licensee to do so in return for a royalty payment, it can be characterized as having received the benefit of the first sale of the patented article, as envisioned by the U.S. patent laws. Should the doctrine of exhaustion apply, releasing the patented article from further control by the patentee, so that subsequent purchasers can import it into the U.S. and resell it in competition with the patentee? Two competing theories have emerged to address this quandary.

The "international exhaustion" theory provides that the doctrine of exhaustion should apply whenever the U.S. patentee sells or authorizes the first sale of the patented article, regardless of whether the article was manufactured or originally sold in the U.S. or abroad. The reasoning, essentially, is that the U.S. patentee has enjoyed the opportunity to control the first sale, which occurred abroad, and can be presumed to have obtained sufficient benefit to maintain an incentive to invest in creative efforts. (Regardless of whether the article is patented in the foreign country, the U.S. patentee's decision to sell there generally suggests that it finds the sale beneficial.) Providing a "second bite of the apple," by granting the opportunity to control foreign purchasers' resale of the article in the United States, is not necessary in order to serve the incentive function of the patent laws. Moreover, it would interfere unnecessarily with the free international movement of goods and the competitive marketplace, depriving consumers of the benefits of competition and greater accessibility of goods. It also arguably would favor patentees selling abroad over patentees whose sales are strictly domestic, since the latter have no comparable opportunity to control resales.

The "territorial" or "domestic" exhaustion theory, in contrast, essentially limits the doctrine of exhaustion to patented articles manufactured and initially sold within the territory of the United States. The reasoning is that the U.S. patent laws only provide rights within the boundaries of the United States, and that the doctrine of exhaustion should extend no further, geographically, than the rights to be exhausted. A U.S. patentee selling patented articles abroad does not benefit from its U.S. patent in the sale. Therefore, it should be able to assert its patent rights (for the first time) when the article enters the United States without the patentee's authorization. It is irrelevant whether the patentee enjoys patent rights comparable to its U.S. rights in the country in which the first sale took place, or otherwise reaped a benefit from

---

37. Parallel imports must be distinguished from counterfeit goods, which are goods that were initially produced and/or sold unlawfully, without the authorization of an intellectual property owner.

the sale abroad. Each country's patent laws provide a separate opportunity to benefit and control patented articles as they enter that country's borders. Moreover, the ability to control the movement of patented articles from one country to another is necessary from a business standpoint, because it permits the U.S. patentee effectively to adapt its price and marketing methods to each country in which it does business, free of competition from parallel imports that it released to the market at a lower price in another country.

A line of cases from the U.S. Court of Appeals for the Second Circuit adopted an international exhaustion doctrine which was modified by the ability of patentees to contract out of it. This was the rule of law in the United States for over a century. See Curtiss Aeroplane & Motor Corp. v. United Aircraft Engineering Corp., 266 F. 71 (2d Cir.1920).

The Court of Appeals for the Federal Circuit effectively reversed the *Curtiss* international exhaustion rule in Jazz Photo Corp. v. International Trade Commission, 264 F.3d 1094 (Fed. Cir. 2001), *cert. denied*, 536 U.S. 950, 122 S.Ct. 2644, 153 L.Ed.2d 823 (2002). The *Jazz Photo* decision arose from a patent infringement action filed with the U.S. International Trade Commission (ITC). The plaintiff, Fuji Photo Film Co., owned U.S. patents for a number of inventions that were incorporated into the disposable camera that it and its licensees sold. Once the film in these disposable cameras was exposed, photoprocessors opened the cameras' plastic shells and removed the film for processing. Though Fuji intended that the camera shells not be reused, third-party firms in China obtained and refurbished (or "reloaded") large numbers of them for reuse. The defendants in *Jazz Photo* purchased the reloaded cameras from the Chinese refurbishers (or in some instances, supplied the film or shells and contracted with the Chinese firms to perform the reloading process), and imported them into the U.S. for resale. All of the imported cameras appear to have been originally manufactured and sold by Fuji or its licensees. Some of the cameras were originally sold in the United States, and some were originally sold abroad. *Jazz Photo, supra*, 264 F.3d at 1105.

The patentee alleged that the imported cameras infringed (that is, were unsheltered by the doctrine of exhaustion) because they had been reconstructed (as opposed to repaired). While the evidence was incomplete regarding the process used by the various Chinese refurbishers, the Court of Appeals for the Federal Circuit recognized eight common steps that the refurbishers employed,[38] and held that as long as the refurbishment process was limited to those steps, the refurbishment would constitute permissible repair and not infringing reconstruction under U.S. precedent.

Fuji had not argued that the doctrine of exhaustion is limited to products sold domestically. It appears that none of the parties distinguished between foreign and domestic camera shells at any point in the litigation before the

---

38. These steps were:

(1) removing the cardboard cover, (2) cutting open the plastic casing, (3) inserting new film and a container to receive the film, (4) replacing the winding wheel for certain cameras, (5) replacing the battery for flash cameras, (6) resetting the counter, (7) resealing the outer case, and (8) adding a new cardboard cover.

Jazz Photo, supra, 264 F.3d at 1098.

ITC or the Federal Circuit, even though they knew through discovery that many of the cameras had first been sold outside of the United States. Nonetheless, the Federal Circuit raised the issue of foreign versus domestic sales *sua sponte*, and held:

> Fuji states that some of the imported * * * cameras originated and were sold only overseas, but are included in the refurbished importations by some of the respondents. The record supports this statement, which does not appear to be disputed. United States patent rights are not exhausted by products of foreign provenance. To invoke the protection of the first sale doctrine, the authorized first sale must have occurred under the United States patent. *See Boesch v. Graff*, 133 U.S. 697, 701–703 (1890)(a lawful foreign purchase does not obviate the need for license from the United States patentee before importation into and sale in the United States). Our decision applies only to [cameras] for which the United States patent right has been exhausted by first sale in the United States. Imported [cameras] of solely foreign provenance are not immunized from infringement of United States patent by the nature of their refurbishment.

Jazz Photo, supra, 264 F.3d at 1105. The court did not acknowledge or attempt to distinguish the significant case precedent to the contrary, or discuss the public policy implications of replacing the international exhaustion rule with the territorial exhaustion rule.

The *Jazz Photo* court cited the Supreme Court's decision in Boesch v. Graff, 133 U.S. 697, 10 S.Ct. 378, 33 L.Ed. 787 (1890), as support for its holding. In *Boesch*, the defendants purchased the plaintiff's patented lamp burners in Germany from a seller who was authorized to sell in Germany by virtue of a "prior user" law,[39] but was not related to the U.S. patentee and derived no rights from him. Although the sale to the defendants in Germany was legal, the U.S. Supreme Court found that the defendants' resale in the United States constituted infringement of the U.S. patent.

> The right which [the German seller] had to make and sell the burners in Germany was allowed him under the laws of that country, and purchasers from him could not be thereby authorized to sell the articles in the United States in defiance of the rights of patentees under a United States patent.... The sale of articles in the United States under a United States patent cannot be controlled by foreign laws.

Id. at 703. Is the finding of infringement in *Boesch* inconsistent with the rule of international exhaustion established in the *Curtiss* line of cases? In *Boesch* the U.S. patentee's rights were not exhausted by the initial sale of the lamps in Germany because the U.S. patentee did not sell them or authorized their sale. The U.S. doctrine of exhaustion is triggered not by a legal first sale, per se, but by a first sale made by the U.S. patentee or its licensees. The U.S. patentee must have received an opportunity to benefit from the initial sale of the patented article before he can be deemed to have exhausted his rights in it.

---

39. The U.S. patentee also owned a German patent, but had no cause of action against the seller for infringement under German law because the seller had already commenced use of the invention in Germany prior to the patentee's application. *Boesch*, 133 U.S. at 701.

Though earlier decisions of the regional Courts of Appeals are generally influential to the Federal Circuit, it is not bound by them. Thus, the court's decision in *Jazz Photo* supersedes the *Curtiss* international exhaustion rule. Which rule makes more sense from a policy standpoint? What are the implications of the *Jazz Photo* decision for foreign purchasers of U.S. goods? For foreign producers who incorporate U.S.-patented parts in their products, pursuant to a license from the U.S patentee? For trade in remanufactured or recycled goods? Is the Federal Circuit's position on parallel imports consistent with the policies that the Supreme Court embraced in *Quanta*?

In 1994, Congress amended the Patent Act to provide patentees an express right of importation, which became effective on January 1, 1996. See 35 U.S.C. § 271(a). Congress added the importation right in order to bring the United States into compliance with Article 28 of the TRIPs Agreement.[40] Does the enactment of this new importation right support movement from an international exhaustion rule to a territorial exhaustion rule? The TRIPs Agreement itself expressly disclaims any position on the the proper rule of exhaustion.[41] Moreover, the legislative history of the Uruguay Round Agreements Act suggests that Congress intended that the amendment would not "affect U.S. law or practice relating to parallel importation of products protected by intellectual property rights." Message from the President of the United States Transmitting the Uruguay Round Trade Agreements, Texts of Agreements Implementing Bill, Statement of Administrative Action and Required Supporting Statements, H.R. Doc. No. 316, 103d Cong., 2d Sess. 981, 990–91 (1994), *reprinted in* 1994 U.S.C.C.A.N. 4040, 4280, 4287.

2. The Right to Exclude Others From Assisting Third Parties to Infringe

DSU MEDICAL CORP. v. JMS CO., LTD.
United States Court of Appeals for the Federal Circuit, 2008.
471 F.3d 1293.

RADER, CIRCUIT JUDGE.

DSU Medical Corporation (DSU) and Medisystems Corporation (MDS) (collectively DSU) sued JMS Company, Limited (JMS) and JMS North

---

40. Under TRIPs art. 28, a product patent must provide the exclusive right "to prevent third parties not having the owner's consent from the acts of: making, using, offering for sale, selling, or importing * * * that product * * *."

Note that Tariff Act § 337 has long enabled U.S. patentees to prevent importation of infringing goods through the International Trade Commission. 19 U.S.C. § 1337. Section 337 authorizes the International Trade Commission to prohibit the importation of articles that "infringe a valid and enforceable United States patent" or "are made, produced, processed or mined under, or by means of, a process patent" by excluding their entry into the country or by means of a cease and desist order.

41. A footnote to TRIPs Article 28 elaborates that the right of importation "is subject to the provisions of Article 6." Article 6, in turn, provides that for the purposes of dispute settlement under the TRIPs Agreement, "nothing in this Agreement shall be used to address the issue of the exhaustion of intellectual property rights." Thus, while the TRIPs Agreement requires adhering nations to provide a right of importation, it deliberately avoids directly addressing the applicability of the doctrine of exhaustion to temper that right. This is because the nations negotiating the TRIPs Agreement were unable to reach agreement about the applicability of the doctrine of exhaustion to goods sold internationally.

America (collectively JMS) and ITL Corporation Pty, Limited (ITL) for patent infringement, inducement to infringe, and contributory infringement of United States Patent Nos. 5,112,311 ('311) and 5,266,072 ('072). After a six-week jury trial produced a unanimous verdict, the United States District Court for the Northern District of California entered a final judgment finding claims 46–47, and 50–52 of the '311 patent invalid as obvious. The trial court also entered a final judgment, pursuant to the unanimous verdict, of infringement against JMS and JMS North American on claims 49, 53, and 54 of the '311 patent, and of non-infringement for ITL. * * * Finding no reversible error, this court affirms.

I.

The '311 and '072 patents claim a guarded, winged-needle assembly. The invention reduces the risk of accidental needle-stick injuries. Needle puncture wounds can transmit blood-borne diseases such as Hepatitis B and AIDS. The '311 and '072 patented inventions effectively guard standard winged-needle-sets to prevent needle-stick injuries.

* * *

Mr. David Utterberg, a co-inventor of the '311 patent, owns DSU and MDS. DSU owns the '311 patent; MDS has an exclusive license to make and sell the '311 invention for large-bore needles * * *. MDS markets AVF needles under the brand names "MasterGuard" and "PointGuard." [Figures 5 and 6, below, illustrate one embodiment of the patented invention.]

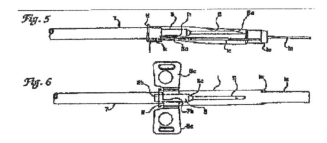

The alleged infringing device, made by ITL (an Australian company) sells under the name Platypus™ Needle Guard (Platypus). ITL manufactures the Platypus in Malaysia and Singapore. The Platypus needle guard is a "stand-alone" product: a small configured piece of plastic. This plastic guard structure is not attached to any other device. In other words, the Platypus does not include a needle, but only a sheathing structure. Some claims of the '311 patent recite both a slotted guard and a guarded winged needle assembly. Before use, the Platypus resembles an open clamshell (open-shell configuration). During use, the halves of the clam shell close to form the needle guard (closed-shell configuration). The following illustration shows the Platypus in open-and closed-shell configuration:

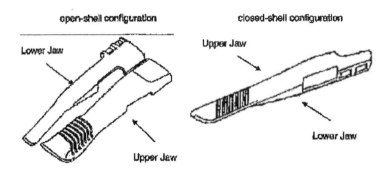

JMS is a large Japanese medical supply business that competes with MDS in the United States market. Beginning in June 1999, JMS purchased Platypus needle guards from ITL, entering into an agreement to distribute the Platypus worldwide (the Supply Agreement). Under the Supply Agreement, JMS bought open-shell configuration Platypus guard units from ITL in Singapore and Malaysia. JMS generally closed the Platypus guards around needle sets before distributing them to customers.

DSU alleges that the Platypus infringes the '311 patent. DSU also alleges that JMS and ITL contributed to and induced each other's infringement. JMS sought to sell ITL's infringing Platypus until it could produce its substitute non-infringing product, the WingEater. ITL offered to supply its infringing Platypus. * * *

     * * *

III.

The jury found that JMS North America and JMS directly and contributorily infringed, and that JMS additionally induced JMS North America to infringe. However, the jury returned a verdict of non-infringement in favor of ITL. The jury entered a verdict finding that ITL did not engage in contributory infringement or inducement to infringe. The trial court denied DSU's motion for new trial on the jury's verdict that ITL did not contributorily infringe or induce infringement. This court reviews a denial of a motion for a new trial after a jury trial for an abuse of discretion.

A.

On appeal, DSU argues that ITL committed contributory infringement. According to DSU, the Platypus, which ITL sold to JMS, had no substantial noninfringing use. Therefore, DSU argues, ITL committed contributory infringement as a matter of law. ITL responds that it made and sold "most Platypus guards" outside of the United States. ITL also contends that the record contains no evidence that the Platypus was used in an infringing manner in the United States.

The Platypus sets that came into the United States fall within three categories:

(1) JMS imported into the United States approximately 30 million Platypus guards that, prior to importation into the United States, it had already assembled into the closed-shell configuration, combined with needle sets. These units accounted for the vast majority of Platypus sales in the United States.

(2) Fresenius purchased approximately 3.5 million Platypus guards, in the open-shell configuration without needle sets. ITL billed JMS for the shipments and shipped them to Fresenius in the United States at JMS's request. Fresenius ultimately decided that guards without needle sets did not meet FDA regulations, and it returned about 3 million.

(3) ITL sent approximately 15,000 Platypus in the open-shell configuration to JMS in San Francisco. DSU introduced no evidence that those units were ever put into the closed-shell configuration in the United States.

Additionally, the record contained evidence that when instructed to do so by JMS, ITL would ship Platypus guard units F.O.B. into the United States. The record also shows, however, that ITL only sold the Platypus in its open-shell configuration.

Therefore, this court must determine whether the jury's verdict is against the clear weight of the evidence. Under § 271(c):

[w]hoever offers to sell or sells *within the United States* ... a component of a patented machine, manufacture, combination or composition ... constituting a material part of the invention, *knowing* the same to be especially made or especially adapted for use in an infringement of such patent, and not a staple article or commodity of commerce *suitable for substantial noninfringing use,* shall be liable as a contributory infringer.

35 U.S.C. § 271(c) (2000) (emphases added). In discussing 35 U.S.C. § 271(c), the Supreme Court stated:

One who makes and sells articles which are only adapted to be used in a patented combination will be presumed to intend the natural consequences of his acts; he will be presumed to intend that they shall be used in the combination of the patent.

Metro-Goldwyn–Mayer Studios, Inc. v. Grokster, Ltd., 545 U.S. 913 (2005). In addition, the patentee always has the burden to show direct infringement for each instance of indirect infringement. * * * Thus, to prevail on contributory infringement, DSU must have shown that ITL made and sold the Platypus, that the Platypus has no substantial non-infringing uses in its closed-shell configuration, that ITL engaged in conduct (made sales) within the United States that contributed to another's direct infringement, and that JMS engaged in an act of direct infringement on those sales that ITL made in the United States.

The trial court properly applied these legal principles. The trial court determined that the record showed that ITL supplied the Platypus, that the Platypus had no substantial non-infringing uses in its closed-shell configuration, and that ITL intended to make the Platypus that resulted in the potential for contributory infringement as a product designed for use in the patented combination. In fact, even beyond the minimal intent requirement for contributory infringement, ITL acted with the knowledge of the '311 patent and knowledge that the component was especially made or adapted for use in an infringing manner. However, the district court denied the motion for a new trial because the record does not show that "the alleged contributory act ha[d] a direct nexus to a specific act of direct infringement." In denying the new trial, the court stated:

> And while it is true that Plaintiffs introduced evidence that "ITL sold and shipped millions of 'stand alone' guards directly to United States customers, including JMS [North America] and end-users like Fresenius," *there was no direct evidence* at trial establishing that these guards were actually closed and used as an act of direct infringement in the United States.

Upon review of the record, this court perceives, as well, an absence of evidence of direct infringement to which ITL contributed *in* the United States. Under the terms of the '311 patent, the Platypus only infringes in the closed-shell configuration. When open, the Platypus, for instance, lacks a "slot" as well as other claimed features. ITL only contributed to placing the Platypus into the closed-shell configuration in Malaysia (category 1, above); not in the United States. Section 271(c) has a territorial limitation requiring contributory acts to occur in the United States. Furthermore, this court cannot reverse a jury verdict of non-infringement on mere inferences that the Platypus guard units sold in the United States (i.e., the open-shell configuration in categories 2 and 3, above) were put into the infringing closed-shell configuration. The record does not show that the Platypus guards ITL shipped into the United States in the open-shell configuration were ever put into an infringing configuration, i.e., closed-shell. On categories 2 and 3, above, the record contains no evidence of direct infringement, i.e., that the open-shell Platypus guards imported by ITL were sold or used in their closed-shell configuration. As a result, the trial court did not abuse its discretion in denying DSU's motion for new trial on ITL's contributory infringement.

On the issue of induced infringement, DSU argues that ITL induced infringement by inducing JMS to sell the closed-shell configuration in the United States. The district court denied DSU's motion for a new trial on the ground that, although JMS directly infringed, ITL did not intend JMS to infringe.

B.

RESOLUTION OF CONFLICTING PRECEDENT
Section III. B., only, is considered en banc.

* * *

This court addresses Part III. B., of this opinion en banc. This section addresses, in the context of induced infringement, "the required intent ... to induce the specific acts of [infringement] or additionally to cause an infringement." *MEMC Elec. Materials, Inc. v. Mitsubishi Materials Silicon Corp.*, 420 F.3d 1369, 1378 n. 4 (Fed.Cir.2005). This section clarifies that intent requirement by holding en banc that, as was stated in *Manville Sales Corp. v. Paramount Systems, Inc.*, 917 F.2d 544, 554 (Fed.Cir.1990), "[t]he plaintiff has the burden of showing that the alleged infringer's actions induced infringing acts and that he knew or should have known his actions would induce actual infringements." The requirement that the alleged infringer knew or should have known his actions would induce actual infringement necessarily includes the requirement that he or she knew of the patent. * * *

* * *

Under section 271(b), "[w]hoever actively induces infringement of a patent shall be liable as an infringer." 35 U.S.C. § 271(b). To establish liability under section 271(b), a patent holder must prove that once the defendants knew of the patent, they "actively and *knowingly* aid[ed] and abett[ed] another's direct infringement." *Water Technologies Corp. v. Calco, Ltd.*, 850 F.2d 660, 668 (Fed.Cir.1988). However, "knowledge of the acts alleged to constitute infringement" is not enough. *Warner-Lambert Co. v. Apotex Corp.*, 316 F.3d 1348, 1363 (Fed.Cir.2003). The "mere knowledge of possible infringement by others does not amount to inducement; specific intent and action to induce infringement must be proven." *Id.* at 1364.

DSU asked the court to instruct the jury, purportedly in accordance with *Hewlett-Packard Co. v. Bausch & Lomb, Inc.*, 909 F.2d 1464 (Fed.Cir. 1990), that to induce infringement, the inducer need only intend to cause the *acts* of the third party that constitute direct infringement. The trial court gave the following instruction to the jury:

> In order to induce infringement, there must first be an act of direct infringement and proof that the defendant knowingly induced infringement with the intent to encourage the infringement. The defendant must have intended to cause the acts that constitute the direct infringement and must have known or should have known than[sic] its action would cause the direct infringement. Unlike direct infringement, which must take place within the United States, induced infringement does not require any activity by the indirect infringer in this country, as long as the direct infringement occurs here.

Thus, the court charged the jury in accordance with *Manville*. The statute does not define whether the purported infringer must intend to induce the infringement or whether the purported infringer must merely intend to engage in the acts that induce the infringement regardless of whether it knows it is causing another to infringe. DSU complains that the instruction is incorrect because it requires that the inducer possess specific intent to encourage another's infringement, and not merely that the inducer had knowledge of the acts alleged to constitute infringement.

In *Grokster,* which was a copyright case, the Supreme Court cited with approval this court's decision in *Water Technologies* when it discussed inducement of infringement, stating:

> The rule on inducement of infringement as developed in the early cases is no different today. Evidence of "active steps ... taken to encourage direct infringement," such as advertising an infringing use or instructing how to engage in an infringing use, show an affirmative intent that the product be used to infringe, and a showing that infringement was encouraged overcomes the law's reluctance to find liability when a defendant merely sells a commercial product suitable for some lawful use.

Grokster, 125 S.Ct. at 2779. As a result, if an entity offers a product with the object of promoting its use to infringe, as shown by clear expression or other affirmative steps taken to foster infringement, it is then liable for the resulting acts of infringement by third parties. *Id.* at 2780. "The inducement rule ... premises liability on purposeful, culpable expression and conduct...." *Id.*

Grokster, thus, validates this court's articulation of the state of mind requirement for inducement. In *Manville,* this court held that the "alleged infringer must be shown ... to have *knowingly* induced infringement," 917 F.2d at 553, not merely knowingly induced the *acts* that constitute direct infringement. This court explained its "knowing" requirement:

> It must be established that the defendant possessed specific intent to encourage another's infringement and not merely that the defendant had knowledge of the acts alleged to constitute inducement. The plaintiff has the burden of showing that the alleged infringer's actions induced infringing acts *and* that he knew or should have known his actions would induce actual infringements.

Id. at 553. In *Water Technologies,* also cited with approval by the Supreme Court, 125 S.Ct. at 2779, this court clarified: "While proof of intent is necessary, direct evidence is not required; rather, circumstantial evidence may suffice." 850 F.2d at 668. Although this court stated "that proof of actual intent to cause the acts which constitute the infringement is a necessary prerequisite to finding active inducement," *Hewlett-Packard,* 909 F.2d at 1469, *Grokster* has clarified that the intent requirement for inducement requires more than just intent to cause the acts that produce direct infringement. Beyond that threshold knowledge, the inducer must have an affirmative intent to cause direct infringement. In the words of a recent decision, inducement requires " 'that the alleged infringer knowingly induced infringement and possessed specific intent to encourage another's infringement.' " *MEMC Elec.,* 420 F.3d at 1378 (Fed.Cir.2005). Accordingly, inducement requires evidence of culpable conduct, directed to encouraging another's infringement, not merely that the inducer had knowledge of the direct infringer's activities. Accordingly, the district court correctly instructed the jury in this case.

C.

The district court denied DSU's motion for a new trial on the issue of inducement to infringe. * * *

The jury heard evidence about the commercial transactions between ITL and JMS, including JMS's intention to sell ITL's Platypus to Fresenius until JMS could get its own WingEater approved by the Food and Drug Administration (FDA) and ready for market. The jury also heard evidence that Mr. Utterberg's lawyer informed ITL in January 1997 that the Platypus infringed the '311 patent. Additionally, the jury learned that ITL contacted an Australian attorney, who concluded that its Platypus would not infringe. JMS and ITL then also obtained letters from U.S. patent counsel advising that the Platypus did not infringe. Mr. William Mobbs, one of the owners of ITL who had participated in the design of the Platypus, testified that ITL had no intent to infringe the '311 patent.

Thus, on this record, the jury was well within the law to conclude that ITL did not induce JMS to infringe by purposefully and culpably encouraging JMS's infringement. To the contrary, the record contains evidence that ITL did not believe its Platypus infringed. Therefore, it had no intent to infringe. Accordingly, the record supports the jury's verdict based on the evidence showing a lack of the necessary specific intent. The trial court certainly did not abuse its discretion.

* * *

NOTES AND QUESTIONS

1. *Contributory infringement.* The Supreme Court stressed, in the *Deepsouth* case and in *Aro Mfg. Co. v. Convertible Top Replacement Co.,* 365 U.S. 336, 81 S.Ct. 599, 5 L.Ed.2d 592 (1961) ("*Aro I*"), that the patent monopoly does not extend to the individual components of a patented combination. However, Patent Act § 271(c) extends the patentee's property rights to unpatented components of her invention in some circumstances. If the sale, offer for sale or importation of an unpatented component leads to direct infringement by purchasers, the component has no substantial noninfringing use, and the other prerequisites of subsection (c) are satisfied, then the patentee may prohibit the sale, offer for sale or importation of the component, and/or recover damages. In some cases, subsection (c) may enable the patentee to completely control the U.S. market for the unpatented component.

The *Aro* case was itself a claim for contributory infringement pursuant to subsection (c). The "combination" patent at issue claimed a top for convertible automobiles. General Motors and the Ford Company both included structures embodying the patented top as original equipment in their 1952–54 convertible models. G.M. was licensed to use the top, but Ford was not. Thus, Ford's manufacture and sale of its automobiles infringed the patent. The defendant Aro, who also was unlicensed, manufactured and sold fabric components especially tailored to replace the fabric in the Ford and G.M. convertible tops when the original fabric wore out. The patentee sued Aro for contributory infringement.

In its first ("*Aro I*") opinion, the Supreme Court dealt only with the G.M. cars. The Court reasoned that Aro could only be liable for contributory infringement in selling the replacement fabric for the G.M. models if its purchasers used the fabric to directly infringe the patent. It found that there was no direct infringement because the purchasers' replacement of the worn fabric constituted permissible "repair," rather than reconstruction.

The Supreme Court addressed Aro's sales of fabric for the Ford convertible models in a later opinion. Aro Manufacturing Co. v. Convertible Top Replacement Co., Inc., 377 U.S. 476, 84 S.Ct. 1526, 12 L.Ed.2d 457 (1964) ("*Aro II*"). In that opinion the majority reasoned that since Ford's tops were unauthorized, the doctrine of exhaustion did not apply, and subsequent purchasers had no right to use them. Thus, the purchasers' use constituted patent infringement. The fact that replacing the fabric constituted "repair" rather than "reconstruction" was irrelevant: "Where use infringes, repair does also, for it perpetuates the infringing use." *Id.*, 377 U.S. at 484. Thus, the legality of the purchasers' repair ultimately depended upon whether the original sale of the tops they repaired was authorized (licensed) by the patentee. Having established direct infringement on the part of the purchasers of Ford convertibles, the majority turned to the claim of contributory infringement against Aro:

> The language of [section 271(c)] fits perfectly Aro's activity of selling "a component of a patented * * * combination * * *, constituting a material part of the invention, * * * especially made or especially adapted for use in an infringement of such patent and not a staple article or commodity of commerce suitable for substantial noninfringing use." Indeed, this is the almost unique case in which the component was hardly suitable for *any* noninfringing use.

Id., 377 U.S. at 487–88. The Court noted that the fabric replacements in question not only were specially designed for the Ford convertibles but would not fit the top structures of any other cars. The majority then turned to the requirement that the defendant know that the component it is selling is "especially made or especially adapted for use in an infringement" of the patent:

> Was Aro "knowing" within the statutory meaning because—as it admits, and as the lower courts found—it knew that its replacement fabrics were especially designed for use in the 1952–54 Ford convertible tops and were not suitable for other use? Or does the statute require a further showing that Aro knew that the tops were patented, and knew also that Ford was not licensed under the patent so that any fabric replacement by a Ford car owner constituted infringement?
>
> On this question a majority of the Court is of the view that § 271(c) does require a showing that the alleged contributory infringer knew that

the combination for which his component was especially designed was both patented and infringing. With respect to many of the replacement-fabric sales involved in this case, Aro clearly had such knowledge. For by letter dated January 2, 1954, [the patentee] informed Aro that it held the * * * patent; that it had granted a license to General Motors but to no one else; and that "It is obvious, from the foregoing and from an inspection of the convertible automobile sold by the Ford Motor Company, that anyone selling ready-made replacement fabrics for these automobiles would be guilty of contributory infringement of said patents." Thus the Court's interpretation of the knowledge requirement affords Aro no defense with respect to replacement-fabric sales made after January 2, 1954. * * * With respect to any sales that were made before that date, however, Aro cannot be held liable in the absence of a showing that at the time it had already acquired the requisite knowledge that the Ford car tops were patented and infringing.

Id., 377 U.S. at 488–91.

Why does the patentee need a cause of action for contributory infringement, given that it already has a cause of action against the direct infringer? Is extension of the patentee's rights to unpatented components in these circumstances consistent with the goal of balancing patent incentives with competition concerns?

Assume that X Company sells a computer program, and a particular subroutine in the program, when run on a computer, infringes Y Company's patented process. That subroutine has no substantial, non-infringing use. All the other components of the program have substantial, non-infringing uses. Assuming that the other prerequisites of contributory infringement are satisfied, should Y's ongoing sale of the program be deemed actionable contributory infringement? See Ricoh Co., Ltd. v. Quanta Computer, Inc., 550 F.3d 1325, 1336–40 (Fed. Cir. 2008).

2. *Active inducement to infringe.* Under § 271(b), a person who actively solicits or assists another to infringe, with the requisite intent, will be liable if the other does in fact directly infringe the patent as a result. What kinds of acts might constitute active inducement? Is there any overlap between subsections (b) and (c), so that a defendant's conduct might simultaneously violate both? Why is the active inducement cause of action needed, given that there will always be a direct infringement, as well?

A cause of action for active inducement to infringe may provide a means of reaching corporate officers and directors (normally protected against liability for corporate acts) who have caused their corporation directly to infringe. An example of an unsuccessful attempt to avoid the corporate shield against officer/director liability occurred in Manville Sales Corp. v. Paramount Systems, Inc., 917 F.2d 544 (Fed.Cir.1990). In *Manville*, Paramount's corporate secretary obtained a copy of a drawing of Manville's patented device that had been submitted to the Florida Department of Transportation, and sent it to Paramount's president. The president gave the drawing to a designer for use in designing Paramount's device. The resulting device was found to infringe the Manville patent. The question before the Court of Appeals for the Federal Circuit was whether the Paramount secretary and president could be held individually liable along with Paramount, either under § 271(a) or (b). With regard to the § 271(a) claim, the court observed:

> [T]here must be evidence to justify piercing the corporate veil. * * * Often a party asking a court to disregard the corporate existence will attempt to show that the corporation was merely the alter ego of its officers. * * * More generally, a court may exert its equitable powers and disregard the corporate entity if it decides that piercing the veil will prevent fraud, illegality, injustice, a contravention of public policy, or prevent the corporation from shielding someone from criminal liability. The court, however, must "start from the general rule that the corporate entity should be recognized and upheld, unless specific, unusual circumstances call for an exception."

Id., 917 F.2d at 552. The court noted that while the facts supported the conclusion that the officers had knowledge of their acts, and the acts assisted the corporation to infringe, the district court had abused its discretion in piercing the veil. The officers' acts were within the scope of their employment. Moreover, the district court had found that the officers were not the alter egos of the corporation, that Paramount and its officers did not know of the patent prior to the suit, and that they had only continued to infringe after the suit was filed on the good faith belief, based on the advice of counsel, that there was no infringement. Nor was there any evidence that the officers were attempting to avoid liability through use of the corporate form. *Id.*, 917 F.2d at 552–3.

> With regard to the § 271(b) active inducement claim, the Court observed:

> Under [subsection (b)], corporate officers who actively assist with their corporation's infringement may be personally liable for inducing infringement regardless of whether the circumstances are such that a court should disregard the corporate entity and pierce the corporate veil. * * * The alleged infringer must be shown, however, to have knowingly induced infringement. * * * It must be established that the defendant possessed specific intent to encourage another's infringement and not merely that the defendant had knowledge of the acts alleged to constitute inducement. The plaintiff has the burden of showing that the alleged infringer's actions induced infringing acts and that he knew or should have known his actions would induce actual infringements.

Id., 917 F.2d at 553. In this case, the court stressed that the officers were not aware of Manville's patent until suit was filed and that Paramount's subsequent infringing acts continued upon the officers' good faith belief, based on advice of counsel, that Paramount's product did not infringe. There was insufficient evidence that the officers had the requisite specific intent. *Id.* For a different result, see Orthokinetics, Inc. v. Safety Travel Chairs, Inc., 806 F.2d 1565 (Fed.Cir.1986).

PROBLEMS

1. X invents and patents a new variety of insulated container for hot foods and liquids. The container keeps its contents hot by insulating them with a special chemical solution suspended in a cavity surrounding the

compartment in which the food is placed. None of the components of the container is novel in itself, and neither is the chemical solution. However, the combination of these elements is novel and non-obvious.

Y begins to manufacture a container with all the same elements as X's, but he does not insert the chemical solution. Instead, he sells the container with instructions to the buyer to purchase the chemical solution from a pharmacy, and explains how to insert the solution into the container.

Z, a homemaker, purchases Y's container, reads the instructions, purchases the chemical solution from P, a local pharmacist, and inserts it into the container as directed. She then uses the container to pack a hot lunch for her daughter to take to school.

What, if any, claims is X likely to have against Y, Z, or P?

2. Acme Company's patented invention consists of two components—component A and component B—both of which are non-staples with no substantial noninfringing use. Acme sells component A and component B separately, rather than in combination. Brown Co. manufactures and sells component B, with no license from Acme. Members of the public purchase component A from Acme, and component B from Brown and combine them to make the patented invention. Assuming that Brown knows of the Acme patent, and that component B has no substantial use other than in Acme's patented invention, is Acme likely to have a cause of action against Brown for contributory infringement or inducement?

F. CLAIM INTERPRETATION

In order to determine whether a defendant has infringed the patented invention, it must be determined exactly what the invention is, through interpretation of the patent claims.

> The scope of every patent is limited to the invention described in the claims contained in it, read in the light of the specification. These so mark where the progress claimed by the patent begins and where it ends that they have been aptly likened to the description in a deed, which sets the bounds to the grant which it contains.

Motion Picture Patents Co. v. Universal Film Manufacturing Co., 243 U.S. 502, 510, 37 S.Ct. 416, 61 L.Ed. 871 (1917). The defendant's product or process must be compared to the patent claims, not to the defendant's commercial embodiment of the invention. To infringe, the defendant's product or process must fall within the bounds of at least one claim, either literally or through the doctrine of equivalents.

GRAVER TANK & MFG. CO. v. LINDE AIR PRODUCTS CO.

United States Supreme Court, 1950.
339 U.S. 605, 70 S.Ct. 854, 94 L.Ed. 1097.

Mr. Justice Jackson delivered the opinion of the Court.

* * *

In determining whether an accused device or composition infringes a valid patent, resort must be had in the first instance to the words of the claim. If accused matter falls clearly within the claim, infringement is made out and that is the end of it.

But courts have also recognized that to permit imitation of a patented invention which does not copy every literal detail would be to convert the protection of the patent grant into a hollow and useless thing. Such a limitation would leave room for—indeed encourage—the unscrupulous copyist to make unimportant and insubstantial changes and substitutions in the patent which, though adding nothing, would be enough to take the copied matter outside the claim, and hence outside the reach of law. One who seeks to pirate an invention, like one who seeks to pirate a copyrighted book or play, may be expected to introduce minor variations to conceal and shelter the piracy. Outright and forthright duplication is a dull and very rare type of infringement. To prohibit no other would place the inventor at the mercy of verbalism and would be subordinating substance to form. It would deprive him of the benefit of his invention and would foster concealment rather than disclosure of inventions, which is one of the primary purposes of the patent system.

The doctrine of equivalents evolved in response to this experience. The essence of the doctrine is that one may not practice a fraud on a patent. Originating almost a century ago in the case of *Winans v. Denmead*, 15 How. 330, it has been consistently applied by this Court and the lower federal courts, and continues today ready and available for utilization when the proper circumstances for its application arise. "To temper unsparing logic and prevent an infringer from stealing the benefit of the invention" a patentee may invoke this doctrine to proceed against the producer of a device "if it performs substantially the same function in substantially the same way to obtain the same result." The theory on which it is founded is that "if two devices do the same work in substantially the same way, and accomplish substantially the same result, they are the same, even though they differ in name, form or shape." The doctrine operates not only in favor of the patentee of a pioneer or primary invention, but also for the patentee of a secondary invention consisting of a combination of old ingredients which produce new and useful results, although the area of equivalence may vary under the circumstances. The wholesome realism of this doctrine is not always applied in favor of a patentee but is sometimes used against him. Thus, where a device is so far changed in principle from a patented article that it performs the same or a similar function in a substantially different way, but nevertheless falls within the literal words of the claim, the doctrine of equivalents may be used to restrict the claim and defeat the patentee's action for infringement. In its early development, the doctrine was usually applied in cases involving devices where there was equivalence in mechanical components. Subsequently, however, the same principles were also applied to compositions, where there was equivalence between chemical ingredients. Today the doctrine is applied to mechanical or chemical equivalents in compositions or devices.

What constitutes equivalency must be determined against the context of the patent, the prior art, and the particular circumstances of the case. Equivalence, in the patent law, is not the prisoner of a formula and is not an absolute to be considered in a vacuum. It does not require complete identity for every purpose and in every respect. In determining equivalents, things equal to the same thing may not be equal to each other and, by the same token, things for most purposes different may sometimes be equivalents. Consideration must be given to the purpose for which an ingredient is used in a patent, the qualities it has when combined with the other ingredients, and the function which it is intended to perform. An important factor is whether persons reasonably skilled in the art would have known of the interchangeability of an ingredient not contained in the patent with one that was.

A finding of equivalence is a determination of fact. Proof can be made in any form: through testimony of experts or others versed in the technology; by documents, including texts and treatises; and, of course, by the disclosures of the prior art. Like any other issue of fact, final determination requires a balancing of credibility, persuasiveness and weight of evidence. It is to be decided by the trial court and that court's decision, under general principles of appellate review, should not be disturbed unless clearly erroneous. Particularly is this so in a field where so much depends upon familiarity with specific scientific problems and principles not usually contained in the general storehouse of knowledge and experience.

* * *

WARNER-JENKINSON CO., INC. v. HILTON DAVIS CHEMICAL CO.

United States Supreme Court, 1997.
520 U.S. 17, 117 S.Ct. 1040, 137 L.Ed.2d 146.

MR. JUSTICE THOMAS delivered the opinion of the Court.

Nearly 50 years ago, this Court in *Graver Tank & Mfg. Co. v. Linde Air Products Co.*, 339 U.S. 605 (1950), set out the modern contours of what is known in patent law as the "doctrine of equivalents." Under this doctrine, a product or process that does not literally infringe upon the express terms of a patent claim may nonetheless be found to infringe if there is "equivalence" between the elements of the accused product or process and the claimed elements of the patented invention. Petitioner, which was found to have infringed upon respondent's patent under the doctrine of equivalents, invites us to speak the death of that doctrine. We decline that invitation. The significant disagreement within the Court of Appeals for the Federal Circuit concerning the application of *Graver Tank* suggests, however, that the doctrine is not free from confusion. We therefore will endeavor to clarify the proper scope of the doctrine.

I

The essential facts of this case are few. Petitioner Warner–Jenkinson Co. and respondent Hilton Davis Chemical Co. manufacture dyes. Impurities in those dyes must be removed. Hilton Davis holds United States Patent No. 4,560,746 ('746 patent), which discloses an improved purification process involving "ultrafiltration." The '746 process filters impure dye through a porous membrane at certain pressures and Ph levels,[1] resulting in a high purity dye product.

The '746 patent issued in 1985. As relevant to this case, the patent claims as its invention an improvement in the ultrafiltration process as follows:

"In a process for the purification of a dye ... the improvement which comprises: subjecting an aqueous solution ... to ultrafiltration through a membrane having a nominal pore diameter of 5–15 Angstroms under a hydrostatic pressure of approximately 200 to 400 p.s.i.g., at a pH from approximately 6.0 to 9.0, to thereby cause separation of said impurities from said dye...."

The inventors added the phrase "at a pH from approximately 6.0 to 9.0" during patent prosecution. At a minimum, this phrase was added to distinguish a previous patent (the "Booth" patent) that disclosed an ultrafiltration process operating at a pH above 9.0. The parties disagree as to why the low-end pH limit of 6.0 was included as part of the claim.[2]

In 1986, Warner–Jenkinson developed an ultrafiltration process that operated with membrane pore diameters assumed to be 5–15 Angstroms, at pressures of 200 to nearly 500 p.s.i.g., and at a pH of 5.0. Warner–Jenkinson did not learn of the '746 patent until after it had begun commercial use of its ultrafiltration process. Hilton Davis eventually learned of Warner–Jenkinson's use of ultrafiltration and, in 1991, sued Warner–Jenkinson for patent infringement.

As trial approached, Hilton Davis conceded that there was no literal infringement, and relied solely on the doctrine of equivalents. Over Warner–Jenkinson's objection that the doctrine of equivalents was an equitable doctrine to be applied by the court, the issue of equivalence was included among those sent to the jury. The jury found that the '746 patent was not invalid and that Warner–Jenkinson infringed upon the patent under the doctrine of equivalents. The jury also found, however, that Warner–Jenkinson had not intentionally infringed, and therefore awarded only 20% of the damages sought by Hilton Davis. The District Court

---

1. The pH, or power (exponent) of Hydrogen, of a solution is a measure of its acidity or alkalinity. A pH of 7.0 is neutral; a pH below 7.0 is acidic; and a pH above 7.0 is alkaline. Although measurement of pH is on a logarithmic scale, with each whole number difference representing a ten-fold difference in acidity, the practical significance of any such difference will often depend on the context.

2. Petitioner contends that the lower limit was added because below a pH of 6.0 the patented process created "foaming" problems in the plant and because the process was not shown to work below that pH level. Respondent counters that the process was successfully tested to pH levels as low as 2.2 with no effect on the process because of foaming, but offers no particular explanation as to why the lower level of 6.0 pH was selected.

denied Warner–Jenkinson's post-trial motions, and entered a permanent injunction prohibiting Warner–Jenkinson from practicing ultrafiltration below 500 p.s.i.g. and below 9.01 pH. A fractured en banc Court of Appeals for the Federal Circuit affirmed.

The majority below held that the doctrine of equivalents continues to exist and that its touchstone is whether substantial differences exist between the accused process and the patented process. The court also held that the question of equivalence is for the jury to decide and that the jury in this case had substantial evidence from which it could conclude that the Warner–Jenkinson process was not substantially different from the ultrafiltration process disclosed in the '746 patent.

There were three separate dissents, commanding a total of 5 of 12 judges. Four of the five dissenting judges viewed the doctrine of equivalents as allowing an improper expansion of claim scope, contrary to this Court's numerous holdings that it is the claim that defines the invention and gives notice to the public of the limits of the patent monopoly. The fifth dissenter, the late Judge Nies, was able to reconcile the prohibition against enlarging the scope of claims and the doctrine of equivalents by applying the doctrine to each element of a claim, rather than to the accused product or process "overall." As she explained it, "[t]he 'scope' is not enlarged if courts do not go beyond the substitution of equivalent elements." All of the dissenters, however, would have found that a much narrowed doctrine of equivalents may be applied in whole or in part by the court.

We granted certiorari, and now reverse and remand.

II

A

Petitioner's primary argument in this Court is that the doctrine of equivalents, as set out in *Graver Tank* in 1950, did not survive the 1952 revision of the Patent Act, because it is inconsistent with several aspects of that Act. In particular, petitioner argues: (1) the doctrine of equivalents is inconsistent with the statutory requirement that a patentee specifically "claim" the invention covered by a patent, 35 U.S.C. § 112; (2) the doctrine circumvents the patent reissue process—designed to correct mistakes in drafting or the like—and avoids the express limitations on that process, 35 U.S.C. §§ 251–252; [and] (3) the doctrine is inconsistent with the primacy of the Patent and Trademark Office (PTO) in setting the scope of a patent through the patent prosecution process * * * [T]hese arguments were made in *Graver Tank* in the context of the 1870 Patent Act, and failed to command a majority.

The 1952 Patent Act is not materially different from the 1870 Act with regard to claiming, reissue, and the role of the PTO. * * * Such minor differences as exist between those provisions in the 1870 and the 1952 Acts have no bearing on the result reached in *Graver Tank*, and thus provide no basis for our overruling it. In the context of infringement, we have already held that pre–1952 precedent survived the passage of the 1952 Act. * * * We see no reason to reach a different result here. * * *

B

We do, however, share the concern of the dissenters below that the doctrine of equivalents, as it has come to be applied since *Graver Tank*, has taken on a life of its own, unbounded by the patent claims. There can be no denying that the doctrine of equivalents, when applied broadly, conflicts with the definitional and public-notice functions of the statutory claiming requirement. Judge Nies identified one means of avoiding this conflict:

> "[A] distinction can be drawn that is not too esoteric between substitution of an equivalent for a component in an invention and enlarging the metes and bounds of the invention beyond what is claimed.
>
> . . . .
>
> "Where a claim to an invention is expressed as a combination of elements, as here, 'equivalents' in the sobriquet 'Doctrine of Equivalents' refers to the equivalency of an element or part of the invention with one that is substituted in the accused product or process.
>
> . . . .
>
> "This view that the accused device or process must be more than 'equivalent' overall reconciles the Supreme Court's position on infringement by equivalents with its concurrent statements that 'the courts have no right to enlarge a patent beyond the scope of its claims as allowed by the Patent Office.' The 'scope' is not enlarged if courts do not go beyond the substitution of equivalent elements."

62 F.3d at 1573–1574 (Nies, J., dissenting).

We concur with this apt reconciliation of our two lines of precedent. Each element contained in a patent claim is deemed material to defining the scope of the patented invention, and thus the doctrine of equivalents must be applied to individual elements of the claim, not to the invention as a whole. It is important to ensure that the application of the doctrine, even as to an individual element, is not allowed such broad play as to effectively eliminate that element in its entirety. So long as the doctrine of equivalents does not encroach beyond the limits just described, or beyond related limits to be discussed *infra*, we are confident that the doctrine will not vitiate the central functions of the patent claims themselves.

III

Understandably reluctant to assume this Court would overrule *Graver Tank*, petitioner has offered alternative arguments in favor of a more restricted doctrine of equivalents than it feels was applied in this case. We address each in turn.

A

Petitioner first argues that *Graver Tank* never purported to supersede a well-established limit on non-literal infringement, known variously as "prosecution history estoppel" and "file wrapper estoppel." According to petitioner, any surrender of subject matter during patent prosecution, regardless of the reason for such surrender, precludes recapturing any part of that subject matter, even if it is equivalent to the matter expressly claimed. Because, during patent prosecution, respondent limited the pH element of its claim to pH levels between 6.0 and 9.0, petitioner would have those limits form bright lines beyond which no equivalents may be claimed. Any inquiry into the reasons for a surrender, petitioner claims, would undermine the public's right to clear notice of the scope of the patent as embodied in the patent file.

We can readily agree with petitioner that *Graver Tank* did not dispose of prosecution history estoppel as a legal limitation on the doctrine of equivalents. But petitioner reaches too far in arguing that the reason for an amendment during patent prosecution is irrelevant to any subsequent estoppel. In each of our cases cited by petitioner and by the dissent below, prosecution history estoppel was tied to amendments made to avoid the prior art, or otherwise to address a specific concern—such as obviousness—that arguably would have rendered the claimed subject matter unpatentable. Thus, in *Exhibit Supply Co. v. Ace Patents Corp.*, Chief Justice Stone distinguished inclusion of a limiting phrase in an original patent claim from the "very different" situation in which "the applicant, in order to meet objections in the Patent Office, based on references to the prior art, adopted the phrase as a substitute for the broader one" previously used. 315 U.S. 126, 136 (1942). Similarly, in *Keystone Driller Co. v. Northwest Engineering Corp.*, 294 U.S. 42 (1935), estoppel was applied where the initial claims were "rejected on the prior art," and where the allegedly infringing equivalent element was outside of the revised claims and within the prior art that formed the basis for the rejection of the earlier claims.

It is telling that in each case this Court probed the reasoning behind the Patent Office's insistence upon a change in the claims. In each instance, a change was demanded because the claim as otherwise written was viewed as not describing a patentable invention at all—typically because what it described was encompassed within the prior art. But, as the United States informs us, there are a variety of other reasons why the PTO may request a change in claim language. And if the PTO has been requesting changes in claim language without the intent to limit equivalents or, indeed, with the expectation that language it required would in many cases allow for a range of equivalents, we should be extremely reluctant to upset the basic assumptions of the PTO without substantial reason for doing so. Our prior cases have consistently applied prosecution history estoppel only where claims have been amended for a limited set of reasons, and we see no substantial cause for requiring a more rigid rule invoking an estoppel regardless of the reasons for a change.[6]

In this case, the patent examiner objected to the patent claim due to a perceived overlap with the Booth patent, which revealed an ultrafiltration process operating at a pH above 9.0. In response to this objection, the phrase "at a pH from approximately 6.0 to 9.0" was added to the claim. While it is undisputed that the upper limit of 9.0 was added in order to distinguish the Booth patent, the reason for adding the lower limit of 6.0 is unclear. The lower limit certainly did not serve to distinguish the Booth patent, which said nothing about pH levels below 6.0. Thus, while a lower limit of 6.0, by its mere inclusion, became a material element of the claim, that did not necessarily preclude the application of the doctrine of equivalents as to that element. * * * Where the reason for the change was not related to avoiding the prior art, the change may introduce a new element, but it does not necessarily preclude infringement by equivalents of that element.[7]

We are left with the problem, however, of what to do in a case like the one at bar, where the record seems not to reveal the reason for including the lower pH limit of 6.0. In our view, holding that certain reasons for a claim amendment may avoid the application of prosecution history estoppel is not tantamount to holding that the absence of a reason for an amendment may similarly avoid such an estoppel. Mindful that claims do indeed serve both a definitional and a notice function, we think the better rule is to place the burden on the patent-holder to establish the reason for an amendment required during patent prosecution. The court then would decide whether that reason is sufficient to overcome prosecution history estoppel as a bar to application of the doctrine of equivalents to the element added by that amendment. Where no explanation is established, however, the court should presume that the PTO had a substantial reason related to patentability for including the limiting element added by amendment. In those circumstances, prosecution history estoppel would bar the application of the doctrine equivalents as to that element. The presumption we have described, one subject to rebuttal if an appropriate reason for a required amendment is established, gives proper deference to the role of claims in defining an invention and providing public notice, and to the primacy of the PTO in ensuring that the claims allowed cover only subject matter that is properly patentable in a proffered patent applica-

---

6. That petitioner's rule might provide a brighter line for determining whether a patentee is estopped under certain circumstances is not a sufficient reason for adopting such a rule. This is especially true where, as here, the PTO may have relied upon a flexible rule of estoppel when deciding whether to ask for a change in the first place. To change so substantially the rules of the game now could very well subvert the various balances the PTO sought to strike when issuing the numerous patents which have not yet expired and which would be affected by our decision.

7. We do not suggest that, where a change is made to overcome an objection based on the prior art, a court is free to review the correctness of that objection when deciding whether to apply prosecution history estoppel. As petitioner rightly notes, such concerns are properly addressed on direct appeal from the denial of a patent, and will not be revisited in an infringement action. What is permissible for a court to explore is the reason (right or wrong) for the objection and the manner in which the amendment addressed and avoided the objection.

tion. Applied in this fashion, prosecution history estoppel places reasonable limits on the doctrine of equivalents, and further insulates the doctrine from any feared conflict with the Patent Act.

Because respondent has not proffered in this Court a reason for the addition of a lower pH limit, it is impossible to tell whether the reason for that addition could properly avoid an estoppel. Whether a reason in fact exists, but simply was not adequately developed, we cannot say. On remand, the Federal Circuit can consider whether reasons for that portion of the amendment were offered or not and whether further opportunity to establish such reasons would be proper.

B

Petitioner next argues that even if *Graver Tank* remains good law, the case held only that the absence of substantial differences was a necessary element for infringement under the doctrine of equivalents, not that it was sufficient for such a result. Relying on *Graver Tank*'s references to the problem of an "unscrupulous copyist" and "piracy," petitioner would require judicial exploration of the equities of a case before allowing application of the doctrine of equivalents. * * *

       * * *

Although *Graver Tank* certainly leaves room for petitioner's suggested inclusion of intent-based elements in the doctrine of equivalents, we do not read it as requiring them. The better view, and the one consistent with *Graver Tank*'s predecessors and the objective approach to infringement, is that intent plays no role in the application of the doctrine of equivalents.

C

Finally, petitioner proposes that in order to minimize conflict with the notice function of patent claims, the doctrine of equivalents should be limited to equivalents that are disclosed within the patent itself. A milder version of this argument, which found favor with the dissenters below, is that the doctrine should be limited to equivalents that were known at the time the patent was issued, and should not extend to after-arising equivalents.

[A] skilled practitioner's knowledge of the interchangeability between claimed and accused elements is not relevant for its own sake, but rather for what it tells the fact-finder about the similarities or differences between those elements. Much as the perspective of the hypothetical "reasonable person" gives content to concepts such as "negligent" behavior, the perspective of a skilled practitioner provides content to, and limits on, the concept of "equivalence." Insofar as the question under the doctrine of equivalents is whether an accused element is equivalent to a claimed element, the proper time for evaluating equivalency—and thus knowledge of interchangeability between elements—is at the time of infringement, not at the time the patent was issued. And rejecting the milder version of petitioner's argument necessarily rejects the more severe proposition that equivalents must not only be known, but must also be actually disclosed in the patent in order for such equivalents to infringe upon the patent.

> * * *

V

All that remains is to address the debate regarding the linguistic framework under which "equivalence" is determined. Both the parties and the Federal Circuit spend considerable time arguing whether the so-called "triple identity" test—focusing on the function served by a particular claim element, the way that element serves that function, and the result thus obtained by that element—is a suitable method for determining equivalence, or whether an "insubstantial differences" approach is better. There seems to be substantial agreement that, while the triple identity test may be suitable for analyzing mechanical devices, it often provides a poor framework for analyzing other products or processes. On the other hand, the insubstantial differences test offers little additional guidance as to what might render any given difference "insubstantial."

In our view, the particular linguistic framework used is less important than whether the test is probative of the essential inquiry: Does the accused product or process contain elements identical or equivalent to each claimed element of the patented invention? Different linguistic frameworks may be more suitable to different cases, depending on their particular facts. A focus on individual elements and a special vigilance against allowing the concept of equivalence to eliminate completely any such elements should reduce considerably the imprecision of whatever language is used. An analysis of the role played by each element in the context of the specific patent claim will thus inform the inquiry as to whether a substitute element matches the function, way, and result of the claimed element, or whether the substitute element plays a role substantially different from the claimed element. With these limiting principles as a backdrop, we see no purpose in going further and micro-managing the Federal Circuit's particular word-choice for analyzing equivalence. We expect that the Federal Circuit will refine the formulation of the test for equivalence in the orderly course of case-by-case determinations, and we leave such refinement to that court's sound judgment in this area of its special expertise.

VI

Today we adhere to the doctrine of equivalents. The determination of equivalence should be applied as an objective inquiry on an element-by-element basis. Prosecution history estoppel continues to be available as a defense to infringement, but if the patent-holder demonstrates that an amendment required during prosecution had a purpose unrelated to patentability, a court must consider that purpose in order to decide whether an estoppel is precluded. Where the patent holder is unable to establish such a purpose, a court should presume that the purpose behind the required amendment is such that prosecution history estoppel would apply. Because the Court of Appeals for the Federal Circuit did not consider all of the requirements as described by us today, particularly as related to prosecution history estoppel and the preservation of some meaning for each element in a claim, we reverse and remand for further proceedings consistent with this opinion.

* * *

JUSTICE GINSBURG, with whom JUSTICE KENNEDY joins, concurring.

I join the opinion of the Court and write separately to add a cautionary note on the rebuttable presumption the Court announces regarding prosecution history estoppel. I address in particular the application of the presumption in this case and others in which patent prosecution has already been completed. The new presumption, if applied woodenly, might in some instances unfairly discount the expectations of a patentee who had no notice at the time of patent prosecution that such a presumption would apply. Such a patentee would have had little incentive to insist that the reasons for all modifications be memorialized in the file wrapper as they were made. Years after the fact, the patentee may find it difficult to establish an evidentiary basis that would overcome the new presumption. The Court's opinion is sensitive to this problem, noting that "the PTO may have relied upon a flexible rule of estoppel when deciding whether to ask for a change" during patent prosecution.

Because respondent has not presented to this Court any explanation for the addition of the lower pH limit, I concur in the decision to remand the matter to the Federal Circuit. On remand, that court can determine—bearing in mind the prior absence of clear rules of the game—whether suitable reasons for including the lower pH limit were earlier offered or, if not, whether they can now be established.

FESTO CORP. v. SHOKETSU KINZOKU KOGYO KABUSHIKI CO., LTD.

United States Supreme Court, 2002.
535 U.S. 722, 122 S.Ct. 1831, 152 L.Ed.2d 944.

KENNEDY, J., delivered the opinion for a unanimous Court.

This case requires us to address once again the relation between two patent law concepts, the doctrine of equivalents and the rule of prosecution history estoppel. The Court considered the same concepts in *Warner-Jenkinson Co. v. Hilton Davis Chemical Co.*, 520 U.S. 17 (1997), and reaffirmed that a patent protects its holder against efforts of copyists to evade liability for infringement by making only insubstantial changes to a patented invention. At the same time, we appreciated that by extending protection beyond the literal terms in a patent the doctrine of equivalents can create substantial uncertainty about where the patent monopoly ends. If the range of equivalents is unclear, competitors may be unable to determine what is a permitted alternative to a patented invention and what is an infringing equivalent.

To reduce the uncertainty, *Warner–Jenkinson* acknowledged that competitors may rely on the prosecution history, the public record of the patent proceedings. In some cases the Patent and Trademark Office (PTO) may have rejected an earlier version of the patent application on the ground that a claim does not meet a statutory requirement for patentability. When the patentee responds to the rejection by narrowing his claims, this prosecution history estops him from later arguing that the subject matter covered by the original, broader claim was nothing more than an equivalent. Competitors may rely on the estoppel to ensure that their own devices will not be found to infringe by equivalence.

In the decision now under review the Court of Appeals for the Federal Circuit held that by narrowing a claim to obtain a patent, the patentee surrenders all equivalents to the amended claim element. Petitioner asserts this holding departs from past precedent in two respects. First, it applies estoppel to every amendment made to satisfy the requirements of the Patent Act and not just to amendments made to avoid pre-emption by an earlier invention, *i.e.,* the prior art. Second, it holds that when estoppel arises, it bars suit against every equivalent to the amended claim element. The Court of Appeals acknowledged that this holding departed from its own cases, which applied a flexible bar when considering what claims of equivalence were estopped by the prosecution history. Petitioner argues that by replacing the flexible bar with a complete bar the Court of Appeals cast doubt on many existing patents that were amended during the application process when the law, as it then stood, did not apply so rigorous a standard.

We granted certiorari to consider these questions.

I

Petitioner Festo Corporation owns two patents for an improved magnetic rodless cylinder, a piston-driven device that relies on magnets to move objects in a conveying system. The device has many industrial uses and has been employed in machinery as diverse as sewing equipment and the Thunder Mountain ride at Disney World. Although the precise details of the cylinder's operation are not essential here, the prosecution history must be considered.

Petitioner's patent applications, as often occurs, were amended during the prosecution proceedings. The application for the first patent, the Stoll Patent (U.S. Patent No. 4,354,125), was amended after the patent examiner rejected the initial application because the exact method of operation was unclear and some claims were made in an impermissible way. (They were multiply dependent.) The inventor, Dr. Stoll, submitted a new application designed to meet the examiner's objections and also added certain references to prior art. The second patent, the Carroll Patent (U.S. Patent No. 3,779,401), was also amended during a reexamination proceeding. The prior art references were added to this amended application as well. Both amended patents added a new limitation—that the inventions contain a pair of sealing rings, each having a lip on one side, which would prevent impurities from getting on the piston assembly. The amended Stoll Patent added the further limitation that the outer shell of the device, the sleeve, be made of a magnetizable material.

After Festo began selling its rodless cylinder, respondents (whom we refer to as SMC) entered the market with a device similar, but not identical, to the ones disclosed by Festo's patents. SMC's cylinder, rather than using two one-way sealing rings, employs a single sealing ring with a two-way lip. Furthermore, SMC's sleeve is made of a nonmagnetizable alloy. SMC's device does not fall within the literal claims of either patent, but petitioner contends that it is so similar that it infringes under the doctrine of equivalents.

SMC contends that Festo is estopped from making this argument because of the prosecution history of its patents. The sealing rings and the magnetized alloy in the Festo product were both disclosed for the first time in the amended applications. In SMC's view, these amendments narrowed the earlier applications, surrendering alternatives that are the very points of difference in the competing devices—the sealing rings and the type of alloy used to make the sleeve. As Festo narrowed its claims in these ways in order to obtain the patents, says SMC, Festo is now estopped from saying that these features are immaterial and that SMC's device is an equivalent of its own.

The United States District Court for the District of Massachusetts disagreed. It held that Festo's amendments were not made to avoid prior art, and therefore the amendments were not the kind that give rise to estoppel. [The Court of Appeals for the Federal Circuit, sitting *en banc*,] reversed, holding that prosecution history estoppel barred Festo from asserting that the accused device infringed its patents under the doctrine of equivalents. The court held, with only one judge dissenting, that estoppel arises from any amendment that narrows a claim to comply with the Patent Act, not only from amendments made to avoid prior art. More controversial in the Court of Appeals was its further holding: When estoppel applies, it stands as a complete bar against any claim of equivalence for the element that was amended. The court acknowledged that its own prior case law did not go so far. Previous decisions had held that prosecution history estoppel constituted a flexible bar, foreclosing some, but not all, claims of equivalence, depending on the purpose of the amendment and the alterations in the text. The court concluded, however, that its precedents applying the flexible-bar rule should be overruled because this case-by-case approach has proved unworkable. In the court's view a complete-bar rule, under which estoppel bars all claims of equivalence to the narrowed element, would promote certainty in the determination of infringement cases.

* * *

II

The patent laws "promote the Progress of Science and useful Arts" by rewarding innovation with a temporary monopoly. The monopoly is a property right; and like any property right, its boundaries should be clear. This clarity is essential to promote progress, because it enables efficient investment in innovation. A patent holder should know what he owns, and the public should know what he does not. For this reason, the patent laws require inventors to describe their work in "full, clear, concise, and exact terms," 35 U.S.C. § 112, as part of the delicate balance the law attempts to maintain between inventors, who rely on the promise of the law to bring the invention forth, and the public, which should be encouraged to pursue innovations, creations, and new ideas beyond the inventor's exclusive rights.

Unfortunately, the nature of language makes it impossible to capture the essence of a thing in a patent application. The inventor who chooses to patent an invention and disclose it to the public, rather than exploit it in secret, bears the risk that others will devote their efforts toward exploiting the limits of the patent's language:

> "An invention exists most importantly as a tangible structure or a series of drawings. A verbal portrayal is usually an afterthought written to satisfy the requirements of patent law. This conversion of machine to words allows for unintended idea gaps which cannot be satisfactorily filled. Often the invention is novel and words do not exist to describe it. The dictionary does not always keep abreast of the inventor. It cannot. Things are not made for the sake of words, but words for things." *Autogiro Co. of America v. United States,* 384 F.2d 391, 397 (1967).

The language in the patent claims may not capture every nuance of the invention or describe with complete precision the range of its novelty. If patents were always interpreted by their literal terms, their value would be greatly diminished. Unimportant and insubstantial substitutes for certain elements could defeat the patent, and its value to inventors could be destroyed by simple acts of copying. For this reason, the clearest rule of patent interpretation, literalism, may conserve judicial resources but is not necessarily the most efficient rule. The scope of a patent is not limited to its literal terms but instead embraces all equivalents to the claims described.

It is true that the doctrine of equivalents renders the scope of patents less certain. It may be difficult to determine what is, or is not, an equivalent to a particular element of an invention. If competitors cannot be certain about a patent's extent, they may be deterred from engaging in legitimate manufactures outside its limits, or they may invest by mistake in competing products that the patent secures. In addition the uncertainty may lead to wasteful litigation between competitors, suits that a rule of literalism might avoid. These concerns with the doctrine of equivalents, however, are not new. Each time the Court has considered the doctrine, it has acknowledged this uncertainty as the price of ensuring the appropriate incentives for innovation, and it has affirmed the doctrine over dissents that urged a more certain rule. * * *

III

Prosecution history estoppel requires that the claims of a patent be interpreted in light of the proceedings in the PTO during the application process. Estoppel is a "rule of patent construction" that ensures that claims are interpreted by reference to those "that have been cancelled or rejected." The doctrine of equivalents allows the patentee to claim those insubstantial alterations that were not captured in drafting the original patent claim but which could be created through trivial changes. When, however, the patentee originally claimed the subject matter alleged to infringe but then narrowed the claim in response to a rejection, he may not argue that the surrendered territory comprised unforeseen subject matter that should be deemed equivalent to the literal claims of the issued patent. On the contrary, "[b]y the amendment [the patentee] recognized and emphasized the difference between the two phrases[,] . . . and [t]he difference which [the patentee] thus disclaimed must be regarded as material."

A rejection indicates that the patent examiner does not believe the original claim could be patented. While the patentee has the right to appeal, his decision to forgo an appeal and submit an amended claim is taken as a concession that the invention as patented does not reach as far as the original claim. See * * * *Wang Laboratories, Inc. v. Mitsubishi Electronics America, Inc.,* 103 F.3d 1571, 1577–1578 (C.A.Fed.1997) ("Prosecution history estoppel . . . preclud[es] a patentee from regaining, through litigation, coverage of subject matter relinquished during prosecution of the application for the patent"). Were it otherwise, the inventor might avoid the PTO's gatekeeping role and seek to recapture in an infringement action the very subject matter surrendered as a condition of receiving the patent.

Prosecution history estoppel ensures that the doctrine of equivalents remains tied to its underlying purpose. Where the original application once embraced the purported equivalent but the patentee narrowed his claims to obtain the patent or to protect its validity, the patentee cannot assert that he lacked the words to describe the subject matter in question. The doctrine of equivalents is premised on language's inability to capture the essence of innovation, but a prior application describing the precise element at issue undercuts that premise. In that instance the prosecution history has established that the inventor turned his attention to the subject matter in question, knew the words for both the broader and narrower claim, and affirmatively chose the latter.

A

The first question in this case concerns the kinds of amendments that may give rise to estoppel. Petitioner argues that estoppel should arise when amendments are intended to narrow the subject matter of the patented invention, for instance, amendments to avoid prior art, but not when the amendments are made to comply with requirements concerning the form of the patent application. In *Warner–Jenkinson* we recognized that prosecution history estoppel does not arise in every instance when a patent application is amended. Our "prior cases have consistently applied prosecution history estoppel only where claims have been amended for a limited set of reasons," such as "to avoid the prior art, or otherwise to address a specific concern—such as obviousness—that arguably would have rendered the claimed subject matter unpatentable." 520 U.S., at 30–32. While we made clear that estoppel applies to amendments made for a "substantial reason related to patentability," we did not purport to define that term or to catalog every reason that might raise an estoppel. Indeed, we stated that even if the amendment's purpose were unrelated to patentability, the court might consider whether it was the kind of reason that nonetheless might require resort to the estoppel doctrine.

Petitioner is correct that estoppel has been discussed most often in the context of amendments made to avoid the prior art. Amendment to accommodate prior art was the emphasis, too, of our decision in *Warner–Jenkinson*. It does not follow, however, that amendments for other purposes will not give rise to estoppel. Prosecution history may rebut the inference that a thing not described was indescribable. That rationale does not cease simply because the narrowing amendment, submitted to secure a patent, was for some purpose other than avoiding prior art.

We agree with the Court of Appeals that a narrowing amendment made to satisfy any requirement of the Patent Act may give rise to an estoppel. As that court explained, a number of statutory requirements must be satisfied before a patent can issue. The claimed subject matter must be useful, novel, and not obvious. 35 U.S.C. §§ 101–103. In addition, the patent application must describe, enable, and set forth the best mode of carrying out the invention. § 112. These latter requirements must be satisfied before issuance of the patent, for exclusive patent rights are given in exchange for disclosing the invention to the public. What is claimed by the patent application must be the same as what is disclosed in the specification; otherwise the patent should not issue. The patent also should not issue if the other requirements of § 112 are not satisfied, and an applicant's failure to meet these requirements could lead to the issued patent being held invalid in later litigation.

Petitioner contends that amendments made to comply with § 112 concern the form of the application and not the subject matter of the invention. The PTO might require the applicant to clarify an ambiguous term, to improve the translation of a foreign word, or to rewrite a dependent claim as an independent one. In these cases, petitioner argues, the applicant has no intention of surrendering subject matter and should not be estopped from challenging equivalent devices. While this may be true in some cases, petitioner's argument conflates the patentee's reason for making the amendment with the impact the amendment has on the subject matter.

Estoppel arises when an amendment is made to secure the patent and the amendment narrows the patent's scope. If a § 112 amendment is truly cosmetic, then it would not narrow the patent's scope or raise an estoppel. On the other hand, if a § 112 amendment is necessary and narrows the patent's scope—even if only for the purpose of better description—estoppel may apply. A patentee who narrows a claim as a condition for obtaining a patent disavows his claim to the broader subject matter, whether the amendment was made to avoid the prior art or to comply with § 112. We must regard the patentee as having conceded an inability to claim the broader subject matter or at least as having abandoned his right to appeal a rejection. In either case estoppel may apply.

B

Petitioner concedes that the limitations at issue—the sealing rings and the composition of the sleeve—were made for reasons related to § 112, if not also to avoid the prior art. Our conclusion that prosecution history estoppel arises when a claim is narrowed to comply with § 112 gives rise to the second question presented: Does the estoppel bar the inventor from asserting infringement against any equivalent to the narrowed element or might some equivalents still infringe? The Court of Appeals held that prosecution history estoppel is a complete bar, and so the narrowed element must be limited to its strict literal terms. Based upon its experience the Court of Appeals decided that the flexible-bar rule is unworkable because it leads to excessive uncertainty and burdens legitimate innovation. For the reasons that follow, we disagree with the decision to adopt the complete bar.

Though prosecution history estoppel can bar a patentee from challenging a wide range of alleged equivalents made or distributed by competitors, its reach requires an examination of the subject matter surrendered by the narrowing amendment. The complete bar avoids this inquiry by establishing a *per se* rule; but that approach is inconsistent with the purpose of applying the estoppel in the first place—to hold the inventor to the representations made during the application process and to the inferences that may reasonably be drawn from the amendment. By amending the application, the inventor is deemed to concede that the patent does not extend as far as the original claim. It does not follow, however, that the amended claim becomes so perfect in its description that no one could devise an equivalent. After amendment, as before, language remains an imperfect fit for invention. The narrowing amendment may demonstrate what the claim is not; but it may still fail to capture precisely what the claim is. There is no reason why a narrowing amendment should be deemed to relinquish equivalents unforeseeable at the time of the amendment and beyond a fair interpretation of what was surrendered. Nor is there any call to foreclose claims of equivalence for aspects of the invention that have only a peripheral relation to the reason the amendment was submitted. The amendment does not show that the inventor suddenly had more foresight in the drafting of claims than an inventor whose application was granted without amendments having been submitted. It shows only that he was familiar with the broader text and with the difference between the two. As a result, there is no more reason for holding the patentee to the literal terms of an amended claim than there is for abolishing the doctrine of equivalents altogether and holding every patentee to the literal terms of the patent.

This view of prosecution history estoppel is consistent with our precedents and respectful of the real practice before the PTO. While this Court has not weighed the merits of the complete bar against the flexible bar in its prior cases, we have consistently applied the doctrine in a flexible way, not a rigid one. We have considered what equivalents were surrendered during the prosecution of the patent, rather than imposing a complete bar that resorts to the very literalism the equivalents rule is designed to overcome.

The Court of Appeals ignored the guidance of *Warner–Jenkinson,* which instructed that courts must be cautious before adopting changes that disrupt the settled expectations of the inventing community. In that case we made it clear that the doctrine of equivalents and the rule of prosecution history estoppel are settled law. The responsibility for changing them rests with Congress. Fundamental alterations in these rules risk destroying the legitimate expectations of inventors in their property. * * * Inventors who amended their claims under the previous regime had no reason to believe they were conceding all equivalents. If they had known, they might have appealed the rejection instead. There is no justification for applying a new and more robust estoppel to those who relied on prior doctrine.

In *Warner–Jenkinson* we struck the appropriate balance by placing the burden on the patentee to show that an amendment was not for purposes of patentability:

> "Where no explanation is established, however, the court should presume that the patent application had a substantial reason related to patentability for including the limiting element added by amendment. In those circumstances, prosecution history estoppel would bar the application of the doctrine of equivalents as to that element." *Id.,* at 33.

When the patentee is unable to explain the reason for amendment, estoppel not only applies but also "bar[s] the application of the doctrine of equivalents as to that element." *Ibid.* These words do not mandate a complete bar; they are limited to the circumstance where "no explanation is established." They do provide, however, that when the court is unable to determine the purpose underlying a narrowing amendment—and hence a rationale for limiting the estoppel to the surrender of particular equivalents—the court should presume that the patentee surrendered all subject matter between the broader and the narrower language.

Just as *Warner–Jenkinson* held that the patentee bears the burden of proving that an amendment was not made for a reason that would give rise to estoppel, we hold here that the patentee should bear the burden of showing that the amendment does not surrender the particular equivalent in question. * * * The patentee, as the author of the claim language, may be expected to draft claims encompassing readily known equivalents. A patentee's decision to narrow his claims through amendment may be presumed to be a general disclaimer of the territory between the original claim and the amended claim. There are some cases, however, where the amendment cannot reasonably be viewed as surrendering a particular equivalent. The equivalent may have been unforeseeable at the time of the application; the rationale underlying the amendment may bear no more than a tangential relation to the equivalent in question; or there may be some other reason suggesting that the patentee could not reasonably be expected to have described the insubstantial substitute in question. In those cases the patentee can overcome the presumption that prosecution history estoppel bars a finding of equivalence.

This presumption is not, then, just the complete bar by another name. Rather, it reflects the fact that the interpretation of the patent must begin with its literal claims, and the prosecution history is relevant to construing those claims. When the patentee has chosen to narrow a claim, courts may presume the amended text was composed with awareness of this rule and that the territory surrendered is not an equivalent of the territory claimed. In those instances, however, the patentee still might rebut the presumption that estoppel bars a claim of equivalence. The patentee must show that at the time of the amendment one skilled in the art could not reasonably be expected to have drafted a claim that would have literally encompassed the alleged equivalent.

IV

On the record before us, we cannot say petitioner has rebutted the presumptions that estoppel applies and that the equivalents at issue have been surrendered. Petitioner concedes that the limitations at issue—the sealing rings and the composition of the sleeve—were made in response to a rejection for reasons under § 112, if not also because of the prior art references. As the amendments were made for a reason relating to patentability, the question is not whether estoppel applies but what territory the amendments surrendered. While estoppel does not effect a complete bar, the question remains whether petitioner can demonstrate that the narrowing amendments did not surrender the particular equivalents at issue. On these questions, SMC may well prevail, for the sealing rings and the composition of the sleeve both were noted expressly in the prosecution history. These matters, however, should be determined in the first instance by further proceedings in the Court of Appeals or the District Court.

The judgment of the Federal Circuit is vacated, and the case is remanded for further proceedings consistent with this opinion.

1. *Claim construction.* The first step in resolving an infringement allegation is to determine exactly what the patented invention is, through construction of the claim language. Once this is done, it can be determined whether the accused product or process falls within the language of the claim and infringes.

Claims are comprised of a series of elements, or "limitations" which in combination define the scope of the invention. To get a sense of this you should study some of the claims set forth in the case opinions in this Chapter, and in the sample patent set forth in the Appendix. The Supreme Court has ruled that interpretation of patent claims, including terms of art within claims, is a matter of law, for the court. Markman v. Westview Instruments, Inc., 517 U.S. 370, 116 S.Ct. 1384, 134 L.Ed.2d 577 (1996). In a patent infringement suit, claim interpretation is generally conducted in a special hearing before the court, called a *"Markman* hearing." There has been considerable confusion in the case law about the proper approach to constructing claim language. In Phillips v. AWH Corp., 415 F.3d 1303 (Fed. Cir. 2005) *cert. denied*, 546 U.S. 1170, 126 S.Ct. 1332, 164 L.Ed.2d 49 (2006), the Court of Appeals for the Federal Circuit, sitting *en banc*, attempted to clarify the rules of claim construction. The primary issue before the court was the proper role of dictionaries and other "external" references in claim construction, and the extent to which a court should resort to and rely on a patent's specification in seeking to construe the claim language. The *Phillips* court explained:

> We have frequently stated that the words of a claim "are generally given their ordinary and customary meaning." We have made clear, moreover, that the ordinary and customary meaning of a claim term is the meaning that the term would have to a person of ordinary skill in the art in question at the time of the invention, i.e., as of the effective filing date of the patent application. * * *
>
>   * * *
>
> Importantly, the person of ordinary skill in the art is deemed to read the claim term not only in the context of the particular claim in which the disputed term appears, but in the context of the entire patent, including the specification. * * *
>
>   * * *
>
> Quite apart from the written description and the prosecution history, the claims themselves provide substantial guidance as to the meaning of particular claim terms. * * *
>
> To begin with, the context in which a term is used in the asserted claim can be highly instructive. To take a simple example, the claim in this case refers to "steel baffles," which strongly implies that the term "baffles" does not inherently mean objects made of steel. * * *
>
> Other claims of the patent in question, both asserted and unasserted, can also be valuable sources of enlightenment as to the meaning of a

claim term. Because claim terms are normally used consistently throughout the patent, the usage of a term in one claim can often illuminate the meaning of the same term in other claims. Differences among claims can also be a useful guide in understanding the meaning of particular claim terms. For example, the presence of a dependent claim that adds a particular limitation gives rise to a presumption that the limitation in question is not present in the independent claim.

* * *

The claims, of course, do not stand alone. Rather, they are part of "a fully integrated written instrument," consisting principally of a specification that concludes with the claims. For that reason, claims "must be read in view of the specification, of which they are a part." As we stated in *Vitronics,* the specification "is always highly relevant to the claim construction analysis. Usually, it is dispositive; it is the single best guide to the meaning of a disputed term."

* * *

The importance of the specification in claim construction derives from its statutory role. The close kinship between the written description and the claims is enforced by the statutory requirement that the specification describe the claimed invention in "full, clear, concise, and exact terms." 35 U.S.C. § 112, para. 1 * * *. In light of the statutory directive that the inventor provide a "full" and "exact" description of the claimed invention, the specification necessarily informs the proper construction of the claims. * * *

Consistent with that general principle, our cases recognize that the specification may reveal a special definition given to a claim term by the patentee that differs from the meaning it would otherwise possess. In such cases, the inventor's lexicography governs. In other cases, the specification may reveal an intentional disclaimer, or disavowal, of claim scope by the inventor. In that instance as well, the inventor has dictated the correct claim scope, and the inventor's intention, as expressed in the specification, is regarded as dispositive.

The pertinence of the specification to claim construction is reinforced by the manner in which a patent is issued. The Patent and Trademark Office ("PTO") determines the scope of claims in patent applications not solely on the basis of the claim language, but upon giving claims their broadest reasonable construction "in light of the specification as it would be interpreted by one of ordinary skill in the art." Indeed, the rules of the PTO require that application claims must "conform to the invention as set forth in the remainder of the specification and the terms and phrases used in the claims must find clear support or antecedent basis in the description so that the meaning of the terms in the claims may be ascertainable by reference to the description." 37 C.F.R. § 1.75(d)(1). It is therefore entirely appropriate for a court, when conducting claim construction, to rely heavily on the written description for guidance as to the meaning of the claims.

* * *

In addition to consulting the specification, we have held that a court "should also consider the patent's prosecution history, if it is in evidence." * * * The prosecution history, which we have designated as part of the "intrinsic evidence," consists of the complete record of the proceedings before the PTO and includes the prior art cited during the examination of the patent. Like the specification, the prosecution history provides evidence of how the PTO and the inventor understood the patent. Furthermore, like the specification, the prosecution history was created by the patentee in attempting to explain and obtain the patent. Yet because the prosecution history represents an ongoing negotiation between the PTO and the applicant, rather than the final product of that negotiation, it often lacks the clarity of the specification and thus is less useful for claim construction purposes. * * * Nonetheless, the prosecution history can often inform the meaning of the claim language by demonstrating how the inventor understood the invention and whether the inventor limited the invention in the course of prosecution, making the claim scope narrower than it would otherwise be.

* * *

Although we have emphasized the importance of intrinsic evidence in claim construction, we have also authorized district courts to rely on extrinsic evidence, which "consists of all evidence external to the patent and prosecution history, including expert and inventor testimony, dictionaries, and learned treatises." However, while extrinsic evidence "can shed useful light on the relevant art," we have explained that it is "less significant than the intrinsic record in determining 'the legally operative meaning of claim language.' "

Within the class of extrinsic evidence, the court has observed that dictionaries and treatises can be useful in claim construction. We have especially noted the help that technical dictionaries may provide to a court "to better understand the underlying technology" and the way in which one of skill in the art might use the claim terms. Because dictionaries, and especially technical dictionaries, endeavor to collect the accepted meanings of terms used in various fields of science and technology, those resources have been properly recognized as among the many tools that can assist the court in determining the meaning of particular terminology to those of skill in the art of the invention. * * *

We have also held that extrinsic evidence in the form of expert testimony can be useful to a court for a variety of purposes, such as to provide background on the technology at issue, to explain how an invention works, to ensure that the court's understanding of the technical aspects of the patent is consistent with that of a person of skill in the art, or to establish that a particular term in the patent or the prior art has a particular meaning in the pertinent field. * * *

We have viewed extrinsic evidence in general as less reliable than the patent and its prosecution history in determining how to read claim terms, for several reasons. First, extrinsic evidence by definition is not part of the patent and does not have the specification's virtue of being created at the time of patent prosecution for the purpose of explaining the patent's scope and meaning. Second, while claims are construed as they would be understood by a hypothetical person of skill in the art, extrinsic publications may not be written by or for skilled artisans and therefore may not reflect the understanding of a skilled artisan in the field of the patent. Third, extrinsic evidence consisting of expert reports and testimony is generated at the time of and for the purpose of litigation and thus can suffer from bias that is not present in intrinsic evidence. The effect of that bias can be exacerbated if the expert is not one of skill in the relevant art or if the expert's opinion is offered in a form that is not subject to cross-examination. Fourth, there is a virtually unbounded universe of potential extrinsic evidence of some marginal relevance that could be brought to bear on any claim construction question. In the course of litigation, each party will naturally choose the pieces of extrinsic evidence most favorable to its cause, leaving the court with the considerable task of filtering the useful extrinsic evidence from the fluff. * * * Finally, undue reliance on extrinsic evidence poses the risk that it will be used to change the meaning of claims in derogation of the "indisputable public records consisting of the claims, the specification and the prosecution history," thereby undermining the public notice function of patents.

In sum, extrinsic evidence may be useful to the court, but it is unlikely to result in a reliable interpretation of patent claim scope unless considered in the context of the intrinsic evidence.

* * *

Id., 415 F.3d at 1312–19 (citations omitted). The court went on to explain how excessive reliance on extrinsic evidence in claim construction could lead to "systemic overbreadth." Why overbreadth? Won't emphasis on the specification in construing the claims create a danger of importing elements, (or "limitations") from the specification into the claim? The Federal Circuit has repeatedly stressed that it is inappropriate to use the specification to add limitations that don't exist in the claim language. Though the specification often describes very specific embodiments of the invention, the claims generally are not confined to those embodiments. As the court noted in *Phillips*, "we have expressly rejected the contention that if a patent describes only a single embodiment, the claims of the patent must be construed as being limited to that embodiment." *Id.* at 1323. In addressing the concern that courts may import limitations from the specification the *Phillips* court noted:

To avoid importing limitations from the specification into the claims, it is important to keep in mind that the purposes of the specification are to teach and enable those of skill in the art to make and use the invention and to provide a best mode for doing so. One of the best ways to teach a person of ordinary skill in the art how to make and use the invention is to provide an example of how to practice the invention in a particular case. Much of the time, upon reading the specification in that context, it will become clear whether the patentee is setting out specific examples of the invention to accomplish those goals, or whether the patentee instead intends for the claims and the embodiments in the specification to be strictly coextensive. The manner in which the patentee uses a term within the specification and claims usually will make the distinction apparent. * * *

Id., at 1323–24. Are the *Phillips* guidelines regarding proper claim construction likely to increase the predictability of claim construction and patent infringement claims?

2. *Infringement–literal infringement and the doctrine of equivalents.* In order to literally infringe, a defendant's process or product must have every limitation, or element, set forth in a claim as construed by the court. The fact that the defendant's product or process has additional elements will not necessarily avoid infringement. If the defendant's process or product does not literally fall within the claim language, the patentee must resort to the doctrine of equivalents, which is described in the cases set forth above.

In *Warner–Jenkinson*, the defendant argued that the doctrine of equivalents is inconsistent with the statutory requirement that a patentee specifically "claim" the invention covered by a patent. How might that be? If it is true, what are the policy implications? The defendant also argued that the doctrine of equivalents circumvents the patent reissue process (which was designed to correct mistakes in drafting) and avoids the express limitations on that process. The reissue procedure is set forth in Patent Act §§ 251–252. How does the doctrine of equivalents differ from the reissue procedure? What are the relative advantages and disadvantages of the two approaches to curing drafting errors from the standpoint of the patentee? From the standpoint of the alleged infringer? From the public's standpoint?

What is Justice Thomas' response to the concern that the doctrine of equivalents may undercut the claiming requirement? Is his solution likely to be effective in limiting the application of the doctrine of equivalents?

The *Warner–Jenkinson* Court states that the doctrine of equivalents applies to permit a finding of infringement if a defendant's differing element "performs substantially the same function in substantially the same way to obtain the same result," or if its difference is "insubstantial." What kinds of evidence will be relevant to make this determination?

In Johnson & Johnston Associates, Inc. v. R.E. Service Co., Inc., 285 F.3d 1046 (Fed. Cir. 2002), an *en banc* Federal Circuit ruled that subject matter that the patentee discloses in the patent specification, but doesn't claim, is dedicated to the public. The patentee cannot claim the disclosed subject matter as equivalent to claimed elements in a doctrine of equivalents argument. In that case, the patent related to the manufacture of printed circuit boards. Though the claim language specifically claimed a sheet of aluminum, its written description explained that "[w]hile aluminum is currently the preferred material * * * other metals, such as stainless steel or nickel alloys, may be used." The accused infringing product was made of stainless steel. The Federal Circuit held that the patent dedicated the alternative material, stainless steel, to the public, and that the defendant's stainless steel product could not infringe the patent as a matter of law. What line of reasoning justifies this result?

3. *Prior art.* Both the *Graver* and the *Warner–Jenkinson* decisions refer to the prior art. Why is the prior art relevant to the question of infringement?

Note that the doctrine of equivalents may never be used to give a patentee rights in the prior art. The patentee may not obtain through the doctrine of equivalents a scope of patent coverage that he could not have obtained directly from the PTO through literal claims. Wilson Sporting Goods Co. v. David Geoffrey & Associates, 904 F.2d 677 (Fed.Cir.), *cert. denied*, 498 U.S. 992, 111 S.Ct. 537, 112 L.Ed.2d 547 (1990). In *Wilson*, the Federal Circuit stated a standard for determining whether the prior art will prohibit a claimed equivalent:

> Whether prior art restricts the range of equivalents of what is literally claimed can be a difficult question to answer. To simplify analysis and bring the issue onto familiar turf, it may be helpful to conceptualize the limitation on the scope of equivalents by visualizing a *hypothetical* patent claim, sufficient in scope to *literally* cover the accused product. The pertinent question then becomes whether that hypothetical claim could have been allowed by the P.T.O. over the prior art. If not, then it would be improper to permit the patentee to obtain that coverage in an infringement suit under the doctrine of equivalents. If the hypothetical claim could have been allowed, then *prior art* is not a bar to infringement under the doctrine of equivalents.

Id., 904 F.2d at 684–85.

4. *The reverse doctrine of equivalents.* In *Graver*, the majority notes that "where a device is so far changed in principle from a patented article that it performs the same or a similar function in a substantially different way, but nevertheless falls within the literal words of the claim, the doctrine of equivalents may be used to restrict the claim and defeat the patentee's action for infringement." This is known as the "reverse doctrine of equivalents." Situations justifying its application arise only rarely. For an example of its application, see SRI Int'l v. Matsushita Elec. Corp. 775 F.2d 1107 (Fed.Cir. 1985) (*en banc*).

5. *Prosecution history estoppel.* "Prosecution history estoppel" is the modern term for what was previously known as "file wrapper estoppel." The earlier name referred to the folder, or "file wrapper," that the PTO used to hold a patent application and the various documents generated in the course of prosecuting the application, including office actions, amendments and other correspondence between the examiner and the applicant or her attorney. The doctrine of prosecution history estoppel limits application of the doctrine of equivalents by binding the patentee to the amendments and representations she made during the course of prosecution. If the patentee expressly relinquished breadth of coverage during prosecution in order to convince the PTO to grant a patent, she is estopped from recovering it in infringement litigation through application of the doctrine of equivalents.[42]

In *Festo*, the Supreme Court ruled that when prosecution history estoppel applies, courts should presume that all equivalents are relinquished. However,

---

42. The Court of Appeals for the Federal Circuit has also held that a patentee's statements to foreign patent offices in proceedings to patent the invention abroad may be considered to limit the scope of a U.S. patent. See Tanabe Seiyaku Co. v. U.S. International Trade Commission, 109 F.3d 726 (Fed.Cir. 1997), *cert. denied*, 522 U.S. 1027, 118 S.Ct. 624, 139 L.Ed.2d 605 (1997)("In evaluating infringement under the doctrine of equivalents, 'representation[s] to foreign patent offices should be considered . . . when [they] comprise relevant evidence.' ").

the patentee may rebut that presumption by demonstrating that: 1) the particular equivalent in question would have been unforeseeable at the time of the narrowing amendment; 2) the rationale underlying the narrowing amendment bore no more than a tangential relation to the equivalent in question; or 3) there was some other reason suggesting that the patentee could not reasonably be expected to have described the alleged equivalent. On remand, the Court of Appeals for the Federal Circuit undertook to provide some guidance to patentees seeking to make such proof:

> Because we cannot anticipate all of the circumstances in which a patentee might rebut the presumption of surrender, we believe that discussion of the relevant factors encompassed by each of the rebuttal criteria is best left to development on a case-by-case basis. However, we provide the following general guidance * * * regarding the application of the three rebuttal criteria.
>
> The first criterion requires a patentee to show that an alleged equivalent would have been "unforeseeable at the time of the amendment and thus beyond a fair interpretation of what was surrendered." This criterion presents an objective inquiry, asking whether the alleged equivalent would have been unforeseeable to one of ordinary skill in the art at the time of the amendment. Usually, if the alleged equivalent represents later-developed technology (*e.g.,* transistors in relation to vacuum tubes, or Velcro® in relation to fasteners) or technology that was not known in the relevant art, then it would not have been foreseeable. In contrast, old technology, while not always foreseeable, would more likely have been foreseeable. Indeed, if the alleged equivalent were known in the prior art in the field of the invention, it certainly should have been foreseeable at the time of the amendment. By its very nature, objective unforeseeability depends on underlying factual issues relating to, for example, the state of the art and the understanding of a hypothetical person of ordinary skill in the art at the time of the amendment. Therefore, in determining whether an alleged equivalent would have been unforeseeable, a district court may hear expert testimony and consider other extrinsic evidence relating to the relevant factual inquiries.
>
> The second criterion requires a patentee to demonstrate that "the rationale underlying the narrowing amendment [bore] no more than a tangential relation to the equivalent in question." In other words, this criterion asks whether the reason for the narrowing amendment was peripheral, or not directly relevant, to the alleged equivalent. * * * Although we cannot anticipate the instances of mere tangentialness that may arise, we can say that an amendment made to avoid prior art that contains the equivalent in question is not tangential; it is central to allowance of the claim. Moreover, much like the inquiry into whether a patentee can rebut the *Warner-Jenkinson* presumption that a narrowing amendment was made for a reason of patentability, the inquiry into whether a patentee can rebut the *Festo* presumption under the "tangential" criterion focuses on the patentee's objectively apparent reason for the narrowing amendment. As we have held in the *Warner-Jenkinson* context, that reason should be discernible from the prosecution history record, if the public notice function of a patent and its prosecution history

is to have significance. * * * Moreover, whether an amendment was merely tangential to an alleged equivalent necessarily requires focus on the context in which the amendment was made; hence the resort to the prosecution history. Thus, whether the patentee has established a merely tangential reason for a narrowing amendment is for the court to determine from the prosecution history record without the introduction of additional evidence, except, when necessary, testimony from those skilled in the art as to the interpretation of that record.

The third criterion requires a patentee to establish "some other reason suggesting that the patentee could not reasonably be expected to have described the insubstantial substitute in question." This category, while vague, must be a narrow one; it is available in order not to totally foreclose a patentee from relying on reasons, other than unforeseeability and tangentialness, to show that it did not surrender the alleged equivalent. Thus, the third criterion may be satisfied when there was some reason, such as the shortcomings of language, why the patentee was prevented from describing the alleged equivalent when it narrowed the claim. When at all possible, determination of the third rebuttal criterion should also be limited to the prosecution history record. For example, as we recently held in *Pioneer Magnetics, Inc. v. Micro Linear Corp.,* 330 F.3d 1352 (Fed.Cir.2003), a patentee may not rely on the third rebuttal criterion if the alleged equivalent is in the prior art, for then "there can be no other reason the patentee could not have described the substitute in question." *Id.* at 1357. We need not decide now what evidence outside the prosecution history record, if any, should be considered in determining if a patentee has met its burden under this third rebuttal criterion.

Festo Corp. v. Shoketsu Kinzoku Kogyo Kabushiki Co., Ltd., 344 F.3d 1359, 1368–70 (Fed. Cir. 2003), *cert. denied,* 541 U.S. 988, 124 S.Ct. 2019, 158 L.Ed.2d 492 (2004). The court also clarified that rebuttal of the presumption of surrender is a question of law to be determined by the court, not a jury. *Id.* at 1367.

What is the practical impact of the *Warner-Jenkinson* and *Festo* decisions likely to be ? How are these decisions likely to affect patent prosecution practice? Did the Supreme Court reach the correct balance of interests? Is the presumption against equivalency essentially a complete bar by another name?

G.   DEFENSES AND REMEDIES

1.   Defenses

a.   *Patent Misuse*

Concern about the potentially anticompetitive effects of patents underlies and shapes patent law throughout, but perhaps most directly through the doctrine of patent misuse. "Patent misuse" may occur when a patentee uses her patent as leverage to obtain more market power than Congress intended to convey through the grant of a patent, and thus causes an anticompetitive effect. Using a patent in a manner that violates the antitrust laws is likely to constitute misuse, but the patent misuse doctrine has not been expressly restricted to antitrust violations.

The doctrine of patent misuse provides an accused patent infringer with a defense that is similar to the "unclean hands" doctrine traditionally applied in courts of equity. If the defendant convinces the court that the plaintiff has engaged in patent misuse, the court will simply refuse to enforce the otherwise valid and infringed patent until the misuse stops and the market effects of the misuse have been dissipated. It is not necessary for the defendant to demonstrate that he himself has been damaged by the alleged misuse.

Perhaps the most common form of patent misuse has been the "tying" arrangement: conditioning a license to make, use or sell the patented invention upon the licensee's purchase of an unpatented product from the patentee, or upon purchase of a license under a separate patent. Courts have reasoned that in imposing such "packaging" arrangements, the patentee unfairly uses the market power conferred by the patent to gain an advantage in sales of things falling outside the scope of the patent claims. For example, the Supreme Court ruled, in Motion Picture Patents Co. v. Universal Film Mfg. Co., 243 U.S. 502, 37 S.Ct. 416, 61 L.Ed. 871 (1917), that a patentee could not condition a license to use its patented film feeder for use in projection of motion pictures on the licensees' agreement only to show films leased from designated sources, since the films were outside the scope of the patent claims. The Court reasoned that enforcement of such a condition would impermissibly extend the scope of the patent monopoly beyond that intended by Congress.

Patent Act § 271(d) imposes some important restrictions on the patent misuse doctrine. Section 271(d)(1)-(3) provides:

> No patent owner otherwise entitled to relief for infringement or contributory infringement of a patent shall be denied relief or deemed guilty of misuse or illegal extension of the patent right by reason of his having done one or more of the following: (1) derived revenue from acts which if performed by another without his consent would constitute contributory infringement of the patent; (2) licensed or authorized another to perform acts which if performed without his consent would constitute contributory infringement of the patent; (3) sought to enforce his patent rights against infringement or contributory infringement * * *.

Since § 271(c) confines the cause of action for contributory infringement to sale of *nonstaple* articles having no substantial, noninfringing use, § 271(d)(1)-(3) effectively limits the patent misuse doctrine in tying arrangements to those cases in which the item tied to the license is a staple article, or has a substantial, noninfringing use.

Dawson Chemical Co. v. Rohm & Haas Co., 448 U.S. 176, 100 S.Ct. 2601, 65 L.Ed.2d 696 (1980), illustrates the effect of § 271(d). That case involved the defendants' sale of propanil, an unpatentable chemical compound. Though propanil had long been known, no use had been found for it until the patentee discovered and patented a method of applying propanil to growing rice crops to kill weeds. The patentee marketed propanil in containers with printed directions for applying it by the patented method. This constituted an implied license permitting farmers who purchased the patentee's propanil to use the method. The patentee did not license persons purchasing propanil from other sources to use the method, however, and refused to license other manufacturers to sell propanil.

The defendants sold propanil to farmers, knowing that the farmers would infringe the patent by applying it through the patented method. The patentee sued them, claiming, among other things, contributory infringement. The defendants admitted that propanil was a "nonstaple" with no substantial noninfringing use, within the meaning of § 271(c), but asserted that the patentee engaged in patent misuse by tying licenses to use the patented method to purchase of the propanil it offered for sale. By limiting licenses to persons purchasing from it, the patentee monopolized the market for propanil, which was an unpatented and unpatentable article.

The Court undertook to construe § 271(d)(1)-(3), finding that § 271(c) and (d)

> effectively confer upon the patentee, as a lawful adjunct of his patent rights, a limited power to exclude others from competition in nonstaple goods. A patentee may sell a nonstaple article himself while enjoining others from marketing that same good without his authorization. By doing so, he is able to eliminate competitors and thereby to control the market for that product. Moreover, his power to demand royalties from others for the privilege of selling the nonstaple item itself implies that the patentee may control the market for the nonstaple good; otherwise, his "right" to sell licenses for the marketing of the nonstaple good would be meaningless, since no one would be willing to pay him for a superfluous authorization.
>
> Rohm & Haas' conduct is not dissimilar in either nature or effect from the conduct that is thus clearly embraced within § 271(d). It sells propanil; it authorizes others to use propanil; and it sues contributory infringers. These are all protected activities. Rohm & Haas does *not* license others to sell propanil, but nothing on the face of the statute requires it to do so. To be sure, the sum effect of Rohm & Haas' actions is to suppress competition in the market for an unpatented commodity. But as we have observed, in this its conduct is no different from that which the statute expressly protects.

Id., 448 U.S. at 201–02. What is the justification for permitting the kind of tying arrangement involved in *Dawson*, and the contributory infringement claim?

In 1988, Congress amended § 271(d) to describe two additional activities that would not constitute patent misuse:

> No patent owner otherwise entitled to relief for infringement or contributory infringement of a patent shall be denied relief or deemed

guilty of misuse or illegal extension of the patent right by reason of his having done one or more of the following * * * (4) refused to license or use any rights to the patent; or (5) conditioned the license of any rights to the patent or the sale of the patented product on the acquisition of a license to rights in another patent or purchase of a separate product, unless, in view of the circumstances, the patent owner has market power in the relevant market for the patent or patented product on which the license or sale is conditioned.

35 U.S.C.A. § 271(d). What is the impact of the 1988 amendments? Why might Congress have deemed them necessary? Taking its cue from Congress' 1988 amendments to § 271(d), the Supreme Court has subsequently ruled that courts should stop presuming that a patent confers market power for purposes of a tying claim under Sherman Act § 1, and that in all tying cases the plaintiff must prove that the defendant has market power in the tying product. Illinois Tool Works v. Independent Ink, 547 U.S. 28, 126 S.Ct. 1281, 164 L.Ed.2d 26 (2006). If a patent gives a "monopoly" in an invention, why shouldn't we presume that it gives the patentee market power for purposes of a misuse or antitrust claim? Would it be possible for a tying arrangement to be procompetitive?

b. *Inequitable Conduct*

The inequitable conduct defense holds that if the patentee intentionally misrepresented or withheld material information concerning the patentability of the invention from the PTO in the course of prosecution, the patent will not be enforceable. The Court of Appeals for the Federal Circuit has explained:

> "Inequitable conduct" is not, or should not be, a magic incantation to be asserted against every patentee. Nor is that allegation established upon a mere showing that art or information having some degree of materiality was not disclosed. To be guilty of inequitable conduct, one must have intended to act inequitably. Thus, one who alleges a "failure to disclose" form of inequitable conduct must offer clear and convincing proof of: (1) prior art or information that is material; (2) knowledge chargeable to applicant of that prior art or information and of its materiality; and (3) failure of the applicant to disclose the art or information resulting from an intent to mislead the PTO.

FMC Corp. v. Manitowoc Co., Inc., 835 F.2d 1411, 1415 (Fed.Cir.1987). The Federal Circuit has clarified that information is "material" for purposes of an inequitable conduct defense if there is a substantial likelihood that a reasonable examiner would have considered it important in deciding whether to allow the application to issue as a patent. Li Second Family Limited Partnership v. Toshiba Corp., 231 F.3d 1373, 1379 (Fed. Cir.2000), *cert. denied*, 533 U.S. 929, 121 S.Ct. 2550, 150 L.Ed.2d 717 (2001). The party asserting inequitable conduct must prove that the patent applicant knew of the prior, material reference. Evidence that the applicant should have known of the reference will not suffice. Nordberg,

Inc. v. Telsmith, Inc., 82 F.3d 394, 397 (Fed.Cir.1996). However, the intent element of an inequitable conduct defense need not be proved by direct evidence. It may be inferred from the facts and circumstances surrounding the applicant's conduct. The more material the omission, the lower the level of intent required. Critikon Inc. v. Becton Dickinson Vascular Access, Inc., 120 F.3d 1253, 1256–58 (Fed.Cir.1997), *cert. denied*, 523 U.S. 1071, 118 S.Ct. 1510, 140 L.Ed.2d 665 (1998).

c. *Patent Invalidity*

Patent invalidity is frequently raised as a defense to an infringement action. In recognition of the PTO's expertise, the Patent Act provides that a patent will be presumed valid. 35 U.S.C.A. § 282. Thus, the challenger bears the burden of proving, with clear and convincing evidence, that the provisions of the Patent Act governing patentability have not been satisfied. Atlas Powder Co. v. E.I. du Pont De Nemours & Co., 750 F.2d 1569, 1573 (Fed.Cir.1984).

Assume that X enters into a license agreement with a patentee, in which the patentee grants X permission to practice the patented invention in return for X's promise to pay royalties. X later stops paying royalties but continues to practice the invention, in violation of the agreement. As a matter of public policy, should X, in a subsequent infringement suit, be estopped from challenging the validity of the patent because he originally agreed to the license? See Lear, Inc. v. Adkins, 395 U.S. 653, 89 S.Ct. 1902, 23 L.Ed.2d 610 (1969) (no licensee estoppel in patent cases); Studiengesellschaft Kohle, M.B.H. v. Shell Oil Co., 112 F.3d 1561 (Fed. Cir.), *cert. denied*, 522 U.S. 996, 118 S.Ct. 560, 139 L.Ed.2d 401 (1997)(even though the licensee is not estopped, it may be liable for compliance with the licensing agreement up until the time that it asserts its claim that the patent is invalid). Why shouldn't the licensee, who initially acquiesced in the patent, be estopped from later challenging its validity?

Assume that A obtains a patent for his invention, and then assigns the patent to B for valuable consideration. Later, A wishes to exploit the patented invention, and challenges the validity of the patent. Should A be estopped? See Mentor Graphics Corp. v. Quickturn Design Systems, Inc., 150 F.3d 1374 (Fed.Cir.1998)(Assignors are estopped from later challenging the validity of the assigned patent, even if the assignor disclaimed any warranty of patent validity in the assignment agreement. The only way an assignor might retain the right to challenge the validity of the assigned patent is to include express language to that effect in the assignment agreement). Why should the assignor be estopped, when the licensee is not?

Assume that X obtains a license from the patentee and later comes to believe that the patent is invalid. Not wishing to risk infringement liability, X continues to pay royalties under the license, but seeks a declaratory judgment that the patent is invalid. Should X's suit be permitted to proceed? In MedImmune Inc. v. Genentech, Inc., 549 U.S.

118, 127 S.Ct. 764, 166 L.Ed.2d 604 (2007), involving similar facts, the Federal Circuit had held that there was no actual controversy to support jurisdiction for a declaratory judgment action, since royalties were fully paid to the licensor and there was no ground upon which the licensor could cancel the license or sue for infringement. The Supreme Court reversed, rejecting this "reasonable apprehension of imminent suit" requirement. The Supreme Court held that the question in each case should be whether the facts alleged, under all the circumstances, show that there is a substantial controversy, between parties having adverse legal interests, of sufficient immediacy and reality to warrant the issuance of a declaratory judgment. Under the facts of that case, this standard was satisfied, even though the plaintiff did not refuse to make royalty payments.

Assume that a patentee sues Y for infringement, and in that action, Y prevails in his defense that the patent is invalid. The patentee then brings suit against Z for infringement. As a matter of policy, should the patentee be permitted to relitigate the issue of patent validity in this new suit, or should it be estopped from asserting the patent? See Blonder–Tongue Laboratories, Inc. v. University of Illinois Foundation, 402 U.S. 313, 91 S.Ct. 1434, 28 L.Ed.2d 788 (1971)(holding that a defendant in an infringement suit is not barred, for lack of mutuality, from pleading collateral estoppel as a defense when the asserted patent had been found invalid in prior litigation. However, the patentee will be able to relitigate the validity of the patent if she can show that she did not have a fair opportunity, substantively and evidentially, to pursue her claim the first time).

d. Prior Use

In the Intellectual Property and Communications Omnibus Reform Act of 1999, Pub. L. No. 106–113, 113 Stat. 1537–513, 547, Congress created a new "prior user" defense to patent infringement claims involving methods of doing business. This defense applies if the defendant, acting in good faith, actually reduced the subject matter to practice at least 1 year before the effective filing date of the asserted business method patent, and commercially used the subject matter before the effective filing date of such patent. 35 U.S.C.A. § 273(b)(1). According to the Congressional Record, the new defense was intended to strike an equitable balance between the interests of earlier U.S. inventors who invented and commercialized business methods, and later U.S. or foreign inventors who patent the methods. 145 Cong. Rec. S14716–17 (daily ed. Nov. 17, 1999)(included in the record at the request of Sen. Lott). As noted earlier in this Chapter, prior to the Federal Circuit's decision in the *State Street* case, it had been generally believed that business methods were unpatentable. Creators of such methods retained them in secrecy. After *State Street*, persons developing the same methods were often able to patent them. Because the earlier users had retained secrecy, the PTO found no evidence of their actions in its prior art search. Congress deemed the new defense necessary under the circumstances to protect earlier users.

Infringement defendants claiming the § 273 defense have the burden of proving it by "clear and convincing evidence." 35 U.S.C.A. § 273(b)(4). A claimant must demonstrate good faith, actual reduction to practice at least one year before the effective patent application filing date, and commercial use before the effective filing date. The defendant must not have derived the method from the patentee. If the defendant invented but later abandoned the business method, it may be limited in establishing the defense to the date it resumed commercial use. *Id.*, at § 273(b)(5). Moreover, the defense is a personal one: It cannot be assigned or transferred to anyone other than the patentee unless the transfer is part of a good-faith transfer of the entire enterprise, or of the line of business to which the defense relates. Even then, the sites at which the transferee may assert the defense are limited. *Id.*, at § 273 (b)(6) & (7).

Section 273(b)(9) provides that "A patent shall not be deemed to be invalid under section 102 or 103 of this title solely because a defense is raised or established under this section." What are the implications of this? Under what circumstances is a defendant availing himself of the § 273 defense likely to have a patent invalidity defense under Patent Act § 102 or 103? Under what circumstances is the defendant not likely to have an invalidity defense? If a defendant has an invalidity defense, is there any reason why he should prefer to rely on the § 273 defense, instead? The legislative history provides the following observation:

> [U]nder current law, although the matter has seldom been litigated, a party who commercially used an invention in secrecy before the patent filing date and who also invented the subject matter before the patent owner's invention may argue that the patent is invalid under section 102(g) of the Patent Act. Arguably, commercial use of an invention in secrecy is not suppression or concealment of the invention within the meaning of section 102(g), and therefore the party's earlier invention could invalidate the patent.

145 Cong. Rec. at S14717. What are the possible policy implications of this new prior user defense? Should the defense be extended to other types of inventions?

2. Remedies

eBAY, INC. v. MERCEXCHANGE, L.L.C.

United States Supreme Court, 2006.
547 U.S. 388, 126 S.Ct. 1837, 164 L.Ed.2d 641.

JUSTICE THOMAS delivered the opinion of the Court.

* * *

Petitioner eBay operates a popular Internet Web site that allows private sellers to list goods they wish to sell, either through an auction or at a fixed price. Petitioner Half.com, now a wholly owned subsidiary of eBay, operates a similar Web site. Respondent MercExchange, L.L.C., holds a number of patents, including a business method patent for an electronic market designed to facilitate the sale of goods between private individuals by establishing a central authority to promote trust among participants. See U.S. Patent No. 5,845,265. MercExchange sought to license its patent to eBay and Half.com, as it had previously done with other companies, but the parties failed to reach an agreement. MercExchange subsequently filed a patent infringement suit against eBay and Half.com in the United States District Court for the Eastern District of Virginia. A jury found that MercExchange's patent was valid, that eBay and Half.com had infringed that patent, and that an award of damages was appropriate.

Following the jury verdict, the District Court denied MercExchange's motion for permanent injunctive relief. The Court of Appeals for the Federal Circuit reversed, applying its "general rule that courts will issue permanent injunctions against patent infringement absent exceptional circumstances." We granted certiorari to determine the appropriateness of this general rule.

II

According to well-established principles of equity, a plaintiff seeking a permanent injunction must satisfy a four-factor test before a court may grant such relief. A plaintiff must demonstrate: (1) that it has suffered an irreparable injury; (2) that remedies available at law, such as monetary damages, are inadequate to compensate for that injury; (3) that, considering the balance of hardships between the plaintiff and defendant, a remedy in equity is warranted; and (4) that the public interest would not be disserved by a permanent injunction. The decision to grant or deny permanent injunctive relief is an act of equitable discretion by the district court, reviewable on appeal for abuse of discretion.

These familiar principles apply with equal force to disputes arising under the Patent Act. As this Court has long recognized, "a major departure from the long tradition of equity practice should not be lightly implied." Nothing in the Patent Act indicates that Congress intended such a departure. To the contrary, the Patent Act expressly provides that injunctions "may" issue "in accordance with the principles of equity." 35 U.S.C. § 283.

To be sure, the Patent Act also declares that "patents shall have the attributes of personal property," § 261, including "the right to exclude others from making, using, offering for sale, or selling the invention," § 154(a)(1). According to the Court of Appeals, this statutory right to exclude alone justifies its general rule in favor of permanent injunctive relief. But the creation of a right is distinct from the provision of remedies for violations of that right. Indeed, the Patent Act itself indicates that patents shall have the attributes of personal property "[s]ubject to the provisions of this title," 35 U.S.C. § 261, including, presumably, the provision that injunctive relief "may" issue only "in accordance with the principles of equity," § 283.

This approach is consistent with our treatment of injunctions under the Copyright Act. * * *

Neither the District Court nor the Court of Appeals below fairly applied these traditional equitable principles in deciding respondent's motion for a permanent injunction. Although the District Court recited the traditional four-factor test, it appeared to adopt certain expansive principles suggesting that injunctive relief could not issue in a broad swath of cases. Most notably, it concluded that a "plaintiff's willingness to license its patents" and "its lack of commercial activity in practicing the patents" would be sufficient to establish that the patent holder would not suffer irreparable harm if an injunction did not issue. But traditional equitable principles do not permit such broad classifications. For example, some patent holders, such as university researchers or self-made inventors, might reasonably prefer to license their patents, rather than undertake efforts to secure the financing necessary to bring their works to market themselves. Such patent holders may be able to satisfy the traditional four-factor test, and we see no basis for categorically denying them the opportunity to do so. To the extent that the District Court adopted such a categorical rule, then, its analysis cannot be squared with the principles of equity adopted by Congress. * * *

In reversing the District Court, the Court of Appeals departed in the opposite direction from the four-factor test. The court articulated a "general rule," unique to patent disputes, "that a permanent injunction will issue once infringement and validity have been adjudged." 401 F.3d, at 1338. The court further indicated that injunctions should be denied only in the "unusual" case, under "exceptional circumstances" and " 'in rare instances ... to protect the public interest.' " *Id.,* at 1338–1339. Just as the District Court erred in its categorical denial of injunctive relief, the Court of Appeals erred in its categorical grant of such relief.

Because we conclude that neither court below correctly applied the traditional four-factor framework that governs the award of injunctive relief, we vacate the judgment of the Court of Appeals, so that the District Court may apply that framework in the first instance. In doing so, we take no position on whether permanent injunctive relief should or should not issue in this particular case, or indeed in any number of other disputes arising under the Patent Act. We hold only that the decision whether to grant or deny injunctive relief rests within the equitable discretion of the district courts, and that such discretion must be exercised consistent with traditional principles of equity, in patent disputes no less than in other cases governed by such standards.

      * * *

CHIEF JUSTICE ROBERTS, with whom JUSTICE SCALIA and JUSTICE GINSBURG join, concurring.

I agree with the Court's holding that "the decision whether to grant or deny injunctive relief rests within the equitable discretion of the district courts, and that such discretion must be exercised consistent with traditional principles of equity, in patent disputes no less than in other cases governed by such standards," and I join the opinion of the Court. * * *

From at least the early 19th century, courts have granted injunctive relief upon a finding of infringement in the vast majority of patent cases. This "long tradition of equity practice" is not surprising, given the difficulty of protecting a right to *exclude* through monetary remedies that allow an infringer to *use* an invention against the patentee's wishes—a difficulty that often implicates the first two factors of the traditional four-factor test. This historical practice, as the Court holds, does not *entitle* a patentee to a permanent injunction or justify a *general rule* that such injunctions should issue. The Federal Circuit itself so recognized in *Roche Products, Inc. v. Bolar Pharmaceutical Co.,* 733 F.2d 858, 865–867 (1984). At the same time, there is a difference between exercising equitable discretion pursuant to the established four-factor test and writing on an entirely clean slate. * * * When it comes to discerning and applying those standards, in this area as others, "a page of history is worth a volume of logic."

JUSTICE KENNEDY, with whom JUSTICE STEVENS, JUSTICE SOUTER, and JUSTICE BREYER join, concurring.

The Court is correct, in my view, to hold that courts should apply the well-established, four-factor test—without resort to categorical rules—in deciding whether to grant injunctive relief in patent cases. THE CHIEF JUSTICE is also correct that history may be instructive in applying this test. The traditional practice of issuing injunctions against patent infringers, however, does not seem to rest on "the difficulty of protecting a right to *exclude* through monetary remedies that allow an infringer to *use* an invention against the patentee's wishes." Both the terms of the Patent Act and the traditional view of injunctive relief accept that the existence of a right to exclude does not dictate the remedy for a violation of that right. To the extent earlier cases establish a pattern of granting an injunction against patent infringers almost as a matter of course, this pattern simply illustrates the result of the four-factor test in the contexts then prevalent. The lesson of the historical practice, therefore, is most helpful and instructive when the circumstances of a case bear substantial parallels to litigation the courts have confronted before.

In cases now arising trial courts should bear in mind that in many instances the nature of the patent being enforced and the economic function of the patent holder present considerations quite unlike earlier cases. An industry has developed in which firms use patents not as a basis for producing and selling goods but, instead, primarily for obtaining licensing fees. For these firms, an injunction, and the potentially serious sanctions arising from its violation, can be employed as a bargaining tool to charge exorbitant fees to companies that seek to buy licenses to practice the patent. When the patented invention is but a small component of the product the companies seek to produce and the threat of an injunction is employed simply for undue leverage in negotiations, legal damages may well be sufficient to compensate for the infringement and an injunction may not serve the public interest. In addition injunctive relief may have different consequences for the burgeoning number of patents over business methods, which were not of much economic and legal significance in earlier times. The potential vagueness and suspect validity of some of these patents may affect the calculus under the four-factor test.

The equitable discretion over injunctions, granted by the Patent Act, is well suited to allow courts to adapt to the rapid technological and legal developments in the patent system. For these reasons it should be recognized that district courts must determine whether past practice fits the circumstances of the cases before them. With these observations, I join the opinion of the Court.

STATE INDUSTRIES, INC. v. MOR–FLO INDUSTRIES, INC.

United States Court of Appeals for the Federal Circuit, 1989.
883 F.2d 1573, *cert. denied,*
493 U.S. 1022, 110 S.Ct. 725, 107 L.Ed.2d 744 (1990).

MAYER, CIRCUIT JUDGE.

Mor–Flo Industries, Inc. and its subsidiary, American Appliance Manufacturing Corporation (Mor–Flo), infringed State Industries, Inc.'s (State) Patent No. 4,447,377, covering a method of insulating water heaters with foam. After the damages trial, the district court awarded State lost profits on approximately 40% of Mor–Flo's infringing sales and a royalty of 3% on the remaining 60%. It concluded that Mor–Flo's infringement was not willful and denied enhanced damages and attorney's fees. We affirm the judgment insofar as it awards lost profits and a 3% royalty, but vacate and remand for a redetermination of the judgment that the infringement was not willful.

BACKGROUND

The '377 patent claims a method of insulating the tank of a water heater by using polyurethane foam. The method includes wrapping the tank with a plastic sheet shaped as an envelope, installing a surrounding jacket and cover, pouring foam through an opening in the cover into the envelope, and then plugging the opening. The method contains the liquid foam while it rises and prevents it from invading areas, such as the electrical components and combustion chamber, which must be kept free of foam. State also has another patent, U.S. Patent No. 4,527,543, not contested here, that claims water heaters using the '377 envelope construction.

Mor–Flo's method found to be infringing used a cylindrical piece of plastic that was pulled over the top of the tank with fiberglass positioned around the combustion chamber at the bottom of the tank. The "sleeve" was taped below the top of the fiberglass. A jacket was then installed over the tank and sleeve, a top was installed, and foam was shot into the sleeve through an opening in the top.

In the liability trial, Mor–Flo maintained that the sleeve was not an "envelope" or " 'wrapped' around the tank" as required by the '377 patent. The sleeve, however, was identical to an embodiment shown in the patent (partial envelope), and was merely secured differently at the bottom of the tank. The illustrated embodiment also revealed a pull-over structure similar to Mor–Flo's sleeve. The district court found that it was especially damaging to Mor–Flo that it did not conceive of its "strikingly similar" sleeve method until after purchasing and disassembling a State foam-insulated water heater. Therefore, the court held that Mor–Flo's method literally infringed the '377. The district court alternatively held that it infringed the patent under the doctrine of equivalents.

The water heater industry is intensely competitive and marked by small profit margins. The invention is pertinent to all water heaters, but the infringement at issue here is restricted to residential gas water heaters, in particular those deemed "energy efficient" by the American Society of Heating, Refrigeration and Air Conditioning Engineers. Foam provides greater insulating capacity than the other alternative, fiberglass; therefore, foam-insulated heaters have cost advantages in terms of material, packaging and freight. The greater insulating capacity enables foam-insulated heaters to meet the energy code requirements imposed by many states by using less space than fiberglass-insulated heaters. The density of foam also strengthens the outer jacket of the water heater and makes it more resistant to denting.

In deciding the damages question, the district court faced three issues: lost profits, reasonable royalty and willful infringement. Infringement occurred between May 8, 1984, when the patent issued, and June 9, 1986, when Mor–Flo switched to the noninfringing method of fiberglass foam stops, which eliminates need for the envelope taught by the patent in suit yet keeps foam from invading the combustion chamber. State produced evidence of lost sales, and took the position that it should recover lost profits for its market share of Mor–Flo's infringing sales and a reasonable royalty for the remainder. It also asked increased damages for willful infringement and attorney fees.

The district court agreed with State in the award of lost profits for part of its damages and a royalty for the rest. The court found there was a growing demand for foam-insulated water heaters, the '377 patent was the first method developed to meet this demand, and there were no other methods available during the pertinent period that were either noninfringing or acceptable as substitutes. Specifically, the court found "that, during the period of infringement, all but one of State's competitors in the United States sold foam insulated water heaters made using State's patented method, or one of a strikingly similar configuration, and/or Denton Patent No. 4,527,543 * * *."

A.O. Smith Corporation, the only clearly noninfringing competitor used the less preferable fiberglass insulation. Hoyt also sold only fiberglass-insulated heaters until 1985 when it added a foam-insulated heater to its inventory. The court found that fiberglass was not an acceptable substitute for foam because of foam's advantages in reducing the size of water heaters, increasing resistance to denting, and meeting governmental energy standards.

The court also found that State was capable of producing during the relevant period, and had sales and distribution capacity to ship and sell, sufficient foam-insulated water heaters to exploit its market share of Mor–Flo's sales. Finding that State has approximately 40% of the gas water heater market nationwide, the court awarded State the profits it lost on 40% of the sales of 754,181 infringing Mor–Flo water heaters.

For the remaining 60% of Mor–Flo's sales, State asked for a royalty of 8 to 10%. Mor–Flo presented no evidence of what it would have paid for a license, but argued that in no event should the royalty rate be above its net profit margin which, for the seventeen months preceding the date infringement began, was 2.1%. The district court awarded a royalty of 3% on the remaining 60% of infringing sales. Finally, the court concluded the infringement was not willful because Mor–Flo relied in good faith on advice of outside counsel that its process was not infringing. Mor–Flo appeals both the award of actual damages and the reasonableness of the royalty. State cross-appeals the reasonableness of the royalty and the court's failure to hold Mor–Flo's infringement willful and to award increased damages and attorney's fees.

DISCUSSION

Deciding how much to award as damages is not an exact science, and the methodology of assessing and computing damages is committed to the sound discretion of the district court. A challenger must show that "the district court abused its discretion by basing its award on clearly erroneous factual findings, legal error, or a manifest error of judgment."

The measure of damages is an amount which will compensate the patent owner for the pecuniary loss sustained because of the infringement. But the floor for a damage award is no less than a reasonable royalty, and the award may be split between lost profits as actual damages to the extent they are proven and a reasonable royalty for the remainder.

A.

To get lost profits as actual damages, the patent owner must demonstrate that there was a reasonable probability that, but for the infringement, it would have made the infringer's sales. But "[t]he patent holder does not need to negate *all* possibilities that a purchaser might have bought a different product or might have foregone the purchase altogether." *Paper Converting Mach. Co. v. Magna–Graphics Corp.*, 745 F.2d 11, 21 (Fed.Cir.1984).

A standard way of proving lost profits, first announced in *Panduit Corp. v. Stahlin Bros. Fibre Works*, 575 F.2d 1152, 1156 (6th Cir.1978), is for the patent owner to prove: "(1) demand for the patented product, (2) absence of acceptable noninfringing substitutes, (3) his manufacturing and marketing capability to exploit the demand, and (4) the amount of the profit he would have made." The district court relied heavily on this test and we have accepted it as a nonexclusive standard for determining lost profits. With only slight modification we think it fits here and confirms the district court's judgment.

Absence of Substitutes and Market Share

This is the first time we have considered whether lost profits can be based on market share. * * *

We start with the presumption that the judgment of the district court is correct, of course, and that the only limit on its discretion in selecting a remedy is that it be adequate to compensate for the damages suffered as a result of the infringement. Any doubt about the correctness of the award is resolved against the infringer.

Frequently, the patent owner and infringer are the only suppliers in the market, and the owner is seeking to recover profits lost through every sale made by the infringer. In the two-supplier market, it is reasonable to assume, provided the patent owner has the manufacturing and marketing capabilities, that it would have made the infringer's sales. In these instances, the *Panduit* test is usually straightforward and dispositive.

Here we have multiple competitors and the patent owner contends that all the competitors infringed or sold a far less preferable alternative—fiberglass. The district court made the absence of acceptable substitutes, *Panduit* item (2), a neutral factor by crediting all the other competitors with their market shares as State requested. If the court is correct in its finding that the other competitors were likely infringers of one or the other of State's patents, State would have been entitled to their shares of the market on top of its own, and a correspondingly greater share of Mor–Flo's sales. If it is wrong in whole or in part, State would have been entitled to its current share or to a lesser increase in share. We need not decide which it is because it would make no difference to the outcome. State would get at least what it asked for, because as discussed further below the district court found, and we agree, that State's share of the market was proven.

But Mor–Flo should not complain because if anything it received a windfall from this approach. To the extent infringing competitors got credit for sales that should have gone to State, the share of the market against which Mor–Flo's damages might be assessed is reduced. So we think that in these circumstances the presence or absence of acceptable noninfringing alternatives does not matter. The question then becomes whether an established market share combined with the other *Panduit* factors is sufficient to show State's loss to a reasonable probability.

Demand

At the infringement phase of this case, the district court said, "Both sides admit that there was a great need to develop foam insulated heaters in the late 1970's. The patented method solved the [ ] problems [of foam leakage and invasion], and was apparently the first to do so in the water heater industry." In a 1979 internal memo, Mor–Flo's own vice president of engineering stated: "With reference to heaters with foam insulation, it was felt that the word foam has a magic sound to it at this time, and even if a fiberglass were available that would be equal to foam, a foam insulated heater would be required."

After the introduction of foam insulation, State's annual sales jumped from less than two hundred thousand to more than four hundred thousand heaters between 1984 and 1986, and accounted for 1,275,525 sales for a net revenue of $155.2 million. Sales of foam heaters by Mor–Flo amounting to more than $83.9 million in total revenue are further evidence of demand. Mor–Flo used the foam insulation feature to "sell up" its entire line of heaters in its trade brochures. Three of the other four competitors used foam insulation. At the damages trial, Mor–Flo presented no evidence on what, if any, unique value any other components of its water heater added.

In describing the demand for State's method, the district court said, "Although there was no demand by customers or consumers of residential gas water heaters that heaters be foamed in accordance with any particular method, during the period of infringement of State's patent, there was no acceptable non-infringing method of satisfactorily foaming gas water heaters in the market place." In effect then, the demand went to the method.

＊　＊　＊

Manufacturing and Marketing

The finding that State has a 40% national market share is unassailable, and Mor–Flo does not seriously contend otherwise, or that State did not have the capacity to produce enough heaters to satisfy at least 40% of Mor–Flo's sales. ＊　＊　＊

＊　＊　＊ We accordingly agree with the court that it is probable, at least, that State could have met the demand.

Amount of Profit

The district court awarded State its incremental profit on foam-insulated gas water heaters reflecting the percentage of sales revenue State lost because of Mor–Flo's infringement that would have been its profit. This approach is well established and appropriate for determining damages for patent infringement. There is some testimony that fixed costs might have varied slightly, but the district court did not abuse its discretion in concluding that any increase in fixed costs was minimal and that award of incremental profits was appropriate. No greater precision is required.

The court based the award on the profit margin of the heater as a unit in accord with the entire market value rule, which permits recovery of damages based on the value of the entire apparatus containing several features, where the patent related feature is the basis for customer demand. In the face of the district court's finding to the contrary, Mor–Flo now argues that foam insulation was not the basis for consumer demand and several unidentified nonpatented components were key. But it did not identify or present evidence of the value of these nonpatented components. In any event, no components can be used separately, except as spare and repair parts for which State does not claim damages. *See Kori Corp. v. Wilco Marsh Buggies & Draglines, Inc.*, 761 F.2d 649, 656 (Fed.Cir.1985) (the entire market rule is properly applied when the nonpatented devices cannot be sold without the patented feature). There is no merit to this argument and we leave undisturbed the district court's adoption of the entire market rule.

In our view, the foregoing discussion compels the conclusion that the district court acted well within its discretion when it awarded damages for Mor–Flo's infringing activity based on State's share of the market. The court had the obligation to decide the case, and to decide it on the evidence and theories the parties proposed. * * * [O]n the record actually made, there was sufficient evidence for the court to find facts and draw inferences that support its damage award.

B.

The only direct evidence on what a reasonable royalty would have been is testimony of State's president that he would have asked for 8 to 10% of Mor–Flo's infringing sales, and its expert's declaration that a reasonable royalty would have been 8% of net infringing sales. Mor–Flo's actual net profit margin was 2.1% for the seventeen months preceding issuance of the patent, and Mor–Flo argues that it should pay a royalty no higher than that. Indeed, it says the rate should be minimal—before the district court it urged an effective rate of .163%.

The determination of a reasonable royalty, however, is based not on the infringer's profit margin, but on what a willing licensor and licensee would bargain for at hypothetical negotiations on the date infringement started. There is no rule that a royalty be no higher than the infringer's net profit margin. State's was a proven process upon which Mor–Flo had already built an established, successful line of heaters, and which it had expanded upon since its introduction in 1981. The value of foam to Mor–Flo was obvious: it never considered fiberglass as an alternative and risked infringement with foam insulation.

The value of collateral sales could also be factored into the royalty rate. Foam insulation was used to promote Mor–Flo's entire line of heaters. And it was not inappropriate for the district court to consider gross profits. Mor–Flo's gross profit during the preceding seventeen months was 19.6% with a net incremental profit of 17.48%. Finally, during the period of infringement, Mor–Flo's net profits varied from 5.9% to 7.3%. In light of all this, it seems to us the district court could very well conclude that a royalty of 3% of Mor–Flo's net sales is reasonable.

Mor–Flo repeats the argument that there were other methods available—the Rheem patented plastic foam belt, the "top-off" method, and the fiberglass foam stop. As discussed earlier, State has not shown that the "top-off" method or fiberglass foam stop were available during the period of infringement. The district court may have overlooked that the Rheem patented plastic foam belt might have provided an alternative way to foam insulate heaters, but Mor–Flo presented no evidence that it could have licensed the Rheem foam belt, and at what cost. Again, the district court could only decide the case on the evidence before it, and we see no objection to its decision not to allow Mor–Flo to rely on the availability of third party patents to mitigate damages.

Turning to State's cross-appeal, the district court found that the water heater industry was intensely competitive with small profit margins and fiberglass was a lesser alternative that manufacturers, however reluctantly, would opt for if the licensing fee for foam was too high. State argues that fiberglass was simply not an alternative, but it is undisputed that fiberglass-insulated heaters were and are sold in direct competition with foam-insulated ones. So, notwithstanding State's asserted hope to license the method in the 8 to 10% range, it was well within the district court's province to conclude it would not have succeeded, that potential licensees would have stayed with lesser alternatives promising some profit, rather than risk losing money by signing on at that high a rate. The award of a 3% royalty may be too low for State and too high for Mor–Flo, but the district court did not abuse its discretion in reaching it.

* * *

[The district court found that the defendant's infringement was not willful, and thus denied an award of enhanced damages under Patent Act § 284. However, the Federal Circuit held that "unresolved conflicting evidence" required that this finding be vacated and remanded to the district court. Because the district court's further findings on willfulness could affect its conclusion regarding award of attorney's fees, the Federal Circuit declined to reach that issue.]

NOTES AND QUESTIONS

1. *Monetary Relief.* Patent Act § 284 provides that upon finding for the claimant, "the court shall award the claimant damages adequate to compensate for the infringement, but in no event less than a reasonable royalty for the use made of the invention by the infringer, together with interest and costs." 35 U.S.C. § 284. Regardless of whether the damages are found by a jury or the court, the court "may increase the damages up to three times the

amount found or assessed." Section 285 adds that the court may, "in exceptional cases," award reasonable attorney fees to the prevailing party.

(a) Compensatory damages. Compensatory damages usually take the form of lost profits or a reasonable royalty. Both measures are illustrated in the *State Industries* case.

(1) Lost profits. According to the *State Industries* opinion, what is the proper standard for proving lost profits? Can you explain why each of the four factors set forth in *Panduit* is relevant to satisfying that standard? Did State Industries ask for too little under this measure? How would you have advised it to approach the lost profits measure?

The Federal Circuit approved the district court's use of the "incremental profit" or "incremental income" approach to computing lost profits. What does this entail? The Federal Circuit has explained:

> The approach recognizes that it does not cost as much to produce unit N + 1 if the first N (or fewer) units produced already have paid the fixed costs. Thus fixed costs—those costs which do not vary with increases in production, such as management salaries, property taxes, and insurance—are excluded when determining profits.

Paper Converting Machine Co. v. Magna–Graphics Corp., 745 F.2d 11, 22 (Fed.Cir.1984).

The *State Industries* court also approved the district court's application of the "entire market value" rule. The *Magna-Graphics* court elaborated on this provision, as well:

> The "entire market value rule" allows for the recovery of damages based on the value of an entire apparatus containing several features, even though only one feature is patented. * * * [U]nder the entire market value rule:
>
> > [I]t is not the physical joinder or separation of the contested items that determines their inclusion in or exclusion from the compensation base, so much as their financial and marketing dependence on the patented item under standard marketing procedures for the goods in question.

Magna-Graphics, 745 F.2d at 23–24. The *Magna-Graphics* court noted that while the unpatented components encompassed by the entire market value rule usually are part of a single machine, physically separate components, such as auxiliary equipment used with the patented invention, can qualify under the rule, even though the patentee could not prevent manufacture or sale of them. The court stressed that the deciding factor is

> whether "[n]ormally the patentee (or its licensee) can anticipate sale of such unpatented components as well as of the patented" ones. If in all reasonable probability the patent owner would have made the sales which the infringer has made, what the patent owner in reasonable probability would have netted from the sales denied to him is the measure of his loss, and the infringer is liable for that.

Id. (quoting Tektronix, Inc. v. United States, 552 F.2d 343, 351 (Ct.Cl.1977)). Are there potential drawbacks to the entire market value rule?

In Rite–Hite Corp. v. Kelley Co., Inc., 56 F.3d 1538 (Fed.Cir.), *cert. denied*, 516 U.S. 867, 116 S.Ct. 184, 133 L.Ed.2d 122 (1995), the Court of Appeals for the Federal Circuit held, in an 8–4 decision *en banc*, that a patentee is entitled to recover lost profits for lost sales of devices that are in direct competition with the infringing devices, but which themselves are not covered by the patent in suit. In that case, the patent in suit covered a device for securing a vehicle to a loading dock to prevent the vehicle from separating from the dock during loading or unloading. In its suit for infringement of the patent, the patentee sought lost profits for two types of vehicle restraints that it made and sold: the MDL–55, which incorporated the patented invention, and the ADL–100, which was not covered by the patent in suit. The district court found that "but for" the defendant's infringement, the patentee would have made 80 more sales of its MDL–55, and 3,243 more sales of its ADL–100, and awarded lost profits accordingly.

In upholding the award of lost profits on the ADL–100, the majority of the Federal Circuit noted the Supreme Court's admonition that a patentee should be "fully compensated" for infringement, and prior precedent providing a "but for" test for determining actual damages. The court characterized the *Panduit* four-factor test as essentially "establishing a patentee's *prima facie* case with respect to 'but for' causation." The court continued:

> Kelley does not challenge that Rite–Hite meets the *Panduit* test and therefore has proven "but for" causation; rather, Kelley argues that damages for the ADL–100, even if in fact caused by the infringement, are not legally compensable because the ADL–100 is not covered by the patent in suit.
>
> Preliminarily, we wish to affirm that the "test" for compensability of damages under § 284 is not solely a "but for" test in the sense that an infringer must compensate a patentee for any and all damages that proceed from the act of patent infringement. Notwithstanding the broad language of § 284, judicial relief cannot redress every conceivable harm that can be traced to an alleged wrongdoing. For example, remote consequences, such as a heart attack of the inventor or loss in value of shares of common stock of a patentee corporation caused indirectly by infringement are not compensable. Thus, along with establishing that a particular injury suffered by a patentee is a "but for" consequence of infringement, there may also be a background question whether the asserted injury is of the type for which the patentee may be compensated.
>
> Judicial limitations on damages, either for certain classes of plaintiffs or for certain types of injuries have been imposed in terms of "proximate cause" or "foreseeability." Such labels have been judicial tools used to limit legal responsibility for the consequences of one's conduct that are too remote to justify compensation. The general principles expressed in the common law tell us that the question of legal compensability is one "to be determined on the facts of each case upon mixed considerations of logic, common sense, justice, policy and precedent."
>
> We believe that under § 284 of the patent statute, the balance between full compensation, which is the meaning that the Supreme Court has attributed to the statute, and the reasonable limits of liability

encompassed by general principles of law can best be viewed in terms of reasonable, objective foreseeability. If a particular injury was or should have been reasonably foreseeable by an infringing competitor in the relevant market, broadly defined, that injury is generally compensable absent a persuasive reason to the contrary. Here, the court determined that Rite–Hite's lost sales of the ADL–100, a product that directly competed with the infringing product, were reasonably foreseeable. We agree with that conclusion. Being responsible for lost sales of a competitive product is surely foreseeable; such losses constitute the full compensation set forth by Congress, as interpreted by the Supreme Court, while staying well within the traditional meaning of proximate cause. Such lost sales should therefore clearly be compensable.

Recovery for lost sales of a device not covered by the patent in suit is not of course expressly provided for by the patent statute. Express language is not required, however. Statutes speak in general terms rather than specifically expressing every detail. Under the patent statute, damages should be awarded "where necessary to afford the plaintiff full compensation for the infringement." *General Motors*, 461 U.S. at 654. Thus, to refuse to award reasonably foreseeable damages necessary to make Rite–Hite whole would be inconsistent with the meaning of § 284.

Kelley asserts that to allow recovery for the ADL–100 would contravene the policy reason for which patents are granted: "[T]o promote the progress of . . . the useful arts." Because an inventor is only entitled to exclusivity to the extent he or she has invented and disclosed a novel, nonobvious, and useful device, Kelley argues, a patent may never be used to restrict competition in the sale of products not covered by the patent in suit. In support, Kelley cites antitrust case law condemning the use of a patent as a means to obtain a "monopoly" on unpatented material. * * *

These cases are inapposite to the issue raised here. The present case does not involve expanding the limits of the patent grant in violation of the antitrust laws; it simply asks, once infringement of a valid patent is found, what compensable injuries result from that infringement, *i.e.*, how may the patentee be made whole. Rite–Hite is not attempting to exclude its competitors from making, using, or selling a product not within the scope of its patent. The Truck Stop restraint was found to infringe the '847 patent, and Rite–Hite is simply seeking adequate compensation for that infringement; this is not an antitrust issue. Allowing compensation for such damage will "promote the Progress of . . . the useful Arts" by providing a stimulus to the development of new products and industries. * * *

> * * *

Id., 56 F.3d at 1545–48. Did the *Rite-Hite* majority expand the rights afforded by a patent? What if the patentee in *Rite-Hite* had sold only the ADL–100, which did not embody the patented invention, and not the MDL–55, which did? Should there be any difference in outcome?

(2) A reasonable royalty. Section 284 states that the damage award shall not be "less than a reasonable royalty." The Federal Circuit has stressed that

the purpose of this alternative is not to provide a simple accounting method, but to set a floor below which the courts are not authorized to go. * * * [An award based on a reasonable royalty] is suited to circumstances where there is an established royalty or licensing program, or if the patentee is not itself in the business, or if profits are too speculative to estimate.

Del Mar Avionics, Inc. v. Quinton Instrument Co., 836 F.2d 1320, 1326, 1328 (Fed.Cir.1987). The fact of infringement itself establishes injury, because the patentee's right to exclude has been violated. Thus, the patentee may recover damages based on a reasonable royalty even if it can show no actual pecuniary loss at all. If the patentee can demonstrate lost profits that exceed the reasonable royalty rate, however, that will be the preferred measure, since the mission of the court is to ensure that the patentee is fully compensated.

According to the *State Industries* court, what is the proper standard for determining a reasonable royalty? What kinds of evidence are likely to be relevant to this determination? See Georgia–Pacific v. U.S. Plywood Corp., 318 F.Supp. 1116 (S.D.N.Y.1970), *modified,* 446 F.2d 295 (2d Cir.), *cert. denied,* 404 U.S. 870, 92 S.Ct. 105, 30 L.Ed.2d 114 (1971).

(3) Prejudgment interest. In General Motors Corp. v. Devex Corp., 461 U.S. 648, 103 S.Ct. 2058, 76 L.Ed.2d 211 (1983), the Supreme Court stressed the importance of prejudgment interest awards, explaining:

Under the pre–1946 statute, the owner of a patent could recover both his own damages and the infringer's profits. A patent owner's ability to recover the infringer's profits reflected the notion that he should be able to force the infringer to disgorge the fruits of the infringement even if it caused him no injury. In 1946 Congress excluded consideration of the infringer's gain by eliminating the recovery of his profits, the determination of which had often required protracted litigation. At the same time, Congress sought to ensure that the patent owner would in fact receive full compensation for "any damages" he suffered as a result of the infringement. Accordingly, Congress expressly provided in § 284 that the court "shall award the claimant damages *adequate to compensate* for the infringement." (Emphasis added.)

The standard governing the award of prejudgment interest under § 284 should be consistent with Congress' overriding purpose of affording patent owners complete compensation. In light of that purpose, we conclude that prejudgment interest should ordinarily be awarded. In the typical case an award of prejudgment interest is necessary to ensure that the patent owner is placed in as good a position as he would have been in had the infringer entered into a reasonable royalty agreement. An award of interest from the time that the royalty payments would have been received merely serves to make the patent owner whole, since his damages consist not only of the value of the royalty payments but also of the foregone use of the money between the time of infringement and the date of the judgment.

Id., 461 U.S. at 654–56.

Prejudgment interest may prove to be a very significant item in the patentee's recovery. In the protracted *Devex* litigation, for example, the lower court determined that the patentee was entitled to a reasonable royalty of $8,813,945.50 for the defendant's infringement. It awarded prejudgment interest of $11,022,854.97.

(b) Enhanced damages and attorney fees. Patent Act § 284 provides that the court may increase the patentee's actual damages up to three times. What is the purpose underlying the enhanced damages provision? According to the *State Industries* court, what is the appropriate standard for determining whether such enhanced damages are warranted? In *In re* Seagate Technology, LLC, 497 F.3d 1360 (Fed. Cir. 2007), *cert. denied*, 552 U.S. 1230, 128 S.Ct. 1445, 170 L.Ed.2d 275 (2008), the Federal Circuit revisited and revised its standard *en banc*:

> Because patent infringement is a strict liability offense, the nature of the offense is only relevant in determining whether enhanced damages are warranted. Although a trial court's discretion in awarding enhanced damages has a long lineage in patent law, the current statute, similar to its predecessors, is devoid of any standard for awarding them. Absent a statutory guide, we have held that an award of enhanced damages requires a showing of willful infringement. * * * This well-established standard accords with Supreme Court precedent. * * * But, a finding of willfulness does not require an award of enhanced damages; it merely permits it.
>
> This court fashioned a standard for evaluating willful infringement in *Underwater Devices Inc. v. Morrison–Knudsen Co.,* 717 F.2d 1380, 1389–90 (Fed.Cir.1983): "Where ... a potential infringer has actual notice of another's patent rights, he has an affirmative duty to exercise due care to determine whether or not he is infringing. Such an affirmative duty includes, *inter alia,* the duty to seek and obtain competent legal advice from counsel *before* the initiation of any possible infringing activity."(citations omitted). This standard was announced shortly after the creation of the court, and at a time "when widespread disregard of patent rights was undermining the national innovation incentive." *Knorr-Bremse Systeme Fuer Nutzfahrzeuge GmbH v. Dana Corp.,* 383 F.3d 1337, 1343 (Fed.Cir.2004) (en banc). Indeed, in *Underwater Devices,* an attorney had advised the infringer that "[c]ourts, in recent years, have—in patent infringement cases—found [asserted patents] invalid in approximately 80% of the cases," and on that basis the attorney concluded that the patentee would not likely sue for infringement. Over time, our cases evolved to evaluate willfulness and its duty of due care under the totality of the circumstances, and we enumerated factors informing the inquiry.
>
> In light of the duty of due care, accused willful infringers commonly assert an advice of counsel defense. Under this defense, an accused willful infringer aims to establish that due to reasonable reliance on advice from counsel, its continued accused activities were done in good faith. Typically, counsel's opinion concludes that the patent is invalid, unenforceable, and/or not infringed. Although an infringer's reliance on favorable advice

of counsel, or conversely his failure to proffer any favorable advice, is not dispositive of the willfulness inquiry, it is crucial to the analysis. * * *

* * *

The term willful is not unique to patent law, and it has a well-established meaning in the civil context. For instance, our sister circuits have employed a recklessness standard for enhancing statutory damages for copyright infringement. Under the Copyright Act, a copyright owner can elect to receive statutory damages, and trial courts have discretion to enhance the damages, up to a statutory maximum, for willful infringement. 17 U.S.C. § 504(c). Although the statute does not define willful, it has consistently been defined as including reckless behavior. * * *

Just recently, the Supreme Court addressed the meaning of willfulness as a statutory condition of civil liability for punitive damages. *Safeco Ins. Co. of Am. v. Burr,* 551 U.S. 47, 127 S.Ct. 2201, 167 L.Ed.2d 1045 (2007). *Safeco* involved the Fair Credit Reporting Act ("FCRA"), which imposes civil liability for failure to comply with its requirements. Whereas an affected consumer can recover actual damages for negligent violations of the FCRA, 15 U.S.C. § 1681 o(a), he can also recover punitive damages for willful ones, 15 U.S.C. § 1681 n(a). Addressing the willfulness requirement in this context, the Court concluded that the "standard civil usage" of "willful" includes reckless behavior. * * *. Significantly, the Court said that this definition comports with the common law usage, "which treated actions in 'reckless disregard' of the law as 'willful' violations."

In contrast, the duty of care announced in *Underwater Devices* sets a lower threshold for willful infringement that is more akin to negligence. This standard fails to comport with the general understanding of willfulness in the civil context * * * and it allows for punitive damages in a manner inconsistent with Supreme Court precedent. Accordingly, we overrule the standard set out in *Underwater Devices* and hold that proof of willful infringement permitting enhanced damages requires at least a showing of objective recklessness. Because we abandon the affirmative duty of due care, we also reemphasize that there is no affirmative obligation to obtain opinion of counsel.

We fully recognize that "the term [reckless] is not self-defining." However, "[t]he civil law generally calls a person reckless who acts ... in the face of an unjustifiably high risk of harm that is either known or so obvious that it should be known." Accordingly, to establish willful infringement, a patentee must show by clear and convincing evidence that the infringer acted despite an objectively high likelihood that its actions constituted infringement of a valid patent. * * * The state of mind of the accused infringer is not relevant to this objective inquiry. If this threshold objective standard is satisfied, the patentee must also demonstrate that this objectively-defined risk (determined by the record developed in the infringement proceeding) was either known or so obvious that it should have been known to the accused infringer. We leave it to future cases to further develop the application of this standard.

Seagate, 497 F.3d at 1368–71. After *Seagate,* what evidence will likely be relevant to the issue of objective recklessness? Would it be appropriate for a patentee to introduce evidence of an accused infringer's failure to obtain opinion of counsel?

Patent Act § 285 permits a court, in its discretion, to award attorney fees to the prevailing party "in exceptional cases." An exceptional case may be found when the losing defendant's infringement was willful, or when the losing party has acted in bad faith—for example, has pursued or conducted the infringement litigation in bad faith.

Review Patent Act § 287(a), which provides for marking goods with notice of patent. Failure properly to mark patented articles may result in denial of damages for infringements occurring before the defendant received actual notice of the infringement.

2. *Injunctive Relief.* What are the practical implications of a general rule that, absent exceptional circumstances, courts must issue permanent injunctions against patent infringement? Is the presence of such a rule likely to change the behavior of parties to business transactions? Is it likely to change the behavior of patent litigants?

Unlike in the case of permanent injunctions, courts historically have been hesitant to grant requests for *preliminary* injunctions to prevent alleged infringement during the course of litigation. A preliminary injunction's potential impact on competition is considerable: an injunction against making, using, offering to sell, selling or importing a product during the course of protracted patent litigation could permanently injure the defendant's competitive position. If the defendant ultimately is acquitted, it may never regain its market share, notwithstanding the plaintiff's posting of a bond to reimburse it for losses incurred as a result of the injunction. The only realistic alternative may be to settle on disadvantageous terms, which also may be injurious to competition.

In Smith Int'l, Inc. v. Hughes Tool Co., 718 F.2d 1573, 1578–79 (Fed. Cir.), *cert. denied*, 464 U.S. 996, 104 S.Ct. 493, 78 L.Ed.2d 687 (1983), the newly created Court of Appeals for the Federal Circuit described the state of the law concerning preliminary injunctions in patent cases as it existed at that time:

> The standard for granting such relief has been characterized as "unusually stringent." * * * The usual requirement of a showing of probability of success on the merits before a preliminary injunction will issue has historically been even stronger in a patent case. Besides having to prove title to the patent, it has been stated as a general proposition that the movant must show that the patent is beyond question valid and infringed. In order to meet the burden of showing validity, the movant has sometimes been required to show either that his patent has previously been adjudicated valid, that there has been public acquiescence to its validity, or that there is conclusive direct technical evidence proving its validity. However, other courts have employed a less stringent standard of proof on the issue of validity. The basis for the more severe rule appears to be both a distrust of and unfamiliarity with patent issues and a belief that the *ex parte* examination by the Patent and Trademark Office is inherently unreliable.

As with preliminary injunctions in other types of cases, the movant is also required to demonstrate in a patent case that he will suffer immediate irreparable harm if the injunction is not granted. Some courts refuse to find irreparable injury where the alleged infringer is solvent and money will adequately compensate the injury. However, at least one court is of the opinion that where the showing on patent validity is very strong, invasion of the inventor's right to exclude granted by the patent laws should be sufficient irreparable harm without a showing that the infringer is financially irresponsible.

Finally, where relevant, the court should take into account both the possibility of harm to other interested persons from the grant or denial of the injunction, and the public interest. In reaching its decision, the district court must consider the above factors and balance all of the elements. No one element will necessarily be dispositive of the case.

In *Smith*, the court adopted the rule that a clear showing of validity and infringement would permit a court to presume irreparable injury. Two years later, in Atlas Powder Co. v. Ireco Chemicals, 773 F.2d 1230, 1233 (Fed.Cir. 1985), the Federal Circuit rejected an argument that validity and infringement must be demonstrated "beyond question:"

> [Defendant] is arguing for a rule, said to be followed by various other circuits, that [the patentee] must prove validity and infringement "beyond question," in order to meet its burden of proof on irreparable harm.

> The burden upon the movant should be no different in a patent case than for other kinds of intellectual property, where, generally, only a "clear showing" is required. Requiring a "final adjudication," "full trial," or proof "beyond question" would support the issuance of a permanent injunction and nothing would remain to establish the liability of the accused infringer. That is not the situation before us. We are dealing with a provisional remedy which provides equitable *preliminary* relief. Thus, when a patentee "clearly shows" that his patent is valid and infringed, a court may, after a balance of all of the competing equities, preliminarily enjoin another from violating the rights secured by the patent.

What competing equities should be balanced, and how? The court's finding in *Atlas* provides some insights. In that case the accused infringer argued that a preliminary injunction would cause it, as well as the mining industry it served, irreparable injury. The allegedly infringing products accounted for 66% of its total sales. It would have to lay off approximately 200 employees as a result of the injunction, though the patent at issue would expire within a year. The Federal Circuit was unimpressed:

> Balancing the equities is within the discretion of the district court. It found, on the basis of Atlas's strong showing of validity and infringement, that the injury to Ireco was not sufficient to outweigh the injury to Atlas's patent rights. We are unpersuaded that the district court abused its discretion in this respect.

The fact that the patent has only one year to run is not a factor in favor of Ireco in the balance of equities. Patent rights do not peter out as the end of the patent term, usually 17 years, is approached.

Atlas, 773 F.2d at 1234. Under what kinds of circumstances might a defendant be able to demonstrate that the balance of equities tips in its favor?

What about the public interest factor? In Hybritech Inc. v. Abbott Laboratories, 849 F.2d 1446, 1458 (Fed.Cir.1988), the court noted that "the focus of the district court's public interest analysis should be whether there exists some critical public interest that would be injured by the grant of preliminary relief." In that case, the court upheld the district court's decision to exclude Abbott's allegedly infringing cancer test kits and hepatitis kits from the preliminary injunction order due to the public interest in having those products readily available. It also upheld the district court's decision to preliminarily enjoin sale of Abbott's other allegedly infringing medical products. In the case of these products, Abbott argued that 1) the diagnostic community relied upon the products; 2) forcing the public to switch vendors would be expensive and time consuming; and 3) supply shortages to the public might result because the patentee allegedly had experienced substantial difficulties in filling orders quickly. After considering these arguments, the district court found that, as to these products, the public interest in enforcing valid patents outweighed the public interest considerations that Abbott invoked.

II. PLANT PATENTS

YODER BROTHERS, INC. v. CALIFORNIA–FLORIDA PLANT CORP.

United States Court of Appeals, Fifth Circuit, 1976.
537 F.2d 1347, *cert. denied,* 429 U.S. 1094, 97 S.Ct. 1108, 51 L.Ed.2d 540 (1977).

GOLDBERG, CIRCUIT JUDGE:

In this clash between two giants of the chrysanthemum business, we confront a myriad of antitrust and plant patent issues. Yoder Brothers (Yoder), plaintiff in the district court, sued, alleging infringement of twenty-one chrysanthemum plant patents by California–Florida Plant Corp. (CFPC) and California–Florida Plant Corp. of Florida (CFPCF) (sometimes referred to collectively as Cal–Florida). CFPC and CFPCF denied the infringement and filed antitrust counterclaims under sections 1 and 2 of the Sherman Act. As to seven of the chrysanthemum plant patents, the lower court directed verdicts for Yoder that the patents were valid and infringed and awarded treble damages. * * *

Because many of the issues in this case turn on the particular nature of the ornamental plant industry and the specific characteristics of chrysanthemums, we shall describe the background facts in some detail before discussing the many complex legal issues presented on this appeal. * * *

I. GENERAL BACKGROUND

A. *The Chrysanthemum Industry*

Chrysanthemums, in their natural state, blossom only during the fall. This is because they are photoperiodic in nature, meaning that their growth is affected by the relative lengths of lightness and darkness in the day. When the days are long, the chrysanthemum plant remains in a vegetative state. As the nights become longer, the initiation process of the chrysanthemum bud begins. Thus, in early August, when the nights achieve a duration of nine and one-half continuous dark hours, the chrysanthemum plant in its natural state will begin the process of developing a flower. During the fall and early winter months, the mature flower appears.

Yoder began doing business in the 1930's as a simple greenhouse operator, specializing in tomatoes. Soon thereafter, because the fall tomato crop was less profitable than the spring crop, it decided to replace the fall crop with chrysanthemums. In 1939 or 1940, Yoder employees began research into out-of-season flowering of chrysanthemums. By applying black cloth shades over the chrysanthemums when dark hours were needed and applying artificial light when light hours were needed, it became possible to flower chrysanthemums on a year-round basis. Yet this breakthrough was not without its problems. For example, the use of black cloth shades resulted in an abnormally high temperature build-up around the plants, which in turn retarded bud initiation. Similarly, when the finishing temperatures were too warm, the chrysanthemums would not hold their color. In an effort to adjust for these conditions and to improve the quality of the chrysanthemum generally, Yoder initiated a breeding program in the early 1940's. One of the most important goals of the breeding program was the development of new varieties for consumers.

* * *

Chrysanthemums have been subject to intensive breeding efforts over the past thirty years; each individual specimen is a genetically unique complex organism. Several definitions of the term "variety" of chrysanthemum were offered at trial. Mr. Duffett, Yoder's head breeder, defined a variety as a group of individual plants which, on the basis of observation by skilled floriculturists and according to reasonable commercial tolerances, display identical characteristics under similar environments. Cal–Florida defined variety in its complaint as "a subspecies or class of chrysanthemums distinguishable from other subspecies or classes of chrysanthemums by distinct characteristics, such as color, hue, shape and size of petal or blossom or any of them."

New varieties of chrysanthemums are developed in two major ways: by sexual reproduction and by mutagenic techniques. Sexual reproduction, the result of self or cross pollination, produces a genetically unique seedling, the characteristics of which are impossible to predict. Mutagenic techniques simply accelerate the natural rate of mutation in the chrysanthemum plant itself. A mutation was defined by Mr. Duffett as "a change in the number of chromosomes or a change in the chromosome position or a specific change in the genes within those chromosomes." Technically, only those mutations that first express themselves as bud variations are properly called "sports"; however, the word is used loosely in the industry as a general synonym for mutation, and we will so use it. Two types of sports can appear: spontaneous sports and radiation sports. The cells of all living things occasionally mutate, and spontaneous sports are simply the result of that process. Radiation sports, on the other hand, are induced artificially, through exposure to such things as gamma radiation from radioactive cobalt and X-rays. These techniques do nothing that could not occur in nature apart from speeding up the natural mutation process. Although most of the mutations induced by radiation are not commercially usable plants, a skilled breeder will select for further development those that display such desirable characteristics as fast response time, temperature tolerance, durability, size, and vigor.

After a breeder has successfully isolated a new variety, the only way he can preserve his creation is by means of asexual reproduction. In the case of chrysanthemums, the most common technique of asexual reproduction is the taking of cuttings from a stock plant. Cuttings, as defined in the Cal–Florida complaint, are "sections or parts of chrysanthemum plants which may be grown into mature plants for sale as cut flowers and/or potted plants or from which additional cuttings may be harvested." According to Yoder's suggested definition, cuttings are simply immature chrysanthemum plants. Since a cutting is genetically identical to the parent plant, it will develop into a plant whose characteristics match the parent's exactly, so long as the same environmental conditions obtain. A central fact of life in the chrysanthemum industry is the ease with which cuttings can be taken from parent plants: from one chrysanthemum, it is theoretically possible to develop an infinitely large stock, by taking cuttings, maturing some into flowered plants, taking more cuttings, and so on.

Over the years since Yoder first entered the chrysanthemum business, the industry has become internally specialized. At the first functional level are the breeders, who create new varieties of chrysanthemums. Breeding is an expensive, complex procedure. The breeder must possess the skill and discrimination to spot potential new varieties and recognize whether they possess desirable traits; facilities for elaborate testing and development must be available. Because chrysanthemums mutate rapidly, a breeder must always be on the lookout for new changes.

At the next level in the industry are the propagator-distributors. The propagator-distributors build up mother stock from sources such as breeders, retail florists, or their existing flowers, and reproduce cuttings from that mother stock. In a sense they are simply mass producers of cuttings. They do not develop cuttings to the mature flower stage (except for purposes of their own testing). Next are the growers, who develop cuttings purchased from propagator-distributors into mature plants either for cut flowers or potted plants. Combining the function of propagator-distributors and growers are the self-propagators. Cal–Florida defined a "self-propagator" as "a person who either buys or establishes stock and takes cuttings for the sole purpose of producing cut flowers and/or potted plants for resale or own use." In other words, the self-propagators are vertically integrated into one step. Finally, the growers (or self-propagators) sell their products to retail florists, who in turn sell to ultimate consumers.

B. The Parties

During the times relevant to this litigation, Yoder operated on two levels in the business: as a substantial (if not the largest) breeder of new varieties of chrysanthemums, and as a large propagator-distributor. * * *

CFPC * * * was a propagator-distributor. CFPCF, a wholly owned subsidiary of CFPC, was also a propagator-distributor. * * *

* * *

IV. PLANT PATENTS

A. Introduction

* * * [T]he only issues before this Court concern the seven patents that the district court ruled valid and infringed as a matter of law: Red Torch, Gold Marble, Morocco, Promenade, Southern Gold, Mountain Snow, and Mountain Sun. After considerable thought, we have decided that the district court correctly ruled that Cal–Florida failed to rebut the statutory presumption of validity with sufficient relevant evidence. * * *

B. Constitutional and Statutory Background

* * *

* * * In its present form, the principal statute allowing patents on plants reads:

> Whoever invents or discovers and asexually reproduces any distinct and new variety of plant, including cultivated sports, mutants, hybrids, and newly found seedlings, other than a tuberpropagated plant or a plant found in an uncultivated state, may obtain a patent therefor, subject to the conditions and requirements of this title.
>
> The provision of this title relating to patents for inventions shall apply to patents for plants, except as otherwise provided.

35 U.S.C. § 161. Since section 161 makes the general patent law applicable to plant patents except as otherwise provided,[32] we take as our starting point the general requisites for patentability, and then apply them as well as we can to plants.

Normally, the three requirements for patentability are novelty, utility, and obviousness. For plant patents, the requirement of distinctness

---

32. The only express provision modifying the applicability of the invention patent statutes for plant patents is contained in 35 U.S.C. § 162, which says that no plant patent will be invalidated for noncompliance with § 112 (description) if the description is as complete as is reasonably possible. No description issue is before us.

replaces that of utility, and the additional requirement of asexual reproduction is introduced.

The concept of novelty refers to novelty of conception, rather than novelty of use; no single prior art structure can exist in which all of the elements serve substantially the same function. In *Beckman Instruments, Inc. v. Chemtronics, Inc.*, 5 Cir., 439 F.2d 1369, 1375, cert. denied, 1970, 400 U.S. 956, 91 S.Ct. 353–54, 27 L.Ed.2d 264, this Court said:

> [S]ection 102, which pertains to novelty, requires that the patentee be the original inventor of the object claimed in his patent, and also that the invention not have been known or used by others before his discovery of it. . . . Furthermore the prior art is to be considered as covering all uses to which it could have been put.

As applied to plants, the Patent Office Board of Appeals held that a "new" plant had to be one that literally had not existed before, rather than one that had existed in nature but was newly found, such as an exotic plant from a remote part of the earth.[34] In *Application of Greer*, Ct.Cust. & Pat.App.1973, 484 F.2d 488, the court indicated that the Board believed that novelty was to be determined by a detailed comparison with other known varieties.

The legislative history of the Plant Patent Act is of considerable assistance in defining "distinctness." The Senate Report said:

> [I]n order for the new variety to be distinct it must have characteristics clearly distinguishable from those of existing varieties and it is immaterial whether in the judgment of the Patent Office the new characteristics are inferior or superior to those of existing varieties. Experience has shown the absurdity of many views held as to the value of new varieties at the time of their creation.
>
> The characteristics that may distinguish a new variety would include, among others, those of habit; immunity from disease; or soil conditions; color of flower, leaf, fruit or stems; flavor; productivity, including ever-bearing qualities in case of fruits; storage qualities; perfume; form; and ease of asexual reproduction. Within any one of the above or other classes of characteristics the differences which would suffice to make the variety a distinct variety, will necessarily be differences of degree.

S.Rep. 315, 71st Cong., 2d Sess. (1930). A definition of "distinctness" as the aggregate of the plant's distinguishing characteristics seems to us a sensible and workable one.

The third requirement, nonobviousness, is the hardest to apply to plants, though we are bound to do so to the best of our ability. The traditional three part test for obviousness, as set out in *John Deere, supra,*

---

34. In order for a plant to have "existed" before in nature, we think that it must have been capable of reproducing itself. Thus, we have concluded that the mere fact that a sport of a plant had appeared in the past would not be sufficient to preclude the patentability of the plant on novelty grounds, since each sport is a one-time phenomenon absent human intervention. See in this connection the discussion on validity, at IV.C., *infra.*

inquires as to (1) the scope and content of the prior art, (2) the differences between the prior art and the claims at issue, and (3) the level of ordinary skill in the prior art. Secondary characteristics such as commercial success, long felt but unsolved needs, and failure of others can be used to illuminate the circumstances surrounding the subject matter sought to be patented.

The Supreme Court has viewed the obviousness requirement of section 103 as Congress' articulation of the constitutional standard of invention. *Dann v. Johnston*, 425 U.S. 219, 225, 96 S.Ct. 1393, 1397, 47 L.Ed.2d 692, 698 (1976). In *Dann*, the Court commented that

> [a]s a judicial test, "invention"—i.e., "an exercise of the inventive faculty," . . . —has long been regarded as an absolute prerequisite to patentability.

425 U.S. at 225, 96 S.Ct. at 1397, 47 L.Ed.2d at 697–98. An "invention" is characterized by a degree of skill and ingenuity greater than that possessed by an ordinary mechanic acquainted with the business. The obviousness requirement appears to presume that if the gap between the prior art and the claimed improvement is small, then an ordinary mechanic skilled in the art would have been able to create the improvement, thus leading to the conclusion that the improvement was obvious and a patentable invention not present. Section 103 requires the determination of obviousness *vel non* to be made with reference to the time the invention was made. Obviousness, like the general question of patent validity, is ultimately a question of law, though factual inquiries are often necessary to its resolution.

Rephrasing the *John Deere* tests for the plant world, we might ask about (1) the characteristics of prior plants of the same general type, both patented and nonpatented, and (2) the differences between the prior plants and the claims at issue. We see no meaningful way to apply the third criterion to plants—*i.e.*, the level of ordinary skill in the prior art. Criteria one and two are reminiscent of the "distinctness" requirement already in the Plant Patent Act. Thus, if we are to give obviousness an independent meaning, it must refer to something other than observable characteristics.

We think that the most promising approach toward the obviousness requirement for plant patents is reference to the underlying constitutional standard that it codifies—namely, invention.

The general thrust of the "invention" requirement is to ensure that minor improvements will not be granted the protection of a seventeen year monopoly by the state. In the case of plants, to develop or discover a new variety that retains the desirable qualities of the parent stock and adds significant improvements, and to preserve the new specimen by asexually reproducing it constitutes no small feat.

This Court's case dealing with the patent on the chemical compound commonly known as the drug "Darvon," *Eli Lilly & Co. v. Generix Drug*

Sales, Inc., 5 Cir.1972, 460 F.2d 1096, provides some insight into the problem of how to apply the "invention" requirement to a new and esoteric subject matter. The court first noted that

> [a]nalogical reasoning is necessarily restricted in many chemical patent cases because of the necessity for physiological experimentation before any use can be determined.

> In fact, such lack of predictability of useful result from the making of even the slightest variation in the atomic structure or spatial arrangement of a complex molecule ... deprives the instant claims of obviousness and anticipation of most of their vitality....

460 F.2d at 1101. The court resolved the apparent dilemma by looking to the therapeutic value of the new drug instead of to its chemical composition:

> [R]eason compels us to agree that novelty, usefulness and non-obviousness inhere in the true discovery that a chemical compound exhibits a new needed medicinal capability, even though it be closely related in structure to a known or patented drug.

460 F.2d at 1103.

The same kind of shift in focus would lead us to a more productive inquiry for plant patents. If the plant is a source of food, the ultimate question might be its nutritive content or its prolificacy. A medicinal plant might be judged by its increased or changed therapeutic value. Similarly, an ornamental plant would be judged by its increased beauty and desirability in relation to the other plants of its type, its usefulness in the industry, and how much of an improvement it represents over prior ornamental plants, taking all of its characteristics together.

Before reaching the issues on appeal, we make a final comment about the requirement of asexual reproduction.[36] It has been described as the "very essence" of the patent. Asexual reproduction is literally the only way that a breeder can be sure he has reproduced a plant identical in every respect to the parent. It is quite possible that infringement of a plant patent would occur only if stock obtained from one of the patented plants is used, given the extreme unlikelihood that any other plant could actually infringe. If the alleged infringer could somehow prove that he had developed the plant in question independently, then he would not be liable in damages or subject to an injunction for infringement.[37] This example illustrates the extreme extent to which asexual reproduction is the heart of the present plant patent system: the whole key to the "invention" of a new plant is the discovery of new traits *plus* the foresight and appreciation to take the step of asexual reproduction.

---

36. Lest the reader fear that Congress neglected to make adequate provision for reproduction of the sexual type, we hasten to note that the Plant Variety Protection statute, 7 U.S.C. §§ 2321–2583, applies only to sexually reproducing plants.

37. Whether he might also be entitled to a patent on his plant is more problematic, although we would not want to rule out the possibility.

C. Yoder's Plant Patents—Validity

During the trial, Cal–Florida offered as evidence certain documents showing that growers had found mutations on the Mandalay variety that were the same as the patented variety Glowing Mandalay—*i.e.*, evidence that the sport Glowing Mandalay had recurred. Although Glowing Mandalay is no longer in the case, Cal–Florida later proffered similar evidence with respect to Gold Marble, Promenade, and Red Torch, which are three of the patents whose validity is challenged on appeal. Gold Marble, Promenade, and Red Torch are all sport patents, meaning that they first appeared as a sport of another plant, in contrast to seedling patents, which develop from seeds. Of the remaining four challenged patents, two were sport patents and two were seedling patents. Cal–Florida never proffered any sport recurrence evidence as to the other two sport patents, Mountain Sun and Southern Gold, nor did it offer any specific evidence attacking the seedling patents, Morocco and Mountain Snow. Since we find that the district court's ruling on the sport recurrence evidence did not preclude Cal–Florida from introducing other types of evidence to attack the validity of the patents, and since no sport recurrence evidence was introduced as to Mountain Sun and Southern Gold, we find no warrant on appeal to disturb the ruling that Mountain Sun, Southern Gold, Morocco, and Mountain Snow were valid and infringed. Plant patents, like others, enjoy a statutory presumption of validity that was not rebutted as to those four.

At the time the court rejected the sport return evidence for Glowing Mandalay, it made a ruling designed to apply to the rest of the trial with respect to that kind of evidence. That ruling is the focus of Cal–Florida's cross appeal on the plant patent validity point. Because of its importance, we set out the pertinent parts in some detail here:

> [I]t seems clear that it was the Congressional intent that a person who discovered an asexually reproduced variety of a new and distinct plant was entitled to a patent.
>
> It was not contemplated, apparently, that he invent, in the term that is used, or in the significance of that term, as we understand it, traditional concept of inventing a machine....
>
> In any event, the issue presented here is a rather narrow one and it has some practical overtones.
>
> I am frank to confess that I think Mr. Foster's [Yoder's counsel's] presentation here ... is very persuasive. In all probability, this will be, or may be, the ultimate result of this trial. It may not be, after we have listened to the testimony, of course, of Mr. Boone's [Cal–Florida's counsel's] other witnesses who are coming in to testify on the genetics of this thing, but on this one narrow limited issue, it would seem that the plaintiffs [Yoder] were entitled to prevail. Therefore, the objection to the introduction of the various letters and documents from ... the growers and plant propagators around the

country, which were forwarded to Yoder Brothers over the years, is sustained.

Cal–Florida construes the above-quoted ruling as an all-encompassing holding that the constitutional standard of invention does not apply to plant patents. It further claims that since the ruling was admittedly intended to apply to the entire trial, it was precluded from offering evidence on the issues of newness, distinctness, and obviousness by the court's action. In fact, it never even tried to introduce the expected expert genetics testimony, although it did make a formal offer of more sport return evidence at a later time in the trial.

Yoder disputes the breadth of the ruling and its effect on any other evidence Cal–Florida might have offered, and notes that the court's actual ruling on the issues of newness and distinctness did not come until some two weeks later. With regard to the ruling on the admissibility of the evidence, Yoder argues that the documents would not have shown lack of distinctness, since the fact that a sport with particular traits recurs says nothing about what those traits are and how they differ from other plants. Furthermore, Yoder argues that the documents would not have shown obviousness, because if sport recurrence were evidence of obviousness, then almost no mutations would be patentable, and that would be contrary to Congress' intent.

We do not construe the district court's evidentiary ruling as anything more than that; in our opinion, it simply held that the sport recurrence evidence was not relevant to any of the patent validity issues. We therefore confine our remarks accordingly.

The only possible probative value of the sport recurrence evidence would be to show that a sport of that particular size, shape, color, or other trait is predictable from a given variety of parent plant. Thus, we must first determine whether Congress intended predictability to negate the possibility of "invention." Next, if Congress considered that factor irrelevant, we must decide if the Constitution is offended by permitting patents on the kinds of sports that recur.[39]

Both the language of the statute and its legislative history persuade us that Congress did not intend to exclude the kind of mutation that might recur from the Act's protection. Instead, both Senate Report 315, 71st Cong., 2d Sess. (1930), on the original bill, and Senate Report 1937, 83d Cong., 2d Sess. (1954), on the 1954 amendment, speak generally about sports and mutations. The 1954 amendment was added to clarify Congress' intention that seedlings should be patentable, but in the process of describing the bill, the report states:

---

39. In this discussion, we are concerned only with the "invention" or obviousness issue. As we have defined novelty, *supra*, the recurrence of a sport of a particular color would be irrelevant. Similarly, sport recurrence says nothing about the new plant's particular characteristics. The testimony at the trial amply established that Yoder's patented chrysanthemums were distinct to those skilled in the field—*i.e.*, those in the breeding business. We note that there is a distinction between looking to the opinion of persons in the industry to prove a feature of patentability and relying on commercial success to prove nonobviousness. Yoder's arguments relied on the former kind of evidence.

The enactment of this legislation will remove any doubt that the legislative intent of the Congress clearly means that sports, mutants, hybrids, and seedlings, discovered by persons engaged in agriculture or horticulture, should be patentable ...

S.Rep. 1937, *supra.*

Although we are willing to assume for purposes of this argument that some mutations may appear that would have been genetically impossible before—*i.e.*, that a fundamental change in the biochemical structure of the chromosome may take place—by far the majority of mutations and sports of chrysanthemums are predictable to some extent for those skilled in the field. For example, the testimony at trial indicated that a yellow sport could be expected from a white chrysanthemum. Indeed, part of the skill required of a chrysanthemum breeder is to know what to look for and to take steps immediately to preserve it by asexual reproduction if the desired trait appears. Given that fact, we think that the purpose of the Plant Patent Act would be frustrated by a requirement that only those rare, never-before-seen, if not genetically impossible sports or mutations would be patentable. That purpose was "to afford agriculture, so far as practicable, the same opportunity to participate in the benefits of the patent system as has been given industry, and thus assist in placing agriculture on a basis of economic equality with industry." S.Rep. 315, *supra.* To make it significantly more difficult to obtain a plant patent than another type of patent would frustrate that purpose.

We therefore find that Congress did not intend to exclude the kind of sport that recurs frequently from the Plant Patent Act. That being the case, the district court correctly ruled that the evidence proffered by Cal–Florida was irrelevant, as a matter of statutory law.

The only way that the Constitution would be offended by permitting patents on recurring sports would be if such leniency indicated that no "invention" was present. We do not think that sport recurrence would negate invention, however. An infinite number of a certain sized sport could appear on a plant, but until someone recognized its uniqueness and difference and found that the traits could be preserved by asexual reproduction in commercial quantities, no patentable plant would exist. An objective judgment of the value of the sport's new and different characteristics—*i.e.*, nutritive value, ornamental value, hardiness, longevity, etc.—would not depend in any way on whether a similar sport had appeared in the past, or whether that particular sport was predictable. We therefore find no reason to disturb our approval of the district court's evidentiary ruling based on the constitutional standard of invention. As that standard applies to plant patents, the proffered evidence was irrelevant.

Viewing the evidence offered on the patent validity question as a whole, we find that Cal–Florida failed to rebut the statutory presumption of validity as to Gold Marble, Promenade, and Red Torch, as well as the other four discussed above. Thus, the lower court's finding of validity must be affirmed on this record.

D. Patent Infringement

On cross appeal, Cal–Florida asserts that the absence of flowering plants grown from the cuttings it had admittedly taken from Yoder's patented plants was fatal to Yoder's infringement counts. This is because the patent claim in each instance describes a mature flowering plant, and it is Cal–Florida's position that only another mature flowering plant could directly infringe. Yoder retorts that the Plant Patent Act provides that

> [i]n the case of a plant patent the grant shall be of the right to exclude others from asexually reproducing the plant or selling or using the plant so reproduced.

35 U.S.C. § 163. The district court ruled that the act of asexual reproduction was complete at the time the cutting was taken. Finally, the pretrial stipulations established that Cal–Florida had taken plant material, or cuttings, from Yoder's patented plants.

We agree with Yoder that it was not necessary to prove that the cuttings actually matured into flowered plants to show infringement. Under such a rule, it would be virtually impossible for a propagator-distributor directly to infringe a patent, despite the vital role he plays in dissemination of plant material. Furthermore, we think section 163 is plain in its statement that a patentee may exclude others from asexually reproducing, selling or using the plant. The negative inference to be drawn from this is that commission of one of those acts would constitute infringement. We therefore affirm the finding of infringement.

* * *

NOTES AND QUESTIONS

1. *Plant patents.* The Plant Patent Act was enacted in 1930, long after utility patents had been established in the United States. It was later codified in the Patent Act of 1952 at 35 U.S.C. §§ 161–64. Section 161 provides that utility patent provisions should apply to plant patents, except as otherwise provided. As the Fifth Circuit's opinion indicates, adapting provisions created and construed with new and useful machines, compositions of matter, manufactures and processes in mind to plants raises some conceptual problems. How does the court adapt the nonobviousness requirement of § 103 to the plant patent context? What about the novelty requirement? Why shouldn't the evidence that the same sports had appeared prior to Yoder's discovery and application be relevant to the court's novelty and nonobviousness determinations? Indeed, could one argue that the evidence that sports recur naturally, with no help from humans, indicates that there was no "invention" on Yoder's part?

What does the "distinctiveness" requirement, set forth in § 161, entail?

Once a plant patent is granted, what conduct will infringe it? Assume that A identifies and preserves a new rose sport and patents it. Shortly thereafter, the patented sport recurs naturally, B discovers it and asexually reproduces it. Will B be liable to A for plant patent infringement? In Imazio

Nursery, Inc. v. Dania Greenhouses, 69 F.3d 1560 (Fed.Cir.1995), *cert. denied*, 518 U.S. 1018, 116 S.Ct. 2549, 135 L.Ed.2d 1069 (1996), the Court of Appeals for the Federal Circuit clarified the scope of plant patents, confirming the view expressed by the Fifth Circuit in *Yoder* that the patent extends only to plants that were derived through asexual reproduction from the original patented plant. Thus, to recover for plant patent infringement, the patentee must prove that the alleged infringing plant is an asexual reproduction, derived directly or indirectly from the original patented plant. Asexually reproducing a plant that has the same essential characteristics, but that is not derived from the patented plant, does not constitute infringement. In this regard, plant patents are narrower than utility and design patents, which extend rights against independently created inventions and designs.

What problems might an applicant for a plant patent have in satisfying the enabling disclosure provisions of § 112? The perceived disclosure problems had been an important obstacle to patenting plants prior to passage of the Plant Patent Act. Congress directly addressed the issue in § 162: "[N]o plant patent shall be declared invalid for noncompliance with section 112 of this title if the description is as complete as is reasonably possible." The disclosure and claiming for plant patents is done primarily through color photographs or drawings. See 37 C.F.R. § 1.165.

Section 162 does not, however, directly address a related problem: What sort of "printed publication" will trigger the one-year statutory bar of § 102(b)? The Court of Customs and Patent Appeals addressed the "printed publication" question in *Application of* LeGrice, 301 F.2d 929 (C.C.P.A.1962). In *LeGrice*, the patent applicant's roses had been depicted and described in English publications more than a year before he filed his United States patent application. The publications included color photographs and descriptions such as the following:

> Glowing dark scarlet with dusky velvety sheen. Single blooms carried in large trusses. Size when open 3–in. in diameter. Very fragrant. Vigorous. Foliage dark green and abundant. Bedding. Trail Ground Certificate, 1945. Prune 34.

Id., 301 F.2d at 931. The *LeGrice* court held that the provisions of § 102(b) were fully applicable, and that they should be interpreted in the same manner for plant patents as for utility patents. Utility patent opinions specified that the printed publication must be sufficiently full, clear and exact to enable a person skilled in the relevant art to make or practice the invention. The English publications did not enable anyone to "make" the applicant's rose. The applicant's roses were the result of cross-pollenization, but even identification of the parent plants would not be sufficiently enabling, since "the principles of heredity and plant genetics introduce such variables that no two seeds from the parent cross can be expected to produce identical plants." *Id.*, 301 F.2d at 938. Thus, the statutory bar had not been triggered.

Forty-two years later, in *In re* Elsner, 381 F.3d 1125 (Fed. Cir. 2004), the Court of Appeals for the Federal Circuit found that a description such as that in *LeGrice*, coupled with foreign sales of the described plant, could be sufficient to trigger the § 102(b) statutory bar. In that case, Elsner, a German plant breeder, had applied for a European Community Plant Variety Rights

Certificate for a new type of geranium. The application was published. Elsner later withdrew the application, but sold the geranium in Europe. Likewise, Zary filed a Plant Breeder's Rights application in South Africa claiming a variety of new rose plant. That application was subsequently published, and the rose was sold in South Africa and Zambia. More than a year after these events took place, both breeders filed applications for U.S. plant patents. In finding a potential § 102(b) bar, the Federal Circuit reasoned:

> Prior art under § 102(b) must sufficiently describe a claimed invention to have placed the public in possession of that invention. The proper test of a publication as a § 102(b) bar is "whether one skilled in the art to which the invention pertains could take the description of the invention in the printed publication and combine it with his own knowledge of the particular art and from this combination be put in possession of the invention on which a patent is sought." *LeGrice,* 301 F.2d at 939. In particular, one must be able to make the claimed invention without undue experimentation.

> It is undisputed that the PBR applications were published more than one year prior to the effective filing dates of Appellants' respective applications and that the applications fully disclose the claimed plants. It is also clear that the foreign sales of the Pendec geranium and the JACopper rose are not themselves § 102(b) prior art against the applications; that is, those foreign sales themselves do not constitute an on-sale bar. Ordinarily, foreign sales of an invention in combination with a publication will not constitute a bar because such a result would circumvent the established rules that neither non-enabling publications nor foreign sales can bar one's right to a patent. What sets this case apart is that it deals with plant patents, which may be granted to "[w]hoever invents or discovers and asexually reproduces any distinct and new variety of plant. . . ." 35 U.S.C. § 161. The grant accompanying a plant patent includes "the right to exclude others from asexually reproducing the plant, and from using, offering for sale, or selling the plant so reproduced, or any of its parts. . . ." *Id.* § 163. * * *

> * * * In the case of plant patents, the touchstone of the statutory subject matter is asexual reproduction of a unique biological organism. When a publication identifies the plant that is invented or discovered and a foreign sale occurs that puts one of ordinary skill in the art in possession of the plant itself, which, based on the level of ordinary skill in the art, permits asexual reproduction without undue experimentation, that combination of facts and events so directly conveys the essential knowledge of the invention that the sale combines with the publication to erect a statutory bar. In any event, the inventor is in control of the activities relating to his invention, and avoidance of a bar is accomplished by making a timely filing at the PTO.

> Appellants' PBR applications disclosed the claimed plant varieties, but concededly do not, by themselves, enable the skilled artisan to practice the claimed inventions or reproduce the plants. However, because the public may have had access to the claimed inventions through the foreign sales of the plants, from which the claimed plants may be

reproduced, it may fairly be said that the PBR applications are adequately enabled. Because the published applications, combined with the foreign sales of the plants, placed the claimed inventions in the possession of the public, we therefore hold that they are proper § 102(b) anticipatory references that may bar patentability.

In re Elsner, 381 F.3d at 1128–30. While the Federal Circuit agreed that the prior publications, coupled with foreign sales *could* trigger the § 102(b) statutory bar, it remanded because the Board had not specifically determined whether a skilled artisan would have known of the foreign sales. The court noted that "[t]he foreign sale must not be an obscure, solitary occurrence that would go unnoticed by those skilled in the art. Its availability must have been known in the art, just as a printed publication must be publicly available." *Id., at 1131*. Moreover, "even if the interested public would readily know of the foreign sales," the Board must determine whether those sales enabled one of ordinary skill in the art to reproduce the claimed plants without undue experimentation. *Id.*

2. *The Plant Variety Protection Act.* Congress excluded sexually reproduced plants (plants reproduced from seeds, rather than through cloning) from the Plant Patent Act because in 1930, it was not clear that new varieties could be reproduced true-to-type through seeds. By 1970, however, it was generally recognized that true-to-type reproduction was in fact possible. This led Congress to enact the Plant Variety Protection Act ("PVPA") to extend patent-like protection to new sexually reproduced varieties of plants. The PVPA, which is codified at 7 U.S.C.A. §§ 2321–2582, protects new varieties through certificates of plant variety protection, issued by the Department of Agriculture.

As subsequently amended, the PVPA extends protection to sexually reproduced and tuberpropagated plant varieties other than fungi and bacteria. 7 U.S.C.A. § 2402. To qualify, the new variety must be new, distinct, uniform, and stable. *Id.* The latter two conditions underscore the need to ensure that the variety reproduces itself true-to-type. Congress declined to include a non-obviousness requirement. There are, however, statutory bar provisions reminiscent of Patent Act § 102(b). 7 U.S.C.A. § 2402.

A certificate of plant variety protection enables the owner to exclude others from selling the variety, offering the variety for sale, reproducing it, importing it, exporting it, or using it in producing (as opposed to developing) a hybrid or different variety. *Id.*, § 2483. The term of protection, previously 18 years, is now 20 years (and in the case of trees and vines, 25 years) from the date of issuance. (The new term measure applies to certificates granted on applications filed after April 4, 1995.). There are opportunities for protection prior to issuance of the certificate, as well. *Id.*, §§ 2541, 2567.

There are some exceptions to liability. Most notably, a "research exemption" permits "use and reproduction of a protected variety for plant breeding or other bona fide research." *Id.*, § 2544. Farmers may save seed descended from seed originally acquired under the certificate owner's authority, and use it to produce new crops. Amendments in 1994 deleted a controversial "farmers exemption," which permitted farmers to sell saved seed in some circumstances for reproductive purposes. This exception will continue to apply, however, in the case of certificates in existence or granted on applications pending on April 4, 1995, the amendments' effective date.

3. *Utility patents for plants.* After the Supreme Court determined, in *Diamond v. Chakrabarty,* that living matter is within the scope of utility patents, it appeared that new plant matter might qualify for utility patent protection even if it also qualified for a plant patent or a certificate of plant variety protection. The PTO's Board of Patent Appeals and Interferences confirmed this in *Ex parte* Hibberd, 227 U.S.P.Q. 443 (PTO Bd. Pat. App. 1985), when it found that plants, plant seeds, and plant tissue cultures constituted patentable subject matter under Patent Act § 101. As of 2001, the PTO had issued 1,800 utility patents for plants. J.E.M. Ag Supply, Inc. v. Pioneer Hi–Bred International, Inc., 534 U.S. 124, 145, 122 S.Ct. 593, 151 L.Ed.2d 508 (2001). In *Pioneer Hi–Bred,* the Supreme Court considered and rejected arguments that the Plant Patent Act of 1930 and the Plant Variety Protection Act set forth the exclusive statutory means for protecting plant life. The Court looked to its decision in *Chakrabarty,* again stressing the broad scope of § 101, and found nothing in the statutory language, the legislative history, or rules of statutory construction to convince it that the narrower plant protection statutes should preclude granting utility patents for plants. The Court found ample precedent for dual or overlapping forms of intellectual property protection. Why might a producer of new plant matter prefer to seek a utility patent, rather than a plant patent or certificate of plant variety protection? See *Pioneer Hi–Bred* at 142–145.

4. *International protection for new varieties of plants.* The TRIPs Agreement permits World Trade Organization members to exclude plants and "essentially biological processes for the production of plants" from patentability. However, members must "provide for the protection of plant varieties either by patents or by an effective *sui generis* system or by any combination thereof." TRIPs art. 27(3). Pursuant to the national treatment principle, each WTO member must afford to the nationals of other members "treatment no less favorable than it accords its own nationals." TRIPs art. 3.

The United States is also a member of the International Convention for the Protection of New Varieties of Plants.[43] The Convention, which is administered by the Union for the Protection of New Varieties of Plants ("UPOV"), in Geneva, provides for national treatment and a filing right of priority, as well as a number of substantive common rules. Among other things, it specifies genera and species that must be protected, standards for protectibility, a minimum term of protection, and minimum rights that must be offered. It provides, however, that member nations may design their protection either in the form of a special title, such as a plant variety protection certificate, or a patent.

PROBLEMS

1. Francine observes a plant that is the subject of a plant patent growing in a neighbor's garden. She takes seeds from the plant and plants

---

43. International Convention for the Protection of New Varieties of Plants, Dec. 2, 1961, *last revised,* 1991, 33 U.S.T. 2703, T.I.A.S. No. 10,199.

them in her own garden, without the permission of the plant patentee. Is the resulting plant an infringement of the plant patent?

2. Plant Co. asexually reproduces X's patented plant in Mexico, grows the cuttings to maturity, harvests the fruit of the plant, and ships it to the United States to sell in competition with X and X's licensees. Is Plant Co. liable under U.S. patent law for infringing X's plant patent?

III. DESIGN PATENTS

A. THE LAW OF DESIGN PATENTS

Congress created design patents in 1842. The present design provisions can be found at 35 U.S.C. §§ 171–173. Section 171 authorizes patents for "any new, original and ornamental design for an article of manufacture," and specifies that the provisions relating "to patents for inventions shall apply to patents for designs, except as otherwise provided." 35 U.S.C.A. § 171. Pursuant to this directive, courts have imposed the "novelty" and "nonobviousness" standards developed in connection with utility patents to judge the patentability of designs. "Ornamentality" replaces "usefulness" as the third standard of design patentability.

According to the Supreme Court:

The acts of Congress which authorize the grant of patents for designs were plainly intended to give encouragement to the decorative arts. They contemplate not so much utility as appearance * * *. [T]he thing invented or produced, for which a patent is given, is that which gives a peculiar or distinctive appearance to the manufacture, or article to which it may be applied, or to which it gives form. The law manifestly contemplates that giving certain new and original appearances to a manufactured article may enhance its salable value, may enlarge the demand for it, and may be a meritorious service to the public. It therefore proposes to secure for a limited time to the ingenious producer of those appearances the advantages flowing from them.

Gorham v. White, 81 U.S. 511 (14 Wall.), 524–25, 20 L.Ed. 731, 736 (1871).

EGYPTIAN GODDESS, INC. v. SWISA, INC.

United States Court of Appeals for the Federal Circuit, 2008.
543 F.3d 665 (en banc).

BRYSON, CIRCUIT JUDGE.

We granted rehearing en banc in this design patent case to address the appropriate legal standard to be used in assessing claims of design patent infringement.

Appellant Egyptian Goddess, Inc., ("EGI") brought this action in the United States District Court for the Northern District of Texas, alleging that Swisa, Inc., and Dror Swisa (collectively, "Swisa") had infringed EGI's U.S. Design Patent No. 467,389 ("the '389 patent"). The patent claimed a design for a nail buffer, consisting of a rectangular, hollow tube having a generally square cross-section and featuring buffer surfaces on three of its four sides. Swisa's accused product consists of a rectangular, hollow tube having a square cross-section, but featuring buffer surfaces on all four of its sides.

The district court first issued an order construing the claim of the '389 patent. In so doing, the district court sought to describe in words the design set forth in Figure 1 of the patent, which is depicted below:

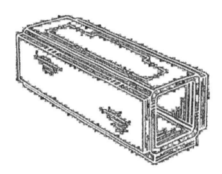

Upon study of the claimed design, the court described it as follows:

> A hollow tubular frame of generally square cross section, where the square has sides of length S, the frame has a length of approximately 3S, and the frame has a thickness of approximately T = 0.1S; the corners of the cross section are rounded, with the outer corner of the cross section rounded on a 90 degree radius of approximately 1.25T, and the inner corner of the cross section rounded on a 90 degree radius of approximately 0.25T; and with rectangular abrasive pads of thickness T affixed to three of the sides of the frame, covering the flat portion of the sides while leaving the curved radius uncovered, with the fourth side of the frame bare.

In the same order, the district court ruled that "Swisa has not shown that the appearance of the Buffer Patent is dictated by its utilitarian purpose." The court therefore held that the patent is not invalid on the ground that the design was governed solely by function.

Swisa then moved for summary judgment of noninfringement. The district court granted the motion. Citing precedent of this court, the district court stated that the plaintiff in a design patent case must prove both (1) that the accused device is "substantially similar" to the claimed design under what is referred to as the "ordinary observer" test, and (2) that the accused device contains "substantially the same points of novelty that distinguished the patented design from the prior art." After comparing the claimed design and the accused product, the court held that Swisa's allegedly infringing product did not incorporate the "point of novelty" of the '389 patent, which the court identified as "a fourth, bare side to the buffer."

The district court noted that the parties disagreed as to the points of novelty in the '389 patent. EGI identified four elements in its design, and for each element it identified prior art that did not embody that element. EGI therefore contended that the point of novelty of the '389 patent is the combination of those four elements. The district court, however, declined to address the question whether the point of novelty could be found in the combination of elements not present in various prior art references, because the court found that a single prior art reference, United States Design Patent No. 416,648 ("the Nailco patent"), contained all but one of the elements of the '389 design. The court described the Nailco Patent as disclosing "a nail buffer with an open and hollow body, raised rectangular pads, and open corners." The only element of the '389 patent design that was not present in the Nailco patent, according to the district court, was "the addition of the fourth side without a pad, thereby transforming the equilateral triangular cross-section into a square." Because the Swisa product does not incorporate the point of novelty of the '389 patent—a fourth side without a pad—the court concluded that there was no infringement.

EGI appealed, and a panel of this court affirmed. The panel agreed with the district court that there was no issue of material fact as to whether the accused Swisa buffer "appropriates the point of novelty of the claimed design." In reaching that conclusion, the panel stated that the point of novelty in a patented design "can be either a single novel design element or a combination of elements that are individually known in the prior art." The panel added, however, that in order for a combination of individually known design elements to constitute a point of novelty, "the combination must be a nontrivial advance over the prior art."

The panel noted that EGI's asserted point of novelty was a combination of four of the claimed design's elements: (1) an open and hollow body, (2) a square cross-section, (3) raised rectangular buffer pads, and (4) exposed corners. The panel agreed with the district court's observation that the Nailco prior art patent contained each of those elements except that the body was triangular, rather than square, in cross-section. In light of the prior art, the panel determined that "no reasonable juror could conclude that EGI's asserted point of novelty constituted a non-trivial advance over the prior art."

The panel further observed that the various design elements of the claimed design "were each individually disclosed in the prior art." The Swisa buffers, the panel noted, have raised, abrasive pads on all four sides, not just on three of the four sides, as in the claimed design, in which the fourth side is bare. The panel then concluded that "[w]hen considering the prior art in the nail buffer field, this difference between the accused design and the patented design cannot be considered minor." The panel therefore concluded that summary judgment was appropriate.

The dissenting judge would not have adopted the "non-trivial advance" test as a way of ascertaining whether a particular feature of the claimed design constituted a point of novelty for infringement purposes. In the view of the dissenting judge, the "nontrivial advance" test was inconsistent with and unsupported by prior precedent; it conflated the criteria for infringement and obviousness; it applied only to designs that involved combinations of design elements; and it improperly focused on the obviousness of each point of novelty, rather than the obviousness of the overall design.

This court granted rehearing en banc and asked the parties to address several questions, including whether the "point of novelty" test should continue to be used as a test for infringement of a design patent; whether the court should adopt the "non-trivial advance test" as a means of determining whether a particular design feature qualifies as a point of novelty; how the point of novelty test should be administered, particularly when numerous features of the design differ from certain prior art designs; and whether district courts should perform formal claim construction in design patent cases.

I

The starting point for any discussion of the law of design patents is the Supreme Court's decision in *Gorham Co. v. White,* 14 Wall. 511, 81 U.S. 511 (1871). That case involved a design patent for the handles of tablespoons and forks. In its analysis of claim infringement, the Court stated that the test of identity of design "must be sameness of appearance, and mere difference of lines in the drawing or sketch . . . or slight variances in configuration . . . will not destroy the substantial identity." Identity of appearance, the Court explained, or "sameness of effect upon the eye, is the main test of substantial identity of design"; the two need not be the same "to the eye of an expert," because if that were the test, "[t]here never could be piracy of a patented design, for human ingenuity has never yet produced a design, in all its details, exactly like another, so like, that an expert could not distinguish them."

The *Gorham* Court then set forth the test that has been cited in many subsequent cases: "[I]f, in the eye of an ordinary observer, giving such attention as a purchaser usually gives, two designs are substantially the same, if the resemblance is such as to deceive such an observer, inducing him to purchase one supposing it to be the other, the first one patented is infringed by the other." In the case before it, the Court concluded that "whatever differences there may be between the plaintiffs' design and those of the defendant in details of ornament, they are still the same in general appearance and effect, so much alike that in the market and with purchasers they would pass for the same thing—so much alike that even persons in the trade would be in danger of being deceived."

Since the decision in *Gorham,* the test articulated by the Court in that case has been referred to as the "ordinary observer" test and has been recognized by lower courts, including both of this court's predecessors, as the proper standard for determining design patent infringement. However, in a series of cases tracing their origins to *Litton Systems, Inc. v. Whirlpool Corp.,* 728 F.2d 1423 (Fed.Cir.1984), this court has held that proof of similarity under the ordinary observer test is not enough to establish design patent infringement. Rather, the court has stated that the accused design must also appropriate the novelty of the claimed design in order to be deemed infringing. The court in *Litton Systems* wrote as follows:

> For a design patent to be infringed . . . no matter how similar two items look, "the accused device must appropriate the novelty in the patented device which distinguishes it from the prior art." That is, even though the court compares two items through the eyes of the ordinary observer, it must nevertheless, to find infringement, attribute their similarity to the novelty which distinguishes the patented device from the prior art.

Litton Systems, 728 F.2d at 1444. After identifying the combination of features in the design that it considered novel, the court in *Litton Systems* held that the accused design had none of those features and therefore did not infringe.

In a number of cases decided after *Litton Systems,* this court has interpreted the language quoted above to require that the test for design patent infringement consider both the perspective of the ordinary observer and the particular novelty in the claimed design. * * *

The extent to which the point of novelty test has been a separate test has not always been clear in this court's case law. In cases decided shortly after *Litton*, the court described the ordinary observer test and the point of novelty test as "conjunctive." *See L.A. Gear, Inc. v. Thom McAn Shoe Co.,* 988 F.2d 1117, 1125 (Fed.Cir.1993). It has not been until much more recently that this court has described the ordinary observer and point of novelty tests as "two distinct tests" and has stated that "[t]he merger of the point of novelty test and the ordinary observer test is legal error." *Unidynamics Corp. v. Automatic Prods. Int'l, Inc.,* 157 F.3d 1311, 1323–24 (Fed. Cir. 1998).

Regardless of the differences in the way it has been characterized, the point of novelty test has proved reasonably easy to apply in simple cases in which the claimed design is based on a single prior art reference and departs from that reference in a single respect. In such cases, it is a simple matter to identify the point of novelty and to determine whether the accused design has appropriated the point of novelty, as opposed to copying those aspects of the claimed design that were already in the prior art. However, the point of novelty test has proved more difficult to apply where the claimed design has numerous features that can be considered points of novelty, or where multiple prior art references are in issue and the claimed design consists of a combination of features, each of which could be found in one or more of the prior art designs. In particular, applying the point of novelty test where multiple features and multiple prior art references are in play has led to disagreement over whether combinations of features, or the overall appearance of a design, can constitute the point of novelty of the claimed design. In light of the questions surrounding the status and application of the point of novelty test, we use this case as a vehicle for reconsidering the place of the point of novelty test in design patent law generally.

II

EGI argues that this court should no longer recognize the point of novelty test as a second part of the test for design patent infringement, distinct from the ordinary observer test established in *Gorham.* Instead of requiring the fact-finder to identify one or more points of novelty in the patented design and then determining whether the accused design has appropriated some or all of those points of novelty, EGI contends that the ordinary observer test can fulfill the purposes for which the point of novelty test was designed, but with less risk of confusion. As long as the ordinary observer test focuses on the "appearance that distinguishes the patented design from the prior art," EGI contends that it will enable the fact-finder to address the proper inquiry, i.e., whether an ordinary observer, familiar with the prior art, would be deceived into thinking that the accused design was the same as the patented design. Relatedly, EGI argues that if the ordinary observer test is performed from the perspective of an ordinary observer who is familiar with the prior art, there is no need for a separate "non-trivial advance" test, because the attention of an ordinary observer familiar with prior art designs will naturally be drawn to the features of the claimed and accused designs that render them distinct from the prior art.

Several of the amici make essentially the same point, referring to the proper approach as calling for a three-way visual comparison between the patented design, the accused design, and the closest prior art. * * *

* * *

[W]e conclude that the point of novelty test, as a second and free-standing requirement for proof of design patent infringement, is inconsistent with the ordinary observer test laid down in *Gorham,* is not mandated by * * * precedent from other courts, and is not needed to protect against unduly broad assertions of design patent rights.

* * *

[The Court discusses a number of early precedents, including the Supreme Court's decision in Smith v. Whitman Saddle Co., 148 U.S. 674 (1893). It then turns to the Sixth Circuit's decision in *Applied Arts Corp. v. Grand Rapids Metalcraft Corp.,* 67 F.2d 428 (6th Cir.1933), which involved a design patent on a combination ash tray and electric lighter.] The district court found infringement by two of the defendant's designs upon finding that the resemblance between the patented design and the accused design was such as to deceive the ordinary observer. In analyzing the case, the court addressed the question whether the ordinary observer test of *Gorham* was in conflict with the principle that "similitude of appearance is to be judged by the scope of the patent in relation to the prior art."

The court explained that the ordinary observer of the *Gorham* test was not one "who has never seen an ash tray or a cigar lighter, but one who, though not an expert, has reasonable familiarity with such objects," and is capable of assessing the similarity of the patented and accused designs in light of the similar objects in the prior art. Viewing the ordinary observer test in that manner, the court stated:

> [W]hile there is some similarity between the patented and alleged infringing designs, which without consideration of the prior art might seem important, yet such similarity as is due to common external configuration is no greater, if as great, between the patented and challenged designs as between the former and the designs of the prior art.

Id. After noting the similarities between the patented design and the prior art designs, the court concluded that the differences between the two "are no greater than those that exist between the patented design and the alleged infringing designs." Accordingly, the court concluded, assuming the patent to be valid "it is quite clear it is entitled to a very limited interpretation and that so limited the defendant's designs do not infringe." The court ruled that while it was aware that similarity "is not to be determined by making too close an analysis of detail," nonetheless, "where in a crowded art the composite of differences presents a different impression to the eye of the average observer (as above defined), infringement will not be found."

That precedent was followed by the Eighth Circuit in *Sears, Roebuck & Co. v. Talge,* 140 F.2d 395 (8th Cir.1944). The district court in that case held that the defendant's home fruit juicer infringed the plaintiff's patents on fruit juicer designs. The court stated that the test for design patent infringement involves two elements: (1) "the identity of appearance, or sameness of effect as a whole upon the eye of an ordinary purchaser must be such as to deceive him, inducing him to purchase one, supposing it to be the other" and (2) "the accused device must appropriate the novelty in the patented device which distinguishes it from the prior art." To make the latter determination, the court explained, "requires a comparison of the features of the patented designs with the prior art and with the accused design." By examining the prior art fruit juicers, the court was able to identify the "novel elements embodied in the [patented] design." The court then determined that there was no identity of appearance with respect to those elements between the claimed designs and the accused products.

The *Sears, Roebuck* and *Applied Arts* cases, in turn, became the principal precedents relied upon by this court in the seminal *Litton Systems* case to which this court's precedents dealing with the point of novelty test trace their origin. In *Litton Systems,* as in *Sears, Roebuck,* the court identified the *Gorham* ordinary observer test as the starting point for design patent infringement. Quoting from *Sears, Roebuck,* the *Litton* court added, however, that "no matter how similar two items look, 'the accused device must appropriate the novelty in the patented device which distinguishes it from the prior art.'" 728 F.2d at 1444. That is, the court added, after comparing two items through the eyes of the ordinary observer, the court must, to find infringement, "attribute their similarity to the novelty which distinguishes the patented device from the prior art." The court then referred to that second test as the point of novelty approach, and that tag has been applied to the second part of the design patent infringement test ever since.

In analyzing the claim of infringement, the court in *Litton Systems* focused on what it characterized as the novelty of the patent in suit, i.e., "the combination on a microwave oven's exterior of a three-stripe door frame, a door without a handle, and a latch release lever on the control panel." Significantly, however, the court quoted from the *Applied Arts* case and stated that the degree of similarity between the accused design and the patented design had to be assessed in light of the designs in the prior art. The court noted that where, as in the case before it, "a field is crowded with many references relating to the design of the same type of appliance, we must construe the range of equivalents very narrowly." Accordingly, the court held that the scope of protection of the patent in that case was limited to "a narrow range" that did not include the accused design.

As noted, this court has cited *Litton Systems* for the proposition that the point of novelty test is separate from the ordinary observer test and requires the patentee to point out the point of novelty in the claimed design that has been appropriated by the accused design. We think, however, that *Litton* and the predecessor cases on which it relied are more properly read as applying a version of the ordinary observer test in which the ordinary observer is deemed to view the differences between the patented design and the accused product in the context of the prior art. When the differences between the claimed and accused design are viewed in light of the prior art, the attention of the hypothetical ordinary observer will be drawn to those aspects of the claimed design that differ from the prior art. And when the claimed design is close to the prior art designs, small differences between the accused design and the claimed design are likely to be important to the eye of the hypothetical ordinary observer. * * *

    * * *

Not only is this approach consistent with the precedents discussed above, but it makes sense as a matter of logic as well. Particularly in close cases, it can be difficult to answer the question whether one thing is like another without being given a frame of reference. The context in which the claimed and accused designs are compared, i.e., the background prior art, provides such a frame of reference and is therefore often useful in the process of comparison. Where the frame of reference consists of numerous similar prior art designs, those designs can highlight the distinctions between the claimed design and the accused design as viewed by the ordinary observer.

Applying the ordinary observer test with reference to prior art designs also avoids some of the problems created by the separate point of novelty test. One such problem is that the point of novelty test has proved difficult to apply in cases in which there are several different features that can be argued to be points of novelty in the claimed design. In such cases, the outcome of the case can turn on which of the several candidate points of novelty the court or fact-finder focuses on. The attention of the court may therefore be focused on whether the accused design has appropriated a single specified feature of the claimed design, rather than on the proper inquiry, i.e., whether the accused design has appropriated the claimed design as a whole.

In addition, the more novel the design, and the more points of novelty that are identified, the more opportunities there are for a defendant to argue that its design does not infringe because it does not copy all of the points of novelty, even though it may copy most of them and even though it may give the overall appearance of being identical to the claimed design. In such cases, a test that asks how an ordinary observer with knowledge of the prior art designs would view the differences between the claimed and accused designs is likely to produce results more in line with the purposes of design patent protection.

This court has characterized the purpose of the point of novelty test as being "to focus on those aspects of a design which render the design different from prior art designs." *Sun Hill Indus., Inc. v. Easter Unlimited, Inc.,* 48 F.3d 1193, 1197 (Fed. Cir. 1995). That purpose can be equally well served, however, by applying the ordinary observer test through the eyes of an observer familiar with the prior art. If the accused design has copied a particular feature of the claimed design that departs conspicuously from the prior art, the accused design is naturally more likely to be regarded as deceptively similar to the claimed design, and thus infringing. At the same time, unlike the point of novelty test, the ordinary observer test does not present the risk of assigning exaggerated importance to small differences between the claimed and accused designs relating to an insignificant feature simply because that feature can be characterized as a point of novelty.

This approach also has the advantage of avoiding the debate over the extent to which a combination of old design features can serve as a point of novelty under the point of novelty test. An ordinary observer, comparing the claimed and accused designs in light of the prior art, will attach importance to differences between the claimed design and the prior art depending on the overall effect of those differences on the design. If the claimed design consists of a combination of old features that creates an appearance deceptively similar to the accused design, even to an observer familiar with similar prior art designs, a finding of infringement would be justified. Otherwise, infringement would not be found.

One function that has been served by the point of novelty test, according to Swisa and its supporting amici, is to cabin unduly broad assertions of design patent scope by ensuring that a design that merely embodies or is substantially similar to prior art designs is not found to infringe. Again, however, we believe that the preferable way to achieve that purpose is to do so directly, by relying on the ordinary observer test, conducted in light of the prior art. Our rejection of the point of novelty test does not mean, of course, that the differences between the claimed design and prior art designs are irrelevant. To the contrary, examining the novel features of the claimed design can be an important component of the comparison of the claimed design with the accused design and the prior art. But the comparison of the designs, including the examination of any novel features, must be conducted as part of the ordinary observer test, not as part of a separate test focusing on particular points of novelty that are designated only in the course of litigation.

On the basis of the foregoing analysis, we hold that the "point of novelty" test should no longer be used in the analysis of a claim of design patent infringement. Because we reject the "point of novelty" test, we also do not adopt the "non-trivial advance" test, which is a refinement of the "point of novelty" test. Instead, in accordance with *Gorham* and subsequent decisions, we hold that the "ordinary observer" test should be the sole test for determining whether a design patent has been infringed. * * *

In some instances, the claimed design and the accused design will be sufficiently distinct that it will be clear without more that the patentee has not met its burden of proving the two designs would appear "substantially the same" to the ordinary observer, as required by *Gorham*. In other instances, when the claimed and accused designs are not plainly dissimilar, resolution of the question whether the ordinary observer would consider the two designs to be substantially the same will benefit from a comparison of the claimed and accused designs with the prior art, as in many of the cases discussed above and in the case at bar. Where there are many examples of similar prior art designs, * * * differences between the claimed and accused designs that might not be noticeable in the abstract can become significant to the hypothetical ordinary observer who is conversant with the prior art.

We emphasize that although the approach we adopt will frequently involve comparisons between the claimed design and the prior art, it is not a test for determining validity, but is designed solely as a test of infringement. Thus, as is always the case, the burden of proof as to infringement remains on the patentee. However, if the accused infringer elects to rely on the comparison prior art as part of its defense against the claim of infringement, the burden of production of that prior art is on the accused infringer. To be sure, we have stated that the burden to introduce prior art under the point of novelty test falls on the patentee. Under the ordinary observer test, however, it makes sense to impose the burden of production as to any comparison prior art on the accused infringer. The accused infringer is the party with the motivation to point out close prior art, and in particular to call to the court's attention the prior art that an ordinary observer is most likely to regard as highlighting the differences between the claimed and accused design. Regardless of whether the accused infringer elects to present prior art that it considers pertinent to the comparison between the claimed and accused design, however, the patentee bears the ultimate burden of proof to demonstrate infringement by a preponderance of the evidence. * * *

III

One of the issues raised by this court in its order granting en banc review was whether trial courts should conduct claim construction in design patent cases. While this court has held that trial courts have a duty to conduct claim construction in design patent cases, as in utility patent cases, the court has not prescribed any particular form that the claim construction must take. To the contrary, the court has recognized that design patents "typically are claimed as shown in drawings," and that claim construction "is adapted accordingly." *Arminak & Assocs., Inc. v. Saint–Gobain Calmar, Inc.*, 501 F.3d 1314, 1319 (Fed. Cir. 2007). For that reason, this court has not required that the trial court attempt to provide a detailed verbal description of the claimed design, as is typically done in the case of utility patents. * * *

* * * Given the recognized difficulties entailed in trying to describe a design in words, the preferable course ordinarily will be for a district court not to attempt to "construe" a design patent claim by providing a detailed verbal description of the claimed design.

With that said, it is important to emphasize that a district court's decision regarding the level of detail to be used in describing the claimed design is a matter within the court's discretion, and absent a showing of prejudice, the court's decision to issue a relatively detailed claim construction will not be reversible error. At the same time, it should be clear that the court is not obligated to issue a detailed verbal description of the design if it does not regard verbal elaboration as necessary or helpful. In addition, in deciding whether to attempt a verbal description of the claimed design, the court should recognize the risks entailed in such a description, such as the risk of placing undue emphasis on particular features of the design and the risk that a finder of fact will focus on each individual described feature in the verbal description rather than on the design as a whole. In this case, for example, the district court came up with a detailed verbal description of the claimed design. We see no inaccuracy in the court's description, and neither party has pointed to any prejudice resulting from the court's interpretation. Yet it is not clear that the considerable effort needed to fashion the verbal description contributed enough to the process of analyzing the case to justify the effort.

While it may be unwise to attempt a full description of the claimed design, a court may find it helpful to point out, either for a jury or in the case of a bench trial by way of describing the court's own analysis, various features of the claimed design as they relate to the accused design and the prior art. In a case such as this one, for example, there would be nothing wrong with the court pointing out to a jury that in the patented design only three sides have buffers attached, while in the accused product (and in the three-sided Nailco patent), all of the sides have buffers attached. It would similarly be permissible for the court to point out that, for example, although the Falley Buffer Block has four sides, it is not hollow, unlike the design of the '389 patent, the Nailco patent, and the accused Swisa product.

Apart from attempting to provide a verbal description of the design, a trial court can usefully guide the finder of fact by addressing a number of other issues that bear on the scope of the claim. Those include such matters as describing the role of particular conventions in design patent drafting, such as the role of broken lines, *see* 37 C.F.R. § 1.152; assessing and describing the effect of any representations that may have been made in the course of the prosecution history; and distinguishing between those features of the claimed design that are ornamental and those that are purely functional, *see OddzOn Prods., Inc. v. Just Toys, Inc.,* 122 F.3d 1396, 1405 (Fed.Cir.1997) ("Where a design contains both functional and non-functional elements, the scope of the claim must be construed in order to identify the non-functional aspects of the design as shown in the patent.").

Providing an appropriate measure of guidance to a jury without crossing the line and unduly invading the jury's fact-finding process is a task that trial courts are very much accustomed to, and any attempt by an appellate court to guide that process in detail is likely to do more harm than good. We therefore leave the question of verbal characterization of the claimed designs to the discretion of trial judges, with the proviso that as a general matter, those courts should not treat the process of claim construction as requiring a detailed verbal description of the claimed design, as would typically be true in the case of utility patents.

IV

We now turn to the facts of this case. It is agreed that the general shape of the accused nail buffer at issue in this case is the same as that of the patented buffer design. The difference between the two is that the accused buffer has raised buffing pads on all four sides, while the patented buffer has buffing pads on only three sides. The two closest prior art nail buffers before the court were the Falley nail buffer, which has a solid, rectangular cross section with slightly raised buffers on all sides, and the

Nailco patent, which shows a nail buffer design having a triangular shape and a hollow cross section, and in which raised buffing pads are located on all three sides. The four nail buffers are pictured below:

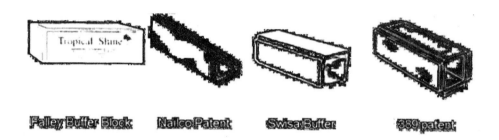

Falley Buffer Block   Nailco Patent   Swisa Buffer   389 patent

The question before this court under the standard we have set forth above is whether an ordinary observer, familiar with the prior art Falley and Nailco designs, would be deceived into believing the Swisa buffer is the same as the patented buffer. EGI argues that such an observer would notice a difference between the prior art and the '389 patent, consisting of "the hollow tube that is square in cross section and that has raised pads with exposed gaps at the corners." To support that contention, EGI invokes the declaration of its expert witness, Kathleen Eaton. After viewing the patented, accused, and Nailco buffers, Ms. Eaton concluded that the patented and accused designs would "confuse an ordinary observer into purchasing the accused buffer thinking it to be the patented buffer design." She reached that conclusion, she explained, because "the substantially similar appearance [between the accused and patented designs] results from both designs having a hollow tube, square in cross section and rectangular in length, with multiple raised rectangular pads mounted on the sides, and that do not cover the corners of the tube." While recognizing that the accused buffer has pads on all four sides and that the claimed design has buffer pads on only three sides, she stated that "I do not believe that, to an ordinary observer and purchaser of nail buffers, the presence of one more buffer pad[s] greatly alters the ornamental effect and appearance of the whole design as compared to the whole patented design."

Swisa counters that the '389 patent closely tracks the design of the Nailco nail buffer, except that it "add[s] a fourth side without an abrasive pad, resulting in square ends." In light of the close prior art buffers, including a number having square cross-sections, Swisa argues that an ordinary observer would notice the difference between the claimed and accused designs. To support that contention, Swisa cites the declaration of its expert, Steve Falley. Mr. Falley addressed the differences among the prior art designs, the accused design, and patented design, and he concluded that

> you could simply add to the Nailco Buffer a fourth side without an abrasive on it. This merely takes the Nailco Buffer to the block shape of the original Falley Buffer Block, while keeping the hollow aspect of the Nailco Buffer. As there had already been on the market for a long time 3–way buffer blocks that had no abrasive on one side, it was also obvious after the Nailco Buffer that you could have a three way hollow buffer that had four sides but with no abrasive on one side.

Mr. Falley added that "four-way" nail buffers having four different abrasive surfaces have been made since 1985, and that four-sided "buffer blocks" have been on the market since 1987. He pointed to catalogs showing three-sided and four-sided buffer blocks that have been offered for sale since at least 1994, and in light of his knowledge of the industry, he stated that the "number of sides with abrasive surface on them would be important to purchasers because it determines whether a buffer is a 'three way buffer' or a 'four way buffer.' " Accordingly, he concluded:

> The difference between a buffer with abrasive on three sides—a "three-way buffer"—and a buffer with abrasive on four sides—a "four-way buffer"—is immediately apparent to any consumer used to buying nail buffers. Even if such a consumer did not have a preference for either three-way or four-way buffers (although they almost always do), they would at a glance be able to tell that a buffer with abrasive on only three sides had abrasive on three sides, and was a three-way buffer, while a buffer with abrasive on four sides had abrasive on all four sides, and was a four-way buffer. I cannot imagine consumers would buy buffers with abrasive on four sides thinking that they were buying buffers with abrasive on three sides.

The problem with Ms. Eaton's declaration is that she characterized the accused and patented designs as similar because they both have square cross sections and "multiple" raised buffer pads, without directly acknowledging that the patented design has three pads while the accused design has four, one on each side. She also failed to address the fact that the design of the Nailco patent is identical to the accused device except that the Nailco design has three sides rather than four. Thus, she could as easily have said that the Nailco buffer design "is like the accused design because both designs have a hollow tube, have multiple rectangular sides with raised rectangular pads mounted on each side that do not cover the corners of the tube," in which case the Nailco prior art buffer would be seen to closely resemble the accused design. Nothing about Ms. Eaton's declaration explains why an ordinary observer would regard the accused design as being closer to the claimed design than to the Nailco prior art patent. In fact, Ms. Eaton's reference to the prior art buffers is limited to the single, and conclusory, comment that an ordinary observer and purchaser of nail buffers would consider the patented design and the accused buffer to be substantially similar, "particularly in light of other nail buffers, such as a solid block buffer and the hollow triangular Nailco buffer."

In light of the similarity of the prior art buffers to the accused buffer, we conclude that no reasonable fact-finder could find that EGI met its burden of showing, by a preponderance of the evidence, that an ordinary observer, taking into account the prior art, would believe the accused design to be the same as the patented design. In concluding that a reasonable fact-finder could not find infringement in this case, we reach the same conclusion that the district court reached, and for many of the same reasons. Although we do so by using the ordinary observer test as informed by the prior art, rather than by applying the point of novelty test, our analysis largely tracks that of the district court. After analyzing the Nailco patent and the claimed design, as they related to the accused design, the district court concluded that "in the context of nail buffers, a fourth side without a pad is not substantially the same as a fourth side with a pad." While the district court focused on the differences in the particular feature at issue rather than the effect of those differences on the appearance of the design as a whole, we are satisfied that the difference on which the district court focused is important, viewed in the context of the prior art.

Finally, although we do not adopt the "non-trivial advance" test employed by the panel in this case, we note that our analysis under the ordinary observer test is parallel to the panel's approach in an essential respect. The panel focused on viewing the difference between the claimed and accused designs in light of the prior art, as we do. The panel wrote: "The Swisa buffers have raised, abrasive pads on *all four* sides. When considering the prior art in the nail buffer field, this difference between the accused design and the patented design cannot be considered minor." That point captures the essence of the rationale of our decision today, even though the panel decision employed a different analytical approach. For the foregoing reasons, we sustain the district court's entry of summary judgment of no infringement, but we do so under the ordinary observer test in the form that we have adopted, and without using the point of novelty test that we have disapproved. In the language used by the Supreme Court in *Gorham,* we hold that the accused design could not reasonably be viewed as so similar to the claimed design that a purchaser familiar with the prior art would be deceived by the similarity between the claimed and accused designs, "inducing him to purchase one supposing it to be the other."

RICHARDSON v. STANLEY WORKS, INC.

United States Court of Appeals for the Federal Circuit, 2010.
597 F.3d 1288.

LOURIE, CIRCUIT JUDGE.

* * *

Richardson owns the '167 patent, a design patent that claims the design for a multi-function carpentry tool that combines a conventional hammer with a stud climbing tool and a crowbar. The tool is known as the "Stepclaw." The only claim of the '167 patent claims the ornamental design of the tool as depicted in figures 1 and 2 of the patent:

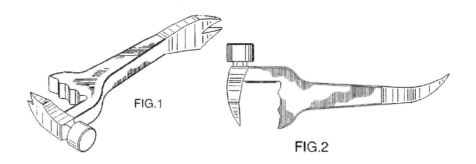

Stanley manufactures and sells construction tools. In 2005, Stanley introduced into the U.S. market a product line of tools by the series name "Fubar." The Fubar is sold in five different versions and is useful in carpentry, demolition, and construction work. Stanley successfully applied for and obtained U.S. Patent D562,101 ("the '101 patent") on the basic Fubar design. All five versions of the tool are built around that same basic Fubar design. Figures 1 and 5 of the '101 patent are illustrative of the Fubar design:

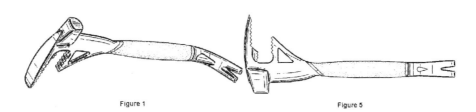

On June 3, 2008, Richardson filed a complaint against Stanley in the district court for the District of Arizona alleging that the Fubar tools infringed his '167 patent. * * * [T]he court conducted a bench trial on Richardson's patent infringement claim and entered judgment of noninfringement in favor of Stanley. In its order, the court first distinguished, as part of its claim construction, the ornamental aspects from the functional aspects of Richardson's design and then determined that an ordinary observer, after discounting the functional elements of Richardson's design, would not be deceived into thinking that any of the Fubar tools were the same as Richardson's Stepclaw. The court therefore concluded that the overall visual effect of the Fubar was not substantially similar to that of the Stepclaw, and that the '167 patent had not been infringed. * * *

DISCUSSION

A. *Claim Construction*

Richardson argues that the district court's approach to evaluating infringement of a design patent was incorrect. Richardson primarily argues that the district court erred in its claim construction by separating the functional aspects of the design from the ornamental ones, rather than considering the design as a whole. Richardson argues that our *Egyptian Goddess* decision requires that the patented design be compared in its entirety with the accused design, and that the comparison be made from the perspective of an ordinary observer. A claim construction such as the one performed by the district court, Richardson argues, is necessary only for designs that contain "purely functional" elements. According to Richardson, a design element is purely functional only when the function encompassed by that element cannot be performed by any other design. Richardson contends that the overall design of the '167 patent is not dictated by the useful elements found in the tool, and that the functional parts of its design remain relevant to the scope of the patented claim.

* * * We disagree with Richardson that the district court erred in its claim construction by separating the functional and ornamental aspects of the '167 patent design. In *OddzOn*, we affirmed a district court's claim construction wherein the court had carefully distinguished the ornamental features of the patented design from the overall "rocket-like" appearance of the design of a football-shaped foam ball with a tail and fin structure. *OddzOn Prods., Inc. v. Just Toys, Inc.,* 122 F.3d 1396, 1405 (Fed.Cir. 1997). We held that "[w]here a design contains both functional and non-functional elements, the scope of the claim must be construed in order to identify the non-functional aspects of the design as shown in the patent."

The issue before us is not very different from that in *OddzOn,* and we are not persuaded by Richardson's argument that our holding in *Egyptian Goddess* mandates a different result here. In *Egyptian Goddess,* we abandoned the point of novelty test for design patent infringement and held that the ordinary observer test should serve as the sole test for infringement. Although we proposed that the preferable course ordinarily will be for a district court not to attempt to construe a design patent claim, we also emphasized that there are a number of claim scope issues on which a court's guidance would be useful to the fact finder. Among them, we specifically noted, is the distinction between the functional and ornamental aspects of a design.

The district court here properly factored out the functional aspects of Richardson's design as part of its claim construction. By definition, the patented design is for a multi-function tool that has several functional components, and we have made clear that a design patent, unlike a utility patent, limits protection to the ornamental design of the article. If the patented design is primarily functional rather than ornamental, the patent is invalid. However, when the design also contains ornamental aspects, it is entitled to a design patent whose scope is limited to those aspects alone and does not extend to any functional elements of the claimed article. * * *

Richardson's multi-function tool comprises several elements that are driven purely by utility. As the district court noted, elements such as the handle, the hammerhead, the jaw, and the crowbar are dictated by their functional purpose. The jaw, for example, has to be located on the opposite end of the hammer head such that the tool can be used as a step. The crowbar, by definition, needs to be on the end of the longer handle such that it can reach into narrow spaces. The handle has to be the longest arm of the tool to allow for maximum leverage. The hammer-head has to be flat on its end to effectively deliver force to the object being struck. As demonstrated by the prior art, those are purely functional elements whose utility has been known and used in the art for well over a century.

Richardson's argument that the court erred in separating out functional aspects of his design essentially is an argument for a claim scope that includes the utilitarian elements of his multi-function tool. We agree with the district court that it would indeed be improper to allow Richardson to do so. * * * A claim to a design containing numerous functional elements, such as here, necessarily mandates a narrow construction. * * *

> * * *

B. *Infringement*

> * * *

We agree with the court's finding of noninfringement. * * * The patentee must establish that an ordinary observer, familiar with the prior art designs, would be deceived into believing that the accused product is the same as the patented design. In our recent *Crocs* decision, we set out in detail how an ordinary observer analysis could be conducted to determine infringement. *See Crocs, Inc. v. International Trade Comm'n,* 598 F.3d 1294, 1303–06 (Fed. Cir. 2010). In analyzing whether a design patent on footwear was infringed, noting the various differences that could be found between the two pieces of footwear in question, we compared their overall effect on the designs. We looked to ornamental elements such as the curves in the design, the strap assembly, and the base portion of the footwear. We concluded that both the claimed design and the accused designs contained those overall ornamental effects, thereby allowing for market confusion.

The ordinary observer test similarly applies in cases where the patented design incorporates numerous functional elements. *See Amini Innovation Corp. v. Anthony Cal., Inc.,* 439 F.3d 1365, 1372 (Fed.Cir.2006) (holding that while it is proper to factor out the functional aspects of various design elements, that discounting of functional elements must not convert the overall infringement test to an element-by-element comparison). In evaluating infringement, we determine whether "the deception that arises is a result of the similarities in the overall design, not of similarities in ornamental features in isolation."

We do not agree with Richardson that the district court failed to apply the ordinary observer test in finding no infringement. The court specifically concluded that "[f]rom the perspective of an ordinary observer familiar with the prior art, the overall visual effect of the Fubar is significantly different from the Stepclaw." It recited the significant differences between the ornamental features of the two designs but, in determining infringement, it mainly focused on whether an ordinary observer would be deceived into thinking that any of the Fubar designs were the same as Richardson's patented design. We therefore find no error in the district court's approach. *See Egyptian Goddess,* 543 F.3d at 681 ("An ordinary observer, comparing the claimed and accused designs in light of the prior art, will attach importance to differences between the claimed design and the prior art depending on the overall effect of those differences on the design.") * * * .

We also agree that, ignoring the functional elements of the tools, the two designs are indeed different. Each of the Fubar tools has a streamlined visual theme that runs throughout the design including elements such as a tapered hammer-head, a streamlined crow-bar, a triangular neck with rounded surfaces, and a smoothly contoured handled. In a side-by-side comparison with the '167 patent design, the overall effect of this streamlined theme makes the Fubar tools significantly different from Richardson's design. Overall, the accused products clearly have a more rounded appearance and fewer blunt edges than the patented design. The court therefore was not clearly erroneous in concluding that the accused products embody an overall effect that cannot be found in the '167 patent design and hence cannot cause market confusion. * * *

    * * *

NOTES AND QUESTIONS

1. *Design patents.* A design patent is not concerned with how an article of manufacture was made or how it works. It is only concerned with how it

looks. The protected design may consist of surface ornamentation, the article's configuration, or a combination of both. Given the purpose of design patents, however, only those design aspects open to human view are eligible for protection. The Court of Appeals for the Federal Circuit has held that an article's design is eligible for protection if, at some point in the life of the article, its appearance is a matter of concern. Thus, for example, if the appearance of an article of manufacture, such as a vitamin tablet or a casket, is designed to attract purchasers, it is patentable even though the appearance will be hidden when the article is put to its intended use. *In re* Webb, 916 F.2d 1553, 1558 (Fed.Cir.1990).

What qualifies as an "article of manufacture" for purposes of the design patent provisions? The term has been defined very broadly: "anything made 'by the hands of man' from raw materials, whether literally by hand or by machinery or by art." *In re* Hruby, 373 F.2d 997, 1000–01 (C.C.P.A.1967) (holding that the pattern of water generated by a water fountain was an eligible article of manufacture).

Do the novelty and non-obviousness standards of patentability, developed in connection with utility patents, seem an appropriate vehicle for judging the protectibility of an ornamental design? The fit is not always clear. For example, design patents are subject to § 102(b), which bars patents on applications filed more than a year after public use or sale of the "invention." But is there a conceivable design patent corollary to the "experimental use" exception to the § 102(b) statutory bar? Compare *In re* Mann, 861 F.2d 1581, 1582 (Fed.Cir.1988) ("[w]e see no way in which an ornamental design for an article of manufacture can be subject to the 'experimental use' exception applicable in the case of functioning machines, manufactures, or processes. Obtaining the reactions of people to a design—whether or not they like it—is not 'experimentation' in that sense.") with Tone Brothers, Inc. v. Sysco Corp., 28 F.3d 1192, 1200 (Fed.Cir.1994), *cert. denied*, 514 U.S. 1015, 115 S.Ct. 1356, 131 L.Ed.2d 214 (1995) ("experimentation directed to functional features of a product also containing an ornamental design may negate what otherwise would be considered a public use within the meaning of section 102(b)"); Continental Plastic Containers, Inc. v. Owens Brockway Plastic Products, Inc., 141 F.3d 1073 (Fed.Cir.1998)(refusing to extend the reasoning in *Tone* (which involved an alleged "public use") to a "sale").

2. *The "ornamentality" requirement.* To qualify for a design patent, the design of an article of manufacture must be primarily ornamental, rather than functional. As the Court of Appeals for the Federal Circuit has explained, "[w]hen function dictates a design, protection would not promote the decorative arts, a purpose of the design patent statute." Avia Group International, Inc. v. L.A. Gear California, Inc., 853 F.2d 1557, 1563 (Fed.Cir.1988). Moreover, protection of functional designs would undermine utility patents. See Lee v. Dayton–Hudson Corp., Matrix International, Inc., 838 F.2d 1186, 1188 (Fed.Cir.1988). In *Lee*, the patented article was a massage device consisting of an elongated handle with two opposing balls at one end, as shown below.

Appellant Lee's patented design for a massage device is shown as follows:

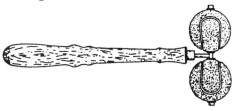

Following is an illustration of one of the accused devices:

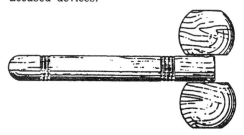

The patentee argued that the scope of the design patent extended to the configuration of the device, and thus that any massage device with that general configuration infringed the patent. The court rejected the argument, limiting the scope of the patent to the surface ornamentation of the device on the ground that the configuration was dictated primarily by functional considerations. The court observed that "by obtaining a design patent, not a utility patent, Mr. Lee limited his patent protection to the ornamental design of the article. * * * Design patents do not and cannot include claims to the structural or functional aspects of the article * * *." *Id.*

The *Avia* case, *supra*, involved two design patents—one claiming an ornamental design for an athletic shoe outer sole (the '420 patent), and the other claiming an ornamental design for the upper part of an athletic shoe (the '301 patent). In finding the designs ornamental and the patents valid, the Court of Appeals for the Federal Circuit explained:

> There is no dispute that shoes are functional and that certain features of the shoe designs in issue perform functions. However, a distinction exists between the functionality of an article or features thereof and the functionality of the particular design of such article or features thereof that perform a function. Were that not true, it would not be possible to obtain a design patent on a utilitarian article of manufacture. * * *

Id., 853 F.2d at 1563. With regard to the ornamentality of the athletic shoe upper, covered by the '301 patent, the defendant had argued that many aspects or features of the upper performed a function. The court found this essentially irrelevant. The court of appeals quoted with approval the district court's findings on this issue:

"If the functional aspect or purpose could be accomplished in many other ways [than are] involved in this very design, that fact is enough to destroy the claim that this design is primarily functional. There are many things in the ['301] patent on the upper which are clearly ornamental and nonfunctional such as the location of perforations and how they are arranged, and the stitching and how it's arranged, and the coloration of elements between black and white colors. The overall aesthetics of the various components and the way they are combined are quite important and are not functional. They are purely aesthetic * * *." *Pensa, Inc.* v. *L.A. Gear California*, 4 U.S.P.Q.2d 1016, 1019 (C.D.Cal.1987).

Avia, 853 F.2d at 1563. The court of appeals likewise found the soles ornamental, again quoting and approving the district court's findings:

"[E]very function which [defendant] says is achieved by one of the component aspects of the sole in this case could be and has been achieved by different components. And that is a very persuasive rationale for the holding that the design overall is not primarily functional. Moreover, there is no function which even defendant assigns to the swirl effect around the pivot point, which swirl effect is a very important aspect of the design. [T]his is a unique and pleasing design and [its patentability] is not offset or destroyed by the fact that the utility patent is utilized and incorporated in this aesthetically pleasing design. Plaintiff has given us evidence of other shoes that incorporate the utility patent and its concavity—others of its own shoes—but with a totally different design, and has thus established that the utility patent does not make the design patent invalid in this case." *Pensa, Inc.*, 4 U.S.P.Q.2d at 1019–20.

Avia, 853 F.2d at 1563.

3. *Infringement.* How would you describe the difference between the infringement standard described in *Egyptian Goddess* and the infringement standard in utility patent cases? Does it make sense that it should differ? Is the "ordinary observer" standard a test for literal infringement or a test for infringement by equivalents? What guideposts does the court provide for making the similarity analysis?

What concerns might have led the Federal Circuit to adopt the "points of novelty" standard? Does the *Egyptian Goddess* "ordinary observer in light of the prior art" standard adequately address those underlying concerns? Who is the "ordinary observer" of a design? What should that person be deemed to know?

How does functionality figure into the infringement evaluation? In light of the *Richardson* decision, how would you describe the appropriate method of accounting for functional features when making the *Gorham* analysis?

How would you describe the relationship between the standard for infringement under *Egyptian Goddess,* and the standard for design patent invalidity due to anticipation or obviousness? In the past, the Federal Circuit applied a dual test for anticipation identical to the then-applicable test for infringement—the ordinary observer and point of novelty tests. In International Seaway Trading Corp. v. Walgreens Corp., 589 F.3d 1233 (Fed. Cir. 2009), a panel of the Court of Appeals for the Federal Circuit held that

"*Egyptian Goddess* necessarily requires a change in the standard for anticipation." The court explained:

> [I]t has been well established for over a century that the same test must be used for both infringement and anticipation. This general rule derives from the Supreme Court's proclamation 120 years ago in the context of utility patents: "[t]hat which infringes, if later, would anticipate, if earlier." Peters v. Active Mfg. Co., 129 U.S. 530, 537, 9 S.Ct. 389, 32 L.Ed. 738 (1889). The same rule applies for design patents. * * *
>
> * * *
>
> In light of Supreme Court precedent and our precedent holding that the same tests must be applied to infringement and anticipation, and our holding in *Egyptian Goddess* that the ordinary observer test is the sole test for infringement, we now conclude that the ordinary observer test must logically be the sole test for anticipation as well. In doing so, we will prevent an inconsistency from developing between the infringement and anticipation analysis, and we will continue our well-established practice of maintaining identical tests for infringement and anticipation.

Id., at 1239–40. The plaintiff in *Seaway* objected that adopting the ordinary observer test for anticipation would "blur the distinction between the tests for obviousness under § 103 and for anticipation under § 102, resulting in jury confusion." The Federal Circuit rejected the argument:

> According to Seaway, the test for invalidity due to obviousness is whether the designer of ordinary skill in the art would have found the patented design, as a whole, obvious in light of the prior art. The test for invalidity due to anticipation, on the other hand, requires the jury to consider the perspective of the ordinary consumer. There is in fact no potential for confusion. For design patents, the role of one skilled in the art in the obviousness context lies only in determining whether to combine earlier references to arrive at a single piece of art for comparison with the potential design or to modify a single prior art reference. Once that piece of prior art has been constructed, obviousness, like anticipation, requires application of the ordinary observer test, not the view of one skilled in the art. And, as noted by Seaway, "[b]oth the ordinary observer test, whether applied for infringement or invalidity, and the obviousness test, applied for invalidity under section 103, focus on the *overall* designs." Under these circumstances, we see no potential for jury confusion.

Id., at 1240–41.

What is the likely impact of the *Egyptian Goddess* ruling on the overall value of design patents and on litigation of design patent infringement claims?

4. *Comparing design patents and utility patents.* Although most of the provisions concerning utility patents are applicable to design patents, there are a few important differences, in addition to those mentioned in Note 2. To begin, the term of design patents is 14 years, commencing on the date of issuance. Design patent applicants enjoy a shorter foreign filing priority period. Design patents are not published 18 months after filing, do not entail "provisional rights" and do not have the benefit of the new provisional application procedure, made available for utility and plant patents under the

Uruguay Round Agreements Act. See 35 U.S.C.A. §§ 172, 122(b)(2). On the other hand, unlike utility and plant patentees, design patentees may recover certain infringing defendants' profits, as well as actual damages, as long as there is no double recovery. 35 U.S.C.A. § 289.

Another important difference lies in the application and claims. While utility patent applications entail detailed written descriptions, the design patent application contains a single claim for the ornamental design "as shown" in the accompanying drawings. 37 C.F.R. § 1.153. Thus, in the case of designs, the drawings define the scope of the patent monopoly.[44] What impact is this difference likely to have on courts' determination of the patentability and infringement issues?

Courts have been careful to ensure that the functions of utility and design patents remain distinct. As demonstrated in the *Lee* case, *supra*, a design patent may not be granted or construed to give rights in utilitarian aspects of an article of manufacture. As the *Avia* opinion suggests, it is possible to obtain both a design patent and a utility patent to protect different aspects of the same article of manufacture.

5. *International design protection.* The TRIPs Agreement obligates WTO members to protect "independently created industrial designs that are new or original," though they may meet this obligation "through industrial design law or through copyright law." TRIPs art. 25. Members may disqualify designs from protection "if they do not significantly differ from known designs or combinations of known design features," or if the design is "dictated essentially by technical or functional considerations." *Id.* Owners of protected industrial designs must have the "right to prevent third parties not having the owner's consent from making, selling or importing articles bearing or embodying a design which is a copy, or substantially a copy, of the protected design, when such acts are undertaken for commercial purposes." TRIPs art. 26. The duration of protection must be at least 10 years. *Id.* The TRIPs national treatment provisions require that WTO members provide nationals of other WTO members protection "no less favorable" than their own nationals receive. TRIPs art. 3.

Many countries have chosen to protect industrial designs through copyright, or a *sui generis* form of design protection, rather than through patent law.

---

44. Due to the nature of the subject matter and the claim, the best mode requirement is not applicable. See Racing Strollers, Inc. v. TRI Industries, Inc., 878 F.2d 1418 (Fed.Cir.1989).

PART THREE

RIGHTS IN ORIGINAL FORMS OF EXPRESSION

■ ■ ■

CHAPTER FOUR

COPYRIGHT

■ ■ ■

I. INTRODUCTION

REPORT OF THE REGISTER OF COPYRIGHTS ON THE GENERAL REVISION OF THE U.S. COPYRIGHT LAW

3–6 (1961).

* * *

B. THE NATURE OF COPYRIGHT

1. In General

In essence, copyright is the right of an author to control the reproduction of his intellectual creation. As long as he keeps his work in his sole possession, the author's absolute control is a physical fact. When he discloses the work to others, however, he makes it possible for them to reproduce it. Copyright is a legal device to give him the right to control its reproduction after it has been disclosed.

Copyright does not preclude others from using the ideas or information revealed by the author's work. It pertains to the literary, musical, graphic, or artistic form in which the author expresses intellectual concepts. It enables him to prevent others from reproducing his individual expression without his consent. But anyone is free to create his own expression of the same concepts, or to make practical use of them, as long as he does not copy the author's form of expression.

2. Copyright as Property

Copyright is generally regarded as a form of property, but it is property of a unique kind. It is intangible and incorporeal. The thing to which the property right attaches—the author's intellectual work—is incapable of possession except as it is embodied in a tangible article such as a manuscript, book, record, or film. The tangible articles containing the work may be in the possession of many persons other than the copyright

402

owner, and they may use the work for their own enjoyment, but copyright restrains them from reproducing the work without the owner's consent.

Justice Holmes, in his famous concurring opinion in White–Smith Music Publishing Co. v. Apollo Co. (209 U.S. 1 (1908)), gave a classic definition of the special characteristics of copyright as property:

> The notion of property starts, I suppose, from confirmed possession of a tangible object and consists in the right to exclude others from interference with the more or less free doing with it as one wills. But in copyright property has reached a more abstract expression. The right to exclude is not directed to an object in possession or owned, but is now in vacuo, so to speak. It restrains the spontaneity of men where, but for it, there would be nothing of any kind to hinder their doing as they saw fit. It is a prohibition of conduct remote from the persons or tangibles of the party having the right. It may be infringed a thousand miles from the owner and without his ever becoming aware of the wrong.

3. *Copyright as a Personal Right*

a. *Generally*

Some commentators, particularly in European countries, have characterized copyright as a personal right of the author, or as a combination of personal and property rights. It is true that an author's intellectual creation has the stamp of his personality and is identified with him. But insofar as his rights can be assigned to other persons and survive after his death, they are a unique kind of personal rights.

b. *Moral rights*

On the theory of personal right, some countries have included in their copyright laws special provisions for ''moral rights'' of authors. These provisions are intended to protect the author against certain acts injurious to his personal identity or reputation. They give the author the following rights:

- To have his name appear on copies of his work;

- To prevent the attribution to him of another person's work;

- To prevent the reproduction of his work in a distorted or degrading form.

These moral rights are regarded as not assignable, but the author may sometimes agree to waive them in particular cases. In some countries the moral rights survive the author's death and may be enforced by his heirs or representatives.

In the United States the moral rights of authors have never been treated as aspects of copyright. But authors have been given much the same protection of personal rights under general principles of the common law such as those relating to implied contracts, unfair competition, misrepresentation, and defamation. * * *

4. Copyright as a Monopoly

Copyright has sometimes been said to be a monopoly. This is true in the sense that the copyright owner is given exclusive control over the market for his work. And if his control were unlimited, it could become an undue restraint on the dissemination of the work.

On the other hand, any one work will ordinarily be competing in the market with many others. And copyright, by preventing mere duplication, tends to encourage the independent creation of competitive works. The real danger of monopoly might arise when many works of the same kind are pooled and controlled together.

C. THE PURPOSES OF COPYRIGHT

1. Constitutional Basis of the Copyright Law

The copyright law of the United States must be founded on the provision of the Constitution (art. I, sec. 8) which empowers Congress—

* * * To Promote the Progress of Science and useful Arts, by securing for limited Times to Authors and Inventors the exclusive Right to their respective Writings and Discoveries.

As reflected in the Constitution, the ultimate purpose of copyright legislation is to foster the growth of learning and culture for the public welfare, and the grant of exclusive rights to authors for a limited time is a means to that end. A fuller statement of these principles was contained in the legislative report (H. Rep. No. 2222, 60th Cong., 2d Sess.) on the Copyright Act of 1909:

The enactment of copyright legislation by Congress under the terms of the Constitution is not based upon any natural right that the author has in his writings, for the Supreme Court has held that such rights as he has are purely statutory rights, but upon the ground that the welfare of the public will be served and the progress of science and useful arts will be promoted by securing to authors for limited periods the exclusive rights to their writings. The Constitution does not establish copyrights, but provides that Congress shall have the power to grant such rights if it thinks best. Not primarily for the benefit of the author, but primarily for the benefit of the public, such rights are given. Not that any particular class of citizens, however worthy, may benefit, but because the policy is believed to be for the benefit of the great body of people, in that it will stimulate writing and invention to give some bonus to authors and inventors.

In enacting the copyright law Congress must consider * * * two questions: First, how much will the legislation stimulate the producer and so benefit the public, and second, how much will the monopoly granted be detrimental to the public? The granting of such exclusive rights, under the proper terms and conditions, confers a benefit upon the public that outweighs the evils of the temporary monopoly.

2. The Rights of Authors and the Public Interest

a. In general

Although the primary purpose of the copyright law is to foster the creation and dissemination of intellectual works for the public welfare, it also has an important secondary purpose: To give authors the reward due them for their contribution to society.

These two purposes are closely related. Many authors could not devote themselves to creative work without the prospect of remuneration. By giving authors a means of securing the economic reward afforded by the market, copyright stimulates their creation and dissemination of intellectual works. Similarly, copyright protection enables publishers and other distributors to invest their resources in bringing those works to the public.

b. Limitations on authors' rights

Within reasonable limits, the interests of authors coincide with those of the public. Both will usually benefit from the widest possible dissemination of the author's works. But it is often cumbersome for would-be users to seek out the copyright owner and get his permission. There are many situations in which copyright restrictions would inhibit dissemination, with little or no benefit to the author. And the interests of authors must yield to the public welfare where they conflict.

Accordingly, the U.S. copyright law has imposed certain limitations and conditions on copyright protection:

- The rights of the copyright owner do not extend to certain uses of the work. * * *

- The term of copyright is limited, as required by the Constitution. * * *

- A notice of copyright in published works has been required. * * * The large mass of published material for which the authors do not wish copyright is thus left free of restrictions.

- The registration of copyrights and the recordation of transfers of ownership have been required. * * * The public thus is given the means of determining the status and ownership of copyright claims.

c. The author's reward

While some limitations and conditions on copyright are essential in the public interest, they should not be so burdensome and strict as to deprive authors of their just reward. Authors wishing copyright protection should be able to secure it readily and simply. And their rights should be broad enough to give them a fair share of the revenue to be derived from the market for their works.

D. SUMMARY

Copyright is a legal device to give authors the exclusive right to exploit the market for their works. It has certain features of property rights, personal rights, and monopolies, but it differs from each of these. The legal principles usually applicable to property, personal rights, or monopolies are not always appropriate for copyright.

The primary purpose of copyright is to stimulate the creation and dissemination of intellectual works, thus advancing "the progress of science and useful arts." The grant of exclusive rights to authors is a means of achieving this end, and of compensating authors for their labors and their contributions to society.

Within limits, the author's interests coincide with those of the public. Where they conflict, the public interest must prevail. The ultimate task of the copyright law is to strike a fair balance between the author's right to control the dissemination of his works and the public interest in fostering their widest dissemination.

NOTES AND QUESTIONS

1. *United States copyright legislation.* The first United States copyright statute was enacted in 1790. Heavily influenced by the English Statute of Anne, 8 Anne C.19, 1710, this first Copyright Act granted protection to maps, charts and books for a term of fourteen years that could be renewed once. Copyright Act of May 31, 1790, 1 Stat. 124. Over time, Congress extended the duration of federal copyright and brought additional subject matter under its protection, including prints (1802); musical compositions (1831); dramatic compositions (1856); photographs (1865); and works of fine art (1870). The landmark Copyright Act of 1909, which remained in effect for 68 years, extended protection to "all the writings of an author," 17 U.S.C.A. § 4 (1909 Act), though this language ultimately was construed not to encompass all the expression that Congress was constitutionally empowered to protect. The Copyright Act of 1909 provided for a term of 28 years, commencing upon publication, which could be renewed once for a total of 56 years. *Id.*, § 24.

The Report of the Register of Copyrights, excerpted above, was prepared in anticipation of the revisions ultimately enacted as the Copyright Act of 1976, which became effective on January 1, 1978, and governs today. 17 U.S.C.A. § 101 *et seq.* Years of study and negotiation went into the formulation of the 1976 Act, and it represented a significant departure from the prior law. Among other things, the 1976 Act terminated the dual system of copyright that had existed under the 1909 Act, in which state common-law copyright protected unpublished works, and federal statutory copyright became available upon publication of the work with proper notice of the author's copyright claim. The 1976 Act unified the law by extending federal copyright protection to both published and unpublished works, commencing on the date the work is first "fixed" in tangible form. The 1976 Act expressly preempted state copyright protection for all works so fixed. 17 U.S.C.A. § 301. In addition, the Act replaced the former system of renewable terms with a single term consisting, for most works, of the life of the author plus 50 years. *Id.*, § 302. (A subsequent amendment has extended the duration of the term an additional twenty years, to life of the author plus 70 years. Sonny Bono Copyright Term Extension Act of 1998, Pub. L. No. 105–298, 12 Stat. 2827.)

2. *International Copyright Agreements.* In October, 1988, after a century of hesitation and debate, the United States ratified the Berne Convention for the Protection of Literary and Artistic Works,[1] a venerable multinational copyright treaty to which approximately 100 nations already adhered. In contrast to the Paris Convention for the Protection of Industrial Property (discussed in Chapter 3, *supra*) and the Universal Copyright Convention (a multinational copyright treaty that the U.S ratified in 1952),[2] the Berne Convention imposes relatively strong substantive standards upon its members.

The Berne Convention is founded on the principle of national treatment: Generally, each member nation must provide essentially as strong copyright protection to other members' authors as it does to its domestic authors.[3] However, the Berne Convention imposes a number of minimum standards for the copyright protection each member must provide to foreign authors. Among other things, the Berne Convention prescribes a minimum term of protection, specifies subject matter that must be protected, and specifies rights that must be provided in connection with that subject matter. The Berne Convention has strong foundations in the civil law "author's right" approach to protection of works of authorship. In contrast to the highly pragmatic view of copyright set forth in the Report of the Register of Copyrights, the author's right, or natural right, approach undertakes to protect an author's inherent, natural right to reap the fruits of his own creation and to control and protect the integrity of his work as a natural extension of his personality.

In order to comply with the provisions of the Berne Convention, the United States was compelled to revise its law in several important respects. Most notably, by virtue of the natural rights influence, the Berne Convention prohibits the conditioning of copyright protection on compliance with formalities such as notice or registration. The U.S. was obliged, in its implementing legislation, to relinquish its long tradition of requiring authors to provide

---

1. The Berne Convention for the Protection of Literary and Artistic Works, Sept. 9, 1886, *as last revised* at Paris July 24, 1971, Treaty Doc. 99–27, 828 U.N.T.S. 221. The Berne Convention, like the Paris Convention for the Protection of Industrial Property, is administered by the World Intellectual Property Organization ("WIPO"), which is a special agency of the United Nations.

2. The Universal Copyright Convention, September 6, 1952, 6 U.S.T. 2731, 216 U.N.T.S. 132 ("UCC"), is administered by the United Nations Educational, Scientific and Cultural Organization (UNESCO). Newer and substantively weaker than the Berne Convention, the Universal Copyright Convention was created in part to permit the United States to join a multinational copyright treaty: At the time, the United States was unwilling to revise its copyright laws to comply with the requirements of the Berne Convention. The United States still depends upon the UCC, with its national treatment provisions and more minimal substantive standards, to govern its copyright relations with nations that have adhered to the UCC but not to the Berne Convention or to the GATT TRIPs Agreement, which incorporates most of the Berne Convention provisions.

3. For a listing of circumstances under which a foreign author is entitled to U.S. copyright protection, see § 104 of the Copyright Act of 1976. 17 U.S.C.A. § 104.

notice of copyright on all published copies of their work, and to revise its registration and renewal requirements. Berne Convention Implementation Act, Pub. L. No. 100–568, 102 Stat. 2853 (1988). Compliance with the Berne also led the United States to introduce a limited version of "moral rights," which the Register describes in the Report, into U.S. copyright law for the first time (Visual Artists Rights Act of 1990, Pub. L. No. 101–650, 104 Stat. 5128), and to expand copyright protection for architectural works (Architectural Works Copyright Protection Act, Pub. L. No. 101–650, 104 Stat. 5133).

The TRIPs Agreement, which brought intellectual property into the framework of international trade negotiations, incorporated the substantive provisions of the Berne Convention, with the exception of the Article 6*bis* moral rights provisions, and made them binding on members of the new World Trade Organization. In addition, it clarified that copyright extends to computer programs and that the original selection and arrangement of data in compilations is copyrightable subject matter. It required member nations to provide copyright owners with the right to control commercial rental of their sound recordings and computer programs and, perhaps most importantly, required members to provide copyright owners with a range of specific enforcement measures. While the United States already complied with most of the TRIPs provisions, Congress found it necessary to restore U.S. copyrights in certain foreign works, which had been forfeited due to the foreign authors' failure to comply with the strict U.S. notice and renewal provisions. Congress also had to enact rights similar to copyright ("neighboring rights") for performers in their live musical performances. Uruguay Round Agreements Act, Pub. L. No. 103–465, 108 Stat. 4809 (1994).

In 1998, Congress ratified two additional copyright-related multinational treaties: the WIPO Copyright Treaty and the WIPO Performances and Phonograms Treaty, both negotiated under the auspices of the World Intellectual Property Organization in 1996. These treaties were designed to augment the Berne Convention and certain international conventions for protecting sound recordings and performers. The new treaties incorporate the advances made in TRIPs, and specifically address rights in works of authorship, sound recordings and performances in digital environments. The new treaties require signatories (1) to provide right-holders a "right of communication to the public ... by wire or wireless means," (2) to prohibit tampering with "electronic rights management information" which right-holders attach to their works, and (3) to prohibit "circumvention of effective technological measures" that right-holders implement to control access to or use of their works. Finally, the WIPO Performances and Phonograms Treaty broke new ground in mandating moral rights for performers in their live aural performances and performances fixed in "phonograms" (sound recordings). In implementing the treaties, the United States Congress enacted anticircumvention and rights management information provisions, but studiously ignored the issue of moral rights for performers. Digital Millennium Copyright Act of 1998, Pub.L. No. 105–304, 112 Stat. 2860.

3. *The nature of copyright.* As you will see in the following sections, the standards for copyright—originality and fixation—are much lower than those for obtaining a patent. Moreover, in contrast to a patent, federal copyright arises automatically, as a matter of law, as soon as a qualifying work of

authorship is fixed in a tangible medium of expression (*e.g.*, a manuscript, canvas, or audiotape). It is unnecessary to apply for a copyright, and registration of an existing copyright with the Copyright Office, when necessary, is relatively simple, entailing little substantive examination. The term of protection is significantly longer for copyrights than for patents, as well.

On the other hand, the level of protection afforded by copyright is lower than that afforded by a patent. Copyright only prohibits copying: Independent creation does not infringe. Moreover, the Copyright Act contains numerous exceptions to infringement liability, permitting the public to make specified unauthorized uses of the copyrighted work. Perhaps most importantly, as the Report of the Register of Copyrights notes, copyright only prevents others from copying the author's particular method of expressing ideas or facts: It gives no rights in the substantive ideas or facts themselves.

Thus, in providing property rights in an individual's expression, Congress has struck a unique balance. Making copyright easier to obtain can be justified because there are usually numerous ways to express a concept: Providing rights in one of those ways takes less from society than granting rights in the concept itself. Moreover, protection of all expression satisfying a minimal originality standard avoids censorship and encourages the creation of a more diverse, robust array of expression, to the ultimate enrichment of society.

At the same time, Congress clearly recognized the need to limit the scope of copyright protection. It is essential to retain in the public domain those basic building blocks—ideas, facts, standard forms of expression—needed for future authorship. Indeed, in order to avoid stagnation, there must be some leeway for new authorship to draw upon preexisting expressive works. As one commentator has observed, it is inappropriate to base copyright law

> on the charming notion that authors create something from nothing, that works owe their origin to the authors who produce them. * * *
>
> The process of authorship * * * is more equivocal than that romantic model admits. To say that every new work is in some sense based on the works that preceded it is such a truism that it has long been a cliche, invoked but not examined. But the very act of authorship in *any* medium is more akin to translation and recombination than it is to creating Aphrodite from the foam of the sea. Composers recombine sounds they have heard before; playwrights base their characters on bits and pieces drawn from real human beings and other playwrights' characters; novelists draw their plots from lives and other plots within their experience; software writers use the logic they find in other software; lawyers transform old arguments to fit new facts; cinematographers, actors, choreographers, architects, and sculptors all engage in the process of adapting, transforming, and recombining what is already "out there" in some other form. This is not parasitism: it is the essence of authorship. And, in the absence of a vigorous public domain, much of it would be illegal.

Litman, *The Public Domain*, 39 Emory L. J. 965, 965–66 (1990).[4] As you proceed through this Chapter, you should evaluate how Congress has bal-

---

4. © Jessica Litman, 1990. Reprinted with permission.

anced the interest of providing rights as an incentive to create against the interest in maintaining the widest possible public access and a viable public domain from which future authors may draw. Has Congress struck the optimal balance?

4. *First Amendment considerations.* By prohibiting the unauthorized use of copyrighted expression, the copyright laws undoubtedly abridge the freedoms of speech and press, to some extent. Can they be applied consistently with the First Amendment?[5]

The First Amendment has not been construed in an absolute, literal sense to prohibit all laws abridging speech. In evaluating the constitutionality of laws under the First Amendment, the Supreme Court has tended to weigh the interest advanced by the law in question against the interest in free speech and press, and to evaluate the extent of the law's interference with First Amendment interests. See, e.g., Zacchini v. Scripps–Howard Broadcasting Co., 433 U.S. 562, 97 S.Ct. 2849, 53 L.Ed.2d 965 (1977). Copyright is limited in ways that minimize its intrusion on the exercise of free speech and press.

First, as noted above, copyright does not prohibit others from copying, discussing or making other uses of an author's ideas. It merely prohibits unauthorized use of his particular mode of expressing the ideas, when those ideas may be expressed in a number of different ways. Second, the fair use defense, codified at 17 U.S.C.A. § 107, and other more specific statutory exceptions to liability, give the public some leeway to use an author's expression when such use promotes the general public interest. Finally, limitations on the duration of copyright undertake to ensure that the author's protection does not extend beyond what is needed to provide the necessary incentive to create and accomplish the legitimate purposes of copyright law.

These limitations on copyright protection, combined with the weight of the interest the copyright laws advance (indeed, the interest—providing an incentive to authors to express and disseminate their ideas—is highly consistent with First Amendment interests), have convinced most courts and commentators that the law's intrusion on free speech withstands First Amendment scrutiny in most, if not all cases. See, e.g., Eldred v. Ashcroft, 537 U.S. 186, 123 S.Ct. 769, 154 L.Ed.2d 683 (2003); Nimmer, *Does Copyright Abridge the First Amendment Guarantees of Free Speech and Press?*, 17 U.C.L.A. L. Rev. 1180 (1970); Denicola, *Copyright and Free Speech: Constitutional Limitations on the Protection of Expression*, 67 Cal. L Rev. 283 (1979); Goldstein, *Copyright and the First Amendment*, 70 Colum. L. Rev. 983 (1970).

5. *Additional resources.* Excellent multi-volume treatises on copyright include Melville B. Nimmer & David Nimmer, Nimmer On Copyright (2008); and P. Goldstein, Copyright (3d ed. 2005 & 2009 supp.). For a discussion of the history and development of the copyright law, see L.R. Paterson & S.W. Lindberg, The Nature of Copyright: A Law of Users' Rights (1991). For an examination of the unusual legislative history of the Copyright Act of 1976 and its implications, see Litman, *Copyright, Compromise, and Legislative History*, 72 Cornell L. Rev. 857 (1987). For an economic evaluation of

---

5. The First Amendment to the United States Constitution provides: "Congress shall make no law * * * abridging the freedom of speech, or of the press * * *."

copyright law, see Landes & Posner, *An Economic Analysis of Copyright*, 18 J. Legal Stud. 325 (1989).

II. THE SUBJECT MATTER OF COPYRIGHT

§ 102. Subject Matter of Copyright: In General

(a) Copyright protection subsists, in accordance with this title, in original works of authorship fixed in any tangible medium of expression, now known or later developed, from which they can be perceived, reproduced, or otherwise communicated, either directly or with the aid of a machine or device. Works of authorship include the following categories:

(1) literary works;

(2) musical works, including any accompanying words;

(3) dramatic works, including any accompanying music;

(4) pantomimes and choreographic works;

(5) pictorial, graphic, and sculptural works;

(6) motion pictures and other audiovisual works;

(7) sound recordings; and

(8) architectural works.

(b) In no case does copyright protection for an original work of authorship extend to any idea, procedure, process, system, method of operation, concept, principle, or discovery, regardless of the form in which it is described, explained, illustrated, or embodied in such work.

17 U.S.C.A. § 102.

Copyright Act § 102 provides protection for "original works of authorship." The Copyright Act of 1909 had provided protection for "all the writings of an author," tracking the Constitutional language empowering Congress to secure to authors exclusive rights in their "writings." U.S. Const. art. I, § 8, cl. 8. The House Report accompanying the bill that was to become the Copyright Act of 1976 explained the change in language:

> In using the phrase "original works of authorship," rather than "all the writings of an author" * * *, the committee's purpose is to avoid exhausting the constitutional power of Congress to legislate in this field, and to eliminate the uncertainties arising from the latter phrase. Since the present statutory language is substantially the same as the empowering language of the Constitution, a recurring question has been whether the statutory and the constitutional provisions are coextensive. If so, the courts would be faced with the alternative of holding copyrightable something that Congress clearly did not intend to protect, or of holding constitutionally incapable of copyright something that Congress might one day want to protect. To avoid these equally undesirable results, the courts have indicated that "all the

writings of an author" under the [1909] statute is narrower in scope than the "writings" of "authors" referred to in the Constitution. The bill avoids this dilemma by using a different phrase—"original works of authorship"—in characterizing the general subject matter of statutory copyright protection.

The history of copyright law has been one of gradual expansion in the types of works accorded protection, and the subject matter affected by this expansion has fallen into two general categories. In the first, scientific discoveries and technological developments have made possible new forms of creative expression that never existed before. In some of these cases the new expressive forms—electronic music, filmstrips, and computer programs, for example—could be regarded as an extension of copyrightable subject matter Congress had already intended to protect, and were thus considered copyrightable from the outset without the need of new legislation. In other cases, such as photographs, sound recordings, and motion pictures, statutory enactment was deemed necessary to give them full recognition as copyrightable works.

Authors are continually finding new ways of expressing themselves, but it is impossible to foresee the forms that these new expressive methods will take. The bill does not intend either to freeze the scope of copyrightable subject matter at the present stage of communications technology or to allow unlimited expansion into areas completely outside the present congressional intent. Section 102 implies neither that that subject matter is unlimited nor that new forms of expression within that general area of subject matter would necessarily be unprotected.

The historic expansion of copyright has also applied to forms of expression which, although in existence for generations or centuries, have only gradually come to be recognized as creative and worthy of protection. The first copyright statute in this country, enacted in 1790, designated only "maps, charts, and books;" major forms of expression such as music, drama, and works of art achieved specific statutory recognition only in later enactments. Although the coverage of the present statute is very broad, and would be broadened further by the explicit recognition of all forms of choreography, there are unquestionably other areas of existing subject matter that this bill does not propose to protect but that future Congresses may want to.

H.R. Rep. No. 1476, 94th Cong., 2d Sess. 51–52 (1976).

Section 102(a) requires that works of authorship be: 1) "fixed in any tangible medium of expression" and 2) "original" in order to qualify for federal copyright. This section of the Chapter will examine the fixation and originality requirements, and then focus on the prohibition, in § 102(b), of copyright protection for ideas and facts (which is sometimes called the "idea/expression dichotomy"). While it is unnecessary to examine each of the eight categories of subject matter set forth in § 102(a), we will examine several of the subject matter areas that have presented courts with particular difficulties in applying the originality requirement and the idea/expression dichotomy, and promoting the policies that underlie them.

A. THE FIXATION REQUIREMENT

§ 101. Definitions

* * *

A work is "fixed" in a tangible medium of expression when its embodiment in a copy or phonorecord, by or under the authority of the author, is sufficiently permanent or stable to permit it to be perceived, reproduced, or otherwise communicated for a period of more than transitory duration. A work consisting of sounds, images, or both, that are being transmitted, is "fixed" for purposes of this title if a fixation of the work is being made simultaneously with its transmission.

17 U.S.C.A. § 101.

HOUSE REPORT ON COPYRIGHT ACT OF 1976

H.R. Rep. No. 1476, 94th Cong., 2d Sess. 52–53 (1976).

Fɪxᴀᴛɪᴏɴ ɪɴ Tᴀɴɢɪʙʟᴇ Fᴏʀᴍ

As a basic condition of copyright protection, the bill perpetuates the existing requirement that a work be fixed in a "tangible medium of expression," and adds that this medium may be one "now known or later developed," and that the fixation is sufficient if the work "can be perceived, reproduced, or otherwise communicated, either directly or with the aid of a machine or device." This broad language is intended to avoid the artificial and largely unjustifiable distinctions, derived from cases such as White–Smith Publishing Co. v. Apollo Co., 209 U.S. 1 (1908), under which statutory copyrightability in certain cases has been made to depend upon the form or medium in which the work is fixed. Under the bill it makes no difference what the form, manner, or medium of fixation may be— whether it is in words, numbers, notes, sounds, pictures, or any other graphic or symbolic indicia, whether embodied in a physical object in written, printed, photographic, sculptural, punched, magnetic, or any other stable form, and whether it is capable of perception directly or by means of any machine or device "now known or later developed."

Under the bill, the concept of fixation is important since it not only determines whether the provisions of the statute apply to a work, but it also represents the dividing line between common law and statutory protection. [A]n unfixed work of authorship, such as an improvisation or an unrecorded choreographic work, performance, or broadcast, would continue to be subject to protection under State common law or statute, but would not be eligible for Federal statutory protection under section 102.

The bill seeks to resolve, through the definition of "fixation" in section 101, the status of live broadcasts—sports, news coverage, live performances of music, etc.—that are reaching the public in unfixed form but that are simultaneously being recorded. When a football game is being covered by four television cameras, with a director guiding the activities of the four cameramen and choosing which of their electronic images are sent out to the public and in what order, there is little doubt that what the cameramen and the director are doing constitutes "authorship." The further question to be considered is whether there has been a fixation. If the images and sounds to be broadcast are first recorded (on a video tape, film, etc.) and then transmitted, the recorded work would be considered a "motion picture" subject to statutory protection against unauthorized reproduction or retransmission of the broadcast. If the program content is transmitted live to the public while being recorded at the same time, the case would be treated the same; the copyright owner would not be forced to rely on common law rather than statutory rights in proceeding against an infringing user of the live broadcast.

Thus, assuming it is copyrightable—as a "motion picture" or "sound recording," for example—the content of a live transmission should be regarded as fixed and should be accorded statutory protection if it is being recorded simultaneously with its transmission. On the other hand, the definition of "fixation" would exclude from the concept purely evanescent or transient reproductions such as those projected briefly on a screen, shown electronically on a television or other cathode ray tube, or captured momentarily in the "memory" of a computer.

Under the first sentence of the definition of "fixed" in section 101, a work would be considered "fixed in a tangible medium of expression" if there has been an authorized embodiment in a copy or phonorecord and if that embodiment "is sufficiently permanent or stable" to permit the work "to be perceived, reproduced, or otherwise communicated for a period of more than transitory duration." * * *

Under this definition "copies" and "phonorecords" together will comprise all of the material objects in which copyrightable works are capable of being fixed. The definitions of these terms in section 101, together with their usage in section 102 and throughout the bill, reflect a fundamental distinction between the "original work" which is the product of "authorship" and the multitude of material objects in which it can be embodied. Thus, in the sense of the bill, a "book" is not a work of authorship, but is a particular kind of "copy." Instead, the author may write a "literary work," which in turn can be embodied in a wide range of "copies" and "phonorecords," including books, periodicals, computer punch cards, microfilm, tape recordings, and so forth. It is possible to have an "original work of authorship" without having a "copy" or "phonorec-ord" embodying it, and it is also possible to have a "copy" or "phonorecord" embodying something that does not qualify as an "original work of authorship." Two essential elements—original work and tangible object— must merge through fixation in order to produce subject matter copyrightable under the statute.

NOTES AND QUESTIONS

1. *"Works of authorship" vs. "copies" and "phonorecords."* As the House Report suggests, copyright law provides rights in works of authorship, which are intangible creations of the mind. Though the existence of a tangible embodiment is a prerequisite to federal copyright protection, the copyright interest in the intangible work of authorship is separate and distinct from the ownership interest in the tangible manuscript, canvas, or audio tape that embodies it. As Copyright Act § 202 explains:

> Ownership of a copyright, or of any of the exclusive rights under a copyright, is distinct from ownership of any material object in which the work is embodied. Transfer of ownership of any material object, including the copy or phonorecord in which the work is first fixed, does not of itself convey any rights in the copyrighted work embodied in the object; nor, in the absence of an agreement, does transfer of ownership of a copyright or of any exclusive rights under a copyright convey property rights in any material object.

17 U.S.C.A. § 202. Copyright Act § 204(a) provides that a transfer of copyright (other than by operation of law) is not valid unless in writing and signed by the owner. Sections 202 and 204(a) superseded an earlier state common-law doctrine that presumed that authors or artists transferred their common-law copyright when they sold their manuscript or canvas, unless they specifically reserved the copyright. See H.R. Rep. No. 1476, 94th Cong., 2d Sess. 124 (1976).

Assume that Artist makes a painting and sells the canvas to X. X obtains personal property rights in the canvas and may prevent others (including Artist) from taking or using the canvas without permission. He may also transfer the canvas to another person. However, Artist's retention of copyright in the intangible work of authorship (the painting), imposes some limits on what X can do with the physical embodiment of it. For example, since Artist, as the owner of copyright, has the exclusive right to reproduce, adapt and publicly distribute the painting to the public, he can create and sell posters depicting the painting. Notwithstanding his ownership of the canvas, X will be liable to Artist for infringement if he does the same. In addition, since Artist owns the exclusive right to display the painting to the public, he can also prevent X from making certain public displays of the canvas. Under the Visual Artists Rights Act of 1990, enacted to bring the U.S. into compliance with the Berne Convention's moral rights provisions, Artist may prevent X from misattributing the painting to a different artist, or intentionally distorting, mutilating or modifying the painting, if doing so is prejudicial to Artist's honor or reputation. See 17 U.S.C.A. § 106A.

Note that works of authorship may be embodied in copies or phonorecords. Review the definitions of these terms in § 101 of the Copyright Act. What is the difference between a copy and a phonorecord?

2. *Fixation.* Review the definition of "fixation" in Copyright Act § 101. Suppose that, in the course of giving a live performance, a dance group improvises, producing a new work of choreography. At that point, would there be federal copyright in the new work? Suppose that a member of the audience, unknown to the dance group, makes a simultaneous video recording of the performance. Would that constitute a fixation sufficient to qualify the new work for federal copyright?

Assume, instead, that a member of the dance group keeps a video recorder nearby on the stage, and records the new work of choreography as it is created. Members of the audience make unauthorized recordings at the same time. Would the dance group have a cause of action for federal copyright infringement against those members of the audience? If your answer is no, why should the dance group's claim be viewed differently from the claim of the producer of a live football game broadcast that is being recorded simultaneously with the broadcast?

For that matter, why have a fixation requirement at all? Note that fixation is deemed necessary to qualify a work as a "writing," and thus to fall within Congress' authority under the Constitution's Copyrights and Patents Clause. See 1 M.B. Nimmer & D. Nimmer, Nimmer on Copyright, § 1.08(C)(2) (2000).

3. *Interactive computer systems.* Are interactive computer programs and their visual displays "fixed" for purposes of copyright protection? Consider, for example, a video game that responds to the specific input of the individual playing the game. The game provides a different set of responses and displays from one game to the next. On what basis might one argue that such works are not fixed? What is the best argument that they are? Courts have generally found interactive computer systems sufficiently fixed to qualify for copyright. See, e.g., Williams Electronics, Inc. v. Artic International, Inc., 685 F.2d 870 (3d Cir.1982).

4. *Temporary reproductions in random access memory.* Does loading a computer program or other digital work into the random access memory ("RAM") of a computer (or creating a work there) create a "copy" for purposes of federal copyright protection? Consider the Copyright Act's definitions of "copy" and "fixed," set forth in Copyright Act § 101, 17 U.S.C. § 101. If so, what are the implications of this?

5. *State protection for unfixed works.* Although the Copyright Act of 1976 preempts state copyright protection for fixed works, 17 U.S.C. § 301, the states remain free to provide rights in unfixed works, such as oral statements and improvised, unrecorded musical compositions or pantomimes. While some states have explicitly asserted an intention to provide such protection, see, e.g., Cal. Civ. Code § 980(a)(1) (West Supp. 2001), there is little case law to define the extent of the protection. As a matter of policy, should unfixed works be protected, and if so, how broad should state protection for unfixed works be? Do you foresee any problems in enforcing such rights? See Hemingway v. Random House, Inc., 23 N.Y.2d 341, 244 N.E.2d 250, 296 N.Y.S.2d 771 (1968).

B. THE ORIGINALITY REQUIREMENT

BURROW-GILES LITHOGRAPHIC CO. v. SARONY

United States Supreme Court, 1884.
111 U.S. 53, 4 S.Ct. 279, 28 L.Ed. 349.

MR. JUSTICE MILLER delivered the opinion of the Court.

* * * The suit was commenced by an action at law in which Sarony was plaintiff and the lithographic company was defendant, the plaintiff charging the defendant with violating his copyright in regard to a photograph, the title of which is "Oscar Wilde, No. 18." A jury being waived, the court made a finding of facts on which a judgment in favor of the plaintiff was rendered * * *.

* * *

Other findings leave no doubt that plaintiff had taken all the steps required by the act of Congress to obtain copyright of this photograph, and section 4952 names photographs, among other things, for which the author, inventor, or designer may obtain copyright, which is to secure him the sole privilege of reprinting, publishing, copying, and vending the same. That defendant is liable, under that section and section 4965, there can be no question if those sections are valid as they relate to photographs.

[The issue is whether Congress has the Constitutional power to protect photographs and negatives by copyright.]

The Constitutional question is not free from difficulty. The eighth section of the first article of the Constitution is the great repository of the powers of Congress, and by the eight clause of that section Congress is authorized "to promote the progress of science and useful arts, by securing, for limited times to authors and inventors the exclusive right to their respective writings and discoveries." The argument here is that a photograph is not a writing nor the production of an author. * * * It is insisted, in argument, that a photograph being a reproduction, on paper, of the exact features of some natural object, or of some person, is not a writing of which the producer is the author. Section 4952 of the Revised Statutes places photographs in the same class as things which may be copyrighted * * * "books, maps, charts, dramatic or musical compositions, engravings, cuts, prints, paintings, drawings, statues, statuary, and models or designs intended to be perfected as works of the fine arts." * * *

* * *

* * * Unless * * * photographs can be distinguished in the classification of this point from the maps, charts, designs, engravings, etchings, cuts, and other prints, it is difficult to see why Congress cannot make them the subject of copyright as well as the others. These statutes certainly answer the objection that books only, or writing, in the limited sense of a book and its author, are within the Constitutional provision. Both these words are susceptible of a more enlarged definition than this.

An author in that sense is "he to whom anything owes its origin; originator; maker; one who completes a work of science or literature." Worcester. So, also, no one would now claim that the word "writing" in this clause of the Constitution, though the only word used as to subjects in regard to which authors are to be secured, is limited to the actual script of the author, and excludes books and all other printed matter. By writings in that clause is meant the literary productions of those authors, and Congress very properly has declared these to include all forms of writing, printing, engravings, etchings, etc., by which the ideas in the mind of the author are given visible expression. The only reason why photographs were not included in the extended list in the Act of 1802 is, probably, that they did not exist, as photography, as an art, was then unknown, and the scientific principle on which it rests, and the chemicals and machinery by which it is operated, have all been discovered long since that statute was enacted. * * *

We entertain no doubt that the Constitution is broad enough to cover an act authorizing copyright of photographs, so far as they are representatives of original intellectual conceptions of the author.

But it is said that an engraving, a painting, a print, does embody the intellectual conception of its author, in which there is novelty, invention, originality, and therefore comes within the purpose of the Constitution in securing its exclusive use or sale to its author, while a photograph is the mere mechanical reproduction of the physical features or outlines of some object, animate or inanimate, and involves no originality of thought or any novelty in the intellectual operation connected with its visible reproduction in shape of a picture. * * * This may be true in regard to the ordinary production of a photograph, and that in such case a copyright is no protection. On the question as thus stated we decide nothing.

* * *

The third finding of facts says, in regard to the photograph in question, that it is a "useful, new, harmonious, characteristic, and graceful picture, and that plaintiff made the same ... entirely from his own original mental conception, to which he gave visible form by posing the said Oscar Wilde in front of the camera, selecting and arranging the costume, draperies, and other various accessories in said photograph, arranging the subject so as to present graceful outlines, arranging and disposing the light and shade, suggesting and evoking the desired expression, and from such disposition, arrangement, or representation, made entirely by plaintiff, he produced the picture in suit." These findings, we think, show this photograph to be an original work of art, the product of plaintiff's intellectual invention, of which plaintiff is the author, and of a class of inventions for which the Constitution intended that Congress should secure to him the exclusive right to use, publish, and sell, as it has done by section 4952 of the Revised Statutes.

* * *

Nᴏᴛᴇs ᴀɴᴅ Qᴜᴇsᴛɪᴏɴs

1. *The originality standard.* How does the *Sarony* Court define "originality?" What, exactly, is original in the photograph of Oscar Wilde? Would all photographs be likely to qualify? For example, instead of a studio photograph, suppose the plaintiff had taken a photograph of a public building and the surrounding city street scene? Would the requisite originality exist? See Pagano v. Chas. Beseler Co., 234 F. 963 (S.D.N.Y.1916). What about a standard driver's license or passport photo?

Should it matter whether a purported "author" intended to make a realistic representation of an existing object? Consider the Supreme Court's remarks in Bleistein v. Donaldson Lithographing Co., 188 U.S. 239, 249–50, 23 S.Ct. 298, 300, 47 L.Ed. 460, 462 (1903), involving chromolithographs advertising a circus, which featured a likeness of the circus owner and of circus performers in action:

Even if [the depictions were] drawn from life, that fact would not deprive them of protection. The opposite proposition would mean that a portrait by Velasquez or Whistler was common property because others might try their hand on the same face. Others are free to copy the original. They are not free to copy the copy. The copy is the personal reaction of an individual upon nature. Personality always contains something unique. It expresses its singularity even in handwriting, and a very modest grade of art has in it something irreducible, which is one man's alone. That something he may copyright unless there is a restriction in the words of the Act.

In *Bleistein*, the Court also addressed the relevance of a work's artistic merit to its "originality" and copyrightability:

It would be a dangerous undertaking for persons trained only to the law to constitute themselves final judges of the worth of pictorial illustrations, outside of the narrowest and most obvious limits. At the one extreme, some works of genius would be sure to miss appreciation. Their very novelty would make them repulsive until the public had learned the new language in which their author spoke. It may be more than doubted, for instance, whether the etchings of Goya or the paintings of Manet would have been sure of protection when seen for the first time. At the other end, copyright would be denied to pictures which appealed to a public less educated than the judge. Yet if they command the interest of any public, they have a commercial value,—it would be bold to say that they have not an aesthetic and educational value,—and the taste of any public is not to be treated with contempt. * * *

Id., 188 U.S. at 251–52. Does the public benefit from affording copyright to advertising materials, and other works of questionable artistic stature? If so, how? Is the benefit sufficient to justify the impediment to free access and competition?

How would you compare the "originality" standard for copyrights with the "novelty" and "non-obviousness" standards for patents? Consider Judge Learned Hand's comments in Sheldon v. Metro–Goldwyn Pictures Corp., 81 F.2d 49, 53–54 (2d Cir.1936), *aff'd*, 309 U.S. 390, 60 S.Ct. 681, 84 L.Ed. 825 (1940), in which the plaintiff claimed copyright infringement of a play:

We are to remember that it makes no difference how far the play was anticipated by works in the public demesne which the plaintiffs did not use. The defendants appear not to recognize this, for they have filled the record with earlier instances of the same dramatic incidents and devices, as though, like a patent, a copyrighted work must be not only original, but new. That is not however the law, as is obvious in the case of maps or compendia, where later works will necessarily be anticipated. * * * Borrowed the work must indeed not be, for a plagiarist is not himself pro tanto an "author;" but if by some magic a man who had never known it were to compose anew Keats' Ode on a Grecian Urn, he would be an "author," and, if he copyrighted it, others might not copy that poem, though they might of course copy Keats'. But though a copyright is for this reason less vulnerable than a patent, the owner's protection is more limited, for just as he is no less an "author" because others have preceded him, so another who follows him, is not a tort-feasor unless he pirates his work.

FEIST PUBLICATIONS, INC. v. RURAL TELEPHONE SERVICE CO., INC.

United States Supreme Court, 1991.
499 U.S. 340, 111 S.Ct. 1282, 113 L.Ed.2d 358.

JUSTICE O'CONNOR delivered the opinion of the Court.

This case requires us to clarify the extent of copyright protection available to telephone directory white pages.

I

Rural Telephone Service Company is a certified public utility that provides telephone service to several communities in northwest Kansas. It is subject to a state regulation that requires all telephone companies operating in Kansas to issue annually an updated telephone directory. Accordingly, as a condition of its monopoly franchise, Rural publishes a typical telephone directory, consisting of white pages and yellow pages. The white pages list in alphabetical order the names of Rural's subscribers, together with their towns and telephone numbers. The yellow pages list Rural's business subscribers alphabetically by category and feature classified advertisements of various sizes. Rural distributes its directory free of charge to its subscribers, but earns revenue by selling yellow pages advertisements.

Feist Publications, Inc., is a publishing company that specializes in area-wide telephone directories. Unlike a typical directory, which covers only a particular calling area, Feist's area-wide directories cover a much larger geographical range, reducing the need to call directory assistance or consult multiple directories. The Feist directory that is the subject of this litigation covers 11 different telephone service areas in 15 counties and contains 46,878 white pages listings—compared to Rural's approximately 7,700 listings. Like Rural's directory, Feist's is distributed free of charge and includes both white pages and yellow pages. Feist and Rural compete vigorously for yellow pages advertising.

As the sole provider of telephone service in its service area, Rural obtains subscriber information quite easily. Persons desiring telephone service must apply to Rural and provide their names and addresses; Rural then assigns them a telephone number. Feist is not a telephone company, let alone one with monopoly status, and therefore lacks independent access to any subscriber information. To obtain white pages listings for its area-wide directory, Feist approached each of the 11 telephone companies operating in northwest Kansas and offered to pay for the right to use its white pages listings.

Of the 11 telephone companies, only Rural refused to license its listings to Feist. Rural's refusal created a problem for Feist, as omitting these listings would have left a gaping hole in its area-wide directory, rendering it less attractive to potential yellow pages advertisers. * * *

Unable to license Rural's white pages listings, Feist used them without Rural's consent. Feist began by removing several thousand listings that fell outside the geographic range of its area-wide directory, then hired personnel to investigate the 4,935 that remained. These employees verified the data reported by Rural and sought to obtain additional information. As a result, a typical Feist listing includes the individual's street address; most of Rural's listings do not. Notwithstanding these additions, however, 1,309 of the 46,878 listings in Feist's 1983 directory were identical to listings in Rural's 1982–1983 white pages. Four of these were fictitious listings that Rural had inserted into its directory to detect copying.

Rural sued for copyright infringement in the District Court for the District of Kansas taking the position that Feist, in compiling its own directory, could not use the information contained in Rural's white pages. Rural asserted that Feist's employees were obliged to travel door-to-door or conduct a telephone survey to discover the same information for themselves. Feist responded that such efforts were economically impractical and, in any event, unnecessary because the information copied was beyond the scope of copyright protection. The District Court granted summary judgment to Rural, explaining that "[c]ourts have consistently held that telephone directories are copyrightable" and citing a string of lower court decisions. In an unpublished opinion, the Court of Appeals for the Tenth Circuit affirmed "for substantially the reasons given by the district court." We granted certiorari, to determine whether the copyright in Rural's directory protects the names, towns, and telephone numbers copied by Feist.

II

A

This case concerns the interaction of two well-established propositions. The first is that facts are not copyrightable; the other, that compilations of facts generally are. Each of these propositions possesses an impeccable pedigree. That there can be no valid copyright in facts is universally understood. The most fundamental axiom of copyright law is that "[n]o author may copyright his ideas or the facts he narrates." *Harper & Row, Publishers, Inc. v. Nation Enterprises*, 471 U.S. 539, 556, 105 S.Ct. 2218, 2228, 85 L.Ed.2d 588 (1985). Rural wisely concedes this point, noting in its brief that "[f]acts and discoveries, of course, are not themselves subject to copyright protection." At the same time, however, it is beyond dispute that compilations of facts are within the subject matter of copyright. Compilations were expressly mentioned in the Copyright Act of 1909, and again in the Copyright Act of 1976.

There is an undeniable tension between these two propositions. Many compilations consist of nothing but raw data—*i.e.*, wholly factual information not accompanied by any original written expression. On what basis may one claim a copyright in such a work? Common sense tells us that 100 uncopyrightable facts do not magically change their status when gathered together in one place. Yet copyright law seems to contemplate that compilations that consist exclusively of facts are potentially within its scope.

The key to resolving the tension lies in understanding why facts are not copyrightable. The *sine qua non* of copyright is originality. To qualify for copyright protection, a work must be original to the author. Original, as the term is used in copyright, means only that the work was independently created by the author (as opposed to copied from other works), and that it possesses at least some minimal degree of creativity. To be sure, the requisite level of creativity is extremely low; even a slight amount will suffice. The vast majority of works make the grade quite easily, as they possess some creative spark, "no matter how crude, humble or obvious" it might be. Originality does not signify novelty; a work may be original even though it closely resembles other works so long as the similarity is fortuitous, not the result of copying. To illustrate, assume that two poets, each ignorant of the other, compose identical poems. Neither work is novel, yet both are original and, hence, copyrightable.

Originality is a constitutional requirement. The source of Congress' power to enact copyright laws is Article I, § 8, cl. 8, of the Constitution, which authorizes Congress to "secur[e] for limited Times to Authors ... the exclusive Right to their respective Writings." In two decisions from the late 19th Century—*The Trade–Mark Cases*, 100 U.S. 82, 25 L.Ed. 550 (1879); and *Burrow–Giles Lithographic Co. v. Sarony*, 111 U.S. 53, 4 S.Ct. 279, 28 L.Ed. 349 (1884)—this Court defined the crucial terms "authors" and "writings." In so doing, the Court made it unmistakably clear that these terms presuppose a degree of originality.

* * *

The originality requirement articulated in *The Trade–Mark Cases* and *Burrow–Giles* remains the touchstone of copyright protection today. It is the very "premise of copyright law." Leading scholars agree on this point. As one pair of commentators succinctly puts it: "The originality requirement is *constitutionally mandated* for all works." Paterson & Joyce, Monopolizing the Law: The Scope of Copyright Protection for Law Reports and Statutory Compilations, 36 UCLA L.Rev. 719, 763, n. 155 (1989). * * *

It is this bedrock principle of copyright that mandates the law's seemingly disparate treatment of facts and factual compilations. "No one may claim originality as to facts." Nimmer, § 2.11[A], p. 2–157. This is because facts do not owe their origin to an act of authorship. The distinction is one between creation and discovery: the first person to find and report a particular fact has not created the fact; he or she has merely discovered its existence. To borrow from *Burrow–Giles*, one who discovers a fact is not its "maker" or "originator." "The discoverer merely finds and records." Census-takers, for example, do not "create" the population figures that emerge from their efforts; in a sense, they copy these figures from the world around them. Census data therefore do not trigger copyright because these data are not "original" in the constitutional sense. The same is true of all facts—scientific, historical, biographical, and news of the day. "[T]hey may not be copyrighted and are part of the public domain available to every person."

Factual compilations, on the other hand, may possess the requisite originality. The compilation author typically chooses which facts to include, in what order to place them, and how to arrange the collected data so that they may be used effectively by readers. These choices as to selection and arrangement, so long as they are made independently by the compiler and entail a minimal degree of creativity, are sufficiently original that Congress may protect such compilations through the copyright laws. Thus, even a directory that contains absolutely no protectible written expression, only facts, meets the constitutional minimum for copyright protection if it features an original selection or arrangement.

This protection is subject to an important limitation. The mere fact that a work is copyrighted does not mean that every element of the work may be protected. Originality remains the *sine qua non*; accordingly, copyright protection may extend only to those components of a work that are original to the author. Thus, if the compilation author clothes facts with an original collocation of words, he or she may be able to claim a copyright in this written expression. Others may copy the underlying facts from the publication, but not the precise words used to present them. In *Harper & Row*, for example, we explained that President Ford could not prevent others from copying bare historical facts from his autobiography, but that he could prevent others from copying his "subjective descriptions and portraits of public figures." Where the compilation author adds no written expression but rather lets the facts speak for themselves, the expressive element is more elusive. The only conceivable expression is the manner in which the compiler has selected and arranged the facts. Thus, if the selection and arrangement are original, these elements of the work are eligible for copyright protection. No matter how original the format, however, the facts themselves do not become original through association.

This inevitably means that the copyright in a factual compilation is thin. Notwithstanding a valid copyright, a subsequent compiler remains free to use the facts contained in another's publication to aid in preparing a competing work, so long as the competing work does not feature the same selection and arrangement. As one commentator explains it: "[N]o matter how much original authorship the work displays, the facts and ideas it exposes are free for the taking.... [T]he very same facts and ideas may be divorced from the context imposed by the author, and restated or reshuffled by second comers, even if the author was the first to discover the facts or to propose the ideas."

It may seem unfair that much of the fruit of the compiler's labor may be used by others without compensation. As Justice Brennan has correctly observed, however, this is not "some unforeseen byproduct of a statutory scheme." It is, rather, "the essence of copyright," and a constitutional requirement. The primary objective of copyright is not to reward the labor of authors, but "[t]o promote the Progress of Science and useful Arts." Art. I, § 8, cl. 8. To this end, copyright assures authors the right to their original expression, but encourages others to build freely upon the ideas and information conveyed by a work. This principle, known as the idea/expression or fact/expression dichotomy, applies to all works of authorship. As applied to a factual compilation, assuming the absence of original written expression, only the compiler's selection and arrangement may be protected; the raw facts may be copied at will. This result is neither unfair nor unfortunate. It is the means by which copyright advances the progress of science and art.

This Court has long recognized that the fact/expression dichotomy limits severely the scope of protection in fact-based works. More than a century ago, the Court observed: "The very object of publishing a book on science or the useful arts is to communicate to the world the useful knowledge which it contains. But this object would be frustrated if the knowledge could not be used without incurring the guilt of piracy of the book." *Baker v. Selden*, 101 U.S. 99, 103, 25 L.Ed. 841 (1880). * * *

This, then, resolves the doctrinal tension: Copyright treats facts and factual compilations in a wholly consistent manner. Facts, whether alone or as part of a compilation, are not original and therefore may not be copyrighted. A factual compilation is eligible for copyright if it features an original selection or arrangement of facts, but the copyright is limited to the particular selection or arrangement. In no event may copyright extend to the facts themselves.

B

As we have explained, originality is a constitutionally mandated prerequisite for copyright protection. The Court's decisions announcing this rule predate the Copyright Act of 1909, but ambiguous language in the 1909 Act caused some lower courts temporarily to lose sight of this requirement.

* * *

[These ambiguities] led some courts to infer erroneously that directories and the like were copyrightable *per se*, "without any further or precise showing of original—personal—authorship."

Making matters worse, these courts developed a new theory to justify the protection of factual compilations. Known alternatively as "sweat of the brow" or "industrious collection," the underlying notion was that copyright was a reward for the hard work that went into compiling facts. The classic formulation of the doctrine appeared in *Jeweler's Circular Publishing Co.*, 281 F., at 88:

"The right to copyright a book upon which one has expended labor in its preparation does not depend upon whether the materials which he has collected consist or not of matters which are publici juris, or whether such materials show literary skill *or originality,* either in thought or in language, or anything more than industrious collection. The man who goes through the streets of a town and puts down the names of each of the inhabitants, with their occupations and their street number, acquires material of which he is the author" (emphasis added).

The "sweat of the brow" doctrine had numerous flaws, the most glaring being that it extended copyright protection in a compilation beyond selection and arrangement—the compiler's original contributions—to the facts themselves. Under the doctrine, the only defense to infringement was independent creation. A subsequent compiler was "not entitled to take one word of information previously published," but rather had to "independently wor[k] out the matter for himself, so as to arrive at the same result from the same common sources of information." "Sweat of the brow" courts thereby eschewed the most fundamental axiom of copyright law—that no one may copyright facts or ideas. * * *

    * * *

Without a doubt, the "sweat of the brow" doctrine flouted basic copyright principles. Throughout history, copyright law has "recognize[d] a greater need to disseminate factual works than works of fiction or fantasy." But "sweat of the brow" courts took a contrary view; they handed out proprietary interests in facts and declared that authors are absolutely precluded from saving time and effort by relying upon the facts contained in prior works. In truth, "[i]t is just such wasted effort that the proscription against the copyright of ideas and facts ... [is] designed to prevent." "Protection for the fruits of such research ... may in certain circumstances be available under a theory of unfair competition. But to accord copyright protection on this basis alone distorts basic copyright principles in that it creates a monopoly in public domain materials without the necessary justification of protecting and encouraging the creation of 'writings' by 'authors.' "

C

    * * *

The definition of "compilation" is found in § 101 of the 1976 Act. It defines a "compilation" in the copyright sense as "a work formed by the collection and assembly of preexisting materials or of data *that* are selected, coordinated, or arranged *in such a way that* the resulting work as a whole constitutes an original work of authorship" (emphasis added).

The purpose of the statutory definition is to emphasize that collections of facts are not copyrightable *per se.* It conveys this message through its tripartite structure, as emphasized above by the italics. The statute identifies three distinct elements and requires each to be met for a work to qualify as a copyrightable compilation: (1) the collection and assembly of pre-existing material, facts, or data; (2) the selection, coordination, or arrangement of those materials; and (3) the creation, by virtue of the particular selection, coordination, or arrangement, of an "original" work of authorship. * * *

* * *

As discussed earlier, however, the originality requirement is not particularly stringent. A compiler may settle upon a selection or arrangement that others have used; novelty is not required. Originality requires only that the author make the selection or arrangement independently (i.e., without copying that selection or arrangement from another work), and that it display some minimal level of creativity. Presumably, the vast majority of compilations will pass this test, but not all will. There remains a narrow category of works in which the creative spark is utterly lacking or so trivial as to be virtually nonexistent. * * *

Even if a work qualifies as a copyrightable compilation, it receives only limited protection. This is the point of § 103 of the Act. Section 103 explains that "[t]he subject matter of copyright ... includes compilations," § 103(a), but that copyright protects only the author's original contributions—not the facts or information conveyed:

"The copyright in a compilation ... extends only to the material contributed by the author of such work, as distinguished from the preexisting material employed in the work, and does not imply any exclusive right in the preexisting material." § 103(b).

As § 103 makes clear, copyright is not a tool by which a compilation author may keep others from using the facts or data he or she has collected. * * * [T]he facts contained in existing works may be freely copied because copyright protects only the elements that owe their origin to the compiler—the selection, coordination, and arrangement of facts.

In summary, the 1976 revisions to the Copyright Act leave no doubt that originality, not "sweat of the brow," is the touchstone of copyright protection in directories and other fact-based works. * * *

III

There is no doubt that Feist took from the white pages of Rural's directory a substantial amount of factual information. At a minimum, Feist copied the names, towns, and telephone numbers of 1,309 of Rural's subscribers. Not all copying, however, is copyright infringement. To establish infringement, two elements must be proven: (1) ownership of a valid copyright, and (2) copying of constituent elements of the work that are original. The first element is not at issue here; Feist appears to concede that Rural's directory, considered as a whole, is subject to a valid copyright because it contains some foreword text, as well as original material in its yellow pages advertisements.

The question is whether Rural has proved the second element. In other words, did Feist, by taking 1,309 names, towns, and telephone numbers from Rural's white pages, copy anything that was "original" to

Rural? Certainly, the raw data does not satisfy the originality require-ment. Rural may have been the first to discover and report the names, towns, and telephone numbers of its subscribers, but this data does not " 'ow[e] its origin' " to Rural. *Burrow–Giles*, 111 U.S., at 58, 4 S.Ct., at 281. Rather, these bits of information are uncopyrightable facts; they existed before Rural reported them and would have continued to exist if Rural had never published a telephone directory. * * *

  * * *

The question that remains is whether Rural selected, coordinated, or arranged these uncopyrightable facts in an original way. As mentioned, originality is not a stringent standard; it does not require that facts be presented in an innovative or surprising way. It is equally true, however, that the selection and arrangement of facts cannot be so mechanical or routine as to require no creativity whatsoever. The standard of originality is low, but it does exist. As this Court has explained, the Constitution mandates some minimal degree of creativity, and an author who claims infringement must prove "the existence of . . . intellectual production, of thought, and conception." *Burrow–Giles, supra,* 111 U.S., at 59–60, 4 S.Ct., at 281–282.

The selection, coordination, and arrangement of Rural's white pages do not satisfy the minimum constitutional standards for copyright protec-tion. As mentioned at the outset, Rural's white pages are entirely typical. Persons desiring telephone service in Rural's service area fill out an application and Rural issues them a telephone number. In preparing its white pages, Rural simply takes the data provided by its subscribers and lists it alphabetically by surname. The end product is a garden-variety white pages directory, devoid of even the slightest trace of creativity.

Rural's selection of listings could not be more obvious: it publishes the most basic information—name, town, and telephone number—about each person who applies to it for telephone service. This is "selection" of a sort, but it lacks the modicum of creativity necessary to transform mere selection into copyrightable expression. Rural expended sufficient effort to make the white pages directory useful, but insufficient creativity to make it original.

We note in passing that the selection featured in Rural's white pages may also fail the originality requirement for another reason. Feist points out that Rural did not truly "select" to publish the names and telephone numbers of its subscribers; rather, it was required to do so by the Kansas Corporation Commission as part of its monopoly franchise. Accordingly, one could plausibly conclude that this selection was dictated by state law, not by Rural.

Nor can Rural claim originality in its coordination and arrangement of facts. The white pages do nothing more than list Rural's subscribers in alphabetical order. This arrangement may, technically speaking, owe its origin to Rural; no one disputes that Rural undertook the task of alphabe-tizing the names itself. But there is nothing remotely creative about arranging names alphabetically in a white pages directory. It is an age-old practice, firmly rooted in tradition and so commonplace that it has come to be expected as a matter of course. It is not only unoriginal, it is practically inevitable. This time-honored tradition does not possess the minimal creative spark required by the Copyright Act and the Constitution.

We conclude that the names, towns, and telephone numbers copied by Feist were not original to Rural and therefore were not protected by the copyright in Rural's combined white and yellow pages directory. As a constitutional matter, copyright protects only those constituent elements of a work that possess more than a *de minimis* quantum of creativity. Rural's white pages, limited to basic subscriber information and arranged alphabetically, fall short of the mark. As a statutory matter, 17 U.S.C. § 101 does not afford protection from copying to a collection of facts that are selected, coordinated, and arranged in a way that utterly lacks originality. Given that some works must fail, we cannot imagine a more likely candidate. Indeed, were we to hold that Rural's white pages pass muster, it is hard to believe that any collection of facts could fail.

Because Rural's white pages lack the requisite originality, Feist's use of the listings cannot constitute infringement. This decision should not be construed as demeaning Rural's efforts in compiling its directory, but rather as making clear that copyright rewards originality, not effort. As this Court noted more than a century ago, " 'great praise may be due to the plaintiffs for their industry and enterprise in publishing this paper, yet the law does not contemplate their being rewarded in this way.' "
* * *

NOTES AND QUESTIONS

1. *Creativity.* As the *Feist* opinion makes clear, modern formulations of the originality requirement tend to break the requirement into two parts: First, the work must be the author's independent creation, and second, the work must demonstrate a minimal, threshold level of creativity. Why impose a creativity requirement? How is creativity to be measured—does creativity turn on the degree of mental process employed by the author, or is creativity to be measured objectively, perhaps through comparison to similar kinds of works? Why was the creativity requirement not satisfied in the *Feist* case? Can you think of any practical way that telephone white page listings might be made sufficiently creative to obtain copyright protection? Are there any aspects of a typical telephone book that are likely to satisfy the creativity requirement? If so, which aspects?

Compilations of facts often have been found sufficiently original to merit copyright. For example, in Eckes v. Card Prices Update, 736 F.2d 859 (2d Cir.1984), the court found the plaintiff's "selection, creativity and judgement in choosing" 5,000 "premium" baseball cards from among 18,000 sufficient to merit copyright protection. In Kregos v. Associated Press, 937 F.2d 700 (2d Cir.1991), the claimant's selection of nine categories of statistics for use in predicting a baseball pitcher's performance sufficed. The court noted, "there are at least scores of available statistics about pitching performance available to be calculated from the underlying data and therefore thousands of combinations of data that a selector can choose to include in a pitching form." Moreover, there were no prior pitching forms which combined the same set of statistics to suggest that the plaintiff's selection was "entirely typical," "garden-variety," or "obvious." *Id.*, 937 F.2d at 704–05.

2. *Originality.* How might one evaluate the copyrightability of computer-generated works? When a human invests intellect and judgement to generate a work, using the computer as a tool, copyright clearly should be available. However, computers are capable today of generating works with little or no human intervention. When all the human has done is essentially turn the computer on, and the computer has generated its own work, should the product be copyrightable? If so, who should own the copyright? The user of the computer? The programmer who designed the software? See Samuelson, *Allocating Ownership Rights in Computer–Generated Works*, 47 U. Pitt. L. Rev. 1185 (1986) Clifford, *Intellectual Property in the Era of the Creative Computer Program: Will the True Creator Please Stand Up?* 71 Tulane L. Rev. 1675 (1997).

Ethnic groups and indigenous peoples often express concern about outsiders' unauthorized commercial reproduction and adaptation of their folklore and other traditional creative works, such as rug designs, and crafts, which have been handed down from one generation to the next. To what extent is copyright likely to assist them in preventing this unwanted commercial exploitation?

3. *Protection for facts.* Are you satisfied with the Supreme Court's explanation of why facts can never be considered "original" to an author? Can one be said to "create" a fact by causing it to occur? If so, could the Telephone Company be deemed to "create" the telephone numbers at issue by accepting customer orders and assigning specific numbers to individual customers? What if the Telephone Company undertook to design special "easy-to-remember" telephone numbers, which it then assigned to customers?

From whose viewpoint should the status of something as "fact" be determined? The author's? The court's? The "typical" member of the audience's? Might the selection of viewpoint make a difference in the outcome of the determination? Are facts strictly objective discoveries, or may they have subjective aspects? If the latter, how should the subjective aspects be treated for purposes of copyright protection? Where should the line be drawn between fact and expression in such cases? See CCC Information Services, Inc. v. Maclean Hunter Market Reports, Inc., 44 F.3d 61 (2d Cir. 1994), *cert. denied*, 516 U.S. 817 (1995); CDN, Inc. v. Kapes, 197 F.3d 1256 (9th Cir. 1999).

Apart from the "discover" vs. "create" distinction, are there other justifications for refusing to afford copyright protection for facts?

Of what relevance is the certainty that the defendant will get a "free ride," possibly at the plaintiff's expense, if permitted to copy the facts the plaintiff has gone to the effort and expense of gathering? From a public policy standpoint, should the plaintiff's investment and effort be protected against such free riding? Given the *Feist* decision, could Congress amend the copyright laws to provide such protection for databases lacking originality? If not, is there any other constitutional provision that would empower Congress to provide such protection? For example, could Congress rely on its Commerce Clause power to provide protection for data bases that are insufficiently original to merit copyright protection? What are the constitutional implications of Congress' use of one enumerated power to circumvent express limitations built into another enumerated power? See U.S. Copyright Office, *Copyright Office Report on Database Protection, Executive Summary* (1997), *reprinted in* 54 Pat., Trademark & Copyright J. (BNA) 369 (1997); Patry, *The Enumerated Powers Doctrine and Intellectual Property: An Imminent Constitutional Collision*, 67 Geo. Wash. L. Rev. 359 (1999).

4. *Words, short phrases, titles, labels and other "minimal" works.* Courts and the Copyright Office generally refuse to recognize copyright in "[w]ords and short phrases such as names, titles, and slogans; familiar symbols or designs; mere variations of typographic ornamentation, lettering or coloring; [and] mere listings of ingredients or contents * * *." 37 C.F.R. § 202.1(a) (2000). There are two justifications for this rule. First, such minimal works are viewed as insufficiently original to merit copyright. See, e.g., Laskowitz v. Marie Designer, Inc., 119 F.Supp. 541, 551 (S.D.Cal.1954) ("I do not think that phrases such as 'This is Nature's most restful posture' or phrases emphasizing 'the relaxing' qualities of the chair, which are so purely descriptive of the product, comply even with the slight requirement of originality in the law of copyright * * * "). In addition, it is often reasoned that granting rights in words or short phrases, in particular, may interfere with others' ability to express the underlying idea. We will examine this latter issue at greater depth later in the Chapter.

Courts occasionally deviate from the general rule in the case of short phrases or slogans. See, e.g., Universal City Studios, Inc. v. Kamar Industries, Inc., 217 U.S.P.Q. 1162, 1166 (S.D.Tex.1982) (recognizing copyright in "I love you E.T." and "E.T. Phone Home"). But they have steadfastly refused to recognize copyright in titles of books, movies, or other works of authorship. Apart from the questionable originality of titles comprised simply of individual words or short phrases, titles "serve mainly to identify and describe the work itself." 1 P. Goldstein, Copyright, § 2.7.3 (1998). Authors wishing to prevent others' use of their titles must seek redress under the trademark and unfair competition laws, which will be explored in a subsequent chapter.

Should news headlines be deemed copyrightable subject matter under this rule? Note that bloggers and news aggregation web sites often copy headlines as a means of commenting on or referring web site visitors to the articles the headlines identify. What are the policy implications of a ruling that holds news headlines are (or are not) copyrightable?

Product labels that do more than list ingredients or contents sometimes raise originality issues. Would you find the following material, printed on the label of a hair care product, sufficiently original to merit protection?

Hair stays wet-looking as long as you like. Brushes out to full-bodied dry look. WET 4 is one step-four choice (finishing) in Sebastian's four step program for a healthy scalp and head of hair. WET is not oily, won't flake and keeps hair wet-looking for hours, allowing you to sculpture, contour, wave or curl. It stays looking wet until it's brushed out. When brushed, hair looks and feels thicker, extra full. Try brushing partly, leaving some parts wet for a different look.

See Sebastian International, Inc. v. Consumer Contact (PTY) Ltd., 664 F.Supp. 909, 913 (D.N.J.1987), *vacated*, 847 F.2d 1093 (3d Cir.1988).

5. *Automated databases*. Automated databases constitute compilations which may qualify for copyright, subject to the same rules that courts have developed for hard-copy compilations. Are the creators of automated databases likely to face any greater problems in obtaining copyrights and reaping their benefits than hard-copy compilers?

PROBLEMS

1. X Company publishes a used car valuation book that sets forth X Company's projections of the values of "average" versions of used cars to be sold in a particular geographic region during a particular period of time. These predicted values are set forth separately for each automobile make, model number, body style, and engine type. The book also provides predicted value adjustments for various options and for mileage in 5,000 mile increments. The valuation figures given in the book are not historical market prices, quotations, or averages; nor are they derived by mathematical formulas from available statistics. They represent X Company's editors' predictions, based on their professional judgment and a wide range of informational sources. Are the valuations, in and of themselves, facts or protectible expression?

2. X creates a book of trivia questions that she calls the "SAT" (*Seinfeld* Aptitude Test). All the trivia questions in the book are based on the *Seinfeld* television show. X gathered the information from watching the show. The SAT contains 643 trivia questions about the events and characters in the show, drawing from 86 *Seinfeld* episodes. The number of questions devoted to each episode varies from one to twenty. Following are two examples of the questions:

(1.) To impress a woman, George passes himself off as

   (a) a gynecologist

   (b) a geologist

   (c) a marine biologist

   (d) a meteorologist

(2.) What candy does Kramer snack on while observing a surgical procedure from an operating-room balcony?

The producer of the *Seinfeld* television show sues X for copyright infringement. Has X taken copyrightable expression?

3. Southco manufactures a variety of products, including "captive fasteners," which are used to fasten two panels together. "Captive screws" are a type of captive fastener. Each captive screw consists of a "knob" (the component that surrounds the screw head), the screw itself, and a "ferrule" (a component that houses the screw). The captive screw is mounted on the

outer panel by means of the ferrule. The other panel contains an internally threaded insert that receives the screw. Captive screws may differ with respect to composition, screw length, screw diameter, thread size, and finish.

To assist employees and customers in identifying and distinguishing among its captive screws, Southco developed a numbering system under which each particular digit or group of digits signifies a relevant characteristic of the product. For example, in the case of part number 47–10–202–10, the first two digits (47) show that the part falls within a particular class of captive screws. Other digits in the part number indicate characteristics such as thread size, composition of the screw (e.g., aluminum), and finish of the knob (e.g., "knurled").

A person who understands the Southco system can use it in two ways. First, he can determine the characteristics of the particular product from the product number. Second, working in reverse, a person who knows the characteristics of the product needed for a particular job can determine the number of the product with the desired characteristics. Southco includes its product numbers in handbooks that it publishes each year.

Kanebridge competes with Southco. It has reproduced Southco's part numbers in comparison charts that demonstrate the Kanbridge part number that corresponded to each of the Southco part numbers, making it clear that the two companies' parts are interchangeable. Kanbridge provides the comparison charts to prospective customers and uses them in advertising. Kanebridge argues that the ability to cross-reference Southco part numbers in an honest, accurate and comparative manner is necessary in order for it to compete for business.

Southco alleges that Kanbridge's actions constitute copyright infringement. Does Southco have a protectable interest?

4. Roulo's *Feeling Sensitive* line of greeting cards features beige, single-face cards containing sentimental verses written in cursive style in brown ink. The verses often contain ellipses (...). The verse is bordered on each side by a series of four stripes in silver foil, brown, and an additional color.

Berrie's cards employ similar types of sentimental verses (complete with ellipses), but not the same verses. The cards are the same size and shape as plaintiff's and are printed on cream-colored paper. The verses are written in cursive style in brown ink, and are flanked by two colored stripes on one side, and one colored stripe on the other. The parties' respective cards are illustrated below.

Roulo wants to sue Berrie for copyright infringement. Has Berrie appropriated any copyrightable subject matter from Roulo?

(Roulo card)

(Berrie card)

1. Originality in Derivative Works

§ 101. Definitions

* * *

A "derivative work" is a work based upon one or more preexisting works, such as a translation, musical arrangement, dramatization, fictionalization, motion picture version, sound recording, art reproduction, abridgment, condensation, or any other form in which a work may be recast, transformed, or adapted. A work consisting of editorial revisions, annotations, elaborations, or other modifications which, as a whole, represent an original work of authorship, is a "derivative work."

17 U.S.C.A. § 101.

SCHROCK v. LEARNING CURVE INTERNATIONAL, INC.

United States Court of Appeals for the Seventh Circuit, 2009.
586 F.3d 513.

SYKES, CIRCUIT JUDGE.

HIT Entertainment ("HIT") owns the copyright to the popular "Thomas & Friends" train characters, and it licensed Learning Curve International ("Learning Curve") to make toy figures of its characters. Learning Curve in turn hired Daniel Schrock, a professional photographer, to take pictures of the toys for promotional materials. Learning Curve used Schrock's services on a regular basis for about four years and thereafter continued to use some of his photographs in its advertising and on product packaging. After Learning Curve stopped giving him work, Schrock registered his photos for copyright protection and sued Learning Curve and HIT for infringement.

The district court granted summary judgment for the defendants, holding that Schrock has no copyright in the photos. The court classified the photos as "derivative works" under the Copyright Act—derivative, that is, of the "Thomas & Friends" characters, for which HIT owns the copyright—and held that Schrock needed permission from Learning Curve (HIT's licensee) not only to make the photographs but also to copyright them. Because Schrock had permission to make but not permission to copyright the photos, the court dismissed his claim for copyright infringement.

We reverse. We assume for purposes of this decision that the district court correctly classified Schrock's photographs as derivative works. It does not follow, however, that Schrock needed authorization from Learning Curve to copyright the photos. As long as he was authorized to make the photos (he was), he owned the copyright in the photos to the extent of their incremental original expression. In requiring permission to make and permission to copyright the photos, the district court relied on language in Gracen v. Bradford Exchange, 698 F.2d 300 (7th Cir.1983), suggesting that both are required for copyright in a derivative work. We have more recently explained, however, that copyright in a derivative work arises by operation of law—not through authority from the owner of the copyright in the underlying work—although the parties may alter this default rule by agreement. Schrock created the photos with permission and therefore owned the copyright to the photos provided they satisfied the other requirements for copyright and the parties did not contract around the default rule.

We also take this opportunity to clarify another aspect of Gracen that is prone to misapplication. Gracen said that "a derivative work must be substantially different from the underlying work to be copyrightable." This statement should not be understood to require a heightened standard of originality for copyright in a derivative work. We have more recently explained that "the only 'originality' required for [a] new work to be copyrightable ... is enough expressive variation from public-domain or other existing works to enable the new work to be readily distinguished from its predecessors." Bucklew v. Hawkins, Ash, Baptie & Co., LLP, 329 F.3d 923, 929 (7th Cir.2003). Here, Schrock's photos of Learning Curve's "Thomas & Friends" toys possessed sufficient incremental original expression to qualify for copyright.

But the record doesn't tell us enough about the agreements between the parties for us to determine whether they agreed to alter the default rule regarding copyright or whether Learning Curve had an implied license to continue to use Schrock's photos. * * *

I. Background

HIT is the owner of the copyright in the "Thomas & Friends" properties, and Learning Curve is a producer and distributor of children's toys. HIT and Learning Curve entered into a licensing agreement granting Learning Curve a license to create and market toys based on HIT's characters. * * *

In 1999 Learning Curve retained Daniel Schrock to take product photographs of its toys, including those based on HIT's characters, for use in promotional materials. On numerous occasions during the next four years, Schrock photographed several lines of Learning Curve's toys, including many of the "Thomas & Friends" toy trains, related figures, and train-set accessories. (We have attached two of the photos as examples, although they are extremely poor copies because the originals are in color.)[Learning Curve paid Schrock more than $400,000 for his work.]

Learning Curve stopped using Schrock's photography services in mid–2003 but continued to use some of his photos in its printed advertising, on packaging, and on the internet. In 2004 Schrock registered his photos for copyright protection and sued HIT and Learning Curve for infringement. [The district court granted summary judgement for the defendants.]

    * * *

II. Discussion

Schrock argues that the district judge mistakenly classified his photos as derivative works and misread or misapplied *Gracen*. He contends that his photos are not derivative works, and even if they are, his copyright is valid and enforceable because he had permission from Learning Curve to photograph the underlying copyrighted works and his photos contained sufficient incremental original expression to qualify for copyright. HIT and Learning Curve defend the district court's determination that the photos are derivative works and argue that the court properly read *Gracen* to require permission to copyright as well as permission to make the derivative works. Alternatively, they maintain that Schrock's photographs contain insufficient originality to be copyrightable and that copyright protection is barred under the scènes à faire or merger doctrines. Finally, the defendants ask us to affirm on the independent ground that Schrock orally granted them an unlimited license to use his works.

As a general matter, a plaintiff asserting copyright infringement must prove: "(1) ownership of a valid copyright, and (2) copying of constituent elements of the work that are original." Feist Publ'ns, Inc. v. Rural Tel. Serv. Co., 499 U.S. 340, 361, 111 S.Ct. 1282, 113 L.Ed.2d 358 (1991). There is no dispute here about copying; Learning Curve used Schrock's photos in its promotional materials. The focus instead is on the validity of Schrock's asserted copyright in the photos. * * * In this circuit, copyrightability is an issue of law for the court.

Much of the briefing on appeal—and most of the district court's analysis—concerned the classification of the photos as derivative works. A "derivative work" is:

> [A] work based upon one or more preexisting works, such as a translation, musical arrangement, dramatization, fictionalization, motion picture version, sound recording, art reproduction, abridgment, condensation, or any other form in which a work may be recast, transformed, or adapted. A work consisting of editorial revisions, annotations, elaborations, or other modifications which, as a whole, represent an original work of authorship, is a "derivative work".

17 U.S.C. § 101. The Copyright Act specifically grants the author of a derivative work copyright protection in the incremental original expression he contributes as long as the derivative work does not infringe the underlying work. See id. § 103(a), (b). The copyright in a derivative work, however, "extends only to the material contributed by the author of such work, as distinguished from the preexisting material employed in the work." 17 U.S.C. § 103(b).

A. Photographs as Derivative Works

Whether photographs of a copyrighted work are derivative works is the subject of deep disagreement among courts and commentators alike. The district court held that Schrock's photos came within the definition of derivative works because they "recast, transformed, or adapted" the three-dimensional toys into a different, two-dimensional medium. For this conclusion the judge relied in part on language in *Gracen* and in the Ninth Circuit's decision in Ets–Hokin v. Skyy Spirits, Inc., 225 F.3d 1068 (9th Cir.2000), recognizing, however, that neither decision directly decided the matter. * * *

* * *

We need not resolve the issue definitively here. The classification of Schrock's photos as derivative works does not affect the applicable legal standard for determining copyrightability, although as we have noted, it does determine the scope of copyright protection. Accordingly, we will assume without deciding that each of Schrock's photos qualifies as a derivative work within the meaning of the Copyright Act.

B. Originality and Derivative Works

As a constitutional and statutory matter, "[t]he sine qua non of copyright is originality." *Feist Publ'ns, Inc.*, 499 U.S. at 345, 111 S.Ct. 1282. Originality in this context "means only that the work was independently created by the author ... and that it possesses at least some minimal degree of creativity." The Supreme Court emphasized in *Feist* that "the requisite level of creativity is extremely low; even a slight amount will suffice." The Court also explained that "[o]riginality does not signify novelty; a work may be original even though it closely resembles other works." *Id.* What is required is "independent creation plus a modicum of creativity."

Federal courts have historically applied a generous standard of originality in evaluating photographic works for copyright protection. In some cases, the original expression may be found in the staging and creation of the scene depicted in the photograph. But in many cases, the photographer does not invent the scene or create the subject matter depicted in it. Rather, the original expression he contributes lies in the rendition of the subject matter—that is, the effect created by the combination of his choices of perspective, angle, lighting, shading, focus, lens, and so on. * * * Most photographs contain at least some originality in their rendition * * *, except perhaps for a very limited class of photographs that can be characterized as "slavish copies" of an underlying work, Bridgeman Art Library, Ltd. v. Corel Corp., 25 F.Supp.2d 421, 427 (S.D.N.Y.1998) (finding no originality in transparencies of paintings where the goal was to reproduce those works exactly and thus to minimize or eliminate any individual expression).

Our review of Schrock's photographs convinces us that they do not fall into the narrow category of photographs that can be classified as "slavish copies," lacking any independently created expression. To be sure, the photographs are accurate depictions of the three-dimensional "Thomas & Friends" toys, but Schrock's artistic and technical choices combine to create a two-dimensional image that is subtly but nonetheless sufficiently his own.[3] This is confirmed by Schrock's deposition testimony describing his creative process in depicting the toys. Schrock explained how he used various camera and lighting techniques to make the toys look more "life like," "personable," and "friendly." He explained how he tried to give the toys "a little bit of dimension" and that it was his goal to make the toys "a little bit better than what they look like when you actually see them on the shelf." The original expression in the representative sample is not particularly great (it was not meant to be), but it is enough under the applicable standard to warrant the limited copyright protection accorded derivative works under § 103(b).

Aside from arguing that the works fail under the generally accepted test for originality, Learning Curve and HIT offer two additional reasons why we should conclude that Schrock's photographs are not original. First, they claim that the photos are intended to serve the "purely utilitarian function" of identifying products for consumers. The purpose of the photographs, however, is irrelevant. See Bleistein v. Donaldson Lithographing Co., 188 U.S. 239, 251–52, 23 S.Ct. 298, 47 L.Ed. 460 (1903) * * *.

The defendants' second and more substantial argument is that it is not enough that Schrock's photographs might pass the ordinary test for originality; they claim that as derivative works, the photos are subject to a higher standard of originality. A leading copyright commentator disagrees. The Nimmer treatise maintains that the quantum of originality required for copyright in a derivative work is the same as that required for copyright in any other work. More particularly, Nimmer says the relevant standard is whether a derivative work contains a "nontrivial" variation from the preexisting work "sufficient to render the derivative work distinguishable from [the] prior work in any meaningful manner." The caselaw generally follows this formulation. See, e.g., Eden Toys, Inc. v. Florelee Undergarment Co., 697 F.2d 27, 34–35 (2d Cir.1982) (holding that numerous minor changes in an illustration of Paddington Bear were

---

3. We note, however, that a mere shift in medium, without more, is generally insufficient to satisfy the requirement of originality for copyright in a derivative work. * * *

sufficiently nontrivial because they combined to give Paddington a "different, cleaner 'look' ''").

Learning Curve and HIT argue that our decision in *Gracen* established a more demanding standard of originality for derivative works. *Gracen* involved an artistic competition in which artists were invited to submit paintings of the character Dorothy from the Metro–Goldwyn–Mayer ("MGM") movie The Wizard of Oz. Participating artists were given a still photograph of Dorothy from the film as an exemplar, and the paintings were solicited and submitted with the understanding that the best painting would be chosen for a series of collector's plates. Plaintiff Gracen prevailed in the competition, but she refused to sign the contract allowing her painting to be used in the collector's plates. The competition sponsor commissioned another artist to create a similar plate, and Gracen sued the sponsor, MGM, and the artist for copyright infringement. We held that Gracen could not maintain her infringement suit because her painting, a derivative work, was not "substantially different from the underlying work to be copyrightable."

Gracen drew this language from an influential Second Circuit decision, L. Batlin & Son, Inc. v. Snyder, 536 F.2d 486 (2d Cir.1976). Read in context, however, the cited language from *L. Batlin* did not suggest that a heightened standard of originality applies to derivative works.[4] To the contrary, the Second Circuit said only that to be copyrightable a work must " 'contain some substantial, not merely trivial originality.' " The court explained that for derivative works, as for any other work, "[t]he test of originality is concededly one with a low threshold in that all that is needed is that the author contributed something more than a merely trivial variation, something recognizably his own."

The concern expressed in *Gracen* was that a derivative work could be so similar in appearance to the underlying work that in a subsequent infringement suit brought by a derivative author, it would be difficult to separate the original elements of expression in the derivative and underlying works in order to determine whether one derivative work infringed another. The opinion offered the example of artists A and B who both painted their versions of the Mona Lisa, a painting in the public domain. "[I]f the difference between the original and A's reproduction is slight, the difference between A's and B's reproductions will also be slight, so that if B had access to A's reproductions the trier of fact will be hard-pressed to decide whether B was copying A or copying the Mona Lisa itself."

No doubt this concern is valid. But nothing in the Copyright Act suggests that derivative works are subject to a more exacting originality requirement than other works of authorship. Indeed, we have explained since *Gracen* that "the only 'originality' required for [a] new work to be copyrightable ... is enough expressive variation from public-domain or

---

4. To the extent that *Gracen's* reading of *L. Batlin* and its "substantial difference" language can be understood as establishing a more demanding standard of originality for derivative works, it has received mixed reviews. Some commentators have suggested that *Gracen* may have inappropriately narrowed the copyrightability of derivative works without a statutory basis. * * *

other existing works to enable the new work to be readily distinguished from its predecessors." *Bucklew*, 329 F.3d at 929. We emphasized in *Bucklew* that this standard does not require a "high degree of [incremental] originality."

We think *Gracen* must be read in light of *L. Batlin*, on which it relied, and *Bucklew*, which followed it. And doing so reveals the following general principles: (1) the originality requirement for derivative works is not more demanding than the originality requirement for other works; and (2) the key inquiry is whether there is sufficient nontrivial expressive variation in the derivative work to make it distinguishable from the underlying work in some meaningful way. This focus on the presence of nontrivial "distinguishable variation" adequately captures the concerns articulated in *Gracen* without unduly narrowing the copyrightability of derivative works. It is worth repeating that the copyright in a derivative work is thin, extending only to the incremental original expression contributed by the author of the derivative work.

As applied to photographs, we have already explained that the original expression in a photograph generally subsists in its rendition of the subject matter. If the photographer's rendition of a copyrighted work varies enough from the underlying work to enable the photograph to be distinguished from the underlying work (aside from the obvious shift from three dimensions to two), then the photograph contains sufficient incremental originality to qualify for copyright. Schrock's photos of the "Thomas & Friends" toys are highly accurate product photos but contain minimally sufficient variation in angle, perspective, lighting, and dimension to be distinguishable from the underlying works; they are not "slavish copies." Accordingly, the photos qualify for the limited derivative-work copyright provided by § 103(b).[5] See *SHL Imaging*, 117 F.Supp.2d at 311 (holding that copyright protection in product-accurate photographs was "thin") * * *. However narrow that copyright might be, it at least protects against the kind of outright copying that occurred here.

---

5. Learning Curve and HIT argue in the alternative that Schrock's photos fall within the scènes à faire [doctrine] and therefore are not copyrightable. The doctrine of scènes à faire (French for "scenes for action") prohibits copyright protection in elements or themes that are "so rudimentary, commonplace, standard, or unavoidable that they do not serve to distinguish one work within a class of works from another." Bucklew, 329 F.3d at 929. * * * The defendants' argument seems to be that because images of its "Thomas & Friends" toys will be common to all product photos of the toys, no product photos can be copyrighted. If this were true, then no derivative work would be copyrightable; by definition, derivative works incorporate the underlying work in some way. In any event, as we explained in Bucklew,

"[e]very expressive work can be decomposed into elements not themselves copyrightable—the cars in a car chase, the kiss in a love scene, the dive bombers in a movie about Pearl Harbor, or for that matter the letters of the alphabet in any written work. The presence of such [common] elements obviously does not forfeit copyright protection of the work as a whole, but infringement cannot be found on the basis of such elements alone; it is the combination of elements, or particular novel twists given to them, that supply the minimal originality required for copyright protection."

329 F.3d at 929. Schrock's contribution of the photographic elements of lighting, angle, perspective, and the like supply the "minimal originality" required for copyright in the photos. * * *

C. Authorization and Derivative Works

To be copyrightable, a derivative work must not be infringing. The owner of the copyright in the underlying work has the exclusive right to "prepare derivative works based upon the copyrighted work," 17 U.S.C. § 106(2), and "it is a copyright infringement to make or sell a derivative work without a license from the owner of the copyright on the work from which the derivative work is derived." This means the author of a derivative work must have permission to make the work from the owner of the copyright in the underlying work; *Gracen* suggested, however, that the author of a derivative work must also have permission to copyright it. * * * The district court relied on this language from *Gracen* to conclude that Schrock has no copyright in his photos because he was not authorized by Learning Curve to copyright them. This was error.

First, *Gracen's* language presupposing a permission-to-copyright requirement was dicta; the case was actually decided on nonoriginality grounds. More importantly, the dicta was mistaken; there is nothing in the Copyright Act requiring the author of a derivative work to obtain permission to copyright his work from the owner of the copyright in the underlying work. To the contrary, the Act provides that copyright in a derivative work, like copyright in any other work, arises by operation of law once the author's original expression is fixed in a tangible medium. * * *

    * * *

[B]ecause the owner of a copyrighted work has the exclusive right to control the preparation of derivative works, the owner could limit the derivative-work author's intellectual-property rights in the contract, license, or agreement that authorized the production of the derivative work. * * * [A]lthough the right to claim copyright in a derivative work arises by operation of law—not by permission of the underlying copyright owner—the parties may alter this general rule by agreement. * * *

    * * *

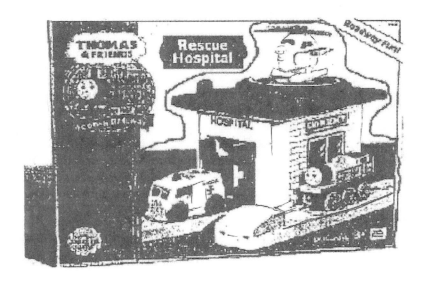

Circled Photo by Dan Schrock Photography
Rescue Hospital   2002

NOTES AND QUESTIONS

1. *The "distinguishable variation" requirement.* What is the purpose of the "distinguishable variation" requirement? Is the requirement a part of the originality requirement, or is it a separate and independent requirement?

In *Schrock,* was it really unnecessary for the court to decide whether photographs of copyrightable subject matter are derivative works of the underlying subject matter or independent works? If an artist sets up her easel in a public park and paints a highly realistic depiction of what she sees, will copyright in the painting be conditioned on the existence of a "distinguishable variation" from the subject matter? Should it?

The *Schrock* court says that a mere change of medium is insufficient to qualify a work for copyright protection. It also finds that there is a "distinguishable variation" between Schrock's photographs and the toys he photographed, so that the photographs qualify for copyright. What is the distinguishable variation? In your opinion, is the variation sufficient to avoid the concerns about harassing litigation expressed in *Gracen*?

Compare *Schrock* with the Ninth Circuit's decision in Entertainment Research Group, Inc. v. Genesis Creative Group, Inc., 122 F.3d 1211 (9th Cir.1997), *cert. denied*, 523 U.S. 1021, 118 S.Ct. 1302, 140 L.Ed.2d 468 (1998). In that case the Ninth Circuit adopted a "two-prong" test for determining whether a derivative work could be copyrighted. First, the derivative work must have original aspects that are "more than trivial." Second, it must appear that granting copyright in the derivative work will not affect the copyright protection in the underlying work.

The derivative works at issue in *Entertainment Research Group* were inflatable three-dimensional costumes, based on the copyrighted two-dimensional cartoon character mascots of various businesses, such as the Pillsbury Dough Boy and the Toys 'R' Us Giraffe. The Ninth Circuit found that these costumes (which were designed by ERG) did not contain a "more than trivial" variation from the original cartoon characters under the first prong of its test. Most of the differences were dictated by functional considerations, and thus could not be protected due to the separability requirement for pictorial, graphic and sculptural features of useful articles. (See pages 483–493, *infra*.) The one truly "artistic" variation the plaintiff could demonstrate was the facial expressions on the costumes. The court deemed this difference insufficient, explaining:

> [B]ecause ERG's costumes are "instantly identifiable as embodiments" of the underlying copyrighted characters in "yet another form," no reasonable juror could conclude that there are any "non-trivial" artistic differences between the underlying cartoon characters and the immediately recognizable costumes that ERG has designed and manufactured.

122 F.3d at 1223.

Moreover, the costumes did not satisfy the second prong of the Ninth Circuit's test because, if the plaintiff obtained a derivative copyright in its costumes, the owners of copyright in the original cartoon characters would be hampered in their ability to exploit their copyrights:

> Given the fact that ERG's costumes are so similar to the well-known copyrighted characters that they are based upon, the district court was correct to conclude that granting ERG a copyright in its costumes would have the practical effect of providing ERG with a *de facto* monopoly on all inflatable costumes depicting the copyrighted characters also in ERG's costumes. Indeed, if ERG had copyrights for its costumes, any future licensee who was hired to manufacture costumes depicting these characters would likely face a strong copyright infringement suit from ERG.

122 F.3d at 1224. Given that a derivative work maker must obtain a license from the owner of copyright in the underlying work in order to avoid infringement liability, is the court's concern about affecting the copyright protection in the underlying work a valid one? Can't the parties reach their own contractual arrangements regarding copyright?

C. PROTECTION OF EXPRESSION vs. IDEA

BAKER v. SELDEN

United States Supreme Court, 1879.
101 U.S. (11 Otto) 99, 25 L.Ed. 841.

MR. JUSTICE BRADLEY delivered the opinion of the court.

Charles Selden, the testator of the complainant in this case, in the year 1859 took the requisite steps for obtaining the copyright of a book, entitled "Selden's Condensed Ledger, or Book-keeping Simplified," the object of which was to exhibit and explain a peculiar system of book-keeping. In 1860 and 1861, he took the copyright of several other books, containing additions to and improvements upon the said system. The bill of complaint was filed against the defendant, Baker, for an alleged infringement of these copyrights. * * *

* * *

The book or series of books of which the complainant claims the copyright consists of an introductory essay explaining the system of book-keeping referred to, to which are annexed certain forms or banks, consisting of ruled lines, and headings, illustrating the system and showing how it is to be used and carried out in practice. This system effects the same results as book-keeping by double entry; but, by a peculiar arrangement of columns and headings, presents the entire operation, of a day, a week, or a month, on a single page, or on two pages facing each other, in an account-book. The defendant uses a similar plan so far as results are concerned; but makes a different arrangement of the columns, and uses different headings. If the complainant's testator had the exclusive right to the use of the system explained in his book, it would be difficult to contend that the defendant does not infringe it, notwithstanding the difference in his form of arrangement; but if it be assumed that the system is open to public use, it seems to be equally difficult to contend that the books made and sold by the defendant are a violation of the copyright of the complainant's book considered merely as a book explanatory of the system. Where the truths of a science or the methods of an art are the common property of the whole world, any author has the right to express the one, or explain and use the other, in his own way. As an author, Selden explained the system in a particular way. It may be conceded that Baker makes and uses account-books arranged on substantially the same system; but the proof fails to show that he has violated the copyright of Selden's book, regarding the latter merely as an explanatory work; or that he has infringed Selden's right in any way, unless the latter became entitled to an exclusive right in the system.

The evidence of the complainant is principally directed to the object of showing that Baker uses the same system as that which is explained and illustrated in Selden's books. It becomes important, therefore, to determine whether, in obtaining the copyright of his books, he secured the exclusive right to the use of the system or method of book-keeping which the said books are intended to illustrate and explain. It is contended that he has secured such exclusive right, because no one can use the system without using substantially the same ruled lines and headings which he was appended to his books in illustration of it. In other words, it is contended that the ruled lines and headings, given to illustrate the system, are a part of the book, and, as such, are secured by the copyright; and that no one can make or use similar ruled lines and headings, or ruled lines and headings made and arranged on substantially the same system, without violating the copyright. And this is really the question to be decided in this case. Stated in another form, the question is, whether the exclusive property in a system of book-keeping can be claimed, under the law of copyright, by means of a book in which that system is explained? The complainant's bill, and the case made under it, are based on the hypothesis that it can be.

* * *

There is no doubt that a work on the subject of book-keeping, though only explanatory of well-known systems, may be the subject of a copyright; but, then, it is claimed only as a book. Such a book may be explanatory either of old systems, or of an entirely new system; and, considered as a book, as the work of an author, conveying information on the subject of book-keeping, and containing detailed explanations of the art, it may be a very valuable acquisition to the practical knowledge of the community. But there is a clear distinction between the book, as such, and the art which it is intended to illustrate. The mere statement of the proposition is so evident, that it requires hardly any argument to support it. The same distinction may be predicated of every other art as well as that of book-keeping. A treatise on the composition and use of medicines, be they old or new; on the construction and use of ploughs, or watches, or churns; or on the mixture and application of colors for painting or dyeing; or on the mode of drawing lines to produce the effect of perspective,—would be the subject of copyright; but no one would contend that the copyright of the treatise would give the exclusive right to the art or manufacture described therein. The copyright of the book, if not pirated from other works, would be valid without regard to the novelty, or want of novelty, of its subject-matter. The novelty of the art or thing described or explained has nothing to do with the validity of the copyright. To give to the author of the book an exclusive property in the art described therein, when no examination of its novelty has ever been officially made, would be a surprise and a fraud upon the public. That is the province of letters-patent, not of copyright. The claim to an invention or discovery of an art or manufacture must be subjected to the examination of the Patent Office before an exclusive right therein can be obtained; and it can only be secured by a patent from the government.

* * *

The copyright of a book on perspective, no matter how many drawings and illustrations it may contain, gives no exclusive right to the modes of drawing described, though they may never have been known or used before. By publishing the book, without getting a patent for the art, the latter is given to the public. The fact that the art described in the book by illustrations of lines and figures which are reproduced in practice in the application of the art, makes no difference. Those illustrations are the mere language employed by the author to convey his ideas more clearly. Had he used words of description instead of diagrams (which merely stand in the place of words), there could not be the slightest doubt that others, applying the art to practical use, might lawfully draw the lines and diagrams which were in the author's mind, and which he thus described by words in his book.

The copyright of a work on mathematical science cannot give to the author an exclusive right to the methods of operation which he propounds, or to the diagrams which he employs to explain them, so as to prevent an engineer from using them whenever occasion requires. The very object of publishing a book on science or the useful arts is to communicate to the world the useful knowledge which it contains. But this object would be frustrated if the knowledge could not be used without incurring the guilt of piracy of the book. And where the art it teaches cannot be used without employing the methods and diagrams used to illustrate the book, or such as are similar to them, such methods and diagrams are to be considered as necessary incidents to the art, and given therewith to the public; not given for the purpose of publication in other works explanatory of the art, but for the purpose of practical application.

Of course, these observations are not intended to apply to ornamental designs, or pictorial illustrations addressed to the taste. Of these it may be said, that their form is their essence, and their object, the production of pleasure in their contemplation. This is their final end. They are as much the product of genius and the result of composition, as are the lines of the poet or the historian's period. On the other hand, the teachings of science and the rules and methods of useful art have their final end in application and use; and this application and use are what the public derive from the publication of a book which teaches them. But as embodied and taught in a literary composition or book, their essence consists only in their statement. This alone is what is secured by the copyright. The use by another of the same methods of statement, whether in words or illustrations, in a book published for teaching the art, would undoubtedly be an infringement of the copyright.

Recurring to the case before us, we observe that Charles Selden, by his books, explained and described a peculiar system of book-keeping, and illustrated his method by means of ruled lines and blank columns, with proper headings on a page, or on successive pages. Now, whilst no one has a right to print or publish his book, or any material part thereof, as a book intended to convey instruction in the art, any person may practice and use the art itself which he has described and illustrated therein. The use of the art is a totally different thing from a publication of the book explaining it. The copyright of a book on book-keeping cannot secure the exclusive right to make, sell, and use account-books prepared upon the plan set forth in such book. Whether the art might or might not have been patented, is a question which is not before us. It was not patented, and is open and free to the use of the public. And, of course, in using the art, the ruled lines and headings of accounts must necessarily be used as incident to it.

The plausibility of the claim put forward by the complainant in this case arises from a confusion of ideas produced by the peculiar nature of the art described in the books which have been made the subject of copyright. In describing the art, the illustrations and diagrams employed happen to correspond more closely than usual with the actual work performed by the operator who uses the art. Those illustrations and diagrams consist of ruled lines and headings of accounts; and it is similar ruled lines and headings of accounts which, in the application of the art, the book-keeper makes with his pen, or the stationer with his press; whilst in most other cases the diagrams and illustrations can only be represented in concrete forms of wood, metal, stone, or some other physical embodiment. But the principle is the same in all. The description of the art in a book, though entitled to the benefit of copyright, lays no foundation for an exclusive claim to the art itself. The object of the one is explanation; the object of the other is use. The former may be secured by copyright. The latter can only be secured, if it can be secured at all, by letters-patent.

* * *

The conclusion to which we have come is, that blank account-books are not the subject of copyright; and that the mere copyright of Selden's book did not confer upon him the exclusive right to make and use account-books, ruled and arranged as designated by him and described and illustrated in said book.

* * *

Selden's Form

NOTES AND QUESTIONS

1. *The* Baker *decision.* How would you characterize the Supreme Court's holding in *Baker*? Which (if any) of the following accurately describes the Court's reasoning?

1) The Court found that the accounting forms did not constitute copyrightable expression because they lacked originality or creativity;

2) The Court found that the forms were not copyrightable expression, but rather were utilitarian objects outside the protection of the copyright laws;

3) The Court found that regardless of whether the forms constituted copyrightable expression, the defendant did not copy that expression—he only copied the underlying idea or accounting system, which was not protected by copyright;

4) The Court assumed that the forms constituted copyrightable expression, and that the defendant copied that expression, but found that the copying did not infringe because it was done for the purpose of using the accounting system, rather than for purposes of explaining the accounting system;

5) The Court found that, regardless of whether forms are copyrightable as a general matter, no copyright in the forms could be enforced in this case because the forms constituted the only means by which the underlying idea or accounting system could be implemented or expressed. Enforcing the copyright would give the plaintiff a *de facto* monopoly in the accounting system.

What are the implications of each interpretation? If alternative 5 is accurate, was there in fact only one way to implement or express the accounting system? Are there likely to be many instances in which there is only one way to implement or express an idea?

2. *The "blank form" rule.* The Copyright Office has adopted the following rule:

> The following are examples of works not subject to copyright and applications for registration of such works cannot be entertained:
>
> * * *
>
> (c) Blank forms, such as time cards, graph paper, account books, diaries, bank checks, scorecards, address books, report forms, order forms and the like, which are designed for recording information and do not in themselves convey information. * * *

37 C.F.R. § 202.1(c) (2000). The rule, which is consistent with modern case law, is frequently attributed to the *Baker* decision. What in *Baker* compels or supports such a rule? Is there any alternative basis for the rule? Are blank forms unprotectible because they lack authorship (are insufficiently original), or because they constitute embodiments of systems for collecting and organizing information?

In implementing this rule, how does one determine whether a form conveys or merely records information? Presumably, a form that contains lengthy, complex instructions for its use and completion conveys information. See, e.g., Edwin K. Williams & Co. v. Edwin K. Williams, 542 F.2d 1053 (9th Cir.1976), *cert. denied*, 433 U.S. 908, 97 S.Ct. 2973, 53 L.Ed.2d 1092 (1977) (account books with several pages of instructions on the use of the forms and advice on the successful management of a service station conveyed information and were therefore copyrightable). Assume that a form provides no significant instructions. Might the manner in which information is solicited in itself convey information? For example, might the questions asked convey information about what is deemed relevant or important? If so, should that finding be sufficient to take the form out of the rule against copyrightability of blank forms? Compare Bibbero Systems, Inc. v. Colwell Systems, Inc., 893 F.2d 1104 (9th Cir.1990), with Kregos v. Associated Press, 937 F.2d 700 (2d Cir.1991).

MORRISSEY v. THE PROCTER & GAMBLE CO.

United States Court of Appeals for the First Circuit, 1967.
379 F.2d 675.

ALDRICH, CHIEF JUDGE.

This is an appeal from a summary judgment for the defendant. The plaintiff, Morrissey, is the copyright owner of a set of rules for a sales promotional contest of the "sweepstakes" type involving the social security numbers of the participants. Plaintiff alleges that the defendant, Procter & Gamble Company, infringed, by copying, almost precisely, Rule 1. In its motion for summary judgment, based upon affidavits and depositions, defendant denies that plaintiff's Rule 1 is copyrightable material * * *. The district court held for the defendant * * *.

* * *

[W]e recite plaintiff's Rule 1, and defendant's Rule 1, the italicizing in the latter being ours to note the defendant's variations or changes.

> "1. Entrants should print name, address and social security number on a boxtop, or a plain paper. Entries must be accompanied by * * * boxtop or by plain paper on which the name * * * is copied from any source. Official rules are explained on * * * packages or leaflets obtained from dealer. If you do not have a social security number you may use the name and number of any member of your immediate family living with you. Only the person named on the entry will be deemed an entrant and may qualify for prize.

> "Use the correct social security number belonging to the person named on entry * * * wrong number will be disqualified."

(Plaintiff's Rule)

> "1. Entrants should print name, address and Social Security number on a Tide boxtop, or *on* [a] plain paper. Entries must be accompanied by Tide boxtop (*any size*) or by plain paper on which the name 'Tide' is copied from any source. Official rules are *available* on Tide Sweepstakes packages, or *on* leaflets *at* Tide dealers, *or you can send a stamped, self-addressed envelope to*: Tide 'Shopping Fling' Sweepstakes, P.O. Box 4459, Chicago 77, Illinois.

> "If you do not have a Social Security number, you may use the name and number of any member of your immediate family living with you. Only the person named on *the* entry will be deemed an entrant and may qualify for a prize.

"Use the correct Social Security number, belonging to the person named on the entry—wrong numbers will be disqualified."

(Defendant's Rule)

The district court * * * took the position that since the substance of the contest was not copyrightable, which is unquestionably correct, *Baker v. Selden*, 1879, 101 U.S. 99, 25 L.Ed. 841, and the substance was relatively simple, it must follow that plaintiff's rule sprung directly from the substance and "contains no original creative authorship." 262 F.Supp. at 738. This does not follow. Copyright attaches to form of expression, and defendant's own proof, introduced to deluge the court on the issue of access, itself established that there was more than one way of expressing even this simple substance. Nor, in view of the almost precise similarity of the two rules, could defendant successfully invoke the principle of a stringent standard for showing infringement which some courts apply when the subject matter involved admits of little variation in form of expression.

Nonetheless, we must hold for the defendant. When the uncopyrightable subject matter is very narrow, so that "the topic necessarily requires," *Sampson & Murdock Co. v. Seaver–Radford Co.*, 1 Cir., 1905, 140 F. 539, 541, if not only one form of expression, at best only a limited number, to permit copyrighting would mean that a party or parties, by copyrighting a mere handful of forms, could exhaust all possibilities of future use of the substance. In such circumstances it does not seem accurate to say that any particular form of expression comes from the subject matter. However, it is necessary to say that the subject matter would be appropriated by permitting the copyrighting of its expression. We cannot recognize copyright as a game of chess in which the public can be checkmated.

Upon examination the matters embraced in Rule 1 are so straightforward and simple that we find this limiting principle to be applicable. Furthermore, its operation need not await an attempt to copyright all possible forms. It cannot be only the last form of expression which is to be condemned, as completing defendant's exclusion from the substance. Rather, in these circumstances, we hold that copyright does not extend to the subject matter at all, and plaintiff cannot complain even if his particular expression was deliberately adopted.

NOTES AND QUESTIONS

1. *The merger doctrine.* A direct outgrowth of the idea/expression dichotomy, the merger doctrine tells us that when there is only one or a limited number of ways to express an idea, the expression "merges" with the idea and becomes unprotectible. The issue of merger often arises in cases such as *Morrissey*, involving straightforward, highly utilitarian or functional works.

In determining the range of alternatives, should one count all conceivable means of expressing the idea? In Matthew Bender & Co., Inc. v. Kluwer Law

Book Publishers, Inc., 672 F.Supp. 107 (S.D.N.Y.1987), the plaintiff published a work documenting the range of personal injury recoveries. The plaintiff organized its illustrative cases according to the body part injured and arranged the body-part categories alphabetically. Within each body-part category plaintiff subdivided the cases according to type and amount of recovery, and by jurisdiction. For each reported case the plaintiff provided information in six categories: "Amount;" "Case;" "Plaintiff;" "Event;" "Injury;" and "Relevant Data."

In an infringement suit against a defendant who used a similar organization and format, the court found the plaintiff's organization and format uncopyrightable on the basis of the merger and the blank form doctrines. With regard to the merger issue, the court observed:

> In this case, the "idea" embodied in Bender's work is to provide attorneys working on a medical malpractice case with a useful guide, in chart form, outlining the results achieved in prior similar cases. The expression of this "idea," it seems, can be achieved in a variety of ways by organizing the charts differently. * * *

> While in theory there are numerous ways to place this information in chart form, from a practical point of view the number of ways to organize this information in a useful and accessible manner is limited. It would make little sense, for example, to arrange the information by listing all of the cases alphabetically or chronologically, or by organizing the cases according to the names of the attorneys listed alphabetically. These arrangements, while possible, would be of little value to a practitioner seeking relevant information.

Id., 672 F.Supp. at 110.

How many practical, effective ways are there to express the idea underlying the sweepstakes rule in *Morrissey*? Would your answer depend upon the range of variations that would infringe the copyright on the plaintiff's rule? Clearly, if loose paraphrasing infringes, there will be fewer alternative methods of expressing the idea than if only close, nearly *verbatim* copying infringes, and a defendant's use of words or phrases commonly used in connection with the concept at issue is overlooked. Some courts, in situations like *Morrissey*, prefer to find a "thin copyright," rather than a merger. While a merger may deny the plaintiff copyright protection altogether, finding an enforceable, but thin copyright entitles the plaintiff to protection against close copying only—permitting closer versions than might be permitted under other circumstances. For example, in Continental Casualty Co. v. Beardsley, 253 F.2d 702 (2d Cir.1958), *cert. denied*, 358 U.S. 816, 79 S.Ct. 25, 3 L.Ed.2d 58 (1958), the court recognized copyright in Beardsley's forms and insurance instruments, but cautioned that it would be strict in finding infringement:

> [I]n the fields of insurance and commerce the use of specific language in forms and documents may be so essential to accomplish a desired result and so integrated with the use of a legal or commercial conception that the proper standard of infringement is one which will protect as far as possible the copyrighted language and yet allow free use of the thought beneath the language.

Id., 253 F.2d at 706. Does the thin copyright approach make better sense than finding a merger, when there are a limited number of ways to express the idea?

If the court in *Morrissey* had taken the thin copyright approach, would the outcome have differed? If so, would this have been a good result?

Might the *Morrissey* court have found plaintiff's Rule 1 insufficiently original to merit copyright protection, as an alternative ground for refusing relief? Might some short phrases and product labels, deemed uncopyrightable because insufficiently original, alternatively be denied copyright by virtue of the merger rule?

While we consider the concept of merger in connection with "copyrightable subject matter" for pedagogical reasons, some courts prefer to entertain arguments regarding merger in the "infringement" phase of litigation, rather than in the course of determining whether the plaintiff has a valid copyright. As the Court of Appeals for the Second Circuit has explained, "[a] court will normally have a 'more detailed and realistic basis' for evaluating the identity between idea and expression if it has all the contested forms of expression before it." *Hart v. Dan Chase Taxidermy Supply Co., Inc.*, 86 F.3d 320, 322 (2d Cir.1996).

2. *Applying the idea/expression dichotomy to non-utilitarian works.* The *Baker* Court stressed that the forms there in issue were utilitarian, rather than "ornamental designs, or pictorial illustrations addressed to the taste." Does this suggest that the concern about granting a *de facto* monopoly in the idea underlying a work is inapplicable in cases involving nonutilitarian works? Consider the following case.

HERBERT ROSENTHAL JEWELRY CORP. v. KALPAKIAN

United States Court of Appeals for the Ninth Circuit, 1971.
446 F.2d 738.

BROWNING, CIRCUIT JUDGE:

Plaintiff and defendants are engaged in the design, manufacture, and sale of fine jewelry.

Plaintiff charged defendants with infringing plaintiff's copyright registration of a pin in the shape of a bee formed of gold encrusted with jewels. * * *

Plaintiff contends that its copyright registration of a jeweled bee entitles it to protection from the manufacture and sale by others of any object that to the ordinary observer is substantially similar in appearance. The breadth of this claim is evident. For example, while a photograph of the copyrighted bee pin attached to the complaint depicts a bee with nineteen small white jewels on its back, plaintiff argues that its copyright is infringed by defendants' entire line of a score or more jeweled bees in three sizes decorated with from nine to thirty jewels of various sizes, kinds, and colors.

Although plaintiff's counsel asserted that the originality of plaintiff's bee pin lay in a particular arrangement of jewels on the top of the pin, the elements of this arrangement were never identified. Defendants' witnesses testified that the "arrangement" was simply a function of the size and form of the bee pin and the size of the jewels used. Plaintiff's counsel, repeatedly pressed by the district judge, was unable to suggest how jewels might be placed on the back of a pin in the shape of a bee without infringing plaintiff's copyright. He eventually conceded, "not being a jeweler, I can't conceive of how he might rearrange the design so it is dissimilar."

If plaintiff's understanding of its rights were correct, its copyright would effectively prevent others from engaging in the business of manufacturing and selling jeweled bees. We think plaintiff confuses the balance Congress struck between protection and competition under the Patent Act and the Copyright Act.

The owner of a patent is granted the exclusive right to exploit for a period of seventeen years (a maximum of fourteen years for design patents) the conception that is the subject matter of the patent. The grant of this monopoly, however, is carefully circumscribed by substantive and procedural protections. To be patentable the subject matter must be new and useful, and represent a nonobvious advance * * *. A patent is granted only after an independent administrative inquiry and determination that these substantive standards have been met. This determination is subject to both administrative and court review.

Copyright registration, on the other hand, confers no right at all to the conception reflected in the registered subject matter. "Unlike a patent, a copyright gives no exclusive right to the art disclosed; protection is given only to the expression of the idea—not the idea itself." *Mazer v. Stein*, 347 U.S. 201, 217, 74 S.Ct. 460, 470, 98 L.Ed. 630 (1954). Accordingly, the prerequisites for copyright registration are minimal. The work offered for registration need only be the product of the registrant. * * * [R]egistration is accomplished simply by filing a claim and depositing copies of the work with the Register of Copyrights. There is no administrative investigation or determination of the validity of the claim. A certificate is refused only if the object falls outside the broad category of matter subject to copyright registration. * * *

Obviously a copyright must not be treated as equivalent to a patent lest long continuing private monopolies be conferred over areas of gainful activity without first satisfying the substantive and procedural prerequisites to the grant of such privileges.

    * * *

* * * A copyright, we have seen, bars use of the particular "expression" of an idea in a copyrighted work but does not bar use of the "idea" itself. Others are free to utilize the "idea" so long as they do not plagiarize its "expression." As the court said in *Trifari, Krussman & Fishel, Inc. v. B. Steinberg–Kaslo Co.*, 144 F.Supp. 577, 580 (S.D.N.Y.

1956), where the copyrighted work was a jeweled pin representing a hansom cab, "though an alleged infringer gets the idea of a hansom cab pin from a copyrighted article there can be no infringement unless the article itself has been copied. The idea of a hansom cab cannot be copyrighted. Nevertheless plaintiff's expression of that idea, as embodied in its pin, can be copyrighted." * * *

The critical distinction between "idea" and "expression" is difficult to draw. As Judge Hand candidly wrote, "Obviously, no principle can be stated as to when an imitator has gone beyond copying the 'idea,' and has borrowed its 'expression.'" *Peter Pan Fabrics, Inc. v. Martin Weiner Corp.*, 274 F.2d 487, 489 (2d Cir.1960). At least in close cases, one may suspect, the classification the court selects may simply state the result reached rather than the reason for it. In our view, the difference is really one of degree as Judge Hand suggested in his striking "abstraction" formulation in *Nichols v. Universal Pictures Corp.*, 45 F.2d 119, 121 (2d Cir.1930). The guiding consideration in drawing the line is the preservation of the balance between competition and protection reflected in the patent and copyright laws.

What is basically at stake is the extent of the copyright owner's monopoly—from how large an area of activity did Congress intend to allow the copyright owner to exclude others? We think the production of jeweled bee pins is a larger private preserve than Congress intended to be set aside in the public market without a patent. A jeweled bee pin is therefore an "idea" that defendants were free to copy. Plaintiff seems to agree, for it disavows any claim that defendants cannot manufacture and sell jeweled bee pins and concedes that only plaintiff's particular design or "expression" of the jeweled bee pin "idea" is protected under its copyright. The difficulty, as we have noted, is that on this record the "idea" and its "expression" appear to be indistinguishable. There is no greater similarity between the pins of plaintiff and defendants than is inevitable from the use of jewel-encrusted bee forms in both.

When the "idea" and its "expression" are thus inseparable, copying the "expression" will not be barred, since protecting the "expression" in such circumstances would confer a monopoly of the "idea" upon the copyright owner free of the conditions and limitations imposed by the patent law. *Baker v. Selden*, 101 U.S. 99, 103, 25 L.Ed. 841 (1879).

Notes and Questions

1. *Distinguishing idea from expression.* What method does the *Kalpakian* court suggest for identifying the idea underlying a work? Once identified, how is the idea to be distinguished from the author's protectible expression of the idea? How easy will the *Kalpakian* court's approach be to apply?

Distinguishing a work's "idea" from its "expression" has proven to be the most difficult aspect of copyright law. The *Kalpakian* court refers to Judge Learned Hand's famous "abstractions" formulation for distinguishing idea from expression, set forth in Nichols v. Universal Pictures Corp., 45 F.2d 119 (2d Cir.1930), *cert. denied*, 282 U.S. 902, 51 S.Ct. 216, 75 L.Ed. 795 (1931). In *Nichols*, the plaintiff claimed that the defendant's motion picture, *The Cohens and the Kellys*, infringed the copyright in her play, *Abie's Irish Rose*. Both works involved a secret marriage of the children of Jewish and Irish Catholic fathers, a quarrel between the fathers, the birth of grandchildren, and an ultimate reconciliation of the fathers. In other respects, the works differed significantly.

In *Abie's Irish Rose*, the prosperous Jewish father, a New York widower, was obsessed with the notion that his only son should marry an orthodox Jewess. The Irish Catholic father, a California widower, was equally obsessed with the notion that his daughter should marry within her faith. The son and daughter secretly married, and a series of scenes ensued in which the children tried to deceive the fathers about their respective religious backgrounds. The fathers ultimately learned the truth, and after trying unsuccessfully to dissolve the marriage, disowned their children. The children subsequently had twins (a boy and a girl), and each father learned that a child had been born. Yearning to see his grandchild, each father went to the children's house, and discovered the other there. Upon meeting, the fathers argued about the gender of what each believed to be a single grandchild. Ultimately learning that there were two grandchildren, and that each had been named for one of their grandparents, the fathers were reconciled with their children and with one another.

The Cohens and the Kellys involved full families, rather than just widowed fathers, who were neighbors in a poor New York neighborhood. Neither the Jewish nor the Irish Catholic family was particularly religious. Rather, the families had a general, on-going personal feud. After the Jewish daughter and the Irish son secretly married, the Jewish father was informed that he had inherited a large sum of money from a great aunt, moved his family to a luxurious home, and began to live in vulgar opulence. When the Irish son sought to visit the Jewish daughter at the new home, the Jewish father chased him away, decrying such a lowly alliance, and then abused the Irish father over the telephone. In so doing, the Jewish father became so upset that he was forced to go to Florida to recuperate. When he returned he learned of the marriage between his daughter and the Irish boy and that the pair had borne a child. An altercation ensued between the Irish and the Jewish fathers, and the Jewish father disowned his daughter. The daughter and her baby went to live with the Irish family. The Jewish father then learned that a mistake had been made: The Irish father, rather than he, had inherited from the great aunt. Rejecting opportunities fraudulently to conceal the fact, the Jewish father went to the Irish father to admit this, and the two were reconciled, with the Irish father offering to share the wealth with the Jew. The grandchild had little, if anything to do with the reconciliation. Rather, the reconciliation was due to the Jew's honesty and the Irishman's generosity.

The problem before the *Nichols* court was to determine whether the defendant had taken copyrightable expression from *Abie's Irish Rose*, or only the idea underlying the play. Only the unauthorized taking of copyrighted expression would constitute infringement. The court thus set out to differentiate the idea underlying the plaintiff's play from the plaintiff's expression of the idea.

Writing for the court, Judge Hand noted that "copyrightable expression" was not limited to the literal words that the plaintiff used. The defendant might infringe if it took an "abstract" of the plaintiff's work as a whole. The problem lay in determining whether the "abstract" consisted only of the idea underlying the plaintiff's work or incorporated "expression" as well:

> Upon any work, and especially upon a play, a great number of patterns of increasing generality will fit equally well, as more and more of the incident is left out. The last may perhaps be no more than the most general statement of what the play is about, and at times might consist only of its title; but there is a point in this series of abstractions where they are no longer protected, since otherwise the playwright could prevent the use of his "ideas," to which, apart from their expression, his property is never extended. Nobody has ever been able to fix that boundary, and nobody ever can. In some cases the question has been treated as though it were analogous to lifting a portion out of the copyrighted work; but the analogy is not a good one, because, though the skeleton is a part of the body, it pervades and supports the whole. In such cases we are rather concerned with the line between expression and what is expressed. As respects plays, the controversy chiefly centers upon the characters and sequence of incident, these being the substance.

> We did not in Dymow v. Bolton, 11 F.2d 690, hold that a plagiarist was never liable for stealing a plot * * *. We found the plot of the second play was too different to infringe, because the most detailed pattern, common to both, eliminated so much from each that its content went into the public domain; and for this reason we said, "this mere subsection of a plot was not susceptible of copyright." But we do not doubt that two plays may correspond in plot closely enough for infringement. How far that correspondence must go is another matter. * * *

> In the two plays at bar we think both as to incident and character, the defendant took no more—assuming that it took anything at all—than the law allowed. The stories are quite different. One is of a religious zealot who insists upon his child's marrying no one outside his faith; opposed by another who is in this respect just like him, and is his foil. Their difference in race is merely an obbligato to the main theme, religion. They sink their differences through grandparental pride and affection. In the other, zealotry is wholly absent; religion does not even appear. It is true that the parents are hostile to each other in part because they differ in race; but the marriage of their son to a Jew does not apparently offend the Irish family at all, and it exacerbates the existing animosity of the Jew, principally because he has become rich, when he learns it. They are reconciled through the honesty of the Jew and the generosity of the Irishman; the grandchild has nothing whatever to do with it. The only matter common to the two is a quarrel between a Jewish and an Irish father, the marriage of their children, the birth of grandchildren and a reconciliation.

If the defendant took so much from the plaintiff, it may well have been because her amazing success seemed to prove that this was a subject of enduring popularity. * * * Though the plaintiff discovered the vein, she could not keep it to herself; so defined, the theme was too generalized an abstraction from what she wrote. It was only a part of her "ideas."

Nichols, 45 F.2d at 121–22.

Judge Hand indicated that taking a portion of a plaintiff's plot could constitute copyright infringement, even in the absence of taking the plaintiff's literal language: What aspects of the plot constitute copyrightable expression?

2. *Copyright in characters.* One issue that has perplexed courts and commentators alike is the extent to which fictitious characters created in literary, dramatic, audiovisual, or other works are copyrightable in themselves, outside of the context in which they were created. Characters such as Sherlock Holmes, Nancy Drew or Captain James T. Kirk have great commercial value. May the owner of the copyright in the original "Star Trek" television series prevent, via copyright law, others from building their own works (such as advertisements, action figures or short stories) around Captain Kirk, if they take no other protectible elements from the series?

The name of the character, by itself, is unlikely to be protectible under copyright law (though trademark or unfair competition protection may be available). With regard to the author's delineation of the character, the basic issue is whether the character, by itself, constitutes merely an idea or protectible expression. Judge Hand addressed the issue in the *Nichols* case, discussed above:

[W]e do not doubt that two plays may correspond in plot closely enough for infringement. * * * Nor need we hold that the same may not be true as to the characters, quite independently of the "plot" proper, though, as far as we know, such a case has never arisen. If Twelfth Night were copyrighted, it is quite possible that a second comer might so closely imitate Sir Toby Belch or Malvolio as to infringe, but it would not be enough that for one of his characters he cast a riotous knight who kept wassail to the discomfort of the household, or a vain and foppish steward who became amorous of his mistress. These would be no more than Shakespeare's "ideas" in the play, as little capable of monopoly as Einstein's Doctrine of Relativity, or Darwin's theory of the Origin of the Species. It follows that the less developed the characters, the less they can be copyrighted; that is the penalty an author must bear for marking them too indistinctly.

Nichols, 45 F.2d at 121. How much development is necessary? Professor Goldstein, in his treatise, has suggested the following rule of thumb: "A literary character can be said to have a distinctive personality, and thus to be protectible, when it has been delineated to the point at which its behavior is relatively predictable so that, when placed in a new plot situation, it will react in ways that are at once distinctive and unsurprising." P. Goldstein, Copyright § 2.7.2 (1998).

The rule in *Nichols* has not been universally followed. Warner Brothers Pictures v. Columbia Broadcasting System, 216 F.2d 945 (9th Cir.1954), *cert.*

denied, 348 U.S. 971, 75 S.Ct. 532, 99 L.Ed. 756 (1955), involved Dashiell Hammett's mystery, *The Maltese Falcon*, and its hero, Sam Spade. The issue was whether Hammett would infringe copyright in *The Maltese Falcon* (now owned by another) if he wrote a new story featuring Sam Spade as the detective. The Ninth Circuit found that the copyright in *The Maltese Falcon* gave no exclusive rights in the character, suggesting that characters *per se* are not protected unless they "constitute the story being told."

> It is conceivable that the character really constitutes the story being told, but if the character is only the chessman in the game of telling the story he is not within the area of the protection afforded by the copyright. * * * [E]ven if the Owners assigned their complete rights in the copyright to the *Falcon*, such assignment did not prevent the author from using the characters used therein, in other stories. The characters were vehicles for the story told, and the vehicles did not go with the sale of the story.

Id., 216 F.2d at 950. This standard will rarely be satisfied. It has not been widely adopted, however, and the Ninth Circuit has subsequently limited its application. See Walt Disney Productions v. Air Pirates, 581 F.2d 751 (9th Cir.1978), *cert. denied,* 439 U.S. 1132, 99 S.Ct. 1054, 59 L.Ed.2d 94 (1979).

The characters at issue in both *Nichols* and *Warner* were strictly literary characters. Characters possessing a visual, as well as a conceptual or literary aspect, such as cartoon or television characters, may be more readily protected because of their more concrete delineation. See, e.g., *Walt Disney, supra* (Mickey Mouse, Donald Duck, Goofy, and other characters protected).

3. *Scenes a faire.* Judge Hand's abstractions test in *Nichols, supra,* suggests that copyrightable "expression" may be found in an author's choice of specific details—scene, characters, setting, incidents, etc.—for use in telling his story. Use of some such details, however, may be excluded from consideration in evaluating whether a defendant's work infringes under the "*scenes a faire*" doctrine:

> *Scenes a faire* refers to "incidents, characters or settings which are as a practical matter indispensable, or at least standard, in the treatment of a given topic." * * * Such stock literary devices are not protectible by copyright.

Atari v. North American Philips Consumer Electronics, 672 F.2d 607, 616 (7th Cir.1982), *cert. denied,* 459 U.S. 880, 103 S.Ct. 176, 74 L.Ed.2d 145 (1982).

For example, in Walker v. Time Life Films, Inc., 784 F.2d 44, 50 (2d Cir.1986), *cert. denied,* 476 U.S. 1159, 106 S.Ct. 2278, 90 L.Ed.2d 721 (1986), the Second Circuit found that

> [e]lements such as drunks, prostitutes, vermin and derelict cars would appear in any realistic work about the work of policemen in the South Bronx. These similarities therefore are unprotectible as "*scenes a faire,*" that is, scenes that necessarily result from the choice of a setting or situation.

Likewise, when the plaintiff's story concerned the crash of the German dirigible Hindenburg in 1937, the court found that scenes of revelry in a German beer hall, use of the greeting "Heil Hitler," and the passionate singing of the German national anthem were unprotectible *scenes a faire*: Their presence in the defendant's story on the same topic did not assist the plaintiff's infringement claim. The court reasoned that it would be "virtually impossible to write" about that period in German history without employing such " 'stock' or standard literary devices." Hoehling v. Universal City Studios, Inc., 618 F.2d 972, 979 (2d Cir.), *cert. denied*, 449 U.S. 841, 101 S.Ct. 121, 66 L.Ed.2d 49 (1980). See also *Atari, supra* (court finds that standard "maze-chase game" devices in the "PAC–MAN" video game, including the maze, scoring table, and tunnel exits, are unprotectible under the *scenes a faire* doctrine).

Stock or standard devices falling under the *scenes a faire* doctrine can be said to merge with the underlying idea, because they are needed by all in order to express the idea. Also, because they are a form of cliche, or generic expression, they may be characterized as lacking originality.

PROBLEMS

1. X Company designed, and now manufactures and sells, highly automated widget production machinery. In the course of designing the machinery, X Company created a series of 5–digit numeric instructions, which it called "command codes." These command codes are used to access the computerized features of the machinery and set them to perform various production tasks. X Company selected many of the command code sequences arbitrarily, although there are certain non-arbitrary aspects to the code sequences:

—X Company identified each production task to be represented by a command code, and then sorted the tasks into logically related categories. It then assigned a separate number to each category. Each command code begins with the general category number of the task that the code represents.

—X Company wrote the command codes so that the higher level tasks within a category have higher numbers in the last two digits of their code, and the lower level tasks have lower numbers in the last two digits of their code.

X Company's widget production machinery was the first of its kind, and is the standard in the industry. Most widget production machinery operators have been trained in the X Company command codes. Y Systems, Inc., has begun to produce competing widget production machinery. It has adopted the same command codes to access the computerized features of its machinery as X Company uses. Has Y Systems taken copyrightable expression from X Company?

2. X, the President of Ickysweet Cola, Inc., hired Y to break into the Justright Cola Company safe and photograph the sole copy of the highly confidential, trade secret Justright Cola product formula kept there. Y successfully did so, and delivered the negatives to X. Is this likely to constitute copyright infringement?

3. Glass-in-glass sculpture is a centuries-old art form that consists of a glass sculpture inside a second glass layer, commonly called the "shroud."

The artist creates an inner glass sculpture and then dips it into molten glass, encasing it in a solid outer glass shroud. The shroud is malleable before it cools, and the artist can manipulate it into any shape he or she desires.

Plaintiff glass artist produces glass-in-glass jellyfish sculptures, which he describes as follows: "vertically oriented, colorful, fanciful jellyfish with tendril-like tentacles and a rounded bell encased in an outer layer of rounded clear glass that is bulbous at the top and tapering toward the bottom to form roughly a bullet shape, with the jellyfish portion of the sculpture filling almost the entire volume of the outer, clear glass shroud." His jellyfish are lifelike, resembling the *pelagia colorata* that live in the Pacific Ocean. Plaintiff sells these sculptures in galleries and gift shops. An example of plaintiff's jellyfish sculpture is on the left-hand side, below.

Defendant glass artist, who has seen photographs and actual examples of plaintiff's jellyfish sculptures, begins making his own glass-in-glass jellyfish sculptures, which look so much like plaintiff's that people confuse them. An example of defendant's jellyfish sculpture is on the right-hand side, below. Plaintiff sues for copyright infringement. Assuming that the defendant copied from plaintiff, has defendant taken copyrightable expression?

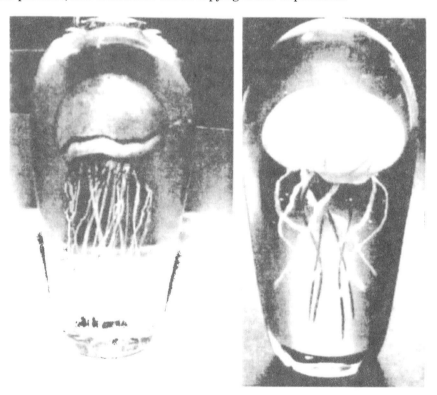

1. Computer Programs

Courts have encountered a number of conceptual dilemmas in the course of applying copyright protection to computer programs. Part of the difficulty arises from the early relegation of programs to the "literary works" category of copyrightable subject matter. Rules and concepts developed for more traditional literary works—such as books, poetry and letters—have often proven a poor fit for highly utilitarian, technical computer programs. In addition, the ever-perplexing task of distinguishing a work's ideas from its expression appears particularly difficult in the case of software.

The Copyright Office began registering computer programs as literary works in the mid–1960s, though the status and scope of the copyright protection remained uncertain. In enacting the Copyright Act of 1976, Congress found the issues surrounding copyright protection for programs insufficiently developed for definitive legislative resolution. Accordingly, in § 117 of the Act, Congress preserved the legal status quo, such as it was, until the recently appointed Commission on New Technological Uses of Copyrighted Works ("CONTU") could study the issue and make specific recommendations. Acting on the Commission's subsequent report, in 1980 Congress amended the Copyright Act to define "computer programs" in § 101 of the Act, and to set forth limitations on the software copyright in § 117. Pub. L. No. 96–517 § 10, 94 Stat. 3028, 3028 (1980).

As amended, § 101 provides: "A 'computer program' is a set of statements or instructions to be used directly or indirectly in a computer in order to bring about a certain result." Congress had already indicated in the 1976 Act legislative history that computer programs should be treated as "literary works." H.R. Rep. No. 1476, 94th Cong., 2d Sess. 54 (1976). The original 1976 Act definition of "literary works" was sufficiently broad to encompass computer programs:

> "Literary works" are works, other than audiovisual works, expressed in words, numbers, or other verbal or numerical symbols or indicia, regardless of the nature of the material objects, such as books, periodicals, manuscripts, phonorecords, film, tapes, disks, or cards, in which they are embodied.

17 U.S.C.A. § 101.

The initial infringement suits involved claims that defendants had copied or closely paraphrased the plaintiffs' program code. Computer programmers write programs in "source code," using computer languages such as C or C++, which consist of words, numbers and symbols that trained humans can read. Once the program is written, the source code is compiled, or translated, into object code—a binary language consisting of ones and zeros that indicate an open or closed switch. The object code communicates directly with the computer hardware—a machine. Humans generally cannot read the program in that form. Programs sold to users on disks or chips are in object code form, ready to be used in computers. Programmers generally do not release the source code version of their programs to the public.

One of the first legal issues to arise was whether copyright protection extended only to the source code version of the program, or to the object code, as well. Infringement defendants argued that "a copyrightable work must be intelligible to human beings and must be intended as a medium of communication to human beings." Williams Electronics, Inc. v. Artic International, Inc., 685 F.2d 870, 876–77 (3d Cir.1982). Courts rejected this argument as contrary to the literal language of the § 101 definitions of "computer program" and "literary works," as well as to the language of § 102(a), which specifies that copyrightable works may be "perceived, reproduced, or otherwise communicated, either directly or with the aid of a machine or device." See Apple Computer, Inc. v. Franklin Computer Corp., 714 F.2d 1240, 1248–49 (3d Cir.1983), *cert. dismissed*, 464 U.S. 1033, 104 S.Ct. 690, 79 L.Ed.2d 158 (1984).

Courts also considered and rejected arguments that programs embedded on a silicon chip (a "read only memory" or "ROM"), as opposed to magnetic disks or tapes, could not be protected. For example, in the *Apple* case, *supra*, the defendants argued that chips—which are incorporated into the circuitry of the computer—are machine parts, not writings. The Third Circuit responded that programs on chips "should no more be considered machine parts than videotapes should be considered parts of projectors or phonorecords parts of sound reproduction equipment." *Id.*, at 1249, 1251. Likewise, courts rejected attempts to distinguish between application programs (which perform a specific task for the user, such as word processing) and operating system programs (which manage the internal operations of the computer and have no direct interaction with the user) for purposes of copyright protection. *Id.*, at 1251.

Later cases raised the issue of whether there could be "non-literal" infringement of computer programs—that is, liability for copying internal structural elements of a program, rather than the code. It was well established that nonliteral, structural elements of a novel, such as the selection and arrangement of plot elements, were protected subject matter. Would protection extend by analogy to the structure or organization of a computer program?

The U.S. Court of Appeals for the Third Circuit was the first appellate court to review this issue, in Whelan Associates, Inc. v. Jaslow Dental Laboratory, Inc., 797 F.2d 1222 (3d Cir.1986), *cert. denied*, 479 U.S. 1031, 107 S.Ct. 877, 93 L.Ed.2d 831 (1987). The program at issue in *Whelan* was a custom computer program written to assist in the business operations of a dental laboratory—processing orders, maintaining inventory, dealing with accounts receivable, etc. The defendants, who were accused of copying structural aspects of this program, but no literal code, argued that the structure constituted the idea of the program, rather than expression, and thus was not copyrightable subject matter. The Third Circuit thus had to distinguish the program's idea from its expression.

The court found that the Supreme Court's opinion in *Baker v. Selden* suggests a way to distinguish idea from expression. Just as *Baker v. Selden* focused on the end sought to be achieved by Selden's book, the line between idea and expression may be drawn with reference to the end sought to be achieved by the work in question. In other words, *the purpose or function of a utilitarian work would be the work's idea, and everything that is not necessary to the purpose or function would be part of the expression of the idea.* * * * Where there are various means of achieving the desired purpose, then the particular means chosen is not necessary to the purpose; hence, there is expression, not idea.

Whelan, 797 F.2d at 1236. Turning to the case before it, the court noted:

it is clear that the purpose of the utilitarian Dentalab program was to aid in the business operations of a dental laboratory. It is equally clear that the structure of the program was not essential to that task: there are other programs on the market * * * that perform the same functions but have different structures and designs.

Id., 797 F.2d at 1238. Thus, the structure of the plaintiff's program was protected subject matter under the plaintiff's copyright.

COMPUTER ASSOCIATES INTERNATIONAL, INC. v. ALTAI, INC.

United States Court of Appeals for the Second Circuit, 1992.
982 F.2d 693.

WALKER, CIRCUIT JUDGE:

* * *

Among other things, this case deals with the challenging question of whether and to what extent the "non-literal" aspects of a computer program, that is, those aspects that are not reduced to written code, are protected by copyright. While a few other courts have already grappled with this issue, this case is one of first impression in this circuit. As we shall discuss, we find the results reached by other courts to be less than satisfactory. Drawing upon long-standing doctrines of copyright law, we take an approach that we think better addresses the practical difficulties embedded in these types of cases. In so doing, we have kept in mind the necessary balance between creative incentive and industrial competition.

* * *

COMPUTER PROGRAM DESIGN

Certain elementary facts concerning the nature of computer programs are vital to the following discussion. The Copyright Act defines a computer program as "a set of statements or instructions to be used directly or indirectly in a computer in order to bring about a certain result." 17 U.S.C. § 101. In writing these directions, the programmer works "from the general to the specific."

The first step in this procedure is to identify a program's ultimate function or purpose. An example of such an ultimate purpose might be the creation and maintenance of a business ledger. Once this goal has been achieved, a programmer breaks down or "decomposes" the program's ultimate function into "simpler constituent problems or 'subtasks,'" which are also known as subroutines or modules. In the context of a business ledger program, a module or subroutine might be responsible for the task of updating a list of outstanding accounts receivable. Sometimes, depending upon the complexity of its task, a subroutine may be broken down further into sub-subroutines.

Having sufficiently decomposed the program's ultimate function into its component elements, a programmer will then arrange the subroutines or modules into what are known as organizational or flow charts. Flow charts map the interactions between modules that achieve the program's end goal.

In order to accomplish these intra-program interactions, a programmer must carefully design each module's parameter list. A parameter list, according to the expert appointed and fully credited by the district court, Dr. Randall Davis, is "the information sent to and received from a subroutine." The term "parameter list" refers to the form in which information is passed between modules (e.g. for accounts receivable, the designated time frame and particular customer identifying number) and the information's actual content (e.g. 8/91–7/92; customer No. 3). With respect to form, interacting modules must share similar parameter lists so that they are capable of exchanging information.

"The functions of the modules in a program together with each module's relationships to other modules constitute the 'structure' of the program." Additionally, the term structure may include the category of modules referred to as "macros." A macro is a single instruction that initiates a sequence of operations or module interactions within the program. Very often the user will accompany a macro with an instruction from the parameter list to refine the instruction (e.g. current total of accounts receivable (macro), but limited to those for 8/91 to 7/92 from customer No. 3 (parameters)).

In fashioning the structure, a programmer will normally attempt to maximize the program's speed, efficiency, as well as simplicity for user operation, while taking into consideration certain externalities such as the memory constraints of the computer upon which the program will be run. "This stage of program design often requires the most time and investment."

Once each necessary module has been identified, designed, and its relationship to the other modules has been laid out conceptually, the resulting program structure must be embodied in a written language that the computer can read. This process is called "coding," and requires two steps. First, the programmer must transpose the program's structural blue-print into a source code. This step has been described as "comparable to the novelist fleshing out the broad outline of his plot by crafting from words and sentences the paragraphs that convey the ideas." The source code may be written in any one of several computer languages, such as COBAL, FORTRAN, BASIC, EDL, etc., depending upon the type of computer for which the program is intended. Once the source code has been completed, the second step is to translate or "compile" it into object code. Object code is the binary language comprised of zeros and ones through which the computer directly receives its instructions.

After the coding is finished, the programmer will run the program on the computer in order to find and correct any logical and syntactical errors. This is known as "debugging" and, once done, the program is complete.

FACTS

[Both Computer Associates ("CA") and Altai are in the computer software industry—designing, developing and marketing various types of computer programs. This litigation concerns one of CA's marketed programs entitled CA–SCHEDULER. CA–SCHEDULER is a job scheduling program designed for IBM mainframe computers. CA–SCHEDULER contains a sub-program entitled ADAPTER, also developed by CA.]

[An "operating system" is a program that manages the resources of the computer, allocating those resources to other programs as needed. Generally, a computer program written to run with one operating system will not, without modification, run with another operating system. ADAPTER is an "operating system compatibility component," or translator, which enables a program written to be compatible with one operating system to run under another operating system. ADAPTER translates the language of the program into the particular language that the computer's operating system can understand.]

[Starting in 1982, Altai began marketing its own job scheduling program entitled ZEKE. In 1983, Williams, then an employee of Altai and now its President, recruited Arney, a computer programmer with CA, to assist Altai in designing a version of ZEKE to run with another operating system. Though Williams did not know it, Arney was intimately familiar with various aspects of ADAPTER. When Arney left CA to work for Altai in January, 1984, he took with him copies of the source code for two versions of ADAPTER. Once at Altai, Arney persuaded Williams that the best way to make the needed modifications was to introduce a "common system interface" component into ZEKE. He did not tell Williams that his idea stemmed from his familiarity with ADAPTER. They decided to name this new component-program OSCAR.]

[Arney went to work creating OSCAR at Altai's offices using the ADAPTER source code. The district court accepted Williams' testimony that no one at Altai, with the exception of Arney, affirmatively knew that Arney had the ADAPTER code, or that he was using it to create OSCAR. Arney copied approximately 30% of OSCAR's code from CA's ADAPTER program.]

[The first generation of OSCAR programs was known as OSCAR 3.4. In 1988, CA first learned that Altai may have appropriated parts of ADAPTER, and brought this copyright action against Altai. Only at this point did Altai learn that Arney had copied much of the OSCAR code from

ADAPTER. Upon obtaining advice of counsel, Williams initiated a rewrite of OSCAR. The project's goal was to save as much of OSCAR 3.4 as legitimately could be used, and to excise those portions which had been copied from ADAPTER. Arney was entirely excluded from the process. Eight new programmers were assigned to rewrite the appropriate code. The resulting program was entitled OSCAR 3.5. From that point on, Altai shipped only OSCAR 3.5 to its new customers. Altai also shipped OSCAR 3.5 as a "free upgrade" to all customers that had previously purchased OSCAR 3.4.]

[In the infringement suit, the court found that Altai's OSCAR 3.4 program infringed CA's copyrighted ADAPTER program, but that the OSCAR 3.5 program was not substantially similar to plaintiff's program, and thus did not infringe. The issue before the court on appeal is whether OSCAR 3.5 infringes ADAPTER.]

I. COPYRIGHT INFRINGEMENT

* * *

As a general matter, and to varying degrees, copyright protection extends beyond a literary work's strictly textual form to its non-literal components. As we have said, "[i]t is of course essential to any protection of literary property ... that the right cannot be limited literally to the text, else a plagiarist would escape by immaterial variations." *Nichols v. Universal Pictures Corp.*, 45 F.2d 119, 121 (2d Cir.1930) (L. Hand, J.), *cert. denied*, 282 U.S. 902, 51 S.Ct. 216, 75 L.Ed. 795 (1931). Thus, where "the fundamental essence or structure of one work is duplicated in another," 3 Melville B. Nimmer & David Nimmer, Nimmer on Copyright § 13.03[A][1], at 13–24, courts have found copyright infringement. This black letter proposition is the springboard for our discussion.

A. *Copyright Protection for the Non-literal Elements of Computer Programs*

* * *

In this case, the hotly contested issues surround OSCAR 3.5. As recounted above, OSCAR 3.5 is the product of Altai's carefully orchestrated rewrite of OSCAR 3.4. After the purge, none of the ADAPTER source code remained in the 3.5 version; thus, Altai made sure that the literal elements of its revamped OSCAR program were no longer substantially similar to the literal elements of CA's ADAPTER.

* * *

CA argues that, despite Altai's rewrite of the OSCAR code, the resulting program remained substantially similar to the *structure* of its ADAPTER program. As discussed above, a program's structure includes its non-literal components such as general flow charts as well as the more specific organization of inter-modular relationships, parameter lists, and macros. In addition to these aspects, CA contends that OSCAR 3.5 is also substantially similar to ADAPTER with respect to the list of services that both ADAPTER and OSCAR obtain from their respective operating systems. We must decide whether and to what extent these elements of computer programs are protected by copyright law.

The statutory terrain in this area has been well explored. The Copyright Act affords protection to "original works of authorship fixed in any tangible medium of expression. . . ." 17 U.S.C. § 102(a). This broad category of protected "works" includes "literary works" * * *. [T]he legislative history leaves no doubt that Congress intended [computer programs] to be considered literary works.

The syllogism that follows from the foregoing premises is a powerful one: if the non-literal structures of literary works are protected by copyright; and if computer programs are literary works, as we are told by the legislature; then the non-literal structures of computer programs are protected by copyright. We have no reservation in joining the company of those courts that have already ascribed to this logic. However, that conclusion does not end our analysis. We must determine the scope of copyright protection that extends to a computer program's non-literal structure.

* * *

1) Idea vs. Expression Dichotomy

It is a fundamental principle of copyright law that a copyright does not protect an idea, but only the expression of the idea. This axiom of common law has been incorporated into the governing statute. Section 102(b) of the Act provides:

In no case does copyright protection for an original work of authorship extend to any idea, procedure, process, system, method of operation, concept, principle, or discovery, regardless of the form in which it is described, explained, illustrated, or embodied in such work.

* * *

Drawing the line between idea and expression is a tricky business. Judge Learned Hand noted that "[n]obody has ever been able to fix that boundary, and nobody ever can." *Nichols*, 45 F.2d at 121. * * *

The essentially utilitarian nature of a computer program further complicates the task of distilling its idea from its expression. In order to describe both computational processes and abstract ideas, its content "combines creative and technical expression." The variations of expression found in purely creative compositions, as opposed to those contained in utilitarian works, are not directed towards practical application. For example, a narration of Humpty Dumpty's demise, which would clearly be a creative composition, does not serve the same ends as, say, a recipe for scrambled eggs—which is a more process oriented text. Thus, compared to aesthetic works, computer programs hover even more closely to the elusive boundary line described in § 102(b).

The doctrinal starting point in analyses of utilitarian works, is the seminal case of *Baker v. Selden*, 101 U.S. 99, 25 L.Ed. 841 (1879). * * *

[From the reasoning in *Baker*,] we conclude that those elements of a computer program that are necessarily incidental to its function are * * * unprotectible.

While *Baker v. Selden* provides a sound analytical foundation, it offers scant guidance on how to separate idea or process from expression, and moreover, on how to further distinguish protectible expression from that expression which "must necessarily be used as incident to" the work's underlying concept. * * *

[The *Altai* court considers and rejects the Third Circuit's approach in *Whelan*, noting that it was wrong to assume that only one "idea"—the program's ultimate purpose—underlies any computer program. The *Altai* court characterizes the *Whelan* approach as overly simplistic.]

2) Substantial Similarity Test for Computer Program Structure: Abstraction–Filtration–Comparison

As discussed herein, we think that district courts would be well-advised to undertake a three-step procedure, based on the abstractions test utilized by the district court, in order to determine whether the non-literal elements of two or more computer programs are substantially similar. This approach breaks no new ground; rather, it draws on such familiar copyright doctrines as merger, *scenes a faire*, and public domain. In taking this approach, however, we are cognizant that computer technology is a dynamic field which can quickly outpace judicial decisionmaking. Thus, in cases where the technology in question does not allow for a literal application of the procedure we outline below, our opinion should not be read to foreclose the district courts of our circuit from utilizing a modified version. In ascertaining substantial similarity under this approach, a court would first break down the allegedly infringed program into its constituent structural parts. Then, by examining each of these parts for such things as incorporated ideas, expression that is necessarily incidental to those ideas, and elements that are taken from the public domain, a court would then be able to sift out all non-protectible material. Left with a kernel, or possible kernels, of creative expression after following this process of elimination, the court's last step would be to compare this material with the structure of an allegedly infringing program. The result of this comparison will determine whether the protectible elements of the programs at issue are substantially similar so as to warrant a finding of infringement. It will be helpful to elaborate a bit further.

STEP ONE: ABSTRACTION

As the district court appreciated, the theoretic framework for analyzing substantial similarity expounded by Learned Hand in the *Nichols* case is helpful in the present context. In *Nichols*, we enunciated what has now become known as the "abstractions" test for separating idea from expression:

Upon any work ... a great number of patterns of increasing generality will fit equally well, as more and more of the incident is left out. The last may perhaps be no more than the most general statement of what the [work] is about, and at times might consist only of its title; but there is a point in this series of abstractions where they are no longer protected, since otherwise the [author] could prevent the use of his "ideas," to which, apart from their expression, his property is never extended.

Nichols v. Universal Pictures, 45 F.2d 119, 121 (2d Cir. 1930), *cert. denied*, 282 U.S. 902, 51 S.Ct. 216, 75 L.Ed. 795 (1931).

While the abstractions test was originally applied in relation to literary works such as novels and plays, it is adaptable to computer programs. In contrast to the *Whelan* approach, the abstractions test "implicitly recognizes that any given work may consist of a mixture of numerous ideas and expressions."

As applied to computer programs, the abstractions test will comprise the first step in the examination for substantial similarity. Initially, in a manner that resembles reverse engineering on a theoretical plane, a court should dissect the allegedly copied program's structure and isolate each level of abstraction contained within it. This process begins with the code and ends with an articulation of the program's ultimate function. Along the way, it is necessary essentially to retrace and map each of the designer's steps—in the opposite order in which they were taken during the program's creation.

As an anatomical guide to this procedure, the following description is helpful:

At the lowest level of abstraction, a computer program may be thought of in its entirety as a set of individual instructions organized into a hierarchy of modules. At a higher level of abstraction, the instructions in the lowest-level modules may be replaced conceptually by the functions of those modules. At progressively higher levels of abstraction, the functions of higher-level modules conceptually replace the implementations of those modules in terms of lower-level modules and instructions, until finally, one is left with nothing but the ultimate function of the program.... A program has structure at every level of abstraction at which it is viewed. At low levels of abstraction, a program's structure may be quite complex; at the highest level it is trivial.

Englund, at 897–98.

STEP TWO: FILTRATION

Once the program's abstraction levels have been discovered, the substantial similarity inquiry moves from the conceptual to the concrete. Professor Nimmer suggests, and we endorse, a "successive filtering method" for separating protectible expression from non-protectible material. This process entails examining the structural components at each level of abstraction to determine whether their particular inclusion at that level was "idea" or was dictated by considerations of efficiency, so as to be necessarily incidental to that idea; required by factors external to the program itself; or taken from the public domain and hence is nonprotectible expression. The structure of any given program may reflect some, all, or none of these considerations. Each case requires its own fact specific investigation.

Strictly speaking, this filtration serves "the purpose of defining the scope of plaintiff's copyright." *Brown Bag Software v. Symantec Corp.*, 960 F.2d 1465, 1475 (9th Cir.) (endorsing "analytic dissection" of computer programs in order to isolate protectible expression), *cert. denied*, 506 U.S. 869, 113 S.Ct. 198, 121 L.Ed.2d 141 (1992). By applying well developed doctrines of copyright law, it may ultimately leave behind a "core of protectible material." Further explication of this second step may be helpful.

(a) *Elements Dictated by Efficiency*

The portion of *Baker v. Selden*, discussed earlier, which denies copyright protection to expression necessarily incidental to the idea being expressed, appears to be the cornerstone for what has developed into the doctrine of merger. The doctrine's underlying principle is that "[w]hen there is essentially only one way to express an idea, the idea and its expression are inseparable and copyright is no bar to copying that expression." Under these circumstances, the expression is said to have "merged" with the idea itself. In order not to confer a monopoly of the idea upon the copyright owner, such expression should not be protected.

   * * *

[W]hen one considers the fact that programmers generally strive to create programs "that meet the user's needs in the most efficient manner," the applicability of the merger doctrine to computer programs becomes compelling. In the context of computer program design, the concept of efficiency is akin to deriving the most concise logical proof or formulating the most succinct mathematical computation. Thus, the more efficient a set of modules are, the more closely they approximate the idea or process embodied in that particular aspect of the program's structure.

While, hypothetically, there might be a myriad of ways in which a programmer may effectuate certain functions within a program,—i.e., express the idea embodied in a given subroutine—efficiency concerns may so narrow the practical range of choice as to make only one or two forms of expression workable options. Of course, not all program structure is informed by efficiency concerns. It follows that in order to determine whether the merger doctrine precludes copyright protection to an aspect of a program's structure that is so oriented, a court must inquire "whether the use of *this particular set* of modules is necessary efficiently to implement that part of the program's process" being implemented. If the answer is yes, then the expression represented by the programmer's choice of a specific module or group of modules has merged with their underlying idea and is unprotected.

* * *

(b) *Elements Dictated By External Factors*

We have stated that where "it is virtually impossible to write about a particular historical era or fictional theme without employing certain 'stock' or standard literary devices," such expression is not copyrightable. *Hoehling v. Universal City Studios, Inc.*, 618 F.2d 972, 979 (2d Cir.), *cert. denied*, 449 U.S. 841, 101 S.Ct. 121, 66 L.Ed.2d 49 (1980). For example, the *Hoehling* case was an infringement suit stemming from several works on the Hindenburg disaster. There we concluded that similarities in representations of German beer halls, scenes depicting German greetings such as "Heil Hitler," or the singing of certain German songs would not lead to a finding of infringement because they were " 'indispensable, or at least standard, in the treatment of' " life in Nazi Germany. This is known as the *scenes a faire* doctrine, and like "merger," it has its analogous application to computer programs.

Professor Nimmer points out that "in many instances it is virtually impossible to write a program to perform particular functions in a specific computing environment without employing standard techniques." This is a result of the fact that a programmer's freedom of design choice is often circumscribed by extrinsic considerations such as (1) the mechanical specifications of the computer on which a particular program is intended to run; (2) compatibility requirements of other programs with which a program is designed to operate in conjunction; (3) computer manufacturers' design standards; (4) demands of the industry being serviced; and (5) widely accepted programming practices within the computer industry.

Courts have already considered some of these factors in denying copyright protection to various elements of computer programs. In the *Plains Cotton* case, the Fifth Circuit refused to reverse the district court's denial of a preliminary injunction against an alleged program infringer because, in part, "many of the similarities between the ... programs [were] dictated by the externalities of the cotton market."

In *Manufacturers Technologies*, the district court noted that the program's method of screen navigation "is influenced by the type of hardware that the software is designed to be used on." 706 F.Supp. at 995. Because, in part, "the functioning of the hardware package impact[ed] and constrain[ed] the type of navigational tools used in plaintiff's screen displays," the court denied copyright protection to that aspect of the program.

* * *

Building upon this existing case law, we conclude that a court must also examine the structural content of an allegedly infringed program for elements that might have been dictated by external factors.

(c) *Elements Taken From the Public Domain*

Closely related to the non-protectibility of *scenes a faire*, is material found in the public domain. Such material is free for the taking and cannot be appropriated by a single author even though it is included in a copyrighted work. We see no reason to make an exception to this rule for elements of a computer program that have entered the public domain by virtue of freely accessible program exchanges and the like. See *Brown Bag Software*, 960 F.2d at 1473 (affirming the district court's finding that " '[p]laintiffs may not claim copyright protection of an ... expression that is, if not standard, then commonplace in the computer software industry.' "). Thus, a court must also filter out this material from the allegedly infringed program before it makes the final inquiry in its substantial similarity analysis.

STEP THREE: COMPARISON

The third and final step of the test for substantial similarity that we believe appropriate for non-literal program components entails a comparison. Once a court has sifted out all elements of the allegedly infringed program which are "ideas" or are dictated by efficiency or external factors, or taken from the public domain, there may remain a core of protectible expression. In terms of a work's copyright value, this is the golden nugget. At this point, the court's substantial similarity inquiry focuses on whether the defendant copied any aspect of this protected expression, as well as an assessment of the copied portion's relative importance with respect to the plaintiff's overall program.

3) Policy Considerations

We are satisfied that the three step approach we have just outlined not only comports with, but advances the constitutional policies underlying the Copyright Act. Since any method that tries to distinguish idea from expression ultimately impacts on the scope of copyright protection afforded to a particular type of work, "the line [it draws] must be a pragmatic one, which also keeps in consideration 'the preservation of the balance between competition and protection....' "

CA and some *amici* argue against the type of approach that we have set forth on the grounds that it will be a disincentive for future computer program research and development. At bottom, they claim that if programmers are not guaranteed broad copyright protection for their work, they will not invest the extensive time, energy and funds required to design and improve program structures. While they have a point, their argument cannot carry the day. The interest of the copyright law is not in simply conferring a monopoly on industrious persons, but in advancing the public welfare through rewarding artistic creativity, in a manner that permits the free use and development of non-protectible ideas and processes.

In this respect, our conclusion is informed by Justice Stewart's concise discussion of the principles that correctly govern the adaptation of the copyright law to new circumstances. In *Twentieth Century Music Corp. v. Aiken*, he wrote:

> The limited scope of the copyright holder's statutory monopoly, like the limited copyright duration required by the Constitution, reflects a balance of competing claims upon the public interest: Creative work is to be encouraged and rewarded, but private motivation must ultimately serve the cause of promoting broad public availability of literature, music, and the other arts.
>
> The immediate effect of our copyright law is to secure a fair return for an "author's" creative labor. But the ultimate aim is, by this incentive, to stimulate artistic creativity for the general public good.... When technological change has rendered its literal terms ambiguous, the Copyright Act must be construed in light of this basic purpose.

422 U.S. 151, 156, 95 S.Ct. 2040, 2043–44, 45 L.Ed.2d 84 (1975).

Recently, the Supreme Court has emphatically reiterated that "[t]he primary objective of copyright is not to reward the *labor* of authors...." *Feist Publications, Inc. v. Rural Tel. Serv. Co.*, 499 U.S. 340, 111 S.Ct. 1282, 1290, 113 L.Ed.2d 358 (1991) (emphasis added). While the *Feist* decision deals primarily with the copyrightability of purely factual compilations, its underlying tenets apply to much of the work involved in computer programming. *Feist* put to rest the "sweat of the brow" doctrine in copyright law. The rationale of that doctrine "was that copyright was a reward for the hard work that went into compiling facts." The Court flatly rejected this justification for extending copyright protection, noting that it "eschewed the most fundamental axiom of copyright law—that no one may copyright facts or ideas."

Feist teaches that substantial effort alone cannot confer copyright status on an otherwise uncopyrightable work. As we have discussed, despite the fact that significant labor and expense often goes into computer program flow-charting and debugging, that process does not always result in inherently protectible expression. * * *

>   * * *

To be frank, the exact contours of copyright protection for non-literal program structure are not completely clear. We trust that as future cases are decided, those limits will become better defined. Indeed, it may well be that the Copyright Act serves as a relatively weak barrier against public access to the theoretical interstices behind a program's source and object codes. This results from the hybrid nature of a computer program, which, while it is literary expression, is also a highly functional, utilitarian component in the larger process of computing.

Generally, we think that copyright registration—with its indiscriminating availability—is not ideally suited to deal with the highly dynamic technology of computer science. Thus far, many of the decisions in this area reflect the courts' attempt to fit the proverbial square peg in a round hole. The district court and at least one commentator have suggested that patent registration, with its exacting up-front novelty and non-obviousness requirements, might be the more appropriate rubric of protection for intellectual property of this kind. In any event, now that more than 12 years have passed since CONTU issued its final report, the resolution of this specific issue could benefit from further legislative investigation— perhaps a CONTU II.

In the meantime, Congress has made clear that computer programs are literary works entitled to copyright protection. Of course, we shall abide by these instructions, but in so doing we must not impair the overall integrity of copyright law. While incentive based arguments in favor of broad copyright protection are perhaps attractive from a pure policy perspective, ultimately, they have a corrosive effect on certain fundamental tenets of copyright doctrine. If the test we have outlined results in narrowing the scope of protection, as we expect it will, that result flows from applying, in accordance with Congressional intent, long-standing principles of copyright law to computer programs. Of course, our decision is also informed by our concern that these fundamental principles remain undistorted.

[The court of appeals reviewed the decision of the district court, which had found no substantial similarity of copyrighted expression, and held that it was not clearly erroneous.]

CONCLUSION

In adopting the above three step analysis for substantial similarity between the non-literal elements of computer programs, we seek to insure two things: (1) that programmers may receive appropriate copyright protection for innovative utilitarian works containing expression; and (2) that non-protectible technical expression remains in the public domain for others to use freely as building blocks in their own work. At first blush, it may seem counter-intuitive that someone who has benefitted to some degree from illicitly obtained material can emerge from an infringement suit relatively unscathed. However, so long as the appropriated material consists of non-protectible expression, "[t]his result is neither unfair nor unfortunate. It is the means by which copyright advances the progress of science and art." *Feist*, 111 S.Ct. at 1290.

* * *

NOTES AND QUESTIONS

1. *Copyright in a program's structure.* Does the *Altai* abstraction-filtration-comparison approach take account of the expression generated by the programmer's selection, coordination and arrangement of uncopyrightable elements? If so, at what point in the analysis?

In Softel, Inc. v. Dragon Medical and Scientific Communications, Inc., 118 F.3d 955 (2d Cir.1997), *cert. denied*, 523 U.S. 1020, 118 S.Ct. 1300, 140

L.Ed.2d 466 (1998), the Second Circuit clarified that a programmer's original selection, coordination and arrangement of uncopyrightable elements will be considered and protected under the *Altai* three-part test:

> [A]n allegation of infringement based on similarities in architecture cannot be ignored merely because many or all of the design elements that make up that architecture are not protectible when considered at a lower level of abstraction. In *Altai*, the district court held many aspects of the program at issue in that case to be not protectible for various reasons (e.g., because they were in the public domain or were computer *scenes a faire*). Nevertheless, the court proceeded to a higher level of abstraction and responded to the plaintiff's claim of infringement based on alleged similarities between the two programs' "organizational charts." In reviewing that claim, the trial court made no effort to remove from its analysis those elements of the program that had been found unprotectible at the lower level of abstraction. * * *
>
> The foregoing approach is consistent with the Supreme Court's decision in *Feist* * * *. In *Feist*, the Court made quite clear that a compilation of non-protectible elements can enjoy copyright protection even though its constituent elements do not.

118 F.3d at 963–64. Thus, individual program elements that are filtered out at one level may nonetheless be considered and protected as part of an aggregate of elements at another level of abstraction.

Circuit Courts of Appeal generally agree that a programmer's original selection and arrangement of uncopyrightable structural elements can constitute original, protectible expression. However, some have been grudging in the level of protection they will afford. Both the Ninth and Eleventh Circuits, for example, have adopted a "bodily appropriation of expression" or "virtual identicality" standard, which is higher than the "substantial similarity" standard which the *Altai* court used in evaluating infringement. See MiTek Holdings, Inc. v. Arce Engineering, 89 F.3d 1548, 1559 (11th Cir.1996) ("This Circuit has not established the standard that should be used in analyzing claims of compilation copyright infringement of nonliteral elements of a computer program. Today, we join the Ninth Circuit in adopting the 'bodily appropriation of expression' or 'virtual identicality' standard."); Apple Computer, Inc. v. Microsoft Corp., 35 F.3d 1435, 1446 (9th Cir.1994), *cert. denied*, 513 U.S. 1184, 115 S.Ct. 1176, 130 L.Ed.2d 1129 (1995) ("there can be no infringement unless the works are virtually identical"); Harper House, Inc. v. Thomas Nelson, Inc., 889 F.2d 197, 205 (9th Cir.1989) ("As with factual compilations, copyright infringement of compilations consisting of largely uncopyrightable elements should not be found in the absence of 'bodily appropriation of expression.' ").

Does the *Altai* approach strike the right balance of competing interests? In discussing its "filtration" step, the *Altai* court specifies that elements necessary to achieve compatibility with a specific computer or with other programs should be deemed unprotectible. What are the practical implications of permitting such elements to be copied?

2. *Alternative methods of protecting computer programs*. We have examined three different means of claiming proprietary rights in computer pro-

grams: trade secret protection, patents, and copyright. From a strategic standpoint, what are the relative advantages and disadvantages of each? See Final Report of the National Commission on New Technological Uses of Copyrighted Works, 16–19 (1978). Is there any objection to businesses pursuing more than one of these forms of protection simultaneously?

As the *Altai* court notes, the National Commission on New Technological Uses of Copyrighted Works ("CONTU") reviewed the various approaches to protecting computer programs and recommended that Congress retain copyright protection. The CONTU Report found that programs fit well into existing copyright doctrine, and that copyright afforded some advantages over existing alternatives. Final Report, *supra*, at 9–26. The *Altai* court questions the continuing validity of the CONTU findings and suggests further legislative investigation. There has been significant criticism of copyright as a vehicle for software protection. What is it about the nature of computer programs that leads the *Altai* court to characterize use of copyright as a "square peg in a round hole"? In your opinion, what, if any, practical or policy problems arise from applying copyright law to computer programs? Are the problems sufficiently great to justify a change? Compare Miller, *Copyright Protection for Computer Programs, Databases, and Computer–Generated Works: Is Anything New Since CONTU?*, 106 Harv. L. Rev. 977 (1993), with Samuelson, *CONTU Revisited: The Case Against Copyright Protection for Computer Programs in Machine–Readable Form*, [1984] Duke L.J. 663.

3. *Protection for a program's user interface.* In a portion of the *Altai* decision not reprinted above, the Second Circuit specified that its decision should not control infringement actions regarding "categorically distinct works," such as a program's screen display. The court explained that screen displays "represent products of computer programs, rather than the programs themselves, and fall under the copyright rubric of audiovisual works." *Altai*, 982 F.2d at 703. Copyright protection for a program's screen display and other aspects of a program's "user interface,"[6] such as the correspondence between particular commands and keys on the keyboard, has also provided courts with conceptual difficulties. The screen display itself is relatively familiar territory, though issues of merger, blank forms and originality may frequently arise. How should one analyze the assignment of particular keys to particular commands? How about the use of a joy stick, a dial, or a power glove?

In Lotus Development Corp. v. Borland International, Inc., 49 F.3d 807 (1st Cir.1995), *aff'd*, 516 U.S. 233, 116 S.Ct. 804, 133 L.Ed.2d 610 (1996),[7] the Court of Appeals for the First Circuit undertook to determine whether the menu command hierarchy of the Lotus 1–2–3 spreadsheet program constituted copyrightable subject matter. The Lotus 1–2–3 program enables users to perform accounting functions electronically on a computer. Users manipulate and control the program via a series of menu commands, such as "Copy," "Print," and "Quit." Users choose commands either by highlighting them on the screen or by typing their first letter. In all, Lotus 1–2–3 has 469

---

6. The term "user interface" generally refers to the visual, tactile and aural elements through which a computer program communicates with its user.

7. The Supreme Court Justices split 4–4 on the merits of the case, which had the technical effect of affirming the First Circuit's decision in *Lotus*.

commands arranged into more than 50 menus and submenus. The defendant, Borland, incorporated a virtually identical copy of the 1–2–3 menu tree into its program, in order to make its program compatible with 1–2–3, and enable spreadsheet users who were already familiar with 1–2–3 to switch to the Borland program without having to learn new commands or rewrite their Lotus macros. Borland did not copy any of Lotus' underlying computer code. It copied only the words and structure of Lotus' menu command hierarchy.

In determining whether Borland had taken copyrightable subject matter, the First Circuit immediately distinguished *Altai*:

> In the instant appeal, we are not confronted with alleged nonliteral copying of computer code. Rather, we are faced with Borland's deliberate, literal copying of the Lotus menu command hierarchy. Thus, we must determine not whether nonliteral copying occurred in some amorphous sense, but rather whether the literal copying of the Lotus menu command hierarchy constitutes copyright infringement.

> While the *Altai* test may provide a useful framework for assessing the alleged nonliteral copying of computer code, we find it to be of little help in assessing whether the literal copying of a menu command hierarchy constitutes copyright infringement. In fact, we think that the *Altai* test in this context may actually be misleading because, in instructing courts to abstract the various levels, it seems to encourage them to find a base level that includes copyrightable subject matter that, if literally copied, would make the copier liable for copyright infringement. While that base (or literal) level would not be at issue in a nonliteral-copying case like *Altai*, it is precisely what is at issue in this appeal. We think that abstracting menu command hierarchies down to their individual word and menu levels and then filtering idea from expression at that stage, as [the *Altai* test requires], obscures the more fundamental question of whether a menu command hierarchy can be copyrighted at all. The initial inquiry should not be whether individual components of a menu command hierarchy are expressive, but rather whether the menu command hierarchy as a whole can be copyrighted.

Lotus, 49 F.3d at 814–15.

The First Circuit found that the menu command hierarchy constituted a "method of operation," which could not be protected under the terms of Copyright Act § 102.

> We think that "method of operation," as that term is used in § 102(b), refers to the means by which a person operates something, whether it be a car, a food processor, or a computer. Thus a text describing how to operate something would not extend copyright protection to the method of operation itself; other people would be free to employ that method and to describe it in their own words. Similarly, if a new method of operation is used rather than described, other people would still be free to employ or describe that method.

> We hold that the Lotus menu command hierarchy is an uncopyrightable "method of operation." The Lotus menu command hierarchy provides the means by which users control and operate Lotus 1–2–3. If users

wish to copy material, for example, they use the "Copy" command. If users wish to print material, they use the "Print" command. Users must use the command terms to tell the computer what to do. Without the menu command hierarchy, users would not be able to access and control, or indeed make use of, Lotus 1–2–3's functional capabilities.

The Lotus menu command hierarchy does not merely explain and present Lotus 1–2–3's functional capabilities to the user; it also serves as the method by which the program is operated and controlled. The Lotus menu command hierarchy is different from the Lotus long prompts, for the long prompts are not necessary to the operation of the program; users could operate Lotus 1–2–3 even if there were no long prompts. The Lotus menu command hierarchy is also different from the Lotus screen displays, for users need not "use" any expressive aspects of the screen displays in order to operate Lotus 1–2–3; because the way the screens look has little bearing on how users control the program, the screen displays are not part of Lotus 1–2–3's "method of operation." The Lotus menu command hierarchy is also different from the underlying computer code, because while code is necessary for the program to work, its precise formulation is not. In other words, to offer the same capabilities as Lotus 1–2–3, Borland did not have to copy Lotus's underlying code (and indeed it did not); to allow users to operate its programs in substantially the same way, however, Borland had to copy the Lotus menu command hierarchy. Thus the Lotus 1–2–3 code is not an uncopyrightable "method of operation."

The district court held that the Lotus menu command hierarchy, with its specific choice and arrangement of command terms, constituted an "expression" of the "idea" of operating a computer program with commands arranged hierarchically into menus and submenus. Under the district court's reasoning, Lotus's decision to employ hierarchically arranged command terms to operate its program could not foreclose its competitors from also employing hierarchically arranged command terms to operate their programs, but it did foreclose them from employing the specific command terms and arrangement that Lotus had used. In effect, the district court limited Lotus 1–2–3's "method of operation" to an abstraction.

Accepting the district court's finding that the Lotus developers made some expressive choices in choosing and arranging the Lotus command terms, we nonetheless hold that that expression is not copyrightable because it is part of Lotus 1–2–3's "method of operation." We do not think that "methods of operation" are limited to abstractions; rather, they are the means by which a user operates something. If specific words are essential to operating something, then they are part of a "method of operation" and, as such, are unprotectible. This is so whether they must be highlighted, typed in, or even spoken, as computer programs no doubt will soon be controlled by spoken words.

The fact that Lotus developers could have designed the Lotus menu command hierarchy differently is immaterial to the question of whether it is a "method of operation." In other words, our initial inquiry is not whether the Lotus menu command hierarchy incorporates any expression. Rather, our initial inquiry is whether the Lotus menu command hierarchy is a "method of operation." Concluding, as we do, that users operate Lotus 1–2–3 by using the Lotus menu command hierarchy, and that the entire Lotus menu command hierarchy is essential to operating Lotus 1–2–3, we do not inquire further whether that method of operation could have been designed differently. The "expressive" choices of what to name the command terms and how to arrange them do not magically change the uncopyrightable menu command hierarchy into copyrightable subject matter.

* * *

In many ways, the Lotus menu command hierarchy is like the buttons used to control, say, a video cassette recorder ("VCR"). A VCR is a machine that enables one to watch and record video tapes. Users operate VCRs by pressing a series of buttons that are typically labeled "Record, Play, Reverse, Fast Forward, Pause, Stop/Eject." That the buttons are arranged and labeled does not make them a "literary work," nor does it make them an "expression" of the abstract "method of operating" a VCR via a set of labeled buttons. Instead, the buttons are themselves the "method of operating" the VCR.

When a Lotus 1–2–3 user choose a command, either by highlighting it on the screen or by typing its first letter, he or she effectively pushes a button. Highlighting the "Print" command on the screen, or typing the letter "P," is analogous to pressing a VCR button labeled "Play."

Just as one could not operate a buttonless VCR, it would be impossible to operate Lotus 1–2–3 without employing its menu command hierarchy. Thus the Lotus command terms are not equivalent to the labels on the VCR's buttons, but are instead equivalent to the buttons themselves. Unlike the labels on a VCR's buttons, which merely make operating a VCR easier by indicating the buttons' functions, the Lotus menu commands are essential to operating Lotus 1–2–3. Without the menu commands, there would be no way to "push" the Lotus buttons, as one could push unlabeled VCR buttons. While Lotus could probably have designed a user interface for which the command terms were mere labels, it did not do so here. Lotus 1–2–3 depends for its operation on use of the precise command terms that make up the Lotus menu command hierarchy.

Lotus, 49 F.3d at 815–17.

Do you agree with the First Circuit's analogy? As a matter of public policy, does the outcome of *Lotus* make sense?

The Court of Appeals for the Tenth Circuit has subsequently rejected the *Lotus* court's reasoning, finding it appropriate to apply the abstraction-filtration-comparison test to alleged literal copying of a set of numeric software command codes, and holding that expressive elements found in a "method of operation" may be protected. Mitel, Inc. v. Iqtel, Inc., 124 F.3d 1366 (10th Cir.1997). The Tenth Circuit explained:

The *Lotus* Court concluded that the question whether a work is excluded from protection under section 102(b) logically precedes consideration of whether the individual components of the work are "expressive." Most significantly, the *Lotus* Court held that otherwise protectible expression that is embodied in a method of operation is excluded under section 102(b) from copyright protection because it is part of the method of operation * * *.

We conclude that although an element of a work may be characterized as a method of operation, that element may nevertheless contain expression that is eligible for copyright protection. Section 102(b) does not extinguish the protection accorded a particular expression of an idea merely because that expression is embodied in a method of operation at a higher level of abstraction. Rather, sections 102(a) and (b) interact to secure ideas for [the] public domain and to set apart an author's particular expression for further scrutiny to ensure that copyright protection will "promote the ... useful Arts." Our abstraction-filtration-comparison approach is directed to achieving this balance. Thus, we decline to adopt the *Lotus* Court's approach to section 102(b), and continue to adhere to our abstraction-filtration-comparison approach.

We are mindful of the concern expressed by the *Lotus* Court that, by its very nature, the abstraction-filtration-comparison approach tends to produce a core of copyrightable protectible expression that, if literally copied, would make the copier liable for infringement. Undoubtedly, the portions of a work to which a court applies abstraction analysis frequently contain a level of abstraction which reveals expression that does not fall within the excluded categories of section 102(b). Although this core of expression is eligible for copyright protection, it is subject to the rigors of filtration analysis which excludes from protection expression that is in the public domain, otherwise unoriginal, or subject to the doctrines of merger and *scenes a faire.*

Mitel, 124 F.3d at 1372. Which approach is preferable?

NOTE: THE SEMICONDUCTOR CHIP PROTECTION ACT

Congress enacted a *sui generis* scheme of protection for one new technology that it deemed insufficiently protected by existing intellectual property doctrines. The Semiconductor Chip Protection Act of 1984 ("SCPA"), 17 U.S.C.A. §§ 901–914, draws elements from both the Copyright and Patent Acts in an attempt to custom-tailor rights in the intricate design lay-outs of semiconductor chips.

Chips consist of a collection of transistors laid out in a single integrated structure to perform an electronic function, such as processing, memory, or logic. Creation of chips entails extensive investment of engineering talent, time and money. The process begins with the creation of drawings setting forth the chip's electronic circuitry design. The drawings are then used to produce stencils, called "masks." The masks are used in connection with a chemical process to produce the various layers of the chip.

The SCPA protects "original" mask works that are "fixed" in chips. 17 U.S.C.A. § 901(a)(3). To be "original," the mask work must be an independent creation, and it must not consist of designs that are staple, commonplace or familiar in the semiconductor industry, or obvious variations of such designs. *Id.*, § 902(b). Protection commences when the work is registered with the Copyright Office or is first commercially exploited anywhere in the world, and lasts for ten years. *Id.*, § 904. The SCPA gives no rights in the ideas, systems or methods underlying or embodied in the mask work—only in the creator's particular means of expressing or implementing them. *Id.*, § 902(c).

Mask work owners are granted the exclusive rights 1) to reproduce the mask work by optical, electronic or any other means; 2) to import or distribute chips embodying the protected mask work; and 3) to induce or knowingly cause another person to do the acts described in 1) and 2). *Id.*, § 905. However, the SCPA imposes several important limitations on the mask work owner's rights. For example, there is an innocent purchaser defense. *Id.*, § 907. In addition, the SCPA permits reverse engineering by expressly providing that others may copy a protected mask work if their purpose is solely to teach, analyze or evaluate it. Concepts or techniques learned from analyzing or evaluating the chip can be incorporated in the reverse engineer's own original chips. *Id.*, § 906(a).

The ten years following enactment of the SCPA produced only one reported infringement case. Why so little litigation under the Act? At least a couple of explanations have been advanced. First, the Act addressed itself to the technology existing in the late 1970's and early 1980's, under which it was relatively easy and inexpensive to copy and manufacture another company's chip. Subsequent advances in technology have rendered piracy less feasible and cost-effective. Second, through its broad exemption for reverse engineering and use of the product of reverse engineering, the SCPA excluded much chip copying from its coverage. See Rauch, *The Realities of Our Times: The Semiconductor Chip Protection Act of 1984 and the Evolution of the Semiconductor Industry*, 75 J. Pat. & Trademark Off. Soc. 93 (1993); Kasch, *The Semiconductor Chip Protection Act: Past, Present, and Future*, 7 High Tech. L.J. 71 (1992).

The TRIPs Agreement requires all adhering countries to provide protection for the "layout designs of integrated circuits" either pursuant to a *sui generis* law or as part of their copyright, patent, or other existing intellectual property laws. Why might the U.S. Congress have deemed *sui generis* protection necessary for chips? Wouldn't copyright provide adequate protection?

2. Pictorial, Graphic and Sculptural Works—Copyright in Useful Articles

§ 101.   Definitions

      * * *

      "Pictorial, graphic, and sculptural works" include two-dimensional and three-dimensional works of fine, graphic, and applied art, photographs, prints and art reproductions, maps, globes, charts, diagrams, models, and technical drawings, including architectural plans. Such works shall include works of artistic craftsmanship insofar as their form but not their mechanical or utilitarian aspects are concerned; the design of a useful article, as defined in this section, shall be considered a pictorial, graphic, or sculptural work only if, and only to the extent that, each such design incorporates pictorial, graphic, or sculptural features that can be identified separately from, and are capable of existing independently of, the utilitarian aspects of the article.

* * *

A "useful article" is an article having an intrinsic utilitarian function that is not merely to portray the appearance of the article or to convey information. An article that is normally a part of a useful article is considered a "useful article."

17 U.S.C.A. § 101.

HOUSE REPORT ON THE COPYRIGHT ACT OF 1976

H.R. Rep. No. 1476, 94th Cong., 2d Sess. 47, 54–55 (1976).

[T]he definition of "pictorial, graphic, and sculptural works" carries with it no implied criterion of artistic taste, aesthetic value, or intrinsic quality. The term is intended to comprise not only "works of art" in the traditional sense but also works of graphic art and illustration, art reproductions, plans and drawings, photographs and reproductions of them, maps, charts, globes, and other cartographic works, works of these kinds intended for use in advertising and commerce, and works of "applied art." * * *

In accordance with the Supreme Court's decision in Mazer v. Stein, 347 U.S. 201 (1954), works of "applied art" encompass all original pictorial, graphic, and sculptural works that are intended to be or have been embodied in useful articles, regardless of factors such as mass production, commercial exploitation, and the potential availability of design patent protection. * * *

The Committee has added language to the definition of "pictorial, graphic, and sculptural works" in an effort to make clearer the distinction between works of applied art protectible under the bill and industrial designs not subject to copyright protection. The declaration that "pictorial, graphic, and sculptural works" include "works of artistic craftsmanship insofar as their form but not their mechanical or utilitarian aspects are concerned" is classic language: it is drawn from Copyright Office regulations promulgated in the 1940's and expressly endorsed by the Supreme Court in the *Mazer* case.

The second part of the amendment states that "the design of a useful article ... shall be considered a pictorial, graphic, or sculptural work only if, and only to the extent that, such design incorporates pictorial, graphic, or sculptural features that can be identified separately from, and are capable of existing independently of, the utilitarian aspects of the article." * * *

In adopting this amendatory language, the Committee is seeking to draw as clear a line as possible between copyrightable works of applied art and uncopyrighted works of industrial design. A two-dimensional painting, drawing, or graphic work is still capable of being identified as such when it is printed on or applied to utilitarian articles such as textile fabrics, wallpaper, containers, and the like. The same is true when a statue or carving is used to embellish an industrial product or, as in the Mazer case, is incorporated into a product without losing its ability to exist independently as a work of art. On the other hand, although the shape of an industrial product may be aesthetically satisfying and valuable, the Committee's intention is not to offer it copyright protection under the bill. Unless the shape of an automobile, airplane, ladies' dress, food processor, television set, or any other industrial product contains some element that, physically or conceptually, can be identified as separable from the utilitarian aspects of that article, the design would not be copyrighted under the bill. The test of separability and independence from "the utilitarian aspects of the article" does not depend upon the nature of the design— that is, even if the appearance of an article is determined by aesthetic (as opposed to functional) considerations, only elements, if any, which can be identified separately from the useful article as such are copyrightable. And, even if the three-dimensional design contains some such element (for example, a carving on the back of a chair or a floral relief design on silver flatware), copyright protection would extend only to that element, and would not cover the over-all configuration of the utilitarian article as such.

BRANDIR INTERNATIONAL, INC. v. CASCADE PACIFIC LUMBER CO.

United States Court of Appeals for the Second Circuit, 1987.
834 F.2d 1142.

OAKES, CIRCUIT JUDGE:

In passing the Copyright Act of 1976 Congress attempted to distinguish between protectible "works of applied art" and "industrial designs not subject to copyright protection." The courts, however, have had difficulty framing tests by which the fine line establishing what is and what is not copyrightable can be drawn. Once again we are called upon to draw such a line, this time in a case involving the "RIBBON Rack," a bicycle rack made of bent tubing that is said to have originated from a wire sculpture. (A photograph of the rack is contained in the appendix to this opinion.) [The Register of Copyright denied copyright. The district court granted summary judgement to the defendant, Cascade Pacific, with regard to the copyright claim.]

＊　＊　＊

As courts and commentators have come to realize, ＊　＊　＊ the line Congress attempted to draw between copyrightable art and noncopyrightable design "was neither clear nor new." Denicola, *Applied Art and Industrial Design: A Suggested Approach to Copyright in Useful Articles*, 67 Minn.L.Rev. 707, 720 (1983). One aspect of the distinction that has drawn considerable attention is the reference in the House Report to "physically *or conceptually* "(emphasis added) separable elements. The District of Columbia Circuit in *Esquire, Inc. v. Ringer*, 591 F.2d 796, 803–04 (D.C.Cir.1978) (holding outdoor lighting fixtures ineligible for copyright), *cert. denied*, 440 U.S. 908, 99 S.Ct. 1217, 59 L.Ed.2d 456 (1979), called this an "isolated reference" and gave it no significance. * * * [I]n *Kieselstein–Cord v. Accessories by Pearl, Inc.*, 632 F.2d 989, 993 (2d Cir.1980), this court accepted the idea that copyrightability can adhere in the "conceptual" separation of an artistic element. Indeed, the court went on to find such conceptual separation in reference to ornate belt buckles that could be and were worn separately as jewelry. * * *

In *Carol Barnhart Inc. v. Economy Cover Corp.*, 773 F.2d 411 (2d Cir.1985), a divided panel of this circuit affirmed a district court grant of summary judgment of noncopyrightability of four life-sized, anatomically correct human torso forms. *Carol Barnhart* distinguished *Kieselstein–Cord*, but it surely did not overrule it. The distinction made was that the ornamented surfaces of the *Kieselstein–Cord* belt buckles "were not in any respect required by their utilitarian functions," but the features claimed to be aesthetic or artistic in the *Carol Barnhart* forms were "inextricably intertwined with the utilitarian feature, the display of clothes." 773 F.2d at 419. As Judge Newman's dissent made clear, the *Carol Barnhart* majority did not dispute "that 'conceptual separability' is distinct from 'physical separability' and, when present, entitles the creator of a useful article to a copyright on its design." 773 F.2d at 420.

"Conceptual separability" is thus alive and well, at least in this circuit. The problem, however, is determining exactly what it is and how it is to be applied. Judge Newman's illuminating discussion in dissent in *Carol Barnhart*, see 773 F.2d at 419–24, proposed a test that aesthetic features are conceptually separable if "the article ... stimulate[s] in the mind of the beholder a concept that is separate from the concept evoked by its utilitarian function." *Id.* at 422. This approach has received favorable endorsement by at least one commentator, W. Patry, Latman's *The Copyright Law* 43–45 (6th ed. 1986), who calls Judge Newman's test the "temporal displacement" test. It is to be distinguished from other possible ways in which conceptual separability can be tested, including whether the primary use is as a utilitarian article as opposed to an artistic work, whether the aesthetic aspects of the work can be said to be "primary," and whether the article is marketable as art, none of which is very satisfactory. But Judge Newman's test was rejected outright by the majority as "a standard so ethereal as to amount to a 'nontest' that would be extremely difficult, if not impossible, to administer or apply." 773 F.2d at 419 n. 5.

Perhaps the differences between the majority and the dissent in *Carol Barnhart* might have been resolved had they had before them the Denicola article on *Applied Art and Industrial Design: A Suggested Approach to Copyright in Useful Articles, supra*. There, Professor Denicola points out that although the Copyright Act of 1976 was an effort " 'to draw as clear a line as possible,' " in truth "there is no line, but merely a spectrum of forms and shapes responsive in varying degrees to utilitarian concerns." 67 Minn.L.Rev. at 741. Denicola argues that "the statutory directive requires a distinction between works of industrial design and works whose origins lie outside the design process, despite the utilitarian environment in which they appear." He views the statutory limitation of copyrightability as "an attempt to identify elements whose form and appearance reflect the unconstrained perspective of the artist," such features not being the product of industrial design. *Id.* at 742. "Copyrightability, therefore, should turn on the relationship between the proffered work and the process of industrial design." *Id.* at 741. He suggests that "the dominant characteristic of industrial design is the influence of nonaesthetic, utilitarian concerns" and hence concludes that copyrightability "ultimately should depend on the extent to which the work reflects artistic expression uninhibited by functional considerations."[2] *Id.* To state the Denicola test in the language of conceptual separability, if design elements reflect a merger of aesthetic and functional considerations, the artistic aspects of a work cannot be said to be conceptually separable from the utilitarian elements. Conversely, where design elements can be identified as reflecting the designer's artistic judgment exercised independently of functional influences, conceptual separability exists.

We believe that Professor Denicola's approach provides the best test for conceptual separability and, accordingly, adopt it here for several reasons. First, the approach is consistent with the holdings of our previous cases. * * * Second, the test's emphasis on the influence of utilitarian concerns in the design process may help, as Denicola notes, to "alleviate the de facto discrimination against nonrepresentational art that has regrettably accompanied much of the current analysis." *Id.* at 745. Finally, and perhaps most importantly, we think Denicola's test will not be too difficult to administer in practice. The work itself will continue to give "mute testimony" of its origins. In addition, the parties will be required to present evidence relating to the design process and the nature of the work, with the trier of fact making the determination whether the aesthetic design elements are significantly influenced by functional considerations.

Turning now to the facts of this case, we note first that Brandir contends, and its chief owner David Levine testified, that the original design of the RIBBON Rack stemmed from wire sculptures that Levine had created, each formed from one continuous undulating piece of wire. These sculptures were, he said, created and displayed in his home as a means of personal expression, but apparently were never sold or displayed elsewhere. He also created a wire sculpture in the shape of a bicycle and states that he did not give any thought to the utilitarian application of any

---

2. Professor Denicola rejects the exclusion of all works created with some utilitarian application in view, for that would not only overturn *Mazer v. Stein*, 347 U.S. 201, 74 S.Ct. 460, 98 L.Ed. 630 (1954), on which much of the legislation is based, but also "a host of other eminently sensible decisions, in favor of an intractable factual inquiry of questionable relevance." 67 Minn.L.Rev. at 741. He adds that "[a]ny such categorical approach would also undermine the legislative determination to preserve an artist's ability to exploit utilitarian markets." *Id.* (citing 17 U.S.C. § 113(a) (1976)).

of his sculptures until he accidentally juxtaposed the bicycle sculpture with one of the self-standing wire sculptures. It was not until November 1978 that Levine seriously began pursuing the utilitarian application of his sculptures, when a friend, G. Duff Bailey, a bicycle buff and author of numerous articles about urban cycling, was at Levine's home and informed him that the sculptures would make excellent bicycle racks, permitting bicycles to be parked under the overloops as well as on top of the underloops. Following this meeting, Levine met several times with Bailey and others, completing the designs for the RIBBON Rack by the use of a vacuum cleaner hose, and submitting his drawings to a fabricator complete with dimensions. The Brandir RIBBON Rack began being nationally advertised and promoted for sale in September 1979.

In November 1982 Levine discovered that another company, Cascade Pacific Lumber Co., was selling a similar product. [Levine attempted to register the RIBBON Rack, but the] Copyright Office refused registration by letter, stating that the RIBBON Rack did not contain any element that was "capable of independent existence as a copyrightable pictorial, graphic or sculptural work apart from the shape of the useful article." * * *

* * * The RIBBON Rack has been featured in *Popular Science, Art and Architecture*, and *Design 384* magazines, and it won an Industrial Designers Society of America design award in the spring of 1980. In the spring of 1984 the RIBBON Rack was selected from 200 designs to be included among 77 of the designs exhibited at the Katonah Gallery in an exhibition entitled "The Product of Design: An Exploration of the Industrial Design Process," an exhibition that was written up in the *New York Times*.

Sales of the RIBBON Rack from September 1979 through January 1985 were in excess of $1,367,000. * * *

Applying Professor Denicola's test to the RIBBON Rack, we find that the rack is not copyrightable. It seems clear that the form of the rack is influenced in significant measure by utilitarian concerns and thus any aesthetic elements cannot be said to be conceptually separable from the utilitarian elements. This is true even though the sculptures which inspired the RIBBON Rack may well have been—the issue of originality aside—copyrightable.

Brandir argues correctly that a copyrighted work of art does not lose its protected status merely because it subsequently is put to a functional use. The Supreme Court so held in *Mazer v. Stein*, 347 U.S. 201, 74 S.Ct. 460, 98 L.Ed. 630 (1954), and Congress specifically intended to accept and codify *Mazer* in section 101 of the Copyright Act of 1976. The district court thus erred in ruling that, whatever the RIBBON Rack's origins, Brandir's commercialization of the rack disposed of the issue of its copyrightability.

Had Brandir merely adopted one of the existing sculptures as a bicycle rack, neither the application to a utilitarian end nor commercialization of that use would have caused the object to forfeit its copyrighted status. Comparison of the RIBBON Rack with the earlier sculptures, however, reveals that while the rack may have been derived in part from one or more "works of art," it is in its final form essentially a product of industrial design. In creating the RIBBON Rack, the designer has clearly adapted the original aesthetic elements to accommodate and further a utilitarian purpose. These altered design features of the RIBBON Rack, including the spacesaving, open design achieved by widening the upper loops to permit parking under as well as over the rack's curves, the straightened vertical elements that allow in-and above-ground installation of the rack, the ability to fit all types of bicycles and mopeds, and the heavy-gauged tubular construction of rustproof galvanized steel, are all features that combine to make for a safe, secure, and maintenance-free system of parking bicycles and mopeds. Its undulating shape is said in *Progressive Architecture*, January 1982, to permit double the storage of conventional bicycle racks. Moreover, the rack is manufactured from 2 3/8–inch standard steam pipe that is bent into form, the six-inch radius of the bends evidently resulting from bending the pipe according to a standard formula that yields bends having a radius equal to three times the nominal internal diameter of the pipe.

Brandir argues that its RIBBON Rack can and should be characterized as a sculptural work of art within the minimalist art movement. Minimalist sculpture's most outstanding feature is said to be its clarity and simplicity, in that it often takes the form of geometric shapes, lines, and forms that are pure and free of ornamentation and void of association. As Brandir's expert put it, "The meaning is to be found in, within, around and outside the work of art, allowing the artistic sensation to be experienced as well as intellectualized." People who use Foley Square in New York City see in the form of minimalist art the "Tilted Arc," which is on the plaza at 26 Federal Plaza. Numerous museums have had exhibitions of such art, and the school of minimalist art has many admirers.

It is unnecessary to determine whether to the art world the RIBBON Rack properly would be considered an example of minimalist sculpture. The result under the copyright statute is not changed. Using the test we have adopted, it is not enough that, to paraphrase Judge Newman, the rack may stimulate in the mind of the reasonable observer a concept separate from the bicycle rack concept. While the RIBBON Rack may be worthy of admiration for its aesthetic qualities alone, it remains nonetheless the product of industrial design. Form and function are inextricably intertwined in the rack, its ultimate design being as much the result of utilitarian pressures as aesthetic choices. Indeed, the visually pleasing proportions and symmetricality of the rack represent design changes made in response to functional concerns. Judging from the awards the rack has received, it would seem in fact that Brandir has achieved with the RIBBON Rack the highest goal of modern industrial design, that is, the harmonious fusion of function and aesthetics. Thus there remains no artistic element of the RIBBON Rack that can be identified as separate and "capable of existing independently, of, the utilitarian aspects of the article." Accordingly, we must affirm on the copyright claim.

* * *

Appendix

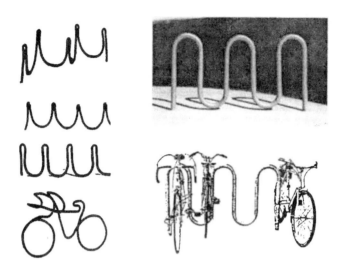

WINTER, CIRCUIT JUDGE, concurring in part and dissenting in part:

* * * I respectfully dissent from the majority's discussion and disposition of the copyright claim.

My colleagues, applying an adaptation of Professor Denicola's test, hold that the aesthetic elements of the design of a useful article are not conceptually separable from its utilitarian aspects if "[f]orm and function are inextricably intertwined" in the article, and "its ultimate design [is] as much the result of utilitarian pressures as aesthetic choices." Applying that test to the instant matter, they observe that the dispositive fact is that "in creating the Ribbon Rack, [Levine] has clearly adapted the *original* aesthetic elements to accommodate and further a utilitarian purpose." (emphasis added). The grounds of my disagreement are that: (1) my colleagues' adaptation of Professor Denicola's test diminishes the statutory concept of "conceptual separability" to the vanishing point; and (2) their focus on the process or sequence followed by the particular designer makes copyright protection depend upon largely fortuitous circumstances concerning the creation of the design in issue.

* * *

[T]he relevant question is whether the design of a useful article, however intertwined with the article's utilitarian aspects, causes an ordinary reasonable observer to perceive an aesthetic concept not related to the article's use. The answer to this question is clear in the instant case because any reasonable observer would easily view the Ribbon Rack as an ornamental sculpture.[2] Indeed, there is evidence of actual confusion over whether it is strictly ornamental in the refusal of a building manager to accept delivery until assured by the buyer that the Ribbon Rack was in fact a bicycle rack. Moreover, Brandir has received a request to use the Ribbon Rack as environmental sculpture, and has offered testimony of art experts who claim that the Ribbon Rack may be valued solely for its artistic features. As one of those experts observed: "If one were to place a Ribbon Rack on an island without access, or in a park and surround the work with a barrier, . . . its status as a work of art would be beyond dispute."

My colleagues also allow too much to turn upon the process or sequence of design followed by the designer of the Ribbon Rack. They thus suggest that copyright protection would have been accorded "had Brandir merely adopted . . . as a bicycle rack" an enlarged version of one of David Levine's original sculptures rather than one that had wider upper loops and straightened vertical elements. I cannot agree that copyright protection for the Ribbon Rack turns on whether Levine serendipitously chose the final design of the Ribbon Rack during his initial sculptural musings or whether the original design had to be slightly modified to accommodate bicycles. Copyright protection, which is intended to generate incentives for designers by according property rights in their creations, should not turn on purely fortuitous events. For that reason, the Copyright Act expressly states that the legal test is how the final article is perceived, not how it was developed through various stages. It thus states in pertinent part:

> the design of a useful article . . . shall be considered a . . . sculptural work only if, and only to the extent that, such design incorporates . . . *sculptural features that can be identified separately from, and are capable of existing independently of, the utilitarian aspects of the article.*

17 U.S.C. § 101 (1982) (emphasis added). * * *

NOTES AND QUESTIONS

1. *The "separability" issue.* In discussing the best means of distinguishing the artistic features of a design from its utilitarian aspects, it is useful to consider why Congress desired to make such a distinction in the first place. What was Congress' purpose? What are the practical implications of construing the separability requirement liberally to permit copyright protection for a wide array of useful article designs?

As the *Brandir* opinion indicates, the Second Circuit has interpreted the House Report to permit copyright upon a showing of *either* physical *or* conceptual separability. There has been relatively little debate about the

---

2. The reasonable observer may be forgiven, however, if he or she does not recognize the Ribbon Rack as an example of minimalist art.

meaning of physical separability. Courts have found a pictorial, graphic, or sculptural feature of a useful article "physically separable" if it can be physically separated from the article and stand alone as a work of art in the traditional sense. *Mazer v. Stein, supra*, the Supreme Court decision that established the applicability of copyright to works of applied art, provides a good example of physical separability. The works in that case were sculptures of dancers used as the base of table lamps, one of which is illustrated below. If the statue were physically detached from the table lamp electrical wiring and shade apparatus, it would stand alone as a sculptural work. In *Mazer*, the Supreme Court found that such a statue did not lose its copyrightable status simply because its creator intended to and did embed it in a useful article and mass produce it.

Conceptual separability, which was at issue in *Brandir*, has proven more difficult. One case in which the Second Circuit *did* find conceptual separability was Kieselstein–Cord v. Accessories by Pearl, Inc., 632 F.2d 989 (2d Cir.1980). The useful articles at issue in that case were belt buckles ornamented with a sculpted metal surface, as depicted below:

Winchester　　　　　　　　　　　　　Vaquero

These buckles, made of precious metals, were sold at jewelry and high-fashion stores, and had been accepted by the Metropolitan Museum of Art for its permanent collection. There was evidence that at least one of the buckles had been worn as ornamentation around the neck, rather than around the waist. In finding that the buckles were protected by copyright, the court stated that "the primary ornamental aspect of the * * * buckles is conceptually separable from their subsidiary utilitarian function." *Id.*, 632 F.2d at 993. Did the court mean to suggest that conceptual separability should depend on whether the aesthetically pleasing aspect of the article is primary and the utilitarian function subsidiary? Unfortunately, the court did not elaborate. In subsequent opinions, panels of the Second Circuit have revisited the case of the belt buckles, and offered other justifications for the finding that their sculpted ornamental metal surfaces were "conceptually separable." For example, in Carol Barnhart Inc. v. Economy Cover Corp., 773 F.2d 411, 419 (2d Cir.1985), the court explained:

> [T]he ornamented surfaces of the buckles were not in any respect required by their utilitarian functions; the artistic and aesthetic features could thus be conceived of as having been added to, or superimposed upon, an otherwise utilitarian article. The unique artistic design was wholly unnecessary to performance of the utilitarian function.

In *Brandir*, the court noted that in *Kieselstein–Cord*, "the artistic aspects of the belt buckles reflected purely aesthetic choices, independent of the buckles' function." 834 F.2d at 1145.

In your opinion, which is the better approach to determining conceptual separability—the approach advocated by the *Brandir* majority, or that advocated by the *Brandir* dissent? Why? Which approach more effectively promotes Congress' underlying purpose in restricting copyright to elements that are physically or conceptually separable from the utilitarian aspects of the useful article? Which approach is easier to apply, or more likely to lead to consistent and fair results?

2. *Developments in other circuits.* In Pivot Point International, Inc. v. Charlene Products, Inc., 372 F.3d 913 (7th Cir. 2004), the Seventh Circuit adopted the *Brandir* court's "proccess-oriented approach" for determining conceptual separability. In the course of doing so, the court characterized the *Brandir* standard as consistent with the "temporal displacement" standard that Judge Newman proposed in his dissent in the *Carol Barnhart* case:

"[T]he requisite 'separateness' exists whenever the design creates in the mind of an ordinary observer two different concepts that are not inevitably entertained simultaneously." 773 F.2d at 422. The *Pivot* court explained:

> When a product has reached its final form as a result of predominantly functional or utilitarian considerations, it necessarily will be more difficult for the observer to entertain simultaneously two different concepts— the artistic object and the utilitarian object. In such circumstances, *Brandir* has the added benefit of providing a more workable judicial methodology by articulating the driving principle behind conceptual separability—the influence of industrial design. When the ultimate form of the object in question is "as much the result of utilitarian pressures as aesthetic choices," "[f]orm and function are inextricably intertwined," and the artistic aspects of the object cannot be separated from its utilitarian aspects for purposes of copyright protection.

372 F.3d at 931. Are these two standards indeed consistent? In *Pivot Point*, the allegedly infringed work consisted of a mannequin head (called "Mara") produced for use by students in beauty schools to practice styling hair and applying makeup. The plaintiff commissioned a German artist to design "Mara" to imitate the "hungry look" of high-fashion runway models. Applying the *Brandir*/temporal displacement standard, the Seventh Circuit found the Mara mannequin's facial features conceptually separable and protectible:

> It certainly is not difficult to conceptualize a human face, independent of all of Mara's specific facial features, i.e., the shape of the eye, the upturned nose, the angular cheek and jaw structure, that would serve the utilitarian functions of a hair stand and, if proven, of a makeup model. Indeed, one is not only able to conceive of a different face than that portrayed on the Mara mannequin, but one easily can conceive of another visage that portrays the "hungry look" on a high-fashion runway model.
> * * *
>
> Mara can be conceptualized as existing independent from its use in hair display or make-up training because it is the product of Heerlein's [the German artist's] artistic judgment. When Passage approached Heerlein about creating the Mara sculpture, Passage did not provide Heerlein with specific dimensions or measurements; indeed, there is no evidence that Heerlein's artistic judgment was constrained by functional considerations. Passage did not require, for instance, that the sculpture's eyes be a certain width to accommodate standard-sized eyelashes, that the brow be arched at a certain angle to facilitate easy make-up application or that the sculpture as a whole not exceed certain dimensional limits so as to fit within Pivot Point's existing packaging system. Such considerations, had they been present, would weigh against a determination that Mara was purely the product of an artistic effort. By contrast, after Passage met with Heerlein to discuss Passage's idea for a "hungry look" model, Heerlein had carte blanche to implement that vision as he saw fit.

Id. at 931–32. Is the Seventh Circuit's analysis consistent with Judge Newman's "temporal displacement" concept?

In Galiano v. Harrah's Operating Co., Inc., 416 F.3d 411 (5th Cir. 2005), the Fifth Circuit declined to apply a *Brandir*/*Pivot Point* process oriented standard in determining the copyrightability of flamboyant casino employee uniform designs. Rather, the court adopted Professor Nimmer's proposed "likelihood of marketability" standard: "[C]onceptual separability exists where there is substantial likelihood that even if the article had no utilitarian use it would still be marketable to some significant segment of the community simply because of its aesthetic qualities." *Id.* at 419 (*quoting* 1 Nimmer on Copyright § 2.08[B][3], at 2–101). Thus, the question was essentially whether the clothing design would have actual or potential market value as a stand-alone piece of artwork. The court characterized this standard as "the implicit standard courts have been using for quite some time," and noted that it was presently only adopting this standard for evaluation of clothing designs, and not for the designs of other kinds of useful articles. *Id.* at 421.

Is the *Galiano* "likelihood of marketability" standard preferable, in the case of clothing designs, to the *Brandir* and *Pivot Point* "process-oriented" standard? Are there any potential problems with it? See *Carol Barnhart, supra,* 773 F.2d at 421 (Newman, J., dissenting). Is it appropriate to apply one standard to evaluate the separability of applied art in clothing designs, and a different standard to evaluate separability in other kinds of useful articles?

3. *Useful articles.* Before reaching the separability issue one must, of course, find that the pictorial, graphic or sculptural work is part of the design of a "useful article." A "useful article" is one "having an intrinsic utilitarian function that is not merely to portray the appearance of the article or to convey information." 17 U.S.C.A. § 101.

Is a toy plane a "useful article?" It could be argued that toys are an important aspect of childhood, and even necessary as stimuli to proper emotional and intellectual development. The district court in Gay Toys, Inc. v. Buddy L Corp., 522 F.Supp. 622 (E.D.Mich.1981), *vacated,* 703 F.2d 970 (6th Cir.1983), accepted such an argument, noting that a toy airplane "permits a child to dream and to let his or her imagination soar." *Id.,* at 625. On appeal, the U.S. Court of Appeals for the Sixth Circuit proved more difficult to persuade:

> [A] toy airplane is merely a model which portrays a real airplane. * * * The intention of Congress was to exclude from copyright protection industrial products such as automobiles, food processors, and television sets. The function of toys is much more similar to that of works of art than it is to the "intrinsic utilitarian function" of industrial products.
>
> Indeed, under the district court's reasoning, virtually any "pictorial, graphic, and sculptural work" would not be copyrightable as a useful article. A painting of Lindbergh's Spirit of St. Louis invites the viewer "to dream and to let his or her imagination soar," and would not be copyrightable under the district court's approach. But the statute clearly intends to extend copyright protection to paintings. The district court would have the "useful article" exception swallow the general rule, and its rationale is incorrect.

703 F.2d 970, 973 (6th Cir.1983).

Much to the regret of high-fashion designers, items of clothing are considered to be useful articles, and thus are subject to the separability analysis. Should the same be true of halloween costumes? Could it not be argued that the function of a ladybug costume is merely to portray the appearance of an insect, and thus is exempted from the useful article category? See Copyright Office, Registrability of Costume Designs, 56 Fed. Reg. 56,530 (Nov. 5, 1991) (Fanciful costumes will be treated as useful articles because they serve the dual purpose of clothing the body and portraying the appearance of something. However, masks will not be treated as useful articles, since they have no inherent utility other than their appearance.).

PROBLEM

1. How would you judge the copyrightability of the design of a set of measuring spoons in which the bowl of each spoon is made in the shape of a heart and the handle is made in the shape of an arrow shaft?

NOTE: ALTERNATIVE FORMS OF PROTECTION FOR THE APPEARANCE OF USEFUL ARTICLES

Copyright is not the only form of protection available for designs of useful articles. For example, in *Brandir*, the plaintiff claimed trademark rights in the configuration of its RIBBON Rack pursuant to Lanham Act § 43(a), 15 U.S.C.A. § 1125(a), and New York unfair competition law, and the court remanded for further findings of fact on these claims. Trademark and unfair competition law may protect surface ornamentation and the configuration of an article if these features are "nonfunctional" and sufficiently distinctive to indicate the commercial source of the article to consumers.

In addition, Brandir might have pursued a design patent for his bike rack. As a practical matter, how would you compare the respective standards for obtaining a design patent and copyright protection? How would you evaluate the respective levels of protection that each provides? What are the practical advantages and disadvantages of each?

Notwithstanding the number of alternative routes to proprietary rights in design features of useful articles, many commercial designers believe that their work receives insufficient protection against the creation and sale of less expensive "knock-offs." Commercial designers have, for many years, lobbied Congress to enact *sui generis* legislation to provide broad-based, readily obtainable protection for the designs of useful articles in the United States, unfettered by considerations of physical or conceptual separability or the demanding non-obviousness standard of design patents.

Bills to create this protection have been introduced in Congress repeatedly over the past several decades, but none has ever been enacted. In 1998, Congress enacted *sui generis* protection for original designs of "useful articles," but limited the definition of "useful articles" for this purpose to "the design of a vessel hull, deck, or combination of a hull and deck, including a plug or mold." 17 U.S.C. § 1301(a)(2)(as amended). While the scope of the new *sui generis* design protection is thus quite limited, the provisions follow the general pattern of broader-scope design protection bills that have been introduced in the past, and may indicate the style of future, more general design protection legislation, should Congress ultimately enact it.

The Digital Millennium Copyright Act's design provisions protect the "original" design of a useful article (as narrowly defined) "which makes the article attractive or distinctive in appearance to the purchasing or using public." 17 U.S.C. § 1301. A design is deemed "original" if "it is the result of the designer's creative endeavor that provides a distinguishable variation over prior work pertaining to similar articles which is more than merely trivial and [was not] copied from another source." *Id.*, § 1301(b)(1). The design may not be "staple or commonplace," *id.*, § 1302(2), or "dictated solely by a utilitarian function of the article that embodies it." *Id.*, § 1302(4). Design claimants must register their designs within two years of making the design public. *Id.*, § 1310. However, the registration process is relatively cursory, consisting only of a determination of "whether or not the application relates to a design which on its face appears to be subject to protection." *Id.*, § 1313(a).

Protection begins when a useful article embodying the design is made public or a registration for the design is published, and lasts ten years. *Id.*, §§ 1304, 1305. The owner enjoys the exclusive right (1) to "make, have made, or import, for sale or for use in trade;" and (2) to "sell or distribute for sale or for use in trade" any useful article embodying the design. *Id.*, § 1309(a). There are some express exceptions to liability, including a provision authorizing reproduction "solely for the purpose of teaching, analyzing, or evaluating the appearance, concepts, or techniques embodied in the design, or the function of the useful article embodying the design." *Id.*, § 1309(g). The new law specifies that the issuance of a design patent will terminate the *sui generis* design protection, but that the new law does not annul or limit rights under the trademark and unfair competition laws. *Id.*, §§ 1329, 1330.

How does this *sui generis* protection differ from existing design patent protection? From copyright protection? What does it borrow from each? Is the law well adapted to the need for useful article design protection? Do you see any potential problems? Should this *sui generis* protection be extended to protect a wider range of useful article designs? If so, what, if any, subject matter limitations should be imposed? There have been numerous arguments made both for and against providing protection to useful article designs that fail to qualify for design patent or copyright protection.

Consumer groups have been among the strongest adversaries of broad, *sui generis* design protection, arguing that it would raise the prices of consumer products, including many that are not truly innovative. Automobile insurers have added their voices, arguing that by protecting automobile replacement parts, a general *sui generis* design protection law would raise the price of automobile repairs (and presumably, automobile insurance). Other opponents of *sui generis* design protection have argued that existing laws are adequate: Through all the years of lobbying for enhanced design protection, American designers have been highly creative and productive, demonstrating that no further legislation-based incentive is needed. They have also argued that the ability to copy design ideas is essential to free competition. Because the number of design choices for many functional products is limited, a few companies could tie up all the practical design alternatives, leading to greater concentration of monopoly power. See *The Industrial Innovation and Technology Act, 1987: Hearings on S.791 Before the Subcomm. On Patents, Copyrights and Trademarks of the Senate Comm. on the Judiciary*, 100th Cong., 1st Sess. 232–35 (1987) (statement of Ralph Oman, Register of Copyrights).

3. Architectural Works

While many countries fully protect works of architecture through copyright, the United States has a history of hesitation, particularly with regard to architectural works as embodied in three-dimensional buildings. Because Berne Convention Art. 2 mandates full copyright protection for works of architecture, Congress enacted the Architectural Works Copyright Protection Act ("AWCPA") in 1990 to bring the United States into compliance. The AWCPA only applies prospectively, however, to architectural works created on or after the effective date (December 1, 1990) and to works that were unconstructed and embodied in unpublished plans or drawings on that date. Existing architectural works falling outside the scope of the Act continue to be governed by the earlier law.

The Law Prior to the AWCPA

The United States traditionally protected architectural plans, or blueprints, as pictorial, graphic and sculptural works. But copyright law has provided significantly less protection for architectural works embodied in buildings, rather than plans. This is because buildings are deemed to be useful articles. Though pictorial, graphic or sculptural aspects of buildings may be protected, they are subject to the "physical or conceptual separability" test discussed in the last section. Thus, most aspects of building design, which integrate form and function, have enjoyed no protection. While a defendant will be liable for making an unauthorized copy of blueprints embodying an architectural work, absent the AWCPA, she is unlikely to be liable if she copies the architectural work by simply viewing the finished building in which the work is embodied.

What if the defendant lawfully obtained authorized copies of blueprints and used them to create an unauthorized building? One could argue that this would constitute the making of an unauthorized copy of the protected plans, since copying generally is prohibited in any medium. Nonetheless, the making of an unauthorized building from copyrighted architectural plans has been deemed not to infringe the copyright in the plans. The building is a useful article. By analogy to the reasoning in *Baker v. Selden*, courts have found that copyright in technical plans can give no rights in the useful article they depict. 17 U.S.C. § 113(b); H.R. Rep. No. 94–1476, 94th Cong., 2d Sess. 105 (1976).

The Architectural Works Copyright Protection Act of 1990

Among other things, the AWCPA amended Copyright Act § 102(a) to add "architectural works" as a new category of copyrightable subject matter. See 17 U.S.C.A. § 102(a)(8). It amended § 101 to define the new category as follows:

An "architectural work" is the design of a building as embodied in any tangible medium of expression, including a building, architectural plans, or drawings. The work includes the overall form as well as the arrangement and composition of spaces and elements in the design, but does not include individual standard features.

17 U.S.C.A. § 101.

COPYRIGHT AMENDMENTS ACT OF 1990

H.R. Rep. No. 101–735, 101st Cong., 2d Sess. 18–21 (1990).

SECTION 202.—DEFINITIONS

* * * The definition [of an "architectural work"] has two components. First, it states what is protected. Second, it specifies the material objects in which the architectural work may be embodied. The protected work is the design of a building. The term "design" includes the overall form as well as the arrangement and composition of spaces and elements in the design. The phrase "arrangement and composition of spaces and elements" recognizes that: (1) creativity in architecture frequently takes the form of a selection, coordination, or arrangement of unprotectible elements into an original, protectible whole; (2) an architect may incorporate new, protectible design elements into otherwise standard, unprotectible building features; and (3) interior architecture may be protected.

Consistent with other provisions of the Copyright Act and Copyright Office regulations, the definition makes clear that protection does not extend to individual standard features, such as common windows, doors, and other staple building components. A grant of exclusive rights in such features would impede, rather than promote, the progress of architectural innovation. The provision is not, however, intended to exclude from the copyright in the architectural work any individual features that reflect the architect's creativity. * * *

SECTION 203.—SUBJECT MATTER OF COPYRIGHT

This provision amends section 102, title 17, United States Code, to create a new category of protected subject matter: "architectural works." By creating a new category of protectible subject matter in new section 102(a)(8), and, therefore, by deliberately not encompassing architectural works as pictorial, graphic, or sculptural works in existing section 102(a)(5), the copyrightability of architectural works shall not be evaluated under the separability test applicable to pictorial, graphic, or sculptural works embodied in useful articles. There is considerable scholarly and judicial disagreement over how to apply the separability test, and the principal reason for not treating architectural works as pictorial, graphic, or sculptural works is to avoid entangling architectural works in this disagreement.

The Committee does not suggest, though, that in evaluating the copyrightability or scope of protection for architectural works, the Copyright Office or the courts should ignore functionality. A two-step analysis is envisioned. First, an architectural work should be examined to determine whether there are original design elements present, including overall shape and interior architecture. If such design elements are present, a second step is reached to examine whether the design elements are functionally required. If the design elements are not functionally required, the work is protectible without regard to physical or conceptual separability. As a consequence, contrary to the Committee's report accompanying the 1976 Copyright Act with respect to industrial products, the aesthetically pleasing overall shape of an architectural work could be protected under this bill.

The proper scope of protection for architectural works is distinct from registrability. Functional considerations may, for example, determine only particular design elements. Protection would be denied for the functionally determined elements, but would be available for the nonfunctionally determined elements. Under such circumstances, the Copyright Office should issue a certificate of registration, letting the courts determine the scope of protection. In each case, the courts must be free to decide the issue upon the facts presented, free of the separability conundrum presented by the useful articles doctrine applicable for pictorial, graphic, and sculptural works. Evidence that there is more than one method of obtaining a given functional result may be considered in evaluating registrability or the scope of protection.

* * *

ORAVEC v. SUNNY ISLES LUXURY VENTURES, L.C.

United States Court of Appeals for the Eleventh Circuit, 2008.
527 F.3d 1218.

WILSON, CIRCUIT JUDGE:

[Oravec developed a design for a high-rise building that featured the use of alternating concave and convex segments and elevator cores protruding through the building's roof line. He registered this design in 1996, and after making certain refinements, obtained an additional copyright registration the following year. He subsequently brought suit, alleging that the newly designed Trump Buildings infringed his copyrights. The district court granted summary judgment to the defendants, holding that no reasonable jury could find that the Trump Buildings were substantially similar to Oravec's 1996 and 1997 designs.]

1. Legal Framework

To establish copyright infringement, "two elements must be proven: (1) ownership of a valid copyright, and (2) copying of constituent elements of the work that are original." *Feist Publ'ns, Inc. v. Rural Tel. Serv. Co.,* 499 U.S. 340, 361, 111 S.Ct. 1282, 1296 (1991). * * * [T]he district court found that Oravec owned valid copyrights in his 1996 and 1997 designs, and that there were disputed issues of fact as to whether certain defendants had access to those designs. Thus, summary judgment turned on the issue of substantial similarity.

We have defined substantial similarity as existing "where an average lay observer would recognize the alleged copy as having been appropriated from the copyrighted work." *Original Appalachian Artworks, Inc. v. Toy Loft, Inc.*, 684 F.2d 821, 829 (11th Cir.1982). Not all copying constitutes infringement, however, and therefore we have emphasized that the substantial similarity analysis "must focus on similarity of expression, *i.e.*, material susceptible of copyright protection." Beal v. Paramount Pictures Corp., 20 F.3d 454, 459 n. 4 (11th Cir.1994). * * *

In identifying the protected elements of a plaintiff's work, the court must be mindful of the fundamental axiom that copyright protection does not extend to ideas but only to particular expressions of ideas. * * * This distinction—known as the idea/expression dichotomy—can be difficult to apply, as there is no bright line separating the ideas conveyed by a work from the specific expression of those ideas. As Judge Learned Hand recognized in an influential opinion: "Obviously, no principle can be stated as to when an imitator has gone beyond copying the 'idea,' and has borrowed its 'expression.' Decisions must therefore inevitably be *ad hoc*." *Peter Pan Fabrics, Inc. v. Martin Weiner Corp.*, 274 F.2d 487, 489 (2d Cir.1960).

Nevertheless, in attempting to distinguish between ideas and expression, it is useful to note the policy purposes served by the distinction. The idea/expression dichotomy seeks to achieve a proper balance between competing societal interests: that of encouraging the creation of original works on the one hand, and that of promoting the free flow of ideas and information on the other. * * * Therefore, "in defining protectable expression, the court should 'neither draw the line so narrowly that authors, composers and artists will have no incentive to produce original literary, musical and artistic works, nor [should the court] draw it so broadly that future authors, composers and artists will find a diminished store of ideas on which to build their works.'" *Meade v. United States*, 27 Fed.Cl. 367, 372 (Fed.Cl.1992), *aff'd*, 5 F.3d 1503 (Fed.Cir.1993).

In addition to the idea/expression dichotomy, certain statutory provisions specific to architectural works further define the scope of available copyright protection. The Copyright Act's definition of "architectural work" excludes "individual standard features" from the protectible elements of the design. 17 U.S.C. § 101. According to legislative history, such features include "common windows, doors, and other staple building components." H.R.Rep. No. 101–735 (1990), *as reprinted in* 1990 U.S.C.C.A.N. 6935, 6949. At the same time, however, the statute includes within the definition of "architectural work" "the arrangement and composition of spaces and elements in the design." 17 U.S.C. § 101. This definition reflects Congress's awareness that "creativity in architecture frequently takes the form of a selection, coordination, or arrangement of unprotectible elements into an original, protectible whole." H.R.Rep. No.

101–735, *as reprinted in* 1990 U.S.C.C.A.N. at 6949. Thus, while individual standard features and architectural elements classifiable as ideas are not themselves copyrightable, an architect's original combination or arrangement of such features may be. * * *

2. *Comparison of Works*

Oravec bases his infringement claims on the following elements that he contends are present in both his designs and the Trump Buildings: (1) alternating concave and convex sections; (2) three prominent elevator shafts that protrude above the roof of the building; (3) rounded building ends; (4) constant radius curves; (5) holes in the building; (6) a twin tower design; (7) see-through floor plans; (8) a circular plaza; (9) a central fountain; and (10) a rooftop pool and landscape elements. Examining these elements individually and collectively, the district court determined that the similarities between the Oravec designs and the Trump Buildings exist only at a conceptual level. Accordingly, the court concluded that no reasonable jury, properly instructed, could find the competing works substantially similar without implicitly finding that Oravec owns a copyright in an idea. For the reasons discussed below, we agree.[1]

As the district court noted, the key distinctive features of Oravec's designs are their use of alternating concave and convex sections and their use of three partially exposed elevator towers extending above the buildings' roof lines. While such features also are present in the Trump Buildings, a comparison of the works reveals numerous significant differences in the expression of these elements. As to the concave/convex concept, one readily apparent difference is the fact that the alternating segments appear on both sides of Oravec's designs but only on one side of the Trump Buildings. Even when viewing the Trump Buildings from that side, however, several other dissimilarities are evident. For example, Oravec's designs contain five alternating segments, while the Trump Buildings have only three. Additionally, the segments in Oravec's designs extend across the entire face of the building, while those in the Trump Buildings appear only in the middle portion between the two outer elevator towers. In Oravec's designs, these segments are long and narrow, and each segment is placed on one side of the three elevator towers so as to create a void throughout the vertical center of the building. In the Trump Buildings, the segments appear only on the façade of the building, and there is no vertical void created. These differences are reflected in the buildings' respective floor plans. Oravec's 1997 design measures 320 feet long and 42 feet wide, and the entire floor plan has a pronounced, "banana-shaped" curve to it. The Trump Buildings have a more rectilinear shape, measuring 260 feet long and 72 feet wide at their narrowest points.

---

1. To illustrate our analysis, we have attached selected images of the designs as appendices to this opinion. Appendix A shows Oravec's 1997design, and Appendix B shows the Trump Palace as constructed.

The expression of the elevator towers also differs significantly. Oravec's elevator towers are free-standing and are located within the space created by the alternating convex and concave sections of the building. The Trump Buildings' elevator towers are located within the solid structure of the building. In addition, in Oravec's designs, a viewer can see only certain sections of the elevator towers because they are partially obstructed by the alternating convex and concave sections. In the Trump Buildings, the viewer can see the exteriors of the outer two elevator towers through the entire length of the building; only the center tower is partially obscured. The towers also differ in shape and orientation. Oravec's elevator towers are cylindrical, while those in the Trump Buildings are ovals. In Oravec's designs, the towers are clustered in the center of the building, and the middle tower is thicker than the two outer two. The towers in the Trump Buildings are spread out evenly, and all three are equal in diameter. Further, the two outer towers in the Trump Buildings "are angled inward so that the leading edge of all three towers orient toward a focal point outside the building." Given that Oravec's towers are cylindrical, this feature is absent in his designs. Finally, the tops of the Trump Buildings' towers are sloped so as to give the effect of smokestacks on a cruise ship. The towers in Oravec's designs are horizontal across the top.

The remaining elements identified by Oravec—the use of rounded building ends, a constant radius on individual floor plans, holes in the building, a twin-tower design, "see-through" units, a circular plaza, a central fountain, and a rooftop pool with landscape elements—are best characterized as either individual standard features or ideas. * * * We agree with the district court that the expression of these elements in the Oravec designs is not substantially similar to their expression in the Trump Buildings. For example, in Oravec's designs, the twin tower concept is expressed such that it appears that one building could fit into the other; the Trump Buildings lack this feature. The holes in the buildings also differ significantly. As noted, Oravec's designs contain a space from the ground through the top of the building. The Trump Buildings have only a small horizontal gap. As to the rounded building ends, Oravec's designs have full wrap-around terraces, which create a visually smooth façade. The Trump Buildings have individual balconies, creating a more jagged appearance in the rounded ends.

With respect to the circular plazas, the district court properly found that these elements are not substantially similar because Oravec's plaza lacks the intricate details expressed in that of the Trump Buildings. The same conclusion applies to the use of a circular fountain in each design. As to the constant radius curves and "see-through" floor plans, we have already noted that the floor plans in the respective designs differ dramatically. Finally, Oravec points to his use of a rooftop pool with landscape elements. However, the Trump Buildings do not have a rooftop pool, and the landscape elements in those buildings are not similar to any such features that are discernible in Oravec's designs.

These differences, as well as others, preclude a finding of substantial similarity. While it is true that Oravec's designs and the Trump Buildings have a number of features in common, those elements are similar only at the broadest level of generality. At the level of protected expression, the differences between the designs are so significant that no reasonable, properly instructed jury could find the works substantially similar. As the district court observed, to conclude otherwise would require a finding that Oravec owns a copyright in the concept of a convex/concave formula or in that of using three external elevator towers that extend above the roof of a building. Such a conclusion would extend the protections of copyright law well beyond their proper scope. * * *

For similar reasons, we also reject Oravec's argument that he can establish substantial similarity on the basis of his selection of design elements. In Oravec's view, the fact that the same combination of elements appears in both his designs and the Trump Buildings should have precluded summary judgment, notwithstanding the differences in the expression of those elements. However, while it is clear that an architect's original selection or combination of elements can warrant copyright protection the selection that Oravec is seeking to protect is too generalized to qualify as protected expression. The copyright claimed by Oravec would encompass any building that combined a concave/convex structure, three external and protruding elevator towers, and various common building features, however any of these elements might be expressed. Were we to grant him such a right, we would effectively bar all other architects from incorporating these concepts into new and original designs. That result would lead to "a diminished store of ideas" available for future works, and thus would be contrary to the fundamental purposes of copyright law.

     * * *

Appendix

A (Oravec Design)   B (Trump Building)

NOTES AND QUESTIONS

1. *Protection for "architectural works."* What in the *Baker v. Selden* opinion prohibits the owner of copyrighted blueprints from asserting copyright against a person who uses the blueprints to create the depicted building?

How would you describe the changes to existing law wrought by the AWCPA? The legislative history of the AWCPA makes it clear that the courts should avoid applying copyright to functional features of architectural works. What is your evaluation of the method the House Report suggests for doing this? How would you compare that method to the "separability" inquiry used in the case of pictorial, graphic, and sculptural works in useful articles?

Should architectural works be the subject of copyright? Are they writings? Is there a policy justification for granting greater copyright protection to building designs than to other useful article designs, such as the design of an automobile or a fine piece of furniture?

2. *What is a "building"?* An architectural work is "the design of a building." But what is a "building," for purposes of the Copyright Act? The Copyright Office has defined "buildings" as "humanly habitable structures that are intended to be both permanent and stationary, such as houses and office buildings and other permanent and stationary structures designed for human occupancy, including but not limited to churches, museums, gazebos, and garden pavilions." Viad Corp. v. Stak Design, Inc., 2005 WL 894853 at 1 (E.D.Tex. 2005)(*quoting* 37 C.F.R. § 202.11(b)(2)). In light of this definition, the district court in *Viad* held that kiosks designed for use in displaying merchandise in shopping centers did not constitute "buildings" because they

were not capable of being occupied by humans *Id.* at 3. Thus the kiosks were not subject to protection as architectural works.

In Yankee Candle Co. v. New England Candle Co., 14 F.Supp.2d 154 (D. Mass.), *vacated by settlement*, 29 F.Supp.2d 44 (1998), the issue was whether a "structure within a structure," such as a store within a mall, constituted a "building." The district court determined that it did not:

> The Court has difficulty concluding that constructing an empty room in a large shopping mall into a candle shop with a colonial motif transforms that room into a "building" within the meaning of the Copyright Act. The entire mall itself, with its interior walled off and divided into separate spaces for stores, easily qualifies as a building, but an individual store does not. Yankee did not design or construct the walls and ceiling in its store, it built within an existing structure.

Id. at 159. If kiosks and stores in malls do not constitute architectural works, does that mean that there can be no copyright protection for their design?

3. *The scope of copyright in architectural works:* In your opinion, did the *Oravec* court succeed in attaining the best balance of competing societal interests? In Intervest Construction, Inc. v. Canterbury Estate Homes, Inc., 554 F.3d 914 (11th Cir. 2008), the Eleventh Circuit noted the similarity between the Copyright Act's definition of "architectural work" and its definition of "compilation." (Copyright Act § 101 defines a compilation as "a work formed by the collection and assembling of preexisting materials * * * that are selected, coordinated, or arranged in such a way that the resulting work as a whole constitutes an original work of authorship.") The *Intervest* court then relied on *Feist* and *Oravec* to reason that in architectural works, as in factual compilations, the copyrightable expression consists of the author's selection and arrangement judgement. Because of this, the copyright in architectural works, like the copyright in factual compilations, should be "thin."

PROBLEM

1. In 1985, X conceived of a new design for a building, drew up blueprints, and built the depicted building, completing the job in 1988. X died in 1990, and his will devised all his blueprints and other papers to the local Architectural Society Library. The will specified that X's son, Y, would be X's residual legatee. In 1998, Z, a member of the Architectural Society, found X's blueprint in the Library, checked it out, and proceeded to build the building depicted in the blueprint. Y has sued for infringement. Is he likely to succeed? Would it make any difference if all the events described above occurred ten years later than specified?

4. Government Works

Subject Matter of Copyright: United States Government Works
17 U.S.C. § 105

Copyright protection under this title is not available for any work of the United States Government, but the United States Government is not precluded from receiving and holding copyrights transferred to it by assignment, bequest, or otherwise.

HOUSE REPORT ON COPYRIGHT ACT OF 1976

H.R. Rep. No. 1476, 94th Cong., 2d Sess. 58–60 (1976).

The general prohibition against copyright in section 105 applies to "any work of the United States Government," which is defined in section 101 as "a work prepared by an officer or employee of the United States Government as part of that person's official duties." Under this definition a Government official or employee would not be prevented from securing copyright in a work written at that person's own volition and outside his or her duties, even though the subject matter involves the Government work or professional field of the official or employee. Although the wording of the definition of "work of the United States Government" differs somewhat from that of the definition of "work made for hire," the concepts are intended to be construed in the same way.

* * *

The bill deliberately avoids making any sort of outright, unqualified prohibition against copyright in works prepared under Government contract or grant. There may well be cases where it would be in the public interest to deny copyright in the writings generated by Government research contracts and the like; it can be assumed that, where a Government agency commissions a work for its own use merely as an alternative to having one of its own employees prepare the work, the right to secure a private copyright would be withheld. However, there are almost certainly many other cases where the denial of copyright protection would be unfair or would hamper the production and publication of important works. Where, under the particular circumstances, Congress or the agency involved finds that the need to have a work freely available outweighs the need of the private author to secure copyright, the problem can be dealt with by specific legislation, agency regulations, or contractual restrictions.

* * *

The effect of section 105 is intended to place all works of the United States Government, published or unpublished, in the public domain. This means that the individual Government official or employee who wrote the work could not secure copyright in it or restrain its dissemination by the Government or anyone else, but it also means that, as far as the copyright law is concerned, the Government could not restrain the employee or official from disseminating the work if he or she chooses to do so. The use of the term "work of the United States Government" does not mean that a work falling within the definition of that term is the property of the U.S. Government.

NOTES AND QUESTIONS

1. *Copyright in government works.* Why prohibit copyright in federal government works? Do the reasons vary depending on the type of work it is? Do the same reasons exist for prohibiting copyright in state and local government works?

Copyright Act § 105 does not address the copyrightability of state and local government works. Nonetheless, while some state and local government works can be and are copyrighted, it is generally accepted that statutes, ordinances, and state judicial opinions are in the public domain. Do you see what distinguishes this category of works from other government-produced works? Does the distinction explain why statutes, ordinances and judicial opinions are deemed uncopyrightable?

Assume that a state adopts a model act, drafted by a private entity. Should the private entity be able to enforce copyright in the model act after it is adopted as state law? See Veeck v. Southern Building Code Congress International, Inc., 293 F.3d 791 (5th Cir.), *cert. denied,* 537 U.S. 1043, 123 S.Ct. 650, 154 LEd.2d 513 (2002).

III. THE EXCLUSIVE RIGHTS OF COPYRIGHT AND THEIR INFRINGEMENT

A. INTRODUCTION

§ 106.   Exclusive rights in copyrighted works

Subject to sections 107 through 121, the owner of copyright under this title has the exclusive rights to do and to authorize any of the following:

(1) to reproduce the copyrighted work in copies or phonorecords;

(2) to prepare derivative works based upon the copyrighted work;

(3) to distribute copies or phonorecords of the copyrighted work to the public by sale or other transfer of ownership, or by rental, lease or lending;

(4) in the case of literary, musical, dramatic, and choreographic works, pantomimes, and motion pictures and other audiovisual works, to perform the copyrighted work publicly;

(5) in the case of literary, musical, dramatic, and choreographic works, pantomimes, and pictorial, graphic, or sculptural works, including the individual images of a motion picture or other audiovisual work, to display the copyrighted work publicly; and

(6) in the case of sound recordings, to perform the copyrighted work publicly by means of a digital audio transmission.

17 U.S.C.A. § 106.

HOUSE REPORT ON COPYRIGHT ACT OF 1976

H.R. Rep. No. 1476, 94th Cong., 2d Sess. 61 (1976).

The five fundamental rights that the bill gives to copyright owners—the exclusive rights of reproduction, adaptation, publication, performance, and display—are stated generally in section 106. These exclusive rights, which comprise the so-called "bundle of rights" that is a copyright, are cumulative and may overlap in some cases. Each of the five enumerated rights may be subdivided indefinitely and, as discussed * * * in connection with section 201, each subdivision of an exclusive right may be owned and enforced separately.

The approach of the bill is to set forth the copyright owner's exclusive rights in broad terms in section 106, and then to provide various limitations, qualifications, or exemptions in the * * * sections that follow. Thus, everything in section 106 is made "subject to sections 107 through [121]," and must be read in conjunction with those provisions.

The exclusive rights accorded to a copyright owner under section 106 are "to do and to authorize" any of the activities specified in the [six] numbered clauses. Use of the phrase "to authorize" is intended to avoid any questions as to the liability of contributory infringers. For example, a person who lawfully acquires an authorized copy of a motion picture would be an infringer if he or she engages in the business of renting it to others for purposes of unauthorized public performance.

———

The exclusive rights set forth in § 106 are sometimes referred to as the copyright owner's "economic rights," since they are geared toward protecting the owner's opportunities to exploit the work commercially. Subsequent to the House Report excerpted above, Congress amended § 106 to add a sixth economic right directed to sound recording copyright owners: the right to perform the copyrighted work publicly by means of digital audio transmission.

United States copyright law traditionally recognized only economic rights. Berne Convention Article 6bis, however, requires its member nations to provide the "moral rights" of attribution and integrity to authors, as well. Moral rights protect the author's personal interests in reputation and self-expression. In 1990, Congress enacted the Visual Artists' Rights Act, which amended the Copyright Act of 1976 to extend these moral rights to authors of a very limited class of works. See 17 U.S.C.A. §§ 101, 106A.

In this Section we will examine the nature and scope of the various economic and moral rights and how they may be infringed. We will also examine some of the more important statutory exceptions to the exclusive rights, as set forth in §§ 108 through 121 of the Copyright Act. The

Copyright Act strikes a balance between the competing interests in promoting public access to works and providing economic incentives to create original, new works of authorship. The need for this balance informed Congress' selection and definition of the rights to be afforded to copyright owners. The exceptions set forth in §§ 108 through 121 represent Congress' attempts to further "fine tune" the balance by singling out and permitting particular types of unauthorized use that promote the public interest but do not unduly interfere with the copyright owner's economic incentive.

At the heart of any infringement action is the allegation that the work the defendant reproduced, adapted, or publicly distributed, performed or displayed was the "copyrighted work." The defendant's work must be copied from the plaintiff's copyrighted work of authorship, and must be "substantially similar" in its expression. Thus, before examining the §§ 106 and 106A exclusive rights and their exceptions, we will review the methods by which the courts determine whether a defendant's work meets the "copied" and "substantially similar" criteria.

B. INFRINGEMENT OF THE COPYRIGHTED WORK

ARNSTEIN v. PORTER

United States Court of Appeals for the Second Circuit, 1946.
154 F.2d 464.

[The plaintiff charged the defendant, Cole Porter, with infringing copyrights in several of his musical compositions.] Defendant then moved for * * * summary judgment. Attached to defendant's motion papers were the depositions, phonograph records of piano renditions of the plaintiff's compositions and defendant's alleged infringing compositions, and the court records of five previous copyright infringement suits brought by plaintiff in the court below against other persons, in which judgments had been entered, after trials, against plaintiff. Defendant also moved for dismissal of the action on the ground of "vexatiousness."

Plaintiff alleged that defendant's "Begin the Beguine" is a plagiarism from plaintiff's "The Lord Is My Shepherd" and "A Mother's Prayer." Plaintiff testified, on deposition, that "The Lord Is My Shepherd" had been published and about 2,000 copies sold, that "A Mother's Prayer" had been published, over a million copies having been sold. In his depositions, he gave no direct evidence that defendant saw or heard these compositions. He also alleged that defendant's "My Heart Belongs to Daddy" had been plagiarized from plaintiff's "A Mother's Prayer."

Plaintiff also alleged that defendant's "I Love You" is a plagiarism from plaintiff's composition "La Priere," stating in his deposition that the latter composition had been sold. He gave no direct proof that plaintiff knew of this composition.

He also alleged that defendant's song "Night and Day" is a plagiarism of plaintiff's song "I Love You Madly," which he testified had not been published but had once been publicly performed over the radio, copies having been sent to divers radio stations but none to defendant; a copy of this song, plaintiff testified, had been stolen from his room. He also alleged that "I Love You Madly" was in part plagiarized from "La Priere." He further alleged that defendant's "You'd Be So Nice To Come Home To" is plagiarized from plaintiff's "Sadness Overwhelms My Soul." He testified that this song had never been published or publicly performed but that copies had been sent to a movie producer and to several publishers. He also alleged that defendant's "Don't Fence Me In" is a plagiarism of plaintiff's song "A Modern Messiah" which has not been published or publicly performed; in his deposition he said that about a hundred copies had been sent to divers radio stations and band leaders but that he sent no copy to defendant. Plaintiff said that defendant "had stooges right along to follow me, watch me, and live in the same apartment with me," and that plaintiff's room had been ransacked on several occasions. Asked how he knew that defendant had anything to do with any of these "burglaries," plaintiff said, "I don't know that he had to do with it, but I only know that he could have." He also said " * * * many of my compositions had been published. No one had to break in to steal them. They were sung publicly."

Defendant in his deposition categorically denied that he had ever seen or heard any of plaintiff's compositions or had had any acquaintance with any persons said to have stolen any of them.

The prayer of plaintiff's original complaint asked "at least one million dollars out of the millions the defendant has earned and is earning out of all the plagiarism." In his amended complaint the prayer is "for judgment against the defendant in the sum of $1,000,000 as damages sustained by the plagiarism of all the compositions named in the complaint." Plaintiff, not a lawyer, appeared pro se below and on this appeal.

FRANK, CIRCUIT JUDGE.

* * *

The principal question on this appeal is whether the lower court, under Rule 56, properly deprived plaintiff of a trial of his copyright infringement action. * * * [I]t is important to avoid confusing two separate elements essential to a plaintiff's case in such a suit: (a) that defendant copied from plaintiff's copyrighted work and (b) that the copying (assuming it to be proved) went so far as to constitute improper appropriation.

As to the first—copying—the evidence may consist (a) of defendant's admission that he copied or (b) of circumstantial evidence—usually evidence of access—from which the trier of the facts may reasonably infer copying. Of course, if there are no similarities, no amount of evidence of access will suffice to prove copying. If there is evidence of access and similarities exist, then the trier of the facts must determine whether the similarities are sufficient to prove copying. On this issue, analysis ("dissection") is relevant, and the testimony of experts may be received to aid the trier of the facts. If evidence of access is absent, the similarities must be so striking as to preclude the possibility that plaintiff and defendant independently arrived at the same result.

If copying is established, then only does there arise the second issue, that of illicit copying (unlawful appropriation). On that issue (as noted more in detail below) the test is the response of the ordinary lay hearer; accordingly, on that issue, "dissection" and expert testimony are irrelevant.

In some cases, the similarities between the plaintiff's and defendant's work are so extensive and striking as, without more, both to justify an inference of copying and to prove improper appropriation. But such double-purpose evidence is not required; that is, if copying is otherwise shown, proof of improper appropriation need not consist of similarities which, standing alone, would support an inference of copying.

Each of these two issues—copying and improper appropriation—is an issue of fact. If there is a trial, the conclusions on those issues of the trier of the facts—of the judge if he sat without a jury, or of the jury if there was a jury trial—bind this court on appeal, provided the evidence supports those findings, regardless of whether we would ourselves have reached the same conclusions. But a case could occur in which the similarities were so striking that we would reverse a finding of no access, despite weak evidence of access (or no evidence thereof other than the similarities); and similarly as to a finding of no illicit appropriation.

We turn first to the issue of copying. After listening to the compositions as played in the phonograph recordings submitted by defendant, we find similarities; but we hold that unquestionably, standing alone, they do not compel the conclusion, or permit the inference, that defendant copied. The similarities, however, are sufficient so that, if there is enough evidence of access to permit the case to go to the jury, the jury may properly infer that the similarities did not result from coincidence.

Summary judgment was, then, proper if indubitably defendant did not have access to plaintiff's compositions. Plainly that presents an issue of fact. On that issue, the district judge, who heard no oral testimony, had before him the depositions of plaintiff and defendant. The judge characterized plaintiff's story as "fantastic"; and, in the light of the references in his opinion to defendant's deposition, the judge obviously accepted defendant's denial of access and copying. Although part of plaintiff's testimony on deposition (as to "stooges" and the like) does seem "fantastic," yet plaintiff's credibility, even as to those improbabilities, should be left to the jury. If evidence is "of a kind that greatly taxes the credulity of the judge, he can say so, or, if he totally disbelieves it, he may announce that fact, leaving the jury free to believe it or not." * * *

But even if we were to disregard the improbable aspects of plaintiff's story, there remain parts by no means "fantastic." On the record now before us, more than a million copies of one of his compositions were sold; copies of others were sold in smaller quantities or distributed to radio stations or band leaders or publishers, or the pieces were publicly performed. If, after hearing both parties testify, the jury disbelieves defendant's denials, it can, from such facts, reasonably infer access. It follows that, as credibility is unavoidably involved, a genuine issue of material fact presents itself. With credibility a vital factor, plaintiff is entitled to a trial where the jury can observe the witnesses while testifying. Plaintiff must not be deprived of the invaluable privilege of cross-examining the defendant—the "crucial test of credibility"—in the presence of the jury. Plaintiff, or a lawyer on his behalf, on such examination may elicit damaging admissions from defendant; more important, plaintiff may persuade the jury, observing defendant's manner when testifying, that defendant is unworthy of belief.

      * * *

With all that in mind, we cannot now say—as we think we must say to sustain a summary judgment—that at the close of a trial the judge could properly direct a verdict.

      * * *

Assuming that adequate proof is made of copying, that is not enough; for there can be "permissible copying," copying which is not illicit. Whether (if he copied) defendant unlawfully appropriated presents, too, an issue of fact. The proper criterion on that issue is not an analytic or other comparison of the respective musical compositions as they appear on paper or in the judgment of trained musicians.[19] The plaintiff's legally protected interest is not, as such, his reputation as a musician but his interest in the potential financial returns from his compositions which derive from the lay public's approbation of his efforts. The question, therefore, is whether defendant took from plaintiff's works so much of what is pleasing to the ears of lay listeners, who comprise the audience for whom such popular music is composed, that defendant wrongfully appropriated something which belongs to the plaintiff.

Surely, then, we have an issue of fact which a jury is peculiarly fitted to determine.[22] Indeed, even if there were to be a trial before a judge, it would be desirable (although not necessary) for him to summon an advisory jury on this question.

We should not be taken as saying that a plagiarism case can never arise in which absence of similarities is so patent that a summary judgment for defendant would be correct. Thus suppose that Ravel's "Bolero" or Shostakovitch's "Fifth Symphony" were alleged to infringe "When Irish Eyes Are Smiling." But this is not such a case. For, after listening to the playing of the respective compositions, we are, at this time, unable to conclude that the likenesses are so trifling that, on the

---

19. Where plaintiff relies on similarities to prove copying (as distinguished from improper appropriation) paper comparisons and the opinions of experts may aid the court.

22. It would, accordingly, be proper to exclude tone-deaf persons from the jury.

issue of misappropriation, a trial judge could legitimately direct a verdict for defendant.

At the trial, plaintiff may play, or cause to be played, the pieces in such manner that they may seem to a jury to be inexcusably alike, in terms of the way in which lay listeners of such music would be likely to react. The plaintiff may call witnesses whose testimony may aid the jury in reaching its conclusion as to the responses of such audiences. Expert testimony of musicians may also be received, but it will in no way be controlling on the issue of illicit copying, and should be utilized only to assist in determining the reactions of lay auditors. The impression made on the refined ears of musical experts or their views as to the musical excellence of plaintiff's or defendant's works are utterly immaterial on the issue of misappropriation; for the views of such persons are caviar to the general—and plaintiff's and defendant's compositions are not caviar.

* * *

CLARK, CIRCUIT JUDGE (dissenting).

* * *

[A]fter repeated hearings of the records, I could not find therein what my brothers found. The only thing definitely mentioned seemed to be the repetitive use of the note e in certain places by both plaintiff and defendant, surely too simple and ordinary a device of composition to be significant. In our former musical plagiarism cases we have, naturally, relied on what seemed the total sound effect; but we have also analyzed the music enough to make sure of an intelligible and intellectual decision. Thus in Arnstein v. Edward B. Marks Music Corp., 2 Cir., 82 F.2d 275, 277, Judge L. Hand made quite an extended comparison of the songs, concluding, inter alia: " * * * the seven notes available do not admit of so many agreeable permutations that we need be amazed at the re-appearance of old themes, even though the identity extend through a sequence of twelve notes." See also the discussion in Marks v. Leo Feist, Inc., 2 Cir., 290 F. 959, and Darrell v. Joe Morris Music Co., 2 Cir., 113 F.2d 80, where the use of six similar bars and of an eight-note sequence frequently repeated were respectively held not to constitute infringement * * *.

[When] we start with an examination of the written and printed material supplied by the plaintiff in his complaint and exhibits, we find at once that he does not and cannot claim extensive copying, measure by measure, of his compositions. He therefore has resorted to a comparative analysis * * * to support his claim of plagiarism of small detached portions here and there, the musical fillers between the better known parts of the melody. And plaintiff's compositions, as pointed out in the cases cited above, are of the simple and trite character where small repetitive sequences are not hard to discover. It is as though we found Shakespeare a plagiarist on the basis of his use of articles, pronouns, prepositions, and adjectives also used by others. The surprising thing, however, is to note the small amount of even this type of reproduction which plaintiff by dint of extreme dissection has been able to find.

Though it is most instructive, it will serve no good purpose for me to restate here this showing as to each of the pieces in issue. As an example of the rest, we may take plaintiff's first cause of action. This involves his "A Modern Messiah" with defendant's "Don't Fence Me In." The first is written in 6/8 time, the second in common or 4/4 time; and there is only one place where there is a common sequence of as many as five consecutive notes, and these without the same values. Thus it goes. The usual claim seems to be rested upon a sequence of three, of four, or of five— never more than five—identical notes, usually of different rhythmical values. Nowhere is there anything approaching the twelve-note sequence of the Marks case, supra. * * *

In the light of these utmost claims of the plaintiff, I do not see a legal basis for the claim of plagiarism. So far as I have been able to discover, no earlier case approaches the holding that a simple and trite sequence of this type, even if copying may seem indicated, constitutes proof either of access or of plagiarism. * * *

NOTES AND QUESTIONS

1. *Similarity.* The issue of "similarity" arises in both parts of the *Arnstein* two-step test for infringement. First, evidence of similarities between the parties' works, coupled with evidence of access, will support a finding that the defendant copied from the plaintiff. In this context, similarities in both the copyrightable and uncopyrightable elements of the works may be relevant. The level of similarity that the plaintiff must demonstrate may vary, depending upon the strength of the evidence of access.

Once "copying in fact" has been demonstrated, the "improper appropriation" step entails deciding whether the defendant has taken too much of the plaintiff's copyrightable expression. Generally, this will turn on whether the audience for whom the works were intended would find the works to be "substantially similar" in their copyrightable expression. The courts sometimes use the term "substantial similarity" in both the "copying in fact" and "improper appropriation" inquiries, and "substantial similarity" is sometimes used as a synonym for the overall "copying/improper appropriation" determination, as well. Do not permit the interchangeable use of the "substantial similarity" terminology to confuse you. Note that the "similarity" inquiry in determining "copying in fact" is not the same as in determining "improper appropriation," and does not entail the same standard.

Copyright infringement entails strict liability: No showing of intent or fault is required. Actionable copying may be entirely unintentional, or subconscious, as was the case in Bright Tunes Music Corp. v. Harrisongs Music, Ltd., 420 F.Supp. 177 (S.D.N.Y.1976), *affirmed sub nom.* ABKCO Music, Inc. v. Harrisongs Music, Ltd., 722 F.2d 988 (2d Cir.1983). In *Bright Tunes*, the court found that former Beatle George Harrison's song, "My Sweet Lord," infringed the plaintiff's "He's So Fine," which had been made popular by The Chiffons. The Chiffons' recording had been a hit in both the United States and England, so that Harrison was highly likely to have heard it. The court fully credited Harrison's testimony that he did not deliberately copy:

What happened? I conclude that the composer, in seeking musical materials to clothe his thoughts, was working with various possibilities. As he tried this possibility and that, there came to the surface of his mind a particular combination that pleased him as being one he felt would be appealing to a prospective listener; in other words, that this combination of sounds would work. Why? Because his subconscious knew it already had worked in a song his conscious mind did not remember. * * * [I]t is clear that My Sweet Lord is the very same song as He's So Fine with different words, and Harrison had access to He's So Fine. This is, under the law, infringement of copyright, and is no less so even though subconsciously accomplished.

Id., 420 F.Supp. at 180–81.

Assuming that a plaintiff has provided sufficient evidence of access and similarity to give rise to an inference of copying, how might the defendant rebut that inference?

2. *Unlawful appropriation/substantial similarity—identifying the appropriate perspective from which to judge.* The *Arnstein* majority advises that "unlawful appropriation," should be determined from the standpoint of the "lay listeners, who comprise the audience" for whom the work was created. This standard, sometimes called the "ordinary observer" or "audience" test, is widely accepted. In Dawson v. Hinshaw Music Inc., 905 F.2d 731 (4th Cir.1990), *cert. denied*, 498 U.S. 981, 111 S.Ct. 511, 112 L.Ed.2d 523 (1990), the Court of Appeals for the Fourth Circuit elaborated on the standard:

Although *Arnstein* established a sound foundation for the appeal to audience reaction, its reference to "lay listeners" may have fostered the development of a rule that has come to be stated too broadly. Under the facts before it, with a popular composition at issue, the *Arnstein* court appropriately perceived "lay listeners" and the works' "audience" to be the same. However, under *Arnstein's* sound logic, the lay listeners are relevant only because they comprise the relevant audience. Although *Arnstein* does not address the question directly, we read the case's logic to require that where the intended audience is significantly more specialized than the pool of lay listeners, the reaction of the intended audience would be the relevant inquiry. In light of the copyright law's purpose of protecting a creator's market, we think it sensible to embrace *Arnstein's* command that the ultimate comparison of the works at issue be oriented towards the works' intended audience.

      * * *

Under the foregoing logic, we state the law to be as follows. When conducting the second prong of the substantial similarity inquiry, a district court must consider the nature of the intended audience of the plaintiff's work. If, as will most often be the case, the lay public fairly represents the intended audience, the court should apply the lay observer formulation of the ordinary observer test. However, if the intended audience is more narrow in that it possesses specialized expertise, relevant to the purchasing decision, that lay people would lack, the court's inquiry should focus on whether a member of the intended audience would find the two works to be substantially similar. Such an inquiry may include, and no doubt in many cases will require, admission of testimony from members of the intended audience or, possibly, from those who possess expertise with reference to the tastes and perceptions of the intended audience.

Id., 905 F.2d at 734–36. Under similar reasoning, courts have held that infringement of works intended for children should be judged by the "impact of the respective works upon the minds and imaginations of young people." Sid & Marty Krofft Television Productions, Inc. v. McDonald's Corp., 562 F.2d 1157, 1166 (9th Cir.1977). What conclusion must the appropriate audience be likely to reach in order to justify a finding of "improper appropriation?" When will two works be "substantially similar" in copyrightable expression?

3. *Improper appropriation/substantial similarity—distinguishing copyrightable expression from uncopyrightable material.* Why not permit expert testimony and dissection in the course of the "improper appropriation" inquiry, as the *Arnstein* dissent would seem to advocate?

Copyright infringement can only be found upon substantial similarity of copied *expression.* Defendants are perfectly free to copy elements of a plaintiff's work that belong to the public domain. Yet the "ordinary observer" or "audience" test seems geared to gauge the intended audience's general, overall impression of the parties' respective works. In the absence of dissection or analysis of the works, what assurance is there that the finder of fact will base its finding on similarity of expression, rather than on similarities in such things as ideas, *scenes a faire*, facts, preexisting material, and other uncopyrightable elements? In Knitwaves, Inc. v. Lollytogs Ltd., 71 F.3d 996 (2d Cir.1995), the Court of Appeals for the Second Circuit addressed this concern:

> In most cases, the test for "substantial similarity" is the so-called "ordinary observer test" * * *: whether "an average lay observer would recognize the alleged copy as having been appropriated from the copyrighted work."
>
> However * * *, where we compare products that contain both protectible and unprotectible elements, our inspection must be "more discerning;" we must attempt to extract the unprotectible elements from our consideration and ask whether the protectible elements, standing alone, are substantially similar.

Id., 71 F.3d at 1002. The court nonetheless rejected arguments that

> in comparing designs for copyright infringement, we are required to dissect them into their separate components, and compare only those elements which are in themselves copyrightable. As the district court noted, if we took this argument to its logical conclusion, we might have to decide that "there can be no originality in a painting because all colors of paint have been used somewhere in the past."
>
> It is commonplace that in comparing works for infringement purposes—whether we employ the traditional "ordinary observer" test or the "more discerning" inquiry—we examine the works' "total concept and feel." As the Supreme Court's decision in Feist Publications, Inc. v. Rural Tel. Serv. Co., 499 U.S. 340, 111 S.Ct. 1282, 113 L.Ed.2d 358 (1991),

makes clear, a work may be copyrightable even though it is entirely a compilation of unprotectible elements.

Id., 71 F.3d at 1003–04. How might the "more discerning ordinary observer" test be implemented through jury instructions?

How might one reconcile the Second Circuit's "abstraction-filtration-comparison" test, which it applied to evaluate infringement of non-literal elements of computer programs, (*Computer Associates International, Inc. v. Altai, Inc.*, *supra*), with its "ordinary observer" test (*Arnstein*) and its "more discerning" test (*Knitwaves*)? Clearly the standard the court employs (and thus the level of dissection and objective measurement) depends at least in part on the court's estimation of the level of originality in the plaintiff's work, and the extent to which the work consists of uncopyrightable elements.

The Second Circuit has adopted its "more discerning" and "abstraction-filtration-comparison" infringement standards in an attempt to ensure that finders of fact do not overprotect works heavy in unprotectible elements. The Court of Appeals for the Eleventh Circuit, in contrast, prefers to avoid overprotection in such cases by giving the infringement analysis to judges, rather than to juries, whenever possible. The Eleventh Circuit explained that in cases involving works with numerous public domain elements (such as architectural works), infringement:

> is often more reliably and accurately resolved in a summary judgment proceeding. This is so because a judge is better able to separate original expression from the non-original elements of a work where the copying of the latter is not protectable and the copying of the former is protectable. The judge understands the concept of the idea/expression dichotomy and how it should be applied in the context of the works before him. * * * Moreover, in examining compilations wherein only the arrangement and coordination of elements which by the nature of the work (here architectural floor plans) are sure to be common to each of the works and are not copyrightable themselves (spacial depictions of rooms, doors, windows, walls, etc.), the already difficult tasks may become even more nuanced. Because a judge will more readily understand that all copying is not infringement, particularly in the context of works that are compilations, the "substantial-similarity" test is more often correctly administered by a judge rather than a jury—even one provided proper instruction. The reason for this is plain—the ability to separate protectable expression from non-protectable expression is, in reality, a question of law or, at the very least, a mixed question of law and fact. It is difficult for a juror, even properly instructed, to conclude, after looking at two works, that there is no infringement where, say, 90% of one is a copy of the other, but only 15% of the work is protectable expression that has not been copied. * * *

Intervest Construction, Inc. v. Canterbury Estate Homes, Inc., 554 F.3d 914, 920 (11th Cir. 2008).

4. *Improper appropriation/substantial similarity—the appropriate level of similarity.* In addition to varying the *standard* for evaluating similarity, courts may also vary the *level* of similarity they will require as a prerequisite to infringement liability, depending on the nature of the works at issue. As Professor Nimmer has noted:

[T]he measure of how substantial a "substantial similarity" must be may vary according to circumstances. Many copyrights represent significant creative effort, and are therefore reasonably robust, whereas others reflect only scant creativity; the Supreme Court labels the latter "thin." It would seem to follow analytically that more similarity is required when less protectible matter is at issue. Thus, if substantial similarity is the normal measure required to demonstrate infringement, "supersubstantial" similarity must pertain when dealing with "thin" works.

4 Melville B. Nimmer & David Nimmer, Nimmer on Copyright § 13.03[A], at 13–28 (2000). In Jacobsen v. Deseret Book Co., 287 F.3d 936, 943–44 (10th Cir.), *cert. denied*, 537 U.S. 1066 123 S.Ct. 623, 154 L.Ed.2d 555 (2002), the Court of Appeals for the Tenth Circuit held that the measure of how substantial a "substantial similarity" must be will vary according to the circumstances. While courts have often applied a supersubstantial similarity test (typically referred to as "virtual identicality" or "bodily appropriation of protectible expression") to fact-based works, this does not require that the supersubstanital similarity test be applied to *all* fact-based works:

Because fact-based works differ "as to the relative proportion of fact and fancy," the quantum of similarity required to establish infringement differs in each case. Merely applying a supersubstantial similarity test to all fact-based works would ignore the differences between "sparsely embellished maps and directories" and "elegantly written biography."

Id. (*quoting* Harper & Row Publishers, Inc. v. Nation Enterprises, 471 U.S. 539, 563 (1985)). The *Jacobsen* court found that the personal memoirs before it involved more creative effort and original expression than a telephone directory, and thus that the plaintiff could prove substantial similarity with "less similarity than we would require if the allegedly infringed work were a telephone directory." *Id.* at 944. However, the court found that the memoirs should receive "less protection than a purely fictional novel." *Id.* at 944 n.6.

SHAW v. LINDHEIM

United States Court of Appeals for the Ninth Circuit, 1990.
919 F.2d 1353.

ALARCON, CIRCUIT JUDGE:

* * *

A. *The Krofft Framework*

The Ninth Circuit employs a two-part test for determining whether one work is substantially similar to another. Established in *Sid & Marty Krofft Television Prods. Inc. v. McDonald's Corp.*, 562 F.2d 1157, 1164 (9th Cir.1977), the test permits a finding of infringement only if a plaintiff proves both substantial similarity of general ideas under the "extrinsic test" and substantial similarity of the protectible expression of those ideas under the "intrinsic test."

1. *Scope of the Krofft Tests*

Krofft defined the extrinsic test as a "test for similarity of ideas" under which "analytic dissection and expert testimony are appropriate."

The intrinsic test, according to *Krofft*, should measure "substantial similarity in expressions … depending on the response of the ordinary reasonable person…. [I]t does not depend on the type of external criteria and analysis which marks the extrinsic test." In decisions under the intrinsic test, "analytic dissection and expert testimony are not appropriate."

Relying on this language, panels applying *Krofft* to literary works have included a lengthy list of concrete elements under the extrinsic test. Whereas *Krofft* listed "the type of art work involved, the materials used, the subject matter, and the setting for the subject" as criteria for consideration under the extrinsic test, a series of [subsequent] opinions * * * have listed "plot, themes, dialogue, mood, setting, pace, [characters] and sequence [of events]" as extrinsic test criteria.

Now that it includes virtually every element that may be considered concrete in a literary work, the extrinsic test as applied to books, scripts, plays, and motion pictures can no longer be seen as a test for mere similarity of ideas. Because the criteria incorporated into the extrinsic test encompass all objective manifestations of creativity, the two tests are more sensibly described as objective and subjective analyses of *expression*, having strayed from *Krofft's* division between expression and ideas. Indeed, a judicial determination under the intrinsic test is now virtually devoid of analysis, for the intrinsic test has become a mere subjective judgment as to whether two literary works are or are not similar.

2. The District Court's Application of Krofft

An example of how the absence of legal analysis may frustrate appellate review of the intrinsic test is the district court's order in this matter. The district court found, after extensive analysis, that reasonable minds might conclude that plaintiffs' and defendants' works were substantially similar as to the objective characteristics of theme, plot, sequence of events, characters, dialogue, setting, mood, and pace. Nevertheless, the court made a subjective determination under the intrinsic test that no reasonable juror could determine that the works had a substantially similar total concept and feel. * * *

The district court's decision to grant summary judgment solely on a subjective assessment under *Krofft's* intrinsic test conflicts with the prescriptions of *Krofft*. In *Krofft*, this court stated that the outcome of the extrinsic test "may often be decided as a matter of law." In contrast, "[i]f there is substantial similarity in ideas, then the *trier of fact* must decide [under the intrinsic test] whether there is substantial similarity in the expressions of the ideas so as to constitute infringement." *Id.* (emphasis added); *see also Id.* at 1166 ("[T]he intrinsic test for expression is uniquely suited for determination by the *trier of fact*." (emphasis added)). * * *

3. Krofft and the Summary Judgment Standard

* * *

We must determine in this matter whether a party that demonstrates a triable issue of fact under the extrinsic test has made a sufficient showing of substantial similarity to defeat a summary judgment motion. As noted above, the extrinsic test focuses on "specific similarities between the plot, theme, dialogue, mood, setting, pace, characters, and sequence of events ... 'the actual concrete elements that make up the total sequence of events and the relationships between the major characters.'" These are the measurable, objective elements that constitute a literary work's expression. Because these elements are embodied in the extrinsic test, we hold that it is improper for a court to find, as the district court did, that there is no substantial similarity as a matter of law after a writer has satisfied the extrinsic test. To conclude otherwise would allow a court to base a grant of summary judgment on a purely subjective determination of similarity. * * *

* * *

Given the variety of possible expression and the objective criteria available under the extrinsic test to analyze a literary work's expression, as distinct from the ideas embodied in it, the intrinsic test cannot be the sole basis for a grant of summary judgment. Once a court has established that a triable question of objective similarity of expression exists, by analysis of each element of the extrinsic test, its inquiry should proceed no further. What remains is a subjective assessment of the "concept and feel" of two works of literature—a task no more suitable for a judge than for a jury. This subjective assessment is not a legal conclusion; rather it involves the audience in an interactive process with the author of the work in question, and calls on us "to transfer from our inward nature a human interest and a semblance of truth sufficient to procure for these shadows of imagination that willing suspension of disbelief for the moment, which constitutes poetic faith." S.T. Coleridge, *Biographia Litera-ria*, ch. 14, *reprinted in 5 English Literature: The Romantic Period* (A. Reed ed. 1929). This interactive assessment is by nature an individualized one that will provoke a varied response in each juror, for what "makes the unskillful laugh, cannot but make the judicious grieve." W. Shakespeare, *Hamlet*, Act III, scene ii, 11. 27–28. It is not the district court's role, in ruling on a motion for a summary judgment, to limit the interpretive judgment of each work to that produced by its own experience.

* * * A comparison of literary works * * * generally requires the reader or viewer to engage in a two-step process. The first step involves the objective comparison of concrete similarities; the second employs the subjective process of comprehension, reasoning, and understanding. The imagery presented in a literary work may also engage the imagination of the audience and evoke an emotional response. Because each of us differs, to some degree, in our capability to reason, imagine, and react emotional-ly, subjective comparisons of literary works that are objectively similar in their expression of ideas must be left to the trier of fact.

For these reasons, a showing of substantial similarity with reference to the eight objective components of expression in the extrinsic test applied to literary works creates a genuine issue for trial. If a district court concludes, after analyzing the objective criteria under the extrinsic test, that reasonable minds might differ as to whether there is substantial similarity between the protected expression of ideas in two literary works, and the record supports the district court's conclusion, there is a triable issue of fact that precludes summary judgment. This rule is necessary because our expansion of the extrinsic test as applied to literary works has incorporated all objective elements of expression, leaving a mere subjective assessment of similarity for the intrinsic test. Because such an assessment may not properly be made as a matter of law, it is for the trier of fact to determine whether the intrinsic test is satisfied. * * *

       * * *

NOTES AND QUESTIONS

1. *The Ninth Circuit's extrinsic/intrinsic test.* Does the Ninth Circuit's test for substantial similarity differ substantively from the *Arnstein* approach? From the *Knitwaves* approach? If so, how would you articulate the difference? Which approach is preferable? Does the extrinsic/intrinsic test resolve the concerns that Judge Clark described in his dissent in *Arnstein*?

As the *Shaw* opinion explains, the Ninth Circuit first stated its extrinsic/intrinsic approach in Sid & Marty Krofft Television Productions, Inc. v. McDonald's Corp., 562 F.2d 1157 (9th Cir.1977). As originally framed in *Krofft*, the extrinsic test was a "test for similarity of ideas," while the intrinsic test measured "substantial similarity in expressions * * * depending on the response of the ordinary reasonable person." What did division of the infringement inquiry in this fashion accomplish?

Given the way the Ninth Circuit has changed the extrinsic test, has its purpose changed? If so, has this change in purpose affected the scope of the intrinsic test, as well? If so, how?

While the *Shaw* court characterized the revised "objective analysis of expression" version of the extrinsic test as applying to "books, scripts, plays and motion pictures," the Ninth Circuit has subsequently extended objective evaluation of expression to the whole substantive range of infringement claims. See, e.g., Brown Bag Software v. Symantec Corp., 960 F.2d 1465 (9th Cir.1992), *cert. denied*, 506 U.S. 869, 113 S.Ct. 198, 121 L.Ed.2d 141 (1992) (alleged infringement of software); Swirsky v. Carey, 376 F.3d 841 (9th Cir. 2004) (alleged infringement of popular song); Cavalier v. Random House, Inc., 297 F.3d 815, 826 (9th Cir. 2002) (alleged infringement of works of art). For each general category of copyrightable subject matter, the Ninth Circuit has formulated a list of concrete elements of expression to be objectively evaluated in the extrinsic test. For example, in the case of musical works, the Ninth Circuit recognized that applying objective factors to analyze musical expression was a "somewhat unnatural task," but justified the objective analysis because it serves "the purpose of permitting summary judgment in clear cases of non-infringement, and it informs the fact-finder of some of the complexities of the medium in issue while guiding attention toward protected elements and away from unprotectible elements of a composition." *Swirsky*, 376 F.3d at 848–49. While noting that music is not capable of ready classification into only five or six constituent elements, the court noted that the plaintiff should address, through expert testimony, some or all of the following elements: melody, harmony, phrasing, structure, chord progression, lyrics, rhythm, pitch, tempo, title hook phrase, cadence, instrumental figures, verse/chorus relationship, melodic contours, meter, timbre, tune, spatial organization, consonance, dissonance, accents, note choice, interplay of instruments, basslines, and new technological sounds. *Id.*, at 849.

Courts outside the Ninth Circuit have sometimes adopted the Ninth Circuit's extrinsic/intrinsic framework for evaluating infringement. See, e.g., Taylor Corp. v. Four Seasons Greetings, LLC, 403 F.3d 958 (8th Cir. 2005) (alleged infringement of greeting card designs); Herzog v. Castle Rock Entertainment, 193 F.3d 1241, 1257 (11th Cir. 1999) (alleged infringement of screen play).

2. *Integrating the "extrinsic-intrinsic" standard with the "thin" copyright standard.* In a recent opinion, the Ninth Circuit demonstrated how the concept of "thin" copyright should be integrated into its "extrinsic-intrinsic" analysis. As Judge Kozinski explained:

At the initial "extrinsic" stage, we examine the similarities between the copyrighted and challenged works and then determine whether the similar elements are protectable or unprotectable. For example, ideas, scenes a faire (standard features) and unoriginal components aren't protectable. When the unprotectable elements are "filtered" out, what's left is an author's particular expression of an idea, which most definitely *is* protectable.

Given that others may freely copy a work's ideas (and other unprotectable elements), we start by determining the breadth of the possible expression of those ideas. If there's a wide range of expression (for example, there are gazillions of ways to make an aliens-attack movie), then copyright protection is "broad" and a work will infringe if it's "substantially similar" to the copyrighted work. If there's only a narrow range of expression (for example, there are only so many ways to paint a red bouncy ball on blank canvas), then copyright protection is "thin" and a work must be "virtually identical" to infringe. * * *

The standard for infringement—substantially similar or virtually identical—determined at the "extrinsic" stage is applied at the "intrinsic" stage. There we ask, most often of juries, whether an ordinary reasonable observer would consider the copyrighted and challenged works substantially similar (or virtually identical). If the answer is yes, then the challenged work is infringing.

Mattel, Inc. v. MGA Entertainment, Inc., 616 F.3d 904, 913–14 (9th Cir., 2010).

3. *Literal vs. non-literal similarity.* Copyright infringement liability may be based either on literal or non-literal similarity, or on a combination of both. For example, a plaintiff may successfully demonstrate substantial similarity of copyrightable expression by showing that the defendant copied the

plaintiff's particular selection and arrangement of plot devices—such as theme, setting, incidents of action, mood, and character—even though the defendant did not copy any of the plaintiff's literal language.

Suppose that the defendant had engaged only in literal copying or close paraphrasing of the plaintiff's script. How much must he have taken in order to infringe? In determining substantial similarity in literal infringement cases, courts examine both the quantity of literal expression taken and the quality, or importance, of the copied portion. Thus, for example, in Harper & Row Publishers, Inc. v. Nation Enterprises, 471 U.S. 539, 105 S.Ct. 2218, 85 L.Ed.2d 588 (1985), the defendant was held liable for the verbatim copying of 300–400 words from President Ford's 200,000-word memoirs. The Court noted that the 300–400 words that the defendant took were essentially "the heart of the book," because they constituted President Ford's explanation of why he pardoned President Nixon. See also Roy Export Co. Establishment v. Columbia Broadcasting System, Inc., 503 F.Supp. 1137 (S.D.N.Y.1980), *affirmed*, 672 F.2d 1095 (2d Cir.1982), *cert. denied*, 459 U.S. 826, 103 S.Ct. 60, 74 L.Ed.2d 63 (1982) (taking 55 seconds out of a one-hour and 29-minute film may be sufficient to infringe).

What, if any, relevance should be assigned to the dissimilarities between the parties' works?

C. SECTION 106(1): THE RIGHT TO REPRODUCE THE COPYRIGHTED WORK IN COPIES OR PHONORECORDS

HOUSE REPORT ON COPYRIGHT ACT OF 1976
H.R. Rep. No. 1476, 94th Cong., 2d Sess. 61–62 (1976).

Read together with the relevant definitions in section 101, the right "to reproduce the copyrighted work in copies or phonorecords" means the right to produce a material object in which the work is duplicated, transcribed, imitated, or simulated in a fixed form from which it can be "perceived, reproduced, or otherwise communicated, either directly or with the aid of a machine or device." As under the present law, a copyrighted work would be infringed by reproducing it in whole or in any substantial part, and by duplicating it exactly or by imitation or simulation. Wide departures or variations from the copyrighted works would still be an infringement as long as the author's "expression" rather than merely the author's "ideas" are taken. An exception to this general principle, applicable to the reproduction of copyrighted sound recordings, is specified in section 114.

"Reproduction" under clause (1) of section 106 is to be distinguished from "display" under clause (5). For a work to be "reproduced," its fixation in tangible form must be "sufficiently permanent or stable to permit it to be perceived, reproduced, or otherwise communicated for a period of more than transitory duration." Thus, the showing of images on a screen or tube would not be a violation of clause (1), although it might come within the scope of clause (5).

Notes and Questions

1. *The exclusive right to reproduce the work.* The reproduction right is the most fundamental of the economic rights, and is applicable to all categories of copyrightable subject matter. It is important, however, to note the "material object" limitation: Copying that produces no material copy or phonorecord, such as unauthorized performance of a work, does not infringe the § 106(1) reproduction right, though it may infringe one of the other exclusive rights.

Each of the § 106 rights is independent. Thus, a defendant may violate the right of reproduction even though he never sells or otherwise transfers the unauthorized copy he makes, and never makes the copy available to the public through display or performance. Likewise, a single act may violate more than one of the § 106 rights. For example, in the *Arnstein* case, the defendant might be found to have violated both the right of reproduction and the right of adaptation, § 106(2), if the portions he took from the plaintiff's musical composition were sufficient to render the works substantially similar. After all, he not only reproduced the plaintiff's expression but also combined it with his own to form a new version.

2. *The reproduction right in sound recordings.* Congress granted sound recordings the status of copyrightable subject matter in the early 1970's. Only those sound recordings "fixed" on or after February 15, 1972, are eligible for federal copyright protection.[8] Sound recordings fixed prior to 1972 may be protected under state law. 17 U.S.C.A. § 301(c).

As the House Report accompanying the 1976 Act explained, "sound recordings are original works of authorship comprising an aggregate of musical, spoken, or other sounds that have been fixed in tangible form." The copyrightable elements in a sound recording generally will consist of expression contributed both by the performers whose performance is captured and by the record producer, who captures and electronically processes the sounds, and compiles and edits them to make the final sound recording. H.R. Rep. No. 1476, 94th Cong., 2d Sess. 55–56 (1976).

It is important to note that the sound recording copyright is separate from any copyright that might exist in the musical, literary or dramatic work that is recorded. The rights afforded the owner of a sound recording copyright are narrower than those afforded owners of copyright in other subject matter, in several respects. Review Copyright Act § 114(a)–(b) carefully. Based on your reading thus far, how would you compare the scope of the right to reproduce sound recordings to the scope of the right to reproduce other types of copyrighted subject matter? What explains or justifies the differential treatment?

Under the terms of § 114(b), will evidence of sound sampling—the mechanical recapture of sounds from a copyrighted sound recording, in itself, be sufficient to demonstrate infringement of the sound recording right of reproduction, or must the plaintiff also demonstrate substantial similarity as

---

8. Some *foreign* sound recordings fixed prior to February 15, 1972 may enjoy U.S. copyright protection. See pp. 668–70, *infra.*

discussed in the prior section? This question may be very important, since many sound samplers take only a small portion of the sampled recording, and may mix the sampled sounds with other sounds or alter them significantly by changing the speed, deleting certain frequencies or tones, or introducing reverberations or echoes, to the point that the average listener would not recognize the taking.

In Bridgeport Music, Inc. v. Dimension Films, 410 F.3d 792 (6th Cir. 2005), the Sixth Circuit held that the act of unauthorized digital sampling, in and of itself, infringes a sound recording copyright. The district court in that case had found that no reasonable juror, even one familiar with the plaintiff's works, would recognize the source of the defendant's digital sample, and that the qualitative and quantitative amount taken in the defendant's sample was "*de minimis*." The Sixth Circuit held these findings irrelevant. While a substantial similarity evaluation would be necessary to determine whether the sample infringed the copyrighted *musical composition* recorded in the sampled sound recording, no such analysis would be needed to determine infringement of the sampled *sound recording*. The court based this finding on its construction of the statutory language in Copyright Act § 114(a) and (b), and on its evaluation of the policy issues:

> To begin with, there is ease of enforcement. Get a license or do not sample. We do not see this as stifling creativity in any significant way. It must be remembered that if an artist wants to incorporate a "riff" from another work in his or her recording, he is free to duplicate the sound of that "riff" in the studio. Second, the market will control the license price and keep it within bounds. The sound recording copyright holder cannot exact a license fee greater than what it would cost the person seeking the license to just duplicate the sample in the course of making the new recording. Third, sampling is never accidental. * * *

> This analysis admittedly raises the question of why one should, without infringing, be able to take three notes from a musical composition, for example, but not three notes by way of sampling from a sound recording. Why is there no *de minimis* taking or why should substantial similarity not enter the equation. Our first answer to this question is what we have earlier indicated. We think this result is dictated by the applicable statute. Second, even when a small part of the sound recording is sampled, the part taken is something of value. No further proof of that is necessary than the fact that the producer of the record or the artist on the record intentionally sampled because it would (1) save costs, or (2) add something to the new recording, or (3) both. For the sound recording copyright holder, it is not the "song" but the sounds that are fixed in the medium of his choice. When those sounds are sampled they are taken directly from that fixed medium. It is a physical taking rather than an intellectual one.

Id., at 801–02. The *Bridgeport* court went on to justify its bright-line rule in terms of judicial economy. While acknowledging that "many of the hip hop artists may view this rule as stifling creativity," the court noted that the record companies and performing artists were not all of one mind on the issue, and many samplers do in fact secure licenses prior to sampling.

Moreover, the record industry would have the ability and know-how to work out guidelines, including a fixed schedule of license fees. *Id.* at 803–05.

Review the language of § 114(a) and (b). Do you agree with the Sixth Circuit's interpretation of that language? Does it seem likely that Congress would have deviated from the long established requirement of substantial similarity without more clearly stating its intent to do so? What, specifically, is the harm to the plaintiff if the intended audience is unlikely to recognize the source of the defendant's sample? Where does the public's interest lie? Is the public better served by a license requirement, or by the imposition of the regular "substantial similarity" prerequisite to infringement liability? Why should it matter whether the defendant's "taking" is physical or intellectual?

NOTE: THE RIGHT OF REPRODUCTION AND DIGITAL WORKS

The right of reproduction is the right "to reproduce the copyrighted work in copies or phonorecords." 17 U.S.C.A. § 106(1). Copyright Act § 101 defines a "copy" as a material object in which a work is "fixed." It provides that a work is "fixed" when its embodiment in a copy "is sufficiently permanent or stable to permit it to be perceived, reproduced, or otherwise communicated for a period of more than transitory duration." Given these definitions, is the loading of a computer program or other copyrightable work into the random access memory ("RAM") of a computer the making of a "copy," and thus a "reproduction" within the meaning of Copyright Act § 106(1)?[9]

In MAI Systems Corp. v. Peak Computer, Inc., 991 F.2d 511 (9th Cir.1993), the Court of Appeals for the Ninth Circuit held that loading a computer program into RAM did constitute a potentially infringing reproduction of the copyrighted program. Other jurisdictions have followed the Ninth Circuit's lead. In *MAI*, the owner of copyright in operating system software licensed others to use the software in their computers, but the license prohibited use by third parties. The copyright owner also offered computer maintenance and repair services to its licensees. Some of its licensees later contracted with Peak, an independent computer service and repair business, to service their computers. The copyright owner then sued Peak for copyright infringement, alleging that its servicing of the licensees' computers resulted in unauthorized reproductions of its copyrighted operating system software.

In finding infringement, the Ninth Circuit reasoned:

---

9. The legislative history is somewhat mixed. See H.R. Rep. No. 1476, 94th Cong., 2d Sess. 53, 62 (1976):

[T]he definition of "fixation" would exclude from the concept purely evanescent or transient reproductions such as those * * * captured momentarily in the "memory" of a computer. * * *

Reproduction under clause (1) of section 106 is to be distinguished from "display" under clause (5). * * * [T]he showing of images on a screen or tube would not be a violation of clause (1), although it might come within the scope of clause (5).

But see Final Report of the National Commission on New Technological Uses of Copyrighted Works 13 (1978):

Because the placement of a work into a computer is the preparation of a copy, the law should provide that persons in rightful possession of copies of programs be able to use them freely without fear of exposure to copyright liability.

Peak concedes that in maintaining its customer's computers, it uses MAI operating software "to the extent that the repair and maintenance process necessarily involves turning on the computer to make sure it is functional and thereby running the operating system." It is also uncontroverted that when the computer is turned on the operating system is loaded into the computer's RAM. As part of diagnosing a computer problem at the customer site, the Peak technician runs the computer's operating system software, allowing the technician to view the systems error log, which is part of the operating system, thereby enabling the technician to diagnose the problem.

Peak argues that this loading of copyrighted software does not constitute a copyright violation because the "copy" created in RAM is not "fixed." However, by showing that Peak loads the software into the RAM and is then able to view the system error log and diagnose the problem with the computer, MAI has adequately shown that the representation created in the RAM is "sufficiently permanent or stable to permit it to be perceived, reproduced, or otherwise communicated for a period of more than transitory duration."

MAI, 991 F.3d at 518.

What are the implications of the *MAI* reasoning for use of the Internet? In its Final Report, the President's Information Infrastructure Task Force observed that the right to reproduce works will be implicated in virtually all transactions over the Internet—uploading documents, downloading documents, transmitting documents from one place to another, and storing documents on servers will all entail making digital copies of them. Information Infrastructure Task Force, Intellectual Property and the National Information Infrastructure, The Report of the Working Group on Intellectual Property Rights 64–66 (1995). These copies may endure for less than a second, a few seconds, a few minutes, a week, or months. The Task Force believed that most, if not all of these transactions should be viewed as potentially infringing "reproduction." Should that be so? What are the implications of such a finding? For provocative discussions, see, e.g., Litman, *The Exclusive Right to Read*, 13 Cardozo Arts & Ent. L.J. 29 (1994); Samuelson, *The NII Intellectual Property Report*, 37 Communications of the ACM 21 (Dec., 1994). If digital reproductions made in the course of transmitting and storing works on the Internet constitute "reproduction" for purposes of Copyright Act § 106(1), who should be liable for them?

In CoStar Group, Inc. v. Loopnet, Inc., 373 F.3d 544 (4th Cir. 2004), the defendant Internet service provider ("ISP") operated a web site that hosted online commercial real estate listings for brokers. Subscribing brokers were permitted to post listings on the site. Although the defendant took some measures to prevent the posting of infringing materials, some of its subscribing brokers made unauthorized postings of the plaintiff's copyrighted photographs of commercial real estate sites. When the photographs were posted, the defendant ISP's computer system automatically made digital copies. The issue was whether the ISP should be liable for directly infringing the plaintiff's reproduction rights in the photographs, pursuant to Copyright Act § 106(1). Adopting the reasoning in Religious Technology Center v. Netcom On–Line

Communication Services, Inc., 907 F.Supp. 1361 (N.D.Cal. 1995), the Fourth Circuit held that the defendant was not liable. The court explained that even though copyright is a strict liability statute, there must still be "some element of volition or causation which is lacking where a defendant's system is merely used to make a copy by a third party." *Id., at 548 (quoting Netcom*, 907 F.Supp. at 1370).

> [C]onstruing the Copyright Act to require some aspect of volition and meaningful causation—as distinct from passive ownership and management of an electronic Internet facility—receives additional support from the Act's concept of "copying." A violation of § 106 requires copying or the making of copies. And the term "copies" refers to "material objects . . . in which a work *is fixed.*" A work is "fixed" in a medium when it is embodied in a copy "sufficiently permanent or stable to permit it to be perceived, reproduced, or otherwise communicated for a period *of more than transitory duration.*" [17 U.S.C. § 101] (emphasis added). When an electronic infrastructure is designed and managed as a *conduit* of information and data that connects users over the Internet, the owner and manager of the conduit hardly "copies" the information and data in the sense that it fixes a copy in its system *of more than transitory duration.* Even if the information and data are "downloaded" onto the owner's RAM or other component as part of the transmission function, that downloading is a temporary, automatic response to the user's request, and the entire system functions solely to transmit the user's data to the Internet. Under such an arrangement, the ISP provides a system that automatically transmits users' material but is itself totally indifferent to the material's content. In this way, it functions as does a traditional telephone company when it transmits the contents of its users' conversations. While temporary electronic copies may be made in this transmission process, they would appear not to be "fixed" in the sense that they are "of more than transitory duration," and the ISP therefore would not be a "copier" to make it directly liable under the Copyright Act. * * *

> In concluding that an ISP has not itself fixed a copy in its system of more than transitory duration when it provides an Internet hosting service to its subscribers, we do not hold that a computer owner who downloads copyrighted software onto a computer cannot infringe the software's copyright. *See, e.g., MAI Systems Corp. v. Peak Computer, Inc.,* 991 F.2d 511, 518–19 (9th Cir.1993). When the computer owner downloads copyrighted software, it possesses the software, which then functions in the service of the computer or its owner, and the copying is no longer of a transitory nature. "Transitory duration" is thus both a qualitative and quantitative characterization. It is quantitative insofar as it describes the period during which the function occurs, and it is qualitative in the sense that it describes the status of transition. Thus, when the copyrighted software is downloaded onto the computer, because it may be used to serve the computer or the computer owner, it no longer remains transitory. This, however, is unlike an ISP, which provides a system that automatically receives a subscriber's infringing material and transmits it to the Internet at the instigation of the subscriber.

Accordingly, we conclude that *Netcom* made a particularly rational interpretation of § 106 when it concluded that a person had to engage in volitional conduct—specifically, the act constituting infringement—to become a direct infringer. As the court in *Netcom* concluded, such a construction of the Act is especially important when it is applied to cyberspace. There are thousands of owners, contractors, servers, and users involved in the Internet whose role involves the storage and transmission of data in the establishment and maintenance of an Internet facility. Yet their conduct is not truly "copying" as understood by the Act; rather, they are conduits from or to would-be copiers and have no interest in the copy itself. *See Doe v. GTE Corp.,* 347 F.3d 655, 659 (7th Cir.2003) ("A web host, like a delivery service or phone company, is an intermediary and normally is indifferent to the content of what it transmits").

Id. at 550–51. Compare Playboy Enterprises, Inc. v. Frena, 839 F.Supp. 1552 (M.D.Fla. 1993)(holding an ISP strictly liable for illegal copying on its computer system). In your view, was the *CoStar* court successful in distinguishing the Ninth Circuit's decision in *MAI?* Does the *CoStar* finding make sense as a matter of policy? The *CoStar* court found the defendant ISP comparable to the owner of a copy machine who makes the machine available to the public (for example, in a drug store or copy shop), charges its customers a fixed amount per copy, and leaves them to operate the machine themselves. Is this an apt analogy? What kind of "volitional" conduct on the part of an ISP would render it a direct infringer, under the *CoStar* reasoning?

The Court of Appeals for the Second Circuit recently relied on the *Netcom and CoStar* decisions in evaluating a new remote storage digital video recorder ("RS–DVR") system that allowed the defendant's cable subscribers to copy television programs and movies being shown via cable. Cartoon Network, LP v. CSC Holdings, Inc., 536 F.3d 121 (2d Cir. 2008). From customers' standpoint, the process of recording and playing back recorded programs through the remote storage system was similar to that of traditional, stand-alone digital video recorders attached to the users' television. However, rather than making copies in a set-top DVR, the defendant's system created and stored the copies on the defendant's central hard drives at a remote location, and played them back at the user's request via cable transmission. The process of recording the programs entailed "buffering" the data stream (somewhat akin to processing data in RAM), creating temporary buffer replicas of copyrighted cable content that lasted up to 1.2 seconds. The plaintiffs (providers of copyrighted content) alleged that these buffer replicas constituted infringing copies, and also argued that the defendant directly infringed their copyrights by creating the longer-term copies that it stored on its hard drives until the customer requested play-back.

The Second Circuit rejected the argument that the 1.2–second buffer replicas constituted infringing copies. The court noted that under Copyright Act § 101, a "copy" is a material object in which a work is "fixed," and that a work will only be "fixed" when it is *embodied* in a tangible medium of expression from which it can be perceived, reproduced, or otherwise communicated for *a period of more than transitory duration.* While the buffer replicas were "embodied" as required, they did not endure for more than a transitory duration. The court distinguished *MAI* on the ground that the Ninth Circuit had had no occasion to address the duration issue:

> [W]e construe *MAI Systems* and its progeny as holding that loading a program into a computer's RAM *can* result in copying that program. We do not read *MAI Systems* as holding that, as a matter of law, loading a program into a form of RAM *always* results in copying. Such a holding would read the "transitory duration" language out of the definition.

Cartoon Network, 536 F.3d at 128.

With regard to the play-back copies stored on the defendant's remote hard drives, the issue was *who made the copy*. If the defendant made the copy, it could be liable for direct infringement. But if the cable subscriber made the copy, the defendant could only be liable, at most, for indirect infringement. Following the reasoning in *Netcom* and *CoStar,* the Second Circuit found that the cable subscriber made the copy:

> When there is a dispute as to the author of an allegedly infringing instance of reproduction, *Netcom* and its progeny direct our attention to the volitional conduct that causes the copy to be made. There are only two instances of volitional conduct in this case: Cablevision's conduct in designing, housing, and maintaining a system that exists only to produce a copy, and a customer's conduct in ordering that system to produce a copy of a specific program. In the case of a VCR, it seems clear * * * that the operator of the VCR, the person who actually presses the button to make the recording, supplies the necessary element of volition, not the person who manufactures, maintains, or, if distinct from the operator, owns the machine. We do not believe that a RS–DVR customer is sufficiently distinguishable from a VCR user to impose liability as a direct infringer on a different party for copies that are made automatically upon that customer's command.

Id., at 131.

NOTES AND QUESTIONS

1. *Exceptions to the right to reproduce computer programs.* Review the provisions of Copyright Act § 117(a) and (b). In enacting these provisions, Congress adopted almost *verbatim* the statutory language recommended in the CONTU Final Report. Final Report of the Commission on New Technological Uses of Copyrighted Works 12 (1979). Thus, the Final Report is frequently consulted in the course of construing § 117. The Final Report justified subsections (a) and (b) as follows:

> Because the placement of a work into a computer is the preparation of a copy, the law should provide that persons in rightful possession of copies of programs be able to use them freely without fear of exposure to copyright liability. Obviously, creators, lessors, licensors, and vendors of copies of programs intend that they be used by their customers, so that rightful users would but rarely need a legal shield against potential copyright problems. It is easy to imagine, however, a situation in which the copyright owner might desire, for good reason or none at all, to force

a lawful owner or possessor of a copy to stop using a particular program. One who rightfully possesses a copy of a program, therefore, should be provided with a legal right to copy it to that extent which will permit its use by that possessor. This would include the right to load it into a computer and to prepare archival copies of it to guard against destruction or damage by mechanical or electrical failure. But this permission would not extend to other copies of the program. Thus, one could not, for example, make archival copies of a program and later sell some while retaining some for use. * * *

Id. at 13.

Courts have encountered several important issues in construing and applying § 117. For example, how strictly should courts construe the language that limits the exemption to copying that is "an essential step" in the use of the program in conjunction with a machine? One court has construed the "essential step" language to exclude a computer manufacturer's practice of copying programs from disks it purchased onto semiconductor chips, to be inserted into its computers. According to the court, "essential" means "indispensable and necessary," not merely "convenient." The court reasoned that the "essential step" requirement limits the § 117 exemption to copies that are "no more permanent than is reasonably necessary." Apple Computer, Inc. v. Formula International, Inc., 594 F.Supp. 617 (C.D.Cal.1984).

Compare Vault Corp. v. Quaid Software Ltd., 847 F.2d 255 (5th Cir.1988). In that case, the plaintiff produced and sold disks containing an anticopying program to prevent users from reproducing other programs on the disk in a useable form. The defendant produced and sold a program designed to "unlock" the plaintiff's anticopying program. In the course of creating its "unlocking" program, the defendant inserted plaintiff's anticopying program into its computer memory in order to study it. The Fifth Circuit found that this reproduction was permitted under § 117 as an essential step in using the program. The court rejected plaintiff's argument that § 117 only permits loading a program into a computer for the use *its creator* intended, in this case preventing the copying of other programs on the disk. *Id.* at 261.

Note that § 117 exempts the "owner of a computer program" from liability, rather than the "rightful possessor," as recommended by the CONTU Final Report. What are the implications of this change in language?

Today, most software venders purport not to transfer title to programs, but merely to grant a license to use them. In the *MAI* case, discussed *supra*, the Court of Appeals for the Ninth Circuit held that the "licensees" of the plaintiff's copyrighted operating system software were not "owners" within the meaning of § 117, and thus that they were not entitled to reproduce the software under any terms other than those spelled out in the license. The license authorized the licensees to reproduce the operating system software in the course of their own internal information processing, but not to have third parties (like the defendant independent computer service and repair business) reproduce it. Thus, when the licensees had their computers serviced by the defendant, rather than by the copyright owner, the reproduction of the software in the course of servicing was not sheltered under either § 117 or the license and constituted infringement. The copyright owner was able to use copyright law to monopolize the business of servicing computers programmed with its operating system software.

Review the provisions of § 117(c). Congress amended § 117 to add this narrow exception to liability in 1998, specifically to prevent the *result* in *MAI*. Does this amendment affect the precedential value of the *MAI* court's reasoning regarding the status of RAM copies as "reproductions" under Copyright Act § 106(1)?

In DSC Communications Corp. v. Pulse Communications, Inc., 170 F.3d 1354 (Fed.Cir.), *cert. denied*, 528 U.S. 923, 120 S.Ct. 286, 145 L.Ed.2d 240 (1999), the Court of Appeals for the Federal Circuit rejected the *MAI* court's blanket characterization of all purported software "licensees" as non-owners. It held that in deciding whether a particular rightful possessor is a licensee or an owner for purposes of § 117, courts should examine the terms of the purported "licensing" transaction. Relevant considerations include whether the possessor obtained its rights in the software through a single payment, whether its rightful possession is perpetual, and whether its right to use the software under the license is heavily encumbered by restrictions that are inconsistent with the status of an owner (such as restrictions on transfer of the copy, or use of the software with particular hardware). After undertaking this analysis, the *DSC* court found that the rightful possessor before it would not qualify as an "owner" for purposes of § 117. Given the restriction against use by third parties in *MAI*, would the Federal Circuit's approach lead to a different result in that case? Given today's marketing practices, how many rightful possessors of software are likely to enjoy the benefits of § 117? See Krause v. Titleserv, Inc., 402 F.3d 119, 122–24 (2d Cir.), *cert. denied*, 126 S.Ct. 622, 163 L.Ed.2d 504 (2005)(Second Circuit, agreeing with the *DSC* reasoning, finds defendant rightful possessor an "owner" for purposes of § 117 because (1) defendant paid the program creator "substantial consideration to develop the programs for its sole benefit;" (2) the creator customized the software to serve defendant's operations; (3) the copies were stored on a server owned by the defendant; (4) the creator never reserved the right to repossess the copies and agreed that defendant had the right to continue to possess and use the programs forever, regardless of whether its relationship with creator terminated; and (5) defendant was free to discard or destroy the copies at any time it wished.).

2. *Other exceptions to the reproduction right.* Copyright Act §§ 108 through 121 contain a number of additional exceptions to the exclusive right of reproduction. Some, like §§ 114 and 117, are specifically directed to a particular category of copyrightable subject matter. Section 113, for example, sets forth exceptions for the pictorial, graphic, and sculptural works category. Among other things, it permits owners of useful articles embodying pictorial, graphic and sculptural works to make, distribute and display drawings and photographs of the useful articles to advertise their sale. Section 120 is directed specifically to architectural works. Among other things, it permits the creation, distribution and public display of photographs and other pictorial representations of protected buildings located in public places. Congress

concluded that such "reproductions" serve an "important public purpose" and "do not interfere with the normal exploitation of architectural works." H.R. Rep. No. 735, 101st Cong., 2d Sess. 22 (1990).

Other exceptions focus on the particular use being made of a protected work, or the identity of the user. For example, § 108 permits libraries and archives to reproduce and distribute protected works for their own non-commercial purposes or for their patrons, as long as specific guidelines are followed. Section 112 gives broadcasters who are otherwise entitled to transmit performances or displays of copyrighted works limited rights to record their transmissions. In 1996, Congress amended the Copyright Act to permit certain non-profit and government organizations to reproduce and distribute designated copyrighted literary works in braille, audio or other specialized formats, for use by persons with disabilities. 17 U.S.C.A. § 121.

3. *Compulsory licenses.* Although compulsory licensing provisions are rare in United States intellectual property law, the Copyright Act expressly provides for compulsory licenses in several situations. For example, § 115 provides a compulsory license to produce and distribute sound recordings ("cover recordings") of non-dramatic musical compositions. This license is sometimes called the "mechanical license." Once the owner of copyright in a nondramatic musical composition has authorized the making and public distribution of a sound recording of the work, others may freely make and distribute their own independent sound recordings of the musical composition, as long as they follow the procedure set out in the statute and pay the prescribed royalty fee to the music copyright owner.

PROBLEMS

1. Assume that Elvina Hardpressed, a pop singer, made a sound recording of the Beatles' old hit, *I Want To Hold Your Hand*, in 2009. Y, an Elvina Hardpressed impersonator, bought a copy of the sound recording, obtained a license to record *I Want To Hold Your Hand* pursuant to Copyright Act § 115, and recorded the song in a manner that sounded exactly like Elvina's recording. Listeners could not tell the difference. Y then put her own recording on the market. Are Y's acts likely to constitute copyright infringement?

2. X created a photograph of San Francisco as seen when one approaches the city over the Golden Gate Bridge. Y set out to create his own, digitally altered image of San Francisco. In the course of doing this, Y scanned X's photograph, creating a "precursor image" in his computer, and proceeded to cut and manipulate six distinctive buildings from that precursor image. He then inserted the six buildings into his own digitized work, and deleted the precursor image of X's photograph. Y's finished image provided a prospect of San Francisco that differed from that offered from the Golden Gate Bridge. In addition to the six buildings taken from X's photograph, it incorporated architectural structures and other features from a number of photographs Y himself had taken over the years. Is Y likely to have infringed X's copyright in his photograph?

D.   SECTION 106(2): THE EXCLUSIVE RIGHT TO PREPARE DERIVATIVE WORKS BASED UPON THE COPYRIGHTED WORK

HOUSE REPORT ON COPYRIGHT ACT OF 1976

H.R. Rep. No. 1476, 94th Cong., 2d Sess. 62 (1976).

The exclusive right to prepare derivative works, specified separately in clause (2) of section 106, overlaps the exclusive right of reproduction to some extent. It is broader than that right, however, in the sense that reproduction requires fixation in copies or phonorecords, whereas the preparation of a derivative work, such as a ballet, pantomime, or improvised performance, may be an infringement even though nothing is ever fixed in tangible form.

To be an infringement the "derivative work" must be "based upon the copyrighted work," and the definition in section 101 refers to "a translation, musical arrangement, dramatization, fictionalization, motion picture version, sound recording, art reproduction, abridgment, condensation, or any other form in which a work may be recast, transformed, or adapted." Thus, to constitute a violation of section 106(2), the infringing work must incorporate a portion of the copyrighted work in some form; for example, a detailed commentary on a work or a programmatic musical composition inspired by a novel would not normally constitute infringements under this clause.

MIRAGE EDITIONS, INC. v. ALBUQUERQUE A.R.T. CO.

United States Court of Appeals for the Ninth Circuit, 1988.
856 F.2d 1341, *cert. denied*
489 U.S. 1018, 109 S.Ct. 1135, 103 L.Ed.2d 196 (1989).

BRUNETTI, CIRCUIT JUDGE:

[Plaintiffs/Appellees Dumas and Mirage own copyrights to Nagel art works. They licensed Van Der Marck Editions, Inc. to publish a commemorative book entitled *NAGEL: The Art of Patrick Nagel*, which includes prints of some of Nagel's works. Defendant/Appellant's primary business is 1) purchasing art work prints or books containing good quality art work prints; 2) gluing each individual print onto a rectangular sheet of black plastic material exposing a narrow black margin around the print; 3) gluing the black sheet with print onto a major surface of a rectangular white ceramic tile; 4) applying a transparent plastic film over the print, black sheet and ceramic tile surface; and 5) offering the tile with art work mounted thereon for sale in the retail market. Defendant acquired the Nagel book and performed this process with some of the prints. The plaintiffs sued, alleging copyright infringement, and the district court granted summary judgement in their favor.]

Appellant contends that there has been no copyright infringement because its tiles are not derivative works * * *.

The Copyright Act of 1976, 17 U.S.C. § 101 defines a derivative work as:

[A] work based upon one or more preexisting works such as a translation, musical arrangement, dramatization, fictionalization, motion picture version, sound recording, art reproduction, abridgment, condensation *or any other form in which a work may be recast, transformed, or adapted.* * * * (emphasis added).

* * *

What appellant has clearly done here is to make another version of Nagel's art works, and that amounts to preparation of a derivative work. By borrowing and mounting the preexisting, copyrighted individual art images without the consent of the copyright proprietors—Mirage and Dumas as to the art works and Van Der Marck as to the book—appellant has prepared a derivative work and infringed the subject copyrights.

Appellant's contention that * * * it has not engaged in "art reproduction" and therefore its tiles are not derivative works is not fully dispositive of this issue. Appellant has ignored the disjunctive phrase "or any other form in which a work may be recast, transformed or adapted." The legislative history of the Copyright Act of 1976 indicates that Congress intended that for a violation of the right to prepare derivative works to occur "the infringing work must incorporate a portion of the copyrighted work in *some form.*" 1976 U.S.Code Cong. & Admin.News 5659, 5675. (emphasis added). The language "recast, transformed or adapted" seems to encompass other alternatives besides simple art reproduction. By removing the individual images from the book and placing them on the tiles, perhaps the appellant has not accomplished reproduction. We conclude, though, that appellant has certainly recast or transformed the individual images by incorporating them into its tile-preparing process.

* * *

LEE v. A.R.T. CO.

United States Court Of Appeals For The Seventh Circuit, 1997.
125 F.3d 580.

EASTERBROOK, CIRCUIT JUDGE.

Annie Lee creates works of art, which she sells through her firm Annie Lee & Friends. Deck the Walls, a chain of outlets for modestly priced art, is among the buyers of her works, which have been registered with the Register of Copyrights. One Deck the Walls store sold some of Lee's note cards and small lithographs to A.R.T. Company, which mounted the works on ceramic tiles (covering the art with transparent epoxy resin in the process) and resold the tiles. Lee contends that these tiles are derivative works, which under 17 U.S.C. § 106(2) may not be prepared without the permission of the copyright proprietor. She seeks both monetary and injunctive relief. Her position has the support of two cases holding that A.R.T.'s business violates the copyright laws. *Munoz v.*

Albuquerque A.R.T. Co., 38 F.3d 1218 (9th Cir.1994), affirming without published opinion, 829 F.Supp. 309 (D.Alaska 1993); *Mirage Editions, Inc. v. Albuquerque A.R.T. Co.*, 856 F.2d 1341 (9th Cir.1988). *Mirage Editions*, the only full appellate discussion, dealt with pages cut from books and mounted on tiles; the court of appeals' brief order in *Munoz* concludes that the reasoning of *Mirage Editions* is equally applicable to works of art that were sold loose. Our district court disagreed with these decisions and entered summary judgment for the defendant.

Now one might suppose that this is an open and shut case under the doctrine of first sale, codified at 17 U.S.C. § 109(a). A.R.T. bought the work legitimately, mounted it on a tile, and resold what it had purchased. Because the artist could capture the value of her art's contribution to the finished product as part of the price for the original transaction, the economic rationale for protecting an adaptation as "derivative" is absent. An alteration that includes (or consumes) a complete copy of the original lacks economic significance. One work changes hands multiple times, exactly what § 109(a) permits, so it may lack legal significance too. But § 106(2) creates a separate exclusive right, to "prepare derivative works", and Lee believes that affixing the art to the tile is "preparation," so that A.R.T. would have violated § 106(2) even if it had dumped the finished tiles into the Marianas Trench. For the sake of argument we assume that this is so and ask whether card-on-a-tile is a "derivative work" in the first place.

"Derivative work" is a defined term:

A "derivative work" is a work based upon one or more preexisting works, such as a translation, musical arrangement, dramatization, fictionalization, motion picture version, sound recording, art reproduction, abridgment, condensation, or any other form in which a work may be recast, transformed, or adapted. A work consisting of editorial revisions, annotations, elaborations, or other modifications which, as a whole, represent an original work of authorship, is a "derivative work".

17 U.S.C. § 101. The district court concluded that A.R.T.'s mounting of Lee's works on tile is not an "original work of authorship" because it is no different in form or function from displaying a painting in a frame or placing a medallion in a velvet case. No one believes that a museum violates § 106(2) every time it changes the frame of a painting that is still under copyright, although the choice of frame or glazing affects the impression the art conveys, and many artists specify frames (or pedestals for sculptures) in detail. *Munoz* and *Mirage Editions* acknowledge that framing and other traditional means of mounting and displaying art do not infringe authors' exclusive right to make derivative works. Nonetheless, the Ninth Circuit held, what A.R.T. does creates a derivative work because the epoxy resin bonds the art to the tile. Our district judge thought this a distinction without a difference, and we agree. If changing the way in which a work of art will be displayed creates a derivative work,

and if Lee is right about what "prepared" means, then the derivative work is "prepared" when the art is mounted; what happens later is not relevant, because the violation of the § 106(2) right has already occurred. If the framing process does not create a derivative work, then mounting art on a tile, which serves as a flush frame, does not create a derivative work. What is more, the Ninth Circuit erred in assuming that normal means of mounting and displaying art are easily reversible. A painting is placed in a wooden "stretcher" as part of the framing process; this leads to some punctures (commonly tacks or staples), may entail trimming the edges of the canvas, and may affect the surface of the painting as well. Works by Jackson Pollock are notoriously hard to mount without damage, given the thickness of their paint. As a prelude to framing, photographs, prints, and posters may be mounted on stiff boards using wax sheets, but sometimes glue or another more durable substance is employed to create the bond.

Lee wages a vigorous attack on the district court's conclusion that A.R.T.'s mounting process cannot create a derivative work because the change to the work "as a whole" is not sufficiently original to support a copyright. Cases such as *Gracen v. The Bradford Exchange, Inc.*, 698 F.2d 300 (7th Cir.1983), show that neither A.R.T. nor Lee herself could have obtained a copyright in the card-on-a-tile, thereby not only extending the period of protection for the images but also eliminating competition in one medium of display. After the Ninth Circuit held that its mounting process created derivative works, A.R.T. tried to obtain a copyright in one of its products; the Register of Copyrights sensibly informed A.R.T. that the card-on-a-tile could not be copyrighted independently of the note card itself. But Lee says that this is irrelevant—that a change in a work's appearance may infringe the exclusive right under § 106(2) even if the alteration is too trivial to support an independent copyright. Pointing to the word "original" in the second sentence of the statutory definition, the district judge held that "originality" is essential to a derivative work. This understanding has the support of both cases and respected commentators. Pointing to the fact that the first sentence in the statutory definition omits any reference to originality, Lee insists that a work may be derivative despite the mechanical nature of the transformation. This view, too, has the support of both cases and respected commentators. * * *

Fortunately, it is not necessary for us to choose sides. Assume for the moment that the first sentence recognizes a set of non-original derivative works. To prevail, then, Lee must show that A.R.T. altered her works in one of the ways mentioned in the first sentence. The tile is not an "art reproduction;" A.R.T. purchased and mounted Lee's original works. That leaves the residual clause: "any other form in which a work may be recast, transformed, or adapted." None of these words fits what A.R.T. did. Lee's works were not "recast" or "adapted". "Transformed" comes closer and gives the Ninth Circuit some purchase for its view that the permanence of the bond between art and base matters. Yet the copyrighted note cards and lithographs were not "transformed" in the slightest. The art was bonded to a slab of ceramic, but it was not changed in the process. It still depicts exactly what it depicted when it left Lee's studio. * * * If mounting works a "transformation," then changing a painting's frame or a photograph's mat equally produces a derivative work. Indeed, if Lee is right about the meaning of the definition's first sentence, then any alteration of a work, however slight, requires the author's permission. We asked at oral argument what would happen if a purchaser jotted a note on one of the note cards, or used it as a coaster for a drink, or cut it in half, or if a collector applied his seal (as is common in Japan); Lee's counsel replied that such changes prepare derivative works, but that as a practical matter artists would not file suit. A definition of derivative work that makes criminals out of art collectors and tourists is jarring despite Lee's gracious offer not to commence civil litigation.

* * * We therefore decline to follow *Munoz* and *Mirage Editions*.

NOTES AND QUESTIONS

1. *The adaptation right.* The right to make derivative works is often called the right to adapt the copyrighted work. In most cases, the same acts that constitute an unauthorized adaptation will also infringe the exclusive right to reproduce the work. A defendant who, without authorization, makes a motion picture based on a novel, creates three-dimensional dolls based on popular two-dimensional cartoon characters, or translates a biography from English to French clearly is making a derivative work. But she is also reproducing the original work in copies. Regardless of which of these two rights a plaintiff alleges to be infringed, the plaintiff must prove that the defendant's work was copied from his own copyrighted work and is substantially similar to it in expression. See Horgan v. Macmillan, Inc., 789 F.2d 157 (2d Cir.1986).

Thus, the adaptation right generally is duplicative and cumulative. Only when the defendant's adaptation fails to create a tangible copy or phonorecord of the copyrighted work will the plaintiff be unable to rely on the reproduction right.[10] This might occur when the defendant physically alters an existing, authorized copy of the original work, as in *Mirage* and *Lee*. As the House Report suggests, it might also occur if the defendant created a performance that borrowed from the plaintiff's copyrighted work. The dancing of an improvised ballet based on a copyrighted work of choreography presumably would constitute the making of a derivative work, but unless the defendant fixed the improvised dance in tangible form—for example, by notation or filming—it would not infringe the right of reproduction. Of course, if the dance occurred in a public place or was performed for the public, it would also infringe the plaintiff's exclusive right of public performance.

In a case like *Mirage* or *Lee*, should it matter whether the defendant would otherwise qualify for a derivative work copyright? Can the *Mirage* and *Lee* decisions be distinguished on their facts? If so, which set of facts presents a more justifiable basis for finding an infringement of the adaptation right?

---

10. Of course, a plaintiff may allege infringement of the adaptation right when it has licensed the defendant to reproduce the work, but not to alter it.

LEWIS GALOOB TOYS, INC. v. NINTENDO
OF AMERICA, INC.

United States Court of Appeals for the Ninth Circuit, 1992.
964 F.2d 965, *cert. denied,*
507 U.S. 985, 113 S.Ct. 1582, 123 L.Ed.2d 149 (1993).

FARRIS, CIRCUIT JUDGE:

[Nintendo appeals the district court's decision that Lewis Galoob Toys' Game Genie does not violate any of Nintendo's copyrights.]

The Nintendo Entertainment System is a home video game system marketed by Nintendo. To use the system, the player inserts a cartridge containing a video game that Nintendo produces or licenses others to produce. By pressing buttons and manipulating a control pad, the player controls one of the game's characters and progresses through the game. The games are protected as audiovisual works under 17 U.S.C. § 102(a)(6).

The Game Genie is a device manufactured by Galoob that allows the player to alter up to three features of a Nintendo game. For example, the Game Genie can increase the number of lives of the player's character, increase the speed at which the character moves, and allow the character to float above obstacles. The player controls the changes made by the Game Genie by entering codes provided by the Game Genie Programming Manual and Code Book. The player also can experiment with variations of these codes.

The Game Genie functions by blocking the value for a single data byte sent by the game cartridge to the central processing unit in the Nintendo Entertainment System and replacing it with a new value. If that value controls the character's strength, for example, then the character can be made invincible by increasing the value sufficiently. The Game Genie is inserted between a game cartridge and the Nintendo Entertainment System. The Game Genie does not alter the data that is stored in the game cartridge. Its effects are temporary.

Discussion

The Copyright Act of 1976 confers upon copyright holders the exclusive right to prepare and authorize others to prepare derivative works based on their copyrighted works. *See* 17 U.S.C. § 106(2). Nintendo argues that the district court erred in concluding that the audiovisual displays created by the Game Genie are not derivative works. * * *

A derivative work must incorporate a protected work in some concrete or permanent "form." The Copyright Act defines a derivative work as follows:

A "derivative work" is a work based upon one or more preexisting works, such as a translation, musical arrangement, dramatization, fictionalization, motion picture version, sound recording, art reproduction, abridgment, condensation, *or any other form in which a work may be recast, transformed, or adapted*. A work consisting of editorial revisions, annotations, elaborations, or other modifications which, as a whole, represent an original work of authorship, is a "derivative work."

17 U.S.C. § 101 (emphasis added). The examples of derivative works provided by the Act all physically incorporate the underlying work or works. The Act's legislative history similarly indicates that "the infringing work must incorporate a portion of the copyrighted work in some form." 1976 U.S.Code Cong. & Admin.News 5659, 5675.

Our analysis is not controlled by the Copyright Act's definition of "fixed." The Act defines copies as "material objects, other than phonorecords, in which a work is *fixed* by any method." 17 U.S.C. § 101 (emphasis added). The Act's definition of "derivative work," in contrast, lacks any such reference to fixation. Further, we have held in a copyright infringement action that "[i]t makes no difference that the derivation may not satisfy certain requirements for statutory copyright registration itself." *Lone Ranger Television v. Program Radio Corp.*, 740 F.2d 718, 722 (9th Cir.1984). A derivative work must be fixed to be *protected* under the Act, see 17 U.S.C. § 102(a), but not to *infringe*.

* * *

The district court's finding that no independent work is created is supported by the record. The Game Genie merely enhances the audiovisual displays (or underlying data bytes) that originate in Nintendo game cartridges. The altered displays do not incorporate a portion of a copyrighted work in some concrete or permanent *form*. Nintendo argues that the Game Genie's displays are as fixed in the hardware and software used to create them as Nintendo's original displays. Nintendo's argument ignores the fact that the Game Genie cannot produce an audiovisual display; the underlying display must be produced by a Nintendo Entertainment System and game cartridge. Even if we were to rely on the Copyright Act's definition of "fixed," we would similarly conclude that the resulting display is not "embodied," *see* 17 U.S.C. § 101, in the Game Genie. It cannot be a derivative work.

Mirage Editions is illustrative. Albuquerque A.R.T. transferred art works from a commemorative book to individual ceramic tiles. We held that "[b]y borrowing and mounting the preexisting, copyrighted individual art images without the consent of the copyright proprietors ... [Albuquerque A.R.T.] has prepared a derivative work and infringed the subject copyrights." The ceramic tiles *physically* incorporated the copyrighted works in a form that could be sold. Perhaps more importantly, sales of the tiles supplanted purchasers' demand for the underlying works. Our holding in *Mirage Editions* would have been much different if Albuquerque A.R.T. had distributed lenses that merely enabled users to view several art works simultaneously.

Nintendo asserted at oral argument that the existence of a $150 million market for the Game Genie indicates that its audiovisual display must be fixed. We understand Nintendo's argument; consumers clearly would not purchase the Game Genie if its display was not "sufficiently permanent or stable to permit it to be perceived . . . for a period of more than transitory duration." 17 U.S.C. § 101. But, Nintendo's reliance on the Act's definition of "fixed" is misplaced. Nintendo's argument also proves too much; the existence of a market does not, and cannot, determine conclusively whether a work is an infringing derivative work. For example, although there is a market for kaleidoscopes, it does not necessarily follow that kaleidoscopes create unlawful derivative works when pointed at protected art work. The same can be said of countless other products that enhance, but do not replace, copyrighted works.

Nintendo also argues that our analysis should focus exclusively on the audiovisual displays created by the Game Genie, *i.e.*, that we should compare the altered displays to Nintendo's original displays. Nintendo emphasizes that " '[a]udiovisual works' are works that consist of a series of related images . . . *regardless of the nature of the material objects . . . in which the works are embodied.*" 17 U.S.C. § 101 (emphasis added). The Copyright Act's definition of "audiovisual works" is inapposite; the *only* question before us is whether the audiovisual displays created by the Game Genie are "derivative works." The Act does not similarly provide that a work can be a derivative work regardless of the nature of the material objects in which the work is embodied. A derivative work must incorporate a protected work in some concrete or permanent form. We cannot ignore the actual source of the Game Genie's display.

* * *

In holding that the audiovisual displays created by the Game Genie are not derivative works, we recognize that technology often advances by improvement rather than replacement. Some time ago, for example, computer companies began marketing spell-checkers that operate within existing word processors by signalling the writer when a word is misspelled. These applications, as well as countless others, could not be produced and marketed if courts were to conclude that the word processor and spell-checker combination is a derivative work based on the word processor alone. The Game Genie is useless by itself, it can only enhance, and cannot duplicate or recast, a Nintendo game's output. It does not contain or produce a Nintendo game's output in some concrete or permanent form, nor does it supplant demand for Nintendo game cartridges. Such innovations rarely will constitute infringing derivative works under the Copyright Act.

* * *

NOTES AND QUESTIONS

1. *Computer-related derivative works.* In the *Galoob* case, Nintendo alleged that persons who used the Game Genie with Nintendo games directly

infringed its adaptation rights in the games. In naming Galoob Toys as its defendant, Nintendo relied on a contributory infringement theory. We will examine the contributory infringement cause of action later.

If the *Galoob* court had found that the Game Genie created infringing derivative works, how might this affect the computer industry? If a computer user brought a copyrighted work into his random access memory and altered it in a material way, would this, in itself, constitute an infringement of the adaptation right under *Galoob*?

In Micro Star v. Formgen, Inc., 154 F.3d 1107 (9th Cir.1998), the Court of Appeals for the Ninth Circuit was more willing to find that "enhancement" infringed. In *Formgen*, the defendant published a CD–ROM containing a number of user-created "game levels" for the popular "Duke Nukem 3D" computer game. The copyrighted game software consisted of a game engine, a source art library, and "MAP" files of instructions that told the game engine what images to take from the source art library and how to arrange them to make the screen display for a particular level of play. The MAP files themselves contained none of the copyrighted art images—all the art that appeared on the game screen came from the art library. The user-created game levels that defendant published were MAP files for new levels of play. The issue was whether the audiovisual displays generated when the copyrighted Duke Nukem 3D game was run with the defendant's MAP files constituted infringing derivative works.

In finding that they did, Judge Kozinski distinguished the Ninth Circuit's decision in *Galoob*, noting that the defendant's MAP files were not simply a more advanced version of the Game Genie:

> [W]hereas the audiovisual displays created by Game Genie were never recorded in any permanent form, the audiovisual displays generated by [Duke Nukem 3D] from the [defendant's] MAP files are in the MAP files themselves. In *Galoob*, the audiovisual display was defined by the original game cartridge, not by the Game Genie; no one could possibly say that the data values inserted by the Game Genie described the audiovisual display. In the present case the audiovisual display that appears on the computer monitor when [defendant's MAP file] is played is described—in exact detail—by [defendant's MAP file].

> This raises the interesting question whether an exact, down to the last detail, description of an audiovisual display (and—by definition—we know that MAP files do describe audiovisual displays down to the last detail) counts as a permanent or concrete form for purposes of *Galoob*. We see no reason it shouldn't. What, after all, does sheet music do but describe in precise detail the way a copyrighted melody sounds? * * * To be copyrighted, pantomimes and dances may be "described in sufficient detail to enable the work to be performed from that description." [*Compendium II of Copyright Office Practices § 463*]. Similarly, the [defendant's] MAP files describe the audiovisual display that is to be generated when the player chooses to play [Duke Nukem 3D] using the [defendant's] levels. Because the audiovisual displays assume a concrete or permanent form in the MAP files, *Galoob* stands as no bar to finding that they are derivative works.

Formgen, 154 F.3d at 1111–12. The defendant argued that the user-generated MAP files failed to incorporate Duke Nukem 3D's protected expression because the MAP files only referenced the source art library, and did not actually contain any art files. The court, however, rejected that argument:

> [Defendant] misconstrues the protected work. The work that [defendant] infringes is the [Duke Nukem 3D] story itself—a beefy commando type named Duke who wanders around post-Apocalypse Los Angeles, shooting Pig Cops with a gun, lobbing hand grenades, searching for medkits and steroids, using a jetpack to leap over obstacles, blowing up gas tanks, avoiding radioactive slime. A copyright owner holds the right to create sequels, and the stories told in [defendant's] MAP files are surely sequels, telling new (though somewhat repetitive) tales of Duke's fabulous adventures. A book about Duke Nukem would infringe for the same reason, even if it contained no pictures.

Id., 154 F.3d at 1112.

What are the implications of *Galoob* and *Formgen* for the practices of hyperlinking to copyrighted works and framing copyrighted works on the Internet? As a matter of policy, should a copyright owner be able to prohibit such actions by asserting infringement of his or her adaptation right?

2. *Exceptions to the exclusive right to adapt computer programs.* To what extent does the *Galoob* opinion permit companies to market add-on or enhancement programs that modify or improve the performance of others' successful programs? If the legality of their acts is uncertain, is § 117 likely to provide any additional shelter?

Section 117(a) provides that the owner of a copy of a computer program may make or authorize an adaptation of a program if the "adaptation is created as an essential step in the utilization of the computer program in conjunction with a machine and * * * is used in no other manner." Just how much leeway does this provision give to copy "owners"?

In Krause v. Titleserv, Inc., 402 F.3d 119 (2d Cir.), *cert. denied,* 546 U.S. 1002, 126 S.Ct. 622, 163 L.Ed.2d 504 (2005), the defendant business made the following categories of modifications to its authorized program copies:

> (1) It corrected programming errors or "bugs," which interfered with the proper functioning of the programs;

> (2) It changed the source code to add new clients, insert changed client addresses, and perform other routine tasks necessary to keep the programs up-to-date and to maintain their usefulness to the business;

> (3) It incorporated the programs into the Windows-based system it subsequently designed and implemented (which may have entailed copying the programs into the new system); and

> (4) It added new capabilities, such as the ability to print checks, and to a limited degree, allow customers direct access to the defendant's records, which made the defendant's copies of the programs more responsive to its business needs.

Id., at 125. The issue was whether these modifications constituted an infringement of the copyright owner's adaptation right, or were authorized under § 117(a). Judge Leval, writing for the Second Circuit, found that each modification was authorized as "an essential step in the utilization of the computer program." The court found it quite clear that the first three categories of modifications fell within the statutory language. The fixing of bugs was done so that the program would continue to function. Modification of the source code to reflect such business changes as the addition of new customers and changed customer address also easily qualified as "essential"—to keep the software in step with changes in the business. Incorporation of the program into the defendant's new Windows system was essential in order for it to continue to function on the new computer system.

With regard to the fourth category, the court acknowledged that the newly added features were not "strictly necessary to keep the programs functioning, but were designed to improve their functionality in serving the business for which they were created." *Id.* at 126. However, after evaluating the meaning of "essential" and "utilization" in light of the legislative history, Judge Leval rejected arguments that § 117 only authorized modifications absolutely necessary to make a program boot and run. Rather, Congress intended to permit a range of modifications that would better enable the program to serve the purposes for which it was both sold and purchased, included the addition of new features such as those added by the defendant. The judge noted that it was unnecessary to address "whether other types of improvements might be too radical, or might fail to qualify because they somehow harm the interests of the copyright owner."

> A different scenario would be presented if [defendant's] alteration some-how interfered with [plaintiff's] access to, or ability to exploit, the copyrighted work that he authored, or if the altered copy of [plaintiff's] work were to be marketed by the owner of the copy. But on our facts, we see no harm whatsoever to [plaintiff's] enjoyment of his copyright.

Id., at 128–29. As a matter of policy, should program owners be entitled to prevent sales of unauthorized program enhancements?

3. *Exceptions to the right to adapt architectural works.* An exception to the right to adapt architectural works can be found in § 120(b):

> Notwithstanding the provisions of section 106(2), the owners of a building embodying an architectural work may, without the consent of the author or copyright owner of the architectural work, make or author-ize the making of alterations to such building, and destroy or authorize the destruction of such building.

17 U.S.C.A. § 120(b). What justifies permitting unauthorized alterations of architectural works when such alterations would not be permitted in the case of other categories of copyrightable works? Should it matter what the building owner's purposes are in making the alterations?

PROBLEMS

1. X owns the copyright in a popular word processing program. The program does not provide a spell-checking feature. Y creates and sells a separate spell-checking program that can, when loaded into the same comput-

er, interact with X's word processing program to provide users with spell checking in the course of word processing. Y's spell checking program does not create a separate copy of the word processing program or permanently alter it. Are Y's actions likely to constitute copyright infringement?

2.   Leo establishes a web page, which he entitles "The Virtual Wine Taster." Among other things, the web page features news stories about wine, and Leo's expert reviews of the products of various California wineries. *Glug* is a magazine that caters to wine and beer fans. Its publisher establishes a web page, and creates a link from its page to Leo's Virtual Wine Taster web page. (The link consists of HTML code which directs visitors' computers to the Virtual Wine Taster web address.) Exercising the link causes the visitor's computer screen to be segmented: The screen shows Leo's Virtual Wine Taster web page in the larger, central portion of the screen. However, the visitor sees the Virtual Wine Taster page "framed" with material from the *Glug* web page: A directory to other features on the *Glug* web site runs along the right side, and a banner advertisement sold by *Glug* runs along the top. Visitors who peruse the Virtual Wine Taster web page do so within the *Glug* frame. Does Leo have a cause of action against the *Glug* publisher (or visitors to the *Glug* site who exercise the link) for infringement of his adaptation right?

E.   SECTION 106(3): THE EXCLUSIVE RIGHT TO DISTRIBUTE COPIES OR PHONORECORDS OF THE COPYRIGHTED WORK TO THE PUBLIC BY SALE OR OTHER TRANSFER OF OWNERSHIP, OR BY RENTAL, LEASE, OR LENDING

The right to distribute copies or phonorecords to the public includes the right of first publication. Like the adaptation right, the right of public distribution overlaps the right of reproduction in many cases. For example, a defendant who makes and sells unauthorized copies of a work to the public will be liable under either right. A defendant may infringe the right of public distribution by itself, however. Assume that A writes a song and B, with A's permission, makes a sound recording in which he performs the song. X makes unauthorized CDs of B's sound recording and sells them to a middle person, who sells them to Y Company. Y Company then sells the CDs to the public through its retail music stores. Regardless of whether Y Company knew that the CDs were bootlegged, it would be liable for infringing both A's and B's exclusive rights to distribute their respective works to the public. In such situations, A and B may sue X (for infringing the rights of reproduction and distribution), and the middle person and Y Company (who both are direct infringers of A's and B's rights of distribution).

What does it take to "distribute" a copy or phonorecord? The Copyright Act provides no definition of "distribute," but the traditional view is that there must be an actual physical transfer of a material copy or phonorecord from one person to another. A mere offer to transfer copies or phonorecords is not a distribution. However, recent case law has introduced some flexibility to the concept. For example, in Hotaling v. Church of Jesus Christ of Latter–Day Saints, 118 F.3d 199 (4th Cir. 1997), the court held that a work is "distributed" within the meaning of § 106(3) if it is "made available" to the public without the authorization of the copyright owner. In that case, the Fourth Circuit found that a publicly accessible library engages in "distribution" of a work whenever it "adds a work to its collection, lists the work in its index or catalog system, and makes the work available to the borrowing or browsing public." *Id.*, at 203. It would not be necessary to show that any library visitors actually took or used the copy. The Fourth Circuit reasoned:

> When a library adds a work to its collection, lists the work in its index or catalog system, and makes the work available to the borrowing or browsing public, it has completed all the steps necessary for distribution to the public. At that point, members of the public can visit the library and use the work. Were this not to be considered distribution within the meaning of § 106(3), a copyright holder would be prejudiced by a library that does not keep records of public use, and the library would unjustly profit by its own omission. * * *

Id. Would the placement of an unauthorized copy on a web site constitute infringing "distribution to the public" under this theory? See Marobie–FL, Inc. v. National Association of Fire Equipment Distributors, 983 F.Supp. 1167 (N.D. Ill. 1997)(reasoning that once the infringing file was posted, it was freely available for downloading by Internet users).

When persons engage in peer-to-peer music file sharing they designate particular digital music files stored on their computer hard drives that they are willing to share. This allows others using the same file-sharing software to access and download those files. In light of the *Hotaling* decision, should making digital flies available for download, in itself, constitute "distribution," or must the copyright owners demonstrate that actual downloading took place? Compare Motown Record Co. v. DePietro, 2007 W.L. 576284 at *3 (E.D. Penn. 2007) ("A plaintiff claiming infringement of the exclusive distribution right can establish infringement by proof of actual distribution or by proof of offers to distribute, that is, proof that the defendant 'made available' the copyrighted work."), with Elektra Entertainment Group, Inc. v. Barker, 551 F.Supp.2d 234, 244–45 (S.D.N.Y. 2008) (finding that a defendant may infringe the distribution right by "offering to distribute phonorecords to a group of persons for purposes of further distribution, public performance or public display," but holding that a such a theory of infringement is not adequately alleged through a claim that the defendant made the copyrighted work "available" on its hard drive), and Atlantic Recording Corp. v. Howell, 554 F.Supp.2d 976 (D.Ariz. 2008) (neither an offer to distribute phonorecords to a group of persons for purposes of further distribution, public performance or public display, nor making a copyrighted work "available" constitutes infringement of the distribution right).

The *Hotaling* and *Marobie* cases involved copies made without the copyright holder's authorization. In the case of lawfully made copies, the doctrine of first sale, which is codified in Copyright Act § 109(a), limits the distribution right:

> Notwithstanding the provisions of section 106(3), the owner of a particular copy or phonorecord lawfully made under this title, or any person authorized by such owner, is entitled, without the authority of the copyright owner, to sell or otherwise dispose of the possession of that copy or phonorecord.

The doctrine of first sale, in turn, is subject to some exceptions that permit the copyright owner to exert some control over copies or phonorecords even after transferring or authorizing their transfer to the public. We turn to the doctrine of first sale and its exceptions below.

1. The Doctrine of First Sale

HOUSE REPORT ON COPYRIGHT ACT OF 1976

H.R. Rep. No. 1476, 94th Cong., 2d Sess. 79 (1976).

Section 109(a) restates and confirms the principle that, where the copyright owner has transferred ownership of a particular copy or phonorecord of a work, the person to whom the copy or phonorecord is transferred is entitled to dispose of it by sale, rental, or any other means. Under this principle, * * * the copyright owner's exclusive right of public distribution would have no effect upon anyone who owns "a particular copy or phonorecord lawfully made under this title" and who wishes to transfer it to someone else or to destroy it.

Thus, for example, the outright sale of an authorized copy of a book frees it from any copyright control over its resale price or other conditions of its future disposition. A library that has acquired ownership of a copy is entitled to lend it under any conditions it chooses to impose. This does not mean that conditions on future dispositions of copies of phonorecords, imposed by a contract between their buyer and seller, would be unenforceable between the parties as a breach of contract, but it does mean that they could not be enforced by an action for infringement of copyright. Under section 202 however, the owner of the physical copy or phonorecord cannot reproduce or perform the copyrighted work publicly without the copyright owner's consent.

To come within the scope of section 109(a), a copy or phonorecord must have been "lawfully made under this title," though not necessarily with the copyright owner's authorization. For example, any resale of any illegally "pirated" phonorecord would be an infringement, but the disposition of a phonorecord legally made under the compulsory licensing provisions of section 115 would not.

NOTES AND QUESTIONS

1. *The doctrine of first sale.* The copyright doctrine of first sale is similar in many respects to the doctrine of first sale, or doctrine of exhaustion, applied in patent law. As you will see, trademark law employs its own counterpart. Are the justifications for the doctrine the same in copyright as in patent law?

Should transmissions of copyrighted works over the Internet be considered "distributions to the public" for purposes of Copyright Act § 106(3)? If so, how should the doctrine of first sale apply to such distributions? Here is what the Information Infrastructure Task Force had to say about the doctrine of first sale in Internet transmissions:

> [T]he doctrine of first sale limits only the copyright owner's distribution right; it in no way affects the reproduction right. Thus, the first sale doctrine does not allow the transmission of a copy of a work (through a computer network, for instance), because under current technology the transmitter retains the original copy of the work while the recipient of the transmission obtains a reproduction of the original copy (*i.e.*, a *new* copy), rather than the copy owned by the transmitter. The language of the Copyright Act, the legislative history and case law make clear that the doctrine is applicable only to those situations where the owner of a particular copy disposes of physical possession of that particular copy.
>
>   * * *
>
> It has * * * been suggested that the scope of the first sale doctrine be *narrowed* to exclude copies obtained via transmission. This would mean, for instance, that if a copy of a literary work is legally purchased on-line and the copy so purchased is downloaded onto the purchaser's disk, the disk could not be resold. Clearly, the first sale doctrine should apply if the particular copy involved is in fact the copy that is further distributed, even if the copy was first obtained by transmission. Further, if the technology utilized allows the transmission of a copy without making an unlawful reproduction—*i.e.*, no copy remains with the original owner—the first sale doctrine would apply and the transmission would not be an infringement.
>
> Some argue that the first sale doctrine should also apply to transmissions, as long as the transmitter destroys or deletes from his or her computer the original copy from which the reproduction in the receiving computer was made. The proponents of this view argue that at the completion of the activity, only one copy would exist between the original owner who transmitted the copy and the person who received it—the same number of copies as at the beginning. However, this zero sum gaming analysis misses the point. The question is not whether there exist the same number of copies at the completion of the transaction or not. The question is whether the transaction when viewed as a whole violates one or more of the exclusive rights, and there is no applicable exception from liability. In this case, without any doubt, a reproduction of the work

takes place in the receiving computer. To apply the doctrine of first sale in such a case would vitiate the reproduction right.

Information Infrastructure Task Force, Intellectual Property and the National Information Infrastructure, The Report of the Working Group on Intellectual Property Rights, 92–94 (1995).

Do you agree with the Task Force's analysis?

2. *Record and software rentals.* In response to concerns voiced by the recording and software industries, Congress amended the Copyright Act in 1984, and again in 1990, to carve out narrow exceptions to the first sale doctrine.

The Record Rental Amendments Act of 1984, codified at 17 U.S.C.A. § 109(b), prevents owners of phonorecords of musical sound recordings from renting the phonorecords to the public commercially without the permission of both the sound recording and the underlying musical work copyright owners. This amendment responded to the advent of commercial record rental establishments that offered records, tapes and compact disks for short-term rental, and often sold blank tapes, as well. These businesses made it extremely easy for renters to engage in home taping to save the price of purchasing recordings. As the House Report noted, "[o]ne such establishment advertised, 'Never, ever buy another record.'" H.R. Rep. No. 987, 98th Cong., 2d Sess. 2 (1984). In the absence of the amendment, of course, the first sale doctrine would permit the owner of an authorized phonorecord of a sound recording to rent it to others. Under the amendment, commercial rental without the permission of the affected copyright owners constitutes copyright infringement in violation of § 106(3).

The Computer Software Rental Amendments Act of 1990 amended section 109(b) to extend a similar prohibition against commercial rentals of computer programs. Section 109(b) expressly permits not-for-profit lending of sound recordings and software by non-profit libraries and educational institutions. It also specifies that its prohibitions against rental do not apply to "a computer program which is embodied in a machine or product and which cannot be copied during the ordinary operation or use of the machine or product." 17 U.S.C.A. § 109(b)(1)(B)(i).

Review the provisions of § 109(b). Should they be extended to other subject matter? For example, should motion picture copyright owners be permitted to control rentals of lawfully purchased video tapes and DVDs of their motion pictures? Should non-profit public lending of books and other works of authorship by public libraries be regulated or made subject to a compulsory royalty payment to compensate copyright owners? Some European nations recognize such a "public lending right" in authors.

3. *The droit de suite.* In a report issued in 1992, the Copyright Office discussed the *droit de suite*, which originated in Europe:

> [T]he *droit de suite*—the right of an artist to collect a part of the price paid when a work is resold—is based on the premise that visual artists are entitled to participate in an increase in the value of their works in ways that are not otherwise adequately addressed by copyright law.

The copyright law's rights of reproduction and distribution are better suited to exploitation of literary or musical works. A visual artist's expression is usually embodied in an end product, sold to a single purchaser. The artist's current work and reputation continue to affect the value of that earlier work. Many European countries, in the event of resale, allow artists to benefit from any increase in value of their works.

* * *

* * * The Berne Convention for the Protection of Literary and Artistic Property contains statements of principle in favor of the *droit de suite.* * * *

Whether the *droit de suite* will make the transition from an idealistic notion to an international norm depends both on commitment to *droit de suite* and creation of practical means to implement the goal of allowing artists to share in the profit of their work once it has left their hands.

Those countries that have most successfully implemented the *droit de suite* share certain characteristics. In France, Germany, and Belgium, for instance, the royalty is collected on the total resale price of the work. Measuring the royalty by the resale price departs from the rationale allowing artists to participate in an *increase* in value, but is considered simpler and more practical. * * *

Auctions are the minimum field of application in all countries which have adopted the *droit de suite*, because auctions sales are easiest to monitor. Including dealer sales increases the administrative challenge and the risk of noncompliance. * * * Although the *droit de suite* is inalienable and non-waivable, in almost all effective systems it may be transferred for purposes of collection through an artists' collecting agency.

* * *

[T]here have been efforts to realize this European concept in the United States since as early as 1940. In the early 1960's, proposals were made to incorporate *droit de suite* into state or federal law in the United States. To date, only California's efforts have resulted in law. * * *

The State of California passed a resale royalty law in 1976. The law mandates a five percent royalty of the resale price to the artist when a work is resold in California or resold anywhere by a California resident. Several artists report significant financial gain under the law. However, the law is widely criticized as underused and underenforced, and a 1986 survey of California artists and dealers was inconclusive. Some commentators claim that the law places California's art market at a competitive disadvantage, but others say that it has had no effect on the California market.

* * * Any state resale royalty scheme may be preempted under section 301 of the 1976 Act because it inhibits the section 106 distribution right as modified by the section 109 "first sale" doctrine (which allows the owner of a lawfully-made copy, including an original, to dispose of that copy as he or she pleases). Given potential problems of preemption, enforcement, and multiple application, any *droit de suite* that is enacted in the United States should be at the federal level.

* * *

U.S. Copyright Office, *Droit de Suite*: The Artist's Resale Royalty, i-iv (1992).

Are visual artists disadvantaged vis-a-vis other authors under the Copyright Act? If so, are resale royalties as described in the Copyright Office Report the best way to level the playing field? If not, what alternatives might Congress consider? After further discussion, the Copyright Office concluded that it was "not persuaded that sufficient economic and copyright policy justifications exist to establish *droit de suite* in the United States." What copyright policies are likely to be implicated in the *droit de suite* debate?

2. The Importation Right

QUALITY KING DISTRIBUTORS, INC. v. L'ANZA RESEARCH INTERNATIONAL, INC.

United States Supreme Court, 1998.
523 U.S. 135, 118 S.Ct. 1125, 140 L.Ed.2d 254.

JUSTICE STEVENS delivered the opinion of the Court.

Section 106(3) of the Copyright Act of 1976 (Act), 17 U.S.C. § 106(3), gives the owner of a copyright the exclusive right to distribute copies of a copyrighted work. That exclusive right is expressly limited, however, by the provisions of §§ 107 through 120. Section 602(a) gives the copyright owner the right to prohibit the unauthorized importation of copies. The question presented by this case is whether the right granted by § 602(a) is also limited by §§ 107 through 120. More narrowly, the question is whether the "first sale" doctrine endorsed in § 109(a) is applicable to imported copies.

I

Respondent, L'anza Research International, Inc. (L'anza), is a California corporation engaged in the business of manufacturing and selling shampoos, conditioners, and other hair care products. L'anza has copyrighted the labels that are affixed to those products. In the United States, L'anza sells exclusively to domestic distributors who have agreed to resell within limited geographic areas and then only to authorized retailers such as barber shops, beauty salons, and professional hair care colleges. L'anza has found that the American "public is generally unwilling to pay the price charged for high quality products, such as L'anza's products, when they are sold along with the less expensive lower quality products that are generally carried by supermarkets and drug stores." App. 54 (declaration of Robert Hall). L'anza promotes the domestic sales of its products with extensive advertising in various trade magazines and at point of sale, and by providing special training to authorized retailers.

L'anza also sells its products in foreign markets. In those markets, however, it does not engage in comparable advertising or promotion; its prices to foreign distributors are 35% to 40% lower than the prices charged to domestic distributors. In 1992 and 1993, L'anza's distributor in the United Kingdom arranged the sale of three shipments to a distributor in Malta; each shipment contained several tons of L'anza products with copyrighted labels affixed. The record does not establish whether the initial purchaser was the distributor in the United Kingdom or the distributor in Malta, or whether title passed when the goods were delivered to the carrier or when they arrived at their destination, but it is undisputed that the goods were manufactured by L'anza and first sold by L'anza to a foreign purchaser.

It is also undisputed that the goods found their way back to the United States without the permission of L'anza and were sold in California by unauthorized retailers who had purchased them at discounted prices from Quality King Distributors, Inc. (petitioner). There is some uncertainty about the identity of the actual importer, but for the purpose of our decision we assume that petitioner bought all three shipments from the Malta distributor, imported them, and then resold them to retailers who were not in L'anza's authorized chain of distribution.

After determining the source of the unauthorized sales, L'anza brought suit against petitioner and several other defendants. The complaint alleged that the importation and subsequent distribution of those products bearing copyrighted labels violated L'anza's "exclusive rights under 17 U.S.C. §§ 106, 501 and 602 to reproduce and distribute the copyrighted material in the United States." The District Court rejected petitioner's defense based on the "first sale" doctrine recognized by § 109 and entered summary judgment in favor of L'anza. Based largely on its conclusion that § 602 would be "meaningless" if § 109 provided a defense in a case of this kind, the Court of Appeals affirmed. Because its decision created a conflict with the Third Circuit, see *Sebastian Int'l, Inc. v. Consumer Contacts (PTY) Ltd.*, 847 F.2d 1093 (1988), we granted the petition for certiorari.

II

This is an unusual copyright case because L'anza does not claim that anyone has made unauthorized copies of its copyrighted labels. Instead, L'anza is primarily interested in protecting the integrity of its method of marketing the products to which the labels are affixed. Although the labels themselves have only a limited creative component, our interpretation of the relevant statutory provisions would apply equally to a case involving more familiar copyrighted materials such as sound recordings or books. Indeed, we first endorsed the first sale doctrine in a case involving a claim by a publisher that the resale of its books at discounted prices infringed its copyright on the books. *Bobbs–Merrill Co. v. Straus*, 210 U.S. 339, 28 S.Ct. 722, 52 L.Ed. 1086 (1908).

In that case, the publisher, Bobbs–Merrill, had inserted a notice in its books that any retail sale at a price under $1.00 would constitute an infringement of its copyright. The defendants, who owned Macy's department store, disregarded the notice and sold the books at a lower price without Bobbs–Merrill's consent. We held that the exclusive statutory right to "vend" applied only to the first sale of the copyrighted work:

> "What does the statute mean in granting 'the sole right of vending the same'? Was it intended to create a right which would permit the holder of the copyright to fasten, by notice in a book or upon one of the articles mentioned within the statute, a restriction upon the subsequent alienation of the subject-matter of copyright after the owner had parted with the title to one who had acquired full dominion over it and had given a satisfactory price for it? It is not denied that one who has sold a copyrighted article, without restriction, has parted with all right to control the sale of it. The purchaser of a book, once sold by authority of the owner of the copyright, may sell it again, although he could not publish a new edition of it.

> "In this case the stipulated facts show that the books sold by the appellant were sold at wholesale, and purchased by those who made no agreement as to the control of future sales of the book, and took upon themselves no obligation to enforce the notice printed in the book, undertaking to restrict retail sales to a price of one dollar per copy."

Id., at 349–350, 28 S.Ct., at 726.

The statute in force when *Bobbs–Merrill* was decided provided that the copyright owner had the exclusive right to "vend" the copyrighted work. Congress subsequently codified our holding in *Bobbs–Merrill* that the exclusive right to "vend" was limited to first sales of the work. Under the 1976 Act, the comparable exclusive right granted in 17 U.S.C. § 106(3) is the right "to distribute copies ... by sale or other transfer of ownership." The comparable limitation on that right is provided not by judicial interpretation, but by an express statutory provision. Section 109(a) provides:

> "Notwithstanding the provisions of section 106(3), the owner of a particular copy or phonorecord lawfully made under this title, or any person authorized by such owner, is entitled, without the authority of the copyright owner, to sell or otherwise dispose of the possession of that copy or phonorecord.... "

The *Bobbs–Merrill* opinion emphasized the critical distinction between statutory rights and contract rights. In this case, L'anza relies on the terms of its contracts with its domestic distributors to limit their sales to authorized retail outlets. Because the basic holding in *Bobbs–Merrill* is now codified in § 109(a) of the Act, and because those domestic distributors are owners of the products that they purchased from L'anza (the labels of which were "lawfully made under this title"), L'anza does not, and could not, claim that the statute would enable L'anza to treat unauthorized resales by its domestic distributors as an infringement of its exclusive right to distribute copies of its labels. L'anza does claim, however, that contractual provisions are inadequate to protect it from the actions of foreign distributors who may resell L'anza's products to American vendors unable to buy from L'anza's domestic distributors, and that § 602(a) of the Act, properly construed, prohibits such unauthorized competition. To evaluate that submission, we must, of course, consider the text of § 602(a).

III

The most relevant portion of § 602(a) provides:

"Importation into the United States, without the authority of the owner of copyright under this title, of copies or phonorecords of a work that have been acquired outside the United States is an infringement of the exclusive right to distribute copies or phonorecords under section 106, actionable under section 501...."[11]

It is significant that this provision does not categorically prohibit the unauthorized importation of copyrighted materials. Instead, it provides that such importation is an infringement of the exclusive right to distribute copies "under section 106." Like the exclusive right to "vend" that was construed in *Bobbs–Merrill*, the exclusive right to distribute is a limited right. The introductory language in § 106 expressly states that all of the exclusive rights granted by that section—including, of course, the distribution right granted by subsection (3)—are limited by the provisions of §§ 107 through 120. One of those limitations, as we have noted, is provided by the terms of § 109(a), which expressly permit the owner of a lawfully made copy to sell that copy "[n]otwithstanding the provisions of section 106(3)."

After the first sale of a copyrighted item "lawfully made under this title," any subsequent purchaser, whether from a domestic or from a foreign reseller, is obviously an "owner" of that item. Read literally, § 109(a) unambiguously states that such an owner "is entitled, without the authority of the copyright owner, to sell" that item. Moreover, since § 602(a) merely provides that unauthorized importation is an infringement of an exclusive right "under section 106," and since that limited right does not encompass resales by lawful owners, the literal text of § 602(a) is simply inapplicable to both domestic and foreign owners of

---

11. The remainder of § 602(a) reads as follows:

"This subsection does not apply to—

"(1) importation of copies or phonorecords under the authority or for the use of the Government of the United States or of any State or political subdivision of a State, but not including copies or phonorecords for use in schools, or copies of any audiovisual work imported for purposes other than archival use;

"(2) importation, for the private use of the importer and not for distribution, by any person with respect to no more than one copy or phonorecord of any one work at any one time, or by any person arriving from outside the United States with respect to copies or phonorecords forming part of such person's personal baggage; or

"(3) importation by or for an organization operated for scholarly, educational, or religious purposes and not for private gain, with respect to no more than one copy of an audiovisual work solely for its archival purposes, and no more than five copies or phonorecords of any other work for its library lending or archival purposes, unless the importation of such copies or phonorecords is part of an activity consisting of systematic reproduction or distribution, engaged in by such organization in violation of the provisions of section 108(g)(2)."

L'anza's products who decide to import them and resell them in the United States.[14]

Notwithstanding the clarity of the text of §§ 106(3), 109(a), and 602(a), L'anza argues that the language of the Act supports a construction of the right granted by § 602(a) as "distinct from the right under Section 106(3) standing alone," and thus not subject to § 109(a). Otherwise, L'anza argues, both the § 602(a) right itself and its exceptions would be superfluous. Moreover, supported by various amici curiae, including the Solicitor General of the United States, L'anza contends that its construction is supported by important policy considerations. We consider these arguments separately.

IV

L'anza advances two primary arguments based on the text of the Act: (1) that § 602(a), and particularly its three exceptions, are superfluous if limited by the first sale doctrine; and (2) that the text of § 501 defining an "infringer" refers separately to violations of § 106, on the one hand, and to imports in violation of § 602. The short answer to both of these arguments is that neither adequately explains why the words "under section 106" appear in § 602(a). The Solicitor General makes an additional textual argument: he contends that the word "importation" in § 602(a).
* * *

The Coverage of § 602(a)

Prior to the enactment of § 602(a), the Act already prohibited the importation of "piratical," or unauthorized, copies. Moreover, that earlier prohibition is retained in § 602(b) of the present Act.[17] L'anza therefore argues (as do the Solicitor General and other amici curiae) that § 602(a) is superfluous unless it covers non-piratical ("lawfully made") copies sold by the copyright owner, because importation nearly always implies a first sale. There are several flaws in this argument.

First, even if § 602(a) did apply only to piratical copies, it at least would provide the copyright holder with a private remedy against the importer, whereas the enforcement of § 602(b) is vested in the Customs Service. Second, because the protection afforded by § 109(a) is available only to the "owner" of a lawfully made copy (or someone authorized by the owner), the first sale doctrine would not provide a defense to a § 602(a) action against any non-owner such as a bailee, a licensee, a consignee, or one whose possession of the copy was unlawful. Third, § 602(a) applies to a category of copies that are neither piratical nor

---

14. Despite L'anza's contention to the contrary, the owner of goods lawfully made under the Act is entitled to the protection of the first sale doctrine in an action in a United States court even if the first sale occurred abroad. Such protection does not require the extraterritorial application of the Act any more than § 602(a)'s "acquired abroad" language does.

17. Section 602(b) provides in relevant part: "In a case where the making of the copies or phonorecords would have constituted an infringement of copyright if this title had been applicable, their importation is prohibited...." The first sale doctrine of § 109(a) does not protect owners of piratical copies, of course, because such copies were not "lawfully made."

"lawfully made under this title." That category encompasses copies that were "lawfully made" not under the United States Copyright Act, but instead, under the law of some other country.

The category of copies produced lawfully under a foreign copyright was expressly identified in the deliberations that led to the enactment of the 1976 Act. We mention one example of such a comment in 1961 simply to demonstrate that the category is not a merely hypothetical one. In a report to Congress, the Register of Copyrights stated, in part:

> "When arrangements are made for both a U.S. edition and a foreign edition of the same work, the publishers frequently agree to divide the international markets. The foreign publisher agrees not to sell his edition in the United States, and the U.S. publisher agrees not to sell his edition in certain foreign countries. It has been suggested that the import ban on piratical copies should be extended to bar the importation of the foreign edition in contravention of such an agreement."

Copyright Law Revision: Report of the Register of Copyrights on the General Revision of the U.S. Copyright Law, 87th Cong., 1st Sess., 125–126 (H.R. Judiciary Comm. Print 1961).

Even in the absence of a market allocation agreement between, for example, a publisher of the U.S. edition and a publisher of the British edition of the same work, each such publisher could make lawful copies. If the author of the work gave the exclusive U.S. distribution rights—enforceable under the Act—to the publisher of the U.S. edition and the exclusive British distribution rights to the publisher of the British edition, however, presumably only those made by the publisher of the U.S. edition would be "lawfully made under this title" within the meaning of § 109(a). The first sale doctrine would not provide the publisher of the British edition who decided to sell in the American market with a defense to an action under § 602(a) (or, for that matter, to an action under § 106(3), if there was a distribution of the copies).

The argument that the statutory exceptions to § 602(a) are superfluous if the first sale doctrine is applicable rests on the assumption that the coverage of that section is co-extensive with the coverage of § 109(a). But since it is, in fact, broader because it encompasses copies that are not subject to the first sale doctrine—e.g., copies that are lawfully made under the law of another country—the exceptions do protect the traveler who may have made an isolated purchase of a copy of a work that could not be imported in bulk for purposes of resale. As we read the Act, although both the first sale doctrine embodied in § 109(a) and the exceptions in § 602(a) may be applicable in some situations, the former does not subsume the latter; those provisions retain significant independent meaning.

Section 501's Separate References to §§ 106 and 602

The text of § 501 does lend support to L'anza's submission. In relevant part, it provides:

"(a) Anyone who violates any of the exclusive rights of the copyright owner as provided by sections 106 through 118 or of the author as provided in section 106A(a), or who imports copies or phonorecords into the United States in violation of section 602, is an infringer of the copyright or right of the author, as the case may be...."

The use of the words *"or* who imports," rather than words such as *"including* one who imports," is more consistent with an interpretation that a violation of § 602 is distinct from a violation of § 106 (and thus not subject to the first sale doctrine set out in § 109(a)) than with the view that it is a species of such a violation. Nevertheless, the force of that inference is outweighed by other provisions in the statutory text.

Most directly relevant is the fact that the text of § 602(a) itself unambiguously states that the prohibited importation is an infringement of the exclusive distribution right "under section 106, actionable under section 501." Unlike that phrase, which identifies § 602 violations as a species of § 106 violations, the text of § 106A, which is also cross-referenced in § 501, uses starkly different language. It states that the author's right protected by § 106A is "independent of the exclusive rights provided in Section 106." The contrast between the relevant language in § 602 and that in § 106A strongly implies that only the latter describes an independent right.

Of even greater importance is the fact that the § 106 rights are subject not only to the first sale defense in § 109(a), but also to all of the other provisions of "sections 107 through 120." If § 602(a) functioned independently, none of those sections would limit its coverage. For example, the "fair use" defense embodied in § 107 would be unavailable to importers if § 602(a) created a separate right not subject to the limitations on the § 106(3) distribution right. Under L'anza's interpretation of the Act, it presumably would be unlawful for a distributor to import copies of a British newspaper that contained a book review quoting excerpts from an American novel protected by a United States copyright. Given the importance of the fair use defense to publishers of scholarly works, as well as to publishers of periodicals, it is difficult to believe that Congress intended to impose an absolute ban on the importation of all such works containing any copying of material protected by a United States copyright.

In the context of this case, involving copyrighted labels, it seems unlikely that an importer could defend an infringement as a "fair use" of the label. In construing the statute, however, we must remember that its principal purpose was to promote the progress of the "useful Arts," U.S.Const., Art. I, § 8, cl. 8, by rewarding creativity, and its principal function is the protection of original works, rather than ordinary commercial products that use copyrighted material as a marketing aid. It is therefore appropriate to take into account the impact of the denial of the fair use defense for the importer of foreign publications. As applied to such publications, L'anza's construction of § 602 "would merely inhibit access to ideas without any countervailing benefit." *Sony Corp. of America v. Universal City Studios, Inc.*, 464 U.S. 417, 450–451, 104 S.Ct. 774, 793, 78 L.Ed.2d 574 (1984).

* * *

V

The parties and their amici have debated at length the wisdom or unwisdom of governmental restraints on what is sometimes described as either the "gray market" or the practice of "parallel importation." In *K Mart Corp. v. Cartier, Inc.*, 486 U.S. 281, 108 S.Ct. 1811, 100 L.Ed.2d 313 (1988), we used those terms to refer to the importation of foreign-manufactured goods bearing a valid United States trademark without the consent of the trademark holder. We are not at all sure that those terms appropriately describe the consequences of an American manufacturer's decision to limit its promotional efforts to the domestic market and to sell its products abroad at discounted prices that are so low that its foreign distributors can compete in the domestic market.[29] But even if they do, whether or not we think it would be wise policy to provide statutory protection for such price discrimination is not a matter that is relevant to our duty to interpret the text of the Copyright Act.

Equally irrelevant is the fact that the Executive Branch of the Government has entered into at least five international trade agreements that are apparently intended to protect domestic copyright owners from the unauthorized importation of copies of their works sold in those five countries. The earliest of those agreements was made in 1991; none has been ratified by the Senate. Even though they are of course consistent with the position taken by the Solicitor General in this litigation, they shed no light on the proper interpretation of a statute that was enacted in 1976.[31]

The judgment of the Court of Appeals is reversed.

JUSTICE GINSBURG, concurring.

This case involves a "round trip" journey, travel of the copies in question from the United States to places abroad, then back again. I join the Court's opinion recognizing that we do not today resolve cases in which the allegedly infringing imports were manufactured abroad. See W. Patry, Copyright Law and Practice 166–170 (1997 Supp.) (commenting that provisions of Title 17 do not apply extraterritorially unless expressly so stated, hence the words "lawfully made under this title" in the "first sale" provision, 17 U.S.C. § 109(a), must mean "lawfully made in the United States"). * * *

---

29. Presumably L'anza, for example, could have avoided the consequences of that competition either (1) by providing advertising support abroad and charging higher prices, or (2) if it was satisfied to leave the promotion of the product in foreign markets to its foreign distributors, to sell its products abroad under a different name.

31. We also note that in 1991, when the first of the five agreements was signed, the Third Circuit had already issued its opinion in *Sebastian Int'l, Inc. v. Consumer Contacts (PTY) Ltd.*, 847 F.2d 1093 (1988), adopting a position contrary to that subsequently endorsed by the Executive Branch.

NOTES AND QUESTIONS

1. *The doctrine of first sale and parallel imports.* The issue of "parallel imports" may arise under patent and trademark law, as well as copyright law. Generally speaking, parallel imports are goods that are legitimately manufactured by or under the authority of the U.S. intellectual property owner and sold in foreign markets. Many U.S. intellectual property owners charge significantly less for their products abroad than they do in the United States. Due to this practice, or to differences in currency values, others may be able to purchase the goods abroad, ship them to the United States and profitably resell them at lower prices than the U.S. intellectual property owner charges U.S. consumers.

When U.S. intellectual property owners sell their goods abroad or license foreign companies to manufacture and sell them abroad, they frequently negotiate contractual provisions that prohibit the foreign purchaser/licensee from bringing the goods into the United States or transferring them to another for the purpose of doing so. If the foreign purchaser/licensee later participates in importing the goods to the U.S., the intellectual property owner will have a cause of action against it for breach of contract. In many cases, however, the goods change hands several times before landing in the hands of the parallel importers. In such instances, the parallel importers are not in privity with the U.S. intellectual property owner, and contract law may provide no redress for the importation.

Needless to say, U.S. intellectual property owners would like to use their intellectual property rights to prohibit the parallel imports. We will consider their ability to rely on trademark law to exclude the goods in a later chapter. As a general matter, apart from the fair use issue the Court discusses in *L'anza*, what are the public policy implications of permitting or prohibiting parallel imports? Is construction of the doctrine of first sale to permit the imports consistent with the underlying purpose of the doctrine? In the long term, will the availability of parallel imports enhance or depress competition in U.S. markets? Does the need for economic incentives require that the goods be excluded from the country?

In *L'anza*, the copyright owner manufactured the hair care products in the United States and distributed them abroad. Given the Supreme Court's discussion, how might it view a situation in which the U.S. copyright owner manufactured the products overseas instead of domestically? What if the U.S. copyright owner did not manufacture the goods itself, but licensed a foreign company to manufacture the goods overseas and sell them, in return for a royalty payment? As a matter of policy, should it make any difference? See Sebastian International, Inc. v. Consumer Contacts (PTY) Ltd., 847 F.2d 1093, 1096–99 (3d Cir.1988).

Justice Ginsburg, in her concurrence, refers to the statutory language that restricts the doctrine of first sale to copies and phonorecords "lawfully made under this title." 17 U.S.C.A. § 109(a). In Columbia Broadcasting System, Inc. v. Scorpio Music Distributors, Inc., 569 F.Supp. 47 (E.D.Pa. 1983), *aff'd*, 738 F.2d 421 (3d Cir.1984), the district court held that this language restricts the doctrine to "copies which have been legally manufactured and sold within the United States." The court explained that "[t]he protection afforded by the United States Code does not extend beyond the borders of this country unless the Code expressly states." 567 F.Supp. at 49–50. Would application of the doctrine of first sale to goods manufactured and sold abroad and later imported into the United States constitute an extraterritorial application of U.S. law? Are there alternative ways to construe the "lawfully made under this title" language, other than as a geographical restriction?

In Omega, S.A. v. Costco Wholesale Corp., 541 F.3d 982 (9th Cir. 2008), the Court of Appeals for the Ninth Circuit held that the Supreme Court's opinion in *L'Anza* was limited to its facts and did not require application of the doctrine of first sale to imported goods that the U.S. copyright owner manufactured and sold abroad. Thus the Omega Company, which manufactured its luxury watches in Switzerland and sold them at varying prices around the world, could assert its U.S. copyright to prohibit Costco from importing authentic Omega watches that it had purchased abroad (for prices appreciably lower than those charged by Omega's authorized U.S. distributors.) The Supreme Court has granted *certiorari* in the case, ___ U.S. ___, 130 S.Ct. 2089, 176 L.Ed.2d 720 (2010), to determine whether the Ninth Circuit's construction is correct.

F. SECTION 106(4): THE RIGHT TO PERFORM THE COPYRIGHTED WORK PUBLICLY

HOUSE REPORT OF COPYRIGHT ACT OF 1976

H.R. Rep. No. 1476, 94th Cong., 2d Sess. 62–65 (1976).

Under the definitions of "perform," "display," "publicly," and "transmit" in section 101, the concepts of public performance and public display cover not only the initial rendition or showing, but also any further act by which that rendition or showing is transmitted or communicated to the public. Thus, for example: a singer is performing when he or she sings a song; a broadcasting network is performing when it transmits his or her performance (whether simultaneously or from records); a local broadcaster is performing when it transmits the network broadcast; a cable television system is performing when it retransmits the broadcast to its subscribers; and any individual is performing whenever he or she plays a phonorecord embodying the performance or communicates the performance by turning on a receiving set. Although any act by which the initial performance or display is transmitted, repeated, or made to recur would itself be a "performance" or "display" under the bill, it would not be actionable as an infringement unless it were done "publicly," as defined in section 101. Certain other performances and displays, in addition to those that are "private," are exempted or given qualified copyright control under sections 107 through 118.

To "perform" a work, under the definition in section 101, includes reading a literary work aloud, singing or playing music, dancing a ballet or other choreographic work, and acting out a dramatic work or pantomime. A performance may be accomplished "either directly or by means of any device or process," including all kinds of equipment for reproducing or amplifying sounds or visual images, any sort of transmitting apparatus, any type of electronic retrieval system, and any other techniques and systems not yet in use or even invented.

* * *

Under clause (1) of the definition of "publicly" in section 101, a performance or display is "public" if it takes place "at a place open to the public or at any place where a substantial number of persons outside of a normal circle of a family and its social acquaintances is gathered." One of the principal purposes of the definition was to make clear that, contrary to the decision in Metro–Goldwyn–Mayer Distributing Corp. v. Wyatt, 21 C.O.Bull. 203 (D.Md.1932), performances in "semipublic" places such as clubs, lodges, factories, summer camps, and schools are "public performances" subject to copyright control. The term "a family" in this context would include an individual living alone, so that a gathering confined to the individual's social acquaintances would normally be regarded as private. Routine meetings of businesses and governmental personnel would be excluded because they do not represent the gathering of a "substantial number of persons."

Clause (2) of the definition of "publicly" in section 101 makes clear that the concepts of public performance and public display include not only performances and displays that occur initially in a public place, but also acts that transmit or otherwise communicate a performance or display of the work to the public by means of any device or process. The definition of "transmit"—to communicate a performance or display "by any device or process whereby images or sound are received beyond the place from which they are sent"—is broad enough to include all conceivable forms and combinations of wires and wireless communications media, including but by no means limited to radio and television broadcasting as we know them. Each and every method by which the images or sounds comprising a performance or display are picked up and conveyed is a "transmission," and if the transmission reaches the public in any form, the case comes within the scope of clauses (4) or (5) of section 106.

Under the bill, as under the present law, a performance made available by transmission to the public at large is "public" even though the recipients are not gathered in a single place, and even if there is no proof that any of the potential recipients was operating his receiving apparatus at the time of the transmission. The same principles apply whenever the potential recipients of the transmission represent a limited segment of the public, such as the occupants of hotel rooms or the subscribers of a cable television service. Clause (2) of the definition of "publicly" is applicable "whether the members of the public capable of receiving the performance or display receive it in the same place or in separate places and at the same time or at different times."

COLUMBIA PICTURES INDUSTRIES, INC. v. AVECO, INC.

United States Court of Appeals for the Third Circuit, 1986.
800 F.2d 59.

STAPLETON, CIRCUIT JUDGE.

Plaintiffs, appellees in this action, are producers of motion pictures ("Producers") and bring this copyright infringement action against the defendant, Aveco, Inc. Producers claim that Aveco's business, which includes renting video cassettes of motion pictures in conjunction with rooms in which they may be viewed, violates their exclusive rights under the Copyright Act of 1976. * * *

* * * The district court found that Aveco had infringed on Producers' exclusive rights to publicly perform and authorize public performances of their copyrighted works and so granted their motion for partial summary judgment. * * *

I

Among their other operations, Producers distribute video cassette copies of motion pictures in which they own registered copyrights. They do so knowing that many retail purchasers of these video cassettes, including Aveco, rent them to others for profit. Aveco also makes available private rooms of various sizes in which its customers may view the video cassettes that they have chosen from Aveco's offerings. For example, at one location, Lock Haven, Aveco has thirty viewing rooms, each containing seating, a video cassette player, and television monitor. Aveco charges a rental fee for the viewing room that is separate from the charge for the video cassette rental.

Customers of Aveco may (1) rent a room and also rent a video cassette for viewing in that room, (2) rent a room and bring a video cassette obtained elsewhere to play in the room, or (3) rent a video cassette for out-of-store viewing.

Aveco has placed its video cassette players inside the individual viewing rooms and, subject to a time limitation, allows the customer complete control over the playing of the video cassettes. Customers operate the video cassette players in each viewing room and Aveco's employees assist only upon request. Each video cassette may be viewed only from inside the viewing room, and is not transmitted beyond the particular room in which it is being played. Aveco asserts that it rents its viewing rooms to individual customers who may be joined in the room only by members of their families and social acquaintances. Furthermore, Aveco's stated practice is not to permit unrelated groups of customers to share a viewing room while a video cassette is being played. For purposes of this appeal we assume the veracity of these assertions.

II

* * * Producers do not, in the present litigation, allege infringement of their exclusive rights "to do and to authorize [the distribution of] copies

or phonorecords of the copyrighted work to the public by sale or other transfer of ownership, or by rental, lease, or lending." Thus, Aveco's rental of video cassettes for at-home viewing is not challenged.

Producers' claim in this litigation is based on the alleged infringement of their "exclusive right ... to perform the copyrighted work publicly" and to "authorize" such performances. Producers assert that Aveco, by renting its viewing rooms to the public for the purpose of watching Producers' video cassettes, is authorizing the public performance of copyrighted motion pictures.

Our analysis begins with the language of the Act. We first observe that there is no question that "performances" of copyrighted materials take place at Aveco's stores. "To perform" a work is defined in the Act as, "in the case of a motion picture or other audiovisual work, to show its images in any sequence or to make the sounds accompanying it audible." As the House Report notes, this definition means that an individual is performing a work whenever he does anything by which the work is transmitted, repeated, or made to recur.

Producers do not argue that Aveco itself performs the video cassettes. They acknowledge that under the Act Aveco's *customers* are the ones performing the works, for it is they who actually place the video cassette in the video cassette player and operate the controls. * * * However, if there is a public performance, Aveco may still be responsible as an infringer even though it does not actually operate the video cassette players. In granting copyright owners the exclusive rights to "authorize" public performances, Congress intended "to avoid any questions as to the liability of contributory infringers. For example, a person who lawfully acquires an authorized copy of a motion picture would be an infringer if he or she engages in the business of renting it to others for purposes of an unauthorized public performance." H.R.Rep. No. 1476, 94th Cong., 2d Sess. 61, *reprinted in* 1976 U.S.Code Cong. & Ad.News at 5674. In our opinion, this rationale applies equally to the person who knowingly makes available other requisites of a public performance. Accordingly, we agree with the district court that Aveco, by enabling its customers to perform the video cassettes in the viewing rooms, authorizes the performances.

The performances of Producers' motion pictures at Aveco's stores infringe their copyrights, however, only if they are "public." The copyright owners' rights do not extend to control over private performances.

* * *

We recently parsed this definition in *Columbia Pictures Industries v. Redd Horne*, 749 F.2d 154 (3d Cir.1984), a case similar to the one at bar. The principal factual distinction is that in Redd Horne's operation, known as Maxwell's Video Showcase, Ltd. ("Maxwell's"), the video cassette players were located in the stores' central areas, not in each individual screening room. Maxwell's customers would select a video cassette from Maxwell's stock and rent a room which they entered to watch the motion picture on a television monitor. A Maxwell's employee would play the video cassette for the customers in one of the centrally-located video cassette players and transmit the performance to the monitor located in the room. Thus, unlike Aveco's customers, Maxwell's clientele had no control over the video cassette players.

The *Redd Horne* court began its analysis with the observation that the two components of clause (1) of the definition of a public performance are disjunctive. "The first category is self-evident; it is 'a place open to the public.' The second category, commonly referred to as a semi-public place, is determined by the size and composition of the audience."

The court then concluded that the performances were occurring at a place open to the public, which it found to be the entire store, including the viewing rooms.

> Any member of the public can view a motion picture by paying the appropriate fee. The services provided by Maxwell's are essentially the same as a movie theater, with the additional feature of privacy. The relevant "place" within the meaning of Section 101 is each of Maxwell's two stores, not each individual booth within each store. Simply because the cassettes can be viewed in private does not mitigate the essential fact that Maxwell's is unquestionably open to the public.

749 F.2d at 159.

The *Redd Horne* court reached this conclusion despite the fact that when a customer watched a movie at Maxwell's, the viewing room was closed to other members of the public. Nevertheless, Aveco asserts that factual differences between Maxwell's stores and its own require a different result in this case.

Aveco first observes that when Maxwell's employees "performed" the video cassettes, they did so in a central location, the store's main area. This lobby was undeniably "open to the public." Aveco suggests that, in *Redd Horne*, the location of the customers in the private rooms was simply irrelevant, for the *performers* were in a public place, the lobby. In the case at bar, Aveco continues, its employees do not perform anything, the customers do. Unlike Maxwell's employees located in the public lobby, Aveco's customers are in private screening rooms. Aveco argues that while these viewing rooms are available to anyone for rent, they are private during each rental period, and therefore, not "open to the public." The performance—the playing of the video cassette—thus occurs not in the public lobby, but in the private viewing rooms.

We disagree. The necessary implication of Aveco's analysis is that *Redd Horne* would have been decided differently had Maxwell's located its video cassette players in a locked closet in the back of the stores. We do not read *Redd Horne* to adopt such an analysis. The Copyright Act speaks of performances at a place open to the public. It does not require that the public place be actually crowded with people. A telephone booth, a taxi cab, and even a pay toilet are commonly regarded as "open to the public," even though they are usually occupied only by one party at a time. Our opinion in *Redd Horne* turned not on the precise whereabouts of the video cassette players, but on the nature of Maxwell's stores. Maxwell's, like Aveco, was willing to make a viewing room and video cassette available to any member of the public with the inclination to avail himself of this service. It is this availability that made Maxwell's stores public places, not the coincidence that the video cassette players were situated in the lobby. Because we find *Redd Horne* indistinguishable from the case at bar, we find that Aveco's operations constituted an authorization of public performances of Producers' copyrighted works.

Aveco's reliance on the first sale doctrine is likewise misplaced. The first sale doctrine, codified at 17 U.S.C. § 109(a), prevents the copyright owner from controlling future transfers of a particular copy of a copyrighted work after he has transferred its "material ownership" to another. When a copyright owner parts with title to a particular copy of his copyrighted work, he thereby divests himself of his exclusive right to vend that particular copy. Accordingly, under the first sale doctrine, Producers cannot claim that Aveco's rentals or sales of lawfully acquired video cassettes infringe on their exclusive rights to vend those cassettes.

* * *

* * * The rights protected by copyright are divisible and the waiver of one does not necessarily waive any of the others. In particular, the transfer of ownership in a particular copy of a work does not affect Producers' Section 106(4) exclusive rights to do and to authorize public performances. It therefore cannot protect one who is infringing Producers' Section 106(4) rights by the public performance of the copyrighted work.

* * *

NOTES AND QUESTIONS

1. *The public performance right.* Is there an alternative theory for finding a "public performance" under the facts of the *Redd Horne* case?

2. *Sound recordings.* By its terms, § 106(4) extends the right of public performance to "literary, musical, dramatic, and choreographic works, pantomimes, and motion pictures and other audiovisual works." Pictorial, graphic and sculptural works and architectural works are excluded. This exclusion is easy to understand, since such works generally are not performed. Pictorial, graphic and sculptural works, at least, are adequately protected by the exclusive right of public display.

Note, however, that § 106(4) also withholds the public performance right in the case of sound recordings. The exclusion is reiterated in § 114(a). Radio stations, night clubs and others who publicly perform sound recordings must pay royalties to the owners of copyright in the musical compositions that they perform by means of sound recordings. Section 106(4) does not, however, oblige them to pay royalties to the owners of copyright in the sound recordings themselves.

The question of performance rights for sound recordings has generated several congressional hearings and considerable lobbying by interested parties. The Copyright Office has recommended that Congress enact a general public performance right for sound recordings, but to date Congress has declined to do so. What interest groups are likely to oppose extending public performance rights to sound recordings, and why? Most developed nations provide a performance right for sound recordings, either through copyright or "neighboring rights." Record producers and performers often share the performance rights under these regimes.

In 1995, Congress enacted the Digital Performance Rights in Sound Recordings Act, which amended Copyright Act §§ 106 and 114 to provide sound recording copyright owners a limited right of public performance "by means of a digital audio transmission." 17 U.S.C.A. § 106(6). The Act, subsequent amendments, and the legislative history make it clear that Congress intended only to provide a very limited right against *digital audio transmissions* of sound recordings. The right does not extend to FCC-regulated terrestrial radio or television broadcasts to the general public, or to most retransmissions of such broadcasts (though it does apply to Internet "webcasts"). Nor does the right apply to digital transmissions of audio-visual works such as music videos, or to forms of digital performance that do not entail transmission, such as live performances of compact discs at night clubs or other public places. The lengthy and complex provisions that define the digital performance right provide a number of additional exceptions and limitations. For example, the Act exempts "storecasts" (transmissions within a business establishment) and transmissions to business establishments for use in the ordinary course of their business. Thus, in most cases, stores, restaurants and offices may use sound recordings as background music free from interference by the sound recording copyright owners, and background music services, like Muzak, can be conducted digitally. 17 U.S.C.A. § 114(d)(1).

Congress enacted the new digital audio transmission performance right due to its concern that digital audio transmissions via cable or the Internet would displace sales of tapes and compact discs, on which sound recording copyright owners depend for their income. It did not find that other types of public performances, such as those by traditional over-the-air broadcasters, posed such a threat.

As a general matter, the Act affords sound recording copyright owners the greatest rights against digital transmissions by "interactive services," which are services, such as "audio-on-demand," "pay-per-listen," and "celestial jukebox" services, that enable a member of the public to request and receive digital transmission of a particular sound recording. Interactive services pose the greatest threat to the recording industry because they enable consumers to hear their choice of sound recording at any time they choose, undercutting their incentive to purchase a material embodiment of the sound recording from the copyright owner. In such cases, the copyright owner has considerable freedom to negotiate digital performance licenses on its own terms, though the Act does impose some restrictions, including a restriction on the duration of exclusive licenses. 117 U.S.C.A. § 114(d)(3)(A). These limited restrictions exist primarily to protect the interests of musical composition copyright owners.[11] Music composition copyright owners had expressed concern that sound recording copyright owners exercising their new rights might become " 'gatekeepers' and limit opportunities for public performances of the musical works embodied in the sound recordings." S. Rep. No. 104–128, 104th Cong., 2d Sess. 25 (1995).

In the case of many non-interactive digital transmissions, the sound recording copyright owner's rights are more limited. In such cases, the rights amount essentially to a right to compensation for performances, which are statutorily authorized under complex compulsory licensing provisions. 17 U.S.C.A. § 114(d)(2), (e)-(f). The Act directs that the royalty payments from these compulsory or "statutory" licenses be allocated 50% to the sound recording copyright owner and 50% to the sound recording performers. 17 U.S.C.A. § 114(g)(2). In the United States, recording companies generally own the copyrights in sound recordings. The Act's allocation of royalty revenues to performers roughly emulates "neighboring rights" provisions in other countries, which provide performers independent rights in their performances.

3. *Rights in performances, as such.* As noted above, many nations provide rights to performers in their performances, frequently through the vehicle of "neighboring rights"—a body of law whose name reflects its close relationship to copyright. In addition to recognizing performers' rights in their recorded performances, neighboring rights provisions may permit performers to prevent unauthorized fixation and/or broadcasting of their live performances.

In the United States, copyright law protects fixed works of authorship, such as sound recordings and audio-visual works, that incorporate a live performance. However, a live performance, as such, does not qualify as copyrightable subject matter. In implementing the TRIPs Agreement, Congress enacted a form of "neighboring rights" in live musical performances. The Uruguay Round Agreements Act added a new § 1101 to Title 17, prohibiting transmission of the sounds and/or images of live musical performances to the public without the performers' authorization. Section 1101 also prohibits unauthorized fixation of the sounds and/or images of live musical performances, and reproduction, distribution, offers to distribute, and "trafficking" of such unauthorized fixations. Persons engaging in these prohibited acts are subject to civil copyright infringement remedies. The Uruguay Round Agreements Act also amended the criminal code to provide criminal penalties. See 18 U.S.C.A. § 2319A. These new federal "anti-bootlegging" remedies were intended to supplement, rather than supersede, existing state-law remedies, such as state right of publicity or unfair competition claims. They have been justified not only as necessary to bring the U.S. into compliance with TRIPs Article 14, but also to provide a uniform, nation-wide cause of action, which could not be obtained through the previously existing state anti-

---

11. It is important to note that a license to perform a sound recording does not extend any rights to perform the copyrighted musical composition that is the subject of the sound recording. An entity wishing to make a digital audio transmission performance must obtain a license from both the sound recording and the musical composition copyright owner. A refusal by the sound recording copyright owner will affect the musical composition copyright owner's ability to exploit his or her work through digital transmission.

bootlegging provisions. See, e.g., S. Rep. No. 412, 103d Cong., 2d Sess. 225 (1994).

Note that these new provisions give rights to performers in their performance, and are independent of any copyright in the musical compositions being performed, which may be simultaneously infringed by the prohibited transmission, reproduction or distribution of the live performance.

The Constitution's Patents and Copyright Clause, U.S. Const., art. 1, § 8, cl. 8, only authorizes Congress to provide rights in an author's "writings," and to provide rights for "limited times." Live musical performances are not "writings" because they are not fixed in any tangible form. Moreover, the new neighboring rights provisions do not limit the duration of performers' rights. Did Congress exceed its constitutional authority in enacting 17 U.S.C. § 1101 and 18 U.S.C. § 2319A? See United States v. Moghadam, 175 F.3d 1269, 1280 (11th Cir.1999), *cert. denied*, 529 U.S. 1036, 120 S.Ct. 1529, 146 L.Ed.2d 344 (2000)("[T]he Copyright Clause does not envision that Congress is positively forbidden from extending copyright-like protection under other constitutional clauses, such as the Commerce Clause, to works of authorship that may not meet the fixation requirement inherent in the term 'Writings.' "); United States v. Martignon, 492 F.3d 140 (2d Cir.2007)(Congress' enactment of criminal penalties for bootlegging live musical performances was constitutional).

4. *Performing rights societies.* Copyrighted musical compositions are publicly performed in numerous ways every day—in live concerts, through radio and television broadcasts and background music services, in night clubs—throughout the country. Individual musical composition copyright owners cannot hope to negotiate separate licenses for every such performance of their works. Nor can they effectively police the marketplace to ensure that performers are obtaining licenses. It is also inefficient for large-scale performers, like radio broadcasters, to negotiate individual licenses for each work they publicly perform.

To manage the licensing of public performances and effectively enforce musical composition copyrights, interested parties formed performing rights societies, such as the American Society of Composers, Authors and Publishers (ASCAP) and Broadcast Music, Inc. (BMI). Today, most domestic musical composition copyright owners are represented by one or the other of these two societies. Each represented copyright owner grants a non-exclusive right to the society to license non-dramatic public performance of his works. By representing large numbers of copyright owners, the societies can issue "blanket licenses" authorizing performance of all the works of a particular type in the society's huge repertoire for a stated period of time. In addition to licensing performances, the societies collect royalties and distribute them among the copyright owners they represent. ASCAP and BMI also send their representatives into the marketplace to monitor compliance with the copyright laws and bring suits on behalf of owners to enforce public performance rights against infringers. For a more detailed description of performing rights society operations and some of the antitrust issues that have surrounded them, see Broadcast Music, Inc. v. Columbia Broadcasting System, Inc., 441 U.S. 1, 99 S.Ct. 1551, 60 L.Ed.2d 1 (1979); Buffalo Broadcasting Co., Inc. v.

American Society of Composers, Authors and Publishers, 744 F.2d 917 (2d Cir.1984), *cert. denied*, 469 U.S. 1211, 105 S.Ct. 1181, 84 L.Ed.2d 329 (1985).

5. *Exceptions to the exclusive right of public performance.* Because many of the statutory exceptions to the public performance right apply to the public display right, as well, these exceptions will be considered in the following section on the right of public display.

Problems

1. Hotel rents DVDs of motion pictures to its guests for a fee of $5 to $7.50. Guests check out DVDs at Hotel's lobby and play them in their rooms, which are equipped with a DVD player and screen. In light of the *Redd Horne* and *Aveco* decisions, are Hotel guests publicly performing the copyrighted motion pictures, giving rise to a cause of action for contributory infringement against Hotel?

2. What if, instead of the arrangement described above, Hotel has a system for electronic delivery of videotaped motion pictures to individual guest rooms? The guest operates the system from her room by remote control. After the television is turned on, the screen lists a menu of available motion pictures. The guest selects one by entering the appropriate code on the remote control. Hotel maintains a bank of video cassette players ("VCPs") in an equipment room. These VCPs are connected to the guest rooms by wiring. Whenever a guest requests a movie, a computer program dedicates the particular VCP containing the tape of the requested motion picture to the appropriate room and starts the video. The video can only be viewed in the room occupied by the guest who selected it. Does this arrangement infringe the right of public performance in the movies?

3. Defendant cable television company markets a new remote storage digital video recorder ("RS-DVR") system that allows its cable subscribers to copy television programs and movies being shown via cable. From customers' standpoint, the process of recording and playing back recorded programs through the remote storage system is similar to that of traditional, stand-alone digital video recorders attached to the users' television. However, rather than making copies in a set-top DVR, the defendant's system creates and stores the copies on the defendant's central hard drives at a remote location, and plays them back at the user's request via cable transmission. An individual copy of the program is made and stored for each customer who instructs the system to record it. The plaintiffs, providers of copyrighted content, bring suit alleging that when customers request play-back of a copy stored on the defendant's remote storage facility, the play-back constitutes an unauthorized public performance of the recorded program. How should a court rule on this argument?

4. Defendant, a provider of cellular telephone services, sells a variety of ringtones to its subscribers, that sound when the subscriber receives a call. Some of the ringtones consist of snippets taken from recordings of copyrighted musical compositions. Is there an actionable "public performance" of the copyrighted musical composition when a subscriber purchases such a ringtone

from the defendant, or when the subscriber subsequently receives a telephone call heralded by the ringtone?

G. SECTION 106(5): THE RIGHT TO DISPLAY THE COPYRIGHTED WORK PUBLICLY

HOUSE REPORT ON COPYRIGHT ACT OF 1976

H.R. Rep. No. 1476, 94th Cong., 2d Sess. 63–64 (1976).

Clause (5) of section 106 represents the first explicit statutory recognition in American copyright law of an exclusive right to show a copyrighted work, or an image of it, to the public. The existence or extent of this right under the present statute is uncertain and subject to challenge. The bill would give the owners of copyright in "literary, musical, dramatic, and choreographic works, pantomimes, and pictorial, graphic, or sculptural works," including the individual images of a motion picture or other audiovisual work, the exclusive right "to display the copyrighted work publicly."

* * *

The corresponding definition of "display" covers any showing of a "copy" of the work, "either directly or by means of a film, slide, television image, or any other device or process." Since "copies" are defined as including the material object "in which the work is first fixed," the right of public display applies to original works of art as well as to reproductions of them. With respect to motion pictures and other audiovisual works, it is a "display" (rather than a "performance") to show their "individual images nonsequentially." In addition to the direct showing of a copy of a work, "display" would include the projection of an image on a screen or other surface by any method, the transmission of an image by electronic or other means, and the showing of an image on a cathode ray tube, or similar viewing apparatus connected with any sort of information storage and retrieval system.

PERFECT 10, INC. v. AMAZON.COM, INC.

Untied States Court of Appeals for the Ninth Circuit, 2007.
508 F.3d 1146.

IKUTA, CIRCUIT JUDGE:

In this appeal, we consider a copyright owner's efforts to stop an Internet search engine from facilitating access to infringing images. Perfect 10, Inc. sued Google Inc., for infringing Perfect 10's copyrighted photographs of nude models, among other claims. Perfect 10 brought a similar action against Amazon.com and its subsidiary A9.com (collectively, "Amazon.com"). * * *

* * *

I

Background

Google's computers, along with millions of others, are connected to networks known collectively as the "Internet." "The Internet is a world-wide network of networks ... all sharing a common communications technology." *Religious Tech. Ctr. v. Netcom On–Line Commc'n Servs., Inc.,* 923 F.Supp. 1231, 1238 n. 1 (N.D.Cal.1995). Computer owners can provide information stored on their computers to other users connected to the Internet through a medium called a webpage. A webpage consists of text interspersed with instructions written in Hypertext Markup Language ("HTML") that is stored in a computer. No images are stored on a webpage; rather, the HTML instructions on the webpage provide an address for where the images are stored, whether in the webpage publisher's computer or some other computer. In general, webpages are publicly available and can be accessed by computers connected to the Internet through the use of a web browser.

Google operates a search engine, a software program that automatically accesses thousands of websites (collections of webpages) and indexes them within a database stored on Google's computers. When a Google user accesses the Google website and types in a search query, Google's software searches its database for websites responsive to that search query. Google then sends relevant information from its index of websites to the user's computer. Google's search engines can provide results in the form of text, images, or videos.

The Google search engine that provides responses in the form of images is called "Google Image Search." In response to a search query, Google Image Search identifies text in its database responsive to the query and then communicates to users the images associated with the relevant text. Google's software cannot recognize and index the images themselves. Google Image Search provides search results as a webpage of small images called "thumbnails," which are stored in Google's servers. The thumbnail images are reduced, lower-resolution versions of full-sized images stored on third-party computers.

When a user clicks on a thumbnail image, the user's browser program interprets HTML instructions on Google's webpage. These HTML instructions direct the user's browser to cause a rectangular area (a "window") to appear on the user's computer screen. The window has two separate areas of information. The browser fills the top section of the screen with information from the Google webpage, including the thumbnail image and text. The HTML instructions also give the user's browser the address of the website publisher's computer that stores the full-size version of the thumbnail.[2] By following the HTML instructions to access the third-party

---

2. The website publisher may not actually store the photographic images used on its webpages in its own computer, but may provide HTML instructions directing the user's browser to some further computer that stores the image. Because this distinction does not affect our analysis, for

webpage, the user's browser connects to the website publisher's computer, downloads the full-size image, and makes the image appear at the bottom of the window on the user's screen. Google does not store the images that fill this lower part of the window and does not communicate the images to the user; Google simply provides HTML instructions directing a user's browser to access a third-party website. However, the top part of the window (containing the information from the Google webpage) appears to frame and comment on the bottom part of the window. Thus, the user's window appears to be filled with a single integrated presentation of the full-size image, but it is actually an image from a third-party website framed by information from Google's website. The process by which the webpage directs a user's browser to incorporate content from different computers into a single window is referred to as "in-line linking." The term "framing" refers to the process by which information from one computer appears to frame and annotate the in-line linked content from another computer.

Google also stores webpage content in its cache.[3] For each cached webpage, Google's cache contains the text of the webpage as it appeared at the time Google indexed the page, but does not store images from the webpage. Google may provide a link to a cached webpage in response to a user's search query. However, Google's cache version of the webpage is not automatically updated when the webpage is revised by its owner. So if the webpage owner updates its webpage to remove the HTML instructions for finding an infringing image, a browser communicating directly with the webpage would not be able to access that image. However, Google's cache copy of the webpage would still have the old HTML instructions for the infringing image. Unless the owner of the computer changed the HTML address of the infringing image, or otherwise rendered the image unavailable, a browser accessing Google's cache copy of the website could still access the image where it is stored on the website publisher's computer. In other words, Google's cache copy could provide a user's browser with valid directions to an infringing image even though the updated webpage no longer includes that infringing image.

* * *

Perfect 10 markets and sells copyrighted images of nude models. Among other enterprises, it operates a subscription website on the Internet. Subscribers pay a monthly fee to view Perfect 10 images in a "members' area" of the site. Subscribers must use a password to log into

---

convenience, we will assume that the website publisher stores all images used on its webpages in the website publisher's own computer.

3. Generally, a "cache" is "a computer memory with very short access time used for storage of frequently or recently used instructions or data." There are two types of caches at issue in this case. A user's personal computer has an internal cache that saves copies of webpages and images that the user has recently viewed so that the user can more rapidly revisit these webpages and images. Google's computers also have a cache which serves a variety of purposes. Among other things, Google's cache saves copies of a large number of webpages so that Google's search engine can efficiently organize and index these webpages.

the members' area. Google does not include these password-protected images from the members' area in Google's index or database. * * *

Some website publishers republish Perfect 10's images on the Internet without authorization. Once this occurs, Google's search engine may automatically index the webpages containing these images and provide thumbnail versions of images in response to user inquiries. When a user clicks on the thumbnail image returned by Google's search engine, the user's browser accesses the third-party webpage and in-line links to the full-sized infringing image stored on the website publisher's computer. This image appears, in its original context, on the lower portion of the window on the user's computer screen framed by information from Google's webpage.

* * *

III

Direct Infringement

[Perfect 10 claims that Google's search engine program directly infringes its exclusive right to publicly display its copyrighted photographs. The district court held that Perfect 10 was not likely to prevail on the merits of its claim and denied its motion for preliminary injunction.]

A. Display Right

In considering whether Perfect 10 made a prima facie case of violation of its display right, the district court reasoned that a computer owner that stores an image as electronic information and serves that electronic information directly to the user ("i.e., physically sending ones and zeroes over the [I]nternet to the user's browser,") is displaying the electronic information in violation of a copyright holder's exclusive display right. Conversely, the owner of a computer that does not store and serve the electronic information to a user is not displaying that information, even if such owner in-line links to or frames the electronic information. The district court referred to this test as the "server test."

Applying the server test, the district court concluded that Perfect 10 was * * * unlikely to succeed in its claim that Google's in-line linking to full-size infringing images constituted a direct infringement. As explained below, because this analysis comports with the language of the Copyright Act, we agree with the district court's resolution of both these issues.

We have not previously addressed the question when a computer displays a copyrighted work for purposes of section 106(5). Section 106(5) states that a copyright owner has the exclusive right "to display the copyrighted work publicly." The Copyright Act explains that "display" means "to show a copy of it, either directly or by means of a film, slide, television image, or any other device or process.... "17 U.S.C. § 101. Section 101 defines "copies" as "material objects, other than phonorecords, in which a work is fixed by any method now known or later developed, and from which the work can be perceived, reproduced, or otherwise communicated, either directly or with the aid of a machine or device." Finally, the Copyright Act provides that "[a] work is 'fixed' in a tangible medium of expression when its embodiment in a copy or phono-record, by or under the authority of the author, is sufficiently permanent or stable to permit it to be perceived, reproduced, or otherwise communicated for a period of more than transitory duration." *Id.*

We must now apply these definitions to the facts of this case. A photographic image is a work that is " 'fixed' in a tangible medium of expression," for purposes of the Copyright Act, when embodied (i.e., stored) in a computer's server (or hard disk, or other storage device). The image stored in the computer is the "copy" of the work for purposes of copyright law. * * * The computer owner shows a copy "by means of a . . . device or process" when the owner uses the computer to fill the computer screen with the photographic image stored on that computer, or by communicating the stored image electronically to another person's computer. 17 U.S.C. § 101. In sum, based on the plain language of the statute, a person displays a photographic image by using a computer to fill a computer screen with a copy of the photographic image fixed in the computer's memory. There is no dispute that Google's computers store thumbnail versions of Perfect 10's copyrighted images and communicate copies of those thumbnails to Google's users.[6] Therefore, Perfect 10 has made a prima facie case that Google's communication of its stored thumbnail images directly infringes Perfect 10's display right.

Google does not, however, display a copy of full-size infringing photographic images for purposes of the Copyright Act when Google frames in-line linked images that appear on a user's computer screen. Because Google's computers do not store the photographic images, Google does not have a copy of the images for purposes of the Copyright Act. In other words, Google does not have any "material objects . . . in which a work is fixed . . . and from which the work can be perceived, reproduced, or otherwise communicated" and thus cannot communicate a copy. 17 U.S.C. § 101.

Instead of communicating a copy of the image, Google provides HTML instructions that direct a user's browser to a website publisher's computer that stores the full-size photographic image. Providing these HTML instructions is not equivalent to showing a copy. First, the HTML instructions are lines of text, not a photographic image. Second, HTML instructions do not themselves cause infringing images to appear on the user's computer screen. The HTML merely gives the address of the image to the user's browser. The browser then interacts with the computer that stores the infringing image. It is this interaction that causes an infringing image to appear on the user's computer screen. Google may facilitate the user's

---

6. Because Google initiates and controls the storage and communication of these thumbnail images, we do not address whether an entity that merely passively owns and manages an Internet bulletin board or similar system violates a copyright owner's display and distribution rights when the users of the bulletin board or similar system post infringing works. *Cf. CoStar Group, Inc. v. LoopNet, Inc.* 373 F.3d 544 (**4th** Cir. 2004).

access to infringing images. However, such assistance raises only contributory liability issues, and does not constitute direct infringement of the copyright owner's display rights.

Perfect 10 argues that Google displays a copy of the full-size images by framing the full-size images, which gives the impression that Google is showing the image within a single Google webpage. While in-line linking and framing may cause some computer users to believe they are viewing a single Google webpage, the Copyright Act, unlike the Trademark Act, does not protect a copyright holder against acts that cause consumer confusion.
* * *

Nor does our ruling that a computer owner does not display a copy of an image when it communicates only the HTML address of the copy erroneously collapse the display right in section 106(5) into the reproduction right set forth in section 106(1). Nothing in the Copyright Act prevents the various rights protected in section 106 from overlapping. Indeed, under some circumstances, more than one right must be infringed in order for an infringement claim to arise. For example, a "Game Genie" device that allowed a player to alter features of a Nintendo computer game did not infringe Nintendo's right to prepare derivative works because the Game Genie did not incorporate any portion of the game itself. *See Lewis Galoob Toys, Inc. v. Nintendo of Am., Inc.,* 964 F.2d 965, 967 (9th Cir.1992). We held that a copyright holder's right to create derivative works is not infringed unless the alleged derivative work "incorporate[s] a protected work in some concrete or permanent 'form.' " In other words, in some contexts, the claimant must be able to claim infringement of its reproduction right in order to claim infringement of its right to prepare derivative works.

Because Google's cache merely stores the text of webpages, our analysis of whether Google's search engine program potentially infringes Perfect 10's display and distribution rights is equally applicable to Google's cache. Perfect 10 is not likely to succeed in showing that a cached webpage that in-line links to full-size infringing images violates such rights. For purposes of this analysis, it is irrelevant whether cache copies direct a user's browser to third-party images that are no longer available on the third party's website, because it is the website publisher's computer, rather than Google's computer, that stores and displays the infringing image.

[The court goes on to agree with the district court's conclusion that Google does not directly infringe Perfect 10's right of distribution to the public. The court reasons that distribution requires an "actual dissemination" of a copy, and since Google does not itself store a "copy" of the images, it does not disseminate, or transmit a copy to its users. Rather, Google's search engine communicates HTML instructions that tell a user's browser where to find full-size images on a website publisher's computer, and the website publisher's computer then distributes copies of the images to users. The court also holds that Google's display of the thumbnail images in its search results is excused under the fair use doctrine.]

NOTES AND QUESTIONS

1. *The right of public display.* The right of public display extends to all copyrightable subject matter except sound recordings and architectural works. Like performances, unauthorized displays must be "public" to infringe. The definition of "public" in § 101, discussed in the prior section, applies equally to displays and performances.

As a general matter, how economically important is the newly recognized right of public display likely to be to copyright owners?

2. *The § 109(c) exception to the public display right.* Section 109(c) provides:

> Notwithstanding the provisions of section 106(5), the owner of a particular copy lawfully made under this title, or any person authorized by such owner, is entitled, without the authority of the copyright owner, to display that copy publicly, either directly or by the projection of no more than one image at a time, to viewers present at the place where the copy is located.

According to the House Report, this exception "adopts the general principle that the lawful owner of a copy of a work should be able to put his copy on public display without the consent of the copyright owner."

> The exclusive right of public display granted by section 106(5) would not apply where the owner of a copy wishes to show it directly to the public, as in a gallery or display case, or indirectly, as through an opaque projector. Where the copy itself is intended for projection, as in the case of a photographic slide, negative, or transparency, the public projection of a single image would be permitted as long as the viewers are "present at the place where the copy is located."

> On the other hand, section 109[(c)] takes account of the potentialities of the new communications media, notably television, cable and optical transmission devices, and information storage and retrieval devices, for replacing printed copies with visual images. First of all, the public display of an image of a copyrighted work would not be exempted from copyright control if the copy from which the image was derived were outside the presence of the viewers. In other words, the display of a visual image of a copyrighted work would be an infringement if the image were transmitted by any method (by closed or open circuit television, for example, or by a computer system) from one place to members of the public located elsewhere.

> Moreover, the exemption would extend only to public displays that are made "either directly or by the projection of no more than one image at a time." Thus, even where the copy and the viewers are located at the same place, the simultaneous projection of multiple images of the work would not be exempted. For example, where each person in a lecture hall is supplied with a separate viewing apparatus, the copyright owner's

permission would generally be required in order to project an image of a work on each individual screen at the same time.

The Committee's intention is to preserve the traditional privilege of the owner of a copy to display it directly, but to place reasonable restrictions on the ability to display it indirectly in such a way that the copyright owner's market for reproduction and distribution of copies would be affected.

H.R. Rep. No. 1476, 94th Cong., 2d Sess. 79–80 (1976).

3. *Section 110 exceptions to the rights of public performance and display.* Copyright Act § 110 provides a number of important exceptions to the rights of public performance and display. Several of the exceptions enable members of the public to make non-profit public performances and displays of works, under various circumstances. To evaluate the scope of these provisions, review the statutory language and then try your hand at applying it to the problems at the end of this section.

Another important exception to the rights of performance and display, sometimes known as the "public reception" or "single, home-style receiver" exception, is set forth in § 110(5). The original subpart (5) was a Congressional response to the fact situation in Twentieth Century Music Corp. v. Aiken, 422 U.S. 151, 95 S.Ct. 2040, 45 L.Ed.2d 84 (1975). In *Aiken*, the defendant, owner and operator of a fast-service food shop in downtown Pittsburgh, played a radio "with outlets to four speakers in the ceiling" in his shop during the business day, for the enjoyment of the shop's employees and customers. The plaintiff claimed that this infringed the public performance rights in its musical works, which were lawfully broadcast by the radio station to which defendant's radio was tuned. The House Report accompanying the Copyright Act of 1976 explained:

> [Section 110(5)] applies to performances and displays of all types of works, and its purpose is to exempt from copyright liability anyone who merely turns on, in a public place, an ordinary radio or television receiving apparatus of a kind commonly sold to members of the public for private use.
>
> The basic rationale of this clause is that the secondary use of the transmission by turning on an ordinary receiver in public is so remote and minimal that no further liability should be imposed. * * *
>
> Under the particular fact situation in the *Aiken* case, assuming a small commercial establishment and the use of a home receiver with four ordinary loudspeakers grouped within a relatively narrow circumference from the set, it is intended that the performances would be exempt under clause (5). However, the Committee considers this fact situation to represent the outer limit of that exemption, and believes that the line should be drawn at that point. Thus, the clause would exempt small commercial establishments whose proprietors merely bring onto their premises standard radio or television equipment and turn it on for their customers' enjoyment, but it would impose liability where the proprietor has a commercial "sound system" installed or converts a standard home receiving apparatus (by augmenting it with sophisticated or extensive

amplification equipment) into the equivalent of a commercial sound system. * * *

H.R. Rep. No. 1476, 94th Cong., 2d Sess. 86–87 (1976). The Conference Report noted that a small commercial establishment of the type involved in *Aiken* "was not of sufficient size to justify, as a practical matter, a subscription to a commercial background music service." H.R. Rep. No. 1733, 94th Cong., 2d Sess. 75 (1976).

Over the years Performing Rights Societies litigated extensively to test the limits of this exception to copyright owners' rights. Indeed, the Performing Rights Societies were so assiduous in asserting the rights of musical composition copyright owners against stores, restaurants and bars that a number of these businesses petitioned Congress for relief. Congress responded in 1998 by amending § 110(5) to give commercial establishments greater leeway to play broadcasts of non-dramatic musical works on their premises. Congress retained the original § 110(5) "single, home-style receiver" exception as § 110(5)(A). It then added a new subpart (B), which permits stores smaller than 2,000 square feet and restaurants and bars smaller than 3,750 square feet to play radio and television broadcasts of non-dramatic musical works, regardless of the type of receiver or number of speakers they use. Subsection (B) permits stores larger than 2,000 square feet and restaurants and bars larger than 3,750 square feet to play broadcasts of non-dramatic musical works, as long as they use no more than six speakers or four televisions with screens smaller than 55 inches. (There are further limitations on the placement of the speakers and televisions.) A study prepared by Dun & Bradstreet, on behalf of ASCAP, estimated that the new subsection (B) would permit approximately 70% of all U.S. drinking and eating establishments, and 45% of all U.S. retail establishments, to play broadcasts of music on their premises without accounting to the copyright owner. *WTO Adopts Ruling Striking Down U.S. Law on Music Licensing*, 14 World Intell. Prop. Rep. (B.N.A.) 307, 308 (2000).

Note that the new subsection (B) only applies in the case of non-dramatic musical works. Public reception of broadcasts of other kinds of copyrighted works (such as broadcast sports events or television comedies) continues to be governed by the original "single, home-style receiver" exemption now codified as subsection (A).

The TRIPs Agreement, Article 13, requires World Trade Organization members to "confine limitations or exceptions to exclusive rights [of copyright] to certain special cases which do not conflict with a normal exploitation of the work and do not unreasonably prejudice the legitimate interests of the right holder." Shortly after Congress enacted the new § 110(5)(B), the European Union challenged both the new subsection (B) and the original "single, home-style receiver" exemption under the dispute resolution provisions of the World Trade Organization, claiming that these exceptions to copyright violate the United States' obligations under TRIPs. The WTO dispute settlement panel ruled that § 110(5)(B) violates TRIPs by exceeding the limitation on copyright exceptions set forth in TRIPs Art. 13. However, the panel rejected the E.U.'s claim that the original "single, home-style receiver" exemption, now codified as § 110(5)(A), also violates TRIPs Art. 13. In so ruling, however, the panel noted its understanding that the scope of the "single, home-style receiver" exemption was narrowed by the addition of subsection (B) to exclude non-dramatic musical works.

The panel ruling does not in itself invalidate or repeal § 110(5)(B). The provision will remain in effect until Congress takes action to remove it. As long as Congress declines to take action, the E.U. may be entitled to collect reparations or impose trade sanctions against the U.S.

4. *Other Exceptions and Compulsory License Provisions.* As the House Report notes, public performance and display include not only the initial rendition or showing of a work, but also "any further act by which that rendition or showing is transmitted or communicated to the public." Accordingly, the Copyright Act includes several provisions addressing the retransmission of broadcast signals. Section 111 creates a complex compulsory licensing system that permits cable systems to pick up broadcasting signals and retransmit them to their subscribers. In addition, § 111 permits hotels, apartment houses, and similar establishments to relay broadcast signals to the private rooms or apartments of guests or residents, and exempts from liability "passive carriers," such as AT & T, that merely provide the wires or cables for retransmissions by others. Section 119 provides a compulsory license for satellite retransmissions. Section 118 provides compulsory licenses to assist public broadcasting stations in transmitting certain public performances and displays of copyrighted works.

PROBLEMS

1. In the course of his basic humanities class, a community college professor has class members perform the first act of a Sam Shepard play. The performance takes place on the stage of the large lecture auditorium where the class regularly meets. There are 250 students enrolled in the class, and most of them are present for the class in which the performance takes place. Directly before the students take the stage, the professor shows the class a photograph of the set used in the original Broadway production of the play. The photograph is in a book that the professor checked out of the library. To enable the whole class to see it, he places the page containing the photograph on an opaque projector. After the performance, the class discusses various dramatic elements of the Shepard play's first act. Assuming that the Shepard play and the photograph are copyrighted, do these activities fall under any of the § 110 exceptions to infringement liability?

2. Assume that the humanities class described above is videotaped and broadcast over the community college television station as part of the college's "College on the Air" program. Through this program, members of the general community can sign up for a course, view the class presentations on their television sets at home, send in the written assignments by mail and receive college credit. The broadcast videotape of the class includes both the performance and the display of the photograph of the set. Does this fall into any of the § 110 exceptions?

3. Assume that the students who perform the first act of the Shepard play enjoy it so much that they decide to present the same performance on the

campus commons during lunch time. They take along the opaque projector, project the photograph of the Broadway set on a screen, and tell the audience to imagine that they are performing on the depicted set. A number of students and college staff sit and eat their lunch on the commons while watching the performance. No admission is charged. Are any of the exceptions applicable?

4. Assume that one of the student actors convinces the others to make the same performance and display at her church's regular Sunday night "Young Adults Group" gathering at the church. The group shares a covered dish supper and then goes to the church sanctuary to view the performance and display. Do any of the § 110 exceptions apply?

5. Assume that a college marching band, led by the faculty member who normally conducts the band, assembles in a park on a sunny afternoon. The band plays songs written by the Beatles, Bob Dylan, and other popular composers for an hour. After a recess, they play a series of tunes from the rock-opera "Tommy." The band displays a sign stating that its performance is for the benefit of AIDS patients, and during the course of the performance band members pass around a bucket for donations from the passers-by who stop to listen. After the performance, the band turns all the donations over to a local charitable organization that assists AIDS patients. Will the band's performance fall under any of the § 110 exceptions?

6. What if a local television reporter and film crew tape the band's performance of one of the Beatles' songs, and their station broadcasts the tape on the evening news. Will the television station's actions be exempted from liability under any of the § 110 exceptions?

7. The owner of a small Italian-style restaurant often brings his accordion to the restaurant and plays popular Italian tunes for the guests' enjoyment when he has a spare moment. He makes no separate charge for this music, and makes no recording or transmission of the performance. Do any of the § 110 exceptions apply?

8. Assume that a little "mom and pop" convenience store keeps a small, inexpensive stereo receiver/tape deck and two small speakers on the back counter of the shop. Its proprietors play compact disks of popular music, purchased at a nearby record shop, for workers and customers during regular business hours. Will § 110(5) apply?

9. Ken subscribes to the popular on-line magazine *Nerd Heat*. Upon perusing the latest issue, he finds an hilarious article about "bit decay." He enjoys the article so much that he posts it to the alt.nerdhumor newsgroup (bulletin board). A number of bulletin board subscribers read it. Which (if any) rights of the "bit decay" article copyright owner have been violated?

10. X Co. operates a web site that features copyrighted photographs. Y Co. operates its own web site. Among other things, Y's web site contains an "in-line link" to one of the photographs on X's web site. Essentially, when a visitor views the relevant page of the Y site, html code prompts the user's computer automatically to retrieve the photograph from X's site. The user's screen displays the photograph from X's site along with the text from Y's site. However, while the text is generated from Y's server, the photograph is generated from X Co.'s server, and does not pass through the Y server. The

visual result on the user's screen is integrated text and photograph. Under these circumstances, is Y liable for directly infringing X's right of public display in its photograph?

H. MORAL RIGHTS AND SECTION 106A

CARTER v. HELMSLEY–SPEAR, INC.

United States Court of Appeals for the Second Circuit, 1995.
71 F.3d 77, *cert. denied*, 517 U.S. 1208, 116 S.Ct. 1824, 134 L.Ed.2d 930 (1996).

CARDAMONE, CIRCUIT JUDGE:

Defendants 474431 Associates and Helmsley–Spear, Inc. (defendants or appellants), as the owner and managing agent respectively, of a commercial building in Queens, New York, appeal from an order of the United States District Court for the Southern District of New York (Edelstein, J.), entered on September 6, 1994 following a bench trial. The order granted plaintiffs, who are three artists, a permanent injunction that enjoined defendants from removing, modifying or destroying a work of visual art that had been installed in defendants' building by plaintiffs-artists commissioned by a former tenant to install the work. See Carter v. Helmsley–Spear, Inc., 861 F.Supp. 303 (S.D.N.Y.1994).* * *

On this appeal we deal with an Act of Congress that protects the rights of artists to preserve their works. One of America's most insightful thinkers observed that a country is not truly civilized "where the arts, such as they have, are all imported, having no indigenous life." 7 Works of Ralph Waldo Emerson, Society and Solitude, Chapt. II Civilization 34 (AMS. ed. 1968). From such reflection it follows that American artists are to be encouraged by laws that protect their works. Although Congress in the statute before us did just that, it did not mandate the preservation of art at all costs and without due regard for the rights of others.

For the reasons that follow, we reverse and vacate * * *.

BACKGROUND

Defendant 474431 Associates (Associates) is the owner of a mixed use commercial building located at 47–44 31st Street, Queens, New York, which it has owned since 1978. * * * Defendant Helmsley–Spear, Inc. is the current managing agent of the property for Associates.

* * *

Plaintiffs John Carter, John Swing and John Veronis (artists or plaintiffs) are professional sculptors who work together and are known collectively as the "Three–J's" or "Jx3." * * *

The art work that is the subject of this litigation is a very large "walk-through sculpture" occupying most, but not all, of the building's lobby. The art work consists of a variety of sculptural elements constructed from recycled materials, much of it metal, affixed to the walls and ceiling, and a vast mosaic made from pieces of recycled glass embedded in the floor and walls. Elements of the work include a giant hand fashioned from an old school bus, a face made of automobile parts, and a number of interactive components. These assorted elements make up a theme relating to environmental concerns and the significance of recycling.

[The artists created the art work pursuant to a contract with the defendants' lessee. The lease subsequently was terminated, and the lessee surrendered the building to defendants.] Representatives of defendants informed the artists that they could no longer continue to install art work at the property, and instead had to vacate the building. These representatives also made statements indicating that defendants intended to remove the art work already in place in the building's lobby.

As a result of defendants' actions, artists commenced this litigation. * * *

[After a bench trial the district court granted artists a] permanent injunction prohibiting defendants from distorting, mutilating, modifying, destroying and removing plaintiffs' art work. The injunction is to remain in effect for the lifetimes of the three plaintiffs. * * *

DISCUSSION

I. Artists' Moral Rights

A. History of Artists' Moral Rights

Because it was under the rubric of the Visual Artists Rights Act of 1990 that plaintiffs obtained injunctive relief in the district court, we must explore, at least in part, the contours of that Act. In doing so it is necessary to review briefly the concept of artists' moral rights and the history and development of those rights in American jurisprudence, which led up to passage of the statute we must now examine.

The term "moral rights" has its origins in the civil law and is a translation of the French *le droit moral*, which is meant to capture those rights of a spiritual, non-economic and personal nature. The rights spring from a belief that an artist in the process of creation injects his spirit into the work and that the artist's personality, as well as the integrity of the work, should therefore be protected and preserved. Because they are personal to the artist, moral rights exist independently of an artist's copyright in his or her work.

While the rubric of moral rights encompasses many varieties of rights, two are protected in nearly every jurisdiction recognizing their existence: attribution and integrity. The right of attribution generally consists of the right of an artist to be recognized by name as the author of his work or to publish anonymously or pseudonymously, the right to prevent the author's work from being attributed to someone else, and to prevent the use of the author's name on works created by others, including distorted editions of the author's original work. The right of integrity allows the author to prevent any deforming or mutilating changes to his work, even after title in the work has been transferred.

In some jurisdictions the integrity right also protects art work from destruction. Whether or not a work of art is protected from destruction represents a fundamentally different perception of the purpose of moral rights. If integrity is meant to stress the public interest in preserving a nation's culture, destruction is prohibited; if the right is meant to empha-size the author's personality, destruction is seen as less harmful than the continued display of deformed or mutilated work that misrepresents the artist and destruction may proceed. * * *

Although moral rights are well established in the civil law, they are of recent vintage in American jurisprudence. Federal and state courts typi-cally recognized the existence of such rights in other nations, but rejected artists' attempts to inject them into U.S. law. Nonetheless, American courts have in varying degrees acknowledged the idea of moral rights, cloaking the concept in the guise of other legal theories, such as copyright, unfair competition, invasion of privacy, defamation, and breach of con-tract. * * *

* * *

B.   Visual Artists Rights Act of 1990

Although bills protecting artists' moral rights had first been intro-duced in Congress in 1979, they had drawn little support. The issue of federal protection of moral rights was a prominent hurdle in the debate over whether the United States should join the Berne Convention, the international agreement protecting literary and artistic works. Article 6*bis* of the Berne Convention protects attribution and integrity, stating in relevant part:

> Independently of the author's economic rights, and even after the transfer of the said rights, the author shall have the right to claim authorship of the work and to object to any distortion, mutilation or other modification of, or other derogatory action in relation to, the said work, which would be prejudicial to his honor or reputation.

Berne Convention for the Protection of Literary and Artistic Works, September 9, 1886, art. 6*bis*, S.Treaty Doc. No. 27, 99th Cong., 2d Sess. 41 (1986).

The Berne Convention's protection of moral rights posed a significant difficulty for U.S. adherence. See [William F. Patry, Copyright Law and Practice], 1022 [1994] ("The obligation of the United States to provide *droit moral* ... was the single most contentious issue surrounding Berne adherence."); [Nimmer on Copyright] 8D–15 [1994] ("During the debate over [the Berne Convention Implementation Act], Congress faced an avalanche of opposition to moral rights, including denunciations of moral rights by some of the bill's most vociferous advocates.") * * *.

Congress passed the Berne Convention Implementation Act of 1988, Pub.L. No. 100–568, 102 Stat. 2853 (1988), and side-stepped the difficult question of protecting moral rights. It declared that the Berne Convention is not self-executing, existing law satisfied the United States' obligations in adhering to the Convention, its provisions are not enforceable through any action brought pursuant to the Convention itself, and neither adherence to the Convention nor the implementing legislation expands or reduces any rights under federal, state, or common law to claim authorship of a work or to object to any distortion, mutilation, or other modification of a work. See *id.* §§ 2, 3.

Two years later Congress enacted the Visual Artists Rights Act of 1990 (VARA or Act), Pub.L. No. 101–650 (tit. VI), 104 Stat. 5089, 5128–33 (1990). Construing this Act constitutes the subject of the present appeal. The Act

> protects both the reputations of certain visual artists and the works of art they create. It provides these artists with the rights of "attribution" and "integrity." . . . These rights are analogous to those protected by Article 6*bis* of the Berne Convention, which are commonly known as "moral rights." The theory of moral rights is that they result in a climate of artistic worth and honor that encourages the author in the arduous act of creation.

H.R.Rep. No. 514 at 5 (internal quote omitted). The Act brings to fruition Emerson's insightful observation.

Its principal provisions afford protection only to authors of works of visual art—a narrow class of art defined to include paintings, drawings, prints, sculptures, or photographs produced for exhibition purposes, existing in a single copy or limited edition of 200 copies or fewer. 17 U.S.C. § 101. With numerous exceptions, VARA grants three rights: the right of attribution, the right of integrity and, in the case of works of visual art of "recognized stature," the right to prevent destruction. 17 U.S.C. § 106A. For works created on or after June 1, 1991—the effective date of the Act—the rights provided for endure for the life of the author or, in the case of a joint work, the life of the last surviving author. The rights cannot be transferred, but may be waived by a writing signed by the author. Copyright registration is not required to bring an action for infringement of the rights granted under VARA, or to secure statutory damages and attorney's fees. All remedies available under copyright law, other than criminal remedies, are available in an action for infringement of moral rights. With this historical background in hand, we pass to the merits of the present litigation.

II. Work of Visual Art

Because VARA is relatively new, a fuller explication of it is helpful. In analyzing the Act, therefore, we will follow in order the definition set forth in § 101, as did the district court when presiding over this litigation. The district court determined that the work of art installed in the lobby of Associates' building was a work of visual art as defined by VARA; that distortion, mutilation, or modification of the work would prejudice plaintiffs' honor and reputations; that the work was of recognized stature, thus protecting it from destruction (including removal that would result in destruction); and that Associates consented to or ratified the installation of the work in its building. The result was that defendants were enjoined from removing or otherwise altering the work during the lifetimes of the three artists.

* * *

B. The Statutory Definition

A "work of visual art" is defined by the Act in terms both positive (what it is) and negative (what it is not). In relevant part VARA defines a work of visual art as "a painting, drawing, print, or sculpture, existing in a single copy" or in a limited edition of 200 copies or fewer. 17 U.S.C. § 101. Although defendants aver that elements of the work are not visual art, their contention is foreclosed by the factual finding that the work is a single, indivisible whole. Concededly, considered as a whole, the work is a sculpture and exists only in a single copy. Therefore, the work satisfies the Act's positive definition of a work of visual art. We next turn to the second part of the statutory definition—what is not a work of visual art.

The definition of visual art excludes "any poster, map, globe, chart, technical drawing, diagram, model, applied art, motion picture or other audio-visual work." 17 U.S.C. § 101. Congress meant to distinguish works of visual art from other media, such as audio-visual works and motion pictures, due to the different circumstances surrounding how works of each genre are created and disseminated. Although this concern led to a narrow definition of works of visual art,

> [t]he courts should use common sense and generally accepted standards of the artistic community in determining whether a particular work falls within the scope of the definition. Artists may work in a variety of media, and use any number of materials in creating their works. Therefore, whether a particular work falls within the definition should not depend on the medium or materials used.

H.R.Rep. No. 514 at 11.

"Applied art" describes "two-and three-dimensional ornamentation or decoration that is affixed to otherwise utilitarian objects." Defendants' assertion that at least parts of the work are applied art appears to rest on the fact that some of the sculptural elements are affixed to the lobby's floor, walls, and ceiling—all utilitarian objects. Interpreting applied art to include such works would render meaningless VARA's protection for works of visual art installed in buildings. A court should not read one part of a statute so as to deprive another part of meaning.

Appellants do not suggest the entire work is applied art. The district court correctly stated that even if components of the work standing alone were applied art, "nothing in VARA proscribes protection of works of visual art that incorporate elements of, rather than constitute, applied art." VARA's legislative history leaves no doubt that "a new and independent work created from snippets of [excluded] materials, such as a collage, is of course not excluded" from the definition of a work of visual art. H.R.Rep. No. 514 at 14. The trial judge correctly ruled the work is not applied art precluded from protection under the Act.

III.   Work Made for Hire

Also excluded from the definition of a work of visual art is any work made for hire. 17 U.S.C. § 1012(B). A "work made for hire" is defined in the Copyright Act, in relevant part, as "a work prepared by an employee within the scope of his or her employment." *Id.* § 101(1). Appellants maintain the work was made for hire and therefore is not a work of visual art under VARA. * * *

[The court of appeals determines that the work is in fact a work made for hire, and thus, for this reason, does not qualify for protection under VARA.]

John Swing, left, John Carter and John Veronis with their sculpture.
Sara Krulwich/The New York Times/Redux. © 1995, New York Times.

NOTES AND QUESTIONS

1. *Moral rights.* American copyright focuses almost exclusively on authors' economic interests, providing financial incentives to induce authors to create and disseminate their works—to the ultimate enrichment of the public. Other countries have taken a less pragmatic view in establishing authors' rights, emphasizing authors' personal, as well as economic, investment in their work. Those rights directed to the author's personal interests are referred to generally as "droit moral," or "moral rights." Moral rights protect the author's personal interest in professional honor, reputation, unfettered self-expression, and privacy. As one scholar has explained: "The notion is that the work of art is an expression of the artist's personality. Distortion, dismemberment or misrepresentation of the work mistreats an expression of the artist's personality, affects his artistic identity, personality, and honor, and thus impairs a legally protected personality interest." Merryman, *The Refrigerator of Bernard Buffet*, 27 Hastings L.J. 1023, 1027 (1976).

What explains the strong opposition to adoption of moral rights in the United States? As the Second Circuit notes in the *Carter* case, when Congress ultimately ratified the Berne Convention, it determined that in combination, a range of existing federal and state law doctrines were sufficient to satisfy the United States' Article 6*bis* obligations, so that no further legislation would be needed:

> [T]here is a composite of laws in this country that provides the kind of protection envisioned by Article 6*bis*. Federal laws include 17 U.S.C. § 106, relating to derivative works; 17 U.S.C. § 115(a)(2), relating to distortions of musical works used under the compulsory license respecting sound recordings; 17 U.S.C. § 203, relating to termination of transfers and licenses; and section 43(a) of the Lanham Act, relating to false designations of origin and false descriptions. State and local laws include those relating to publicity, contractual violations, fraud and misrepresentation, unfair competition, defamation, and invasion of privacy. In addition, eight states have recently enacted specific statutes protecting the rights of integrity and paternity in certain works of art. * * *

Berne Convention Implementation Act of 1988, H.R. Rep. No. 609, 100th Cong., 2d Sess. 33–34 (1988).

While Congress appears to have relied on the availability of Lanham Act § 43(a) (which prohibits "false designations of origin" in connection with goods) in determining that the United States fulfilled its Berne obligation to provide moral rights, a subsequent Supreme Court decision has undercut the ability of authors to rely on § 43(a) for protection of their attribution interests. In *Dastar Corp. v. Twentieth Century Fox Film Corp.*, 539 U.S. 23, 123 S.Ct. 2041, 156 L.Ed.2d 18 (2003), the Court found that Lanham Act § 43(a) should be construed narrowly to avoid providing moral rights-like protection to authors. Ironically, the Court reasoned that to do otherwise would undercut Congress' purpose in limiting moral rights protection, under VARA, to a very narrow range of subject matter and situations.

State statutory moral rights provisions tend to be limited to works of "visual art" or "fine art," as defined under each state's law, and vary significantly in their scope and focus. Some of the statutes focus on the artist's (or the public's) interest in the preservation of works of art, and thus prevent destruction of original works. Other statutes protect both original works and reproductions, but do not necessarily prevent destruction. Rather, they restrict unauthorized alterations of works, and/or the subsequent publication or public display of altered works. The primary focus of these statutes is protection of the artist's reputation and interest in self-expression. For example, the New York statute, N.Y. Art & Cult. Aff. Law § 14.03 (McKinney Supp. 1999–2000), prohibits knowing, unauthorized publication or public display of a mutilated work of fine art if the publication or display expressly or impliedly indicates that the work is that of the artist and is reasonably likely to damage the artist's reputation. *Id.*, § 14.03(1). Compare the California statute, Cal. Civ. Code § 987 (West Supp. 2000). This statute provides that "the physical alteration or destruction of fine art, which is an expression of the artist's personality, is detrimental to the artist's reputation," and that there is "a public interest in preserving the integrity of cultural and artistic creations." *Id.*, § 987(a). It prohibits persons other than the artist from intentionally committing or authorizing "any physical defacement, mutilation, alteration, or destruction of a work of fine art." *Id.*, § 987(c). Note that many of the statutes also recognize the fine artist's right of attribution. For example, the New York statute grants the artist the right to claim authorship, or, "for just and valid reason," to disclaim authorship of a work. *Id.*, § 14.03(2). Because Congress has subsequently enacted the narrow moral rights provision for works of visual art in VARA, causes of action under these state moral rights statutes may be preempted. See 17 U.S.C.A. § 301(f).

2. *The Visual Artists Rights Act of 1990.* Even though Congress concluded that the United States complied with the requirements of Berne Convention Article 6*bis*, it continued to consider the issue of moral rights and, just two years after implementing the Berne Convention, enacted the Visual Artists Rights Act of 1990, Pub. L. No. 101–650, 104 Stat. 5128–5133 ("VARA"), which is codified in Copyright Act §§ 101 (definition of "a work of visual art"), 106A and 113(d). VARA constituted the first express recognition of moral rights in United States copyright law. Congress justified its decision in the accompanying House Report:

> "The theory of moral rights is that they result in a climate of artistic worth and honor that encourages the author in the arduous act of creation." Artist's rights are consistent with the purpose behind the copyright laws and the Constitutional provision they implement: "To promote the Progress of Science and useful Arts." * * *

> * * * These rights:

> promote * * * the interests of artists and public alike. [T]hey benefit artists by assuring their rights to recognition for the works they have created and by protecting the works themselves against destruction or mutilation. These safeguards may enhance the creative environment in which artists labor. Equally important, these safeguards enhance our cultural heritage. The attribution right not only affords

basic fairness to artists, it promotes the public interest by increasing available information concerning art works and their provenance, and by helping ensure that information is accurate. The integrity right helps preserve art works intact for all of us to enjoy.

H.R. Rep. No. 514, 101st Cong., 2d Sess. 5, 14 (1990) (*quoting The Visual Artists Rights Act of 1989: Hearings on H.R. 2690 Before the Subcommittee on Courts, Intellectual Property, and the Administration of Justice of the House Committee on the Judiciary*, 101st Cong., 1st Sess. (Statement of the Honorable Ralph Oman) (1989); U.S. Const. Art. I, § 8, cl. 8; *Hearings on H.R. 2690, supra,* (statement of Prof. Jane C. Ginsburg)).

3. *Works of "visual art."* Study the Copyright Act § 101 definition of "works of visual art." Why should VARA's protection be restricted to original and limited edition copies? Why should protection be denied in the case of works of applied art and works for hire? The § 101 definition of "works of visual art" specifies that a work of visual art "does not include" any "merchandising item or advertising, promotional or descriptive" material. How is one to determine whether a painting, for example, is a "work of visual art" or "promotional" material?

In *Pollara v. Seymour*, 344 F.3d 265, 269 (2d Cir. 2003), the Court of Appeals for the Second Circuit held that resolution of the latter issue must turn on the intended purpose of the work:

> Protection of a work under VARA will often depend * * * upon the work's objective and evident purpose. VARA does not protect advertising, promotional, or utilitarian works, and does not protect works for hire, regardless of their artistic merit, their medium, or their value to the artist or the market. VARA may protect a sculpture that looks like a piece of furniture, but it does not protect a piece of utilitarian furniture, whether or not it could arguably be called a sculpture. Drawings and paintings are protected, but only if they do not advertise or promote.

Id. In *Pollara*, the work at issue was a 10' x 30' banner depicting a tableau of two dozen stylized people, standing in line against a background of shut doors labeled "Public Defender," "Legal Aid" and "Prisoners' Legal Services." The people patiently awaited entry to an open door marked "Lawyer," inside of which sat a person at a desk. Many of the diverse mix of people waiting in line were holding rectangles of paper. Large lettering across the top and left read: "Executive Budget Threatens Right to Counsel" and "Preserve the Right to Counsel–Now More than Ever." The artist painted this banner for a non-profit group that provided legal services to the poor. The group set it up behind an information table in a downtown plaza as part of its annual one-day legislative effort known as "Lobbying Day." The Second Circuit found that while the banner might be "visually appealing" and demonstrate "a great deal of artistic ability and creativity," it did not constitute a work of visual art for purposes of VARA protection, because it was created for the primary purpose of promoting or advertising. *Id.* at 271. The court reasoned that the banner "was created for the purpose of drawing attention to an information desk, as part of a lobbying effort, and the banner overtly promotes in word and picture a lobbying message." *Id.* at 270. While the banner did not provide the name of the organization that commissioned it, the court found it relevant that the organization had itself determined the banner's content.

4. *The § 106A rights.* Study the provisions of Copyright Act § 106A. What is the relationship between the artist's inalienable right of integrity and the copyright owner's right to make derivative works? Are these rights likely to conflict? How might an artist establish prejudice to his honor or reputation, as required in § 106A(a)(2) and (3)(A), or that his work is of recognized stature, as required in 106A(a)(3)(B)? The district court in *Carter v. Helmsley–Spear* undertook to provide the first judicial answers to some of these questions. Since the Second Circuit did not address these questions in reversing the district court, the district court's reasoning remains influential.

The district court first considered whether "intentional distortion, mutilation, or modification" of the plaintiffs' work would be "prejudicial to plaintiffs' honor or reputation." It found that the drafters of VARA intended courts to apply the ordinary dictionary meanings of "prejudice," "honor" and "reputation." The question was whether "alteration would cause injury to plaintiffs' good name, public esteem, or reputation in the artistic community." *Id.*, 861 F.Supp. at 323. The court rejected the defendants' expert witness' testimony that "alteration of the work would not adversely impact plaintiffs' reputation because, in his opinion, the artists have no reputation." *Id.*, at 324. The court observed that the artist need not have a reputation independent of the particular work of art at issue—Congress intended to protect less-known or appreciated artists, as well as famous ones. Thus, the court found, the appropriate framework is to focus on the professional honor or reputation of the plaintiff "as embodied in the work that is protected." *Id.*

The district court then turned to the issue of whether the work at issue was one of "recognized stature." The court observed:

> The phrase "recognized stature" is not defined in VARA. In light of the preservative goal of this Section, however, the recognized stature requirement is best viewed as a gate-keeping mechanism—protection is afforded only to those works that art experts, the art community, or society in general views as possessing stature. A plaintiff need not demonstrate that his or her art work is equal in stature to that created by artists such as Picasso, Chagall, or Giacometti. As one commentator has noted, "The advantages of the 'of recognized stature' qualification include barring nuisance law suits, such as [a law suit over] the destruction of a five-year-old's finger painting by her class mate. . . ." Damich, *The Visual Artists Rights Act of 1990: Toward a Federal System of Moral Rights Protection for Visual Art*, 39 Cath.U.L.Rev. 945, 954 (1990). Nor must the trier of fact personally find the art to be aesthetically pleasing; indeed, courts have persistently shunned the role of art critic.

> The recognized stature requirement must be interpreted in such manner as to maintain the preservative purpose of 17 U.S.C. § 106(a)(3)(B) and in light of this Section's plain meaning. Thus, for a work of visual art to be protected under this Section, a plaintiff must make a two-tiered showing: (1) that the visual art in question has "stature," i.e. is viewed as meritorious, and (2) that this stature is "recognized" by art experts, other members of the artistic community, or

by some cross-section of society. In making this showing, plaintiffs generally, but not inevitably, will need to call expert witnesses to testify before the trier of fact. * * *

Id., 861 F.Supp. at 324–25.

PROBLEMS

1. Comedy Group creates scripts, which the British Broadcasting Corp. (BBC) uses to make a television series. The agreement between Comedy Group and BBC provides that the BBC can make no major changes to a script in the course of producing the series without consulting first with Comedy Group. Nothing in the agreement authorizes the BBC to make changes in a program after it is recorded. The BBC has the right to license broadcast of the television series programs overseas, but the agreement specifies that Comedy Group retains all other rights in the scripts.

BBC licenses American Broadcasting Corp. (ABC) to broadcast several of the television series programs to the U.S. public. The BBC/ABC licensing agreement permits editing for "insertion of commercials, applicable censorship or governmental rules and regulations, and National Association of Broadcasters and time segment requirements." Pursuant to this agreement, ABC edits the programs prior to showing them, taking out "obscene and objectionable" material and making time for advertisements. All told, ABC chops over 1/4 of the original material out of the programs. Some of the deleted material is crucial to the plots and punch lines of the skits. ABC then broadcasts some of the programs. Comedy Group sues. Can it state a cause of action?

2. In 1995, A, a fine-art photographer, took a photograph of an elderly woman gazing at children in an urban park. Due to A's method of capturing the sunlight, her composition and her use of special filters, the photograph had a highly artistic, spiritual quality. A titled the photograph "Time Passes," and created three copies, which she signed and numbered and displayed for sale in galleries.

The following year, A sold the negative of "Time Passes" and the copyright in the photograph to B, a publisher who wished to include the photograph in a high quality "coffee table" book of photographs of urban scenes. Due to a mix-up, when the book was published it identified Z as the photographer of "Time Passes."

B later sold the negative and copyright to C, a manufacturer of nick-knacks. C used the negative to produce ash trays. "Time Passes" was laminated onto the bottom of each ash tray, where users would stub out their cigarette butts. Because of the lamination process and the cheap materials C used, the colors were very different than the colors in the negative.

Meanwhile, the gallery sold one of A's copies of "Time Passes" to X. X died, and his heir, D, inherited the copy of "Time Passes." D, a multimedia artist, cut the elderly woman's face out of the copy and combined it with cuttings from other photographs and materials to make his own work.

Have there been any violations of § 106A?

3. The owner of an original metal sculpture allows it to rust through lack of proper maintenance. Under VARA, is this a violation of the artist's right of integrity in the sculpture?

4. Shopping mall owns an original sculpture of geese in flight. During the Christmas shopping season it ties red ribbons around the geese's necks. Does this constitute a violation of VARA?

5. Church commissions an artist to create a mural on the back wall of the church sanctuary in 1993. The reaction of the congregation to the finished product is mixed. Some members think it is merely ugly and lacking in artistic merit. Others find it generally offensive, and the rest find it sacrilegious. They would all like to remove it from their sanctuary wall. Under what circumstances will VARA permit it?

I. INDIRECT INFRINGEMENT

FONOVISA, INC. v. CHERRY AUCTION, INC.

United States Court of Appeals, Ninth Circuit, 1996.
76 F.3d 259.

SCHROEDER, CIRCUIT JUDGE:

This is a copyright and trademark enforcement action against the operators of a swap meet, sometimes called a flea market, where third-party vendors routinely sell counterfeit recordings that infringe on the plaintiff's copyrights and trademarks. The district court dismissed on the pleadings, holding that the plaintiffs, as a matter of law, could not maintain any cause of action against the swap meet for sales by vendors who leased its premises.

BACKGROUND

The plaintiff and appellant is Fonovisa, Inc., a California corporation that owns copyrights and trademarks to Latin/Hispanic music recordings. Fonovisa filed this action in district court against defendant-appellee, Cherry Auction, Inc., and its individual operators (collectively "Cherry Auction"). For purposes of this appeal, it is undisputed that Cherry Auction operates a swap meet in Fresno, California, similar to many other swap meets in this country where customers come to purchase various merchandise from individual vendors. The vendors pay a daily rental fee to the swap meet operators in exchange for booth space. Cherry Auction supplies parking, conducts advertising and retains the right to exclude any vendor for any reason, at any time, and thus can exclude vendors for patent and trademark infringement. In addition, Cherry Auction receives an entrance fee from each customer who attends the swap meet.

There is also no dispute for purposes of this appeal that Cherry Auction and its operators were aware that vendors in their swap meet were selling counterfeit recordings in violation of Fonovisa's trademarks and copyrights. Indeed, it is alleged that in 1991, the Fresno County Sheriff's Department raided the Cherry Auction swap meet and seized more than 38,000 counterfeit recordings. The following year, after finding that vendors at the Cherry Auction swap meet were still selling counterfeit recordings, the Sheriff sent a letter notifying Cherry Auction of the on-going sales of infringing materials, and reminding Cherry Auction that they had agreed to provide the Sheriff with identifying information from each vendor. In addition, in 1993, Fonovisa itself sent an investigator to the Cherry Auction site and observed sales of counterfeit recordings.

* * *

The copyright claims are brought pursuant to 17 U.S.C. §§ 101 *et seq.* Although the Copyright Act does not expressly impose liability on anyone other than direct infringers, courts have long recognized that in certain circumstances, vicarious or contributory liability will be imposed. *See Sony Corp. of America v. Universal City Studios, Inc.*, 464 U.S. 417, 435, 104 S.Ct. 774, 785, 78 L.Ed.2d 574 (1984) (explaining that "vicarious liability is imposed in virtually all areas of the law, and the concept of contributory infringement is merely a species of the broader problem of identifying circumstances in which it is just to hold one individually accountable for the actions of another").

* * *

VICARIOUS COPYRIGHT INFRINGEMENT

The concept of vicarious copyright liability was developed in the Second Circuit as an outgrowth of the agency principles of respondeat superior. The landmark case on vicarious liability for sales of counterfeit recordings is *Shapiro, Bernstein and Co. v. H.L. Green Co.*, 316 F.2d 304 (2d Cir.1963). In *Shapiro*, the court was faced with a copyright infringement suit against the owner of a chain of department stores where a concessionaire was selling counterfeit recordings. Noting that the normal agency rule of respondeat superior imposes liability on an employer for copyright infringements by an employee, the court endeavored to fashion a principle for enforcing copyrights against a defendant whose economic interests were intertwined with the direct infringer's, but who did not actually employ the direct infringer.

The *Shapiro* court looked at the two lines of cases it perceived as most clearly relevant. In one line of cases, the landlord-tenant cases, the courts had held that a landlord who lacked knowledge of the infringing acts of its tenant and who exercised no control over the leased premises was not liable for infringing sales by its tenant. In the other line of cases, the so-called "dance hall cases," the operator of an entertainment venue was held liable for infringing performances when the operator (1) could control the premises and (2) obtained a direct financial benefit from the audience, who paid to enjoy the infringing performance.

From those two lines of cases, the *Shapiro* court determined that the relationship between the store owner and the concessionaire in the case before it was closer to the dance-hall model than to the landlord-tenant model. It imposed liability even though the defendant was unaware of the infringement. *Shapiro* deemed the imposition of vicarious liability neither unduly harsh nor unfair because the store proprietor had the power to cease the conduct of the concessionaire, and because the proprietor derived an obvious and direct financial benefit from the infringement. The test was more clearly articulated in a later Second Circuit case as follows: "even in the absence of an employer-employee relationship one may be vicariously liable if he has the right and ability to supervise the infringing activity and also has a direct financial interest in such activities." *Gershwin Publishing Corp. v. Columbia Artists Management, Inc.,* 443 F.2d 1159, 1162 (2d Cir.1971). * * *

The district court in this case agreed with defendant Cherry Auction that Fonovisa did not, as a matter of law, meet either the control or the financial benefit prong of the vicarious copyright infringement test articulated in *Gershwin, supra.* Rather, the district court concluded that based on the pleadings, "Cherry Auction neither supervised nor profited from the vendors' sales." In the district court's view, with respect to both control and financial benefit, Cherry Auction was in the same position as an absentee landlord who has surrendered its exclusive right of occupancy in its leased property to its tenants.

This analogy to absentee landlord is not in accord with the facts as alleged in the district court and which we, for purposes of appeal, must accept. The allegations below were that vendors occupied small booths within premises that Cherry Auction controlled and patrolled. According to the complaint, Cherry Auction had the right to terminate vendors for any reason whatsoever and through that right had the ability to control the activities of vendors on the premises. In addition, Cherry Auction promoted the swap meet and controlled the access of customers to the swap meet area. In terms of control, the allegations before us are strikingly similar to those in *Shapiro* and *Gershwin.*

In *Shapiro,* for example, the court focused on the formal licensing agreement between defendant department store and the direct infringer-concessionaire. There, the concessionaire selling the bootleg recordings had a licensing agreement with the department store (H.L. Green Company) that required the concessionaire and its employees to "abide by, observe and obey all regulations promulgated from time to time by the H.L. Green Company," and H.L. Green Company had the "unreviewable discretion" to discharge the concessionaires' employees. In practice, H.L. Green Company was not actively involved in the sale of records and the concessionaire controlled and supervised the individual employees. Nevertheless, H.L. Green's ability to police its concessionaire—which parallels Cherry Auction's ability to police its vendors under Cherry Auction's similarly broad contract with its vendors—was sufficient to satisfy the control requirement.

In *Gershwin,* the defendant lacked the formal, contractual ability to control the direct infringer. Nevertheless, because of defendant's "pervasive participation in the formation and direction" of the direct infringers, including promoting them (i.e. creating an audience for them), the court found that defendants were in a position to police the direct infringers and held that the control element was satisfied. As the promoter and organizer of the swap meet, Cherry Auction wields the same level of control over the direct infringers as did the *Gershwin* defendant. * * *

The district court's dismissal of the vicarious liability claim in this case was therefore not justified on the ground that the complaint failed to allege sufficient control.

We next consider the issue of financial benefit. The plaintiff's allegations encompass many substantive benefits to Cherry Auction from the infringing sales. These include the payment of a daily rental fee by each of the infringing vendors; a direct payment to Cherry Auction by each customer in the form of an admission fee, and incidental payments for parking, food and other services by customers seeking to purchase infringing recordings.

Cherry Auction nevertheless contends that these benefits cannot satisfy the financial benefit prong of vicarious liability because a commission, directly tied to the sale of particular infringing items, is required. They ask that we restrict the financial benefit prong to the precise facts presented in *Shapiro*, where defendant H.L. Green Company received a 10 or 12 per cent commission from the direct infringers' gross receipts. Cherry Auction points to the low daily rental fee paid by each vendor, discounting all other financial benefits flowing to the swap meet, and asks that we hold that the swap meet is materially similar to a mere landlord. The facts alleged by Fonovisa, however, reflect that the defendants reap substantial financial benefits from admission fees, concession stand sales and parking fees, all of which flow directly from customers who want to buy the counterfeit recordings at bargain basement prices. The plaintiff has sufficiently alleged direct financial benefit.

Our conclusion is fortified by the continuing line of cases, starting with the dance hall cases, imposing vicarious liability on the operator of a business where infringing performances enhance the attractiveness of the venue to potential customers. * * *

Plaintiffs have stated a claim for vicarious copyright infringement.

CONTRIBUTORY COPYRIGHT INFRINGEMENT

Contributory infringement originates in tort law and stems from the notion that one who directly contributes to another's infringement should be held accountable. * * * Contributory infringement has been described as an outgrowth of enterprise liability, and imposes liability where one person knowingly contributes to the infringing conduct of another. The classic statement of the doctrine is in *Gershwin*, 443 F.2d 1159, 1162: "[O]ne who, with knowledge of the infringing activity, induces, causes or materially contributes to the infringing conduct of another, may be held liable as a 'contributory' infringer."

There is no question that plaintiff adequately alleged the element of knowledge in this case. The disputed issue is whether plaintiff adequately alleged that Cherry Auction materially contributed to the infringing activity. We have little difficulty in holding that the allegations in this case are sufficient to show material contribution to the infringing activity. Indeed, it would be difficult for the infringing activity to take place in the massive quantities alleged without the support services provided by the swap meet. These services include, inter alia, the provision of space, utilities, parking, advertising, plumbing, and customers.

Here again Cherry Auction asks us to ignore all aspects of the enterprise described by the plaintiffs, to concentrate solely on the rental of space, and to hold that the swap meet provides nothing more. Yet Cherry Auction actively strives to provide the environment and the market for counterfeit recording sales to thrive. Its participation in the sales cannot be termed "passive," as Cherry Auction would prefer.

The district court apparently took the view that contribution to infringement should be limited to circumstances in which the defendant "expressly promoted or encouraged the sale of counterfeit products, or in some manner protected the identity of the infringers." 847 F.Supp. 1492, 1496. Given the allegations that the local sheriff lawfully requested that Cherry Auction gather and share basic, identifying information about its vendors, and that Cherry Auction failed to comply, the defendant appears to qualify within the last portion of the district court's own standard that posits liability for protecting infringers' identities. Moreover, we agree with the Third Circuit's analysis in *Columbia Pictures Industries, Inc. v. Aveco, Inc.*, 800 F.2d 59 (3d Cir.1986) that providing the site and facilities for known infringing activity is sufficient to establish contributory liability.

NOTES AND QUESTIONS

1. *Vicarious liability.* The vicarious liability doctrine is based on principles similar to those underlying the tort doctrine of *respondeat superior*, but, as the *Fonovisa* decision demonstrates, it requires no strict employment relationship. How does a landlord's position differ from that of a dance hall operator? Why should the courts reason that a landlord does not stand to benefit from its tenant's copyright infringement?

Some case opinions have found officers and directors of closely held corporations vicariously liable for their corporation's direct copyright infringement, when it is demonstrated that they had the ability to control the corporation's actions and stood to gain financially—for example, through salary bonuses, increased dividends or increased share value. In some cases, courts have found such vicarious liability even when the officer did not herself participate in the infringement, or know of it. See, e.g., Mallven Music v. 2001 VIP of Lexington, Inc., 230 U.S.P.Q. 543 (E.D.Ky.1986). Does this give copyright plaintiffs an advantage over plaintiffs seeking to hold officers and directors personally liable for other types of corporate wrongs, such as corporate breaches of contract or personal injuries? Should it?

METRO–GOLDWYN–MAYER STUDIOS, INC. v. GROKSTER

United States Supreme Court, 2005.
545 U.S. 913, 125 S.Ct. 2764, 162 L.Ed.2d 781.

JUSTICE SOUTER delivered the opinion of the Court.

The question is under what circumstances the distributor of a product capable of both lawful and unlawful use is liable for acts of copyright infringement by third parties using the product. * * *

I

A

Respondents, Grokster, Ltd., and StreamCast Networks, Inc., * * * distribute free software products that allow computer users to share electronic files through peer-to-peer networks, so called because users' computers communicate directly with each other, not through central servers. * * *

* * * A group of copyright holders (MGM for short, but including motion picture studios, recording companies, songwriters, and music publishers) sued Grokster and StreamCast for their users' copyright infringements, alleging that they knowingly and intentionally distributed their software to enable users to reproduce and distribute the copyrighted works in violation of the Copyright Act, 17 U.S.C. § 101 *et seq.*

* * *

* * * Grokster and StreamCast use no servers to intercept the content of the search requests or to mediate the file transfers conducted by users of the software, there being no central point through which the substance of the communications passes in either direction.

Although Grokster and StreamCast do not therefore know when particular files are copied, a few searches using their software would show what is available on the networks the software reaches. MGM commissioned a statistician to conduct a systematic search, and his study showed that nearly 90% of the files available for download on the FastTrack system were copyrighted works. Grokster and StreamCast dispute this figure * * *. They also argue that potential noninfringing uses of their software are significant in kind, even if infrequent in practice. Some musical performers, for example, have gained new audiences by distributing their copyrighted works for free across peer-to-peer networks, and some distributors of unprotected content have used peer-to-peer networks to disseminate files, Shakespeare being an example. Indeed, StreamCast has given Morpheus users the opportunity to download the briefs in this very case, though their popularity has not been quantified.

As for quantification, the parties' anecdotal and statistical evidence entered thus far to show the content available on the FastTrack and

Gnutella networks does not say much about which files are actually downloaded by users, and no one can say how often the software is used to obtain copies of unprotected material. But MGM's evidence gives reason to think that the vast majority of users' downloads are acts of infringement, and because well over 100 million copies of the software in question are known to have been downloaded, and billions of files are shared across the FastTrack and Gnutella networks each month, the probable scope of copyright infringement is staggering.

Grokster and StreamCast concede the infringement in most downloads, and it is uncontested that they are aware that users employ their software primarily to download copyrighted files, even if the decentralized FastTrack and Gnutella networks fail to reveal which files are being copied, and when. From time to time, moreover, the companies have learned about their users' infringement directly, as from users who have sent e-mail to each company with questions about playing copyrighted movies they had downloaded, to whom the companies have responded with guidance. And MGM notified the companies of 8 million copyrighted files that could be obtained using their software.

Grokster and StreamCast are not, however, merely passive recipients of information about infringing use. The record is replete with evidence that from the moment Grokster and StreamCast began to distribute their free software, each one clearly voiced the objective that recipients use it to download copyrighted works, and each took active steps to encourage infringement.

After the notorious file-sharing service, Napster, was sued by copyright holders for facilitation of copyright infringement, *A & M Records, Inc. v. Napster, Inc.,* 114 F.Supp.2d 896 (N.D.Cal.2000), aff'd in part, rev'd in part, 239 F.3d 1004 (C.A.9 2001), StreamCast gave away a software program of a kind known as OpenNap, designed as compatible with the Napster program and open to Napster users for downloading files from other Napster and OpenNap users' computers. Evidence indicates that "[i]t was always [StreamCast's] intent to use [its OpenNap network] to be able to capture email addresses of [its] initial target market so that [it] could promote [its] StreamCast Morpheus interface to them,"; indeed, the OpenNap program was engineered " 'to leverage Napster's 50 million user base.' "

StreamCast monitored both the number of users downloading its OpenNap program and the number of music files they downloaded. It also used the resulting OpenNap network to distribute copies of the Morpheus software and to encourage users to adopt it. Internal company documents indicate that StreamCast hoped to attract large numbers of former Napster users if that company was shut down by court order or otherwise, and that StreamCast planned to be the next Napster. A kit developed by StreamCast to be delivered to advertisers, for example, contained press articles about StreamCast's potential to capture former Napster users, and it introduced itself to some potential advertisers as a company "which is similar to what Napster was." It broadcast banner advertisements to users of other Napster-compatible software, urging them to adopt its OpenNap. An internal e-mail from a company executive stated: " 'We have put this network in place so that when Napster pulls the plug on their free service . . . or if the Court orders them shut down prior to that . . . we will be positioned to capture the flood of their 32 million users that will be actively looking for an alternative.' "

Thus, StreamCast developed promotional materials to market its service as the best Napster alternative. * * * StreamCast even planned to flaunt the illegal uses of its software; when it launched the OpenNap network, the chief technology officer of the company averred that "[t]he goal is to get in trouble with the law and get sued. It's the best way to get in the new[s]."

The evidence that Grokster sought to capture the market of former Napster users is sparser but revealing, for Grokster launched its own OpenNap system called Swaptor and inserted digital codes into its Web site so that computer users using Web search engines to look for "Napster" or "[f]ree filesharing" would be directed to the Grokster Web site, where they could download the Grokster software. And Grokster's name is an apparent derivative of Napster.

StreamCast's executives monitored the number of songs by certain commercial artists available on their networks, and an internal communication indicates they aimed to have a larger number of copyrighted songs available on their networks than other file-sharing networks. The point, of course, would be to attract users of a mind to infringe, just as it would be with their promotional materials developed showing copyrighted songs as examples of the kinds of files available through Morpheus. Morpheus in fact allowed users to search specifically for "Top 40" songs, which were inevitably copyrighted. Similarly, Grokster sent users a newsletter promoting its ability to provide particular, popular copyrighted materials.

In addition to this evidence of express promotion, marketing, and intent * * *, the business models employed by Grokster and StreamCast confirm that their principal object was use of their software to download copyrighted works. Grokster and StreamCast receive no revenue from users, who obtain the software itself for nothing. Instead, both companies generate income by selling advertising space, and they stream the advertising to Grokster and Morpheus users while they are employing the programs. As the number of users of each program increases, advertising opportunities become worth more. While there is doubtless some demand for free Shakespeare, the evidence shows that substantive volume is a function of free access to copyrighted work. Users seeking Top 40 songs, for example, or the latest release by Modest Mouse, are certain to be far more numerous than those seeking a free Decameron, and Grokster and StreamCast translated that demand into dollars.

Finally, there is no evidence that either company made an effort to filter copyrighted material from users' downloads or otherwise impede the sharing of copyrighted files. Although Grokster appears to have sent e-mails warning users about infringing content when it received threatening notice from the copyright holders, it never blocked anyone from continuing to use its software to share copyrighted files. StreamCast not only rejected another company's offer of help to monitor infringement, but blocked the Internet Protocol addresses of entities it believed were trying to engage in such monitoring on its networks.

B

After discovery, the parties on each side of the case cross-moved for summary judgment. * * * The District Court held that those who used the Grokster and Morpheus software to download copyrighted media files directly infringed MGM's copyrights, a conclusion not contested on appeal, but the court nonetheless granted summary judgment in favor of Grokster and StreamCast as to any liability arising from distribution of the then current versions of their software. Distributing that software gave rise to no liability in the court's view, because its use did not provide the distributors with actual knowledge of specific acts of infringement.

The Court of Appeals affirmed. In the court's analysis, a defendant was liable as a contributory infringer when it had knowledge of direct infringement and materially contributed to the infringement. But the court read *Sony Corp. of America v. Universal City Studios, Inc.,* 464 U.S. 417, 104 S.Ct. 774, 78 L.Ed.2d 574 (1984), as holding that distribution of a commercial product capable of substantial noninfringing uses could not give rise to contributory liability for infringement unless the distributor had actual knowledge of specific instances of infringement and failed to act on that knowledge. The fact that the software was capable of substantial noninfringing uses in the Ninth Circuit's view meant that Grokster and StreamCast were not liable, because they had no such actual knowledge, owing to the decentralized architecture of their software. The court also held that Grokster and StreamCast did not materially contribute to their users' infringement because it was the users themselves who searched for, retrieved, and stored the infringing files, with no involvement by the defendants beyond providing the software in the first place.

The Ninth Circuit also considered whether Grokster and StreamCast could be liable under a theory of vicarious infringement. The court held against liability because the defendants did not monitor or control the use of the software, had no agreed-upon right or current ability to supervise its use, and had no independent duty to police infringement.

II

* * *

B

[T]his Court has dealt with secondary copyright infringement in only one recent case, and because MGM has tailored its principal claim to our opinion there, a look at our earlier holding is in order. In *Sony Corp. v.*

Universal City Studios, supra, this Court addressed a claim that secondary liability for infringement can arise from the very distribution of a commercial product. There, the product, novel at the time, was what we know today as the videocassette recorder or VCR. Copyright holders sued Sony as the manufacturer, claiming it was contributorily liable for infringement that occurred when VCR owners taped copyrighted programs because it supplied the means used to infringe, and it had constructive knowledge that infringement would occur. At the trial on the merits, the evidence showed that the principal use of the VCR was for " 'time-shifting,' " or taping a program for later viewing at a more convenient time, which the Court found to be a fair, not an infringing, use. There was no evidence that Sony had expressed an object of bringing about taping in violation of copyright or had taken active steps to increase its profits from unlawful taping. Although Sony's advertisements urged consumers to buy the VCR to " 'record favorite shows' " or " 'build a library' " of recorded programs, neither of these uses was necessarily infringing.

On those facts, with no evidence of stated or indicated intent to promote infringing uses, the only conceivable basis for imposing liability was on a theory of contributory infringement arising from its sale of VCRs to consumers with knowledge that some would use them to infringe. But because the VCR was "capable of commercially significant noninfringing uses," we held the manufacturer could not be faulted solely on the basis of its distribution.

This analysis reflected patent law's traditional staple article of commerce doctrine, now codified, that distribution of a component of a patented device will not violate the patent if it is suitable for use in other ways. 35 U.S.C. § 271(c). The doctrine was devised to identify instances in which it may be presumed from distribution of an article in commerce that the distributor intended the article to be used to infringe another's patent, and so may justly be held liable for that infringement. "One who makes and sells articles which are only adapted to be used in a patented combination will be presumed to intend the natural consequences of his acts; he will be presumed to intend that they shall be used in the combination of the patent."

In sum, where an article is "good for nothing else" but infringement, there is no legitimate public interest in its unlicensed availability, and there is no injustice in presuming or imputing an intent to infringe. Conversely, the doctrine absolves the equivocal conduct of selling an item with substantial lawful as well as unlawful uses, and limits liability to instances of more acute fault than the mere understanding that some of one's products will be misused. It leaves breathing room for innovation and a vigorous commerce.

The parties and many of the *amici* in this case think the key to resolving it is the *Sony* rule and, in particular, what it means for a product to be "capable of commercially significant noninfringing uses." *Sony Corp. v. Universal City Studios, supra,* at 442. MGM advances the argument that granting summary judgment to Grokster and StreamCast as to their current activities gave too much weight to the value of innovative technology, and too little to the copyrights infringed by users of their software, given that 90% of works available on one of the networks was shown to be copyrighted. Assuming the remaining 10% to be its noninfringing use, MGM says this should not qualify as "substantial," and the Court should quantify *Sony* to the extent of holding that a product used "principally" for infringement does not qualify. As mentioned before, Grokster and StreamCast reply by citing evidence that their software can be used to reproduce public domain works, and they point to copyright holders who actually encourage copying. Even if infringement is the principal practice with their software today, they argue, the noninfringing uses are significant and will grow.

We agree with MGM that the Court of Appeals misapplied *Sony,* which it read as limiting secondary liability quite beyond the circumstances to which the case applied. *Sony* barred secondary liability based on presuming or imputing intent to cause infringement solely from the design or distribution of a product capable of substantial lawful use, which the distributor knows is in fact used for infringement. The Ninth Circuit has read *Sony's* limitation to mean that whenever a product is capable of substantial lawful use, the producer can never be held contributorily liable for third parties' infringing use of it; it read the rule as being this broad, even when an actual purpose to cause infringing use is shown by evidence independent of design and distribution of the product, unless the distributors had "specific knowledge of infringement at a time at which they contributed to the infringement, and failed to act upon that information." Because the Circuit found the StreamCast and Grokster software capable of substantial lawful use, it concluded on the basis of its reading of *Sony* that neither company could be held liable, since there was no showing that their software, being without any central server, afforded them knowledge of specific unlawful uses.

This view of *Sony,* however, was error, converting the case from one about liability resting on imputed intent to one about liability on any theory. Because *Sony* did not displace other theories of secondary liability, and because we find below that it was error to grant summary judgment to the companies on MGM's inducement claim, we do not revisit *Sony* further, as MGM requests, to add a more quantified description of the point of balance between protection and commerce when liability rests solely on distribution with knowledge that unlawful use will occur. It is enough to note that the Ninth Circuit's judgment rested on an erroneous understanding of *Sony* and to leave further consideration of the *Sony* rule for a day when that may be required.

C

Sony's rule limits imputing culpable intent as a matter of law from the characteristics or uses of a distributed product. But nothing in *Sony* requires courts to ignore evidence of intent if there is such evidence, and the case was never meant to foreclose rules of fault-based liability derived from the common law.[10] * * * Thus, where evidence goes beyond a product's characteristics or the knowledge that it may be put to infringing uses, and shows statements or actions directed to promoting infringement, *Sony's* staple-article rule will not preclude liability.

* * *

* * * Evidence of "active steps . . . taken to encourage direct infringement," such as advertising an infringing use or instructing how to engage in an infringing use, show an affirmative intent that the product be used to infringe, and a showing that infringement was encouraged overcomes the law's reluctance to find liability when a defendant merely sells a commercial product suitable for some lawful use. * * *

For the same reasons that *Sony* took the staple-article doctrine of patent law as a model for its copyright safe-harbor rule, the inducement rule, too, is a sensible one for copyright. We adopt it here, holding that one who distributes a device with the object of promoting its use to infringe copyright, as shown by clear expression or other affirmative steps taken to foster infringement, is liable for the resulting acts of infringement by third parties. We are, of course, mindful of the need to keep from trenching on regular commerce or discouraging the development of technologies with lawful and unlawful potential. Accordingly, just as *Sony* did not find intentional inducement despite the knowledge of the VCR manufacturer that its device could be used to infringe, mere knowledge of infringing potential or of actual infringing uses would not be enough here to subject a distributor to liability. Nor would ordinary acts incident to product distribution, such as offering customers technical support or product updates, support liability in themselves. The inducement rule, instead, premises liability on purposeful, culpable expression and conduct, and thus does nothing to compromise legitimate commerce or discourage innovation having a lawful promise.

III

A

The only apparent question about treating MGM's evidence as sufficient to withstand summary judgment under the theory of inducement goes to the need on MGM's part to adduce evidence that StreamCast and Grokster communicated an inducing message to their software users. The classic instance of inducement is by advertisement or solicitation that broadcasts a message designed to stimulate others to commit violations. MGM claims that such a message is shown here. It is undisputed that StreamCast beamed onto the computer screens of users of Napster-compatible programs ads urging the adoption of its OpenNap program, which was designed, as its name implied, to invite the custom of patrons of Napster, then under attack in the courts for facilitating massive

---

10.   Nor does the Patent Act's exemption from liability for those who distribute a staple article of commerce, 35 U.S.C. § 271(c), extend to those who induce patent infringement, § 271(b).

infringement. Those who accepted StreamCast's OpenNap program were offered software to perform the same services, which a factfinder could conclude would readily have been understood in the Napster market as the ability to download copyrighted music files. Grokster distributed an electronic newsletter containing links to articles promoting its software's ability to access popular copyrighted music. And anyone whose Napster or free file-sharing searches turned up a link to Grokster would have understood Grokster to be offering the same file-sharing ability as Napster, and to the same people who probably used Napster for infringing downloads; that would also have been the understanding of anyone offered Grokster's suggestively named Swaptor software, its version of OpenNap. And both companies communicated a clear message by responding affirmatively to requests for help in locating and playing copyrighted materials.

In StreamCast's case, of course, the evidence just described was supplemented by other unequivocal indications of unlawful purpose in the internal communications and advertising designs aimed at Napster users ("When the lights went off at Napster ... where did the users go?") Whether the messages were communicated is not to the point on this record. The function of the message in the theory of inducement is to prove by a defendant's own statements that his unlawful purpose disqualifies him from claiming protection (and incidentally to point to actual violators likely to be found among those who hear or read the message). Proving that a message was sent out, then, is the preeminent but not exclusive way of showing that active steps were taken with the purpose of bringing about infringing acts, and of showing that infringing acts took place by using the device distributed. Here, the summary judgment record is replete with other evidence that Grokster and StreamCast, unlike the manufacturer and distributor in *Sony,* acted with a purpose to cause copyright violations by use of software suitable for illegal use.

Three features of this evidence of intent are particularly notable. First, each company showed itself to be aiming to satisfy a known source of demand for copyright infringement, the market comprising former Napster users. * * *

Second, this evidence of unlawful objective is given added significance by MGM's showing that neither company attempted to develop filtering tools or other mechanisms to diminish the infringing activity using their software. While the Ninth Circuit treated the defendants' failure to develop such tools as irrelevant because they lacked an independent duty to monitor their users' activity, we think this evidence underscores Grokster's and StreamCast's intentional facilitation of their users' infringement.[12]

Third, there is a further complement to the direct evidence of unlawful objective. * * * StreamCast and Grokster make money by selling

---

12. Of course, in the absence of other evidence of intent, a court would be unable to find contributory infringement liability merely based on a failure to take affirmative steps to prevent infringement, if the device otherwise was capable of substantial noninfringing uses. Such a holding would tread too close to the *Sony* safe harbor.

advertising space, by directing ads to the screens of computers employing their software. As the record shows, the more the software is used, the more ads are sent out and the greater the advertising revenue becomes. [T]he commercial sense of their enterprise turns on high-volume use, which the record shows is infringing. This evidence alone would not justify an inference of unlawful intent, but viewed in the context of the entire record its import is clear.

The unlawful objective is unmistakable.

B

In addition to intent to bring about infringement and distribution of a device suitable for infringing use, the inducement theory of course requires evidence of actual infringement by recipients of the device, the software in this case. As the account of the facts indicates, there is evidence of infringement on a gigantic scale, and there is no serious issue of the adequacy of MGM's showing on this point in order to survive the companies' summary judgment requests. * * *

    * * *

NOTES AND QUESTIONS

1. *Inducement liability.* How should the respective interests in copyright protection and development of new technologies be balanced in cases such as this? Did the Supreme Court reach the right balance in *Grokster*? Does it make sense to transplant doctrines developed in connection with patent law into the copyright realm? Given that the parties framed the case as turning on the *Sony* doctrine, why do you think the *Grokster* Court resolved it by importing an inducement cause of action for copyright? Do you think the new inducement cause of action will be effective to control infringing peer-to-peer file sharing in the future?

Are there ways to control peer-to-peer file sharing infringement other than through infringement litigation? A number of approaches have been suggested and discussed in the literature. One approach, sometimes called the "non-commercial use levy," would have Congress enact a statute modeled after the Audio Home Recording Act. The statute would permit unlimited peer-to-peer file sharing of copyrighted music for non-commercial purposes, but impose a levy on the sale of products and services whose value is enhanced by the file sharing (for example, peer-to-peer software, computers, consumer electronics like MP3 players, and Internet access services). The proceeds of the levy would be distributed to copyright owners proportionate to the popularity of their works among file sharers.

Another approach (sometimes called the "voluntary license model") would create a voluntary licensing system, fashioned after that of the performing rights societies. The music industry would form a collecting society that would sell (possibly through middlemen, like Internet service providers) blanket licenses to engage in peer-to-peer file sharing of copyrighted music. For example, Internet service providers might sell a license to engage in peer-to-peer file sharing of all the musical works in a defined category for a flat payment of $5.00 per month. Music consumers would be inclined to purchase the license because of its low cost. The collecting society would then distribute the licensing revenues among the copyright owners.

How effective would such alternative approaches be? Is it likely that they would be appealing to the music and sound recording industries? To the public?

2. *The Sony rule.* Should a 10% non-infringing use, plus the possibility of greater noninfringing uses in the future, be sufficient to shield a technology producer from contributory infringement liability, absent evidence of an intent to induce infringement? Why not limit protection to technologies whose *primary use* is non-infringing, as advocated by the *Grokster* plaintiffs? Why not adopt a balancing test that takes multiple factors into account, such as the percentage of use that is infringing, the defendant's attempts to design against infringing uses, and the cost-effectiveness of alternative (less infringing) designs? Why not just adopt a rule that technology producers must act reasonably to design their new technologies to minimize the possibility of infringing uses, and make indirect infringement liability turn on whether they acted reasonably to do so?

3. *Indirect liability and the Internet.* As noted *supra*, reproductions of copyrightable works are likely to be made whenever the works are uploaded or downloaded on the Internet. Internet service providers (ISPs)—such as access providers and web hosting services—may make numerous additional temporary reproductions of the works as they transmit them from computer to computer or store them on behalf of their users. Any of these actions may infringe copyright in the works, if they are unauthorized by the copyright owner. Indeed, they may infringe several of the copyright owner's exclusive rights—reproduction, adaptation, distribution to the public, public performance, public display—depending on the circumstances. The ISP involved in the acts may be either directly or indirectly liable for the infringement. What are the implications of the *Fonovisa* decision for Internet service providers? Can you think of scenarios in which the *Fonovisa* decision might lead to a finding that an ISP is vicariously or contributorily liable for its user's direct infringement of works on the Internet? Under what, if any circumstances might the *Sony* rule shelter the ISP?

As a matter of policy, should Internet service providers be held liable, either directly or indirectly, for their actions in connection with copyrighted works that their users have placed on the Internet? If so, under what circumstances?

Congress addressed ISP concerns about copyright liability in the Digital Millennium Copyright Act, in 1998. The Act created a new § 512 of the Copyright Act, entitled "Limitations on liability relating to material online." Section 512 provides safe harbors for several categories of activity that might otherwise render a "service provider" directly, contributorily or vicariously liable for copyright infringement: 1) transmission and transient storage of copyrighted material; 2) system caching (temporary reproduction and storage of copies of copyrighted material to facilitate efficient delivery to users); 3) storing material for users; and 4) providing information location tools. Each safe harbor imposes a series of specific conditions that a service provider must satisfy in order to qualify. As a general matter, these conditions are directed toward ensuring that the service provider acted through automatic technological processes at users' behest, and did not alter the copyrighted material or actively participate in the selection of material or recipients; that the service provider acted without knowledge of the infringement; that it made reasonable efforts to accommodate the copyright owner's use of standard technological means to monitor and control uses of the work (such as cookies, digital watermarks, and access prerequisites); that it acted expeditiously to remove infringing material upon proper notice of the infringement; that it implemented a policy of terminating services to users who repeatedly infringe; and that it receives no financial benefit that is directly attributable to the infringement.

As the House Conference Report stresses, the safe harbor provisions were not intended to define what does and does not constitute infringement on the Internet. Thus, failure to qualify for a safe harbor in itself does not indicate that the service provider has engaged in direct or indirect infringement. "Rather, the limitations of liability apply if the provider is found to be liable under existing principles of law." H.R. Conf. Rep. No. 105–796, 105th Cong., 2d Sess. 73 (1998). If a service provider qualifies for a safe harbor, it will be immune from all forms of monetary relief, and can face only limited injunctive remedies, regardless of whether it was charged with direct or indirect infringement.

PROBLEMS

1. Perfect 10 provides adult entertainment services, including a web site featuring photographs of nude models. It owns the copyrights in the photos. Several other commercial web sites publish photographs that infringe the plaintiff's copyrights (the "stolen content sites"). The Visa and Mastercard Companies provide financial services to the stolen content sites, allowing the sites to process Visa and Mastercard credit card payments for their goods and services.

Visa and Mastercard are entities owned by associations of banks, that process hundreds of millions of credit transactions over their networks each day. Two types of banks are associated with Visa and Mastercard—acquiring banks and issuing banks. Acquiring banks contract with merchants to allow those merchants to accept Visa and Mastercard cards as payment. Issuing banks provide credit cards to consumers. When a merchant processes a customer's Visa or Mastercard account number, the merchant electronically relays the transaction to its acquiring bank. The bank then presents the transaction to Visa or Mastercard. The issuing bank for the card notifies Visa or Mastercard whether it authorizes the transaction, and Visa or Mastercard relays that information back to the acquiring bank, which then provides the information to the merchant. The entire process takes a matter of seconds. Visa and Mastercard receive a fee for each transaction processed using their cards. Visa has certain internal regulations regarding the conduct of its member banks. It prohibits its banks from providing services to entities involved in illegal activity, and requires its acquiring banks to investigate and terminate merchant accounts if the merchant is engaging in illegal activity.

Perfect 10 sends letters to the Visa and Mastercard Companies informing them of the stolen content sites' alleged infringing conduct and demands that the credit card companies terminate their provision of financial services to those web sites. When the Companies do not comply, Perfect brings suit against them, alleging indirect copyright infringement under both a contributory infringement and vicarious liability theory. Under these facts, is Perfect likely to prevail on its claim?

IV. FAIR USE

HARPER & ROW, PUBLISHERS, INC. v. NATION ENTERPRISES

United States Supreme Court, 1985.
471 U.S. 539, 105 S.Ct. 2218, 85 L.Ed.2d 588.

JUSTICE O'CONNOR delivered the opinion of the Court.

This case requires us to consider to what extent the "fair use" provision of the Copyright Revision Act of 1976, (hereinafter the Copyright Act) 17 U.S.C. § 107, sanctions the unauthorized use of quotations from a public figure's unpublished manuscript. * * *

I

In February 1977, shortly after leaving the White House, former President Gerald R. Ford contracted with petitioners Harper & Row and Reader's Digest, to publish his as yet unwritten memoirs. The memoirs were to contain "significant hitherto unpublished material" concerning the Watergate crisis, Mr. Ford's pardon of former President Nixon and "Mr. Ford's reflections on this period of history, and the morality and personalities involved." In addition to the right to publish the Ford memoirs in book form, the agreement gave petitioners the exclusive right to license prepublication excerpts, known in the trade as "first serial rights." Two years later, as the memoirs were nearing completion, petitioners negotiated a prepublication licensing agreement with Time, a weekly news magazine. Time agreed to pay $25,000, $12,500 in advance and an additional $12,500 at publication, in exchange for the right to excerpt 7,500 words from Mr. Ford's account of the Nixon pardon. The issue featuring the excerpts was timed to appear approximately one week before shipment of the full length book version to bookstores. Exclusivity was an important consideration; Harper & Row instituted procedures designed to maintain the confidentiality of the manuscript, and Time retained the right to renegotiate the second payment should the material appear in print prior to its release of the excerpts.

Two to three weeks before the Time article's scheduled release, an unidentified person secretly brought a copy of the Ford manuscript to Victor Navasky, editor of The Nation, a political commentary magazine.

Mr. Navasky knew that his possession of the manuscript was not authorized and that the manuscript must be returned quickly to his "source" to avoid discovery. He hastily put together what he believed was "a real hot news story" composed of quotes, paraphrases, and facts drawn exclusively from the manuscript. Mr. Navasky attempted no independent commentary, research or criticism, in part because of the need for speed if he was to "make news" by "publish[ing] in advance of publication of the Ford book." The 2,250–word article * * * appeared on April 3, 1979. As a result of The Nation's article, Time canceled its piece and refused to pay the remaining $12,500.

[The Petitioners brought suit, alleging copyright infringement. The district court found The Nation liable for infringement and rejected its argument that its article constituted a fair use. The Court of Appeals for the Second Circuit reversed.] The Court of Appeals was especially influenced by the "politically significant" nature of the subject matter and its conviction that it is not "the purpose of the Copyright Act to impede that harvest of knowledge so necessary to a democratic state" or "chill the activities of the press by forbidding a circumscribed use of copyrighted words."

II

We agree with the Court of Appeals that copyright is intended to increase and not to impede the harvest of knowledge. But we believe the Second Circuit gave insufficient deference to the scheme established by the Copyright Act for fostering the original works that provide the seed and substance of this harvest. * * * The book at issue here, for example, was two years in the making, and began with a contract giving the author's copyright to the publishers in exchange for their services in producing and marketing the work. In preparing the book, Mr. Ford drafted essays and word portraits of public figures and participated in hundreds of taped interviews that were later distilled to chronicle his personal viewpoint. It is evident that the monopoly granted by copyright actively served its intended purpose of inducing the creation of new material of potential historical value.

* * *

[T]here is no dispute that the unpublished manuscript of "A Time to Heal," as a whole, was protected by § 106 from unauthorized reproduction. Nor do respondents dispute that verbatim copying of excerpts of the manuscript's original form of expression would constitute infringement unless excused as fair use. * * *

* * * The Nation has admitted to lifting verbatim quotes of the author's original language totaling between 300 and 400 words and constituting some 13% of The Nation article. In using generous verbatim excerpts of Mr. Ford's unpublished manuscript to lend authenticity to its account of the forthcoming memoirs, The Nation effectively arrogated to itself the right of first publication, an important marketable subsidiary

right. For the reasons set forth below, we find that this use of the copyrighted manuscript, even stripped to the verbatim quotes conceded by The Nation to be copyrightable expression, was not a fair use within the meaning of the Copyright Act.

III

A

Fair use was traditionally defined as "a privilege in others than the owner of the copyright to use the copyrighted material in a reasonable manner without his consent." H. Ball, Law of Copyright and Literary Property 260 (1944) (hereinafter Ball). The statutory formulation of the defense of fair use in the Copyright Act reflects the intent of Congress to codify the common-law doctrine. Section 107 requires a case-by-case determination whether a particular use is fair, and the statute notes four nonexclusive factors to be considered. This approach was "intended to restate the [pre-existing] judicial doctrine of fair use, not to change, narrow, or enlarge it in any way." H.R.Rep. No. 94–1476, p. 66 (1976) (hereinafter House Report).

"[T]he author's consent to a reasonable use of his copyrighted works ha[d] always been implied by the courts as a necessary incident of the constitutional policy of promoting the progress of science and the useful arts, since a prohibition of such use would inhibit subsequent writers from attempting to improve upon prior works and thus ... frustrate the very ends sought to be attained." Ball 260. * * *

As early as 1841, Justice Story gave judicial recognition to the doctrine in a case that concerned the letters of another former President, George Washington.

> "[A] reviewer may fairly cite largely from the original work, if his design be really and truly to use the passages for the purposes of fair and reasonable criticism. On the other hand, it is as clear, that if he thus cites the most important parts of the work, with a view, not to criticize, but to supersede the use of the original work, and substitute the review for it, such a use will be deemed in law a piracy." *Folsom v. Marsh*, 9 F.Cas. 342, 344–345 (No. 4,901) (CC Mass.)

As Justice Story's hypothetical illustrates, the fair use doctrine has always precluded a use that "supersede[s] the use of the original." *Ibid.*

Perhaps because the fair use doctrine was predicated on the author's implied consent to "reasonable and customary" use when he released his work for public consumption, fair use traditionally was not recognized as a defense to charges of copying from an author's as yet unpublished works. Under common-law copyright, "the property of the author ... in his intellectual creation [was] absolute until he voluntarily part[ed] with the same." This absolute rule, however, was tempered in practice by the equitable nature of the fair use doctrine. In a given case, factors such as implied consent through *de facto* publication or performance or dissemination of a work may tip the balance of equities in favor of prepublication use. * * * But it has never been seriously disputed that "the fact that the plaintiff's work is unpublished ... is a factor tending to negate the defense of fair use." 3 M. Nimmer, Copyright § 13.05, at 13–62, n.2 (1984). Publication of an author's expression before he has authorized its dissemination seriously infringes the author's right to decide when and whether it will be made public, a factor not present in fair use of published works. Respondents contend, however, that Congress, in including first publication among the rights enumerated in § 106, which are expressly subject to fair use under § 107, intended that fair use would apply *in pari materia* to published and unpublished works. The Copyright Act does not support this proposition.

The Copyright Act represents the culmination of a major legislative reexamination of copyright doctrine. Among its other innovations, it eliminated publication "as a dividing line between common law and statutory protection," extending statutory protection to all works from the time of their creation. It also recognized for the first time a distinct statutory right of first publication, which had previously been an element of the common-law protections afforded unpublished works. The Report of the House Committee on the Judiciary confirms that "Clause (3) of section 106, establishes the exclusive right of publications.... Under this provision the copyright owner would have the right to control the first public distribution of an authorized copy ... of his work."

Though the right of first publication, like the other rights enumerated in § 106, is expressly made subject to the fair use provision of § 107, fair use analysis must always be tailored to the individual case. The nature of the interest at stake is highly relevant to whether a given use is fair. From the beginning, those entrusted with the task of revision recognized the "overbalancing reasons to preserve the common law protection of undisseminated works until the author or his successor chooses to disclose them." The right of first publication implicates a threshold decision by the author whether and in what form to release his work. First publication is inherently different from other § 106 rights in that only one person can be the first publisher; as the contract with Time illustrates, the commercial value of the right lies primarily in exclusivity. Because the potential damage to the author from judicially enforced "sharing" of the first publication right with unauthorized users of his manuscript is substantial, the balance of equities in evaluating such a claim of fair use inevitably shifts.

* * *

* * * We conclude that the unpublished nature of a work is "[a] key, though not necessarily determinative, factor" tending to negate a defense of fair use. S. Rep. No. 94–473, 64 (1975).

We also find unpersuasive respondents' argument that fair use may be made of a soon-to-be-published manuscript on the ground that the author has demonstrated he has no interest in nonpublication. This argument assumes that the unpublished nature of copyrighted material is only relevant to letters or other confidential writings not intended for dissemination. It is true that common-law copyright was often enlisted in the service of personal privacy. In its commercial guise, however, an author's right to choose when he will publish is no less deserving of protection. The period encompassing the work's initiation, its preparation, and its grooming for public dissemination is a crucial one for any literary endeavor. The Copyright Act, which accords the copyright owner the "right to control the first public distribution" of his work, echoes the common law's concern that the author or copyright owner retain control throughout this critical stage. The obvious benefit to author and public alike of assuring authors the leisure to develop their ideas free from fear of expropriation outweighs any short-term "news value" to be gained from premature publication of the author's expression. * * * The author's control of first public distribution implicates not only his personal interest in creative control but his property interest in exploitation of prepublication rights, which are valuable in themselves and serve as a valuable adjunct to publicity and marketing. * * * Under ordinary circumstances, the author's right to control the first public appearance of his undisseminated expression will outweigh a claim of fair use.

B

Respondents, however, contend that First Amendment values require a different rule under the circumstances of this case. The thrust of the decision below is that "[t]he scope of [fair use] is undoubtedly wider when the information conveyed relates to matters of high public concern." Respondents advance the substantial public import of the subject matter of the Ford memoirs as grounds for excusing a use that would ordinarily not pass muster as a fair use—the piracy of verbatim quotations for the purpose of "scooping" the authorized first serialization. Respondents explain their copying of Mr. Ford's expression as essential to reporting the news story it claims the book itself represents. In respondents' view, not only the facts contained in Mr. Ford's memoirs, but "the precise manner in which [he] expressed himself [were] as newsworthy as what he had to say." Respondents argue that the public's interest in learning this news as fast as possible outweighs the right of the author to control its first publication.

The Second Circuit noted, correctly, that copyright's idea/expression dichotomy "strike[s] a definitional balance between the First Amendment and the Copyright Act by permitting free communication of facts while still protecting an author's expression." No author may copyright his ideas or the facts he narrates. * * * But copyright assures those who write and publish factual narratives such as "A Time to Heal" that they may at least enjoy the right to market the original expression contained therein as just compensation for their investment.

Respondents' theory, however, would expand fair use to effectively destroy any expectation of copyright protection in the work of a public figure. Absent such protection, there would be little incentive to create or profit in financing such memoirs, and the public would be denied an important source of significant historical information. The promise of copyright would be an empty one if it could be avoided merely by dubbing the infringement a fair use "news report" of the book.

Nor do respondents assert any actual necessity for circumventing the copyright scheme with respect to the types of works and users at issue here. Where an author and publisher have invested extensive resources in creating an original work and are poised to release it to the public, no legitimate aim is served by pre-empting the right of first publication. The fact that the words the author has chosen to clothe his narrative may of themselves be "newsworthy" is not an independent justification for unauthorized copying of the author's expression prior to publication. * * *

In our haste to disseminate news, it should not be forgotten that the Framers intended copyright itself to be the engine of free expression. By establishing a marketable right to the use of one's expression, copyright supplies the economic incentive to create and disseminate ideas. * * *

It is fundamentally at odds with the scheme of copyright to accord lesser rights in those works that are of greatest importance to the public. Such a notion ignores the major premise of copyright and injures author and public alike. * * * And as one commentator has noted: "If every volume that was in the public interest could be pirated away by a competing publisher, ... the public [soon] would have nothing worth reading." Sobel, Copyright and the First Amendment: A Gathering Storm?, 19 ASCAP Copyright Law Symposium 43, 78 (1971).

Moreover, freedom of thought and expression "includes both the right to speak freely and the right to refrain from speaking at all." We do not suggest this right not to speak would sanction abuse of the copyright owner's monopoly as an instrument to suppress facts. But in the words of New York's Chief Judge Fuld:

> "The essential thrust of the First Amendment is to prohibit improper restraints on the *voluntary* public expression of ideas; it shields the man who wants to speak or publish when others wish him to be quiet. There is necessarily, and within suitably defined areas, a concomitant freedom not to speak publicly, one which serves the same ultimate end as freedom of speech in its affirmative aspect." *Estate of Hemingway v. Random House, Inc.*, 23 N.Y.2d 341, 348, 296 N.Y.S.2d 771, 776, 244 N.E.2d 250, 255 (1968).

Courts and commentators have recognized that copyright, and the right of first publication in particular, serve this countervailing First Amendment value.

In view of the First Amendment protections already embodied in the Copyright Act's distinction between copyrightable expression and uncopyrightable facts and ideas, and the latitude for scholarship and comment traditionally afforded by fair use, we see no warrant for expanding the doctrine of fair use to create what amounts to a public figure exception to copyright. Whether verbatim copying from a public figure's manuscript in a given case is or is not fair must be judged according to the traditional equities of fair use.

IV

[W]hether The Nation article constitutes fair use under § 107 must be reviewed in light of the principles discussed above. The factors enumerated in the section are not meant to be exclusive: "[S]ince the doctrine is an equitable rule of reason, no generally applicable definition is possible, and each case raising the question must be decided on its own facts." House Report, at 65. The four factors identified by Congress as especially relevant in determining whether the use was fair are: (1) the purpose and character of the use; (2) the nature of the copyrighted work; (3) the substantiality of the portion used in relation to the copyrighted work as a whole; (4) the effect on the potential market for or value of the copyrighted work. We address each one separately.

Purpose of the Use. The Second Circuit correctly identified news reporting as the general purpose of The Nation's use. News reporting is one of the examples enumerated in § 107 to "give some idea of the sort of activities the courts might regard as fair use under the circumstances." Senate Report, at 61. This listing was not intended to be exhaustive, or to single out any particular use as presumptively a "fair" use. The drafters resisted pressures from special interest groups to create presumptive categories of fair use, but structured the provision as an affirmative defense requiring a case-by-case analysis. * * * The fact that an article arguably is "news" and therefore a productive use is simply one factor in a fair use analysis.

* * * The Nation has every right to seek to be the first to publish information. But The Nation went beyond simply reporting uncopyrightable information and actively sought to exploit the headline value of its infringement, making a "news event" out of its unauthorized first publication of a noted figure's copyrighted expression.

The fact that a publication was commercial as opposed to nonprofit is a separate factor that tends to weigh against a finding of fair use. "[E]very commercial use of copyrighted material is presumptively an unfair exploitation of the monopoly privilege that belongs to the owner of the copyright." *Sony Corp. of America v. Universal City Studios, Inc.*, 464 U.S., at 451, 104 S.Ct., at 793. In arguing that the purpose of news reporting is not purely commercial, The Nation misses the point entirely. The crux of the profit/nonprofit distinction is not whether the sole motive of the use is monetary gain but whether the user stands to profit from exploitation of the copyrighted material without paying the customary price.

In evaluating character and purpose we cannot ignore The Nation's stated purpose of scooping the forthcoming hardcover and Time abstracts. The Nation's use had not merely the incidental effect but the *intended purpose* of supplanting the copyright holder's commercially valuable right of first publication. * * * Also relevant to the "character" of the use is "the propriety of the defendant's conduct." 3 Nimmer § 13.05[A], at 13–72. "Fair use presupposes 'good faith' and 'fair dealing.' " The trial court found that The Nation knowingly exploited a purloined manuscript. Unlike the typical claim of fair use, The Nation cannot offer up even the fiction of consent as justification. Like its competitor newsweekly, it was free to bid for the right of abstracting excerpts from "A Time to Heal." Fair use "distinguishes between 'a true scholar and a chiseler who infringes a work for personal profit.' "

Nature of the Copyrighted Work. Second, the Act directs attention to the nature of the copyrighted work. "A Time to Heal" may be characterized as an unpublished historical narrative or autobiography. The law generally recognizes a greater need to disseminate factual works than works of fiction or fantasy.

> "[E]ven within the field of fact works, there are gradations as to the relative proportion of fact and fancy. One may move from sparsely embellished maps and directories to elegantly written biography. The extent to which one must permit expressive language to be copied, in order to assure dissemination of the underlying facts, will thus vary from case to case." Gorman, Fact or Fancy? The Implications for Copyright, 29 J. Copyright Soc. 560, 563 (1982).

Some of the briefer quotes from the memoirs are arguably necessary adequately to convey the facts; for example, Mr. Ford's characterization of the White House tapes as the "smoking gun" is perhaps so integral to the idea expressed as to be inseparable from it. But The Nation did not stop at isolated phrases and instead excerpted subjective descriptions and portraits of public figures whose power lies in the author's individualized expression. Such use, focusing on the most expressive elements of the work, exceeds that necessary to disseminate the facts.

The fact that a work is unpublished is a critical element of its "nature." Our prior discussion establishes that the scope of fair use is narrower with respect to unpublished works. While even substantial quotations might qualify as fair use in a review of a published work or a news account of a speech that had been delivered to the public or disseminated to the press, the author's right to control the first public appearance of his expression weighs against such use of the work before its release. The right of first publication encompasses not only the choice whether to publish at all, but also the choices of when, where, and in what form first to publish a work.

In the case of Mr. Ford's manuscript, the copyright holders' interest in confidentiality is irrefutable; the copyright holders had entered into a contractual undertaking to "keep the manuscript confidential" and required that all those to whom the manuscript was shown also "sign an agreement to keep the manuscript confidential." While the copyright holders' contract with Time required Time to submit its proposed article seven days before publication, The Nation's clandestine publication afforded no such opportunity for creative or quality control. It was hastily patched together and contained "a number of inaccuracies." A use that so clearly infringes the copyright holder's interests in confidentiality and creative control is difficult to characterize as "fair."

Amount and Substantiality of the Portion Used. Next, the Act directs us to examine the amount and substantiality of the portion used in relation to the copyrighted work as a whole. In absolute terms, the words actually quoted were an insubstantial portion of "A Time to Heal." The District Court, however, found that "[T]he Nation took what was essentially the heart of the book." We believe the Court of Appeals erred in overruling the District Judge's evaluation of the qualitative nature of the taking. A Time editor described the chapters on the pardon as "the most interesting and moving parts of the entire manuscript." The portions actually quoted were selected by Mr. Navasky as among the most powerful passages in those chapters. He testified that he used verbatim excerpts because simply reciting the information could not adequately convey the "absolute certainty with which [Ford] expressed himself," or show that "this comes from President Ford," or carry the "definitive quality" of the original. In short, he quoted these passages precisely because they qualitatively embodied Ford's distinctive expression.

As the statutory language indicates, a taking may not be excused merely because it is insubstantial with respect to the *infringing* work. As Judge Learned Hand cogently remarked, "no plagiarist can excuse the wrong by showing how much of his work he did not pirate." *Sheldon v. Metro–Goldwyn Pictures Corp.*, 81 F.2d 49, 56 (CA2), *cert. denied*, 298 U.S. 669, 56 S.Ct. 835, 80 L.Ed. 1392 (1936). Conversely, the fact that a substantial portion of the infringing work was copied verbatim is evidence of the qualitative value of the copied material, both to the originator and to the plagiarist who seeks to profit from marketing someone else's copyrighted expression.

Stripped to the verbatim quotes, the direct takings from the unpublished manuscript constitute at least 13% of the infringing article. The Nation article is structured around the quoted excerpts which serve as its dramatic focal points. In view of the expressive value of the excerpts and their key role in the infringing work, we cannot agree with the Second Circuit that the "magazine took a meager, indeed an infinitesimal amount of Ford's original language."

Effect on the Market. Finally, the Act focuses on "the effect of the use upon the potential market for or value of the copyrighted work." This last factor is undoubtedly the single most important element of fair use.[9] "Fair use, when properly applied, is limited to copying by others which does not

---

9. Economists who have addressed the issue believe the fair use exception should come into play only in those situations in which the market fails or the price the copyright holder would ask is near zero. As the facts here demonstrate, there is a fully functioning market that encourages the creation and dissemination of memoirs of public figures. In the economists' view, permitting "fair use" to displace normal copyright channels disrupts the copyright market without a commensurate public benefit.

materially impair the marketability of the work which is copied." The trial court found not merely a potential but an actual effect on the market. Time's cancellation of its projected serialization and its refusal to pay the $12,500 were the direct effect of the infringement. The Court of Appeals rejected this factfinding as clearly erroneous, noting that the record did not establish a causal relation between Time's nonperformance and respondents' unauthorized publication of Mr. Ford's *expression* as opposed to the facts taken from the memoirs. We disagree. Rarely will a case of copyright infringement present such clear-cut evidence of actual damage. * * *

More important, to negate fair use one need only show that if the challenged use "should become widespread, it would adversely affect the *potential* market for the copyrighted work." This inquiry must take account not only of harm to the original but also of harm to the market for derivative works. * * *

It is undisputed that the factual material in the balance of The Nation's article, besides the verbatim quotes at issue here, was drawn exclusively from the chapters on the pardon. The excerpts were employed as featured episodes in a story about the Nixon pardon—precisely the use petitioners had licensed to Time. The borrowing of these verbatim quotes from the unpublished manuscript lent The Nation's piece a special air of authenticity—as Navasky expressed it, the reader would know it was Ford speaking and not The Nation. Thus it directly competed for a share of the market for prepublication excerpts. The Senate Report states:

> "With certain special exceptions ... a use that supplants any part of the normal market for a copyrighted work would ordinarily be considered an infringement." Senate Report, at 65.

Placed in a broader perspective, a fair use doctrine that permits extensive prepublication quotations from an unreleased manuscript without the copyright owner's consent poses substantial potential for damage to the marketability of first serialization rights in general. "Isolated instances of minor infringements, when multiplied many times, become in the aggregate a major inroad on copyright that must be prevented." *Ibid.*

V

The Court of Appeals erred in concluding that The Nation's use of the copyrighted material was excused by the public's interest in the subject matter. It erred, as well, in overlooking the unpublished nature of the work and the resulting impact on the potential market for first serial rights of permitting unauthorized prepublication excerpts under the rubric of fair use. Finally, in finding the taking "infinitesimal," the Court of Appeals accorded too little weight to the qualitative importance of the quoted passages of original expression. In sum, the traditional doctrine of fair use, as embodied in the Copyright Act, does not sanction the use made by The Nation of these copyrighted materials. Any copyright infringer may claim to benefit the public by increasing public access to the copyrighted work. But Congress has not designed, and we see no warrant for judicially imposing, a "compulsory license" permitting unfettered access to the unpublished copyrighted expression of public figures.

The Nation conceded that its verbatim copying of some 300 words of direct quotation from the Ford manuscript would constitute an infringement unless excused as a fair use. Because we find that The Nation's use of these verbatim excerpts from the unpublished manuscript was not a fair use, the judgment of the Court of Appeals is reversed, and the case is remanded for further proceedings consistent with this opinion.

NOTES AND QUESTIONS

1. *The fair use defense.* Fair use is an affirmative defense. It does not become relevant until the plaintiff has made a *prima facie* case of infringement. At that point, the defendant must bear the burden of establishing that its use is privileged under the fair use doctrine. What is the purpose of the fair use defense? In cases in which copyright owners generally would not be expected to object to the defendant's use, but the transaction costs of obtaining a license are prohibitive, the fair use defense may facilitate uses of copyrighted matter that benefit the public and would not otherwise be made. However, the fair use doctrine might play an important and beneficial role in other situations. Judge Pierre Leval has described the purpose of the defense as follows:

Notwithstanding the need for monopoly protection of intellectual creators to stimulate creativity and authorship, excessively broad protection would stifle, rather than advance, the objective.

First, all intellectual creative activity is in part derivative. There is no such thing as a wholly original thought or invention. Each advance stands on building blocks fashioned by prior thinkers. Second, important areas of intellectual activity are explicitly referential. Philosophy, criticism, history, and even the natural sciences require continuous reexamination of yesterday's theses.

Monopoly protection of intellectual property that impeded referential analysis and the development of new ideas out of old would strangle the creative process. Three judicially created copyright doctrines have addressed this problem: first, the rule that the copyright does not protect *ideas*, but only the manner of expression; second, the rule that *facts* are not within the copyright protection, notwithstanding the labor expended by the original author in uncovering them; and finally, the fair use doctrine, which protects secondary creativity as a legitimate concern of the copyright. * * *

Fair use should not be considered a bizarre, occasionally tolerated departure from the grand conception of the copyright monopoly. To the contrary, it is a necessary part of the overall design. Although no simple definition of fair use can be fashioned, and inevitably disagreement will arise over individual applications, recognition of the function of fair use as integral to copyright's objectives leads to a coherent and useful set of principles. Briefly stated, the use must be of a character that serves the copyright objective of stimulating productive thought and public instruction without excessively diminishing the incentives for creativity. One must assess each of the issues that arise in considering a fair use defense in light of the governing purpose of copyright law.

Leval, *Toward a Fair Use Standard*, 103 Harv. L. Rev. 1105, 1109–1110 (1990).[12]

What is the relationship of the fair use defense to the statutory exemptions to copyright infringement, found in Copyright Act §§ 108–121?

2. *The four factors.* The *Harper & Row* opinion considered each of the four factors specified in Copyright Act § 107. How are these factors to be weighted in deciding whether a defendant's use was fair? Was the Court influenced by any additional factors apart from the four listed in § 107?

a. *Factor one: the purpose and character of the use.* How does this factor relate to the purpose of the fair use doctrine, as described by Judge Leval in the prior note?

The preamble to § 107 provides several examples of potentially proper "purposes" for using copyrighted material: "criticism, comment, news reporting, teaching (including multiple copies for classroom use), scholarship, or research." The statutory language suggests that Congress did not intend for this list to be exclusive. Is Congress' selection of the particular examples set forth in the preamble useful in evaluating whether other purposes are proper? If so, how? The *Harper & Row* majority refers to "productive" uses of copyrighted material, suggesting that productive uses are more likely to be deemed fair uses. What is a productive use? The term "transformative use" is sometimes used interchangeably with the term "productive use." To make a "transformative" use of a work, must one change the work itself? What if the fair use claimant used the plaintiff's work unchanged, but in a new context, or for a new purpose? Should this weigh in favor of a finding of fair use for purposes of factor one?

Section 107's preamble expressly refers to "teaching (including multiple copies for classroom use)," and factor one directs courts to consider whether a use was made for "nonprofit educational purposes." The permissibility of reproduction for educational purposes, and particularly photocopying for classroom use, generated considerable debate while § 107 was being drafted and enacted. The House Committee ultimately concluded that "a specific exemption freeing certain reproductions of copyrighted works for educational and scholarly purposes from copyright control is not justified." H.R. Rep. No. 1476, 94th Cong., 2d Sess. 66 (1976). Nonetheless, the Committee acknowledged that there was a "need for greater certainty and protection for teachers." *Id.*, at 67. At the Committee's urging, representatives of the interested parties—educators, authors, and publishers—met independently to discuss permissible educational uses of copyrighted material. They ultimately drafted an "Agreement on Guidelines for Classroom Copying in Not–For–Profit Educational Institutions," which set forth guidelines for "fair use" reproduction of books and periodicals for classroom use. Among other things, the guidelines look to the "brevity," "spontaneity," and cumulative effect of

---

12. © Pierre N. Leval, 1990. Reprinted by permission of the copyright owner.

the copying. The Committee incorporated the Agreement into the House Report. See *id.*, at 67–70.[13] While incorporation into the House Report does not give the guidelines the status of law, it undoubtedly is persuasive to courts, thus providing a "semi-safe harbor" for teachers who confine their copying to that approved by the guidelines.[14] Since the guidelines only purport to set forth minimum standards for fair use, reproduction beyond that approved in the guidelines should not be automatically disqualified from a finding of fair use. For an application of the guidelines, see Marcus v. Rowley, 695 F.2d 1171 (9th Cir.1983).

Why was The Nation's news reporting deemed "commercial" in nature? Does the *Harper & Row* majority's emphasis on the commercial nature of The Nation's article undercut Congress' intent in listing news reporting as an example of fair use in the preamble? See *Harper & Row*, 471 U.S. at 592, 105 S.Ct. at 2247, 85 L.Ed.2d at 627 (Justice Brennan, dissenting). Why should a defendant's commercial purpose, as defined by the Court, weigh against a finding of fair use?

b. Factor two: the nature of the copyrighted work. Apart from the published or unpublished status of the plaintiff's work, why is the *type* of the plaintiff's work relevant to the fair use inquiry?

In *Harper & Row*, the Court placed considerable importance on the fact that the plaintiff's work was not yet published. Does the opinion create a presumption against a finding of fair use when the plaintiff's work is unpublished? Should it matter whether the plaintiff intended eventually to publish the work? See Leval, *Toward a Fair Use Standard*, 103 Harv. L. Rev. 1105, 1116–22 (1990).

The Court of Appeals for the Second Circuit interpreted *Harper & Row* to provide that "unpublished letters normally enjoy insulation from fair use copying" and "complete protection." Salinger v. Random House, Inc., 811 F.2d 90, 95, 97 (2d Cir.1987), *cert. denied*, 484 U.S. 890, 108 S.Ct. 213, 98 L.Ed.2d 177 (1987). In accordance with this interpretation, the court enjoined publication of a biography of J.D. Salinger that incorporated quotes and paraphrases from Salinger's letters which, while "unpublished," were lawfully available to scholars in libraries. Historians, biographers and other authors who rely on unpublished letters and other documents in their work protested strongly, arguing that the absence of a fair use defense would make it difficult or impossible for them to write effectively, to the ultimate detriment of the public. They also argued that the Second Circuit's interpretation would permit copyright to be used as a tool for censorship and suppression. Judge Leval stated the concern as follows:

> A ban on fair use of unpublished documents establishes a new despotic potentate in the politics of intellectual life—the "widow censor." A historian who wishes to quote personal papers of deceased public figures

---

13. The Committee also incorporated negotiated "Guidelines for Educational Uses of Music." *Id.* at 70–772.

14. The Committee stated: "The Committee believes the guidelines are a reasonable interpretation of the minimum standards of fair use. Teachers will know that copying within the guidelines is fair use. Thus, the guidelines serve the purpose of fulfilling the need for greater certainty and protection for teachers."*Id.*, at 72.

now must satisfy heirs and executors for fifty years after the subject's death. When writers ask permission, the answer will be, "show me what you write. Then we'll talk about permission." If the manuscript does not exude pure admiration, permission will be denied.

Leval, *Toward a Fair Use Standard, supra*, at 1118.[15]

In response to the controversy, Congress amended Section 107 to provide: "The fact that a work is unpublished shall not itself bar a finding of fair use if such finding is made upon consideration of all of the above factors." Pub.L. No. 102–492, 106 Stat. 3145 (1992).

c. *Factor three: the amount and substantiality of the portion used in relation to the copyrighted work as a whole.* Given that the defendant took enough to infringe, what does further assessment of the amount taken add to the fair use analysis?

In *Harper & Row*, the Court found that the 300–400 words the defendant took from the plaintiff's 200,000–word manuscript constituted a substantial portion of the manuscript for purposes of factor three. Could reproduction of the plaintiff's entire work ever be found to constitute a fair use? See Sony Corp. of America v. Universal City Studios, Inc., 464 U.S. 417, 442, 104 S.Ct. 774, 789, 78 L.Ed.2d 574, 592 (1984) (fair use found even though members of the public taped entire television programs for purposes of time shifting.).

Courts have sometimes considered the amount and substantiality of the portion the defendant used in relation to the *defendant's* work as a whole, though § 107 does not specifically list that as a factor. Why might it be relevant?

d. *Factor four: the effect of the use upon the potential market for or value of the copyrighted work.* In *Harper & Row*, the Supreme Court stated that this factor was the "single most important element of fair use." Why should this be so?

Is this factor relevant in the case of works, such as private letters, that the plaintiff has no intention to publish? In the *Salinger* case, *supra*, the Second Circuit held that it was:

> [T]he need to assess the effect on the market for Salinger's letters is not lessened by the fact that their author has disavowed any intention to publish them during his lifetime. First, the proper inquiry concerns the "potential market" for the copyrighted work. Second, Salinger has the right to change his mind. He is entitled to protect his *opportunity* to sell his letters, an opportunity estimated by his literary agent to have a current value in excess of $500,000.

Id., 811 F.2d at 98.

Suppose that the defendant publishes a scathingly negative review of the plaintiff's novel, which impermissibly quotes from the novel and thus infringes. In response to the defendant's fair use defense, plaintiff demonstrates that the defendant's sarcastically critical review has brought the novel into public contempt, decreasing readership and sales. Should this evidence be deemed relevant to the factor four inquiry?

---

15. © Pierre N. Leval, 1990. Reprinted by permission of the copyright owner.

3. *Parody.* The Supreme Court first addressed application of the fair use defense to parody in Campbell v. Acuff–Rose Music, Inc., 510 U.S. 569, 114 S.Ct. 1164, 127 L.Ed.2d 500 (1994). In *Campbell*, Campbell, a member of the popular rap music group 2 Live Crew, wrote a song entitled "Pretty Woman," which he described as intended, "through comical lyrics, to satirize" the song "Oh, Pretty Woman," made popular by Roy Orbison. The words of the 2 Live Crew song copied the original's first line, but then degenerated into a play on words, substituting shocking lyrics, derisively demonstrating the "blandness" of the Orbison original. In addition to the first line of lyrics, Campbell copied the striking opening bass riff (or musical phrase) of the Orbison original and repeated it throughout. 2 Live Crew sent a recording of Campbell's song to Acuff–Rose, the owner of copyright in the Orbison song, and attempted to obtain a license. Acuff–Rose refused. 2 Live Crew then released recordings of Campbell's song for sale to the public.

When Acuff–Rose sued for infringement, 2 Live Crew asserted the fair use defense. The district court granted summary judgment to 2 Live Crew, and the Court of Appeals for the Sixth Circuit reversed. When the case reached the Supreme Court, the Court undertook a factor-by-factor analysis, as it did in *Harper & Row.*

With regard to the "purpose and character of the use," the Court first stressed that a productive, or "transformative" use is favored:

> The central purpose of this investigation is to see, in Justice Story's words, whether the new work merely "supersede[s] the objects" of the original creation, or instead adds something new, with a further purpose or different character, altering the first with new expression, meaning, or message; it asks, in other words, whether and to what extent the new work is "transformative." Although such transformative use is not absolutely necessary for a finding of fair use, the goal of copyright, to promote science and the arts, is generally furthered by the creation of transformative works. Such works thus lie at the heart of the fair use doctrine's guarantee of breathing space within the confines of copyright, and the more transformative the new work, the less will be the significance of other factors, like commercialism, that may weigh against a finding of fair use.

Id., 510 U.S. at 579. The Court found that parody had "an obvious claim to transformative value." The Court emphasized that parodies generally imitate the work or style of another author for comic effect or ridicule. "Like less ostensibly humorous forms of criticism, [parody] can provide social benefit, by shedding light on an earlier work, and, in the process, creating a new one." *Id.*

The Court stressed, however, that a defendant's parody should be aimed at the plaintiff's work, at least in part, in order to justify copying it. A parody of an existing work "needs to mimic [the] original to make its point, and so has some claim to use the creation of its victim's (or victims') imagination." "If, on the contrary, the commentary has no critical bearing on the substance or style of the original composition, which the alleged infringer merely uses to get attention or to avoid the drudgery in working up something fresh, the claim to fairness in borrowing from another's work diminishes accordingly (if it does not vanish), and other factors, like the extent of its commerciality, loom larger." *Id.*, 510 U.S. at 580. While the Court of Appeals had questioned whether the Campbell song was a parody of the Orbison original, the Supreme Court found that it "reasonably could be perceived as commenting on the original or criticizing it, to some degree." *Id.*

In its factor one inquiry, the Court of Appeals had relied on the Supreme Court's statement in Sony Corp. of America v. Universal City Studios, Inc., 464 U.S. 417, 104 S.Ct. 774, 78 L.Ed.2d 574 (1984), that "every commercial use of copyrighted material is presumptively unfair," and had given "virtually dispositive effect" to the commercial nature of 2 Live Crew's use of the Orbison song. The Supreme Court found this to be error.

> The language of the statute makes clear that the commercial or nonprofit educational purpose of a work is only one element of the first factor inquiry into its purpose and character. * * * As we explained in *Harper & Row*, Congress resisted attempts to narrow the ambit of this traditional inquiry by adopting categories of presumptively fair use, and it urged courts to preserve the breadth of their traditionally ample view of the universe of relevant evidence. * * * If, indeed, commerciality carried presumptive force against a finding of fairness, the presumption would swallow nearly all of the illustrative uses listed in the preamble paragraph of § 107, including news reporting, comment, criticism, teaching, scholarship, and research, since these activities "are generally conducted for profit in this country."

Id., 510 U.S. at 584.

In discussing the third factor, "the amount and substantiality of the portion used in relation to the copyrighted work as a whole," the Court emphasized the interrelationship of all the factors. According to the Court, the third factor asks whether the amount of the defendant's taking is "reasonable in relation to the purpose of the copying."

> Here, attention turns to the persuasiveness of a parodist's justification for the particular copying done, and the inquiry will harken back to the first of the statutory factors, for, as in prior cases, we recognize that the extent of permissible copying varies with the purpose and character of the use. The facts bearing on this factor will also tend to address the fourth, by revealing the degree to which the parody may serve as a market substitute for the original or potentially licensed derivatives.

Id., 510 U.S. at 587.

In finding that the third factor weighed against the defendants, the Court of Appeals had emphasized the extent of the defendants' *verbatim* copying and the quality of the material copied, opining that the defendants had taken "the heart of the original" and made it "the heart of a new work." The Supreme Court disagreed with the Court of Appeals' method of applying these considerations to parody:

> Parody presents a difficult case. Parody's humor, or in any event its comment, necessarily springs from recognizable allusion to its object through distorted imitation. Its art lies in the tension between a known original and its parodic twin. When parody takes aim at a particular

original work, the parody must be able to "conjure up" at least enough of that original to make the object of its critical wit recognizable. What makes for this recognition is quotation of the original's most distinctive or memorable features, which the parodist can be sure the audience will know. Once enough has been taken to assure identification, how much more is reasonable will depend, say, on the extent to which the song's overriding purpose and character is to parody the original or, in contrast, the likelihood that the parody may serve as a market substitute for the original. But using some characteristic features cannot be avoided.

[I]f quotation of the opening riff and the first line [of the Orbison original] may be said to go to the "heart" of the original, the heart is also what most readily conjures up the song for parody, and it is the heart at which parody takes aim. Copying does not become excessive in relation to parodic purpose merely because the portion taken was the original's heart. If 2 Live Crew had copied a significantly less memorable part of the original, it is difficult to see how its parodic character would have come through.

This is not, of course, to say that anyone who calls himself a parodist can skim the cream and get away scot free. In parody, as in news reporting, context is everything, and the question of fairness asks what else the parodist did besides go to the heart of the original. It is significant that 2 Live Crew not only copied the bass riff and repeated it, but also produced otherwise distinctive sounds, interposing "scraper" noise, overlaying the music with solos in different keys, and altering the drum beat. This is not a case, then, where "a substantial portion" of the parody itself is composed of a "verbatim" copying of the original. It is not, that is, a case where the parody is so insubstantial, as compared to the copying, that the third factor must be resolved as a matter of law against the parodists.

Id., 510 U.S. at 588–89.

In turning to the fourth and final factor, the effect of the use upon the potential market for the copyrighted work, the Court noted that the degree to which the defendant's work transforms the appropriated expression may be relevant:

Indeed, as to parody pure and simple, it is * * * more likely that the new work will not affect the market for the original in a way cognizable under this factor, that is, by acting as a substitute for it * * *. This is so because the parody and the original usually serve different market functions.

We do not, of course, suggest that a parody may not harm the market at all, but when a lethal parody, like a scathing theater review, kills demand for the original, it does not produce a harm cognizable under the Copyright Act. Because "parody may quite legitimately aim at garroting the original, destroying it commercially as well as artistically," B. Kaplan, An Unhurried View of Copyright 69 (1967), the role of the courts is to distinguish between "[b]iting criticism [that merely] suppresses demand [and] copyright infringement, [which] merely usurps it." Fisher v. Dees, 794 F.2d at 438.

Id., 510 U.S. at 590–92.

The Court stressed the importance of evaluating the effect of the defendant's copying both on the market for the original work and on the potential market for adaptations. However, the Court recognized that the defendant's use would not undermine any potential market for *parodies* of the plaintiff's work:

> The market for potential derivative uses includes only those that creators of original works would in general develop or license others to develop. [T]he unlikelihood that creators of imaginative works will license critical reviews or lampoons of their own productions removes such uses from the very notion of a potential licensing market. * * *

Id., at 592–93. Justice Souter noted, however, that 2 Live Crew's song comprised not only parody but also rap music, so that the derivative market for rap music would be a proper focus of enquiry under factor four. Evidence of substantial harm to the market for rap versions of "Oh, Pretty Woman" would weigh against a finding of fair use, because the opportunity to license derivatives is an important component of copyright's economic incentive. The Court remanded for further findings on the extent to which the defendant's song interfered with a market for a non-parody, rap version of "Oh, Pretty Woman," and to permit evaluation of the amount taken, in light of the song's parodic purpose and character and its transformative elements.

A copy of the lyrics of the Orbison and Campbell songs can be found in an Appendix to the Court's opinion. Does it appear that the Campbell Court afforded a wider fair use privilege for parody than exists for other types of uses, such as that in Harper & Row? Would a wider fair use privilege be justified?

Justice Kennedy, in his concurring opinion, expressed concern that

> [a]lmost any revamped modern version of a familiar composition can be construed as a "comment on the naivete of the original," because of the difference in style and because it will be amusing to hear how the old tune sounds in the new genre. Just the thought of a rap version of Beethoven's Fifth Symphony or "Achy, Breaky Heart" is bound to make people smile. If we allow any weak transformation to qualify as parody, however, we weaken the protection of copyright. * * *

> * * * As future courts apply our fair use analysis, they must take care to ensure that not just any commercial take-off is rationalized post hoc as a parody.

Id., 510 U.S. at 599–600. Does the Court's test for parody (whether "a parodic character may reasonably be perceived"), coupled with its instructions for applying the four factors in the case of parody, adequately alleviate this concern? In Suntrust Bank v. Houghton Mifflin Co., 268 F.3d 1257, 1269 (11th Cir. 2001), the Eleventh Circuit sought to further clarify the definition of parody:

> The Supreme Court's definition of parody in Campbell * * * is somewhat vague. On the one hand, the Court suggests that the aim of parody is "comic effect or ridicule," but it then proceeds to discuss parody more expansively in terms of its "commentary" on the original. In light of the

admonition in Campbell that courts should not judge the quality of the work or the success of the attempted humor in discerning its parodic character, we choose to take the broader view. For purposes of our fair-use analysis, we will treat a work as a parody if its aim is to comment upon or criticize a prior work by appropriating elements of the original in creating a new artistic, as opposed to scholarly or journalistic, work.

Is the fact that 2 Live Crew sought and was denied a license relevant to the fair use inquiry? If so, how?

4. *Fair use on the Internet and "market failure."* How is the fair use defense likely to fare in the world of the Internet? As the Supreme Court stressed in *Harper & Row*, the fourth § 107 factor—the effect of the defendant's use upon the potential market for the copyrighted work—carries particular weight in fair use determinations. In the concrete world, unauthorized uses of copyrighted works have often been deemed fair because there was no established market for licenses to make those uses. If no market exists, the defendant's unauthorized use would not preempt significant marketing opportunities the copyright owner otherwise might have had. Whether a "market" exists for this purpose might depend on how efficiently the parties might engage in a licensing transaction. If the transaction costs are so high that they are likely to discourage socially beneficial uses, courts may find that no market exists, and treat the defendant's unauthorized use as a non-infringing fair use. On the other hand, if the transaction costs of obtaining a license are relatively low, courts are more likely to find that a "market" exists, and require users to obtain a license.

The transaction costs of obtaining licenses may be greatly reduced in the Internet context, leading courts to be less sympathetic to unlicensed uses. In the future, an Internet user seeking to use a copyrighted work may automatically be confronted with a "click-wrap" license when she attempts to access the work on the Internet. The screen will state the uses for which the work is available, and the terms on which the copyright owner will license the use, so that all the user need do is click on the "I agree" button to obtain a license. The cost can readily be paid on the spot by entering the licensee's credit card number. Or, in the alternative, new electronic permission clearing houses may be created, representing numerous authors and dispensing licenses quickly and efficiently over the Internet. In American Geophysical Union v. Texaco, 60 F.3d 913, 930–31 (2d Cir.1994), the Court of Appeals for the Second Circuit considered the ready availability of photocopying licenses through the Copyright Clearance Center, Inc. ("CCC") to be relevant in evaluating a scientist's unlicensed photocopying of scientific journal articles, which he wanted to have handy for reference in his office and in the lab. The court reasoned:

> [I]t is not unsound to conclude that the right to seek payment for a particular use tends to become legally cognizable under the fourth fair use factor when the means for paying for such a use is made easier. This notion is not inherently troubling: it is sensible that a particular unauthorized use should be considered "more fair" when there is no ready market or means to pay for the use, while such an unauthorized use should be considered "less fair" when there is a ready market or means to pay for the use.

See also Information Infrastructure Task Force, Intellectual Property and the National Information Infrastructure: The Report of the Working Group on Intellectual Property Rights, 82 (1995)("[I]t may be that technological means of tracking transactions and licensing will lead to reduced application and scope of the fair use doctrine [on the Internet]"). For a fuller discussion of this "market failure" approach to fair use analysis, see Wendy Gordon, *Fair Use as Market Failure: A Structural Analysis of the Betamax Case and Its Predecessors*, 82 Columbia L. Rev. 1600 (1993).

Apart from potentially affecting courts' evaluation of the fourth fair use factor, how might copyright owners' widespread adoption of "mass market" or "click-wrap" licenses affect the availability of the fair use defense on the Internet? Might copyright owners use such electronic licenses (in combination with anticircumvention laws described below) to contractually prohibit fair uses altogether? What would the implications of this be? Should such contractual provisions be enforced? See Davidson & Associates, d/b/a/ Blizzard Entertainment Inc. v. Jung, 422 F.3d 630 (8th Cir. 2005).

5. *Copyright misuse.* The copyright misuse defense has emerged from the case law during the last couple of decades. The doctrine of copyright misuse is an equitable doctrine that renders a copyright unenforceable if the copyright owner has engaged in misconduct in licensing or enforcing the copyright, impermissibly broadening the scope of his monopoly right, contrary to the policies underlying copyright law. The copyright will remain unenforceable until the misuse ends and its effects have dissipated.

Although copyright misuse is doctrinally related to the patent misuse defense, discussed in Chapter 3, it does not appear to be as closely affiliated with antitrust law. Some earlier case decisions suggested that an antitrust violation on the copyright owner's part would not necessarily constitute a valid defense to infringement, while several recent decisions indicate that the scope of the copyright misuse doctrine exceeds the prohibitions of antitrust law.

For example, in Lasercomb America, Inc. v. Reynolds, 911 F.2d 970 (4th Cir.1990), the plaintiff used a standard licensing agreement for its software that prohibited the licensee and all of its employees from developing any kind of software competitive with the plaintiff's for 99 years. The defendant in a subsequent copyright infringement suit prevailed in a copyright misuse defense even though he was not himself subject to the license restriction. The Court of Appeals for the Fourth Circuit explained:

> [W]hile it is true that the attempted use of a copyright to violate antitrust law probably would give rise to a misuse of copyright defense, the converse is not necessarily true—a misuse need not be a violation of antitrust law in order to comprise an equitable defense to an infringement action. The question is not whether the copyright is being used in a manner violative of antitrust law (such as whether the licensing agreement is "reasonable"), but whether the copyright is being used in a manner violative of the public policy embodied in the grant of the copyright.

Id. at 978.

PROBLEMS

1. Assume that the plaintiff manufactures and sells a video entertainment console and video game cartridges designed to play in the console. The defendant develops and sells video game cartridges that are compatible with several computer systems. While the plaintiff licenses some independent companies to develop and sell video games that are compatible with its console, it has not licensed the defendant to do so.

In an effort to render its video games compatible with the plaintiff's console, defendant "reverse engineers" several of plaintiff's video game programs in order to discover the requirements for compatibility with the console. This entails translating the machine-readable object code of commercially available copies of plaintiff's games into human-readable source code through a process called "disassembly" or "decompilation." Playing the games in one of plaintiff's commercially available consoles, defendant wires a decompiler into the console circuitry and generates printouts of the resulting source code. Defendant studies and annotates the printouts in order to identify areas of commonality among the video games it has decompiled. Defendant then loads the disassembled code back into a computer and experiments to discover the interface specifications for the console by modifying the programs and studying the results.

At the end of the process, defendant creates a development manual that incorporates the information it has discovered about the requirements for a game to be compatible with the plaintiff's console. The manual contains only functional descriptions of the interface requirements and none of plaintiff's code. Defendant then creates its own games for the console. At this stage it does not copy any of plaintiff's programs, relying only on the information concerning interface specifications for the console contained in the manual. None of the code in defendant's programs is derived from plaintiff's programs, except for the interface specifications.

The plaintiff sues defendant for infringement, claiming that defendant's intermediate copying of its games during the process of reverse engineering to learn the console interface specifications violates its copyrights. Should the defendant's copying be privileged under the fair use defense?

2. Professor Keene selected a range of materials for students in his State University humanities class to read. These materials included excerpts of approximately 20–40 pages each from four different text books, two articles of approximately 10 pages each from two different scholarly journals, one newspaper article from the New York Times, two newspaper articles from the Chicago Tribune, an article of approximately five pages from the Atlantic Magazine, and an article of approximately 7 pages from the New Yorker Magazine. After compiling this class "reader," the Professor took the manuscript to Curly's Copy Shop, a privately-owned, commercial photocopying shop located at the edge of the University campus. Pursuant to Professor Keene's instructions, Curley's photocopied the various components of the reader, bound them together with a cover page, and provided them for sale to students in Keene's humanities class. The materials were assigned reading for

the class. Curley's charged students its standard price for photocopied materials.

The publishers/copyright owners of three of the text books from which excerpts were taken sued Curley's for copyright infringement. Curley's acknowledges copying, but asserts the fair use defense. Should the court find the defense applicable in this case?

3. Jennifer Jones, a successful artist, painted an oil painting of a church picnic, which she entitled "Sunday in the Park." Museum is currently the owner of the original painting. While Jones retained copyright in the painting, she granted Museum a non-exclusive license to reproduce the painting as a poster, and to sell the posters. The poster sells for $20.00 a copy. Thousands of copies of the poster have been sold. Directly below the poster's reproduction of the painting are some words identifying the artist and the painting by name, followed by an identification of Museum.

Television Network, Inc. produces and broadcasts a situation comedy entitled "Praise the Lord." In one episode of "Praise the Lord," a "Sunday in the Park" poster, presumably sold by Museum, was used as part of the set decoration for a particular scene. The scene is five minutes long. In that scene, at least a portion of the poster is shown a total of nine times. In some of those nine segments, the poster is at the center of the screen, although nothing in the dialogue, action, or camera work particularly calls the viewer's attention to the poster. The nine segments in which a portion of the poster is visible range in duration from 1.86 to 4.16 seconds. The aggregate duration of all nine segments is 26.75 seconds. In the longest segment (4.16 seconds), 80% of the poster is visible. Characters on the set, standing in front of the poser, partially obscure the lower right and lower left quadrants, and the top edge of the poster is not within the camera's "framing" of the scene. Since the camera focuses precisely on the characters, the poster is not in perfect focus. All the other segments are of lesser duration and/or contain smaller and less distinct portions of the poster. However, their repetitive effect somewhat reenforces the visual effect of the observable 4.16–second segment described above. The words on the poster indicating the title and author of the work are not distinguishable to the viewer in any of the segments.

This episode of "Praise the Lord" was originally shown over Network in 2000. The series was repeated in 2001, at which time Jones happened to see the episode in which the poster appeared. Jones sued Network for copyright infringement. Network asserted the fair use defense. How would you evaluate the merits of the defense?

V. DIGITAL RIGHTS MANAGEMENT

The Digital Millennium Copyright Act ("DMCA"), codified at 17 U.S.C. §§ 1201–1205, was enacted to encourage and facilitate copyright owners' use of technological measures (such as password systems, digital watermarking or encryption) to protect themselves from infringement in digital environments. The DMCA prohibits circumvention of technological measures used to control access to a copyrighted work, and prohibits manufacturing and trafficking in devices or services that enable circumvention either of access controls or of controls on uses of the work, once access is gained. Although United States law already provided remedies for copyright infringement in digital environments, and acts that enable it, Congress believed that the additional anticircumvention provisions were necessary in order to encourage copyright owners to make their works available in digital form. Congress also deemed the provisions necessary in order to bring the United States into compliance with the new WIPO Copyright Treaty[16] and the WIPO Performances and Phonograms Treaty,[17] which set international standards for recognizing and enforcing copyright and neighboring rights in the digital environment.[18]

The DMCA added a new chapter to Title 17 of the United States Code. 17 U.S.C.A. §§ 1201–1205. Section 1201 sets forth the substantive anticircumvention prohibitions, § 1203 provides civil remedies for violations of § 1201, and § 1204 provides criminal sanctions. It is important to note that the anticircumvention provisions provide copyright owners with a new cause of action that is separate from a copyright infringement cause of action.

Section 1201(a)(1) generally prohibits the act of circumventing a technological measure "that effectively controls access to a work" protected under the Copyright Act. Examples of such measures include encryption and password protection systems. As one commentator put it more colloquially, subsection (a)(1) prohibits "the electronic equivalent of breaking into a locked room in order to obtain a copy of a book." Nimmer, *A Riff on Fair Use in the Digital Millennium Copyright Act*, 148 U. Pa. L. Rev. 673, 685 (2000). Liability arises from the invasion, and does not depend on any showing of subsequent copyright infringement.[19]

---

16. WIPO Copyright Treaty, adopted by the World Intellectual Property Organization Diplomatic Conference on Dec. 20, 1996. The WIPO Copyright Treaty is a protocol to the Berne Convention. As such, it augments the level of copyright protection that adhering Berne Convention member nations must provide.

17. WIPO Performances and Phonograms Treaty, adopted by the Diplomatic Conference on Dec. 20, 1996. The Performances and Phonograms Treaty is free-standing, and enhances international standards for protecting sound recording producers' and performers' interests in their sound recordings (which many nations protect through "neighboring rights," rather than copyright).

18. Article 11 of the WIPO Copyright Treaty provides:

Contracting Parties shall provide adequate legal protection and effective legal remedies against the circumvention of effective technological measures that are used by authors in connection with the exercise of their rights under this Treaty or the Berne Convention and that restrict acts, in respect of their works, which are not authorized by the authors concerned or permitted by law.

The WIPO Performances and Phonograms Treaty, Article 18, sets forth essentially the same provision in connection with technological measures used by producers and performers of sound recordings.

19. In response to concerns that the § 1201(a)(1) prohibition would impair the public's ability to make fair uses of copyrighted works, Congress delayed activating subsection (a)(1) for two years after the DMCA's enactment. During those two years, Congress directed the Librarian of Congress to investigate the effect on fair uses, and to employ rulemaking procedures to designate any "classes of works" for which fair uses would be adversely affected. Such a designation is effective for three years. Persons circumventing technological measures to gain access to works in a designated class are immune from liability under Subpart (a)(1). 17 U.S.C. § 1201(a)(1)(A)-(E). Subsection (a)(1)(E) specifies, however, that this immunity only extends to liability for the act of

Section 1201(a)(2) and (b)(1) are "anti-device and service" provisions—regulating the creation and provision of electronic "crowbars" and infiltration strategies for use in circumventing technological measures. Subsection (a)(2) is directed to devices and services that circumvent technological measures controlling *access* to a work (those devices and services that might be used to violate subsection (a)(1), discussed above). Subsection (b)(1) is directed to devices and services that circumvent technological measures controlling *uses* of works (that is, measures that control the ability of persons having access to a work to reproduce, adapt, distribute, publicly perform or publicly display it. Such measures might include software embedded in a digital work that limits the number of times the work can be performed, or the number of copies that can be made of it). In both cases, the Act prohibits manufacture, importation, offering or trafficking in the devices, services or components. However, to ensure that multi-purpose devices, services and components can continue to be made and distributed to the public, the prohibition is limited to devices, services and components that: 1) are primarily designed or produced for the purpose of circumventing; 2) have only limited commercially significant purposes or uses other than to circumvent; or 3) are marketed for use in circumventing. The Act clarifies that to "circumvent" a technological measure is "to descramble a scrambled work, to decrypt an encrypted work, or otherwise to avoid, bypass, remove, deactivate, or impair a technological measure, without the authority of the copyright owner." 17 U.S.C.A. § 1201(a)(3)(A), (b)(2)(A).

There was considerable opposition to early drafts of the anti-circumvention provisions, generally because of concerns that they would interfere with lawful, fair uses of copyrighted works (thus disrupting the balance of interests achieved under the Copyright Act). More specifically, concerns were expressed that the provisions would interfere with lawful security testing, encryption research, and other technological development. See generally Samuelson, *Intellectual Property and the Digital Economy: Why the Anti–Circumvention Regulations Need to Be Revised*, 14 Berkeley Tech. L.J. 519 (1999). Congress declined to enact a flexible, general "fair use" type of exception to liability. However, Congress attempted to accommodate certain specific concerns by adding a series of narrow statutory exceptions to liability. These include exceptions: to permit software developers to reverse engineer technologically protected software in order to achieve interoperability with those programs; to permit deactivation of "cookies" for privacy purposes; to permit police and intelligence agents to circumvent for law enforcement purposes; to permit researchers to engage in good-faith encryption research; and to permit persons to engage in testing the security of a computer system or network.

---

circumventing an access control. It does not extend to the creation or provision of services or devices for accomplishing such circumvention. Thus, as a practical matter, only those persons with the technical expertise to accomplish the circumvention on their own will enjoy the advantage of this provision.

To date, the Librarian of Congress has only approved exceptions for very narrow, specific categories of works.

As noted above, these exceptions are very narrowly drafted. Some of them only apply to the act of circumvention to obtain access, providing no exception to permit the manufacture or distribution of devices or services to accomplish the circumvention. Others extend beyond the act of circumvention itself to authorize certain devices and services.

CHAMBERLAIN GROUP, INC. v. SKYLINK TECHNOLOGIES, INC.

Court of Appeals for the Federal Circuit, 2004.
381 F.3d 1178, *cert. denied*, 544 U.S. 923, 125 S.Ct. 1669, 161 L.Ed.2d 481 (2005).

GAJARSA, CIRCUIT JUDGE:

The Chamberlain Group, Inc. ("Chamberlain") appeals the November 13, 2003 summary judgment of the United States District Court for the Northern District of Illinois ("District Court") in favor of Skylink Technologies, Inc. ("Skylink"), finding that Skylink is not violating the anti-trafficking provisions of the Digital Millennium Copyright Act ("DMCA"), 17 U.S.C. § 1201 et seq. * * *.

* * *

The technology at issue involves Garage Door Openers (GDOs). A GDO typically consists of a hand-held portable transmitter and a garage door opening device mounted in a homeowner's garage. The opening device, in turn, includes both a receiver with associated signal processing software and a motor to open or close the garage door. In order to open or close the garage door, a user must activate the transmitter, which sends a radio frequency (RF) signal to the receiver located on the opening device. Once the opener receives a recognized signal, the signal processing software directs the motor to open or close the garage door.

When a homeowner purchases a GDO system, the manufacturer provides both an opener and a transmitter. Homeowners who desire replacement or spare transmitters can purchase them in the aftermarket. Aftermarket consumers have long been able to purchase "universal transmitters" that they can program to interoperate with their GDO system regardless of make or model. Skylink and Chamberlain are the only significant distributors of universal GDO transmitters. Chamberlain places no explicit restrictions on the types of transmitter that the homeowner may use with its system at the time of purchase. Chamberlain's customers therefore assume that they enjoy all of the rights associated with the use of their GDOs and any software embedded therein that the copyright laws and other laws of commerce provide.

This dispute involves Chamberlain's Security+ line of GDOs and Skylink's Model 39 universal transmitter. Chamberlain's Security+ GDOs incorporate a copyrighted "rolling code" computer program that constantly changes the transmitter signal needed to open the garage door. Skylink's Model 39 transmitter, which does not incorporate rolling code, nevertheless allows users to operate Security+ openers. Chamberlain alleges that Skylink's transmitter renders the Security+ insecure by allowing unauthorized users to circumvent the security inherent in rolling codes. Of greater legal significance, however, Chamberlain contends that because of this property of the Model 39, Skylink is in violation of the anti-trafficking clause of the DMCA's anticircumvention provisions, specifically § 1201(a)(2).

* * *

Skylink began marketing and selling universal transmitters in 1992. Skylink designed its Model 39, launched in August 2002, to interoperate with common GDOs, including both rolling code and non-rolling code GDOs. Although Chamberlain concedes that the Model 39 transmitter is capable of operating many different GDOs, it nevertheless asserts that Skylink markets the Model 39 transmitter for use in circumventing its copyrighted rolling code computer program. Chamberlain supports this allegation by pointing to the Model 39's setting that operates *only* Chamberlain's rolling code GDOs.

* * *

[I]t is * * * noteworthy that Chamberlain *has not* alleged either that Skylink infringed its copyright or that Skylink is liable for contributory copyright infringement. What Chamberlain *has* alleged is that because its opener and transmitter both incorporate computer programs "protected by copyright" and because rolling codes are a "technological measure" that "controls access" to those programs, Skylink is prima facie liable for violating § 1201(a)(2). In the District Court's words, "Chamberlain claims that the rolling code computer program has a protective measure that protects itself. Thus, only one computer program is at work here, but it has two functions: (1) to verify the rolling code; and (2) once the rolling code is verified, to activate the GDO motor, by sending instructions to a microprocessor in the GDO."

C. *The Summary Judgment Motions*

* * *

According to undisputed facts, a homeowner who purchases a Chamberlain GDO owns it and has a right to use it to access his or her own garage. At the time of sale, Chamberlain does not place any explicit terms or condition on use to limit the ways that a purchaser may use its products. A homeowner who wishes to use a Model 39 must first program it into the GDO. Skylink characterizes this action as the homeowner's authorization of the Model 39 to interoperate with the GDO. In other words, according to Skylink, Chamberlain GDO consumers who purchase a Skylink transmitter have Chamberlain's implicit permission to purchase and to use any brand of transmitter that will open their GDO. The District Court agreed that Chamberlain's unconditioned sale implied authorization.

* * *

The District Court further noted that under Chamberlain's proposed construction of the DMCA, not only would Skylink be in violation of § 1201(a)(2) (prohibiting trafficking in circumvention devices), but Chamberlain's own customers who used a Model 39 would be in violation of § 1201(a)(1) (prohibiting circumvention). The District Court declined to adopt a construction with such dire implications. * * *

DISCUSSION

* * *

D. *The Statute and Liability under the DMCA*

The essence of the DMCA's anticircumvention provisions is that §§ 1201(a),(b) establish causes of action for liability. They do not establish a new property right. The DMCA's text indicates that circumvention is not infringement, 17 U.S.C. § 1201(c)(1) ("Nothing in this section shall affect rights, remedies, limitations, or defenses to copyright infringement, including fair use, under this title."), and the statute's structure makes the point even clearer. This distinction between property and liability is critical. Whereas copyrights, like patents, are property, liability protection from unauthorized circumvention merely creates a new cause of action under which a defendant may be liable. The distinction between property and liability goes straight to the issue of authorization, the issue upon which the District Court both denied Chamberlain's and granted Skylink's motion for summary judgment.

[U]nder Seventh Circuit copyright law, a [copyright infringement] plaintiff only needs to show that the defendant has used her property; the burden of proving that the use was authorized falls squarely on the defendant. The DMCA, however, *defines* circumvention as an activity undertaken "without the authority of the copyright owner." 17 U.S.C. § 1201(a)(3)(A). The plain language of the statute therefore requires a plaintiff alleging circumvention (or trafficking) to prove that the defendant's access was unauthorized—a significant burden where, as here, the copyright laws authorize consumers to use the copy of Chamberlain's software embedded in the GDOs that they purchased. The premise underlying this initial assignment of burden is that the copyright laws authorize members of the public to access a work, but not to copy it. The law therefore places the burden of proof on the party attempting to establish that the circumstances of its case deviate from these normal expectations; defendants must prove authorized copying and plaintiffs must prove unauthorized access.

The distinction between property and liability also addresses an important policy issue that Chamberlain puts into stark focus. * * * Chamberlain [claims] that the DMCA overrode all pre-existing consumer expectations about the legitimate uses of products containing copyrighted embedded software. Chamberlain contends that Congress empowered manufacturers to prohibit consumers from using embedded software products in conjunction with competing products when it passed § 1201(a)(1).

According to Chamberlain, *all* such uses of products containing copyrighted software to which a technological measure controlled access are now per se illegal under the DMCA unless the manufacturer provided consumers with *explicit* authorization. Chamberlain's interpretation of the DMCA would therefore grant manufacturers broad exemptions from both the antitrust laws and the doctrine of copyright misuse.

Such an exemption, however, is only plausible if the anticircumvention provisions established a new property right capable of conflicting with the copyright owner's other legal responsibilities—which as we have already explained, they do not. The anticircumvention provisions convey no additional property rights in and of themselves; they simply provide property owners with new ways to secure their property. Like all property owners taking legitimate steps to protect their property, however, copyright owners relying on the anticircumvention provisions remain bound by all other relevant bodies of law. Contrary to Chamberlain's assertion, the DMCA emphatically *did not* "fundamentally alter" the legal landscape governing the reasonable expectations of consumers or competitors; *did not* "fundamentally alter" the ways that courts analyze industry practices; and *did not* render the pre-DMCA history of the GDO industry irrelevant.

What the DMCA did was introduce new grounds for liability in the context of the unauthorized access of copyrighted material. The statute's plain language requires plaintiffs to prove that those circumventing their technological measures controlling access did so "without the authority of the copyright owner." 17 U.S.C. § 1201(3)(A). Our inquiry ends with that clear language. We note, however, that the statute's structure, legislative history, and context within the Copyright Act all support our construction.
* * *

E.   *Statutory Structure and Legislative History*

* * *

* * * Statutory structure and legislative history both make it clear that § 1201 applies only to circumventions reasonably related to protected rights. Defendants who traffic in devices that circumvent access controls in ways that facilitate infringement may be subject to liability under § 1201(a)(2). Defendants who use such devices may be subject to liability under § 1201(a)(1) whether they infringe or not. Because all defendants who traffic in devices that circumvent rights controls necessarily facilitate infringement, they may be subject to liability under § 1201(b). Defendants who use such devices may be subject to liability for copyright infringement. And finally, defendants whose circumvention devices do not facilitate infringement are not subject to § 1201 liability.

The key to understanding this relationship lies in § 1201(b),[12] which prohibits trafficking in devices that circumvent technological measures

---

12. "No person shall manufacture, import, offer to the public, provide, or otherwise traffic in any technology, product, service, device, component, or part thereof, that . . . [circumvents] a

tailored narrowly to protect an individual right of the copyright owner while nevertheless allowing access to the protected work. Though § 1201(b) parallels the anti-trafficking ban of § 1201(a)(2), there is no narrowly tailored ban on direct circumvention to parallel § 1201(a)(1). This omission was intentional.

> The prohibition in 1201(a)(1) [was] necessary because prior to [the DMCA], the conduct of circumvention was never before made unlawful. The device limitation in 1201(a)(2) enforces this new prohibition in conduct. The copyright law has long forbidden copyright infringements, so no new prohibition was necessary. The device limitation in 1201(b) enforces the longstanding prohibitions on infringements.

S.Rep. No. 105–90 at 12 (1998).

Prior to the DMCA, a copyright owner would have had no cause of action against anyone who circumvented any sort of technological control, but did not infringe. The DMCA rebalanced these interests to favor the copyright owner; the DMCA created circumvention liability for "digital trespass" under § 1201(a)(1). It also created trafficking liability under § 1201(a)(2) for facilitating such circumvention and under § 1201(b) for facilitating infringement (both subject to the numerous limitations and exceptions outlined throughout the DMCA).[13]

      * * *

The most significant and consistent theme running through the entire legislative history of the anticircumvention and anti-trafficking provisions of the DMCA, §§ 1201(a)(1), (2), is that Congress attempted to balance competing interests, and "endeavored to specify, with as much clarity as possible, how the right against anti-circumvention would be qualified to maintain balance between the interests of content creators and information users." H.R.Rep. No. 105–551, at 26 (1998). The Report of the House Commerce Committee concluded that § 1201 "fully respects and extends into the digital environment the bedrock principle of 'balance' in American intellectual property law for the benefit of both copyright owners and users." *Id.*

      * * *

* * * We must understand that balance to resolve this dispute.

F. *Access and Protection*

Congress crafted the new anticircumvention and anti-trafficking provisions here at issue to help bring copyright law into the information age. Advances in digital technology over the past few decades have stripped

---

technological measure that effectively protects *a right of a copyright owner* under this title in a work or a portion thereof." 35 U.S.C. § 1201(b)(1) (emphasis added).

13. For obvious reasons, § 1201(a)(2) trafficking liability cannot exist in the absence of § 1201(a)(1) violations—much as this court has often explained that "indirect [patent] infringement, whether inducement to infringe or contributory infringement, can only arise in the presence of direct infringement, though the direct infringer is typically someone other than the defendant accused of indirect infringement." *Dynacore Holdings Corp. v. U.S. Philips Corp.*, 363 F.3d 1263, 1272 (Fed.Cir.2004).

copyright owners of much of the technological and economic protection to which they had grown accustomed. Whereas large-scale copying and distribution of copyrighted material used to be difficult and expensive, it is now easy and inexpensive. * * * Congress therefore crafted legislation restricting some, but not all, technological measures designed either to access a work protected by copyright, § 1201(a), or to infringe a right of a copyright owner, § 1201(b).

Though as noted, circumvention *is not* a new form of infringement but rather a new violation prohibiting actions or products that facilitate infringement, it is significant that virtually every clause of § 1201 that mentions "access" links "access" to "protection." The import of that linkage may be less than obvious. Perhaps the best way to appreciate the necessity of this linkage—and the disposition of this case—is to consider three interrelated questions inherent in the DMCA's structure: What does § 1201(a)(2) prohibit above and beyond the prohibitions of § 1201(b)? What is the relationship between the sorts of "access" prohibited under § 1201(a) and the rights "protected" under the Copyright Act? And what is the relationship between anticircumvention liability under § 1201(a)(1) and anti-trafficking liability under § 1201(a)(2)? The relationships among the new liabilities that these three provisions, §§ 1201(a)(1), (a)(2), (b), create circumscribe the DMCA's scope-and therefore allow us to determine whether or not Chamberlain's claim falls within its purview. And the key to disentangling these relationships lies in understanding the linkage between access and protection.

Chamberlain urges us to read the DMCA as if Congress simply created a new protection for copyrighted works without any reference at all either to the protections that copyright owners already possess or to the rights that the Copyright Act grants to the public. Chamberlain has not alleged that Skylink's Model 39 infringes its copyrights, nor has it alleged that the Model 39 contributes to third-party infringement of its copyrights. Chamberlain's allegation is considerably more straightforward: The only way for the Model 39 to interoperate with a Security + GDO is by "accessing" copyrighted software. Skylink has therefore committed a per se violation of the DMCA. Chamberlain urges us to conclude that no necessary connection exists between access and *copyrights*. Congress could not have intended such a broad reading of the DMCA. * * *

Chamberlain's proposed construction of the DMCA ignores the significant differences between defendants whose accused products enable copying and those, like Skylink, whose accused products enable only legitimate uses of copyrighted software. * * *

* * *

* * * Were § 1201(a) to allow copyright owners to use technological measures to block *all* access to their copyrighted works, it would effectively create two distinct copyright regimes. In the first regime, the owners of a typical work protected by copyright would possess only the rights enumerated in 17 U.S.C. § 106, subject to the additions, exceptions, and

limitations outlined throughout the rest of the Copyright Act—notably but not solely the fair use provisions of § 107.[14] Owners who feel that technology has put those rights at risk, and who incorporate technological measures to protect those rights from technological encroachment, gain the additional ability to hold traffickers in circumvention devices liable under § 1201(b) for putting their rights back at risk by enabling circumventors who use these devices to infringe.

Under the second regime that Chamberlain's proposed construction implies, the owners of a work protected by *both* copyright *and* a technological measure that effectively controls access to that work per § 1201(a) would possess *unlimited* rights to hold circumventors liable under § 1201(a) *merely for accessing that work,* even if that access enabled *only* rights that the Copyright Act grants to the public. This second implied regime would be problematic for a number of reasons. First, as the Supreme Court recently explained, "Congress' exercise of its Copyright Clause authority must be rational." *Eldred v. Ashcroft,* 537 U.S. 186, 205 n. 10, 123 S.Ct. 769, 154 L.Ed.2d 683 (2003). In determining whether a particular aspect of the Copyright Act "is a rational exercise of the legislative authority conferred by the Copyright Clause ... we defer substantially to Congress. It is Congress that has been assigned the task of defining the scope of the limited monopoly that should be granted to authors ... *in order to give the public appropriate access* to their work product." *Id.* at 204–05, 123 S.Ct. 769 (emphasis added). Chamberlain's proposed construction of § 1201(a) implies that in enacting the DMCA, Congress attempted to "give the public appropriate access" to copyrighted works by allowing copyright owners to deny all access to the public. Even under the substantial deference due Congress, such a redefinition borders on the irrational.

That apparent irrationality, however, is not the most significant problem that this second regime implies. Such a regime would be hard to reconcile with the DMCA's statutory prescription that "[n]othing in this section shall affect rights, remedies, limitations, or defenses to copyright infringement, including fair use, under this title." 17 U.S.C. § 1201(c)(1). A provision that prohibited access without regard to the rest of the Copyright Act would clearly affect rights and limitations, if not remedies and defenses. Justice Souter has remarked that "[n]o canon of statutory construction familiar to me specifically addresses the situation in which two simultaneously enacted provisions of the same statute flatly contradict one another. We are, of course, bound to avoid such a dilemma if we can, by glimpsing some uncontradicted meaning for each provision." *Reno v. American–Arab Anti–Discrimination Comm.,* 525 U.S. 471, 509, 119

---

14. We do not reach the relationship between § 107 fair use and violations of § 1201. The District Court in *Reimerdes* rejected the DeCSS defendants' argument that fair use was a *necessary* defense to § 1201(a), *Reimerdes,* 111 F.Supp.2d at 317; because *any* access enables some fair uses, any act of circumvention would embody its own defense. We leave open the question as to when § 107 might serve as an affirmative defense to a prima facie violation of § 1201. For the moment, we note only that though the traditional fair use doctrine of § 107 remains unchanged as a defense to copyright infringement under § 1201(c)(1), circumvention is not infringement.

S.Ct. 936, 142 L.Ed.2d 940 (1999) (Souter, J., dissenting). Chamberlain's proposed construction of § 1201(a) would flatly contradict § 1201(c)(1)—a simultaneously enacted provision of the same statute. We are therefore bound, if we can, to obtain an alternative construction that leads to no such contradiction.

Chamberlain's proposed severance of "access" from "protection" in § 1201(a) creates numerous other problems. Beyond suggesting that Congress enacted *by implication* a new, highly protective alternative regime for copyrighted works; contradicting other provisions of the same statute including § 1201(c)(1); and ignoring the explicit immunization of interoperability from anticircumvention liability under § 1201(f);[15] the broad policy implications of considering "access" in a vacuum devoid of "protection" are both absurd and disastrous. Under Chamberlain's proposed construction, explicated at oral argument, disabling a burglar alarm to gain "access" to a home containing copyrighted books, music, art, and periodicals would violate the DMCA; anyone who did so would unquestionably have "circumvent[ed] a technological measure that effectively controls access to a work protected under [the Copyright Act]." § 1201(a)(1). The appropriate deterrents to this type of behavior lie in tort law and criminal law, *not* in copyright law. Yet, were we to read the statute's "plain language" as Chamberlain urges, disabling a burglar alarm would be a per se violation of the DMCA.

In a similar vein, Chamberlain's proposed construction would allow any manufacturer of any product to add a single copyrighted sentence or software fragment to its product, wrap the copyrighted material in a trivial "encryption" scheme, and thereby gain the right to restrict consumers' rights to use its products in conjunction with competing products. In other words, Chamberlain's construction of the DMCA would allow virtually any company to attempt to leverage its sales into aftermarket monopolies—a practice that both the antitrust laws, and the doctrine of copyright misuse, normally prohibit.

* * *

Finally, the requisite "authorization," on which the District Court granted Skylink summary judgment, points to yet another inconsistency in Chamberlain's proposed construction. The notion of authorization is central to understanding § 1201(a). * * * Underlying Chamberlain's argument on appeal that it has not granted such authorization lies the necessary assumption that Chamberlain is entitled to prohibit legitimate purchasers of its embedded software from "accessing" the software by using it. * * * Chamberlain's proposed construction would * * * allow any copyright owner, through a combination of contractual terms and technological measures, to repeal the fair use doctrine with respect to an

---

15. Amicus CCIA expanded on this argument in its amicus briefs to both the District Court and this court. Though the District Court found this argument at least superficially persuasive, it did not reach it. On the facts of this case, neither can we. Because § 1201(f) is an affirmative defense, it becomes relevant only if Chamberlain can prove a prima facie case and shift the burden of proof to Skylink.

individual copyrighted work—or even selected copies of that copyrighted work. Again, this implication contradicts § 1201(c)(1) directly. Copyright law itself authorizes the public to make certain uses of copyrighted materials. Consumers who purchase a product containing a copy of embedded software have the inherent legal right to use that copy of the software. What the law authorizes, Chamberlain cannot revoke.[17]

Chamberlain's proposed severance of "access" from "protection" is entirely inconsistent with the context defined by the total statutory structure of the Copyright Act, other simultaneously enacted provisions of the DMCA, and clear Congressional intent. * * * The statutory structure and the legislative history both make it clear that the DMCA granted copyright holders additional legal protections, but neither rescinded the basic bargain granting the public noninfringing and fair uses of copyrighted materials, § 1201(c), nor prohibited various beneficial uses of circumvention technology, such as those exempted under §§ 1201(d), (f), (g), (j).

We therefore reject Chamberlain's proposed construction in its entirety. We conclude that 17 U.S.C. § 1201 prohibits only forms of access that bear a reasonable relationship to the protections that the Copyright Act otherwise affords copyright owners. While such a rule of reason may create some uncertainty and consume some judicial resources, it is the only meaningful reading of the statute. Congress attempted to balance the legitimate interests of copyright owners with those of consumers of copyrighted products. The courts must adhere to the language that Congress enacted to determine how it attempted to achieve that balance.

* * * Were we to interpret Congress's words in a way that eliminated all balance and granted copyright owners carte blanche authority to preclude all use, Congressional intent would remain unrealized.

[The statute] instructs the courts explicitly *not* to construe the anticircumvention provisions in ways that would effectively repeal longstanding principles of copyright law. *See* § 1201(c). The courts must decide where the balance between the rights of copyright owners and those of the broad public tilts subject to a fact-specific rule of reason. Here, Chamberlain can point to no protected property right that Skylink imperils. The DMCA cannot allow Chamberlain to retract the most fundamental right that the Copyright Act grants consumers: the right to use the copy of Chamberlain's embedded software that they purchased.

G. *Chamberlain's DMCA Claim*

The proper construction of § 1201(a)(2) therefore makes it clear that Chamberlain cannot prevail. A plaintiff alleging a violation of § 1201(a)(2) must prove: (1) ownership of a valid *copyright* on a work, (2) effectively controlled by a *technological measure,* which has been circumvented, (3)

---

17. It is not clear whether a consumer who circumvents a technological measure controlling access to a copyrighted work in a manner that enables uses permitted under the Copyright Act but prohibited by contract can be subject to liability under the DMCA. Because Chamberlain did not attempt to limit its customers use of its product by contract, however, we do not reach this issue.

that third parties can now *access* (4) *without authorization,* in a manner that (5) infringes or facilitates infringing a right *protected* by the Copyright Act, because of a product that (6) the defendant either (i) *designed or produced* primarily for circumvention; (ii) made available despite only *limited commercial significance* other than circumvention; or (iii) *marketed* for use in circumvention of the controlling technological measure. A plaintiff incapable of establishing any one of elements (1) through (5) will have failed to prove a prima facie case. A plaintiff capable of proving elements (1) through (5) need prove only one of (6)(i), (ii), or (iii) to shift the burden back to the defendant. At that point, the various affirmative defenses enumerated throughout § 1201 become relevant.

     * * *

Chamberlain * * * has failed to show not only the requisite lack of authorization, but also the necessary fifth element of its claim, the critical nexus between access and protection. Chamberlain neither alleged copyright infringement *nor explained how the access provided by the Model 39 transmitter facilitates the infringement of any right that the Copyright Act protects.* There can therefore be no reasonable relationship between the access that homeowners gain to Chamberlain's copyrighted software when using Skylink's Model 39 transmitter and the protections that the Copyright Act grants to Chamberlain. The Copyright Act authorized Chamberlain's customers to use the copy of Chamberlain's copyrighted software embedded in the GDOs that they purchased. Chamberlain's customers are therefore immune from § 1201(a)(1) circumvention liability. In the absence of allegations of either copyright infringement or § 1201(a)(1) circumvention, Skylink cannot be liable for § 1201(a)(2) trafficking. The District Court's grant of summary judgment in Skylink's favor was correct. Chamberlain failed to allege a claim under 17 U.S.C. § 1201.

     * * *

NOTES AND QUESTIONS

1. *Construction of the anti-circumvention provisions.* Why did Congress prohibit the act of circumventing a technological measure that controls *access* to a work, but not the act of circumventing a technological measure that controls *use* of a work, once access is gained? With regard to the trafficking provisions, why isn't the rule set forth in Sony Corp. v. Universal City Studios, Inc., 464 U.S. 417, 104 S.Ct. 774, 78 L.Ed.2d 574 (1984), providing contributory infringement liability for knowing sale of a device that has no substantial non-infringing use, adequate to protect copyright owners against sale of circumvention devices? If you feel that it is not adequate in itself, is the *Sony* rule, in combination with the new *Grokster* inducement theory of indirect infringement liability sufficient?

Do you agree with the *Chamberlain* court's interpretation of the statutory language? The Court of Appeals for the Fifth Circuit has subsequently adopted a similar construction. MGE UPS Systems, Inc. v. GE Consumer and Industrial, Inc., 612 F.3d 760 (5th Cir. 2010). But compare Universal City

Studios, Inc. v. Corley, 273 F.3d 429, 443 (2d Cir. 2001)("[T]he DMCA targets the *circumvention* of digital walls guarding copyrighted material (and trafficking in circumvention tools), but does not concern itself with the *use* of those materials after circumvention has occurred")(emphasis in original). Under the *Chamberlain* court's interpretation, must use of the defendant's access control circumvention device actually result in copyright infringement, or will it be sufficient to demonstrate that the device makes it possible for the user to infringe? What if the device facilitates both infringing and noninfringing access? For further insights concerning the Federal Circuit's views on these issues, see Storage Technology Corp. v. Custom Hardware Engineering & Consulting, Inc., 421 F.3d 1307, 1318–19 (Fed. Cir. 2005). Why, according to the *Chamberlain* court, does the distinction between property and liability "go straight to the issue of authorization?" Can a meaningful distinction be drawn between "property" and "liability"?

Under the Federal Circuit's reasoning, what would happen if Chamberlain began marketing its garage doors with an express restriction, printed on the packaging and in the instruction manual, prohibiting purchasers from using the garage door with other producers' transmitter/openers? Would it then have a cause of action against Skylink under § 1201(a)(2)?

2. *"Circumvention."* What does it take to "circumvent" a technological measure that controls access to a work, and what kinds of devices or services are likely to accomplish such circumvention? The DMCA provides that "to 'circumvent a technological measure' means to descramble a scrambled work, to decrypt an encrypted work, or otherwise to avoid, bypass, remove, deactivate, or impair a technological measure, without the authority of the copyright owner." 17 U.S.C.A. § 1201(a)(3)(A).

What if the copyright owner implemented a password system, assigning an individualized user identification and password to each person authorized to access digital copyrighted material on its web site, and barring access to all those lacking user identifications and passwords. A password system clearly is a technological measure that controls access to the copyrighted work. The DMCA provides: "A technological measure 'effectively controls access to a work' if the measure, in the ordinary course of its operation, requires the application of information, or a process or a treatment, with the authority of the copyright owner, to gain access to the work." 17 U.S.C.A. § 1201(a)(3)(B). Assume that, without the copyright owner's authorization, an authorized user provides her user identification and password to a third party, who uses it to access the copyrighted material. Has there been an actionable "circumvention" of the password system? Compare I.M.S. Inquiry Management Systems, Ltd. v. Berkshire Information Systems, Inc., 307 F.Supp.2d 521, 531–33 (S.D.N.Y. 2004), and Egilman v. Keller & Heckman, LLP, 401 F.Supp.2d 105, 112–14 (D.D.C. 2005), with 321 Studios v. Metro Goldwyn Mayer Studios, Inc., 307 F.Supp.2d 1085, 1097 (N.D. Ca. 2004).

3. *The meaning of DMCA § 1201(c)(1).* In *Chamberlain*, the Federal Circuit found that construing § 1201(a) to apply to circumventions that do not facilitate infringement would conflict with § 1201(c)(1), which provides: "Nothing in this section shall affect rights, remedies, limitations, or defenses to copyright infringement, including fair use, under this title." The court

reasoned that application of the anticircumvention provisions to prevent all unauthorized access, regardless of whether the access facilitated infringement, would

> allow any copyright owner, through a combination of contractual terms and technological measures, to repeal the fair use doctrine with respect to an individual copyrighted work—or even selected copies of that copyrighted work. [T]his implication contradicts § 1201(c)(1) directly. Copyright law itself authorizes the public to make certain uses of copyrighted materials. * * * The statutory structure and the legislative history both make it clear that the DMCA granted copyright holders additional legal protections, but [did not rescind] the basic bargain granting the public noninfringing and fair uses of copyrighted materials, § 1201(c)(1) * * *.

381 F.3d at 1202.

Compare the Second Circuit's opinion in Universal City Studios, Inc. v. Corley, 273 F.3d 429, 433 (2d Cir. 2001), which involved alleged trafficking in software to unlock the encryption system employed by copyright owners to prevent unauthorized copying of their movies on DVD:

> [Appellants] contend that subsection 1201(c)(1) * * * can be read to allow the circumvention of encryption technology protecting copyrighted material when the material will be put to "fair uses" exempt from copyright liability. We disagree that subsection 1201(c)(1) permits such a reading. Instead, it simply clarifies that the DMCA targets the *circumvention* of digital walls guarding copyrighted material (and trafficking in circumvention tools), but does not concern itself with the *use* of those materials after circumvention has occurred. Subsection 1201(c)(1) ensures that the DMCA is not read to prohibit the "fair use" of information just because that information was obtained in a manner made illegal by the DMCA. The Appellants' much more expansive interpretation of subsection 1201(c)(1) is not only outside the range of plausible readings of the provision, but is also clearly refuted by the statute's legislative history.

Id. at 443–44. In a footnote, the Second Circuit explained why it believed that the legislative history supported its interpretation of § 1201(c)(1):

> The legislative history of the enacted bill makes quite clear that Congress intended to adopt a "balanced" approach to accommodating both piracy and fair use concerns, eschewing the quick fix of simply exempting from the statute all circumventions for fair use. H.R.Rep. No. 105–551, pt.2, at 25 (1998). It sought to achieve this goal principally through the use of what it called a "fail-safe" provision in the statute, authorizing the Librarian of Congress to exempt certain users from the anti-circumvention provision when it becomes evident that in practice, the statute is adversely affecting certain kinds of fair use. * * *
>
> Congress also sought to implement a balanced approach through statutory provisions that leave limited areas of breathing space for fair use. A good example is subsection 1201(d), which allows a library or educational institution to circumvent a digital wall in order to determine whether it wishes legitimately to obtain the material behind the wall. It would be strange for Congress to open small, carefully limited windows

for circumvention to permit fair use in subsection 1201(d) if it then meant to exempt in subsection 1201(c)(1) *any* circumvention necessary for fair use.

Id., at 444 n. 13. Are the *Chamberlain* and *Corley* decisions reconcilable? If not, which one seems the correct reading of the statutory language? Which one seems the correct reading from the standpoint of public policy?

4. *Copyright management information.* In addition to its anticircumvention provisions, the DMCA also prohibits persons from intentionally removing or altering copyright management information, or knowingly distributing copies or phonorecords with illegally modified or deleted copyright management information. 17 U.S.C.A. § 1202. "Copyright management information" is defined in § 1202(c) to include, information about the author, the work, the copyright owner, terms and conditions for use of the work, and in some instances, information about the performer, writer, or director of the work. Congress believed it particularly important to prevent tampering with such information in the digital environment because the information will be digitally encoded in copyrighted works and used in automated licensing and tracking of the works on the Internet.

Review the language of § 1202. How broad are the rights it creates? For example, assume that Textile Co. creates a new fabric design, and prints notice of copyright (the symbol ©, followed by the copyright owner's name and the date of first publication) along the selvage (the edge or border of the fabric that is intended to be cut off and discarded when the fabric is made into clothing). Fashion Co. creates an infringing fabric, which it uses to manufacture clothing for sale. Fashion Co. does not place Textile Co.'s copyright notice on its infringing fabric. Should Textile Co. have a cause of action against Fashion Co. under the Digital Millennium Copyright Act for "deleting" copyright management information? In Textile Secrets International, Inc. v. Ya–Ya Brand, Inc., 524 F.Supp.2d 1184, 1201–02 (C.D.Ca. 2007), the court held that it did not, explaining that § 1202 was not

> intended to apply to circumstances that have no relation to the Internet, electronic commerce, automated copyright protection or management systems, public registers, or other technological measures or processes as contemplated in the DMCA as a whole. In other words, although the parties do not dispute that the FEATHERS fabric contained TSI's copyright information, there are no facts showing that any technological process as contemplated in the DMCA was utilized by plaintiff in placing the copyright information onto the FEATHERS fabric, or that defendants employed any technological process in either their removal of the copyright information from the design or in their alleged distribution of the design. In short, the court finds that, in light of the legislative intent behind the DMCA to facilitate electronic and Internet commerce, the factors of this case do not trigger § 1202.

For a contrasting construction of § 1202, see Associated Press v. All Headline News Corp., 608 F.Supp.2d 454, 462 (S.D.N.Y. 2009)(finding "no textual support for limiting the DMCA's application to 'the technological measures of automated systems'—a phrase that appears nowhere in the statute.")

PROBLEMS

1. Publisher collects rare copies of 19th century public domain books. It writes a new introduction to each book, and digitizes and uploads each book with new introduction onto its commercial web site, subject to a technological protection measure. It then charges for access to and use of each book. Scholar, writing a Ph.D. thesis, hacks the technological protection measure to obtain access to one of the books (which is relevant to her thesis topic) without paying. She locates four lines of text from the body of the book, which are important to support her scholarly argument, and reproduces them in her thesis. Publisher sues. Will Scholar be liable, pursuant to § 1201? What if Scholar lacked hacking expertise, and thus hired her acquaintance, Computer Whiz, to design a device that she can use to obtain the access? Will Computer Whiz be liable?

2. Plaintiff motion picture copyright owners have released some of their copyrighted films for home viewing in DVD (digital versatile disk) format. The films in DVD format are protected through an encryption scheme (called "CSS") that allows the DVD only to be viewed on players or computer drives equipped with licensed technology that permits decryption and playing—but not copying—of the films. X developed a computer program called "DeCSS," which circumvents the plaintiff's encryption system. To do this, X reverse engineered a licensed DVD player and discovered the plaintiffs' encryption algorithm and keys. He then used this information to create DeCSS, which decrypts or "rips" encrypted DVDs, thereby allowing playback on non-compliant computers, as well as the copying of decrypted files to computer hard drives. Although X's particular purpose in creating DeCSS was to permit DVDs to run on his Linux operating system, he knew that DeCSS could be used on computers with other operating systems, and that the copyrighted motion picture files, once decrypted, could be copied like any other computer files. X posted his DeCSS program code on his web site.

Y, learning of X's DeCSS program, posted a copy of the DeCSS code on his web site. Z did not post the program code himself, but provided links from his web site to other web sites that offered the DcCSS code. There is no evidence available to show that any person has relied on Y's posting or Z's links to circumvent plaintiff's encryption system or to infringe any of plaintiff's copyrights.

Please evaluate X, Y and Z's liability under § 1201. What are the policy implications of holding them liable?

VI. OWNERSHIP OF COPYRIGHT

Copyright initially vests in the "author" of a work. 17 U.S.C.A. § 201. Generally, the "author" is the person who conceives of the copyrightable expression and fixes or causes it to be fixed in tangible form. *Andrien v. Southern Ocean County Chamber of Commerce,* 927 F.2d 132 (3d Cir. 1991). When a work is "made for hire," however, the employer or commissioning party, who finances creation of the work and takes the economic risk of it, is deemed the "author," rather than the employee or commissioned party who actually conceives and fixes the expression. 17 U.S.C.A. § 201(b).

Subsection A will discuss when a work is made "for hire," so that the employer or commissioning party is deemed the "author." Subsection B will address the difficulties that arise in determining when a claimant will qualify as a "joint author" of a work, and thus a co-owner of the copyright in it. Subsection C will discuss the divisibility and transfer of copyright ownership.

A. WORKS MADE FOR HIRE

COMMUNITY FOR CREATIVE NON–VIOLENCE v. REID

United States Supreme Court, 1989.
490 U.S. 730, 109 S.Ct. 2166, 104 L.Ed.2d 811.

JUSTICE MARSHALL delivered the opinion of the Court.

In this case, an artist and the organization that hired him to produce a sculpture contest the ownership of the copyright in that work. To resolve this dispute, we must construe the "work made for hire" provisions of the Copyright Act of 1976 (Act or 1976 Act), 17 U.S.C. §§ 101 and 201(b), and in particular, the provision in § 101, which defines as a "work made for hire" a "work prepared by an employee within the scope of his or her employment" (hereinafter § 101(1)).

I

Petitioners are the Community for Creative Non–Violence (CCNV), a nonprofit unincorporated association dedicated to eliminating homelessness in America, and Mitch Snyder, a member and trustee of CCNV. In the fall of 1985, CCNV decided to participate in the annual Christmastime Pageant of Peace in Washington, D.C., by sponsoring a display to dramatize the plight of the homeless. As the District Court recounted:

> "Snyder and fellow CCNV members conceived the idea for the nature of the display: a sculpture of a modern Nativity scene in which, in lieu of the traditional Holy Family, the two adult figures and the infant would appear as contemporary homeless people huddled on a streetside steam grate. The family was to be black (most of the homeless in Washington being black); the figures were to be life-sized, and the steam grate would be positioned atop a platform 'pedestal,' or base, within which special-effects equipment would be enclosed to emit simulated 'steam' through the grid to swirl about the figures. They also settled upon a title for the work—'Third World America'—and a legend for the pedestal: 'and still there is no room at the inn.' "

Snyder made inquiries to locate an artist to produce the sculpture. He was referred to respondent James Earl Reid, a Baltimore, Maryland, sculptor. In the course of two telephone calls, Reid agreed to sculpt the three human figures. CCNV agreed to make the steam grate and pedestal for the statue. Reid proposed that the work be cast in bronze, at a total cost of approximately $100,000 and taking six to eight months to complete. Snyder rejected that proposal because CCNV did not have sufficient funds, and because the statue had to be completed by December 12 to be included in the pageant. Reid then suggested, and Snyder agreed, that the sculpture would be made of a material known as "Design Cast 62," a synthetic substance that could meet CCNV's monetary and time constraints, could be tinted to resemble bronze, and could withstand the elements. The parties agreed that the project would cost no more than $15,000, not including Reid's services, which he offered to donate. The parties did not sign a written agreement. Neither party mentioned copyright.

After Reid received an advance of $3,000, he made several sketches of figures in various poses. At Snyder's request, Reid sent CCNV a sketch of a proposed sculpture showing the family in a creche like setting: the mother seated, cradling a baby in her lap; the father standing behind her, bending over her shoulder to touch the baby's foot. Reid testified that Snyder asked for the sketch to use in raising funds for the sculpture. Snyder testified that it was also for his approval. Reid sought a black family to serve as a model for the sculpture. Upon Snyder's suggestion, Reid visited a family living at CCNV's Washington shelter but decided that only their newly born child was a suitable model. While Reid was in Washington, Snyder took him to see homeless people living on the streets. Snyder pointed out that they tended to recline on steam grates, rather than sit or stand, in order to warm their bodies. From that time on, Reid's sketches contained only reclining figures.

Throughout November and the first two weeks of December 1985, Reid worked exclusively on the statue, assisted at various times by a dozen different people who were paid with funds provided in installments by CCNV. On a number of occasions, CCNV members visited Reid to check on his progress and to coordinate CCNV's construction of the base. CCNV rejected Reid's proposal to use suitcases or shopping bags to hold the family's personal belongings, insisting instead on a shopping cart. Reid and CCNV members did not discuss copyright ownership on any of these visits.

On December 24, 1985, 12 days after the agreed-upon date, Reid delivered the completed statue to Washington. There it was joined to the steam grate and pedestal prepared by CCNV and placed on display near the site of the pageant. Snyder paid Reid the final installment of the $15,000. The statue remained on display for a month. In late January 1986, CCNV members returned it to Reid's studio in Baltimore for minor repairs. Several weeks later, Snyder began making plans to take the statue on a tour of several cities to raise money for the homeless. Reid objected, contending that the Design Cast 62 material was not strong enough to withstand the ambitious itinerary. He urged CCNV to cast the statue in bronze at a cost of $35,000, or to create a master mold at a cost of $5,000. Snyder declined to spend more of CCNV's money on the project.

In March 1986, Snyder asked Reid to return the sculpture. Reid refused. He then filed a certificate of copyright registration for "Third World America" in his name and announced plans to take the sculpture on a more modest tour than the one CCNV had proposed. Snyder, acting in his capacity as CCNV's trustee, immediately filed a competing certificate of copyright registration.

Snyder and CCNV then commenced this action against Reid and his photographer, Ronald Purtee, seeking return of the sculpture and a determination of copyright ownership. [With regard to copyright ownership, the district court found that "Third World America" was a "work made for hire" under § 101 of the Copyright Act and that Snyder, as trustee for CCNV, was the exclusive owner of the copyright in the sculpture. The Court of Appeals for the District of Columbia Circuit reversed and remanded, holding that Reid owned the copyright because "Third World America" was not a work for hire. However, the circuit court suggested that the sculpture might have been jointly authored by CCNV and Reid, and remanded for a determination whether the sculpture was a joint work under the Act.]

We granted *certiorari* to resolve a conflict among the Courts of Appeals over the proper construction of the "work made for hire" provisions of the Act. We now affirm.

II

A

The Copyright Act of 1976 provides that copyright ownership "vests initially in the author or authors of the work." 17 U.S.C. § 201(a). As a general rule, the author is the party who actually creates the work, that is, the person who translates an idea into a fixed, tangible expression entitled to copyright protection. The Act carves out an important exception, however, for "works made for hire." If the work is for hire, "the employer or other person for whom the work was prepared is considered the author" and owns the copyright, unless there is a written agreement to the contrary. § 201(b). Classifying a work as "made for hire" determines not only the initial ownership of its copyright, but also the copyright's duration, § 302(c), and the owners' renewal rights, § 304(a), termination rights, § 203(a), and right to import certain goods bearing the copyright, § 601(b)(1). The contours of the work for hire doctrine therefore carry profound significance for freelance creators—including artists, writers, photographers, designers, composers, and computer programmers—and for the publishing, advertising, music, and other industries which commission their works.

Section 101 of the 1976 Act provides that a work is "for hire" under two sets of circumstances:

"(1) a work prepared by an employee within the scope of his or her employment; or

(2) a work specially ordered or commissioned for use as a contribution to a collective work, as a part of a motion picture or other audiovisual work, as a translation, as a supplementary work, as a compilation, as an instructional text, as a test, as answer material for a test, or as an atlas, if the parties expressly agree in a written instrument signed by them that the work shall be considered a work made for hire."

Petitioners do not claim that the statue satisfies the terms of § 101(2). Quite clearly, it does not. Sculpture does not fit within any of the nine categories of "specially ordered or commissioned" works enumerated in that subsection, and no written agreement between the parties establishes "Third World America" as a work for hire.

The dispositive inquiry in this case therefore is whether "Third World America" is "a work prepared by an employee within the scope of his or her employment" under § 101(1). The Act does not define these terms. In the absence of such guidance, four interpretations have emerged. The first holds that a work is prepared by an employee whenever the hiring party[6] retains the right to control the product. Petitioners take this view. A second, and closely related, view is that a work is prepared by an employee under § 101(1) when the hiring party has actually wielded control with respect to the creation of a particular work. This approach was formulated by the Court of Appeals for the Second Circuit, Aldon Accessories Ltd. v. Spiegel, Inc., 738 F.2d 548, *cert. denied*, 469 U.S. 982, 105 S.Ct. 387, 83 L.Ed.2d 321 (1984), and adopted by the Fourth Circuit, Brunswick Beacon, Inc. v. Schock–Hopchas Publishing Co., 810 F.2d 410 (1987), the Seventh Circuit, Evans Newton, Inc. v. Chicago Systems Software, 793 F.2d 889, *cert. denied*, 479 U.S. 949, 107 S.Ct. 434, 93 L.Ed.2d 383 (1986), and, at times, by petitioners. A third view is that the term "employee" within § 101(1) carries its common-law agency law meaning. This view was endorsed by the Fifth Circuit in Easter Seal Society for Crippled Children & Adults of Louisiana, Inc. v. Playboy Enterprises, 815 F.2d 323 (1987), and by the Court of Appeals below. Finally, respondent and numerous *amici curiae* contend that the term "employee" only refers to "formal, salaried" employees. The Court of Appeals for the Ninth Circuit recently adopted this view. See Dumas v. Gommerman, 865 F.2d 1093 (1989).

The starting point for our interpretation of a statute is always its language. The Act nowhere defines the terms "employee" or "scope of employment." It is, however, well established that "[w]here Congress uses terms that have accumulated settled meaning under ... the common law, a court must infer, unless the statute otherwise dictates, that Congress means to incorporate the established meaning of these terms." In the past, when Congress has used the term "employee" without defining it, we have concluded that Congress intended to describe the conventional

---

6. By "hiring party," we mean to refer to the party who claims ownership of the copyright by virtue of the work for hire doctrine.

master-servant relationship as understood by common-law agency doctrine. Nothing in the text of the work for hire provisions indicates that Congress used the words "employee" and "employment" to describe anything other than " 'the conventional relation of employer and employee.' " On the contrary, Congress' intent to incorporate the agency law definition is suggested by § 101(1)'s use of the term, "scope of employment," a widely used term of art in agency law.

In past cases of statutory interpretation, when we have concluded that Congress intended terms such as "employee," "employer," and "scope of employment" to be understood in light of agency law, we have relied on the general common law of agency, rather than on the law of any particular State, to give meaning to these terms. This practice reflects the fact that "federal statutes are generally intended to have uniform nation-wide application." Establishment of a federal rule of agency, rather than reliance on state agency law, is particularly appropriate here given the Act's express objective of creating national, uniform copyright law by broadly pre-empting state statutory and common-law copyright regulation. We thus agree with the Court of Appeals that the term "employee" should be understood in light of the general common law of agency.

In contrast, neither test proposed by petitioners is consistent with the text of the Act. The exclusive focus of the right to control the product test on the relationship between the hiring party and the product clashes with the language of § 101(1), which focuses on the relationship between the hired and hiring parties. The right to control the product test also would distort the meaning of the ensuing subsection, § 101(2). Section 101 plainly creates two distinct ways in which a work can be deemed for hire: one for works prepared by employees, the other for those specially ordered or commissioned works which fall within one of the nine enumerated categories and are the subject of a written agreement. The right to control the product test ignores this dichotomy by transforming into a work for hire under § 101(1) any "specially ordered or commissioned" work that is subject to the supervision and control of the hiring party. Because a party who hires a "specially ordered or commissioned" work by definition has a right to specify the characteristics of the product desired, at the time the commission is accepted, and frequently until it is completed, the right to control the product test would mean that many works that could satisfy § 101(2) would already have been deemed works for hire under § 101(1). Petitioners' interpretation is particularly hard to square with § 101(2)'s enumeration of the nine specific categories of specially ordered or commissioned works eligible to be works for hire, e.g., "a contribution to a collective work," "a part of a motion picture," and "answer material for a test." The unifying feature of these works is that they are usually prepared at the instance, direction, and risk of a publisher or producer. By their very nature, therefore, these types of works would be works by an employee under petitioners' right to control the product test.

* * *

We therefore conclude that the language and structure of § 101 of the Act do not support either the right to control the product or the actual control approaches. The structure of § 101 indicates that a work for hire can arise through one of two mutually exclusive means, one for employees and one for independent contractors, and ordinary canons of statutory interpretation indicate that the classification of a particular hired party should be made with reference to agency law.

* * *

* * * To determine whether a work is for hire under the Act, a court first should ascertain, using principles of general common law of agency, whether the work was prepared by an employee or an independent contractor. After making this determination, the court can apply the appropriate subsection of § 101.

B

We turn, finally, to an application of § 101 to Reid's production of "Third World America." In determining whether a hired party is an employee under the general common law of agency, we consider the hiring party's right to control the manner and means by which the product is accomplished. Among the other factors relevant to this inquiry are the skill required; the source of the instrumentalities and tools; the location of the work; the duration of the relationship between the parties; whether the hiring party has the right to assign additional projects to the hired party; the extent of the hired party's discretion over when and how long to work; the method of payment; the hired party's role in hiring and paying assistants; whether the work is part of the regular business of the hiring party; whether the hiring party is in business; the provision of employee benefits; and the tax treatment of the hired party. See Restatement [(Second) of Agency] § 220(2) [1958] (setting forth a nonexhaustive list of factors relevant to determining whether a hired party is an employee). No one of these factors is determinative.

Examining the circumstances of this case in light of these factors, we agree with the Court of Appeals that Reid was not an employee of CCNV but an independent contractor. True, CCNV members directed enough of Reid's work to ensure that he produced a sculpture that met their specifications. But the extent of control the hiring party exercises over the details of the product is not dispositive. Indeed, all the other circumstances weigh heavily against finding an employment relationship. Reid is a sculptor, a skilled occupation. Reid supplied his own tools. He worked in his own studio in Baltimore, making daily supervision of his activities from Washington practically impossible. Reid was retained for less than two months, a relatively short period of time. During and after this time, CCNV had no right to assign additional projects to Reid. Apart from the deadline for completing the sculpture, Reid had absolute freedom to decide when and how long to work. CCNV paid Reid $15,000, a sum dependent on "completion of a specific job, a method by which independent contractors are often compensated." Reid had total discretion in hiring and paying assistants. "Creating sculptures was hardly 'regular business' for CCNV." Indeed, CCNV is not a business at all. Finally, CCNV did not pay payroll or Social Security taxes, provide any employee benefits, or contribute to unemployment insurance or workers' compensation funds.

Because Reid was an independent contractor, whether "Third World America" is a work for hire depends on whether it satisfies the terms of § 101(2). This petitioners concede it cannot do. Thus, CCNV is not the author of "Third World America" by virtue of the work for hire provisions of the Act. However, as the Court of Appeals made clear, CCNV nevertheless may be a joint author of the sculpture if, on remand, the District Court determines that CCNV and Reid prepared the work "with the intention that their contributions be merged into inseparable or interdependent parts of a unitary whole." 17 U.S.C. § 101. In that case, CCNV and Reid would be co-owners of the copyright in the work. See § 201(a).

NOTES AND QUESTIONS

1. *Works for hire.* The *C.C.N.V. v. Reid* decision lists a number of factors that are relevant in determining whether the creator of a work is an employee or an independent contractor. Can you explain why each of these factors may be relevant? In Aymes v. Bonelli, 980 F.2d 857 (2d Cir.1992), the Court of Appeals for the Second Circuit reversed a district court that had given each of the factors equal weight and simply counted the number of factors favoring each claimant to determine who should win.

> [T]he *Reid* test can be easily misapplied, since it consists merely of a list of possible considerations that may or may not be relevant in a given case. *Reid* established that no one factor was dispositive, but gave no direction concerning how the factors were to be weighed. It does not necessarily follow that because no one factor is dispositive all factors are equally important, or indeed that all factors will have relevance in every case. The factors should not merely be tallied but should be weighed according to their significance in the case.
>
> For example, the factors relating to the authority to hire assistants will not normally be relevant if the very nature of the work requires the hired party to work alone. In such a case, that factor should be accorded no weight in applying the *Reid* test. * * *
>
> [T]here are some factors that will be significant in virtually every situation. These include: (1) the hiring party's right to control the manner and means of creation; (2) the skill required; (3) the provision of employee benefits; (4) the tax treatment of the hired party; and (5) whether the hiring party has the right to assign additional projects to the hired party. These factors will almost always be relevant and should be given more weight in the analysis, because they will usually be highly probative of the true nature of the employment relationship.

Id., 980 F.2d at 861.

In *Reid*, the Supreme Court described the law regarding works for hire prior to enactment of the Copyright Act of 1976:

In 1955, when Congress decided to overhaul copyright law, the existing work for hire provision was § 62 of the 1909 Copyright Act. It provided that "the word 'author' shall include an employer in the case of works made for hire." Because the 1909 Act did not define "employer" or "works made for hire," the task of shaping these terms fell to the courts. They concluded that the work for hire doctrine codified in § 62 referred only to works made by employees in the regular course of their employment. As for commissioned works, the courts generally presumed that the commissioned party had impliedly agreed to convey the copyright, along with the work itself, to the hiring party.

Id., 490 U.S. at 743–44. See Estate of Burne Hogarth v. Edgar Rice Burroughs, Inc., 342 F.3d 149, 156–62 (2d Cir. 2003)(explaining how, in the Second Circuit, this implied conveyance reasoning evolved into a presumption that all works created at the instance and expense of a commissioning party were works for hire, vesting ownership in the commissioning party, regardless of whether they were created by an employee or an independent contractor.). The earlier standard is still applicable in determining the ownership of copyright in works created before January 1, 1978, the effective date of the Copyright Act of 1976. Serious due process issues might arise if the new '76 Act standard were applied retroactively to alter the ownership of works created before the Act became effective.

PROBLEMS

1. X plans to make a map of a particular area for tourists. He pulls together some existing maps and designates information on each of them that should be transferred onto the new map. He then collects some additional data through personal observation (street names and other features of local interest, such as local shipwrecks of interest to divers, and fishing areas). X determines the scale to be used on the new map, and the color scheme, and then takes all this information to a printer. The printer physically puts all the information together into a new, finished map under X's supervision. Who is the author of the map?

2. X, a real estate agent, goes to United Printing Services and contracts with United to create a map of a particular area for new residents, complete with the name and logo of X's real estate agency on the front. United in turn assigns the job to Y, who is one of its employees. Y pulls together material from a number of existing maps, and designs the new map. Pursuant to the contract, United prints 500 copies of the map and delivers them to X. X registers copyright in the map and begins to distribute the copies to his clients. Later X learns that Z has reproduced a copy of the map without authorization and is selling it in his store. X brings a suit for copyright infringement. Is X likely to prevail?

3. Mary, a student at State University, enrolled in Professor Smart's Anthropology 101 class, and took careful written notes of all of Professor Smart's lectures. She then posted her notes on a student-run web site that was devoted to distribution of student notes from the University's courses. Once posted, the notes were available not only to other University students, but also to anyone with access to the Internet and an interest in anthropolo-

gy. The web site did not charge for access to the notes, though it did sell advertising space. Professor Smart is a tenured, full-time member of the State University faculty. Professor Smart did not consent to Mary's actions, and upon learning of them, brought suit against Mary and the web site operators, alleging copyright infringement. Is the professor likely to prevail?

B. JOINT WORKS

AALMUHAMMED v. LEE

United States Court of Appeals, Ninth Circuit, 2000.
202 F.3d 1227.

KLEINFELD, CIRCUIT JUDGE:

This is a copyright case involving a claim of coauthorship of the movie *Malcolm X*. We reject the "joint work" claim but remand for further proceedings on a quantum meruit claim.

I. FACTS

In 1991, Warner Brothers contracted with Spike Lee and his production companies to make the movie *Malcolm X*, to be based on the book, *The Autobiography of Malcolm X*. Lee co-wrote the screenplay, directed, and co-produced the movie, which starred Denzel Washington as Malcolm X. Washington asked Jefri Aalmuhammed to assist him in his preparation for the starring role because Aalmuhammed knew a great deal about Malcolm X and Islam. Aalmuhammed, a devout Muslim, was particularly knowledgeable about the life of Malcolm X, having previously written, directed, and produced a documentary film about Malcolm X.

Aalmuhammed joined Washington on the movie set. The movie was filmed in the New York metropolitan area and Egypt. Aalmuhammed presented evidence that his involvement in making the movie was very extensive. He reviewed the shooting script for Spike Lee and Denzel Washington and suggested extensive script revisions. Some of his script revisions were included in the released version of the film; others were filmed but not included in the released version. Most of the revisions Aalmuhammed made were to ensure the religious and historical accuracy and authenticity of scenes depicting Malcolm X's religious conversion and pilgrimage to Mecca.

Aalmuhammed submitted evidence that he directed Denzel Washington and other actors while on the set, created at least two entire scenes with new characters, translated Arabic into English for subtitles, supplied his own voice for voice-overs, selected the proper prayers and religious practices for the characters, and edited parts of the movie during post production. Washington testified in his deposition that Aalmuhammed's contribution to the movie was "great" because he "helped to rewrite, to make more authentic." * * *

Aalmuhammed never had a written contract with Warner Brothers, Lee, or Lee's production companies, but he expected Lee to compensate him for his work. * * * Aalmuhammed ultimately received a check for $25,000 from Lee, which he cashed, and a check for $100,000 from Washington, which he did not cash.

During the summer before *Malcolm X*'s November 1992 release, Aalmuhammed asked for a writing credit as a co-writer of the film, but was turned down. When the film was released, it credited Aalmuhammed only as an "Islamic Technical Consultant," far down the list. * * * * * *

II. ANALYSIS

* * *

Aalmuhammed claimed that the movie *Malcolm X* was a "joint work" of which he was an author, thus making him a co-owner of the copyright. He sought a declaratory judgment to that effect, and an accounting for profits. He is not claiming copyright merely in what he wrote or contributed, but rather in the whole work, as a co-author of a "joint work." The district court granted defendants summary judgment against Mr. Aalmuhammed's copyright claims. We review de novo.

* * *

Aalmuhammed argues that he established a genuine issue of fact as to whether he was an author of a "joint work," *Malcolm X*. The Copyright Act does not define "author," but it does define "joint work":

A "joint work" is a work prepared by two or more authors with the intention that their contributions be merged into inseparable or interdependent parts of a unitary whole. [17 U.S.C. § 101.]

"When interpreting a statute, we look first to the language." The statutory language establishes that for a work to be a "joint work" there must be (1) a copyrightable work, (2) two or more "authors," and (3) the authors must intend their contributions be merged into inseparable or interdependent parts of a unitary whole. A "joint work" in this circuit "requires each author to make an independently copyrightable contribution" to the disputed work. *Malcolm X* is a copyrightable work, and it is undisputed that the movie was intended by everyone involved with it to be a unitary whole. It is also undisputed that Aalmuhammed made substantial and valuable contributions to the movie * * *. Aalmuhammed has * * * submitted evidence that he rewrote several specific passages of dialogue that appeared in *Malcolm X,* and that he wrote scenes relating to Malcolm X's Hajj pilgrimage that were enacted in the movie. If Aalmuhammed's evidence is accepted, as it must be on summary judgment, these items would have been independently copyrightable. Aalmuhammed, therefore, has presented a genuine issue of fact as to whether he made a copyrightable contribution.

All persons involved intended that Aalmuhammed's contributions would be merged into interdependent parts of the movie as a unitary whole. Aalmuhammed maintains that he has shown a genuine issue of fact for each element of a "joint work."

But there is another element to a "joint work." A "joint work" includes "two or more authors." Aalmuhammed established that he contributed substantially to the film, but not that he was one of its "authors." We hold that authorship is required under the statutory definition of a joint work, and that authorship is not the same thing as making a valuable and copyrightable contribution. We recognize that a contributor of an expression may be deemed to be the "author" of that expression for purposes of determining whether it is independently copyrightable. The issue we deal with is a different and larger one: is the contributor an author of the joint work within the meaning of 17 U.S.C. § 101.

By statutory definition, a "joint work" requires "two or more authors." The word "author" is taken from the traditional activity of one person sitting at a desk with a pen and writing something for publication. It is relatively easy to apply the word "author" to a novel. It is also easy to apply the word to two people who work together in a fairly traditional pen-and-ink way, like, perhaps, Gilbert and Sullivan. In the song, "I Am the Very Model of a Modern Major General," Gilbert's words and Sullivan's tune are inseparable, and anyone who has heard the song knows that it owes its existence to both men, Sir William Gilbert and Sir Arthur Sullivan, as its creative originator. But as the number of contributors grows and the work itself becomes less the product of one or two individuals who create it without much help, the word is harder to apply.

Who, in the absence of contract, can be considered an author of a movie? The word is traditionally used to mean the originator or the person who causes something to come into being * * *. For a movie, that might be the producer who raises the money. Eisenstein thought the author of a movie was the editor. The "auteur" theory suggests that it might be the director, at least if the director is able to impose his artistic judgments on the film. Traditionally, by analogy to books, the author was regarded as the person who writes the screenplay, but often a movie reflects the work of many screenwriters. Grenier suggests that the person with creative control tends to be the person in whose name the money is raised, perhaps a star, perhaps the director, perhaps the producer, with control gravitating to the star as the financial investment in scenes already shot grows. Where the visual aspect of the movie is especially important, the chief cinematographer might be regarded as the author. And for, say, a Disney animated movie like "The Jungle Book," it might perhaps be the animators and the composers of the music.

The Supreme Court dealt with the problem of defining "author" in new media in *Burrow-Giles Lithographic Co. v. Sarony.* * * * The Court said that an "author," in the sense that the Founding Fathers used the term in the Constitution, was " 'he to whom anything owes its origin; originator; maker; one who completes a work of science or literature.' "

Answering a different question, what is a copyrightable "work," as opposed to who is the "author," the Supreme Court held in *Feist Publications* that "some minimal level of creativity" or "originality" suffices. But that measure of a "work" would be too broad and indeterminate to be useful if applied to determine who are "authors" of a movie. So many people might qualify as an "author" if the question were limited to whether they made a substantial creative contribution that that test would not distinguish one from another. Everyone from the producer and director to casting director, costumer, hairstylist, and "best boy" gets listed in the movie credits because all of their creative contributions really do matter. It is striking in *Malcolm X* how much the person who controlled the hue of the lighting contributed, yet no one would use the word "author" to denote that individual's relationship to the movie. A creative contribution does not suffice to establish authorship of the movie.

Burrow–Giles, in defining "author," requires more than a minimal creative or original contribution to the work. * * * *Burrow-Giles* defines author as the person to whom the work owes its origin and who superintended the whole work, the "master mind." In a movie this definition, in the absence of a contract to the contrary, would generally limit authorship to someone at the top of the screen credits, sometimes the producer, sometimes the director, possibly the star, or the screenwriter—someone who has artistic control. * * *

The Second and Seventh Circuits have likewise concluded that contribution of independently copyrightable material to a work intended to be an inseparable whole will not suffice to establish authorship of a joint work.[24] Although the Second and Seventh Circuits do not base their decisions on the word "authors" in the statute, the practical results they reach are consistent with ours. These circuits have held that a person claiming to be an author of a joint work must prove that both parties intended each other to be joint authors. In determining whether the parties have the intent to be joint authors, the Second Circuit looks at who has decision making authority, how the parties bill themselves, and other evidence.

In *Thomson v. Larson,* an off-Broadway playwright had created a modern version of *La Boheme,* and had been adamant throughout its creation on being the sole author. He hired a drama professor for "dramaturgical assistance and research," agreeing to credit her as "dramaturg" but not author, but saying nothing about "joint work" or copyright. The playwright tragically died immediately after the final dress rehearsal, just before his play became the tremendous Broadway hit, *Rent.* The dramaturg then sued his estate for a declaratory judgment that she was an author of *Rent* as a "joint work," and for an accounting. The Second Circuit noted that the dramaturg had no decision making authority, had neither sought nor was billed as a co-author, and that the defendant

---

24. *Thomson v. Larson,* 147 F.3d 195 (2d Cir.1998); *Erickson v. Trinity Theatre, Inc.,* 13 F.3d 1061 (7th Cir.1994); *Childress v. Taylor,* 945 F.2d 500 (2d Cir.1991).

entered into contracts as the sole author. On this reasoning, the Second Circuit held that there was no intent to be joint authors by the putative parties and therefore it was not a joint work.

Considering *Burrow-Giles,* the recent cases on joint works, * * * and the Gilbert and Sullivan example, several factors suggest themselves as among the criteria for joint authorship, in the absence of contract. First, an author "superintend[s]" the work by exercising control. This will likely be a person "who has actually formed the picture by putting the persons in position, and arranging the place where the people are to be—the man who is the effective cause of that," or "the inventive or master mind" who "creates, or gives effect to the idea." Second, putative coauthors make objective manifestations of a shared intent to be coauthors, as by denoting the authorship of *The Pirates of Penzance* as "Gilbert and Sullivan." We say objective manifestations because, were the mutual intent to be determined by subjective intent, it could become an instrument of fraud, were one coauthor to hide from the other an intention to take sole credit for the work. Third, the audience appeal of the work turns on both contributions and "the share of each in its success cannot be appraised." Control in many cases will be the most important factor.

The best objective manifestation of a shared intent, of course, is a contract saying that the parties intend to be or not to be co-authors. In the absence of a contract, the inquiry must of necessity focus on the facts. * * *

Aalmuhammed did not at any time have superintendence of the work. Warner Brothers and Spike Lee controlled it. Aalmuhammed was not the person "who has actually formed the picture by putting the persons in position, and arranging the place...." Spike Lee was, so far as we can tell from the record. Aalmuhammed, like Larson's dramaturg, could make extremely helpful recommendations, but Spike Lee was not bound to accept any of them, and the work would not benefit in the slightest unless Spike Lee chose to accept them. Aalmuhammed lacked control over the work, and absence of control is strong evidence of the absence of co-authorship.

Also, neither Aalmuhammed, nor Spike Lee, nor Warner Brothers, made any objective manifestations of an intent to be coauthors. Warner Brothers required Spike Lee to sign a "work for hire" agreement, so that even Lee would not be a co-author and co-owner with Warner Brothers. It would be illogical to conclude that Warner Brothers, while not wanting to permit Lee to own the copyright, intended to share ownership with individuals like Aalmuhammed who worked under Lee's control, especially ones who at the time had made known no claim to the role of co-author. No one, including Aalmuhammed, made any indication to anyone prior to litigation that Aalmuhammed was intended to be a co-author and co-owner.

* * *

The Constitution establishes the social policy that our construction of the statutory term "authors" carries out. The Founding Fathers gave Congress the power to give authors copyrights in order "[t]o promote the progress of Science and useful arts." Progress would be retarded rather than promoted, if an author could not consult with others and adopt their useful suggestions without sacrificing sole ownership of the work. Too open a definition of author would compel authors to insulate themselves and maintain ignorance of the contributions others might make. Spike Lee could not consult a scholarly Muslim to make a movie about a religious conversion to Islam, and the arts would be the poorer for that.

The broader construction that Aalmuhammed proposes would extend joint authorship to many "overreaching contributors," like the dramaturg in *Thomson,* and deny sole authors "exclusive authorship status simply because another person render[ed] some form of assistance." Claimjumping by research assistants, editors, and former spouses, lovers and friends would endanger authors who talked with people about what they were doing, if creative copyrightable contribution were all that authorship required.

* * *

NOTES AND QUESTIONS

1. *Joint authors.* Why shouldn't each individual who contributes copyrightable expression to a work be deemed a joint author? Note that absent a contractual provision to the contrary, each joint author owns an equal, undivided interest in the joint work's copyright, regardless of the magnitude of the contribution she actually made to the joint work. And each joint author has the right to exploit the work herself, and grant nonexclusive licenses to others, subject only to an accounting to the other co-owners for any profits she makes. All of the co-owners must agree to assign the copyright or to grant an exclusive license.

The Ninth Circuit finds that while Aalmuhammed was not a joint author of Malcolm X, he did contribute copyrightable expression to the film. Under these circumstances, what is his status? Does he own copyright in the individual parts he contributed? Could he hold Warner Bros. liable for infringement if it exploits the film (complete with his individual contributions) without his permission?

As the *Aalmuhammed* court explains, other circuits have not undertaken to define "author," beyond requiring that the purported joint author contribute copyrightable expression, as opposed to uncopyrightable elements, such as ideas or facts. Rather, they have limited joint authorship claims by requiring that each alleged joint author intend to be a joint author with the others at the time the work is created. What kinds of evidence might be useful to demonstrate the existence of such an intent?

Why require that each joint author contribute copyrightable expression? Why shouldn't the contribution of creative ideas entitle one to ownership rights in the resulting work? How does the producer of a film contribute copyrightable expression to the film?

2. *Joint works, derivative works, collective works.* How would you articulate the difference between joint works, derivative works and contributions to collective works?

In Shapiro, Bernstein & Co. v. Jerry Vogel Music Co., 221 F.2d 569 (2d Cir.1955), *modified*, 223 F.2d 252 (2d Cir.1955) (the "12th Street Rag" case), X composed an instrumental piece for solo piano, intending it to be complete as it was. Two years later he assigned his copyright in the piece to Y and two years after that, Y had Z write lyrics to accompany the instrumental. The Court of Appeals for the Second Circuit held that the resulting song, comprised of music and lyrics, constituted a joint work, even though X had not intended to contribute to a unified whole at the time he created the music. The court found it sufficient that Y, the subsequent copyright holder, had later formed that intent.

This result was much criticized and Congress explicitly rejected it in enacting the Copyright Act of 1976. The 1976 Act defines a joint work as one "*prepared* by two or more authors *with the intention* that their contributions be merged into inseparable or interdependent parts of a unitary whole." 17 U.S.C.A. § 101 (emphasis added). The House Report specifies that the touchstone "is the intention, *at the time the writing is done*, that the parts be absorbed or combined into an integrated unit." H.R. Rep. No. 1476, 94th Cong., 2d Sess. 120 (1976) (emphasis added). Why should the Second Circuit's acceptance of an intent formed after creation be considered problematic?

3. *Rights in collective works.* A "collective work" is "a work, such as a periodical issue, anthology, or encyclopedia, in which a number of contributions, constituting separate and independent works in themselves, are assembled into a collective whole." 17 U.S.C. § 101. Copyright Act § 201(c) provides:

> Copyright in each separate contribution to a collective work is distinct from copyright in the collective work as a whole, and vests initially in the author of the contribution. In the absence of an express transfer of the copyright or of any rights under it, the owner of copyright in the collective work is presumed to have acquired only the privilege of reproducing and distributing the contribution as part of that particular collective work, any revision of that collective work, and any later collective work in the same series.

17 U.S.C. § 201(c). Assume that a newspaper that publishes the work of freelance authors wishes to post daily editions of its paper on its web site, so that Internet users may read it. Absent express contractual arrangement with the freelance authors regarding this use, is the use authorized under § 201(c)? Does § 201(c) authorize the newspaper to publish a CD–ROM collection of all of its daily newspapers, including freelance articles, for the past 20 years? See Faulkner v. National Geographic Enterprises, Inc., 409 F.3d 26 (2d Cir.), *cert. denied*, 126 S.Ct. 833, 163 L.Ed.2d 707 (2005)(CD–ROM collection containing all previous issues of magazine is an authorized revision under § 201(c)). Does § 201(c) authorize the newspaper to make its daily editions, including freelance articles, available for inclusion in electronic databases, such as NEXIS,

that give subscribers access to articles from a vast number of periodicals? In New York Times Co., Inc. v. Tasini, 533 U.S. 483, 121 S.Ct. 2381, 150 L.Ed.2d 500 (2001), the Supreme Court said that it did not. How might you distinguish the second and third situations?

PROBLEMS

1.   Based on the facts available in the Supreme Court's opinion in *CCNV v. Reid, supra,* should the district court, on remand, find that *CCNV* was a joint author of the "Third World America" sculpture?

2.   Dr. X and Dr. Y work closely together to write a scholarly paper. Dr. X later revises the paper unilaterally, without input from Dr. Y. Then Dr. Y, without Dr. X's authorization, reproduces the revised paper. Is Dr. Y liable to Dr. X for copyright infringement?

C.   DIVISIBILITY AND TRANSFER OF OWNERSHIP

Copyright Act § 201(d) provides the first explicit statutory recognition of copyright divisibility. As the House Report explained:

> This provision, which has long been sought by authors and their representatives, and which has attracted wide support from other groups, means that any of the exclusive rights that go to make up a copyright, including those enumerated in section 106 and any subdivision of them, can be transferred and owned separately. The definition of "transfer of copyright ownership" in section 101 makes clear that the principle of divisibility applies whether or not the transfer is "limited in time or place of effect," and another definition in the same section provides that the term "copyright owner," with respect to any one exclusive right, refers to the owner of that particular right. The last sentence of section 201(d)(2) adds that the owner, with respect to the particular exclusive right he or she owns, is entitled "to all of the protection and remedies accorded to the copyright owner by this title." It is thus clear, for example, that a local broadcasting station holding an exclusive license to transmit a particular work within a particular geographic area and for a particular period of time, could sue, in its own name as copyright owner, someone who infringed that particular exclusive right.

H.R. Rep. No. 1476, 94th Cong., 2d Sess. 123 (1976).

Copyright Act § 204(a) provides that the transfer of any ownership right (that is, any exclusive, as opposed to non-exclusive right), other than by operation of law, must be made by means of a writing signed by the transferor or his agent. Congress made doubly sure, in § 202, that there would be no implied transfers of copyright ownership: "Transfer of ownership of any material object, including the copy or phonorecord in which the work is first fixed, does not of itself convey any rights in the copyrighted work embodied in the object * * *." 17 U.S.C.A. § 202. As the House Report explained:

> As a result of the interaction of this section and the provisions of section 201(a) and 301, the bill would change a common law doctrine exemplified by the decision in *Pushman v. New York Graphic Society, Inc.*, 287 N.Y. 302, 39 N.E.2d 249 (1942). Under that doctrine, authors or artists are generally presumed to transfer common law literary property rights when they sell their manuscript or work of art, unless those rights are specifically reserved. This presumption would be reversed under the bill, since a specific written conveyance of rights would be required in order for sale of any material object to carry with it a transfer of copyright.

H.R. Rep. No. 1476, *supra*, at 124. Bear in mind that the 1976 Act's ownership provisions do not apply retroactively. The ramifications of a transaction are judged under the law in effect when the transaction occurred. Thus, for example, if the creator of an unpublished oil painting sold the canvas on which the painting was fixed, without an express reservation of copyright, prior to January 1, 1978 (the effective date of the 1976 Act) in a state that followed the *Pushman* doctrine, then it is likely that the buyer obtained the artist's common-law copyright. The buyer or his successors would continue to own the copyright, which, under the 1976 Act, was subsequently transformed into a federal copyright. See 17 U.S.C. § 303.

Even though assignments of exclusive rights cannot be implied under the Copyright Act of 1976, non-exclusive licenses may be granted by implication. Thus, for example, the Court of Appeals for the Ninth Circuit has held that an implied license may be found if:

> (1) a person (the licensee) requests the creation of a work, (2) the creator (the licensor) makes that particular work and delivers it to the licensee who requested it; and (3) the licensor intends that the licensee-requestor copy and distribute his work [or, in the case of computer programs, use, retain, and modify the programs].

Asset Marketing Systems, Inc. v. Gagnon, 542 F.3d 748, 754–55 (9th Cir. 2008), *cert. denied*, ___ U.S. ___, 129 S.Ct. 2442, 174 L.Ed.2d 228 (2009). In *Asset Marketing*, the court found that the first two factors were satisfied when Gagnon created and later modified custom software at AMS' request, AMS paid for Gagnon's work in drafting the programs, and Gagnon installed the programs onto AMS' computers and stored the source code on-site at AMS. With regard to the third factor, the court emphasized that Gagnon's intent should be evaluated as of the time he created and delivered the software (as opposed to a later time when the parties terminated their working relationship), as manifested by the parties' conduct. The court adopted several factors developed in the First and Fourth Circuits for evaluating this intent:

> (1) whether the parties were engaged in a short-term discrete transaction as opposed to an ongoing relationship; (2) whether the creator

utilized written contracts . . . providing that copyrighted materials could only be used with the creator's future involvement or express permission; and (3) whether the creator's conduct during the creation or delivery of the copyrighted material indicated that use of the material without the creator's involvement or consent was permissible.

Id., at 756. In applying these factors, the Ninth Circuit emphasized that in addition to creating custom software for AMS, Gagnon had an on-going service relationship with AMS, providing technical support for all AMS' computer-related problems for several years. It also considered documents, including drafts of contracts that were never signed, none of which indicated any intent on Gagnon's part to prohibit AMS' ongoing use of the programs after the parties' relationship terminated. The court noted:

> Gagnon was well paid for his services. Under the circumstances, it defies logic that AMS would have paid Gagnon for his programming services if AMS could not have used the programs without further payment pursuant to a separate licensing arrangement that was never mentioned in the [service agreement], and never otherwise requested at the time. This is especially so because custom software is far less valuable without the ability to modify it and because the [service agreement] was set to expire in one year; one would expect some indication of the need for future licensing if the custom programs were to become unusable after the [service agreement] expired.

Id., at 756–57. Thus, the court held that Gagnon granted AMS an unlimited, nonexclusive license to retain, use, and modify the software. Moreover, because AMS paid consideration, this license was irrevocable. A non-exclusive, implied license supported by consideration is a contract, and binding in the same manner that any implied-in-fact contract is.

PROBLEMS

1. In 1992, Nike Inc. granted to Sony Music Entertainment Corp. an exclusive license to use a Nike-created cartoon character called "MC Teach." The grant was made in exchange for 15% of the profits earned from any use of MC Teach in connection with merchandise. The agreement expressly provided that Nike remained the copyright owner, but did not specify whether Sony had a right to assign its rights under the license. Four years later, Sony assigned all its rights in the exclusive license to Gardner, in exchange for a share of the proceeds Gardner derived from exploitation of MC Teach. Nike sues, alleging that Sony's transfer to Gardner is invalid. What are the parties' respective rights under Copyright Act § 201(d)?

2. Problems sometimes arise in determining whether an existing license grants rights to exploit the licensed work through new technologies. Assuming that nothing else in the license agreement bears on the issue, how would you construe the scope of the following examples of license language?

a) The license (executed in 1930) grants the right to make a motion picture version of a work and "to copyright, vend, license and exhibit such motion picture . . . throughout the world." Does this license grant the right to televise the movie?

b) The license (executed in 1939) grants the right to include the copyrighted musical work in a movie. The license language specifies that the right is "to record [the copyrighted musical composition] in any manner, medium or form for use in a motion picture." The licensee later distributes the motion picture in video format. Does this use fall within the scope of the license?

c) The license authorizes X to "print, publish, and sell" the licensors' novels "in book form." Does this license extend to publication in e-books?

VII.   COPYRIGHT FORMALITIES: NOTICE, REGISTRATION AND DEPOSIT

A.   NOTICE OF COPYRIGHT

Contrary to the practice in most other developed nations, the United States has emphasized the placement of copyright notice on published copies of works. From 1802 until 1989, United States copyright law provided that all authorized published copies of works *must* bear copyright notice, in a specified form, as a condition of copyright protection. Publication of copies lacking such notice would result in forfeiture of copyright in the work.

Nations following civil law traditions tend to view copyright as a natural right in an author flowing from the act of authorship. The notion of imposing conditions on its enjoyment, such as notice or registration, is inconsistent with that view. Influenced by civil law traditions, the Berne Convention for the Protection of Literary and Artistic Works, Article 5(2), specifically directs that the enjoyment and exercise of copyright in member nations "shall not be subject to any formality."

In the United States, which has traditionally viewed copyright as a statutory privilege afforded to authors for the purpose of promoting the general public welfare, conditions to enjoyment of copyright, such as notice, are deemed appropriate whenever they appear to promote the general welfare. Congress justified the notice requirement on essentially two grounds. First, notice informed the public whether a particular work was copyrighted and assisted those seeking to use copyrighted works by identifying the copyright owner and the date of first publication (which might be important in determining whether the copyright was still in effect). Second, notice had "the effect of placing in the public domain a substantial body of published material that no one [was] interested in copyrighting." H.R. Rep. No. 1476, 94th Cong., 2d Sess. 143 (1976).

The study of United States copyright notice provisions must be divided into three "epochs:" (1) the Copyright Act of 1909; (2) January 1, 1978 to March 1, 1989; and (3) March 1, 1989 through the present.

The Copyright Act of 1909. Prior to enactment of the Copyright Act of 1976, a dual system of copyright protection existed in the United States. State common-law copyright protected unpublished works. When the work was published, common-law protection ceased. Federal statutory copyright protection commenced at that point if all the authorized published copies of the work bore notice of copyright in the statutorily prescribed form and location. See 17 U.S.C.A. §§ 10, 19–21 (1909 Act).[20] In the absence of proper notice, the published work fell into the public domain.

The 1909 Act's notice provisions were rather technical, and unintentional omissions or errors in the notice often led to forfeiture of copyright. While § 21 of the Act provided some reprieve in the case of omissions "by accident or mistake," this provision was construed and applied very narrowly. Omissions due to negligence or mistake of law were not excused. Generally, the only excused omissions of notice were those attributable to mechanical accidents, such as damage to printing equipment, when only a relatively small number of copies were involved. See 1 P. Goldstein, Copyright § 3.7.2 (1998).

January 1, 1978 to March 1, 1989. When Congress enacted the Copyright Act of 1976, it provided that federal copyright would commence upon a work's creation, rather than upon publication, and preempted state protection for copyrightable subject matter fixed in tangible form. 17 U.S.C.A. §§ 301, 302. While relaxing some of the 1909 Act's technical rules regarding the form, position, and content of notice, the 1976 Act still required that authorized published copies and phonorecords of the work bear proper copyright notice. *Id.*, §§ 401–402. Failure to comply with the notice requirements would still result in loss of the copyright, though Congress tempered the impact of this consequence through broader "saving" provisions, set forth in §§ 405–406. The House Report explained:

> One of the strongest arguments for revision of the present statute has been the need to avoid the arbitrary and unjust forfeitures now resulting from unintentional or relatively unimportant omissions or errors in the copyright notice. It has been contended that the disadvantages of the notice requirement out-weigh its values and that it should therefore be eliminated or substantially liberalized.
>
> The fundamental principle underlying the notice provisions of the bill is that the copyright notice has real value which should be preserved, and that this should be done by inducing use of notice without causing outright forfeiture for errors or omissions. Subject to certain safeguards for innocent infringers, protection would not be lost by the complete omission of copyright notice from large numbers of copies or from a whole edition, if registration for the work is made before or within 5 years after publication. Errors in the name or date in the notice could be corrected without forfeiture of copyright.

H.R. Rep. No. 1476, 94th Cong., 2d Sess. 143–44 (1976).

---

20. Section 12 of the 1909 Act permitted common-law copyright owners to obtain federal copyright protection for unpublished works. This provision, however, was not widely used.

March 1, 1989 through the present. When the United States finally joined the Berne Convention, it had to relinquish its notice requirement in order to comply with the Berne provision that copyright "not be subject to any formality." The Berne Convention Implementation Act amended the 1976 Act notice provisions to make compliance voluntary rather than mandatory for copies and phonorecords distributed to the public after March 1, 1989, the effective date of the Implementation Act. See 17 U.S.C.A. §§ 401(a), 402(a). In order to encourage voluntary compliance with the notice provisions, the Act further provided:

> If a notice of copyright in the form and position specified by this section appears on the published copy or copies to which a defendant in a copyright infringement suit had access, then no weight shall be given to such a defendant's interposition of a defense based on innocent infringement in mitigation of actual or statutory damages, except as provided in the last sentence of section 504(c)(2).

17 U.S.C.A. § 401(d) (as amended). See also *id.*, § 402(d) (same provision, except "copy or copies" is replaced by "phonorecord or phonorecords").

Neither the 1976 Copyright Act's notice provisions nor the Berne Convention Implementation Act amendments apply retroactively. Thus, when it appears that copies or phonorecords were publicly distributed without proper notice, the consequences must be judged by the law in effect at the time of the distribution. If the publication occurred prior to January 1, 1978 (the effective date of the Copyright Act of 1976), then the copyright is likely to be forfeited unless the narrow provisions of § 21 of the 1909 Act apply. If the distribution occurred between January 1, 1978 and March 1, 1989, §§ 405 and 406 of the 1976 Act will be available to save the work from forfeiture of copyright if the copyright owner falls within their requirements. The Berne Convention Implementation Act does not resurrect copyrights lost for lack of proper notice prior to its effective date. If the copyright was forfeited under the law applicable at the time of the distribution, then it remains invalid and unenforceable, unless it falls within the provisions of Copyright Act § 104A, which restores copyright in certain *foreign* (but not domestic) works. See note 4, *infra.* If the distribution was made after the effective date of the Berne Convention Implementation Act (March 1, 1989), then there will be no forfeiture of copyright. However, the copyright owner may be deprived of remedies for infringement that would otherwise be available.

NOTES AND QUESTIONS

1. *Publication.* "Publication" is an important concept in U.S. copyright law. Under the 1909 Act, publication marked the end of common-law copyright protection and (if proper notice was given) the beginning of federal statutory copyright. Publication without proper notice resulted in complete loss of copyright protection. Even though the 1976 Act dispensed with publication as the starting point for federal copyright, and the Berne Convention Implementation Act did away with mandatory notice on published copies

and phonorecords, publication remains important for a number of other purposes. Among other things, the date of publication must be given as a part of proper (voluntary) notice, and is used in measuring the duration of copyright in works for hire, anonymous and pseudonymous works. Publication is also relevant with regard to deposit and registration requirements, and in determining the applicability of the fair use defense and some of the statutory exceptions to copyright infringement.

a. The Copyright Act of 1909. The 1909 Act left definition of "publication" to the courts. In their hands the issue became highly complex. One thing, however, was clear: The fact that a work had been made public, or commercially exploited, did not necessarily mean that it had been "published."

There was general agreement that publication entailed physically distributing tangible copies of the work to members of the public. However, the circumstances under which such a distribution would constitute a publication varied. Faced with the desire to avoid finding forfeiture of copyright in compelling cases, the courts began to distinguish between "divestive" and "investive" publications. If the issue was whether a distribution divested the owner of copyright protection, the courts required a greater distribution than if the issue was whether the distribution invested the owner with federal statutory copyright. As Judge Frank explained:

> [C]ourts apply different tests of publication depending on whether plaintiff is claiming protection because he did not publish and hence has a common law claim of infringement—in which case the distribution must be quite large to constitute "publication"—or whether he is claiming under the copyright statute—in which case the requirements for publication are quite narrow.

American Visuals Corp. v. Holland, 239 F.2d 740, 744 (2d Cir.1956).

In the course of finding that not every public distribution of copies constituted "publication," courts developed the concept of "limited publication," which, as a legal matter, did not constitute publication at all. As one court described it, a limited publication is a distribution of copies "to a definitely selected group and for a limited purpose, and without the right of diffusion, reproduction, distribution or sale * * *." White v. Kimmell, 193 F.2d 744, 746–47 (9th Cir.1952), *cert. denied*, 343 U.S. 957, 72 S.Ct. 1052, 96 L.Ed. 1357 (1952). The limited purpose could be express or implied.

A good discussion of limited publication can be found in Academy of Motion Picture Arts and Sciences v. Creative House Promotions, Inc., 944 F.2d 1446 (9th Cir., 1991). In that case, the court found that the Academy's coveted "Oscar" statuette had not been subject to a general (divestive) publication prior to 1941, when it obtained federal statutory copyright. Citing the rule set forth in the *White* case, *supra*, the court noted that the plaintiff had certainly limited its distribution of copies of the Oscar to a "selected group": "The Academy distributes the coveted Oscar to performers and members of the motion picture industry selected for outstanding achievement." *Id.*, 944 F.2d at 1453. The Academy had never sold or distributed the award to the general public. The court then found that the Academy's purpose in distributing the Oscar—to honor distinguished recipients and to promote the film industry—was limited. In so finding, the court stressed that at most, any commercial benefit the Academy received in distributing the statuettes was indirect, and indirect commercial benefit was not sufficient to undermine a claim of limited purpose. *Id.* Finally, the court found an implied restriction on recipients' right to further distribute the Oscars: Each Oscar was personalized with the name of the individual winner, reflecting the Academy's expectation that the trophy would belong to the recipient alone. Moreover, the Academy had never given permission or otherwise suggested that it was permissible for recipients to sell or distribute the Oscars to the general public, and none had. Since the Academy's distributions qualified as "limited publication," it was not divested of its common-law copyright in the statuette, and continued to be protected. Compare *American Visuals, supra* (unsupervised distribution of approximately two hundred copies of a book at a convention of persons potentially interested in using it is an investive publication).[21]

Since public performance of a work generally entails no distribution of tangible copies of the work to the public, it did not constitute a "publication" for purposes of the 1909 Act. Similarly, a public display did not constitute a publication, though there is some authority that it would if persons were freely permitted to take photographs of the work and to publish them. See Letter Edged in Black Press, Inc. v. Public Building Commission of Chicago, 320 F.Supp. 1303 (N.D.Ill.1970).

King v. Mister Maestro, Inc., 224 F.Supp. 101 (S.D.N.Y.1963), is a famous example of how far courts were willing to go in some cases to avoid a forfeiture of copyright. The case involved Martin Luther King's "I Have A Dream" speech. Dr. King distributed copies of his speech to numerous members of the press in advance, to assist their reporting. He delivered the speech orally to an audience of thousands, certainly realizing that members of the audience were recording or transcribing it, and that radio and television stations were broadcasting it throughout the nation. Dr. King's public performance of the speech did not constitute a publication, and the court found that his distribution of copies to the press constituted a limited publication, notwithstanding that the reporters undoubtedly would, through their reporting, reproduce and distribute the speech to the general public.

The Court of Appeals for the Eleventh Circuit recently revisited the copyrighted status of the "I Have a Dream" speech and concurred with the findings in the earlier decision. Estate of Marten Luther King, Jr., Inc. v. CBS, Inc., 194 F.3d 1211, 1216-17 (11th Cir. 1999). The Eleventh Circuit stressed:

> The case law indicates that distribution to the news media, as opposed to the general public, for the purpose of enabling the reporting of a contemporary newsworthy event, is only a limited publication. * * * This rule comports with common sense; it does not force an author whose message happens to be newsworthy to choose between obtaining news coverage for his work and preserving his common-law copyright.

---

21. Congress has recently stepped in to identify an additional situation in which physical distribution of a work would not constitute "publication" of the work under the pre–1976 Act law: "The distribution before January 1, 1978, of a phonorecord shall not for any purpose constitute a publication of the musical work embodied therein." 17 U.S.C. § 303(b).

b. The Copyright Act of 1976. The current Copyright Act provides:

"Publication" is the distribution of copies or phonorecords of a work to the public by sale or other transfer of ownership, or by rental, lease, or lending. The offering to distribute copies or phonorecords to a group of persons for purposes of further distribution, public performance, or public display, constitutes publication. A public performance or display of a work does not of itself constitute publication.

17 U.S.C.A. § 101. Does this statutory definition change or clarify the pre–1976 Act law, as described above? If so, how?

2. *The mechanics of notice.* Review the provisions of 1976 Act §§ 401 through 404. Sections 401 and 402, as amended by the Berne Convention Implementation Act, are essentially the same as the original 1976 Act notice provisions, except that they are now permissive, rather than mandatory, and provide (at subsections (d)) that use of notice may avoid an innocent infringer defense.

How useful is the required notice information—the symbol of copyright, name of copyright owner, year of first publication—to someone seeking to determine the status of the copyright or obtain a license to use the work? Note that under the Copyright Act of 1976, the duration of copyright in most works other than works made for hire is measured by the life of the author plus seventy years. Under the 1909 Copyright Act, the duration of copyright depended on whether a proper renewal was made. See pages 672–76, 683–86, *infra.* Was mandating provision of the notice information worth the numerous inadvertent forfeitures of copyright to which it led, or the delay in the United States' joining the Berne Convention?

3. *The Berne Convention Implementation Act amendments.* Lawyers appear to be advising their clients to continue applying notice to the copies and phonorecords of works they distribute to the public. Are the "innocent infringer" incentives the Berne Convention Implementation Act provided in §§ 401(d) and 402(d) a sufficient reason to do so? Are there other reasons why copyright owners might wish to continue giving notice?

4. *Foreign Copyright Restoration.* Review the complex provisions of Copyright Act § 104A, as amended by the Uruguay Round Agreements Act in 1994. The Senate Report on the Uruguay Round Agreements Act explained:

The legislation includes language to restore copyright protection to certain foreign works from countries that are members of the Berne Convention or WTO [World Trade Organization] that have fallen into the public domain for reasons other than the normal expiration of their term of protection.

The [Uruguay Round TRIPs] Agreement requires WTO countries to comply with Article 18 of the Berne Convention. While the United States declared its compliance with the Berne Convention in 1989, it never addressed or enacted legislation to implement Article 18 of the Convention. Article 18 requires that the terms of the Convention apply to all works that have fallen into the public domain by reasons other than the expiration of its term of protection. (Examples include failure to file a timely renewal application and failure to affix a copyright notice.)

The bill would automatically restore copyright protection for qualifying works of authors from Berne or WTO countries one year after the WTO comes into being. In order for the restored copyright to be enforced against a "reliance party," [a "reliance party" is essentially a person who commenced exploitation of the work while it was in the public domain, prior to its copyright restoration] it is necessary for the author or copyright owner (rightholder) of the foreign work to either file a "notice of intent" with the Copyright Office during the 24 months after the effective date of the Uruguay Round Agreement or provide actual notice (for the life of the copyright term) directly by notifying the reliance party. Reliance parties then have one year from publication of the constructive notice or receipt of the actual notice to continue to use or sell off copies of the work that has been restored to a foreign author or rightholder. Reproduction of the work during this period is not permitted. After this period, reliance parties are subject to remedies for infringement, except in certain cases.

Section 104A(d)(3) provides additional protection to a reliance party who used a restored foreign work to create a derivative work because a one year sell off period might have been an inadequate period to recoup the investment. In the case of a derivative work that was created based upon a foreign work that was in the public domain but has been restored, the reliance party may continue to sell the derivative work in exchange for providing reasonable compensation to the owner of the restored copyright. In the event that an agreement cannot be reached regarding compensation a district court may determine reasonable compensation, based upon the contribution made by the reliance party as well as the author of the underlying restored work. The court is to take into consideration any damage to the market for the restored work.

S. Rep. No. 412, 103d Cong., 2d Sess. 225–26 (1994). Pursuant to the Uruguay Round Agreements Act, copyright was restored effective January 1, 1996 for eligible works whose source country participated in the Berne Convention or the World Trade Organization at that time. Copyright in works from countries who later adhere to the Berne or WTO, or that are extended protection by Presidential proclamation, will be restored on the date of adherence or proclamation. 17 U.S.C.A. § 104A(h)(2)(A). The restored copyright lasts for the remainder of the term that the work would have enjoyed in the United States had copyright not been lost. See *id.*, § 104A(a)(1)(B).

The amended § 104A restores copyright in works from eligible countries if the works fell into the U.S. public domain because

1) the copyright owner failed to comply with U.S. copyright formalities, such as notice or renewal;

2) they constituted sound recordings fixed prior to February 15, 1972 (and thus did not constitute copyrightable subject matter under U.S. copyright law); or

3) their source country did not have copyright relations with the U.S. at the time they were published.

Thus, § 104A actually does more than just "restore" lost copyrights—it provides copyright in some foreign works that never before enjoyed copyright in the United States. See *id.*, § 104A(h)(6).

The restored copyright is enforceable immediately against infringers who are not "reliance parties." See *id.*, § 104A(d)(1). However, as the Senate Report explains, notice of intent to enforce the restored copyright must be given before reliance parties will be liable. Do the elaborate notice requirements imposed by § 104A, as amended, condition foreign owners' enjoyment and exercise of copyright on compliance with formalities, in violation of the Berne Convention Article 5(2)? Does restoring foreign copyrights constitute an unconstitutional "taking" of private property without just compensation, in violation of reliance parties' Fifth Amendment rights? Does restoration of foreign works from the public domain exceed Congress' authority under the Patents and Copyrights Clause, U.S. Const. art. 1, § 8, cl. 8, or violate the First Amendment? See Golan v. Gonzales, 501 F.3d 1179 (10th Cir. 2007); Golan v. Holder, 609 F.3d 1076 (10th Cir. 2010).

Note that § 104A does not restore domestic copyrights that were lost due to failure to comply with notice or renewal formalities. Nor does it provide federal copyright for domestic sound recordings fixed prior to February 15, 1972. However, U.S. copyright owners may benefit by reciprocal restoration of copyright for their works in other Berne and World Trade Organization countries.

B. DEPOSIT AND REGISTRATION

1. The Deposit Requirement

Within three months of publishing a work in the United States, "the owner of copyright or of the exclusive right of publication" in the work must deposit two copies or phonorecords of the "best edition" of the work with the Copyright Office. 17 U.S.C.A. § 407. Failure to comply may be penalized by fine, but does not lead to forfeiture of copyright. The deposited copies and phonorecords are for the use of the Library of Congress—the express purpose of § 407 is to enrich the Library of Congress' collection. Given this end, the Register of Copyrights has flexibility to adjust the deposit requirement for various categories of works to conform with the Library's needs and housing capabilities. In addition, the Register may adjust the deposit requirements to avoid causing undue practical or financial hardship to copyright owners. See 17 U.S.C.A. § 407(c). The exemptions to deposit set forth by the Register can be found at 37 C.F.R. §§ 202.19–20.

Congress reviewed the mandatory deposit provisions in the course of enacting the Berne Convention Implementation Act. It determined to maintain the requirement, notwithstanding suggestions that it would subjugate "enjoyment and exercise of copyright" to compliance with formalities, in violation of the Berne Convention. The House Report explained: "Since noncompliance with the mandatory deposit requirement does not result in forfeiture of any copyright protection, mandatory deposit is compatible with Berne." H.R. Rep. No. 609, 100th Cong., 2d Sess. 44 (1988).

2. The Registration Requirement

The Copyright Act's registration provisions are meant to create a comprehensive record of copyright claims throughout the country. The Copyright Office keeps extensive files of registration documents, as well as records of transfers of ownership and other matters relevant to copyright ownership. The public is free to search these records to determine the status of works in which they are interested, or avail themselves of the search service which the Copyright Office offers for a modest fee.

Copyright arises automatically upon fixation of a qualifying work, and is not conditioned on registration. However, the 1976 Act makes registration, preregistration, or an unsuccessful attempt to register a prerequisite to a civil suit for infringement. See 17 U.S.C.A. §§ 408(a), 411(a). Once the Copyright office receives a completed registration form the owner may sue for events that occurred prior to the registration.

While a copyright owner is permitted to register at any time during the copyright term (and may never register, if she never seeks to enforce the copyright), Congress designed § 408 through 412 to encourage owners to register and register early. Section 410(c) provides:

> In any judicial proceedings the certificate of a registration made before or within five years after first publication of the work shall constitute prima facie evidence of the validity of the copyright and of the facts stated in the certificate. The evidentiary weight to be accorded the certificate of a registration made thereafter shall be within the discretion of the court.

17 U.S.C.A. § 410(c).

Section 412 also encourages early registration by prohibiting award of statutory damages and attorneys' fees to copyright owner/plaintiffs who failed to register their works before the infringement at suit began (in the case of unpublished works) or within three months after first publication. 17 U.S.C.A. § 412. Copyright owners failing to register within the § 412 time frame are not denied the "ordinary" remedies of injunctive relief, actual damages and applicable profits.

Copyright registration is relatively simple and inexpensive. The registration process consists of completing a printed form and sending it, the applicable fee, and a copy of the work for deposit to the Copyright Office. 17 U.S.C.A. §§ 408, 409. Pursuant to § 410(a), the Copyright Office will issue a certificate of registration if "the material deposited constitutes copyrightable subject matter and * * * the other legal and formal requirements * * * have been met." The Copyright Office reviews the application for obvious errors, but does not attempt to verify the facts set forth in it, or search prior art.

Arguably, the 1976 Act made the formality of registration a prerequisite to enjoyment and exercise of copyright, contrary to Berne Convention requirements. Reluctant to give up its record-keeping system, Congress adopted a compromise position, taking advantage of its latitude under the Berne Convention to restrict copyrights for domestic works in ways that copyrights for works originating in other member nations may not be restricted. The Berne Convention Implementation Act amended § 411 to delete the registration requirement for works of qualifying foreign origin, while retaining it for works whose country of origin is the United States. See 17 U.S.C.A. § 411(a). As a general matter, a work's country of origin is the United States if it was first published in the United States (or simultaneously published in the United States and another country) or, in the case of unpublished works, was created entirely by United States authors. See 17 U.S.C.A. § 101 (describing when a Berne Convention work's "country of origin" is the United States). Congress retained the §§ 410 and 412 incentives for early registration for foreign works, in the hopes that foreign copyright owners would continue to register voluntarily.

VIII. DURATION OF COPYRIGHT

Under the Copyright Act of 1909, federal copyright protection commenced on the date of publication and continued for 28 years. The copyright could be renewed for a second 28–year term, giving a total potential term of 56 years in all cases.[22] That general means of measurement—a definite number of years with a renewal feature—had been a part of United States Copyright law since the first copyright statute in 1790.

In the Copyright Act of 1976 (which became effective on January 1, 1978), Congress changed the means by which the copyright term would be measured—from a fixed, renewable term to a single term consisting of the author's life plus 50 years (or, in the case of anonymous or pseudonymous works or works for hire, a roughly comparable term of 75 years from publication or 100 years from creation, whichever was shorter). It was expected that the new measurement would provide a term that was, on the average, about 19 or 20 years longer than under the previous method of measurement. While Congress only applied the new method of measurement to copyrights coming into existence after the effective date of the 1976 Act, it provided for existing federal copyrights to share in the benefit of the new longer term by extending their renewal term an additional 19 years. Thus, pre–1976 Act copyrights that existed on January 1, 1978 and were renewed would enjoy a renewal term of 47 years, giving a total copyright term of 75 years.

---

22. In the years preceding enactment of the 1976 Act, Congress anticipated that the new Copyright Act would extend the term of copyrights, and wished to give copyrights still existing on Sept. 19, 1962 and thereafter the benefit of that extension. It thus enacted a series of provisions extending the renewal terms of copyrights that would otherwise expire between September 19, 1962 and the effective date of the new Copyright Act.

The House Report accompanying the 1976 Act explained why Congress deemed it important to change to this new form of term measurement. Among other things, increased life expectancy was forcing more authors to compete with their own earlier works, which had fallen into the public domain. Moreover, the growth in communications media had extended the commercial life of many works—the Report noted that a short term was "particularly discriminatory against serious works of music, literature and art, whose value may not be recognized until after many years." H.R. Rep. No. 1476, 94th Cong., 2d Sess. 133–36 (1976). The Report also cited the confusion and uncertainty that arose from basing the copyright term of the a vague concept such as "publication," suggesting that the new method of measuring duration would be simpler and easier to apply. Copyright protection for all of a particular author's works would end at the same time, avoiding the necessity of determining the publication date of successive revisions of a work, and distinguishing old and new matter in later editions. Perhaps most importantly, the Report noted that a large majority of the world's nations had adopted a copyright term of life of the author plus 50 years, and this term was required under the Berne Convention. Changing to the life plus 50 norm would facilitate international business transactions and smooth the way for eventual U.S. adherence to the Berne Convention. *Id.*

The House Report noted a point raised by educational groups in favor of retaining a renewable term configuration:

> [S]ince a large majority (now about 85 percent) of all copyrighted works are not renewed, a life-plus–50 year term would tie up a substantial body of material that is probably of no commercial interest but that would be more readily available for scholarly use if free of copyright restrictions. A statistical study of renewal registrations made by the Copyright Office in 1966 supports the generalization that most material which is considered to be of continuing or potential commercial value is renewed. Of the remainder, a certain proportion is of practically no value to anyone, but there are a large number of unrenewed works that have scholarly value to historians, archivists, and specialists in a variety of fields. * * *

Id. at 135–36. The Report acknowledged that "today's ephemera represent tomorrow's social history, and that works of scholarly value, which are now falling into the public domain after 28 years, would be protected much longer under the bill." *Id.* However, the Report concluded that "the advantages of a basic term of copyright enduring for the life of the author and for 50 years after the author's death outweigh any possible disadvantages." *Id.*

In the Sonny Bono Copyright Term Extension Act of 1998, Congress extended the copyright term again, by an additional 20 years. Congress provided that both new copyrights and copyrights existing on the Act's effective date (October 27, 1998) would enjoy the benefit of the extension.

While no House or Senate Report explains Congress' purpose in extending the copyright term to life of the author plus 70 years in the Sonny Bono Act, Representative Howard Coble, the Chairman of the House of Representatives Subcommittee on Courts and Intellectual Property, provided the following explanation in Hearings on the proposed extension:

> In 1995, the European Union, the EU, extended the copyright term for all of its member states from life of the author plus 50 years to life of the author plus 70 years. As the world leader in the export of intellectual property, this has potential serious trade implications for the United States.

> The United States and the EU nations are all signatories of the Berne Convention, which includes the so-called rule of the shorter term. Under that rule * * * a member country need only extend protection of a work of foreign authors to the extent that they would be protected in their own country. Therefore, U.S. works will only be granted copyright protection for the shorter life plus 50–year term before falling into the public domain.

> The main reasons for this extension of term are fairness and economics. If the United States does not extend to Americans the same copyright protection afforded their counterparts in Europe, Americans will have 20 years less protection than their European counterparts, 20 years during which time Europeans will not be paying Americans for their copyrighted works. EU countries are huge markets for U.S. intellectual property, and the United States would lose millions of dollars in export revenues. Any imbalance would be harmful to the United States and would, therefore, work a hardship on American creators and their families.

Pre–1978 Distribution of Recordings Containing Musical Compositions; Copyright Term Extension; and Copyright Per Program Licenses: Hearing before the Subcomm. on Courts and Intellectual Property of the House Comm. on the Judiciary, 105th Cong., 1st Sess. 3 (1997).

NOTES AND QUESTIONS

1. *The duration of copyright.* The Constitution empowers Congress to "promote the Progress of Science and useful Arts, by securing *for limited times* to Authors and Inventors the exclusive Right to their respective Writings and Discoveries." U.S. Const. art. I, § 8, cl. 8 (emphasis added). Federal copyright may not be perpetual. Presumably, it should last for the period best calculated to "promote the Progress of Science and useful Arts"—long enough to provide a sufficient incentive to authors, but not longer, so that works move into the public domain, becoming accessible to all (including future authors, who may want to draw from them), as quickly as possible. How long is that?

Are the justifications for the 1976 Act and Sonny Bono Act term extensions persuasive? As a general matter, are there convincing arguments *against* a long copyright term? Consider Lord Macaulay's famous argument against a long posthumous copyright monopoly:

[T]he evil effects of the monopoly are proportioned to the length of its duration. But the good effects for the sake of which we bear with the evil effects are by no means proportioned to the length of its duration. A monopoly of sixty years produces twice as much evil as a monopoly of thirty years, and thrice as much evil as a monopoly of twenty years. But it is by no means the fact that a posthumous monopoly of sixty years gives to an author thrice as much pleasure and thrice as strong a motive as a posthumous monopoly of twenty years. On the contrary, the difference is so small as to be hardly perceptible. We all know how faintly we are affected by the prospect of very distant advantages, even when they are advantages which we may reasonably hope that we shall ourselves enjoy. But an advantage that is to be enjoyed more than half a century after we are dead, by somebody, we know not by whom, perhaps by somebody unborn, by somebody utterly unconnected with us, is really no motive at all to action. . . . Considered as a boon to [authors, long posthumous duration of the copyright monopoly] is a mere nullity; but, considered as an impost on the public, it is no nullity, but a very serious and pernicious reality. I will take an example. Dr. Johnson died fifty-six years ago. If the law [prolonged the copyright for sixty years after the author's death], somebody would now have the monopoly of Dr. Johnson's works. Who that somebody would be is impossible to say; but we may venture to guess. I guess, then, that it would have been some bookseller, who was the assign of another bookseller, who was the grandson of a third bookseller, who had bought the copyright from Black Frank, the Doctor's servant and residuary legatee, in 1785 or 1786. Now, would the knowledge that this copyright would exist in 1841 have been a source of gratification to Johnson? Would it have stimulated his exertions? Would it have once drawn him out of his bed before noon? Would it have once cheered him under a fit of the spleen? Would it have induced him to give us one more allegory, one more life of a poet, one more imitation of Juvenal? I firmly believe not. I firmly believe that a hundred years ago, when he was writing our debates for the Gentleman's Magazine, he would very much rather have had twopence to buy a plate of shin of beef at a cook's shop underground. Considered as a reward to him, the difference between a twenty years' term and a sixty years' term of posthumous copyright would have been nothing or next to nothing. But is the difference nothing to us? I can buy Rassselas for sixpence; I might have had to give five shillings for it. I can buy the Dictionary, the entire genuine Dictionary, for two guineas, perhaps for less; I might have had to give five or six guineas for it. Do I grudge this to a man like Dr. Johnson? Not at all. Show me that the prospect of this boon roused him to any vigorous effort, or sustained his spirits under depressing circumstances, and I am quite willing to pay the price of such an object, heavy as that price is. But what I do complain of is that my circumstances are to be worse, and Johnson's none the better; that I am to give five pounds for what to him was not worth a farthing.

8 Macaulay, Works, 199–201 (Trevelyan ed. 1879), *reprinted* in Chaffee, *Reflections on the Law of Copyright: II*, 45 Colum. L. Rev. 719, 719–20 (1945). In your opinion, how much is the posthumous duration of copyright likely to affect an author's incentive to create? How much is it likely to affect the amount that a publisher is willing to pay the author for assignment of the copyright? See Chaffee, *supra*, at 720–21. Assuming that posthumous copyright protection would be an incentive to authors wishing to provide for a surviving spouse and children, does the protection need to last 70 years after the author's death? Is augmentation of the term of an existing copyright, after the work has been created, likely to affect the author's incentive? Are there other important considerations, beyond the need to provide an incentive to create, that should be entertained in determining the duration of copyright?

Review §§ 302 through 305 of the Copyright Act of 1976, as amended. In what way does extending the terms of *existing* copyrights (as opposed to copyrights arising after the Act's effective date) benefit the public? Congress also converted common-law copyrights existing on the effective date of the 1976 Act to federal copyrights. Even works that had enjoyed common-law copyright protection for more than 50 years after the author's death received federal copyright to endure through the year 2002. Why should Congress do this?

ELDRED v. ASHCROFT

United States Supreme Court, 2003.
537 U.S. 186, 123 S.Ct. 769, 154 L.Ed.2d 683.

JUSTICE GINSBURG delivered the opinion of the Court.

This case concerns the authority the Constitution assigns to Congress to prescribe the duration of copyrights. The Copyright and Patent Clause of the Constitution, Art. I, § 8, cl. 8, provides as to copyrights: "Congress shall have Power ... [t]o promote the Progress of Science ... by securing [to Authors] for limited Times ... the exclusive Right to their ... Writings." In 1998, in the measure here under inspection, Congress enlarged the duration of copyrights by 20 years. Copyright Term Extension Act (CTEA). As in the case of prior extensions, principally in 1831, 1909, and 1976, Congress provided for application of the enlarged terms to existing and future copyrights alike.

Petitioners are individuals and businesses whose products or services build on copyrighted works that have gone into the public domain. They seek a determination that the CTEA fails constitutional review under both the Copyright Clause's "limited Times" prescription and the First Amendment's free speech guarantee. Under the 1976 Copyright Act, copyright protection generally lasted from the work's creation until 50 years after the author's death. Under the CTEA, most copyrights now run from creation until 70 years after the author's death. 17 U.S.C. § 302(a). Petitioners do not challenge the "life-plus–70–years" timespan itself. "Whether 50 years is enough, or 70 years too much," they acknowledge, "is not a judgment meet for this Court." Congress went awry, petitioners maintain, not with respect to newly created works, but in enlarging the term for published works with existing copyrights. The "limited Tim[e]" in effect when a copyright is secured, petitioners urge, becomes the constitutional boundary, a clear line beyond the power of Congress to extend. As to the First Amendment, petitioners contend that the CTEA is a content-neutral regulation of speech that fails inspection under the heightened judicial scrutiny appropriate for such regulations.

* * *

I

A

We evaluate petitioners' challenge to the constitutionality of the CTEA against the backdrop of Congress' previous exercises of its authority under the Copyright Clause. The Nation's first copyright statute, enacted in 1790, provided a federal copyright term of 14 years from the date of publication, renewable for an additional 14 years if the author survived the first term. Act of May 31, 1790 (1790 Act). The 1790 Act's renewable 14–year term applied to existing works (*i.e.*, works already published and works created but not yet published) and future works alike. Congress expanded the federal copyright term to 42 years in 1831 (28 years from publication, renewable for an additional 14 years), and to 56 years in 1909 (28 years from publication, renewable for an additional 28 years). Both times, Congress applied the new copyright term to existing and future works * * *.

In 1976, Congress altered the method for computing federal copyright terms. For works created by identified natural persons, the 1976 Act provided that federal copyright protection would run from the work's creation, not—as in the 1790, 1831, and 1909 Acts—its publication; protection would last until 50 years after the author's death. § 302(a). In these respects, the 1976 Act aligned United States copyright terms with the then-dominant international standard adopted under the Berne Convention for the Protection of Literary and Artistic Works. For anonymous works, pseudonymous works, and works made for hire, the 1976 Act provided a term of 75 years from publication or 100 years from creation, whichever expired first. § 302(c).

These new copyright terms, the 1976 Act instructed, governed all works not published by its effective date of January 1, 1978, regardless of when the works were created. §§ 302–303. For published works with existing copyrights as of that date, the 1976 Act granted a copyright term of 75 years from the date of publication, §§ 304(a) and (b), a 19–year increase over the 56–year term applicable under the 1909 Act.

The measure at issue here, the CTEA, installed the fourth major duration extension of federal copyrights. Retaining the general structure of the 1976 Act, the CTEA enlarges the terms of all existing and future copyrights by 20 years. For works created by identified natural persons, the term now lasts from creation until 70 years after the author's death. 17 U.S.C. § 302(a). This standard harmonizes the baseline United States copyright term with the term adopted by the European Union in 1993. For anonymous works, pseudonymous works, and works made for hire, the term is 95 years from publication or 120 years from creation, whichever expires first. 17 U.S.C. § 302(c).

Paralleling the 1976 Act, the CTEA applies these new terms to all works not published by January 1, 1978. For works published before 1978 with existing copyrights as of the CTEA's effective date, the CTEA extends the term to 95 years from publication. Thus, in common with the 1831, 1909, and 1976 Acts, the CTEA's new terms apply to both future and existing copyrights.

     * * *

II

A

We address first the determination of the courts below that Congress has authority under the Copyright Clause to extend the terms of existing copyrights. Text, history, and precedent, we conclude, confirm that the Copyright Clause empowers Congress to prescribe "limited Times" for copyright protection and to secure the same level and duration of protection for all copyright holders, present and future.

The CTEA's baseline term of life plus 70 years, petitioners concede, qualifies as a "limited Tim[e]" as applied to future copyrights. Petitioners contend, however, that existing copyrights extended to endure for that same term are not "limited." Petitioners' argument essentially reads into the text of the Copyright Clause the command that a time prescription, once set, becomes forever "fixed" or "inalterable." The word "limited," however, does not convey a meaning so constricted. At the time of the Framing, that word meant what it means today: "confine[d] within certain bounds," "restrain[ed]," or "circumscribe[d]." S. Johnson, A Dictionary of the English Language (7th ed. 1785) * * *. Thus understood, a timespan appropriately "limited" as applied to future copyrights does not automatically cease to be "limited" when applied to existing copyrights. And as we observe, *infra*, there is no cause to suspect that a purpose to evade the "limited Times" prescription prompted Congress to adopt the CTEA.

To comprehend the scope of Congress' power under the Copyright Clause, "a page of history is worth a volume of logic." History reveals an unbroken congressional practice of granting to authors of works with existing copyrights the benefit of term extensions so that all under copyright protection will be governed evenhandedly under the same regime. * * *

Because the Clause empowering Congress to confer copyrights also authorizes patents, congressional practice with respect to patents informs our inquiry. We count it significant that early Congresses extended the duration of numerous individual patents as well as copyrights. The courts saw no "limited Times" impediment to such extensions; renewed or extended terms were upheld in the early days, for example, by Chief Justice Marshall and Justice Story sitting as circuit justices. * * *

Further, although prior to the instant case this Court did not have occasion to decide whether extending the duration of existing copyrights complies with the "limited Times" prescription, the Court has found no constitutional barrier to the legislative expansion of existing patents. * * *

Congress' consistent historical practice of applying newly enacted copyright terms to future and existing copyrights reflects a judgment stated concisely by Representative Huntington at the time of the 1831 Act: "[J]ustice, policy, and equity alike forb[id]" that an "author who had sold his [work] a week ago, be placed in a worse situation than the author who should sell his work the day after the passing of [the] act." 7 Cong. Deb. 424 (1831). * * * The CTEA follows this historical practice by keeping the duration provisions of the 1976 Act largely in place and simply adding 20 years to each of them. Guided by text, history, and precedent, we cannot agree with petitioners' submission that extending the duration of existing copyrights is categorically beyond Congress' authority under the Copyright Clause.

Satisfied that the CTEA complies with the "limited Times" prescription, we turn now to whether it is a rational exercise of the legislative authority conferred by the Copyright Clause. On that point, we defer substantially to Congress. * * *

The CTEA reflects judgments of a kind Congress typically makes, judgments we cannot dismiss as outside the Legislature's domain. As respondent describes, a key factor in the CTEA's passage was a 1993 European Union (EU) directive instructing EU members to establish a copyright term of life plus 70 years. Consistent with the Berne Convention, the EU directed its members to deny this longer term to the works of any non-EU country whose laws did not secure the same extended term. By extending the baseline United States copyright term to life plus 70 years, Congress sought to ensure that American authors would receive the same copyright protection in Europe as their European counterparts. The CTEA may also provide greater incentive for American and other authors to create and disseminate their work in the United States. * * *

In addition to international concerns, Congress passed the CTEA in light of demographic, economic, and technological changes,[14] and rationally credited projections that longer terms would encourage copyright holders to invest in the restoration and public distribution of their works. * * *

---

14. Members of Congress expressed the view that, as a result of increases in human longevity and in parents' average age when their children are born, the pre-CTEA term did not adequately secure "the right to profit from licensing one's work during one's lifetime and to take pride and comfort in knowing that one's children—and perhaps their children—might also benefit from one's posthumous popularity." 141 Cong. Rec. 6553 (1995) (statement of Sen. Feinstein) * * * Also cited was "the failure of the U.S. copyright term to keep pace with the substantially increased commercial life of copyrighted works resulting from the rapid growth in communications media." *Ibid.* (statement of Sen. Hatch) * * *

In sum, we find that the CTEA is a rational enactment; we are not at liberty to second-guess congressional determinations and policy judgments of this order, however debatable or arguably unwise they may be. Accordingly, we cannot conclude that the CTEA—which continues the unbroken congressional practice of treating future and existing copyrights in parity for term extension purposes—is an impermissible exercise of Congress' power under the Copyright Clause.

* * *

[P]etitioners contend that the CTEA's extension of existing copyrights does not "promote the Progress of Science" as contemplated by the preambular language of the Copyright Clause. Art. I, § 8, cl. 8. To sustain this objection, petitioners do not argue that the Clause's preamble is an independently enforceable limit on Congress' power. * * * Rather, they maintain that the preambular language identifies the sole end to which Congress may legislate; accordingly, they conclude, the meaning of "limited Times" must be "determined in light of that specified end." The CTEA's extension of existing copyrights categorically fails to "promote the Progress of Science," petitioners argue, because it does not stimulate the creation of new works but merely adds value to works already created.

As petitioners point out, we have described the Copyright Clause as "both a grant of power and a limitation," and have said that "[t]he primary objective of copyright" is "[t]o promote the Progress of Science." The "constitutional command," we have recognized, is that Congress, to the extent it enacts copyright laws at all, create a "system" that "promote[s] the Progress of Science."

We have also stressed, however, that it is generally for Congress, not the courts, to decide how best to pursue the Copyright Clause's objectives. * * * The justifications we earlier set out for Congress' enactment of the CTEA, *supra,* provide a rational basis for the conclusion that the CTEA "promote[s] the Progress of Science."

On the issue of copyright duration, Congress, from the start, has routinely applied new definitions or adjustments of the copyright term to both future works and existing works not yet in the public domain. Such consistent congressional practice is entitled to "very great weight, and when it is remembered that the rights thus established have not been disputed during a period of [over two] centur[ies], it is almost conclusive." Indeed, "[t]his Court has repeatedly laid down the principle that a contemporaneous legislative exposition of the Constitution when the founders of our Government and framers of our Constitution were actively participating in public affairs, acquiesced in for a long term of years, fixes the construction to be given [the Constitution's] provisions." Congress' unbroken practice since the founding generation thus overwhelms petitioners' argument that the CTEA's extension of existing copyrights fails *per se* to "promote the Progress of Science."

Closely related to petitioners' preambular argument, or a variant of it, is their assertion that the Copyright Clause "imbeds a quid pro quo."

They contend, in this regard, that Congress may grant to an "Autho[r]" an "exclusive Right" for a "limited Tim[e]," but only in exchange for a "Writin[g]." Congress' power to confer copyright protection, petitioners argue, is thus contingent upon an exchange: The author of an original work receives an "exclusive Right" for a "limited Tim[e]" in exchange for a dedication to the public thereafter. Extending an existing copyright without demanding additional consideration, petitioners maintain, bestows an unpaid-for benefit on copyright holders and their heirs, in violation of the *quid pro quo* requirement.

We can demur to petitioners' description of the Copyright Clause as a grant of legislative authority empowering Congress "to secure a bargain— this for that." * * * But the legislative evolution earlier recalled demonstrates what the bargain entails. Given the consistent placement of existing copyright holders in parity with future holders, the author of a work created in the last 170 years would reasonably comprehend, as the "this" offered her, a copyright not only for the time in place when protection is gained, but also for any renewal or extension legislated during that time. Congress could rationally seek to "promote ... Progress" by including in every copyright statute an express guarantee that authors would receive the benefit of any later legislative extension of the copyright term. Nothing in the Copyright Clause bars Congress from creating the same incentive by adopting the same position as a matter of unbroken practice.

       * * *

III

Petitioners separately argue that the CTEA is a content-neutral regulation of speech that fails heightened judicial review under the First Amendment. We reject petitioners' plea for imposition of uncommonly strict scrutiny on a copyright scheme that incorporates its own speech-protective purposes and safeguards. The Copyright Clause and First Amendment were adopted close in time. This proximity indicates that, in the Framers' view, copyright's limited monopolies are compatible with free speech principles. Indeed, copyright's purpose is to *promote* the creation and publication of free expression. As *Harper & Row* observed: "[T]he Framers intended copyright itself to be the engine of free expression. By establishing a marketable right to the use of one's expression, copyright supplies the economic incentive to create and disseminate ideas." 471 U.S., at 558, 105 S.Ct. 2218.

In addition to spurring the creation and publication of new expression, copyright law contains built-in First Amendment accommodations. First, it distinguishes between ideas and expression and makes only the latter eligible for copyright protection. * * * As we said in *Harper & Row,* this "idea/expression dichotomy strike[s] a definitional balance between the First Amendment and the Copyright Act by permitting free communication of facts while still protecting an author's expression." Due to this distinction, every idea, theory, and fact in a copyrighted work becomes instantly available for public exploitation at the moment of publication.

Second, the "fair use" defense allows the public to use not only facts and ideas contained in a copyrighted work, but also expression itself in certain circumstances. * * * The fair use defense affords considerable "latitude for scholarship and comment," and even for parody.

The CTEA itself supplements these traditional First Amendment safeguards. First, it allows libraries, archives, and similar institutions to "reproduce" and "distribute, display, or perform in facsimile or digital form" copies of certain published works "during the last 20 years of any term of copyright . . . for purposes of preservation, scholarship, or research" if the work is not already being exploited commercially and further copies are unavailable at a reasonable price. 17 U.S.C. § 108(h). Second, Title II of the CTEA, known as the Fairness in Music Licensing Act of 1998, exempts small businesses, restaurants, and like entities from having to pay performance royalties on music played from licensed radio, television, and similar facilities. 17 U.S.C. § 110(5)(B).

* * *

* * * The First Amendment securely protects the freedom to make—or decline to make—one's own speech; it bears less heavily when speakers assert the right to make other people's speeches. To the extent such assertions raise First Amendment concerns, copyright's built-in free speech safeguards are generally adequate to address them. We recognize that the D.C. Circuit spoke too broadly when it declared copyrights "categorically immune from challenges under the First Amendment." 239 F.3d, at 375. But when, as in this case, Congress has not altered the traditional contours of copyright protection, further First Amendment scrutiny is unnecessary.

IV

If petitioners' vision of the Copyright Clause held sway, it would do more than render the CTEA's duration extensions unconstitutional as to existing works. Indeed, petitioners' assertion that the provisions of the CTEA are not severable would make the CTEA's enlarged terms invalid even as to tomorrow's work. The 1976 Act's time extensions, which set the pattern that the CTEA followed, would be vulnerable as well.

As we read the Framers' instruction, the Copyright Clause empowers Congress to determine the intellectual property regimes that, overall, in that body's judgment, will serve the ends of the Clause. Beneath the facade of their inventive constitutional interpretation, petitioners forcefully urge that Congress pursued very bad policy in prescribing the CTEA's long terms. The wisdom of Congress' action, however, is not within our province to second-guess. Satisfied that the legislation before us remains inside the domain the Constitution assigns to the First Branch, we affirm the judgment of the Court of Appeals.

NOTES AND QUESTIONS

1. *Extending existing terms.* Did Congress make a good policy judgment in extending the term for new copyrights to life plus seventy years? Did it make a good policy judgment in extending the term of existing copyrights by a comparable twenty years? Which is more inequitable—depriving earlier works of later enacted term extensions, or depriving members of the public of access to works that they expected to enter the public domain at the end of the original term? Assuming that copyright is a form of *quid pro quo*, or bargain between the government (acting on behalf of the public) and the copyright owner, is it appropriate to change the terms of the bargain after it has gone into effect? Does the public enjoy a constitutionally protected interest in the public domain? In his dissent, Justice Stevens argued that *"Ex post facto* extensions of copyrights result in a gratuitous transfer of wealth from the public to authors, publishers, and their successors in interest." *Eldred*, 537 U.S. at 227, 123 S.Ct. at 793.

Works first federally copyrighted on or after 1923 have now enjoyed two subsequent extensions of their original copyright term and remain under copyright. Assume that Congress, at the urging of U.S. copyright industries, enacted another 20-year extension to existing copyrights in 2018, and again in 2038? Given the Supreme Court's opinion, would the extensions be subject to constitutional challenge? If the Supreme Court had held the Sonny Bono Act invalid, what would the practical effect have been? What, if anything, does the *Eldred* decision tell us about Congress' authority to restore foreign copyrights from the public domain?

While Justice Stevens' dissent focused on Congress' power under the Patents and Copyrights Clause, Justice Breyer's dissent argued that the Sonny Bono term extension violated the First Amendment. He argued that a statute that regulates expression lacks the constitutionally required rational basis:

> (1) if the significant benefits that it bestows are private, not public; (2) if it threatens seriously to undermine the expressive values that the Copyright Clause embodies; and (3) if it cannot find justification in any significant Clause-related objective.

Eldred, 537 U.S. 245, 123 S.Ct. at 802. Justice Breyer then argued at length that the Sonny Bono Act failed this standard, characterizing the term extension as providing "virtually nonexistent public benefit" and "serious public harm." *Id.*, 537 U.S. at 266, 123 S.Ct. 813. Among other things, he emphasized two costs the term extension imposed on the public. First, for the small percentage of works still retaining commercial value 50 years after the author's death, extended terms will enable copyright proprietors to charge higher prices, and potentially restrict their work's dissemination. Second, in the case of the large majority of works (which retain no further commercial value) extended terms will require educators, researchers, data base creators and other potential users to incur tremendous search costs to track down copyright owners and obtain permission. The prospect of these prohibitive search costs may as effectively deprive the public of these works as an outright denial of permission by the copyright owner. *Id.*, 537 U.S. at 248–53, 123 S.Ct. 804–07. Justice Breyer rejected as irrational the justifications that the attorney general offered as potentially offsetting these costs. What is your evaluation of the argument that extension of existing terms will provide incentives to publishers to republish and redistribute older copyrighted works? Is republication more or less likely if the work goes into the public domain? Why is the argument that people live longer and have children later in life relevant to the issue of whether copyrights should extend fifty or seventy years after the author's death? Why is the growth of new communication technologies relevant?

The *Eldred* majority suggests that when Congress alters "the traditional contours of copyright protection" greater First Amendment scrutiny may be necessary. What sort of legislation might alter the traditional contours of copyright protection? Would the Digital Millennium Copyright Act's anticircumvention provisions fit that description? How about legislation to provide rights in databases that lack originality?

2. *Renewal of copyright.* The 1909 Copyright Act provided for a 28–year copyright term that could (if a proper filing was made) be renewed for a second 28–year term, to give a total of 56 years of protection. Failure to make a proper filing for renewal placed the work in the public domain at the end of the first 28–year term.[23] In enacting the 1976 Act, Congress retained the renewable term configuration for federal copyrights already in existence on the effective date of the new Act (January 1, 1978). The only important change Congress made with regard to the term of existing copyrights was to add 19 years to the second ("renewal") term (and, in 1998, add an additional 20 years). Case law construing the 1909 Act renewal provisions remains relevant not only to interpret the effect of acts occurring before the effective date of the 1976 Act, but also to interpret the 1976 Act renewal provisions for federal copyrights existing on January 1, 1978.

Copyright Act § 304, like its predecessor in the 1909 Act, specifies that in most cases the *author (or the author's statutory successors)*, as opposed to the person owning the copyright at the end of the first term, has the right to renew the copyright and enjoy the renewal term. Upon proper renewal during the last year of the first term, the author (or his statutory successors) takes a whole new term, rather than a continuance of the old term. The renewal term operates much like a future estate in land: When it vests in possession, the recipient takes the copyright free of any assignments or licenses made in the first copyright term.

Congress created this renewal term in the author or her successors in order to give authors and their families a second opportunity to market the copyright. Works often are incapable of accurate monetary valuation before they are exploited and public reaction to them can be gauged. Unknown authors, in particular, may be in a poor bargaining position when first seeking to sell rights in a work. The renewal procedure gives the author, or if the author is dead, her family, an opportunity to renegotiate earlier assignments

---

23. As discussed *supra*, qualifying foreign copyrights forfeited for failure to renew are restored under the provisions of Uruguay Round Agreements Act § 514. 17 U.S.C.A. § 104A.

and licenses once the real value of the work has been ascertained, and obtain the benefit of any increase over the initial estimated value.

Just as the renewal term operates like a future estate, the expectancy of the right to renew and take the renewal term is like a contingent future interest in the succession of persons specified in § 304(a)(1)(C). The author is entitled to renew the copyright and enjoy the renewal term if he is still living when the renewal right vests. If the author is not living, the author's widow, widower, and/or children (as defined in § 101) are entitled to take the renewal term. If there are no surviving spouse or children, the author's executor is entitled to take the renewal term on behalf of the author's legatees.[24] In the absence of a will, the interest vests directly in the author's next of kin, as determined by the intestacy laws of the author's domicile.[25]

In Fred Fisher Music Co. v. M. Witmark & Sons, 318 U.S. 643, 63 S.Ct. 773, 87 L.Ed. 1055 (1943), the Supreme Court held that the author (and, by implication, the author's statutory successors) may convey her expectancy of renewal, if she clearly indicates her intention to do so. Thus, for example, if a publisher requires an author to assign both her present and renewal term, and the author's written assignment makes it clear that she intends to assign her rights in the renewal term, the assignment will be honored. If the author is alive when the renewal term is to vest, the publisher/assignee may make the renewal in the author's name, and retain the rights to the work during the second term. If, on the other hand, the author is deceased at vesting time, the publisher/assignee will take nothing. The author could not assign more than she had—a contingent future interest whose contingency has not been satisfied. The surviving spouse and children will receive the renewal interest, and if they do not exist, the executor or next of kin will take (unless, of course, these individuals also assigned their contingent renewal rights to the publisher). See Miller Music Corp. v. Charles N. Daniels, Inc., 362 U.S. 373, 80 S.Ct. 792, 4 L.Ed.2d 804 (1960). Does permitting assignment of the renewal right make sense in light of Congress' purpose to benefit the author and her family?

Prior to the Copyright Amendments Act of 1992, renewal term claimants were required to file an application for renewal with the Copyright Office during the 28th year of the first copyright term. Failure to do so cast the work into the public domain when the first term ended. Through ignorance or inattentiveness, some qualified claimants lost their right to a renewal term.

---

24. Note that the Copyright Act gives the renewal term to surviving spouse and children if they exist, regardless of what the author has provided in his will. See Saroyan v. William Saroyan Foundation, 675 F.Supp. 843 (S.D.N.Y.1987), *aff'd*, 862 F.2d 304 (2d Cir.1988) (author's express attempt to leave all his copyrights to charity would not defeat his estranged children's renewal rights under § 304). Only if there are no surviving spouse or children can the author direct who the recipient will be.

25. Section 304(a)(1)(B) specifies some categories of works for which the copyright proprietor (the person owning the copyright at the end of the first term), *rather than the author or her successors*, has the right to renew. These include:

1) posthumous works (A "posthumous work" is a work for which there was no assignment or contract for exploitation made during the author's life);

2) periodical, cyclopedic, or other composite works originally copyrighted by the proprietor;

3) works for hire.

What justification exists for exempting each of these categories of works from the general rule?

Apart from leading to unintended forfeitures, the renewal filing requirement arguably was inconsistent with the Berne Convention's prohibition of formalities as a precondition to copyright. In 1992, Congress amended § 304 to dispense with the filing requirement and provide for automatic renewal of all remaining first-term copyrights (those secured after January 1, 1964).

The amendment nonetheless seeks to encourage voluntary filings for renewal. Among other things, the amended § 304 provides that registration through a proper application to renew will "constitute prima facie evidence as to the validity of the copyright during its renewal and extended term and of the facts stated in the certificate." Moreover, if a person who is entitled to renew (or his renewal right assignee) registers the renewal term by filing a voluntary application to renew, the renewal interest will vest in that person as of the date of application (*during* the 28th year of the first term). If the renewal is automatic, the interest will vest in the person entitled to renew (or his renewal right assignee) at *the end* of the 28th year. *Id.*, § 304 (a)(2)(B). Thus, for example, assume that the author assigned his renewal rights to X. X files and renews at the beginning of the 28th year of the first term, while the author is still alive. The author dies a month later, prior to the end of the first term. X will take the renewal term. If X had relied on automatic renewal, he would have lost the term to the author's surviving spouse and children.

PROBLEMS

1. Assume that an author writes the first chapter of a novel in 1982. He writes four more chapters in 1983. He then puts the novel aside for several years to work on another project. In 1989, he writes the remainder of the first draft of the novel. In 1991, he completes revisions and sends the manuscript to publishers. In 1992 a publisher accepts the manuscript and edits it. The finished novel is published with notice in 1994. When does copyright commence? See 17 U.S.C.A. § 101 (definition of "created").

2. Carefully review Copyright Act §§ 302–305, and calculate the duration of the copyright in each of the problems below:

> a) Allen writes a poem on April 3, 1990, and publishes it with proper notice on April 8, 1994. She dies on August 4, 2009. When will copyright in the poem expire? What if Allen never publishes the poem?

> b) Brown writes a letter on June 1, 1948. He never publishes it, and dies on August 10, 2003. When will copyright in the letter expire?

> c) Chin composes a song on June 1, 1911. She never publishes it, and dies on October 17, 1917. When will copyright in the song expire?

> d) Donald and Delores Doe collaborate to write a novel, which is completed on April 4, 1982. They publish the novel with proper notice of copyright in 1984. Donald dies on September 8, 1993. Delores dies December 10, 2020. When will copyright in the novel expire?

> e) Edwards takes a photograph in his capacity as staff photographer for the local newspaper in 1962. The newspaper publishes the photograph with proper notice of copyright in 1968. Edwards dies in 1988. When will copyright in the photograph expire?

f) Fernandez creates art work for an advertising brochure in her capacity as a staff artist of the X advertising firm in 1979. X firm publishes the art work in a brochure with proper copyright notice in 1987. Fernandez dies in 2018. When will copyright in the art work expire?

g) Grosskoff writes a play in 1932, publishes it in 1934 with proper copyright notice, and properly renews the copyright in 1962. He dies in 1971. When does the copyright in the play expire?

3. Insbrook creates an oil painting on February 14, 1993. She sells the painting in 1994, and assigns all her rights in the copyright in 1998. She dies in 2019. When do her moral rights in the painting expire? See 17 U.S.C.A. § 106A(d).

4. Assume that X wrote a play and published it, with proper copyright notice, in 1923. He properly renewed copyright in the play in 1951. In 1938, X licensed Y to produce a motion picture based on the play. The motion picture received federal copyright in 1940. Because Y failed properly to renew copyright in the motion picture, it fell into the public domain in 1968. What, if any, rights should X have against Z if, in 1970, Z wishes to reproduce and sell copies of the motion picture?

5. Assume that A writes a story prior to January 1, 1978, and obtains federal copyright. While the copyright is in its first term, A grants to B Company the exclusive right to make and commercially exploit a movie based on the story. B does so. A dies. At the end of the first term of copyright in the story, A's widow successfully renews and obtains the renewal term. Is B free to reproduce, publicly distribute, perform and display its movie during the second term?

A. TERMINATION OF TRANSFERS

Review the complex provisions of Copyright Act §§ 203 and 304(c) and (d). According to the House Report, provisions of this sort are needed "because of the unequal bargaining position of authors, resulting in part from the impossibility of determining a work's value until it has been exploited." H.R. Rep. No. 1476, 94th Cong., 2d Sess. 124 (1976). Section 203, which applies to all *inter vivos* licenses and assignments of copyright executed by a work's author after 1977, serves much the same purpose as the old renewal provisions did: it permits the author or his statutorily designated successors to benefit from the work's appreciation in value by terminating the author's earlier licenses and assignments and reselling rights in the work. The House Report explains:

> Instead of being automatic, as is theoretically the case under the present renewal provision, the termination of a transfer or license under section 203 would require the serving of an advance notice within specified time limits and under specified conditions. However, although affirmative action is needed to effect a termination, the right to take this action cannot be waived in advance or contracted away.
> * * *

The right of termination would be confined to inter vivos transfers or licenses executed by the author, and would not apply to transfers by the author's successors in interest or to the author's own bequests. The scope of the right would extend not only to any "transfer of copyright ownership," as defined in section 101, but also to nonexclusive licenses. The right of termination would not apply to "works made for hire" * * *.

* * * With respect to the ultimate effective date, section 203(a)(3) provides, as a general rule, that a grant may be terminated during the 5 years following the expiration of a period of 35 years from the execution of the grant. As an exception to this basic 35–year rule, the bill also provides that "if the grant covers the right of publication of the work, the period begins at the end of 35 years from the date of publication of the work under the grant or at the end of 40 years from the date of execution of the grant, whichever term ends earlier." This alternative method of computation is intended to cover cases where years elapse between the signing of a publication contract and the eventual publication of the work.

The effective date of termination, which must be stated in the advance notice, is required to fall within the 5 years following the end of the applicable 35– or 40–year period, but the advance notice itself must be served earlier. Under section 203(a)(4)(A), the notice must be served "not less than two or more than ten years" before the effective date stated in it.

* * *

Section 203(b) makes clear that, unless effectively terminated within the applicable 5–year period, all rights covered by an existing grant will continue unchanged, and that rights under other Federal, State, or foreign laws are unaffected. * * *

H.R. Rep. No. 1476, 94th Cong., 2d Sess. 124–27 (1976). In your opinion, is § 203 likely to be more successful than the old renewal regime?

Section 304(c) permits authors and their statutorily designated successors to terminate pre–1978 transfers of rights in the renewal term in order to recapture and enjoy the bonus years that Congress subsequently added to the renewal term. According to the House Report:

Subsection (c) of section 304 is a close but not exact counterpart of section 203. In the case of either a first-term or renewal copyright already subsisting when the new statute becomes effective, any grant of the rights covering the renewal copyright in the work, executed before the effective date [of the 1976 Act], may be terminated under conditions and limitations similar to those provided in section 203. * * * [T]he 5–year period during which termination could be made effective would start 56 years after copyright was originally secured.

* * * Instead of being limited to transfers and licensees executed by the author, the right of termination under section 304(c) also

extends to grants executed by those beneficiaries of the author who can claim renewal under the present law: his or her widow or widower, children, executors, or next of kin. * * *

Id., at 140.

Section 304(d), added by the Sonny Bono Copyright Term Extension Act, permits authors or their successors to recapture that Act's 20–year extension through a termination of transfer, if they have not already done so as provided under § 304(c). Section 304(d) provides that if the copyright is still in its renewal term on the effective date of the Sonny Bono Act (October 27, 1998), but the termination right set forth in § 304(c) has expired without being exercised, then the author or his successors will have a new right to terminate during a five-year period commencing 75 years from the date the copyright was originally secured.

Instead of imposing the § 304(c) and (d) termination procedures, why not just provide that the additional years added to the renewal term automatically vest in the author or her designated successors?

PROBLEMS

1. Assume that Author creates a novel in 1985. He assigns exclusive rights to publish the novel to Publishing, Inc. in 1986, and Publishing, Inc. publishes the novel in 1987. In 1990, Author assigns the exclusive right to make a motion picture based on the novel to Movie Co., and the assignment agreement includes an express waiver of Author's right to terminate the assignment, assuring Movie Co. rights "for the full term of the copyright." Describe Author's termination rights in the case of each assignment. If Author is successful in terminating the assignment to Movie Co., will Movie Co. be forced to stop exploiting the movie it made based on the novel prior to the termination?

2. Author creates a play in 1980. In 1986 he grants a 50–year exclusive license to publicly perform the play to X. Author dies in 2013, survived by his wife, one living son (who has two children) and three grandchildren who are the offspring of a deceased daughter. In 2022, the author's survivors grant an exclusive right to publish the play in print to Y. The Author's survivors wish to terminate the transfer of performance rights prior to the 50–year term specified in the license to X. When may they terminate? Who must join in the notice of termination? Who will own the performance right once the transfer to X is terminated? May the survivors also terminate the assignment of publication rights to Y?

3. Author creates and publishes a play in 1940. She conveys all her rights in the first and renewal terms of copyright to First Publishing, Inc. Author dies in 1959, leaving a husband and three sons. She leaves all of her real and personal property by will to X Foundation. In 1968, husband and the three sons renew copyright in the play and assign it to Second Publishing, Inc. One of the sons dies shortly thereafter, leaving two daughters. Is the grant by the husband and three sons to Second Publishing, Inc. subject to termination?

If so, who has the right to terminate? When could the termination right be exercised?

4. Author creates and publishes a novel in 1930, and renews his copyright in 1958. In 1960 he grants the exclusive right to base a motion picture on the novel to Movie Co. Author dies in 1990. In 2002 his successors in interest want to terminate the assignment to Movie Co. What are their rights?

IX. REMEDIES

ABESHOUSE v. ULTRAGRAPHICS, INC.

United States Court of Appeals for the Second Circuit, 1985.
754 F.2d 467.

FEINBERG, CHIEF JUDGE:

* * *

In September 1981, Tevin and Matthew Abeshouse obtained a copyright for a large poster entitled "The Cube Solution," which described in great detail the solution to the popular puzzle known as "Rubik's Cube." Shortly before, Tevin Abeshouse, acting for Amity Products, Ltd.—the partnership under whose name he and his brother Matthew did business—entered into an exclusive distribution agreement with Ultragraphics, which was represented by its president, Richard Calio. The agreement took effect immediately and ran until December 31, 1981; under it, Ultragraphics became the exclusive North American distributor of "The Cube Solution" poster, which would be supplied by Amity at the rate of $0.90 per poster for the first 10,000 posters and $0.75 per poster thereafter.

This arrangement, however, soon broke down. In early October, apparently fearing that Amity would be unable to provide Ultragraphics with enough posters to meet customer demand, Calio placed an order with D & M, a printer, for 20,000 posters. Although these posters were slightly modified, they were substantially based on "The Cube Solution" poster. Calio also ordered two "separations" (negatives), to be used in the production of the poster overseas. It appears that D & M delivered 21,500 posters to Ultragraphics and that the latter distributed them at a wholesale price of $2.00 per poster until it had exhausted its supply. D & M also provided the two separations to Ultragraphics, which shipped them to two English publishing companies; for these separations, Ultragraphics received $2,500 credited to its account. At the expiration of the agreement with Ultragraphics, the Abeshouses entered into an agreement licensing Ideal Toy Co. to produce and sell their poster.

In September 1982, plaintiffs Abeshouses brought suit against Ultragraphics, Calio and D & M for copyright infringement, unfair competition, breach of contract and unjust enrichment. * * * On the copyright infringement claim, the jury found Ultragraphics and D & M jointly and severally liable for $55,368 and $2,441.53 respectively. * * * The district court awarded attorney's fees pursuant to 17 U.S.C. § 505 against Ultragraphics but refused to do so against D & M. These appeals and the cross-appeal followed.

II.   The Appeal of Ultragraphics

The Copyright Act of 1976 entitles a copyright owner to choose between statutory damages, as defined in 17 U.S.C. § 504(c), or "the actual damages suffered by him or her as a result of the infringement, and any profits of the infringer that are attributable to the infringement and are not taken into account in computing the actual damages," 17 U.S.C. § 504(b). In this respect, the 1976 Act clearly departs from the previous copyright statute, under which a copyright holder could receive a cumulative award of his own damages, including profits the owner would have earned on lost sales, and the infringer's actual profits, regardless of the latter's relationship to the holder's damages. The House Report that preceded the 1976 Act reasoned:

> Damages are awarded to compensate the copyright owner for losses from the infringement, and profits are awarded to prevent the infringer from unfairly benefiting from a wrongful act. Where the defendant's profits are nothing more than a measure of the damages suffered by the copyright owner, it would be inappropriate to award damages and profits cumulatively, since in effect they amount to the same thing. However, in cases where the copyright owner has suffered damages not reflected in the infringer's profits, or where there have been profits attributable to the copyrighted work but not used as a measure of damages, subsection (b) authorizes the award of both.

H.R. Rep. No. 1476, 94th Cong., 2d Sess. 161, reprinted in 1976 U.S. Code Cong. & Ad. News 5659, 5777.

In reviewing an award made under § 504(b), we must therefore ensure that it was not based upon undue speculation, and that it does not entail the double-counting of profits and damages expressly barred by that provision. Ultragraphics argues that the jury engaged in both undue speculation and improper double-counting in finding it liable for $55,368.

With regard to the profits component of § 504(b), we believe that the jury had before it a sufficient basis from which to calculate Ultragraphics' profits from sales of the modified "Cube Solution" posters produced by D & M. While Calio testified that he had ordered 20,000 of these posters, Robert Davidson, the president of D & M, recalled having actually delivered 21,500; the jury was entitled to use the larger number in computing Ultragraphics' profits. Since Calio testified that Ultragraphics had distributed all of the "Cube Solution" posters in its inventory, and the evidence suggested that the wholesale price for these posters was $2.00 per poster, the jury could fairly calculate Ultragraphics' gross revenues from the infringing posters to be $43,000. Once a copyright owner has shown evidence of an infringer's gross revenues, § 504(b) places upon the infringer the burden of proving his deductible expenses. Ultragraphics met that burden here by presenting evidence that its printing costs were

$7,932. The jury thus could have found that Ultragraphics' profits on infringing posters distributed domestically were $35,068. Adding to this sum the $2,500 in credit that Ultragraphics received for the separations it sold to the English publishers, but deducting the $300 that Ultragraphics paid D & M for these separations, the jury was entitled to fix Ultragraphics' profits from infringement at $37,268.

Since the jury found Ultragraphics liable for $18,100 beyond this amount, we may assume that the additional amount represents the jury's assessment of the actual damages suffered by appellees. Appellees argue that the jury's award of $55,368 against Ultragraphics represents actual damages, in the form of compensation for profits appellees would have earned by selling 20,000 of their own posters directly to the public for between $4.50 and $5.50. However, during the period in which Ultragraphics sold most of the infringing posters, appellees were bound by the agreement making Ultragraphics the exclusive distributor of "The Cube Solution" poster in North America. Furthermore, upon the expiration of this agreement, appellees granted Ideal Toy Co. a two-year license to produce and market the poster. Appellees failed to present any evidence that under these two agreements they would have been allowed to make direct sales themselves or that, even if permitted, they would have been equipped to do so. Similarly, appellees failed to offer any evidence suggesting they might actually have done business in foreign markets.

Appellees also contend that the jury awarded them actual damages, by compensating them for "damage to the reputation of the posters resulting from the inferior quality of the infringing posters" and for damage to their ability to sell their posters in the future caused by the absence of a copyright notice on the infringing posters. However, appellees did not offer any proof that the terms of their two-year exclusive license to Ideal Toy had been affected by Ultragraphics' conduct; nor did appellees make any effort to assess the marketability of their copyright during any time following that sale. These claims were thus too speculative to support any award of actual damages.

The only actual damages for which appellees did adduce sufficient evidence were for the profits they would have earned on sales to their distributor, Ultragraphics, had Ultragraphics not sought out an alternative source of supply for "The Cube Solution" posters. If appellees, rather than D & M, had supplied Ultragraphics with 21,500 posters pursuant to the exclusive distribution agreement, appellees would have received $0.75 per poster. Out of this sum, they would have had to pay printing costs that the jury could have found to be as low as $0.22 per poster, leaving appellees with damages in the form of lost profits of $11,395. In charging Ultragraphics with these damages, the jury would not have been engaging in the double-counting forbidden by § 504(b), even though the jury also awarded to appellees Ultragraphics' profits of $37,268. Double-counting may occur when an infringing seller has to disgorge profits on sales that a copyright holder might have made and for which he may therefore claim damages in the form of lost profits.[3] But here, appellees could not have sold their posters domestically to anyone but their exclusive distributor, Ultragraphics, at $0.75 apiece. Ultragraphics sold to wholesalers at $2.00 per poster. Appellees could not properly have made the latter sales and therefore cannot claim any lost profits on them. Thus, requiring Ultragraphics to disgorge to appellees its profits on those sales contains no element of double-counting, even though appellees are also recovering damages of $11,395.

In the absence of any consideration of joint and several liability, appellees thus appear to have been entitled to an award of only $48,663 against Ultragraphics. This figure represents the total of Ultragraphics' profits of $37,268 and appellees' damages of $11,395. Since appellees were awarded $55,368 by the jury, a remittitur would therefore seem appropriate. * * *

* * *

Finally, we find that the district court did not abuse the discretion given to it by 17 U.S.C. § 505 when it refused to award attorney's fees against D & M. The court reasoned that D & M had acted at the direction of Ultragraphics, had made only a small profit from the infringement and had diligently pursued settlement. We cannot say that the court should not have been swayed by these considerations.

* * *

RSO RECORDS, INC. v. PERI

United States District Court, Southern District of New York, 1984.
596 F.Supp. 849.

HAIGHT, DISTRICT JUDGE:

This is a civil action for willful copyright infringement. Plaintiffs are the producers, manufacturers, and distributors of some thirty-five copyrighted sound recordings which they claim have been infringed by the defendants. The corporate defendants are Creative Disc, Inc. ("Creative"), which manufactured and packaged phonograph records, and Dynasty Graphics, Inc. ("Dynasty"), which prepared photographic materials used in the printing of labels and paper packaging for phonograph records and prerecorded cassette and eight-track tapes. * * * The individual defendants have all been involved in the manufacture of sound recordings. Defendants Joseph Peri ("Joe Peri") and Carl Feuerstein have admitted being officers and shareholders in Dynasty, and the evidence demonstrates that both were also in control of operations at Creative. Salvatore "Sam" Peri ("Sam Peri") worked in a cassette and eight-track tape duplicating facility called Delmonico Audio Sounds, Inc. ("Delmonico"), which was housed in the same building as Creative. Plaintiffs accuse defendants of

---

3. Double-counting would occur in this case, for example, if appellees were to recover both the profits D & M made on its sales to Ultragraphics and the profits appellees lost because Ultragraphics sought out D & M as an alternative supplier.

copying plaintiffs' copyrighted sound recordings and the packaging of those recordings—in essence, of record counterfeiting. They have requested damages, attorney's fees, and destruction of various tools of reproduction seized from the corporate defendants' places of business. The action was tried to the Court sitting without a jury over the course of seven trial days. This opinion constitutes the Court's findings of fact and conclusions of law pursuant to Rule 52(a), Fed.R.Civ.P.

[The court finds that the defendants engaged in two varieties of infringement. First, they produced counterfeit copies of the plaintiffs' copyrighted sound recordings. Counterfeit records and tapes are exact copies of sound recordings made without the permission of the copyright holder. Second, the defendants contributed to the production of counterfeit records and tapes by producing materials essential to printing packaging for the counterfeits. In order to make successful counterfeits, the packaging materials ("graphics")—labels and jackets for records, labels and cardboard boxes for tapes—must look exactly like those of the original. This is done by photographing a legitimate copy of the graphics of a sound recording and producing "color separations"—a series of four negative or positive photographs, each in a different color, of the same set of graphics. These four photographs are used to reproduce four-color printed copies of the original graphics. The court finds that the defendants produced separations for their own use and also produced and sold them to other record producers, both legitimate and counterfeit.]

[In the course of a criminal investigation, the FBI had found on the Creative and Dynasty premises copies of color separations for the graphics of twenty-seven sound recordings copyrighted by the plaintiffs. There was also direct evidence that the defendants had manufactured copies of three of the plaintiffs' copyrighted sound recordings—"Breezin' " by George Benson (records), "Bat Out of Hell" by Meatloaf (records), and "Saturday Night Fever" (tapes). The plaintiffs had copies of production records seized by the FBI from Creative, as well as some copies of counterfeit phonorecords seized on the premises. The defendants refused to answer virtually all questions and refused to produce documents at their depositions, invoking their Fifth Amendment right to avoid self-incrimination. They also declined to testify at trial. They did, however, present witnesses who established that a significant amount of Creative's output was produced for legitimate record production companies.]

[While the corporate defendants made the infringing color separations and counterfeit copies, the court found that the individual defendants all either personally participated or were vicariously liable for at least some of the companies' infringements. The court also found that the defendants' infringement was willful.]

[The plaintiffs were unable to quantify their actual damages because the defendants refused to turn over any further production records, aid in the interpretation of the records which had already been seized, or provide information about how the color separations were to be used. The court found the available evidence only sufficient to establish a sum of damages and profits totalling $42,239.85—$29,964.85 for "Breezin'," $5,875.00 for "Bat Out of Hell," $4,700.00 for "Saturday Night Fever," and $2,700.00 for the twenty-seven color separations. The court noted that the actual profits and damages were likely much higher.]

B.   Statutory Damages

Statutory damages are the other option. Section 504(c)(2) permits an award of statutory damages of up to $50,000 per infringed work[16] when, as in this case, the infringement was willful. The statute leaves the exact amount of the award to the discretion of the Court, to be set "as the court deems just." 17 U.S.C. § 504(c)(1). The case law on statutory damages is still in its formative stages. Undoubtedly assessed statutory damages should bear some relation to actual damages suffered. Because statutory damages are often used in cases where actual damages cannot be precisely calculated, however, they cannot be expected to correspond exactly. Further, courts have also recognized that Congress's provision for a greater award in cases of willful infringement indicates that statutory damages may in such cases exceed the amount of documented damages. By taking on a partially punitive character, such awards serve the Copyrights Act's twofold purpose of compensation and deterrence. For example, after finding actual damages of $5,000, Judge Duffy in *Lauratex Textile Corp. v. Allton Knitting Mills Inc.*, 519 F.Supp. 730, 733 (S.D.N.Y.1981) awarded $40,000 in statutory damages because of defendant's willful and repeated infringements. * * * An additional factor must be considered in setting statutory damages in this action. Any information which may be available on the exact amount of profits or damages is entirely in the hands of the defendants. They are the only ones capable of interpreting their own production records and specifying how the infringing color separations were used. They have chosen to remain silent. Plaintiffs should not be penalized thereby.

The one incident of infringement on which partial information on damages is available demonstrates that defendants made a minimum of $30,000 in illicit profits. It is likely that the other infringed phonograph record, "Bat Out of Hell," and the infringed tape, "Saturday Night Fever," were produced in quantities similar to "Breezin'," since all were very popular recordings. Defendants, in any event, have not shown "Breezin' " to have been exceptional. The probable size of the damages combined with the large-scale and willful infringing activity of defendants thus makes appropriate an award of maximum statutory damages of

---

16. The language of § 504(c)(1) makes it clear that plaintiffs may not recover multiple statutory awards where they have copyrighted both graphics for a recording and the recording itself. Nor can they recover separate statutory damages for record and tape infringement. Each "work" is entitled to only one award of damages. House Report No. 94–1476, at 162, quoted in 1976 U.S. Code Cong. & Admin. News 565, 577. Inasmuch as graphics simply complement the recording and have no separate economic value, whatever their artistic value, they must be considered part of the musical "work" for purposes of the copyright statute. A separate award for their infringement is not permitted. Similarly, tape and phonograph record are simply two media for presenting the same "work," precluding separate awards.

$50,000 for each infringement. Plaintiffs will recover a total of $150,000 for these three infringements.

For similar reasons, I reach the same conclusion as to the color separation infringements. Joe Peri admitted selling color separations to Jerry Pettus, regarded as the most active counterfeiter in the nation. Another Dynasty customer was Murry Kaplan, who was also under investigation by the FBI for counterfeiting. Thus, it is clear that Dynasty provided color separations not only for their own counterfeiting operations but those of others. In this manner Dynasty likely contributed to the making of thousands of counterfeit records and tapes. Again, the information which would indicate the scope of this activity is wholly in defendants' hands, and they have not disclosed it. Because it is likely that Dynasty's color separations each contributed to the counterfeiting of thousands of records and tapes, thus depriving plaintiffs of thousands of sales and was undertaken in a wholly willful manner, the maximum statutory award is again appropriate. Statutory damages of $50,000 are awarded for each of the [27 works for which color separations were produced] except "Saturday Night Fever," which was already the subject of a maximum award. See footnote 16, *supra*.

If plaintiffs elect statutory damages, the total award will be $1,450,000. * * *

* * *

I will require plaintiffs to file a notice of election stating which type of damages they prefer. If they elect actual damages and profits, final judgment for $42,239.85 plus costs and attorney's fees will be entered. If plaintiffs elect statutory damages, final judgment of $1,450,000, plus costs and attorney's fees will be entered. * * *

NOTES AND QUESTIONS

1. *Actual damages and profits.* Since proving actual damages can be difficult, plaintiffs frequently focus on recovering the defendant's profits, instead. Under § 504(b), a plaintiff must only prove an infringer's gross revenues. The defendant/infringer must prove his costs in generating the revenues in order to deduct them from the award. If the profits are not totally attributable to the infringement, the defendant bears the burden of proving what portion of the profit is attributable to other factors, and thus not subject to recovery. For example, assume that the defendant makes a movie that borrows impermissibly from the plot of plaintiff's novel. The defendant adds its own creative elements to the plot, hires popular stars to play the leading roles, and promotes the movie heavily through advertising. It is unlikely that all of the defendant's profit from the movie is attributable to its infringement of the plaintiff's novel. How might the defendant prove the amount of profit that is attributable to the other factors mentioned above? See generally Sheldon v. Metro–Goldwyn Pictures Corp., 309 U.S. 390, 60 S.Ct. 681, 84 L.Ed. 825 (1940) (court credits expert testimony, and, giving plaintiff the

"benefit of every doubt," finds that twenty percent of the defendant's net profit was attributable to the infringement.).

Suppose that the floor show at defendant's Las Vegas gambling casino infringed the plaintiff's work. How should the profits attributable to the infringement be calculated? Should plaintiff be able to recover a portion of the defendant's overall hotel and gambling revenues on the theory that the infringing floor show brought more guests and gamblers to the casino? See Frank Music Corp. v. Metro–Goldwyn–Mayer, Inc., 772 F.2d 505, 516–17 (9th Cir.1985) (indirect profits from the hotel and gaming operations, as well as direct profits from the show itself, are recoverable).

Should plaintiffs be able to collect prejudgment interest on damage awards? The Copyright Act makes no express provision for this. The Circuit Courts have disagreed. Compare Kleier Advertising Inc. v. Premier Pontiac, Inc., 921 F.2d 1036, 1041–2 (10th Cir.1990) ("it would be 'anomalous' to hold that a plaintiff would be entitled to recover profits flowing from infringement but not revenue generated by the *use* of the profits"), with Robert R. Jones Associates v. Nino Homes, 858 F.2d 274, 282 (6th Cir.1988) (the damages granted were sufficient to serve the purposes of promoting innovation and deterring unauthorized exploitation of others' creative expression. A grant of prejudgment interest was thus unnecessary.).

2. *Statutory damages*. Recall that the statutory damages option is only available to those copyright owners who registered their copyright before the defendant's infringement commenced or, in the case of published works, within three months of first publication. 17 U.S.C.A. § 412. Congress has raised the monetary limits for statutory damages since the decision in *RSO*, in order to heighten the allure of statutory damages as an incentive to register. For causes of action arising after December 9, 1999, Copyright Act § 504(c), as amended, provides for awards ranging from $750 to $30,000. The ceiling is $150,000 in the case of willful infringement. "Willful" infringement occurs when the defendant knows or should know that his actions constitute infringement, or acts with reckless disregard of whether his acts constitute infringement.

Section 504(c)(2) also provides that "[i]n a case where the infringer sustains the burden of proving, and the court finds, that such infringer was not aware and had no reason to believe that his or her acts constituted an infringement of copyright, the court in its discretion may reduce the award of statutory damages to a sum of not less than $200." As an incentive for copyright owners to continue providing notice of copyright, the Berne Convention Implementation Act amended Copyright Act §§ 401 and 402 to deny an innocent infringer defense when notice was properly given on the published copy or phonorecord to which the defendant had access. How effective is this incentive likely to be?

In *RSO Records*, the court found that the plaintiffs were only entitled to one $50,000 award in connection with the "Saturday Night Fever" infringement, even though the defendants infringed both the sound recording and the copyrighted graphics accompanying the recording. Why should the plaintiffs not be entitled to two awards? Review the language of § 504(c).

Assume that the defendants made unauthorized reproductions of "Saturday Night Fever" on three different occasions during a period of three years. Would plaintiffs be entitled to three separate awards?

Assume that a plaintiff owned the exclusive right to reproduce the sound recordings, but another party, X, owned the exclusive right to distribute the sound recordings to the public. The defendants infringed both rights. Would plaintiff and X each be entitled to recover a separate award of statutory damages?

Assume that the plaintiff published a book of photographs it had taken of emerging seedlings of various plants. Defendants, in the business of selling seeds, reproduced 122 of the photographs without the plaintiff's authorization and featured them on their seed packages. Under § 504(c), would the plaintiff be entitled to 122 awards of damages or only one? See Stokes Seeds Ltd. v. Geo. W. Park Seed Co., Inc., 783 F.Supp. 104, 108–09 (W.D.N.Y.1991) (only one award could be made).

In Feltner v. Columbia Pictures Television, Inc., 523 U.S. 340, 118 S.Ct. 1279, 140 L.Ed.2d 438 (1998), the Supreme Court found that Copyright Act § 504(c) itself provides no right to have a jury determine statutory damages. However, the Seventh Amendment does provide a right to a jury on all issues pertinent to an award of statutory damages under § 504(c), including the amount of statutory damages to be awarded. Are juries well suited to use the discretion called for under § 504(c)?

3. *Injunctions.* Copyright Act § 502 authorizes both preliminary and permanent injunctive relief in copyright actions.

Courts have traditionally granted permanent injunctions liberally upon a finding of copyright infringement. In e-Bay, Inc. v. MercExchange, 547 U.S. 388, 126 S.Ct. 1837, 164 L.Ed.2d 641 (2006), however, the Supreme Court significantly curbed that practice. In *e-Bay,* the Supreme Court held that *patent* infringement should only be enjoined when a four-factor standard is satisfied: 1) the plaintiff has suffered an irreparable injury; 2) the remedies available at law are inadequate to compensate for that injury; 3) considering the balance of hardships between the plaintiff and defendant, a remedy in equity is warranted; and 4) the public interest would not be disserved by a permanent injunction. The Circuit Courts of Appeal have subsequently determined that the *e-Bay* decision applies with equal force in the copyright context. See, e.g., Christopher Phelps & Associates LLC v. Galloway, 492 F.3d 532, 543 (4th Cir. 2007)(Finding that the Supreme Court's four-factor standard in *eBay* applies equally to permanent injunctions against patent infringement and copyright infringement). Indeed, the Second Circuit has recently held that *e-Bay* sets the appropriate standard for evaluating motions for *preliminary* injunctions in copyright infringement cases, as well as for permanent injunctions. Salinger v. Colting, 607 F.3d 68 (2d Cir. 2010). The *Salinger* court stressed that under the *e-Bay* standard, it is inappropriate for courts to make assumptions of irreparable harm upon a showing of a likelihood of success on the merits, as had been done in the past:

> a district court must undertake the following inquiry in determining whether to grant a plaintiff's motion for a preliminary injunction in a copyright case. First, as in most other kinds of cases in our Circuit, a

court may issue a preliminary injunction in a copyright case only if the plaintiff has demonstrated "either (a) a likelihood of success on the merits or (b) sufficiently serious questions going to the merits to make them a fair ground for litigation and a balance of hardships tipping decidedly in the [plaintiff]' s favor." Second, the court may issue the injunction only if the plaintiff has demonstrated "that he is likely to suffer irreparable injury in the absence of an injunction." The court must not adopt a "categorical" or "general" rule or presume that the plaintiff will suffer irreparable harm * * *. Instead, the court must actually consider the injury the plaintiff will suffer if he or she loses on the preliminary injunction but ultimately prevails on the merits, paying particular attention to whether the "remedies available at law, such as monetary damages, are inadequate to compensate for that injury." Third, a court must consider the balance of hardships between the plaintiff and defendant and issue the injunction only if the balance of hardships tips in the plaintiff's favor. Finally, the court must ensure that the "public interest would not be disserved" by the issuance of a preliminary injunction.

Id., at 80.

4. *Costs and attorney's fees.* Copyright Act § 505 authorizes courts to award costs to any party, and "a reasonable attorney's fee to the prevailing party." The "prevailing party" may be either the plaintiff or the defendant, though § 412 conditions fee awards on copyright claimants' timely registration. Unlike its Patent Act counterpart, § 505 does not reserve fee awards for exceptional cases.

Several Circuit Courts of Appeals imposed a dual standard for fee awards, in which prevailing plaintiffs were awarded attorney's fees as a matter of course, while prevailing defendants were required to show that the original suit was frivolous or brought in bad faith. See Fogerty v. Fantasy, Inc., 510 U.S. 517, 114 S.Ct. 1023, 127 L.Ed.2d 455 (1994). They justified this distinction on policy grounds: A more generous standard for plaintiffs would encourage the bringing of meritorious infringement claims. In *Fogerty, supra,* the Supreme Court rejected this dual standard, adopting instead an "evenhanded" approach. The Court specifically discredited the policy justification that had been given for the dual standard:

> We think the argument is flawed because it expresses a one-sided view of the purposes of the Copyright Act. While it is true that *one* of the goals of the Copyright Act is to discourage infringement, it is by no means the *only* goal of that Act. In the first place, it is by no means always the case that the plaintiff in an infringement action is the only holder of a copyright; often times, defendants hold copyrights too * * *.
>
> More importantly, the policies served by the Copyright Act are more complex, more measured, than simply maximizing the number of meritorious suits for copyright infringement. * * * We have often recognized the monopoly privileges that Congress has authorized, while "intended to motivate the creative activity of authors and inventors by the provision of a special reward," are limited in nature and ultimately must serve the public good. * * *

* * *

Because copyright law ultimately serves the purpose of enriching the general public through access to creative works, it is peculiarly important that the boundaries of copyright be demarcated as clearly as possible. To that end, defendants who seek to advance a variety of meritorious copyright defenses should be encouraged to litigate them to the same extent that plaintiffs are encouraged to litigate meritorious claims of infringement. * * * Thus a successful defense of a copyright infringement action may further the policies of the Copyright Act every bit as much as a successful prosecution of an infringement claim by the holder of a copyright.

Id., 510 U.S. at 526–27.

The Court likewise rejected arguments that § 505 was intended to adopt the "British Rule" that both prevailing plaintiffs and defendants should be awarded attorney's fees as a matter of course, absent exceptional circumstances. The Court stressed that there was no precise rule or formula for making the fee determination. Rather, courts should exercise equitable discretion in each case, in light of all the circumstances. *Id.*, 510 U.S. at 534.

5. *Criminal sanctions.* The Copyright Act provides for criminal sanctions against persons who infringe a copyright willfully and "for purposes of commercial advantage or private financial gain." 17 U.S.C § 506(a)(1)(A).

In United States v. La Macchia, 871 F.Supp. 535 (D.Mass.1994), the defendant computer bulletin board operator provided Internet users with free infringing copies of software. The court held that criminal penalties were unauthorized, because the defendant's activities lacked the necessary element of commercial advantage or private financial gain required by § 506(a). This decision led Congress to enact the No Electronic Theft Act in 1997. Among other things, this Act authorized criminal penalties when the defendant, during a 180–day period, willfully reproduces or distributes infringing copies or phonorecords with a total retail value exceeding $1,000. 17 U.S.C. § 506(a)(1)(B). At the same time, Congress provided that "financial gain," for purposes of § 506(a)(1), includes "receipt, or expectation of receipt, of anything of value, including the receipt of other copyrighted works." 17 U.S.C. § 101.

The Artists' Rights and Theft Prevention Act, signed into law in 2005, further amends § 506 by providing criminal penalties for willful and knowing distribution (via computer network) of a work being prepared for commercial distribution. § 506(a)(1)(c). This provision addresses the growing problem of pre-release infringement, which occurs when an individual obtains a copy of a movie, sound recording or computer program that is being prepared for commercial distribution, and undercuts the copyright owner by distributing it (often for free) over the Internet. The amendments make it clear that the criminal provisions extend to distribution of movies that have been released in theaters, but have not yet been released in video tapes or DVDs for non-theater viewing. Related amendments impose criminal penalties for the act of making unauthorized recordings of movies in theaters. 18 U.S.C. § 2319B.

PART FOUR

RIGHTS IN CONSUMER GOOD WILL AND RELATED TRADE VALUES

■ ■ ■

CHAPTER FIVE

TRADEMARKS AND OTHER INDICATIONS OF ORIGIN

■ ■ ■

I. INTRODUCTION

NOTE: THE HISTORICAL DEVELOPMENT OF THE LAW OF TRADEMARKS AND UNFAIR COMPETITION

Trademark and unfair competition laws have their origin in the common law. Throughout their development, courts recognized the need to balance a range of conflicting interests. In order to have an efficient, competitive marketplace, consumers must have the means to easily and quickly distinguish the goods[1] of competing producers and exercise their purchasing preferences. Thus, each producer must be able to adopt a word or symbol (a "mark" or "trademark") that readily identifies it as the source of its goods, and prohibit other producers from adopting a confusingly similar mark that may mislead consumers and cause them to make mistaken purchases. Affording merchants exclusive rights in the marks they adopt provides multiple benefits: It reduces consumer search costs, promotes marketplace efficiency, and protects both consumers and producers against deceptive and fraudulent practices. It also encourages producers to invest in product quality because, to the extent that trademark protection enables consumers to exercise their preferences, producers can expect to recoup such investments through repeat patronage.

On the other hand, an efficient, competitive marketplace requires that competing producers be able to communicate the nature, qualities and characteristics of their products to interested consumers without unwarranted interference. Thus, it is problematic to permit individual merchants to assert exclusive rights in words or symbols that others may legitimately need for this purpose. If merchants are granted trademark rights in descriptive words or symbols they may be able, individually or collectively, to prevent others from

---

1. This historical note refers to the "goods," "merchandise" or "products" of marketplace actors. Early case law focused primarily on marks for tangible goods, and the law of technical trademarks was limited to protecting marks that distinguished goods, as were the early federal trademark acts. Today, of course, marks indicating the source of intangible *services* are also routinely protected.

702

effectively describing their competing goods to prospective purchasers, and thus impair competition. They may be able to claim exclusive rights in their surnames, and thus prevent others with the same name from using it to identify goods of their own personal manufacture. A single producer of goods in a desirable geographic area may be able to assert trademark rights in the geographic name of the place, and thus deny its neighbors the benefits arising from associating their own goods with it. Moreover, overly generous trademark rights in *any kind* of word or symbol may enable mark owners to block others from referring to their products in the course of comparative advertising, to the detriment of consumers. They might also assert trademark rights to censor critical product critiques and commentary, not only by their competitors, but also by dissatisfied consumers and the media. This, of course, would impair First Amendment interests, as well as impair competition by choking the essential flow of useful marketplace information to consumers.

In developing the common law, American courts reconciled these conflicting concerns by crafting two separate causes of action to regulate interests in product marks: 1) the cause of action for technical trademark infringement; and 2) the unfair competition cause of action for *trade name* (or "secondary meaning mark")[2] *infringement.* Courts correlated the contours of these two causes of action to the comparative social impact of permitting merchants to appropriate *fanciful, coined or arbitrary words or symbols* to their exclusive use, on one hand, and allowing them to appropriate *surnames and descriptive and geographically descriptive words and symbols,* on the other. The technical trademark infringement cause of action provided merchants with strong, property-like rights in the fanciful, coined or arbitrary ("inherently distinctive") marks they adopted to identify their goods. In contrast, the unfair competition cause of action only purported to enforce rights in surnames or descriptive or geographically descriptive words or symbols when the merchant claiming them could demonstrate that the defendant used them in their "secondary" (trademark) sense, rather than their "primary" (surname, descriptive, or geographically descriptive) sense, and acted with fraudulent intent to deceive consumers about the source of its goods.

---

2. Prior to 1946, when the Lanham Act was enacted, courts generally described the unfair competition cause of action as providing rights in *trade names.* "Trade name" was a broad term, encompassing both ordinary, descriptive, geographically descriptive, and surname marks for products and services, *and* the names of businesses. When Congress enacted the Lanham Act, it defined the term "trademark" to include words, names, symbols or devices (or combinations thereof) used to identify the source of the user's product. 15 U.S.C. § 1127. It provided for "service marks," which it defined as including words, names, symbols and devices (and combinations thereof) used to identify the source of the user's services. *Id.* It *redefined* the term "trade name" to refer *only* to the name of a business. *Id.* That is the terminology that most modern trademark practitioners and scholars use today.

To avoid potential confusion, we can use the term *secondary meaning mark* to refer to common, descriptive, geographically descriptive and surname marks that might be protected under the common-law cause of action for unfair competition, rather than the (once broader) term "trade name."

A. The Unfair Competition Cause of Action for
Secondary Meaning Mark Infringement

The early common law declined to afford merchants exclusive rights in words or symbols (or combinations of words or symbols) that described their product, described the product's geographical origin, or constituted a surname or designation common to the trade. Numerous marketplace actors might legitimately want or need to use such words and symbols in communicating the nature and qualities of their own goods to consumers, and a robust, efficient marketplace depended on their ability to do so freely. Thus, the early common law relegated such words and symbols to the public domain, for use by all. While a business might adopt such a word or symbol to identify its product, it had no right to expect exclusivity. The courts made it clear that the interest in unfettered, truthful use of language in its ordinary or descriptive meaning outweighed concerns about potential consumer confusion about product source.

However, courts came to recognize that when a merchant heavily stressed a surname or descriptive word or symbol in marketing its goods, or employed such a word or symbol for a long period of time, consumers might come to associate it with the user's product, and upon encountering it in connection with similar goods, believe it to indicate source in the heavy or long-term user. In such cases (when the surname or descriptive word or symbol had acquired a "secondary meaning" to consumers as an indication of source), unregulated use by competitors could lead to problematic consumer deception. Recognizing *limited* rights in such words or symbols ("secondary meaning marks") might be in order to minimize confusion, notwithstanding the counter interest in retaining competitor access to descriptive, geographically descriptive, and surname words and symbols.

Courts reasoned that while the common law permitted all competitors to employ surnames and descriptive words and symbols in their ordinary meaning, it did not permit them to use such words or symbols *for the purpose of committing fraud*.[3] Thus, when competitors used a surname or descriptive word or symbol for its *secondary meaning* (as a mark, to indicate source), rather than for its non-trademark "primary" meaning, *for the purpose* of confusing consumers and diverting trade from an earlier user, courts would intervene. They did not intervene on the ground that the plaintiff had property rights in the surname or descriptive word or symbol (as might be the case with regard to a technical trademark), but because the defendant/competitor was engaged in fraudulent conduct.

Thus, the unfair competition cause of action for infringement of secondary meaning marks represented a judicial balancing of the compet-

---

3. As the Eighth Circuit put it:

Everyone has the right to use and enjoy the rays of the sun, but no one may lawfully focus them to burn his neighbor's house.... Everyone has the right to use pen, ink and paper, but no one may apply them to the purpose of defrauding his neighbor of his property, or making counterfeit money, or of committing forgery.

Shaver v. Heller & Merz Co., 108 F. 821, 827 (8th Cir. 1901).

ing social interests in: 1) preventing consumer confusion; 2) regulating fraudulent conduct; and 3) retaining general marketplace access to common and descriptive words and symbols. When a descriptive, geographically descriptive, surname or other common word or symbol acquired secondary (trademark) meaning by virtue of its claimant's long and/or heavy use, competitors could continue to employ the word or symbol in its "primary" sense (that is, in its non-trademark descriptive, geographic or surname sense), but they would not be permitted fraudulently to use it in its secondary (trademark, or source-indicating) sense.

B. The Technical Trademark Infringement Cause of Action

"Technical trademarks," as recognized in the common law, were marks that we would consider "inherently distinctive" today—words or symbols that were non-descriptive, fanciful or arbitrary in relation to the products they were used to identify.

In crafting the cause of action for technical trademark infringement, courts reasoned that a business could legitimately appropriate a fanciful or arbitrary word or symbol to its sole, exclusive use, with no great harm to competition. A technical trademark, by definition, was either made up (and thus had no meaning) or had a meaning that bore no descriptive or other apparent relationship to the user's product. Thus, competitors had no legitimate reason to adopt a similar word or symbol to identify or describe their similar goods. If they did adopt a similar mark, it could be assumed that they did so for the purpose of perpetrating a fraud on the mark owner and the public.

Because protection of technical trademarks threatened no significant interference with competitors' ability to describe their products to consumers, courts provided stronger, exclusive rights, to enable technical trademark owners to protect the source-indicating function of their marks. To acquire rights in a technical trademark, the claimant need only be the first to "affix" the mark to its products and offer them for sale in the ordinary course of business. And if a *defendant* affixed a similar mark to similar merchandise, courts would *presume* that the defendant acted with fraudulent intent, and might also presume a likelihood of consumer confusion resulting from the defendant's actions. Upon finding infringement, courts typically granted injunctive relief prohibiting the defendant from all uses of the word or symbol at issue.

Notwithstanding courts' frequent characterization of technical trademark rights as "property" rights and "exclusive," however, it was clear that the law did not give technical trademark owners exclusive rights to *all* uses of their inherently distinctive words or symbols. Rather, it gave them the exclusive right to use the word or symbol *as an indication of product source*. In the 1800's, technical trademark infringement could only be asserted against a defendant who *"affixed" a similar mark to similar types of goods*. See, e.g., Postal Tel. Cable Co. v. Netter, 102 F. 691 (E.D.Pa. 1900). See also Trademark Act of 1881, 21 Stat. 502, § 7. Affixation ensured that the defendant's use of the contested word or symbol would be likely to signal source to consumers, and thus cause a likelihood of consumer confusion about the origin of the defendant's similar goods. Prior to the advent of modern mass market advertising practices, which commenced in the earlier half of the twentieth century, affixation to products undoubtedly was the primary way that merchants communicated product source.

While "affixation" was originally a rather rigid limitation, the affixation requirement was relaxed in the early 1900's to require that the defendant affix the allegedly infringing mark *either* to its merchandise *or* to labels, signs, prints, packages, wrappers or receptacles intended to be used upon or in connection with the sale of the product. New York Mackintosh Co. v. Flam, 198 F. 571, 573 (D.C.N.Y. 1912). This more relaxed "affixation or other close association" requirement was codified in the federal Trademark Act of 1905,[4] and again in the Trademark Act of 1920. 41 Stat. 533 § 4 (1920). Courts also found that a defendant's application of the contested mark *in advertising* similar kinds of goods would constitute actionable trademark use. See, e.g., Mishawaka Rubber & Woolen Mfg. Co. v. Panther–Panco Rubber Co., Inc., 153 F.2d 662 (1st Cir.), *cert. denied,* 329 U.S. 722 (1946). Thus, during the first half of the twentieth century, the original restrictive "defendant affixation" requirement evolved into a more general requirement that the defendant *closely or directly associate* the mark with similar goods that it was advertising or offering for sale. In effect, this "affixation or other close association" requirement ensured that the infringement defendant used the allegedly infringing word or symbol "as a trademark," or in a manner that was likely to indicate the source of its goods to consumers. Only such uses were likely to cause a serious possibility of consumer confusion, and thus justify judicial intervention.

C. Consolidation of the Common-Law Trademark Infringement and Unfair Competition Doctrines in the Lanham Act

As noted earlier, courts in unfair competition cases specifically required the plaintiff to demonstrate that the defendant used the allegedly

---

4. 33 Stat. 724 § 16 (1905). More fully, § 16 imposed liability on:

Any person who shall, without the consent of the owner thereof, reproduce, counterfeit, copy or colorably imitate any such trademark and affix the same to merchandise of substantially the same descriptive properties as those set forth in the registration, or to labels, signs, prints, packages, wrappers, or receptacles intended to be used upon or in connection with the sale of merchandise of substantially the same descriptive properties as those set forth in such registration, and shall use, or shall have used, such reproduction, counterfeit, copy, or colorable imitation in commerce among the several states, or with a foreign nation, or with the Indian tribes....

Prior to enactment of the Lanham Act in 1946, federal trademark acts were strictly "registration" provisions: They permitted persons owning *technical trademarks* under the common law to register the marks and thereby obtain procedural advantages and the right to bring infringement suits in federal court. The acts provided no substantive advantages beyond what was already available under the common law. Walgreen Drug Stores, Inc. v. Obear–Nester Glass Co., 113 F.2d 956, 960 (8th Cir. 1940). The later (1905 and 1920) acts permitted registration of some secondary meaning marks under limited circumstances. In the 1940's, when Congress undertook to draft and enact the Lanham Act, it determined, for the first time, to augment the *substantive* rights of persons who register their common-law marks, beyond the substantive rights afforded under contemporary common law.

infringing word or symbol for its secondary (trademark) meaning and acted fraudulently, with bad-faith intent to pass off its business, goods or services as those of the plaintiff. The Supreme Court emphasized these requirements in a number of its decisions. See, e.g., McLean v. Fleming, 96 U.S. 245 (1877); Elgin National Watch Co. v. Illinois Watch Co., 179 U.S. 665, 674 (1901); Thaddeus Davids Co. v. Davids, 233 U.S. 461, 471 (1914). However, as the United States progressed into the twentieth century, courts and commentators increasingly criticized the fraud requirement, reasoning that technical trademark infringement and infringement of secondary meaning marks caused the same injury to business good will and consumer reliance interests, and that all infringement cases should focus on the *effect* of the defendant's acts, rather than on the defendant's intent. Indeed, some commentators began to call for elimination of *all* distinctions between technical trademark infringement and infringement of secondary meaning marks, and for unification of the technical trademark infringement and unfair competition causes of action. In unfair competition cases, courts began to more readily *infer* the requisite fraudulent intent from circumstantial evidence—such as the defendant's adoption of a print style or color that simulated the plaintiff's presentation of the mark, or the defendant's emphasis on or placement of the mark—that might suggest an intent to use the contested word or symbol in its secondary (source indicating) sense, and thus to confuse consumers.

Pressure grew to modernize federal trademark protection in other ways, too. By the late 1930's the Trademark Act of 1905 had been frequently amended, resulting in a confusing array of statutory provisions. Practitioners argued that registration opportunities should be provided for service marks, and that the limited opportunities to register secondary meaning marks under the Trademark Acts of 1905 and 1920 should be liberalized.

In 1938, Congress began seriously to focus on drafting a new, more modern and comprehensive federal trademark act. It completed the task in 1946, and the resulting act (called the "Lanham Act" in honor of the Congressman primarily credited with its drafting and enactment) went into effect in 1947. 15 U.S.C. §§ 1051 *et seq.* It is generally understood that the Lanham Act *primarily* codified contemporary common-law doctrine, just as the prior federal trademark acts had done. However, the Lanham Act did introduce some new concepts[5] (which we will study in the course of this Chapter), and modernize and liberalize features of the earlier trademark acts.[6] For present purposes, the Lanham Act did three

---

5. For example, it introduced the doctrine of constructive notice, which enabled mark registrants to enhance the geographic scope of their rights, 15 U.S.C. § 1072, and incontestability status to shelter mark registrants from certain challenges and defenses after five years of registration. 15 U.S.C. §§ 1065, 1115. It officially recognized and provided federal registration and protection for service marks, collective marks and certification marks. 15 U.S.C. §§ 1053, 1054, 1127.

6. For example, as critics had advocated, Congress deleted the earlier statutory language that limited infringement liability to cases in which the defendant affixed the mark to "merchandise of

important things. First, the Lanham Act *liberalized registration of secondary meaning marks.* Lanham Act § 2 provides that words, names, symbols or devices that are merely descriptive, primarily geographically descriptive or constitute surnames can be registered upon a showing that they have "become distinctive" of the applicant's goods or services (that is, have acquired a secondary meaning). It authorizes the Patent and Trademark Office to accept proof of "substantially exclusive and continuous use of the mark" for five years as *prima facie* evidence of secondary meaning.[7]

Second, the Lanham Act continued the practice (begun in the 1905 Act) of applying a *uniform infringement standard* that did not distinguish between registered technical trademarks and registered secondary meaning marks. It also provided a federal cause of action for infringement of *unregistered* marks, applying essentially the same eligibility and infringement standards as for registered marks. 15 U.S.C. § 1125(a); Two Pesos, Inc. v. Taco Cabana, Inc., 505 U.S. 763 (1992). This uniform infringement standard required that (1) infringement defendants "use in commerce" a reproduction, counterfeit, copy, or colorable imitation of a mark "in connection with" the sale, offering for sale, distribution, or advertising of goods or services, and (2) that the use caused a likelihood of consumer confusion. 15 U.S.C. §§ 32(1)(a), 43(a). It defined "use in commerce" essentially to entail "affixation or other close association" of the mark with the defendant's goods or services, as was required in the common-law cause of action for technical trademark infringement and in the Trademark Acts of 1905 and 1920. 15 U.S.C. § 1127. Like the Trademark Act of 1905, the Lanham Act infringement provisions imposed no requirement that the plaintiff demonstrate the defendant's fraudulent intent, regardless of whether the mark at issue was inherently distinctive or distinctive through secondary meaning. Moreover, it imposed no fraud requirement in the case of unregistered marks.

Finally, the Lanham Act codified the unfair competition law's longstanding distinction between a defendant's use of a surname, descriptive, or geographically descriptive word for its *primary* (surname or descriptive) meaning, and its use of the word for its *secondary* (trademark) meaning. Under Lanham Act § 33(b)(4), 15 U.S.C. § 1115(b)(4), a defendant will

---

substantially the same descriptive properties" as those set forth in the plaintiff's certificate of registration. 15 U.S.C. § 1114(1)(a). This enabled mark owners to recover against defendants who were not direct competitors. Moreover, the Lanham Act's statutory language defining a "trademark" and describing what marks could be registered, 15 U.S.C. §§ 1052, 1127, opened the way for businesses to claim rights in a broader range of symbols and devices than had been recognized in the past. See Qualitex Co. v. Jacobson Products Co., Inc., 514 U.S. 159 (1995).

7. 15 U.S.C. § 1052(e) & (f). The Lanham Act defines "trademarks" broadly, to include "any word, name, symbol or device or any combination thereof" used "to identify and distinguish [the claimant's] goods . . . from those manufactured or sold by others and to indicate the source of the goods, even if that source is unknown." 15 U.S.C. § 1127. Thus, the Lanham Act *denominates both kinds of common-law marks* (technical marks and secondary meaning marks) (aka "trade names") *as "trademarks."* It provides that "trademarks" can be registered *unless* they are specifically disqualified under one of the provisions of Lanham Act § 2. 15 U.S.C. § 1052. While § 2(e) disqualifies surname, descriptive, and geographically descriptive marks, subsection (f) provides that such marks may nonetheless be registered if they have "become distinctive of the applicant's goods in commerce." *Id.,* § 1052(f). This standard for determining secondary meaning is much more liberal and flexible than the rigid ten years of exclusive use required under the Trademark Act of 1905.

not be liable for infringement if his use of an allegedly infringing word or symbol was a use "otherwise than as a mark, of [his] individual name in his own business * * * or of a term or device which is descriptive of and used fairly and in good faith only to describe [his] goods or services, or their geographic origin." While the common law required the *plaintiff* to demonstrate that the defendant used the surname or descriptive mark for its secondary (trademark) meaning, § 33(b)(4) shifts the burden to the defendant to demonstrate that it used the word or symbol in good faith for its *primary* (non-trademark) meaning, as an affirmative defense.

NOTES AND QUESTIONS

1. *The purposes of trademark law.* A trademark, when affixed to a product, is an important piece of information: It identifies the "origin" or "source" of the product. This is not to say that it *literally* notifies the consumer of the producer's identity—the trademark may differ from the name of the company that owns and uses it on its products. Rather, it notifies the consumer that the product comes from the *same* source (whatever that source may be[8]) as other products of a similar type bearing the same mark. Since the consumer assumes that products from the same source will have similar characteristics, he is able to relate whatever experience he has had with other products bearing the mark to the present product. If the source provided a satisfying product in the past, or the consumer has heard good things about the products bearing that mark, he will be moved to buy. If the contrary is true, the consumer will avoid making the purchase. The mark enables the consumer to make meaningful choices in the marketplace, and thereby enables producers to compete effectively for his business. This process only works, however, as long as the consumer can safely assume that products bearing the same mark in fact come from the same source. The purpose of trademark law and related unfair competition doctrines is essentially to ensure that this assumption can be made. By providing that assurance, trademark and unfair competition law protect both the consumer and the business that owns the mark.

How is the business benefited? Assume that Acme Company places a new product—for example, a soda—on the market, under the trademark "Whatacola." Acme invests considerable money and effort in promoting the soda to the public through advertising and marketing, and maintains high standards of quality in its production and packaging process. Over the years, consumers become familiar with the Whatacola mark and associate it with a high quality soda. Many consumers develop brand loyalty, repeatedly choosing the Whatacola drink over competing brands. This reputation and expectation of repeat patronage is known as "good will." Good will is intangible, but it can be extremely valuable, and it is directly tied to the product trademark.[9] If a competitor takes the mark, it also takes the good will.

---

8. In this context, we use the term "source" broadly, to include not only manufacturers of goods, but also others, such as distributors, retailers, or endorsers of the goods, who may apply their own mark.

9. For example, see *Coca-Cola: Things Better Go Better*, The Economist, May 10, 1986, at 98:

Assume that Beta Company puts its own soda on the market, with the same or a confusingly similar trademark (for example, "Watacola"). Consumers who mean to purchase Whatacola are confused and buy Beta's product by mistake. Beta gets a free ride on Acme's investment and reputation, but more importantly, Acme's good will is injured in two respects. First, Beta diverted sales that were meant for Acme. Second, Acme has lost the opportunity to control the quality of the product being sold as its own. If Beta's soda is of inferior quality, and consumers believe (mistakenly) that it came from Acme, Acme's reputation will be injured. Consumers may refuse to buy from Acme in the future. In preventing Beta from using a confusingly similar mark, the trademark law protects Acme's good will, and by protecting the good will, it encourages Acme and other businesses to invest in the development and promotion of high-quality products.

Trademark law gives businesses a cause of action for infringement, and they are diligent to bring it in order to protect their good will. However, when businesses bring meritorious claims of trademark infringement, this protects consumers, as well. How, exactly, are consumers protected? Obviously if Beta's cola is of lower quality than Acme's, consumers' interests will be promoted when Acme sues to enjoin Beta's use of a mark that tricks them into buying the lower quality product. However, assume that Beta's cola is exactly the same as Acme's, but Beta sells it at half the price. Acme loyalists who mistakenly buy Beta's drink will be better off, financially, but the law still permits Acme to enjoin the infringement. In Eastern Wine Corp. v. Winslow–Warren, Ltd., 137 F.2d 955 (2d Cir.1943), *cert. denied,* 320 U.S. 758, 64 S.Ct. 65, 88 L.Ed. 452 (1943), the Court of Appeals for the Second Circuit acknowledged this fact, and explained:

> [There] is an assumed social interest in safeguarding consumers from being deceived even if the deception may be to their financial benefit. There appears to be a related judicial policy of protecting snobbism; as this court recently put it, "People like to get what they think they are getting, and courts have steadfastly refused in this class of cases to demand justification for their preferences. * * * If the buyers wish to be snobs, the law will protect them in their snobbery." Benton Announcements, Inc. v. Federal Trade Commission, 130 F.2d 254. In other words, "the public is entitled to get what it chooses, though the choice may be dictated by caprice or by fashion or perhaps by ignorance." Federal Trade Commission v. Algoma Lumber Co., 291 U.S. 67, 54 S.Ct. 315, 78 L.Ed. 655.

Id., 137 F.2d at 958.

Wall Street now values the [Coca–Cola] company at $14 billion—$7 billion more than the value of the company's assets (machinery, buildings, etc.). That, roughly, is what the trademark is worth.

Julius R. Lunsford, Jr., a lawyer for the Coca–Cola Company, has stated:

The production plants and inventories of The Coca–Cola Company could go up in flames overnight. Yet, on the following morning there is not a bank in Atlanta, New York, or anywhere else, that would not lend this Company the funds necessary for rebuilding, accepting as security only the inherent good will in its trademarks "Coca–Cola" and "Coke."

Drescher, *The Transformation and Evolution of Trademarks—From Signals to Symbols to Myth,* 82 Trademark Rep. 301, 301–02 (1992).

2. *The relationship between trademark law and the law of unfair competition.* Today, "unfair competition" is a term that covers several related legal doctrines, all aimed at prohibiting improper conduct in the marketplace. Trademark infringement is one of the doctrines in this family. Closely related doctrines of unfair competition protect a business' name (known in modern parlance as the company's "trade name"), and product or service "trade dress" (which may consist of a variety of things, including the business' product packaging, the distinctive features of the product itself, or the overall look and feel of the business' premises). Just as consumers rely on trademarks to provide information about the source, sponsorship or affiliation of a product or service, they may also rely on a business establishment's trade name or trade dress for the same information. Thus, modern unfair competition law provides the same general kind of protection against competitors' use of confusingly similar trade names and trade dress as it does against their use of confusingly similar trademarks.(We sometimes refer to marks, trade names and trade dress as "indications of origin.")

3. *The Lanham Act and the common law.* In enacting the Lanham Act, Congress primarily codified common-law doctrine, but enhanced it in several important ways. First, Congress provided a system for registering trademarks and service marks on the Lanham Act's Principal Register. Registration of a mark on the Principal Register provides a number of benefits, such as rights in a broader geographic area than would be available at common law, legal presumptions of mark validity, immunity from certain state causes of action, and the opportunity to obtain the assistance of the U.S. Customs Service in excluding infringing imports from the country. Second, Congress provided a federal cause of action for infringement of unregistered indications of origin, including unregistered marks, trade dress, and trade names, in Lanham Act § 43(a). 15 U.S.C.A. § 1125(a). While unregistered indications of origin do not enjoy the benefits of registration mentioned above, § 43(a) provides a federal forum for claims of unregistered mark, trade dress, and trade name infringement, and the same generous federal infringement remedies that owners of registered marks enjoy.

Enactment of the Lanham Act did not preempt the state common-law cause of action for unfair competition. Nor did it prohibit the states from enacting their own statutory trademark registration systems, as most have. Thus, the owner of a qualifying indication of origin (trademark, trade dress, trade name) may sue infringers pursuant to the Lanham Act registered mark or unregistered indication of origin provisions, or may pursue a state law cause of action for the same conduct. Congress anticipated that trademark, trade dress and trade name owners might wish to allege both a Lanham Act claim and a state cause of action in the same suit, and expressly provided for pendant jurisdiction in the federal district courts to hear state claims brought with related Lanham Act infringement claims. 28 U.S.C.A. § 1338(b). As we will see, today, most infringement claims are litigated in federal court, under the Lanham Act, rather than pursuant to state law.

This Chapter focuses on the Lanham Act provisions for registering trademarks on the Principal Register, the legal rights of Lanham Act registrants, and the rights in unregistered indications of origin provided under Lanham Act § 43(a). The next Chapter will examine several other unfair competition doctrines—false advertising, product disparagement, and misappropriation—that exist in state law and/or under Lanham Act § 43(a), but do not necessarily entail the unauthorized use of indications of origin.

Congress relied on its Commerce Clause powers (U.S. Const. Art. I, § 8, cl. 3) to enact the Lanham Act. Thus, only those indications of origin used "in interstate commerce" are eligible to receive the benefits of Lanham Act protection. The United States Patent and Trademark Office ("PTO") administers the Lanham Act's registration system. PTO decisions regarding trademark registrations may be appealed directly to the Court of Appeals for the Federal Circuit, 28 U.S.C.A. § 1295(a)(4)(B), but unlike appeals from patent infringement cases, appeals from Lanham Act infringement cases are taken to the regional United States Circuit Courts of Appeals.

4. *Comparing trademarks with copyrights and patents.* Trademark and unfair competition law do not serve the same purpose as copyright and patent law. Trademark rights are not given as an economic incentive to create or invent, and so they are tailored much more narrowly than the rights afforded by copyrights and patents. Rather than giving businesses exclusive rights in the words, symbols or devices they claim as marks, trademark law usually gives only the limited right to prohibit commercial use by others *when that use is likely to cause consumer confusion about the source, sponsorship or affiliation of goods or services.* The rights are narrowly drawn to avoid potential First Amendment issues, and to ensure that other merchants' ability to communicate useful information about their products and to adopt useful product features are not undermined.

5. *Additional resources.* J.T. McCarthy's McCarthy on Trademarks and Unfair Competition (4th ed., 1996)(regularly supplemented) is an excellent multi–volume resource on trademarks and related unfair competition doctrines. J. Gilson, Trademark Protection and Practice (1976)(regularly supplemented), is another valuable reference. For information abut state statutory trademark provisions, see International Trademark Assn., State Trademark and Unfair Competition Law (1999)(regularly supplemented).

II. THE SPECTRUM OF "INDICATIONS OF ORIGIN"

A. MARKS

1. *Types of Marks*

The Lanham Act recognizes and authorizes registration of four different types of marks: trademarks, service marks, certification marks and collective marks. Of these, trademarks and service marks are the more prevalent. This Subsection will briefly describe each of the different types of marks. However, since most of the principles governing the validity of a mark and its infringement remain constant regardless of the type of mark involved, the remainder of the Chapter generally will focus on trademarks and service marks. Unless indicated otherwise, the terms "mark," "indication of origin," or "trademark" can be understood to include all of the different types of marks.

a. Trademarks

Lanham Act § 45, 15 U.S.C. § 1127, provides that the term "trademark" includes "any word, name, symbol, or device, or any combination thereof" which is used to identify and distinguish one person's goods (including unique products) from goods manufactured or sold by others. It adds that a trademark is used to "indicate the source of the goods, even if that source is unknown."

As discussed earlier, the common law originally recognized rights in "technical trademarks"—words or symbols that were arbitrary or fanciful in relation to the goods being identified or distinguished. (The mark "tango" has a meaning, but when it is used to distinguish or identify ball bearings, it is *arbitrary* because it does not describe the product or any of its characteristics. The mark "ked–4" for ball bearings is *fanciful*, because it has no meaning at all, apart from its meaning as a trademark.) Such words and symbols received the earliest and strongest protection because it can be assumed that consumers will understand them to indicate the origin of the goods—they serve no other apparent purpose. Also, competitors have significantly less need to use such words or symbols in identifying and describing their own products to consumers.

The early common law protected descriptive, geographically descriptive, surname, and other words or symbols commonly used in connection with particular products through a cause of action for "unfair competition." Such marks could only be protected on a showing that they had acquired "secondary meaning" (that is, consumers had come to understand the word or symbol not only in its *primary,* descriptive geographically descriptive or surname meaning in the language, but also in its *secondary* meaning as an indicator of product source) and that the defendant had used the word or symbol for its secondary (trademark) meaning. Examples of such words and symbols include "Durable," "Johnson's," "Great Lakes," or "Superior" to identify ball bearings. This latter category of words or symbols was called "trade names" or "secondary meaning marks" at common law. The Lanham Act, however, united the law governing the two categories of words and symbols and refers to them all as "trademarks."

b. Service Marks

Under modern law, service marks are essentially the same as trademarks, except that they consist of words, names, symbols or devices used to identify and distinguish their owners' intangible services, rather than products. 15 U.S.C. § 1127. Thus a service mark may identify and distinguish transportation services (for example, "Delta" Airlines), restaurant services (for example, "McDonalds"), or insurance services (for example, "Aetna" Insurance). The Lanham Act does not define the term "service," but the term has generally been construed broadly: "The performance of labor for the benefit of another." Morningside Group, Ltd. v. Morningside Capital Group, 182 F.3d 133, 137 (2d Cir. 1999).

The courts have, however, imposed one important limitation on recognition of marks for "services:" The service to be identified must consist of something more than actions that are expected or routine in connection with the sale of one's own goods, such as quoting prices for the goods, promoting sale of the goods, demonstrating how the goods work, or providing routine warranties or repairs. Thus, for example, in *In re Dr. Pepper Co.*, 836 F.2d 508 (Fed. Cir. 1987), the Court of Appeals for the Federal Circuit held that an applicant could not register a service mark for the alleged "service" of conducting a contest with prizes to promote the sale of its own goods. The court explained:

> Appellant argues that the exclusion of services ordinarily or routinely rendered in connection with the sale of goods will preclude registration of marks for a vast array of activities currently recognized as services under the Act, such as those provided by retail department stores, mail order companies, and gasoline stations. Contrary to appellant's view, this consequence does not follow. Appellant leaves out the key element which is that the activities being questioned here relate to promotion of *its own goods*. Department stores and gasoline stations are service businesses and provide precisely the types of services intended to be brought under the Act. Indeed, advertising agency services as well as the service of conducting contests *for others* are within the Act. A parallel nonregistrability situation with a service business would be a refusal to register an asserted service of offering "free" glassware to customers who have made a certain level of purchases at a gasoline station, the service of providing "free" bags for purchasers at a grocery store, or a lottery contest by a new shopping mall. Registration of the marks identifying the services of service businesses is not endangered by continuing to apply the principle that services which are ordinary or routine in the sale of goods (or services), such as promotional activities for one's own business, are not services within the meaning of the Act.

Id. at 511. The rule applied in *Dr. Pepper* has led one court to define a "service" as "the performance of labor for the benefit of another." The Morningside Group Ltd. v. Morningside Capital Group, L.L.C., 182 F.3d 133, 137–38 (2d Cir.1999). The *Morningside* court elaborated that "services must not be 'solely for the benefit of the performer; the services must be rendered to others.' " *Id.*, at 138.

Lanham Act § 3, 15 U.S.C.A. § 1053, specifies that service marks shall be registrable in the same manner and with the same effect as trademarks. What is the difference between a service mark and a trade name (as defined in Lanham Act § 45, 15 U.S.C. § 1127)? Why should a service mark be registrable when a trade name is not?

c. *Certification Marks*

A certification mark is a word, name, symbol or device that is used by a person other than its owner "to certify regional or other origin, material, mode of manufacture, quality, accuracy, or other characteristics of such person's goods or services or that the work or labor on the goods or services was performed by members of a union or other organization." 15 U.S.C.A. § 1127. Thus, unlike trademarks and service marks, certification marks do not indicate the *source* of the goods or services with which they are used. Rather, certification marks are owned by one person and used by others to certify that those others' goods or services have certain specified qualities or characteristics. For example, the Underwriters Laboratory (UL) mark certifies that users' consumer products comply with the safety standards prescribed by the certification mark owner.

Lanham Act § 4, 15 U.S.C.A. § 1054, provides that certification marks, including indications of regional origin, are registerable in the same manner and with the same effect as trademarks. However, certification marks are subject to some special requirements: Lanham Act § 14 provides that the owner of a certification mark must exercise control over others' use of its mark; must refrain from using the mark in connection with any of its own goods or services; must prohibit use of the mark for purposes other than certification; and must not discriminately refuse to certify or continue to certify goods or services that meet its specified standards for certification. Failure to comply with these requirements may lead to cancellation of the certification mark's registration. 15 U.S.C. § 1064.

What was Congress seeking to accomplish in imposing these restrictions on registered certification marks?

d. *Collective Marks*

A collective mark is a trademark or service mark used by members of a cooperative, association, or other collective group or organization to identify their goods or services, or to indicate their membership, and includes a mark used to indicate membership in a union, an association or other organization. 15 U.S.C. § 1127. As the Trademark Trial and Appeal Board has explained:

> There are two basic types of collective marks. A *collective trademark or collective service mark* is a mark adopted by a "collective" (i.e., an association, union, cooperative, fraternal organization, or other organized collective group) for use only by its members, who in turn use the mark to identify their goods or services and distinguish them from those of nonmembers. The "collective" itself neither sells goods nor performs services under a collective trademark or collective service mark, but the collective may advertise or otherwise promote the goods or services sold or rendered by its members under the mark. A *collective membership mark* is a mark adopted for the purpose of indicating membership in an organized collective group, such as a union, an association, or other organization. Neither the collective nor its members uses the collective membership mark to identify and distinguish goods or services; rather, the sole function of such a mark is to indicate that the person displaying the mark is a member of the organized collective group. For example, if the collective group is a

fraternal organization, members may display the mark by wearing pins or rings upon which the mark appears, by carrying membership cards bearing the mark, etc. Of course, a collective group may itself be engaged in the marketing of its own goods or services under a particular mark, in which case the mark is not a collective mark but is rather a trademark for the collective's goods or service mark for the collective's services.

Aloe Creme Laboratories, Inc. v. American Society for Aesthetic Plastic Surgery, Inc., 192 U.S.P.Q. 170 (T.T.A.B. 1976).

How do collective trademarks and service marks differ from regular trademarks and service marks? What if one company owns and registers a trademark or service mark, and then licenses other companies to use it in connection with their own goods or services? See 15 U.S.C.A. §§ 1055, 1127 (definition of "related company"). What is the difference between the licensed mark and a collective trademark or service mark?

How do collective trademarks and service marks differ from certification marks? For example, compare the following two situations.

1) A citrus producers' organization in Florida adopts the mark "Florida Fresh" as a certification mark, and permits Florida citrus producers to apply the mark to certify that their citrus comes from Florida.

2) A citrus producers' organization comprised of Florida citrus growers adopts the mark "Florida Fresh" as a collective trademark, which each member of the organization uses to identify the citrus it produces and sells.

2. The Composition of Marks

QUALITEX CO. v. JACOBSON PRODUCTS CO., INC.

United States Supreme Court, 1995.
514 U.S. 159, 115 S.Ct. 1300, 131 L.Ed.2d 248.

JUSTICE BREYER delivered the opinion of the Court.

The question in this case is whether the Trademark Act of 1946 (Lanham Act) permits the registration of a trademark that consists, purely and simply, of a color. We conclude that, sometimes, a color will meet ordinary legal trademark requirements. And, when it does so, no special legal rule prevents color alone from serving as a trademark.

I

The case before us grows out of petitioner Qualitex Company's use (since the 1950's) of a special shade of green-gold color on the pads that it makes and sells to dry cleaning firms for use on dry cleaning presses. In 1989, respondent Jacobson Products (a Qualitex rival) began to sell its own press pads to dry cleaning firms; and it colored those pads a similar green gold. In 1991, Qualitex registered the special green-gold color on press pads with the Patent and Trademark Office as a trademark. Qualitex subsequently added a trademark infringement count, 15 U.S.C. § 1114(1), to an unfair competition claim, § 1125(a), in a lawsuit it had already filed challenging Jacobson's use of the green-gold color.

Qualitex won the lawsuit in the District Court. But, the Court of Appeals for the Ninth Circuit set aside the judgment in Qualitex's favor on the trademark infringement claim because, in that Circuit's view, the Lanham Act does not permit Qualitex, or anyone else, to register "color alone" as a trademark.

The Courts of Appeals have differed as to whether or not the law recognizes the use of color alone as a trademark. Compare NutraSweet Co. v. Stadt Corp., 917 F.2d 1024, 1028 (C.A.7 1990) (absolute prohibition against protection of color alone), with In re Owens–Corning Fiberglas Corp., 774 F.2d 1116, 1128 (C.A.Fed.1985) (allowing registration of color pink for fiberglass insulation), and Master Distributors, Inc. v. Pako Corp., 986 F.2d 219, 224 (C.A.8 1993) (declining to establish per se prohibition against protecting color alone as a trademark). Therefore, this Court granted certiorari. We now hold that there is no rule absolutely barring the use of color alone, and we reverse the judgment of the Ninth Circuit.

II

The Lanham Act gives a seller or producer the exclusive right to "register" a trademark, and to prevent his or her competitors from using that trademark. Both the language of the Act and the basic underlying principles of trademark law would seem to include color within the universe of things that can qualify as a trademark. The language of the Lanham Act describes that universe in the broadest of terms. It says that trademarks "includ[e] any word, name, symbol, or device, or any combination thereof." § 1127. Since human beings might use as a "symbol" or "device" almost anything at all that is capable of carrying meaning, this language, read literally, is not restrictive. The courts and the Patent and Trademark Office have authorized for use as a mark a particular shape (of a Coca–Cola bottle), a particular sound (of NBC's three chimes), and even a particular scent (of plumeria blossoms on sewing thread). If a shape, a sound, and a fragrance can act as symbols why, one might ask, can a color not do the same?

A color is also capable of satisfying the more important part of the statutory definition of a trademark, which requires that a person "us[e]" or "inten[d] to use" the mark

> "to identify and distinguish his or her goods, including a unique product, from those manufactured or sold by others and to indicate the source of the goods, even if that source is unknown."

15 U.S.C. § 1127.

True, a product's color is unlike "fanciful," "arbitrary," or "suggestive" words or designs, which almost automatically tell a customer that they refer to a brand. The imaginary word "Suntost," or the words "Suntost Marmalade," on a jar of orange jam immediately would signal a brand or a product "source"; the jam's orange color does not do so. But, over time, customers may come to treat a particular color on a product or its packaging (say, a color that in context seems unusual, such as pink on a firm's insulating material or red on the head of a large industrial bolt) as signifying a brand. And, if so, that color would have come to identify and distinguish the goods—i.e., "to indicate" their "source"—much in the way that descriptive words on a product (say, "Trim" on nail clippers or "Car–Freshner" on deodorizer) can come to indicate a product's origin. In this circumstance, trademark law says that the word (e.g., "Trim"), although not inherently distinctive, has developed "secondary meaning." * * * Again, one might ask, if trademark law permits a descriptive word with secondary meaning to act as a mark, why would it not permit a color, under similar circumstances, to do the same?

We cannot find in the basic objectives of trademark law any obvious theoretical objection to the use of color alone as a trademark, where that color has attained "secondary meaning" and therefore identifies and distinguishes a particular brand (and thus indicates its "source"). In principle, trademark law, by preventing others from copying a source-identifying mark, "reduce[s] the customer's costs of shopping and making purchasing decisions," for it quickly and easily assures a potential customer that this item—the item with this mark—is made by the same producer as other similarly marked items that he or she liked (or disliked) in the past. At the same time, the law helps assure a producer that it (and not an imitating competitor) will reap the financial, reputation-related rewards associated with a desirable product. The law thereby "encourage[s] the production of quality products," and simultaneously discourages those who hope to sell inferior products by capitalizing on a consumer's inability quickly to evaluate the quality of an item offered for sale. It is the source-distinguishing ability of a mark—not its ontological status as color, shape, fragrance, word, or sign—that permits it to serve these basic purposes. And, for that reason, it is difficult to find, in basic trademark objectives, a reason to disqualify absolutely the use of a color as a mark.

Neither can we find a principled objection to the use of color as a mark in the important "functionality" doctrine of trademark law. The functionality doctrine prevents trademark law, which seeks to promote competition by protecting a firm's reputation, from instead inhibiting legitimate competition by allowing a producer to control a useful product feature. It is the province of patent law, not trademark law, to encourage invention by granting inventors a monopoly over new product designs or functions for a limited time, after which competitors are free to use the innovation. If a product's functional features could be used as trademarks, however, a monopoly over such features could be obtained without regard to whether they qualify as patents and could be extended forever (because trademarks may be renewed in perpetuity). * * * Functionality doctrine therefore would require, to take an imaginary example, that even if customers have come to identify the special illumination-enhancing shape of a new patented light bulb with a particular manufacturer, the manufacturer may not use that shape as a trademark, for doing so, after the patent had expired, would impede competition—not by protecting the reputation of the original bulb maker, but by frustrating competitors' legitimate efforts to produce an equivalent illumination-enhancing bulb. * * * This Court consequently has explained that, "[i]n general terms, a product feature is functional," and cannot serve as a trademark, "if it is essential to the use or purpose of the article or if it affects the cost or quality of the article," that is, if exclusive use of the feature would put competitors at a significant non-reputation-related disadvantage. Although sometimes color plays an important role (unrelated to source identification) in making a product more desirable, sometimes it does not. And, this latter fact—the fact that sometimes color is not essential to a product's use or purpose and does not affect cost or quality—indicates that the doctrine of "functionality" does not create an absolute bar to the use of color alone as a mark. See *Owens-Corning*, 774 F.2d, at 1123 (pink color of insulation in wall "performs no nontrademark function").

It would seem, then, that color alone, at least sometimes, can meet the basic legal requirements for use as a trademark. It can act as a symbol that distinguishes a firm's goods and identifies their source, without serving any other significant function. * * * See 1 McCarthy §§ 3.01[1], 7.26, pp. 3–2, 7–113 ("requirements for qualification of a word or symbol as a trademark" are that it be (1) a "symbol," (2) "use[d] . . . as a mark," (3) "to identify and distinguish the seller's goods from goods made or sold by others," but that it not be "functional"). Indeed, the District Court, in this case, entered findings (accepted by the Ninth Circuit) that show Qualitex's green-gold press pad color has met these requirements. The green-gold color acts as a symbol. Having developed secondary meaning (for customers identified the green-gold color as Qualitex's), it identifies the press pads' source. And, the green-gold color serves no other function. (Although it is important to use some color on press pads to avoid noticeable stains, the court found "no competitive need in the press pad industry for the green-gold color, since other colors are equally usable.") Accordingly, unless there is some special reason that convincingly militates against the use of color alone as a trademark, trademark law would protect Qualitex's use of the green-gold color on its press pads.

III

Respondent Jacobson Products says that there are four special reasons why the law should forbid the use of color alone as a trademark. We shall explain, in turn, why we, ultimately, find them unpersuasive.

First, Jacobson says that, if the law permits the use of color as a trademark, it will produce uncertainty and unresolvable court disputes about what shades of a color a competitor may lawfully use. Because lighting (morning sun, twilight mist) will affect perceptions of protected color, competitors and courts will suffer from "shade confusion" as they try to decide whether use of a similar color on a similar product does, or does not, confuse customers and thereby infringe a trademark. Jacobson adds that the "shade confusion" problem is "more difficult" and "far different from" the "determination of the similarity of words or symbols."

We do not believe, however, that color, in this respect, is special. Courts traditionally decide quite difficult questions about whether two words or phrases or symbols are sufficiently similar, in context, to confuse buyers. They have had to compare, for example, such words as "Bonamine" and "Dramamine" (motion-sickness remedies); "Huggies" and "Dougies" (diapers); "Cheracol" and "Syrocol" (cough syrup); "Cyclone" and "Tornado" (wire fences); and "Mattres" and "1–800–Mattres" (mattress franchisor telephone numbers). Legal standards exist to guide courts in making such comparisons. * * * We do not see why courts could not apply those standards to a color, replicating, if necessary, lighting conditions under which a colored product is normally sold. Indeed, courts already have done so in cases where a trademark consists of a color plus a design, i.e., a colored symbol such as a gold stripe (around a sewer pipe), a yellow strand of wire rope, or a "brilliant yellow" band (on ampules).

Second, Jacobson argues, as have others, that colors are in limited supply. Jacobson claims that, if one of many competitors can appropriate a particular color for use as a trademark, and each competitor then tries to do the same, the supply of colors will soon be depleted. Put in its strongest form, this argument would concede that "[h]undreds of color pigments are manufactured and thousands of colors can be obtained by mixing." But, it would add that, in the context of a particular product, only some colors are usable. By the time one discards colors that, say, for reasons of customer appeal, are not usable, and adds the shades that competitors cannot use lest they risk infringing a similar, registered shade, then one is left with only a handful of possible colors. And, under these circumstances, to permit one, or a few, producers to use colors as trademarks will "deplete" the supply of usable colors to the point where a competitor's inability to find a suitable color will put that competitor at a significant disadvantage.

This argument is unpersuasive, however, largely because it relies on an occasional problem to justify a blanket prohibition. When a color serves as a mark, normally alternative colors will likely be available for similar use by others. Moreover, if that is not so—if a "color depletion" or "color scarcity" problem does arise—the trademark doctrine of "functionality" normally would seem available to prevent the anticompetitive consequences that Jacobson's argument posits, thereby minimizing that argument's practical force.

The functionality doctrine, as we have said, forbids the use of a product's feature as a trademark where doing so will put a competitor at a significant disadvantage because the feature is "essential to the use or purpose of the article" or "affects [its] cost or quality." The functionality doctrine thus protects competitors against a disadvantage (unrelated to recognition or reputation) that trademark protection might otherwise impose, namely, their inability reasonably to replicate important non-reputation-related product features. For example, this Court has written that competitors might be free to copy the color of a medical pill where that color serves to identify the kind of medication (e.g., a type of blood medicine) in addition to its source. * * *

* * *

Third, Jacobson points to many older cases—including Supreme Court cases—in support of its position. * * *

These Supreme Court cases, however, interpreted trademark law as it existed *before* 1946, when Congress enacted the Lanham Act. The Lanham Act significantly changed and liberalized the common law to "dispense with mere technical prohibitions," S.Rep. No. 1333, 79th Cong., 2d Sess., 3 (1946), most notably, by permitting trademark registration of descriptive words (say, "U–Build–It" model airplanes) where they had acquired "secondary meaning." The Lanham Act extended protection to descriptive marks by making clear that (with certain explicit exceptions not relevant here)

> "nothing ... shall prevent the registration of a mark used by the applicant which has become distinctive of the applicant's goods in commerce."

15 U.S.C. § 1052(f) (1988 ed., Supp. V).

This language permits an ordinary word, normally used for a non-trademark purpose (e.g., description), to act as a trademark where it has gained "secondary meaning." Its logic would appear to apply to color as well. Indeed, in 1985, the Federal Circuit considered the significance of the Lanham Act's changes as they related to color and held that trademark protection for color was consistent with the

> "jurisprudence under the Lanham Act developed in accordance with the statutory principle that if a mark is capable of being or becoming distinctive of [the] applicant's goods in commerce, then it is capable of serving as a trademark."

Owens-Corning, 774 F.2d, at 1120.

In 1988, Congress amended the Lanham Act, revising portions of the definitional language, but left unchanged the language here relevant. It enacted these amendments against the following background: (1) the Federal Circuit had decided *Owens-Corning*; (2) the Patent and Trademark Office had adopted a clear policy (which it still maintains) permitting registration of color as a trademark; and (3) the Trademark Commission had written a report, which recommended that "the terms 'symbol, or device' ... not be deleted or narrowed to preclude registration of such things as a color, shape, smell, sound, or configuration which functions as a mark." * * * This background strongly suggests that the language "any word, name, symbol, or device," 15 U.S.C. § 1127, had come to include color. And, when it amended the statute, Congress retained these terms. Indeed, the Senate Report accompanying the Lanham Act revision explicitly referred to this background understanding, in saying that the "revised definition intentionally retains ... the words 'symbol or device' so as not to preclude the registration of colors, shapes, sounds or configurations where they function as trademarks." S.Rep. No. 100–515, at 44 U.S.Code Cong. & Admin.News, 1988, p. 5607. (In addition, the statute retained language providing that "[n]o trademark by which the goods of the applicant may be distinguished from the goods of others shall be refused registration ... on account of its nature" (except for certain specified reasons not relevant here). 15 U.S.C. § 1052.)

* * *

IV

Having determined that a color may sometimes meet the basic legal requirements for use as a trademark and that respondent Jacobson's arguments do not justify a special legal rule preventing color alone from serving as a trademark (and, in light of the District Court's here undisputed findings that Qualitex's use of the green-gold color on its press pads meets the basic trademark requirements), we conclude that the Ninth Circuit erred in barring Qualitex's use of color as a trademark.

NOTES AND QUESTIONS

1. *Multiple marks.* A number of different marks can be used to identify one product or service, even on the same label or package:

> The salient question is whether the designation in question, as used, will be recognized in and of itself as an indication of origin for this particular product. That is, does this component or designation create a commercial impression separate and apart from the other material appearing on the label?

Procter & Gamble Co. v. Keystone Automotive Warehouse, Inc., 191 U.S.P.Q. 468, 474 (T.T.A.B.1976). In Chun King Corp. v. Genii Plant Line, Inc., 403 F.2d 274 (C.C.P.A.1968), the Court of Customs and Patent Appeals considered whether Genii had used the words "Living Earth" in such a manner that consumers would regard them as a trademark for its potting soil. Genii's package design featured the word "Genii" in large red letters appearing above the head of a genie with smoke emanating from a lamp. The words "Living Earth" appeared across the top of the package in smaller but prominent letters. The Court rejected Chun King's argument that the display of "Living Earth" jointly with "GENII" and in much smaller print negated its status as a trademark:

> "No authority has been cited, and none has been found to the effect that a trademark use requires a display of a design of any particular size or prominence. The important question is not how readily the mark will be noticed but whether, when it is noticed it will be understood as indicating origin of the goods." And considering that "LIVING EARTH" is wholly arbitrary and has always been a separate and distinct, albeit subservient, feature of petitioner's containers, it is our opinion that it would be regarded as a trademark by purchasers of petitioner's goods.

Id., 403 F.2d at 276.

Can ornamental designs on products or their packaging be registered as trademarks? It depends on whether consumers are likely to perceive the design as an indication of origin or merely as decoration. If the former, the fact that the design is also ornamental will not preclude registration. For example, in Application of Swift & Co., 223 F.2d 950 (C.C.P.A.1955), the applicant sought to register two bands of red with white polka dots, which it used on the label of a can of cleanser:

The examiner had determined that this banding was merely background ornamentation, and thus could not function as a mark. The Court of Customs and Patent Appeals disagreed:

> Since the line distinguishing between mere ornamentation and ornamentation which is merely an incidental quality of a trade-mark is not always clearly ascertainable, the application of legal principles to fit one situation or the other requires proper reflection upon the impression likely to govern the ordinary purchaser in the market place. For that reason, the merits of each case of the character here presented must be individually and accordingly adjudged.

> In its brief on appeal, appellant refers to the fact that a great deal of purchasing in retail outlets is of a casual nature (particularly in self-service types of stores) and, with regard thereto, it makes this observation:

> " * * * Here the purchasers often engage in 'impulse' buying. If their attention is caught by an item for which they have a need or

have been induced to believe they have a need, as for example by advertising, they will pick up the item on this impulse even though the item was not one for which they entered the store to buy.

"In order for this to happen, however, it is imperative that their attention be focused on the item sufficiently for the 'impulse' to occur. The focusing process often takes place at a time when the individual is too distant from the object to read any wording thereon. If the individual sees the item at a distance and is able to identify it by some symbol or device on the object that stands out at such a distance where the wording cannot, that symbol or device becomes the means by which the object is identified and the factor by which the impulse to purchase it is induced or occasioned.

"This identification at a distance can be one or a combination of two kinds of identification. In the first place, it can be an identification of the nature of the product. Naturally the trade-mark function of indicating origin does not become a part of this identification of the product. However, in addition to the identification of the product, the symbols or devices may be such as to distinguish the product of a particular manufacturer from similar products of other manufacturers and thus serve as an indication of origin. When this is possible, * * * that symbol or device clearly responds to the definition of a 'trade mark'." * * *

Id., 223 F.2d at 954. The court concluded:

It is axiomatic, of course, that a trade-mark must be distinctive in order to accomplish its function of indicating the producer of the article to which it is applied, and, with particular regard to symbols and devices, should be displayed with such prominence as will enable easy recognition. * * * We think a definite and lasting impression will be created by use of the design in association with appellant's product whereby the average consumer will regard it as an unmistakable, certain, and primary means of identification pointing distinctly to the commercial origin of such product. The fact that the design may incidentally add to the attractiveness of appellant's label, and hence impart a certain distinctive appearance thereto, does not, in our opinion, vitiate its primary significance.

Id., 223 F.2d at 955.

Slogans can be effective trademarks, too. Who can doubt that "It's the real thing" and "Hair color so natural only her hairdresser knows for sure" indicate the origin of the goods with which they are used? What special problems might one encounter in demonstrating that a slogan will be perceived as indicating origin?

PROBLEM

1. In your view, should the following things qualify for protection as trademarks?

a) The creators of Superman comics and cartoons claim rights in the word "Kryptonite." [Kryptonite is the name for a fictitious green material that deprives Superman of his super strength, x-ray vision and other special powers. In Superman comics, cartoons and movies, bad guys routinely manage to find and use kryptonite in an attempt to foil the super hero.]

b) A cherry scent, which is added to race car fuel, causing the race car exhaust to smell like cherries.

c) The flavor of chocolate for toothbrushes.

d) The sound of a duck quacking.

B.　TRADE DRESS

TWO PESOS, INC. v. TACO CABANA, INC.

United States Supreme Court, 1992.
505 U.S. 763, 112 S.Ct. 2753, 120 L.Ed.2d 615.

JUSTICE WHITE delivered the opinion of the Court.

The issue in this case is whether the trade dress[1] of a restaurant may be protected under § 43(a) of the Trademark Act of 1946 (Lanham Act), 15 U.S.C. § 1125(a),* based on a finding of inherent distinctiveness, without proof that the trade dress has secondary meaning.

* * *

I

Respondent Taco Cabana, Inc., operates a chain of fast-food restaurants in Texas. The restaurants serve Mexican food. The first Taco Cabana restaurant was opened in San Antonio in September 1978, and five more restaurants had been opened in San Antonio by 1985. Taco Cabana describes its Mexican trade dress as

> a festive eating atmosphere having interior dining and patio areas decorated with artifacts, bright colors, paintings and murals. The patio includes interior and exterior areas with the interior patio

---

1.　The District Court instructed the jury: " '[T]rade dress' is the total image of the business. Taco Cabana's trade dress may include the shape and general appearance of the exterior of the restaurant, the identifying sign, the interior kitchen floor plan, the decor, the menu, the equipment used to serve food, the servers' uniforms and other features reflecting on the total image of the restaurant." The Court of Appeals accepted this definition and quoted from *Blue Bell Bio–Medical v. Cin–Bad, Inc.*, 864 F.2d 1253, 1256 (C.A.5 1989): "The 'trade dress' of a product is essentially its total image and overall appearance." It "involves the total image of a product and may include features such as size, shape, color or color combinations, texture, graphics, or even particular sales techniques." *John H. Harland Co. v. Clarke Checks, Inc.*, 711 F.2d 966, 980 (C.A.11 1983).

* [By the editor: Lanham Act § 43(a) provides for protection of *unregistered* indications of origin:

(1) Any person who, on or in connection with any goods or services, or any container for goods, uses in commerce any word, term, name, symbol, or device, or any combination thereof, or any false designation of origin * * * which—

(A) is likely to cause confusion, or to cause mistake, or to deceive as to the affiliation, connection, or association of such person with another person, or as to the origin, sponsorship, or approval of his or her goods, services, or commercial activities by another person * * *

shall be liable in a civil action by any person who believes that he or she is or is likely to be damaged by such act.]

capable of being sealed off from the outside patio by overhead garage doors. The stepped exterior of the building is a festive and vivid color scheme using top border paint and neon stripes. Bright awnings and umbrellas continue the theme.

In December 1985, a Two Pesos, Inc., restaurant was opened in Houston. Two Pesos adopted a motif very similar to the foregoing description of Taco Cabana's trade dress. Two Pesos restaurants expanded rapidly in Houston and other markets, but did not enter San Antonio. In 1986, Taco Cabana entered the Houston and Austin markets and expanded into other Texas cities, including Dallas and El Paso, where Two Pesos was also doing business.

In 1987, Taco Cabana sued Two Pesos in the United States District Court for the Southern District of Texas for trade dress infringement under § 43(a) of the Lanham Act, 15 U.S.C. § 1125(a) * * *. The case was tried to a jury, which was instructed to return its verdict in the form of answers to five questions propounded by the trial judge. The jury's answers were: Taco Cabana has a trade dress; taken as a whole, the trade dress is nonfunctional; the trade dress is inherently distinctive; the trade dress has not acquired a secondary meaning in the Texas market; and the alleged infringement creates a likelihood of confusion on the part of ordinary customers as to the source or association of the restaurant's goods or services. Because, as the jury was told, Taco Cabana's trade dress was protected if it either was inherently distinctive or had acquired a secondary meaning, judgment was entered awarding damages to Taco Cabana. In the course of calculating damages, the trial court held that Two Pesos had intentionally and deliberately infringed Taco Cabana's trade dress.

The Court of Appeals ruled that the instructions adequately stated the applicable law and that the evidence supported the jury's findings. In particular, the Court of Appeals rejected petitioner's argument that a finding of no secondary meaning contradicted a finding of inherent distinctiveness.

In so holding, the court below followed precedent in the Fifth Circuit. In *Chevron Chemical Co. v. Voluntary Purchasing Groups, Inc.*, 659 F.2d 695, 702 (C.A.5 1981), the court noted that trademark law requires a demonstration of secondary meaning only when the claimed trademark is not sufficiently distinctive of itself to identify the producer; the court held that the same principles should apply to protection of trade dresses. The Court of Appeals noted that this approach conflicts with decisions of other courts, particularly the holding of the Court of Appeals for the Second Circuit in *Vibrant Sales, Inc. v. New Body Boutique, Inc.*, 652 F.2d 299 (1981), *cert. denied*, 455 U.S. 909, 102 S.Ct. 1257, 71 L.Ed.2d 448 (1982), that § 43(a) protects unregistered trademarks or designs only where secondary meaning is shown. We granted certiorari to resolve the conflict among the Courts of Appeals on the question whether trade dress which is inherently distinctive is protectible under § 43(a) without a showing that it has acquired secondary meaning. We find that it is, and we therefore affirm.

II

The Lanham Act was intended to make "actionable the deceptive and misleading use of marks" and "to protect persons engaged in ... commerce against unfair competition." § 45, 15 U.S.C. § 1127. Section 43(a) prohibits a broader range of practices than does § 32, which applies to registered marks, but it is common ground that § 43(a) protects qualifying unregistered trademarks and that the general principles qualifying a mark for registration under § 2 of the Lanham Act are for the most part applicable in determining whether an unregistered mark is entitled to protection under § 43(a).

* * * In order to be registered, a mark must be capable of distinguishing the applicant's goods from those of others. Marks are often classified in categories of generally increasing distinctiveness; following the classic formulation set out by Judge Friendly, they may be (1) generic; (2) descriptive; (3) suggestive; (4) arbitrary; or (5) fanciful. See Abercrombie & Fitch Co. v. Hunting World, Inc., 537 F.2d 4, 9 (C.A.2 1976). The Court of Appeals followed this classification and petitioner accepts it. The latter three categories of marks, because their intrinsic nature serves to identify a particular source of a product, are deemed inherently distinctive and are entitled to protection. * * *

Marks which are merely descriptive of a product are not inherently distinctive. When used to describe a product, they do not inherently identify a particular source, and hence cannot be protected. However, descriptive marks may acquire the distinctiveness which will allow them to be protected under the Act. Section 2 of the Lanham Act provides that a descriptive mark that otherwise could not be registered under the Act may be registered if it "has become distinctive of the applicant's goods in commerce." §§ 2(e), (f), 15 U.S.C. §§ 1052(e), (f). This acquired distinctiveness is generally called "secondary meaning." The concept of secondary meaning has been applied to actions under § 43(a).

The general rule regarding distinctiveness is clear: an identifying mark is distinctive and capable of being protected if it *either* (1) is inherently distinctive *or* (2) has acquired distinctiveness through secondary meaning. It is also clear that eligibility for protection under § 43(a) depends on nonfunctionality. It is, of course, also undisputed that liability under § 43(a) requires proof of the likelihood of confusion.

The Court of Appeals determined that the District Court's instructions were consistent with the foregoing principles and that the evidence supported the jury's verdict. Both courts thus ruled that Taco Cabana's trade dress was not descriptive but rather inherently distinctive, and that it was not functional. None of these rulings is before us in this case, and for present purposes we assume, without deciding, that each of them is correct. In going on to affirm the judgment for respondent, the Court of

Appeals, following its prior decision in *Chevron*, held that Taco Cabana's inherently distinctive trade dress was entitled to protection despite the lack of proof of secondary meaning. It is this issue that is before us for decision, and we agree with its resolution by the Court of Appeals. There is no persuasive reason to apply to trade dress a general requirement of secondary meaning which is at odds with the principles generally applicable to infringement suits under § 43(a). * * *

Petitioner argues that the jury's finding that the trade dress has not acquired a secondary meaning shows conclusively that the trade dress is not inherently distinctive. The Court of Appeals' disposition of this issue was sound:

> Two Pesos' argument—that the jury finding of inherent distinctiveness contradicts its finding of no secondary meaning in the Texas market—ignores the law in this circuit. While the necessarily imperfect (and often prohibitively difficult) methods for assessing secondary meaning address the empirical question of current consumer association, the legal recognition of an inherently distinctive trademark or trade dress acknowledges the owner's legitimate proprietary interest in its unique and valuable informational device, regardless of whether substantial consumer association yet bestows the additional empirical protection of secondary meaning.

> * * *

This brings us to the line of decisions by the Court of Appeals for the Second Circuit that would find protection for trade dress unavailable absent proof of secondary meaning, * * *. In *Vibrant Sales, Inc. v. New Body Boutique, Inc.*, 652 F.2d 299 (C.A.2 1981), the plaintiff claimed protection under § 43(a) for a product whose features the defendant had allegedly copied. The Court of Appeals held that unregistered marks did not enjoy the "presumptive source association" enjoyed by registered marks and hence could not qualify for protection under § 43(a) without proof of secondary meaning. The court's rationale seemingly denied protection for unregistered but inherently distinctive marks of all kinds, whether the claimed mark used distinctive words or symbols or distinctive product design. The court thus did not accept the arguments that an unregistered mark was capable of identifying a source and that copying such a mark could be making any kind of a false statement or representation under § 43(a).

This holding is in considerable tension with the provisions of the Act. If a verbal or symbolic mark or the features of a product design may be registered under § 2, it necessarily is a mark "by which the goods of the applicant may be distinguished from the goods of others," and must be registered unless otherwise disqualified. Since § 2 requires secondary meaning only as a condition to registering descriptive marks, there are plainly marks that are registrable without showing secondary meaning. These same marks, even if not registered, remain inherently capable of distinguishing the goods of the users of these marks. Furthermore, the copier of such a mark may be seen as falsely claiming that his products may for some reason be thought of as originating from the plaintiff.

Some years after *Vibrant*, the Second Circuit announced in *Thompson Medical Co. v. Pfizer Inc.*, 753 F.2d 208 (C.A.2 1985), that in deciding whether an unregistered mark is eligible for protection under § 43(a), it would follow the classification of marks set out by Judge Friendly in *Abercrombie & Fitch*, 537 F.2d, at 9. Hence, if an unregistered mark is deemed merely descriptive, which the verbal mark before the court proved to be, proof of secondary meaning is required; however, "[s]uggestive marks are eligible for protection without any proof of secondary meaning, since the connection between the mark and the source is presumed." The Second Circuit has nevertheless continued to deny protection for trade dress under § 43(a) absent proof of secondary meaning, despite the fact that § 43(a) provides no basis for distinguishing between trademark and trade dress.

The Fifth Circuit was quite right in *Chevron*, and in this case, to follow the *Abercrombie* classifications consistently and to inquire whether trade dress for which protection is claimed under § 43(a) is inherently distinctive. If it is, it is capable of identifying products or services as coming from a specific source and secondary meaning is not required. This is the rule generally applicable to trademark, and the protection of trademarks and trade dress under § 43(a) serves the same statutory purpose of preventing deception and unfair competition. There is no persuasive reason to apply different analysis to the two. * * *

It would be a different matter if there were textual basis in § 43(a) for treating inherently distinctive verbal or symbolic trademarks differently from inherently distinctive trade dress. But there is none. The section does not mention trademarks or trade dress, whether they be called generic, descriptive, suggestive, arbitrary, fanciful, or functional. Nor does the concept of secondary meaning appear in the text of § 43(a). Where secondary meaning does appear in the statute, 15 U.S.C. § 1052, it is a requirement that applies only to merely descriptive marks and not to inherently distinctive ones. We see no basis for requiring secondary meaning for inherently distinctive trade dress protection under § 43(a) but not for other distinctive words, symbols, or devices capable of identifying a producer's product.

Engrafting onto § 43(a) a requirement of secondary meaning for inherently distinctive trade dress also would undermine the purposes of the Lanham Act. Protection of trade dress, no less than of trademarks, serves the Act's purpose to "secure to the owner of the mark the goodwill of his business and to protect the ability of consumers to distinguish among competing producers. National protection of trademarks is desirable, Congress concluded, because trademarks foster competition and the maintenance of quality by securing to the producer the benefits of good reputation."

        * * *

III

We agree with the Court of Appeals that proof of secondary meaning is not required to prevail on a claim under § 43(a) of the Lanham Act where the trade dress at issue is inherently distinctive, and accordingly the judgment of that court is affirmed.

NOTES AND QUESTIONS

1. *The nature of "trade dress."* While some trade dress is registered as a mark, § 43(a) has become an especially important vehicle for trade dress infringement claims. What exactly is "trade dress?" The term originally was understood primarily to refer to the combination of elements in product packaging, but it came to encompass nonfunctional features of the product, as well. As the district court in *Two Pesos* noted, trade dress now is understood to include the "total image" of a product or service, which may include visual aspects as well as sales techniques. In Hartford House, Ltd. v. Hallmark Cards, Inc., 846 F.2d 1268 (10th Cir.1988), *cert. denied,* 488 U.S. 908, 109 S.Ct. 260, 102 L.Ed.2d 248 (1988), the court found enforceable trade dress rights in the overall "look" of the plaintiff's line of greeting cards. This "look" consisted of

  1.   A two-fold card containing poetry on the first and third pages.

  2.   Unprinted surfaces on the inside three panels.

  3.   A deckle edge on the right side of the first page.

  4.   A rough-edge stripe of color, or wide stripe, on the outside of the deckle edge of the first page.

  5.   A high-quality, uncoated, and textured art paper for the cards.

  6.   Fluorescent ink for some of the colors printed on the cards.

  7.   Lengthy poetry, written in free verse, typically with a personal message.

  8.   Appearance of hand-lettered calligraphy on the first and third pages with the first letter of the words often enlarged.

  9.   An illustration that wraps around the card and is spread over three pages, including the back of the card.

  10.   The look of the cards primarily characterized by backgrounds of soft colors done with air brush blends or light watercolor strokes, usually depicting simple contrasting foreground scenes superimposed in the background.

Id., 846 F.2d at 1270. The court explained that its ruling did not grant the claimant, Blue Mountain,

> exclusive rights in an artistic style or in some concept, idea, or theme of expression. Rather, it is Blue Mountain's specific artistic expression, in combination with other features to produce an overall Blue Mountain look, that is being protected. This protection does not extend the protection available under trademark law and does not conflict with the policy of copyright law.

Id., 846 F.2d at 1274. Study the court's description of Taco Cabana's trade dress in *Two Pesos*. Could it be argued that this trade dress constitutes a "concept, idea, or theme of expression?" Why should it matter? How might one draw the line between protectible trade dress and concepts or themes?

What justification might exist for requiring that trade dress have secondary meaning in all cases before it can be protected? Should it matter what kind of trade dress is involved?

PROBLEM

1. Should the following things be protectible as trade dress?

a) An artist's distinctive artistic style, as displayed in his works of fine art.

b) The following configuration for cinnamon buns:

c) The following style of container for cheese and other dairy products:

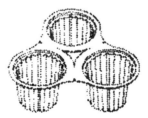

d) The following design of a building for restaurant services:

e) Advertisements featuring actors posing as vampires, and other vampire-related marketing for sun glasses.

C. TRADE NAMES

Trademarks and trade names are technically distinct. Trade names are symbols used to distinguish companies, partnerships and businesses. Trade names symbolize the reputation of a business as a whole. In contrast, trademarks and service marks are designed to identify and distinguish a company's goods and services.

Accuride International, Inc. v. Accuride Corp., 871 F.2d 1531, 1534 (9th Cir.1989). Though trade name infringement litigation has focused primarily on profit-seeking businesses, other entities, such as charitable organizations, educational institutions, and fraternal groups may also avail themselves of trade name protection.

The same rationales exist for protecting trade names as for protecting trademarks and trade dress: Protection of a business' trade name prevents infringers from unfairly appropriating its identity and good will, and jeopardizing its reputation. Trade name protection may encourage businesses to invest in quality by insuring the opportunity to reap the benefits of the favorable reputation that such investment generates. Perhaps most importantly, prevention of trade name infringement protects consumers from confusion concerning the identity or "source" of the business.

The common law of unfair competition traditionally protected trade names under the same basic principles as trademarks, and Lanham Act § 43(a) continues this tradition. Accordingly, trade names must satisfy the same standards of distinctiveness as marks—they typically are categorized in the same way: generic, descriptive, suggestive, arbitrary or fanciful. Moreover, the same standard of infringement—a likelihood of consumer confusion—applies. The same basic rules regarding geographic rights and priority apply as for unregistered marks and trade dress.

What, if any impact do state statutes governing incorporation and registration of corporate names have on rights in trade names? Exclusive rights in trade names, like exclusive rights in trademarks, are obtained through use of the name in the ordinary course of business. Registration or incorporation under a name pursuant to state corporate statutes, in the absence of actual use of the name in trade, generally gives no exclusive right in the name for purposes of an infringement suit against others. In some states, however, persons incorporating or registering under a name receive indirect trade name protection through statutory provisions precluding businesses from registering or incorporating under a name that is deceptively similar to that of a corporation already authorized to transact business in that state. See Restatement (Third) of Unfair Competition § 12 cmt c (1995). In most states, however, the fact that the state has accepted registration of a name does not shield the registrant against infringement liability to a senior user. *Id.*

A trade name, in itself, may not be registered on the Lanham Act Principal Register. Of course, a business that uses a word or symbol both as its trade name and as a mark for its goods or services may register the word or symbol in the latter capacity. Note that a defendant's unauthorized use of a plaintiff's trade name as a mark may infringe the plaintiff's rights in the name, if the use leads to a likelihood of confusion. Indeed, prior continuing use of a word or symbol as a trade name may prevent another from registering a confusingly similar word or symbol as a mark under Lanham Act § 2(d). 15 U.S.C.A. § 1052(d).

III. THE DISTINCTIVENESS REQUIREMENT

ABERCROMBIE & FITCH CO. v. HUNTING WORLD, INC.

United States Court of Appeals for the Second Circuit, 1976.
537 F.2d 4.

FRIENDLY, CIRCUIT JUDGE:

* * *

The cases, and in some instances the Lanham Act, identify four different categories of terms with respect to trademark protection. Arrayed in an ascending order which roughly reflects their eligibility to trademark status and the degree of protection accorded, these classes are (1) generic, (2) descriptive, (3) suggestive, and (4) arbitrary or fanciful. The lines of demarcation, however, are not always bright. Moreover, the difficulties are compounded because a term that is in one category for a particular product may be in quite a different one for another,[6] because a term may shift from one category to another in light of differences in usage through time,[7] because a term may have one meaning to one group of users and a different one to others, and because the same term may be put to different uses with respect to a single product. * * *

A generic term is one that refers, or has come to be understood as referring, to the genus of which the particular product is a species. At common law neither those terms which were generic nor those which were merely descriptive could become valid trademarks * * *. The same was true under the Trademark Act of 1905, except for marks which had been the subject of exclusive use for ten years prior to its enactment, 33 Stat. 726.[10] While * * * the Lanham Act makes an important exception with respect to those merely descriptive terms which have acquired secondary meaning, see § 2(f), 15 U.S.C. § 1052(f), it offers no such exception for

---

6. To take a familiar example "Ivory" would be generic when used to describe a product made from the tusks of elephants but arbitrary as applied to soap.

7. *See, e.g., Haughton Elevator Co. v. Seeberger*, 85 U.S.P.Q. 80 (1950), in which the coined word "Escalator", originally fanciful, or at the very least suggestive, was held to have become generic.

10. Some protection to descriptive marks which had acquired a secondary meaning was given by the law of unfair competition. The Trademark Act of 1920 permitted registration of certain descriptive marks which had acquired secondary meaning.

generic marks. The Act provides for the cancellation of a registered mark if at any time it [becomes generic], § 14(c). This means that even proof of secondary meaning, by virtue of which some "merely descriptive" marks may be registered, cannot transform a generic term into a subject for trademark. As explained in *J. Kohnstam, Ltd. v. Louis Marx and Company*, 280 F.2d 437, 440, 47 CCPA 1080 (1960), no matter how much money and effort the user of a generic term has poured into promoting the sale of its merchandise and what success it has achieved in securing public identification, it cannot deprive competing manufacturers of the product of the right to call an article by its name. * * * The pervasiveness of the principle is illustrated by a series of well known cases holding that when a suggestive or fanciful term has become generic as a result of a manufacturer's own advertising efforts, trademark protection will be denied save for those markets where the term still has not become generic and a secondary meaning has been shown to continue. A term may thus be generic in one market and descriptive or suggestive or fanciful in another.

The term which is descriptive but not generic[11] stands on a better basis. Although § 2(e) of the Lanham Act, 15 U.S.C. § 1052, forbids the registration of a mark which, when applied to the goods of the applicant, is "merely descriptive," § 2(f) removes a considerable part of the sting by providing that "except as expressly excluded in paragraphs (a)–(d) of this section, nothing in this chapter shall prevent the registration of a mark used by the applicant which has become distinctive of the applicant's goods in commerce" and that the Commissioner may accept, as prima facie evidence that the mark has become distinctive, proof of substantially exclusive and continuous use of the mark applied to the applicant's goods for five years preceding the application. * * * In the [case of generic terms] any claim to an exclusive right must be denied since this in effect would confer a monopoly not only of the mark but of the product by rendering a competitor unable effectively to name what it was endeavoring to sell. In the [case of descriptive terms] the law strikes the balance, with respect to registration, between the hardships to a competitor in hampering the use of an appropriate word and those to the owner who, having invested money and energy to endow a word with the good will adhering to his enterprise, would be deprived of the fruits of his efforts.

The category of "suggestive" marks was spawned by the felt need to accord protection to marks that were neither exactly descriptive on the one hand nor truly fanciful on the other—a need that was particularly acute because of the bar in the Trademark Act of 1905, 33 Stat. 724, 726,

---

11. A commentator has illuminated the distinction with an example of the "Deep Bowl Spoon":

> "Deep Bowl" identifies a significant characteristic of the article. It is "merely descriptive" of the goods, because it informs one that they are deep in the bowl portion. . . . It is not, however, "the common descriptive name" of the article [since] the implement is not a deep bowl, it is a spoon. . . . "Spoon" is not merely descriptive of the article—it identifies the article—[and therefore] the term is generic.

Fletcher, *Actual Confusion as to Incontestability of Descriptive Marks*, 64 Trademark Rep. 252, 260 (1974). On the other hand, "Deep Bowl" would be generic as to a deep bowl.

(with an exceedingly limited exception noted above) on the registration of merely descriptive marks regardless of proof of secondary meaning. Having created the category the courts have had great difficulty in defining it. Judge Learned Hand made the not very helpful statement:

> It is quite impossible to get any rule out of the cases beyond this: That the validity of the mark ends where suggestion ends and description begins.

Franklin Knitting Mills, Inc. v. Fashionit Sweater Mills, Inc., 297 F. 247, 248 (2 Cir.1923), *aff'd per curiam*, 4 F.2d 1018 (2 Cir.1925)—a statement amply confirmed by comparing the list of terms held suggestive with those held merely descriptive in 3 Callmann, Unfair Competition, Trademarks and Monopolies § 71.2 (3d ed.). Another court has observed, somewhat more usefully, that:

> A term is suggestive if it requires imagination, thought and perception to reach a conclusion as to the nature of goods. A term is descriptive if it forthwith conveys an immediate idea of the ingredients, qualities or characteristics of the goods.

Stix Products, Inc. v. United Merchants & Manufacturers Inc., 295 F.Supp. 479, 488 (S.D.N.Y.1968) * * *. Also useful is the approach taken by this court in *Aluminum Fabricating Co. of Pittsburgh v. Season–All Window Corp.*, 259 F.2d 314 (2 Cir.1958), that the reason for restricting the protection accorded descriptive terms, namely the undesirability of preventing an entrant from using a descriptive term for his product, is much less forceful when the trademark is a suggestive word since, as Judge Lumbard wrote, 259 F.2d at 317:

> The English language has a wealth of synonyms and related words with which to describe the qualities which manufacturers may wish to claim for their products and the ingenuity of the public relations profession supplies new words and slogans as they are needed.

If a term is suggestive, it is entitled to registration without proof of secondary meaning. Moreover, as held in the *Season-All* case, the decision of the Patent Office to register a mark without requiring proof of secondary meaning affords a rebuttable presumption that the mark is suggestive or arbitrary or fanciful rather than merely descriptive.

It need hardly be added that fanciful or arbitrary terms[12] enjoy all the rights accorded to suggestive terms as marks without the need of debating whether the term is "merely descriptive" and with ease of establishing infringement.

* * *

---

12. [T]he term "fanciful," as a classifying concept, is usually applied to words invented solely for their use as trademarks. When the same legal consequences attach to a common word, i. e., when it is applied in an unfamiliar way, the use is called "arbitrary."

NOTES AND QUESTIONS

1. *The distinctiveness requirement.* In order to qualify for trademark or unfair competition protection, a word, name, symbol or device must be distinctive. That is, it must indicate the source of the product or service to consumers, distinguishing the source from that of other goods or services. As the *Abercrombie & Fitch* opinion indicates, arbitrary words or symbols (such as "Ivory" for soap or "Tea Rose" for flour) and made-up or fanciful words or symbols (such as "Kodak" for camera film and equipment and "Exxon" for gasoline) are viewed as "inherently distinctive." It can be assumed that consumers perceiving such words or symbols in the context of product or service sales will understand them to indicate source. What other purpose could they serve?

Such an assumption cannot be made in the case of words or symbols that describe characteristics of the good or service (such as "World Book" for encyclopedias, "Beef & Brew" for restaurant services, or "Easyload" for tape recorders). Thus, descriptive words and symbols are not inherently distinctive. They are merely *capable* of becoming distinctive if, through exposure through extensive use on labels and in advertising, consumers come to understand them as indications of source. If a descriptive word or symbol has not become distinctive, then it is unlikely that its use by other competitors will lead to consumer confusion about the source of goods or services, or loss of good will. Moreover, as discussed in the Introduction, there are very good reasons not to recognize exclusive rights in descriptive words in one business enterprise too readily: Other competitors may legitimately need to use such words or symbols to describe their own products or services. As Judge Posner has stated:

> [I]t is no purpose of trademark protection to allow a firm to prevent its competitors from informing consumers about the attributes of the competitors' brands. * * * To allow a firm to use as a trademark a generic word, or a descriptive word still understood by the consuming public to describe, would make it difficult for competitors to market their own brands of the same product.

Blau Plumbing, Inc. v. S.O.S. Fix–It, Inc., 781 F.2d 604, 609 (7th Cir.1986). Accordingly, modern trademark and unfair competition law permit descriptive words and symbols to be protected, and the Lanham Act permits them to be registered, *if* the user is able to demonstrate that consumers do, in fact, recognize the word or symbol as an indication of source. In such cases, the descriptive word has acquired "secondary meaning." Only then will limiting competitors' use of a descriptive word or symbol be justified by concerns about consumer confusion and protection of business good will.

Suggestive words (such as "Coppertone" for suntan cream, or "Roach Motel" for insect traps), like arbitrary and fanciful words, are considered inherently distinctive, and can be protected and registered without the necessity of demonstrating secondary meaning. How does one determine whether a word or symbol is descriptive or suggestive? Is the *Abercrombie* discussion helpful? The court refers to policy considerations that justify protecting and registering suggestive marks without a showing of secondary meaning. Do those policy considerations suggest an additional test for determining which classification is appropriate in a given case?

We will examine two of the categories identified by Judge Friendly—generic marks and descriptive marks—in greater detail in the following subsections.

2. *Categorization of design and other nonverbal marks.* The four *Abercrombie* mark classifications are best suited for word marks. While some nonverbal marks, such as representational drawings of a product or of persons using it, may readily be classified as "descriptive" (as opposed to "suggestive" or "arbitrary"), many nonverbal marks, such as abstract designs and packaging shapes, cannot readily be characterized by those terms. In such cases, as a practical matter the four categories can be collapsed into two: marks that are inherently distinctive and marks that are merely capable of becoming distinctive through acquisition of secondary meaning. Marks in the first category can be protected or registered without any demonstration of secondary meaning. How is the distinctiveness determination made?

In Wiley v. American Greetings Corp., 762 F.2d 139 (1st Cir.1985), the plaintiff manufactured and sold stuffed teddy bears, each of which had a red heart shape permanently affixed to its left breast. The defendants began using a similar heart on their teddy bears, and plaintiff sued for trademark infringement. The Court of Appeals for the First Circuit upheld summary judgement for the defendants, finding that the heart was not inherently distinctive as a matter of law, and that the plaintiff had not demonstrated secondary meaning. The court explained:

> Whether a design is "inherently distinctive," *i.e.*, whether it is arbitrary or merely descriptive, is ordinarily a question of fact that is decided by reference to the following factors:
>
>> Whether [the design] was a "common basic shape or design," whether it was unique or unusual in a particular field, whether it was a mere refinement of a commonly-adopted and well-known form of ornamentation for a particular class of goods viewed by the public as dress or ornamentation for the goods, or whether it was capable of creating a commercial impression distinct from the accompanying words.
>
> Seabrook Foods, Inc. v. Bar–Well Foods, Ltd., 568 F.2d 1342, 1344 (C.C.P.A.1977). Evaluating the record here in the light most favorable to Wiley, however, leads us to conclude that no genuine issue exists for the trier of fact, since we see no proper basis on which a trier could determine that Wiley's heart is commensurate with the above standards.
>
> Wiley's red heart is a "common" basic shape, similar to a geometrical design. It is hornbook law that "[o]rdinary geometric shapes such as circles, ovals, squares, etc., even when not used as background for other marks, are regarded as non-distinctive and protectible only upon proof of secondary meaning." *McCarthy, Trademarks and Unfair Competition*, § 7:12, at 172. A plain heart shape, like an "[o]rdinary geometric shape," carries no distinctive message of origin to the consumer, and could not carry such a message (absent establishment of a secondary meaning) given the heart shape's widespread use as decoration for any number of products put out by many different companies.

Using a red heart as ornamentation for stuffed animals is also far from unique or unusual. The record contains pictures of, and references to, an abundance of plush animals, including many teddy bears, that sport heart designs on their chests or other parts of their anatomy. * * *

The fact that Wiley's alleged mark is a red heart, *permanently* affixed to the *left* breast of a *teddy bear* does not, as she claims, serve to distinguish her use of the design from others' uses of hearts on other stuffed animals. These characteristics, even if they in combination could be deemed unique, are "mere refinement[s] of a commonly-adopted and well-known form of ornamentation for a particular class of goods viewed by the public as dress or ornamentation for a particular class of goods." *Seabrook Foods*, 568 F.2d at 1344.

Id., 762 F.2d at 141–42. See also Restatement (Third) of Unfair Competition § 13, cmt d (1995) ("unless the symbol or design is striking, unusual, or otherwise likely to differentiate the products of a particular producer, the designation is not inherently distinctive.").

In contrast to the red heart in *Wiley*, the red and white polka-dot bands on Swift cleanser, depicted in the prior section, were held inherently distinctive. See also *In re* Esso Standard Oil Co., 305 F.2d 495 (C.C.P.A.1962) (red, white and blue "Esso" label held inherently distinctive); Sicilia Di R. Biebow & Co. v. Cox, 732 F.2d 417 (5th Cir.1984) (tear-shape-on-a-pedestal design for bottle may be inherently distinctive).

How would you assess the distinctiveness of "Mr. Peanut," the peanut with stick arms and legs, a top hat, spats, cane and monocle, used as a mark for Planters' peanuts? How would you evaluate the distinctiveness of the following sound mark, claimed to identify a "personal security alarm in the nature of a child's bracelet to deter and prevent child abductions": "a descending frequency sound pulse (from 2.3 kHz to approximately 1.5 kHz) that follows an exponential, RC charging curve, wherein said descending frequency sound pulse occurs four to five times per second, and that over a one second period of time, there is alternating sound pulses and silence with each occurring approximately 50% of the time during a one second period of time"? See *In re* Vertex Group LLC, 89 U.S.P.Q.2d 1694 (T.T.A.B. 2009).

3. *Secondary meaning.* The classic definition of secondary meaning comes from G. & C. Merriam Co. v. Saalfield, 198 F. 369, 373 (6th Cir.1912):

[A] word or phrase originally, and in that sense primarily, incapable of exclusive appropriation with reference to an article on the market, because geographically or otherwise descriptive, might nevertheless have been used so long and so exclusively by one producer with reference to his article that, in that trade and to that branch of the purchasing public, the word or phrase had come to mean that the article was his product; in other words, had come to be, to them, his trademark. So it was said that the word had come to have a secondary meaning, although this phrase, "secondary meaning," seems not happily chosen, because, in the limited field, this new meaning is primary rather than secondary: that is to say, it is, in that field, the natural meaning.

Persons seeking to demonstrate that their non-inherently distinctive marks have attained secondary meaning often rely on consumer surveys, which undertake to ascertain whether consumers perceive the claimed word, symbol or device as an indication of source. In order to be accepted and accorded weight as evidence, however, a consumer survey must be formulated and conducted scientifically. See, e.g., Brooks Shoe Mfg. Co. v. Suave Shoe Corp., 716 F.2d 854 (11th Cir.1983). Mark claimants may also call consumers as witnesses to testify about their understanding. In addition, a wide array of circumstantial evidence may be useful. Particularly, the claimant may demonstrate that it has used the word, symbol or device as a mark exclusively and extensively for a substantial period of time. This permits an inference that consumers have been sufficiently exposed to the use to understand its trademark significance. Evidence of extensive advertising that features the mark is effective for the same reason. In infringement suits, courts have sometimes found that a defendant's intentional copying constitutes circumstantial evidence of secondary meaning. See, e.g., Ideal Toy Corp. v. Plawner Toy Manufacturing Corp., 685 F.2d 78 (3d Cir.1982). As the *Abercrombie* court notes, the Lanham Act permits (but does not require) the PTO to accept as *prima facie* evidence of secondary meaning "proof of substantially exclusive and continuous use" by the applicant in commerce "for the five years before the date on which the claim of distinctiveness is made." 15 U.S.C.A. § 1052(f). The degree of proof of secondary meaning that will be required may vary according to the perceived "strength" of the mark. For example, the PTO or a court may require stronger evidence of secondary meaning in the case of a highly descriptive term than in the case of a term which is descriptive, but only slightly so.

How many consumers must understand the word, symbol or device's trademark significance? Many courts have stated that a "substantial segment" or a "substantial number" of prospective purchasers of the good or service will suffice. See, e.g., Centaur Communications, Ltd. v. A/S/M Communications, Inc., 830 F.2d 1217, 1222 (2d Cir.1987). This requirement can be satisfied with less than fifty percent of the potential consumers. *In re* Owens–Corning Fiberglas Corp., 774 F.2d 1116, 1127 (Fed.Cir.1985); Restatement (Third) of Unfair Competition § 13, cmt e (1995)("A person attempting to prove the existence of secondary meaning is not required to [prove] that the designation is recognized as distinctive by all [consumers], or even by a majority of them.").

A. GENERIC WORDS AND SYMBOLS

THE MURPHY DOOR BED CO., INC. v. INTERIOR SLEEP SYSTEMS, INC.

Unites States Court of Appeals for the Second Circuit, 1989.
874 F.2d 95.

MINER, CIRCUIT JUDGE:

Defendants-appellants appeal from a judgment entered in the United States District Court for the Eastern District of New York (Mishler, J.), awarding plaintiff, the Murphy Door Bed Company ("Murphy" or "Murphy Co.''), * * * damages for breach of contract [and] trademark infringement and unfair competition. The judgment includes a permanent injunction enjoining all defendants from use of the Murphy name.

* * *

We hold that ''Murphy bed'' is a generic term, having been appropriated by the public to designate generally a type of bed. Consequently, defendants could not have infringed on plaintiff's trademark, alleged to be Murphy bed, and the district court erred in finding trademark infringement. * * *

BACKGROUND

At the turn of this century, William Lawrence Murphy invented and manufactured a bed that when not in use could be concealed in a wall closet. By using a counter-balancing mechanism, the bed could be lowered from or raised to a closet in a wall to which the bed is hinged. In 1918, the United States Patent Office granted Mr. Murphy a patent for a ''pivot bed,'' which was substantially similar to the wall bed. Mr. Murphy incorporated in New York in 1925 as the Murphy Door Bed Company and began to sell the wall bed under the name of ''Murphy bed.'' Since its inception, the Murphy Co. has used the words Murphy and Murphy bed as its trademark for concealed beds. Other manufacturers of wall beds generally describe their products as ''wall beds,'' ''concealed beds,'' ''disappearing beds,'' ''authentic adjustable hydraulic beds'' and the like, but rarely as Murphy beds. In fact, at least twice, when independent companies marketed their products as Murphy beds, Murphy complained to them and, as a result, the companies refrained from further deliberate use of the term Murphy bed.

On March 23, 1981, and again on November 16, 1982, the Patent and Trademark Office (''PTO'') denied the Murphy Co.'s application to register the Murphy bed trademark. The PTO examining attorney explained that the words ''Murphy bed'' had become generic and that the phrase Murphy bed was ''merely descriptive of a characteristic of the goods.'' In August 1984, the Trademark Trial and Appeal Board (''TTAB'') affirmed the denial of registration. The TTAB noted that ''Murphy bed has for a long period of time been used by a substantial segment of the public as a generic term for a bed which folds into a wall or a closet.''

In December 1981, Frank Zarcone, on behalf of ISS and himself, entered into a distributorship agreement with the Murphy Co. and became the exclusive distributor of the Murphy bed in the four Florida counties of Broward, Dade, Palm Beach and Monroe. The agreement, in the form of a letter signed by both Murphy and Zarcone, provided in part that:

4) ... Interior Sleep Systems will pay for material purchased within 30 days of date of Murphy's invoice....

5)—Whenever the Murphy name is used, it must be in capital letters and identified by the word trademark or TM adjacent to

Murphy. Cabinets or other material not furnished by Murphy will not be promoted or sold as Murphy products.

* * *

8)—Upon termination of this agreement Interior Sleep Systems, Inc. agrees to discontinue the use of the name "Murphy bed".

After learning of the TTAB's 1984 decision denying Murphy's application for trademark registration, Zarcone formed MBCA Ga. in December 1985, and MBCA Fl. in February 1986. In addition, Zarcone obtained a telephone listing in New York City under the name "Murphy Bed Company."

On March 20, 1986, Magnolia Builders ("Magnolia") of Pensacola, Florida ordered 109 Murphy beds, Model SL 60/80, from MBCA Fl. Zarcone previously had filled similar Magnolia orders with beds of the Murphy Co. To fill this order, however, Zarcone delivered beds designated as Murphy bed Model SL 60/80 but that were, in fact, manufactured by one of his companies.

Thereafter, Zarcone ordered from the Murphy Co. forty-eight Murphy beds, which were delivered with an invoice on May 21, 1986. [Zarcone did not pay for these beds in accordance with his distributorship agreement. Murphy then notified Zarcone that it was cancelling the distributorship agreement and] that in keeping with paragraph 8 of the agreement, Zarcone was within "ten (10) days from receipt of this letter to remove the name 'Murphy Bed' from all signs, vehicles, billboards, and all advertising." * * * Zarcone continued to advertise regularly in south Florida using the Murphy name, including describing his product as "Murphy Bed Co. of America, Inc.—Original Wall–Bed Systems" and "The New Murphy Beds ... Original Wall Bed Systems."

Murphy initiated this action on December 19, 1986, seeking compensation, punitive damages, and injunctive relief based on claims of: (i) trademark infringement, (ii) unfair competition and (iii) breach of contract. * * *

* * *

DISCUSSION

1. Trade-mark Infringement

The district court found that Murphy had shown that the term Murphy bed had secondary meaning—i.e. that the term symbolized a particular business, product or company—and thus was protectible. As a result, the court assigned to defendants the burden of proving that the term somehow had been transformed into a generic phrase. The defendants did not sustain their burden, in the view of the court. Defendants now claim that the court improperly placed the burden of proof upon them, arguing that, instead, Murphy should have been required to prove that the trademark was not generic.

A term or phrase is generic when it is commonly used to depict a genus or type of product, rather than a particular product. When a term is generic, "trademark protection will be denied save for those markets where the term still has not become generic and a secondary meaning has been shown to continue." We have held that "the burden is on plaintiff to prove that its mark is a valid trademark ... [and] that its unregistered mark is not generic." *Reese Publishing Co. v. Hampton Int'l Communications, Inc.*, 620 F.2d 7, 11 (2d Cir.1980).

As the Murphy mark is unregistered, *Reese* suggests that the district court erred in shifting the burden of proof to the defendants. However, the words at issue in *Reese*, "Video Buyer's Guide," were of common use before the product developer applied them to his product, whereas here, the term Murphy bed was created for its purpose by the manufacturer and only thereafter was it adopted by the public as a matter of common use. * * * It was this genericness of an "invented" term that Learned Hand addressed when determining whether "aspirin," a coined word, had been so adopted by the lay public as to become generic. *See Bayer Co. v. United Drug Co.*, 272 F. 505, 509 (S.D.N.Y.1921); *see also King–Seeley Thermos Co. v. Aladdin Indus., Inc.*, 321 F.2d 577, 579 (2d Cir.1963) (wide-spread use of the word "thermos," despite having been invented by plaintiff for description of vacuum bottle, created genericness); *DuPont Cellophane Co. v. Waxed Products Co.*, 85 F.2d 75, 81 (2d Cir.) (expropriation by public of word "cellophane" created genericness), *cert. denied*, 299 U.S. 601, 57 S.Ct. 194, 81 L.Ed. 443 (1936). We find this distinction important and hold that where the public is said to have expropriated a term established by a product developer, the burden is on the defendant to prove genericness. Thus, critical to a trial court's allocation of proof burdens is a determination of whether the term at issue is claimed to be generic by reason of common usage or by reason of expropriation. * * *

The Murphy Co. was the first to employ the word Murphy to describe a bed that could be folded into a wall closet. It is claimed that over time the public adopted, or, rather, expropriated, the term Murphy bed as a synonym for any bed that folds into a closet. Accordingly, the district court was correct in placing the burden of proof of genericness upon the defendants. We find, however, that Zarcone did indeed establish the genericness of the term Murphy bed.

The following factors combined lead us to conclude that Zarcone showed at trial that today the term Murphy bed, in the eyes of "a substantial majority of the public," *King-Seeley*, 321 F.2d at 579, refers to a species of bed that can fold into a wall enclosure. First, the decision of the PTO, and certainly the TTAB, is to be accorded great weight. The district court explicitly rejected the decisions of the PTO and TTAB finding genericness, despite acknowledging their persuasive force. Second, the term Murphy bed is included in many dictionaries as a standard description of a wall-bed. *See, e.g.*, Webster's Third New International Dictionary 1489 (1981). While dictionary definitions are not conclusive proof of a mark's generic nature, they are influential because they reflect the general public's perception of a mark's meaning and implication. Third, Zarcone introduced as evidence numerous examples of newspaper and magazine use of the phrase Murphy bed to describe generally a type of bed. Again, such evidence is not proof positive, but it is a strong indication of the general public's perception that Murphy bed connotes something other than a bed manufactured by the Murphy Co.

In finding a lack of genericness, the district court was influenced by Murphy's efforts at policing its mark. The court noted with approval instances where Murphy complained to those who had used the term Murphy bed to describe beds not necessarily produced by Murphy. However, when, as here, the mark has "entered the public domain beyond recall," policing is of no consequence to a resolution of whether a mark is generic. *King-Seeley*, 321 F.2d at 579.[2]

Because we find that the evidence presented at trial demonstrated the genericness of the term Murphy bed, the claim for trademark infringement must fail. Neither statutory law, namely the Lanham Act, nor common law supports a claim for trademark infringement when the mark in question is generic. * * *

NOTES AND QUESTIONS

1. *Loss of a valuable trademark.* What is the rationale underlying the rule that there can be no trademark rights in generic words and symbols? How does one determine whether a mark has become generic? Would consumer surveys be an effective way to prove or disprove genericness?

In determining whether a trademark has become the generic name of a product or service, should it matter whether the product or service already has one or more generic names? In light of the test discussed in *Murphy*, what is the likely status of the mark "Xerox" for photocopiers, "Kleenex" for facial tissues, "Band–Aids" for self-adhesive bandages, or "Q–Tips" for cotton swabs? What can a business do to avoid losing a valuable trademark through public appropriation? Is there any cause of action that would permit a trademark owner to enjoin generic uses of its mark, for example, in the media or in dictionaries? Compare Lucasfilm Ltd. v. High Frontier, 622 F.Supp. 931 (D.D.C.1985) (owner of service mark "Star Wars" cannot enjoin public interest groups from using the term "star wars" in advertisements to describe the Reagan Administration's Strategic Defense Initiative) with Selchow & Righter Co. v. McGraw–Hill Book Co., 580 F.2d 25 (2d Cir.1978) (owner of "Scrabble" trademark is entitled to preliminary injunction against unauthorized publication of dictionary entitled "The Complete Scrabble Dictionary." Irreparable harm is demonstrated by fact that publication might render the "Scrabble" trademark generic.). Should there be?

---

2. Indeed, the only evidence that even arguably supports the view that the mark was not generic is the circumstance that other manufacturers did not use the term Murphy bed to describe their beds. However, that fact is not sufficient to support a conclusion that the mark is not generic, especially since Murphy's action in policing the mark might well have deterred other manufacturers from using the term Murphy bed in describing their products.

2. *The Lanham Act.* If the plaintiff's "Murphy Bed" mark had been registered on the Lanham Act Principal Register, allocation of the burden of proof would have been clear. One of the advantages of registration is that it constitutes *"prima facie* evidence of the validity of the registered mark and of the registration of the mark." 15 U.S.C.A. § 1057(b). This would have placed the burden of proof on the defendant to rebut the presumption of validity.

Lanham Act § 2, 15 U.S.C.A. § 1052, sets forth the grounds on which registration of marks can be refused. There is no express reference to generic words or symbols. Is there any language in § 2 that can be interpreted to disqualify an application to register a mark on the ground that it is generic?

3. *Residual trademark significance.* In some cases, public appropriation of a once-arbitrary or fanciful mark may not be complete. For example, while 75% of the relevant public understands the term to be the generic name of the product, the remaining 25% may still view the term as an indication that the product (which may have other generic names) comes from one particular source. Since the primary significance is generic, the term must be adjudged generic, 15 U.S.C.A. § 1064(3), and competitors must be allowed to use it. What, if anything, can be done to prevent confusion of the remaining 25% of the public that still accords the term trademark significance?

4. *Determining the relevant "genus."* A generic term is generally defined as the name of a class or "genus" of products or services. See Park 'N Fly, Inc. v. Dollar Park & Fly, Inc., 469 U.S. 189, 194, 105 S.Ct. 658, 661, 83 L.Ed.2d 582, 587 (1985) (a generic term is one that refers to the genus, while each producer's particular product is a species within the genus). As a first step in determining whether a term is the common name of a genus, therefore, the relevant class or "genus" of product or service must be defined. In *Murphy,* the Second Circuit defined the relevant genus as "concealed" or "wall" beds. The issue was not controversial in that case, and often is not.

One case in which genus definition proved controversial is A.J. Canfield Co. v. Honickman, 808 F.2d 291 (3d Cir.1986). In that case, the court had to decide, in the course of reviewing the denial of a preliminary injunction, whether the term "chocolate fudge" was generic for the plaintiff's diet soda. The court found that the issue hinged on whether the relevant product genus was chocolate soda (in which case the composite "chocolate fudge soda" might be deemed descriptive or even suggestive of chocolate soda) or chocolate fudge soda. This in turn depended on whether "fudge" denoted a separate flavor or flavor variation of chocolate. After considerable discussion, the court determined:

> [W]hen a producer introduces a product that differs from an established product class in a significant, functional characteristic, and uses the common descriptive term of that characteristic as its name, that new product becomes its own genus, and the term denoting the genus becomes generic if there is no commonly used alternative that effectively communicates the same functional information.

Id., 808 F.2d at 293. Applying this test to the case at hand, the *Canfield* court noted that the plaintiff's advertising emphasized the difference between soda tasting like chocolate fudge and mere chocolate soda, chocolate fudge sodas having "a particular full and rich chocolate flavor." Thus, a soda tasting like chocolate fudge did differ from chocolate soda with respect to a significant, functional characteristic, and constituted a separate product genus. The term "fudge" denoted that different characteristic. Since the court knew of no commonly used alternative to communicate the flavor variation, it determined that the name "chocolate fudge" must be viewed as the generic name of this new genus of soda. Giving the plaintiff exclusive rights in the term would make it difficult, if not impossible, for a competing producer to convey to the public that its product shared this functional flavor characteristic. This, in turn, would effectively give the plaintiff an undeserved monopoly in the functional, unpatented product characteristic itself.

5. *Misspellings, abbreviations and foreign-language equivalents.* Merchants cannot avoid a finding of genericness by simply misspelling the word at issue, as long as the public can still recognize the generic meaning. Likewise, an abbreviation of a generic term is generic, if it still conveys the original generic connotation. For example, in National Conference of Bar Examiners v. Multistate Legal Studies, Inc., 692 F.2d 478 (7th Cir.1982), *cert. denied*, 464 U.S. 814, 104 S.Ct. 69, 78 L.Ed.2d 83 (1983), the court found both the term "Multistate Bar Examination" and its abbreviation, "MBE" to be generic, and available for use by a business that prepared students to take the exam.

Under the doctrine of foreign equivalents, foreign words are treated as generic when, if translated, they would be the generic name of the product or service they identify. On this basis, for example, the Trademark Trial and Appeal Board has refused to register the French words "le sorbet" as a mark for fruit ice, *In re* Le Sorbet, Inc., 228 U.S.P.Q. 27 (T.T.A.B. 1985). In Weiss Noodle Co. v. Golden Cracknel & Specialty Co., 290 F.2d 845 (C.C.P.A.1961), the Court of Customs and Patent Appeals found the term "Ha-Lush-ka" to be a hyphenated, phonetically spelled version of the Hungarian word "haluska," which means egg noodles. For that reason, it was generic and could not be registered as a trademark for egg noodle products. What is the justification for this rule?

The fact that a generic term is incorporated into a composite mark does not preclude registration or common-law protection of the composite mark, as long as the combination of elements is itself distinctive. Recognition of rights in the composite mark, however, gives no rights in the generic term by itself. Thus, the mark "Coca–Cola" is an enforceable mark, though the Coca-Cola Company has no right to prevent others from using the word "cola" by itself or in their own composite marks. Likewise, the user of a distinctive decorative design that incorporates a generic term may prevent use of the term only as it is incorporated into the design.

6. *Non-verbal generic marks.* Most judicial decisions finding alleged marks to be generic involve verbal marks. However, non-verbal symbols or devices may also be found generic. For example, in Kendall–Jackson Winery, Ltd. v. E. & J. Gallo Winery, 150 F.3d 1042 (9th Cir.1998), Kendall–Jackson claimed that Gallo's use of a multicolored grape leaf design on its wine label, which allegedly resembled a similarly colored leaf design used by Kendall–Jackson, constituted trademark infringement. The court rejected the claim, reasoning that the grape leaf symbol itself was generic for wine, and thus was not protectible as a mark. The court explained:

The use of a grape leaf as a mark for wine would normally be inherently distinctive because it suggests, rather than describes, the product. One has to go through two or three steps to associate the leaf with the product—i.e., a grape leaf comes from a grapevine, which has grapes from which wine is produced. Under the standard test, a grape leaf could be suggestive and thus inherently distinctive. * * *

The difference in the present case is that because wine bottlers other than Kendall–Jackson have long used grape leaves to decorate their labels, that emblem has become generic. * * * By itself, a grape leaf cannot differentiate one brand from another because precisely the same reasoning links the same emblem to the product in each case: A grape leaf suggests a grapevine, which suggests a grape, which suggests wine. Because the grape leaf is used widely in the industry, it has lost the power to differentiate brands. * * *

A producer's depiction of a grape leaf, may, however, be so distinctive as to warrant protection from copying. * * * If a particular rendering of a grape leaf has the power to distinguish one brand from another, it is the rendering that should be evaluated for its distinctiveness. * * *

There is no jury question on the copying of any of the distinctive characteristics of Kendall–Jackson's leaf. The most distinctive feature of the Kendall–Jackson grape leaf is that it is separated by a space in the middle where the name of the winery is printed. Less distinctive features are the leaf's downward pointing orientation, and the arguably unusual coloration. Gallo did not, however, depict a bifurcated leaf with its brand name printed in a space between the segments. Gallo's leaf is folded and turns at an angle rather than pointing straight down. Also, the intensity of the coloration is markedly different from that of the original Kendall–Jackson leaf. When viewed in its entirety, we do not see how any distinctive feature of the Kendall–Jackson mark has been duplicated so as to present a jury issue of trademark infringement.

Id., at 1048–49.

PROBLEM

1. Should the following be deemed generic in light of the authorities discussed in this section?

(a) The word "Tas-tee" as a mark for salad dressing.

(b) The word "Otokoyama" as a mark for sake imported from Japan. (The literal interpretation of the word from Japanese to English is "man/mountain." However, in Japan "otokoyama" is understood to designate a particular variety of sake.)

(c) The words "Filipino Yellow Pages" as a mark for a business telephone directory designed to serve the Filipino–American community in Southern California.

(d) The term "1–800–M-A-T-R-E-S-S" as a mark for retail mattress sales by telephone.

(e) The term "mattress.com" as a mark for online retail sales of mattresses, beds and bedding.

B. DESCRIPTIVE MARKS AND LANHAM ACT § 2(e)

The language of the Lanham Act § 2 preamble could be understood to prevent registration of non-distinctive marks. Nonetheless, subsections 2(e) and (f), read together, specifically provide that descriptive, deceptively misdescriptive, geographically descriptive, and surname marks, which traditionally have been viewed as non-distinctive at common law, cannot be registered without a demonstration of secondary meaning (or, in the language of subsection (f), a demonstration that the mark "has become distinctive.") 15 U.S.C. § 1052(e)–(f). A review of these "secondary meaning mark" categories is useful.

1. Marks That Are Merely Descriptive or Deceptively Misdescriptive

GIMIX, INC. v. JS & A GROUP, INC.

United States Court of Appeals, Seventh Circuit, 1983.
699 F.2d 901.

CUDAHY, CIRCUIT JUDGE.

* * * Appellant Gimix, Inc. ("Gimix") sued defendants Iwata Electric Co. ("Iwata"), Auto Page, Inc., and JS & A Group, Inc. ("JS & A") for trademark infringement * * *. The district court granted the defendants' motion for summary judgment on the grounds that the term in question—"Auto Page"—was generic and thus that Gimix had no protectible rights in it * * *. We affirm the district court's order, although we do so on grounds other than those relied on below.

I.

Plaintiff-appellant, Gimix, is a manufacturer of telephone products and computers. In 1975 Gimix began to market an automatic dialing device. The most common use of this device, although not the only use, is to connect an automatic telephone answering service with a paging terminal; the machine responds to a message left with an answering service by automatically dialing a paging terminal, causing it to notify the user, via the user's "beeper," that a message has been left on the telephone answering machine. * * *

On April 26, 1976, Gimix applied for a patent on this product, which it described in the application variously as an "automatic dialer" or as an "automatic page." The device has been advertised both under the name of "Gimix Auto Page" and under the name of "Gimix," although only the word "Gimix" was registered as a trademark. Gimix contends that it nonetheless holds trademark rights in the word "Auto Page."

[Defendant-appellee Iwata, a Japanese manufacturer and exporter, commenced use of "Auto Page" in marketing its car theft warning device in 1978, and registered "Auto Page" as the mark for that device in 1980. Shortly thereafter, Iwata began manufacturing and selling a wireless portable paging system consisting of a short-range transmitter and receiver for use in paging persons inside buildings or within a one-mile radius. Auto Page, Inc. is Iwata's United States distributor for this product, which is also marketed under the name "Auto Page."]

On December 10, 1980, Gimix filed a complaint charging Iwata, Auto Page, Inc. and JS & A with trademark infringement under federal trademark law and at common law * * *. On April 9, 1981, Auto Page, Inc. and Iwata moved for summary judgment on the ground that "Auto Page" was a generic name for the plaintiff's product and thus not an interest protectible at law. * * * They argued, as well, that Gimix would not be able to establish secondary meaning and that there was no likelihood of confusion, since the products were different and non-competing. In response to the motion for summary judgment, Gimix argued that the generic name for its product was an automatic dialer and that confusion was likely because the end result of all the products involved in the lawsuit was the same: paging. * * *

[The Seventh Circuit concluded that the term "auto page" was not generic.]

B. DESCRIPTIVENESS

Our holding that "Auto Page" is not a generic term does not dispose of the question whether it is a protectible trademark, for a term which is found to be merely descriptive is also incapable of being the subject of a valid trademark. This court has defined such a mark as being one which is "merely descriptive of the ingredients, qualities, or characteristics of an article of trade." Such terms are "unsuited to the function of marks both because they are poor means of distinguishing one source of services from another and because they are often necessary to the description of all goods or services of a similar nature."

Thus our initial inquiry here must be whether the term "Auto Page" is reasonably descriptive of the characteristics of the article in relation to which Gimix asserts a trademark. We hold that it is. As we have already discussed, one common use of the term "page" is to signify an individual whose role it is to summon another person, frequently because that person has received a telephone call. As a verb, "to page" is commonly understood (in a context apart from books) as meaning to locate a person via some sort of signalling system for the purpose of reaching her with an incoming telephone call. "Auto" in all of its manifestations retains some sense of self-activating or self-operating. As a combined term, therefore, "Auto Page" is a very apt description of Gimix' product, which is capable of paging a person in response to the receipt of an incoming telephone call, without the intervention of any independent agent or actor.

The rationale for prohibiting the appropriation of such a descriptive term as a trademark rests upon the equal right of another individual producing and marketing a similar product to describe his or her product with similar accuracy. Were this right not protected by the law, elements of the language could be monopolized in such a way as to impoverish others' ability to communicate. In recognition of the need to protect the language against incremental monopolization, this court has held that the terms "Auto Shampoo" and "Car Shampoo" were merely descriptive of the nature of a product used in cleaning and washing automobiles, and that "Telemed" merely described a process by which electrocardiograms were analyzed by computer over the telephone. In like fashion, we now hold that "Auto Page" is descriptive of the plaintiff's product here.

C. SECONDARY MEANING

Having found "Auto Page" to be a merely descriptive term, Gimix' alleged trademark could be upheld only if it were established that the term had acquired secondary meaning in the mind of the public. In other words, although the term's "primary" meaning was merely descriptive, if through use the public had come to identify the term with plaintiff's product in particular, the words would have become a valid trademark.

The factors which this court has indicated it will consider on the issue of secondary meaning include "[t]he amount and manner of advertising, volume of sales, the length and manner of use, direct consumer testimony and consumer surveys." These factors are relevant because they shed light upon the ultimate issue: how does the public regard the mark in question? Consumer testimony and consumer surveys are the only direct evidence on this question, and the existence of neither has been suggested here. The other factors are relevant in a more circumstantial fashion. Advertising is relevant because it is the means by which a manufacturer establishes its trademark in the minds of consumers as an indication of origin from one particular source; it is especially persuasive if the exposure has been "massive." In this case, however, far from creating an issue of fact as to a massive advertising campaign to establish "Auto Page" in the minds of the public as its exclusive mark, Gimix has failed to counter the impression that it in fact used the term inconsistently. Some Gimix flyers tout the product as "Gimix"; others as "Gimix Auto Page." Moreover, the period of time involved here, from the introduction of plaintiff's product in 1975 until the introduction of Iwata's similar product in 1980, is so brief as to cast serious doubt upon the very possibility of having established a strong secondary meaning * * *.

The only arguably relevant evidence Gimix has presented on this question is an affidavit and a letter by one dealer, a Mr. Sheldon Epstein, alleging that "Auto Page" was well-known as a trademark for Gimix' product and saying that he thought its use by JS & A was confusing. Even if evidence to this effect were presented at trial, however, it is not probative of a strong connection in the mind of the consuming public between the term and its source. Epstein was a Gimix dealer and his affidavit and letter were conclusory in nature and did not adequately place the question of secondary meaning to consumers in issue. Gimix, as the owner of an alleged mark we have found to be descriptive, has the burden of establishing a genuine issue of material fact as to whether its mark has attained secondary meaning in the mind of the public. Gimix has made no showing that sufficiently establishes such an issue of fact. We therefore hold that summary judgment was properly granted.

NOTES AND QUESTIONS

1. *The overall commercial impression.* To judge whether a mark is descriptive, one must consider the overall commercial impression the mark would make on the average prospective purchaser. When the mark contains more than one element (that is, when the mark is a "composite mark"), then one must evaluate the impression made by the mark as a whole, resisting the urge to break it into its constituent elements. It is not unusual to find that combining two or more descriptive elements results in a mark that is more than the sum of its elements and is inherently distinctive. See, e.g., Minnesota Mining and Manufacturing Co. v. Johnson & Johnson, 454 F.2d 1179 (C.C.P.A.1972) ("skinvisible" not merely descriptive of transparent medical tape). Moreover, combining descriptive elements with design elements often makes the mark as a whole non-descriptive. See, e.g., *In re* Clutter Control Inc., 231 U.S.P.Q. 588 (T.T.A.B. 1986) (descriptive words "Construct–A–Closet" combined with tube-like rendition of a double "C" for shelf components held not merely descriptive). Since rights in composite marks are in the mark as a whole, competitors need not be deprived of the individual descriptive components.

When a mark has two possible connotations, one descriptive and the other not, it is less likely to be deemed descriptive. For example, the phrase "sugar and spice" for bakery products not only describes ingredients of the products but also invokes the nursery rhyme, "sugar and spice and everything nice." In *In re* Colonial Stores, Inc., 394 F.2d 549 (C.C.P.A.1968), the court found this phrase not merely descriptive, because of its "reminiscent, suggestive, or associative connotation" with a non-descriptive idea.

As discussed in connection with generic terms, for purposes of classifying a mark, foreign words are translated into English and then judged for descriptiveness or genericness. Recognizable abbreviations are treated as though they were the abbreviated words. Misspelled words are treated as though properly spelled, as long as the phonetic identity between the misspelled word and the descriptive word remains. For example, the mark "C-thru" has been treated as the equivalent of the descriptive term "see-through." C–Thru Ruler Co. v. Needleman, 190 U.S.P.Q. 93 (E.D.Pa.1976).

2. *Descriptive vs. suggestive.* Could a reasonable argument have been made in *Gimix* that the mark "Auto Page" was suggestive, and thus inherently distinctive? How would you judge the mark "Security Center" for a business that provides private storage vaults, offers pick-up and delivery services, leases office space, and provides mail services? In Security Center, Ltd. v. First National Security Centers, 750 F.2d 1295 (5th Cir. 1985), the

Court of Appeals for the Fifth Circuit reversed the district court's finding that the mark was suggestive, finding instead that it was descriptive. The court explained:

> From the caselaw we distill two overarching questions to be considered in determining whether a mark is descriptive or suggestive. First, we must inquire how much imagination is required on the consumer's part in trying to cull some indication from the mark about the qualities, characteristics, effect, purpose, or ingredients of the product or service. Second, we determine whether sellers of similar products are likely to use, or actually do use, the term in connection with their goods. * * * The weight of these two considerations, taken together, determines the proper classification of the mark.

> On the issue of imaginativeness, we read "security center[s]" without saddling the phrase with unlikely meanings to demonstrate that it is ambiguous, hence imaginative, hence suggestive. A plausible interpretation of the phrase—not in vacuo, but in its natural setting—would be "a center where security is afforded one's property." To arrive at this definition, one must jettison all patently extraneous definitions of either "security" or "center." Even so, the phrase is not unambiguous. It is less ambiguous, however, when one adds into the equation the context and environment in which the mark is used—the natural environment in which the consumer would meet with the phrase. Nevertheless, there is no reason why a descriptive phrase could not be ambiguous—many, if not most, are.

> To be descriptive, a term need only describe the essence of a business, rather than to spell out comprehensively all its adjunct services. The essence of both the Security Center and First National Security Centers is that they provide secured storage facilities. They also engage in various related activities, but safekeeping is the gist of the trade. No English word would "describe" all the activities engaged in; and yet this fact alone would not make the uncomprehensive term "security" suggestive, merely because it might take imagination to deduce that the other activities play a part in the business. Indeed, even the most fecund imagination might not arrive at such a conclusion, though it might readily surmise accurately about certain characteristics of the business. For instance "center," modified as it is by "security," must needs be a place, probably a building. And "security," vague though it is, does connote certain qualities and characteristics about this "center." We conclude, then, that the mark, though hardly transparent, does give the unknowing consumer some idea of the function, quality, or components of the business. Still, we note that "security center" is just as likely to suggest a jail as a private vault.

> The imagination test might usefully be reversed by inquiring whether the first user has devised a term of some creativity or cleverness, as opposed to merely selecting a term that anyone might readily have chosen. (Any dunce could come up with a generic term, for example.) Creativity on the part of the mark's inventor is a correlative of imagination on the part of the consumer. With this correlative in mind, we have

no hesitation in stating that only a modicum of creativity was needed to arrive at "security center" as a name for the business in question. The name is merely a coupling of two quite common English words, and the coupling itself exhibits little originality.

We turn now to the issue whether those engaged in similar businesses have used the phrase, or are likely to do so. [Mr. Drummond testified that a number of members of the trade association to which the parties belong use the words "security" and/or "center" in their title.] [H]e stated that *both* words appear in twelve of the names in his files * * *. Nine of these use the phrase "security center," and three others have intervening words. [There are] twenty-six other private vault operations that use in their names "security" (in some form), and seven more that use "center." It is unclear from the testimony whether the roster of forty-five businesses using either "security" or "center" is to be compared against a total of ninety-nine extant businesses, or against the sixty-five that are members of Mr. Drummond's trade association. We do not think it matters; First National succeeded in demonstrating both likelihood of use and actual use.

Before leaving this point, we should spell out the policy underlying this particular prong of the investigation and demonstrate how our outcome serves that policy. We look into actual and likely use of a mark in order to determine whether its protection, i.e., its exclusion from the language freely available for commercial use, interferes with competition among providers of the same product or service. The more users there are of a term, the more its protection in a given case would be commercially disruptive and unfair to competitors. Under our jurisprudence, the same holds true even for *likelihood* of use. Given the number of enterprises throughout the nation that use "security center" in some form, the burgeoning nature of the industry, and the evidently increasingly common generic use of the term in some form, it would disserve the public to sanction use of the term by only one business in a given region, when other words can readily be affixed to the term for purposes of differentiation and clarity as to source. When we consider the net effect of our two paramount concerns within the descriptive/suggestive paradigm—imaginativeness, and actual and likely use of the mark—we are convinced that the scales are tipped decisively on the side of descriptiveness, hence nondistinctiveness.

3. *Deceptively misdescriptive marks.* When will a mark be "deceptively misdescriptive?" How does a deceptively misdescriptive mark differ from a deceptive mark, for which registration is prohibited under Lanham Act § 2(a), 15 U.S.C.A. § 1052(a)? Why require secondary meaning to register deceptively misdescriptive marks? Why recognize or register them at all?

PROBLEM

1. How would you classify the distinctiveness of the following marks?

    (a) "Platinum" as a mark for home mortgages;

    (b) "First Bank" as a mark for banking services;

(c) "Bed & Bath" as a mark for stores selling linens, bedding, towels and the like;

(d) "Season–All" for aluminum storm windows;

(e) "Volkswagen" for cars;

(f) "Kwix–Tart" for electric storage batteries;

(g) "Patents.com" as a mark for Internet-based software for tracking patents;

(h) "One Minute" as a mark for washing machines;

(i) "Nuhide" as a mark for dungarees.

2. *Marks That Are Primarily Geographically Descriptive or Deceptively Misdescriptive*

IN RE CALIFORNIA INNOVATIONS, INC.

United States Court of Appeals, Federal Circuit, 2003.
329 F.3d 1334.

RADER, CIRCUIT JUDGE.

California Innovations, Inc. (CA Innovations), a Canadian-based corporation, appeals the Trademark Trial and Appeal Board's refusal to register its mark—CALIFORNIA INNOVATIONS. Citing section 2(e)(3) of the Lanham Act, 15 U.S.C. § 1052(e)(3) (2000), the Board concluded that the mark was primarily geographically deceptively misdescriptive. Because the Board applied an outdated standard in its analysis under § 1052(e)(3), this court vacates the Board's decision and remands.

CA Innovations filed an intent-to-use trademark application, Serial No. 74/650,703, on March 23, 1995, for the composite mark CALIFORNIA INNOVATIONS and Design. The application sought registration for [a range of goods, including thermal insulated bags for food and beverages, thermal insulated tote bags for food or beverages, and thermal insulated wraps for cans to keep the containers cold or hot in International Class 21].

II.

The Lanham Act addresses geographical marks in three categories. The first category, § 1052(a), identifies geographically deceptive marks:

No trademark by which the goods of the applicant may be distinguished from the goods of others shall be refused registration on the principal register on account of its nature unless it—(a) Consists of or comprises immoral, *deceptive,* or scandalous matter; or matter which may disparage or falsely suggest a connection with persons, living or dead, institutions, beliefs, or national symbols, or bring them into contempt, or disrepute.

15 U.S.C. § 1052(a) (2000) (emphasis added). Although not expressly addressing geographical marks, § 1052(a) has traditionally been used to

reject geographic marks that materially deceive the public. A mark found to be deceptive under § 1052(a) cannot receive protection under the Lanham Act. To deny a geographic mark protection under § 1052(a), the PTO must establish that (1) the mark misrepresents or misdescribes the goods, (2) the public would likely believe the misrepresentation, and (3) the misrepresentation would materially affect the public's decision to purchase the goods. This test's central point of analysis is materiality because that finding shows that the misdescription deceived the consumer.

The other two categories of geographic marks are (1) "primarily geographically descriptive" marks and (2) "primarily geographically deceptively misdescriptive" marks under § 1052(e). The North American Free Trade Agreement [hereinafter NAFTA], as implemented by the NAFTA Implementation Act in 1993, has recently changed these two categories. Before the NAFTA changes, § 1052(e) and (f) stated:

> No trademark by which the goods of the applicant may be distinguished from the goods of others shall be refused registration on the principal register on account of its nature unless it—
>
> (e) Consists of a mark which ...
>
>> (2) when used on or in connection with the goods of the applicant is primarily geographically descriptive or deceptively misdescriptive of them. * * *
>
> (f) Except as expressly excluded in paragraphs (a)–(d) of this section, nothing in this chapter shall prevent the registration of a mark used by the applicant which has become distinctive of the applicant's goods in commerce.

15 U.S.C. § 1052(e)(2) and (f) (1988). The law treated these two categories of geographic marks identically. Specifically, the PTO generally placed a "primarily geographically descriptive" or "deceptively misdescriptive" mark on the supplemental register. Upon a showing of acquired distinctiveness, these marks could qualify for the principal register.

Thus, in contrast to the permanent loss of registration rights imposed on deceptive marks under § 1052(a), pre-NAFTA § 1052(e)(2) only required a temporary denial of registration on the principal register. Upon a showing of distinctiveness, these marks could acquire a place on the principal register. * * *

In the pre-NAFTA era, the focus on distinctiveness overshadowed the deceptiveness aspect of § 1052(e)(2) and made it quite easy for the PTO to deny registration on the principal register to geographically deceptively misdescriptive marks under § 1052(e)(2). On the other hand, the deception requirement of § 1052(a) protected against fraud and could not be overlooked. Therefore, the PTO had significantly more difficulty denying registration based on that higher standard.

[The court discusses the pre-NAFTA decision in *In re Nantucket, Inc.*, 677 F.2d 95 (CCPA 1982). In that case the Court of Customs and Patent Appeals established a two-part standard for identifying geographically descriptive or misdescriptive marks for purposes of Lanham Act § 2(e): 1) does the mark convey to a meaningful segment of the purchasing public primarily or immediately a geographical connotation? If so, 2) are those persons likely to think that the goods or services in fact come from that place (is there a "goods-place association")? If the answer to both questions is yes, then the mark is either primarily geographically descriptive or primarily geographically deceptively misdescriptive, depending on whether the goods came from the place indicated by the mark. However, the *California Innovations* court stresses that status as geographically descriptive or geographically deceptively misdescriptive made little difference prior to the NAFTA amendments: Either way, the mark could be registered on a showing of secondary meaning.]

As noted, the Lanham Act itself does not expressly require different tests for geographically misleading marks. In order to implement the Lanham Act prior to the NAFTA amendments, the PTO used a low standard to reject marks for geographically deceptive misdescriptiveness under pre-NAFTA § 1052(e), which was relatively simple to meet. In contrast, the PTO required a much more demanding finding to reject for geographical deception under § 1052(a). This distinction was justified because rejection under subsection (a) was final, while rejection under pre-NAFTA subsection (e)(2) was only temporary, until the applicant could show that the mark had become distinctive. The more drastic consequence establishes the propriety of the elevated materiality test in the context of a permanent ban on registration under § 1052(a).

NAFTA and its implementing legislation obliterated the distinction between geographically deceptive marks and primarily geographically deceptively misdescriptive marks. Article 1712 of NAFTA provides:

> 1. Each party [United States, Mexico, Canada] shall provide, in respect of geographical indications, the legal means for interested persons to prevent:
>
> > (a) the use of any means in the designation or presentation of a good that indicates or suggests that the good in question originates in a territory, region or locality other than the true place of origin, in a manner that misleads the public as to the geographical origin of the good....

See NAFTA, Dec. 17, 1992, art. 1712, 32 I.L.M. 605, 698. This treaty shifts the emphasis for geographically descriptive marks to prevention of any public deception. Accordingly, the NAFTA Act amended § 1052(e) to read:

> No trademark by which the goods of the applicant may be distinguished from the goods of others shall be refused registration on the principal register on account of its nature unless it–
>
> > (e) Consists of a mark which (1) when used on or in connection with the goods of the applicant is merely descriptive or deceptively misdescriptive of them, (2) when used on or in connection with the goods of the applicant is primarily geographically descriptive

of them, except as indications of regional origin may be registrable under section 4 [15 USCS § 1054], (3) when used on or in connection with the goods of the applicant is primarily geographically deceptively misdescriptive of them, (4) is primarily merely a surname, or (5) comprises any matter that, as a whole, is functional.

(f) Except as expressly excluded in subsections (a), (b), (c), (d), (e)(3), and (e)(5) of this section, nothing herein shall prevent the registration of a mark used by the applicant which has become distinctive of the applicant's goods in commerce.

15 U.S.C. § 1052(e)–(f) (2000).

Recognizing the new emphasis on prevention of public deception, the NAFTA amendments split the categories of geographically descriptive and geographically deceptively misdescriptive into two subsections (subsections (e)(2) and (e)(3) respectively). Under the amended Lanham Act, subsection (e)(3)—geographically deceptive misdescription—could no longer acquire distinctiveness under subsection (f). Accordingly, marks determined to be primarily geographically deceptively misdescriptive are permanently denied registration, as are deceptive marks under § 1052(a).

Thus, § 1052 no longer treats geographically deceptively misdescriptive marks differently from geographically deceptive marks. Like geographically deceptive marks, the analysis for primarily geographically deceptively misdescriptive marks under § 1052(e)(3) focuses on deception of, or fraud on, the consumer. The classifications under the new § 1052 clarify that these two deceptive categories both receive permanent rejection. Accordingly, the test for rejecting a deceptively misdescriptive mark is no longer simple lack of distinctiveness, but the higher showing of deceptiveness.

The legislative history of the NAFTA Act confirms the change in standard for geographically deceptively misdescriptive marks. In a congressional record statement, which appears to be the equivalent of a committee report, the Senate Judiciary Committee acknowledges the new standard for these marks:

[T]he bill creates a distinction in subsection 2(e) of the Trademark Act between geographically "descriptive" and "misdescriptive" marks and amends subsections 2(f) and 23(a) of the Act to preclude registration of "primarily geographically deceptively misdescriptive" marks on the principal and supplemental registers, respectively. The law as it relates to "primarily geographically descriptive" marks would remain unchanged.

139 Cong. Rec. S 16,092 (1993).

The amended Lanham Act gives geographically deceptively misdescriptive marks the same treatment as geographically deceptive marks under § 1052(a). Because both of these categories are subject to permanent denial of registration, the PTO may not simply rely on lack of distinctiveness to deny registration, but must make the more difficult showing of public deception. In other words, by placing geographically deceptively misdescriptive marks under subsection (e)(3) in the same fatal circumstances as deceptive marks under subsection (a), the NAFTA Act also elevated the standards for identifying those deceptive marks.

Before NAFTA, the PTO identified and denied registration to a primarily geographically deceptively misdescriptive mark with a showing that (1) the primary significance of the mark was a generally known geographic location, and (2) "the public was likely to believe the mark identified the place from which the goods originate and that the goods did not come from there." *In re Loew's*, 769 F.2d at 768. The second prong of the test represents the "goods-place association" between the mark and the goods at issue. This test raised an inference of deception based on the likelihood of a goods-place association that did not reflect the actual origin of the goods. A mere inference, however, is not enough to establish the deceptiveness that brings the harsh consequence of non-registrability under the amended Lanham Act. As noted, NAFTA and the amended Lanham Act place an emphasis on actual misleading of the public.

Therefore, the relatively easy burden of showing a naked goods-place association without proof that the association is material to the consumer's decision is no longer justified, because marks rejected under § 1052(e)(3) can no longer obtain registration through acquired distinctiveness under § 1052(f). To ensure a showing of deceptiveness and misleading before imposing the penalty of non-registrability, the PTO may not deny registration without a showing that the goods-place association made by the consumer is material to the consumer's decision to purchase those goods. This addition of a materiality inquiry equates this test with the elevated standard applied under § 1052(a). * * *

　　　　* * *

Thus, due to the NAFTA changes in the Lanham Act, the PTO must deny registration under § 1052(e)(3) if (1) the primary significance of the mark is a generally known geographic location, (2) the consuming public is likely to believe the place identified by the mark indicates the origin of the goods bearing the mark, when in fact the goods do not come from that place, and (3) the misrepresentation was a material factor in the consumer's decision.

As a result of the NAFTA changes to the Lanham Act, geographic deception is specifically dealt with in subsection (e)(3), while deception in general continues to be addressed under subsection (a). Consequently, this court anticipates that the PTO will usually address geographically deceptive marks under subsection (e)(3) of the amended Lanham Act rather than subsection (a). While there are identical legal standards for deception in each section, subsection (e)(3) specifically involves deception involving geographic marks.

III.

* * *

The parties agree that CA Innovations' goods do not originate in California. Under the first prong of the test—whether the mark's primary significance is a generally known geographic location—a composite mark such as the applicant's proposed mark must be evaluated as a whole. It is not erroneous, however, for the examiner to consider the significance of each element within the composite mark in the course of evaluating the mark as a whole.

The Board found that "the word CALIFORNIA is a prominent part of applicant's mark and is not overshadowed by either the word INNOVATIONS or the design element." Although the mark may also convey the idea of a creative, laid-back lifestyle or mindset, the Board properly recognized that such an association does not contradict the primary geographic significance of the mark. Even if the public may associate California with a particular life-style, the record supports the Board's finding that the primary meaning remains focused on the state of California. * * *

The second prong of the test requires proof that the public is likely to believe the applicant's goods originate in California. The Board stated that the examining attorney submitted excerpts from the Internet and the NEXIS database showing "some manufacturers and distributors of backpacks, tote bags, luggage, computer cases, and sport bags ... headquartered in California." * * *

* * *

CA Innovations argues that the examining attorney provided no evidence at all concerning insulated bags for food and wraps for cans in California. The Government contends that the evidence shows some examples of a lunch bag, presumed to be insulated, and insulated backpacks. According to the government, the evidence supports a finding of a goods-place association between California and insulated bags and wraps. This court has reviewed the publications and listings supplied by the examining attorney. At best, the evidence of a connection between California and insulated bags and wraps is tenuous. Even if the evidence supported a finding of a goods-place association, the PTO has yet to apply the materiality test in this case. This court declines to address that issue and apply the new standard in the first instance. Accordingly, this court vacates the finding of the Board that CA Innovations' mark is primarily geographically deceptively misdescriptive, and remands the case for further proceedings. On remand, the Board shall apply the new three-prong standard.

* * *

NOTES AND QUESTIONS

1. *Primarily geographically descriptive.* What is the purpose of conditioning rights in geographically descriptive marks on a showing of secondary meaning?

In rejecting an application for registration, the PTO must make a *prima facie* showing that the mark fails to qualify for registration under one of the provisions of Lanham Act § 2. In the case of rejections on the ground that the mark is primarily geographically descriptive or misdescriptive, the PTO must make a *prima facie* showing that the mark conveys primarily or immediately a geographical connotation and that the public understands the mark to indicate the geographic origin of the goods (makes a "goods-place association"). What evidence might be available for this purpose, and what should be deemed sufficient to shift the burden of proof to the applicant?

In re Loew's Theatres, Inc., 769 F.2d 764 (Fed.Cir.1985), addressed the "goods-place association" issue. In *Loew's*, the applicant sought to register "Durango" as a mark for chewing tobacco. The PTO rejected the application on the ground that the mark was primarily geographically deceptively misdescriptive of the goods (since they did not come from Durango). In support of the rejection, the examiner cited references indicating that Durango was a populous state and city in Mexico and that tobacco was an important crop of the Durango, Mexico area. Based on this evidence, he found that it would be reasonable for the purchasing public to expect chewing tobacco bearing the name Durango to have its origin in that area. The court of appeals found the evidence that tobacco was a crop of Durango a sufficient *prima facie* showing of a public goods/place association:

> While the [*Nantucket* decision] requires a goods/place association to support a refusal to register under § 2(e)(2), it does not follow that such association embraces only instances where the place is well-known or noted for the goods * * *. Rather, * * * the PTO must show only a reasonable basis for concluding that the public is likely to believe the mark identifies the place from which the goods originate. * * *

> [The applicant] attacks the sufficiency of the evidence of record on several grounds:

>> 1.　The Gazetteer relied upon by the PTO shows that Durango is also the name of towns in Colorado and in Spain. Therefore, per appellant, Durango would not be associated with Mexico's tobacco region of that name.

>> 2.　The PTO produced no evidence that the public would actually make the asserted association.

> Contrary to LTI's position, we conclude that the PTO made a prima facie showing of a goods/place association between tobacco and the geographic name Durango. Durango (Mexico) is not an obscure place name to the Mexican population of this country nor to reasonably informed non-Mexicans. The cited Gazetteer shows tobacco to be one in a short list of principal crops of the region. No more can be expected from

the PTO in the way of proof. The PTO does not have means to conduct a marketing survey as LTI would require. The practicalities of the limited resources available to the PTO are routinely taken into account in reviewing its administrative action. * * * We affirm that a prima facie case can be established by the type of evidence of record here where the question concerns the registrability of a geographic name.

Finally, it does not detract from the prima facie case made by the PTO that there are a few other uses of Durango as a geographic name, such as Durango, Colorado. The PTO's burden is simply to establish that there is a reasonable predicate for its conclusion that the public would be likely to make the particular goods/place association on which it relies. That there is more than one place bearing the name or that one place is better known than another is not dispositive. The issue is not the fame or exclusivity of the place name, but the likelihood that a particular place will be associated with particular goods. Thus, the mark DURANGO for skis might also be barred (without proof of secondary meaning) if it were shown that Durango, Colorado, is a ski resort.

Id., 769 F.2d at 767–69.

2. *The California Innovations construction of the NAFTA amendments.* Do you agree with the Federal Circuit's construction of the NAFTA amendments to Lanham Act 2(e) and (f)? Is it likely that Congress intended to permit registration of geographically deceptively misdescriptive marks whose misdescription would not be material to consumers' purchase decision? If that was Congress' intention, why did Congress enact the amendments? Is the court's interpretation consistent with general rules of statutory interpretation? Under the *California Innovations* construction, if a mark primarily conveys a geographic connotation, consumers are likely to believe that the goods come from the indicated place, the goods don't come from that place, but the misdescription of geographic origin is not material to consumers, can the mark be registered without a showing of secondary meaning? If so, does that make sense as a matter of policy?

3. *Materiality.* In *In re* Spirits International, N.V., 563 F.3d 1347 (Fed. Cir. 2009), the Court of Appeals for the Federal Circuit more closely considered when a geographic misdescription should be deemed "material." In that case the applicant sought to register the mark "Moskovskaya" for vodka that had no connection with the city of Moscow. The examiner and T.T.A.B. rejected the application as primarily geographically deceptively misdescriptive under Lanham Act § 2(e)(3). When translated from Russian to English, as required under the doctrine of foreign equivalents, the mark meant "of or from Moscow." The T.T.A.B. reasoned that Moscow is a generally known geographic location, and that there is a goods/place association between Moscow and vodka. Thus, prospective purchasers would be likely to believe that the mark indicates geographic origin in Moscow. Since Moscow is reputed for high quality vodka, the mark would materially influence their purchase decision.

The Federal Circuit rejected this conclusion, noting that under early common law, as well as more recent case precedent, a finding of materiality requires evidence that the misdescription would materially deceive a "significant" or "substantial" portion of prospective purchasers. Russian speakers (who would be able to make the translation "of or from Moscow") do not constitute a substantial portion of the entire U.S. population. (2000 census data show approximately 706,000 Russian speakers in the U.S.—.25% of the U.S. population.) To reject the application, the P.T.O. would need to make a prima facie showing that Russian speakers nonetheless constitute a substantial portion of vodka-consuming Americans (the relevant consuming public), or that some number of non-Russian speakers would understand the mark to suggest that the vodka came from Moscow, and that these two groups would together constitute a substantial portion of prospective purchasers.

PROBLEMS

1. How would you evaluate the mark "Rodeo Drive" as a mark for perfume? Is it likely to be disqualified or subject to a showing of secondary meaning under Lanham Act § 2(e) and (f)?

2. How would you evaluate the mark "Le Marais" as a service mark for a New York restaurant that serves a French Kosher cuisine? (Le Marais is the name of an upscale Jewish neighborhood in Paris, which has a number of fine restaurants.)

3. Marks that Are Primarily Merely a Surname

LANE CAPITAL MANAGEMENT, INC. v. LANE CAPITAL MANAGEMENT, INC.

United States Court of Appeals, Second Circuit, 1999.
192 F.3d 337.

PARKER, CIRCUIT JUDGE:

Defendant-appellant Lane Capital Management, Inc. appeals from an order of the United States District Court for the Southern District of New York * * * granting in part the motion for summary judgment by plaintiff-appellee Lane Capital Management, Inc., and enjoining appellant from using the service mark "Lane Capital Management," or any confusingly similar mark, in connection with its services on a nationwide basis.

    * * *

I. BACKGROUND

A. *The Parties*

Paul Fulenwider founded appellee and is the firm's manager and owner. Appellee was incorporated in Delaware on December 23, 1993, and immediately began business as an investment advisor. Appellee manages three investment funds which have $200 million in equity. * * * Fulenwider chose the name "Lane Capital Management" at the suggestion of his wife. Lane was his father's nickname and middle name, and is his son's middle name. Fulenwider also asserts that he chose the name because "it's like a narrow path or channel. It's a relatively straight and narrow path. You know, it can be a shipping lane, an air lane, or a bowling lane. And in the context of being a risk management type firm, the idea of having a channel or a path or a tightly controlled thing had a very interesting meaning."

Douglas C. Lane is the president and majority shareholder of appellant, which manages stock portfolios and provides investment advice for individuals. Appellant was incorporated in New York on July 6, 1994. Douglas Lane began soliciting clients the first week of July 1994 and began providing investment advisor services to clients on July 25, 1994. Appellant has 700 clients with portfolios or accounts valued at $700 million. At the suggestion of his wife, Douglas C. Lane chose the name "Lane Capital Management" because Lane is his surname and he wished to benefit from the good will he had built in his name over the course of his career as an investment advisor.

* * *

C. *The Suit*

Appellee commenced this action on February 14, 1997. Appellee alleged service mark infringement under 15 U.S.C. § 1125(a) * * *.

On January 27, 1998, the PTO granted appellee's application for a service mark for the principal register for "financial services, namely investment management in the field of securities, commodities and other investment media...." On February 11, 1998, appellee moved for summary judgment.

As relevant to this appeal, appellant raised two grounds in opposition to the motion. First, appellant contended that a genuine issue of material fact existed as to whether appellee's service mark was inherently distinctive. Appellant contended that the fact-finder could find that the purchasing public perceived appellee's mark to be primarily merely a surname. If the fact-finder did so find, then appellant's mark would not be inherently distinctive, and appellant would prevail on the infringement claim because there had been no showing of acquired distinctiveness. Appellant proffered three pieces of evidence in support of its argument that a genuine issue of material fact existed on this point. As an initial matter, appellant produced evidence that Lane is the 170th most popular surname in the United States and that in the New York City area there are almost 1,000 residential listings for individuals with the surname "Lane." Appellant also proffered evidence that there are numerous companies in New York City, nationwide, and on the Internet, who use Lane in their business names. Specifically, appellant pointed to over 125 business listings in the New York City area for companies with the name "Lane"; to a trademark research report that indicates "many more" companies who use the word "Lane" as a trade name in connection with financial services, insurance, or related businesses nationwide; and, to five companies that do business on the Internet under the name "Lane." Finally, appellant alleged that it

is a common industry practice for financial institutions to employ surnames in their trade names. * * *.

* * *

B.   The Protectibility of Appellee's Mark

1.   Basic Principles

The purpose of a mark is to identify the source of products—a word
which we use in this opinion as a synonym for goods and services—to
prospective consumers.[2]

To prevail on an infringement claim, a plaintiff must establish that it
possesses a valid, legally protectible mark and that defendant's subsequent use of a similar mark is likely to create confusion as to the origin of
the product at issue.

To be valid and protectible, a mark must be capable of distinguishing
the products it marks from those of others. There are five different
categories of terms with respect to the protection of a mark: generic,
descriptive, suggestive, arbitrary, and fanciful. * * *

The classification of a mark is a factual question. The factual issue
presented is how the purchasing public views the mark. The fact-finder is
not the designated representative of the purchasing public, and the fact-
finder's own perception of the mark is not the object of the inquiry.
Rather, the fact-finder's function is to determine, based on the evidence
before it, what the perception of the purchasing public is. * * *

Further, the relevant purchasing public is not the population at large,
but prospective purchasers of the product.

A certificate of registration with the PTO is prima facie evidence that
the mark is registered and valid (i.e., protectible), that the registrant owns
the mark, and that the registrant has the exclusive right to use the mark
in commerce. See 15 U.S.C. § 1115(a). Registration by the PTO without
proof of secondary meaning creates the presumption that the mark is
more than merely descriptive, and, thus, that the mark is inherently
distinctive. As a result, when a plaintiff sues for infringement of its
registered mark, the defendant bears the burden to rebut the presumption
of mark's protectibility by a preponderance of the evidence.

* * *

2.   Surnames

Marks that are "primarily merely surnames" constitute a specific
subcategory of descriptive marks, in that they describe the fact that the
named individual is affiliated with the firm. Whether a mark is primarily
merely a surname is a question of fact.

---

2. "[I]dentical standards" generally govern trademark claims and service mark claims. West
& Co. v. Arica Inst., Inc., 557 F.2d 338, 340 n. 1 (2d Cir. 1977); see 15 U.S.C. § 1053. Except
where otherwise noted, we make no distinction between the law governing these different marks.

A mark is primarily merely a surname if the primary significance of the mark to the purchasing public is that of a surname. In this context, "merely" is synonymous with "only," meaning that the question is whether the significance of the mark is "primarily only a surname." As stated in *In re* Rivera Watch Corp., 106 U.S.P.Q. 145, 149, 1955 WL 6450 (Comm'r Pat.1955):

> A trademark is a trademark only if it is used in trade. When it is used in trade it must have some impact upon the purchasing public, and it is that impact or impression which should be evaluated in determining whether or not the primary significance of a word when applied to a product is a surname significance. If it is, and it is only that, then it is primarily merely a surname.

Applying this principle, *Rivera Watch* noted that surnames such as "Reeves," "Higgins," and "Wayne" are primarily merely surnames whereas "King" and "Cotton" are not, because the latter have "well known meanings as a word in the language." *Id.* However, the mere fact that a word has a dictionary definition does not exclude the possibility that it is primarily merely a surname. See *In re* Nelson Souto Major Piquet, 5 U.S.P.Q.2d 1367, 1368, 1987 WL 123866 (T.T.A.B.1987) (dictionary reference to "obscure card game" did not rebut prima facie showing that "N. Piquet" was primarily merely a surname; affirming refusal to register).

Further, when the mark at issue is a composite mark consisting of personal names and additional words, the question becomes what the purchasing public would think when confronted with the mark as a whole.

3.   Judge Chin Correctly Granted Summary Judgment for Appellee

To defeat appellee's motion for summary judgment, appellant had to produce evidence from which the fact-finder could reasonably find that the mark was primarily merely a surname. * * *

As noted, to defeat appellee's motion for summary judgment, appellant proffered evidence that Lane is a popular surname, that people named Lane have named their businesses after themselves, and that it is common knowledge that this practice is particularly common in the financial services industry. This evidence is insufficient to create a genuine issue for trial.

The evidence that a mark is a common surname, in the absence of a dictionary definition, is evidence towards establishing a prima facie case of unprotectibility in a registration proceeding. Compare *In re* Harris–Intertype Corp., 518 F.2d 629, 631 (C.C.P.A.1975) (unusually large number of telephone directory listings established prima facie case that "Harris" was primarily merely a surname) with *In re* Kahan & Weisz Jewelry Mfg. Corp., 508 F.2d 831, 833 (C.C.P.A.1975) (listings in telephone directly cannot, standing alone, meet PTO's burden of showing that "Ducharme" is primarily merely a surname, particularly because there were relatively few listings). However, evidence that Lane is a common surname does not meet the burden of proving that it is primarily only a surname, especially since Lane—unlike, for example, Harris—does have a dictionary definition.

Appellant does not explain what it considers to be the evidentiary significance of the fact that businesses in New York City, nationwide, and on the Internet incorporate Lane in their names. The Federal Circuit has held that these types of listings can be admissible and probative of the strength of a service mark for the purposes of determining likelihood of confusion. * * * The common use of a term can reduce its effectiveness in distinguishing products. * * * However, the issue in this case is not likelihood of confusion, but the inherent distinctiveness of Lane Capital Management. To rebut the presumption of inherent distinctiveness, rather than undermine the strength of the mark for likelihood of confusion purposes, the listings must show that the use of Lane in other business names renders it more likely than not that consumers view Lane Capital Management as a surname. The proffered listings do not reasonably permit this inference. Many of the businesses on the lists patently use Lane as a surname. For example, in the list of nationwide companies containing Lane, a substantial number of the listings are people named Lane who are in business under their own name, or who have named their business after themselves (e.g., Kenneth S. Lane MD, Linda Lane Insurance). It is obvious that Lane is used as a surname in that context. However, it is unclear—and appellant has not produced evidence that tends to show—how consumers will rely on those examples when they encounter marks like "Lane Capital Management," in which Lane is not patently used as a surname.

For similar reasons, we see no genuine issue of material fact created by the evidence that it is common knowledge that financial service companies frequently employ surnames in their trade names. We basically agree with Judge Chin's analysis of this issue. As Judge Chin noted, Lane has a readily recognizable dictionary meaning that other surnamed financial institutions lack, does not contain additional markers pointing to its surname significance (e.g., " & Sons"), and does not dilute the dictionary meaning of Lane by including more than one apparent surname in the mark. Further, with little effort we could construct a competing list of financial services institutions that do not use surnames (Fidelity, Vanguard, Janus, and Citigroup come quickly to mind). * * *

In sum, all that this evidence tends to show is that Lane has been used in business names as a surname, and that the use of surnames in business names has often occurred in the parties' industry. This highly circumstantial evidence appears to be somewhat probative of the ultimate fact that appellant must prove. It may help to contextualize and bolster other, more direct evidence of consumer perception. It does not, however, appropriately support a conclusion that Lane is primarily merely a surname. We hold that, by itself, this evidence is too weak to create a genuine issue for trial.

    * * *

NOTES AND QUESTIONS

1. *Primarily merely a surname.* What other evidence might the appellant in *Lane* have introduced to overcome the statutorily created presumption of distinctiveness?

2. *The reasons underlying the rule.* Two considerations have been cited to justify conditioning rights in surnames on a showing of secondary meaning. First, as the Second Circuit notes in *Lane*, surname marks, like other kinds of marks addressed in Lanham Act § 2(e), may be viewed as descriptive of the goods or services, indicating that someone of that name has something to do with the product but not necessarily serving as a brand.

Second, there is a traditional interest in permitting individuals to use their own names in connection with their business. Courts have reasoned that this interest should be accommodated as fully as possible: no user should be able to exclude others from using a surname unless he has acquired secondary meaning, which makes exclusive rights necessary in order to avoid consumer confusion and appropriation of good will. As the Court of Appeals for the District of Columbia Circuit has explained:

> A seller's right to use his family name might have carried the day against a risk of buyer confusion in an era when the role of personal and localized reputation gave the right a more exalted status. In *Burgess v. Burgess*, 3 De G.M. & G. 896, 903–04, 43 Eng.Rep. 351, 354 (1853), the plaintiff's son had followed him into the trade of making anchovy paste; Lord Justice Bruce said: "All the Queen's subjects have a right, if they will, to manufacture and sell pickles and sauces, and not the less that their fathers have done so before them. All the Queen's subjects have a right to sell these articles in their own names, and not the less so that they bear the same name as their fathers." * * * But even quite old decisions have enjoined a second comer's use of his name where necessary to prevent confusion. * * * True, even recent decisions have invoked the right to use one's name, at least as an interest against which the senior user's are balanced. But its weight has decidedly diminished. The courts are now consistent in imposing tighter restrictions on the second comer in the face of possible confusion. * * *
>
> This trend in the law unsurprisingly reflects trends in the marketplace. In a world of primarily local trade, the goodwill of an anchovy paste seller may well have depended on his individual reputation within the community. Indeed, one elderly decision tells us that an entrepreneur's failure to use his family name once risked "the reproach of doing business under false colors." *Hat Corp.*, 4 F.Supp. at 623. By contrast, the court went on, "[i]n an age when by corporate activity, mass production, and national distribution, the truly personal element has been so largely squeezed out of business, there is naturally less legitimate pecuniary value in a family name." That was in 1933 and the point is more obvious today. Other than understandable pride and sense of identity, the modern businessman loses nothing by losing the name. A junior user's right to

use his name thus must yield to the extent its exercise causes confusion with the senior user's mark.

Basile, S.p.A. v. Basile, 899 F.2d 35, 39 (D.C.Cir.1990).

In addition to justifying a requirement of secondary meaning, the interest in using one's name also may influence the formulation of relief in trademark infringement cases. The Second Circuit's opinion in Taylor Wine Co. v. Bully Hill Vineyards, Inc., 569 F.2d 731 (2d Cir.1978), is illustrative. In that case the well established plaintiff, founded in 1880 and the owner of thirteen federally registered "Taylor" trademarks for wine, sued Bully Hill Vineyards, owned by Walter S. Taylor, claiming that the defendant's use of the mark "Walter S. Taylor" for a new line of wines infringed its registered marks. In addition to featuring the name "Walter S. Taylor" in large letters, the defendant's labels also featured the words "original," "Owner of the Taylor Family Estate," and "Bully Hill." The Court of Appeals had no doubt that the defendant's use infringed the plaintiff's trademarks, and that it should be enjoined. The issue was how broad the injunction should be.

Noting the traditional judicial respect for an individual's use of his name in business, the court recited what it regarded as the "guiding principle" in trademark surname cases: "Once an individual's name has acquired a secondary meaning in the marketplace, a later competitor who seeks to use the same or similar name must take 'reasonable precautions to prevent * * * mistake.' " Id., 569 F.2d at 734. The court elaborated that

> the fact that an alleged infringer has previously sold his business with its goodwill to the plaintiff makes a sweeping injunction more tolerable. So, too, if an individual enters a particular line of trade for no apparent reason other than to use a conveniently confusing surname to his advantage, the injunction is likely to be unlimited.
>
> If, however, the second comer owns the company himself and evinces a genuine interest in establishing an enterprise in which his own skill or knowledge can be made known to the public, that argues in favor of allowing him to use his own name in some restricted fashion. * * *
>   * * *
>
> Speaking generally, when the defendant demonstrates a genuine desire to build a business under his own name, courts have been reluctant to proscribe all surname use whatever even though the defendant's conduct has been less than exemplary. * * * [T]he courts have given qualified relief which reflects "a judicious balancing of the countervailing interests of protecting an individual's use of his own name and the avoiding of confusion."

Id., 569 F.2d at 735–36. The court ultimately concluded that the defendant could not use the "Taylor" name as a trademark, as such, but that it could show Walter S. Taylor's personal connection with Bully Hill. It could use Walter S. Taylor's signature on a Bully Hill label or advertisement, but only with an appropriate disclaimer that he was not connected with, or a successor to, the Taylor Wine Company. It must also be restrained from using such words as "original" or "Owner of the Taylor Family Estate." Id., 569 F.2d at 736.

PROBLEM

1. How would you evaluate the following marks for widgets:

    (a) "Schaub–Lorenz;"

    (b) "Mr. King;"

    (c) "Hutchinson Technology;"

    (d) "Da Vinci."

C. SPECIAL CONSIDERATIONS CONCERNING TRADE DRESS

In Two Pesos, Inc. v. Taco Cabana, Inc., 505 U.S. 763, 112 S.Ct. 2753, 120 L.Ed.2d 615 (1992), reprinted earlier in the Chapter, the Supreme Court held that inherently distinctive trade dress could be protected under Lanham Act § 43(a) without a showing of secondary meaning. (Recall that the trade dress at issue in that case consisted of the festive atmosphere of a Mexican restaurant, "having interior dining and patio areas decorated with artifacts, bright colors, paintings and murals.") However, in *Two Pesos*, the Supreme Court offered little guidance in determining *when* trade dress is inherently distinctive. Courts have recognized two general categories of protectible trade dress: product packaging and product features (or "product configuration"). The following two Subsections will discuss the courts' approach to evaluating the distinctiveness of trade dress in each category.

1. *Product Packaging Trade Dress*

In Paddington Corp. v. Attiki Importers & Distributors, Inc., 996 F.2d 577 (2d Cir.1993), the Court of Appeals for the Second Circuit undertook to determine when "packaging" trade dress is inherently distinctive. The court described the packaging trade dress before it (for imported Greek ouzo) as follows:

> No. 12 Ouzo is sold in a clear glass bottle with a large label on its side and a second, smaller label on its neck. Both labels are red, white, and black. The large label consists of a white background, inside of which is a rectangle consisting of a white top half and a red lower half, bordered by a thin black line. In the white half, there is a small "No" and a very large "12" in black block letters made to resemble a stencilled number on a crate or barrel. In the red lower half the word "ouzo" appears in white block letters with black shadowing, under which the word "Kaloyannis" is found in small, thin black letters, along with some other information in fine print. The neck label mirrors the large label in layout, except that a circle is used in place of the rectangle. The overall appearance of the bottle is simple, even stark.

Id., 996 F.2d at 581.

Turning to the issue of distinctiveness, the court observed:

> Since the choices that a producer has for packaging its products are * * * almost unlimited, typically a trade dress will be arbitrary or fanciful and thus inherently distinctive, and the only real question for the courts will be whether there is a likelihood of confusion between the products, provided, of course, the trade dress is not functional.

> However, where it is the custom of an industry to package products in a particular manner, a trade dress in that style would be generic and therefore not inherently distinctive. * * * Descriptive trade dresses also are not inherently distinctive. In Blau Plumbing, Inc. v. S.O.S. Fix–It, Inc., 781 F.2d 604, 609 (7th Cir.1986), the court found that an advertisement for a sewer service company containing four boxes labeled north, south, east, and west, each containing the locations and phone numbers of different branches of the company within that area of the city, was a trade dress descriptive of the company's ability to service the entire city. Similarly, a trade dress featuring an illustration of a shining car on a bottle of car wax likely would be descriptive.

> Trade dresses often utilize commonly used lettering styles, geometric shapes, or colors, or incorporate descriptive elements, such as an illustration of the sun on a bottle of sun tan lotion. While each of these elements individually would not be inherently distinctive, it is the combination of elements and the total impression that the dress gives to the observer that should be the focus of a court's analysis of distinctiveness. If the overall dress is arbitrary, fanciful, or suggestive, it is inherently distinctive despite its incorporation of generic or descriptive elements. One could no more deny protection to a trade dress for using commonly used elements than one could deny protec-

tion to a trademark because it consisted of a combination of commonly used letters of the alphabet.

> The No. 12 Ouzo bottle is inherently distinctive. There is no evidence in the record of any industry practice of using a design like the one that appears on the bottle's labels. There is nothing descriptive about the bottle and label design that conveys anything about its particular contents, except for the use of the trademark "No. 12 Ouzo," * * * and the fact that the bottle is of a style such that it indicates to the observer that it contains a liquid that probably is potable. The tone and layout of the colors, the style and size of the lettering, and, most important, the overall appearance of the bottle's labeling, are undeniably arbitrary. They were selected from an almost limitless supply of patterns, colors and designs. Since the No. 12 trade dress is arbitrary, and therefore protectible under the Lanham Act, the secondary meaning analysis is unnecessary * * *.

Id., 996 F.2d at 583–84.

What if a court finds that the individual elements of a plaintiff's trade dress are commonplace in the industry, but that no product possesses those same elements in combination? Should this compel a finding that the trade dress is inherently distinctive? The district court in Turtle Wax, Inc. v. First Brands Corp., 781 F.Supp. 1314, 1321 (N.D.Ill.1991), rejected such an argument:

> [S]uch a rule essentially would extend trade dress protection to every new compilation of elements in a particular field and would run afoul of the [tenet in Seabrook Foods, Inc. v. Bar–Well Foods Ltd., 568 F.2d 1342 (C.C.P.A.1977)] that a trade dress is not unique and distinctive if it merely refines common forms of ornamentation utilized in a particular field of goods. Presumably, it could be said about the trade dress of any new product that no competitive product combines precisely the same elements in its trade dress * * * However, that fact alone does not make the product's trade dress inherently distinctive. Any other rule essentially would require a finding of inherent distinctiveness whenever a new product enters the market.

2. *Product Feature Trade Dress*

In recent years many business entities have turned to § 43(a) trade dress claims as a means of prohibiting competitors from marketing knockoffs of their products. They have argued that consumers identify the goods of a particular producer and distinguish them from the goods of competitors not only through trademarks on product labels and product packaging, but also through the appearance of the products themselves. Thus, if competitors are permitted to copy the appearance of a plaintiff's product, consumers may be confused about the source, sponsorship or affiliation of the parties' respective products.

Some courts have expressed hesitation to embrace such claims due to concern that § 43(a) product feature trade dress claims might interfere unduly with competition, undercutting the careful limitations built into the patent and copyright laws. These courts have reasoned that if courts readily accept the plaintiffs' arguments and enjoin the copying, the plaintiffs may be able to avoid the rigors of competition without the necessity of satisfying the novelty and non-obviousness standards imposed by patent law, or the separability requirement imposed for pictorial, graphic or sculptural design features of useful articles under the copyright law.

While virtually all lower courts construed *Two Pesos* to mandate protection for inherently distinctive product feature trade dress without a showing of secondary meaning, the Circuits split rather dramatically on the proper method of determining when product feature trade dress is inherently distinctive. The concerns described above led some of the Circuits—particularly the Second and Third—to hold that the traditional *Abercrombie & Fitch* distinctiveness classification system was inappropriate for product feature trade dress. They held that a different, and more rigorous, standard should be imposed as a prerequisite to finding product feature trade dress inherently distinctive, and thus protected without a showing of secondary meaning. Other Circuits, including the Eighth and Fourth, maintained that *Two Pesos* mandated equal treatment for all forms of trade dress, and that the *Abercrombie & Fitch* classification system should be used in assessing the distinctiveness of all types of trade dress.

In the *Wal-Mart* case, reproduced below, the Supreme Court addressed this issue.

WAL-MART STORES, INC. v. SAMARA BROTHERS, INC.

United States Supreme Court, 2000.
529 U.S. 205, 120 S.Ct. 1339, 146 L.Ed.2d 182.

JUSTICE SCALIA delivered the opinion of the Court.

In this case, we decide under what circumstances a product's design is distinctive, and therefore protectible, in an action for infringement of unregistered trade dress under § 43(a) of the Trademark Act, 15 U.S.C. § 1125(a).

I

Respondent Samara Brothers, Inc., designs and manufactures children's clothing. Its primary product is a line of spring/summer one-piece seersucker outfits decorated with appliques of hearts, flowers, fruits, and the like. A number of chain stores, including JCPenney, sell this line of clothing under contract with Samara.

Petitioner Wal–Mart Stores, Inc., is one of the nation's best known retailers, selling among other things children's clothing. In 1995, Wal–Mart contracted with one of its suppliers, Judy–Philippine, Inc., to manufacture a line of children's outfits for sale in the 1996 spring/summer season. Wal–Mart sent Judy–Philippine photographs of a number of garments from Samara's line, on which Judy–Philippine's garments were to be based; Judy–Philippine duly copied, with only minor modifications, 16 of Samara's garments, many of which contained copyrighted elements. In 1996, Wal–Mart briskly sold the so-called knockoffs, generating more than $1.15 million in gross profits.

[After sending cease-and-desist letters, Samara brought this action against Wal-Mart, Judy-Philippine, and others for copyright infringement and infringement of unregistered trade dress under § 43(a) of the Lanham Act, 15 U.S.C. § 1125(a). The jury found in favor of Samara on all counts, and the trial judge denied Wal-Mart's motion for judgment as a matter of law on the issue of trade dress infringement. The Second Circuit affirmed the denial.]

II

The Lanham Act provides for the registration of trademarks, which it defines in § 45 to include "any word, name, symbol, or device, or any combination thereof [used or intended to be used] to identify and distinguish [a producer's] goods ... from those manufactured or sold by others and to indicate the source of the goods...." 15 U.S.C. § 1127. * * * In addition to protecting registered marks, the Lanham Act, in § 43(a), gives a producer a cause of action for the use by any person of "any word, term, name, symbol, or device, or any combination thereof ... which ... is likely to cause confusion ... as to the origin, sponsorship, or approval of his or her goods...." 15 U.S.C. § 1125(a). * * *

The breadth of the definition of marks registrable under § 2, and of the confusion-producing elements recited as actionable by § 43(a), has been held to embrace not just word marks, such as "Nike," and symbol marks, such as Nike's "swoosh" symbol, but also "trade dress"—a category that originally included only the packaging, or "dressing," of a product, but in recent years has been expanded by many courts of appeals to encompass the design of a product. These courts have assumed, often without discussion, that trade dress constitutes a "symbol" or "device" for purposes of the relevant sections, and we conclude likewise. "Since human beings might use as a 'symbol' or 'device' almost anything at all that is capable of carrying meaning, this language, read literally, is not restrictive." Qualitex Co. v. Jacobson Products Co., 514 U.S. 159, 162, 115 S.Ct. 1300, 131 L.Ed.2d 248 (1995). This reading of § 2 and § 43(a) is buttressed by a recently added subsection of § 43(a), § 43(a)(3), which refers specifically to "civil action[s] for trade dress infringement under this chapter for trade dress not registered on the principal register."

The text of § 43(a) provides little guidance as to the circumstances under which unregistered trade dress may be protected. It does require that a producer show that the allegedly infringing feature is not "functional," see § 43(a)(3), and is likely to cause confusion with the product for which protection is sought, see § 43(a)(1)(A), 15 U.S.C. § 1125(a)(1)(A). Nothing in § 43(a) explicitly requires a producer to show that its trade dress is distinctive, but courts have universally imposed that requirement, since without distinctiveness the trade dress would not "cause confusion ... as to the origin, sponsorship, or approval of [the] goods," as the section requires. Distinctiveness is, moreover, an explicit prerequisite for registration of trade dress under § 2, and "the general principles qualifying a mark for registration under § 2 of the Lanham Act are for the most part applicable in determining whether an unregistered mark is entitled to protection under § 43(a)." Two Pesos, Inc. v. Taco Cabana, Inc., 505 U.S. 763, 768, 112 S.Ct. 2753, 120 L.Ed.2d 615 (1992).

In evaluating the distinctiveness of a mark under § 2 (and therefore, by analogy, under § 43(a)), courts have held that a mark can be distinctive in one of two ways. First, a mark is inherently distinctive if "[its] intrinsic nature serves to identify a particular source." Ibid. In the context of word marks, courts have applied the now-classic test originally formulated by Judge Friendly, in which word marks that are "arbitrary" ("Camel" cigarettes), "fanciful" ("Kodak" film), or "suggestive" ("Tide" laundry detergent) are held to be inherently distinctive. Second, a mark has acquired distinctiveness, even if it is not inherently distinctive, if it has developed secondary meaning, which occurs when, "in the minds of the public, the primary significance of a [mark] is to identify the source of the product rather than the product itself." Inwood Laboratories, Inc. v. Ives Laboratories, Inc., 456 U.S. 844, 851, n. 11, 102 S.Ct. 2182, 72 L.Ed.2d 606 (1982).[1]

The judicial differentiation between marks that are inherently distinctive and those that have developed secondary meaning has solid foundation in the statute itself. Section 2 requires that registration be granted to any trademark "by which the goods of the applicant may be distinguished from the goods of others"—subject to various limited exceptions. 15 U.S.C. § 1052. It also provides, again with limited exceptions, that "nothing in this chapter shall prevent the registration of a mark used by the applicant which has become distinctive of the applicant's goods in commerce"—that is, which is not inherently distinctive but has become so only through secondary meaning. § 2(f), 15 U.S.C. § 1052(f). Nothing in § 2, however, demands the conclusion that every category of mark necessarily includes some marks "by which the goods of the applicant may be distinguished from the goods of others" without secondary meaning—that in every category some marks are inherently distinctive.

Indeed, with respect to at least one category of mark—colors—we have held that no mark can ever be inherently distinctive. In Qualitex, [we] held that a color could be protected as a trademark, but only upon a showing of secondary meaning. Reasoning by analogy to the Abercrombie & Fitch test developed for word marks, we noted that a product's color is

---

1. The phrase "secondary meaning" originally arose in the context of word marks, where it served to distinguish the source-identifying meaning from the ordinary, or "primary," meaning of the word. "Secondary meaning" has since come to refer to the acquired, source-identifying meaning of a non-word mark as well. it is often a misnomer in that context, since non-word marks ordinarily have no "primary" meaning. Clarity might well be served by using the term "acquired meaning" in both the word-mark and the non-word-mark contexts–but in this opinion we follow what has become the conventional terminology.

unlike a "fanciful," "arbitrary," or "suggestive" mark, since it does not "almost automatically tell a customer that [it] refer[s] to a brand," and does not "immediately . . . signal a brand or a product 'source,' " *Qualitex*, 514 U.S. at 163, 115 S.Ct. 1300. However, we noted that, "over time, customers may come to treat a particular color on a product or its packaging . . . as signifying a brand." *Id.*, at 162–163, 115 S.Ct. 1300. Because a color, like a "descriptive" word mark, could eventually "come to indicate a product's origin," we concluded that it could be protected upon a showing of secondary meaning.

It seems to us that design, like color, is not inherently distinctive. The attribution of inherent distinctiveness to certain categories of word marks and product packaging derives from the fact that the very purpose of attaching a particular word to a product, or encasing it in a distinctive packaging, is most often to identify the source of the product. Although the words and packaging can serve subsidiary functions—a suggestive word mark (such as "Tide" for laundry detergent), for instance, may invoke positive connotations in the consumer's mind, and a garish form of packaging (such as Tide's squat, brightly decorated plastic bottles for its liquid laundry detergent) may attract an otherwise indifferent consumer's attention on a crowded store shelf—their predominant function remains source identification. Consumers are therefore predisposed to regard those symbols as indication of the producer, which is why such symbols "almost automatically tell a customer that they refer to a brand," *Id.*, at 162–163, 115 S.Ct. 1300, and "immediately . . . signal a brand or a product 'source,' " *Id.*, at 163, 115 S.Ct. 1300. And where it is not reasonable to assume consumer predisposition to take an affixed word or packaging as indication of source—where, for example, the affixed word is descriptive of the product ("Tasty" bread) or of a geographic origin ("Georgia" peaches)—inherent distinctiveness will not be found. That is why the statute generally excludes, from those word marks that can be registered as inherently distinctive, words that are "merely descriptive" of the goods, § 2(e)(1), 15 U.S.C. § 1052(e)(1), or "primarily geographically descriptive of them," see § 2(e)(2), 15 U.S.C. § 1052(e)(2). In the case of product design, as in the case of color, we think consumer predisposition to equate the feature with the source does not exist. Consumers are aware of the reality that, almost invariably, even the most unusual of product designs—such as a cocktail shaker shaped like a penguin—is intended not to identify the source, but to render the product itself more useful or more appealing.

The fact that product design almost invariably serves purposes other than source identification not only renders inherent distinctiveness problematic; it also renders application of an inherent-distinctiveness principle more harmful to other consumer interests. Consumers should not be deprived of the benefits of competition with regard to the utilitarian and aesthetic purposes that product design ordinarily serves by a rule of law that facilitates plausible threats of suit against new entrants based upon alleged inherent distinctiveness. How easy it is to mount a plausible suit depends, of course, upon the clarity of the test for inherent distinctiveness, and where product design is concerned we have little confidence that a reasonably clear test can be devised. Respondent and the United States as *amicus curiae* urge us to adopt for product design relevant portions of the test formulated by the Court of Customs and Patent Appeals for product packaging in Seabrook Foods, Inc. v. Bar–Well Foods, Ltd., 568 F.2d 1342 (1977). That opinion, in determining the inherent distinctiveness of a product's packaging, considered, among other things, "whether it was a 'common' basic shape or design, whether it was unique or unusual in a particular field, [and] whether it was a mere refinement of a commonly-adopted and well-known form of ornamentation for a particular class of goods viewed by the public as a dress or ornamentation for the goods." *Id.*, at 1344. Such a test would rarely provide the basis for summary disposition of an anticompetitive strike suit. Indeed, at oral argument, counsel for the United States quite understandably would not give a definitive answer as to whether the test was met in this very case, saying only that "[t]his is a very difficult case for that purpose."

It is true, of course, that the person seeking to exclude new entrants would have to establish the nonfunctionality of the design feature—a showing that may involve consideration of its aesthetic appeal. Competition is deterred, however, not merely by successful suit but by the plausible threat of successful suit, and given the unlikelihood of inherently source-identifying design, the game of allowing suit based upon alleged inherent distinctiveness seems to us not worth the candle. That is especially so since the producer can ordinarily obtain protection for a design that is inherently source identifying (if any such exists), but that does not yet have secondary meaning, by securing a design patent or a copyright for the design—as, indeed, respondent did for certain elements of the designs in this case. The availability of these other protections greatly reduces any harm to the producer that might ensue from our conclusion that a product design cannot be protected under § 43(a) without a showing of secondary meaning.

Respondent contends that our decision in *Two Pesos* forecloses a conclusion that product-design trade dress can never be inherently distinctive. In that case, we held that the trade dress of a chain of Mexican restaurants, which the plaintiff described as "a festive eating atmosphere having interior dining and patio areas decorated with artifacts, bright colors, paintings and murals," could be protected under § 43(a) without a showing of secondary meaning. *Two Pesos* unquestionably establishes the legal principle that trade dress can be inherently distinctive, but it does not establish that product-design trade dress can be. *Two Pesos* is inapposite to our holding here because the trade dress at issue, the decor of a restaurant, seems to us not to constitute product design. It was either product packaging—which, as we have discussed, normally is taken by the consumer to indicate origin—or else some *tertium quid* that is akin to product packaging and has no bearing on the present case.

Respondent replies that this manner of distinguishing *Two Pesos* will force courts to draw difficult lines between product-design and product-packaging trade dress. There will indeed be some hard cases at the margin: a classic glass Coca–Cola bottle, for instance, may constitute packaging for those consumers who drink the Coke and then discard the bottle, but may constitute the product itself for those consumers who are bottle collectors, or part of the product itself for those consumers who buy Coke in the classic glass bottle, rather than a can, because they think it more stylish to drink from the former. We believe, however, that the frequency and the difficulty of having to distinguish between product design and product packaging will be much less than the frequency and the difficulty of having to decide when a product design is inherently distinctive. To the extent there are close cases, we believe that courts should err on the side of caution and classify ambiguous trade dress as product design, thereby requiring secondary meaning. The very closeness will suggest the existence of relatively small utility in adopting an inherent-distinctiveness principle, and relatively great consumer benefit in requiring a demonstration of secondary meaning.

* * *

We hold that, in an action for infringement of unregistered trade dress under § 43(a) of the Lanham Act, a product's design is distinctive, and therefore protectible, only upon a showing of secondary meaning. * * *

NOTES AND QUESTIONS

1. *Product configuration trade dress.* Can the Supreme Court's decision in *Wal-Mart* really be reconciled with its decision in *Two Pesos*? How would you articulate the policy concerns underlying the Court's opinion in *Wal-Mart*? Do you agree that they justify the Court's holding? What are the long-term implications of the *Wal-Mart* decision?

Will copyright and patent laws provide adequate protection to businesses against knock-offs? If not, is Lanham Act § 43(a) an appropriate way to augment that protection, or should some other route be taken?

After *Wal-Mart*, will secondary meaning be required in every case to register product configuration trade dress on the Principal Register?

What makes product configuration comparable to color, for purposes of the distinctiveness determination? Why was the restaurant decor at issue in *Two Pesos* more akin to product packaging than to product design? Apart from "erring on the side of caution," what standard should courts use to determine whether a particular trade dress is "packaging" trade dress (which can be inherently distinctive) or "product" trade dress (which cannot)?

PROBLEMS

1. Applicant wants to register a mark for pants, shorts, and skirts on the Principal Register. The mark consists of a label with the words "FLASH

DARE!'' in a V-shaped background, and cut-out areas located on each side of the label. The cut-out areas consist of a hole in the garment and a flap attached to the garment with a closure device. An illustration follows. Assuming that the applicant cannot demonstrate secondary meaning, should the mark be registered?

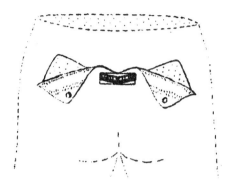

2. The applicant (an adult entertainment provider) employs male exotic dancers, who routinely wear shirt cuffs and a shirt collar with bow tie (and little else) while performing. Applicant now seeks to register its "cuffs and collar mark" for adult entertainment services. The application includes the drawing reproduced below and describes the mark as follows: "The mark consists of a three-dimensional nude, male torso with cuffs around the wrists and neck collar comprising of (sic) a bow tie. The dotted lines in the drawing indicate placement of the mark. The matter shown by the dotted lines is not claimed as part of the mark and serves only to show the position of the mark."

Should the applicant be required to demonstrate secondary meaning as a prerequisite to registration?

IV. DECEPTIVE MARKS AND LANHAM ACT § 2(a)

§ 1052. (§ 2) Trademarks Registrable on Principal Register; Concurrent Registration

No trademark by which the goods of the applicant may be distinguished from the goods of others shall be refused registration on the principal register on account of its nature unless it—

(a) Consists of or comprises immoral, deceptive, or scandalous matter; or matter which may disparage or falsely suggest a connection with persons, living or dead, institutions, beliefs, or national symbols, or bring them into contempt, or disrepute; or a geographical indication which, when used on or in connection with wines or spirits, identifies a place other than the origin of the goods and is first used on or in connection with wines or spirits by the applicant on or after one year after the date on which the WTO Agreement (as defined in section 3501(9) of Title 19) enters into force with respect to the United States. [January 1, 1996.]

15 U.S.C.A. § 1052(a).

IN RE BUDGE MANUFACTURING CO. INC.

United States Court of Appeals, Federal Circuit, 1988.
857 F.2d 773.

Nies, Circuit Judge.

Budge Manufacturing Co., Inc., appeals from the final decision of the United States Trademark Trial and Appeal Board refusing registration of LOVEE LAMB for "automotive seat covers," application Serial No. 507,-974 filed November 9, 1984. The basis for rejection is that the term LAMB is deceptive matter within the meaning of section 2(a) of the Lanham Act, 15 U.S.C. § 1052(a) (1982), as applied to Budge's goods which are made wholly from synthetic fibers. We affirm.

Opinion

Section 2(a) of the Lanham Act bars registration of a mark which: "Consists of or comprises ... deceptive ... matter...." As stated in *In re Automatic Radio Mfg. Co.*, 404 F.2d 1391, 1396 (CCPA 1969): "The proscription [of section 2(a)] is not against misdescriptive terms unless they are also deceptive." Thus, that a mark or part of a mark may be inapt or misdescriptive as applied to an applicant's goods does not make it "deceptive." *Id.* (AUTOMATIC RADIO not a deceptive mark for air conditioners, ignition systems, and antennas). Recognizing that premise, the Trademark Trial and Appeal Board has sought to articulate a standard by which "deceptive matter" under section 2(a) can be judged. In this case, the board applied the three-part test which was stated in *In re*

Shapely, Inc., 231 USPQ 72, 73 (TTAB 1986): (1) whether the term is misdescriptive as applied to the goods, (2) if so, whether anyone would be likely to believe the misrepresentation, and (3) whether the misrepresentation would materially affect a potential purchaser's decision to buy the goods.

Budge argues that the board was bound to follow the standard articulated in *In re Simmons, Inc.*, 192 USPQ 331 (TTAB 1976). Per Budge, *Simmons* sets forth a different standard in that it requires as a minimum that "the mark convey some information, upon which an intended customer may reasonably rely, concerning something about the character, quality, function, composition or use of the goods to induce the purchase thereof, but which information, in fact, is misleadingly false."

The standard applied by the board for determining deceptive matter in section 2(a) cases has not been uniformly articulated in some material respects. For example, in at least one opinion an intent to mislead was required to establish section 2(a) deceptiveness. However, while phrased differently, we discern no material difference between the standard set forth in *Shapely* and that in *Simmons*. Budge points to no substantive difference and, indeed, merely quarrels over the different result here from that in *Simmons*. Thus, we need not address the question of the extent to which panels of the board are required to follow prior decisions of other board panels.

What is more significant, in any event, is that this court is bound only by its own precedent, none of which Budge discusses. Although we will give deference in appropriate circumstances to a board's decision on a question of law, we are, of course, not bound by such rulings. Where the issue relates to deceptive misdescriptiveness within the meaning of 2(a), we are in general agreement with the standard set out by the board in *Shapely*, with the following amplification in part drawn from *Simmons*:

(1) Is the term misdescriptive of the character, quality, function, composition or use of the goods?

(2) If so, are prospective purchasers likely to believe that the misdescription actually describes the goods?

(3) If so, is the misdescription likely to affect the decision to purchase?

In *ex parte* prosecution, the burden is initially on the Patent and Trademark Office (PTO) to put forth sufficient evidence that the mark for which registration is sought meets the above criteria of unregistrability. Mindful that the PTO has limited facilities for acquiring evidence—it cannot, for example, be expected to conduct a survey of the marketplace or obtain consumer affidavits—we conclude that the evidence of record here is sufficient to establish a *prima facie* case of deceptiveness. That evidence shows with respect to the three-pronged test:

(1) Budge admits that its seat covers are not made from lamb or sheep products. Thus, the term LAMB is misdescriptive of its goods.

(2) Seat covers for various vehicles can be and are made from natural lambskin and sheepskin. Applicant itself makes automobile seat covers of natural sheepskin. Lambskin is defined, *inter alia*, as fine-grade sheep skin. See Webster's Third New International Dictionary 639 (unabr. 1976). The board's factual inference is reasonable that purchasers are likely to believe automobile seat covers denominated by the term LAMB or SHEEP are actually made from natural sheep or lamb skins.

(3) Evidence of record shows that natural sheepskin and lambskin is more expensive than simulated skins and that natural and synthetic skins have different characteristics. Thus, the misrepresentation is likely to affect the decision to purchase.

Faced with this *prima facie* case against registration, Budge had the burden to come forward with countering evidence to overcome the rejection. It wholly failed to do so.

Budge argues that its use of LAMB as part of its mark is not misdescriptive when considered in connection with the text in its advertising, which states that the cover is of "simulated sheepskin." Some, but not all, of Budge's specimen labels also have this text. This evidence is unpersuasive. In *R. Neumann & Co. v. Overseas Shipments, Inc.*, 326 F.2d 786 (1964), a similar argument was made that the mark DURA–HYDE on shoes was not deceptive as an indication of leather because of tags affixed to the shoes proclaiming the legend "Outwears leather." In discounting the evidence, the court stated: "The legends constitute advertisement material separate and apart from any trademark significance." To the same effect is *In re Bonide Chemical Co.*, 46 F.2d 705 (1931). There the court held, with respect to a clarifying statement made in advertising circulars, which the applicant urged negated the deceptive nature of the mark, "This argument is beside the issue. It is the word of the mark, not the statement of an advertising circular which appellant seeks to register. . . ."

Thus, we conclude that the board properly discounted Budge's advertising and labeling which indicate the actual fabric content. Misdescriptiveness of a term may be negated by its meaning in the context of the whole mark inasmuch as the combination is seen together and makes a unitary impression. *A.F. Gallun & Sons Corp. v. Aristocrat Leather Prods., Inc.*, 135 USPQ 459, 460 (TTAB 1962) (COPY CALF not misdescriptive, but rather suggests imitation of calf skin). The same is not true with respect to explanatory statements in advertising or on labels which purchasers may or may not note and which may or may not always be provided. The statutory provision bars registration of a mark comprising deceptive matter. Congress has said that the advantages of registration may not be extended to a mark which deceives the public. Thus, the mark standing alone must pass muster, for that is what the applicant seeks to register, not extraneous explanatory statements.

Budge next argues that no reasonable purchaser would expect to purchase lambskin automobile seat covers because none made of lambskin are on the market. Only sheepskin automobile seat covers are being made, per Budge. Not only was no evidence submitted on the point Budge seeks to make, only statements of Budge's attorney, but also the argument is without substance. The board properly equated sheepskin and lambskin based on the dictionary definition which indicates that the terms may be used interchangeably. In addition, while Budge would discount the evidence presented that bicycle and airline seat coverings are made of lambskin, we conclude that it does support the board's finding that there is nothing incongruous about automobile seat covers being made from lambskin. We also agree with the board's conclusion that any differences between sheepskin and lambskin would not be readily apparent to potential purchasers of automobile seat covers. The board's finding here that purchasers are likely to believe the misrepresentation is not clearly erroneous.

To overturn the board's finding that misdescribing synthetic fabric as "lamb" would affect a purchaser's decision to purchase the item, Budge merely reiterates its argument that its advertising negates the possibility of misdescriptiveness. We find that argument no more persuasive in this context than previously and, in any event, wholly unresponsive to this issue.

* * *

Conclusion

None of the facts found by the board have been shown to be clearly erroneous nor has the board erred as a matter of law. Accordingly, we affirm the board's decision that Budge's mark LOVEE LAMB for automobile seat covers made from synthetic fibers is deceptive within the meaning of 15 U.S.C. § 1052(a) and is, thus, barred from registration.

Notes and Questions

1. *Deceptive marks.* How does the standard the Federal Circuit states for "deceptive misdescriptiveness within the meaning of 2(a)" differ from the standard for determining whether a mark is "deceptively misdescriptive" for purposes of § 2(e)? Why have both provisions?

2. *Immoral or scandalous marks.* In *In re* Old Glory Condom Corp., 26 U.S.P.Q.2d 1216 (T.T.A.B. 1993), the applicant for registration sought to register its mark for condoms which, as shown below, consisted of the words, "Old Glory Condom Corp." and a pictorial representation of a condom decorated with stars and stripes, suggesting the American flag.

OLD GLORY CONDOM CORP

The examiner had refused registration on the ground that the mark constituted scandalous matter within the meaning of Lanham Act § 2(a). She argued that the mark was likely to offend a substantial component of the general public because of its use of American flag imagery to promote products associated with sexual activity. On appeal, the Trademark Trial and Appeal Board reversed.

> Taking as our starting point the definitions of "scandalous" to which the Board has in previous cases looked for assistance in applying Section 2(a), we have considered whether "OLD GLORY CONDOM CORP" (and flag design) can be characterized as "[g]iving offense to the conscience or moral feelings" or "shocking to the sense of decency or propriety." If any pattern can be discerned from the most recent cases * * * where the Board or its reviewing court found marks to be scandalous (viz., a mark for newsletters comprising a photograph of a man and woman kissing and embracing in a manner appearing to expose the man's genitalia, *In re* McGinley, 660 F.2d 481 (C.C.P.A.1981); "BULLSHIT," for handbags, wallets, etc., *In re* Tinseltown, Inc., 212 U.S.P.Q. 863 (T.T.A.B. 1981); and the design of a defecating dog, for shirts, Greyhound Corp. v. Both Worlds Inc., 6 U.S.P.Q.2d 1635 (T.T.A.B. 1988)), that pattern seems to describe marks that convey, in words or in pictures, vulgar imagery.

> As applicant has asserted (and as the examining attorney seems to concede), this Office has registered many trademarks and service marks that include imagery of the American flag. While we realize that there may be citizens of this country who disapprove of *any* commercial use of the American flag or American flag imagery, such uses have been sufficiently common that there can be no justification for refusing registration of applicant's mark simply on the basis of the presence in that mark of flag imagery. Nor do we find any evidence in this case that convinces us that a mark containing a pictorial representation of a condom should, simply because of that fact, be refused registration as scandalous. The particular pictorial presentation featured in applicant's composite mark was not found by the examining attorney to be vulgar, nor do we find it so. The examining attorney's objection to applicant's mark seems to be directed to the mark's linking of flag imagery and a pictorial representation of a condom, each of which, in itself, she apparently finds unobjectionable. * * *

Id., at 1221. As evidence that a substantial component of the public would be offended by the applicant's mark, the examining attorney alluded to an unsuccessful proposed amendment to the U.S. Constitution to prohibit flag burning and to a comment by Chief Justice Rehnquist in a dissent that many Americans have an "almost mystical reverence" for the American flag. She also introduced printouts of several news stories describing some persons' disapproval of a video public service announcement promoting voter registration that featured rock star Madonna, scantily clad and wrapped in an American flag. The Board was unimpressed.

> We are not willing, based solely on the examining attorney's opinion, the evidence of the reaction to the Madonna video, and the unsuccessful effort to amend the U.S. Constitution to prohibit the burning of the flag, to presume that the flag imagery of applicant's mark would give offense in a manner that must be deemed "scandalous" under Section 2(a).

Id. What sort of evidence might the PTO rely on to make a prima facie showing that a mark is unregisterable because immoral or scandalous? In *In re* Boulevard Entertainment, Inc., 334 F.3d 1336 (Fed.Cir. 2003), the Federal Circuit upheld the PTO's rejection of the marks "Jack–Off" and "1–800–JACK–OFF" as scandalous for "entertainment in the nature of adult-oriented conversations by telephone." As evidence to support its rejection, the PTO had relied on definitions of the term "jack-off" in four dictionaries, all of which identified the term as "vulgar." The issue was whether these dictionary references, by themselves, were sufficient to satisfy the PTO's burden of proof. The Federal Circuit held that they were, noting that "dictionary definitions represent an effort to distill the collective understanding of the community with respect to language." *Id.* at 1340. The court concluded that "in a case in which the evidence shows that the mark has only one pertinent meaning, dictionary evidence alone can be sufficient to satisfy the PTO's burden." The fact that dictionaries provide a second, non-vulgar meaning for the word will not undermine the PTO's showing, if the vulgar meaning is clearly the one invoked by the applicant's use, given the context of the marketplace and the goods or services described in the application to register.

If the PTO examiner approves an arguably "immoral" or "scandalous" mark for registration, who then has standing to file an opposition to prevent the registration from being carried out? In Ritchie v. Simpson, 170 F.3d 1092 (Fed.Cir.1999), O.J. Simpson filed to register the marks "O.J. Simpson," "O.J.," and "The Juice" for a range of goods including figurines, trading cards, sportswear, toys and prepaid telephone cards. The PTO examiner approved the marks and they were published for opposition. Ritchie, a lawyer and law school professor, filed an opposition, alleging that the marks comprised immoral or scandalous matter. The Trademark Trial and Appeal Board dismissed the opposition, finding that as a general member of the public, Ritchie lacked standing to oppose the registration. The Federal Circuit reversed, noting that "the policy behind the procedure for determining whether a mark is scandalous encourages, if not requires, participation by members of the general public who seek to participate through opposition proceedings." *Id.* at 1094. Looking to the language of Lanham Act § 13, the court held that an opposer must meet two requirements in order to have standing: The opposer must have a "real interest in the proceedings" and must have a "reasonable basis for his belief that he will be damaged by the registration."

The court went on to find that Ritchie had satisfied both of these requirements for purposes of a motion to dismiss. Ritchie alleged, among other things, that "the marks disparage[d] his values, especially those values relating to his family," because the marks were "synonymous with wife-beater and wife-murderer;" and "attempt to justify physical violence against women." *Id.*, at 1097. The Federal Circuit found that these allegations (which must be assumed to be true for purposes of the motion) were sufficient to establish a real interest on Ritchie's part. The court found that Ritchie alleged a reasonable basis for his belief that he would be damaged, as well, because he alleged that other members of the public shared the same belief of harm. Ritchie alleged that he had obtained "petitions signed by people from all over the United States who agree with him that the marks at issue are scandalous, denigrate their values, encourage spousal abuse and minimize the problem of domestic violence." *Id.*, at 1098.

3. *Matter which may disparage.* In Greyhound Corp. v. Both Worlds Inc., 6 U.S.P.Q.2d 1635 (T.T.A.B. 1988), which the Board cited in *Old Glory Condom*, the mark depicting a defecating dog (a greyhound) was found not only to be scandalous but also to disparage the Greyhound Bus Company, whose corporate symbol is a running greyhound. The Board explained:

> Disparagement is essentially a violation of one's right of privacy—the right to be "let alone" from contempt or ridicule. It has been defined as the publication of a statement which the publisher intends to be understood, or which the recipient reasonably should understand, as tending "to cast doubt upon the quality of another's land, chattels, or intangible things." Restatement (Second) of Torts § 629 (1977). The two elements of such a claim are (1) that the communication reasonably would be understood as referring to the plaintiff; and (2) that the communication is disparaging, that is, would be considered offensive or objectionable by a reasonable person of ordinary sensibilities.

Id. at 1639.

More recently, the Trademark Trial and Appeal Board relied on the Lanham Act § 2(a) "disparagement" prohibition to cancel registration of the "Redskins" mark, owned by the Washington Redskins football team. The Board found that the mark was disparaging to Native Americans. In its lengthy opinion, the Board explained that when a non-profit group (as opposed to an individual or a commercial entity) has allegedly been disparaged, the disparagement issue should be evaluated from the standpoint of a substantial component of the group (here, Native Americans) as of the time of the registration. The Board rejected suggestions of an intent requirement. Harjo v. Pro–Football, Inc., 50 U.S.P.Q.2d 1705 (T.T.A.B. 1999). The Board also found that the Redskins mark brought Native Americans into "contempt and disrepute," within the meaning of § 2(a), for the same reasons as it found the mark disparaging. However, the Board rejected arguments that the mark was also scandalous within the meaning of Lanham Act § 2(a). The Board noted that the proper measure for scandalousness is the reaction of a substantial component of American society as a whole, and found that there was general acceptance of "Redskins" as a mark for the football team.

The owner of the "Redskins" mark subsequently sought judicial review of the Trademark Trial and Appeal Board's decision to cancel the mark. The U.S. District Court for the District of Columbia found that the TTAB had correctly stated the standard for disparagement for purposes of Lanham Act § 2(a), but held (among other things) that the Board's decision to cancel on that ground was not supported by substantial evidence. Pro–Football, Inc. v. Harjo, 284 F.Supp.2d 96 (D.D.C. 2003), *remanded on other grounds*, 415 F.3d 44 (D.C. Cir. 2005).

4. *Matter which may falsely suggest a connection with persons, living or dead, institutions, beliefs, or national symbols.* In University of Notre Dame Du Lac v. J.C. Gourmet Food Imports Co., Inc., 703 F.2d 1372 (Fed.Cir.1983), the University opposed Gourmet's registration of the mark "Notre Dame" with design for its imported cheese on the ground that the mark falsely suggested a connection between the cheese and the University. The TTAB dismissed the opposition, and the Court of Appeals for the Federal Circuit affirmed. The court found it unlikely that Gourmet's use of the mark would lead purchasers to think that the cheese came from or was otherwise affiliated with the University. However, for purposes of § 2(a), a showing of likelihood of confusion was unnecessary. The drafters of § 2(a) intended to protect privacy interests, and a mark might violate a person's privacy interests even if it did not cause a likelihood of confusion about source, sponsorship or affiliation. The court determined that in order to demonstrate that an applicant's mark falsely suggests a connection with a person or institution, it must be shown that the mark is unmistakably associated with a particular personality or "persona." *Id.*, 703 F.2d at 1376. In this case, the court decided, such a showing could not be made.

> As the board noted, "Notre Dame" is not a name solely associated with the University. It serves to identify a famous and sacred religious figure and is used in the names of churches dedicated to Notre Dame, such as the Cathedral of Notre Dame in Paris, France. Thus, it cannot be said that the only "person" which the name possibly identifies is the University and that the mere use of NOTRE DAME by another appropriates its identity.

Id., 703 F.2d at 1377. The court suggested that its conclusion would differ if there were evidence that Gourmet had intended to identify the University with its mark. Evidence of such intent would be highly persuasive that the public would in fact make the intended false association. No such evidence, however, had been presented.

In *ex parte* proceedings, the Trademark Trial and Appeal Board applies the following four-part test to determine whether an applicant's mark "falsely suggests a connection" with a person:

1. The mark is the same as, or a close approximation of, the name or identity previously used by the other person;

2. The mark would be recognized as such, in that it points uniquely and unmistakably to that person;

3. The person is not connected to the goods sold by the applicant; and

4. The fame or reputation of the person is such that consumers of applicant's goods will presume a connection between her and the applicant's goods.

In re MC MC S.r.l., 88 U.S.P.Q.2d 1378 (2008).

5. *Geographic indications as marks for wines and spirits.* The Uruguay Round Agreements Act amended Lanham Act § 2(a) to prohibit registration of marks consisting of

> a geographical indication which, when used on or in connection with wines or spirits, identifies a place other than the origin of the goods and is first used on or in connection with wines or spirits by the applicant [on or after January 1, 1996].

15 U.S.C. § 1052(a). This change was necessary in order to comply with Article 23 of the TRIPs Agreement. The Senate Report on the Uruguay Round Agreements Act explained:

> As amended, section 2 of the Trademark Act will prohibit the registration of marks for wines and spirits that contain a geographical indication which refers to a place other than where a good actually originates. "Geographical indications" are defined in TRIPs as "indications which identify a good as originating in the territory of a Member, or a region or locality in that territory, where a given quality, reputation or other characteristic of the good is essentially attributable to its geographical origin." It is intended that this definition will be applied in the context of trademark registration and that a "geographical indication" as used in this provision will be interpreted to comprise only those areas which have a reputation for being associated with the specific goods at issue. Obscure areas or those that do not have a reputation or other characteristics generally associated with wines or spirits should not be prohibited from registration.

S. Rep. No. 412, 103d Cong., 2d Sess. 226–27 (1994). Marks containing geographical indications that are registered or in use prior to January 1, 1996 may be maintained. *Id.*

What does this new statutory language prohibit that would not already have been prohibited under the existing § 2(a) language? After the Uruguay Round and NAFTA amendments to Lanham Act § 2(a), (e) and (f), under what circumstances can a word or symbol with geographic connotations be registered?

PROBLEMS

1. Jimmy Buffett is a singer who is often associated in the public mind with the song "Wasting Away in Margaritaville." If X Company applied to register "Margaritaville" as a mark for restaurant services, could Buffett successfully oppose the registration under Lanham Act § 2(a)?

2. Would use of the marks "Da Vinci" for inexpensive jewelry or "Beethoven" for musical instruments falsely suggest a connection with the famous Leonardo or Ludwig, in violation of § 2(a)?

3. How would you evaluate the words "National Collection & Credit Control," shown with a drawing of an American eagle superimposed on an outline of the shape of the United States, for a collection agency?

4. How would you evaluate the words "Lo Fat Yumm" as a mark for deep-fried Chinese noodles?

5. How would you evaluate an application to register "Just Like Champagne" as a mark for sparkling wine made in California?

V. NON–FUNCTIONALITY

TRAFFIX DEVICES, INC. v. MARKETING DISPLAYS, INC.

United States Supreme Court, 2001.
532 U.S. 23, 121 S.Ct. 1255, 149 L.Ed.2d 164.

JUSTICE KENNEDY delivered the opinion of the Court.

Temporary road signs with warnings like "Road Work Ahead" or "Left Shoulder Closed" must withstand strong gusts of wind. An inventor named Robert Sarkisian obtained two utility patents for a mechanism built upon two springs (the dual-spring design) to keep these and other outdoor signs upright despite adverse wind conditions. The holder of the now-expired Sarkisian patents, respondent Marketing Displays, Inc. (MDI), established a successful business in the manufacture and sale of sign stands incorporating the patented feature. MDI's stands for road signs were recognizable to buyers and users (it says) because the dual-spring design was visible near the base of the sign.

This litigation followed after the patents expired and a competitor, TrafFix Devices, Inc., sold sign stands with a visible spring mechanism that looked like MDI's. MDI and TrafFix products looked alike because they were. When TrafFix started in business, it sent an MDI product abroad to have it reverse engineered, that is to say copied. * * *

MDI brought suit under the Trademark Act of 1964 (Lanham Act), 15 U.S.C. § 1051 *et seq.*, against TrafFix for * * * trade dress infringement (based on the copied dual-spring design) and unfair competition. * * *

I

* * * The District Court ruled against MDI on its trade dress claim. After determining that the one element of MDI's trade dress at issue was the dual-spring design, it held that "no reasonable trier of fact could determine that MDI has established secondary meaning" in its alleged trade dress. * * * As a second, independent reason to grant summary judgment in favor of TrafFix, the District Court determined the dual-spring design was functional. * * * In ruling on the functional aspect of the design, the District Court noted that Sixth Circuit precedent indicated that the burden was on MDI to prove that its trade dress was nonfunctional, and not on TrafFix to show that it was functional (a rule since

adopted by Congress, see 15 U.S.C. § 1125(a)(3)), and then went on to consider MDI's arguments that the dual-spring design was subject to trade dress protection. Finding none of MDI's contentions persuasive, the District Court concluded MDI had not "proffered sufficient evidence which would enable a reasonable trier of fact to find that MDI's vertical dual-spring design is *non*-functional." Summary judgment was entered against MDI on its trade dress claims.

The Court of Appeals for the Sixth Circuit reversed the trade dress ruling. The Court of Appeals held the District Court had erred in [finding that] the alleged trade dress was * * * a functional product configuration. The Court of Appeals suggested the District Court committed legal error by looking only to the dual-spring design when evaluating MDI's trade dress. Basic to its reasoning was the Court of Appeals' observation that it took "little imagination to conceive of a hidden dual-spring mechanism or a tri or quad-spring mechanism that might avoid infringing [MDI's] trade dress." The Court of Appeals explained that "[i]f TrafFix or another competitor chooses to use [MDI's] dual-spring design, then it will have to find *some other way* to set its sign apart to avoid infringing [MDI's] trade dress." It was not sufficient, according to the Court of Appeals, that allowing exclusive use of a particular feature such as the dual-spring design in the guise of trade dress would "hinde[r] competition somewhat." Rather, "[e]xclusive use of a feature must 'put competitors at a *significant* non-reputation-related disadvantage' before trade dress protection is denied on functionality grounds." In its criticism of the District Court's ruling on the trade dress question, the Court of Appeals took note of a split among Courts of Appeals in various other Circuits on the issue whether the existence of an expired utility patent forecloses the possibility of the patentee's claiming trade dress protection in the product's design. * * *

II

It is well established that trade dress can be protected under federal law. The design or packaging of a product may acquire a distinctiveness which serves to identify the product with its manufacturer or source; and a design or package which acquires this secondary meaning, assuming other requisites are met, is a trade dress which may not be used in a manner likely to cause confusion as to the origin, sponsorship, or approval of the goods. In these respects protection for trade dress exists to promote competition. As we explained just last Term, various Courts of Appeals have allowed claims of trade dress infringement relying on the general provision of the Lanham Act which provides a cause of action to one who is injured when a person uses "any word, term name, symbol, or device, or any combination thereof ... which is likely to cause confusion ... as to the origin, sponsorship, or approval of his or her goods." 15 U.S.C. § 1125(a)(1)(A). Congress confirmed this statutory protection for trade dress by amending the Lanham Act to recognize the concept. Title 15 U.S.C. § 1125(a)(3) provides: "In a civil action for trade dress infringement under this chapter for trade dress not registered on the principal register, the person who asserts trade dress protection has the burden of proving that the matter sought to be protected is not functional." This burden of proof gives force to the well-established rule that trade dress protection may not be claimed for product features that are functional. And in *Wal-Mart, supra,* we were careful to caution against misuse or over-extension of trade dress. We noted that "product design almost invariably serves purposes other than source identification."

Trade dress protection must subsist with the recognition that in many instances there is no prohibition against copying goods and products. In general, unless an intellectual property right such as a patent or copyright protects an item, it will be subject to copying. As the Court has explained, copying is not always discouraged or disfavored by the laws which preserve our competitive economy. *Bonito Boats, Inc. v. Thunder Craft Boats, Inc.,* 489 U.S. 141, 160, 109 S.Ct. 971, 103 L.Ed.2d 118 (1989). Allowing competitors to copy will have salutary effects in many instances. * * *

The principal question in this case is the effect of an expired patent on a claim of trade dress infringement. A prior patent, we conclude, has vital significance in resolving the trade dress claim. A utility patent is strong evidence that the features therein claimed are functional. If trade dress protection is sought for those features the strong evidence of functionality based on the previous patent adds great weight to the statutory presumption that features are deemed functional until proved otherwise by the party seeking trade dress protection. Where the expired patent claimed the features in question, one who seeks to establish trade dress protection must carry the heavy burden of showing that the feature is not functional, for instance by showing that it is merely an ornamental, incidental, or arbitrary aspect of the device.

In the case before us, the central advance claimed in the expired utility patents (the Sarkisian patents) is the dual-spring design; and the dual-spring design is the essential feature of the trade dress MDI now seeks to establish and to protect. The rule we have explained bars the trade dress claim, for MDI did not, and cannot, carry the burden of overcoming the strong evidentiary inference of functionality based on the disclosure of the dual-spring design in the claims of the expired patents.

    * * *

The rationale for the rule that the disclosure of a feature in the claims of a utility patent constitutes strong evidence of functionality is well illustrated in this case. The dual-spring design serves the important purpose of keeping the sign upright even in heavy wind conditions; and, as confirmed by the statements in the expired patents, it does so in a unique and useful manner. As the specification of one of the patents recites, prior art "devices, in practice, will topple under the force of a strong wind." The dual-spring design allows sign stands to resist toppling in strong winds. Using a dual-spring design rather than a single spring achieves important operational advantages. For example, the specifications of the patents note that the "use of a pair of springs ... as opposed to the use of a single spring to support the frame structure prevents canting or twisting of the sign around a vertical axis," and that, if not prevented, twisting "may cause damage to the spring structure and may result in tipping of the device." In the course of patent prosecution, it was said that "[t]he use of a pair of spring connections as opposed to a single spring connection ... forms an important part of this combination" because it "forc[es] the sign frame to tip along the longitudinal axis of the elongated ground-engaging members." The dual-spring design affects the cost of the device as well; it was acknowledged that the device "could use three springs but this would unnecessarily increase the cost of the device." These statements made in the patent applications and in the course of procuring the patents demonstrate the functionality of the design. MDI does not assert that any of these representations are mistaken or inaccurate, and this is further strong evidence of the functionality of the dual-spring design.

III

In finding for MDI on the trade dress issue the Court of Appeals gave insufficient recognition to the importance of the expired utility patents, and their evidentiary significance, in establishing the functionality of the device. The error likely was caused by its misinterpretation of trade dress principles in other respects. As we have noted, even if there has been no previous utility patent the party asserting trade dress has the burden to establish the nonfunctionality of alleged trade dress features. MDI could not meet this burden. Discussing trademarks, we have said " '[i]n general terms, a product feature is functional,' and cannot serve as a trademark, 'if it is essential to the use or purpose of the article or if it affects the cost or quality of the article.' " *Qualitex*, 514 U.S., at 165, 115 S.Ct. 1300 (quoting *Inwood Laboratories, Inc. v. Ives Laboratories, Inc.*, 456 U.S. 844, 850, n. 10, 102 S.Ct. 2182, 72 L.Ed.2d 606 (1982)). Expanding upon the meaning of this phrase, we have observed that a functional feature is one the "exclusive use of [which] would put competitors at a significant non-reputation-related disadvantage." 514 U.S., at 165, 115 S.Ct. 1300. The Court of Appeals in the instant case seemed to interpret this language to mean that a necessary test for functionality is "whether the particular product configuration is a competitive necessity." * * * This was incorrect as a comprehensive definition. As explained in *Qualitex, supra,* and *Inwood, supra,* a feature is also functional when it is essential to the use or purpose of the device or when it affects the cost or quality of the device. The *Qualitex* decision did not purport to displace this traditional rule. Instead, it quoted the rule as *Inwood* had set it forth. It is proper to inquire into a "significant non-reputation-related disadvantage" in cases of aesthetic functionality, the question involved in *Qualitex*. Where the design is functional under the *Inwood* formulation there is no need to proceed further to consider if there is a competitive necessity for the feature. In *Qualitex*, by contrast, aesthetic functionality was the central question, there having been no indication that the green-gold color of the laundry press pad had any bearing on the use or purpose of the product or its cost or quality.

The Court has allowed trade dress protection to certain product features that are inherently distinctive. In *Two Pesos*, however, the Court at the outset made the explicit analytic assumption that the trade dress features in question (decorations and other features to evoke a Mexican theme in a restaurant) were not functional. The trade dress in those cases did not bar competitors from copying functional product design features. In the instant case, beyond serving the purpose of informing consumers that the sign stands are made by MDI (assuming it does so), the dual-spring design provides a unique and useful mechanism to resist the force of the wind. Functionality having been established, whether MDI's dual-spring design has acquired secondary meaning need not be considered.

There is no need, furthermore, to engage, as did the Court of Appeals, in speculation about other design possibilities, such as using three or four springs which might serve the same purpose. Here, the functionality of the spring design means that competitors need not explore whether other spring juxtapositions might be used. The dual-spring design is not an arbitrary flourish in the configuration of MDI's product; it is the reason the device works. Other designs need not be attempted.

Because the dual-spring design is functional, it is unnecessary for competitors to explore designs to hide the springs, say by using a box or framework to cover them, as suggested by the Court of Appeals. The dual-spring design assures the user the device will work. If buyers are assured the product serves its purpose by seeing the operative mechanism that in itself serves an important market need. It would be at cross-purposes to those objectives, and something of a paradox, were we to require the manufacturer to conceal the very item the user seeks.

In a case where a manufacturer seeks to protect arbitrary, incidental, or ornamental aspects of features of a product found in the patent claims, such as arbitrary curves in the legs or an ornamental pattern painted on the springs, a different result might obtain. There the manufacturer could perhaps prove that those aspects do not serve a purpose within the terms of the utility patent. The inquiry into whether such features, asserted to be trade dress, are functional by reason of their inclusion in the claims of an expired utility patent could be aided by going beyond the claims and examining the patent and its prosecution history to see if the feature in question is shown as a useful part of the invention. No such claim is made here, however. MDI in essence seeks protection for the dual-spring design alone. The asserted trade dress consists simply of the dual-spring design, four legs, a base, an upright, and a sign. MDI has pointed to nothing arbitrary about the components of its device or the way they are assembled. The Lanham Act does not exist to reward manufacturers for their innovation in creating a particular device; that is the purpose of the patent law and its period of exclusivity. The Lanham Act, furthermore, does not protect trade dress in a functional design simply because an investment has been made to encourage the public to associate a particular functional feature with a single manufacturer or seller. The Court of Appeals erred in viewing MDI as possessing the right to exclude competitors from using a design identical to MDI's and to require those competitors to adopt a different design simply to avoid copying it. MDI cannot gain the exclusive right to produce sign stands using the dual-spring design by asserting that consumers associate it with the look of the invention itself. Whether a utility patent has expired or there has been no utility patent at all, a product design which has a particular appearance may be functional because it is "essential to the use or purpose of the article" or "affects the cost or quality of the article." *Inwood*, 456 U.S., at 850, n. 10, 102 S.Ct. 2182.

TrafFix and some of its *amici* argue that the Patent Clause of the Constitution, Art. I, § 8, cl. 8, of its own force, prohibits the holder of an expired utility patent from claiming trade dress protection. We need not resolve this question. If, despite the rule that functional features may not be the subject of trade dress protection, a case arises in which trade dress becomes the practical equivalent of an expired utility patent, that will be time enough to consider the matter. The judgment of the Court of Appeals is reversed, and the case is remanded for further proceedings consistent with this opinion.

NOTES AND QUESTIONS

1. *Utilitarian functionality.* The issue of functionality arises primarily when a business asserts trademark or trade dress rights in product packaging or in features of the product itself. Functionality questions generally do not

arise in connection with word marks, though the prohibition of rights in generic matter, which is regularly applied to word and some symbol marks, serves some of the same purposes as the functionality doctrine. The rule that functional features cannot serve as marks developed in the common law of unfair competition, and for years courts applied it in determining the enforceability and registrability of marks and trade dress under the Lanham Act, even though the Lanham Act itself made no mention of the rule. In 1998, Congress amended the Lanham Act specifically to enumerate functionality as a ground for denying registration, 15 U.S.C.A. § 1052(e)(5), and as a ground for canceling a registration. 15 U.S.C.A. § 1064(3). As the *TrafFix* Court notes, Congress has also amended Lanham Act § 43(a) expressly to incorporate the rule that functional matter cannot be protected. 15 U.S.C.A. § 1125(a).

Why should a business be prohibited from relying on trademark or unfair competition law to gain exclusive rights in a functional product feature, especially when the public has come to view the feature as an indication of origin? The Court of Customs and Patent Appeals has explained that the functionality doctrine:

> has as its genesis the judicial theory that there exists a fundamental right to compete through imitation of a competitor's product, which right can only be *temporarily* denied by the patent or copyright laws:
>
>> If one manufacturer should make an advance in effectiveness of operation, or in simplicity of form, or in utility of color; and if that advance did not entitle him to a monopoly by means of a machine or process or a product or a design patent; and if by means of unfair trade suits he could shut out other manufacturers who plainly intended to share in the benefits of unpatented utilities * * * he would be given gratuitously a monopoly more effective than that of the unobtainable patent in the ratio of eternity to seventeen years. [*Pope Automatic Merchandising Co. v. McCrum–Howell Co.*, 191 F. 979, 981–82 (7th Cir.1911).]
>
> An exception to the right to copy exists, however, where the product or package design under consideration is "nonfunctional" and serves to identify its manufacturer or seller * * *. Thus, when a design is "nonfunctional," the right to compete through imitation gives way, presumably upon balance of that right with the originator's right to prevent others from infringing upon an established symbol of trade identification.

In re Morton–Norwich Products, Inc., 671 F.2d 1332, 1336–37 (C.C.P.A. 1982).

Determining when a product feature is "functional" has proven difficult for the courts. In *Morton-Norwich*, the Court of Customs and Patent Appeals distinguished between "*de facto* functionality" and "*de jure* functionality," and this distinction was adopted in the case law of other jurisdictions. As the *Morton-Norwich* court explained, the term "*de facto* functionality" merely denotes functionality in the lay sense, indicating that the product or container design feature is directed to performance of a function—that it serves a utilitarian purpose. The *Morton-Norwich* court held that *de facto* functionality does not prevent protection of a product or container feature as an indication of origin. Only if the feature is deemed *de jure* functional should it be denied protection. The court then explained that *de jure* functionality depends on the extent to which competitors legitimately need to copy the product or container feature. The greater the legitimate need to copy, the more readily the feature should be deemed *de jure* functional and unprotectible. Thus, a court should ask whether the feature in question gives a utilitarian competitive advantage—whether it is superior in function or in economy of manufacture over the available alternatives, or is one of the few superior designs available. *Id.*, 671 F.2d at 1337, at 1339–40.

Under *TrafFix*, should inclusion in a design patent be treated in the same way as inclusion in the claims of a utility patent? Assuming that the applicant already has a design patent (or qualifies for one or has had one in the past) that covers the features the applicant seeks to protect as a mark or trade dress, what justification is there for providing trademark protection? Does recognizing trademark rights undercut Congress's purpose in limiting design patent protection to 14 years? Suppose that the applicant claims copyright in the design features described in the application. Should that be relevant?

After the Supreme Court's decision in *TrafFix*, is the *Morton-Norwich* distinction between *de facto* and *de jure* functionality still viable? Under what circumstances will the availability of alternative designs be relevant under the *TrafFix* decision? After *TrafFix*, what is the distinction between "utilitarian functionality" and "aesthetic functionality?" As the following two cases demonstrate, the Circuit Courts have not been able to agree on the meaning of *TrafFix*.

VALU ENGINEERING, INC. v. REXNORD CORP.

United States Court of Appeals, Federal Circuit, 2002.
278 F.3d 1268.

DYK, CIRCUIT JUDGE.

Valu Engineering, Inc. ("Valu") appeals a decision of the Trademark Trial and Appeal Board ("Board") sustaining Rexnord Corporation's ("Rexnord") opposition to registration of Valu's cross-sectional designs of conveyor guide rails as trademarks on the Principal Register. * * * Because the Board correctly concluded that Valu's cross-sectional designs of conveyor guide rails are *de jure* functional, we *affirm* the Board's refusal to register Valu's designs * * *.

BACKGROUND

On February 25, 1993, Valu filed three applications seeking registration of conveyor guide rail configurations in ROUND, FLAT, and TEE cross-sectional designs as trademarks on the Principal Register. Conveyor guide rails are rails positioned along the length of the sides of a conveyor to keep containers or objects that are traveling on the conveyor from falling off the conveyor. Valu's ROUND, FLAT, and TEE cross-sectional designs are shown below.

 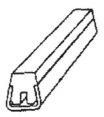 

* * *

The Board concluded that Valu's cross-sectional shapes were functional and not registrable, and sustained Rexnord's opposition on May 9, 2000. The Board analyzed the functionality of Valu's guide rail configurations by applying the factors outlined by this court's predecessor in *In re Morton–Norwich Products, Inc.,* 671 F.2d 1332, 1340–41 (CCPA 1982). The Board focused its functionality analysis on the utilitarian advantages of Valu's guide rail configurations [and] determined that all four *Morton-Norwich* factors weighed in favor of a finding of functionality. Specifically, the Board found that: an abandoned utility patent application filed by Valu but rejected under 35 U.S.C. § 103 "disclose[d] certain utilitarian advantages of [Valu's] guide rail designs, and that those advantages . . . result from the shape of the guide rail designs," Valu's advertising materials "tout the utilitarian advantages of [Valu's] guide rail design[s]," the "limited number of basic guide rail designs . . . should not be counted as 'alternative designs' " because they are "dictated solely by function," and Valu's guide rail designs "result[ ] in a comparatively simple or cheap method of manufacturing." Accordingly, the Board sustained Rexnord's opposition and refused to register Valu's guide rail designs.

    * * *

DISCUSSION

    * * *

Beginning at least with the decisions in *Kellogg Co. v. National Biscuit Co.,* 305 U.S. 111, 119–120 (1938), and *Morton-Norwich,* 671 F.2d at 1336–37, the Supreme Court and this court's predecessor have held that a mark is not registerable if the design described is functional, because "patent law, not trade dress law, is the principal means for providing exclusive rights in useful product features." The First Circuit likewise has noted that "[t]rademark and trade dress law cannot be used to evade the requirements of utility patents, nor the limits on monopolies imposed by the Patent Clause of the Constitution." Commentators share this view: "trademark law cannot properly make an 'end run' around the strict requirements of utility patent law by giving equivalent rights to exclude." J. Thomas McCarthy, *1 McCarthy on Trademarks and Unfair Competition* § 7:64, 7–147 (4th ed.2001).

The functionality doctrine thus accommodates trademark law to the policies of patent law:

> The functionality doctrine prevents trademark law, which seeks to promote competition by protecting a firm's reputation, from instead inhibiting legitimate competition by allowing a producer to control a useful product feature. It is the province of patent law, not trademark law, to encourage invention by granting inventors a monopoly over new product designs or functions for a limited time, 35 U.S.C. §§ 154,173, after which competitors are free to use the innovation. If a product's functional features could be used as trademarks, however, a monopoly over such features could be obtained without regard to whether they qualify as patents and could be extended forever (because trademarks may be renewed in perpetuity).

Qualitex Co. v. Jacobson Prods. Co., 514 U.S. 159, 165 (1995).

Our decisions distinguish *de facto* functional features, which may be entitled to trademark protection, from *de jure* functional features, which are not. "In essence, *de facto* functional means that the design of a product has a function, *i.e.,* a bottle of any design holds fluid." *De facto* functionality does not necessarily defeat registerability. * * * *De jure* functionality means that the product has a particular shape "because it works better in this shape."

* * *

III

Definition of "functionality"

To determine whether a particular product design is *de jure* functional, we have applied the *"Morton-Norwich* factors": (1) the existence of a utility patent disclosing the utilitarian advantages of the design; (2) advertising materials in which the originator of the design touts the design's utilitarian advantages; (3) the availability to competitors of functionally equivalent designs; and (4) facts indicating that the design results in a comparatively simple or cheap method of manufacturing the product.

Because we have an obligation to apply the case law in effect at the time of decision, we must determine whether the Supreme Court's recent decision in *TrafFix Devices, Inc. v. Marketing Displays, Inc.,* 532 U.S. 23 (2001) altered the *Morton-Norwich* factors. * * *

[In *TrafFix,* the] court of appeals criticized the district court for finding functionality where granting MDI exclusive use of the design would only hinder competition "somewhat," stating: "[t]he appropriate question is whether the particular product configuration is a competitive necessity," and that "[h]aving any effect on cost or quality is not enough. Exclusive use of a feature must 'put competitors at a *significant* non-reputation-related disadvantage' before trade dress protection is denied on functionality grounds."

The Supreme Court reversed, finding that the court of appeals gave insufficient evidentiary weight to the expired utility patents in analyzing the functionality of the dual-spring design, and that it overread *Qualitex:* "the Court of Appeals ... seemed to interpret [*Qualitex*] to mean that a necessary test for functionality is 'whether the particular product configuration is a competitive necessity.' ... This was incorrect as a comprehensive definition." The Court then reaffirmed the "traditional rule" of *Inwood* that "a product feature is functional if it is essential to the use or purpose of the article or if it affects the cost or quality of the article." The Court further held that once a product feature is found to be functional under this "traditional rule," "there is no need to proceed further to consider if there is competitive necessity for the feature," and consequently "[t]here is no need ... to engage ... in speculation about other design possibilities.... Other designs need not be attempted."[4]

We do not understand the Supreme Court's decision in *TrafFix* to have altered the *Morton-Norwich* analysis. As noted above, the *Morton-Norwich* factors aid in the determination of whether a particular feature is functional, and the third factor focuses on the availability of "other alternatives." We did not in the past under the third factor require that the opposing party establish that there was a "competitive necessity" for the product feature. Nothing in *TrafFix* suggests that consideration of alternative designs is not properly part of the overall mix, and we do not read the Court's observations in *TrafFix* as rendering the availability of alternative designs irrelevant. Rather, we conclude that the Court merely noted that once a product feature is found functional based on other considerations[5] there is no need to consider the availability of alternative designs, because the feature cannot be given trade dress protection merely because there are alternative designs available. But that does not mean that the availability of alternative designs cannot be a legitimate source of evidence to determine whether a feature is functional in the first place. We find it significant that neither party argues that *TrafFix* changed the law of functionality, and that scholarly commentary has reached exactly the same conclusion that we have:

> In the author's view, the observations by the Supreme Court in *TrafFix* do not mean that the availability of alternative designs cannot be a legitimate source of evidence to determine in the first instance if a particular feature is in fact "functional." Rather, the Court merely said that once a design is found to be functional, it

4. *TrafFix* suggests that there may be a requirement under *Qualitex* to inquire into a "significant non-reputation-related disadvantage" in aesthetic functionality cases, because aesthetic functionality was "the question involved in *Qualitex*." 121 S.Ct. at 1262. This statement has been criticized because "aesthetic functionality was *not* the central question in the *Qualitex* case." J. Thomas McCarthy, *1 McCarthy on Trademarks and Unfair Competition* § 7:80, 7–198 (4th ed.2001). We need not decide what role, if any, the determination of a "significant non-reputation-related disadvantage" plays in aesthetic functionality cases, because aesthetic functionality is not at issue here.

5. For example, a feature may be found functional where the feature "affects the cost or quality of the device." *TrafFix,* 121 S.Ct. at 1263.

cannot be given trade dress status merely because there are alternative designs available. . . .

. . . .

. . . The existence of actual or potential alternative designs that work equally well strongly suggests that the particular design used by plaintiff is not needed by competitors to effectively compete on the merits.

J.Thomas McCarthy, *1 McCarthy on Trademarks and Unfair Competition,* § 7:75, 7–180–1 (4th ed.2001). In sum, *TrafFix* does not render the Board's use of the *Morton-Norwich* factors erroneous.

* * *

[Turning to the particular product features before it, the court finds that the Board did not err in finding that the conveyor guide rail designs were functional.]

An important policy underlying the functionality doctrine is the preservation of competition. As this court's predecessor noted in *Morton-Norwich,* the "effect upon competition 'is really the crux' " of the functionality inquiry, and, accordingly, the functionality doctrine preserves competition by ensuring competitors "the right to compete effectively." As we stated in *Brunswick Corp. v. British Seagull Ltd.,* 35 F.3d 1527, 1531 (Fed.Cir.1994), "functionality rests on 'utility,' which is determined in light of 'superiority of design,' and rests upon the foundation of 'effective competition.' " The importance of competition was reaffirmed in *Qualitex,* in which the Supreme Court focused on whether a feature "would put competitors at a significant non-reputation-related disadvantage." And when discussing the policy behind limiting trade dress protection, the Supreme Court in *TrafFix* noted that "[a]llowing competitors to copy will have salutary effects in many instances."

Thus, in determining "functionality," the Board must assess the effect registration of a mark would have on competition. * * *

* * *

EPPENDORF–NETHELER–HINZ GMBH v. RITTER GMBH

United States Court of Appeals, Fifth Circuit, 2002.
289 F.3d 351, *cert. denied,* 537 U.S. 1071, 123 S.Ct. 671, 154 L.Ed.2d 565.

EDITH H. JONES, CIRCUIT JUDGE:

Defendants–Appellants Ritter GMBH and RK Manufacturing, Inc., appeal the district court's judgment that they infringed upon Eppendorf–Netheler–Hinz GMBH's trade-dress rights in violation of the Lanham Act, 15 U.S.C. § 1125(a). For the reasons discussed below, we conclude that Eppendorf failed to carry its burden of proof on the issue of non-functionality, and reverse the judgment of the district court.

I. BACKGROUND

Eppendorf is a German company which manufactures medical and laboratory equipment. At issue in this case is Eppendorf's line of disposable pipette tips and dispenser syringes capable of accurate and rapid "multiple dispensing" of liquids. Eppendorf's disposable pipette tips are sold in the United States marked with the word-marks "COMBITIPS," "EPPENDORF" and "EPPENDORF COMBITIPS" (hereinafter referred to as "Combitips"). Eppendorf manufactures eight Combitip sizes, from .05 milliliters to 50 milliliters. All eight sizes are designed to fit into the "Combitip Dispenser Syringe". By attaching a Combitip to the dispenser syringe, a user can rapidly dispense liquids in precisely measured aliquots.

Ritter is a German manufacturer specializing in injection-molded plastic products. In the early 1990s, Ritter began manufacturing disposable pipettes virtually identical to the Combitips. At that time, there was a large American market for disposable pipettes, and the market was dominated by Eppendorf. Ritter, through its American distributor, RK Manufacturing, Inc., entered the American market in March of 1994. Ritter's disposable pipettes were marked with the word-mark "RITIPS" (hereinafter "Ritips") and distributed in boxes marked with Ritips and Ritter's name. Ritter also introduced its own dispenser syringe, known in the market as the "Ripette". However, the Ritips were compatible with Eppendorf's Combitip Dispenser Syringe, and the Ritips were marketed as a "direct replacement" for Combitips. Ritter priced its Ritips below Eppendorf's Combitips in an attempt to acquire market share from Eppendorf.

* * * Eppendorf alleges that Ritter infringed on its trade dress rights by "slavishly mimick[ing]" the design and trade dress of the "entire family of Eppendorf [Combitips]." Eppendorf contends that Ritter infringed upon eight elements of the Combitips's trade dress: (1) the flange on top of the tip; (2) the fins connecting the flange to the body of the tip; (3) the plunger head; (4) the plunger; (5) the length of the tips; (6) the eight sizes of the tips; (7) the coloring scheme on the tips; and (8) the angle of the stump on the tips. * * *

* * *

II. DISCUSSION

* * *

Trade dress protection * * * is not intended to create patent-like rights in innovative aspects of product design. Trade dress protection, unlike patent law, does not foster innovation by preventing reverse engineering or copying of innovative product design features. * * * "Trade dress protection must subsist with the recognition that in many instances there is no prohibition against copying goods and products." *TrafFix,* 532 U.S. at 29. Therefore, trade dress protection extends only to incidental, arbitrary or ornamental product features which identify the source of the product. If a product feature is functional, it cannot be protected trade dress. Unless protected by patent or copyright, functional product features may be copied freely by competitors in the marketplace. "Allowing competitors to copy will have salutary effects in many instances. 'Reverse engineering ... often leads to significant advances in technology.'" *Id.* (citing *Bonito Boats, Inc. v. Thunder Craft Boats, Inc.,* 489 U.S. 141, 160 (1989)).

* * *

It is clear that functional product features do not qualify for trade dress protection. However, the definition of "functionality" has not enjoyed such clarity. In *TrafFix,* the Supreme Court recognized two tests for functionality. First, the Court recognized the "traditional" definition of functionality: "a product feature is functional, and cannot serve as a trademark, 'if it is essential to the use or purpose of the article or if it affects the cost or quality of an article.'" Under this traditional definition, if a product feature is "the reason the device works," then the feature is functional. The availability of alternative designs is irrelevant.

In addition to the traditional definition, *TrafFix* recognized a second test for functionality: "a functional feature is one the 'exclusive use of which would put competitors at a significant non-reputation-related disadvantage.'" This "competitive necessity" test for functionality is an expansion of the traditional test. The Court emphasized, however, that the "competitive necessity" test is not "a comprehensive definition" of functionality. The primary test for functionality is the traditional test, and there is no need to consider the "competitive necessity" test where a product feature is functional under the traditional definition.

Eppendorf correctly argues that before *TrafFix,* this circuit had adopted a "utilitarian" test of functionality. Under this utilitarian test, "[t]he ultimate inquiry concerning functionality [ ] is whether characterizing a feature or configuration as protected 'will hinder competition or impinge upon the rights of others to compete effectively in the sale of goods.'" *Sicilia Di R. Biebow & Co. v. Cox,* 732 F.2d 417, 429 (5th Cir.1984). This court's "utilitarian" test, with its focus on the ability of competitors to compete effectively in the marketplace, is virtually identical to the "competitive necessity" test discussed in *TrafFix.* Accordingly, *TrafFix* supersedes the definition of functionality previously adopted by this court. The "utilitarian" test, although still valid as a secondary test, is not a comprehensive definition of functionality. In light of *TrafFix,* the primary test for determining whether a product feature is functional is whether the feature is essential to the use or purpose of the product or whether it affects the cost or quality of the product.[4]

---

4. This court noted in *Sunbeam* that the utilitarian definition of functionality "lowers the threshold for trade dress protection." 123 F.3d at 255 n. 18. This broad definition of functionality is not consistent with the Court's recent discussion of functionality. The Court, in *TrafFix,* cautioned against "misuse or over-extension of trade dress [protection]." A product feature that satisfies the traditional definition of functionality is not shielded from functional status merely because the feature is not a competitive necessity.

B.

The crucial issue presented by this appeal is whether the eight design elements of the Eppendorf Combitips are functional as a matter of law. This case was tried in June of 2000, almost ten months before the Supreme Court decided *TrafFix*. The district court, correctly applying this circuit's utilitarian test of functionality, instructed the jury as follows:

> A design or characteristic is nonfunctional if there are reasonably effective and efficient alternatives possible. Hence, a product's trade dress is functional only, one, if competitors need to incorporate it in order to compete effectively because it is essential to the product's use, or, two, if it significantly affects the cost or quality of the article. A design is functional and thus unprotectable if it is one of a limited number of equally efficient options available to competitors and free competition would be significantly disadvantaged by according the design trademark protection.

Relying on this instruction, the jury determined that the Combitips were non-functional. * * *

* * *

Eppendorf contends that the evidence supports the jury's finding of non-functionality because "[t]he evidence clearly established that there were alternative designs to each of the eight non-functional features." Indeed, there is extensive testimony in the record regarding available alternative designs for each of the eight elements. For example, Eppendorf's expert testified that the number of fins under the flange "could be increased or decreased or their appearance could be changed." Thus, Eppendorf argues that the fins are non-functional because alternative designs are available to competitors in the marketplace.

Eppendorf's argument, while consistent with this circuit's utilitarian definition of functionality, is unpersuasive in light of the Court's discussion of functionality in *TrafFix*. As explained above, the primary test for functionality is whether the product feature is essential to the use or purpose of the product or if it affects the cost or quality of the product. In *TrafFix,* the Court determined that the dual-spring design on a wind-resistant road sign was functional because the dual-spring design "provides a unique and useful mechanism to resist the force of the wind." The Court rejected the argument that the springs were non-functional because a competitor could use three or four springs which would serve the same purpose. The Court explained,

> There is no need, furthermore, to engage, as did the Court of Appeals, in speculation about other design possibilities, such as using three or four springs which might serve the same purpose. . . . The dual-spring design is not an arbitrary flourish in the configuration of [the road sign]; it is the reason the device works. Other designs need not be attempted.

Accordingly, the design features for which Eppendorf seeks trade dress rights are functional if they are essential to the use or purpose of the Combitips or affect the cost or quality of the Combitips. The availability of alternative designs is irrelevant.

In this case it is undisputed that the Combitips's fins provide necessary support for the flange. Without the fins, the flange is subject to deformation. The only testimony offered by Eppendorf to prove nonfunctionality of the fins related to the existence of alternative design possibilities. Eppendorf's functionality expert testified that the appearance and number of fins could be changed without affecting the function of the fins. Eppendorf did not prove, however, that the fins are an arbitrary flourish which serve no purpose in the Combitips. Rather, Eppendorf's experts concede that fins of some shape, size or number are necessary to provide support for the flange and to prevent deformation of the product. Thus, the fins are design elements necessary to the operation of the product.[5] Because the fins are essential to the operation of the Combitips, they are functional as a matter of law, and it is unnecessary to consider design alternatives available in the marketplace. *TrafFix*, 532 U.S. at 33–34.

Likewise, a careful review of the record demonstrates that Eppendorf failed to prove that the remaining Combitip design elements are unnecessary, non-essential design elements. It is undisputed that: (1) The flange is necessary to connect the Combitip to the dispenser syringe; (2) The rings on the plunger head are necessary to lock the plunger into a cylinder in the dispenser syringe; (3) The plunger is necessary to push liquids out of the tip, and the ribs on the plunger stabilize its action; (4) The tips at the lower end of the Combitips are designed to easily fit into test tubes and other receptacles; (5) The size of the Combitip determines the dispensed volume, and size is essential to accurate and efficient dispensing; (6) The color scheme used on the Combitip—clear plastic with black lettering—enables the user easily to see and measure the amount of liquid in the Combitip, and black is standard in the medical industry; and (7) The stumps of the larger Combitips must be angled to separate air bubbles from the liquid and ensure that the full volume of liquid is dispensed. Thus, all eight design elements identified by Eppendorf are essential to the operation of the Combitips.

Eppendorf's theory of non-functionality focused on the existence of alternative designs. Eppendorf's design expert summarized Eppendorf's approach to functionality: "My conclusion was that to achieve the same functional purpose, [the design elements identified by Eppendorf] can be changed significantly, considerably without affecting the overall intended purpose." Although alternative designs are relevant to the utilitarian test of functionality, alternative designs are not germane to the traditional test for functionality. Each of the eight design elements identified by Eppen-

---

5. Additionally, Eppendorf's experts concede that some of the suggested alternative designs would slightly increase the cost of the product. This provides further support for the conclusion that the fins are functional under the traditional definition of functionality.

dorf is essential to the use or purpose of the Combitips, and is not arbitrary or ornamental features. Therefore, no reasonable juror could conclude that Eppendorf carried its burden of proving non-functionality.

* * *

NOTES AND QUESTIONS

1. *Construing TrafFix.* Which construction—the Federal Circuit's construction in *Valu Engineering* or the Fifth Circuit's construction in *Eppendorf*—more nearly reflects the Supreme Court's intent in *TrafFix*? Essentially three different approaches to functionality existed in the pre-*TrafFix* case precedent.

Under the first, which might be called the "role of the feature" approach, functionality turns on the relationship of the claimed feature (or combination of features) to the product, or on the role that the feature plays within the product. Does the feature contribute in a significant way to the use or purpose of the product? Does the feature affect the product's cost or quality? If so, it is functional. On the other hand, if the feature is merely incidental or arbitrary in the context of the product, or serves only to identify the source of the product, it is non-functional. Courts applying this standard essentially assume that if the product feature contributes significantly to the function of the product, or to the ease of its manufacture or use, competition will be impaired if the feature becomes the subject of exclusive trade dress rights. This standard is consistent with the Restatement of Torts § 742, which provides:

> A feature of goods is functional * * * if it affects their purpose, action or performance, or the facility or economy of processing, handling, or using them; it is non-functional if it does not have any of such effects.

Restatement of Torts § 742 (1938). The Restatement adds that "[w]hen goods are bought largely for their aesthetic value, their features may be functional because they definitely contribute to that value and thus aid the performance of an object for which the goods are intended." *Id.* The availability of alternative features does not appear to be a consideration at any point in the Restatement of Torts' functionality determination. This represents a strict approach to functionality that significantly restricts trade dress protection for product features.

The second approach, which might be called the "practical effect" approach, is much more lenient. Unlike the "role of the feature" approach, which emphasizes the interest in permitting competitors to copy unpatented, utilitarian product features, the "practical effect" standard assumes that consumers' interest in avoiding confusion and producers' economic interest in their chosen identifiers ("the trademark interests") are as important as competitors' interest in copying unpatented utilitarian product features. Thus a product feature will only be deemed functional if it appears that protection will in fact significantly interfere with other producers' ability to compete. Accordingly, courts undertake to evaluate the actual, practical effect of protecting the product feature under the particular circumstances of the case. One of the primary considerations they entertain in making this determination is whether there are sufficient, equally good alternative product features available to competitors. If there are, it is assumed that protecting the plaintiff's particular feature will not significantly interfere with competition, and the trademark interests should predominate. Thus, to be functional under the "practical effect" approach, the product feature at issue must be superior to the available alternatives, or give some unique advantage. This standard leads to much greater trade dress protection for product features than the "role of the feature" approach. The American Law Institute gave this approach a boost in the Restatement (Third) of Unfair Competition. The Restatement provides that a design is functional if it:

> affords benefits in the manufacturing, marketing, or use of the goods or services with which the design is used, apart from any benefits attributable to the design's significance as an indication of source, that are important to effective competition by others and that are not practically available through the use of alternative designs.

Restatement (Third) of Unfair Competition § 17 (1995). Comment b emphasizes that: "A packaging or product feature is not functional merely because the feature serves a utilitarian purpose. The recognition of trademark rights is precluded only when the particular design affords benefits that are not practically available through alternative designs."

The third approach, which might be called the "important ingredient" approach, asks whether the product feature is an important ingredient in the commercial success of the product. This approach appears to rely on consumer perceptions and motivation in purchasing the product at issue. See, e.g., Insty*Bit, Inc. v. Poly–Tech Indus., Inc., 95 F.3d 663, 673 (8th Cir. 1996).

Which, (if any) of these three approaches does the *TrafFix* opinion endorse? Which approach does the *Valu Engineering* court seem to advocate? Which approach does the *Eppendorf* court seem to adopt? Which makes more sense, as a matter of policy? Assuming that the Supreme Court intended to adopt a "role of the feature" standard for measuring functionality in *TrafFix*, is there any room left for consideration of alternative design features? For discussion of these issues, see Barrett, *Consolidating the Diffuse Paths to Trade Dress Functionality: Encountering TrafFix on the Way to Sears*, 61 Wash. & Lee L.Rev 79 (2004).

2. *Aesthetic functionality.* Both the *Valu Engineering* and the *Eppendorf* decisions purported to apply the *Inwood Laboratories* standard (which the *TrafFix* decision held to be the "traditional" or primary standard for evaluating functionality), and found the product features at issue functional. Recall that in *TrafFix*, the Court held that even if a product feature is non-functional under the *Inwood Laboratories* standard, it must also be found non-functional under the *Qualitex* standard before it can be protected as trade dress. Thus, even if the feature is merely "arbitrary, incidental or ornamental" it might be deemed functional if its protection would put competitors at a "significant non-reputation-related disadvantage" (or if it is a "competitive necessity"). The Supreme Court referred to the *Qualitex* standard as a test for "aesthetic functionality." The existence and nature of "aesthetic functionality" had been highly controversial and uncertain in the Circuit Courts of Appeals. Some circuits had rejected the notion that purely aesthetic product features could be deemed functional. See, e.g., Sicilia Di R. Biebow & Co. v.

Cox, 732 F.2d 417, 429 (5th Cir. 1984); Clicks Billiards, Inc. v. Sixshooters, Inc., 251 F.3d 1252, 1260 (9th Cir. 2001). Why might the concept of "aesthetic functionality" be controversial? For criticism of the aesthetic functionality concept, see 1 J.T. McCarthy, McCarthy on Trademarks and Unfair Competition § 7.81 (4th ed. 1996).

3. *Alternative means for protecting product designs.* We have reviewed three intellectual property doctrines–copyright, design patents, and trademark/unfair competition law–that may afford rights in product designs. How does each approach compare, with regard to eligibility for protection, strength of protection, and efficiency? From a designer's standpoint, is one approach preferable to the others? Do the three alternatives, in combination, provide sufficient protection for industrial designs, or is a new, *sui generis* approach to protection needed, as many advocates have argued? Is trademark/unfair competition law an appropriate way to protect industrial designs, as a matter of policy?

As we will see in the last chapter, a line of Supreme Court decisions, including Sears, Roebuck & Co. v. Stiffel Co., 376 U.S. 225 (1964), Compco Corp. v. Day–Brite Lighting, Inc., 376 U.S. 234 (1964), and Bonito Boats, Inc. v. Thunder Craft Boats, Inc., 489 U.S. 141 (1989), casts doubt upon the availability of *state* trademark or unfair competition causes of action to prevent the copying of product features, suggesting that these state causes of action may be preempted pursuant to the Supremacy Clause of the United States Constitution. The *Sears/Compco/Bonito Boats* decisions reasoned that in enacting the Patent Act, Congress specifically intended that inventions failing to qualify for a patent, and inventions for which the patent has expired, remain in the public domain, available for competitors to copy. Use of state trademark and unfair competition laws to prevent competitors from copying features of such invention/products would frustrate this Congressional purpose. While the *Sears/Compco/Bonito Boats* line of cases does not purport to address the propriety of federal trademark and trade dress causes of action to protect unpatented product features, should those cases nonetheless be influential to federal courts in construing the scope of Lanham Act protection? See Dastar Corp. v. Twentieth Century Fox Film Corp., 539 U.S. 23 (2003).

VI.   ACQUISITION OF RIGHTS IN MARKS

A.   THE USE REQUIREMENT

BLUE BELL, INC. v. FARAH MANUFACTURING CO., INC.

United States Court of Appeals for the Fifth Circuit, 1975.
508 F.2d 1260.

Gewin, Circuit Judge:

In the spring and summer of 1973 two prominent manufacturers of men's clothing created identical trademarks for goods substantially identical in appearance. Though the record offers no indication of bad faith in the design and adoption of the labels, both Farah Manufacturing Company (Farah) and Blue Bell, Inc. (Blue Bell) devised the mark "Time Out" for new lines of men's slacks and shirts. Both parties market their goods on a national scale, so they agree that joint utilization of the same trademark would confuse the buying public. Thus, the only question presented for our review is which party established prior use of the mark in trade. A response to that seemingly innocuous inquiry, however, requires us to define the chameleonic term "use" as it has developed in trademark law.

After a full development of the facts in the district court both parties moved for summary judgment. The motion of Farah was granted and that of Blue Bell denied. * * * For the reasons hereinafter stated we affirm.

Farah conceived of the Time Out mark on May 16, after screening several possible titles for its new stretch menswear. Two days later the firm adopted an hourglass logo and authorized an extensive advertising campaign bearing the new insignia. Farah presented its fall line of clothing, including Time Out slacks, to sales personnel on June 5. In the meantime, patent counsel had given clearance for use of the mark after scrutiny of current federal registrations then on file. One of Farah's top executives demonstrated samples of the Time Out garments to large customers in Washington, D.C. and New York, though labels were not attached to the slacks at that time. Tags containing the new design were completed June 27. With favorable evaluations of marketing potential from all sides, Farah sent one pair of slacks bearing the Time Out mark to each of its twelve regional sales managers on July 3. Sales personnel paid for the pants, and the garments became their property in case of loss.

Following the July 3 shipment, regional managers showed the goods to customers the following week. Farah received several orders and production began. Further shipments of sample garments were mailed to the rest of the sales force on July 11 and 14. Merchandising efforts were fully operative by the end of the month. The first shipments to customers, however, occurred in September.

Blue Bell, on the other hand, was concerned with creating an entire new division of men's clothing, as an avenue to reaching the "upstairs" market. * * * On June 18 Blue Bell management arrived at the name Time Out to identify both its new division and its new line of men's sportswear. Like Farah, it received clearance for use of the mark from counsel. Like Farah, it inaugurated an advertising campaign. Unlike Farah, however, Blue Bell did not ship a dozen marked articles of the new line to its sales personnel. Instead, Blue Bell authorized the manufacture of several hundred labels bearing the words Time Out and its logo shaped like a referee's hands forming a T. When the labels were completed on June 29, the head of the embryonic division flew them to El Paso. He instructed shipping personnel to affix the new Time Out labels to slacks that already bore the 'Mr. Hicks' trademark. The new tags, of varying sizes and colors, were randomly attached to the left hip pocket button of slacks and the left hip pocket of jeans. Thus, although no change occurred in the design or manufacture of the pants, on July 5 several hundred pair left El Paso with two tags.

Blue Bell made intermittent shipments of the doubly-labeled slacks thereafter, though the out-of-state customers who received the goods had ordered clothing of the Mr. Hicks variety. Production of the new Time Out merchandise began in the latter part of August, and Blue Bell held a sales meeting to present its fall designs from September 4–6. Sales personnel solicited numerous orders, though shipments of the garments were not scheduled until October.

By the end of October Farah had received orders for 204,403 items of Time Out sportswear, representing a retail sales value of over $2,750,000. Blue Bell had received orders for 154,200 garments valued at over $900,000. Both parties had commenced extensive advertising campaigns for their respective Time Out sportswear.

Soon after discovering the similarity of their marks, Blue Bell sued Farah for common law trademark infringement and unfair competition, seeking to enjoin use of the Time Out trademark on men's clothing. Farah counter-claimed for similar injunctive relief. The district court found that Farah's July 3 shipment and sale constituted a valid use in trade, while Blue Bell's July 5 shipment was a mere "token" use insufficient at law to create trademark rights. While we affirm the result reached by the trial court as to Farah's priority of use, the legal grounds upon which we base our decision are somewhat different from those undergirding the district court's judgment.

Federal jurisdiction is predicated upon diversity of citizenship, since neither party has registered the mark pursuant to the Lanham Act. Given the operative facts surrounding manufacture and shipment from El Paso, the parties agree the Texas law of trademarks controls. In 1967 the state legislature enacted a Trademark Statute.[5] Section 16.02 of the Act explains that a mark is "used" when it is affixed to the goods and "the goods are sold, displayed for sale, or otherwise publicly distributed." Thus the question whether Blue Bell or Farah established priority of trademark use depends upon interpretation of the cited provision. Unfortunately, there are no Texas cases construing 16.02. This court must therefore determine what principles the highest state court would utilize in deciding such a question. In view of the statute's stated purpose to preserve common law rights, we conclude the Texas Supreme Court would apply the statutory provision in light of general principles of trademark law.

A trademark is a symbol (word, name, device or combination thereof) adopted and used by a merchant to identify his goods and distinguish them from articles produced by others. Ownership of a mark requires a combination of both appropriation and use in trade. Thus, neither conception of the mark, nor advertising alone establishes trademark rights at common law. Rather, ownership of a trademark accrues when goods bearing the mark are placed on the market.

---

5.   Vernon's Tex. Code Ann., Bus. & Comm. 16.01–16.28 (1968).

The exclusive right to a trademark belongs to one who first uses it in connection with specified goods. Such use need not have gained wide public recognition, and even a single use in trade may sustain trademark rights if followed by continuous commercial utilization.

The initial question presented for review is whether Farah's sale and shipment of slacks to twelve regional managers constitutes a valid first use of the Time Out mark. Blue Bell claims the July 3 sale was merely an internal transaction insufficiently public to secure trademark ownership. After consideration of pertinent authorities, we agree.

Secret, undisclosed internal shipments are generally inadequate to support the denomination "use." Trademark claims based upon shipments from a producer's plant to its sales office, and vice versa, have often been disallowed. Though none of the cited cases dealt with sales to intra-corporate personnel, we perceive that fact to be a distinction without a difference. The sales were not made to customers, but served as an accounting device to charge the salesmen with their cost in case of loss. The fact that some sales managers actively solicited accounts bolsters the good faith of Farah's intended use, but does not meet our essential objection: that the "sales" were not made to the public.

The primary, perhaps singular purpose of a trademark is to provide a means for the consumer to separate or distinguish one manufacturer's goods from those of another. Personnel within a corporation can identify an item by style number or other unique code. A trademark aids the public in selecting particular goods. As stated by the First Circuit:

> But to hold that a sale or sales are the *sine qua non* of a use sufficient to amount to an appropriation would be to read an unwarranted limitation into the statute, for so construed registration would have to be denied to any manufacturer who adopted a mark to distinguish or identify his product, and perhaps applied it thereon for years, if he should in practice lease his goods rather than sell them, as many manufacturers of machinery do. It seems to us that although evidence of sales is highly persuasive, the question of use adequate to establish appropriation remains one to be decided on the facts of each case, and that evidence showing, first, adoption, and, second, *use in a way sufficiently public to identify or distinguish the marked goods in an appropriate segment of the public mind as those of the adopter of the mark*, is competent to establish ownership. . . .

New England Duplicating Co. v. Mendes, 190 F.2d 415, 418 (1st Cir.1951). Similarly, the Trademark Trial and Appeal Board has reasoned:

> To acquire trademark rights there has to be an "open" use, that is to say, a use has to be made to the relevant class of purchasers or prospective purchasers since a trademark is intended to identify goods and distinguish those goods from those manufactured or sold by others. There was no such "open" use—rather the use can be said to be an "internal" use, which cannot give rise to trademark rights.

Sterling Drug, Inc. v. Knoll A. G. Chemische Fabriken, *supra* at 631.

Farah nonetheless contends that a recent decision of the Board so undermines all prior cases relating to internal use that they should be ignored. In Standard Pressed Steel Co. v. Midwest Chrome Process Co., 183 U.S.P.Q. 758 (TTAB 1974) the agency held that internal shipment of marked goods from a producer's manufacturing plant to its sales office constitutes a valid "use in commerce" for registration purposes.

An axiom of trademark law has been that the right to register a mark is conditioned upon its actual use in trade. Theoretically, then, common law use in trade should precede the use in commerce upon which Lanham Act registration is predicated. Arguably, since only a trademark owner can apply for registration, any activity adequate to create registrable rights must perforce also create trademark rights. A close examination of the Board's decision, however, dispels so mechanical a view. The tribunal took meticulous care to point out that its conclusion related solely to registration use rather than ownership use.

> It has been recognized and especially so in the last few years that, in view of the expenditures involved in introducing a new product on the market generally and the attendant risk involved therein prior to the screening process involved in resorting to the federal registration system and in the absence of an "intent to use" statute, a token sale or a single shipment in commerce *may be sufficient to support an application to register a trademark* in the Patent Office notwithstanding that the evidence may not show what disposition was made of the product so shipped. That is, the fact that a sale or a shipment of goods bearing a trademark was *designed primarily to lay a foundation for the filing of an application for registration* does not, per se, invalidate any such application or subsequent registration issued thereon. * * * Inasmuch as it is our belief that a most liberal policy should be followed in a situation of this kind [*in which dispute as to priority of use and ownership of a mark is not involved*], applicant's initial shipment of fasteners, although an intra-company transaction in that it was to a company sales representative, was a bona fide shipment....

Standard Pressed Steel Co. v. Midwest Chrome Process Co., *supra* at 764–65.

Priority of use and ownership of the Time Out mark are the only issues before this court. The language fashioned by the Board clearly indicates a desire to leave the common law of trademark ownership intact. The decision may demonstrate a reversal of the presumption that ownership rights precede registration rights, but it does not affect our analysis of common law use in trade. Farah had undertaken substantial preliminary steps toward marketing the Time Out garments, but it did not establish ownership of the mark by means of the July 3 shipment to its sales managers. The gist of trademark rights is actual use in trade.

Though technically a "sale," the July 3 shipment was not "publicly distributed" within the purview of the Texas statute.

Blue Bell's July 5 shipment similarly failed to satisfy the prerequisites of a bona fide use in trade. Elementary tenets of trademark law require that labels or designs be affixed to the merchandise actually intended to bear the mark in commercial transactions. Furthermore, courts have recognized that the usefulness of a mark derives not only from its capacity to identify a certain manufacturer, but also from its ability to differentiate between different classes of goods produced by a single manufacturer. Here customers had ordered slacks of the Mr. Hicks species, and Mr. Hicks was the fanciful mark distinguishing these slacks from all others. Blue Bell intended to use the Time Out mark on an entirely new line of men's sportswear, unique in style and cut, though none of the garments had yet been produced. While goods may be identified by more than one trademark, the use of each mark must be bona fide. Mere adoption of a mark without bona fide use, in an attempt to reserve it for the future, will not create trademark rights. In the instant case Blue Bell's attachment of a secondary label to an older line of goods manifests a bad faith attempt to reserve a mark. We cannot countenance such activities as a valid use in trade. Blue Bell therefore did not acquire trademark rights by virtue of its July 5 shipment.

We thus hold that neither Farah's July 3 shipment nor Blue Bell's July 5 shipment sufficed to create rights in the Time Out mark. Based on a desire to secure ownership of the mark and superiority over a competitor, both claims of alleged use were chronologically premature. Essentially, they took a time out to litigate their differences too early in the game. The question thus becomes whether we should continue to stop the clock for a remand or make a final call from the appellate bench. While a remand to the district court for further factual development would not be improper in these circumstances, we believe the interests of judicial economy and the parties' desire to terminate the litigation demand that we decide, if possible, which manufacturer first used the mark in trade.

Careful examination of the record discloses that Farah shipped its first order of Time Out clothing to customers in September of 1973. Blue Bell, approximately one month behind its competitor at other relevant stages of development, did not mail its Time Out garments until at least October. Though sales to customers are not the *sine qua non* of trademark use, they are determinative in the instant case. These sales constituted the first point at which the public had a chance to associate Time Out with a particular line of sportswear. Therefore, Farah established priority of trademark use; it is entitled to a decree permanently enjoining Blue Bell from utilization of the Time Out trademark on men's garments.

* * *

NOTES AND QUESTIONS

1. *Use in trade.* As the *Farah* opinion indicates, ownership of a mark or trade name at common law, and the right to register a mark on the Lanham Act Principal Register, both depend upon a claimant's use of the mark in trade. As we will see in the next section, 1988 amendments to the Lanham Act made it possible for the first time to *apply* to register a mark based only on a *bona fide intent* to use the mark in the future. Nonetheless, the registration will not be *granted* until the requisite use is made. Thus, even after the amendments, "use" continues to be the foundation of U.S. trademark protection.

The *Farah* court, in discussing the Trademark Trial and Appeal Board's *Standard Pressed Steel* decision, suggests that "use" for purposes of federal registration might be more readily found than "use" for purposes of determining priority and ownership. What could explain such a dual standard? When Congress implemented the "intent to use" application procedure, referred to above, it also expressly rejected a "token use" standard for registration, amending Lanham Act § 45 to provide: "The term 'use in commerce' means the bona fide use of a mark in the ordinary course of trade, and not made merely to reserve a right in a mark." 15 U.S.C. § 1127.

What is the rationale for conditioning ownership rights and registration of marks on use in trade? Why not provide that the first business to register a mark becomes its owner, regardless of use, as is done in most other countries?

2. *Priority in the case of inherently distinctive indications of origin.* As the *Farah* opinion illustrates, when two or more parties claim the same inherently distinctive indication of origin, or two that are confusingly similar, the first to "use" the indication of origin in trade has superior rights. Thus, the law of trademarks and unfair competition adopts the "first in time, first in right" philosophy that exists in other areas of property law.

How much "use" is required to establish priority? In Allard Enterprises, Inc. v. Advanced Programming Resources, Inc., 146 F.3d 350 (6th Cir.1998), the Court of Appeals for the Sixth Circuit explained that mark ownership can be established even if the first use was not extensive and did not result in deep market penetration or widespread recognition. Even a single use in trade could establish rights if it was genuine and was followed by continuous commercial use. In that case, Heagren founded defendant company to provide employment placement services, and ran it as a side-line to his regular job. He alleged that his use of the "APR" mark in the defendant business during 1993 and early 1994 made him the prior user. During that time he had attempted to place several acquaintances in jobs, and in the course of this, had used the "APR" mark on at least one fax, on at least one resume, and in other communications with potential employers in Ohio. He had not succeeded in making any placements or earning any revenues prior to the plaintiff's first use date. However, the court found his use sufficient to establish priority:

> On appeal, plaintiff discredits defendants' uses of the APR mark as part of a "word-of-mouth" marketing plan that targeted "personal friends," and asserts that such "secretive," "minimal," and "sporadic"

uses are neither sufficiently commercial nor public to qualify as *bona fide* uses of a service mark. For the following reasons we disagree. First, we agree with the magistrate judge's finding that "whether or not this ... word-of-mouth or 'relationship' marketing is the preferred or optimal way to conduct this type of business, it is not so atypical that no reasonable person could view it as 'commercial.' " [Defendants] used the APR mark on at least one fax, on at least one resume, and in numerous other solicitations, as they offered * * * services to several employers doing business in Ohio. Defendants were not engaged in "pre-marketing maneuvers," the disingenuous uses of a trademark, or the mere attempt to reserve the APR mark for later utilization. Defendants used the APR mark as they attempted to complete genuine commercial transactions, with the understanding that they would be paid if an employee was hired. Second, these commercial uses also were sufficiently public to qualify for protection. The use of the mark "need not have gained wide public recognition" to establish priority, *Blue Bell, Inc.*, 508 F.2d at 1265, and there was evidence in this case that several large companies that did business in Ohio identified the APR mark with [defendant] and his permanent employee placement service. Finally, we find that defendant's use of the APR mark over the course of 1993 and into 1994 was consistent and continuous, if not high-volume. Defendant's "trademark usage, although limited, was a part of an ongoing program to exploit the mark commercially." *La Societe Anonyme des Parfums Le Galion*, 495 F.2d at 1272. For these reasons, we conclude that defendants established both the *bona fide* use in commerce of the APR mark before plaintiff's first use * * * and the continuous use of that mark since then.

Id., 146 F.3d at 359–60.

Compare Lucent Information Management, Inc. v. Lucent Technologies, Inc., 186 F.3d 311 (3d Cir.), *cert. denied*, 528 U.S. 1106, 120 S.Ct. 845, 145 L.Ed.2d 714 (2000). In *Lucent*, plaintiff business, a small start-up, selected the "Lucent" mark in the summer of 1995 and, in September, used the mark in a letter to about 50 people to announce the services it would offer. In October, it made one sale, for $323.50. In November, it made several sales presentations, none of which led to any sales. In the following months, plaintiff made several more sales presentations, continued to seek clients (on a word-of-mouth basis) from existing contacts and referrals, but did no public or paid advertising. It made one additional sale. The question was whether plaintiff had made sufficient use to acquire priority in the Lucent mark as of November 30. The Court of Appeals for the Third Circuit found that it had not.

The court found that plaintiff must "introduce evidence to show its trademark 'has achieved market penetration that is significant enough to pose the real likelihood of confusion among * * * consumers,' " and applied a "four-factor test" to evaluate whether the market penetration of the trademark was sufficient to warrant protection: (1) the volume of sales of the trademarked product; (2) the growth trends (both positive and negative) in the area; (3) the number of persons actually purchasing the product in relation to the potential number of customers; and (4) the amount of product advertising in the area. *Id.*, at 317. The court noted that plaintiff's "volume of sales," consisting of a single sale for $323.50, was *de minimis*. The court continued:

> [Plaintiff] asks us to consider *Blue Bell*, in which the Court of Appeals for the Fifth Circuit held that "even a single use in trade may sustain trademarks rights if followed by continuous commercial utilization." There, though, if we look for "continuous commercial utilization" beyond the first sale, as required under *Blue Bell*, we do not find that the continuous use—the further promotional efforts—"sufficiently public to identify or distinguish the marked goods in an appropriate segment of the public mind as those of the adopter of the mark."
>
> * * *
>
> [Plaintiff] existed for only about three months before [the defendant's November 30 priority date], had made but one sale in that period, had not invested any monies in public advertising or expanded beyond its initial set-up, and had made a relatively small number of sales presentations. * * * [Plaintiff] wants to protect its intention to create goodwill and a successful business, and not the goodwill and business itself. Certainly any new business will need time to get off the ground, but the courts cannot aid that effort by awarding trademark rights in an unregistered mark that the business hopes or anticipates will be used but had not been used.

Id., at 318. Can the *Allard Enterprises* and *Lucent* decisions be meaningfully distinguished on their facts? If not, which result makes more sense as a matter of policy? For a third approach, see Zazu Designs v. L'Oreal, S.A., 979 F.2d 499 (7th Cir. 1992). In that case, the Seventh Circuit suggested that the use requirement exists in part to ensure that other potential users of a mark have notice of the claimant's earlier use, and thus can avoid inefficient investment in marks that have already been spoken for. Accordingly, at least when the claimant has not filed to register the mark, the claimant's use must be sufficiently active and notorious to provide reasonable notice of his claim to competitors.

When the issue of "first use" is a close one in a priority contest, more than strictly chronological considerations may come into play. Consider the Second Circuit's opinion in Manhattan Industries, Inc. v. Sweater Bee by Banff, Ltd., 627 F.2d 628 (2d Cir.1980). In that case, competitors were trying to snatch up the valuable "Kimberly" trademark directly after it was formally abandoned by its owner. Essentially, each began shipping products bearing the "Kimberly" mark within a day of the other. Given this closeness in time, the court refused to recognize that the first shipper had gained the right to completely prohibit the other from using the mark—especially since the second shipper had expended considerable amounts on the mark in good faith:

> We have previously stated that "the concept of priority in the law of trademarks is applied 'not in its calendar sense' but on the basis of 'the equities involved.'" Given the evenly balanced equities in this case, it would be inequitable to allow only the appellees to use the "Kimberly" mark.

Id., 627 F.2d at 630. Refusing to enjoin either party's use of the mark, the court found that each party must differentiate its label from that of the other and from the original "Kimberly" mark, in order to avoid consumer confusion. Is this a satisfactory solution?

3. *Priority and indications of origin that are not inherently distinctive.* While the first to use an *inherently distinctive* mark in trade has priority over others (as long as she uses it continuously thereafter), a different rule exists for marks, trade names and trade dress that are not inherently distinctive. As we have already noted, some indications of origin that are not inherently distinctive (such as descriptive words and symbols, surnames, and common designs) may become distinctive, and thus qualify for protection, through acquisition of secondary meaning. Ownership rights in such cases arise upon the acquisition of secondary meaning. Thus, for example, assume that a producer of ball bearings commences use of the mark "durable" to identify the source of the ball bearings in 2005. He acquires no rights from that use because the mark is descriptive and not inherently distinctive. However, assume that the producer continues his use, featuring the mark in sales and advertising of the ball bearings, and acquires secondary meaning in 2010. At that point (in 2010) the producer will acquire rights in the "durable" mark. For purposes of determining priority among conflicting claimants in such cases, the first user to acquire secondary meaning will have priority over subsequent users.

4. *Priority and Lanham Act § 2(d).* Lanham Act § 2(d) incorporates the common-law "first in time, first in right" rule of priority into the Lanham Act's registration scheme. 15 U.S.C.A. § 1052(d). Section 2(d) provides:

> No trademark by which the goods of the applicant may be distinguished from the goods of others shall be refused registration on the principal register on account of its nature unless it—
>
> * * *
>
> (d) Consists of or comprises a mark which so resembles a mark registered in the Patent and Trademark Office, or a mark or trade name previously used in the United States by another and not abandoned, as to be likely, when used on or in connection with the goods of the applicant, to cause confusion, or to cause mistake, or to deceive * * *.

It is important to note that a "previous use" that will prohibit an applicant's registration under § 2(d) can consist of a trademark or service mark use or a use of the word, symbol or device as a trade name—the name of a business. Since a trade name, as such, cannot be registered, it is obvious that the previous user need not have registered the trade name or mark. It is sufficient that the previous user acquired proprietary rights in the mark or trade name at common law—through use in trade or (in the case of words, names, symbols or devices that are not inherently distinctive) acquisition of secondary meaning—prior to the applicant, and that she is continuing her use.

The standard for determining whether the applicant's mark is sufficiently similar to the prior user's to cause a likelihood of consumer confusion, when used in connection with the applicant's goods, is similar to the standard used to determine whether a defendant's mark infringes a plaintiff's mark. We will examine the latter standard at some length later in the chapter. Another factor that may figure into the § 2(d) likelihood of confusion inquiry is the parties' agreement to concurrent use. For example, in *Application of* E.I. DuPont DeNemours & Co., 476 F.2d 1357 (C.C.P.A. 1973), Horizon, the prior user of the "Rally" mark for an automobile cleaning product, assigned the automotive cleaner portion of its business, along with the "Rally" mark, to DuPont. However, it continued to use the "Rally" mark for its all-purpose household detergent. As a part of their transaction, Horizon and DuPont entered into an agreement designed to facilitate concurrent use of the "Rally" mark while avoiding consumer confusion about the source of their respective products. Among other things, the agreement provided that neither party could promote its product as "especially suited for use" in the other's market. The parties also agreed to "take any further actions and execute any further agreements needed to carry out the spirit and intent" of the agreement. The court accorded this agreement considerable weight in finding DuPont's subsequent application to register "Rally" appropriate under § 2(d):

> In considering agreements, a naked "consent" may carry little weight. Absent more, the consenter may continue or expand his use. The consent may be based on ignorance or misconception of the law. The facts may show, on the other hand, that consent could exist only in the absence of any real likelihood of confusion.
>
> The weight to be given more detailed agreements of the type presented here should be substantial. It can be safely taken as fundamental that reputable businessmen-users of valuable trademarks have no interest in *causing* public confusion. The genius of the free competitive system is the paralleling of the interest of the entrepreneur and the consuming public so far as possible. Altruism aside, it is in his *pecuniary* interest, indeed a matter of economic survival, that the businessman obtain and retain customers, the very purpose and function of a trademark, and that he avoid and preclude confusion. Millions of advertising dollars are spent daily for that precise purpose. The history of trademark litigation and the substantial body of law to which it relates demonstrate the businessman's alertness in seeking to enjoin confusion. In so doing he guards both his pocketbook and the public interest.
>
> Thus when those most familiar with use in the marketplace and most interested in precluding confusion enter agreements designed to avoid it, the scales of evidence are clearly tilted. It is at least difficult to maintain a subjective view that confusion will occur when those directly concerned say it won't. A mere *assumption* that confusion is likely will rarely prevail against uncontroverted evidence from those on the firing line that it is not.

Id., at 1362–63.

5. *Affixation.* "Using a mark in trade" entails "affixation" or other close association of the mark with the product or service it is to identify. Lanham Act § 45, 15 U.S.C.A. § 1127, provides that a mark will be deemed to be in use in connection with goods when:

it is placed in any manner on the goods or their containers or the displays associated therewith or on the tags or labels affixed thereto, or if the nature of the goods makes such placement impracticable, then on documents associated with the goods or their sale * * *.

Obviously a mark cannot be physically attached to a service, so the Lanham Act finds affixation in the case of service marks when the mark is "used or displayed in the sale or advertising of services * * *." *Id.*

6. *Use in commerce.* Because Congress relied upon its Commerce Clause power to enact the Lanham Act, an indication of origin must be "used in commerce" in order to qualify for registration, or for protection under Lanham Act § 43(a). Section 45 defines "commerce" as "all commerce which may lawfully be regulated by Congress." 15 U.S.C.A. § 1127. The interstate commerce requirement is generally easy to meet. For example, in the case of products, courts have held that strictly intrastate sales are "in commerce" for jurisdictional purposes if the goods at issue were shipped to the seller from another state or country.

Services that are offered strictly intrastate may qualify, if they "affect" interstate commerce. For example, in *In re* Gastown, 326 F.2d 780 (C.C.P.A. 1964), the Court of Customs and Patent Appeals found that though the registration applicant's service stations were all located in one state, its services qualified as "rendered in commerce" because the stations (some of which were located on federal highways) serviced interstate travelers, who themselves were engaged in interstate commerce. The stations also extended credit to out-of-state customers and billed them in their respective domiciliary states.

More recently, in Larry Harmon Pictures Corp. v. The Williams Restaurant Corp., 929 F.2d 662 (Fed.Cir.), *cert. denied,* 502 U.S. 823, 112 S.Ct. 85, 116 L.Ed.2d 58 (1991), Bozo the Clown opposed the registration of "Bozo's" as the service mark of a single-location Tennessee restaurant, claiming that the restaurant's services were not rendered in interstate commerce. The findings of fact revealed that the restaurant was about an hour's drive from Memphis, "a major commercial center for the Mid–South region." The Memphis metropolitan statistical area comprised not only a portion of Tennessee, but also portions of Mississippi and Arkansas. The restaurant had been at least mentioned in publications originating in Memphis, New York City, the District of Columbia, Dallas, Gila Bend, Arizona, and Palm Beach, Florida. Some interstate travelers patronized the restaurant, though the number of such travelers was in dispute. (The restaurant owner estimated that 15% of its business consisted of out-of-state customers.) In finding that the commerce requirement was satisfied, the Court of Appeals for the Federal Circuit specifically rejected arguments that single-location restaurants should not be permitted to register service marks unless they are located on an interstate highway, at least 50 percent of their meals are served to interstate travelers, or they regularly advertise in out-of-state media.

PROBLEMS

1. X began to use the word "Carnival" as a mark for boxed raw shrimp, sold fresh and frozen to wholesalers, retailers, food suppliers, and restaurants, in 1980. In 1996, X expanded its product market to include prepared, ready-to-eat entrees, such as cooked shrimp, which it also sold under the "Carnival" mark. In 1990, Y began selling prepared food products like seafood gumbo, shrimp cakes, and crab cakes under the "Carnival" mark. Which party has priority in the "Carnival" mark for prepared, "ready-to-eat" seafood products?

2. X, a non-profit group formed to disseminate information about spinal injuries, registers the domain name "Argos.com" with an Internet registry and sets up a web site that provides free information about various spinal injuries and diseases, and about a range of medications and surgical procedures that address these problems. Assuming that this is the only use X has made of "Argos.com," is it likely to have acquired trademark rights in the term?

NOTE: COMPLICATIONS OF THE NEW GLOBAL ECONOMY

What if a mark claimant uses the mark to advertise services in the United States, but only renders the services in a foreign country? Will that constitute a sufficient use in trade and commerce to give ownership of the mark and standing to sue under the Lanham Act? In Buti v. Impressa Perosa, S.R.L., 139 F.3d 98 (2d Cir.1998), *cert. denied*, 525 U.S. 826, 119 S.Ct. 73, 142 L.Ed.2d 57 (1998), an Italian business promoted its "Fashion Cafe," located in Milan, in the United States before the plaintiff began its use of the "Fashion Cafe" mark for U.S. restaurant services. The Court of Appeals for the Second Circuit rejected the Italian business' claims that this gave it superior rights in the "Fashion Cafe" mark in the U.S. The court explained that "trademark rights exist only as rights 'appurtenant to an established business or trade in connection with which the mark is employed.' " 139 F.3d at 105. The restaurant services must themselves have been rendered in U.S. commerce in order for the Italian business' U.S. advertising and promotion of its mark to give it priority over the domestic restaurant.

Compare the Fourth Circuit's opinion in International Bancorp, LLC v. Societe des Bains de Mer et du Cercle des Estrangers a Monaco, 329 F.3d 359 (4th Cir. 2003), *cert. denied,* 540 U.S. 1106, 124 S.Ct. 1052, 157 L.Ed.2d 891 (2004). In that case, a Monaco casino ("SBM") that operated solely in Monaco but advertised in the U.S. sought Lanham Act infringement relief against a defendant who used allegedly infringing domain names in connection with its online gambling web sites. The Fourth Circuit found that SMB met the "use in commerce" requirement, and thus was entitled to recover under the Lanham Act, although it only provided its casino services abroad. The court stressed the language of Lanham Act § 45, which provides that a mark is used "on services when it is used or displayed in the sale or advertising of services *and the services are rendered in commerce.*" *Id.* at 364. In this case, SMB used the mark in the U.S. to advertise its services, and it rendered its casino services "in commerce." The court found that "commerce," for purposes of the Lanham Act, was all commerce that Congress may regulate under the Commerce Clause, which includes "foreign trade" ("trade between subjects of the United States and subjects of a foreign nation.") Here, the casino's services were rendered in foreign trade because U.S. citizens went to and gambled at the Monaco casino. Thus:

> "while SBM's promotions within the United States do not on their own constitute a use in commerce of the 'Casino de Monte Carlo' mark, the mark is nonetheless used in commerce because United States citizens purchase casino services sold by a subject of a foreign nation, which purchases constitute trade with a foreign nation that Congress may regulate under the Commerce Clause. And SBM's promotions 'use[] or display[] [the mark] in the sale or advertising of [these] services ... rendered in commerce.' "

Id. at 366. The court stressed:

> [Section 45] defines the term "use in commerce" with respect to services as being when a mark is "used or displayed in the sale or advertising of services *and* the services are rendered in commerce." As a consequence of the *conjunctive* command, it is not enough for a mark owner simply to render services in foreign commerce for it to be eligible for trademark protection. Nor is it enough for a mark owner simply to use or display a mark in the sale or advertising of services to United States consumers. *Both* elements are required, and *both* elements must be distinctly analyzed.

Id. at 373. The court distinguished *Buti, supra,* on the ground that the Italian business claiming the "Fashion Cafe" mark conceded in oral argument that its restaurant services were not a part of U.S.–Italy trade. *Id.* at 369.

Compare General Healthcare, Ltd. v. Qashat, 364 F.3d 332 (1st Cir. 2004). In that case the mark claimant manufactured goods (a cosmetic cream) in the U.S., shipped them to the United Kingdom for final assembly, and then sold them from the U.K. to purchasers in the Middle East. The claimant argued that these actions gave rise to Lanham Act rights in the mark it used to identify the goods. It relied on the Lanham Act § 45 definition of "use in commerce," which provides that a mark is used in commerce in connection with goods when it is affixed to the goods and the goods are "sold or transported in commerce." 15 U.S.C. § 1127.

The First Circuit rejected the argument. While interstate transportation alone would satisfy the jurisdictional "in commerce" requirement, it was not sufficient under the circumstances to give rise to ownership rights: "In assessing rights stemming from transportation, courts and commentators have required an element of public awareness of the use." *Id.* at 336. Here, no members of the U.S. public were exposed to the shipment, or had an opportunity to associate the mark with the claimant as the source of the product. The court explained that:

> [T]he fact that GHL follows intra-corporate shipments (serving no source identifying function) with overseas sales is * * * insufficient to garner trademark protection in the United States. The subsequent sales between

the United Kingdom and the Middle East are not a "use in commerce" within the purview of the Lanham Act. *See Buti v. Perosa, S.R.L.*, 139 F.3d 98, 103 (2d Cir. 1998)(promotional activities in the United States did not merit Lanham Act protection for a mark associated entirely with ongoing business overseas).

Id. at 337.

Further International Complications—"Well–Known Marks"

The Paris Convention for the Protection of Industrial Property (to which the United States adheres) provides:

> The countries of the Union undertake, ex officio if their legislation so permits, or at the request of an interested party, to refuse or to cancel the registration, and to prohibit the use, of a trademark which constitutes a reproduction, an imitation, or a translation, liable to create confusion, of a mark considered by the competent authority of the country of registration or use to be well known in that country as being already the mark of a person entitled to the benefits of this convention and used for identical or similar goods.

Paris Convention, Art. **6***bis*. The TRIPs Agreement (to which the U.S. also adheres) incorporates the provisions of Paris Convention Art. **6***bis*, extends its "well-known mark" requirement to service marks, and provides that the parties' goods or services do not have to be similar, as long as the domestic use of the well-known mark would indicate a connection with the foreign mark owner. TRIPs Art. 16(2) & (3).

Suppose that a chain of stores operates throughout Mexico and Central America, but not in the United States. The chain's mark is widely known in the countries in which it operates, and is well-known to persons in the U.S. who have ties to Mexico and/or Central America. A U.S. resident opens a similar kind of store in Southern California with the same mark, causing a likelihood of confusion with the well-known Mexican/Central American mark. Will the foreign chain have a federal cause of action to prohibit the use, as contemplated under Paris Convention Art 6*bis* and TRIPs Art. 16? Note that the Mexican/Central American chain was the first to use the mark in an absolute sense, but has not used it in the United States (or obtained a U.S. mark registration), even though its mark is well-known to a substantial segment of the United States population.

In Grupo Gigante SA De CV v. Dallo & Co., 391 F.3d 1088 (9th Cir. 2004), the Ninth Circuit recognized a "famous mark" exception to the territoriality principle (the principle that marks have a separate legal existence in each country, and that use in one country gives no rights in another), based on policy considerations:

> Commerce crosses borders. In this nation of immigrants, so do people. Trademark is, at its core, about protecting against consumer confusion and 'palming off.' There can be no justification for using trademark law to fool immigrants into thinking that they are buying from the store they liked back home.

Id., at 1904. In sharp contrast, the Second Circuit has rejected a federal cause of action for infringement of "well-known" foreign marks:

> The principle of territoriality is basic to American trademark law. As our colleague, Judge Leval, has explained, this principle recognizes that
>
>> a trademark has a separate legal existence under each country's laws, and that its proper lawful function is not necessarily to specify the origin or manufacture of a good (although it may incidentally do that), but rather to symbolize the domestic goodwill of the domestic markholder so that the consuming public may rely with an expectation of consistency on the domestic reputation earned for the mark by its owner, and the owner of the mark may be confident that his goodwill and reputation (the value of the mark) will not be injured through use of the mark by others in domestic commerce.
>
> Precisely because a trademark has a separate legal existence under each country's laws, ownership of a mark in one country does not automatically confer upon the owner the exclusive right to use that mark in another country.

ITC Ltd., Inc. v. Punchgini, Inc., 482 F.3d 135, 155 (2d Cir.), *cert. denied*, 522 U.S. 827, 128 S.Ct. 288, 169 L.Ed.2d 38 (2007). The court noted that neither the Paris Convention nor the TRIPs Agreement is self-executing, and reasoned that since Congress had expressly enacted legislation (Lanham Act § 44, 15 U.S.C. § 1126) to implement U.S. international trademark treaty obligations, it would be inappropriate simply to find a "famous mark" cause of action based on policy concerns, as the Ninth Circuit had done. Turning to the provisions of § 44 itself, the court found that the statutory language created no exception to the doctrine of territoriality that would permit the foreign famous mark owner's cause of action. In particular, the court rejected arguments that such an exception could be found in subsections 44(b) and 44(h). Review the language of these subsections. Do you agree with the court's construction? What, exactly, do those subsections provide?

B. REGISTRATION PROCEDURE

1. *Applications Based on Use and Intent to Use in Commerce*

Lanham Act § 1, 15 U.S.C.A. § 1051, sets forth two alternative procedures for registering marks on the Principal Register: 1) the original method of registration, based on use of the mark in commerce ("use applications"); and 2) the method enacted in 1988, based on a *bona fide* intent to use the mark in commerce ("intent-to-use applications").

Under either method, the applicant must send a written application to the Patent and Trademark Office that includes a drawing of the mark and the filing fee. Use applicants must also send information about their use of the mark in commerce in connection with the specified goods or services. Intent-to-use applicants need only assert a *bona fide*, good faith intention to use the mark in commerce in connection with the specified goods or services. The PTO staff reviews the application documents to ensure that they meet the minimum requirements, and if they do, assigns a filing date.

Subsequently, a PTO examining attorney reviews the application and determines whether the mark may be registered. (Factors that may render the mark unregistrable are set forth in Lanham Act § 2, 15 U.S.C.A. § 1052.) If the examining attorney has objections to the mark, she will notify the applicant, who may then respond to the objections and make corrections. See 15 U.S.C.A. § 1062. If the applicant's response does not overcome the examining attorney's objections, the examining attorney will issue a final refusal, and the applicant may appeal her decision to the Trademark Trial and Appeal Board. See 15 U.S.C.A. § 1070.

If the examining attorney has no objections, or the applicant overcomes them, the examining attorney will approve the mark for publication in the PTO's Official Gazette. See 15 U.S.C.A. § 1062. Interested persons who oppose registration of the published mark have thirty days from the date of publication to file an opposition. See 15 U.S.C.A. § 1063. Oppositions may be based on any of the grounds for refusing registration set forth in Lanham Act § 2, and are heard in a proceeding before the Trademark Trial and Appeal Board. See 15 U.S.C.A. § 1067.

If no opposition is filed, the next step in the process will depend on whether the applicant has filed a use application or an intent-to-use application. If the former, the PTO will register the mark and issue a registration certificate. Notice of the registration will be published in the Official Gazette. See 15 U.S.C.A. § 1063(b)(1). The certificate of registration is

> prima facie evidence of the validity of the registered mark and of the registration of the mark, of the registrant's ownership of the mark, and of the registrant's exclusive right to use the registered mark in commerce on or in connection with the goods or services specified in the certificate, subject to any conditions or limitations stated in the certificate.

15 U.S.C.A. § 1057(b). Thus, registration creates a rebuttable presumption of mark validity, which assists the registrant in the event of litigation.

If the application was based on a *bona fide* intent to use the mark in the future, the PTO will issue a Notice of Allowance. See 15 U.S.C.A. § 1063(b)(2). The applicant then has six months to either 1) use the mark in commerce and file a verified statement affirming that use has been made, along with specimens of the use; or 2) request a six-month extension of time. This first extension is granted as a matter of course. Additional six-month extensions may be granted upon a showing of good cause, for up to an additional 24 months. See 15 U.S.C.A. § 1051(d). Assuming that the applicant ultimately files a timely and acceptable statement of use, the PTO will then issue a registration certificate, as described above, and publish notice of the registration. *Id.*

The Lanham Act seeks to ensure that only marks actually in use are and remain registered. Accordingly, between the fifth and sixth year following registration, the registrant must file an affidavit verifying that the mark is still being used in commerce in connection with the goods or services set forth in the registration, or showing that non-use is due to special circumstances that excuse it. The PTO will cancel the mark at the end of the sixth year if this filing is not made. See 15 U.S.C.A. § 1058. Assuming that the affidavit is filed, the registration is good for ten years, *id.*, and can be renewed for periods of ten years. See 15 U.S.C.A. § 1059. However, the registrant must continue to file affidavits of continued use periodically as specified in Lanham Act § 8. 15 U.S.C. § 1058.

Applicants for registration, parties to opposition proceedings, parties who have been denied renewal of registrations, and others who are dissatisfied with the Commissioner's or the Trademark Trial and Appeal Board's disposition of their claims may seek judicial review. Lanham Act § 21, 15 U.S.C.A. § 1071, provides two alternative routes. Under subsection (a), a direct appeal may be taken to the United States Court of Appeals for the Federal Circuit, which will review the disputed PTO decision on the record before the PTO. Under subsection (b), a party may seek *de novo* review in a United States district court. Appeals from the district court are taken to the appropriate regional circuit court of appeals.

NOTES AND QUESTIONS

1. *Advantages of intent-to-use applications.* Congress amended the Lanham Act to provide the intent-to-use route to registration in 1988, after considerable public debate. Why was this avenue to registration deemed necessary? Consider the following:

> The Lanham Act's preapplication use requirement * * * creates unnecessary legal uncertainty for a U.S. business planning to introduce products or services into the marketplace. It simply has no assurance after selecting and adopting a mark, and possibly making a sizeable investment in packaging, advertising and marketing, it will not learn that its use of the mark infringes the rights of another acquired through earlier use. In an age of national, if not global, marketing, this has a chilling effect on business investment. This effect is not merely theoretical, but is real. And it can be costly: Marketing a new product domestically often exceeds $30 million for a large company and can consume the life-savings of an individual or small entrepreneur.

> Partially in recognition of the difficulties companies face in launching new products and services, and the sizable investments that may be at stake, regardless of a company's or individual's resources, the courts have sanctioned the practice of "token use." Token use is a contrived and commercially transparent practice—nothing more than a legal fiction. At the same time, token use is essential under current law because it recognizes present day marketing costs and realities; it reduces some of the legal and economic risks associated with entering the marketplace; and it nominally achieves the threshold "use" required to apply for federal registration and the creation of trademark rights in advance of commercial use.

> Unfortunately, token use is not available to all businesses and industries. For example, it is virtually impossible to make token use of a

trademark on a large or expensive product such as an airplane. The same is true for service industries (that is, hotels, restaurants, and banks) prior to opening for business. Similarly, it is difficult for small business and individuals to avail themselves of token use because they frequently lack the resources or the knowledge to engage in the practice.

Token use is also troublesome for another reason. It allows companies to obtain registration based on minimal use. Often these companies change their marketing plans and subsequently do not make commercial use. The result is that the trademark register is clogged with unused marks, making the clearance of new marks more difficult and discouraging others from adopting and using marks which should otherwise be available.

Trademark Law Revision Act of 1988, S. Rep. No. 515, 100th Cong., 2d Sess. 5–6 (1988).

Given that registration is not granted, even on intent-to-use applications, until the mark is used in trade and commerce, how does the intent-to-use application assist businesses who wish to "reserve a mark" for future use? Lanham Act § 7(c) provides:

Contingent on the registration of a mark on the principal register provided by this Act, the filing of the application to register such mark shall constitute constructive use of the mark, conferring a right of priority, nationwide in effect, on or in connection with the goods or services specified in the registration against any other person except for a person whose mark has not been abandoned and who, prior to such filing—

(1) has used the mark;

(2) has filed an application to register the mark which is pending or has resulted in registration of the mark; or

(3) has filed a foreign application to register the mark on the basis of which he or she has acquired a right of priority, and timely files an application under section 1126(d) of this title to register the mark which is pending or has resulted in registration of the mark.

15 U.S.C.A. § 1057(c).

This provision is tempered somewhat by the fact that the Lanham Act, as amended, provides the intent-to-use applicant with no judicial remedy for infringement prior to her actual use of the mark. See Fila Sport, S.p.A. v. Diadora America, Inc., 141 F.R.D. 74 (N.D.Ill.1991). Should an interim remedy be provided?

2. *Rights by use vs. rights by registration.* Even after enactment of the intent-to-use application procedure, the Lanham Act, like American common law, is firmly committed to the notion that rights in trademarks arise from adoption and use, not from the mere act of registration. In this respect, United States law differs from that of most nations, who impose no use requirement on persons seeking to register marks, and provide that the act of registration in itself confers ownership rights in marks. Which system is

preferable—one based on use, such as the United States', or a "race to the trademark office" system, which bases rights on being the first to register?

3. *Other registration-related proceedings before the TTAB.* In addition to the "opposition" proceeding discussed above, it is useful to know about a couple of other *inter partes* proceedings that are adjudicated before the PTO's Trademark Trial and Appeal Board. First, a "concurrent use" proceeding arises when an applicant for registration claims a right to use a mark that is concurrent with another user's right, rather than claiming an exclusive right. The circumstances in which this might occur will be explored more fully in later sections, but include situations in which two parties obtained the right to use the same or similar marks in different parts of the country under the common law, before either registered or applied to register. Lanham Act § 2(d) authorizes issuance of a concurrent registration in such situations if it appears that "confusion, mistake, or deception is not likely to result from the continued use by more than one person." In order to ensure that confusion does not occur, the PTO, in issuing the concurrent registration, may impose "conditions or limitations" regarding the mode or place of use of the mark. 15 U.S.C.A. § 1052(d).

The second *inter partes* proceeding arises when the TTAB determines petitions to cancel existing registrations. "[A]ny person who believes that he is or will be damaged by the registration of a mark on the principal register" may file a petition to cancel the registration. *Id.,* at § 1064. During the first five years of registration, a mark can be canceled on any of the grounds for refusing registration in the first place. *Id.,* at § 1052. The grounds for cancellation are reduced thereafter. *Id.,* at § 1064.

4. *The Supplemental Register.* The PTO maintains a second trademark register, known as the "Supplemental Register." Lanham Act § 23 provides that "[a]ll marks *capable* of distinguishing applicant's goods or services and not registrable on the principal register * * * which are in lawful use in commerce by the owner thereof * * * may be registered on the supplemental register"[10] 15 U.S.C.A. § 1091(a) (emphasis added). As a general matter, this means that persons using words, symbols and devices that are capable of becoming distinctive (as opposed to inherently distinctive) but have not yet acquired secondary meaning may register them on the Supplemental Register.

The intent-to-use registration procedure is not available to register marks on the Supplemental Register, *id.* at § 1094, and the registration procedure based on use is abbreviated. *Id.* at § 1092. Most of the advantages flowing from registration on the Principal Register are unavailable. See *id.* at § 1094. What, then, is the purpose of the Supplemental Register?

The primary purpose is to assist United States businesses to obtain registration of their marks abroad, in countries that condition registration of foreign marks on the mark's registration in the applicant's home country. Registration on the Supplemental Register also gives registrants access to the federal courts for infringement claims, assuming that their marks have become distinctive enough to support a claim of ownership rights. Such

10. Marks declared unregistrable under Lanham Act § 2(a)–(d) and (in most cases) (e)(3) are excluded from the Supplemental Register. See 15 U.S.C.A. § 1091(a).

jurisdiction would be available in any event for infringement of unregistered marks under Lanham Act § 43(a). 15 U.S.C.A. § 1125(a).

Registration on the Supplemental Register does not preclude later registration on the Principal Register, once the mark has become sufficiently distinctive through use.

PROBLEMS

1. A Company selects a mark and files an intent-to-use application to register it in June, 1999. The application is allowed in January of 2000. In July, 2000, A Company files for an extension of time. A Company completes its preparations and introduces goods bearing the mark to the market in November, 2000. A Company then files an affidavit of use and registration is granted. B Company begins using the same mark on similar goods in August, 1999. After obtaining registration, A Company sues B Company for infringement. Who has priority?

2. X Company files an intent-to-use application to register the mark "Real Wheels" on January 1, 2000, and commences preparations to launch a toy on the market with that mark. The application is allowed in July, 2000. However, in September, 2000, before X has made its use of the "Real Wheels" mark and completed its registration, Y Company introduces its own new toy to the market, using the mark "Real Wheels." Y Company then sues X Company for infringement, seeking a preliminary injunction to prevent X Company from making its planned use of the "Real Wheels" mark, perfecting its registration, and obtaining registration and the benefit of its application date as a constructive use date. How should the court rule?

NOTE: TRADEMARK INCONTESTABILITY AND IMMUNITY FROM CANCELLATION

Creating a central, nationwide register of trademark interests is efficient: it gives notice of business' trademark claims throughout the country and thus enables others to locate and evaluate prior uses of the marks they wish to adopt before investing in them. The register reduces search costs and helps to avoid unnecessary post-adoption litigation. Congress undertook to encourage businesses to register their marks in several ways when it enacted the Lanham Act. As we will see in the next section, Congress introduced "constructive notice" (and later, "constructive use") provisions, which enable mark registrants to attain rights in a broader geographic area than would be possible under the common law. It also adopted "incontestability" and "cancellation immunity" provisions, which serve as a kind of statute of limitations. If the validity and registration of a mark are not successfully challenged during the first five years of registration, certain grounds of challenge are thereafter foreclosed. The owner can invest in promotion of the mark with confidence that the investment will not be lost through a challenge to the mark's validity down the line.

To understand "incontestability," one must understand the interaction of Lanham Act §§ 14, 15, and 33(b). 15 U.S.C.A. §§ 1064, 1065, 1115(b). First, study the provisions of § 14. This section sets forth the grounds on which the registration of a mark can be cancelled. Within the first five years of registration, a "person who believes that he is or will be damaged by the registration of a mark" may seek cancellation on any ground that would have precluded registration in the first place. After five years, the grounds for cancellation are narrowed. Subsections (3) through (5) list the grounds that may still be asserted to cancel a registration after five years. 15 U.S.C.A. § 1064(3)–(5).

While § 14 addresses the registration of a mark, § 15 addresses the right to use a registered mark. Review the language of § 15. Five years after registration, the registrant who complies with the "continuous use" and other listed requirements may attain an "incontestable" right to use its mark in commerce. If the right to use the mark is incontestable, then others cannot prevent the registrant from using it in connection with the goods or services specified in the registration—except on a ground that would expose the mark to cancellation under § 14(3)–(5), and except to the extent that the registrant is infringing a valid state right predating the registration. Thus, §§ 14 and 15 are "defensive" in nature. Section 14 applies to assist the registrant of five years against a petition to cancel its registration, while § 15 applies to protect an incontestable registrant against an infringement suit to enjoin the registrant's continuing use of the mark.

Subsection 33(a), as amended, provides that registration shall be

prima facie evidence of the validity of the registered mark and of the registration of the mark, of the registrant's ownership of the mark, and of the registrant's exclusive right to use the registered mark in commerce on or in connection with the goods or services specified in the registration * * *.

15 U.S.C.A. § 1115(a). Thus, pursuant to subsection (a), registration creates a rebuttable presumption of validity, ownership and exclusive right. While "any defense or defect" that might have been asserted in the absence of registration may still be asserted, the burden of proof is on the person contesting the registrant's rights.

Subsection (b) provides that "to the extent the mark has become incontestable" under Lanham Act § 15, the presumption of validity, ownership and exclusive right set forth in subsection (a) becomes conclusive—no longer subject to challenge by others. However, subsection (b) then provides that this "conclusive evidence" is subject to a list of nine "defenses or defects" that may be asserted against the registrant.[11] Note also that in limiting its provisions to incontestable marks, the language of subsection (b) incorporates

---

11. Note that the literal language of § 33(b) suggests that proof of one of the nine enumerated defenses or defects is not a defense on the merits, but merely eliminates the conclusive evidentiary status of the incontestable registration, so that common-law legal and equitable defenses may be asserted as provided under § 33(a). See *Park 'N Fly*, 469 U.S. at 199 n.6, 105 S.Ct. at 669 n.6, 83 L.Ed.2d at 591 n.6. As a technical matter, this would require that the defendant establish a defense twice—first to eliminate the conclusive effect of the incontestable registration and then to establish his defense to the infringement claim. To the extent that the § 33(b) "defenses and defects" differ from the corresponding common-law defenses, this two step procedure makes sense. Since they generally do not, the two-step procedure is duplicative in most cases. For this reason, courts usually collapse the process into one step, so that proof of the § 33(b) defense or defect serves immediately as a defense on the merits against the infringement claim.

the exceptions to incontestability set forth in § 15, which in turn incorporate the grounds for challenge "at any time" set forth in §§ 14(3) and (5). As the Supreme Court held in Park 'N Fly, Inc. v. Dollar Park and Fly, Inc., 469 U.S. 189, 105 S.Ct. 658, 83 L.Ed.2d 582 (1985), § 33(b) applies "offensively," to assist the registrant when it sues another for infringement. The advantage, however, is limited. As Justice Stevens points out in his dissent, there are numerous defenses that can still be asserted against the owner of an "incontestable" mark, in addition to a defense of no likelihood of confusion. Apart from the defense that the incontestable mark is merely descriptive and lacks secondary meaning, what additional defenses are precluded under § 33(b)? Is the term "incontestable" an accurate description of the qualifying registrant's rights?

2. *Applications Pursuant to International Treaty Provisions*

The Paris Convention for the Protection of Industrial Property regulates both international trademark and patent protection. Under its provisions, each of the over 160 member nations agrees to the principle of national treatment. That is, each undertakes to register and protect the trademarks of other members' nationals on essentially the same basis that it registers and protects its own. Each also agrees to afford certain minimal trademark rights. In addition, Paris Convention Article 4 provides a six-month filing priority period. This permits nationals of member nations who apply to register a mark in one member nation to obtain the benefit of that first filing date for applications filed in other member countries during the next six months. This benefit can be substantial, since most nations accord priority to the first person to file or register, rather than the first person to use a mark. Foreign applicants filing in the United States benefit, as well, since the earlier foreign filing date will become the applicant's constructive use date in the United States under Lanham Act § 7(c), once U.S. registration is granted. This will give the foreign applicant priority over U.S. applicants who make their first use or file an intent-to-use application at any time after the foreign priority filing date. The Lanham Act implements the Paris Convention priority filing date provisions in § 44(d). 15 U.S.C.A. § 1126(d).

Since the United States adheres to the Paris Convention, nationals of other member countries may, under national treatment principles, choose to register their marks on the Lanham Act Principal Register on the same basis as U.S. nationals—that is, by complying with the use or intent-to-use registration provisions described in the prior section. In the alternative, by virtue of article 6^{quinquies} of the Paris Convention, these foreign applicants may choose simply to rely on the fact that their marks have been registered in their countries of origin.[12] Article 6^{quinquies} sets forth what is

---

12. Article 6^{quinquies}(A)(2) defines the "country of origin" as:

[T]he country of the Union where the applicant has a real and effective industrial or commercial establishment, or, if he has no such establishment within the Union, the country of the Union where he has his domicile, or, if he has no domicile within the Union but is a national of a country of the Union, the country of which he is a national.

Given this definition, it is possible for an applicant to have more than one country of origin.

known as the *telle quelle* principle: Registration in one's country of origin entitles one to registration in other Paris Convention member nations, unless one of the exceptions enumerated in article 6*quinquies* applies.[13] Since most member nations register marks without any showing that they have been used in trade or commerce, this means that the United States must register foreign marks that have never been used—in the United States, or anywhere at all—even though it would not register unused marks on a domestic application. Lanham Act § 44(e), 15 U.S.C.A. § 1126(e), which implements the United States' *telle quelle* obligations, provides:

> A mark duly registered in the country of origin of the foreign applicant may be registered on the principal register if eligible, otherwise on the supplemental register * * *. Such applicant shall submit, within such time period as may be prescribed by the Commissioner, a certification or a certified copy of the registration in the country of origin of the applicant. The application must state the applicant's bona fide intention to use the mark in commerce, but use in commerce shall not be required prior to registration.

NOTES AND QUESTIONS

1. *An unequal playing field?* The U.S. system of imposing preapplication use requirements on domestic applicants, but no use requirements on foreign *telle quelle* applicants, was criticized as unfair. The perceived unfairness was a key factor in Congress' decision in 1988 to enact the intent-to-use application process. How does implementation of the intent-to-use application procedure address the disparity? What, if any, advantage do foreign applicants now have over domestic applicants?

2. *Trademark registration filing treaties.* In 1998, the United States implemented the Trademark Law Treaty[14], which was designed to harmonize

---

13. Marks are excepted when 1) "they are of such a nature as to infringe rights acquired by third parties in the country where protection is claimed;" 2) "they are devoid of any distinctive character, or consist exclusively of signs or indications which may serve, in trade, to designate the kind, quality, quantity, intended purpose, value, place of origin, of the goods, or the time of production, or have become customary in the current language or in the bona fide and established practices of the trade of the country where protection is claimed;" or 3) "they are contrary to morality or to public order and, in particular, of such a nature as to deceive the public." Paris Convention, *supra*, article 6*quinquies*(B).

The Court of Appeals for the Federal Circuit has held that *telle quelle* marks must satisfy the requirements of Lanham Act § 2 in order to be registered. Thus, a surname mark registered in Germany was not entitled to be registered on the Principal Register absent a showing of secondary meaning. The court reasoned that the Paris Convention is not self-executing, and construed Lanham Act § 44(e), which implements the provisions of the Paris Convention, only to authorize *telle quelle* registrations when the marks are "eligible"–that is, when they satisfy the provisions of Lanham Act § 2. *In re* Rath, 402 F.3d 1207 (Fed. Cir. 2005). Judge Bryson filed a concurring opinion arguing that the majority's construction of § 44(e) to trump the provisions of article 6*quinquies* was unnecessary, since the Paris Convention's exception for marks "devoid of any distinctive character" would justify the PTO's rejection of the *telle quelle* application in this particular case.

14. Trademark Law Treaty Implementation Act of 1998, Pub. L. No. 105–30, 112 Stat. 3064. The Trademark Law Treaty was negotiated under the auspices of the World Intellectual Property Organization, adopted at Geneva on October 27, 1994, and entered into force on August 1, 1996.

treaty members' requirements for applications to register marks and registration maintenance. A few years later, the U.S. ratified and passed legislation to implement the Protocol Relating to the Madrid Agreement Concerning the International Registration of Marks (the "Madrid Protocol"). The Protocol, which became effective in the U.S. in November, 2003, provides U.S. trademark owners an opportunity to register their marks in numerous other countries through use of a single, standardized application in English, and a single payment of fees in U.S. dollars.

U.S. mark owners may apply for international registration at the time that they apply for U.S. registration, or if they have already applied or registered in the U.S., they can file a subsequent international application with the U.S. Patent and Trademark Office. The international application designates the other Madrid Protocol member nations in which the applicant wishes to register. Since an international registration is based on the applicant's U.S. application or registration, the PTO must certify that the international application accurately reflects the substance of the U.S. application or registration. The PTO then forwards the Protocol application to the International Bureau of the World Intellectual Property Organization ("WIPO"). The International Bureau checks to ensure that the application complies with certain formalities, but does not perform a substantive examination. It records the mark on the International Register and then sends requests for extensions of protection to the registering authority in each member country that the applicant designated. The international registration, in itself, confers no substantive rights. The registering authority in each designated country follows its own examination procedure and applies its own substantive trademark laws to determine whether it will "extend" the international registration to that country. The scope of examination varies greatly from one country to the next. If the country issues a certificate of extension, the WIPO international registration is "extended" to that country. The international registration is good for ten years, and can be renewed in all countries with a single application to renew, filed with the WIPO International Bureau. Likewise, mark assignments can be recorded through a central filing.

This streamlined process may prove easier and more cost-effective for U.S. businesses than filing individual applications to register in each country, though the extent of savings may depend in part on the number of countries designated in the international application, and the identity of the designated nations. While the applicant may avoid the necessity of hiring foreign counsel to prosecute the application in countries with relatively lax registration laws and procedures, it may still be necessary to do so in the member nations that have stricter examination procedures and substantive rules. Moreover, there are some perceived disadvantages in the Madrid Protocol's international

The United States is also a party to the Nice Agreement Concerning the International Classification of Goods and Services to which Trademarks are Applied, June 15, 1957, 23 U.S.T. 1336, 550 U.N.T.S. 45. The Nice Agreement is a classification treaty, also meant to simplify the process of registering trademarks in a number of nations. Many nations, including the United States, require that registration applicants designate the class in which their goods or services fall, for administrative purposes. When the classifications of goods and services differ from one country to the next, applicants may experience difficulty and expense in determining the proper classes to designate in each country. By setting up a uniform classification system, the Nice Agreement makes it easier to make multiple registration applications in the more than 60 nations that adhere to its system.

registration. First, because the international registration is based on the application or registration in the applicant's country of origin, it will reflect any limitations in scope imposed by the applicant's domestic law. Since the United States imposes relatively strict limitations on the range of goods or services for which a mark may be registered, international registrants may find that their international registration provides a narrower scope of protection abroad than they could obtain through individual applications in each foreign country, which are tailored to take the fullest advantage of that country's rules. A second perceived problem is the "central attack" feature of the Madrid Protocol. For the first five years, the international registration remains dependent on the mark's registration in its country of origin. If registration is refused or canceled there during this period, then the mark's international registration and all the member country extensions will fall as well, even if the basis for the domestic refusal or cancellation would not have posed an obstacle to registration in the foreign countries. Because the U.S. tends to impose greater restrictions on registration than most other countries, this leaves the U.S. international registrant vulnerable: A challenge in the U.S. Patent and Trademark Office may have the effect not only of blocking or cancelling the company's domestic registration, but also of transforming all the company's international extensions to individual national applications! Accordingly, U.S. trademark owners are likely to be selective in their use of the Madrid Protocol procedure, and continue to file individual applications to register abroad in at least some cases.

What, if any impact is the Madrid Protocol likely to have on domestic trademark searches?

C. THE GEOGRAPHIC SCOPE OF RIGHTS

1. *The Common–Law Rule*

SWEET SIXTEEN CO. v. SWEET "16" SHOP, INC.

United States Court of Appeals for the Eighth Circuit, 1926.
15 F.2d 920.

FARIS, DISTRICT JUDGE.

This is an action in equity * * * based on the alleged infringement of plaintiff's trade-mark and trade-name. The decree below went for defendant, and plaintiff appealed in conventional mode.

* * * In the year 1916, plaintiff began business in San Francisco, as a dealer in women's ready-to-wear clothing, under the name of Sweet Sixteen Company, a corporation. In its business and advertisements it referred to many of its garments and goods as "Sweet Sixteens," it designated its system of dealing as the "Sweet Sixteen System," and it sold many of the garments kept for sale by it at $16 per garment. In the beginning it had but one store. It prospered in such wise as that, by the year 1921, it was the owner of five stores, two in San Francisco, and the others in three other cities of the coast states, namely, Los Angeles, Portland and Seattle, and also an office and general purchasing agency in

New York. It was advertising its business in divers trade journals and in the daily newspapers of the several cities in which its stores were located. Some 75 of these newspapers were daily sold and read in Utah. Its annual advertising expenditures in the year in which this suit was begun, amounted to more than $120,000. It had a very considerable mail order business, through which it sold some goods in some 12 or 15 different states, among which was the state of Utah. While the business done thus in the state of Utah was, in proportion to its total business, negligible, it was making efforts to increase it, and to this end, in the year 1921, it sent some 1,500 of its printed catalogues into that state. In the year 1922 it supplemented this selling and advertising campaign in the state of Utah by distributing therein pictures and drawings of many of the articles kept by it for sale.

Prior to 1923, and about the year 1921, it put on foot tentative plans to rent and establish a store in Salt Lake City, Utah. These plans were not consummated, however, up to April 3, 1923, when defendant started in Salt Lake City a wholly similar business, (save that it does not particularly cater to the mail order business), dealing in like merchandise, which defendant ran and operated under the name of the Sweet "16" Shop, Inc. Defendant was incorporated in the state of Utah on the 17th day of May, 1923. Prior to such incorporation, and on April 3, 1923, defendants Provol and Wrigley procured the issuance to them, as copartners, of a certificate of trade-mark from the secretary of state of the state of Utah, carrying the designation "Sweet '16' Shop." Some four days prior to the issuance of this certificate, and a like period before defendants Provol and Wrigley began business, Provol, one of the copartners, was advised by wire from plaintiff of the existence of plaintiff corporation and was warned not to use the name "Sweet 16" in defendants' business. Thereupon defendants took legal advice as to their right to use this name. While this advice was favorable to them, there is left no question in the case that defendants assumed this name with full knowledge of its use by plaintiff, if such fact shall be of controlling importance.

The record discloses fairly numerous instances wherein dealers, customers, and potential customers were misled by the similarity of names into mistaking defendants' business for that of plaintiff. * * *

[B]oth [parties] largely rely on the same cases to sustain their respective contentions. These cases are Hanover Star Milling Co. v. Metcalf, 240 U.S. 403, 36 S.Ct. 357, 60 L.Ed. 713, and United Drug Co. v. Rectanus Co., 248 U.S. 90, 39 S.Ct. 48, 63 L.Ed. 141. * * * The one decisive question here, broadly stated, is whether, on the facts, this case is within the rule announced in the above cases, or within the exceptions which plaintiff insists are clearly noted in these cases.

The brief and salient facts in the Rectanus case are that, about the year 1877, Mrs. Regis began to use the word "Rex" as a trade-mark for certain medicinal preparations made by her in Haverhill, Mass. Thereafter, through mesne assignments and continued use, this trade-mark came, about the year 1911, into the hands of the United Drug Company. During all of the years between 1877 and 1911 the sales of this medicinal preparation were confined to the New England states, with inconsiderable sales in New York, New Jersey, Canada, and Nova Scotia. In the meantime, and in the year 1889, one Rectanus, familiarly known as "Rex," began at Louisville, Ky., to use the word "Rex" as a trade-mark for another sort of medicinal preparation, which he sold and advertised in Kentucky. In 1912 the United Drug Company for the first time extended the sale of its medicines, bearing its "Rex" trade-mark, into the state of Kentucky. When it did so, and prior thereto, it had notice that the assignee of Rectanus was using the identical trade-mark in Kentucky on its medicines. These facts and all of them notwithstanding the United Drug Company sued the Rectanus Company for the infringement of its trade-mark. In the Supreme Court the decree went for defendant; the court saying, among other things, this:

> "Undoubtedly, the general rule is that, as between the conflicting claimants to the right to use the same mark, priority of appropriation determines the question. But the reason is that purchasers have come to understand the mark as indicating the origin of the wares, so that its use by a second producer amounts to an attempt to sell his goods as those of his competitor. The reason for the rule does not extend to a case where the same trade-mark happens to be employed simultaneously by two manufacturers, in different markets separate and remote from each other, so that the mark means one thing in one market, an entirely different thing in another. It would be a perversion of the rule of priority to give it such an application in our broadly extended country that an innocent party, who had in good faith employed a trade-mark in one state, and by the use of it had built up a trade there, being the first appropriator in that jurisdiction, might afterwards be prevented from using it, with consequent injury to his trade and good will, at the instance of one who theretofore had employed the same mark, but only in other and remote jurisdictions, upon the ground that its first employment happened to antedate that of the first-mentioned trader. * * *

> "The same point was involved in Hanover Milling Co. v. Metcalf, 240 U.S. 403, 415, 36 S.Ct. 357, 60 L.Ed. 713, where we said: 'In the ordinary case of parties competing under the same mark in the same market, it is correct to say that prior appropriation settles the question. But where two parties independently are employing the same mark upon goods of the same class, but in separate markets wholly remote the one from the other, the question of prior appropriation is legally insignificant, unless at least it appear that the second adopter has selected the mark with some design inimical to the interests of the first user, such as to take the benefit of the reputation of his goods to forestall the extension of his trade, or the like.'

> "In this case, as already remarked, there is no suggestion of a sinister purpose on the part of Rectanus or the Rectanus Company;

hence the passage quoted correctly defines the status of the parties prior to the time when they came into competition in the Kentucky market. And it results, as a necessary inference from what we have said, that petitioner, being the newcomer in that market, must enter it subject to whatever rights had previously been acquired there in good faith by the Rectanus Company and its predecessor. To hold otherwise—to require Rectanus to retire from the field upon the entry of Mrs. Regis' successor—would be to establish, the right of the latter as a right in gross, and to extend it to territory wholly remote from the furthest reach of the trade to which it was annexed, with the effect not merely of depriving Rectanus of the benefit of the good will resulting from his long-continued use of the mark in Louisville and vicinity, and his substantial expenditures in building up his trade, but of enabling petitioner to reap substantial benefit from the publicity that Rectanus has thus given to the mark in that locality, and of confusing if not misleading the public as to the origin of goods thereafter sold in Louisville under the Rex mark, for, in that market, until petitioner entered it, 'Rex' meant the Rectanus product, not that of Regis.''

The facts in the case of Allen & Wheeler Co. v. Hanover Star Milling Co., *sub nomine* Hanover Milling Co. v. Metcalf, 240 U.S. 403, 36 S.Ct. 357, 60 L.Ed. 713, are very similar to those in the Rectanus Case, *supra.* In the Metcalf Case, Allen & Wheeler Company had first adopted and used the trade-mark "Tea Rose," on a certain sort of flour made by it, and which it sold wholly, in that part of the United States north of the Ohio river; "while the Hanover Company had adopted 'Tea Rose' as its mark in perfect good faith with no knowledge that anybody else was using or had used those words in such a connection, and during many years it had built up and extended its trade in the southeastern territory, comprising Georgia, Florida, Alabama, and Mississippi, so that in the flour trade in that territory the mark 'Tea Rose' had come to mean the Hanover Company's flour and nothing else." The Circuit Court of Appeals held, and the Supreme Court concurred substantially in the holding, "that the right to protection in the exclusive use of a trade-mark extends only to those markets where the trader's goods have become known and identified by his use of the mark; and because of the nonoccupancy by the Allen & Wheeler Company of the Southeastern markets it had no ground of relief in equity." It need scarcely be added that the alleged infringement, above complained of, occurred in the "Southeastern markets."

Confessedly, then, the general rule is that, while the first appropriator and user of a trade-mark owns such mark and is entitled to protection by the courts in the use thereof, against subsequent users on the same class of goods, such protection will not be afforded as against a subsequent user and appropriator, who in good faith adopts and uses the mark in territory into which the goods of the first appropriator have not penetrated and have not been used or sold. [A]ppellant frankly concedes the general rule to be substantially as stated, but it urges that the instant case falls upon the facts within the exceptions held in mind by the Supreme Court * * *.

* * *

[T]he exceptions to the general rule, which appellant contends differentiate on the facts the case at bar from both the Metcalf Case and the Rectanus Case, are found in this language in the above quoted excerpts from these two opinions:

> (a) "But where two parties independently are employing the same mark upon goods of the same class, but in separate markets wholly remote the one from the other, the question of prior appropriation is legally insignificant, *unless at least it appear that the second adopter has selected the mark with some design inimical to the interests of the first user, such as to take the benefit of the reputation of his goods, to forestall the extension of his trade, or the like.*"

(Italics ours.) United Drug Co. v. Rectanus Co., 248 U.S. loc.cit. 101, 39 S.Ct. 52 (63 L.Ed. 141).

> (b) "*We are not dealing with a case where the junior appropriator of a trade-mark is occupying territory that would probably be reached by the prior user in the natural expansion of his trade, and need pass no judgment upon such a case.*"

(Italics ours.) Hanover Milling Co. v. Metcalf, 240 U.S. loc.cit. 420, 36 S.Ct. 363 (60 L.Ed. 713).

In the instant case defendants Provol and Wrigley, while they were copartners, before they organized defendant corporation and before they actually began business, had notice of plaintiff's prior adoption, appropriation, and use of the words "Sweet Sixteen" to designate its business, and as a trade-mark on the goods in which plaintiff was dealing. The trial court so found, and the facts in evidence conclusively so disclose. Not only is this conclusively shown by the telegram sent to Provol, notice to whom as a partner was notice to Wrigley, but it is corroborated by other evidence in the case, some of which is suggestive, if not sinister. For example, they saw fit to make a slight change in the manner of representing the expression "Sixteen" by the use of quoted numerals, instead of spelling the word out, as plaintiff does; before they began business, and before they had ever actually used this mark, they registered it as a trade-mark with the secretary of state of Utah. Aside from the finding of the trial court, and of the conclusive evidence of prior notice, the two latter precautions are such as would not ordinarily be taken by those who were wholly innocent of plaintiff's existence and of its use of the mark in controversy.

Apposite to the exception of prior appropriation of the field of trade and of the right to a natural expansion into such field, the facts, as already said, are that plaintiff in 1921, and some two years before defendant began business under the style complained of here, had sent some 1,500 of its catalogues into Utah and to Salt Lake City; in 1922 it supplemented these catalogues by sending into that state pictures and drawings of many of the goods kept and sold by it; and it had sold to citizens of Utah at Salt Lake City some goods and had filled some mail orders there; in all, making some six or eight sales in one or the other of the above ways. Newspapers containing its advertisements had constantly been sold in Salt Lake City for a number of years before defendants did the act here complained of. Plaintiff avers, and the evidence discloses, its intention to establish a store in Utah, and to this end it had already taken tentative steps till the acts of defendants forestalled it.

* * * Not only, we repeat, are we of the opinion that the instant case is within what seem to be the very plain exceptions to the general rule as pointed out in the above cases, but that the above facts of notice of prior use, the quantum of such use, the solicitation of trade, and the advertisements of plaintiff in the Salt Lake City territory of trade, bring the case within settled rules not at all disturbed by the above-cited leading cases. For we are dealing here with a trade-mark clearly within the category of odd and fanciful marks, and not with a mark within the public domain, in which latter the user required must be such, and so long and so expansively used, as to acquire a secondary meaning.

In a case then like the instant one, the rule laid down in the very excellent and able work of Mr. Nims, seems yet applicable:

"In considering the question of extent of use, careful distinction must be drawn between technical and pure trade-marks and marks which are not technical, but are in the public domain. Where the name or device chosen is fanciful and may become a technical trade-mark, very slight use will, in addition to adoption create a trade-mark. * * *"

Nims, The Law of Unfair Competition and Trade–Marks, 415.

Obviously, the trade-marks under discussion in the Hanover and Rectanus Cases were likewise technical trade-marks, but in neither of the latter cases had there been any sales, advertisements of goods, or user whatever by complainants therein in the territory there in controversy. In case of a technical trade-mark as here dealt with, while there must, of course, be some user in trade in the disputed field of trade, the quantum thereof need not be large. * * * [I]t would seem to follow inevitably, that if "a single instance of user, with accompanying circumstances evidencing an intent to establish the right to a trade-mark" (Hopkins on Trade-marks), be sufficient to establish such right in San Francisco, as against an alleged infringer in that city, then six or eight instances of such use, by sales of trade-marked goods, accompanied by fairly extensive advertisements in certain newspapers circulated and read in Salt Lake City, and the distribution therein of many catalogues ought, certeris paribus, to be sufficient user, as against a subsequent appropriator, to constitute infringement by the latter in Salt Lake City.

[W]e are of opinion that the case should be reversed and remanded, with directions to grant to plaintiff the relief for which it prays. * * *

NOTES AND QUESTIONS

1. *The remote, good-faith user.* What policy underlies the *Rectanus/Hanover Star Milling* rule? As a practical matter, in today's world of modern communications, transportation and travel, is one as likely to encounter local, remote markets of the type involved in those cases? As you will see in the following subsection, the Lanham Act alters the impact of the remote, good-faith user rule for marks registered on the Principal Register. The rule still controls, however, in the case of common-law and § 43(a) claims for infringement of unregistered marks, trade dress and trade names.

Why, exactly, did the defendants in *Sweet Sixteen* fail to qualify as remote, good-faith users under the *Rectanus/Hanover Star Milling* rule? Were the defendants the first to use the "Sweet 16" mark in Utah? Did the defendants lack good faith? Were they not in a "remote" geographic area? Suppose that the defendants had convinced the court that they qualified as remote, good-faith first users in Utah. Does it follow under the Supreme Court's reasoning in *Rectanus* and *Hanover Star Milling* that they could enjoin the plaintiff's use of the mark in Utah?

2. *Good faith.* In order to qualify as a remote, good faith user under the *Rectanus/Hanover Star Milling* rule, a "junior" (subsequent) user must demonstrate that she had "good faith" at the time that she began her use of the mark. There has been some dispute over the nature of the good faith requirement. At points, the Supreme Court in *Rectanus* and *Hanover Star Milling* spoke of a "lack of knowledge" of the senior user's mark. However, the Court also spoke of a "design inimical to the interests of the first user, such as to take the benefit of the reputation of his goods, to forestall the extension of his trade, or the like." *Hanover Star Milling*, 240 U.S. at 415. The majority view today is that knowledge of the prior user's mark at the time the junior user commences use negates good faith. Indeed, in the case of registered marks, constructive knowledge of the registrant's use, imputed by the fact of registration, is sufficient to negate good faith.

A minority of case opinions and commentators have favored the "design inimical to the interests of the first user" test, suggesting that it would be possible for a junior user with knowledge of the senior user to adopt the mark in good faith. Under this view, knowledge will support an inference of bad faith, but the ultimate question is whether the junior user had the intent to benefit from the reputation or good will of the first user. See Restatement (Third) of Unfair Competition § 19, cmt d (1995). Which view makes the most sense?

3. *A remote area.* The fact that the senior user does no business with the mark in an area does not guarantee that the area is "remote." Given modern communications and travel, consumers may be familiar with a mark used in other parts of the country. For example, the mark of a famous department store or hotel in New York City might be well known in Omaha by virtue of national advertising, media coverage, and the travel of Omaha residents, even though the owner does no business there. If the senior user's mark is so well known in an area at the time of the junior user's first use that the junior use

will lead to a likelihood of consumer confusion, then the junior use will not be deemed remote, and the *Rectanus/Hanover Star Milling* doctrine will afford no protection. See Restatement (Third) of Unfair Competition § 19 cmt d (1995). (As discussed in the prior section, however, historically, the senior famous use must be within United States territory.)

4. *"Technical trademarks" vs. secondary meaning marks.* In *Sweet Sixteen*, the court made a point of stressing that it was dealing "with a trademark clearly within the category of odd and fanciful marks, and not with a mark within the public domain, in which latter the user required must be such, and so long and so expansively used, as to acquire a secondary meaning." Why is that relevant?

5. *The zone of natural expansion.* In *Sweet Sixteen*, the plaintiff argued that the following statement from the *Hanover Star Milling* case supported its claim: "We are not dealing with a case where the junior appropriator of a trade-mark is occupying territory that would probably be reached by the prior user in the natural expansion of his trade * * *." 240 U.S. at 420. This implied exception to the general remote, good-faith user rule has served as the foundation for the somewhat dubious "zone of natural expansion" doctrine.

This doctrine may provide superior rights to the senior user in a geographic area that was not otherwise within his market territory at the time the junior user began its good faith use. To gain such rights, the senior user must demonstrate that at the time the junior user began its use in the area, it was natural and foreseeable that the senior user would expand into that area. The doctrine has been justified as giving a senior user some "breathing space" and room to expand. Case opinions relying on the zone of natural expansion doctrine are relatively rare, however. Some authorities have rejected it altogether. See, e.g., Restatement (Third) of Unfair Competition § 19, cmt c (1995).

PROBLEM

1. Alice, an Ohio homemaker, conceived of a business venture in which she, with the help of her daughter and a neighbor, would design and manufacture "superhero capes" for children. The capes would be fashioned after the capes worn by such superheros as Superman and Batman, would be available in a range of colors, and would bear a large initial on the back to represent the wearer's first name. Alice then registered the domain name "Alscapes.com" and in January, 2005, set up a web site over which shoppers could order personalized capes for their children. During the first six months of operations, she sold 160 capes to purchasers in various parts of the world, but by the seventh month her web site had attracted some notice, and she was beginning to get increased sales. In August, 2005, Al, a businessman in Montana, opened a small costume shop which he called "Alscapes." Al was not aware of Alice's business. Assuming that "Alscapes.com" and "Alscapes" are confusingly similar, what are the parties' respective rights?

2. *The Lanham Act and Constructive Use and Notice*

DAWN DONUT COMPANY, INC. v.
HART'S FOOD STORES, INC.

United States Court of Appeals for the Second Circuit, 1959.
267 F.2d 358.

Lumbard, Circuit Judge.

The principal question is whether the plaintiff, a wholesale distributor of doughnuts and other baked goods under its federally registered trademarks "Dawn" and "Dawn Donut," is entitled under the provisions of the Lanham Trade–Mark Act to enjoin the defendant from using the mark "Dawn" in connection with the retail sale of doughnuts and baked goods entirely within a six county area of New York State surrounding the city of Rochester. The primary difficulty arises from the fact that although plaintiff licenses purchasers of its mixes to use its trademarks in connection with the retail sales of food products made from the mixes, it has not licensed or otherwise exploited the mark at the retail level in defendant's market area for some thirty years.

We hold that because no likelihood of public confusion arises from the concurrent use of the mark in connection with retail sales of doughnuts and other baked goods in separate trading areas, and because there is no present likelihood that plaintiff will expand its retail use of the mark into defendant's market area, plaintiff is not now entitled to any relief under the Lanham Act, 15 U.S.C.A. 1114. Accordingly, we affirm the district court's dismissal of plaintiff's complaint.

This is not to say that the defendant has acquired any permanent right to use the mark in its trading area. On the contrary, we hold that because of the effect of the constructive notice provision of the Lanham Act, should the plaintiff expand its retail activities into the six county area, upon a proper application and showing to the district court, it may enjoin defendant's use of the mark.

* * *

Plaintiff, Dawn Donut Co., Inc., of Jackson, Michigan since June 1, 1922 has continuously used the trademark "Dawn" upon 25 to 100 pound bags of doughnut mix which it sells to bakers in various states, including New York, and since 1935 it has similarly marketed a line of sweet dough mixes for use in the baking of coffee cakes, cinnamon rolls and oven goods in general under that mark. In 1950 cake mixes were added to the company's line of products. Dawn's sales representatives call upon bakers to solicit orders for mixes and the orders obtained are filled by shipment to the purchaser either directly from plaintiff's Jackson, Michigan plant, where the mixes are manufactured, or from a local warehouse within the customer's state. For some years plaintiff maintained a warehouse in Jamestown, New York, from which shipments were made, but sometime prior to the commencement of this suit in 1954 it discontinued this warehouse and has since then shipped its mixes to its New York customers directly from Michigan.

Plaintiff furnishes certain buyers of its mixes, principally those who agree to become exclusive Dawn Donut Shops, with advertising and packaging material bearing the trademark "Dawn" and permits these bakers to sell goods made from the mixes to the consuming public under that trademark. These display materials are supplied either as a courtesy or at a moderate price apparently to stimulate and promote the sale of plaintiff's mixes.

The district court found that with the exception of one Dawn Donut Shop operated in the city of Rochester, New York during 1926–27, plaintiff's licensing of its mark in connection with the retail sale of doughnuts in the state of New York has been confined to areas not less than 60 miles from defendant's trading area. The court also found that for the past eighteen years plaintiff's present New York state representative has, without interruption, made regular calls upon bakers in the city of Rochester, N.Y., and in neighboring towns and cities, soliciting orders for plaintiff's mixes and that throughout this period orders have been filled and shipments made of plaintiff's mixes from Jackson, Michigan into the city of Rochester. But it does not appear that any of these purchasers of plaintiff's mixes employed the plaintiff's mark in connection with retail sales.

The defendant, Hart Food Stores, Inc., owns and operates a retail grocery chain within the New York counties of Monroe, Wayne, Livingston, Genesee, Ontario and Wyoming. The products of defendant's bakery, Starhart Bakeries, Inc., a New York corporation of which it is the sole stockholder, are distributed through these stores, thus confining the distribution of defendant's product to an area within a 45 mile radius of Rochester. Its advertising of doughnuts and other baked products over television and radio and in newspapers is also limited to this area. Defendant's bakery corporation was formed on April 13, 1951 and first used the imprint "Dawn" in packaging its products on August 30, 1951. The district court found that the defendant adopted the mark "Dawn" without any actual knowledge of plaintiff's use or federal registration of the mark, selecting it largely because of a slogan "Baked at midnight, delivered at Dawn" which was originated by defendant's president and used by defendant in its bakery operations from 1929 to 1935. Defendant's president testified, however, that no investigation was made prior to the adoption of the mark to see if anyone else was employing it. Plaintiff's marks were registered federally in 1927, and their registration was renewed in 1947. Therefore by virtue of the Lanham Act, 15 U.S.C.A. 1072, the defendant had constructive notice of plaintiff's marks as of July 5, 1947, the effective date of the Act.

Defendant's principal contention is that because plaintiff has failed to exploit the mark "Dawn" for some thirty years at the retail level in the

Rochester trading area, plaintiff should not be accorded the exclusive right to use the mark in this area.

We reject this contention as inconsistent with the scope of protection afforded a federal registrant by the Lanham Act.

Prior to the passage of the Lanham Act courts generally held that the owner of a registered trademark could not sustain an action for infringement against another who, without knowledge of the registration, used the mark in a different trading area from that exploited by the registrant so that public confusion was unlikely. Hanover Star Milling Co. v. Metcalf, 1916, 240 U.S. 403, 36 S.Ct. 357, 60 L.Ed. 713. By being the first to adopt a mark in an area without knowledge of its prior registration, a junior user of a mark could gain the right to exploit the mark exclusively in that market.

But the Lanham Act, 15 U.S.C.A. 1072, provides that registration of a trademark on the principal register is constructive notice of the registrant's claim of ownership. Thus, by eliminating the defense of good faith and lack of knowledge, 1072 affords nationwide protection to registered marks, regardless of the areas in which the registrant actually uses the mark.

That such is the purpose of Congress is further evidenced by 15 U.S.C.A. 1115(a) and (b) which make the certificate of registration evidence of the registrant's "exclusive right to use the * * * mark in commerce." "Commerce" is defined in 15 U.S.C.A. 1127 to include all the commerce which may lawfully be regulated by Congress. These two provisions of the Lanham Act make it plain that the fact that the defendant employed the mark "Dawn," without actual knowledge of plaintiff's registration, at the retail level in a limited geographical area of New York state before the plaintiff used the mark in that market, does not entitle it either to exclude the plaintiff from using the mark in that area or to use the mark concurrently once the plaintiff licenses the mark or otherwise exploits it in connection with retail sales in the area.

Plaintiff's failure to license its trademarks in defendant's trading area during the thirty odd years that have elapsed since it licensed them to a Rochester baker does not work an abandonment of the rights in that area. We hold that 15 U.S.C.A. 1127, which provides for abandonment in certain cases of non-use,[3] applies only when the registrant fails to use his mark, within the meaning of 1127, anywhere in the nation. Since the Lanham Act affords a registrant nationwide protection, a contrary holding would create an insoluble problem of measuring the geographical extent of the abandonment. * * *

---

3. 15 U.S.C.A. 1127 provides:

"A mark shall be deemed to be 'abandoned'—

"(a) When its use has been discontinued with intent not to resume. Intent not to resume may be inferred from circumstances. Nonuse for two consecutive years shall be prima facie abandonment.

"(b) When any course of conduct of the registrant, including acts of omission as well as commission, causes the mark to lose its significance as an indication of origin."

Accordingly, since plaintiff has used its trademark continuously at the retail level, it has not abandoned its federal registration rights even in defendant's trading area.

* * *

[W]e turn to the question of whether on this record plaintiff has made a sufficient showing to warrant the issuance of an injunction against defendant's use of the mark "Dawn" in a trading area in which the plaintiff has for thirty years failed to employ its registered mark.

The Lanham Act, 15 U.S.C.A. 1114, sets out the standard for awarding a registrant relief against the unauthorized use of his mark by another. It provides that the registrant may enjoin only that concurrent use which creates a likelihood of public confusion as to the origin of the products in connection with which the marks are used. Therefore if the use of the marks by the registrant and the unauthorized user are confined to two sufficiently distinct and geographically separate markets, with no likelihood that the registrant will expand his use into defendant's market, so that no public confusion is possible, then the registrant is not entitled to enjoin the junior user's use of the mark.

As long as plaintiff and defendant confine their use of the mark "Dawn" in connection with the retail sale of baked goods to their present separate trading areas it is clear that no public confusion is likely.

The district court took note of what it deemed common knowledge, that "retail purchasers of baked goods, because of the perishable nature of such goods, usually make such purchases reasonably close to their homes, say within about 25 miles, and retail purchases of such goods beyond that distance are for all practical considerations negligible." No objection is made to this finding and nothing appears in the record which contradicts it as applied to this case.

Moreover, we note that it took plaintiff three years to learn of defendant's use of the mark and bring this suit, even though the plaintiff was doing some wholesale business in the Rochester area. This is a strong indication that no confusion arose or is likely to arise either from concurrent use of the marks at the retail level in geographically separate trading areas or from its concurrent use at different market levels, viz. retail and wholesale in the same area.

The decisive question then is whether plaintiff's use of the mark "Dawn" at the retail level is likely to be confined to its current area of use or whether in the normal course of its business, it is likely to expand the retail use of the mark into defendant's trading area. If such expansion were probable, then the concurrent use of the marks would give rise to the conclusion that there was a likelihood of confusion.

* * *

We note not only that plaintiff has failed to license its mark at the retail level in defendant's trading area for a substantial period of time, but also that the trend of plaintiff's business manifests a striking decrease in the number of licensees employing its mark at the retail level in New York state and throughout the country. In the 1922–1930 period plaintiff had 75 to 80 licensees across the country with 11 located in New York. At the time of the trial plaintiff listed only 16 active licensees not one of which was located in New York.

The normal likelihood that plaintiff's wholesale operations in the Rochester area would expand to the retail level is fully rebutted and overcome by the decisive fact that plaintiff has in fact not licensed or otherwise exploited its mark at retail in the area for some thirty years.

Accordingly, because plaintiff and defendant use the mark in connection with retail sales in distinct and separate markets and because there is no present prospect that plaintiff will expand its use of the mark at the retail level into defendant's trading area, we conclude that there is no likelihood of public confusion arising from the concurrent use of the marks and therefore the issuance of an injunction is not warranted. *A fortiori* plaintiff is not entitled to any accounting or damages. However, because of the effect we have attributed to the constructive notice provision of the Lanham Act, the plaintiff may later, upon a proper showing of an intent to use the mark at the retail level in defendant's market area, be entitled to enjoin defendant's use of the mark. * * *

NOTES AND QUESTIONS

1. *The effect of registration on the Lanham Act Principal Register.* Why did the defendant in *Dawn Donut* not have a remote, good-faith user defense? What is the practical impact of Lanham Act § 22, 15 U.S.C.A. § 1072, on the geographic rights of registrants? Why is this result desirable?

Given the provisions of § 22, why did the court refuse to enjoin the defendant's continued use of the "Dawn" mark? What are the practical implications of the court's decision for the defendant? Does the rule set forth in *Dawn Donut* adequately protect the public against confusion?

Some courts have rejected the absolute rule set forth in *Dawn Donut*, opting instead to consider the geographic remoteness of the parties' use as just one factor in the multi-factor standard for determining whether the junior user's actions cause a likelihood of consumer confusion. See, e.g., Circuit City Stores, Inc. v. CarMax, Inc., 165 F.3d 1047 (6th Cir. 1999)(Judge Jones concurring).

Lanham Act § 22 provides nationwide priority in a mark as of the date of registration by providing that registration on the Principal Register constitutes constructive notice of the registrant's claim of ownership. 15 U.S.C.A. § 1072. Section 7(c), as amended by the Trademark Revision Act of 1988, provides:

> Contingent on the registration of a mark on the principal register provided by this Act, the filing of the application to register such mark shall constitute constructive use of the mark, *conferring a right of priority, nationwide in effect, on or in connection with the goods or services specified in the registration against any other person* except for a

person whose mark has not been abandoned and who, prior to such filing—

> (1) has used the mark;
>
> (2) has filed an application to register the mark which is pending or has resulted in registration of the mark; or
>
> (3) has filed a foreign application to register the mark on the basis of which he or she has acquired a right of priority, and timely files an application under section 1126(d) of this title to register the mark which is pending or has resulted in registration of the mark.

15 U.S.C.A. § 1057(c) (emphasis added). Accordingly, for all registered marks whose registration is based on an application filed on or after the effective date of the 1988 Amendments (November 16, 1989), nationwide priority is moved back from the date of registration to the date the application to register was filed, against persons who do not fall within the three enumerated exceptions.

2. *"Intermediate" junior users.* Assume that X begins using a mark in South Carolina in December, 1990. He files an application to register the mark on the Principal Register in December, 1992, and the mark is registered in December, 1993. Y begins using the same mark on similar products in Oregon in December, 1991, having no knowledge of X. X later decides to expand his business to Oregon. Assuming that Y continues to use the mark there, what are the respective rights of X and Y?

While X is the senior user, with nationwide priority by virtue of his registration, Y has the benefit of the "limited area defense." This defense, which is similar to the common-law remote, good-faith user defense, is described in Lanham Act § 33(b)(5), as amended, 15 U.S.C.A. § 1115(b)(5), which provides that "incontestable" marks are subject to the following defense:

> That the mark whose use by a party is charged as an infringement was adopted without knowledge of the registrant's prior use and has been continuously used by such party or those in privity with him from a date prior to (A) the date of the constructive use of the mark established pursuant to section 1057(c) of this title, (B) the registration of the mark under this Act if the application for registration is filed before the effective date of the Trademark Law Revision Act of 1988, or (C) publication of the registered mark under subsection (c) of section 1062 of this title: *Provided, however,* That this defense or defect shall apply only for the area in which such continuous prior use is proved * * *.

Section 33(a), 15 U.S.C.A. § 1115(a), makes this same defense available against marks that are not incontestable.

Y enjoys priority in those areas in which he has continuously used the mark since before X's application date. He may continue his use there, and may enjoin X from entering that territory, even though X has superior rights throughout the rest of the country. Note, however, that Y's territory is "frozen" to that which he occupied on the date of X's application and has occupied continuously ever since—Oregon, or if he only occupied parts of Oregon, those parts. For example, if Y had expanded his use of the mark to

Idaho in 1994, he would be subject to an injunction against further use there, once X decided to enter the Idaho market with the mark.

What if, instead of commencing use of the mark on December 1, 1991, Y began use in January, 1993?

The provisions discussed above attempt to balance the conflicting interests in providing for nationwide trademark rights and accommodating the interests traditionally protected by the common-law rules. Assuming (under the first fact situation) that Y continues his use in Oregon (or the part of Oregon that he occupied on X's application date), and X expands to use the mark throughout the rest of the nation, what are the practical implications? Will X be able to advertise in the national media?

3. *When the junior user is the registrant.* Suppose that A begins using a mark in Texas and continuously uses it in Texas thereafter. B begins using the same mark in connection with similar products in Maine two years after A commences use in Texas, with no knowledge of A's use, and registers the mark on the Principal Register. B later expands her business and seeks to enter Texas with her mark. What result?

If B's registered mark has not attained incontestability status, A can rely on her senior use and enjoin B from entering Texas (or that part of Texas in which A was using the mark when B applied to register). Whether and to what extent A may assert superior rights beyond that geographic area will depend on the particular circumstances of the case and a balancing of the equities. See Weiner King, Inc. v. Wiener King Corp., 615 F.2d 512, 522, 525–26 (C.C.P.A.1980).

If B's mark has become incontestable, the language of Lanham Act §§ 15 and 33(b), 15 U.S.C.A. §§ 1065, 1115(b), becomes relevant. Can you identify the relevant language? Assuming that A is able to demonstrate prior, continuous use of the mark, she will be able to continue using the mark on those goods for which she establishes the prior use, in those geographic areas that she occupied at the time of B's application or registration. She may enjoin B's use in those areas, but B will retain incontestable rights in the rest of the country. What policy justifies freezing A's rights when A is the senior user?

4. *Concurrent registration.* As noted earlier, Lanham Act § 2(d), 15 U.S.C.A. § 1052(d), provides for concurrent registration when more than one party is legally entitled to use a mark. Review subsection (d). As the statutory language suggests, concurrent registration may be obtained when the PTO determines that it is appropriate in a concurrent use proceeding, or pursuant to a court determination that dual parties have a right to use the mark. The Court of Customs and Patent Appeals set forth guidelines for the PTO in making concurrent use determinations in *Application of* Beatrice Foods Co., 429 F.2d 466 (C.C.P.A.1970). With regard to registration pursuant to a court determination, see Holiday Inn v. Holiday Inns, Inc., 534 F.2d 312 (C.C.P.A. 1976).

PROBLEM

1. In August, 1998, X Paper Co. selected the mark "Pencils" for its new line of paper pads for artists' use in pencil, charcoal and pastel sketching. X

Paper Co. filed an application to register the mark with the PTO the same month, alleging a good-faith intent to use the mark in commerce. The PTO allowed the application in January, 1999. X Paper Co. filed a request for an extension in July, 1999, and then used the mark in sales of artists' pads the following November. X Paper Co. filed an affidavit of use and obtained registration the following month (December, 1999). At that time, X Paper Co.'s sales territory consisted of the states of Alabama, Georgia and Florida.

In October, 1998, Y Paper, Inc. began to use the mark "Pencils" in connection with sketching pads it sold in Oregon, Washington and Idaho. Y Paper, Inc. had no knowledge of X Paper Co.'s plans or later use of the mark.

In February, 2002, X Paper Co. started offering its products—including its "Pencils" sketching pads—for sale throughout the nation. Y Paper, Inc. would like to enjoin X Paper Co. from entering Oregon, Washington and Idaho with the "Pencils" mark. Will it be successful?

D. ASSIGNMENTS AND TRADEMARK ABANDONMENT

MONEY STORE v. HARRISCORP FINANCE, INC.

United States Court of Appeals for the Seventh Circuit, 1982.
689 F.2d 666.

Pell, Circuit Judge.

[The plaintiff (whom the court refers to as "Modern Acceptance") began using the mark "THE MONEY STORE" on January 2, 1972, at its New Jersey and Pennsylvania offices and in newspaper and radio advertisements. Plaintiff applied to register the mark on February 4, 1972, and obtained registration on April 2, 1974. The plaintiff's business increased dramatically after adoption of the mark, both in terms of the volume of business and the geographic area in which it operated under "THE MONEY STORE" mark.]

Defendant-appellee Harriscorp is a Delaware corporation. * * * In 1972, Theodore Roberts, the principal Harris executive responsible for the Harriscorp Finance retail lending project, selected "THE MONEY STORE" as his preferred name for money-lending service facilities the Bank planned to open in the metropolitan Chicago area. A trademark search conducted in mid–1973 disclosed [among other things, Modern Acceptance's pending application to register]. Because Harris found no evidence of any use of "THE MONEY STORE" in the Chicago area, it tentatively decided to use the mark.

In September 1972, Roberts learned that United Bank in Chicago was using "THE MONEY STORE" mark. United had first used the mark in August, 1972, eight months after the plaintiff's first use. In January, 1974, United assigned its rights in the mark to Harris. Although the evidence indicated that United had decided to discontinue use of the mark, it similarly indicated that United was still using "THE MONEY STORE" at the time of the assignment. In fact, at the time of the assignment,

United was featuring the marks on three billboards located on major Chicago streets. The assignment recited that "for good and valuable consideration, the receipt of which is hereby acknowledged ... [the mark is assigned] together with the goodwill of the business symbolized by the mark." Harris did not acquire customer lists, real estate, receivables, accounts or any other tangible assets in return for the one dollar consideration it actually paid to United.

Having obtained the assignment from United, Harris made a final decision to use the mark and in December, 1974, Harriscorp opened three lending offices in the Chicago area utilizing the mark "THE MONEY STORE."

In January, 1975, Modern Acceptance sent Harriscorp a letter requesting it to cease and desist from using the mark [and later brought the present suit].

    * * *

V. ASSIGNMENT FROM UNITED

Harriscorp asserts the defense of a good faith junior user based on the January, 1974 assignment from United Bank. A good faith junior user is one who begins using a mark with no knowledge that someone else is already using it. The innocent junior user retains the right to use the mark in an area remote from where the senior user is operating.

United began using the mark, "THE MONEY STORE," in the metropolitan Chicago area in August, 1972, approximately eight months after the plaintiff's first use in New Jersey and Pennsylvania. United's use preceded issuance of the plaintiff's federal registration, however, by approximately twenty months. United could not be charged, therefore, with constructive knowledge of the plaintiff's use of "THE MONEY STORE" as a service mark. 15 U.S.C. § 1072 (1976). Similarly, there is no evidence that United had actual knowledge of the usage of the mark by Modern Acceptance. United therefore was a good faith junior user. This status would give United, were it still using the mark, the right to enjoin the plaintiff's use of the identical mark in the Chicago area.

Whether Harriscorp can assert the good faith junior user defense turns on three factors: (1) whether United had abandoned use of the mark at the time of the assignment; (2) whether the assignment included a transfer of goodwill; and (3) whether the assignment is invalid as a sham transaction.

Before addressing these three points, we note that the fact Harris actually paid only one dollar to United is not dispositive. The exchange of a nominal sum, like the recitation that the assignment was for "good and valuable consideration," is customary in many contracts and does not in itself make the assignment ineffective. The amount actually paid is relevant only insofar as it might indicate either that United had abandoned the mark or that no goodwill was associated with "THE MONEY

STORE" mark and therefore could not be transferred pursuant to the assignment. Each of these points is discussed below.

An abandoned trademark is not capable of assignment because such a mark is subject to cancellation by the Patent Office or by the courts and is therefore invalid. 15 U.S.C. §§ 1064(c), 1119 (1976). Section 45 of the Lanham Act defines when a mark shall be deemed abandoned. The subsection relevant to United's use of "THE MONEY STORE" mark states:

> (a) When its use has been discontinued with intent not to resume. Intent not to resume may be inferred from circumstances. Nonuse for two consecutive years shall be prima facie abandonment.

15 U.S.C. § 1127 (1976). The district court found that United Bank was still using the mark at the time of the assignment and had not abandoned it. The plaintiff argues in its brief that "(a)bandonment is a matter of intent" and points to evidence suggesting that United intended to abandon use of the mark. The statutory definition makes clear, however, that abandonment requires *discontinuance of use* as well as intent to abandon. Such discontinuance of use was not found by the district court and we find nothing in the record suggesting that the court below was incorrect. * * * We conclude that the judge below correctly found that United had not abandoned the mark at the time of the assignment to Harriscorp.

The assignment conferred no rights on Harriscorp under the Lanham Act, however, unless the goodwill of the business was assigned along with the mark. 15 U.S.C. § 1060 (1976). The judge below found that no goodwill had been transferred in the assignment. First, we recognize that, although the assignment stated that the mark was assigned "together with the good will of the business symbolized by the mark," such a recitation is not necessarily dispositive.

Second, we find that it is not necessary to the continuing validity of the mark that tangible assets of the assignor pass to the assignee. * * *

It is admittedly difficult to determine when a transfer of goodwill has occurred. This is particularly so in the case of a service mark. Before turning to other cases relied upon by the parties, it is important to recognize why the common law and Lanham Act prohibitions on a transfer of a mark unassociated with any goodwill exist:

> A sale of a trademark divorced from its good will is characterized as an "assignment in gross." If one obtains a trademark through an assignment in gross, divorced from the good will of the assignor, the assignee obtains the symbol, but not the reality. Any subsequent use of the mark by the assignee will necessarily be in connection with a different business, a different good will and a different type of product. The continuity of the things symbolized by the mark is broken. Use of the mark by the assignee in connection with a different good will and different product would result in a fraud on the purchasing public, who reasonably assume that the mark signified

the same things, whether used by one person or another.... The fundamental policy of consumer protection must always be kept in mind. The central purpose of the technical rules regarding the assignment of trademarks is to protect consumers and these rules were "not evolved for the purpose of invalidating all trademark assignments which do not satisfy a stereo-typed set of formalities."

McCarthy, *Trademarks and Unfair Competition*, § 18.1, at 607.

Application of this reasoning is apparent in *PepsiCo, Inc. v. Grapette Co.*, 416 F.2d 285 (8th Cir.1969). In that case, the mark "Peppy" had been used for many years on a cola-based drink. The mark was assigned to Grapette Co. Grapette acquired no tangible assets from the assignor, nor any process or formula for producing the beverage. Grapette then used the "Peppy" mark on a pepper-type beverage. The *PepsiCo* court noted the possibility of public deceit if the assignment were considered valid, and stated:

> It seems fundamental that either the defendant did not acquire any "goodwill" as required by law or if it did, assuming as defendant argues the mark itself possesses "goodwill," by use of the mark on a totally different product, Grapette intended to deceive the public. Either ground is untenable to the validity of the assignment.

Id. at 290.

* * *

Perhaps the strongest case in support of Harriscorp's contention is *Hy-Cross Hatchery, Inc. v. Osborne*, 303 F.2d 947 (C.C.P.A.1962). In *Hy-Cross*, the assignor held a valid registration of the mark "HY–CROSS" and had used it for some time to identify the baby chicks that he sold. He assigned the mark, along with a recitation of goodwill. The assignor continued in the business of selling chicks. The court held that the assignment was effective, stating that "by assigning the goodwill, [the assignor] gave up the right to sell 'HY–CROSS' chicks. This had been a part of his 'business.'"

Modern Acceptance argues that *Hy-Cross* is weak support because of then Judge Blackmun's concurrence in *PepsiCo, Inc. v. Grapette Co.*, 416 F.2d 285 (8th Cir.1969). As discussed *supra*, the assignee in that case had used the mark on an entirely different type of beverage from that made by the assignor. The majority of the court had mentioned the *Hy-Cross* case, characterizing it as involving a naked assignment, but had decided the appeal on the ground that an assignment is valid only if the assignee's product has the same characteristics as that of the assignor. In his concurrence, Judge Blackmun noted that *Hy-Cross* was a peculiar case in that live baby chicks were the product of both the assignor and assignee. He read *Hy-Cross* as attaching little significance to the absence of any assignment of the chicks themselves only in that particular context. Judge Blackmun stated that he would be opposed to any broader interpretation of the *Hy-Cross* rule.

We do not believe that Judge Blackmun's concurrence casts doubt upon the applicability of *Hy-Cross* to the instant case. The circumstances in this case are also "peculiar" in that United and Harriscorp offered the identical service. A customer who was drawn first to United and later to Harriscorp because of the "MONEY STORE" mark would not be misled as to the nature of the services offered. United's use of the mark in advertising, including highly visible billboards, strongly suggests that the mark carried with it a degree of goodwill. What United gave up in assigning the mark was the right to attract customers through use of the mark. The fact that one cannot say with certainty how many customers might have gone to a Harriscorp office, rather than a United office, because they recognized the mark does not compel the conclusion that no goodwill passed with the assignment.

The cases cited by both sides of this controversy are consistent with the underlying purpose of why a transfer of goodwill is required in order for an assignment of a mark to be effective. The cases all seek to protect customers from deception and confusion. In the case of a service mark, such confusion would result if an assignee offered a service different from that offered by the assignor of the mark. Such is not the case here.

We similarly do not believe that there was a lack of continuity in the usage of the mark. The mark was utilized by Harris Bank in the short period between the assignment and the opening of the Harriscorp offices. It was used both before and after the assignment in connection with money-lending services.

One final point remains. The plaintiff claims that the assignment is ineffective because it was a sham transaction, initiated by Harris for the sole purpose of obtaining superior rights to the mark in the Chicago area. Presumably, Harris sought the assignment because it knew of the plaintiff's prior rights in the mark. Harris did in fact know of the plaintiff's pending registration and it would be naive to conclude that that knowledge was completely irrelevant to its decision to seek an assignment from United. It is also true, however, that so long as United retained any rights in the mark, that institution was itself an impediment to the defendant's usage of the mark. Obtaining the assignment from United is consistent with the defendant's documented belief that the plaintiff could not successfully assert nationwide rights in the mark, and therefore another institution was free to use the mark in the Chicago area. We do not believe that an assignment motivated at least in part by sound business judgment should be set aside as a sham transaction.

We conclude that the assignment from United to Harris was effective. The mark had not been abandoned at the time of the assignment and whatever goodwill was associated with the mark passed to the defendant pursuant to the assignment.

* * *

* * * Harriscorp is entitled * * * to assert the rights of a good faith junior user in its market area, as that area shall be determined by the district court on remand. * * *

NOTES AND QUESTIONS

1. *Assignment of marks.* "Unlike patents or copyrights, trademarks are not separate property rights. They are integral and inseparable elements of the good will of the business or services to which they pertain." Visa U.S.A., Inc. v. Birmingham Trust National Bank, 696 F.2d 1371, 1375 (Fed.Cir.1982), *cert. denied,* 464 U.S. 826, 104 S.Ct. 98, 78 L.Ed.2d 104 (1983). Thus, assignment of the mark alone, without the attendant good will, is meaningless in the eyes of the law and invalid. This was the rule at common law, and it is codified in Lanham Act § 10, 15 U.S.C.A. § 1060:

> A registered mark or a mark for which application to register has been filed shall be assignable with the good will of the business in which the mark is used, or with that part of the good will of the business connected with the use of and symbolized by the mark.

In determining whether a mark was assigned with the good will it represented, courts traditionally looked for evidence that assets associated with the assignor's product or business—such as plant, product formula or inventory—were assigned along with the mark. If such things were assigned, there was some assurance that the assignee would continue to offer a similar product or service under the mark. The more modern trend, as exemplified in *Money Store*, is to cast aside formulaic requirements and find a passing of good will even in the absence of such assets, as long as it is demonstrated that the assignee continued to sell goods or services of the same kind as the assignor.

As the *Money Store* opinion suggests, the main purpose of the good will requirement is to avoid consumer deception or confusion. In this sense, trademark law undertakes to guarantee the consistency of products or services offered under the same mark. The court in *Money Store* found that the assignee and assignor offered similar services—money lending—and thus that this purpose was fulfilled. The court did not, however, examine the specifics of the parties' respective services. For example, what if the terms or circumstances under which the parties loaned money differed significantly? Should a finding to that effect lead to the conclusion that the assignment was invalid?

What, exactly, does it mean to find that the assignment of a mark is invalid? Does the invalidity mean that the assignee may not use the mark? Does it mean that the purported assignor retains rights in the mark?

2. *Abandonment.* Proof of "trademark abandonment" provides a defense against infringement liability as well as grounds for canceling the abandoning party's registration. See 15 U.S.C.A. § 1064(3). The *Money Store* and *Dawn Donut* defendants both raised abandonment defenses based upon the first definition of abandonment set forth in Lanham Act § 45, 15 U.S.C.A. § 1127:

> A mark shall be deemed to be "abandoned" * * *

(1) When its use has been discontinued with intent not to resume such use. Intent not to resume may be inferred from circumstances. Nonuse for three consecutive years shall be prima facie evidence of abandonment. "Use" of a mark means the bona fide use of such mark made in the ordinary course of trade, and not made merely to reserve a right in a mark.[15]

Section 45 provides a second important basis for finding abandonment, which was also raised in *Dawn Donut*:

A mark shall be deemed to be "abandoned" * * *

(2) When any course of conduct of the owner, including acts of omission as well as commission, causes the mark to * * * lose its significance as a mark.

This second form of abandonment may arise when trademark owners license others to use their mark, but fail to supervise and control the licensees' use. The court in *Dawn Donut* explained:

[T]he Lanham Act places an affirmative duty upon a licensor of a registered trademark to take reasonable measures to detect and prevent misleading uses of his mark by his licensees or suffer cancellation of his federal registration. * * *

> * * *

The Lanham Act [provides] that controlled licensing does not work an abandonment of the licensor's registration, while a system of naked licensing does. * * *

Without the requirement of control, the right of a trademark owner to license his mark separately from the business in connection with which it has been used would create the danger that products bearing the same trademark might be of diverse qualities. If the licensor is not compelled to take some reasonable steps to prevent misuses of his trademark in the hands of others the public will be deprived of its most effective protection against misleading uses of a trademark. The public is hardly in a position to uncover deceptive uses of a trademark before they occur and will be at best slow to detect them after they happen. Thus, unless the licensor exercises supervision and control over the operations of its licensees the risk that the public will be unwittingly deceived will be increased and this is precisely what the Act is in part designed to prevent. Clearly the only effective way to protect the public where a trademark is used by licensees is to place on the licensor the affirmative duty of policing in a reasonable manner the activities of his licensees.

Dawn Donut, 267 F.2d at 366–67.

Permitting controlled trademark licensing made modern franchising practices possible. Typically, franchise and licensing agreements impose express restrictions on the licensee's use of the licensed mark and call for ongoing licensor supervision. Though the presence or absence of contractual provisions for control is relevant, however, the ultimate issue is the licensor's *actual*

---

15. Prior to 1996, this definition provided that nonuse for *two* consecutive years would be *prima facie* evidence of abandonment.

exercise of control over the licensees. With regard to the degree of control that the licensor must exercise, the Restatement (Third) of Unfair Competition advocates a flexible standard that takes into account consumers' likely expectations, given the particular product and circumstances. Those expectations may differ, depending on how similar the goods and services sold by the licensee are to those sold by the mark owner. The closer the goods or services, the higher the expectations of consistency. In some cases, due to a long-term relationship or the licensee's experience and expertise, the trademark owner may be justified in relying on the licensee's contractual undertaking to maintain standards, with no additional control mechanism. In other cases, where the licensee is not as reliable, or the goods or services are complex or pose particular health hazards to the public if not properly produced, the mark owner may be required to undertake a more active supervisory role. Restatement (Third) of Unfair Competition § 33, cmt c (1995). From a practical standpoint, why might courts hesitate to impose strong control obligations on licensors?

VII. RIGHTS IN INDICATIONS OF ORIGIN

A. DIRECT INFRINGEMENT

The ultimate purpose of trademark protection is to foster an efficient, competitive marketplace. It achieves this purpose by preventing misleading uses of marks that may confuse consumers about the source, sponsorship, or affiliation of the products or services they buy. This reduces consumer search costs, and by enabling consumers effectively to exercise their purchasing preferences, encourages producers to vie for their patronage by investing in product quality and business good will. As the Senate Report accompanying the Lanham Act stressed, trademark law (unlike the law of patents and copyrights) was not created to provide an incentive to innovate, and thus does not convey monopoly rights in words and symbols. Rather, businesses have rights in their trademarks only to the extent necessary to prevent unauthorized uses that cause a likelihood of consumer confusion about source, sponsorship or affiliation, and thus increase search costs and undermine fair and efficient marketplace competition. S. Rep. No. 1333, 79th Cong., 2d Sess., 1–17 (1946). The origins of trademark law are in the law of deceit, rather than in trespass.

The trademark infringement cause of action is tailored only to accomplish these limited purposes, because it is generally understood that overprotection of marks may in itself impair competition, as well as interfere with First Amendment interests. As we have seen, trademark law only protects "distinctive" marks, because distinctive marks are most likely to signify product source to consumers, and effective competition requires that competitors have access to commonplace, descriptive, and generic words and symbols. Trademark law only protects non-functional marks, to ensure that trademark rights are not used to monopolize useful product and packaging features that the patent and copyright laws relegate to the public domain. Moreover, the infringement cause of action is limited to cases in which defendant (1) *used the mark in commerce in connection with goods or services* (2) in a manner that *causes a likelihood of consumer confusion* about the source, sponsorship or affiliation of the parties' goods or services.

Lanham Act § 32(1)(a) defines direct infringement of registered marks, imposing liability on any person who, without authorization,

> use[es] in commerce any reproduction, counterfeit, copy, or colorable imitation of a registered mark in connection with the sale, offering for sale, distribution, or advertising of any goods or services on or in connection with which such use is likely to cause confusion, or to cause mistake, or to deceive.

15 U.S.C. § 1114(1)(a). Lanham Act § 43(a) defines direct infringement of unregistered indications of origin, imposing liability on

> any person who, on or in connection with any goods or services, or any container for goods, uses in commerce any word, term, name, symbol, or device, or any combination thereof, or any false designation of origin * * * which * * * is likely to cause confusion, or to cause mistake, or to deceive as to the affiliation, connection, or association of such person with another person, or as to the origin, sponsorship, or approval of his or her goods, services, or commercial activities by another person * * *.

15 U.S.C. § 1125(a). Thus, assuming that an infringement claimant owns a valid mark, she must demonstrate two essential things in order to make out a case of direct infringement under *either* Lanham Act provision: She must demonstrate 1) that the defendant "used" a mark in the manner described (made a "use in commerce" "in connection with" goods or services); and 2) that the use caused a likelihood of consumer confusion. Subsection 1 will examine the "use" requirement and Subsection 2 will examine the "likelihood of confusion" requirement. Subsection 3 will examine how courts have construed and applied these requirements in a special context–the Internet.

1. *Trademark Use*

Trademark law's "use" requirement tailors the infringement cause of action to ensure that it effectively serves its purpose (ensuring that consumers can rely on marks for accurate information about product source) without interfering unduly with the free flow of useful marketplace information to consumers. It permits courts to identify "non-trademark" uses of words or symbols that are unlikely to communicate product or service source to consumers, and permit them to be made without the necessity of litigating the fact-intensive issue of consumer perception and likelihood of confusion. In addition, the trademark use requirement minimizes use of trademark rights to interfere with First Amendment-protected speech by confining the infringement cause of action primarily to commercial transactions (and thus to commercial speech). The Lanham Act's requirement that uses be made "in commerce" also ensures that infringement claims fall within Congress's Commerce Clause powers.

Early common-law decisions and federal trademark acts clearly required that infringement defendants use contested words or symbols *in the manner of a trademark*, to identify the source of goods the defendant was offering or advertising for sale. Originally, a defendant could only infringe a "technical" (inherently distinctive) trademark by placing it on the article it was selling. The Trademark Act of 1881 provided for infringement liability only when a defendant reproduced, counterfeited, copied or colorably imitated a plaintiff's registered mark and *"affixed"* it to "merchandise of substantially the same descriptive properties" as the merchandise described in the plaintiff's registration. An Act To Authorize the Registration of Trade-marks and Protect the Same, 46th Cong., § 7 (1881).

The Trademark Act of 1905 expanded on this definition of infringing use, providing liability when a defendant *affixed* a reproduction, counterfeit, copy or colorable imitation of the plaintiff's mark to merchandise that was substantially similar to that listed in the plaintiff's registration, *or to labels, signs, prints, packages, wrappers, or receptacles intended to be used upon or in connection with the sale of such merchandise*, and used the allegedly infringing mark in commerce. Trademark Act of 1905, ch. 592, § 16, 33 Stat. 742 (1905)(formerly codified at 15 U.S.C. § 96). Courts construed this provision to extend to a defendant's use of the mark in advertising its goods, as well. See, e.g., Mishawaka Rubber & Woolen Mfg. Co. v. Panther–Panco Rubber Co., 153 F.2d 662, 666–67 (1st Cir.), *cert. denied*, 329 U.S. 722, 67 S.Ct. 64, 91 L.Ed. 626 (1946).

Pre–Lanham Act case law regarding infringement of technical trademarks routinely recited the requirement that the defendant "affix" the allegedly infringing mark to its own goods or their packaging, or apply it in advertisements of its goods. This "affixation" or other close association of mark to product ensured that consumers would be likely to associate the contested word or symbol with a specific product the defendant was offering to the public, and rely on it to indicate the source of that product.

The unfair competition "passing off" cause of action (which encompassed infringement of trade dress, business names and "secondary meaning marks") was broader than technical trademark infringement. A defendant could "pass off" his goods as those of the plaintiff without using a confusingly similar mark at all—for example, by stating to consumers that its goods were "the original" when the plaintiff was the original producer, and defendant had only recently entered the field. However, in those common-law passing off cases specifically involving alleged infringement of "non-technical" ("secondary meaning") marks, the courts came to apply essentially the same "use" rules as they applied in the case of technical trademarks. See Restatement of Torts § 717(1), 727 (1938).

When the Lanham Act was enacted in 1946, it provided new statutory definitions of infringement (reproduced above) that expressly require a defendant's "use in commerce" "in connection with" goods or services. Lanham Act § 45 provides an express definition of "use in commerce:" A mark will be used in commerce:

(1) on goods when–

(A) it is placed in any manner on the goods or their containers, or the displays associated therewith or on the tags or labels affixed thereto, or if the nature of the goods makes such placement impracticable, then on documents associated with the goods or their sale, and

(B) the goods are sold or transported in commerce, and

(2) on services when it is used or displayed in the sale or advertising of services and the services are rendered in commerce * * *.

15 U.S.C. § 1127. A number of courts have found that this definition defines the kind of use an infringement defendant must make in order to be liable. See, e.g., 1–800–Contacts, Inc., v. WhenU.Com, Inc., 414 F.3d 400, 407 (2d Cir. 2005); DaimlerChrysler AG v. Bloom, 315 F.3d 932, 936 (8th Cir. 2003). This construction is supported by the Lanham Act's legislative history, and is consistent with pre-Lanham Act statutory provisions and case decisions. See Margreth Barrett, *Finding Trademark Use: The Historical Foundation for Limiting Infringement Liability to Uses "In the Manner of a Mark,"* 43 Wake Forest L. Rev. 893, 943–957 (2008). However, a number of other courts have held that the § 45 definition only applies for purposes of determining whether a claimant has acquired rights in a mark. See, e.g., Playboy Enterprises, Inc. v. Netscape Communications Corp., 354 F.3d 1020, 1024 n. 11 (9th Cir. 2004); Utah Lighthouse Ministry v. Foundation for Apologetic Information & Research, 527 F.3d 1045, 1054 (10th Cir. 2008). This latter group of courts has held that the requisite "use" an infringement defendant must make is described in the more general §§ 32 (1)(a) and 43(a) "in connection with" language. As noted earlier, Lanham Act § 32(1)(a) requires that the defendant use the mark "in connection with the sale, offering for sale, distribution or advertising of goods or services," and § 43(a) requires that the defendant use the mark "on or in connection with any goods or services, or any container for goods." Note that under either statutory construction, the Lanham Act "use" requirement consists of two separate components. First, the defendant must associate the allegedly infringing mark with products, product containers, or services. Second, the defendant's actions must be "in commerce," thus bringing them within Congress' jurisdiction under the Commerce Clause.

In the years following enactment of the Lanham Act, the case decisions have stressed that the defendant must use the mark to identify the source of goods or services, rather than to serve some other purpose, and have repeatedly emphasized that the infringement cause of action provides only limited rights in marks. As the Tenth Circuit recently put it:

The Lanham Act addresses the specific problem of consumer confusion about the source of goods and services created by the unauthorized use of trademarks. * * * Unless there is a competing good or service labeled or associated with the plaintiff's trademark, the concerns of the Lanham Act are not invoked. "[T]he Lanham Act seeks to prevent consumer confusion that enables a seller to pass off his goods as the goods of another ... [T]rademark infringement protects only against mistaken purchasing decisions and not against confusion generally."

Utah Lighthouse, supra, 1053–54 (citations omitted).

As demonstrated both by the evolution of the pertinent statutory language and by the case opinions, Congress and the courts have eased the rigidity of the "affixation" or "trademark use" requirement over the years, moving from physical attachment of the mark to the good being offered for sale to a wider array of applications. However, given the limited purpose of trademark protection, common-law precedent and federal statutory language, courts have *generally* limited infringing uses to those that consumers are able to perceive, and that closely and directly associate the allegedly infringing mark with goods or services the defendant is offering for sale or other distribution. Thus, infringing use of a trademark might be described as application of a confusingly similar word or symbol in a manner that invites consumers to associate the mark with goods or services the user is offering for sale or distribution, and to rely on the word or symbol for information about the source, sponsorship or affiliation of those goods or services. See, e.g., Interactive Products Corp. v. a2z Mobile Office Solutions, Inc., 326 F.3d 687, 695 (6th Cir. 2003)(stating that trademark infringement and false designation of origin laws do not apply if defendants are only using plaintiff's trademark in a "nontrademark" way—that is, in a way that does not identify source of product). In addition, the use must affect interstate commerce.

In Subsection 3, *infra*, we will see how courts sometimes lose sight of this precedent in evaluating new forms of trademark application in the Internet context.

NOTES AND QUESTIONS

1. *Trademark rights in gross.* A mark is a word, name, symbol or device that a business uses to identify its goods or services and to distinguish those goods or services from those offered by others. The legal significance of the mark lies in its relationship to the product or service it identifies—its role in signifying the business good will associated with that product. The law undertakes to protect the effectiveness of the mark to inform consumers that the product it identifies comes from a particular source (which in turn permits consumers to infer the quality and characteristics of the product or service). Divorced from its role in identifying the source of a product or service, a mark has no legal significance. United Drug Co. v. Theodore Rectanus Co., 248 U.S. 90, 97 (1918). As a general matter, the courts have made it clear that there

are no "rights in gross" or "rights at large" in a word or symbol. As noted *supra*, the purpose of trademark protection differs from that of patent and trademark protection: Trademark law was not intended to give monopoly rights in a word or symbol, as such.

The Fifth Circuit's decision in *Boston Professional Hockey Assn., Inc. v. Dallas Cap & Emblem Mfg., Inc.*, 510 F.2d 1004 (5th Cir.), *cert. denied*, 423 U.S. 868, 96 S.Ct. 132, 46 L.Ed.2d 98 (1975), has sometimes been cited for the contrary proposition that a sale of the mark, by itself, can constitute an infringing "use" of the mark in commerce. *Boston Professional* involved a defendant who manufactured and sold embroidered cloth emblems, or patches, resembling the registered trademarks and service marks of professional sports teams, to be sewed on fans' hats or other clothing. The teams, who had licensed some manufacturers (but not the defendant) to place the team symbols on merchandise sued, alleging trademark infringement under both Lanham Act § 32 and § 43(a) and the common law of unfair competition.

Early in its decision, the Fifth Circuit observed that the case was difficult because "a reproduction of the trademark itself [was] being sold, unattached to any other goods or services." *Id.*, 510 F.2d at 1010. However, notwithstanding this initial characterization, the court ultimately determined that the case involved separate marks and products. The court characterized the issues raised by the case as: 1) whether the defendant "used" the plaintiffs' marks "in connection with the sale of goods," and 2) whether that use was likely to cause a likelihood of consumer confusion. In finding the requisite "use in connection with the sale of goods," the Fifth Circuit rejected the lower court's finding that the mark was, in effect, the product being sold. The Fifth Circuit reasoned that the patch was the "product," and that the defendant used the mark to sell that product when it embroidered the mark onto the patch. The court explained:

> Defendant is in the business of manufacturing and marketing emblems for wearing apparel. These emblems are the products, or goods, which defendant sells. When defendant causes plaintiffs' marks to be embroidered upon emblems which it later markets, defendant uses those marks in connection with the sale of goods as surely as if defendant had embroidered the marks upon knit caps. * * * The fact that the symbol covers the entire face of defendant's product does not alter the fact that the trademark symbol is used in connection with the sale of the product. * * * Were defendant to embroider the same fabric with the same thread in other designs, the resulting products would still be emblems for wearing apparel but they would not give trademark identification to the customer. * * *

Id., at 1011–1012. Thus, upon careful examination, the *Boston Professional Hockey* case does not ultimately support claims to marks "in gross." Nonetheless, that decision has subsequently influenced courts to afford mark owners greater control over uses of their marks in "mark merchandising" cases like *Boston Hockey*. See, e.g., Boston Athletic Ass'n v. Sullivan, 867 F.2d 22 (1st Cir. 1989); Processed Plastic Co. v. Warner Communications, Inc., 675 F.2d

852 (7th Cir. 1982). And as we will see later, these mark merchandising decisions have, in turn, sometimes influenced courts to expand owners' control over marks in Internet contexts.

2. *Predatory intent and trademark use.* Several Circuit-level decisions have emphasized that a defendant's predatory intent (that is, his intent to benefit from the plaintiff's business good will) cannot substitute for trademark use. The Sixth Circuit's decision in Holiday Inns, Inc. v. 800 Reservation, Inc., 86 F.3d 619 (6th Cir. 1996), *cert. denied,* 519 U.S. 1093 (1997), is a good example. In that case, the plaintiff claimed trademark rights in its mark "Holiday Inns," and also in its vanity telephone number, "1–800–HOLIDAY," which it featured in its advertisements. Customers could dial the 1–800–HOLIDAY number (which translated to the numbers 1–800–465–4329) to obtain information and reserve hotel rooms. The defendants secured and used a number that potential Holiday Inn customers frequently dialed by mistake when attempting to reach the plaintiff. (It was well known that customers often substitute a zero for the letter "o" in dialing vanity numbers: the number the defendants used–1–800–405–4329–represented that variation from the plaintiff's vanity number. This kind of variation is known as a "complimentary number.") The defendants used the complimentary number in their business of making reservations for customers with a number of hotel chains, including Holiday Inns. Holiday Inns sued, alleging trademark infringement and unfair competition.

The Court of Appeals for the Sixth Circuit assumed that the plaintiff had trademark rights in its vanity number, and noted that the defendants' "sole purpose" in choosing the complementary number was "to intercept calls from misdialing consumers who were attempting to reach Holiday Inns," and thus to free-ride on the plaintiff's business good will. *Id.*, 86 F.3d at 621. Nonetheless, the Court rejected Holiday Inns' infringement claim as a matter of law, on the ground that the defendants did not "use" the Holiday Inns trademark or any variant of it within the meaning of the Lanham Act infringement provisions. The Court reasoned that the defendants only used a phone number that was neither phonetically nor visually similar to the 1–800–HOLIDAY mark. The Court stressed that the defendants never advertised or otherwise publicized either the Holiday Inns or the 1–800–Holiday mark. The fact that the defendants used the complimentary number with the *intent* to intercept calls meant for the plaintiff was not sufficient to constitute the necessary "trademark use:" *Id.*, 86 F.3d at 625. The Court of Appeals for the Eighth Circuit subsequently adopted the Sixth Circuit's reasoning in a somewhat factually similar case. DaimlerChrysler AG v. Bloom, 315 F.3d 932 (8th Cir. 2003).

Under these cases, the defendant must expose the public to the mark in the course of selling, disseminating, or advertising goods or services. A showing that the defendant had a predatory intent will not, in itself, satisfy this requirement. Such a rule is consistent with the limited purpose of trademark protection. Trademark laws were not designed to prevent all forms of free-riding on a mark owner's business good will. Indeed, we have long recognized that in many instances free riding may be pro-competitive.

2. *Likelihood of Consumer Confusion*

AMF INC. v. SLEEKCRAFT BOATS

United States Court of Appeals for the Ninth Circuit, 1979.
599 F.2d 341.

J. BLAINE ANDERSON, CIRCUIT JUDGE:

In this trademark infringement action, the district court, after a brief non-jury trial, found appellant AMF's trademark was valid, but not infringed, and denied AMF's request for injunctive relief.

AMF and appellee Nescher both manufacture recreational boats. AMF uses the mark Slickcraft, and Nescher uses Sleekcraft. The crux of this appeal is whether concurrent use of the two marks is likely to confuse the public. The district judge held that confusion was unlikely. We disagree and remand for entry of a limited injunction.

I. FACTS

AMF's predecessor used the name Slickcraft Boat Company from 1954 to 1969 when it became a division of AMF. The mark Slickcraft was federally registered on April 1, 1969, and has been continuously used since then as a trademark for this line of recreational boats.

Slickcraft boats are distributed and advertised nationally. AMF has authorized over one hundred retail outlets to sell the Slickcraft line. For the years 1966–1974, promotional expenditures for the Slickcraft line averaged approximately $200,000 annually. Gross sales for the same period approached $50,000,000.

After several years in the boat-building business, appellee Nescher organized a sole proprietorship, Nescher Boats, in 1962. This venture failed in 1967. In late 1968 Nescher began anew and adopted the name Sleekcraft. Since then Sleekcraft has been the Nescher trademark. The name Sleekcraft was selected without knowledge of appellant's use. After AMF notified him of the alleged trademark infringement, Nescher adopted a distinctive logo and added the identifying phrase "Boats by Nescher" on plaques affixed to the boat and in much of its advertising. (See Appendix A). The Sleekcraft mark still appears alone on some of appellee's stationery, signs, trucks, and advertisements.

The Sleekcraft venture succeeded. Expenditures for promotion increased from $6,800 in 1970 to $126,000 in 1974. Gross sales rose from $331,000 in 1970 to over $6,000,000 in 1975. Like AMF, Nescher sells his boats through authorized local dealers.

Slickcraft boats are advertised primarily in magazines of general circulation. Nescher advertises primarily in publications for boat racing enthusiasts. Both parties exhibit their product line at boat shows, sometimes the same show.

* * *

IV.   FACTORS RELEVANT TO LIKELIHOOD OF CONFUSION

When the goods produced by the alleged infringer compete for sales with those of the trademark owner, infringement usually will be found if the marks are sufficiently similar that confusion can be expected.[9] When the goods are related,[10] but not competitive, several other factors are added to the calculus. If the goods are totally unrelated, there can be no infringement because confusion is unlikely.

AMF contends these boat lines are competitive. Both lines are comprised of sporty, fiberglass boats often used for water skiing; the sizes of the boats are similar as are the prices. Nescher contends his boats are not competitive with Slickcraft boats because his are true high performance boats intended for racing enthusiasts.

The district court found that although there was some overlap in potential customers for the two product lines, the boats "appeal to separate sub-markets." Slickcraft boats are for general family recreation, and Sleekcraft boats are for persons who want high speed recreation; thus, the district court concluded, competition between the lines is negligible. Our research has led us to only one case in which a similarly fine distinction in markets has been recognized. Yet, after careful review of all the exhibits introduced at trial, we are convinced the district court's finding was warranted by the evidence.

The Slickcraft line is designed for a variety of activities: fishing, water skiing, pleasure cruises, and sunbathing. The promotional literature emphasizes family fun. Sleekcraft boats are not for families. They are low-profile racing boats designed for racing, high speed cruises, and water skiing. Seating capacity and luxury are secondary. Unlike the Slickcraft line, handling capability is emphasized. The promotional literature projects an alluring, perhaps flashier, racing image; absent from the pictures are the small children prominently displayed in the Slickcraft brochures.

Even though both boats are designed for towing water skiers, only the highly skilled enthusiast would require the higher speeds the Sleekcraft promises. We therefore affirm the district court's finding that, despite the potential market overlap, the two lines are not competitive. Accordingly, we must consider all the relevant circumstances in assessing the likelihood of confusion.

V.   FACTORS RELEVANT TO LIKELIHOOD OF CONFUSION

In determining whether confusion between related goods is likely, the following factors are relevant:[11]

---

9. The alleged infringer's intent in adopting the mark is weighed, both as probative evidence of the likelihood of confusion and as an equitable consideration.

10. Related goods are those "products which would be reasonably thought by the buying public to come from the same source if sold under the same mark." *Standard Brands, Inc. v. Smidler*, 151 F.2d 34, 37 (C.A.2 1945).

11. The list is not exhaustive. Other variables may come into play depending on the particular facts presented.

1. strength of the mark;

2. proximity of the goods;

3. similarity of the marks;

4. evidence of actual confusion;

5. marketing channels used;

6. type of goods and the degree of care likely to be exercised by the purchaser;

7. defendant's intent in selecting the mark; and

8. likelihood of expansion of the product lines.

We discuss each serially.

1. Strength of the mark

A strong mark is inherently distinctive, for example, an arbitrary or fanciful mark; it will be afforded the widest ambit of protection from infringing uses. A descriptive mark tells something about the product; it will be protected only when secondary meaning is shown.[12] In between lie suggestive marks which subtly connote something about the products. Although less distinctive than an arbitrary or fanciful mark and therefore a comparatively weak mark, a suggestive mark will be protected without proof of secondary meaning.

Slickcraft is, AMF asserts, a fanciful mark and therefore entitled to wide protection. This assertion is incorrect. The issue, as we view it, is whether Slickcraft is descriptive or suggestive of appellant's boats.

* * *

Although the distinction between descriptive and suggestive marks may be inarticulable, several criteria offer guidance. The primary criterion is "the imaginativeness involved in the suggestion": that is, how immediate and direct is the thought process from the mark to the particular product. From the word Slickcraft one might readily conjure up the image of appellant's boats, yet a number of other images might also follow. A secondary criterion is whether granting the trademark owner a limited monopoly will in fact inhibit legitimate use of the mark by other sellers. There is no evidence here that others have used or desire to use Slickcraft in describing their goods. Another criterion is whether the mark is actually viewed by the public as an indication of the product's origin or as a self-serving description of it. We think buyers probably will understand that Slickcraft is a trademark, particularly since it is generally used in conjunction with the mark AMF. (See Appendix A). Based on the above criteria and our reading of the district court's findings, we hold that Slickcraft is a suggestive mark when applied to boats.

---

12. Once secondary meaning is established, though, the protection afforded should be commensurate with the degree of consumer association proven.

Although appellant's mark is protectible and may have been strengthened by advertising, it is a weak mark entitled to a restricted range of protection. Thus, only if the marks are quite similar, and the goods closely related, will infringement be found.

2. *Proximity of the goods*

For related goods, the danger presented is that the public will mistakenly assume there is an association between the producers of the related goods, though no such association exists. The more likely the public is to make such an association, the less similarity in the marks is requisite to a finding of likelihood of confusion. Thus, less similarity between the marks will suffice when the goods are complementary, the products are sold to the same class of purchasers, or the goods are similar in use and function.

Although these product lines are non-competing, they are extremely close in use and function. In fact, their uses overlap. Both are for recreational boating on bays and lakes. Both are designed for water skiing and speedy cruises. Their functional features, for the most part, are also similar: fiberglass bodies, outboard motors, and open seating for a handful of people. Although the Sleekcraft boat is for higher speed recreation and its refinements support the market distinction the district court made, they are so closely related that a diminished standard of similarity must be applied when comparing the two marks.

3. *Similarity of the marks*

The district court found that "the two marks are easily distinguishable in use either when written or spoken." * * *

Similarity of the marks is tested on three levels: sight, sound, and meaning. Each must be considered as they are encountered in the marketplace. Although similarity is measured by the marks as entities, similarities weigh more heavily than differences.

Standing alone the words Sleekcraft and Slickcraft are the same except for two inconspicuous letters in the middle of the first syllable. To the eye, the words are similar.

In support of the district court's finding, Nescher points out that the distinctive logo on his boats and brochures negates the similarity of the words. We agree: the names appear dissimilar when viewed in conjunction with the logo, but the logo is often absent. The exhibits show that the word Sleekcraft is frequently found alone in trade journals, company stationery, and various advertisements.

Nescher also points out that the Slickcraft name is usually accompanied by the additional trademark AMF. As a result of this consistent use, Nescher argues, AMF has become the salient part of the mark indicative of the product's origin.

Although Nescher is correct in asserting that use of a house mark can reduce the likelihood of confusion, the effect is negligible here even though AMF is a well-known house name for recreational equipment. The exhibits show that the AMF mark is down-played in the brochures and advertisements; the letters AMF are smaller and skewed to one side. Throughout the promotional materials, the emphasis is on the Slickcraft name. Accordingly, we find that Slickcraft is the more conspicuous mark and serves to indicate the source of origin to the public.

Another argument pressed by Nescher is that we should disregard the common suffix "craft" and compare Slick and Sleek alone. Although these are the salient parts of the two marks, we must consider the entire mark. Craft, a generic frequently used in trademarks on boats, is not itself protectible, yet the common endings do add to the marks' similarity. The difference between Slick and Sleek is insufficient to overcome the overall visual similarity.

Sound is also important because reputation is often conveyed word-of-mouth. We recognize that the two sounds can be distinguished, but the difference is only in a small part of one syllable. In *G. D. Searle & Co. v. Chas. Pfizer & Co.*, 265 F.2d 385 (C.A.7 1959), *cert. denied*, 361 U.S. 819, 80 S.Ct. 64, 4 L.Ed.2d 65 (1959), the court reversed the trial court's finding that Bonamine sounded "unlike" Dramamine, stating that: "Slight differences in the sound of trademarks will not protect the infringer." The difference here is even slighter. * * *

Neither expert testimony nor survey evidence was introduced below to support the trial court's finding that the marks were easily distinguishable to the eye and the ear. The district judge based his conclusion on a comparison of the marks. After making the same comparison, we are left with a definite and firm conviction that his conclusion is incorrect.

The final criterion reinforces our conclusion. Closeness in meaning can itself substantiate a claim of similarity of trademarks. Nescher contends the words are sharply different in meaning. This contention is not convincing; the words are virtual synonyms.

Despite the trial court's findings, we hold that the marks are quite similar on all three levels.

4. *Evidence of actual confusion*

Evidence that use of the two marks has already led to confusion is persuasive proof that future confusion is likely. Proving actual confusion is difficult, however, and the courts have often discounted such evidence because it was unclear or insubstantial.

AMF introduced evidence that confusion had occurred both in the trade and in the mind of the buying public. A substantial showing of confusion among either group might have convinced the trial court that continued use would lead to further confusion.

The district judge found that in light of the number of sales and the extent of the parties' advertising, the amount of past confusion was negligible. We cannot say this finding is clearly erroneous though we might have viewed the evidence more generously.

Because of the difficulty in garnering such evidence, the failure to prove instances of actual confusion is not dispositive. Consequently, this factor is weighed heavily only when there is evidence of past confusion or, perhaps, when the particular circumstances indicate such evidence should have been available.

5. *Marketing channels*

Convergent marketing channels increase the likelihood of confusion. There is no evidence in the record that both lines were sold under the same roof except at boat shows; the normal marketing channels used by both AMF and Nescher are, however, parallel. Each sells through authorized retail dealers in diverse localities. The same sales methods are employed. The price ranges are almost identical. Each line is advertised extensively though different national magazines are used; the retail dealers also promote the lines, by participating in smaller boat shows and by advertising in local newspapers and classified telephone directories. Although different submarkets are involved, the general class of boat purchasers exposed to the products overlap.

6. *Type of goods and purchaser care*

Both parties produce high quality, expensive goods. According to the findings of fact, the boats "are purchased only after thoughtful, careful evaluation of the product and the performance the purchaser expects."

In assessing the likelihood of confusion to the public, the standard used by the courts is the typical buyer exercising ordinary caution. Although the wholly indifferent may be excluded, the standard includes the ignorant and the credulous. When the buyer has expertise in the field, a higher standard is proper though it will not preclude a finding that confusion is likely. Similarly, when the goods are expensive, the buyer can be expected to exercise greater care in his purchases; again, though, confusion may still be likely.

The parties vigorously dispute the validity of the trial court's finding on how discriminating the average buyer actually is. Although AMF presented expert testimony to the contrary, the court's finding is amply supported by the record. The care exercised by the typical purchaser, though it might virtually eliminate mistaken purchases, does not guarantee that confusion as to association or sponsorship is unlikely.

The district court also found that trademarks are unimportant to the average boat buyer. Common sense and the evidence indicate this is not the type of purchase made only on "general impressions." This inattention to trade symbols does reduce the possibilities for confusion.

The high quality of defendant's boats is also relevant in another way. The hallmark of a trademark owner's interest in preventing use of his mark on related goods is the threat such use poses to the reputation of his own goods. When the alleged infringer's goods are of equal quality, there is little harm to the reputation earned by the trademarked goods. Yet this is no defense, for present quality is no assurance of continued quality. The wrong inheres in involuntarily entrusting one's business reputation to another business; AMF, of course, cannot control the quality of Sleekcraft boats. In addition, what may be deemed a beneficial feature in a racing boat may be seen as a deficiency to a person seeking a craft for general-purpose recreation; the confused consumer may then decide, without even perusing one, that a Slickcraft boat will not suit his needs. Finally, equivalence in quality may actually contribute to the assumption of a common connection.

7. Intent

The district judge found that Nescher was unaware of appellant's use of the Slickcraft mark when he adopted the Sleekcraft name. There was no evidence that anyone attempted to palm off the latter boats for the former. And after notification of the purported infringement, Nescher designed a distinctive logo. (See Appendix A.) We agree with the district judge: appellee's good faith cannot be questioned.

When the alleged infringer knowingly adopts a mark similar to another's, reviewing courts presume that the defendant can accomplish his purpose: that is, that the public will be deceived. Good faith is less probative of the likelihood of confusion, yet may be given considerable weight in fashioning a remedy.

8. Likelihood of expansion

Inasmuch as a trademark owner is afforded greater protection against competing goods, a "strong possibility" that either party may expand his business to compete with the other will weigh in favor of finding that the present use is infringing. When goods are closely related, any expansion is likely to result in direct competition. The evidence shows that both parties are diversifying their model lines. The potential that one or both of the parties will enter the other's submarket with a competing model is strong.

VI. Remedy

Based on the preceding analysis, we hold that Nescher has infringed the Slickcraft mark. Since Nescher's use is continuing, an injunction should have been entered. Several considerations, however, convince us that a limited injunction will suffice.

Both parties have used their trademarks for over a decade. AMF has a substantial investment in the Slickcraft name, yet a complete prohibition against appellee's use of the Sleekcraft name is unnecessary to protect against encroachment of appellant's mark, or to eliminate public confusion. Appellee has also expended much effort and money to build and preserve the goodwill of its mark.

There is little doubt both parties honestly desire to avoid confusion of their products. Nescher adopted the Sleekcraft name in good faith and has subsequently taken steps to avoid confusion. Use of the Nescher logo in all facets of the business would ensure that confusion would not occur. The exhibits, particularly the yellow pages advertisements, convince us that this is not being done.

Thus, in "balancing the conflicting interests both parties have in the unimpaired continuation of their trade-mark use," and the interest the public and the trade have in avoiding confusion, we conclude that a limited mandatory injunction is warranted. Upon remand the district court should consider the above interests in structuring appropriate relief. At minimum, the logo should appear in all advertisements, signs, and promotional materials prepared either by appellee or by his retail dealers, and on all appellee's business forms except those intended for strictly internal use. A specific disclaimer of any association with AMF or the Slickcraft line seems unnecessary, nor do we think it necessary to enjoin Nescher from expanding his product line. * * *

Appendix A

NOTES AND QUESTIONS

1. *The standard of review.* There has been some dispute regarding the proper standard of review to apply when a district court's determination regarding likelihood of confusion is challenged on appeal. In *AMF,* the Court of Appeals for the Ninth Circuit stated that it would review a district court's determination *de novo* if it was based upon undisputed facts. However, when disputed facts were involved, it would apply the clearly erroneous standard to the underlying "foundational facts" and give *de novo* review to the "legal conclusion" regarding likelihood of confusion. Several years later, in Levi Strauss & Co. v. Blue Bell, Inc., 778 F.2d 1352, 1355 (9th Cir.1985), the court reevaluated the standard of review, and decided that the "clearly erroneous" standard was the more appropriate standard of review for the likelihood of confusion determination. While a few of the Circuits continue to treat the ultimate likelihood of confusion issue as one of law, as in *AMF,* the majority of Circuits today treat it as an issue of fact, as in *Levi Strauss,* and apply the clearly erroneous standard. See J.T. McCarthy, 3 McCarthy on Trademarks and Unfair Competition, § 23.73.

2. *Who must be confused, and about what?* The *AMF* opinion states that in assessing the likelihood of confusion, courts apply the standard of the typical buyer of such goods exercising ordinary caution. To find a defendant liable for infringement, it must appear that a significant, or appreciable number of prospective purchasers are likely to be confused by the defendant's use of its mark. However, it is usually safe to assume that if the typical buyer exercising ordinary caution would be confused, a significant or appreciable number of prospective purchasers would be confused. See Restatement (Third) of Unfair Competition § 20, cmt g (1995).

Courts are rarely specific about what will constitute a "significant" or "appreciable" number of prospective purchasers for purposes of infringement liability. In most cases, it would be impossible to measure the exact extent of confusion in any event. The cases do make it clear, however, that the number need not constitute the majority of potential customers for the parties' goods. Indeed, survey evidence indicating that ten or fifteen percent would be confused may be sufficient, when supported by other evidence. *Id.*

About what must this significant or appreciable number of prospective purchasers be confused? While earlier trademark and unfair competition law specified that they must be confused about the goods' or services' *origin*, or *source*, modern law also protects against confusion as to *affiliation, connection, approval or sponsorship*. See Lindy Pen Co., Inc. v. Bic Pen Corp., 725 F.2d 1240, 1246 (9th Cir.1984), *cert. denied*, 469 U.S. 1188, 105 S.Ct. 955, 83 L.Ed.2d 962 (1985). This broadening of the confusion standard has fostered the growing business of trademark licensing, or merchandising. For example, assume that a clothing manufacturer makes and sells tee-shirts featuring a large replica of the mark of a popular sports team on the front. Consumers, seeing the shirt in a store, may not think that the team is the *source* of the shirt, since most teams are not in the clothing manufacturing and sales business. They might, however, believe that the team has affiliated itself with the producer in some fashion, approving or sponsoring the shirt. Bringing such situations into the trademark infringement cause of action gives mark owners greater control over the use of their marks and provides lucrative opportunities to sell the right to use them. It is, of course, a question of fact in each case whether a significant number of prospective customers will understand the mark to be an indication of sponsorship or affiliation with the mark owner or merely decoration. For an excellent discussion of the present status of the law on this issue, see J.T. McCarthy, 3 McCarthy on Trademarks and Unfair Competition, § 23.5.

The trademark law has also broadened with regard to *when* prospective customers are likely to be confused. Confusion at the point of purchase has been the traditional focus. However, assume that plaintiff manufactures and sells an expensive, prestige product, and the defendant manufactures and sells an inexpensive replica, using a similar trademark. Given the discrepancy in price and sales outlet, purchasers of the defendant's product may be unlikely to think that the product comes from the plaintiff. But after the sale, other prospective purchasers may see the defendant's product (with its mark) outside of the sales context—in the purchaser's home or on his person—and think it comes from the plaintiff. Under modern trademark law, this *post-sale* likelihood of confusion may serve as the basis for a finding of infringement. In such cases, what is the plaintiff's injury? How is the public injured? See Restatement (Third) of Unfair Competition § 20 cmt b (1995).

What if the defendant's similar mark is likely to cause initial consumer confusion, when consumers first encounter it, but the circumstances or nature of the sales process ensure that the confusion will be dissipated prior to the actual time to purchase? Should that temporary pre-sale likelihood of confusion support a finding of infringement? What, if any, injury does it cause the plaintiff? Does this initial interest confusion injure the public? See Mobil Oil Corp. v. Pegasus Petroleum Corp., 818 F.2d 254 (2d Cir.1987).

Most trademark infringement cases arise when a subsequent (junior) mark user creates a likelihood that purchasers will think *its* goods or services come from (or are associated with) a prior (senior) user of the mark. In some cases, however, the junior user is so much larger or more famous than the senior user, or so extensively promotes its mark, that it overshadows the senior user, leading consumers to think that *the senior user's goods come from (or are associated with) the junior user.* This is known as "reverse confusion." This reverse confusion will sustain the senior user's trademark infringement claim against the junior user. See, e.g., Big O Tire Dealers, Inc. v. Goodyear Tire & Rubber Co., 561 F.2d 1365 (10th Cir.1977). In such cases, what is the nature of the senior user's injury?

3. *The multiple factor test for likelihood of confusion.* The *AMF* opinion differentiated between infringement cases in which the goods are "competitive" and those in which the goods are "related," and upheld the district court's determination that the *AMF* parties' boats were "related" goods. If the defendant's goods do not compete with the plaintiff's, why should the plaintiff be entitled to enjoin the defendant's use of a confusingly similar mark? How is the plaintiff harmed? How is the public harmed?

Every Circuit Court of Appeals has developed its own variation of the multiple factor test set forth in *AMF.* While these multiple factor tests originally were applied only in cases of *related* goods, today they routinely are applied *in all infringement cases, including those involving directly competing goods.*

(a) *Strength of the mark.* The *AMF* court states that the "stronger" or more distinctive the mark, the greater the scope of protection it will be afforded. Why should this be the case? See Restatement (Third) of Unfair Competition § 21 and cmt i (1995). What makes a mark "strong?"

(b) *Proximity of the goods.* The more similar the parties' respective goods or services, the less similar the marks must be. How should similarity of goods be determined? Do the goods perform the same function? Are the goods often used together? Are they of the same general type, so that consumers might expect that they come from the same producer? Are consumers likely to believe that lamps and light bulbs come from the same source? How about light bulbs and heavy earth moving equipment?

(c) *Similarity of the marks.* Courts have often admonished that the similarity of the parties' marks is not to be judged simply through a side-by-side comparison:

The marks must be compared in the light of what occurs in the market-place, not in the courtroom. A prospective purchaser does not ordinarily carry a sample or specimen of the article he knows well enough to call by its trade name, he necessarily depends upon the mental picture of that which symbolizes origin and ownership of the thing desired. * * * Therefore, the court must determine whether the alleged infringing mark will be confusing to the public when singly presented.

Beer Nuts, Inc. v. Clover Club Foods Co., 711 F.2d 934, 941 (10th Cir.1983). Indeed, "it is sufficient if one adopts a trade-name or a trade-mark so like another in form, spelling or sound that one, *with a not very definite or clear recollection as to the real trade-mark*, is likely to become confused or misled." Northam Warren Corp. v. Universal Cosmetic Co., 18 F.2d 774, 775 (7th Cir.1927) (emphasis added).

The *AMF* court discusses the "sight, sound and meaning" test, set forth in Restatement of Torts § 729. As one might imagine, the "sight" test is quite subjective: Given the wide variety of design, word, and device marks, there can be no uniformly applicable rule for determining when two marks "look alike." Nonetheless, especially for picture and design marks, similarity of appearance can be an extremely important factor. It may also be important in the case of foreign words. For example, are the following words confusingly similar: "Senorita," "Si Senor" and "Senioral"? See Myrurgia, S.A. v. Comptoir De La Parfumerie S.A. Ancienne Maison Tschanz, 441 F.2d 673 (C.C.P.A. 1971).

As the Second Circuit has observed, "[t]rademarks, like small children, are not only seen but heard." Grotrian, Helfferich, Schulz, Th. Steinweg Nachf. v. Steinway & Sons, 523 F.2d 1331, 1340 (2d Cir.1975). In assessing the phonetic similarity of the "Slickcraft" and "Sleekcraft" marks, the *AMF* court looked to the Seventh Circuit's opinion in G.D. Searle & Co. v. Chas. Pfizer & Co., 265 F.2d 385 (7th Cir.), *cert. denied*, 361 U.S. 819, 80 S.Ct. 64, 4 L.Ed.2d 65 (1959). The *Searle* court's opinion, which found "Bonamine" phonetically similar to "Dramamine," demonstrates one of the more scientific judicial approaches to the similarity issue:

> DRAMAMINE and BONAMINE contain the same number of syllables; they have the same stress pattern, with primary accent on the first syllable and secondary accent on the third; and the last two syllables of DRAMAMINE and BONAMINE are identical. The initial sounds of DRAMAMINE and BONAMINE ["d" and "b"] are both what are known as "voiced plosives," and are acoustically similar; the consonants "m" and "n" are nasal sounds and are acoustically similar. The only dissimilar sound in the two trademarks is the "r" in DRAMAMINE. Slight differences in the sound of similar trademarks will not protect the infringer.

Id., 265 F.2d at 387. How would you evaluate the phonetic similarity of the following marks:

(1) "Coca Cola" and "Cup–O'-Cola" (see Coca–Cola Co. v. Clay, 324 F.2d 198 (C.C.P.A.1963));

(2) "Coca–Cola" and "Polar Cola" (see Coca–Cola Co. v. Snow Crest Beverages, Inc., 162 F.2d 280 (1st Cir.), *cert. denied,* 332 U.S. 809, 68 S.Ct. 110, 92 L.Ed. 386 (1947));

(3) "Beck's Beer" and "Ex Bier" (see Beck & Co. v. Package Distributors of America, Inc., 198 U.S.P.Q. 573 (T.T.A.B. 1978)).

Under the "meaning" prong of the Restatement test, one must consider the mental imagery evoked by the marks. For example, how would you compare a drawing of a winged horse with the word mark "Pegasus?" See Mobil Oil Corp. v. Pegasus Petroleum Corp., 818 F.2d 254, 257–58 (2d Cir.1987) (approving district court's finding that "the word 'Pegasus' evokes the symbol of the flying red horse * * *. In other words, the symbol of the flying horse and its name 'Pegasus' are synonymous.") How would you compare the word marks "Cyclone" and "Tornado" for wire fencing? See Hancock v. American Steel & Wire Co., 203 F.2d 737 (C.C.P.A.1953). How about "Gravel" and "On the Rocks" for men's cologne? See Gravel Cologne, Inc. v. Lawrence Palmer, Inc., 469 F.2d 1397 (C.C.P.A.1972).

Another point to bear in mind under the "meaning" test is that, under the doctrine of foreign equivalents, words from common foreign languages may be held confusingly similar to their English translation. See, e.g., *In re* American Safety Razor Co., 2 U.S.P.Q.2d 1459 (T.T.A.B. 1987) (finding "Good Morning" for shaving cream confusingly similar to "Buenos Dias" for soap). It must appear, however, that a significant number of consumers would be likely to make the translation.

(d) Evidence of actual confusion. As the *AMF* court notes, evidence of actual consumer confusion is not required to prove that the defendant's use of its mark causes a likelihood of consumer confusion. On the other hand, such evidence, if reliable, can be very persuasive. How might one go about proving the existence of actual confusion?

(e) Marketing channels used. Does the evidence on this factor weigh for or against a likelihood of confusion in *AMF?* Why should it matter whether the parties' goods are sold through similar retail outlets, or advertised in the same media? See Restatement (Third) of Unfair Competition § 21 cmt g (1995).

(f) Type of goods and the degree of care likely to be exercised by the purchaser. If the goods are expensive, like boats, or the purchasers are sophisticated (for example, professional purchasers for institutions), then it generally can be expected that the purchasers will devote some care and attention to selecting the goods. They are only likely to be confused by highly similar marks. What level of care are self-service grocery-store customers likely to use in selecting a jar of pickles? It has been suggested that "the average purchaser undergoes, while in a supermarket, an experience not unlike that of hypnosis." Pikle–Rite Co. v. Chicago Pickle Co., 171 F.Supp. 671, 676 (N.D.Ill.1959). In such circumstances a much lesser degree of similarity may lead to confusion.

(g) Defendant's intent in selecting the mark. Trademark law has its origins in the tort of deceit, but the modern common-law and Lanham Act trademark causes of action do not require any showing of wrongful intent. On

the other hand, as the *AMF* opinion acknowledges, evidence of an intent to confuse consumers may give rise to an inference (or in some Circuits, a rebuttable presumption) that the defendant succeeded in accomplishing what she set out to do.

An intent to *copy* the plaintiff's mark, however, is not necessarily an intent to *confuse*. For example, in Jordache Enterprises, Inc. v. Hogg Wyld, Ltd., 828 F.2d 1482 (10th Cir.1987), the defendants intentionally copied plaintiff's prestigious "Jordache" mark when they adopted the mark "Lardashe" for large women's jeans. The court found that their purpose in copying was to parody, not to confuse. Thus, there was no basis for inferring a likelihood of confusion under the rule stated above:

> Given the unlimited number of possible names and symbols that could serve as a trademark, it is understandable that a court generally presumes one who chooses a mark similar to an existing mark intends to confuse the public. However, where a party chooses a mark as a parody of an existing mark, the intent is not necessarily to confuse the public but rather to amuse. * * *

> In one sense, a parody is an attempt "to derive benefit from the reputation" of the owner of the mark, *Sicilia*, 732 F.2d at 431, if only because no parody could be made without the initial mark. The benefit to the one making the parody, however, arises from the humorous association, not from public confusion as to the source of the marks. A parody relies upon a difference from the original mark, presumably a humorous difference, in order to produce its desired effect.

Id., 828 F.2d at 1486.

(h) Likelihood of expansion of the product lines. This factor is sometimes referred to as the likelihood that the senior user will "bridge the gap." As one court has explained,

> In the likelihood of confusion context, "bridging the gap" refers to two distinct possibilities. The first is that the senior user presently intends to expand his sales efforts to compete directly with the junior user; likelihood of confusion is created by the likelihood that the two products will be directly competitive. The second possibility is that, while there is no present intention to bridge the gap, consumers will assume otherwise and conclude, in this era of corporate diversification, that the parties are related companies.

Lambda Electronics Corp. v. Lambda Technology, Inc., 515 F.Supp. 915, 926 (S.D.N.Y.1981).

4. *Families of marks.* A business that uses the same prefix or suffix in a number of marks may establish a "family of marks," which effectively gives it rights in the common element itself: "A family of marks may have a synergistic recognition that is greater than the sum of each mark." Quality Inns International, Inc. v. McDonald's Corp., 695 F.Supp. 198, 212 (D.Md. 1988). The Court of Appeals for the Federal Circuit has explained:

> A family of marks is a group of marks having a recognizable common characteristic, wherein the marks are composed and used in such a way that the public associates not only the individual marks, but the common

characteristic of the family, with the trademark owner. Simply using a series of similar marks does not of itself establish the existence of a family. There must be a recognition among the purchasing public that the common characteristic is indicative of a common origin of the goods.

J & J Snack Foods Corp. v. McDonald's Corp., 932 F.2d 1460, 1462 (Fed.Cir. 1991).

Perhaps the most famous mark family is the "Mc" family, owned by the McDonald's fast food chain. McDonald's has registered numerous marks consisting of the prefix "Mc" and a generic term, such as "McMuffin," "Chicken McNuggets," etc. As a result of McDonald's tremendous volume of sales and advertising, the public has come to associate the prefix "Mc" in combination with a generic term with McDonald's, even though McDonald's has not registered or used "Mc" by itself. McDonald's has repeatedly convinced courts and the TTAB that others' use of "Mc" with the name of food items will create a likelihood of confusion. Thus, for example, in *J & J Snack Foods*, cited above, the Court of Appeals for the Federal Circuit upheld McDonald's successful opposition to J & J Snack Foods Corporation's registration of "McPretzel" for frozen soft pretzels sold in bulk to food service retailers. McDonald's business activities have not been limited to the food business, however, and neither have its trademark claims. In McDonald's Corp. v. McKinley, 13 U.S.P.Q.2d 1895 (T.T.A.B. 1989), McDonald's successfully opposed registration of "McTeddy" for teddy bears. In the *Quality Inns* case, cited above, it convinced the judge to enjoin the use of "McSleep" for economy motels. In McDonald's Corp. v. Druck and Gerner DDS, P.C., 814 F.Supp. 1127 (N.D.N.Y.1993), McDonald's successfully enjoined the use of "McDental" for dental services.

Note that the term "Mc" has taken on a life of its own, however. Terms such as "McNews," "McPaper," and even "McLaw" appear with some regularity in the media and common speech. What, if any, impact is this likely to have on McDonalds' trademark rights? See *Quality Inns*, 695 F.Supp. at 212.

5. *Infringement of product configuration trade dress.* The central inquiry in a trade dress infringement suit is whether the defendant's packaging, product configuration, business decor, or other trade dress is so similar to the plaintiff's that it causes a likelihood of consumer confusion about the source, sponsorship or affiliation of the parties' products or services. In determining likelihood of confusion, the alleged trade dress must be considered as a whole: "It is the 'combination of features as a whole rather than a difference in some of the details which must determine whether the competing product is likely to cause confusion in the mind of the public.'" Perfect Fit Industries, Inc. v. Acme Quilting Co., 618 F.2d 950, 955 (2d Cir.1980). Courts typically consider the same factors in evaluating likelihood of confusion, regardless of whether the claim is for trademark or trade dress infringement.

However, some Circuit Courts of Appeals have suggested that the likelihood of confusion issue, like the distinctiveness issue, should be handled somewhat differently in the particular case of product configuration, or product feature trade dress. The Third Circuit made the strongest statement to this effect in Versa Products Co., Inc. v. Bifold Co., Ltd., 50 F.3d 189 (3d Cir.1995), *cert. denied*, 516 U.S. 808, 116 S.Ct. 54, 133 L.Ed.2d 19 (1995).

In *Versa*, the Third Circuit reviewed the usual factors for evaluating the likelihood of confusion and held that the factors should be weighted differently in product feature trade dress cases. First, a strong similarity of appearance should not carry the same weight as it traditionally has in trademark and packaging trade dress cases:

> Consumers have grown accustomed to relying on trademarks as trustworthy indicators of the source of the product: that is the point of a trademark. Perhaps to a somewhat lesser extent, consumers also rely on other aspects of product packaging to identify the manufacturer. * * *

> In a product configuration trade dress infringement case, by contrast, consumers do not have to rely on a potentially distinctive configuration to identify the source of the product; rather, they can generally look to the packaging, trademarks, and advertising used to market the product, which are typically much less ambiguous. Consumers therefore have less need, and so are much less likely, to rely on a product configuration as an indicator of the product's source. Accordingly, they are less likely to be confused as to the sources of two products with substantially similar configurations. Thus, in trade dress infringement suits where the dress inheres in a product configuration, the primary factors to be considered in assessing likelihood of confusion are the product's labeling, packaging, and advertisements. * * *

> Indeed, except where consumers ordinarily exercise virtually no care in selecting a particular type of product (as may be the case with inexpensive disposable or consumable items * * *), clarity of labeling in packaging and advertising will suffice to preclude almost all possibility of consumer confusion as to source stemming from the product's configuration.

Id. at 202–03.

The *Versa* court added that evidence that the plaintiff's mark is strong should only count in favor of a likelihood of confusion if consumers *rely* on the product's configuration to identify the producer of the good. A mere showing that large numbers of consumers are able to identify the configuration as coming from a particular source should not be deemed sufficient. *Id.*, at 203. The court reasoned that to hold otherwise would "sanction too much reliance by consumers on product designs that, lacking the protection of a patent, are in large measure copyable at will." *Id.* To avoid this,"courts should require evidence of actual reliance by consumers on a particular product configuration as a source indicator before crediting that configuration's 'strength' toward likelihood of confusion." *Id.*, at 204.

Finally, the *Versa* court considered the issue of the defendant's intent in product configuration trade dress cases. The court noted that it is the defendant's intent to confuse, not a mere intent to copy, that is probative of the likelihood of confusion issue. While it might be justifiable in some settings to *infer* an intent to confuse from the defendant's intentional copying, such an inference could not be justified in the case of product features.

Where product configurations are concerned, we must be especially wary of undermining competition. Competitors have broad rights to copy successful product designs when those designs are not protected by utility or design patents. It is not unfair competition for someone to trade off the good will of a product, it is only unfair to deceive consumers as to the origin of one's goods and thereby trade off the good will of a prior producer.

Id., at 207. Thus, the Third Circuit held that "in the product configuration context, a defendant's intent weighs in favor of a finding of likelihood of confusion only if intent to confuse or deceive is demonstrated by clear and convincing evidence, and only where the product's labeling and marketing are also affirmatively misleading." *Id.*, at 208.

The *Versa* court justified all of the limitations discussed above on the reasoning that "the penumbra of the federal patent laws restricts the degree to which courts may grant legal recognition of consumer reliance on product configurations as source indicators." *Id.*, at 204. The court referred to "the federal policy, found in Art. I, § 8, cl. 8, of the Constitution and in the implementing federal statutes, of allowing free access to copy whatever the federal patent and copyright laws leave in the public domain." *Id.* For somewhat similar views from other Circuits, see Dorr–Oliver, Inc. v. Fluid–Quip, Inc., 94 F.3d 376, 381, 383–84 (7th Cir.1996); Sunbeam Products, Inc. v. West Bend Co., 123 F.3d 246 (5th Cir.1997).

Is the *Versa* court assuming that consumers will have the opportunity to see the product labeling and packaging along with the product configuration? How might the Third Circuit handle a "post-sale" confusion claim, where it is alleged that potential consumers encounter the product in the purchaser's home or on her person, stripped of its packaging and label?

In Gibson Guitar Corp. v. Paul Reed Smith Guitars, L.P., 423 F.3d 539, 550–52 (6th Cir. 2005), the Court of Appeals for the Sixth Circuit expressed strong doubt that it could ever justify finding product configuration trade dress infringement on an initial interest (or "pre-sale") confusion theory, reasoning that doing so would have an unacceptable anticompetitive effect. Why might that be so?

6. *The use of disclaimers.* How effective is a disclaimer, such as "not associated with * * * "likely to be as a means of avoiding consumer confusion? In most cases, courts accord little weight to use of disclaimers. For example, see Justice Holmes' opinion in Jacobs v. Beecham, 221 U.S. 263, 272, 31 S.Ct. 555, 556, 55 L.Ed. 729, 732 (1911):

To call pills Beecham's pills is to call them the plaintiff's pills. The statement that the defendant makes them does not save the fraud. That is not what the public would notice or is intended to notice, and, if it did, its natural interpretation would be that the defendant had bought the original business out and was carrying it on.

7. *Trademark counterfeiting.* Trademark counterfeiting is hard-core, willful infringement. It entails intentional, knowing use of "a spurious mark which is identical with, or substantially indistinguishable from, a registered mark," on the same kind of goods or services for which the mark is registered.

15 U.S.C.A. § 1127. The problem of counterfeiting became epidemic in the late 1970's and 1980's. As one commentator has explained:

> [Counterfeiting ranges] from infringement of designer labels to crude imitations of carefully crafted, life-sustaining heart valves and crucial airplane parts threatening the public safety. After this threat became known, Congress began scrutinizing the problem more carefully and finally acknowledged that counterfeiting was an insidious crime which had ramifications to the trademark holder and the public far beyond what was readily apparent.

> Congress was then forced to intervene primarily because legal remedies to deter this conduct were inadequate. Counterfeiting was not a crime and many counterfeiters would simply destroy the evidence of their activity once receiving notice of the filing of a civil suit. Still, courts continued to apply notice requirements blindly without fully grasping the unique problems associated with this form of street-level commercial vandalism.

> Another problem in fighting counterfeiting was that judges were often influenced by the spectacle in court of a huge multinational conglomerate suing an individual wide-eyed street peddler. Consequently many did not take the cases seriously because they were shut off from the larger picture.

> Moreover, the picture that was playing outside the courtroom told the tale of bands of transient peddlers, "fly-by-night" distributors, and retail operators that were selling cheap knock-offs and slashing prices far below those of authentic, quality goods. Not only were they deceiving consumers and eroding the value of commercial property, but they were thwarting the judicial process with fictitious identities, disappearing merchandise and bogus invoices. Consequently, simply proving the existence of an actionable claim against an identifiable defendant became a legal nightmare.

Bainton, *Reflections on The Trademark Counterfeiting Act of 1984: Score a Few for the Good Guys*, 82 Trademark Rep. 1, 3–4 (1992).[16] Congress ultimately responded to the problem by passing the Trademark Counterfeiting Act of 1984, Pub.L. No. 98–473, 98 Stat. 2178, which attempted to deter counterfeiters, provide more effective relief to legitimate mark owners, and encourage private owners to police counterfeiting by filing civil infringement suits.

The Lanham Act already provided civil relief against use of a counterfeit mark. However, the Trademark Counterfeiting Act augmented it by providing for attorney's fees and treble damages when a defendant intentionally uses a mark, knowing it to be counterfeit. See 15 U.S.C.A. § 1117(b). It also provided for *ex parte* orders to seize goods bearing counterfeit marks, *Id.*, at § 1116(d), and for destruction of such goods. *Id.*, at § 1118. In addition, the Trademark Counterfeiting Act amended the criminal code to provide criminal sanctions

---

16. Copyright © 1992, The International Trademark Association. Excerpts reprinted with permission from 82 TMR 1, January–February, 1992, The Trademark Reporter®.

against persons who intentionally traffic or attempt to traffic in goods through use of marks they know to be counterfeit. See 18 U.S.C.A. § 2320.

In 1996, Congress further augmented the penalties for counterfeiting by enacting The Anti–Counterfeiting Consumer Protection Act of 1996, Pub. L. No. 104–153, 110 Stat. 1386. Among other things, the Act subjected traffickers in counterfeit goods to liability under the Racketeer Influenced and Corrupt Organizations Act ("RICO"), 18 U.S.C.A. § 1961, which allows law enforcement officials to seize not only counterfeit goods, but also the property associated with the counterfeiting enterprise. The Act also provided statutory damages as an alternative to actual damages in civil counterfeiting litigation. Courts may now award statutory damages ranging from $500 to $100,000 per counterfeit mark for each type of offending good, and up to $1,000,000 if the violation is "willful." The amendments shore up government efforts to stop imports of counterfeit goods, further facilitate seizures of counterfeit goods, and give trademark owners greater control over their disposal. The Act was prompted in part by perceptions that organized crime was becoming increasingly involved in counterfeiting activities.

In 2006 Congress enacted further amendments to criminalize trafficking in "labels, patches, stickers, wrappers, badges, emblems, medallions, charms, boxes, containers, cans, cases, hangtags, documentation, or packaging of any type or nature, knowing that a counterfeit mark has been applied thereto." 18 U.S.C. § 2320. Thus, it is no longer necessary, for purposes of criminal sanctions, to demonstrate that the defendant attached the counterfeit mark to goods or services.

A mark is not counterfeit if the producer or manufacturer lawfully applied it to the good or service at the time of production or manufacture. See 15 U.S.C.A. § 1116(d)(1). Thus, dealing in "grey market" goods (defined as "trademarked goods legitimately manufactured and sold overseas and then imported into the United States outside the trademark owner's desired distribution channels") does not constitute counterfeiting. *Joint Statement on Trademark Counterfeiting Legislation,* 130 Cong. Rec. 31673, 31676 (Oct. 10, 1984). The legal implications of "gray marketeering" will be discussed later in the Chapter.

PROBLEMS

1. Starbucks sells coffee from thousands of retail locations throughout the world, with billions of dollars in annual revenues. It is the largest and best known coffee seller in North America, where it serves coffee to over 20 million customers each week. Please evaluate whether Starbucks would have a cause of action for trademark infringement in the two cases described below.

a) Defendant, doing business as Black Bear Micro Roastery, sells roasted coffee beans and related goods via mail order, internet order and through a limited number of New England supermarkets. It also sells coffee products from a retail outlet called "The Den" in New Hampshire. Black Bear developed a dark roasted blend of coffee that it named "Charbucks Blend," and a blend of dark roasted coffee called "Mr. Charbucks." At the time that it named its blends, it was aware of the Starbucks mark and knew that Starbucks tended to roast its product more darkly than other major roasters.

b) Defendant Samantha Lundberg owns and operates a business in Oregon under the name "Sambuck's Coffeehouse," which sells coffee and coffee-related products. At the time she named her business, Samantha was aware of the Starbucks mark. A consumer survey demonstrated that "Sambuck's Coffeehouse" made the majority of consumers think of Starbucks.

2. Plaintiff Dream Cloud, Inc. is a Florida corporation that organizes and runs conventions for *Star Trek* fans around the country. It began using "Dream Cloud" in advertising, selling and rendering its services in 1990 and has been using it ever since. It registered the Dream Cloud mark for its services in 1995. In 2001, X, a famous movie producer, set up a studio, which he called "Dream Cloud Studios." Since then Dream Cloud Studios has produced a number of blockbuster films, including several that were nominated for Academy Awards. The name "Dream Cloud Studios" is featured prominently in the credits of the movies X produces. Moreover, X uses the name "Dream Cloud" in advertising his films, and those advertisements, along with the tremendous free press coverage the films and the Studio receive, have made "Dream Cloud Studios" a household term in the United States. By contrast, only people who work in the *Star Trek* convention business or attend *Star Trek* conventions are familiar with the plaintiff's registered Dream Cloud mark.

Plaintiff's employees have encountered numerous situations in which members of the public assumed that plaintiff was a part of the Dream Cloud Studio enterprise, even though there is in fact no relationship. Plaintiff would like to sue to enjoin X from further use of the "Dream Cloud" mark. On what theory might it proceed?

3. Plaintiff sells expensive, prestigious leather handbags under the registered mark "Coach & Four." Plaintiff's Coach & Four bags are only sold at fine boutiques and department stores. The defendant sells leather handbags at flea markets and street fairs. The defendant's handbags look very similar to one of the plaintiff's most popular styles, and bear the name "Coach & Four" in the same style as plaintiff's handbags. The defendant sells his handbags for approximately 1/10 of the price that plaintiff charges, and he specifically tells each purchaser that his handbags are not produced by the plaintiff, even though they look very much like plaintiff's bags. Is the plaintiff likely to have any remedy for trademark infringement?

4. Conopco has been marketing Vaseline Intensive Care Lotion ("VICL") for 20 years. It decides to "relaunch" VICL to enhance the product's therapeutic image and to distance it from private label brands, which have been eroding its sales. Accordingly, it develops a new bottle shape and label for the product.

Venture manufactures and sells private label hand lotions. It becomes aware of Conopco's plans to relaunch VICL, and develops a private label product to compete with the revised VICL product. The evidence suggests that it deliberately imitates aspects of the new VICL trade dress. Venture begins marketing its product soon after the VICL relaunch. Conopco sues Venture for trade dress infringement, under Lanham Act § 43(a).

Photographs of the original VICL and Venture Bottles, and of the revised VICL and Venture bottles are reproduced below. How would you evaluate the claim?

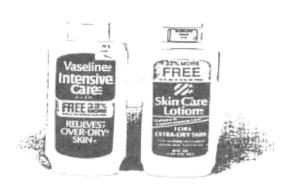

COMPARISON OF REVISED VICL AND VENTURE BOTTLES

5. Plaintiff holds federal registrations for various "Frito–Lay" marks for its snack foods, which enjoy a 50% market share in the multi-billion dollar domestic snack food industry. Defendant sells natural dog treats under the "Fido–Lay" mark in Birmingham, Alabama. Plaintiff sues defendant for infringement. What is your analysis?

NOTE: THE EXTRATERRITORIAL REACH OF UNITED STATES TRADEMARK INTERESTS

We've considered the extent to which businesses can rely on their actions abroad to establish U.S. trademark ownership. This note examines the corollary question: To what extent can a U.S. trademark owner assert its U.S. rights against actions taken abroad? The Lanham Act can, in some circumstances, be applied to reach extraterritorial conduct: Actions abroad may impact U.S. trademark rights, and Congress intended the Lanham Act to apply to all commerce that is within Congress' power to regulate. Steele v. Bulova Watch Co., 344 U.S. 280, 73 S.Ct. 252, 97 L.Ed. 319 (1952).

A traditional test for extraterritorial application of the Lanham Act is set forth in Vanity Fair Mills v. T. Eaton Co., 234 F.2d 633, 642–43 (2d Cir. 1956). The *Vanity Fair* test considers three factors: (1) whether the defendant is an American citizen, (2) whether the defendant's actions have a substantial effect on United States commerce, and (3) whether relief would create a conflict with foreign law. While acknowledging that all three of these inquiries are relevant, the Court of Appeals for the First Circuit has recently opted to disaggregate them:

Our framework asks first whether the defendant is an American citizen; that inquiry is different because a separate constitutional basis for jurisdiction exists for control of activities, even foreign activities, of an American citizen. Further, when the Lanham Act plaintiff seeks to enjoin sales in the United States, there is no question of extraterritorial application; the court has subject matter jurisdiction.

In order for a plaintiff to reach *foreign activities of foreign defendants* in American courts, however, we adopt a separate test. We hold that subject matter jurisdiction under the Lanham Act is proper only if the complained-of activities have a substantial effect on United States commerce, viewed in light of the purposes of the Lanham Act. If this "substantial effects" question is answered in the affirmative, then the court possesses subject matter jurisdiction.

We reject the notion that a comity analysis is part of subject matter jurisdiction. Comity considerations, including potential conflicts with foreign trademark law, are properly treated as questions of whether a court should, in its discretion, decline to exercise subject matter jurisdiction that it already possesses.

McBee v. Delica, 417 F.3d 107 (1st Cir. 2005) (emphasis added). In *McBee*, the plaintiff, a famous American jazz bassist, had a strong following throughout the world, including Japan. The defendant, Delica, was a Japanese corporation that had registered and was using the mark "Cecil McBee" to identify its line of clothing for adolescent girls. The defendant only sold its clothing in Japan, and had specifically adopted a policy of refusing sale or shipment to the United States. However, it maintained a website that was accessible throughout the world, including in the United States, under the web address "www.cecilmcbee.net." The website was created and hosted in Japan and was written primarily in Japanese characters (although it contained some English words). The site contained photographs and information about the defendant's "Cecil McBee" fashions, but made no on-line sales. An on-line search for "Cecil McBee" would generally turn up both the defendant's Japanese web site and sites having to do with the plaintiff and his music in the first ten results. Sometimes the Japanese site was ranked above the sites related to plaintiff. While there was some evidence that defendant's "Cecil McBee" clothing had been sold on e-Bay, there was virtually no evidence that "Cecil McBee" clothing had entered the United States.

Plaintiff objected to the defendant's use, and challenged its registration of the Cecil McBee mark in the Japanese Patent Office. When Japanese courts ultimately upheld the defendant's registration, McBee brought suit in United States District Court, alleging that the defendant's use constituted a false claim of endorsement under Lanham Act § 43(a), creating a likelihood of confusion over whether McBee sponsored, approved or endorsed the defendant's products. The district court dismissed his claims for lack of subject matter jurisdiction and the First Circuit affirmed:

We hold that the Lanham Act grants subject matter jurisdiction over extraterritorial conduct by foreign defendants only where the conduct has a substantial effect on United States commerce. Absent a showing of such a substantial effect, at least as to foreign defendants, the court lacks jurisdiction over the Lanham Act claim. * * * The goal of the jurisdictional test is to ensure that the United States has a sufficient interest in the litigation, as measured by the interests protected by the Lanham Act, to assert jurisdiction.

417 F.3d at 120–21. The court noted that there would be jurisdiction to enjoin the defendant's sales of infringing goods in the United States, because such sales would be deemed "domestic acts." Moreover, if a court had jurisdiction to enjoin sales of goods within the U.S. it might also have jurisdiction to enjoin the website through which the sales were made, or at least those parts of the website necessary to carry out those sales. However, it would constitute an extraterritorial application of the Lanham Act to enjoin the defendant from simply posting its website in a manner visible to United States consumers, as McBee sought to do.

> Delica's website, although hosted from Japan and written in Japanese, happens to be reachable from the United States just as it is reachable from other countries. That is the nature of the Internet. The website is hosted and managed overseas; its visibility within the United States is more in the nature of an effect, which occurs only when someone in the United States decides to visit the website. To hold that any website in a foreign language, wherever hosted, is automatically reachable under the Lanham Act so long as it is visible in the United States would be senseless. The United States often will have no real interest in hearing trademark lawsuits about websites that are written in a foreign language and hosted in other countries. * * *

> [A]llowing subject matter jurisdiction under the Lanham Act to automatically attach whenever a website is visible in the United States would eviscerate the territorial curbs on judicial authority that Congress is, quite sensibly, presumed to have imposed in this area.

Id., at 123–24. To prevail, McBee would need to demonstrate that the defendant's website had a substantial effect on U.S. commerce. However, McBee had failed to do that: The court particularly stressed that the defendant's website was written almost entirely in Japanese characters, making it unlikely that many Americans would visit it or understand it to be related to the plaintiff. The court discounted McBee's arguments that the defendant's site made it more difficult for Americans to find information about him or his music on the web. Moreover, McBee had produced no evidence of confused American consumers.

The court likewise found that there was no subject matter jurisdiction for McBee's claim for damages arising from the defendant's Japanese sales. There was no evidence that American consumers had been exposed to Delicia's products in Japan, or that defendant's products had entered the United States in substantial quantities, either new or post-purchase. Nor was there convincing evidence that the Japanese use of the mark had caused economic harm to McBee's reputation or career, either in the U.S. or Japan. *Id.*, at 125–26.

Since it had found a lack of subject matter jurisdiction for both of McBee's claims, the court found it unnecessary to reach the issue of whether it should decline jurisdiction because of comity concerns. It noted in a footnote, however, that if it were to reach comity principles, they would most likely counsel for dismissal of McBee's claims. *Id.*, at 126 n. 15. Why might that be?

3. *Trademark Use and Likelihood of Confusion in the Internet Context*

The technology underlying the Internet has provided a host of new opportunities for businesses and individuals to promote their own agendas through unauthorized use of others' marks: to divert on-line customers; to free-ride on the mark owner's business good will; to notify consumers that their own products or services are comparable to, compatible with, or second-hand versions of the mark owner's product; to air their grievances about the mark owner's product or service; or to parody, criticize or argue with the mark owner's social, political or religious views. These new digital applications may not directly, or even indirectly associate the plaintiff's mark with goods or services that the defendant is marketing, and in some cases the defendant's use may be completely hidden from consumers' view. Following are some examples of how courts have approached the infringement claims that these new uses have inevitably invoked. In reviewing them, think about whether courts have remained true to the limited purposes of trademark protection, and whether there might be better ways to evaluate the defendants' unauthorized uses of the plaintiff's mark.

a. *Classic Cybersquatting*

INTERMATIC, INC. v. TOEPPEN

United States District Court, Northern District of Illinois, 1996.
947 F.Supp. 1227.

[Toeppen registered hundreds of marks as domain names in the ".com" top level domain, including the plaintiff's "Intermatic" mark for electronic products. Toeppen subsequently set up a web page under the "intermatic.com" domain name that featured a map of Champaign–Urbana, the town where Toeppen lived. When the plaintiff contacted Toeppen about it, Toeppen offered to sell the registration to the plaintiff for a profit. Intermatic sued for trademark infringement and dilution. The court specifically found that Toeppen had not used "intermatic" or "intermatic.com" in connection with the sale or advertisement of goods or services.* The court denied Toeppen's motion for summary judgment and Intermatic's motion for summary judgment on the infringement claim, but granted Intermatic summary judgment on the dilution claim.]

Toeppen is what is commonly referred to as a cyber-squatter. These individuals attempt to profit from the Internet by reserving and later reselling or licensing domain names back to the companies that spent millions of dollars developing the goodwill of the trademark. While many may find patently offensive the practice of reserving the name or mark of a federally registered trademark as a domain name and then attempting to sell the name back to the holder of the trademark, others may view it as a service. Regardless of one's views as to the morality of such conduct, the legal issue is whether such conduct is illegal. Cyber-squatters such as

---

* [Toeppen initially set up a web page regarding a software program he was developing and intended to call "Intermatic," but when contacted by Intermatic, Toeppen agreed to remove that page, which had been available for less than a week. He also dropped the proposed name for his software. He then set up the web page featuring the map of Champaign–Urbana. Toeppen never sold any software.]

Toeppen contend that because they were the first to register the domain name through NSI it is theirs. Intermatic argues that it is entitled to protect its valuable trademark by preventing Toeppen from using "intermatic.com" as a domain name.

The practical effect of Toeppen's conduct is to enjoin Intermatic from using its trademark as its domain name on the Internet. Unlike the typical trademark dispute, where both parties are using the name simultaneously and arguing whether confusion exists, the current configuration of the Internet allows only one party to use the "intermatic.com" domain name. Because the Internet assigns the top-level domain name .com to commercial and non-commercial users, there does not currently appear to be a way in which both Intermatic and Toeppen can both use the intermatic.com name.

* * *

* * * In order to prevail under the federal trademark infringement claim, the federal unfair competition claim, and the state deceptive trade practices and unfair competition claims, * * * Intermatic need only prove that: 1) it owns prior rights in the INTERMATIC mark; and 2) Toeppen's use of "intermatic.com" is likely to cause consumer confusion, deception or mistake.

* * *

Intermatic's name and prior rights over Toeppen to use the INTERMATIC name are clear. Intermatic's first use of the INTERMATIC name and mark predates Toeppen's first use of "intermatic.com" by more than fifty years. Also, it is undisputed that Intermatic holds a valid registration for the trademark INTERMATIC.

The Seventh Circuit has held that the following seven factors should be weighed to determine if there is a likelihood of confusion: 1) the degree of similarity between the marks in appearance and suggestion; 2) the similarity of products or services for which the name is used; 3) the area and manner of concurrent use; 4) the degree of care likely to be exercised by consumers; 5) the strength of the complainant's mark; 6) actual confusion; and 7) an intent on the part of the alleged infringer to palm off his products as those of another. The test is not whether the public would confuse the marks, but whether the viewer of an accused mark would be likely to associate the product or service with which it is connected with the source of products or services with which an earlier mark is connected. * * *

[The court proceeds to apply the "likelihood of confusion" factors, noting that the "Intermatic" mark is strong and that "Intermatic" and "intermatic.com" are similar, but that there is no similarity between the parties' respective products or services: Plaintiff sells electronics, while Toeppen displays a city map. The court notes that Toeppen is "willing to be enjoined from using the website for the sale of any product or service, thereby guaranteeing that his use will be entirely dissimilar from Intermatic's use." The court also finds that factor 3 (the area and manner of use) weighs against a likelihood of confusion, since Toeppen will not be selling any goods or services through his website. It emphasizes, however, that Intermatic, like other companies, wants to establish a presence in cyberspace and to register its trademark as its domain name, to assist consumers to find it easily on the Internet.]

[The court denies summary judgment based on the need for further fact finding on three issues: 1) actual confusion (will use of the "intermatic.com" domain name, in and of itself, confuse consumers?); 2) the degree of care likely to be exercised by consumers; and 3) the defendant's intent.]

[The court does not specifically consider whether Toeppen's actions constitute an actionable use "in connection with" goods or services or "use in commerce" in evaluating the infringement claim. The court does, however, consider the "use" issue in evaluating Intermatic's dilution claim. That discussion is reproduced below, because courts have generally construed the dilution cause of action as imposing the same "use" requirement as does the infringement cause of action.]

Toeppen argues that there has been no violation of the Federal Trademark Dilution Act because his use of the Intermatic mark is not a commercial use. Intermatic asserts that Toeppen's use is commercial because the Internet designation ".com" is short for commercial * * *.

The use of the first level domain designation ".com" does not in and of itself constitute a commercial use. The Internet is constantly changing and evolving. Currently the ".com" designation is the only one available for both commercial and private use. In the future perhaps other first level domain designations will be available solely for private or commercial uses. However, the Court is not here to set policy guidelines for the Internet, but rather the Court must apply the law to the Internet as it exists today. Therefore, the Court holds that the ".com" designation alone does not establish commercial use.

      * * *

Toeppen's intention to arbitrage the "intermatic.com" domain name constitutes a commercial use. At oral argument Toeppen's counsel candidly conceded that one of Toeppen's intended uses for registering the Intermatic mark was to eventually sell it back to Intermatic or to some other party. Toeppen's desire to resell the domain name is sufficient to meet the "commercial use" requirement of the Lanham Act.

      * * *

* * * Toeppen also argues that he has not violated the Act because his use of the "intermatic.com" domain name was not in commerce. This argument misses the mark. "Because Internet communications transmit instantaneously on a worldwide basis there is little question that the 'in commerce' requirement would be met in a typical Internet message, be it trademark infringement or false advertising." 1 Gilson, *Trademark Protection and Practice*, § 5.11[2], p. 5–234 (1996). * * *

NOTES AND QUESTIONS

1. *Actionable "use?"* Does the *Intermatic* court's finding conform to the pre-Internet construction of the "use" requirement discussed *supra*? Why or why not? As a matter of policy, did the court reach the *"right"* result on this issue? Does finding an actionable "use" in this case further the purposes of trademark law?

Would it have made any difference in the court's analysis if Toeppen had simply held the "Intermatic.com" registration and not set up his token web site? Did Toeppen's posting of the map constitute provision of a "service" for purposes of the Lanham Act?

The Court of Appeals for the Ninth Circuit found actionable use in a later case with similar facts and the same defendant. Panavision International, L.P. v. Toeppen, 141 F.3d 1316 (9th Cir. 1998). There the court emphasized that Toeppen (who had registered "panavision.com" as a domain name)

> traded on the value of Panavision's marks. So long as he held the Internet registrations, he curtailed Panavision's exploitation of the value of its trademarks on the Internet, a value which Toeppen then used when he attempted to sell the Panavision.com domain name to Panavision.

> * * *

> Toeppen made a commercial use of Panavision's trademarks. It does not matter that he did not attach the marks to a product. Toeppen's commercial use was his attempt to sell the trademarks themselves.

Id. at 1325. The court cited the *Boston Professional Hockey* decision in support of this proposition, characterizing that case as establishing that sale of a mark by itself—that is, in gross—is actionable under the Lanham Act. *Id.* at 1326 n. 5. The court thus disassociated the mark from goods or services and from its role of identifying product or service source, recognizing a property interest in the word/symbol in and of itself. Was it necessary for the court to take this extreme measure in order to reach the result it did? What are the implications of the court's finding?

2. *A likelihood of confusion.* In your view, was there a meaningful issue regarding the likelihood of consumer confusion in this case? If so, how would you describe it? Assuming that the plaintiff could still set up a web site under the domain name "Intermaticinc.com" or "Intermaticelectronics.com," did Toeppen's actions cause the company any meaningful harm? If so, how would you characterize the harm? Is it a harm the trademark infringement laws were meant to address?

3. *Subsequent developments.* Though relatively few courts found Mr. Toeppen's style of cybersquatting to constitute infringement, a number of courts followed the *Intermatic* and *Panasonic* courts' lead and found that it constituted actionable dilution. Congress has subsequently enacted the Anti-cybersquatting Consumer Protection Act, codified at 15 U.S.C. § 1125(d), which expressly targets cybersquatting, making it generally unnecessary for courts to evaluate whether classic cybersquatters like Toeppen engage in trademark infringement or dilution. However, the *Intermatic/Panasonic* line

of cases remains influential in courts' evaluation of actionable use and confusion in other Internet settings.

Of course, cybersquatters like Toeppen are not the only problems mark owners encounter when they try to establish a web site identified by a domain name that consists of their mark and the ".com" top level domain. Under trademark law, a number of different businesses can use the same word or symbol as a mark, as long as they are selling unrelated products or services, or are operating in separate geographical areas, so that the use does not create a likelihood of consumer confusion. For example, "Ritz" may lawfully designate both crackers and hotels, and "United" may lawfully designate furniture moving services, airlines, and movie theaters, all within the United States. Moreover, different entities may operate under the "United" and "Ritz" marks in different countries, since trademark rights are territorial in nature. By contrast, there can be only one "United.com" address on the Internet, anywhere in the world. And businesses generally prefer to register in the .com top level domain, where consumers are most likely to search for commercial entities.

One answer to this concern has been to create additional generic top-level domains for use by commercial entities, including ".biz," ".info," and ".pro." This will, for example, permit several businesses operating under the "United" mark to register and use the "United" mark in a top-level "commercial" generic domain. What are the pros and cons of this approach, from the standpoint of trademark owners?

b. *Incorporation of Marks in Metatags*

Metatags consist of HTML code integrated into a web site that is invisible to web site visitors but can be read by search engines. The metatags are meant to communicate the contents of the web site to Internet search engines by means of a short description and "keywords." Search engines operate in different ways and continue to evolve. However, particularly during the late 1990's, search engines often relied on keywords in metatags to formulate and rank their search results. Thus, if X, the operator of a web site, entered "acme" as a keyword into her metatags, persons entering "acme" as a search term in the hopes of finding the Acme Company might find X's web site listed in their search results, even though the word "acme" does not appear in visible text on X's web site, and the site has no relation to the Acme Company or its products or services. If X were to enter "acme" multiple times in her metatags, she might be able to get the search engine to rank her site high in its search result listings, thus increasing the chance that the person searching for Acme Company might visit her site.

The practice of entering others' trademarks in web site metatags evoked a number of Lanham Act claims such as the one below. Search engine designers have since moved away from heavy reliance on metatags in formulating search results. Nonetheless the judicial decisions addressing use of marks in metatags continue to be influential in other Internet contexts.

BROOKFIELD COMMUNICATIONS, INC. v. WEST COAST ENTERTAINMENT CORP.

United States Court of Appeals for the Ninth Circuit, 1999.
174 F.3d 1036.

[Plaintiff Brookfield sold entertainment industry information software and database services under the mark "MovieBuff," both through retail stores and over its web site, which offered access to its database for a fee. Defendant West Coast, a large video rental chain, set up a web site under the domain name *"moviebuff.com,"* and included "moviebuff" as a keyword in its metatags. The defendant's web site offered videos and other entertainment-related merchandise for sale, along with a free searchable database of entertainment industry information. Upon learning of the defendant's use of its mark, Brookfield brought suit to enjoin the defendant's actions under Lanham Act §§ 32(1)(a) and 43(a). The Ninth Circuit applied the *Sleekcraft* factors for determining likelihood of confusion, and found that Brookfield was likely to succeed on the merits of its argument that West Coast's use of its *"moviebuff.com"* domain name infringed Brookfield's "MovieBuff" mark for entertainment information databases and software. The court explained:]

Given the virtual identity of "moviebuff.com" and "MovieBuff," the relatedness of the products and services accompanied by those marks, and the companies' simultaneous use of the Web as a marketing and advertising tool, many forms of consumer confusion are likely to result. People surfing the Web for information on "MovieBuff" may confuse "MovieBuff" with the searchable entertainment database at "moviebuff.com" and simply assume that they have reached Brookfield's web site. In the Internet context, in particular, entering a web site takes little effort—usually one click from a linked site or a search engine's list; thus, Web surfers are more likely to be confused as to the ownership of a web site than traditional patrons of a brick-and-mortar store would be of a store's ownership. Alternatively, they may incorrectly believe that West Coast licensed "MovieBuff" from Brookfield, or that Brookfield otherwise sponsored West Coast's database. Other consumers may simply believe that West Coast bought out Brookfield or that they are related companies.

Yet other forms of confusion are likely to ensue. Consumers may wrongly assume that the "MovieBuff" database they were searching for is no longer offered, having been replaced by West Coast's entertainment database, and thus simply use the services at West Coast's web site. And even where people realize, immediately upon accessing "moviebuff.com," that they have reached a site operated by West Coast and wholly unrelated to Brookfield, West Coast will still have gained a customer by appropriating the goodwill that Brookfield has developed in its "MovieBuff" mark. A consumer who was originally looking for Brookfield's products or services may be perfectly content with West Coast's database (especially as it is offered free of charge); but he reached West Coast's site because of its use of Brookfield's mark as its second-level domain name, which is a misappropriation of Brookfield's goodwill by West Coast.

[The court then turned to the question of West Coast's use of "moviebuff" in its metatags.]

* * *

At first glance, our resolution of the infringement issues in the domain name context would appear to dictate a similar conclusion of likelihood of confusion with respect to West Coast's use of "moviebuff.com" in its metatags. Indeed, all eight likelihood of confusion factors outlined in Part V–A—with the possible exception of purchaser care, which we discuss below—apply here as they did in our analysis of domain names; we are, after all, dealing with the same marks, the same products and services, the same consumers, etc. Disposing of the issue so readily, however, would ignore the fact that the likelihood of confusion in the domain name context resulted largely from the associational confusion between West Coast's domain name "moviebuff.com" and Brookfield's trademark "MovieBuff." The question in the metatags context is quite different. Here, we must determine whether West Coast can use "Movie-Buff" or "moviebuff.com" in the metatags of its web site at "westcoastvideo.com" or at any other domain address other than "moviebuff.com" (which we have determined that West Coast may not use).

Although entering "MovieBuff" into a search engine is likely to bring up a list including "westcoastvideo.com" if West Coast has included that term in its metatags, the resulting confusion is not as great as where West Coast uses the "moviebuff.com" domain name. First, when the user inputs "MovieBuff" into an Internet search engine, the list produced by the search engine is likely to include both West Coast's and Brookfield's web sites. Thus, in scanning such list, the Web user will often be able to find the particular web site he is seeking. Moreover, even if the Web user chooses the web site belonging to West Coast, he will see that the domain name of the web site he selected is "westcoastvideo.com." Since there is no confusion resulting from the domain address, and since West Coast's initial web page prominently displays its own name, it is difficult to say that a consumer is likely to be confused about whose site he has reached or to think that Brookfield somehow sponsors West Coast's web site.

Nevertheless, West Coast's use of "moviebuff.com" in metatags will still result in what is known as initial interest confusion. Web surfers looking for Brookfield's "MovieBuff" products who are taken by a search engine to "westcoastvideo.com" will find a database similar enough to "MovieBuff" such that a sizeable number of consumers who were originally looking for Brookfield's product will simply decide to utilize West Coast's offerings instead. Although there is no source confusion in the sense that consumers know they are patronizing West Coast rather than Brookfield, there is nevertheless initial interest confusion in the sense that, by using "moviebuff.com" or "MovieBuff" to divert people looking for "MovieBuff" to its web site, West Coast improperly benefits from the goodwill that Brookfield developed in its mark. Recently in *Dr. Seuss*, we explicitly recognized that the use of another's trademark in a manner calculated "to capture initial consumer attention, even though no actual sale is finally completed as a result of the confusion, may be still an infringement." *Dr. Seuss*, 109 F.3d at 1405 (citing *Mobil Oil Corp. v. Pegasus Petroleum Corp.*, 818 F.2d 254, 257–58 (2d Cir.1987)).[24]

* * *

Using another's trademark in one's metatags is much like posting a sign with another's trademark in front of one's store. Suppose West Coast's competitor (let's call it "Blockbuster") puts up a billboard on a highway reading—"West Coast Video: 2 miles ahead at Exit 7"—where West Coast is really located at Exit 8 but Blockbuster is located at Exit 7. Customers looking for West Coast's store will pull off at Exit 7 and drive around looking for it. Unable to locate West Coast, but seeing the Blockbuster store right by the highway entrance, they may simply rent there. Even consumers who prefer West Coast may find it not worth the trouble to continue searching for West Coast since there is a Blockbuster right there. Customers are not confused in the narrow sense: they are fully aware that they are purchasing from Blockbuster and they have no reason to believe that Blockbuster is related to, or in any way sponsored by, West Coast. Nevertheless, the fact that there is only initial consumer confusion does not alter the fact that Blockbuster would be misappropriating West Coast's acquired goodwill.

* * *

Consistently with *Dr. Seuss* * * * we conclude that the Lanham Act bars West Coast from including in its metatags any term confusingly similar with Brookfield's mark.

* * *

NOTES AND QUESTIONS

1. *Use in commerce.* Did the *Brookfield* court assume that West Coast's use of "moviebuff" in its metatags constituted a "trademark use" or "use in commerce?" Metatags are generally invisible to human Internet users. How can they be said to indicate the source or affiliation of the web site or its products or services to consumers, when consumers never see them?

The *Brookfield* court analogized placing a plaintiff's mark in metatags to placing a billboard on the freeway advising travelers that the plaintiff's

---

24. The *Dr. Seuss* court discussed initial interest confusion within its purchaser care analysis. As a district court within our circuit recognized in a recent case involving a claim of trademark infringement via metatags usage, "[t]his case . . . is not a standard trademark case and does not lend itself to the systematic application of the eight factors." *Playboy Enters. v. Welles*, 7 F.Supp.2d 1098 (S.D.Cal.1998). Because we agree that the traditional eight-factor test is not well-suited for analyzing the metatags issue, we do not attempt to fit our discussion into one of the *Sleekcraft* factors.

business is at Exit 7, when it really is at Exit 8 and the defendant's business is at Exit 7. Assuming that this analogy is correct, does it demonstrate actionable trademark use? Is the analogy in fact accurate? Whether accurate or not, it has been influential.

2. *The likelihood of confusion.* What is the justification for permitting a finding of infringement based on a showing of "initial interest confusion" that is dissipated prior to any actual sales? How broadly should application of the initial interest confusion doctrine reach in the Internet context? Under the Ninth Circuit's reasoning, is it necessary that the defendant using plaintiff's mark in metatags sell or disseminate competing products? What if the defendant sells products that are complementary to the plaintiff's products, but don't compete with them? What if the only similarity between the plaintiff's and defendant's products is that "upscale" consumers will be interested in them, and defendant uses plaintiff's very popular mark in its metatags as a means of attracting more of the right kind of consumers to its web page? Should the plaintiff have a cause of action?

Did West Coast's metatagging action even create a likelihood of initial interest confusion, given that Brookfield and West Coast were assumed to be operating under entirely different domain names? Assume that a consumer in the concrete world goes into a grocery store to buy a six-pack of Cokes. However, approaching the soft drink shelves, she encounters a wide range of colas and other soft drinks sitting alongside the Cokes, and seeing this range of choices, she decides instead to buy a six-pack of Pepsi. Does arranging the competing products side-by-side on the store shelves constitute actionable trademark use? Is it likely to confuse consumers about product source, sponsorship or affiliation? Can the grocery store's actions be distinguished from a situation in which Pepsi sets up a web site under the domain name "*pepsi.com*," which sells Pepsi, and includes the "Coke" mark in its metatags?

What is the impact of metatagging from the consumer's point of view? Is it a detriment or a benefit? Could one argue that it actually assists efficient consumer product searches?

What if the defendant sells no products at all, but is a dissatisfied customer of the plaintiff who sets up a web page for the purpose of criticizing plaintiff's product or service and publicizing her displeasure? If the defendant includes the plaintiff's mark repeatedly in her metatags, should this result in infringement liability under the reasoning in *Brookfield*?

c. *Incorporation of Marks in "Forum" Web Site Domain Names*

PEOPLE FOR THE ETHICAL TREATMENT OF ANIMALS v. DOUGHNEY

United States Court of Appeals for the Fourth Circuit, 2001.
263 F.3d 359.

[People for the Ethical Treatment of Animals ("PETA") is an animal rights organization that opposes the exploitation of animals for food, clothing, entertainment and vivisection. Michael Doughney is a former internet executive who has registered a number of domain names, such as "dubyadot.com," "dubyadot.net," "RandallTerry.org" (Not Randall Terry for Congress), and "pmrc.org." ("People's Manic Repressive Church"). At the time in question, Doughney owned 50–60 domain name registrations.]

[Doughney registered the domain name "peta.org" and used it to identify a web site entitled "People Eating Tasty Animals." Doughney claims he created the web site as a parody of PETA. A viewer accessing the web site would see the title "People Eating Tasty Animals" in large, bold type, followed by a statement that the web site was a "resource for those who enjoy eating meat, wearing fur and leather, hunting, and the fruits of scientific research." The web site contained links to various meat, fur, leather, hunting, animal research, and other organizations, all of which held views generally antithetical to PETA's views. Another statement on the web site asked the viewer whether he/she was "Feeling lost? Offended? Perhaps you should, like, *exit immediately*." The phrase "exit immediately" contained a hyperlink to PETA's official web site.]

[PETA sued, claiming, among other things, service mark infringement and unfair competition under Lanham Act §§ 32(1)(a) and 43(a) and Virginia common law. In a subsequent media interview about the suit, Doughney was quoted as saying "[i]f they [PETA] want one of my domains, they should make me an offer." Doughney also posted a message on his web site stating that PETA had no legal grounds for its suit, and that it should negotiate a settlement. The district court granted PETA's motion for summary judgment, and Doughney appeals.]

A plaintiff alleging causes of action for trademark infringement and unfair competition must prove (1) that it possesses a mark; (2) that the defendant used the mark; (3) that the defendant's use of the mark occurred "in commerce"; (4) that the defendant used the mark "in connection with the sale, offering for sale, distribution, or advertising" of goods or services; and (5) that the defendant used the mark in a manner likely to confuse consumers.

There is no dispute here that PETA owns the "PETA" Mark, that Doughney used it, and that Doughney used the Mark "in commerce." Doughney disputes the district court's findings that he used the Mark in connection with goods or services and that he used it in a manner engendering a likelihood of confusion.

1.

To use PETA's mark "in connection with" goods or services, Doughney need not have actually sold or advertised goods or services on the *www.peta.org* website. Rather, Doughney need only have prevented users from obtaining or using PETA's goods or services, or need only have connected the website to other's goods or services.

While sparse, existing caselaw on infringement and unfair competition in the Internet context clearly weighs in favor of this conclusion. For example, in *OBH, Inc. v. Spotlight Magazine, Inc.,* the plaintiffs owned the "The Buffalo News" registered trademark used by the newspaper of the same name. 86 F.Supp.2d 176 (W.D.N.Y.2000). The defendants registered the domain name *thebuffalonews.com* and created a website parodying The Buffalo News and providing a public forum for criticism of the newspaper. The site contained hyperlinks to other local news sources and a site owned by the defendants that advertised Buffalo-area apartments for rent.

The court held that the defendants used the mark "in connection with" goods or services because the defendants' website was "likely to prevent or hinder Internet users from accessing plaintiffs' services on plaintiffs' own web site."

> Prospective users of plaintiffs' services who mistakenly access defendants' web site may fail to continue to search for plaintiffs' web site due to confusion or frustration. Such users, who are presumably looking for the news services provided by the plaintiffs on their web site, may instead opt to select one of the several other news-related hyperlinks contained in defendants' web site. These news-related hyperlinks will directly link the user to other news-related web sites that are in direct competition with plaintiffs in providing news-related services over the Internet. Thus, defendants' action in appropriating plaintiff's mark has a connection to plaintiffs' distribution of its services.

Id. at 183. Moreover, the court explained that defendants' use of the plaintiffs' mark was in connection with goods or services because it contained a link to the defendants' apartment-guide website.

Similarly, in *Planned Parenthood Federation of America, Inc. v. Bucci,* the plaintiff owned the "Planned Parenthood" mark, but the defendant registered the domain name *plannedparenthood.com.* 42 U.S.P.Q.2d 1430 (S.D.N.Y.1997). Using the domain name, the defendant created a website containing information antithetical to the plaintiff's views. The court ruled that the defendant used the plaintiff's mark "in connection with" the distribution of services

> because it is likely to prevent some Internet users from reaching plaintiff's own Internet web site. Prospective users of plaintiff's services who mistakenly access defendant's web site may fail to continue to search for plaintiff's own home page, due to anger, frustration, or the belief that plaintiff's home page does not exist.

Id. at 1435.

The same reasoning applies here. * * *

* * * Moreover, Doughney's web site provides links to more than 30 commercial operations offering goods and services. By providing links to these commercial operations, Doughney's use of PETA's Mark is "in connection with" the sale of goods or services.

2.

* * *

Doughney does not dispute that the *peta.org* domain name engenders a likelihood of confusion between his web site and PETA. Doughney claims, though, that the inquiry should not end with his domain name. Rather, he urges the Court to consider his website in conjunction with the domain name because, together, they purportedly parody PETA and, thus, do not cause a likelihood of confusion.

A "parody" is defined as a "simple form of entertainment conveyed by juxtaposing the irreverent representation of the trademark with the idealized image created by the mark's owner." A parody must "convey two simultaneous—and contradictory—messages: that it is the original, but also that it is *not* the original and is instead a parody." To the extent that an alleged parody conveys only the first message, "it is not only a poor parody but also vulnerable under trademark law, since the customer will be confused." While a parody necessarily must engender some initial confusion, an effective parody will diminish the risk of consumer confusion "by conveying [only] just enough of the original design to allow the consumer to appreciate the point of parody."

Looking at Doughney's domain name alone, there is no suggestion of a parody. The domain name *peta.org* simply copies PETA's mark, conveying the message that it is related to PETA. The domain name does not convey the second, contradictory message needed to establish a parody—a message that the domain name is not related to PETA, but that it is a parody of PETA.

Doughney claims that this second message can be found in the content of his website. Indeed, the website's content makes it clear that it is not related to PETA. However, this second message is not conveyed *simultaneously* with the first message, as required to be considered a parody. The domain name conveys the first message; the second message is conveyed only when the viewer reads the content of the website. As the district court explained, "an internet user would not realize that they were not on an official PETA web site until after they had used PETA's Mark to access the web page 'www.peta.org.' " Thus, the messages are not conveyed simultaneously and do not constitute a parody. * * * The district court properly rejected Doughney's parody defense and found that Doughney's use of the *peta.org* domain name engenders a likelihood of confusion. Accordingly, Doughney failed to raise a genuine issue of material fact regarding PETA's infringement and unfair competition claims.

* * *

NOTES AND QUESTIONS

1. *"Forum site."* As used in this Subsection, the term "forum site" refers to a web site that primarily states the personal views of the site operator and does not itself offer goods or services for sale.

2. The "use" requirement. Earlier, in considering general (non-Internet) case law, we noted that potentially infringing Lanham Act "use" consists of two components: 1) affixation or other close association of the mark with the defendant's goods or services (or "use in connection with goods or services," as the Fourth Circuit calls it) and 2) a connection with interstate commerce sufficient to support federal regulation. Under this definition, would use of a mark in a domain name for a web site that sells or distributes goods or services constitute the requisite "use?" If so, should potentially infringing Lanham Act "use" also be found if the domain name identifies a "forum" web site that neither sells nor advertises goods or services, but merely sets forth the site operator's personal religious, political or consumer opinions?

In *PETA*, the Fourth Circuit provides two alternative explanations of how Doughney made the requisite "use in connection with goods or services" in that case. First, the court reasoned that "Doughney need not have actually sold or advertised goods or services on the *www.peta.org* website. Rather, Doughney need only have prevented users from obtaining or using PETA's goods or services." Is the court suggesting that it is appropriate to combine the *defendant's* application of the mark with the *plaintiff's* sale of goods or services to get the requisite trademark use or use "in connection with the sale of goods or services?" Is actionable Lanham Act "use" determined by the existence of negative impact on the plaintiff's sales? Is such an approach consistent with the purpose of trademark law? Assuming that it is, how much impact is the existence of a parody site at *www.peta.org* likely to have on PETA's sales or distribution of goods or services? Not all courts have accepted the *PETA* court's line of reasoning. See, e.g., Bosley Medical Institute v. Kremer, 403 F.3d 672, 678–79 (9th Cir. 2005)(noting that this approach "would place most critical, otherwise protected consumer commentary under the restrictions of the Lanham Act"); Utah Lighthouse Ministry v. Foundation for Apologetic Information and Research, 527 F.3d 1045, 1053 (10th Cir. 2008)(connecting defendant's application of mark with plaintiff's sales "eliminates the requirement of an economic competitor and is therefore inconsistent with the purpose of the Lanham Act 'to protect the ability of consumers to distinguish among competing producers.' * * * In our view, the defendant in a trademark infringement and unfair competition case must use the mark in connection with the goods or services of a competing producer, not merely to make a comment on the trademark owner's goods or services.").

Second, the *PETA* court reasoned that Doughney's use of PETA's mark as the domain name for a web site that includes links to other, commercial sites provided the requisite trademark use: By providing links to these commercial operations, Doughney's use of PETA's mark was "in connection with" the other sites' sale of goods or services. Thus, the court combined Doughney's application of the PETA mark with third parties' sales of goods or services. Does the mere existence of links on a forum web site provide the requisite "affixation or other close association" of mark to goods? Does the defendant's use of the mark in his domain name invite consumers to rely on the mark for information about the source of goods or services being offered on the linked sites? What are the implications of the *PETA* reasoning for the growth and development of the Internet? Are there First Amendment implications? Again, not all courts have agreed to rely on links to establish actionable

Lanham Act "use". See, e.g., Bally Total Fitness Holding Corp. v. Faber, 29 F.Supp.2d 1161, 1168 (C.D.Ca. 1998)("Looking beyond the 'Bally sucks' site to other sites within the domain or to other linked sites would, to an extent, include the Internet in its entirety. The essence of the Internet is that sites are connected to facilitate access to information. Including linked sites as grounds for finding commercial use * * * would extend the statute far beyond its intended purpose"); *Utah Lighthouse, supra*, 527 F.3d at 1052 (holding that direct links to commercial sites might support a finding of actionable trademark use in some cases, but each case must be evaluated on its facts–in the case before the court, the defendant's links provided too roundabout and attenuated a connection with goods and services).

Some courts have relied on a third line of reasoning to find that incorporating a mark into a forum site domain name constitutes actionable Lanham Act "use." For example, in Planned Parenthood Federation of America, Inc. v. Bucci, 1997 W.L. 133313 (S.D.N.Y.), *aff'd*, 152 F.3d 920 (2d Cir. 1997) (cited by the *PETA* court), the defendant set up a web site under the domain name "plannedparenthood.com" and used it as a forum to state his personal anti-abortion views, which conflicted with the plaintiff mark owner's views. The court justified finding that the defendant used the Planned Parenthood mark "in connection with" goods or services by reasoning that the defendant's anti-abortion statements constituted "informational services for use in convincing people that certain activities, including the use of plaintiff's services, are morally wrong." Thus, the defendant used the plaintiff's mark "in connection with the distribution of those services over the Internet." Likewise, the district court in the *PETA* case held that the term "services" should be "interpreted broadly, to include the dissemination of information, including purely ideological information." 113 F.Supp.2d 915, 919. Under this view, Doughney's ridicule of the PETA organization constituted an "information service," which the "*peta.org*" domain name identified. The Lanham Act provides no definition of "services." Were the district courts in *Planned Parenthood* and *PETA* correct to find that the defendants were engaged in the distribution of Lanham Act services through use of the plaintiffs' marks? Are there any First Amendment implications to such a finding?

   3. *The likelihood of consumer confusion.* On what basis did Doughney's use of the "*peta.org*" domain name cause a likelihood of confusion? The court specifically finds that the web site's contents made it clear that the site was not related to PETA. Did Doughney's use cause initial interest confusion? That is the basis on which a number of courts appear to have found infringement in forum site domain name cases. See, e.g., OBH, Inc. v. Spotlight Magazine, Inc., 86 F.Supp.2d 176, 190 (W.D.N.Y. 2000). Regardless of whether the defendant claims that he is parodying the plaintiff, should the issue of likelihood of confusion be evaluated solely on the similarity of the domain name to the mark, without reference to the contents of the defendant's web site?

   In Lamparello v. Falwell, 420 F.3d 309 (4th Cir. 2005), Lamparello took issue with views about homosexuality expressed by Rev. Jerry Falwell, a well-known minister and commentator on politics and public affairs. Accordingly, he registered the domain name "*fallwell.com*" and set up a web site to respond to those views. Lamparello's web site included headlines such as "Bible verses that Dr. Falwell chooses to ignore," and "Jerry Falwell has been bearing false witness (Exodus 20:16) against his gay and lesbian neighbors for a long time," and in-depth criticism of Falwell's views. The site's home page prominently stated, "This website is NOT affiliated with Jerry Falwell or his ministry" and advised that "If you would like to visit Rev. Falwell's website you may click here," providing a hyperlink to the plaintiff's own site. The district court granted Falwell's motion for summary judgment on his §§ 32(1)(a) and 43(a) claims, but the Fourth Circuit reversed, finding no likelihood of consumer confusion. The court explained:

> Reverend Falwell's mark is distinctive, and the domain name of Lamparello's website, www.fallwell.com, closely resembles it. But, although Lamparello and Reverend Falwell employ similar marks online, Lamparello's website looks nothing like Reverend Falwell's; indeed, Lamparello has made no attempt to imitate Reverend Falwell's website. Moreover, Reverend Falwell does not even argue that Lamparello's website consititues advertising or a facility for business, let alone a facility or advertising similar to that of Reverend Falwell. Furthermore, Lamparello clearly created his website intending only to provide a forum to criticize ideas, not to steal customers.

> Most importantly, Reverend Falwell and Lamparello do not offer similar goods or services. Rather, they offer opposing ideas and commentary. Reverend Falwell's mark identifies his spiritual and political views; the website at www.fallwell.com criticizes those very views. After even a quick glance at the content of the website at www.fallwell.com, no one seeking Reverend Falwell's guidance would be misled by the domain name—www.falwell.com–into believing Reverend Falwell authorized the content of that website. No one would believe that Reverend Falwell sponsored a site criticizing himself, his positions, and his interpretations of the Bible. * * *

>   * * *

> Nevertheless, Reverand Falwell argues that he is entitled to prevail under the "initial interest confusion doctrine." * * * According to Reverend Falwell, this doctrine requires us to compare his mark with Lamparello's website domain name, www.fallwell.com, *without* considering the content of Lamparello's website. Reverend Falwell argues that some people who misspell his name may go to www.fallwell.com assuming it is his site, thus giving Lamparello an unearned audience—albeit one that quickly disappears when it realizes it has not reached Reverend Falwell's site. This argument fails for two reasons.

> First, we have never adopted the initial interest confusion theory; rather, we have followed a very different mode of analysis, requiring courts to determine whether a likelihood of confusion exists by "examin[ing] the allegedly infringing use *in the context in which it is seen by the ordinary consumer.*"

> Contrary to Reverend Falwell's arguments, we did not abandon this approach in *PETA*. Our inquiry in *PETA* was limited to whether Doughney's use of the domain name "www.peta.org" constituted a successful

enough parody of People for the Ethical Treatment of Animals that no one was likely to believe www.peta.org was sponsored or endorsed by that organization. * * *

PETA simply outlines the parameters of the parody defense; it does not adopt the initial interest confusion theory or otherwise diminish the necessity of examining context when determining whether a likelihood of confusion exists. * * * When dealing with domain names, this means a court must evaluate an allegedly infringing domain name in conjunction with the content of the website identified by the domain name.

Moreover, even if we did endorse the initial interest confusion theory, that theory would not assist Reverend Falwell here because it provides no basis for liability in circumstances such as these. The few appellate courts that have followed the Ninth Circuit and imposed liability under this theory for using marks on the Internet have done so only in cases involving a factor utterly absent here–one business' use of another's mark for its own financial gain.

Profiting financially from initial interest confusion is thus a key element for imposition of liability under this theory. When an alleged infringer does not compete with the markholder for sales, "some initial confusion will not likely facilitate free riding on the goodwill of another mark, or otherwise harm the user claiming infringement. Where confusion has little or no meaningful effect in the marketplace, it is of little or no consequence in our analysis."

This critical element—use of another firm's mark to capture the markholder's customers and profits—simply does not exist when the alleged infringer establishes a gripe site that criticizes the markholder. * * * Applying the initial interest confusion theory to gripe sites like Lamparello's would enable the markholder to insulate himself from criticism—or at least to minimize access to it. We have already condemned such uses of the Lanham Act, stating that a markholder cannot "shield itself from criticism by forbidding the use of its name in commentaries critical of its conduct."

420 F.3d at 315–18. In your opinion, does the *Lamparello* panel adequately distinguish *PETA*?

4. *An administrative alternative to infringement litigation in the case of "bad faith" registration of domain names.* In 1998, the U.S. Department of Commerce reviewed a number of Internet-related issues and recommended formation of a new non-profit private corporation to take over global administration of the Internet name and address system. United States Department of Commerce, Management of Internet Names and Addresses, 63 Fed. Reg. 31741 (1998)("White Paper"). The Internet Corporation for Assigned Names and Numbers ("ICANN") has since been formed to perform this administrative function. Located in Los Angeles, ICANN is governed by an elected board of directors drawn from a range of Internet constituencies. It has contracted with a number of domain name registrars, which now compete in registering domain names in the generic top level domains. It has also adopted a dispute resolution policy to assist in resolving disputes between trademark owners and persons registering domain names. This policy offers an administrative

alternative to litigation in the case of "bad faith registration" of domain names that are similar to established marks. This Uniform Domain Name Dispute Resolution Policy ("UDRP") is discussed further *infra,* at pages 985–86.

d.   Use of Marks in Contextual Advertising

1–800 CONTACTS, INC. v. WHENU.COM, INC.

United States Court of Appeals for the Second Circuit, 2005.
414 F.3d 400.

[WhenU.com installs its "SaveNow" software onto users' computers with the users' consent. The SaveNow program tracks the user's use of the web, examining the search terms and web site URLs the user enters. It compares these terms and URLs to its directory, which lists a large number of web addresses, keywords, and search terms, categorized in much the same way that telephone directories categorize businesses. If it finds a match for the user's search term or URL, it identifies the relevant product or service category and causes an ad to appear on the user's screen pertaining to that category. For example, if the user is browsing the 1–800 Contacts web site at *www.1800contacts.com*, the SaveNow software checks its directory, finds the 1–800 Contacts URL in its assigned category (perhaps eye care), and pops up an ad for a WhenU.Com advertising client whose product or service also falls into the eye care category (perhaps a competing seller of contact lenses, like Vision Direct, Inc., who is a co-defendant in the present case). The ads vary in their format and placement, but some of them appear in front of, and partially obscure, the window the user has open at the time. The user must then either click the ad closed or use the keystrokes "Alt–F4" to get rid of it. The ads are displayed in separate, conspicuously branded windows and specifically advise the user that they are from WhenU.Com and are not sponsored by whatever web site the user may be viewing. The user may click on the ad to visit the advertiser's web site. In some cases, the ad may offer a coupon good for discounts on the advertiser's web site.

Plaintiff 1–800–Contacts sued WhenU.Com for trademark infringement under Lanham Act §§ 32(1)(a) and 43(a). The district court granted the plaintiff a preliminary injunction. Defendant WhenU.Com has appealed from that order. In its opinion, the Second Circuit refers to computer users as "C-users."]

* * *

DISCUSSION

WhenU challenges the district court's finding that WhenU "uses" 1–800's trademarks within the meaning of the Lanham Act, 15 U.S.C. § 1127. In the alternative, WhenU argues that the district court erred in finding that WhenU's pop-up ads create a likelihood of both source confusion and "initial interest confusion," as to whether WhenU is "somehow associated with [1–800] or that [1–800] has consented to [WhenU's] use of the pop-up ad[s]." Because we agree with WhenU that it does not "use" 1–800's trademarks, we need not and do not address the issue of likelihood of confusion.

[The court relies on Lanham Act § 45's definition of "use in commerce" for the requisite standard of actionable trademark use. 15 U.S.C. § 1127. In issuing the preliminary injunction, the district court held that WhenU "used" the plaintiff's "1–800 Contacts" mark in two actionable ways. First, by causing computers to superimpose its ads over part of the screen that displayed plaintiff's web site, WhenU "displayed" plaintiff's mark (which was on the web site) in the advertising of defendant Vision Direct's services. Second, WhenU included plaintiff's web address, which incorporated the plaintiff's mark, in its proprietary directory of terms to trigger pop-up ads—thus using the mark in advertising a competitor's goods or services.]

A. *The SaveNow Directory*

* * * WhenU does not "use" 1–800's trademark in the manner ordinarily at issue in an infringement claim: it does not "place" 1–800 trademarks on any goods or services in order to pass them off as emanating from or authorized by 1–800. The fact is that WhenU does not reproduce or display 1–800's trademarks at all, nor does it cause the trademarks to be displayed to a C-user. Rather, WhenU reproduces 1–800's website address, www.1800contacts. com., which is similar, but not identical, to 1–800's 1–800 CONTACTS trademark.

The district court found that the differences between 1–800's trademarks and the website address utilized by WhenU were insignificant because they were limited to the addition of the "www." and ".com" and the omission of the hyphen and a space. We conclude that, to the contrary, the differences between the marks are quite significant because they transform 1–800's trademark—which is entitled to protection under the Lanham Act—into a word combination that functions more or less like a public key to 1–800's website.

Moreover, it is plain that WhenU is using 1–800's website address precisely because it is a website address, rather than because it bears any resemblance to 1–800's trademark, because the only place WhenU reproduces the address is in the SaveNow directory. Although the directory resides in the C-user's computer, it is inaccessible to both the C-user and the general public. Thus, the appearance of 1–800's website address in the directory does not create a possibility of visual confusion with 1–800's mark. More important, a WhenU pop-up ad cannot be triggered by a C-user's input of the 1–800 trademark or the appearance of that trademark on a webpage accessed by the c-user. Rather, in order for WhenU to capitalize on the fame and recognition of 1–800's trademark—the improper motivation both 1–800 and the district court ascribe to WhenU—it would have needed to put the actual trademark on the list.[11]

In contrast to some of its competitors, moreover, WhenU does not disclose the proprietary contents of the SaveNow directory to its advertising clients nor does it permit these clients to request or purchase specified keywords to add to the directory. * * *

A company's internal utilization of a trademark in a way that does not communicate it to the public is analogous to a individual's private thoughts about a trademark. Such conduct simply does not violate the Lanham Act, which is concerned with the use of trademarks in connection with the sale of goods or services in a manner likely to lead to consumer confusion as to the source of such goods or services. *See* 15 U.S.C. § 1127; *see also* Louis Altman, *4 Callmann on Unfair Competition, Trademarks and Monopolies* § 22:25 n.1 (4th ed. 2004) ("A fortiori, a defendant who does not sell, but merely uses internally within his own company, the trademarked product of another, is not a trademark infringer or unfair competitor by virtue of such use.").

Accordingly, we conclude that WhenU's inclusion of the 1–800 website address in its SaveNow directory does not infringe on 1–800's trademark.

B.   *The Pop-up Advertisements*

The primary issue to be resolved by this appeal is whether the placement of pop-up ads on a C-user's screen contemporaneously with either the 1–800 website or a list of search results obtained by the C-user's input of the 1–800 website address constitutes "use" under the Lanham Act. * * *

The fatal flaw with [the district court's] holding is that WhenU's pop-up ads do *not* display the 1–800 trademark. * * * As we explained above, the WhenU pop-up ads appear in a separate window that is prominently branded with the WhenU mark; they have absolutely no tangible effect on the appearance or functionality of the 1–800 website.

More important, the appearance of WhenU's pop-up ad is not contingent upon or related to 1–800's trademark, the trademark's appearance on 1–800's website, or the mark's similarity to 1–800's website address. Rather, the contemporaneous display of the ads and trademarks is the result of the happenstance that 1–800 chose to use a mark similar to its trademark as the address to its web page and to place its trademark on its website. The pop-up ad, which is triggered by the C-user's input of 1–800's website address, would appear even if 1–800's trademarks were not displayed on its website. A pop-up ad could also appear if the C-user typed the 1–800 website address, not as an address, but as a search term in the browser's search engine, and then accessed 1–800's website by using the hyperlink that appeared in the list of search results.

---

11. This observation, however, is not intended to suggest that inclusion of a trademark in the directory would necessarily be an infringing "use." We express no view on this distinct issue.

In addition, 1–800's website address is not the only term in the SaveNow directory that could trigger a Vision Direct ad to "pop up" on 1–800's website. For example, an ad could be triggered if a C-user searched for "contacts" or "eye care," both terms contained in the directory, and then clicked on the listed hyperlink to 1–800's website.

Exemplifying the conceptual difficulty that inheres in this issue, the district court's decision suggests that the crux of WhenU's wrongdoing—and the primary basis for the district court's finding of "use"—is WhenU's alleged effort to capitalize on a C-user's specific attempt to access the 1–800 website. As the court explained it,

> WhenU.com is doing far more than merely "displaying" Plaintiff's mark. WhenU's advertisements are delivered to a SaveNow user when the user directly accesses Plaintiff's website—thus allowing Defendant Vision Direct to profit from the goodwill and reputation in Plaintiff's website that led the user to access Plaintiff's website in the first place.

Absent improper use of 1–800's trademark, however, such conduct does not violate the Lanham Act. * * * Indeed, it is routine for vendors to seek specific "product placement" in retail stores precisely to capitalize on their competitors' name recognition. For example, a drug store typically places its own store-brand generic products next to the trademarked products they emulate in order to induce a customer who has specifically sought out the trademarked product to consider the store's less-expensive alternative. WhenU employs this same marketing strategy by informing C-users who have sought out a specific trademarked product about available coupons, discounts, or alternative products that may be of interest to them.

* * *

In addition, unlike several other internet advertising companies, WhenU does not "sell" keyword trademarks to its customers or otherwise manipulate which category-related advertisement will pop up in response to any particular terms on the internal directory. * * * In other words, WhenU does not link trademarks to any particular competitor's ads, and a customer cannot pay to have its pop-up ad appear on any specific website or in connection with any particular trademark. Instead, the SaveNow directory terms trigger categorical associations (e.g., www.1800Contacts.com might trigger the category of "eye care"), at which point, the software will randomly select one of the pop-up ads contained in the eye-care category to send to the C-user's desktop.

Perhaps because ultimately 1–800 is unable to explain precisely how WhenU "uses" its trademark, it resorts to bootstrapping a finding of "use" by alleging other elements of a trademark claim. For example, 1–800 invariably refers to WhenU's pop-up ads as "unauthorized" in an effort, it would seem, to establish by sheer force of repetition the element of unauthorized use of a trademark. Not surprisingly, 1–800 cites no legal authority for the proposition that advertisements, software applications, or any other visual image that can appear on a C-user's computer screen must be authorized by the owner of any website that will appear contemporaneously with that image. The fact is that WhenU does not need 1–800's authorization to display a separate window containing an ad any more than Corel would need authorization from Microsoft to display its WordPerfect word-processor in a window contemporaneously with a Word word-processing window. Moreover, contrary to 1–800's repeated admonitions, WhenU's pop-up ads *are* authorized—if unwittingly—by the C-user who has downloaded the SaveNow software.

1–800 also argues that WhenU's conduct is "use" because it is likely to confuse C-users as to the source of the ad. It buttresses this claim with a survey it submitted to the district court that purportedly demonstrates, *inter alia,* that (1) a majority of C-users believe that pop-up ads that appear *on* websites are sponsored by those websites, and (2) numerous C-users are unaware that they have downloaded the SaveNow software. 1–800 also relies on several cases in which the court seemingly based a finding of trademark "use" on the confusion such "use" was likely to cause. * * * Again, this rationale puts the cart before the horse. Not only are "use," "in commerce," and "likelihood of confusion" three distinct elements of a trademark infringement claim, but "use" must be decided as a threshold matter because, while any number of activities may be "in commerce" or create a likelihood of confusion, no such activity is actionable under the Lanham Act absent the "use" of a trademark. Because 1–800 has failed to establish such "use," its trademark infringement claims fail.

* * *

RESCUECOM CORP. v. GOOGLE, INC.

United States Court of Appeals for the Second Circuit, 2009.
562 F.3d 123.

LEVAL, CIRCUIT JUDGE:

[Rescuecom Corp. appeals from the district court's dismissal of its §§ 32 and 43(a) infringement claims against Google for failure to state a cause of action. The district court believed that dismissal was compelled by the Second Circuit's opinion in *1–800 Contacts v. WhenU.com, supra.*] We believe this misunderstood the holding of *1–800.* While we express no view as to whether Rescuecom can prove a Lanham Act violation, an actionable claim is adequately alleged in its pleadings. * * *

BACKGROUND

* * * Rescuecom is a national computer service franchising company that * * * conducts a substantial amount of business over the Internet and receives between 17,000 to 30,000 visitors to its website each month. It also advertises over the Internet, using many web-based services, including those offered by Google. Since 1998, "Rescuecom" has been a registered federal trademark, and there is no dispute as to its validity.

Google operates a popular Internet search engine, which users access by visiting www.google.com. Using Google's website, a person searching for the website of a particular entity in trade (or simply for information about it) can enter that entity's name or trademark into Google's search engine and launch a search. Google's proprietary system responds to such a search request in two ways. First, Google provides a list of links to websites, ordered in what Google deems to be of descending relevance to the user's search terms based on its proprietary algorithms. Google's search engine assists the public not only in obtaining information about a provider, but also in purchasing products and services. If a prospective purchaser, looking for goods or services of a particular provider, enters the provider's trademark as a search term on Google's website and clicks to activate a search, within seconds, the Google search engine will provide on the searcher's computer screen a link to the webpage maintained by that provider (as well as a host of other links to sites that Google's program determines to be relevant to the search term entered). By clicking on the link of the provider, the searcher will be directed to the provider's website, where the searcher can obtain information supplied by the provider about its products and services and can perhaps also make purchases from the provider by placing orders.

The second way Google responds to a search request is by showing context-based advertising. When a searcher uses Google's search engine by submitting a search term, Google may place advertisements on the user's screen. Google will do so if an advertiser, having determined that its ad is likely to be of interest to a searcher who enters the particular term, has purchased from Google the placement of its ad on the screen of the searcher who entered that search term. What Google places on the searcher's screen is more than simply an advertisement. It is also a link to the advertiser's website, so that in response to such an ad, if the searcher clicks on the link, he will open the advertiser's website, which offers not only additional information about the advertiser, but also perhaps the option to purchase the goods and services of the advertiser over the Internet. Google uses at least two programs to offer such context-based links: AdWords and Keyword Suggestion Tool.

AdWords is Google's program through which advertisers purchase terms (or keywords). When entered as a search term, the keyword triggers the appearance of the advertiser's ad and link. An advertiser's purchase of a particular term causes the advertiser's ad and link to be displayed on the user's screen whenever a searcher launches a Google search based on the purchased search term. Advertisers pay Google based on the number of times Internet users "click" on the advertisement, so as to link to the advertiser's website. For example, using Google's AdWords, Company Y, a company engaged in the business of furnace repair, can cause Google to display its advertisement and link whenever a user of Google launches a search based on the search term, "furnace repair." Company Y can also cause its ad and link to appear whenever a user searches for the term "Company X," a competitor of Company Y in the furnace repair business.

Thus, whenever a searcher interested in purchasing furnace repair services from Company X launches a search of the term X (Company X's trademark), an ad and link would appear on the searcher's screen, inviting the searcher to the furnace repair services of X's competitor, Company Y. And if the searcher clicked on Company Y's link, Company Y's website would open on the searcher's screen, and the searcher might be able to order or purchase Company Y's furnace repair services.

In addition to AdWords, Google also employs Keyword Suggestion Tool, a program that recommends keywords to advertisers to be purchased. The program is designed to improve the effectiveness of advertising by helping advertisers identify keywords related to their area of commerce, resulting in the placement of their ads before users who are likely to be responsive to it. Thus, continuing the example given above, if Company Y employed Google's Keyword Suggestion Tool, the Tool might suggest to Company Y that it purchase not only the term "furnace repair" but also the term "X," its competitor's brand name and trademark, so that Y's ad would appear on the screen of a searcher who searched Company X's trademark, seeking Company X's website.

Once an advertiser buys a particular keyword, Google links the keyword to that advertiser's advertisement. The advertisements consist of a combination of content and a link to the advertiser's webpage. Google displays these advertisements on the search result page either in the right margin or in a horizontal band immediately above the column of relevance-based search results. These advertisements are generally associated with a label, which says "sponsored link." Rescuecom alleges, however, that a user might easily be misled to believe that the advertisements which appear on the screen are in fact part of the relevance-based search result and that the appearance of a competitor's ad and link in response to a searcher's search for Rescuecom is likely to cause trademark confusion as to affiliation, origin, sponsorship, or approval of service. This can occur, according to the Complaint, because Google fails to label the ads in a manner which would clearly identify them as purchased ads rather than search results. The Complaint alleges that when the sponsored links appear in a horizontal bar at the top of the search results, they may appear to the searcher to be the first, and therefore the most relevant, entries responding to the search, as opposed to paid advertisements.

Google's objective in its AdWords and Keyword Suggestion Tool programs is to sell keywords to advertisers. Rescuecom alleges that Google makes 97% of its revenue from selling advertisements through its AdWords program. Google therefore has an economic incentive to increase the number of advertisements and links that appear for every term entered into its search engine.

Many of Rescuecom's competitors advertise on the Internet. Through its Keyword Suggestion Tool, Google has recommended the Rescuecom trademark to Rescuecom's competitors as a search term to be purchased. Rescuecom's competitors, some responding to Google's recommendation, have purchased Rescuecom's trademark as a keyword in Google's Ad-Words program, so that whenever a user launches a search for the term "Rescuecom," seeking to be connected to Rescuecom's website, the competitors' advertisement and link will appear on the searcher's screen. This practice allegedly allows Rescuecom's competitors to deceive and divert users searching for Rescuecom's website. According to Rescuecom's allegations, when a Google user launches a search for the term "Rescuecom" because the searcher wishes to purchase Rescuecom's services, links to websites of its competitors will appear on the searcher's screen in a manner likely to cause the searcher to believe mistakenly that a competitor's advertisement (and website link) is sponsored by, endorsed by, approved by, or affiliated with Rescuecom.

[The district court dismissed Rescuecom's claims on the ground that Google's actions did not constitute "use in commerce" as required by the Lanham Act. This was because the competitors' advertisements triggered by Google's programs did not exhibit Rescuecom's trademark to consumers. The court rejected the argument that Google engaged in actionable "use" by displaying Rescuecom's mark to advertising clients when recommending and selling it as a keyword to trigger their advertisements. The Court of Appeals reverses.]

I. Google's Use of Rescuecom's Mark Was a "Use in Commerce"
          * * *

At the outset, we note two significant aspects of our holding in *1–800,* which distinguish it from the present case. A key element of our court's decision in *1–800* was that under the plaintiff's allegations, the defendant did not use, reproduce, or display the plaintiff's mark *at all.* The search term that was alleged to trigger the pop-up ad was the plaintiff's *website address. 1–800* noted, notwithstanding the similarities between the website address and the mark, that the website address was not used or claimed by the plaintiff as a trademark. Thus, the transactions alleged to be infringing were not transactions involving use of the plaintiff's trademark. *1–800* suggested in dictum that is highly relevant to our case that had the defendant used the plaintiff's *trademark* as the trigger to pop-up an advertisement, such conduct might, depending on other elements, have been actionable.

Second, as an alternate basis for its decision, *1–800* explained why the defendant's program, which might randomly trigger pop-up advertisements upon a searcher's input of the plaintiff's website address, did not constitute a "use in commerce," as defined in § 1127. In explaining why the plaintiff's mark was not "used or displayed in the sale or advertising of services,"*1–800* pointed out that, under the defendant's program, advertisers could not request or purchase keywords to trigger their ads. Even if an advertiser wanted to display its advertisement to a searcher using the plaintiff's trademark as a search term, the defendant's program did not offer this possibility. In fact, the defendant "did not disclose the proprietary contents of [its] directory to its advertising clients...." In addition to not selling trademarks of others to its customers to trigger these ads, the defendant did not "otherwise manipulate which category-related advertisement will pop up in response to any particular terms on the internal directory." The display of a particular advertisement was controlled by the category associated with the website or keyword, rather than the website or keyword itself. The defendant's program relied upon categorical associations such as "eye care" to select a pop-up ad randomly from a predefined list of ads appropriate to that category. To the extent that an advertisement for a competitor of the plaintiff was displayed when a user opened the plaintiff's website, the trigger to display the ad was not based on the defendant's sale or recommendation of a particular trademark.

The present case contrasts starkly with those important aspects of the *1–800* decision. First, in contrast to *1–800,* where we emphasized that the defendant made no use whatsoever of the plaintiff's trademark, here what Google is recommending and selling to its advertisers is Rescuecom's trademark. Second, in contrast with the facts of *1–800* where the defendant did not "use or display," much less sell, trademarks as search terms to its advertisers, here Google displays, offers, and sells Rescuecom's mark to Google's advertising customers when selling its advertising services. In addition, Google encourages the purchase of Rescuecom's mark through its Keyword Suggestion Tool. Google's utilization of Rescuecom's mark fits literally within the terms specified by 15 U.S.C. § 1127. According to the Complaint, Google uses and sells Rescuecom's mark "in the sale ... of [Google's advertising] services ... rendered in commerce." § 1127.

Google, supported by amici, argues that *1–800* suggests that the inclusion of a trademark in an internal computer directory cannot constitute trademark use. Several district court decisions in this Circuit appear to have reached this conclusion. * * * This over-reads the *1–800* decision. First, regardless of whether Google's use of Rescuecom's mark in its internal search algorithm could constitute an actionable trademark use, Google's recommendation and sale of Rescuecom's mark to its advertising customers are not internal uses. Furthermore, *1–800* did not imply that use of a trademark in a software program's internal directory precludes a finding of trademark use. Rather, influenced by the fact that the defendant was not using the plaintiff's trademark at all, much less using it as the basis of a commercial transaction, the court asserted that the particular use before it did not constitute a use in commerce. We did not imply in *1–800* that an alleged infringer's use of a trademark in an internal software program insulates the alleged infringer from a charge of infringement, no matter how likely the use is to cause confusion in the marketplace. If we were to adopt Google and its amici's argument, the operators of search engines would be free to use trademarks in ways designed to deceive and cause consumer confusion.[3] This is surely neither within the intention nor the letter of the Lanham Act.

---

3. For example, instead of having a separate "sponsored links" or paid advertisement section, search engines could allow advertisers to pay to appear at the top of the "relevance" list based on

Google and its amici contend further that its use of the Rescuecom trademark is no different from that of a retail vendor who uses "product placement" to allow one vender to benefit from a competitors' name recognition. An example of product placement occurs when a store-brand generic product is placed next to a trademarked product to induce a customer who specifically sought out the trademarked product to consider the typically less expensive, generic brand as an alternative. Google's argument misses the point. From the fact that proper, non-deceptive product placement does not result in liability under the Lanham Act, it does not follow that the label "product placement" is a magic shield against liability, so that even a deceptive plan of product placement designed to confuse consumers would similarly escape liability. It is not by reason of absence of a use of a mark in commerce that benign product placement escapes liability; it escapes liability because it is a benign practice which does not cause a likelihood of consumer confusion. In contrast, if a retail seller were to be paid by an off-brand purveyor to arrange product display and delivery in such a way that customers seeking to purchase a famous brand would receive the off-brand, believing they had gotten the brand they were seeking, we see no reason to believe the practice would escape liability merely because it could claim the mantle of "product placement." The practices attributed to Google by the Complaint, which at this stage we must accept as true, are significantly different from benign product placement that does not violate the Act.

Unlike the practices discussed in *1–800,* the practices here attributed to Google by Rescuecom's complaint are that Google has made use in commerce of Rescuecom's mark. Needless to say, a defendant must do more than use another's mark in commerce to violate the Lanham Act. The gist of a Lanham Act violation is an unauthorized use, which "is likely to cause confusion, or to cause mistake, or to deceive as to the affiliation, ... or as to the origin, sponsorship, or approval of ... goods [or] services." *See* 15 U.S.C. § 1125(a). We have no idea whether Rescuecom can prove that Google's use of Rescuecom's trademark in its AdWords program causes likelihood of confusion or mistake. Rescuecom has alleged that it does, in that would-be purchasers (or explorers) of its services who search for its website on Google are misleadingly directed to the ads and websites of its competitors in a manner which leads them to believe mistakenly that these ads or websites are sponsored by, or affiliated with Rescuecom. * * * Whether Google's actual practice is in fact benign or confusing is not for us to judge at this time. We consider at the 12(b)(6) stage only what is alleged in the Complaint.

---

a user entering a competitor's trademark—a functionality that would be highly likely to cause consumer confusion. Alternatively, sellers of products or services could pay to have the operators of search engines automatically divert users to their website when the users enter a competitor's trademark as a search term. Such conduct is surely not beyond judicial review merely because it is engineered through the internal workings of a computer program.

NOTES AND QUESTIONS

1. Trademark use: Did the Second Circuit reach the right decision in *WhenU*? Did it reach the right result in *Rescuecom?* Can the two decisions be meaningfully reconciled?

Why should it matter that the *WhenU* defendant availed itself of the plaintiff's web address, rather than the plaintiff's mark, given that the plaintiff's web address ("1800contacts.com") was highly similar to its mark ("1–800 Contacts")? Wouldn't "1800contacts.com" be deemed a "reproduction, counterfeit, copy, or colorable imitation" of the plaintiff's registered mark, as required in Lanham Act § 32(1)(a)? What if, instead of selling its advertising clients the right to have their sponsored links appear whenever users input a competitor's mark as a search term, Google sold its advertising clients the right to have their sponsored links appear whenever their competitor's web address (which typically incorporates the competitor's mark) appeared in one of the first three search result listings? Should that change the outcome of an infringement claim?

From a trademark law standpoint, should liability turn on whether an Internet service provider sells the right to key ads to a group (or category) of words or symbols that includes the plaintiff's mark, or sells advertisers the right to have ads keyed directly to the plaintiff's mark? Is one practice more likely than the other to cause the kind of harm that trademark law is designed to prevent?

What if the defendant does not sell keying rights at all, but simply causes banner or pop-up ads to appear randomly on users' computer screens? If a competitor's ad happens to appear on users' computer screens when they are searching for or visiting the plaintiff's web site, are consumers any more or less likely to be misled by its appearance? Is the defendant's hidden, internal use of the plaintiff's mark (or something confusingly similar to it) the potentially deceptive act, or does the potential deception lie in the nature of the defendant's screen display? If the latter, should the plaintiff's cause of action be for trademark infringement, or for some other form of unfair competition? (For that matter, is trademark infringement the appropriate cause of action to address the nefarious events described in the *Rescuecom* court's footnote 3? If not, what might a more appropriate cause of action entail?) Could keying ads to trademarks be deemed productive or useful, from consumers' standpoint? (In considering these questions, it may be relevant to note that Google routinely prohibited its advertisers from reproducing keyword/competitor marks in their displayed ads.)

If consumers are never exposed to the defendant's "use" of the plaintiff's mark, how can it confuse them? Judge Leval holds that the Lanham Act § 45 definition of "use in commerce" is applicable in determining whether Google's use of the Rescuecom mark constitutes actionable use. On what basis does he find that Google's actions, as pled, fall within the § 45 definition?

Does the *Rescuecom* court mean to say that placing competing brands next to one another on store shelves constitutes actionable trademark use? Assume that a customer enters the store and asks a clerk where he can find

Bayer aspirin. The clerk answers: "Aisle 6." The customer proceeds to Aisle 6, where he finds not only Bayer aspirin, but several other brands of aspirin as well. Upon reading the labels and comparing prices, the customer decides to buy one of the competing brands. Should the store be deemed to have engaged in actionable trademark use by putting the brands together on a shelf? Should the law discourage stores from locating competing goods together, where it is convenient for consumers to comparison shop? What if a Shell gas station sets up directly across the street from a Union 76 gas station? Consumers traveling to the Union 76 station notice the new Shell station across the street, along with a sign indicating that Shell gas is 10¢ cheaper per gallon than Union 76 gas, and decide to fill up at the Shell, rather than the Union 76. Has Shell engaged in actionable trademark use? If not, how does the practical effect of its actions differ from the practical effect of the defendant's actions in *Rescuecom*?

PROBLEMS

1. Assume that Acme Company manufactures and sells hiking and camping equipment throughout the United States. It has registered the mark "Acme" on the Lanham Act Principal Register for its goods. How would you apply Lanham Act §§ 32 to resolve the following conflicts?

a. Acme Co. wants to register "acme.com" as the domain name for a web site that will provide information about its hiking and camping equipment, and the means for consumers to order equipment directly from Acme and pay for it in an on-line transaction. However, when it seeks to register the name, it finds that the name is already registered to A.M.E. Corp., which has also used the "Acme" mark for some years in sales of instant oatmeal, and has registered "Acme" as a mark for breakfast cereals on the Lanham Act Principal Register.

b. Same facts as above, except that the entity that has registered the "acme.com" domain name is Acme's chief competitor, Gear, Inc., which normally sells its hiking and camping equipment under the "Gear" mark. Gear has set up a web page under the "acme.com" domain name which greets the user with the large, colorful heading:

Hi! Welcome to the world of Gear hiking and camping equipment. Gear is not related to Acme Co.—its products compete with Acme products.

The home page goes on to provide information about "Gear" hiking and camping equipment, pointing out how superior "Gear" equipment is to "Acme" equipment, setting out comparative prices, and providing a link to the gear.com website, from which consumers can order and pay for "Gear" products.

c. Same facts as in subpart a, except the person who has registered the "acme.com" domain name is a dissatisfied customer who has set up a web site that is highly critical of Acme's products.

d. Assume instead that Acme is successful in setting up its web page with the "acme.com" domain name. Shortly thereafter, it receives a "cease and desist" letter from a South African Company that sells camping equipment under the "Acme" mark in South Africa and several neighboring

African nations, and has registered the "Acme" mark in each of the African nations in which it sells. Since setting up its website, the U.S. Acme has made a couple of online sales to South African customers. Could the South African Company state a claim for trademark infringement? Where would jurisdiction be proper? Which country's law should apply?

2. Goodreads, Inc. is a well-established, successful book seller, with stores in a number of major U.S. cities. Jones Books, a small book store in West Virginia, set up a web page under the domain name "Booksforsale.com." It then repeated the following phrase 100 times in metatags: "Booksforsale.com is not in any way affiliated with Goodreads, Inc." As a result, when Internet users input "Goodreads," as a search term in the hopes of finding a Goodreads, Inc. web site, the search results include Jones' Booksforsale.com site. Could Goodreads state a trademark infringement cause of action against Jones for this use of its mark?

B. CONTRIBUTORY INFRINGEMENT

INWOOD LABORATORIES, INC. v. IVES LABORATORIES, INC.

United States Supreme Court, 1982.
456 U.S. 844, 102 S.Ct. 2182, 72 L.Ed.2d 606.

JUSTICE O'CONNOR delivered the opinion of the Court.

This action requires us to consider the circumstances under which a manufacturer of a generic drug, designed to duplicate the appearance of a similar drug marketed by a competitor under a registered trademark, can be held vicariously liable for infringement of that trademark by pharmacists who dispense the generic drug.

I

In 1955, respondent Ives Laboratories, Inc. (Ives), received a patent on the drug cyclandelate, a vasodilator used in long-term therapy for peripheral and cerebral vascular diseases. Until its patent expired in 1972, Ives retained the exclusive right to make and sell the drug, which it did under the registered trademark CYCLOSPASMOL. Ives marketed the drug, a white powder, to wholesalers, retail pharmacists, and hospitals in colored gelatin capsules. Ives arbitrarily selected a blue capsule, imprinted with "Ives 4124," for its 200 mg dosage and a combination blue-red capsule, imprinted with "Ives 4148," for its 400 mg dosage.

After Ives' patent expired, several generic drug manufacturers, including petitioners Premo Pharmaceutical Laboratories, Inc., Inwood Laboratories, Inc., and MD Pharmaceutical Co., Inc. (collectively the generic manufacturers), began marketing cyclandelate. They intentionally copied the appearance of the CYCLOSPASMOL capsules, selling cyclandelate in 200 mg and 400 mg capsules in colors identical to those selected by Ives.[3]

---

3. Initially, the generic manufacturers did not place any identifying mark on their capsules. After Ives initiated this action, Premo imprinted "Premo" on its capsules and Inwood imprinted "Inwood 258."

The marketing methods used by Ives reflect normal industry practice. Because cyclandelate can be obtained only by prescription, Ives does not direct its advertising to the ultimate consumer. Instead, Ives' representatives pay personal visits to physicians, to whom they distribute product literature and "starter samples." Ives initially directed these efforts toward convincing physicians that CYCLOSPASMOL is superior to other vasodilators. Now that its patent has expired and generic manufacturers have entered the market, Ives concentrates on convincing physicians to indicate on prescriptions that a generic drug cannot be substituted for CYCLOSPASMOL.[4]

The generic manufacturers also follow a normal industry practice by promoting their products primarily by distribution of catalogs to wholesalers, hospitals, and retail pharmacies, rather than by contacting physicians directly. The catalogs truthfully describe generic cyclandelate as "equivalent" or "comparable" to CYCLOSPASMOL. In addition, some of the catalogs include price comparisons of the generic drug and CYCLOSPASMOL and some refer to the color of the generic capsules. The generic products reach wholesalers, hospitals, and pharmacists in bulk containers which correctly indicate the manufacturer of the product contained therein.

A pharmacist, regardless of whether he is dispensing CYCLOSPASMOL or a generic drug, removes the capsules from the container in which he receives them and dispenses them to the consumer in the pharmacist's own bottle with his own label attached. Hence, the final consumer sees no identifying marks other than those on the capsules themselves.

II

A

Ives instituted this action in the United States District Court for the Eastern District of New York under §§ 32 and 43(a) of the Trademark Act of 1946 (Lanham Act). * * *.

Ives' claim under * * * 15 U.S.C. § 1114 derived from its allegation that some pharmacists had dispensed generic drugs mislabeled as CYCLOSPASMOL. Ives contended that the generic manufacturers' use of look-alike capsules and of catalog entries comparing prices and revealing the colors of the generic capsules induced pharmacists illegally to substitute a generic drug for CYCLOSPASMOL and to mislabel the substitute drug CYCLOSPASMOL. Although Ives did not allege that the petitioners themselves applied the Ives trademark to the drug products they produced and distributed, it did allege that the petitioners contributed to the infringing activities of pharmacists who mislabeled generic cyclandelate.

* * *

---

4. Since the early 1970's, most States have enacted laws allowing pharmacists to substitute generic drugs for brand name drugs under certain conditions. * * *

Contending that pharmacists would continue to mislabel generic drugs as CYCLOSPASMOL so long as imitative products were available, Ives asked that the court enjoin the petitioners from marketing cyclandelate capsules in the same colors and form as Ives uses for CYCLOSPAS-MOL. * * *

B

The District Court denied Ives' request for an order preliminarily enjoining the petitioners from selling generic drugs identical in appearance to those produced by Ives. * * * The Court of Appeals for the Second Circuit affirmed. To assist the District Court in the upcoming trial on the merits, the appellate court defined the elements of a claim based upon § 32 in some detail. [T]he court stated that the petitioners would be liable under § 32 either if they suggested, even by implication, that retailers fill bottles with generic cyclandelate and label the bottle with Ives' trademark or if the petitioners continued to sell cyclandelate to retailers whom they knew or had reason to know were engaging in infringing practices.

C

After a bench trial on remand, the District Court entered judgment for the petitioners. Applying the test approved by the Court of Appeals to the claim based upon § 32, the District Court found that the petitioners had not suggested, even by implication, that pharmacists should dispense generic drugs incorrectly identified as CYCLOSPASMOL.[12]

In reaching that conclusion, the court first looked for direct evidence that the petitioners intentionally induced trademark infringement. Since the petitioners' representatives do not make personal visits to physicians and pharmacists, the petitioners were not in a position directly to suggest improper drug substitutions. Therefore, the court concluded, improper suggestions, if any, must have come from catalogs and promotional materials. The court determined, however, that those materials could not "fairly be read" to suggest trademark infringement.

The trial court next considered evidence of actual instances of mislabeling by pharmacists, since frequent improper substitutions of a generic drug for CYCLOSPASMOL could provide circumstantial evidence that the petitioners, merely by making available imitative drugs in conjunction with comparative price advertising, implicitly had suggested that pharmacists substitute improperly. After reviewing the evidence of incidents of mislabeling, the District Court concluded that such incidents occurred too infrequently to justify the inference that the petitioners' catalogs and use of imitative colors had "impliedly invited" druggists to mislabel. Moreover, to the extent mislabeling had occurred, the court found it resulted from pharmacists' misunderstanding of the requirements of the New York

---

12. The District Court also found that the petitioners did not continue to provide drugs to retailers whom they knew or should have known were engaging in trademark infringement. * * *

Drug Substitution Law, rather than from deliberate attempts to pass off generic cyclandelate as CYCLOSPASMOL.

* * *

Without expressly stating that the District Court's findings were clearly erroneous, and for reasons which we discuss below, the Court of Appeals concluded that the petitioners violated § 32. * * * We granted certiorari, and now reverse the judgment of the Court of Appeals.

III

A

As the lower courts correctly discerned, liability for trademark infringement can extend beyond those who actually mislabel goods with the mark of another. Even if a manufacturer does not directly control others in the chain of distribution, it can be held responsible for their infringing activities under certain circumstances. Thus, if a manufacturer or distributor intentionally induces another to infringe a trademark, or if it continues to supply its product to one whom it knows or has reason to know is engaging in trademark infringement, the manufacturer or distributor is contributorily responsible for any harm done as a result of the deceit.

It is undisputed that those pharmacists who mislabeled generic drugs with Ives' registered trademark violated § 32. However, whether these petitioners were liable for the pharmacists' infringing acts depended upon whether, in fact, the petitioners intentionally induced the pharmacists to mislabel generic drugs or, in fact, continued to supply cyclandelate to pharmacists whom the petitioners knew were mislabeling generic drugs. The District Court concluded that Ives made neither of those factual showings.

* * *

[A]fter completing its own review of the evidence, the Court of Appeals concluded that the evidence was "clearly sufficient to establish a § 32 violation." In reaching its conclusion, the Court of Appeals was influenced by several factors. First, it thought the petitioners reasonably could have anticipated misconduct by a substantial number of the pharmacists who were provided imitative, lower priced products which, if substituted for the higher priced brand name without passing on savings to consumers, could provide an economic advantage to the pharmacists. Second, it disagreed with the trial court's finding that the mislabeling which did occur reflected confusion about state law requirements. Third, it concluded that illegal substitution and mislabeling in New York are neither *de minimis* nor inadvertent. Finally, the Court of Appeals indicated it was further influenced by the fact that the petitioners did not offer "any persuasive evidence of a legitimate reason unrelated to CYCLOS-PASMOL" for producing an imitative product.[20]

---

20. The Court of Appeals reached that conclusion despite the District Court's express finding that, for purposes of § 43(a), the capsule colors were functional. * * * By establishing to the

Each of those conclusions is contrary to the findings of the District Court. An appellate court cannot substitute its interpretation of the evidence for that of the trial court simply because the reviewing court "might give the facts another construction, resolve the ambiguities differently, and find a more sinister cast to actions which the District Court apparently deemed innocent." *United States v. Real Estate Boards*, 339 U.S. 485, 495, 70 S.Ct. 711, 717, 94 L.Ed. 1007 (1950).

* * *

NOTES AND QUESTIONS

1. *Contributory infringement.* Given the Supreme Court's definition of contributory infringement in the trademark context, is it possible to allege a contributory infringement cause of action against an actor who did not supply products to the direct infringer or induce her infringement? In Hard Rock Café Licensing Corp. v. Concession Services, Inc., 955 F.2d 1143 (7th Cir. 1992), Hard Rock sought to hold CSI, the operator of flea markets, liable for the direct infringement of a booth operator named Parvez, who sold allegedly infringing t-shirts at the markets.

The booth operators rented space from CSI for a flat fee, and paid an additional fee if they wanted CSI to reserve a particular space for them from month to month or provide storage for their goods. CSI advertised the flea market (but not the presence of any individual vendors or any particular goods), provided security and crowd control, and ran concession stands inside the market. It charged shoppers an admission fee. CSI did relatively little to supervise the flea market: It posted a sign prohibiting vendors from selling "illegal goods" and had "Rules for Sellers" which prohibited the sale of certain items, such as alcohol, weapons, drugs, fireworks, and live animals. The CSI manager walked around the flea market several times a day to look for problems or rule violations, but no one inspected vendor's wares before they were offered for sale, or engaged in any in-depth or systematic inspection thereafter.

The Seventh Circuit considered how a claim against CSI would fit with the Supreme Court's definition of contributory infringement in *Inwood Labs*:

> [I]t is not clear how the doctrine applies to people who do not actually manufacture or distribute the good that is ultimately palmed off as made by someone else. A temporary help service, for example, might not be liable if it furnished Parvez the workers he employed to erect his stand, even if the help service knew that Parvez would sell counterfeit goods. Thus we must ask whether the operator of a flea market is more like the manufacturer of a mislabled good or more like a temporary help service supplying the purveyor of goods. To answer questions of this sort, we have treated trademark infringement as a species of tort and have turned

District Court's satisfaction that uniform capsule colors served a functional purpose, the petitioners offered a legitimate reason for producing an imitative product. Nor was the Court of Appeals entitled simply to dismiss the District Court's finding of functionality as not "persuasive." If the District Court erred as a matter of law, the Court of Appeals should have identified the District Court's legal error. If the Court of Appeals disagreed with the District Court's factual findings, it should not have dismissed them without finding them clearly erroneous.

to the common law to guide our inquiry into the appropriate boundaries of liability.

CSI characterizes its relationship with Parvez as that of landlord and tenant. Hard Rock calls CSI a licensor, not a landlord. Ether way, the Restatement of Torts tells us that CSI is responsible for the torts of those it permits on its premises "knowing or having reason to know that the other is acting or will act tortiously ...". Restatement (Second) of Torts § 877(c) & cmt d (1979). The common law, then, imposes the same duty on landlords and licensors that the Supreme Court has imposed on manufacturers and distributors. In the absence of any suggestion that a trademark violation should not be treated as a common law tort, we believe that the *Inwood Labs* test for contributory liability applies. CSI may be liable for trademark violations by Parvez if it knew or had reason to know of them.

* * *

* * * CSI has no affirmative duty to take precautions against the sale of counterfeits. Although the "reason to know" part of the standard for contributory liability requires CSI (or its agents) to understand what a reasonably prudent person would understand, it does not impose any duty to seek out and prevent violations. We decline to extend the protection * * * to require CSI, and other landlords, to be more dutiful guardians of Hard Rock's commercial interests.

Id., 955 F.2d at 1148–49. Do you agree with the Seventh Circuit's reasoning? Why is providing booth space more like providing a product (per *Inwood Labs*) than providing temporary help? Is this extension of the *Inwood Labs* standard justified? Why shouldn't the temporary help service be liable for Parvez' infringement? If this were a copyright infringement claim, would the same standard be imposed? See the *Fonovisa* decision, *supra*, at pages 591–95.

2. *Vicarious infringement.* Is there such a thing as vicarious liability for trademark infringement? The *Hard Rock* court noted:

[A] joint tortfeasor may bear vicarious liability for trademark infringement by another. This theory of liability requires a finding that the defendant and the infringer have an apparent or actual partnership, have authority to bind one another in transactions with third parties or exercise joint ownership or control over the infringing product.

Hard Rock, 955 F.2d at 1150. Clearly CSI did not fit this description. However, Hard Rock urged the court to apply the more expansive doctrine of vicarious liability applicable in copyright infringement cases. Under copyright law, a defendant will be vicariously liable for another's direct infringement if it has the right and ability to supervise the infringing activity and a direct financial interest in it. CSI would probably be liable under this standard, just as the flea market operator in the *Fonovisa* decision was. However, the Seventh Circuit declined to incorporate this more liberal theory of liability into trademark law, nothing that "the Supreme Court tells us that secondary liability for trademark infringement should * * * be more narrowly drawn than secondary liability for copyright infringement." 955 F.2d at 1150. Why should that be? Do you agree?

PROBLEMS

1. eBay operates an on-line marketplace that allows users to purchase and sell goods. More than 6 million new listings are posted on its site daily. At any given time it has nearly 100 million listings. eBay provides the venue for sale, and supports the sales transactions, but dos not itself sell the items listed on its site. Nor does it ever have physical possession of the items. eBay generates revenue by charging sellers for use of its listing services and through its Pay Pal Company, which assists users to pay for their purchases. eBay promotes use of its site by advertising the availability of various items, including "Tiffany" jewelry.

Many eBay sellers list items of "Tiffany" jewelry for sale, but in fact a significant portion of the "Tiffany" jewelry listed on eBay is counterfeit. eBay maintains a "notice and takedown" system, and whenever the owner of the "Tiffany" mark notifies eBay of a specific listing of counterfeit jewelry, eBay acts promptly to remove the listing. eBay also operates a "fraud engine" which is devoted to ferreting out illegal listings, and periodically conducts manual reviews of listings in an effort to remove those that might be counterfeit. eBay has also set up a "Buyer Protection Plan" which reimburses purchasers of counterfeit goods in some cases, and engages in other activities to prevent or minimize sale of counterfeit goods and accommodate mark owners.

It appears that eBay knows that there are many listings for sale of counterfeit Tiffany jewelry beyond the specific cases identified in notice and takedown claims. It knows this by virtue of general survey evidence provided by Tiffany, the thousands of notice and takedown claims Tiffany has filed over the past few years, and complaints from buyers.

The owner of the Tiffany mark sues eBay for contributory infringement. How should the court rule?

2. When someone wants to set up a web site, he must choose a domain name for the site and submit a registration form to Domain Name Registry Service (DNRS). Once the registration is confirmed, an Internet Protocol ("IP") address (essentially a string of numbers) which gives the actual location of the web site can be associated with the registered domain name. DNRS enters the domain name and corresponding IP address into its database and thus causes Internet users who enter the domain name to be routed to the corresponding IP address for the registrant's web site. DNRS charges a fee for the registration.

DNRS processes thousands of registrations per month, most of them electronically. Ten percent of the time, an employee of DNRS reviews the registration application, due, for example, to an error in filling out the form or because the applied-for domain name includes a prohibited character string, such as "Olympic," "Red Cross," "NASA," or certain obscene words. It also performs a conflict check on all applications, which compares an application to other registered domain names. However, DNRS does not consult third parties during the registration process, check for a registrant's legal right to use a particular word in a domain name, or monitor the use of a domain name once it is registered. It does, however, maintain a post-registration dispute resolution procedure. Anyone who feels that his or her trademark rights are violated by a registrant's domain name can submit a certified copy of a trademark registration to DNRS. DNRS then requires the registrant to obtain a declaratory judgement that he has a right to maintain the domain name. If the registrant fails to do this, DNRS terminates the registration.

Lockheed owns and operates "The Skunk Works," an aircraft design and construction laboratory. It has registered "Skunk Works" as a service mark for this laboratory, and the registration is incontestable. Lockheed learns that third parties have registered domain names with DNRS that incorporate Lockheed's mark, including "skunkworks.com" and "skunkworks.net." Lockheed notifies DNRS of these allegedly infringing registrations and requests that it cancel them and cease registering domain names that incorporate its mark. DNRS takes no action on Lockheed's requests, informing Lockheed that it has failed to comply with the terms of its dispute resolution policy. It subsequently permits a new registrant to register a domain name that incorporates the words "skunk works."

Lockheed sues DNRS, alleging contributory trademark infringement. Assuming that the third party domain name registrants have in fact infringed the Skunk Works mark, how should the court resolve the claim?

3. Acme Company leases paper towel dispensers that prominently display the "Acme" mark. It also sells bundles of "Acme" brand paper towels to lessees to place in the dispensers. Although the towel packaging displays the "Acme" mark, the individual towels themselves do not. When it leases a dispenser, Acme contractually requires the lessee to use only Acme paper towels with the dispenser.

Cheapco sells bundles of its competing (and less expensive, lower quality) paper towels in wrappers prominently displaying the "Cheapco" mark. It sells its towels to lessees of Acme dispensers, knowing that the purchasers will use the towels in Acme dispensers.

Acme sues Cheapco, alleging contributory infringement. Is it likely to prevail?

C. COLLATERAL USES OF MARKS AND GRAY MARKET GOODS

CHAMPION SPARK PLUG CO. v. SANDERS

United States Supreme Court, 1947.
331 U.S. 125, 67 S.Ct. 1136, 91 L.Ed. 1386.

MR. JUSTICE DOUGLAS delivered the opinion of the Court.

Petitioner is a manufacturer of spark plugs which it sells under the trade mark "Champion." Respondents collect the used plugs, repair and recondition them, and resell them. Respondents retain the word "Champion" on the repaired or reconditioned plugs. The outside box or carton in which the plugs are packed has stamped on it the word "Champion," together with the letter and figure denoting the particular style or type.

They also have printed on them "Perfect Process Spark Plugs Guaranteed Dependable" and "Perfect Process Renewed Spark Plugs." Each carton contains smaller boxes in which the plugs are individually packed. These inside boxes also carry legends indicating that the plug has been renewed.[1] But respondent company's business name or address is not printed on the cartons. It supplies customers with petitioner's charts containing recommendations for the use of Champion plugs. On each individual plug is stamped in small letters, blue on black, the word "Renewed," which at times is almost illegible.

Petitioner brought this suit in the District Court, charging infringement of its trade mark and unfair competition. The District Court found that respondents had infringed the trade mark. It enjoined them from offering or selling any of petitioner's plugs which had been repaired or reconditioned unless (a) the trade mark and type and style marks were removed, (b) the plugs were repainted with a durable grey, brown, orange, or green paint, (c) the word "REPAIRED" was stamped into the plug in letters of such size and depth as to retain enough white paint to display distinctly each letter of the word, (d) the cartons in which the plugs were packed carried a legend indicating that they contained used spark plugs originally made by petitioner and repaired and made fit for use up to 10,000 miles by respondent company.[2] * * *

The Circuit Court of Appeals held that respondents not only had infringed petitioner's trade mark but also were guilty of unfair competition. It likewise denied an accounting but modified the decree in the following respects: (a) it eliminated the provision requiring the trade mark and type and style marks to be removed from the repaired or reconditioned plugs; (b) it substituted for the requirement that the word "REPAIRED" be stamped into the plug, etc., a provision that the word "REPAIRED" or "USED" be stamped and baked on the plug by an electrical hot press in a contrasting color so as to be clearly and distinctly visible, the plug having been completely covered by permanent aluminum paint or other paint or lacquer; and (c) it eliminated the provision specifying the precise legend to be printed on the cartons and substituted therefor a more general one.[3] The case is here on a petition for certiorari * * *.

1.

"The process used in renewing this plug has been developed through 10 years continuous experience. This Spark Plug has been tested for firing under compression before packing."

"This Spark Plug is guaranteed to be a selected used Spark Plug, thoroughly renewed and in perfect mechanical condition and is guaranteed to give satisfactory service for 10,000 miles."

2. The prescribed legend read:

"Used spark plug(s) originally made by Champion Spark Plug Company repaired and made fit for use up to 10,000 miles by Perfect Recondition Spark Plug Co., 1133 Bedford Avenue, Brooklyn, N.Y."

The decree also provided:

"the name and address of the defendants to be larger and more prominent than the legend itself, and the name of plaintiff may be in slightly larger type than the rest of the body of the legend."

3. "The decree shall permit the defendants to state on cartons and containers, selling and advertising material, business records, correspondence and other papers, when published, the

There is no challenge here to the findings as to the misleading character of the merchandising methods employed by respondents, nor to the conclusion that they have not only infringed petitioner's trade mark but have also engaged in unfair competition. The controversy here relates to the adequacy of the relief granted, particularly the refusal of the Circuit Court of Appeals to require respondents to remove the word "Champion" from the repaired or reconditioned plugs which they resell.

We put to one side the case of a manufacturer or distributor who markets new or used spark plugs of one make under the trade mark of another. Equity then steps in to prohibit defendant's use of the mark which symbolizes plaintiff's good will and "stakes the reputation of the plaintiff upon the character of the goods." *Bourjois & Co. v. Katzel*, 260 U.S. 689, 692, 43 S.Ct. 244, 245, 67 L.Ed. 464.

We are dealing here with second-hand goods. The spark plugs, though used, are nevertheless Champion plugs and not those of another make. There is evidence to support what one would suspect, that a used spark plug which has been repaired or reconditioned does not measure up to the specifications of a new one. But the same would be true of a second-hand Ford or Chevrolet car. And we would not suppose that one could be enjoined from selling a car whose valves had been reground and whose piston rings had been replaced unless he removed the name Ford or Chevrolet. *Prestonettes, Inc. v. Coty*, 264 U.S. 359, 44 S.Ct. 350, 68 L.Ed. 731, was a case where toilet powders had as one of their ingredients a powder covered by a trade mark and where perfumes which were trade marked were rebottled and sold in smaller bottles. The Court sustained a decree denying an injunction where the prescribed labels told the truth. Mr. Justice Holmes stated, "A trade-mark only gives the right to prohibit the use of it so far as to protect the owner's good will against the sale of another's product as his. * * * When the mark is used in a way that does not deceive the public we see no such sanctity in the word as to prevent its being used to tell the truth. It is not taboo." 264 U.S. at page 368, 44 S.Ct. at page 351, 68 L.Ed. 731.

Cases may be imagined where the reconditioning or repair would be so extensive or so basic that it would be a misnomer to call the article by its original name, even though the words "used" or "repaired" were added. But no such practice is involved here. The repair or reconditioning of the plugs does not give them a new design. It is no more than a restoration, so far as possible, of their original condition. The type marks attached by the manufacturer are determined by the use to which the plug is to be put. But the thread size and size of the cylinder hole into which the plug is fitted are not affected by the reconditioning. The heat range also has relevance to the type marks. And there is evidence that the reconditioned plugs are inferior so far as heat range and other qualities are concerned. But inferiority is expected in most second-hand articles.

original make and type numbers provided it is made clear that any plug referred to therein is used and reconditioned by the defendants, and that such material contains the name and address of defendants."

Indeed, they generally cost the customer less. That is the case here. Inferiority is immaterial so long as the article is clearly and distinctively sold as repaired or reconditioned rather than as new. The result is, of course, that the second-hand dealer gets some advantage from the trade mark. But under the rule of *Prestonettes, Inc. v. Coty*, that is wholly permissible so long as the manufacturer is not identified with the inferior qualities of the product resulting from wear and tear or the reconditioning by the dealer. Full disclosure gives the manufacturer all the protection to which he is entitled.

The decree as shaped by the Circuit Court of Appeals is fashioned to serve the requirements of full disclosure. We cannot say that of the alternatives available the ones it chose are inadequate for that purpose. * * *

NOTES AND QUESTIONS

1. *Use of marks in the resale of genuine goods.* Why does the plaintiff in *Champion Spark Plug* object to the defendant's use of its mark? As a practical matter, what harm can the use do to the plaintiff? Assuming that there is injury, why is the Court unwilling to prevent it?

Why does the Court require that the defendant indicate clearly that it had repaired or reconditioned the plugs? In the *Prestonettes* case, discussed in *Champion*, why did the defendant have to indicate that it had rebottled the plaintiff's perfume, as long as it was the same perfume, and had not been altered? Would it constitute trademark infringement if the defendant had, in addition to transferring plaintiff's perfume to different bottles, diluted the perfume with water?

2. *The doctrine of exhaustion.* The doctrine of exhaustion underlies the reasoning in *Champion Spark Plug* and *Prestonettes*. This doctrine tracks the patent and copyright doctrines of exhaustion or first sale. The doctrine provides, essentially, that once the trademark owner permits goods bearing its mark to enter the stream of commerce, it generally cannot prevent or control resale of the goods with the mark, and truthful advertising that goods bearing that mark are for sale. Others may further distribute the goods under the mark, as long as the use is truthful and does not confuse consumers about the immediate source of the goods. Trademark rights are thus "exhausted" as to a given good upon its first authorized sale.

PROBLEMS

1. Adolph Glug Co. sells its beer only in the western states, and imposes quality control requirements on its authorized distributors to ensure that its beer remains fresh for consumers. Among other things, Glug requires its distributors to refrigerate the beer as much as possible and remove from retail stores and destroy any beer that has been on the shelf for more than 60 days after packaging. The defendant buys large quantities of Glug beer from authorized retailers in the western states, transports it to Maryland and resells it to retailers and other distributors in that state in its original

packaging. Defendant advertises that it has beer for sale, including Glug, but does not represent to third persons that it is an authorized distributor of Glug beer. Defendant does not refrigerate the beer, and leaves it on the shelf for longer than 60 days before it is sold to the ultimate consumers. As a result, the Glug beer that Maryland consumers get often is inferior, with a deteriorated taste. Under the principles set forth in *Champion Spark Plug*, should the defendant be liable for trademark infringement?

2. Defendant purchases Volkswagen badges (consisting of the familiar Volkswagen logo comprised of the letters "VW" inside a circle) from the Volkswagen Company. Volkswagen sells the badges as replacements for the badges found on trunks or hoods of Volkswagen automobiles. After purchasing the badges, defendant alters them by removing prongs from the back and mounting them on marquee license plates. It sells the marquee license plates packaged with labels that explain that the plates are not produced or sponsored by the Volkswagen Co.

The Volkswagen Company sues defendant for trademark infringement, and provides evidence that defendant's actions create a likelihood of post-sale confusion. That is, Volkswagen argues that while purchasers will not be confused about the source or sponsorship of the license plates, other persons who view the plates mounted on cars may be. How should the court rule?

1. *Gray Market Goods/Parallel Imports*

The doctrine of exhaustion and the question of liability for resale of genuinely marked goods lead naturally to the issue of "gray market goods" or "parallel imports." Gray market goods are products that are lawfully manufactured and marked with trademarks identical to U.S. trademarks, but are intended for sale in foreign countries. Cheaper foreign sales prices and/or exchange rate differences sometimes make it profitable for arbitragers to buy the goods abroad, ship them to the United States, and sell them in competition with the entity that owns the mark in the U.S. If, for example, an importer can purchase genuine Minolta cameras for significantly less in Taiwan than in the United States, it can ship the Taiwanese cameras to the United States, and sell them for less than the price charged by the U.S. entity that owns the domestic mark registration, and still make a profit. Needless to say, this practice has not been popular with U.S. mark registrants.

The gray market issue can arise in a variety of contexts. However, in K Mart Corp. v. Cartier, Inc., 486 U.S. 281, 108 S.Ct. 1811, 100 L.Ed.2d 313 (1988), the Supreme Court described the three contexts in which the issue most frequently arises:

> The prototypical gray-market victim (case 1) is a domestic firm that purchases from an independent foreign firm the rights to register and use the latter's trademark as a United States trademark and to sell its foreign-manufactured products here. * * * If the foreign manufacturer could import the trademarked goods and distribute them here, despite having sold the trademark to a domestic firm, the domestic firm would be forced into sharp intrabrand competition involving the

very trademark it purchased. Similar intrabrand competition could arise if the foreign manufacturer markets its wares outside the United States, as is often the case, and a third party who purchases them abroad could legally import them. In either event, the parallel importation, if permitted to proceed, would create a gray market that could jeopardize the trademark holder's investment.

The second context (case 2) is a situation in which a domestic firm registers the United States trademark for goods that are manufactured abroad by an affiliated manufacturer. In its most common variation (case 2a), a foreign firm wishes to control distribution of its wares in this country by incorporating a subsidiary here. The subsidiary then registers under its own name (or the manufacturer assigns to the subsidiary's name) a United States trademark that is identical to its parent's foreign trademark. The parallel importation by a third party who buys the goods abroad (or conceivably even by the affiliated foreign manufacturer itself) creates a gray market. Two other variations on this theme occur when an American-based firm establishes abroad a manufacturing subsidiary corporation (case 2b) or its own unincorporated manufacturing division (case 2c) to produce its U.S. trademarked goods, and then imports them for domestic distribution. If the trademark holder or its foreign subsidiary sells the trademarked goods abroad, the parallel importation of the goods competes on the gray market with the holder's domestic sales.

In the third context (case 3), the domestic holder of a United States trademark authorizes an independent foreign manufacturer to use it. Usually the holder sells to the foreign manufacturer an exclusive right to use the trademark in a particular foreign location, but conditions the right on the foreign manufacturer's promise not to import its trademarked goods into the United States. Once again, if the foreign manufacturer or a third party imports into the United States, the foreign-manufactured goods will compete on the gray market with the holder's domestic goods.

Id., 486 U.S. at 286–87.

U.S. mark registrants advocating construction of the trademark laws to prohibit unauthorized import of gray market goods argue that a trademark has a separate legal existence under each country's laws. The lawful function of the mark in each country is to symbolize the *domestic source* of the product, and that domestic source's reputation, consistency and good will. The domestic source is the domestic registrant, whoever that may be. If the product was manufactured abroad, the U.S. registrant is likely to be a U.S. entity that owns exclusive rights to distribute the foreign-made good in the U.S. Thus, under these circumstances, the registered mark symbolizes the U.S. distributor, not the foreign manufacturer. Under this theory, unauthorized importation of goods bearing the same mark will cause a likelihood of confusion about the immediate, domestic source of the goods (even if the gray market goods were manufactured and marked by the same foreign manufacturer as the domestically distributed goods), and thus will constitute an infringement.

Advocates of free movement of gray market goods across international borders argue that a mark generally symbolizes the original manufacturer of the good to consumers, not the domestic distributor. If a good is lawfully manufactured and marked in one country, it may carry that mark lawfully wherever it goes. Subsequent resales, no matter where they occur, should not give rise to infringement liability. Concurrent domestic sales by gray market importers and the domestic mark owner will not lead to consumer confusion about the source of the good.

A. Bourjois & Co., Inc. v. Katzel, 260 U.S. 689, 43 S.Ct. 244, 67 L.Ed. 464 (1923), is a key case in the development of United States law governing the unauthorized import of gray market goods. In that case Bourjois, a United States company, purchased from a French powder manufacturer the manufacturer's established United States face powder business and good will, and the registered trademark "Java," under which the business had been conducted. Bourjois imported powder in bulk from the French manufacturer, packaged and sold it domestically under the "Java" mark. Bourjois and the French manufacturer were completely unrelated entities. While the French manufacturer assigned all its rights in the "Java" mark in the United States, it retained rights in the mark abroad and continued to manufacture and sell powder under the "Java" mark in other countries. The defendant bought a large quantity of the manufacturer's "Java" powder in France and imported it into the United States for sale in competition with Bourjois. The French manufacturer's packaging was similar in appearance to Bourjois'.

In upholding an injunction against the defendant's sales, the Supreme Court explained:

> We are of opinion that the plaintiff's rights are infringed. After the sale the French manufacturers could not have come to the United States and have used their old marks in competition with the plaintiff. That plainly follows from the statute authorizing assignments. If for the purpose of evading the effect of the transfer it had arranged with the defendant that she should sell with the old label, we suppose that no one would doubt that the contrivance must fail. There is no such conspiracy here, but apart from the opening of a door to one, the vendors could not convey their goods free from the restriction to which the vendors were subject. Ownership of the goods does not carry the right to sell them with a specific mark. It does not necessarily carry the right to sell them at all in a given place. * * * It is said that the trade-mark here is that of the French house and truly indicates the origin of the goods. But that is not accurate. It is the trade-mark of the plaintiff only in the United States and indicates in law, and, it is found, by public understanding, that the goods come from the plaintiff although not made by it. It was sold and could only

be sold with the good will of the business that the plaintiff bought. It stakes the reputation of the plaintiff upon the character of the goods.

Id., 260 U.S. at 691–92.

At about the same time that the Supreme Court rendered its decision in *Katzel,* Congress enacted Tariff Act § 526, 19 U.S.C.A. § 1526. Section 526 makes it unlawful

> to import into the United States any merchandise of foreign manufacture if such merchandise * * * bears a trademark owned by a citizen of, or by a corporation or association created or organized within, the United States, and registered in the Patent and Trademark Office by a person domiciled in the United States * * * unless written consent of the owner of such trademark is produced at the time of making entry.

19 U.S.C.A. § 1526(a). Under this provision, a trademark owner may have the Customs Service stop offending goods at the border or bring a private cause of action for relief. 19 U.S.C.A. § 1526(c).

The Customs Service, in promulgating regulations to implement § 526, construed that provision as prohibiting only the importation of some, not all, gray market goods. 19 C.F.R. § 133.21(c) provided:

> (c) *Restrictions not applicable.* The restrictions set forth in * * * this section do not apply to imported articles when:
>
> (1) Both the foreign and the U.S. trademark or trade name are owned by the same person or business entity;
>
> (2) The foreign and domestic trademark or trade name owners are parent and subsidiary companies or are otherwise subject to common ownership or control; or
>
> (3) The articles of foreign manufacture bear a recorded trademark or trade name applied under the authorization of the U.S. owner.

In *K Mart Corp. v. Cartier, supra,* an association of U.S. trademark owners challenged the validity of this Customs regulation, arguing that it was inconsistent with § 526. A majority of the Supreme Court held that the exceptions set forth in subsections (c)(1) and (2) constituted reasonable constructions of the ambiguous language of § 526, and were consistent with the statute's intent. A separate majority found that the third exception, subsection (c)(3), was invalid as contrary to the clear language of § 526. Thus, domestic mark registrants who are under common control or are in a parent/subsidiary relationship with the foreign manufacturer are excluded from the benefits of Customs Service protection under § 526.[17] (Returning to the *K Mart* Court's description of the three general

---

17. Technically, the *K Mart* opinion only considered the reasonableness of the Customs Service's interpretation of § 526. The Court did not itself undertake to interpret the scope of § 526 for purposes of civil suits between private parties. As a practical matter, however, the approved Customs interpretation is likely to be applied in both contexts, as in the *Weil* opinion, *infra.*

contexts in which gray market goods most frequently arise, excerpted above, § 526 will prohibit the import of gray market goods in "case 1," which is the *Katzel* case, and "case 3," but not in "case 2.")

Note that when the U.S. mark owner and the foreign manufacturer are subject to common control or are in a parent/subsidiary relationship, they can be viewed as the "same person." In upholding clauses (1) and (2) of the Customs regulation and voiding clause (3), the *K Mart* decision can be viewed as distinguishing between goods marked and sold abroad by the U.S. registrant (which, as a related entity, is deemed the "same" entity as the foreign manufacturer) and goods marked and sold abroad by a foreign manufacturer that is unrelated to the U.S. registrant.

Deprived of a § 526 remedy, "case 2" U.S. trademark owners seeking to exclude gray market goods turned to the Lanham Act, which generated the following opinion, among others.

WEIL CERAMICS AND GLASS, INC. v. DASH

United States Court of Appeals for the Third Circuit, 1989.
878 F.2d 659, *cert. denied,* 493 U.S. 853, 110 S.Ct. 156, 107 L.Ed.2d 114 (1989).

A. Leon Higginbotham, Jr., Circuit Judge.

On this appeal we are asked to determine the availability of trademark * * * protection to an American company—which is owned by the same entity that owns the foreign manufacturer of a good, but which holds a valid American trademark for the foreign manufactured good—against parallel imports or so-called "gray-market" goods. Specifically, we are asked to determine whether § 32 of the Lanham Act, 15 U.S.C. § 1114 (1982), makes damages available to the American trademark holder for trademark infringement and if § 42 of that Act, 15 U.S.C. § 1124 (1982), may be employed on behalf of the American company to prohibit the importation of gray-market goods.

This appeal also raised the question of whether § 526 of the Tariff Act, 19 U.S.C. § 1526 (1982), could be employed to preclude the importation of gray-market goods. That section has been construed by the Customs agency in its regulations as allowing the importation of gray-market goods in those cases where the American trademark holder is owned by, or owns, the foreign manufacturer of the good. See 19 C.F.R. § 133.21 (1987). [The Court notes that this portion of the cited customs regulation was upheld by the Supreme Court in *K Mart*, and that this disposes of the § 526 claim.] *K Mart* is also instructive to the disposition of the Appellee/Cross–Appellant's contentions regarding §§ 42 and 32. We conclude that neither of these sections provides the relief sought * * *.

* * *

I. Background

* * * Appellee/Cross–Appellant, Weil Ceramics & Glass, Inc., ("Weil"), is the wholly owned subsidiary of Lladro Exportadora, S.A., a

Spanish corporation that is a sister corporation to Lladro, S.A., which manufactures fine porcelain in Spain.[2] The porcelain is handmade and each piece bears the trademark "LLADRO," accompanied by a flower logo.

[In 1966 Weil, an independent New York corporation, became the exclusive U.S. distributor of Lladro porcelain. It obtained a valid U.S. registration of the Lladro mark the following year. The Lladro group subsequently purchased 50% of Weil's stock and reacquired the U.S. trademark registration. In 1977, Lladro Exportadora acquired 100% of Weil's stock. In 1983 it reassigned the U.S. trademark registration to Weil.]

In 1982, Appellants/Cross–Appellees Jalyn Corporation * * * ("Jalyn"), began importing LLADRO porcelain. Jalyn legally obtained the porcelain in Spain from distributors of Lladro, S.A. and sold it in the United States without the consent of Weil. In 1984, Weil filed a complaint in the federal district court for the district of New Jersey seeking declaratory and injunctive relief against Jalyn's continued import of Lladro porcelain and money damages for trademark infringement.

[The district court granted Weil's motion for summary judgement, finding that Jalyn's use of the Lladro mark caused a likelihood of confusion, in violation of the Lanham Act. The Court of Appeals reverses.]

III. SECTIONS 42 AND 32

Weil argues that even if § 526 does not bar importation by Jalyn of the LLADRO porcelain, § 42—which was not specifically addressed in *K Mart*—does. Moreover, Weil contends that nothing in *K Mart* precludes its recovery of damages for infringement under § 32 for Jalyn's distribution of the LLADRO porcelain in the United States. We are persuaded, however, because of the relationship that Weil has with Lladro, S.A., that the protections afforded by §§ 42 and 32 of the Lanham Act are also inapplicable.

Weil's argument on this point has two components: first, it asserts that it owns the United States LLADRO trademark independently of its foreign parent and, pursuant to the territoriality theory attributed to *Katzel*, it is entitled to the full measure of trademark protection provided by the Lanham Act. In that light, Weil contends that § 42's preclusion of goods that "copy or simulate" a trademark and that § 32's preclusion of marks that "imitate" a registered trademark are applicable—notwithstanding the fact that the goods are genuine and bear the trademark of the manufacturer—because Jalyn's importation of LLADRO porcelain into the United States, without Weil's permission, represents a "copying" of the registered United States trademark.

a. The "territoriality" theory

Weil's argument relies in large measure upon a theoretical concept of trademark law, attributed to the Supreme Court's decision in *Katzel*, that

2. The specific character of the relationship between Lladro, S.A. and Weil is that they share a common parent corporation * * *.

is the subject of significant debate in the courts * * *. [T]hat theory recognizes the separate existence of a trademark in each territory in which it has been registered. * * *

In reaching its decision, the district court relied significantly upon the rationale of the Supreme Court's decision in *Katzel*. * * *

That case, however, does not present the same scenario as the present case. First, and perhaps most significantly, Bourjois was completely independent from the foreign manufacturer. It entered into an arms-length exchange to acquire the rights to the trademark with the clear intent that the foreign manufacturer would not market the trademarked good in the United States. Moreover, Bourjois obtained control over the quality of the product and, presumably, could have improved the quality of the product that it marketed in the United States while retaining use of the trademark. It had no control over the goods that the foreign manufacturer sold abroad which were imported into the United states and sold with the same trademark.

In the present case, no such compelling circumstances exist. Weil is not independent of the foreign manufacturer. Although it was not incorporated by Lladro, S.A., it nonetheless benefits from the corporate relationship that exits. Thus, even if Weil loses some share of its United States market to Jalyn, it nonetheless benefits from the profits it received as part of the corporate entity from which Jalyn purchased the goods abroad. Moreover, if that corporate entity decides that the profit margin from the sale of the goods to Jalyn abroad is not as significant as would be the profit margin from a United States market in which Jalyn did not compete, it has an obvious self-help mechanism: it can cease the sale to Jalyn abroad and thereby eliminate effectively its United States competition with Weil. We do not read the Lanham Act, however, to protect a foreign manufacturer—that either owns or is owned by a domestic trademark holder—from competition in the sale of its product in the United States by a domestic importer that it has supplied. Moreover, the LLADRO porcelain that Jalyn imports is *identical* to the porcelain that Weil distributes.[11] Weil has made no contention that, pursuant to its agreement with Lladro, S.A., Weil is entitled to, and does in fact, alter the quality of the porcelain that it distributes in the United States.

In our view, the Court's conclusion in *Katzel* does not represent the establishment of a broad "territoriality theory" applicable to every instance in which a domestic company acquires the United States trademark for a foreign manufactured good. We read that decision as creating an

---

11. This is the conclusion reached by the district court. The fact that it made no finding that the porcelain distributed by Jalyn and that distributed by Weil are materially different is significant to our disposition of this appeal. Weil has contended on this appeal that the porcelain imported by Jalyn was of a materially different grade and quality from the porcelain imported by Weil. If true, that fact would provide a stronger argument for Weil's claim of trademark infringement. * * * However, we cannot reach that conclusion on the findings of record, and we premise our decision on the assumption that the porcelain imported by Jalyn was essentially identical to that imported by Weil.

exception to the general application of trademark law in order to protect adequately the interests of domestic trademark holders such as Bourjois.

Our conclusion is consonant with both *K Mart* and *Katzel*, and illustrates the synthesis between those Supreme Court decisions. If placed within the context of the scenarios identified by the Court in *K Mart*, *Katzel* would be described as case 1. *K Mart* clearly held that § 526 was intended to protect domestic trademark holders in that type of case * * *.

b. Goods that "copy," "simulate," "counterfeit," or "imitate"

Having concluded that *Katzel* did not create a broad territoriality principle that is applicable to every instance of parallel imports, we can more easily resolve the remainder of Weil's argument regarding § 42 and § 32. Essentially, Weil argues that our reading of § 42's prohibition of goods that "copy or simulate" a United States trademark, and of § 32's similar proscription of the commercial distribution of goods that "counterfeit" or "imitate" a valid United States trademark, should be informed by the principle attributed to *Katzel*. Accordingly, it argues, Weil's registration of the LLADRO trademark in the United States should be viewed as having created a trademark in the United States that is distinct from any other mark (even the identical mark placed by the same manufacturer) and that that mark should be accorded the full measure of United States trademark law. Weil contends, therefore, that its trademark is "copied" by *any* unauthorized use. In that light, Weil argues that, notwithstanding the fact that the porcelain imported by Jalyn is genuine and that the marks affixed to the porcelain are placed by the manufacturer just as the marks affixed to the porcelain sold by Weil, the porcelain that Jalyn imports "copies" Weil's trademark.

Because of our conclusion that nothing in *Katzel* extends the trademark act protections to the circumstances of this case, we need not attempt the strained interpretation of the language of § 42 or § 32 that Weil advocates. Our inquiry is only to discern the plain meaning of the language of those sections and, on that review, we do not reach the conclusion urged by Weil.

As the starting point for our analysis, we must ascertain the appropriate definition to be given to the terms employed by § 42 and § 32 of the Lanham Act. In pertinent part § 42 provides that

> no article of imported merchandise ... which shall copy or simulate a trademark registered in accordance with the provisions of this chapter ... shall be admitted to entry at any custom house of the United States.

15 U.S.C. § 1124 (1982). Section 32(1)(a) provides that

> (1) [a]ny person who shall, without the consent of the registrant—
>
> > (a) use in commerce any reproduction, counterfeit, copy, or colorable imitation of a registered mark in connection with the

sale, offering for sale, distribution, or advertising of any goods or services on or in connection with which such use is likely to cause confusion, or to cause a mistake or to deceive; ... shall be liable in a civil action by the registrant for the remedies hereinafter provided.

15 U.S.C. § 1114(1)(a) (1982). Weil urges that § 42 is applicable to provide injunctive relief against importation even if § 526 does not and that § 32 is applicable to make damages available, and to provide injunctive relief against distribution, even if neither § 526 or § 42 bar importation. It contends that "the words 'copy or simulate' are neutral terms and are only directed to the physical and visual similarity between the registered mark and the mark on the imported product." Consequently, it argues, "[w]hether or not the act of importation is a violation of § 42 depends on whether the importation is *with or without* the consent of the registrant." *Id.* we can perceive of no basis, either in the specific language of the statute or in its underlying intent that supports such a reading.

In this inquiry of statutory construction, we are assisted again by the Supreme Court's decision in *K Mart* which noted that "[i]n ascertaining the plain meaning of [a] statute, the court must look to the particular statutory language at issue, as well as [to] the language and design of the statute as a whole." *K Mart*, 108 S.Ct. at 1817. In the light of these precedents, we look first to the plain language of the statute, which we do not find to be ambiguous. In our view, the language of these sections reflects Congress' intent to provide a remedy only to the domestic trademark holder who is injured by the distribution of *like* goods, which bear facsimile marks, that result in confusion to consumers or detriment to the goodwill developed by the trademark holder in the trademarked goods. "Trademark law generally does not reach the sale of *genuine* goods bearing a true mark even though such sale is without the owner's consent." *NEC Electronics*, 810 F.2d at 1509.

The terms "copy," "simulate," "counterfeit" and "imitate" have readily comprehensible ordinary meanings. They are used commonly to refer to items that resemble, but are not themselves, the original or genuine artifacts. We are convinced that the Congress understood this commonly held meaning of these terms and intended to apply them literally in §§ 42 and 32. We are, therefore, unpersuaded that those sections are properly applied to the present case.

Our analysis of the "design of the statute as a whole" compels us even more to the conclusion that we have reached. * * * [W]e discern two broad policy goals that Congress sought to foster by this legislation: (1) protection against consumer deception (i.e. purchase of a good that is not what the consumer intended to purchase, but because of packaging or other deceptive imitation of the trademark appears to be the genuine trademarked good); (2) protection of the trademark holder's investment in goodwill and noteworthiness that has been generated by the holder's advertisements and quality from imitative goods over which the trademark holder has no control of quality. Sections 42 and 32 advance these policy goals but neither of the goals is undermined by the importation of genuine goods as in this case. Consumers who purchase Jalyn imported LLADRO porcelain get precisely what they believed that they were purchasing. For that same reason, Weil's investment in and sponsorship of its trademark is not adversely affected because the goodwill that stands behind its product is not diminished by an association with goods of a lesser quality.

The only "injury" that we perceive Weil endures is the uncompensated for benefit that its advertisement and promotion of the trademark confers upon Jalyn. That loss to Weil is not inconsequential or insignificant. The remedy for it, however, is not properly found in the trademark law, particularly not in this case. Moreover, as we noted earlier, that "injury" is not completely uncompensated because Weil's parent corporation profits by the sale [to] Jalyn abroad.

* * * In this case * * * for all intents and purposes, the trademark holder and the manufacturer are the same and there is no reason that compels us to read anything in the language of the act and extend further the protections of the trademark act to this circumstance.[19]

* * *

NOTES AND QUESTIONS

1. *Trademark infringement.* Under the reasoning in *Weil*, how do you know when the mark on gray goods *is* the plaintiff's mark, as opposed to a "copy," "simulation," "imitation" or "counterfeit?" Putting aside the explicit language of Lanham Act §§ 32 and 42, what is the best argument that the defendant's use of the Lladro mark in this case caused a likelihood of consumer confusion?

As a practical matter, how does the rule in *Weil* compare to the Supreme Court's ruling in the *Quality King* case, *supra*, Ch. 4, construing the applicability of copyright law to parallel imports? How does it compare to the Federal Circuit's decision in *Jazz Photo*, *supra*, Ch. 3, regarding the application of U.S. patent law to parallel imports? Do the variations represented by these rulings make sense?

What are the economic and public policy implications of gray market goods? From a public policy perspective, should *K Mart* "case 2" U.S. trademark registrants be permitted to prohibit the sale of gray market goods in the U.S.? In all circumstances? In some circumstances? Would your view

---

19. We are aware that our conclusion results in the seeming anomaly that the language of the trademark act will be read one way in light of the circumstances of some cases (i.e., case 1) and that that same language will be read another way in all other circumstances. This result, however, we believe is correct and mandated by the decision of the Supreme Court in *Katzel*. The seeming conflict is made scrutable, however, with the recognition that the source of the added protection to trademark holders in the case 1 scenario is *Katzel* and § 526 (as that statute has been construed by the Customs Agency)—not in a subjectively different reading given to the text of the statute.

differ with regard to registrants in *K Mart* "case 3" situations? "Case 1" situations?

2. *Differing goods.* In *Weil*, the court stressed that the Lladro porcelain the defendant imported was identical to the porcelain the plaintiff distributed. It noted that if the plaintiff had demonstrated that the defendant's porcelain was of a materially different grade and quality, that fact would provide a stronger argument for finding trademark infringement. A number of Courts of Appeal have found trademark infringement in "case 2" gray market settings when the goods imported by the defendant differed materially from those sold by the plaintiff.

In Lever Brothers Co. v. United States, 877 F.2d 101 (D.C.Cir.1989), both the plaintiff and an affiliated company in the United Kingdom used the marks "Shield" for soap and "Sunlight" for dish detergent which they produced and sold in their respective countries. The soap and dish detergent each sold differed, however, in order to accommodate local tastes and conditions. For example, due to the preference for showers in the U.S., the U.S. Shield soap contained a higher concentration of coconut soap and fatty acids to generate lather quickly. Since the British prefer baths, which permit more time for lather to develop, the U.K. Shield had less of these ingredients. The U.K. Sunlight detergent was designed for water with a higher mineral content than is generally found in the U.S., and therefore did not perform as well as U.S. Sunlight in the soft water typical of U.S. metropolitan areas. Third parties imported U.K. Shield and Sunlight into the U.S. to sell in competition with the plaintiff.

The plaintiff asked the Customs Service to stop the U.K. Shield and Sunlight from entering the country, pursuant to Lanham Act § 42. The Customs Service declined to do so, invoking the "common control" exception to gray market protection, 19 C.F.R. § 133.21(c)(2), which the *K Mart* decision upheld in connection with Tariff Act § 526. The plaintiff argued that Customs could make no exception under § 42 when the goods being imported *differ* from the goods sold by the U.S. mark registrant. It argued that "where affiliated domestic and foreign firms produce goods bearing the same trademark, but different in physical content, the foreign products 'copy or simulate' the domestic trademark, so that § 42 forbids their importation, notwithstanding the fact of affiliation." *Lever Bros.*, 877 F.2d at 103–04. The Court of Appeals for the District of Columbia "tentatively" agreed with that view, remanding to the district court for further findings regarding legislative history and Customs' administrative practice.[18] The court noted that

> In Britain a request for "beer" will yield "bitter," a sort of ale with no exact equivalent here; an American seeking our "beer" over there must ask for "lager." Because of the differing conditions in the United States and United Kingdom, and the Lever affiliates' response to these conditions in the design of their products, Shield and Sunlight likewise have different meanings in the two countries. Thus the use of the trademarks

---

18. The District Court ultimately found that "section 42 of the Lanham Act prohibits the importation of foreign goods that bear a trademark identical to a valid United States trademark but which are physically different, regardless of the validity of the foreign trademark or the existence of an affiliation between the U.S. and foreign markholders." 796 F.Supp. 1, 5–6 (D.D.C.1992). The Court of Appeals affirmed this finding. 981 F.2d 1330 (D.C.Cir.1993).

for the UK versions in the United States is simply not truthful. The reasons that persuaded Holmes to deny relief in *Prestonettes* point toward granting it here.

Id., 877 F.2d at 108. The court concluded:

> We think the natural, virtually inevitable reading of § 42 is that it bars foreign goods bearing a trademark identical to a valid U.S. trademark but physically different, regardless of the trademarks' genuine character abroad or affiliation between the producing firms. On its face the section appears to aim at deceit and consumer confusion; when identical trademarks have acquired different meanings in different countries, one who imports the foreign version to sell it under that trademark will (in the absence of some specially differentiating feature) cause the confusion Congress sought to avoid. The fact of affiliation between the producers in no way reduces the probability of that confusion; it is certainly not a constructive consent to the importation. * * *

Id., 877 F.2d at 111.

In denying relief in *Weil*, the court stressed that the plaintiff had the means to prevent the gray market situation of which it complained. Would the same argument be applicable in *Lever Bros.*? See *Lever Bros.*, 877 F.2d at 101. Given that gray market goods provide consumers with lower price opportunities, could means other than prohibiting importation be found to avoid confusion caused by product differences? For example, could the problem of product differences be more appropriately resolved by requiring full disclosure of the differences at the point of sale?

In response to the Court of Appeals for the District of Columbia's decision in *Lever Bros.*, the U.S. Customs Service has revised its regulations to provide that "physically and materially different" goods bearing a genuine mark applied under the authority of the U.S. mark owner or its affiliate will be prohibited from entering the country *unless*:

> the merchandise or its packaging bears a conspicuous and legible label designed to remain on the product until the first point of sale to a retail consumer in the United States stating that: "This product is not a product authorized by the United States trademark owner for importation and is physically and materially different from the authorized product." The label must be in close proximity to the trademark as it appears in its most prominent location on the article itself or the retail package or container. Other information designed to dispel consumer confusion may also be added.

19 C.F.R. § 133.23(b). Will this precaution adequately dispel the consumer confusion issues identified in *Lever Bros.*? Are U.S. trademark owners likely to be satisfied with this action on the part of the Customs Service?

When should gray goods be deemed "different" for purposes of the *Lever Bros.* rule? In Societe Des Produits Nestle, S.A. v. Casa Helvetia, Inc., 982 F.2d 633 (1st Cir.1992), the Court of Appeals for the First Circuit reasoned that physical differences are not the only relevant differences. Other sorts of differences, such as warranty protection or service commitments, should also be considered. *Id.*, 982 F.2d at 638 n.7. The court concluded that when dealing with the importation of gray goods, a reviewing court must necessarily be concerned with subtle differences, for it is by subtle differences that consumers are most easily confused. For that reason, the threshold of materiality must be kept low enough to take account of potentially confusing differences—differences that are not blatant enough to make it obvious to the average consumer that the origin of the product differs from his or her expectations.

[T]he existence of any difference between the registrant's product and the allegedly infringing gray good that consumers would likely consider to be relevant when purchasing a product creates a presumption of consumer confusion sufficient to support a Lanham Trade–Mark Act claim.

Id., 982 F.2d at 641.

PROBLEMS

1. Crossley, Inc., a German manufacturer of fine writing instruments, sells its ball point and fountain pens under the "Crossley" mark throughout the world. In 2010, Crossley, Inc. purchased 55% of the stock of Pens & Such, a Delaware Corporation that was and remains the exclusive distributor of Crossley pens in the United States. Pens & Such was and remains the U.S. registered owner of the "Crossley" mark for pens in the U.S.

Grace Garcia, an international businesswoman, has purchased a large shipment of genuine "Crossley" ball point and fountain pens in Africa and shipped them to the U.S. for resale. Because the price of the pens in Africa was substantially lower than the price that Pens & Such charges in the U.S., Garcia has been able to undersell Pens & Such and still make a tidy profit. The pens Garcia sells are identical to those which Pens & Such sells in the U.S. However, the instructions and other written material accompanying the pens are in French, rather than in English. The pens that Pens & Such distributes under the Crossley mark have accompanying materials in English. Otherwise, the pens are packaged in the same way.

Pens & Such has brought suit against Garcia, alleging trademark infringement pursuant to Lanham Act §§ 32(a) and 42. What are the merits of its cause of action?

2. Lester Co., a Hungarian corporation that makes high-quality porcelain figurines, sells its figurines under the "Lester" mark throughout the world. It's wholly-owned subsidiary, Martin Imports, is the exclusive distributor of Lester figurines in the U.S., and has registered the "Lester" mark on the Lanham Act Principal Register. Martin does not import all of the styles of figurines that Lester manufactures and sells. Rather, it selects only some of those figurines for importation, based on its evaluation of the U.S. market, its desire to control the nature of the products on which the Lester mark is affixed, and the overall image of Lester products it wants to create in the U.S.

Nells, Inc., an American corporation, purchases genuine Lester products in other countries and imports them into the U.S. Some of the figurines that it imports and sells are the same as those imported and sold by Martin, but others are among those that Martin has decided not to import into the U.S.

Martin brings suit for trademark infringement against Nells, claiming that all of the Lester products it is importing are "materially different" from those that Martin sells under the Lester mark in the U.S. In the case of the figurines that are the same style as those imported by Martin, Martin argues that there is a material difference because it inspects the figurines as a matter of quality control before placing them on the retail market. Any cracked or broken figurines are discarded before they reach retail stores. Nells does not engage in such an inspection. How should the Court rule?

2. *Competitors' Use of Marks for Comparison Purposes*

SMITH v. CHANEL, INC.

United States Court of Appeals for the Ninth Circuit, 1968.
402 F.2d 562.

BROWNING, CIRCUIT JUDGE:

Appellant R. G. Smith, doing business as Ta'Ron, Inc., advertised a fragrance called "Second Chance" as a duplicate of appellees' "Chanel No. 5," at a fraction of the latter's price. Appellees were granted a preliminary injunction prohibiting any reference to Chanel No. 5 in the promotion or sale of appellants' product. This appeal followed.

The action rests upon a single advertisement published in "Specialty Salesmen," a trade journal directed to wholesale purchasers. The advertisement offered "The Ta'Ron Line of Perfumes" for sale. It gave the seller's address as "Ta'Ron Inc., 26 Harbor Cove, Mill Valley, Calif." It stated that the Ta'Ron perfumes "duplicate 100% perfect the exact scent of the world's finest and most expensive perfumes and colognes at prices that will zoom sales to volumes you have never before experienced." It repeated the claim of exact duplication in a variety of forms.

The advertisement suggested that a "Blindfold Test" be used "on skeptical prospects," challenging them to detect any difference between a well known fragrance and the Ta'Ron "duplicate." One suggested challenge was, "We dare you to try to detect any difference between Chanel #5 (25.00) and Ta'Ron's 2nd Chance. $7.00."

In an order blank printed as part of the advertisement each Ta'Ron fragrance was listed with the name of the well known fragrance which it purportedly duplicated immediately beneath. Below "Second Chance" appeared " *(Chanel #5)." The asterisk referred to a statement at the bottom of the form reading "Registered Trade Name of Original Fragrance House."

Appellees conceded below and concede here that appellants "have the right to copy, if they can, the unpatented formula of appellees' product." Moreover, for the purposes of these proceedings, appellees assume that "the products manufactured and advertised by [appellants] are *in fact* equivalents of those products manufactured by appellees." Finally, appellees disclaim any contention that the packaging or labeling of appellants' "Second Chance" is misleading or confusing.[4]

I

The principal question presented on this record is whether one who has copied an unpatented product sold under a trademark may use the trademark in his advertising to identify the product he has copied. We hold that he may, and that such advertising may not be enjoined under either the Lanham Act, 15 U.S.C. 1125(a) (1964), or the common law of unfair competition, so long as it does not contain misrepresentations or create a reasonable likelihood that purchasers will be confused as to the source, identity, or sponsorship of the advertiser's product.

* * *

The rule rests upon the traditionally accepted premise that the only legally relevant function of a trademark is to impart information as to the source or sponsorship of the product. Appellees argue that protection should also be extended to the trademark's commercially more important function of embodying consumer good will created through extensive, skillful, and costly advertising. The courts, however, have generally confined legal protection to the trademark's source identification function for reasons grounded in the public policy favoring a free, competitive economy.

Preservation of the trademark as a means of identifying the trademark owner's products, implemented both by the Lanham Act and the common law, serves an important public purpose.[13] It makes effective competition possible in a complex, impersonal marketplace by providing a means through which the consumer can identify products which please him and reward the producer with continued patronage. Without some such method of product identification, informed consumer choice, and hence meaningful competition in quality, could not exist.

On the other hand, it has been suggested that protection of trademark values other than source identification would create serious anti-competitive consequences with little compensating public benefit. This is said to be true for the following reasons.

The object of much modern advertising is "to impregnate the atmosphere of the market with the drawing power of a congenial symbol" rather than to communicate information as to quality or price. The primary value of the modern trademark lies in the "conditioned reflex developed in the buyer by imaginative or often purely monotonous selling of the mark itself." To the extent that advertising of this type succeeds, it

---

4. Appellants' product was packaged differently from appellees', and the only words appearing on the outside of appellants' packages were "Second Chance Perfume by Ta'Ron." The same words appeared on the front of appellants' bottles; the words "Ta'Ron trademark by International Fragrances, Inc., of Dallas and New York" appeared on the back.

13. It also serves two substantial private interests of the owner: It protects him from diversion of sales through a competitor's use of his trademark or one confusingly similar to it; and it protects his reputation from the injury that could occur if the competitor's goods were inferior.

is suggested, the trademark is endowed with sales appeal independent of the quality or price of the product to which it is attached; economically irrational elements are introduced into consumer choices; and the trademark owner is insulated from the normal pressures of price and quality competition. In consequence the competitive system fails to perform its function of allocating available resources efficiently.

Moreover, the economically irrelevant appeal of highly publicized trademarks is thought to constitute a barrier to the entry of new competition into the market. "The presence of irrational consumer allegiances may constitute an effective barrier to entry. Consumer allegiances built over the years with intensive advertising, trademarks, trade names, copyrights and so forth extend substantial protection to firms already in the market. In some markets this barrier to entry may be insuperable." High barriers to entry tend, in turn, to produce "high excess profits and monopolistic output restriction" and "probably * * * high and possibly excessive costs of sales promotion."

A related consideration is also pertinent to the present case. Since appellees' perfume was unpatented, appellants had a right to copy it, as appellees concede. There was a strong public interest in their doing so, "for imitation is the life blood of competition. It is the unimpeded availability of substantially equivalent units that permits the normal operation of supply and demand to yield the fair price society must pay for a given commodity." But this public benefit might be lost if appellants could not tell potential purchasers that appellants' product was the equivalent of appellees' product. "A competitor's chief weapon is his ability to represent his product as being equivalent and cheaper * * *." The most effective way (and, where complex chemical compositions sold under trade names are involved, often the only practical way) in which this can be done is to identify the copied article by its trademark or trade name. To prohibit use of a competitor's trademark for the sole purpose of identifying the competitor's product would bar effective communication of claims of equivalence. Assuming the equivalence of "Second Chance" and "Chanel No. 5," the public interest would not be served by a rule of law which would preclude sellers of "Second Chance" from advising consumers of the equivalence and thus effectively deprive consumers of knowledge that an identical product was being offered at one third the price.

As Justice Holmes wrote in Saxlehner v. Wagner, 216 U.S. 375, 30 S.Ct. 298, 54 L.Ed. 525 (1910), the practical effect of such a rule would be to extend the monopoly of the trademark to a monopoly of the product. The monopoly conferred by judicial protection of complete trademark exclusivity would not be preceded by examination and approval by a governmental body, as is the case with most other government-granted monopolies. Moreover, it would not be limited in time, but would be perpetual.

Against these considerations, two principal arguments are made for protection of trademark values other than source identification.

The first of these, as stated in the findings of the district court, is that the creation of the other values inherent in the trademark require "the expenditure of great effort, skill and ability," and that the competitor should not be permitted "to take a free ride" on the trademark owner's "widespread goodwill and reputation."

A large expenditure of money does not in itself create legally protectible rights. Appellees are not entitled to monopolize the public's desire for the unpatented product, even though they themselves created that desire at great effort and expense. As we have noted, the most effective way (and in some cases the only practical way) in which others may compete in satisfying the demand for the product is to produce it and tell the public they have done so, and if they could be barred from this effort appellees would have found a way to acquire a practical monopoly in the unpatented product to which they are not legally entitled.

Disapproval of the copyist's opportunism may be an understandable first reaction, "but this initial response to the problem has been curbed in deference to the greater public good." By taking his "free ride," the copyist, albeit unintentionally, serves an important public interest by offering comparable goods at lower prices. On the other hand, the trademark owner, perhaps equally without design, sacrifices public to personal interests by seeking immunity from the rigors of competition.

Moreover, appellees' reputation is not directly at stake. Appellants' advertisement makes it clear that the product they offer is their own. If it proves to be inferior, they, not appellees, will bear the burden of consumer disapproval.[25]

The second major argument for extended trademark protection is that even in the absence of confusion as to source, use of the trademark of another "creates a serious threat to the uniqueness and distinctiveness" of the trademark, and "if continued would create a risk of making a generic or descriptive term of the words" of which the trademark is composed.

The contention has little weight in the context of this case. Appellants do not use appellees' trademark as a generic term. They employ it only to describe appellees' product, not to identify their own. They do not label their product "Ta'Ron's Chanel No. 5," as they might if appellees' trademark had come to be the common name for the product to which it is applied. Appellants' use does not challenge the distinctiveness of appellees' trademark, or appellees' exclusive right to employ that trademark to indicate source or sponsorship. For reasons already discussed, we think appellees are entitled to no more. The slight tendency to carry the mark into the common language which even this use may have is outweighed by

---

25. In addition, if appellants' specific claims of equivalence are false, appellees may have a remedy under 43(a) of the Lanham Act, 15 U.S.C. 1125(a) (1964), which provides a civil remedy to a person injured by "any false description or representation, including words or other symbols * * * "of goods in interstate commerce. A common-law remedy may also be available. * * *

the substantial value of such use in the maintenance of effective competition.

We are satisfied, therefore, that both authority and reason require a holding that in the absence of misrepresentation or confusion as to source or sponsorship a seller in promoting his own goods may use the trademark of another to identify the latter's goods. * * *

* * *

NOTES AND QUESTIONS

1. *Use of the mark by competitors and others for comparison purposes.* In *Smith*, how does the defendant's use of the "Chanel No. 5" mark harm the plaintiff? Why is the defendant's "free ride" on the plaintiff's good will an insufficient basis for granting relief? Is the trademark law's acceptance of free riding consistent with the view taken in other intellectual property doctrines?

2. *The anti-competitive effects of marks.* Marks may be viewed as performing both an informative function and a persuasive function. In their informative function, marks identify the source of goods, and thus enable consumers to predict the goods' quality and characteristics and choose those goods that they prefer. Moreover, by enabling consumers to identify producers and reward quality through repeat patronage, marks encourage producers to provide quality goods. Marks in their informative function are clearly pro-competitive and beneficial to society as a whole. Since unauthorized use of a mark that causes a likelihood of confusion undermines the informative function of marks, courts are quick to prevent such uses.

In their persuasive function, marks provide the vehicle for persuasive advertising. While advertising can be informative, much of advertising is geared toward associating illusions of romance, success, adventure, glamour, patriotism, or other desired elements of "the good life" with the mark, and contains little or no actual informative content. Consumers are assured, directly or by implication, that the woman who buys Chanel perfume will be sexy, pursued by handsome men; the man who wears Foster Grant sunglasses will appear sophisticated; the young career person who drives a Toyota automobile will successfully climb the corporate ladder; the family that eats Jell-o gelatin for dessert will be a happy family. Inducing consumers to associate a mark with such illusions, via advertising, greatly enhances the selling power of the mark and consumer good will for the product the mark identifies. The plaintiff in *Smith* can be characterized as seeking protection for the persuasive, rather than the informative aspect of its prestigious Chanel mark: The parties assumed for purposes of the appeal that the defendant's use did not misinform the public, it merely capitalized on the fruits of the plaintiff's persuasive advertising via the mark. Should marks be protected strictly in their persuasive function? Will doing so ultimately benefit the public?

Some commentators have argued that persuasive advertising introduces economically irrational elements into consumer decision making and interferes with marketplace efficiency. The court in *Smith* refers to some of these arguments. How might mark advertising and promotion insulate the mark owner "from normal pressures of price and quality competition?" Will permitting the kind of mark use that occurred in *Smith* eliminate or reduce this problem? What about the argument that enjoining the defendant's use would encourage the defendant to market a new scent, which would be preferable to having two brands of the same scent? What is your assessment of the argument that the economically irrelevant appeal of highly publicized trademarks constitutes a barrier to the entry of new producers into the market? For excellent discussions of these issues see Brown, *Advertising and the Public Interest: Legal Protection of Trade Symbols*, 57 Yale L.J. 1165 (1948) (Considering "the economic waste and distortion of consumer choice growing out of large-scale persuasive advertising, it should be clear that the persuasive function of trade symbols is of dubious social utility. There seems little reason why the courts should recognize or protect interests deriving from it."); Landes & Posner, *Trademark Law: An Economic Perspective*, 30 J.L. & Econ. 265, 275 (1987) ("The hostile view of brand advertising has been largely and we think correctly rejected by economists. The fact that two goods have the same chemical formula does not make them of equal value to even the most coolly rational consumer."); 1 J.T. McCarthy, McCarthy on Trademarks and Unfair Competition § 2.38 (4th ed. 1996) ("[A]ntipathy towards 'irrational' advertising should be irrelevant in legal disputes over trademarks. If there is a problem, it should be met head on and directly debated as an issue of controlling advertising content, not used as a rationale to limit or deny trademark protection...."). Assuming that you agree with the proposition that the persuasive use of marks, through advertising, has anticompetitive effects, can you identify any offsetting positive effects?

Do you agree with the *Smith* Court's statement that "a large expenditure of money does not in itself create legally protectible rights"?

PROBLEMS

1. An automobile repair shop displays a sign stating: "Independent Volkswagen–Porsche Service." The owner of the Volkswagen mark for cars and for authorized service for the cars sues for trademark infringement. What is your evaluation?

2. Two of your clients are producing "knock-off" perfumes (perfumes that copy the scent of other, brand-name perfumes) and plan to sell them through drug stores and discount stores with the following packaging. What, if any, problems are the clients likely to encounter?

3.   *The Fair Use Defense*

a.   *"Classic" Fair Use*

As discussed in the introduction to this chapter, the common law of unfair competition required that persons claiming rights in descriptive and surname marks not only demonstrate that they had acquired secondary meaning, but also that the defendant had used its allegedly infringing word or symbol for that secondary (trademark) meaning, rather than for its "primary," descriptive, geographically descriptive or surname meaning, and had done so in bad faith. This requirement was meant to ensure that businesses could not use the law to monopolize words or symbols that other marketplace actors might legitimately need to use in their own marketing activities, and thus interfere improperly with the free flow of useful product information to consumers. When Congress enacted the Lanham Act, it codified this common-law limitation on rights in secondary meaning marks, but set it as a defense, rather than as a part of the plaintiff's case-in-chief. Lanham Act § 33(b)(4) provides a defense to infringement if the defendant's use

> is a use, otherwise than as a mark, of the [defendant's] individual name in his own business, or of the individual name of anyone in privity with [the defendant], or of a term or device which is descriptive of and used fairly and in good faith only to describe the goods or services of [the defendant], or their geographic origin.

15 U.S.C.A. § 1115(b)(4). This provision is generally known as the "fair use" defense. As Judge Leval explained in United States Shoe Corp. v. Brown Group, Inc., 740 F.Supp. 196 (S.D.N.Y.1990):

> * * * [T]he fact that one [candy producer] might acquire trademark rights over a descriptive identifier like "chewy" or "lemon flavored" cannot deprive society of the opportunity to be advised by other manufacturers that their candy is chewy or lemon flavored. Therefore, notwithstanding the establishment of trademark rights over a descriptive term by a showing that it has acquired secondary meaning, the statute preserves in others the right to the use of such terms "fairly and in good faith only to describe [and not to designate] the goods or services." 15 U.S.C. § 1115(b)(4).

Id., 740 F.Supp. at 198–99.

In evaluating a fair use defense, courts undertake to determine what the defendant's likely purpose was in using the contested word or symbol. They rely on circumstantial evidence to make that evaluation. Factors that courts typically consider include how the defendant employed the word or symbol—its prominence, style, and placement on the defendant's labels, packaging or advertising—and whether the defendant has emulated the plaintiff's style of presenting the mark or the plaintiff's packaging. They also consider whether the defendant prominently displayed its own, differentiating mark; the relevance or accuracy of the word or symbol's primary meaning in describing the defendant's product or service; and whether the defendant took precautionary measures to avoid consumer confusion. For example, in finding that the defendant's use of the words "dentists' choice" in advertisements for Crest toothpaste constituted a fair use of the plaintiff's registered mark, "Dentists' Choice," the court emphasized that the defendant always used the words along with its "Crest" mark, prominently displayed, which indicated the source of its product. Moreover, the defendant always displayed the words "dentists' choice" in conjunction with other text, so that the words did not stand out unduly. Wonder Labs, Inc. v. Procter & Gamble Co., 728 F.Supp. 1058, 1064 (S.D.N.Y.1990).

How does a finding of fair use differ from a finding that the defendant did not make a "trademark use" or "use in commerce" of the mark? How does a finding of fair use differ from a finding that the defendant's use is unlikely to cause confusion? For in-depth discussion of the historical development and meaning of the fair use defense, see Barrett, *Reconciling Fair Use and Trademark Use,* 28 Cardozo J. L. & Arts 1 (2010).

KP PERMANENT MAKE–UP, INC. v. LASTING IMPRESSION I, INC.

United States Supreme Court, 2004.
543 U.S. 111, 125 S.Ct. 542, 160 L.Ed.2d 440.

JUSTICE SOUTER delivered the opinion of the Court.

The question here is whether a party raising the statutory affirmative defense of fair use to a claim of trademark infringement, 15 U.S.C. § 1115(b)(4), has the burden to negate any likelihood that the practice complained of will confuse consumers about the origin of the goods or services affected. We hold it does not.

[The Circuit Courts of Appeals had split over the ability of a trademark infringement defendant to successfully assert a fair use defense if his use caused a likelihood of confusion. The Ninth, Sixth, and Fifth Circuits had all held that a likelihood of confusion bars a fair use defense. The Second, Fourth, and Seventh Circuits had held that a fair use defense could succeed even if the defendant's use did cause a likelihood of confusion. In siding with the latter group of Circuits, the Supreme Court discussed how imposing a duty on the defendant to prove an *absence* of likely confusion conflicts with the relevant statutory language and common-law traditions: The plaintiff bears the burden to demonstrate a likelihood of confusion by a preponderance of the evidence. Moreover, to hold that an affirmative defense is only available when the plaintiff is unable to bear his burden of proof would make no sense.]

Since the burden of proving likelihood of confusion rests with the plaintiff, and the fair use defendant has no free-standing need to show confusion unlikely, it follows (contrary to the Court of Appeals' view) that some possibility of consumer confusion must be compatible with fair use, and so it is. The common law's tolerance of a certain degree of confusion on the part of consumers followed from the very fact that in cases like this one an originally descriptive term was selected to be used as a mark, not to mention the undesirability of allowing anyone to obtain a complete monopoly on use of a descriptive term simply by grabbing it first. The Lanham Act adopts a similar leniency, there being no indication that the statute was meant to deprive commercial speakers of the ordinary utility of descriptive words. "If any confusion results, that is a risk the plaintiff accepted when it decided to identify its product with a mark that uses a well known descriptive phrase." * * * This right to describe is the reason that descriptive terms qualify for registration as trademarks only after taking on secondary meaning as "distinctive of the applicant's goods," 15 U.S.C. § 1052(f), with the registrant getting an exclusive right not in the original, descriptive sense, but only in the secondary one associated with the markholder's goods, 2 McCarthy, *supra,* § 11:45 ("The only aspect of the mark which is given legal protection is that penumbra or fringe of secondary meaning which surrounds the old descriptive word").

While we thus recognize that mere risk of confusion will not rule out fair use, we think it would be improvident to go further in this case, for deciding anything more would take us beyond the Ninth Circuit's consideration of the subject. It suffices to realize that our holding that fair use can occur along with some degree of confusion does not foreclose the relevance of the extent of any likely consumer confusion in assessing whether a defendant's use is objectively fair. Two Courts of Appeals have found it relevant to consider such scope, and commentators and *amici* here have urged us to say that the degree of likely consumer confusion bears not only on the fairness of using a term, but even on the further question whether an originally descriptive term has become so identified as a mark that a defendant's use of it cannot realistically be called descriptive. * * *

Since we do not rule out the pertinence of the degree of consumer confusion under the fair use defense, we likewise do not pass upon the position of the United States, as *amicus,* that the "used fairly" requirement in § 1115(b)(4) demands only that the descriptive term describe the goods accurately. Accuracy of course has to be a consideration in assessing fair use, but the proceedings in this case so far raise no occasion to evaluate some other concerns that courts might pick as relevant, quite apart from attention to confusion. The Restatement raises possibilities like commercial justification and the strength of the plaintiff's mark. Restatement § 28. As to them, it is enough to say here that the door is not closed.

* * *

b. *"Nominative" Fair Use*

The Court of Appeals for the Ninth Circuit has devised a second fair use doctrine, which it calls "nominative fair use." The nominative fair use doctrine "acknowledges that 'it is often virtually impossible to refer to a particular product for purposes of comparison, criticism, point of reference or any other purpose without using the mark'." Horphag Research Ltd. v. Pellegrini, 337 F.3d 1036, 1041 (9th Cir. 2003). The nominative fair use doctrine permits such referential use of a plaintiff's mark, as long as the use "does not attempt to capitalize on consumer confusion or to appropriate the cachet of one product for a different one." New Kids on the Block v. News America Publishing, Inc., 971 F.2d 302 (9th Cir. 1992). The Ninth Circuit looks to three factors to determine whether the defendant's use is a non-infringing nominative fair use:

(1) The plaintiff's product must not be readily identifiable without use of the mark;

(2) Only so much of the plaintiff's mark may be used as is reasonably necessary to identify the plaintiff's product; and

(3) The defendant must do nothing that would, in conjunction with the mark, suggest sponsorship or endorsement by the trademark holder.

New Kids, supra, 971 F.2d at 308. The court has explained that

> In cases in which the defendant raises a nominative use defense, the [*New Kids*] three-factor test should be applied instead of the test for likelihood of confusion set forth in *Sleekcraft*. The three-factor test better evaluates the likelihood of confusion in nominative use cases. When a defendant uses a trademark nominally, the trademark will be identical to the plaintiff's mark, at least in terms of the words in question. Thus, application of the *Sleekcraft* test, which focuses on the similarity of the mark used by the plaintiff and the defendant, would lead to the incorrect conclusion that virtually all nominative uses are confusing. The three-factor test—with its requirements that the defendant use marks only when no descriptive substitute exists, use no more of the mark than necessary, and do nothing to suggest sponsorship or endorsement by the mark holder—better addresses concerns regarding the likelihood of confusion in nominative use cases.

Playboy Enterprises, Inc. v. Welles, 279 F.3d 796, 801 (9th Cir. 2002). In response to the Supreme Court's opinion in *KP Permanent,* the Ninth Circuit has recently clarified that a defendant seeking to assert nominative fair use does not carry the burden of demonstrating no likelihood of confusion under the three-factor test. It must only demonstrate that it used the plaintiff's mark to refer to the plaintiff or its goods or services. At that point the plaintiff acquires the burden of proving that the defendant's use was *not* a nominative fair use under the three factors. Toyota Motor Sales, U.S.A., Inc. v. Tabari, 610 F.3d 1171 (9th Cir. 2010).

The Third Circuit has adopted its own version of nominative fair use—a bifurcated standard. Century 21 Real Estate Corp. v. LendingTree, Inc., 425 F.3d 211 (3d Cir. 2005). First, the plaintiff must prove likelihood of confusion under a "modified version" of the traditional likelihood of confusion test, which ignores the strength of the plaintiff's mark and the similarity of the marks, and emphasizes the degree of consumer care, length of time the defendant has used the mark without evidence of actual confusion, defendant's intent in adopting the mark, and evidence of actual confusion. If the plaintiff is able to prove a likelihood of confusion under this modified test, the burden then shifts to the defendant to demonstrate fairness under a "three-pronged test" "derived to a great extent" from the Ninth Circuit's nominative fair use standard:

1) Is the use of plaintiff's mark necessary to describe both the plaintiff's product or service and the defendant's product or service?

2) Does the defendant use only so much of the plaintiff's mark as is necessary to describe plaintiff's product?

3) Does the defendant's conduct or language reflect the true and accurate relationship between plaintiff and defendant's products or services?

Id., 425 F.3d at 222.

NOTES AND QUESTIONS

1. *The proper approach to nominative fair use.* Which approach to evaluating nominative use seems better, the Ninth Circuit's or the Third Circuit's? What advantage do multi-factor tests such as those adopted by the Ninth and Third Circuits provide over the more traditional, *ad hoc* evaluation of nominative use, as exemplified by *Smith v. Chanel, supra*? Is there any detriment that might arise from setting up a concrete, multi-part nominative fair use evaluation?

2. *Incorporation of marks in domain names and nominative fair use.* The Court of Appeals for the Ninth Circuit has reasoned that the nominative fair use defense should extend to business defendants who truthfully incorporate a plaintiff's a mark into their domain name to indicate that they buy, sell, repair, or otherwise deal with the plaintiff's goods or services. According to the court:

> [T]he wholesale prohibition of nominative use in domain names * * * would be unfair. It would be unfair to merchants seeking to communicate the nature of the service or product offered at their sites. And it would be unfair to consumers, who would be deprived of an increasingly important means of receiving such information. [T]his would have serious First Amendment implications. The only winners would be [trademark owners], which would acquire greater control over the markets for goods and services related to their trademarked brands, to the detriment of competition and consumers. The nominative fair use doctrine is designed to prevent this type of abuse of the rights granted by the Lanham Act.

Toyota Motor Sales, U.S.A., Inc. v. Tabari, 610 F.3d 1171, 1180 (9th Cir. 2010). The court suggested that the third nominative fair use factor (whether the defendant does something that would, in conjunction with reference to the mark, suggest sponsorship or endorsement by the trademark holder) might preclude a finding of nominative fair use if the defendant simply adopts "trademark.com" (or ".org" or ".net") as its domain name, because that will usually suggest to consumers that the defendant's site is the trademark owner's official site. This might also be true if the defendant adopts additional words, like "trademark-USA.com," "trademark-of-cleveland.com," "etrademark.com," "officialtrademark.com," or "wearetrademark.com." Such additional words affirmatively suggest sponsorship or endorsement by the trademark holder. However, in most cases, adding additional words will pass muster under the third factor. In *Tabari*, the court suggested that the defendants, who were independent automobile brokers who specialized in arranging sales of Toyota's "Lexus" cars, could, consistently with the nominative fair use doctrine, use domain names such as "lexusbroker.com," "buy-a-lexus.com," or "buyorleaselexus.com." The court dismissed concerns about consumer confusion in such cases:

> When a domain name making nominative use of a mark does not actively suggest sponsorship or endorsement, the worst that can happen is that some consumers may arrive at the site uncertain as to what they will find. But in the age of FIOS, cable modems, DSL and T1 lines, reasonable, prudent and experienced internet consumers are accustomed to such exploration by trial and error. They skip from site to site, ready to hit the back button whenever they're not satisfied with a site's contents. They fully expect to find some sites that aren't what they imagine based on a glance at the domain name or search engine summary. Outside the special case of trademark.com, or domains that actively claim affiliation with the trademark holder, consumers don't form any firm expectations about the sponsorship of a website until they've seen the landing page—if then. This is sensible agnosticism, not consumer confusion. So long as the site as a whole does not suggest sponsorship or endorsement by the trademark holder, such momentary uncertainty does not preclude a finding of nominative fair use.

Id., at 1179.

3. *Nominative fair use vs. classic fair use.* What is the difference between classic fair use and nominative fair use? The Ninth Circuit addressed this question in the *Horphag* case:

> The nominative fair use analysis is appropriate where a defendant has used the plaintiff's mark to describe the plaintiff's product, even if the defendant's ultimate goal is to describe his own product. Conversely, the classic fair use analysis is appropriate where a defendant has used the plaintiff's mark only to describe his own product, and not at all to describe the plaintiff's product.

> * * *

> The classic fair use defense "applies only to marks that possess both a primary meaning and a secondary meaning—and only when the mark is used in its primary descriptive sense rather than in its trademark sense."

Horphag, 337 F.3d at 1040–41.

PROBLEMS

1. Plaintiff manufactures and sells air fresheners for cars in the shape of a pine tree. Its air fresheners are made of flat scented cardboard and come in a variety of colors and odors, including a green pine-scented version. They have a string attached to the top of the tree, so that they can be hung from the rear-view mirror of an automobile. Plaintiff has been found to have trademark rights in the pine-tree shape of its product: The court has found the mark to be suggestive, and thus inherently distinctive.

Defendant sells air fresheners under the trademark "Glade." One of the products in its line, the "Plug–In," is designed to be plugged into electrical outlets. The Plug–Ins have a plastic casing that holds a replaceable fragrance cartridge of scented gel. When the unit is plugged in, the electrical current warms the gel, causing release of the fragrance into the air. During the Christmas holiday season, defendant sells a pine-tree-shaped plug-in air freshener called "Holiday Pine Potpourri." This product comes in boxes bearing the "Glade Plug–Ins" trademark, as well defendant's corporate logo. Each unit has "Glade" imprinted across the front of the product itself.

Plaintiff sues defendant, claiming that defendant's pine-tree-shaped plug-in freshener infringes plaintiff's trademark rights in the pine-tree shape for air fresheners. Does the defendant have a viable fair use defense?

2. Plaintiff Playboy Enterprises, Inc. owns the federally registered marks "Playboy," "Playmate," "Playmate of the Month," and "Playmate of the Year." Plaintiff often uses the abbreviation "PMOY" for the term "Playmate of the Year."

Defendant Terri Welles is a self-employed model who began her modeling career with plaintiff's Playboy magazine in 1980. In May of 1980, Ms. Welles appeared on the cover of Playboy magazine and was subsequently featured as the Playmate of the Month in the December 1980 issue. Ms. Welles received plaintiff's Playmate of the Year award in June, 1981. Since 1980, Welles has appeared in thirteen issues of Playboy magazine and eighteen newsstand specials published by the plaintiff.

In 1997, Welles created a web site, which includes photographs of herself (both nude and clothed), a fan club posting board, an autobiography section, a listing of current events and personal appearances, links to other erotic, adult-oriented web sites, and some advertising banners. The domain name for the site is "terriwelles.com," the heading for the web site is "Terri Welles— Playmate of the Year 1981," and the title of the link page is "Terri Welles— Playboy Playmate of the Year 1981." Each of the pages uses "PMOY 1981" as a repeating watermark in the background. Eleven of the fifteen free web pages include a disclaimer at the bottom of the page which indicates that the web site is not endorsed by plaintiff. Defendant also uses the terms "Playboy" and "Playmate," along with other terms, in the keywords section of her metatags.

Plaintiff sues for trademark infringement, seeking to enjoin defendant from 1) using the term "Playmate of the Year" in the title of her home page and link page; 2) using the watermark "PMOY 1981" in the background; and 3) using the terms "Playboy" and "Playmate" in the web site's metatags. Does defendant have a viable fair use defense?

3. Acme and Zeta are direct competitors in the market for widgets. Zeta sets up a web site under the domain name "Zeta.com." It repeatedly places the following phrases both in its metatags and throughout the text of the web site: "We are not Acme—we're better," "We sell widgets for less than Acme," "Compare our low prices with Acme's high prices," and "We sell better quality widgets than Acme." All in all, the word "Acme" appears hundreds of times in this form, both in Zeta's metatags and in visible text on Zeta's site. Acme sues Zeta for infringement. Should Zeta be held liable?

D. TRADEMARK DILUTION

STARBUCKS CORP. v. WOLFE'S BOROUGH COFFEE, INC.

United States Court of Appeals, Second Circuit, 2009.
588 F.3d 97.

MINER, CIRCUIT JUDGE:

[Starbucks appeals from the district court's judgment in favor of the defendant, Wolfe's Borough Coffee, Inc., d/b/a Black Bear Micro Roastery ("Black Bear"). The district court found that Starbucks failed to demonstrate entitlement to relief on its federal trademark infringement and dilution claims. The court of appeals affirms the district court's finding of no trademark infringement, but vacates and remands on the issue of whether Starbucks demonstrated a likelihood of dilution by "blurring."]

A. Preliminary Facts

Starbucks, a company primarily engaged in the sale of coffee products, was founded in Seattle, Washington in 1971. Since its founding, Starbucks has grown to over 8,700 retail locations in the United States, Canada, and 34 foreign countries and territories. In addition to operating its retail stores, Starbucks supplies its coffees to hundreds of restaurants, supermarkets, airlines, sport and entertainment venues, motion picture theaters, hotels, and cruise ship lines. Starbucks also maintains an internet site that generates over 350,000 "hits" per week from visitors.

In conducting all of its commercial activities, Starbucks prominently displays its registered "Starbucks" marks (the "Starbucks Marks") on its products and areas of business. The Starbucks Marks include, *inter alia,* the tradename "Starbucks" and its logo, which is circular and generally contains a graphic of a mermaid-like siren encompassed by the phrase "Starbucks Coffee." Starbucks "has been the subject of U.S. trademark registrations continuously since 1985" and has approximately 60 U.S. trademark registrations. Starbucks also has foreign trademark registrations in 130 countries.

From fiscal years 2000 to 2003, Starbucks spent over $136 million on advertising, promotion, and marketing activities. * * *

    * * *

Black Bear, also a company engaged in the sale of coffee products, has its principal place of business in Tuftonboro, New Hampshire. In contrast to Starbucks, Black Bear is a relatively small company owned by Jim Clark and his wife. It is a family-run business that "manufactures and sells ... roasted coffee beans and related goods via mail order, internet order, and at a limited number of New England supermarkets." Black Bear also sold coffee products from a retail outlet called "The Den," in Portsmouth, New Hampshire. * * *

In April 1997, Black Bear began selling a "dark roasted blend" of coffee called "Charbucks Blend" and later "Mister Charbucks" (together, the "Charbucks Marks"). Charbucks Blend was sold in a packaging that showed a picture of a black bear above the large font "BLACK BEAR MICRO ROASTERY." The package informed consumers that the coffee was roasted and "Air Quenched" in New Hampshire and, in fairly large font, that "You wanted it dark ... You've got it dark!" Mister Charbucks was sold in a packaging that showed a picture of a man walking above the large font "Mister Charbucks." The package also informed consumers that the coffee was roasted in New Hampshire by "The Black Bear Micro Roastery" and that the coffee was "ROASTED TO THE EXTREME ... FOR THOSE WHO LIKE THE EXTREME."

Not long after [Black Bear made] its first sale of Charbucks Blend, in August 1997, Starbucks demanded that Black Bear cease use of the Charbucks Marks. Having felt wrongly threatened by Starbucks, and believing that "[w]e hadn't done anything wrong," Black Bear ultimately decided to continue selling its "Charbucks Blend" and "Mister Charbucks." Mr. Clark later testified, "[m]y main objection was that basically this was a large corporation coming at me and saying, telling us what to do, and, oh, by the way you're going to pay for it, too.... [S]ome of the requests that they were making were really off the wall."

* * *

B. Federal Trademark Dilution

Under federal law, an owner of a "famous, distinctive mark" is entitled to an "injunction against the user of a mark that is 'likely to cause dilution' of the famous mark." Although the requirement that the mark be "famous" and "distinctive" significantly limits the pool of marks that may receive dilution protection, that the Starbucks Marks are "famous" within the meaning of 15 U.S.C. § 1125(c) is not disputed by the parties in this case. Rather, the focus of this appeal is on dilution itself. As specified by statute, federal dilution is actionable in two situations: (1) dilution by "blurring" and (2) dilution by "tarnishment." 15 U.S.C. § 1125(c).

1. Dilution by Blurring

Dilution by blurring is an "association arising from the similarity between a mark or trade name and a famous mark that impairs the distinctiveness of the famous mark," 15 U.S.C. § 1125(c)(2)(B), and may be found "regardless of the presence or absence of actual or likely confusion, of competition, or of actual economic injury," 15 U.S.C. § 1125(c)(1). Some classic examples of blurring include "hypothetical anomalies as Dupont shoes, Buick aspirin tablets, Schlitz varnish, Kodak pianos, Bulova gowns, and so forth." *See Mead Data Cent., Inc. v. Toyota Motor Sales, U.S.A., Inc.,* 875 F.2d 1026, 1031 (2d Cir.1989); *see also id.* (stating that the primary concern in blurring actions is preventing "the whittling away of an established trademark's selling power through its unauthorized use by others.'").

Federal law specifies six non-exhaustive factors for the courts to consider in determining whether there is dilution by blurring:

(i) The degree of similarity between the mark or trade name and the famous mark.

(ii) The degree of inherent or acquired distinctiveness of the famous mark.

(iii) The extent to which the owner of the famous mark is engaging in substantially exclusive use of the mark.

(iv) The degree of recognition of the famous mark.

(v) Whether the user of the mark or trade name intended to create an association with the famous mark.

(vi) Any actual association between the mark or trade name and the famous mark.

15 U.S.C. § 1125(c)(2)(B)(i)–(vi). The District Court found that the second, third, and fourth factors favored Starbucks, and those findings are not challenged in this appeal.

With respect to the first factor—the degree of similarity between the marks—the District Court did not clearly err in finding that the Charbucks Marks were minimally similar to the Starbucks Marks. Although "Ch"arbucks is similar to "St"arbucks in sound and spelling, it is evident from the record that the Charbucks Marks—as they are presented to consumers—are minimally similar to the Starbucks Marks. The Charbucks line of products are presented as either "Mister Charbucks" or "Charbucks Blend" in packaging that displays the "Black Bear" name in no subtle manner, and the packaging also makes clear that Black Bear is a "Micro Roastery" located in New Hampshire. * * * Moreover, Black Bear's package design for Charbucks coffee is "different in imagery, color, and format from Starbucks' logo and signage." For example, either a graphic of a bear or a male person is associated with Charbucks, and those marks are not comparable to the Starbucks graphic of a siren in pose, shape, art-style, gender, or overall impression. Indeed, the Starbucks siren appears nowhere on the Charbucks package. To the extent the Charbucks Marks are presented to the public through Black Bear's website, the dissimilarity between the marks is still evident as the Charbucks brand of coffee is accompanied by Black Bear's domain name, www.blackbearcoffee.com, and other products, such as shirts and cups, displaying Black Bear's name.

* * *

Upon its finding that the marks were not substantially similar, however, the District Court concluded that "[t]his dissimilarity alone is sufficient to defeat [Starbucks'] blurring claim, and in any event, this factor at a minimum weighs strongly against [Starbucks] in the dilution analysis." We conclude that the District Court erred to the extent it required "substantial" similarity between the marks, and, in this connection, we note that the court may also have placed undue significance on the similarity factor in determining the likelihood of dilution in its alternative analysis.

Prior to the [Trademark Dilution Reform Act of 2006—"TDRA"], this Court has held that "[a] plaintiff cannot prevail on a state or federal dilution claim unless the marks at issue are 'very' or 'substantially similar.'" *Playtex Prods., Inc v. Georgia–Pacific Corp.*, 390 F.3d 158, 167 (2d Cir. 2004). Notably, under the pre-TDRA law, the federal statute provided a remedy for dilution of famous marks but did not define "dilution," much less inform the courts of the importance of "similarity" in the dilution analysis.

> The owner of a famous mark shall be entitled, subject to the principles of equity and upon such terms as the court deems reasonable, to an injunction against another person's commercial use in commerce of a mark or trade name, if such use begins after the mark has become famous and causes dilution of the distinctive quality of the mark....

15 U.S.C. § 1125(c) (2000). Our adoption of a "substantially similar" requirement for federal dilution claims can likely be attributed to the lack of guidance under the former federal statute and the existence of a "substantially similar" requirement under state dilution statutes, which were better defined.

The post-TDRA federal dilution statute, however, provides us with a compelling reason to discard the "substantially similar" requirement for federal trademark dilution actions. The current federal statute defines dilution by blurring as an "association arising from the similarity between a mark ... and a famous mark that impairs the distinctiveness of the famous mark," and the statute lists six non-exhaustive factors for determining the existence of an actionable claim for blurring. 15 U.S.C. § 1125(c)(2)(B). Although "similarity" is an integral element in the definition of "blurring," we find it significant that the federal dilution statute does not use the words "very" or "substantial" in connection with the similarity factor to be considered in examining a federal dilution claim. * * *

Indeed, one of the six statutory factors informing the inquiry as to whether the allegedly diluting mark "impairs the distinctiveness of the famous mark" is "[t]he *degree* of similarity between the mark or trade name and the famous mark." 15 U.S.C. § 1125(c)(2)(B)(i) (emphasis added). Consideration of a "degree" of similarity as a factor in determining the likelihood of dilution does not lend itself to a requirement that the similarity between the subject marks must be "substantial" for a dilution claim to succeed. Moreover, were we to adhere to a substantial similarity requirement for all dilution by blurring claims, the significance of the remaining five factors would be materially diminished because they would have no relevance unless the degree of similarity between the marks are initially determined to be "substantial." Such requirement of substantial similarity is at odds with the federal dilution statute, which lists "degree of similarity" as *one* of several factors in determining blurring. * * * Accordingly, the District Court erred to the extent it focused on the absence of "substantial similarity" between the Charbucks Marks and the Starbucks Marks to dispose of Starbucks' dilution claim. We note that the court's error likely affected its view of the importance of the other factors in analyzing the blurring claim, which must ultimately focus on whether an *association,* arising from the similarity between the subject marks, "impairs the distinctiveness of the famous mark." 15 U.S.C. § 1125(c)(2)(B).

Turning to the remaining two disputed factors—(1) whether the user of the mark intended to create an association with the famous mark, and (2) whether there is evidence of any actual association between the mark and the famous mark—we conclude that the District Court also erred in considering these factors.

The District Court determined that Black Bear possessed the requisite intent to associate Charbucks with Starbucks but that this factor did not weigh in favor of Starbucks because Black Bear did not act in "bad faith." The determination of an "intent to associate," however, does not require the additional consideration of whether bad faith corresponded with that intent. The plain language of section 1125(c) requires only the consideration of "[w]hether the user of the mark or trade name intended to create an association with the famous mark." *See* 15 U.S.C. § 1125(c)(2)(B)(v). * * * Thus, where, as here, the allegedly diluting mark was created with an intent to associate with the famous mark, this factor favors a finding of a likelihood of dilution.

The District Court also determined that there was not an "actual association" favoring Starbucks in the dilution analysis. Starbucks, however, submitted the results of a telephone survey where 3.1% of 600 consumers responded that Starbucks was the possible source of Charbucks. The survey also showed that 30.5% of consumers responded "Starbucks" to the question: "[w]hat is the first thing that comes to mind when you hear the name 'Charbucks.' " In rejecting Starbucks' claim of actual association, the District Court referred to evidence supporting the absence of "actual *confusion*" to conclude that "the evidence is insufficient to make the ... factor weigh in [Starbucks'] favor to any significant degree." This was error, as the absence of actual or even of a likelihood of confusion does not undermine evidence of trademark dilution. * * *

      * * *

2. Dilution by Tarnishment

Dilution by tarnishment is an "association arising from the similarity between a mark or trade name and a famous mark that harms the reputation of the famous mark." 15 U.S.C. § 1125(c)(2)(C). "A trademark may be tarnished when it is linked to products of shoddy quality, or is portrayed in an unwholesome or unsavory context, with the result that the public will associate the lack of quality or lack of prestige in the defendant's goods with the plaintiff's unrelated goods." *Hormel Foods Corp. v. Jim Henson Productions, Inc.*, 73 F.3d 497, 507 (2d Cir.1996). A trademark may also be diluted by tarnishment if the mark loses its ability to serve as a "wholesome identifier" of plaintiff's product. *Id.; accord Chemical Corp. v. Anheuser–Busch, Inc.*, 306 F.2d 433 (5th Cir.1962) (finding that use of exterminator's slogan "where there's life, ... there's Bugs" tarnished the use of beer company's slogan "where there's life, ... there's Bud.") * * *.

Starbucks argues that the District Court "erred by failing to find that 'Charbucks' damages the positive reputation of Starbucks by evoking both 'Starbucks' and negative impressions in consumers, including the image of bitter, over-roasted coffee." Starbucks reasons that it has shown dilution by tarnishment because, pursuant to its survey, (1) 30.5% of persons surveyed "immediately associated 'Charbucks' with 'Starbucks' "; and (2) 62% of those surveyed who associated "Charbucks" with "Starbucks" "indicated that they would have a negative impression" of a "coffee named 'Charbucks.' " We are unpersuaded by Starbucks' reasoning.

To the extent Starbucks relies on the survey, a mere association between "Charbucks" and "Starbucks," coupled with a negative impression of the name "Charbucks," is insufficient to establish a likelihood of dilution by tarnishment. That a consumer may associate a negative-sounding junior mark with a famous mark says little of whether the consumer views the junior mark as harming the reputation of the famous mark. The more relevant question, for purposes of tarnishment, would have been how a hypothetical coffee named either "Mister Charbucks" or "Charbucks Blend" would affect the positive impressions about the coffee sold by Starbucks. We will not assume that a purportedly negative-sounding junior mark will likely harm the reputation of the famous mark by mere association when the survey conducted by the party claiming dilution could have easily enlightened us on the matter. Indeed, it may even have been that "Charbucks" would strengthen the positive impressions of Starbucks because it brings to the attention of consumers that the "Char" is absent in "Star"bucks, and, therefore, of the two "bucks," Starbucks is the "un-charred" and more appealing product. Juxtaposition may bring to light more appealing aspects of a name that otherwise would not have been brought to the attention of ordinary observers.

* * *

Moreover, that the Charbucks line of coffee is marketed as a product of "[v]ery high quality"—as Starbucks also purports its coffee to be—is inconsistent with the concept of "tarnishment." *See Hormel Foods Corp.*, 73 F.3d at 507 (citing cases finding tarnishment where challenged marks were either "seamy" or substantially of lesser quality than the famous mark). Certainly, the similarity between Charbucks and Starbucks in that they are both "[v]ery high quality" coffees may be relevant in determining dilution, but such similarity in this case undercuts the claim that Charbucks *harms* the reputation of Starbucks. * * * Accordingly, we conclude that the District Court did not err in rejecting Starbucks' claim of dilution by tarnishment.

     * * *

LOUIS VUITTON MALLETIER S.A.
v. HAUTE DIGGITY DOG, LLC.

United States Court of Appeals for the Fourth Circuit, 2007.
507 F.3d 252.

NIEMEYER, CIRCUIT JUDGE:

Louis Vuitton Malletier S.A., a French corporation located in Paris, that manufactures luxury luggage, handbags, and accessories, commenced this action against Haute Diggity Dog, LLC, a Nevada corporation that manufactures and sells pet products nationally, alleging trademark infringement under 15 U.S.C. § 1114(1)(a) [and] trademark dilution under 15 U.S.C. § 1125(c) * * *. Haute Diggity Dog manufactures, among other things, plush toys on which dogs can chew, which, it claims, parody famous trademarks on luxury products, including those of Louis Vuitton Malletier. The particular Haute Diggity Dog chew toys in question here are small imitations of handbags that are labeled "Chewy Vuiton" and that mimic Louis Vuitton Malletier's LOUIS VUITTON handbags.

On cross-motions for summary judgment, the district court concluded that Haute Diggity Dog's "Chewy Vuiton" dog toys were successful parodies of Louis Vuitton Malletier's trademarks, designs, and products, and on that basis, entered judgment in favor of Haute Diggity Dog on all of Louis Vuitton Malletier's claims.

On appeal, we agree with the district court that Haute Diggity Dog's products are not likely to cause confusion with those of Louis Vuitton Malletier * * *. On the trademark dilution claim, however, we reject the district court's reasoning but reach the same conclusion through a different analysis. * * *

I

Louis Vuitton Malletier S.A. ("LVM") is a well known manufacturer of luxury luggage, leather goods, handbags, and accessories, which it markets and sells worldwide. In connection with the sale of its products, LVM has adopted trademarks and trade dress that are well recognized and have become famous and distinct. Indeed, in 2006, *BusinessWeek* ranked LOUIS VUITTON as the 17th "best brand" of all corporations in the world and the first "best brand" for any fashion business.

LVM has registered trademarks for "LOUIS VUITTON," in connection with luggage and ladies' handbags (the "LOUIS VUITTON mark"); for a stylized monogram of "LV," in connection with traveling bags and other goods (the "LV mark"); and for a monogram canvas design consisting of a canvas with repetitions of the LV mark along with four-pointed stars, four-pointed stars inset in curved diamonds, and four-pointed flowers inset in circles, in connection with traveling bags and other products (the "Monogram Canvas mark"). In 2002, LVM adopted a brightly-colored version of the Monogram Canvas mark in which the LV mark and the designs were of various colors and the background was white (the "Multicolor design"), created in collaboration with Japanese artist Takashi Murakami. * * *

As LVM points out, the Multicolor design * * * attracted immediate and extraordinary media attention and publicity in magazines such as *Vogue, W, Elle, Harper's Bazaar, Us Weekly, Life and Style, Travel & Leisure, People, In Style,* and *Jane.* The press published photographs showing celebrities carrying these handbags, including Jennifer Lopez, Madonna, Eve, Elizabeth Hurley, Carmen Electra, and Anna Kournikova, among others. When the Multicolor design first appeared in 2003, the magazines typically reported, "The Murakami designs for Louis Vuitton, which were the hit of the summer, came with hefty price tags and a long waiting list." *People Magazine* said, "the wait list is in the thousands." The handbags retailed in the range of $995 for a medium handbag to $4500 for a large travel bag. The medium size handbag that appears to be the model for the "Chewy Vuiton" dog toy retailed for $1190. * * *

[The LOUIS VUITTON, LV, and Monogram Canvas marks have been used as identifiers of LVM products continuously since 1896.]

During the period 2003–2005, LVM spent more than $48 million advertising products using its marks and designs, including more than $4 million for the Multicolor design. It sells its products exclusively in LVM stores and in its own in-store boutiques that are contained within department stores such as Saks Fifth Avenue, Bloomingdale's, Neiman Marcus, and Macy's. LVM also advertises its products on the Internet through the specific websites www.louisvuitton.com and www.eluxury.com.

Although better known for its handbags and luggage, LVM also markets a limited selection of luxury pet accessories—collars, leashes, and dog carriers—which bear the Monogram Canvas mark and the Multicolor design. These items range in price from approximately $200 to $1600. LVM does not make dog toys.

Haute Diggity Dog, LLC, which is a relatively small and relatively new business located in Nevada, manufactures and sells nationally— primarily through pet stores—a line of pet chew toys and beds whose names parody elegant high-end brands of products such as perfume, cars, shoes, sparkling wine, and handbags. These include—in addition to Chewy Vuiton (LOUIS VUITTON)—Chewnel No. 5 (Chanel No. 5), Furcedes (Mercedes), Jimmy Chew (Jimmy Choo), Dog Perignonn (Dom Perignon), Sniffany & Co. (Tiffany & Co.), and Dogior (Dior). The chew toys and pet beds are plush, made of polyester, and have a shape and design that loosely imitate the signature product of the targeted brand. They are mostly distributed and sold through pet stores, although one or two

Macy's stores carries Haute Diggity Dog's products. The dog toys are generally sold for less than $20, although larger versions of some of Haute Diggity Dog's plush dog beds sell for more than $100.

Haute Diggity Dog's "Chewy Vuiton" dog toys, in particular, loosely resemble miniature handbags and undisputedly evoke LVM handbags of similar shape, design, and color. In lieu of the LOUIS VUITTON mark, the dog toy uses "Chewy Vuiton"; in lieu of the LV mark, it uses "CV"; and the other symbols and colors employed are imitations, but not exact ones, of those used in the LVM Multicolor * * * designs.

     * * *

II

     * * *

Because Haute Diggity Dog's arguments * * * depend to a great extent on whether its products and marks are successful parodies, we consider first whether Haute Diggity Dog's products, marks, and trade dress are indeed successful parodies of LVM's marks and trade dress.

For trademark purposes, "[a] 'parody' is defined as a simple form of entertainment conveyed by juxtaposing the irreverent representation of the trademark with the idealized image created by the mark's owner." *People for the Ethical Treatment of Animals v. Doughney* ("*PETA*"), 263 F.3d 359, 366 (4th Cir.2001). "A parody must convey two simultaneous—and contradictory—messages: that it is the original, but also that it is *not* the original and is instead a parody." *Id.* This second message must not only differentiate the alleged parody from the original but must also communicate some articulable element of satire, ridicule, joking, or amusement. Thus, "[a] parody relies upon a difference from the original mark, presumably a humorous difference, in order to produce its desired effect." *Jordache Enterprises, Inc. v. Hogg Wyld, Ltd.,* 828 F.2d 1482, 1486 (10th Cir.1987) (finding the use of "Lardashe" jeans for larger women to be a successful and permissible parody of "Jordache" jeans).

When applying the *PETA* criteria to the facts of this case, we agree with the district court that the "Chewy Vuiton" dog toys are successful parodies of LVM handbags and the LVM marks and trade dress used in connection with the marketing and sale of those handbags. First, the pet chew toy is obviously an irreverent, and indeed intentional, representation of an LVM handbag, albeit much smaller and coarser. The dog toy is shaped roughly like a handbag; its name "Chewy Vuiton" sounds like and rhymes with LOUIS VUITTON; its monogram CV mimics LVM's LV mark; the repetitious design clearly imitates the design on the LVM handbag; and the coloring is similar. In short, the dog toy is a small, plush imitation of an LVM handbag carried by women, which invokes the marks and design of the handbag, albeit irreverently and incompletely. No one can doubt that LVM handbags are the target of the imitation by Haute Diggity Dog's "Chewy Vuiton" dog toys.

At the same time, no one can doubt also that the "Chewy Vuiton" dog toy is not the "idealized image" of the mark created by LVM. The differences are immediate, beginning with the fact that the "Chewy Vuiton" product is a dog toy, not an expensive, luxury LOUIS VUITTON handbag. The toy is smaller, it is plush, and virtually all of its designs differ. Thus, "Chewy Vuiton" is not LOUIS VUITTON ("Chewy" is not "LOUIS" and "Vuiton" is not "VUITTON," with its two Ts); CV is not LV; the designs on the dog toy are simplified and crude, not detailed and distinguished. The toys are inexpensive; the handbags are expensive and marketed to be expensive. And, of course, as a dog toy, one must buy it with pet supplies and cannot buy it at an exclusive LVM store or boutique within a department store. In short, the Haute Diggity Dog "Chewy Vuiton" dog toy undoubtedly and deliberately conjures up the famous LVM marks and trade dress, but at the same time, it communicates that it is not the LVM product.

Finally, the juxtaposition of the similar and dissimilar—the irreverent representation and the idealized image of an LVM handbag—immediately conveys a joking and amusing parody. The furry little "Chewy Vuiton" imitation, as something to be *chewed by a dog*, pokes fun at the elegance and expensiveness of a LOUIS VUITTON handbag, which must *not* be chewed by a dog. The LVM handbag is provided for the most elegant and well-to-do celebrity, to proudly display to the public and the press, whereas the imitation "Chewy Vuiton" "handbag" is designed to mock the celebrity and be used by a dog. The dog toy irreverently presents haute couture as an object for casual canine destruction. The satire is unmistakable. The dog toy is a comment on the rich and famous, on the LOUIS VUITTON name and related marks, and on conspicuous consumption in general. This parody is enhanced by the fact that "Chewy Vuiton" dog toys are sold with similar parodies of other famous and expensive brands—"Chewnel No. 5" targeting "Chanel No. 5"; "Dog Perignonn" targeting "Dom Perignon"; and "Sniffany & Co." targeting "Tiffany & Co."

We conclude that the *PETA* criteria are amply satisfied in this case and that the "Chewy Vuiton" dog toys convey "just enough of the original design to allow the consumer to appreciate the point of parody," but stop well short of appropriating the entire marks that LVM claims. [The Court applies likelihood of confusion factors and determines that the "Chewy Vuiton" dog toy does not create a likelihood of confusion about the source, sponsorship or affiliation of the parties' products.]

III

LVM also contends that Haute Diggity Dog's advertising, sale, and distribution of the "Chewy Vuiton" dog toys dilutes its LOUIS VUITTON, LV, and Monogram Canvas marks, which are famous and distinctive, in violation of the Trademark Dilution Revision Act of 2006 ("TDRA"), 15 U.S.C.A. § 1125(c). It argues, "Before the district court's decision, Vuitton's famous marks were unblurred by any third party trademark use."

"Allowing defendants to become the first to use similar marks will obviously blur and dilute the Vuitton Marks." * * *

Haute Diggity Dog urges that, in applying the TDRA to the circumstances before us, we reject LVM's suggestion that a parody "automatically" gives rise to "actionable dilution." Haute Diggity Dog contends that only marks that are "identical or substantially similar" can give rise to actionable dilution, and its "Chewy Vuiton" marks are not identical or sufficiently similar to LVM's marks. It also argues that "[its] spoof, like other obvious parodies,"" 'tends to increase public identification' of [LVM's] mark with [LVM]," rather than impairing its distinctiveness, as the TDRA requires. * * *

* * *

[T]o state a dilution claim under the TDRA, a plaintiff must show:

(1) that the plaintiff owns a famous mark that is distinctive;

(2) that the defendant has commenced using a mark in commerce that allegedly is diluting the famous mark;

(3) that a similarity between the defendant's mark and the famous mark gives rise to an association between the marks; and

(4) that the association is likely to impair the distinctiveness of the famous mark or likely to harm the reputation of the famous mark.

In the context of blurring, distinctiveness refers to the ability of the famous mark uniquely to identify a single source and thus maintain its selling power. * * * In proving a dilution claim under the TDRA, the plaintiff need not show actual or likely confusion, the presence of competition, or actual economic injury.

The TDRA creates three defenses based on the defendant's (1) "fair use" (with exceptions); (2) "news reporting and news commentary"; and (3) "noncommercial use." *Id.* § 1125(c)(3).

A

* * *

The first three elements of a trademark dilution claim are not at issue in this case. LVM owns famous marks that are distinctive; Haute Diggity Dog has commenced using "Chewy Vuiton," "CV," and designs and colors that are allegedly diluting LVM's marks; and the similarity between Haute Diggity Dog's marks and LVM's marks gives rise to an association between the marks, albeit a parody. The issue for resolution is whether the association between Haute Diggity Dog's marks and LVM's marks is likely to impair the distinctiveness of LVM's famous marks.

* * *

The TDRA prohibits a person from using a junior mark that is likely to dilute (by blurring) the famous mark, and blurring is defined to be an impairment to the famous mark's distinctiveness. "Distinctiveness" in turn refers to the public's recognition that the famous mark identifies a single source of the product using the famous mark.

To determine whether a junior mark is likely to dilute a famous mark through blurring, the TDRA directs the court to consider all factors relevant to the issue, including six factors that are enumerated in the statute:

> (i) The degree of similarity between the mark or trade name and the famous mark.
>
> (ii) The degree of inherent or acquired distinctiveness of the famous mark.
>
> (iii) The extent to which the owner of the famous mark is engaging in substantially exclusive use of the mark.
>
> (iv) The degree of recognition of the famous mark.
>
> (v) Whether the user of the mark or trade name intended to create an association with the famous mark.
>
> (vi) Any actual association between the mark or trade name and the famous mark.

15 U.S.C.A. § 1125(c)(2)(B). Not every factor will be relevant in every case, and not every blurring claim will require extensive discussion of the factors. But a trial court must offer a sufficient indication of which factors it has found persuasive and explain why they are persuasive so that the court's decision can be reviewed. The district court did not do this adequately in this case. Nonetheless, after we apply the factors as a matter of law, we reach the same conclusion reached by the district court.

We begin by noting that parody is not automatically a complete *defense* to a claim of dilution by blurring where the defendant uses the parody as its own designation of source, i.e., *as a trademark*. Although the TDRA does provide that fair use is a complete defense and allows that a parody can be considered fair use, it does not extend the fair use defense to parodies used as a trademark. As the statute provides:

> The following shall not be actionable as dilution by blurring or dilution by tarnishment under this subsection:
>
> > (A) Any fair use ... *other than as a designation of source for the person's own goods or services,* including use in connection with ... parodying....

15 U.S.C.A. § 1125(c)(3)(A)(ii) (emphasis added). Under the statute's plain language, parodying a famous mark is protected by the fair use defense only if the parody is *not* "a designation of source for the person's own goods or services."

The TDRA, however, does not require a court to ignore the existence of a parody that is used as a trademark, and it does not preclude a court from considering parody as part of the circumstances to be considered for determining whether the plaintiff has made out a claim for dilution by blurring. Indeed, the statute permits a court to consider "all relevant factors," including the six factors supplied in § 1125(c)(2)(B).

Thus, it would appear that a defendant's use of a mark as a parody is relevant to the overall question of whether the defendant's use is likely to impair the famous mark's distinctiveness. Moreover, the fact that the defendant uses its marks as a parody is specifically relevant to several of the listed factors. For example, factor (v) (whether the defendant intended to create an association with the famous mark) and factor (vi) (whether there exists an actual association between the defendant's mark and the famous mark) directly invite inquiries into the defendant's intent in using the parody, the defendant's actual use of the parody, and the effect that its use has on the famous mark. While a parody intentionally creates an association with the famous mark in order to be a parody, it also intentionally communicates, if it is successful, that it is *not* the famous mark, but rather a satire of the famous mark. That the defendant is using its mark as a parody is therefore relevant in the consideration of these statutory factors.

Similarly, factors (i), (ii), and (iv)—the degree of similarity between the two marks, the degree of distinctiveness of the famous mark, and its recognizability—are directly implicated by consideration of the fact that the defendant's mark is a successful parody. Indeed, by making the famous mark an object of the parody, a successful parody might actually enhance the famous mark's distinctiveness by making it an icon. The brunt of the joke becomes yet more famous. *See Hormel Foods Corp. v. Jim Henson Prods., Inc.,* 73 F.3d 497, 506 (2d cir. 1996)(observing that a successful parody "tends to increase public identification" of the famous mark with its source) * * *.

In sum, while a defendant's use of a parody as a mark does not support a "fair use" defense, it may be considered in determining whether the plaintiff-owner of a famous mark has proved its claim that the defendant's use of a parody mark is likely to impair the distinctiveness of the famous mark.

In the case before us, when considering factors (ii), (iii), and (iv), it is readily apparent, indeed conceded by Haute Diggity Dog, that LVM's marks are distinctive, famous, and strong. The LOUIS VUITTON mark is well known and is commonly identified as a brand of the great Parisian fashion house, Louis Vuitton Malletier. So too are its other marks and designs, which are invariably used with the LOUIS VUITTON mark. It may not be too strong to refer to these famous marks as icons of high fashion.

While the establishment of these facts satisfies essential elements of LVM's dilution claim, the facts impose on LVM an increased burden to demonstrate that the distinctiveness of its famous marks is likely to be impaired by a successful parody. Even as Haute Diggity Dog's parody mimics the famous mark, it communicates simultaneously that it is not the famous mark, but is only satirizing it. And because the famous mark is particularly strong and distinctive, it becomes more likely that a parody will not impair the distinctiveness of the mark. In short, as Haute Diggity Dog's "Chewy Vuiton" marks are a successful parody, we conclude that they will not blur the distinctiveness of the famous mark as a unique identifier of its source.

It is important to note, however, that this might not be true if the parody is so similar to the famous mark that it likely could be construed as actual use of the famous mark itself. Factor (i) directs an inquiry into the "degree of similarity between the junior mark and the famous mark." If Haute Diggity Dog used the actual marks of LVM (as a parody or otherwise), it could dilute LVM's marks by blurring, regardless of whether Haute Diggity Dog's use was confusingly similar, whether it was in competition with LVM, or whether LVM sustained actual injury. Thus, "the use of DUPONT shoes, BUICK aspirin, and KODAK pianos would be actionable" under the TDRA because the unauthorized use of the famous marks *themselves* on unrelated goods might diminish the capacity of these trademarks to distinctively identify a single source. This is true even though a consumer would be unlikely to confuse the manufacturer of KODAK film with the hypothetical producer of KODAK pianos.

But in this case, Haute Diggity Dog mimicked the famous marks; it did not come so close to them as to destroy the success of its parody and, more importantly, to diminish the LVM marks' capacity to identify a single source. Haute Diggity Dog designed a pet chew toy to imitate and suggest, but not *use,* the marks of a high-fashion LOUIS VUITTON handbag. It used "Chewy Vuiton" to mimic "LOUIS VUITTON"; it used "CV" to mimic "LV"; and it adopted *imperfectly* the items of LVM's designs. We conclude that these uses by Haute Diggity Dog were not so similar as to be likely to impair the distinctiveness of LVM's famous marks.

In a similar vein, when considering factors (v) and (vi), it becomes apparent that Haute Diggity Dog intentionally associated its marks, but only partially and certainly imperfectly, so as to convey the simultaneous message that it was not in fact a source of LVM products. Rather, as a parody, it separated itself from the LVM marks in order to make fun of them.

In sum, when considering the relevant factors to determine whether blurring is likely to occur in this case, we readily come to the conclusion, as did the district court, that LVM has failed to make out a case of trademark dilution by blurring by failing to establish that the distinctiveness of its marks was likely to be impaired by Haute Diggity Dog's marketing and sale of its "Chewy Vuiton" products.

* * *

V SECRET CATALOGUE, INC. v. MOSELEY

United States Court of Appeals for the Sixth Circuit, 2010.
605 F.3d 382.

MERRITT, CIRCUIT JUDGE.

In this trademark "dilution by tarnishment" case, brought under the Trademark Dilution Revision Act of 2006, the question is whether the plaintiff, an international lingerie company that uses the trade name designation "Victoria's Secret" has a valid suit for injunctive relief against the use of the name "Victor's Little Secret" or "Victor's Secret" by the defendants, a small retail store in a mall in Elizabethtown, Kentucky, that sells assorted merchandise, including "sex toys" and other sexually oriented products. * * * The District Court concluded that even though the two parties do not compete in the same market, the "Victor's Little Secret" mark—because it is sex related—disparages and tends to reduce the positive associations and the "selling power" of the "Victoria's Secret" mark. The question is whether the plaintiff's case meets the definitions and standards for "dilution by tarnishment" set out in the new Act which amended the old Act, *i.e.,* the Federal Trademark Dilution Act of 1995.

The new Act was expressly intended to overrule the Supreme Court interpretation of the old Act in this very same case, *Moseley v. V Secret Catalogue, Inc.,* 537 U.S. 418, 123 S.Ct. 1115, 155 L.Ed.2d 1 (2003). The Supreme Court reversed a panel of this Court that had affirmed an injunction against "Victor's Little Secret" issued by the District Court. On remand to the District Court from the Supreme Court after the 2003 reversal, no new evidence was introduced, and the District Court reconsidered the case based on the same evidence but used the new language in the new Act which overrules the Supreme Court in this case. We will first brief the Supreme Court opinion and the reasons Congress overruled the Supreme Court in this case. We will then outline our understanding of the new standards for measuring trademark "dilution by tarnishment" and apply them to this case. We conclude that the new Act creates a kind of rebuttable presumption, or at least a very strong inference, that a new mark used to sell sex related products is likely to tarnish a famous mark if there is a clear semantic association between the two. That presumption has not been rebutted in this case.

I. The Supreme Court Opinion and the New Act

The Supreme Court explained that this case started when an Army Colonel at Fort Knox saw an ad for "Victor's Secret" in a weekly publication. It advertised that the small store in Elizabethtown sold adult videos and novelties and lingerie. There was no likelihood of confusion between the two businesses or the two marks, but the Army Colonel was offended because the sexually-oriented business was semantically associating itself with "Victoria's Secret." The Court explained that the concepts of "dilution by blurring" and "dilution by tarnishment" originated with an article in the Harvard Law Review, Frank Schechter, "Rational Basis of Trademark Protection," 40 HARV. L.REV. 813 (1927), and that the history and meaning of the concepts were further well explained in Restatement (Third) of Unfair Competition, Section 25 (1995). The Restatement section referred to by the Supreme Court explains this new intellectual property tort and contains in § 25 a comprehensive statement of "Liability Without Proof of Confusion: Dilution and Tarnishment."[4] "Tarnishment," as distinguished from "dilution by blurring" was the only claim before the Supreme Court and is the only claim before us in this new appeal. * * *

* * *

[The Supreme] Court held that "actual harm" rather than merely a "likelihood" of harm must be shown by Victoria's Secret in order to prevail and that this means that Victoria's Secret carries the burden of proving an actual "lessening of the capacity of the Victoria's Secret mark to identify and distinguish goods or services sold in Victoria's Secret stores or advertised in its catalogs." In the new law Congress rejected the Court's view that a simple "likelihood" of an association in the consum-

---

4. c. *Interests protected.* The antidilution statutes have been invoked against two distinct threats to the interests of a trademark owner. First, a mark may be so highly distinctive and so well advertised that it acts as a powerful selling tool. Such a mark may evoke among prospective purchasers a positive response that is associated exclusively with the goods or services of the trademark owner. To the extent that others use the trademark to identify different goods, services or businesses, a dissonance occurs that blurs this stimulant effect of the mark. The antidilution statutes protect against this dilution of the distinctiveness and selling power of the mark.

The selling power of a trademark also can be undermined by a use of the mark with goods or services such as illicit drugs or pornography that "tarnish" the mark's image through inherently negative or unsavory associations, or with goods or services that produce a negative response when linked in the minds of prospective purchasers with the goods or services of the prior user, such as the use on insecticide of a trademark similar to one previously used by another on food products.

Tarnishment and dilution of distinctiveness, although conceptually distinct, both undermine the selling power of a mark, the latter by disturbing the conditioned association of the mark with the prior user and the former by displacing positive with negative associations. Thus, tarnishment and dilution of distinctiveness reduce the value of the mark to the trademark owner.

* * *

er's mind of the Victoria's Secret mark with the sexually-oriented videos and toys of "Victor's Secret" is insufficient for liability.

The House Judiciary Committee Report states the purpose of the new 2006 legislation as follows:

> The *Moseley* standard *creates an undue burden* for trademark holders who contest diluting uses and should be revised.
>
> . . .
>
> The new language in the legislation [provides] . . . specifically that the standard for proving a dilution claim is "likelihood of dilution" and that both dilution by blurring and dilution by tarnishment are actionable.

(Emphasis added.) U.S. Code Cong. & Adm. News, 109th Cong. 2d Sess. 2006, Vol. 4, pp. 1091, 1092, 1097. * * * The drafters of the Committee Report also called special attention to the "burden" of proof or persuasion placed on "trademark holders" by the Supreme Court's opinion in *Moseley,* suggesting a possible modification in the burden of proof. The question for us then is whether "Victor's Little Secret" with its association with lewd sexual toys creates a "likelihood of dilution by tarnishment" of [the] Victoria's Secret mark.

II.   Application of Statutory Standard

The specific question in this case is whether, without consumer surveys or polls or other evidence, a semantic "association" is equivalent to a liability-creating mental "association" of a junior mark like "Victor's Little Secret" with a famous mark like "Victoria's Secret" that constitutes dilution by tarnishment when the junior mark is used to sell sexual toys, videos and similar soft-core pornographic products. There appears to be a clearly emerging consensus in the case law, aided by the language of § 25 of the Restatement of Trademarks 3d, that the creation of an "association" between a famous mark and lewd or bawdy sexual activity disparages and defiles the famous mark and reduces the commercial value of its selling power. This consensus stems from an economic prediction about consumer taste and how the predicted reaction of conventional consumers in our culture will affect the economic value of the famous mark.

There have been at least eight federal cases in six jurisdictions that conclude that a famous mark is tarnished when its mark is semantically associated with a new mark that is used to sell sex-related products. We find no exceptions in the case law that allow such a new mark associated with sex to stand. * * *

The phrase "likely to cause dilution" used in the new statute significantly changes the meaning of the law from "causes actual harm" under the preexisting law. The word "likely" or "likelihood" means "probably." It is important to note also that the Committee Report quoted above seeks to reduce the "burden" of evidentiary production on the trademark holder. The burden-of-proof problem, the developing case law, and the

Restatement (Third) of Trademarks in § 25 (particularly subsection g) should now be interpreted, we think, to create a kind of rebuttable presumption, or at least a very strong inference, that a new mark used to sell sex-related products is likely to tarnish a famous mark if there is a clear semantic association between the two. This *res ipsa loquitur*-like effect is not conclusive but places on the owner of the new mark the burden of coming forward with evidence that there is no likelihood or probability of tarnishment. The evidence could be in the form of expert testimony or surveys or polls or customer testimony.

In the present case, the Moseleys have had two opportunities in the District Court to offer evidence that there is no real probability of tarnishment and have not done so. They did not offer at oral argument any suggestion that they could make such a showing or wanted the case remanded for that purpose. The fact that Congress was dissatisfied with the *Moseley* result and the *Moseley* standard of liability, as well as apparently the *Moseley* burden of proof, supports the view of Victoria's Secret that the present record—in the eyes of the legislative branch— shows a likelihood of tarnishment. Without evidence to the contrary or a persuasive defensive theory that rebuts the presumption, the defendants have given us no basis to reverse the judgment of the District Court. We do not find sufficient the defendants' arguments that they should have the right to use Victor Moseley's first name and that the effect of the association is *de minimis*. The Moseleys do not have a right to use the word "secret" in their mark. They use it only to make the association with the Victoria's Secret mark. We agree that the tarnishing effect of the Moseley's mark on the senior mark is somewhat speculative, but we have no evidence to overcome the strong inference created by the case law, the Restatement, and Congressional dissatisfaction with the burden of proof used in this case in the Supreme Court. The new law seems designed to protect trademarks from any unfavorable sexual associations. Thus, any new mark with a lewd or offensive-to-some sexual association raises a strong inference of tarnishment. The inference must be overcome by evidence that rebuts the probability that some consumers will find the new mark both offensive and harmful to the reputation and the favorable symbolism of the famous mark.

* * * It seems clear that the new Act demonstrates that Congress intended that a court should reach a different result in this case if the facts remain the same. We do not necessarily disagree with our dissenting colleague that the policy followed by the Supreme Court in such cases may be better. We simply believe that the will of Congress is to the contrary with regard to the proof in this case and with regard to the method of allocating the burden of proof.

* * *

KAREN NELSON MOORE, CIRCUIT JUDGE, dissenting.

Because I believe that Victoria's Secret has failed to produce sufficient evidence to show that the Moseleys' use of the name "Victor's Little

Secret" is likely to tarnish the VICTORIA'S SECRET mark, I would reverse the judgment of the district court and must respectfully dissent.

Under the Trademark Dilution Revision Act of 2006 ("TDRA"), Victoria's Secret is entitled to injunctive relief if the Moseleys' use of "Victor's Little Secret" as the name of their adult-oriented novelty store "is likely to cause dilution ... by tarnishment of the" VICTORIA'S SECRET mark. 15 U.S.C. § 1125(c)(1). "[D]ilution by tarnishment" is defined as an "association arising from the similarity between a mark or trade name and a famous mark that harms the reputation of the famous mark." *Id.* § 1125(c)(2)(C). Thus, under the terms of the statute, to determine whether the VICTORIA'S SECRET mark is likely to be tarnished by the Moseleys' use, this court must inquire as to both the "association" between the two marks and the "harm" that the association causes to the senior mark.

Because I agree that there is a clear association between the two marks, the determinative inquiry in this dilution-by-tarnishment case is whether that association is likely to harm Victoria's Secret's reputation. Contrary to the majority's conclusion, however, given the record before the panel, I would hold that Victoria's Secret has failed to meet its burden to show that the Moseleys' use of "Victor's Little Secret" is likely to dilute Victoria's Secret's mark.[2]

Victoria's Secret's evidence of tarnishment includes nothing more than the following: (1) an affidavit from Army Colonel John E. Baker stating that he "was ... offended by [the] defendants' use of [Victoria's Secret's] trademark to promote ... unwholesome, tawdry merchandise," such as " 'adult' novelties and gifts," and that since his "wife ... and ... daughter ... shop at Victoria's Secret, [he] was further dismayed by [the] defendants' effort to associate itself with, trade off on the image of, and in fact denigrate a store frequented by members of [his] family," and (2) a statement from one of Victoria's Secret's corporate officers that Victoria's Secret strives to "maintain[ ] an image that is sexy and playful" and one that "avoid[s] sexually explicit or graphic imagery."

Reviewing Baker's affidavit, I believe that it is plain that Baker made a "mental association" between "Victor's Little Secret" and "Victoria's Secret." It is also clear that Baker held a negative impression of "Victor's Little Secret." But despite the clear negative association of this *one* individual when confronted with "Victor's Little Secret," Victoria's Secret has presented *no* evidence that Baker's, or anyone else's, distaste or dislike of "Victor's Little Secret" is likely to taint their positive opinion or perception of Victoria's Secret. Yet evidence that the junior mark is likely to undermine or alter the positive associations of the senior mark—i.e.,

---

2. I respectfully disagree with the majority's conclusion that in dilution-by-tarnishment cases involving new marks "with lewd or offensive-to-some sexual association[s]" the TDRA establishes a presumption or inference of tarnishment that the Moseleys must rebut. To be sure, the House Judiciary Committee Report highlights Congress's concern with the pre-TDRA actual-dilution standard, but I do not read its concern that the previous standard created "an undue burden" to mean that Congress envisioned a modification of the party that bears the burden of proof as opposed to simply a lightening of the evidentiary showing. * * *

evidence that the junior mark is likely to harm the reputation of the senior mark—is precisely the showing required under the plain language of 15 U.S.C. § 1125(c)(2)(C) to prove dilution by tarnishment. * * *

     * * *

     * * * Instead of developing a record on remand that contains at least some evidence that Victoria's Secret's reputation is likely to suffer because of the negative response that "Victor's Little Secret" engendered, the record before the panel indicates only that a single individual thinks poorly of "Victor's Little Secret." On this record, it is simply no more probable that Victoria's Secret will suffer reputational harm as a result of the Moseleys' use of "Victor's Little Secret" than it is probable that those who are offended by "Victor's Little Secret" will limit their negative impressions to the Moseleys and refrain from projecting those negative associations upon Victoria's Secret. Baker's affidavit does nothing to contradict this conclusion, and given the absence of any indication that his or his family's opinion of Victoria's Secret changed following the Moseleys' use of "Victor's Little Secret," his affidavit may, in fact, provide evidence that individuals are likely to confine their distaste to the Moseleys. * * *

     Certainly, it is *possible* that the Moseleys' use of "Victor's Little Secret" to sell adult-oriented material and other novelties could reflect poorly on the VICTORIA'S SECRET mark and could cause Victoria's Secret to suffer damage to its "sexy and playful" reputation, but the evidentiary standard set forth in the statute is one of likelihood *not* mere possibility. Likelihood is based on probable consequence and amounts to more than simple speculation as to what might possibly happen. * * *

NOTES AND QUESTIONS

     1. *The state dilution cause of action.* State dilution statutes preceded the federal dilution cause of action. Like the federal cause of action, the state dilution cause of action was created through legislative enactment, rather than through common law. Massachusetts enacted the first antidilution statute in 1947. Since then, at least half of the states have adopted similar statutes. Initially there was significant judicial reluctance to apply antidilution statutes literally and grant dilution relief in the absence of a likelihood of consumer confusion. Why might that be? What interest does the dilution cause of action protect? Does protecting against dilution in the absence of a likelihood of confusion promote any public interest, or is it solely a benefit for trademark owners? Could anti-dilution protection *harm* consumer interests? First Amendment interests?

     Courts applying state dilution statutes have differed over whether a plaintiff must demonstrate mark fame and distinctiveness throughout the general U.S. population or whether "local" fame and distinctiveness or "niche" fame and distinctiveness is sufficient. What are the practical implications of providing a dilution cause of action for a mark that is only famous in one relatively small geographic locale, like eastern Washington County, Oregon? Should Oregon courts enjoin national retailers from entering that geographic locale with a similar mark (albeit dissimilar products)? Would this be efficient? Should efficiency be relevant? What if the plaintiff can demonstrate that its mark is "famous" among one percent of the general population—for example, florists and morticians. Should the plaintiff (in order to protect the selling power of its own mark) be able to prevent a defendant from adopting a similar mark to identify a new model of car?

2. *The federal dilution cause of action—Lanham Act § 43(c).* Over the years, advocates of dilution protection made several attempts to create a federal cause of action for dilution. In late 1995, these efforts came to fruition with enactment of the Federal Trademark Dilution Act of 1995, which added a new subsection (c) to Lanham Act § 43. 15 U.S.C. § 1125(c). The House Report accompanying the Act justified the new federal dilution cause of action in the name of national uniformity. Famous marks ordinarily are used on a nationwide basis and dilution protection was only available in approximately half of the states. And the protection provided in those states was not uniform. The House Report reasoned that protection for famous marks should not depend on the forum in which the suit is filed, because that encourages forum shopping and increases litigation.[19]

During the ten years following enactment of the Federal Trademark Dilution Act, the Circuit Courts of Appeals split repeatedly over its construction and scope. Among other things, they disagreed over: 1) whether the federal cause of action was available to plaintiffs whose marks enjoyed "niche fame" or only to marks that were famous throughout the general population; 2) whether protection was restricted to inherently distinctive marks that were famous, or applied to all famous distinctive marks, regardless of whether they were inherently distinctive or distinctive through acquisition of secondary meaning; 3) the extent to which federal dilution relief should be available to product feature trade dress; and 4) the proper factors to consider in evaluating the dilutive impact of the defendant's use. Perhaps most importantly, the Circuits split over whether the statutory language of the Federal Trademark Dilution Act required a plaintiff to prove "actual dilution" or only "a likelihood of dilution."

In Moseley v. V Secret Catalogue, Inc., 537 U.S. 418, 123 S.Ct. 1115, 155 L.Ed.2d 1 (2003), the Supreme Court construed the statutory language narrowly, to require a showing of "actual dilution," rather than a mere "likelihood of dilution."

> [T]hat does not mean that the consequences of dilution, such as an actual loss of sales or profits, must also be proved. * * * We do agree,

---

19. H.R. Rep. No. 347, 104th Cong., 2d Sess. (1995). The House Report also justified the federal dilution cause of action on grounds of international relations:

[T]he recently concluded Agreement on Trade–Related Aspects of Intellectual Property Rights, including Trade in Counterfeit Goods ("TRIPs") which was part of the Uruguay Round of the GATT Agreement, includes a provision designed to provide dilution protection to famous marks. Thus, enactment of this bill will be consistent with the terms of [TRIPs], as well as the Paris Convention, of which the U.S. also is a member. Passage of a federal dilution statute would also assist the executive branch in its bilateral and multilateral negotiations with other countries to secure greater protection for the famous marks owned by U.S. companies. Foreign countries are reluctant to change their laws to protect famous U.S. marks if the U.S. itself does not afford special protection for such marks.

H.R. Rep. No. 374, *supra*, at 4.

however, * * * that, at least where the marks at issue are not identical, the mere fact that consumers mentally associate the junior user's mark with a famous mark is not sufficient to establish actionable dilution. [S]uch mental association will not necessarily reduce the capacity of the famous mark to identify the goods of its owner, the statutory requirement for dilution under the FTDA. * * * "Blurring" is not a necessary consequence of mental association. (Nor, for that matter, is "tarnishing.")

537 U.S. at 432–34. In another part of the opinion, the Supreme Court strongly questioned whether the statutory language of the 1995 Federal Trademark Dilution Act actually provided for tarnishment claims.

The Supreme Court's decision substantially reduced the scope of the federal dilution cause of action, leading displeased trademark owners to lobby Congress for an amendment that would legislatively reverse the *Moseley* decision. Their efforts resulted in the Trademark Dilution Revision Act of 2006, which replaced the original § 43(c) language (as well as the definition of "dilution," which the FTDA had added to Lanham Act § 45) with newly drawn dilution provisions.

Review the provisions of Lanham Act § 43(c), as amended. The new provisions clarify a number of the issues over which courts applying the original § 43(c) provisions had split. They expressly enable the owner of a "famous" mark that is distinctive (inherently *or* by acquisition of secondary meaning) to enjoin a defendant's "use in commerce" of a mark or trade name that is *likely to cause dilution by blurring or by tarnishment*, if the defendant's use began after the plaintiff's mark became famous. Relief is limited to an injunction unless the plaintiff can demonstrate: 1) that the defendant first used its diluting mark in commerce after the Trademark Dilution Revision Act of 2006 was enacted, and 2) that the defendant's acts were willful. The defendant's acts will be willful in the case of a blurring claim if the defendant "willfully intended to trade on the recognition of the famous mark." They will be willful in the case of a tarnishment claim if the defendant "willfully intended to harm the reputation of the famous mark." 15 U.S.C. § 1125(c)(5). If the plaintiff can make this showing, it may recover its damages, the defendant's profits, costs and attorney fees as provided under Lanham Act § 35(a), and may qualify for other relief set forth in Lanham Act § 36.

Similar to its predecessor provision, the amended § 43(c)(6) provides that federal registration of a mark will *bar any state claim* that the mark dilutes or otherwise harms "the distinctiveness or reputation of a mark, label or form of advertisement." This provides an additional incentive to register: To the extent that state dilution laws are broader than the federal, registration removes them as an obstacle.

3. *Blurring dilution.* "Blurring" dilution occurs when the defendant's use of a similar mark diminishes or "whittles away" the individuality and uniqueness of the plaintiff's mark and the strong, immediate public association of the mark with the plaintiff and the positive imagery the plaintiff has associated with the mark through persuasive advertising. This is the form of dilution primarily alleged in the *Starbucks* and *Louis Vuitton* cases, and is the more prevalent form. How should the plaintiff go about proving that the defendant's acts are likely to dilute its famous mark? Should it be sufficient to

provide survey evidence that the defendant's mark "reminds" thirty percent of respondents of the plaintiff's mark? Is widespread public association of the marks enough to prove a likelihood of dilution, or is something more needed? If more is needed, what, exactly, is it? Does the presence of a mental association ensure that there is blurring?

The *Louis Vuitton* court addresses allegations that mark parodies dilute the distinctiveness of their target marks. Do you agree with the court's reasoning? Did the court reach the right result? Could the defendant's "Charbucks" mark, in the *Starbucks* case, be deemed a non-diluting parody? How about the "Victor's Little Secret" mark in *Moseley*?

4. *Tarnishment dilution.* Tarnishment dilution may occur when the defendant places a similar mark in an "unwholesome" context or in a context that is "out-of-keeping with plaintiff's high-quality image." The plaintiff's claim is not simply that the defendant's use will diminish the distinctiveness of its mark or name, but that it will actively impair the selling power and allure of the plaintiff's mark or name through negative or unsavory association. For example, in Coca–Cola Co. v. Gemini Rising, Inc., 346 F.Supp. 1183, 1189 (E.D.N.Y.1972), the court found that the defendant's use of the distinctive red-and-white script design of the Coca–Cola trademark on a poster admonishing viewers to "Enjoy Cocaine" was likely to tarnish the Coca–Cola mark. Likewise, in Eastman Kodak Co. v. Rakow, 739 F.Supp. 116 (W.D.N.Y. 1989), the defendant comedian's use of the stage name "Kodak" in comedy routines featuring crude language and raunchy jokes about bodily functions and sex tarnished the camera and film company's wholesome "Kodak" mark. Compare Tetley, Inc. v. Topps Chewing Gum, Inc., 556 F.Supp. 785, 794 (E.D.N.Y.1983) ("Petley Flea Bags" does not tarnish "Tetley Tea Bags"). In Steinway & Sons v. Robert Demars & Friends, 210 U.S.P.Q. 954 (C.D.Cal. 1981), the court found that the defendants' adoption of the mark "Stein–Way" for their clip-on handles for beer cans tarnished the prestigious "Steinway" mark for pianos. The court explained:

> Defendants' use of the designation STEIN–WAY in connection with its business and on its products, unless enjoined, will associate or tend to associate plaintiff's high quality pianos and plaintiff's business and cultural activities with defendants' inexpensive, mass-produced products and with the retail liquor stores, supermarkets and similar merchandising concerns which sell defendants' products. Such association will inevitably tarnish plaintiff's reputation and image with the public of manufacturing and/or sponsoring only products and activities of taste, quality and distinction.

Id., 210 U.S.P.Q. at 961.

In the *Starbucks* case, why does the court find the evidence insufficient to support a finding of tarnishment? What further evidence would suffice? In *Moseley,* who makes the more convincing argument—the majority or the dissent? Should association with sex-related products give rise to a presumption of tarnishment? What if the plaintiff's famous mark was not "Victoria's Secret," but "Playboy" or "Hustler" for magazines, or "Trojan" for condoms? If the plaintiff uses its famous mark to identify sex-related products, is it capable of being tarnished?

Is there a reasonable argument that the defendant's "Chewy Vuiton" dog toy tarnished Louis Vuitton's famous mark for women's handbags?

5. *Fame.* As amended, § 43(c) clarifies that a mark is famous "if it is widely recognized by the general consuming public of the United States as a designation of source of the goods or services of the mark's owner." The 2006 revisions provide a list of non-exclusive factors that courts should consider in determining whether a mark possesses the requisite degree of fame:

(i) The duration, extent, and geographic reach of advertising and publicity of the mark, whether advertised or publicized by the owner or third parties.

(ii) The amount, volume, and geographic extent of sales of goods or services offered under the mark.

(iii) The extent of actual recognition of the mark.

(iv) Whether the mark was registered under the Act of March 3, 1881, or the Act of February 20, 1905, or on the principal register.

15 U.S.C. § 1125(c)(2)(A). In a prepared statement included in the House Report, Representative Howard Berman, Ranking Member of the Subcommittee on Courts, the Internet, and Intellectual Property stressed:

Protection against trademark dilution seems, in some ways, more akin to property protection than consumer protection. Thus, any anti-dilution legislation should be carefully and narrowly crafted. The goal must be to protect only the most famous trademarks * * *. Dilution should once again be used sparingly as an "extraordinary" remedy, one that requires a significant showing of fame. * * * [I]t is our hope that the dilution remedy will be used in the rare circumstance and not as the alternative pleading.

H.Rep. No. 109–23, *supra*, at 16.

The Restatement (Third) of Unfair Competition suggests that a mark will be famous if it "retains its source significance when encountered outside the context of the goods or services with which the mark is used by the trademark owner." Restatement (Third) of Unfair Competition § 25, cmt e (1995). For example, if people think "a source of cameras" when they hear or see the word "Kodak," even in a context other than sale of cameras, the mark is sufficiently famous. If the mark only evokes a source association when used in connection with the goods or services it identifies, then it is not sufficiently famous. *Id.*

6. *Cybersquatter dilution.* Shortly after the Federal Trademark Dilution Act of 1995 was enacted, trademark owners began bringing federal dilution suits against "cybersquatters" who had registered the plaintiffs' allegedly famous marks as domain names (usually in the ".com" top level domain) and offered the registrations for sale The courts often found a cause of action. In doing so, the courts relied on the Act's definition of the term "dilution" in Lanham Act § 45:

[T]he lessening of the capacity of a famous mark to identify and distinguish goods or services, regardless of the presence or absence of (1) competition between the owner of the famous mark and other parties, or (2) likelihood of confusion, mistake or deception.

15 U.S.C. § 1127. The courts reasoned that a defendant's registration of a famous mark as a domain name lessened the capacity of the famous mark to identify and distinguish the mark owner's goods or services by means of the Internet, because the registration effectively prevented the mark owner from using the same combination of mark and top level domain itself. Web surfers who assumed that "X.com" would lead to the web site of X Company (the owner of the X mark) would be misled and might fail to continue to search for the X Company's actual web address. See, e.g., Panavision International, L.P. v. Toeppen, 945 F.Supp. 1296 (C.D.Cal. 1996), aff'd, 141 F.3d 1316 (9th Cir.1998). In its decision in the *Panavision* case, the Ninth Circuit noted that the defendant cybersquatter's conduct varied from that envisioned under the two standard dilution theories of blurring and tarnishment, and added that it was unnecessary to rely on those two standard theories in finding dilution under § 43(c). The Ninth Circuit subsequently referred to the type of dilution found in *Panavision* as "cybersquatter dilution."

In the Trademark Dilution Revision Act of 2006, Congress deleted the original definition of dilution quoted above and substituted the more specific definitions of blurring and tarnishment discussed in Notes 3 and 4, *supra*. What are the implications of this change for the "cybersquatter dilution" cause of action?

7. *Product configuration dilution.* Since product configurations can serve as marks, it follows that product configurations can be diluted under § 43(c). Indeed, the Trademark Dilution Revision Act of 2006 expressly confirmed this understanding by addressing the burden of proof in § 43(c) claims alleging dilution of unregistered trade dress. 15 U.S.C. § 1125(c)(4). However, some have questioned the constitutionality of extending dilution protection to product feature trade dress. For example, in I.P. Lund Trading ApS v. Kohler Co., 163 F.3d 27 (1st Cir. 1998), the plaintiff claimed that the defendant's water faucet configuration diluted the source-indicating configuration of its popular "Falling Water" faucet. The First Circuit characterized the claim as a questionable strategy to circumvent compliance with the design patent laws, and expressed concerns about the constitutionality of applying dilution protection to product designs. The Constitution's Patents and Copyrights Clause only authorizes Congress to provide patent protection for a "limited duration." Applying the Federal Trademark Dilution Act to product designs would grant the products patent-like protection for an unlimited period of time, and constitute use of Congress' Commerce Clause power (which is the basis of trademark and unfair competition protection) to "trump" the limitations on Congressional power set forth in the Patents and Copyrights Clause.

Are the *Lund* court's misgivings well founded? What, if any, implications might the Supreme Court's decisions in the *Wal–Mart* and *TrafFix* cases, *supra*, have for application of § 43(c) in product configuration cases? In the Trademark Dilution Revision Act of 2006, Congress added the following "Savings Clause:" "Nothing in this subsection shall be construed to impair, modify, or supersede the applicability of the patent laws of the United States." 15 U.S.C. § 1125(c)(7).

8. *Express exceptions to § 43(c) dilution liability.* As amended by the Trademark Dilution Revision Act of 2006, Lanham Act § 43(c)(3) provides:

> The following shall not be actionable as dilution by blurring or dilution by tarnishment under this subsection:
>
>> (A) Any fair use, including a nominative or descriptive fair use, or facilitation of such fair use, of a famous mark by another person other than as a designation of source for the person's own goods or services, including use in connection with—
>>
>>> (i) advertising or promotion that permits consumers to compare goods or services; or
>>>
>>> (ii) identifying and parodying, criticizing, or commenting upon the famous mark owner or the goods or services of the famous mark owner.
>>
>> (B) All forms of news reporting and news commentary.
>>
>> (C) Any noncommercial use of a mark.

15 U.S.C. § 1125(c)(3). The original § 43(c) language likewise excluded "noncommercial use of the mark," and courts have routinely construed this language (in light of the legislative history) to restrict the federal dilution cause of action to unauthorized uses of marks in "commercial speech," as that term is understood under the Supreme Court's First Amendment jurisprudence. See, e.g., Mattel, Inc. v. MCA Records, Inc., 296 F.3d 894, 904–06 (9th Cir. 2002).

Subpart (3)(A) expands the original § 43(c) language, which excluded "[f]air use of a famous mark by another person in comparative commercial advertising or promotion to identify the competing goods or services of the owner of the famous mark." What does the new, expanded subpart (3)(A) language add? Assuming that the plaintiff in People for the Ethical Treatment of Animals v. Doughney (reproduced *supra*) alleged a § 43(c) trademark dilution claim, how would the new subpart (3)(A) apply? In *Louis Vuitton*, the Fourth Circuit holds that parodies used as marks for the defendant's products or services are not exempted from dilution liability under § 43(c)(A). Might they nonetheless be exempted as "non-commercial" under subsection (C)? See Smith v. Wal-Mart Stores, 537 F.Supp.2d 1302 (N.D.Ga. 2008).

9. *Dilution and the mark selection and registration process.* What, if any, impact is the Federal Trademark Dilution Act likely to have on business' selection of new marks? After enacting the Federal Trademark Dilution Act, Congress amended the Lanham Act specifically to permit opposition and cancellation of trademark registrations on grounds of dilution. See 15 U.S.C. §§ 1052(f), 1063(a), 1064, 1092. It did not, however, amend § 2(a) to authorize the PTO ex parte to reject an application to register on dilution grounds.

Problems

1. Defendant, an antiabortion activist, sets up a web site under the domain name "plannedparenthood.com." The web site reproduces the cover of an antiabortion book entitled "The Cost of Abortion," by Lawrence Roberge, under which appear several links: "Forward" (links to the Forward of Roberge's book); "Afterword" (links to the Afterword of Roberge's book); "About the Author" (links to information about Roberge); "Book Review" (links to other readers' comments about the book); and "Biography" (links to more information about Roberge's background). The owner of the "Planned Parenthood" mark is a nonprofit reproductive health care organization that, among other things, provides abortions.

Assume that the defendant's motive in setting up his web site under the "plannedparenthood.com" domain name is to attract web users seeking the plaintiff's web page to his own site and to the antiabortion message provided there. The defendant admits that he is trying to criticize the plaintiff, and that he wants to help Roberge "plug" his book. However, the defendant is not being compensated for his actions in connection with the Roberge book and has no profit motive.

The plaintiff has brought a § 43(c) dilution claim against the defendant. How would you evaluate the claim?

What if, instead of the web site described above, the defendant set up a site under the domain name "www.plannedparenthood.com" which consisted simply of horrifying photographs of aborted fetuses. Would this affect the outcome of the case?

2. eBay is the proprietor of an online marketplace, through which users sell and buy goods. eBay does not itself sell goods—it merely provides the site and facilities for others' sales. It makes money by charging sellers to use its listing services and through its "PayPal" service, which assists buyers to pay sellers for their purchases. "Tiffany" is a famous, highly distinctive mark for expensive jewelry. A number of eBay users sell "Tiffany" jewelry on the eBay site. To promote its online marketplace, eBay purchases sponsored-link advertisements on various search engines. Among other things, eBay buys the right to have its ad shown when search engine users enter "Tiffany" as a search term. The ad states: "**Tiffany** on eBay. Find **Tiffany** items at low prices. With over 5 million items for sale every day, you'll be sure to find whatever you are seeking on eBay."

The owner of the "Tiffany" mark for jewelry sues eBay, alleging dilution by blurring. How should the court evaluate the claim?

3. Defendant runs "eVisa," a multilingual education and information business that operates exclusively on the Internet at "www.evisa.com." The "eVisa" name is derived from an earlier English-language tutoring service called "Eikaiwa Visa" that defendant ran while in Japan. "Eikaiwa" is Japanese for "English conversation." According to defendant, the "e" in "eVisa" is short for "Eikaiwa." The use of "visa" in both names is meant to suggest the ability to travel, both linguistically and physically, through the English-speaking world.

Plaintiff, the owner of the famous, distinctive "Visa" mark for credit card services, sues defendant, alleging blurring dilution. How should the court rule?

E. THE ANTICYBERSQUATTING CONSUMER PROTECTION ACT

In 1999, Congress enacted the Anticybersquatting Consumer Protection Act ("Anticybersquatting Act"), which adds a new subsection (d) to Lanham Act § 43, prohibiting the bad-faith registration, trafficking in, or use of a domain name that is confusingly similar to, or dilutive of the mark of another. While the courts had demonstrated that relief against such "cybersquatting" could be provided through the existing trademark infringement and dilution causes of action, Congress found these remedies to be "expensive and uncertain." H.Rep. No. 106–412, 106th Cong., 1st Sess., 6 (1999).

The Anticybersquatting Act (codified at 15 U.S.C. § 1125(d)) provides trademark owners with a narrow cause of action specifically tailored to address the problem of cybersquatting. This cause of action augments, but does not replace, the existing causes of action for infringement and/or dilution, which might be alleged as well in the same suit. The Act makes the remedies of forfeiture or cancellation of the domain name registration, or transfer of the registration to the owner of the mark, available in all cases, regardless of whether the domain name was registered before or after the effective date of the Act. 15 U.S.C.A. § 1125(d)(1)(C). Actual or statutory damages (ranging from $1,000 to $100,000 per domain name) may be awarded for violations, but not in the case of registration, trafficking or use of a domain name that occurred prior to the effective date of the Act.

The Anticybersquatting Act adds another important weapon to the trademark owner's arsenal through provision of *in rem* jurisdiction to seek forfeiture, cancellation, or transfer of an infringing domain name registration when the registrant cannot be located or is not subject to personal jurisdiction.[20]

The key to liability under the Act is the defendant's *bad faith intent to profit* from the mark's good will. In introducing the bill that became the Anticybersquatting Act, Senator Lott submitted a section-by-section anal-

---

20. The Anticybersquatting Act also created a new cause of action for individuals whose names may not qualify for protection as marks:

> Any person who registers a domain name that consists of the name of another living person, or a name substantially and confusingly similar thereto, without that person's consent, with the specific intent to profit from such name by selling the domain name for financial gain to that person or any third party, shall be liable in a civil action by such person.

15 U.S.C. § 1129(1)(A). In such cases, a court may award injunctive relief, including forfeiture or cancellation of the domain name, or the transfer of the domain name to the plaintiff. There are also provisions for costs and attorney fees to the prevailing party. However, unlike the provisions protecting marks against cybersquatting, the individual name provisions do not provide for damages or *in rem* jurisdiction. Moreover, they only apply to domain names registered on or after November 29, 1999. 15 U.S.C. § 1129(2)–(4).

ysis to be printed in the Congressional Record. The following excerpt from that analysis provides useful background information about the Act, the bad faith limitation, and the provisions for *in rem* jurisdiction.

TRADEMARK CYBERPIRACY PREVENTION

145 Cong. Rec. S14713–S14715 (daily ed. Nov. 17, 1999).

Subsection (a). In General. This subsection amends the Trademark Act to provide an explicit trademark remedy for cybersquatting under a new section 43(d). Under paragraph (1)(A) of the new section 43(d), actionable conduct would include the registration, trafficking in, or use of a domain name that is identical or confusingly similar to, or dilutive of, the mark of another, including a personal name that is protected as a mark under section 43 of the Lanham Act, provided that the mark was distinctive (*i.e.*, enjoyed trademark status) at the time the domain name was registered, or in the case of trademark dilution, was famous at the time the domain name was registered. The bill is carefully and narrowly tailored, however, to extend only to cases where the plaintiff can demonstrate that the defendant registered, trafficked in, or used the offending domain name with bad-faith intent to profit from the goodwill of the mark belonging to someone else. Thus, the bill does not extend to innocent domain name registrations by those who are unaware of another's use of the name, or even to someone who is aware of the trademark status of the name but registers a domain name containing the mark for any reason other than with bad faith intent to profit from the goodwill associated with that mark.

 * * *

Paragraph (1)(B)(i) of the new section 43(d) sets forth a number of nonexclusive, nonexhaustive factors to assist a court in determining whether the required bad-faith element exists in any given case. These factors are designed to balance the property interests of trademark owners with the legitimate interests of Internet users and others who seek to make lawful uses of others' marks, including for purposes such as comparative advertising, comment, criticism, parody, news reporting, fair use, etc. The bill suggests a total of nine factors a court may wish to consider. The first four suggest circumstances that may tend to indicate an absence of bad-faith intent to profit from the goodwill of a mark, and the next four suggest circumstances that may tend to indicate that such bad-faith intent exists. The last factor may suggest either bad-faith or an absence thereof depending on the circumstances.

First, under paragraph (1)(B)(i)(I), a court may consider whether the domain name registrant has trademark or any other intellectual property rights in the name. This factor recognizes, as does trademark law in general, that there may be concurring uses of the same name that are noninfringing, such as the use of the "Delta" mark for both air travel and sink faucets. Similarly, the registration of the domain name "delta-force.com" by a movie studio would not tend to indicate a bad-faith intent on the part of the registrant to trade on Delta Airlines or Delta Faucets' trademarks.

Second, under paragraph (1)(B)(i)(II), a court may consider the extent to which the domain name is the same as the registrant's own legal name or a nickname by which that person is commonly identified. This factor recognizes, again as does the concept of fair use in trademark law, that a person should be able to be identified by their own name, whether in their business or on a web site. Similarly, a person may bear a legitimate nickname that is identical or similar to a well-known trademark, such as in the well-publicized case of the parents who registered the domain name "pokey.org" for their young son who goes by that name, and these individuals should not be deterred by this bill from using their name online. This factor is not intended to suggest that domain name registrants may evade the application of this act by merely adopting Exxon, Ford, or other well-known marks as their nicknames. It merely provides a court with the appropriate discretion to determine whether or not the fact that a person bears a nickname similar to a mark at issue is an indication of an absence of bad-faith on the part of the registrant.

Third, under paragraph (1)(B)(i)(III), a court may consider the domain name registrant's prior use, if any, of the domain name in connection with the bona fide offering of goods or services. Again, this factor recognizes that the legitimate use of the domain name in online commerce may be a good indicator of the intent of the person registering that name. Where the person has used the domain name in commerce without creating a likelihood of confusion as to the source or origin of the goods or services and has not otherwise attempted to use the name in order to profit from the goodwill of the trademark owner's name, a court may look to this as an indication of the absence of bad faith on the part of the registrant.

Fourth, under paragraph (1)(B)(i)(IV), a court may consider the person's bona fide noncommercial or fair use of the mark in a web site that is accessible under the domain name at issue. This factor is intended to balance the interests of trademark owners with the interest of those who would make lawful noncommercial or fair uses of others' marks online, such as in comparative advertising, comment, criticism, parody, news reporting, etc. Under the bill, the mere fact that the domain name is used for purposes of comparative advertising, comment, criticism, parody, news reporting, etc. would not alone establish a lack of bad-faith intent. The fact that a person uses a mark in a site in such a lawful manner may be an appropriate indication that the person's registration or use of the domain name lacked the required element of bad-faith. This factor is not intended to create a loophole that otherwise might swallow the bill, however, by allowing a domain name registrant to evade application of the Act by merely putting up a noninfringing site under an infringing domain name. For example, in the well known case of Panavision Int'l v. Toeppen, 141 F.3d 1316 (9th Cir.1998), a well known cybersquatter had registered a host of domain names mirroring famous trademarks, including names for

Panavision, Delta Airlines, Neiman Marcus, Eddie Bauer, Lufthansa, and more than 100 other marks, and had attempted to sell them to the mark owners for amounts in the range of $10,000 to $15,000 each. His use of the "panavision.com" and "panaflex.com" domain names was seemingly more innocuous, however, as they served as addresses for sites that merely displayed pictures of Pana Illinois and the word "Hello" respectively. This bill would not allow a person to evade the holding of that case—which found that Mr. Toeppen had made a commercial use of the Panavision marks and that such uses were, in fact, diluting under the Federal Trademark Dilution Act—merely by posting noninfringing uses of the trademark on a site accessible under the offending domain name, as Mr. Toeppen did. Similarly, the bill does not affect existing trademark law to the extent it has addressed the interplay between First Amendment protections and the rights of trademark owners. Rather, the bill gives courts the flexibility to weigh appropriate factors in determining whether the name was registered or used in bad faith, and it recognizes that one such factor may be the use the domain name registrant makes of the mark.

Fifth, under paragraph (1)(B)(i)(V), a court may consider whether, in registering or using the domain name, the registrant intended to divert consumers away from the trademark owner's website to a website that could harm the goodwill of the mark, either for purposes of commercial gain or with the intent to tarnish or disparage the mark, by creating a likelihood of confusion as to the source, sponsorship, affiliation, or endorsement of the site. This factor recognizes that one of the main reasons cybersquatters use other people's trademarks is to divert Internet users to their own sites by creating confusion as to the source, sponsorship, affiliation, or endorsement of the site. This is done for a number of reasons, including to pass off inferior goods under the name of a well-known mark holder, to defraud consumers into providing personally identifiable information, such as credit card numbers, to attract "eyeballs" to sites that price online advertising according to the number of "hits" the site receives, or even just to harm the value of the mark. Under this provision, a court may give appropriate weight to evidence that a domain name registrant intended to confuse or deceive the public in this manner when making a determination of bad-faith intent.

Sixth, under paragraph (1)(B)(i)(VI), a court may consider a domain name registrant's offer to transfer, sell, or otherwise assign the domain name to the mark owner or any third party for financial gain, where the registrant has not used, and did not have any intent to use, the domain name in the bona fide offering of any goods or services. A court may also consider a person's prior conduct indicating a pattern of such conduct. This factor is consistent with the court cases, like the Panavision case mentioned above, where courts have found a defendant's offer to sell the domain name to the legitimate mark owner as being indicative of the defendant's intent to trade on the value of a trademark owner's marks by engaging in the business of registering those marks and selling them to the rightful trademark owners. It does not suggest that a court should consider the mere offer to sell a domain name to a mark owner or the failure to use a name in the bona fide offering of goods or services as sufficient to indicate bad faith. Indeed, there are cases in which a person registers a name in anticipation of a business venture that simply never pans out. And someone who has a legitimate registration of a domain name that mirrors someone else's domain name, such as a trademark owner that is a lawful concurrent user of that name with another trademark owner, may, in fact, wish to sell that name to the other trademark owner. This bill does not imply that these facts are an indication of bad-faith. It merely provides a court with the necessary discretion to recognize the evidence of bad-faith when it is present. In practice, the offer to sell domain names for exorbitant amounts to the rightful mark owner has been one of the most common threads in abusive domain name registrations. Finally, by using the financial gain standard, this paragraph allows a court to examine the motives of the seller.

Seventh, under paragraph (1)(B)(i)(VII), a court may consider the registrant's intentional provision of material and misleading false contact information in an application for the domain name registration, the person's intentional failure to maintain accurate contact information, and the person's prior conduct indicating a pattern of such conduct. Falsification of contact information with the intent to evade identification and service of process by trademark owners is also a common thread in cases of cybersquatting. This factor recognizes that fact, while still recognizing that there may be circumstances in which the provision of false information may be due to other factors, such as mistake, or, as some have suggested in the case of political dissidents, for purposes of anonymity. This bill balances those factors by limiting consideration to the person's contact information, and even then requiring that the provision of false information be material and misleading. As with other factors, this factor is nonexclusive and a court is called upon to make a determination based on the facts presented whether or not the provision of false information does, in fact, indicate bad-faith.

Eighth, under paragraph (1)(B)(i)(VIII), a court may consider the domain name registrant's acquisition of multiple domain names which the person knows are identical or confusingly similar to, or dilutive of, others' marks. This factor recognizes the increasingly common cybersquatting practice known as "warehousing," in which a cybersquatter registers multiple domain names—sometimes hundreds, even thousands—that mirror the trademarks of others. By sitting on these marks and not making the first move to offer to sell them to the mark owner, these cybersquatters have been largely successful in evading the case law developed under the Federal Trademark Dilution Act. This bill does not suggest that the mere registration of multiple domain names is an indication of bad faith, but it allows a court to weigh the fact that a person has registered multiple domain names that infringe or dilute the trademarks of others as part of its consideration of whether the requisite bad-faith intent exists.

Lastly, under paragraph (1)(B)(i)(IX), a court may consider the extent to which the mark incorporated in the person's domain name registration is or is not distinctive and famous within the meaning of subsection (c)(1) of section 43 of the Trademark Act of 1946. The more distinctive or famous a mark has become, the more likely the owner of that mark is deserving of the relief available under this act. At the same time, the fact that a mark is not well-known may also suggest a lack of bad-faith.

Paragraph (1)(B)(ii) underscores the bad-faith requirement by making clear that bad-faith shall not be found in any case in which the court determines that the person believed and had reasonable grounds to believe that the use of the domain name was a fair use or otherwise lawful.

* * *

Paragraph (2)(A) provides for in rem jurisdiction, which allows a mark owner to seek the forfeiture, cancellation, or transfer of an infringing domain name by filing an in rem action against the name itself, where the mark owner has satisfied the court that it has exercised due diligence in trying to locate the owner of the domain name but is unable to do so, or where the mark owner is otherwise unable to obtain in personam jurisdiction over such person. As indicated above, a significant problem faced by trademark owners in the fight against cybersquatting is the fact that many cybersquatters register domain names under aliases or otherwise provide false information in their registration applications in order to avoid identification and service of process by the mark owner. This bill will alleviate this difficulty, while protecting the notions of fair play and substantial justice, by enabling a mark owner to seek an injunction against the infringing property in those cases where, after due diligence, a mark owner is unable to proceed against the domain name registrant because the registrant has provided false contact information and is otherwise not to be found, or where a court is unable to assert personal jurisdiction over such person, provided the mark owner can show that the domain name itself violates substantive federal trademark law (i.e., that the domain name violates the rights of the registrant of a mark registered in the Patent and Trademark Office, or section 43(a) or (c) of the Trademark Act). Under the bill, a mark owner will be deemed to have exercised due diligence in trying to find a defendant if the mark owner sends notice of the alleged violation and intent to proceed to the domain name registrant at the postal and e-mail address provided by the registrant to the registrar and publishes notice of the action as the court may direct promptly after filing the action. * * *

* * *

LAMPARELLO v. FALWELL

United States Court of Appeals for the Fourth Circuit, 2006.
420 F.3d 309, *cert. denied*, 126 S.Ct. 1772, 164 L.Ed.2d 516 (2006).

DIANA GRIBBON MOTZ, CIRCUIT JUDGE.

Christopher Lamparello appeals the district court's order enjoining him from maintaining a gripe website critical of Reverend Jerry Falwell. For the reasons stated below, we reverse.

I.

Reverend Falwell is "a nationally known minister who has been active as a commentator on politics and public affairs." He holds the common law trademarks "Jerry Falwell" and "Falwell," and the registered trademark "Listen America with Jerry Falwell." Jerry Falwell Ministries can be found online at "www.falwell.com," a website which receives 9,000 hits (or visits) per day.

Lamparello registered the domain name "www.fallwell.com" on February 11, 1999, after hearing Reverend Falwell give an interview "in which he expressed opinions about gay people and homosexuality that [Lamparello] considered ... offensive." Lamparello created a website at that domain name to respond to what he believed were "untruths about gay people." Lamparello's website included headlines such as "Bible verses that Dr. Falwell chooses to ignore" and "Jerry Falwell has been bearing false witness (Exodus 20:16) against his gay and lesbian neighbors for a long time." The site also contained in-depth criticism of Reverend Falwell's views. For example, the website stated:

> Dr. Falwell says that he is on the side of truth. He says that he will preach that homosexuality is a sin until the day he dies. But we believe that if the reverend were to take another thoughtful look at the scriptures, he would discover that they have been twisted around to support an anti-gay political agenda ... at the expense of the gospel.

Although the interior pages of Lamparello's website did not contain a disclaimer, the homepage prominently stated, "This website is NOT affiliated with Jerry Falwell or his ministry"; advised, "If you would like to visit Rev. Falwell's website, you may click here"; and provided a hyperlink to Reverend Falwell's website.

At one point, Lamparello's website included a link to the Amazon.com webpage for a book that offered interpretations of the Bible that Lamparello favored, but the parties agree that Lamparello has never sold goods or services on his website. The parties also agree that "Lamparello's domain name and web site at www.fallwell.com," which received only 200 hits per day, "had no measurable impact on the quantity of visits to [Reverend Falwell's] web site at www.falwell.com."

Nonetheless, Reverend Falwell sent Lamparello letters in October 2001 and June 2003 demanding that he cease and desist from using www.fallwell.com or any variation of Reverend Falwell's name as a domain name. Ultimately, Lamparello filed this action against Reverend Falwell and his ministries (collectively referred to hereinafter as "Reverend Falwell"), seeking a declaratory judgment of noninfringement. Reverend Falwell counter-claimed, alleging trademark infringement under 15 U.S.C.

§ 1114 (2000), false designation of origin under 15 U.S.C. § 1125(a), * * * and cybersquatting under 15 U.S.C. § 1125(d).

The parties stipulated to all relevant facts and filed cross-motions for summary judgment. The district court granted summary judgment to Reverend Falwell, enjoined Lamparello from using Reverend Falwell's mark at www.fallwell.com, and required Lamparello to transfer the domain name to Reverend Falwell. * * *

* * *

III.

* * * To prevail on a cybersquatting claim, Reverend Falwell must show that Lamparello: (1) "had a bad faith intent to profit from using the [www.fallwell.com] domain name," and (2) the domain name www. fallwell.com "is identical or confusingly similar to, or dilutive of, the distinctive and famous [Falwell] mark." *PETA*, 263 F.3d at 367.

"The paradigmatic harm that the ACPA was enacted to eradicate" is "the practice of cybersquatters registering several hundred domain names in an effort to sell them to the legitimate owners of the mark." *Lucas Nursery & Landscaping, Inc. v. Grosse,* 359 F.3d 806, 810 (6th Cir.2004). The Act was also intended to stop the registration of multiple marks with the hope of selling them to the highest bidder, "distinctive marks to defraud consumers" or "to engage in counterfeiting activities," and "well-known marks to prey on consumer confusion by misusing the domain name to divert customers from the mark owner's site to the cybersquatter's own site, many of which are pornography sites that derive advertising revenue based on the number of visits, or 'hits,' the site receives." S.Rep. No. 106–140, 1999 WL 594571, at *5–6. The Act was not intended to prevent "noncommercial uses of a mark, such as for comment, criticism, parody, news reporting, etc.," and thus they "are beyond the scope" of the ACPA. *Id.* at *9.

To distinguish abusive domain name registrations from legitimate ones, the ACPA directs courts to consider nine nonexhaustive factors:

(I) the trademark or other intellectual property rights of the person, if any, in the domain name;

(II) the extent to which the domain name consists of the legal name of the person or a name that is otherwise commonly used to identify that person;

(III) the person's prior use, if any, of the domain name in connection with the bona fide offering of any goods or services;

(IV) the person's bona fide noncommercial or fair use of the mark in a site accessible under the domain name;

(V) the person's intent to divert consumers from the mark owner's online location to a site accessible under the domain name that could harm the goodwill represented by the mark, either for commercial gain or with the intent to tarnish or disparage the mark, by creating a likelihood of confusion as to the source, sponsorship, affiliation, or endorsement of the site;

(VI) the person's offer to transfer, sell, or otherwise assign the domain name to the mark owner or any third party for financial gain without having used, or having an intent to use, the domain name in the bona fide offering of any goods or services, or the person's prior conduct indicating a pattern of such conduct;

(VII) the person's provision of material and misleading false contact information when applying for the registration of the domain name, the person's intentional failure to maintain accurate contact information, or the person's prior conduct indicating a pattern of such conduct;

(VIII) the person's registration or acquisition of multiple domain names which the person knows are identical or confusingly similar to marks of others that are distinctive at the time of the registration of such domain names, or dilutive of famous marks of others that are famous at the time of registration of such domain names, without regard to the goods or services of the parties; and

(IX) the extent to which the mark incorporated in the person's domain name registration is or is not distinctive and famous within the meaning of subsection (c)(1) of this section.

15 U.S.C. § 1125(d)(1)(B)(i).

These factors attempt "to balance the property interests of trademark owners with the legitimate interests of Internet users and others who seek to make lawful uses of others' marks, including for purposes such as comparative advertising, *comment, criticism,* parody, news reporting, fair use, etc." H.R. Rep. No. 106–412, 1999 WL 970519, at *10 (emphasis added). * * * "There is no simple formula for evaluating and weighing these factors. For example, courts do not simply count up which party has more factors in its favor after the evidence is in." In fact, because use of these listed factors is permissive, "[w]e need not ... march through" them all in every case. "The factors are given to courts as a guide, not as a substitute for careful thinking about whether the conduct at issue is motivated by a bad faith intent to profit."

After close examination of the undisputed facts involved in this case, we can only conclude that Reverend Falwell cannot demonstrate that Lamparello "had a bad faith intent to profit from using the [www.fallwell. com] domain name." Lamparello clearly employed www.fallwell.com simply to criticize Reverend Falwell's views. Factor IV of the ACPA counsels against finding a bad faith intent to profit in such circumstances because "use of a domain name for purposes of ... comment, [and] criticism" constitutes a "bona fide noncommercial or fair use" under the statute. That Lamparello provided a link to an Amazon.com webpage selling a book he favored does not diminish the communicative function of his website. The use of a domain name to engage in criticism or commentary "even where done for profit" does not alone evidence a bad faith intent to profit, and Lamparello did not even stand to gain financially from sales of the book at Amazon.com. Thus factor IV weighs heavily in favor of finding that Lamparello lacked a bad faith intent to profit from the use of the domain name.

Equally important, Lamparello has not engaged in the type of conduct described in the statutory factors as typifying the bad faith intent to profit essential to a successful cybersquatting claim. First, we have already held that Lamparello's domain name does not create a likelihood of confusion as to source or affiliation. Accordingly, Lamparello has not engaged in the type of conduct—"creating a likelihood of confusion as to the source, sponsorship, affiliation, or endorsement of the site,"—described as an indicator of a bad faith intent to profit in factor V of the statute.

Factors VI and VIII also counsel against finding a bad faith intent to profit here. Lamparello has made no attempt—or even indicated a willingness—"to transfer, sell, or otherwise assign the domain name to [Reverend Falwell] or any third party for financial gain." Similarly, Lamparello has not registered "multiple domain names"; rather, the record indicates he has registered only one. Thus, Lamparello's conduct is not of the suspect variety described in factors VI and VIII of the Act.

Notably, the case at hand differs markedly from those in which the courts have found a bad faith intent to profit from domain names used for websites engaged in political commentary or parody. For example, in *PETA* we found the registrant of www.peta.org engaged in cybersquatting because www.peta.org was one of *fifty* to *sixty* domain names Doughney had registered, and because Doughney had evidenced a clear intent to sell www.peta.org to PETA, stating that PETA should try to " 'settle' with him and 'make him an offer.' " Similarly, in *Coca-Cola Co. v. Purdy,* 382 F.3d 774 (8th Cir.2004), the Eighth Circuit found an anti-abortion activist who had registered domain names incorporating famous marks such as "Washington Post" liable for cybersquatting because he had registered almost *seventy* domain names, had offered to stop using the Washington Post mark if the newspaper published an opinion piece by him on its editorial page, and posted content that created a likelihood of confusion as to whether the famous markholders sponsored the anti-abortion sites and "ha[d] taken positions on hotly contested issues." *Id.* at 786. In contrast, Lamparello did not register multiple domain names, he did not offer to transfer them for valuable consideration, and he did not create a likelihood of confusion.

Instead, Lamparello, like the plaintiffs in two cases recently decided by the Fifth and Sixth Circuits, created a gripe site. Both courts expressly refused to find that gripe sites located at domain names nearly identical to the marks at issue violated the ACPA. In *TMI, Inc. v. Maxwell,* 368 F.3d 433, 434–35 (5th Cir.2004), Joseph Maxwell, a customer of homebuilder TMI, registered the domain name "www.trendmakerhome.com," which differed by only one letter from TMI's mark, TrendMaker Homes, and its domain name, "www.trendmakerhomes.com." Maxwell used the site to complain about his experience with TMI and to list the name of a contractor whose work pleased him. After his registration expired, Maxwell registered "www.trendmakerhome.info." TMI then sued, alleging cybersquatting. The Fifth Circuit reversed the district court's finding that Maxwell violated the ACPA, reasoning that his site was noncommercial and designed only "to inform potential customers about a negative experience with the company."

Similarly, in *Lucas Nursery & Landscaping,* a customer of Lucas Nursery registered the domain name "www.lucasnursery.com" and posted her dissatisfaction with the company's landscaping services. Because the registrant, Grosse, like Lamparello, registered a single domain name, the Sixth Circuit concluded that her conduct did not constitute that which Congress intended to proscribe—i.e., the registration of multiple domain names. Noting that Grosse's gripe site did not create any confusion as to sponsorship and that she had never attempted to sell the domain name to the markholder, the court found that Grosse's conduct was not actionable under the ACPA. The court explained: "One of the ACPA's main objectives is the protection of consumers from slick internet peddlers who trade on the names and reputations of established brands. The practice of informing fellow consumers of one's experience with a particular service provider is surely not inconsistent with this ideal." *Id.* at 811.

Like Maxwell and Grosse before him, Lamparello has not evidenced a bad faith intent to profit under the ACPA. To the contrary, he has used www.fallwell.com to engage in the type of "comment[ ][and] criticism" that Congress specifically stated militates against a finding of bad faith intent to profit. And he has neither registered multiple domain names nor attempted to transfer www.fallwell.com for valuable consideration. We agree with the Fifth and Sixth Circuits that, given these circumstances, the use of a mark in a domain name for a gripe site criticizing the markholder does not constitute cybersquatting.

      * * *

Notes and Questions

1. *Bad faith intent to profit.* What is "profit" for purposes of the Anticybersquatting Act? Must the defendant intend financial profit, as opposed to some other, more personal benefit? For example, what if Falwell demonstrated that Lamparello registered and used the "fallwell.com" domain name with the intent to benefit himself by exposing what he believed to be dangerous propaganda against himself and other gays? Would it be sufficient if Lamparello acted with the intent to obtain personal satisfaction by creating an outlet through which he could effectively express his strongly felt views and feelings? Must the defendant's intent be to profit or benefit *himself,* or would it be sufficient if he intends to benefit another person or entity? For example, what if Lamparello registered and used the "fallwell.com" domain name for a site that solicited financial contributions for his own church or for Aids relief in Africa?

In *Lamparello v. Falwell*, should the magnitude of impact on the plaintiff's site matter? For example, what if instead of 200 hits per day, Lamparello's site got 4,000 hits per day, and Falwell's site dwindled from 9,000 hits per day to 6,000 hits per day? Should that affect the court's evaluation of Factor IV? For purposes of Factor IV, when is a web site "noncommercial"? For example, what if Lamparello registered and used his domain name with the intent to interfere with Falwell's sales of goods or services, but not to sell or advertise any goods or services himself? Should that render his actions "commercial?" What if his intent was to solicit contributions for a charitable cause? What if, in addition to the web site content described in the opinion, Lapmarello sold caps and tee-shirts emblazoned with the statement "Falwell misreads the Bible" through his web site? Should any of these additional facts render his site "commercial" for purposes of Factor IV?

Assume that a dissatisfied customer registers business's mark in a domain name and sets up a web site that harshly criticizes business's services, charging that they are of the lowest quality, and that business refuses to listen to customer concerns or complaints or to remedy the detrimental effects of its shoddy work. The dissatisfied customer warns others to avoid using business's services for these reasons, but does not herself sell any goods or services or make any other form of financial profit from her site. Should Factor V cut for or against a finding of bad-faith intent to profit?

2. *In rem jurisdiction.* After carefully parsing the statutory language of Lanham Act § 43(d)(1) and (2), the Court of Appeals for the Fourth Circuit has held that the Anticybersquatter Act's *in rem* provisions are available not only for bad faith registration/use/trafficking claims under § 43(d) but also provide *in rem* jurisdiction for claims of infringement and dilution under §§ 32(1)(a), 43(a) and 43(c). 15 U.S.C. §§ 1114(1)(a), 1125(a), (c), (d). Harrods Ltd. v. Sixty Internet Domain Names, 302 F.3d 214 (4th Cir. 2002).

3. *The ICANN Uniform Domain Name Dispute Resolution Policy.* As discussed *supra*, the Internet Corporation for Assigned Names and Numbers ("ICANN") has undertaken global administration of the Internet name and address system. ICANN has approved the creation of additional generic top level domains, and has contracted with a number of domain name registrars, who now compete in registering domain names in the generic top level domains. It has also adopted a dispute resolution policy to assist in resolving disputes between trademark owners and persons registering domain names with its authorized registrars.

The Uniform Domain Name Dispute Resolution Policy ("U.D.R.P."), adopted by ICANN, is incorporated by reference into all domain name registration agreements made by ICANN–accredited registrars. Under the policy, registrants must agree to mandatory administrative proceedings when a third party (a "complainant") asserts that: 1) the registered domain name is identical or confusingly similar to a trademark or service mark in which the complainant has rights; 2) the registrant has no rights or legitimate interests in respect of the domain name; and 3) the domain name has been registered and is being used in bad faith.

Under the U.D.R.P., a registrant may have the requisite bad faith if he or she registered and used the domain name 1) primarily to sell or rent the domain name for profit; 2) primarily to disrupt a competitor's business; 3) intentionally to create a likelihood of confusion with the complainant's mark and thus lure Internet users to his or her web site for commercial gain; or 4) in order to prevent the mark owner from registering and using the mark as its own domain name (provided there has been a pattern of such conduct). A registrant may rebut a claim of bad faith by showing that he used or prepared to use the domain name in selling goods or services prior to notice of the dispute; that he had been commonly known by the domain name; or that he is making a legitimate, noncommercial or fair use of the domain name, without intent for commercial gain.

Dispute panels to resolve these claims are drawn from dispute resolution organizations approved by ICANN. Remedies against a bad-faith registrant are limited to cancellation of the domain name registration or transfer of the registration to the complainant. The existence of the mandatory administrative proceeding will not prevent either party from submitting the dispute to a court for independent resolution. A U.S. mark owner who is dissatisfied with U.D.R.P. findings can still bring a cybersquatting claim against the domain name registrant pursuant to Lanham Act 43(d), and may join infringement and/or dilution claims. While the dispute panel's findings may be influential, they are not binding on the court, and may be disregarded.

A domain name registrant who has lost her registration by virtue of a panel ruling may seek redress under Lanham Act § 32(2)(D)(v), 15 U.S.C. § 1114(2)(D)(v), which provides:

> A domain name registrant whose name has been suspended, disabled, or transferred under a policy described under clause (ii)(II) may, upon notice to the mark owner, file a civil action to establish that the registration or use of the domain name by such registrant is not unlawful under this chapter. The court may grant injunctive relief to the domain name registrant, including the reactivation of the domain name or transfer of the domain name to the domain name registrant.

The "policy described under clause (ii)(II)," referred to above, is "a reasonable policy by [a] registrar, registry, or authority prohibiting the registration of a domain name that is identical to, confusingly similar to, or dilutive of another's mark," *Id.*, at § 1114(2)(D)(ii)(II). This description encompasses the ICANN Uniform Dispute Resolution Policy. See Sallen v. Corinthians Licenciamentos LTDA, 273 F.3d 14 (1st Cir. 2001). In order to establish that the domain name registration "is not unlawful under this chapter," the plaintiff must demonstrate that that it does not violate *any* of the mark owner's Lanham Act rights—that is, does not constitute infringement, dilution, *or* cybersquatting.

Note that the ICANN Uniform Domain Name Dispute Resolution Policy provides an administrative remedy in many of the same cases that might be brought under the new Anticybersquatting Consumer Protection Act cause of action. What are the relative advantages and disadvantages of the ICANN administrative procedure and a suit under § 43(d), from the standpoint of a U.S. mark owner faced with a cybersquatter's bad-faith registration of its mark as a domain name?

PROBLEMS

1.　The plaintiff, Harrods UK, is the owner of the well-known Harrods of London department store. The defendant Harrods BA was once affiliated with plaintiff, but for many years has been a completely separate corporate entity that until recently operated a "Harrods" department store in Buenos Aires, Argentina. Harrods BA owns the rights to the "Harrods" mark in South America, and Harrods UK owns the rights throughout most of the rest of the world, including the U.S., where it uses the mark in retail catalog and Internet sales. Since 1999 Harrods UK has operated a web site under the domain name "harrods.com," that functions as an online retail store.

Over the years, Harrods BA's business has declined until now it's former department store is vacant, and it only earns revenue from the continued operation of the building's parking garage.

In 1999, Harrods BA hired a consultant to prepare a proposal for an online business, and registered 50 domain names that incorporated the Harrods mark, including harrodsamerica, cyberharrods, harrodsservices, harrodsstore, shoppingharrods, and harrodsshopping, each in three different generic top-level domains (the .com, .net. and .org top-level domains). The consultant's proposal suggested using the Harrods-related domain names that Harrods BA had registered to set up a web site portal where users could shop at various vendors' stores within the Harrods BA web site. Under the proposal, Harrods BA would not sell any merchandise itself but would simply earn commissions from vendors that it sponsored. The proposal thus treated the well-known Harrods name as the primary asset that Harrods BA could offer vendors to induce them to join the Harrods portal site and pay commissions. The proposal included an illustration of a transaction occurring through the proposed Harrods BA web site. The illustration showed an online shopper designated as a "UK citizen" purchasing a Burberry sweater (a British brand) at the Harrods BA web site and paying for the purchase with funds from Barclays Bank (a British bank). The "Harrods" logo on the web page illustration was not the distinct "Harrods" logo used by Harrods BA; instead, it was identical to the script logo used by Harrods U.K.

Harrods BA used this proposal to solicit potential investors and partners in Argentina, the U.S. and Europe, but no party expressed interest. Therefore, Harrods BA dropped the proposal and solicited a different consultant to draft a new proposal. In the meanwhile, Harrods UK brought an *in rem* anticyberspuatting action against the Harrods-related domain names in the U.S. district court for the district where NSI, the domain name registry that had registered the Harrods BA domain names, was located. (Harrods UK was not able to obtain personal jurisdiction over Harrods BA in the U.S.).

How should the court resolve the "bad faith intent to profit" issue?

2.　Defendant registered domain names incorporating the marks of a number of different American corporations and law firms. He set up web sites containing derogatory remarks about lawyers and links to other, offensively named web sites, such as "LetsDoSomeIllegalSteroids.com," and "NoIrishNeedApply.com." When one of the law firms brought an anticybersquatting action against him, he testified that he began registering the domain names to "get even" with a company he worked for that allegedly reneged on a contract with him. He thus registered domain names of businesses representing "Corporate America" and law firms, who represent "Corporate America," and set up sites containing "parody" and "jokes" at the firms' expense. The defendant testified that he intended to "mess with" these entities and get them "pissed off." Should the court find a violation of the Anticybersquatting Act?

3. Plaintiff Electronics Boutique Holding Corp. sells video games and software over the Internet under the registered marks "EB" and "Electronics Boutique." Its on-line store can be accessed under the domain names "eb-world.com" and "electronicsboutique.com." Defendant registered the domain names "electronicboutique.com," "electronicbotique.com," "ebwold.com," and "ebworl.com." Internet users attempting to access plaintiff's web site who mistakenly type one of defendant's misspelled variations of plaintiff's domain names are "mousetrapped" in a barrage of advertising windows for a variety of products. They cannot exit without clicking on the succession of ads. Advertisers pay defendant between 10 and 25 cents each time an Internet user clicks on one of their posted ads.

After the plaintiff files suit, the defendant transforms the sites to political protest sites, posting protests about the plaintiff, against ICANN domain name policies, and against the Anticybersquatting Act. Assuming that the plaintiff's marks are distinctive and were distinctive prior to the defendant's actions, how would you assess the defendant's potential liability under § 43(d)?

F. FIRST AMENDMENT LIMITATIONS ON TRADEMARK RIGHTS

Commercial Speech vs. Fully Protected Speech

Understanding the limitations that the First Amendment places on trademark protection[21] entails understanding the distinction between commercial speech and "fully protected" (noncommercial) speech. "Fully protected" speech includes political speech; speech of a philosophical, social, literary, artistic, scientific or ethical nature; and speech that addresses other matters of public concern. Commercial speech is entitled to a lower level of constitutional protection than non-commercial, or fully protected, speech.[22] Thus, assertion of trademark rights against unautho-

---

21. The First Amendment provides that "Congress shall make no law ... abridging the freedom of speech, or of the press...." U.S. Const. Amend. I. Although the First Amendment states that "*Congress* shall make no law ... abridging the freedom of speech, or of the press," this restriction also applies to the States under the Due Process Clause of the Fourteenth Amendment. 44 Liquormart, Inc. v. Rhode Island, 517 U.S. 484, 489 n.1, 116 S.Ct. 1495, 134 L.Ed.2d 711 (1996). When private parties invoke either federal or state statutes in court to restrict speech, this constitutes sufficient government action to trigger First Amendment scrutiny. New York Times Co. v. Sullivan, 376 U.S. 254, 265, 84 S.Ct. 710, 11 L.Ed.2d 686 (1964).

22. In providing a lower level of protection for commercial speech, courts have reasoned that commercial speech, though important, is less likely to be chilled by regulation because of the speaker's economic stake in it. As the Supreme Court has explained:

rized use of a mark in commercial speech is more likely to be consistent with the First Amendment than assertion of trademark rights against unauthorized use of the mark in non-commercial speech.

The Supreme Court has held that "core" commercial speech is speech that does "no more than propose a commercial transaction." Bolger v. Youngs Drug Products Corp., 463 U.S. 60, 66, 103 S.Ct. 2875, 77 L.Ed.2d 469 (1983).[23] Under this definition, application of a mark to a product being offered for sale clearly constitutes commercial speech. Use of the mark in straightforward advertising of products or services fits well under this definition, too.

Mixed messages, which simultaneously propose a commercial transaction and address social, political or other issues of public interest, may also be deemed "commercial speech," and thus subjected to lesser First Amendment protection, in some cases. For example, in Bolger, the Supreme Court held that advertising pamphlets that linked their promotion of the defendant's product (condoms) to information about prophylactics generally and to prevention of venereal disease, constituted commercial speech. The Bolger Court reasoned that the mere fact that the pamphlets were conceded to be advertisements did not compel the conclusion that they were commercial speech. Nor did the fact that the pamphlets referred to a specific product by name. Finally, the fact that the speaker had an economic motivation for distributing the pamphlets would be insufficient by itself to identify the materials as commercial speech. However, the combination of all these characteristics provided "strong support" for the conclusion that they were properly characterized as commercial speech.[24] Generally, if the "primary purpose" of the speech is "informational," as opposed to "commercial," full First Amendment protection applies. Bolger, 463 U.S. at 67–68. Speech is not commercial just because it concerns a

---

There are commonsense differences between speech that does "no more than propose a commercial transaction," and other varieties. Even if the differences do not justify the conclusion that commercial speech is valueless, and thus subject to complete suppression by the State, they nonetheless suggest that a different degree of protection is necessary to insure that the flow of truthful and legitimate commercial information is unimpaired.... [C]ommercial speech may be more durable than other kinds. Since advertising is the *sine qua non* of commercial profits, there is little likelihood of its being chilled by proper regulation and foregone entirely.

Virginia State Bd. of Pharmacy v. Virginia Citizens Consumer Council, Inc., 425 U.S. 748, 772 n. 24, 96 S.Ct. 1817, 48 L.Ed.2d 346 (1976).

23. Another definition that the Supreme Court has used for commercial speech is "expression related solely to the economic interests of the speaker and its audience." Central Hudson Gas & Electric Corp. v. Public Service Comm'n of New York, 447 U.S. 557, 561, 100 S.Ct. 2343, 65 L.Ed.2d 341 (1980). However, in subsequent decisions the Court has suggested that this somewhat broader definition is not the favored definition.

24. Subsequent decisions have drawn a three-part test for commercial speech from *Bolger*, for use in cases of "mixed messages": 1) whether the speech takes place in an advertisement; 2) whether it refers to a specific product or service; and 3) whether the speaker has an economic motivation for the speech. However, the decisions have stressed that the "commercial speech" determination is not a mechanical one: Rather, the difference between commercial and noncommercial speech in mixed message cases is one of degree, to be determined through careful examination of the speech as a whole "to ensure that speech deserving of greater constitutional protection is not inadvertently suppressed." *City of Cincinnati v. Discovery Network, Inc.,* 507 U.S. 410, 423, 113 S.Ct. 1505, 123 L.Ed.2d 99 (1993).

commercial subject. City of Cincinnati v. Discovery Network, Inc., 507 U.S. 410, 421, 113 S.Ct. 1505, 123 L.Ed.2d 99 (1993).

Of course, commercial speech itself is entitled to First Amendment protection (albeit a lower standard of protection that "fully protected speech"). Central Hudson Gas & Electric Corp. v. Public Service Comm'n, 447 U.S. 557, 563–66, 100 S.Ct. 2343, 65 L.Ed.2d 341 (1980). The Supreme Court has recognized that the free flow of truthful commercial information is of vital interest to the public. Under current standards, in order to be protected, commercial speech must concern lawful activity and not be misleading. Thompson v. Western States Medical Ctr., 535 U.S. 357, 366, 122 S.Ct. 1497, 152 L.Ed.2d 563 (2002). If it meets this criterion, courts should ask "whether the asserted governmental interest is substantial." *Central Hudson*, 447 U.S. at 566. If it is, then they must "determine whether the regulation directly advances the governmental interest asserted," and "whether [the regulation] is not more extensive than is necessary to serve that interest." *Id.* Each of these inquiries must be answered in the affirmative for the regulation to be found constitutional.

Trademark Protection and the First Amendment

Protecting marks entails restricting others' use of words and symbols, and thus may impair important First Amendment interests in freedom of expression. As Judge Kozinski has explained:

> [T]rademarks play a significant role in our public discourse. They often provide some of our most vivid metaphors, as well as the most compelling imagery in political campaigns. Some ideas—"it's the Rolls Royce of its class," for example—are difficult to express any other way. That's no accident. Trademarks are often selected for their effervescent qualities, and then injected into the stream of communication with the pressure of a fire hose by means of mass media campaigns. Where trademarks come to carry so much communicative freight, allowing the trademark holder to restrict their use implicates our collective interest in free and open communication.

Alex Kozinski, *Trademarks Unplugged*, 68 N.Y.U. L. Rev. 960, 973 (1993). The Supreme Court has explained that one cannot "forbid particular words without also running a substantial risk of suppressing ideas in the process." Cohen v. California, 403 U.S. 15, 26, 91 S.Ct. 1780, 29 L.Ed.2d 284 (1971) In particular, suppressing unauthorized use of marks may seriously undermine the public's ability to discuss or criticize the mark owner and its products.

As we have discussed, trademark protection serves a limited purpose—primarily to prevent misleading uses of marks that may confuse consumers about the source, quality or characteristics of goods or services, and lead them to make mistaken purchases. The law has been tailored to accomplish that purpose while avoiding undue interference and with First Amendment interests. Thus, trademark protection is limited to "distinctive" marks. Words and symbols that are not distinctive are relegated to the public domain because they are not likely to signify product source to consumers, and are more likely to be needed by other market actors to communicate the characteristics of their own goods or services. In addition, trademark law provides the fair use defenses to allow use of words or symbols strictly in their nontrademark, descriptive capacity, or to identify the owner or the owner's product or service.

The likelihood of confusion requirement has also played an important role in protecting First Amendment interests—it ensures that courts will only apply the trademark law to regulate deceptive or misleading commercial speech, which enjoys little or no First Amendment protection. However, as we have seen, the likelihood of confusion requirement has been watered down considerably through the years. Originally a plaintiff was required to demonstrate a likelihood of confusion about the *source* of goods or services, but now a likelihood of confusion about the sponsorship, affiliation or association of the goods or their producers suffices. Moreover, courts have come to accept a likelihood of initial interest confusion or post-sale confusion, in addition to confusion at the point of sale. And, of course, the relatively new cause of action for dilution requires no evidence of consumer confusion at all. Thus, in the name of trademark infringement or dilution law, courts today may and do penalize essentially truthful, non-misleading speech. That being the case, it seems clear that the likelihood of confusion requirement, in itself, may not ensure that First Amendment interests are adequately protected.

The final limitation that may reconcile trademark protection with the First Amendment is the "use in commerce" (or "trademark use") requirement, which applies to all the Lanham Act infringement and dilution causes of action. As traditionally conceived, this "use" limitation requires that the defendant apply the mark in a manner that invites consumers to associate the mark with the goods or services the defendant is offering for sale or distribution, and to rely on the mark for information about the source, sponsorship or affiliation of those goods or services. As so defined, the "use" requirement prevents use of trademark rights to interfere with First Amendment-protected speech by confining the infringement cause of action to commercial transactions, and generally, to commercial speech. However, as we noted in the section on Internet infringement cases, *supra*, recent court decisions have stretched the understanding of trademark "use" well beyond its traditional meaning, finding that "in gross" sales of domain name registrations (in cybersquatting cases), uses of marks as domain names and in metatags for forum web sites that sell no goods or services, and hidden uses of marks as keywords for banner advertising may constitute the requisite infringing "use" of a mark. This relaxation of the "use" requirement may open more non-commercial speech to trademark regulation.

Explicit Restriction of Dilution Claims to Commercial Speech

Courts have uniformly construed Lanham Act § 43(c)(4)(B) (which provides that there can be no dilution cause of action against "noncommercial use of a mark") to prohibit dilution relief against uses of marks in noncommercial speech. As the Ninth Circuit explained in Mattel, Inc. v. MCA Records, 296 F.3d 894, 904–05 (9th Cir. 2002), *cert. denied*, 537 U.S. 1171, 123 S.Ct. 993, 154 L.Ed.2d 912 (2003), the First Amendment is an especially great concern in the dilution context. First Amendment concerns:

> apply with greater force in the dilution context because dilution lacks two very significant limitations that reduce the tension between trademark law and the First Amendment.
>
> First, depending on the strength and distinctiveness of the mark, trademark law grants relief only against uses that are likely to confuse. * * * A trademark injunction is usually limited to uses within one industry or several related industries. Dilution is the antithesis of trademark law in this respect, because it seeks to protect the mark from association in the public's mind with wholly unrelated goods or services. The more remote the good or service associated with the junior use, the more likely it is to cause dilution rather than trademark infringement. A dilution injunction, by contrast to a trademark injunction, will generally sweep across broad vistas of the economy.
>
> Second, a trademark injunction, even a very broad one, is premised on the need to prevent consumer confusion. This consumer protection rationale—averting what is essentially a fraud on the consuming public—is wholly consistent with the theory of the First Amendment, which does not protect commercial fraud. * * * Moreover, avoiding harm to consumers is an important interest that is independent of the senior user's interest in protecting its business.
>
> Dilution, by contrast, does not require a showing of consumer confusion, * * * and dilution injunctions therefore lack the built-in First Amendment compass of trademark injunctions. In addition, dilution law protects only the distinctiveness of the mark, which is inherently less weighty than the dual interest of protecting trademark owners, and avoiding harm to consumers that is at the heart of every trademark claim.

Id. In *Mattel*, the Ninth Circuit found that the dilution cause of action only applies in cases of "core" commercial speech, and not to "mixed message" commercial speech. Not all courts have restricted the dilution cause of action to "core" commercial speech, however. And while most courts have agreed that the dilution cause of action is restricted to "commercial speech," a significant number of courts have construed "commercial speech" for this purpose in a manner that is inconsistent with the Supreme Court definitions discussed above. For example, in some Internet cases, courts have found that defendants using marks in "forum sites" or "gripe sites" were engaged in commercial speech, even though they proposed no commercial transaction, and had no economic interest in the use. The courts found the use to be "commercial speech" because the defendants' use was intended to have, or potentially could have, a negative impact on the plaintiff's sales. See, e.g., Planned Parenthood Federation of America, Inc. v. Bucci, 1997 WL 133313 (S.D.N.Y.), aff'd, 152 F.3d 920 (2d Cir. 1998); Jews for Jesus v. Brodsky, 993 F.Supp. 282 (D.N.J.), aff'd, 159 F.3d 1351 (3rd Cir. 1998).

Judicial Approaches to Infringement Claims Involving Non–Commercial Speech

There are numerous case decisions that have applied Lanham Act infringement provisions to fully protected, non-commercial speech, as defined by the Supreme Court. In most cases the primary issue has not been whether the unauthorized use of a mark in fully-protected speech *can* be prohibited, but what special safeguards or standards the courts should apply in determining whether to prohibit it.

The courts' analysis is by no means uniform. However, there are three general categories into which most of the decisions can be sorted: 1) a straight "likelihood of confusion" approach, with no special attention to First Amendment concerns; 2) the "alternative avenues" approach; and 3) a balancing of interests approach.

1. The straight "likelihood of confusion" analysis. Some of the decisions in the first category, which apply a straight likelihood of confusion analysis in cases of fully protected speech, may simply stem from the defendants' failure to raise a First Amendment defense, or the court's wish to avoid constitutional (First Amendment) issues when there are alternative, non-constitutional grounds for holding for the defendant. Other decisions in this category may reflect the courts' expectation that the safeguards built into the trademark infringement cause of action (the requirements of "use in commerce," a likelihood of confusion, and distinctiveness, along with the fair use defenses) are sufficient in themselves to protect First Amendment interests, regardless of whether the infringement claim is asserted against commercial or non-commercial speech. Whatever the reason, the trend appears to be away from reliance on a straight likelihood of confusion analysis in cases of non-commercial speech.

2. The "alternative avenues" approach. The second category of cases, embracing the "alternative avenues" approach, stems primarily from a 1979 Second Circuit decision which the Second Circuit has subsequent renounced. In *Dallas Cowboys Cheerleaders, Inc. v. Pussycat Cinema, Ltd.*, 604 F.2d 200 (2d Cir. 1979), the owner of the Dallas Cowboys Cheerleaders sued the producer of a "gross and revolting" pornographic movie, *Debbie Does Dallas*, featuring a heroine who wore a costume similar to that worn by the plaintiff's cheerleaders. The Second Circuit affirmed a preliminary injunction on Lanham Act § 43(a) grounds, and rejected the defendant's First Amendment arguments:

> [F]irst amendment doctrine [does not] protect defendant's infringement of plaintiff's trademark. That defendants' movie may convey a

barely discernible message does not entitle them to appropriate plaintiff's trademark in the process of conveying that message. . . . Plaintiff's trademark is in the nature of a property right . . . , and as such it need not "yield to the exercise of First Amendment rights under circumstances where adequate alternative avenues of communication exist." Lloyd v. Tanner, 407 U.S. 551, 567 (1972). Because there are numerous ways in which defendants may comment on "sexuality in athletics" without infringing plaintiff's trademark, the district court did not encroach upon their first amendment rights in granting a preliminary injunction.

Id. at 206.

The Court of Appeals for the Eighth Circuit picked up on the *Dallas Cowboys* "alternative avenues" approach in *Mutual of Omaha Insurance Co. v. Novak*, 836 F.2d 397, 402 (8th Cir. 1987), *cert. denied*, 488 U.S. 933, 109 S.Ct. 326, 102 L.Ed.2d 344 (1988). In that case the owner of the "Mutual of Omaha" and "Indian Head" logo marks for insurance alleged infringement against an anti-nuclear activist who produced and sold tee-shirts, coffee mugs, caps and buttons featuring the words "Mutant of Omaha" and a "feather-bonneted, emaciated human head," along with the words "Nuclear Holocaust Insurance." *Id.* at 398. However, while the Eighth Circuit relied on the *Dallas Cowboys/Lloyd Corp. v. Tanner* "alternative avenues" analysis in affirming a finding of infringement against the defendant activist, it appeared to rely in part on the fact that the defendant was placing his message on tee-shirts, mugs, and buttons, rather than in more traditional media. The court expressly suggested that a finding for the plaintiff would infringe "upon the constitutional protection [of] the First Amendment" if the defendant were to present an editorial parody in a book, magazine, or film. *Id.* at 402. In a subsequent case involving a trademark parody in a humor magazine, the Eighth Circuit purported to adopt and apply a form of the balancing test discussed in the next subsection, rather than the "alternative avenues" approach. Anheuser–Busch, Inc. v. Balducci, 28 F.3d 769, 776 (8th Cir. 1994). *cert. denied*, 513 U.S. 1112, 115 S.Ct. 903, 130 L.Ed.2d 787 (1995). Thus, it is unclear whether any of the Circuit Courts of Appeals presently endorse the "alternative avenues" approach. However, a number of district courts have applied it. For example, in American Dairy Queen Corp. v. New Line Productions, Inc., 35 F.Supp.2d 727, 734 (D.Minn. 1998), the district court held that the title "Dairy Queens" for a mock documentary satirizing beauty contests in rural Minnesota (where the dairy business is prevalent) infringed on the plaintiff's mark for frozen desserts. The court reasoned that alternative titles, such as "Dairy Princesses," or "Milk Maids," were available, making the defendant's use of the plaintiff's mark unnecessary. *Id.* at 734.

The majority of authority has rejected the "alternative avenues" approach. As noted earlier, the Second Circuit disowned that approach in 1989, holding that it did "not read *Dallas Cowboys Cheerleaders* as generally precluding all consideration of First Amendment concerns whenever an allegedly infringing author has 'alternative avenues of communication.' " The court explained that in the case of literary titles (which the court had before it)

> this "no alternative" standard provides insufficient leeway for literary expression. In *Lloyd*, the issue was whether the First Amendment provided war protesters with the right to distribute leaflets on a shopping center owner's property. The Supreme Court held that it did not. But a restriction on the *location* of a speech is different from a restriction on the *words* the speaker may use. As the Supreme Court has noted, albeit in a different context, "[W]e cannot indulge the facile assumption that one can forbid particular words without running a substantial risk of suppressing ideas in the process."

Rogers v. Grimaldi, 875 F.2d 994, 998–999 (2d Cir. 1989). The First, Fifth, Sixth, and Tenth Circuits have likewise expressly rejected the alternative avenues standard for evaluating trademark law restrictions on non-commercial speech, all reasoning that the analogy of trademark rights to real property rights is inappropriate, that restraints on the use of particular words do not constitute "time, place or manner" restrictions like the restraint at issue in *Lloyd*, and expressing concern about the impact of such an approach on the public interest in the free flow of ideas and information.

3. *The "balancing of interests" approach.* The third approach to infringement claims against non-commercial speech, sometimes referred to as the "balancing approach," was established by the Second Circuit in *Rogers v. Grimaldi, supra*. In that case the Second Circuit reasoned that while movies, plays, books and songs are products being offered for sale, they are also expressive works which are entitled to full First Amendment protection. Thus, when a mark owner claims that the title of an expressive work infringes his mark, First Amendment interests must be balanced against trademark interests in evaluating whether relief should be granted. 875 F.2d at 999. After balancing the public's interest in avoiding confusion against the public's interest in free expression, the court concluded that the balance "will normally not support application of the [Lanham Act] unless the title has no artistic relevance to the underlying work whatsoever," or, if it has some artistic relevance, "unless the title explicitly misleads as to the source or the content of the work." *Id.* The court suggested that the title would not be deemed "explicitly misleading" for this purpose unless the defendant did something more to denote authorship, sponsorship or endorsement by the plaintiff than simply include the plaintiff's mark in the title.[25] Subsequent Second Circuit

---

25. The court explained:

> To illustrate, some titles—such as "Nimmer on Copyright" and "Jane Fonda's Workout Book"—explicitly state the author of the work or at least the name of the person the publisher is entitled to associate with the preparation of the work. Other titles contain words explicitly signifying endorsement, such as the phrase in a subtitle "an authorized biography." If such explicit references were used in a title and were false as applied to the underlying work, the consumer interest in avoiding deception would warrant application of the Lanham Act, even if the title had some relevance to the work.

opinions have suggested that in order to determine whether the defendant's use is explicitly misleading under *Rogers*, courts should apply the regular multifactor test for likelihood of confusion, but withhold relief unless the evidence of likely confusion is "particularly compelling," and thus outweighs the competing First Amendment interests. Twin Peaks Productions, Inc. v. Publications International, Ltd., 996 F.2d 1366, 1379–80 (2d Cir. 1993).

Courts in the Fifth, Sixth, and Ninth Circuits have expressly adopted the Second Circuit's approach to evaluating infringement claims involving the titles to expressive works. Moreover, subsequent decisions have adopted the reasoning underlying *Rogers* in resolving infringement claims against other forms of non-commercial speech. For example, in *Cliffs Notes, Inc. v. Bantam Doubleday Dell Publishing Group, Inc.*, 886 F.2d 490 (2d Cir. 1989), the Court of Appeals for the Second Circuit found that the defendant's unauthorized use of the plaintiff's trade dress on its magazine cover (in order to parody the plaintiff) was protected under the First Amendment. The Second Circuit again described the "competing considerations of allowing artistic expression and preventing consumer confusion," and held:

> We believe that the overall balancing approach of *Rogers* and its emphasis on construing the Lanham Act "narrowly" when First Amendment values are involved are both relevant in this case. That is to say, in deciding the reach of the Lanham Act in any case where an expressive work is alleged to infringe a trademark, it is appropriate to weigh the public interest in free expression against the public interest in avoiding consumer confusion.

Id. at 494–95. While undertaking a traditional likelihood of consumer confusion analysis, the court made it clear that even if some likelihood of confusion were demonstrated, the plaintiff could not prevail unless the risk of confusion outweighed the public interest in free expression under the particular facts of the case. *Id.*[26]

Many titles, however, include a well-known name without any overt indication of authorship or endorsement—for example, the hit song "Bette Davis Eyes," and the recent film "Come back to the Five and Dime, Jimmy Dean, Jimmy Dean." To some people, these titles might implicitly suggest that the named celebrity had endorsed the work or had a role in producing it. Even if that suggestion is false, the title is artistically relevant to the work. In these circumstances, the slight risk that such use of a celebrity's name might implicitly suggest endorsement or sponsorship to some people is outweighed by the danger of restricting artistic expression, and the Lanham Act is not applicable.

Id., at 999–1000.

26. *Id.* See also ETW Corp. v. Jireh Pub., Inc., 332 F.3d 915, 929 & n. 11 (6th Cir. 2003) (Rejecting argument that balancing test is limited to titles of expressive works and holding that the balancing test developed in *Rogers, Cliff Notes* and *Mattel* is generally available "to all cases involving literary or artistic works" where the defendant has made a colorable showing of First Amendment protection.); E.S.S. Entertainment 2000, Inc. v. Rock Star Videos, Inc., 547 F.3d 1095, 1099 (9th Cir. 2008) (Although balancing test "traditionally applies to uses of a trademark in the title of an artistic work, there is no principled reason why it ought not also apply to a use of the trademark in the body of the work.")

NOTES AND QUESTIONS

1. *Trademark parodies.* Parody is frequently sheltered under the intellectual property laws, as illustrated in the *Cliff Notes* case, discussed above. As most college students know, Cliffs Notes are condensed versions of short stories, plays and books. The cover of a typical Cliffs Notes book is yellow with black diagonal stripes and black lettering. It lists the name of the work that is to be condensed on the cover and typically displays a clay sculpture of a mountain.

The defendants, in conjunction with Spy magazine, decided to write and publish a double parody of Cliff Notes and three novels—Tama Janowitz's *Slaves of New York*, Brett Ellis's *Less Than Zero* and Jay McInerney's *Bright Lights, Big City*—which a Spy editor described as being well known to the intended audience and noted for their literary shortcomings. The defendants thought that the Cliff's Notes study guide would provide an ideal vehicle for a parody of these works, because "[t]he flat, straightforward, academic style" of Cliffs Notes "would appear incongruous with the cool, ironic, sophisticated, urbane novels and thus greatly enhance the humor of the satire."

The defendants admitted that they copied the prominent features of the Cliffs Notes trade dress in order to make Spy Notes an effective parody. Thus, Spy Notes replicated the yellow and black striped design of the Cliff Notes cover, and listed the works it condensed on the cover. There were, however, some important differences between the two books. For example, the Spy notes cover featured the words "A Satire" repeated five times in bright red lettering, the notation "A Spy Book" with the logo of Spy magazine against a bright red background, and a clay sculpture of New York City rather than of a mountain.

The owner of the Cliff Notes trade dress sued for infringement, alleging that the defendants' book would give consumers the false impression that Spy Notes was actually appellee's product. The district court granted a preliminary injunction but the Second Circuit reversed. As noted above, the Second Circuit held that the parody was a work of artistic expression, fully protected under the First Amendment. Upon balancing the public's interest in avoiding confusion with the public's interest in expressive freedom, the court found that the interest in expressive freedom should prevail under the particular facts of the case.

Should courts take this approach in evaluating all trademark parodies? For example, suppose that the defendants used the marks "Dogiva" and "Cativa" for their dog and cat treats, and wrapped the treats in foil similar to the foil used to wrap the prestigious "Godiva" chocolates. Should the special First Amendment considerations discussed in *Cliffs Notes* come into play when the owner of the Godiva mark sues for infringement?

2. *The medium or the message?* For purposes of First Amendment analysis, should it matter whether the defendant placed her political protest (which incorporates the plaintiff's mark without authorization) in an essay or on a tee-shirt, mug, or hat? If so, why?

3. *Forum site domain names.* Suppose that Jones, a customer of Acme Co., had a very bad experience with Acme's services and was so infuriated that he registered the domain name "Acme.com" and used it to identify a web

site in which he described his bad experience and provided a place for other dissatisfied Acme customers to share their own bad experiences. Jones' "gripe site" did not offer any goods or services for sale. For purposes of Acme's ensuing infringement/dilution suit, how should the court evaluate the status of Jones' domain name use of Acme's mark? Is it commercial speech, or fully protected speech?

4. *Protection against genericide.* As a matter of policy, should a mark owner have a "blurring" dilution cause of action to prevent *generic* uses of its mark by the media or dictionary publishers in non-commercial speech? See Restatement (Third) of Unfair Competition § 25, cmt i (1995); Ty Inc. v. Perryman, 306 F.3d 509, 513–14 (7th Cir. 2002), *cert. denied,* 538 U.S. 971, 123 S.Ct. 1750, 155 L.Ed.2d 531 (2003).

5. *The Anticybersquatter Consumer Protection Act and the First Amendment.* Review the provisions of the Anticybersquatting Consumer Protection Act, 15 U.S.C.A. § 1125(d). What measures did Congress take in that Act to accommodate First Amendment interests? Are those measures adequate, in your opinion?

PROBLEMS

1. Defendant "adult entertainment" magazine publishes a two-page article entitled "L.L. Bea*m*'s Back–To–School–Sex–Catalog." (Emphasis added.) The article is labeled on the magazine's contents page as "humor" and "parody." The article displays a facsimile of L.L. Bean's trademark and features pictures of nude models in sexually explicit positions using "products" that are described in a crudely humorous fashion. L.L. Bean seeks relief, alleging (among other things) infringement and a state-law cause of action for tarnishment dilution. Would relief violate the First Amendment?

2. Public interest group adopts the term "Star Wars" to identify President Reagan's Strategic Defense Initiative, and incorporates it into a number of aural and written political commentaries. The owner of the valuable "Star Wars" mark for movies and related products sues, alleging infringement and state dilution claims. Would relief violate the First Amendment?

3. Defendant registers the domain name "jewsforjesus.org" and sets up a web site consisting of a single page, which states the defendant's opposition to the religious views promulgated by the Jews for Jesus organization. He includes a link to a web site created and maintained by the Outreach Judaism organization, which also opposes the plaintiff's religious views and activities. In addition to stating its opposition to the Jews for Jesus organization, the Outreach Judaism site describes the organization's own religious views and offers some items for sale, such as audio tapes and books. The entire text of the defendant's site follows:

Jews for Jesus?

Are you interested in learning about Jews and Jesus?

Want to know why one cannot believe in Jesus and be a Jew?

The answers you seek already exist within your faith.

Come home to the truth and beauty of Judaism.

Don't be fooled.

Click here to learn more about how the Jews for Jesus cult is founded upon deceit and distortion of fact.

PLEASE NOTE

This website is an independent project which reflects the personal opinion of its owner, and is in no way affiliated with the Jewish organization Outreach Judaism, or the Christian organization Jews for Jesus.

Send all correspondence to stevebro@worldnet.att.net

The plaintiff Jews for Jesus organization brings suit for Lanham Act dilution and infringement. Will providing relief violate the First Amendment?

G. LANHAM ACT § 43(a): MORAL RIGHTS AND REVERSE PASSING OFF

Lanham Act § 43(a) is capable of considerable flexibility, due to the breadth of its statutory language. It has often been invoked to "fill the gaps," and protect private interests beyond the reach of other intellectual property doctrines. For example, authors might turn to § 43(a) for protection of their literary characters, for whom copyright protection has been uncertain. Unauthorized use of a literary character might falsely suggest sponsorship by or affiliation with the character's creator or copyright owner. See, e.g., Walt Disney Co. v. Powell, 698 F.Supp. 10 (D.D.C.1988), *affirmed in part, vacated in part,* 897 F.2d 565 (D.C.Cir.1990).

Section 43(a)'s protection of unregistered trade dress might serve as an alternative to a design patent or copyright for a product's appearance, providing rights against copying in some cases when neither of the other doctrines would afford relief. (Of course, the Supreme Court's recent decisions in the *Wal-Mart* and *TrafFix* cases, *infra*, have greatly limited this opportunity.) Moreover, a § 43(a) "false endorsement" claim may be used as an alternative to the common-law right of publicity cause of action, to protect a celebrity's interest in controlling commercial exploitation of his or her identity. The right of publicity will be discussed in a later chapter.

Section 43(a) has also played an important role in vindicating artists' and authors' moral right of attribution. However, the following Supreme Court decision has sharply curtailed this practice.

DASTAR CORP. v. TWENTIETH CENTURY FOX FILM CORP.

United States Supreme Court, 2003.
539 U.S. 23, 123 S.Ct. 2041, 156 L.Ed.2d 18.

JUSTICE SCALIA delivered the opinion of the Court.

In this case, we are asked to decide whether § 43(a) of the Lanham Act, 15 U.S.C. § 1125(a), prevents the unaccredited copying of a work
* * *.

In 1948, three and a half years after the German surrender at Reims, General Dwight D. Eisenhower completed Crusade in Europe, his written account of the allied campaign in Europe during World War II. Doubleday published the book, registered it with the Copyright Office in 1948, and granted exclusive television rights to an affiliate of respondent Twentieth Century Fox Film Corporation (Fox). Fox, in turn, arranged for Time, Inc., to produce a television series, also called Crusade in Europe, based on the book, and Time assigned its copyright in the series to Fox. The television series, consisting of 26 episodes, was first broadcast in 1949. It combined a soundtrack based on a narration of the book with film footage from the United States Army, Navy, and Coast Guard, the British Ministry of Information and War Office, the National Film Board of Canada, and unidentified "Newsreel Pool Cameramen." In 1975, Doubleday renewed the copyright on the book as the " 'proprietor of copyright in a work made for hire.' " Fox, however, did not renew the copyright on the Crusade television series, which expired in 1977, leaving the television series in the public domain.

In 1988, Fox reacquired the television rights in General Eisenhower's book, including the exclusive right to distribute the Crusade television series on video and to sublicense others to do so. Respondents SFM Entertainment and New Line Home Video, Inc., in turn, acquired from Fox the exclusive rights to distribute Crusade on video. SFM obtained the negatives of the original television series, restored them, and repackaged the series on videotape; New Line distributed the videotapes.

Enter petitioner Dastar. In 1995, Dastar decided to expand its product line from music compact discs to videos. Anticipating renewed interest in World War II on the 50th anniversary of the war's end, Dastar released a video set entitled World War II Campaigns in Europe. To make Campaigns, Dastar purchased eight beta cam tapes of the *original* version of the Crusade television series, which is in the public domain, copied them, and then edited the series. Dastar's Campaigns series is slightly more than half as long as the original Crusade television series. Dastar substituted a new opening sequence, credit page, and final closing for those of the Crusade television series; inserted new chapter-title sequences and narrated chapter introductions; moved the "recap" in the Crusade television series to the beginning and retitled it as a "preview"; and removed references to and images of the book. Dastar created new packaging for its Campaigns series and (as already noted) a new title.

Dastar manufactured and sold the Campaigns video set as its own product. The advertising states: "Produced and Distributed by: *Entertainment Distributing*" (which is owned by Dastar), and makes no reference to the Crusade television series. Similarly, the screen credits state "DASTAR CORP presents" and "an ENTERTAINMENT DISTRIBUTING Production," and list as executive producer, producer, and associate producer employees of Dastar. The Campaigns videos themselves also make no reference to the Crusade television series, New Line's Crusade videotapes, or the book. Dastar sells its Campaigns videos to Sam's Club, Costco, Best

Buy, and other retailers and mail-order companies for $25 per set, substantially less than New Line's video set.

In 1998, respondents Fox, SFM, and New Line brought this action alleging that Dastar's sale of its Campaigns video set infringes Doubleday's copyright in General Eisenhower's book and, thus, their exclusive television rights in the book. Respondents later amended their complaint to add claims that Dastar's sale of Campaigns "without proper credit" to the Crusade television series constitutes "reverse passing off"[1] in violation of § 43(a) of the Lanham Act, 15 U.S.C. § 1125(a), and in violation of state unfair-competition law. On cross-motions for summary judgment, the District Court found for respondents on all three counts, treating its resolution of the Lanham Act claim as controlling on the state-law unfair-competition claim because "the ultimate test under both is whether the public is likely to be deceived or confused." * * *

The Court of Appeals for the Ninth Circuit affirmed the judgment for respondents on the Lanham Act claim, but reversed as to the copyright claim and remanded. * * * With respect to the Lanham Act claim, the Court of Appeals reasoned that "Dastar copied substantially the entire *Crusade in Europe* series created by Twentieth Century Fox, labeled the resulting product with a different name and marketed it without attribution to Fox[, and] therefore committed a 'bodily appropriation' of Fox's series." It concluded that "Dastar's 'bodily appropriation' of Fox's original [television] series is sufficient to establish the reverse passing off."[2] * * *

II

The Lanham Act was intended to make "actionable the deceptive and misleading use of marks," and "to protect persons engaged in ... commerce against unfair competition." 15 U.S.C. § 1127. While much of the Lanham Act addresses the registration, use, and infringement of trademarks and related marks, § 43(a), 15 U.S.C. § 1125(a) is one of the few provisions that goes beyond trademark protection. * * *[4]

---

1. Passing off (or palming off, as it is sometimes called) occurs when a producer misrepresents his own goods or services as someone else's. "Reverse passing off," as its name implies, is the opposite: The producer misrepresents someone else's goods or services as his own.

2. As for the copyright claim, the Ninth Circuit held that the tax treatment General Eisenhower sought for his manuscript of the book created a triable issue as to whether he intended the book to be a work for hire, and thus as to whether Doubleday properly renewed the copyright in 1976. The copyright issue is still the subject of litigation, but is not before us. We express no opinion as to whether petitioner's product would infringe a valid copyright in General Eisenhower's book.

4. Section 43(a) of the Lanham Act now provides:

"Any person who, on or in connection with any goods or services, or any container for goods, uses in commerce any word, term, name, symbol, or device, or any combination thereof, or any false designation of origin, * * * which—

"(A) is likely to cause confusion, or to cause mistake, or to deceive as to the affiliation, connection, or association of such person with another person, or as to the origin, sponsorship, or approval of his or her goods, services, or commercial activities by another person, * * *

shall be liable in a civil action by any person who believes that he or she is or is likely to be damaged by such act."

[A]s it comes to us, the gravamen of respondents' claim is that, in marketing and selling Campaigns as its own product without acknowledging its nearly wholesale reliance on the Crusade television series, Dastar has made a "false designation of origin, false or misleading description of fact, or false or misleading representation of fact, which … is likely to cause confusion … as to the origin … of his or her goods." § 43(a). That claim would undoubtedly be sustained if Dastar had bought some of New Line's Crusade videotapes and merely repackaged them as its own. Dastar's alleged wrongdoing, however, is vastly different: It took a creative work in the public domain—the Crusade television series—copied it, made modifications (arguably minor), and produced its very own series of videotapes. If "origin" refers only to the manufacturer or producer of the physical "goods" that are made available to the public (in this case the videotapes), Dastar was the origin. If, however, "origin" includes the creator of the underlying work that Dastar copied, then someone else (perhaps Fox) was the origin of Dastar's product. At bottom, we must decide what § 43(a)(1)(A) of the Lanham Act means by the "origin" of "goods."

III

The dictionary definition of "origin" is "[t]he fact or process of coming into being from a source," and "[t]hat from which anything primarily proceeds; source." Webster's New International Dictionary 1720–1721 (2d ed.1949). And the dictionary definition of "goods" (as relevant here) is "[w]ares; merchandise." We think the most natural understanding of the "origin" of "goods"—the source of wares—is the producer of the tangible product sold in the marketplace, in this case the physical Campaigns videotape sold by Dastar. The concept might be stretched (as it was under the original version of § 43(a)) to include not only the actual producer, but also the trademark owner who commissioned or assumed responsibility for ("stood behind") production of the physical product. But as used in the Lanham Act, the phrase "origin of goods" is in our view incapable of connoting the person or entity that originated the ideas or communications that "goods" embody or contain. Such an extension would not only stretch the text, but it would be out of accord with the history and purpose of the Lanham Act and inconsistent with precedent.

Section 43(a) of the Lanham Act prohibits actions like trademark infringement that deceive consumers and impair a producer's goodwill. It forbids, for example, the Coca–Cola Company's passing off its product as Pepsi–Cola or reverse passing off Pepsi–Cola as its product. But the brand-loyal consumer who prefers the drink that the Coca–Cola Company or PepsiCo sells, while he believes that that company produced (or at least stands behind the production of) that product, surely does not necessarily believe that that company was the "origin" of the drink in the sense that it was the very first to devise the formula. The consumer who buys a branded product does not automatically assume that the brand-name company is the same entity that came up with the idea for the product, or designed the product—and typically does not care whether it is. The words of the Lanham Act should not be stretched to cover matters that are typically of no consequence to purchasers.

It could be argued, perhaps, that the reality of purchaser concern is different for what might be called a communicative product—one that is valued not primarily for its physical qualities, such as a hammer, but for the intellectual content that it conveys, such as a book or, as here, a video. The purchaser of a novel is interested not merely, if at all, in the identity of the producer of the physical tome (the publisher), but also, and indeed primarily, in the identity of the creator of the story it conveys (the author). And the author, of course, has at least as much interest in avoiding passing off (or reverse passing off) of his creation as does the publisher. For such a communicative product (the argument goes) "origin of goods" in § 43(a) must be deemed to include not merely the producer of the physical item (the publishing house Farrar, Straus and Giroux, or the video producer Dastar) but also the creator of the content that the physical item conveys (the author Tom Wolfe, or—assertedly—respondents).

The problem with this argument according special treatment to communicative products is that it causes the Lanham Act to conflict with the law of copyright, which addresses that subject specifically. The right to copy, and to copy without attribution, once a copyright has expired, like "the right to make [an article whose patent has expired]—including the right to make it in precisely the shape it carried when patented—passes to the public." *Sears, Roebuck & Co. v. Stiffel Co.,* 376 U.S. 225, 230, 84 S.Ct. 784, 11 L.Ed.2d 661 (1964). "In general, unless an intellectual property right such as a patent or copyright protects an item, it will be subject to copying." *TrafFix Devices, Inc. v. Marketing Displays, Inc.,* 532 U.S. 23, 29, 121 S.Ct. 1255, 149 L.Ed.2d 164 (2001). The rights of a patentee or copyright holder are part of a "carefully crafted bargain," *Bonito Boats, Inc. v. Thunder Craft Boats, Inc.,* 489 U.S. 141, 150–151, 109 S.Ct. 971, 103 L.Ed.2d 118 (1989), under which, once the patent or copyright monopoly has expired, the public may use the invention or work at will and without attribution. Thus, in construing the Lanham Act, we have been "careful to caution against misuse or over-extension" of trademark and related protections into areas traditionally occupied by patent or copyright. *TrafFix,* 532 U.S., at 29, 121 S.Ct. 1255. "The Lanham Act," we have said, "does not exist to reward manufacturers for their innovation in creating a particular device; that is the purpose of the patent law and its period of exclusivity." Federal trademark law "has no necessary relation to invention or discovery," but rather, by preventing competitors from copying "a source-identifying mark," "reduce[s] the customer's costs of shopping and making purchasing decisions," and "helps assure a producer that it (and not an imitating competitor) will reap the financial, reputation-related rewards associated with a desirable product," *Qualitex Co. v. Jacobson Products Co.,* 514 U.S. 159, 163–164, 115 S.Ct. 1300, 131 L.Ed.2d 248 (1995). Assuming for the sake of argument that Dastar's representation of itself as the "Producer" of its videos amounted to a representation that it originated the creative work conveyed by the videos, allowing a cause of action under § 43(a) for that representation would create a species of mutant copyright law that limits the public's "federal right to 'copy and to use'" expired copyrights, *Bonito Boats, supra,* at 165, 109 S.Ct. 971.

When Congress has wished to create such an addition to the law of copyright, it has done so with much more specificity than the Lanham Act's ambiguous use of "origin." The Visual Artists Rights Act of 1990 provides that the author of an artistic work "shall have the right ... to claim authorship of that work." 17 U.S.C. § 106A(a)(1)(A). That express right of attribution is carefully limited and focused: It attaches only to specified "work[s] of visual art," § 101, is personal to the artist, §§ 106A(b) and (e), and endures only for "the life of the author," § 106A(d)(1). Recognizing in § 43(a) a cause of action for misrepresentation of authorship of noncopyrighted works (visual or otherwise) would render these limitations superfluous. A statutory interpretation that renders another statute superfluous is of course to be avoided.

Reading "origin" in § 43(a) to require attribution of uncopyrighted materials would pose serious practical problems. Without a copyrighted work as the basepoint, the word "origin" has no discernable limits. A video of the MGM film Carmen Jones, after its copyright has expired, would presumably require attribution not just to MGM, but to Oscar Hammerstein II (who wrote the musical on which the film was based), to Georges Bizet (who wrote the opera on which the musical was based), and to Prosper Merimee (who wrote the novel on which the opera was based). In many cases, figuring out who is in the line of "origin" would be no simple task. Indeed, in the present case it is far from clear that respondents have that status. Neither SFM nor New Line had anything to do with the production of the Crusade television series—they merely were licensed to distribute the video version. While Fox might have a claim to being in the line of origin, its involvement with the creation of the television series was limited at best. Time, Inc., was the principal, if not the exclusive, creator, albeit under arrangement with Fox. And of course it was neither Fox nor Time, Inc., that shot the film used in the Crusade television series. Rather, that footage came from the United States Army, Navy, and Coast Guard, the British Ministry of Information and War Office, the National Film Board of Canada, and unidentified "Newsreel Pool Cameramen." If anyone has a claim to being the *original* creator of the material used in both the Crusade television series and the Campaigns videotapes, it would be those groups, rather than Fox. We do not think the Lanham Act requires this search for the source of the Nile and all its tributaries.

Another practical difficulty of adopting a special definition of "origin" for communicative products is that it places the manufacturers of those products in a difficult position. On the one hand, they would face Lanham Act liability for *failing* to credit the creator of a work on which their lawful copies are based; and on the other hand they could face Lanham Act liability for *crediting* the creator if that should be regarded as implying the creator's "sponsorship or approval" of the copy, 15 U.S.C. § 1125(a)(1)(A). In this case, for example, if Dastar had simply "copied [the television series] as Crusade in Europe and sold it as Crusade in Europe," without changing the title or packaging (including the original credits to Fox), it is hard to have confidence in respondents' assurance that they "would not be here on a Lanham Act cause of action."

Finally, reading § 43(a) of the Lanham Act as creating a cause of action for, in effect, plagiarism—the use of otherwise unprotected works and inventions without attribution—would be hard to reconcile with our previous decisions. For example, in *Wal-Mart Stores, Inc. v. Samara Brothers, Inc.,* 529 U.S. 205, 120 S.Ct. 1339, 146 L.Ed.2d 182 (2000), we considered whether product-design trade dress can ever be inherently distinctive. Wal–Mart produced "knockoffs" of children's clothes designed and manufactured by Samara Brothers, containing only "minor modifications" of the original designs. We concluded that the designs could not be protected under § 43(a) without a showing that they had acquired "secondary meaning," so that they " 'identify the source of the product rather than the product itself.' " This carefully considered limitation would be entirely pointless if the "original" producer could turn around and pursue a reverse-passing-off claim under exactly the same provision of the Lanham Act. Samara would merely have had to argue that it was the "origin" of the designs that Wal–Mart was selling as its own line. It was not, because "origin of goods" in the Lanham Act referred to the producer of the clothes, and not the producer of the (potentially) copyrightable or patentable designs that the clothes embodied.

Similarly under respondents' theory, the "origin of goods" provision of § 43(a) would have supported the suit that we rejected in *Bonito Boats,* 489 U.S. 141, 109 S.Ct. 971, where the defendants had used molds to duplicate the plaintiff's unpatented boat hulls (apparently without crediting the plaintiff). And it would have supported the suit we rejected in *TrafFix*: The plaintiff, whose patents on flexible road signs had expired, and who could not prevail on a trade-dress claim under § 43(a) because the features of the signs were functional, would have had a reverse-passing-off claim for unattributed copying of his design.

In sum, reading the phrase "origin of goods" in the Lanham Act in accordance with the Act's common-law foundations (which were *not* designed to protect originality or creativity), and in light of the copyright and patent laws (which *were*), we conclude that the phrase refers to the producer of the tangible goods that are offered for sale, and not to the author of any idea, concept, or communication embodied in those goods. To hold otherwise would be akin to finding that § 43(a) created a species of perpetual patent and copyright, which Congress may not do.

The creative talent of the sort that lay behind the Campaigns videos is not left without protection. The original film footage used in the Crusade television series could have been copyrighted, as was copyrighted (as a compilation) the Crusade television series, even though it included material from the public domain. Had Fox renewed the copyright in the Crusade television series, it would have had an easy claim of copyright infringement. And respondents' contention that Campaigns infringes Doubleday's copyright in General Eisenhower's book is still a live question on remand. If, moreover, the producer of a video that substantially copied the Crusade series were, in advertising or promotion, to give purchasers the impression that the video was quite different from that series, then one or more of the respondents might have a cause of action—not for reverse passing off under the "confusion ... as to the origin" provision of § 43(a)(1)(A), but for misrepresentation under the "misrepresents the nature, characteristics [or] qualities" provision of § 43(a)(1)(B). For merely saying it is the producer of the video, however, no Lanham Act liability attaches to Dastar.

* * *

NOTES AND QUESTIONS

1. *Section 43(a) as a substitute for moral rights.* As a matter of policy, should creators of expressive works have an enforceable right to attribution? In *Dastar*, the Supreme Court suggests that use of Lanham Act § 43(a) to protect moral rights would render superfluous Congress' attempt to limit moral rights to a narrow category of works in the Visual Artists Rights Act (VARA). Harkening back to our examination of VARA (and the circumstances of its passage) in the Copyright Chapter, is it likely that Congress intended VARA to be the only means of protecting moral rights under U.S. law? Assuming that it intended to permit other forms of moral rights protection, such as Lanham Act § 43(a), are there constitutional reasons for prohibiting this construction of § 43(a)?

PROBLEMS

1. Architect A and Architect B were finalists in a publicly bid competition to design a new parking garage for University. The University favored the aesthetic aspects of Architect A's design, but granted the contract to Architect B because it preferred other aspects of B's bid. After granting the job to B, the University asked B to change some of the aesthetic aspects of his garage design to look more like A's losing design, and he did so. B later posted drawings of his revised design (which looked quite a bit like A's design) on his firm's web site, claiming the design as his own. When A learned of this, she brought a Lanham Act § 43(a) "false designation of origin" claim against B. How should the court rule, in light of the *Dastar* decision?

2. Ken Follett, while still relatively unknown, edits the English translation of a French book about a famous bank robbery for publication in Britain. Follett goes beyond normal editing, restructuring the story, enhancing the writing style, developing the characters and filling in gaps. The published British edition credits the French author only on the cover, and credits the

French author, followed by "with Ken Follett," on the title page. After Follett becomes a best-selling novelist, an American edition is readied for publication, which highlights Follett's name, reducing the original French author to a secondary role. Only Follett's name appears on the spine of the book. At that point, Follett does not wish to have principle authorship attributed to him. Does he have a cause of action under Lanham Act § 43(a)?

3. Plaintiff manufactures tables with a single leg on each side shaped like a "Y." This Y shape facilitates adjusting the height of the table. A horizontal bar attaching the two legs near the bottom gives the table further support.

The defendant begins manufacturing tables with a similar design. A prospective customer asks defendant to see some sample tables. Because defendant rejected the last batch of legs made by a supplier as unsatisfactory, it has no legs on hand. Defendant therefore takes legs from some of plaintiff's tables and uses them to make samples for the customer's inspection. Defendant does not tell the prospective customer that the sample tables incorporate legs from the plaintiff's tables.

Plaintiff brings suit, alleging reverse passing off under Lanham Act § 43(a). What result?

VIII. REMEDIES

BRUNSWICK CORP. v. SPINIT REEL CO.

Unites States Court of Appeals for the Tenth Circuit, 1987.
832 F.2d 513.

McKAY, CIRCUIT JUDGE.

[Appellant Brunswick Corporation, through its Zebco division, manufactures and sells the Zebco Model 33 "closed face" spin-cast fishing reel. The Zebco Model 33 has a distinctive profile with a chrome, cone-shaped front cover, a "stubby" back cover and a black and chrome finish. Appellee Spinit Reel manufactured and sold the SR 210 closed face spin-cast reel, which was similar in appearance to the Zebco Model 33. Brunswick filed suit against Spinit under Lanham Act § 43(a), 15 U.S.C.A. § 1125(a), claiming infringement of its trademark rights in the distinctive appearance of its reel. The district court found that the SR 210 violated the Lanham Act and enjoined Spinit from further manufacture of the SR 210 or anything identical or confusingly similar to the Zebco Model 33. It also ordered Spinit to recall all models of the SR 210, but declined to award Brunswick damages or attorney's fees.]

[On appeal, the Tenth Circuit found that the reel configuration was entitled to trademark protection and that Brunswick had established a likelihood of confusion through evidence of actual confusion and a survey of potential customers. The court then turned to the issue of relief.]

Spinit argues that the injunction should be vacated because it was granted for the wrong reason and because Spinit has rectified the design problem and is not likely to repeat it. * * * Spinit asserts that it was enjoined as punishment. The court, however, explained its reasoning in the Amended Findings of Fact and Conclusions of Law: an injunction is warranted if consumers are likely to confuse a Spinit SR 210 with a Zebco 33, and consumers are likely to believe that the Spinit SR 210 is manufactured by Zebco because of the similarity of the reels. The trial court applied the appropriate test for issuing an injunction in this case. We find no basis for Spinit's claim of punishment.

* * * Spinit argues that injunctive relief is unnecessary because by drastically altering the SR 210 cover, it solved the confusion problem in the design. Regardless of whether the unfair conduct has stopped and is not likely to recur, the trial court still has the discretion to grant or deny an injunction against such conduct. The district court ruled that the two models of the SR 210 that Spinit had manufactured at the time the suit was brought were likely to confuse customers that they were made by Zebco. We find no abuse of discretion in the court's granting of an injunction.

* * *

The district court found that, although Brunswick established a legal basis for damages, it failed to establish clear proof of damages. * * *

[T]he award [of damages] is distinguishable from injunctive relief, because plaintiff bears a greater burden of proof of entitlement. Likelihood of confusion is insufficient; to recover damages plaintiff must prove it has been damaged by actual consumer confusion or deception resulting from the violation. Actual consumer confusion may be shown by direct evidence, a diversion of sales or direct testimony from the public, or by circumstantial evidence such as consumer surveys.

> Although the quantum of damages, as distinguished from entitlement, must be demonstrated with specificity, courts may engage in "some degree of speculation in computing the amount of damages, particularly when the inability to compute them is attributable to the defendant's wrongdoing."

PPX Enters. Inc. v. Audiofidelity Enters., Inc., 818 F.2d 266, 271 (2d Cir.1987).

The district court found that there was actual confusion among consumers and retailers, and that Zebco and Spinit sell reels in the same marketing channels, in direct competition with each other. Those findings support the court's determination that Brunswick established a legal basis for the recovery of damages, indicating that actual consumer confusion resulted from Spinit's violation of section 43(a). Nevertheless, by adding that Brunswick did not establish clear proof of damages, the court implies that Brunswick presented insufficient proof of actual damages. The court more likely meant that, although Brunswick established entitlement to damages, it failed to show that it suffered damages in fact.

Brunswick submitted evidence that in the fiscal year ending July 1983 sales of all Zebco spin-cast products dropped off by five percent, sales of spin-cast reels generally had decreased by six percent due to the recession. Sales for the Zebco 33, however, dropped sixteen percent. Spinit introduced testimony that the introduction of other new reels on the market might have contributed to the decrease in Zebco's sales. However, in light of the trial court's finding of actual confusion and direct competition between the reels, we are not persuaded that other reels were the sole cause of the substantial reduction in the sale of the Zebco 33. Thus, the evidence does not indicate that Brunswick failed to show it suffered any actual damages.

A defendant whose wrongful conduct has caused the difficulty in assessing damages cannot complain that the damages are somewhat speculative. Evidence of the amount of damages may be circumstantial and inexact.

> [I]n a case such as this, where the wrong is of such a nature as to preclude exact ascertainment of the amount of damages, plaintiff may recover upon a showing of the extent of the damages as a matter of just and reasonable inference, although the result may be only an approximation.

Bangor Punta Operations, Inc. v. Universal Marine Co., 543 F.2d 1107, 1110–11 (5th Cir.1976).

Brunswick bases its claim for damages on the theory that Zebco lost one sale of a Model 33 as a result of each Spinit SR 210 reel sold. While this court does not necessarily believe that each Spinit sale resulted in a corresponding loss of sale by Zebco, the theory provides an upper range for an award of damages. The district court may also look to the difference in the decline of Model 33 sales as compared with the decline in sales of Zebco's other spin-cast reels. Those items of evidence provide the court a broad basis from which it may arrive at a fair, if not precise, amount with which to compensate Brunswick for wrongful infringement. We reverse the trial court's finding on damages and remand for findings of the amount of damages due.

     * * *

Attorney's fees may be awarded, under certain circumstances, under the Lanham Act. Prior to 1975, the Lanham Act (15 U.S.C. §§ 1051–1127) contained no provision for the awarding of attorney's fees, and the United States Supreme Court had ruled that the judicial granting of attorney's fees was improper under the Lanham Act because the granting of fees was not contained in the language of the Act and because "Congress intended § 35 of the Lanham Act to mark the boundaries of the power to award monetary relief in cases arising under the Act." *Fleischmann Distilling Corp. v. Maier Brewing Co.*, 386 U.S. 714, 721, 87 S.Ct. 1404, 1409, 18 L.Ed.2d 475 (1967).

In 1975, Congress responded to the *Fleischmann* ruling and amended section 35 to permit "[t]he court in exceptional cases [to] award reasonable attorney fees to the prevailing party." * * *

* * * This court has previously ruled that an exceptional case "is one in which the trademark infringement can be characterized as 'malicious,' 'fraudulent,' 'deliberate,' or 'willful.' " *VIP Foods, Inc. v. Vulcan Pet, Inc.,* 675 F.2d 1106, 1107 (10th Cir.1982); *but see USM, Inc.,* 810 F.2d at 116 (exceptional means less than "bad faith"; it means "uncommon, not run-of-the-mine"). [T]he element of being "exceptional" i.e. willful, etc., is not present in Spinit's actions. We thus rule that Brunswick is not entitled to attorney's fees under section 43(a) of the Lanham Act.

* * *

NOTES AND QUESTIONS

1. *Lanham Act remedies.* Registration on the Lanham Act Principal Register offers several important advantages to trademark owners: the constructive use and notice provisions for establishing priority and geographic rights throughout the United States; the six-month "grace" period for filing foreign registration applications pursuant to the Paris Convention; U.S. Customs assistance in excluding infringing imports at the border; *prima facie* evidence of mark validity and the registrant's ownership and exclusive right to use; incontestability status; and immunity to state dilution suits. Another valued feature of the Lanham Act is its generous remedy provisions. However, the Lanham Act remedies are available both for owners of registered marks and for owners of unregistered marks, trade dress and other indications of origin claiming infringement pursuant to Lanham Act § 43, 15 U.S.C.A. § 1125.

In addition to injunctive relief, which is authorized in § 34, 15 U.S.C.A. § 1116, Lanham Act § 35(a) provides:

> When a violation of any right of the registrant of a mark registered in the Patent and Trademark Office, a violation under section 1125(a) or (d), or a willful violation under section 1125(c) of this title shall have been established * * * the plaintiff shall be entitled, subject to the provisions of sections 1111 [notice requirements] and 1114 [limitations on the liability of printers and publishers], and subject to the principles of equity, to recover (1) defendant's profits, (2) any damages sustained by the plaintiff, and (3) the costs of the action. * * * In assessing profits the plaintiff shall be required to prove defendant's sales only: defendant must prove all elements of cost or deduction claimed. In assessing damages the court may enter judgment, according to the circumstances of the case, for any sum above the amount found as actual damages, not exceeding three times such amount. If the court shall find that the amount of the recovery based on profits is either inadequate or excessive the court may in its discretion enter judgment for such sum as the court shall find to be just, according to the circumstances of the case. Such sum in either of the above circumstances shall constitute compensation and not a penalty. The court in exceptional cases may award reasonable attorney fees to the prevailing party.

15 U.S.C.A. § 1117(a). Lanham Act § 35(b) provides special, enhanced remedies in counterfeiting cases, including treble damages and attorney fees. 15

U.S.C.A. § 1117(b). Section 35(c) provides that infringement plaintiffs may elect statutory damages of up to $200,000 per counterfeit mark per type of good or service (or up to $2,000,000 in cases of willful counterfeiting) in lieu of actual damages or profits. 15 U.S.C. § 1117(c).

Plaintiffs alleging violation of the anticybersquatting provisions of Lanham Act § 43(d) may also elect to recover an award of statutory damages in lieu of actual damages and profits. These statutory damages may range from $1,000 to $100,000 per domain name, as the court considers just. 15 U.S.C.A. § 1117(d).

2. *Injunctive relief.* In trademark cases, like patent and copyright cases, courts have traditionally granted permanent injunctive relief as a matter of course, once the plaintiff has demonstrated a likelihood of consumer confusion. However, the Supreme Court's recent decision in eBay Inc. v. MercExchange, L.L.C., 547 U.S. 388, 126 S.Ct. 1837, 164 L.Ed.2d 641 (2006) (reprinted in Ch. 3, *supra*), has had its influence in trademark litigation, as it has in patent and copyright litigation, leading courts to adhere more strictly to the four-factor test for permanent injunctive relief set forth in that case. See, e.g., North American Medical Corp. v. Axiom Worldwide, Inc., 522 F.3d 1211, 1227–28 (11th Cir. 2008)(finding *eBay* relevant in evaluating the right both to permanent and preliminary injunctions against trademark infringement).

3. *Actual damages.* The *Brunswick* opinion illustrates the problems plaintiffs may encounter in establishing actual damages. Did the court hold the plaintiff to different standards for proving the *fact* of damage and the specific *amount* of damage? If so, does this make sense? Do the standards of proof that the court imposed provide adequate safeguards for defendants? Is there sufficient guidance for the district court? How should the district court proceed in determining a specific damage amount on remand in *Brunswick*? Would it make more sense to impose a "reasonable royalty" measure of damages as a default standard for use when the plaintiff is unable to prove the specific amount of its loss with certainty, as is done in patent law? Or should Congress enact a general provision for statutory damages, as it has in the Copyright Act? What other means of measuring damages might a court adopt? Apart from lost sales, what items of pecuniary loss might be subject to recovery as actual damages? See Restatement (Third) of Unfair Competition § 36(2) (1995).

Note the Lanham Act's provision for notice of registration in § 29, 15 U.S.C.A. § 1111. A registrant who fails to give such notice is prohibited from recovering either damages or profits unless it can demonstrate that the defendant had actual notice of the registration. What are the implications of this provision for plaintiffs with unregistered marks, such as the plaintiff in *Brunswick*?

4. *The defendant's profits.* In Banjo Buddies, Inc. v. Renosky, 399 F.3d 168 (3d Cir. 2005), the Court of Appeals for the Third Circuit considered the proper standard for awarding an accounting of profits, in light of recent amendments to Lanham Act § 35(a).

> Renosky [the defendant] argues that the District Court erred by awarding profits from the Bionic Minnow project to Banjo Buddies under section 35(a) of the Lanham Act because Renosky's violation of section

43(a) of that statute was not willful or intentional. Renosky relies on *SecuraComm Consulting, Inc. v. Securacom, Inc.,* 166 F.3d 182 (3d Cir.1999), in which this court held that "a plaintiff must prove that an infringer acted willfully before the infringer's profits are recoverable" under § 35(a) of the Lanham Act. *Id.* at 190. * * * [W]e conclude that *SecuraComm'*s bright-line willfulness requirement has been superseded by statute and that, based on all the relevant equitable factors, the District Court did not abuse its discretion by ordering an accounting of Renosky's profits.

*SecuraComm'*s bright-line rule was the dominant view when *SecuraComm* was issued in January 1999. In August 1999, however, Congress amended § 35. Prior to the amendment, that section provided as follows:

> When a violation of any right of the registrant of a mark registered in the Patent and Trademark Office, or a violation under section 43(a) [15 U.S.C. § 1125(a)], shall have been established ... the plaintiff shall be entitled ..., subject to the principles of equity, to recover (1) defendant's profits, (2) any damages sustained by the plaintiff, and (3) the costs of the action.

The 1999 amendment replaced "or a violation under section 43(a)" with "a violation under section 43(a), or a *willful* violation under section 43(c)." The plain language of the amendment indicates that Congress intended to condition monetary awards for § 43(c) violations, but not § 43(a) violations, on a showing of willfulness.

We presume Congress was aware that most courts had consistently required a showing of willfulness prior to disgorgement of an infringer's profits in Lanham Act cases, despite the absence of the word "willful" in the statutory text prior to 1999. * * * By adding this word to the statute in 1999, but limiting it to § 43(c) violations, Congress effectively superseded the willfulness requirement as applied to § 43(a). * * *

This conclusion is supported by *Quick Technologies, Inc. v. Sage Group PLC*, 313 F.3d 338, 349 (5th Cir. 2002), the only other appellate decision to reach the issue. The Fifth Circuit in *Quick Technologies* considered the effect of the 1999 amendment and held that, based on earlier decisions of that court as well as "the plain language of [§ 43(a)]," willful infringement was not a prerequisite to an accounting of the infringer's profits. *Id.* The court noted the wealth of contrary authority, including *SecuraComm,* but pointed out that all of those cases preceded the statutory change. The *Quick Technologies* court reaffirmed the factor-based approach elaborated in prior Fifth Circuit cases, including *Pebble Beach Co. v. Tour 18 I Limited,* 155 F.3d 526, 554 (5th Cir.1998), explaining that the infringer's intent was an important—but not indispensable—factor in evaluating whether equity supports disgorging the infringer's profits. These factors "include, but are not limited to (1) whether the defendant had the intent to confuse or deceive, (2) whether sales have been diverted, (3) the adequacy of other remedies, (4) any unreasonable delay by the plaintiff in asserting his rights, (5) the public interest in making the misconduct unprofitable, and (6) whether it is a case of palming off." *Id.*

399 F.3d at 173–75. The Third Circuit then adopted the *Quick Technologies* multifactor standard and applied it to the facts of the case before it.

Lanham Act § 35(a) provides that "[i]n assessing profits the plaintiff shall be required to prove defendant's sales only; defendant must prove all elements of cost or deduction claimed." What sorts of costs and deductions might the defendant successfully assert in order to reduce the amount it must pay? See Restatement (Third) of Unfair Competition § 37, cmts d, g, and h (1995).

In some cases courts permit a plaintiff to recover both its actual damages and the defendant's profits, though they are careful not to permit the plaintiff to recover twice for the same loss. In what sorts of settings would imposing both forms of recovery be most appropriate? When would it be most likely to lead to double recovery? See Restatement (Third) of Unfair Competition § 36, cmt c (1995).

CHAPTER SIX

UNFAIR COMPETITION

■ ■ ■

I. INTRODUCTION

As discussed in the prior chapter, the law of unfair competition has deep roots in tort doctrine, and particularly in the law of deceit. In its earliest stages, the unfair competition cause of action solely addressed misrepresentations about the source of goods or services. Concepts of "unfair competition" have since expanded, as we will see in this chapter. Today, the "misrepresentation of source" branch of the law of unfair competition is sometimes called "passing off" or "palming off," and includes the modern causes of action for trademark, trade dress, and trade name infringement that we studied in the prior chapter.

"Passing off" occurs when a business makes a false or misleading representation that is likely to cause consumers to believe that its business, product, or service is or is affiliated with that of the plaintiff. That false representation may take a number of different forms. Most commonly, passing off occurs when a defendant uses a mark, trade name, or trade dress that is confusingly similar to the plaintiff's. However, other kinds of false representations may give rise to a cause of action for passing off. For example, a defendant who copies the plaintiff's product may expressly tell the buyer at the point of sale that his product is "the original," thus implying that the plaintiff (who was the "original" producer) produced it. Passing off may also occur when a retailer represents that the products or services of one third party are those of a different third party. This would occur, for example, when a restaurant defendant fills orders for a brand of cola manufactured by X with a brand manufactured by Y without notifying consumers of the switch. Lanham Act § 43(a)(1)(A) has been construed to provide a federal cause of action for all forms of passing off, regardless of whether they involve use of protected marks, trade names, or trade dress, or some other form of misleading action. Dastar Corp. v. Twentieth Century Fox Film Corp., 539 U.S. 23, 123 S.Ct. 2041, 156 L.Ed.2d 18 (2003).

Courts later recognized causes of action to address merchants' misrepresentations about aspects of goods or services *other than* their source. The common-law false advertising cause of action addresses a competitor's misrepresentations about the *nature or characteristics of its own goods or services,* when the plaintiff can demonstrate resulting harm to its own business good will. The common-law commercial disparagement cause of action redresses a defendant's misrepresentations about the *nature or character of the plaintiff's goods or services.*

Each of these two newer causes of action remains available to competitors under state common law and by virtue of state statutes that have codified and modernized the original common-law doctrines. In addition, Lanham Act § 43(a)(1)(B) provides a modernized, federal cause of action for false advertising and commercial disparagement. Section 43(a)(1) provides:

> (a)(1) Any person who, on or in connection with any goods or services, or any container for goods, uses in commerce any word, term, name, symbol, or device, or any combination thereof, or any false designation of origin, false or misleading description of fact, or false or misleading representation of fact, which—
>
> > (A) is likely to cause confusion, or to cause mistake, or to deceive as to the affiliation, connection, or association of such person with another person, or as to the origin, sponsorship, or approval of his or her goods, services, or commercial activities by another person, or
> >
> > (B) in commercial advertising or promotion, misrepresents the nature, characteristics, qualities, or geographic origin of his or her or another person's goods, services, or commercial activities,
>
> shall be liable in a civil action by any person who believes that he or she is or is likely to be damaged by such act.

15 U.S.C.A. § 1125(a)(1). Because the Lanham Act causes of action modernize and expand the common-law doctrines, and provide the same liberal remedies as are available for infringement of registered marks, the § 43(a) causes of action have become popular and have tended to eclipse the state causes of action.

In the twentieth century, the common law of unfair competition extended beyond its origins in the law of deceit, to embrace a rationale more nearly akin to trespass or conversion. In particular, a number of state courts adopted and developed the controversial cause of action for "misappropriation," originally conceived by the United States Supreme Court in International News Service v. Associated Press, 248 U.S. 215, 39 S.Ct. 68, 63 L.Ed. 211 (1918), as pre-*Erie Railroad* federal common law. The misappropriation doctrine may recognize a property right in the product of one's investment, labor or skill, and prevent others from taking that product in a manner that constitutes "free-riding," or "reaping where they have not sown." There is no general federal statutory counterpart to the misappropriation doctrine.

While the four causes of action discussed above do not comprise the whole of modern unfair competition law, they comprise the bulk of it. We have explored the underlying tenets of passing off doctrine in our examination of trademarks and other indications of origin in the prior chapter. In this chapter, we will briefly review the false advertising, commercial disparagement and misappropriation doctrines.

NOTES AND QUESTIONS

1. *International Considerations.* Article 10*bis* of the Paris Convention provides:

> 1. The countries of the Union are bound to assure to nationals of such countries effective protection against unfair competition.

> 2. Any act of competition contrary to honest practices in industrial or commercial matters constitutes an act of unfair competition.

> 3. The following in particular shall be prohibited:

>> (1) all acts of such a nature as to create confusion by any means whatever with the establishment, the goods, or the industrial or commercial activities, of a competitor;

>> (2) false allegations in the course of trade of such a nature as to discredit the establishment, the goods, or the industrial or commercial activities, of a competitor;

>> (3) indications or allegations the use of which in the course of trade is liable to mislead the public as to the nature, the manufacturing process, the characteristics, the suitability for their purpose, or the quantity, of the goods.[1]

Lanham Act § 44, 15 U.S.C.A. § 1126, implements the United States' treaty obligations to protect nationals of other countries against unfair competition. While there has been some debate about the scope of § 44, the courts have tended to construe the § 44 provisions narrowly. As the Eleventh Circuit recently explained: "[S]ection 44 of the Lanham Act gives foreign nationals the same rights and protections provided to United States citizens by the Lanham Act. As such, foreign nationals * * * may seek protection in the United States for violations of the Lanham Act. But the Paris Convention, as incorporated by section 44 of the Lanham Act, creates no new cause of action for unfair competition. Any cause of action based on unfair competition must be grounded in the substantive provisions of the Lanham Act." International Café, S.A.L. v. Hard Rock Café International, Inc., 252 F.3d 1274, 1278–79 (11th Cir.2001). See also L'Aiglon Apparel, Inc. v. Lana Lobell, Inc., 214 F.2d 649, 652 (3d Cir.1954) (Section 44 gives U.S. citizens "reciprocal rights against foreign nationals where foreign nationals compete unfairly with them. It does not aim to create a federal law of unfair competition available to [U.S.] citizens one against the other nor does it grant the federal courts any new authority to hear such controversies between citizens.").

---

1. Paris Convention for the Protection of Industrial Property, March 20, 1883, as most recently revised at Stockholm on July 14, 1967, 21 U.S.T. 1629, 828 U.N.T.S. 107.

2. *Additional resources.* The leading treatises on unfair competition are J.T. McCarthy, McCarthy on Trademarks and Unfair Competition, and J. Gilson, Trademark Protection and Practice, both of which are regularly supplemented. The new Restatement (Third) of Unfair Competition (1995) is also an invaluable resource.

II. FALSE ADVERTISING

ELY–NORRIS SAFE CO. v. MOSLER SAFE CO.

United States Court of Appeals for the Second Circuit, 1925.
7 F.2d 603, *reversed on other grounds,* 273 U.S. 132, 47 S.Ct. 314, 71 L.Ed. 578 (1927).

The jurisdiction of the District Court depended upon diverse citizenship, and the suit was for unfair competition. The bill alleged that the plaintiff manufactured and sold safes under certain letters patent, which had as their distinctive feature an explosion chamber, designed for protection against burglars. Before the acts complained of, no one but the plaintiff had ever made or sold safes with such chambers, and, except for the defendant's infringement, the plaintiff has remained the only manufacturer and seller of such safes. By reason of the plaintiff's efforts the public has come to recognize the value of the explosion chamber and to wish to purchase safes containing them. Besides infringing the patent, the defendant has manufactured and sold safes without a chamber, but with a metal band around the door, in the same place where the plaintiff put the chamber, and has falsely told its customers that this band was employed to cover and close an explosion chamber. Customers have been thus led to buy safes upon the faith of the representation, who in fact wished to buy safes with explosion chambers, and would have done so, but for the deceit.

The bill prayed an injunction against selling safes with such metal bands, and against representing that any of its safes contained an explosion chamber. From the plaintiff's answers to interrogatories it appeared that all the defendant's safes bore the defendant's name and address, and were sold as its own. Furthermore, that the defendant never gave a customer reason to suppose that any safe sold by it was made by the plaintiff.

HAND, CIRCUIT JUDGE (after stating the facts as above).

This case is not the same as that before Mr. Justice Bradley in New York & Rosendale Co. v. Coplay Cement Co. (C.C.) 44 F. 277, 10 L.R.A. 833. The plaintiffs there manufactured cement at Rosendale, N.Y., but it did not appear that they were the only persons making cement at that place. There was no reason, therefore, to assume that a customer of the defendant, deceived as to the place of origin of the defendant's cement, and desiring to buy only such cement, would have bought of the plaintiffs. It resulted that the plaintiffs did not show any necessary loss of trade through the defendant's fraud upon its own customers. * * *

American Washboard Co. v. Saginaw Mfg. Co., 103 F. 281 (C.C.A.6), 43 C.C.A. 233, 50 L.R.A. 609, was, however, a case in substance like that at bar, because there the plaintiff alleged that it had acquired the entire output of sheet aluminum suitable for washboards. It necessarily followed that the plaintiff had a practical monopoly of this metal for the articles in question, and from this it was a fair inference that any customer of the defendant, who was deceived into buying as an aluminum washboard one which was not such, was a presumptive customer of the plaintiff, who had therefore lost a bargain. This was held, however, not to constitute a private wrong, and so the bill was dismissed.

* * *

We must concede, therefore, that on the cases as they stand the law is with the defendant, and the especially high authority of the court which decided American Washboard Co. v. Saginaw Mfg. Co., supra, makes us hesitate to differ from their conclusion. Yet there is no part of the law which is more plastic than unfair competition, and what was not reckoned an actionable wrong 25 years ago may have become such today. We find it impossible to deny the strength of the plaintiff's case on the allegations of its bill. As we view it, the question is, as it always is in such cases, one of fact. While a competitor may, generally speaking, take away all the customers of another that he can, there are means which he must not use. One of these is deceit. The false use of another's name as maker or source of his own goods is deceit, of which the false use of geographical or descriptive terms is only one example. But we conceive that in the end the questions which arise are always two: Has the plaintiff in fact lost customers? And has he lost them by means which the law forbids? The false use of the plaintiff's name is only an instance in which each element is clearly shown.

In the case at bar the means are as plainly unlawful as in the usual case of palming off. It is as unlawful to lie about the quality of one's wares as about their maker; it equally subjects the seller to action by the buyer. * * * The reason, as we think, why such deceits have not been regarded as actionable by a competitor, depends only upon his inability to show any injury for which there is a known remedy. In an open market it is generally impossible to prove that a customer, whom the defendant has secured by falsely describing his goods, would have bought of the plaintiff, if the defendant had been truthful. Without that, the plaintiff, though aggrieved in company with other honest traders, cannot show any ascertainable loss. He may not recover at law, and the equitable remedy is concurrent. The law does not allow him to sue as a vicarious avenger of the defendant's customers.

But, if it be true that the plaintiff has a monopoly of the kind of wares concerned, and if to secure a customer the defendant must represent his own as of that kind, it is a fair inference that the customer wants those and those only. Had he not supposed that the defendant could supply him, presumably he would have gone to the plaintiff, who alone could. At least, if the plaintiff can prove that in fact he would, he shows a direct loss, measured by his profits on the putative sale. If a tradesman falsely foists on a customer a substitute for what the plaintiff alone can supply, it can scarcely be that the plaintiff is without remedy, if he can show that the customer would certainly have come to him, had the truth been told.

Yet that is in substance the situation which this bill presents. It says that the plaintiff alone could lawfully make such safes, and that the defendant has sold others to customers who asked for the patented kind. It can make no difference that the defendant sold them as its own. The sale by hypothesis depended upon the structure of the safes, not on their maker. To be satisfied, the customer must in fact have gone to the plaintiff, or the defendant must have infringed. Had he infringed, the plaintiff could have recovered his profit on the sale; had the customer gone to him, he would have made that profit. Any possibilities that the customers might not have gone to the plaintiff, had they been told the truth, are foreclosed by the allegation that the plaintiff in fact lost the sales. It seems to us * * * that, if this can be proved, a private suit will lie.

NOTES AND QUESTIONS

1. *The common-law cause of action for false advertising.* Prior to the Second Circuit's *Mosler* opinion, the cause of action for unfair competition had consisted almost exclusively of relief for misrepresentations about the source of goods or services. As the *Mosler* court suggests, the courts had strongly resisted expanding the law to provide redress for other misrepresentations a competitor might make about his own goods or services. The *American Washboard* court, cited in *Mosler*, explained:

> If the doctrine contended for by complainant in this case was to be carried to its legitimate results, we should, as suggested by Mr. Justice Bradley in the case of New York & R. Cement Co. v. Coplay Cement Co., (C.C.) 44 Fed. 277, open a Pandora's box of litigation. A person who undertook to manufacture a genuine article could suppress the business of all untruthful dealers, although they were in no wise undertaking to pirate his trade. Says Mr. Justice Bradley:
>
>> The principle for which counsel for complainant contends would enable any crockery merchant of Dresden or elsewhere interested in the particular trade to sue a dealer of New York or Philadelphia who should sell an article as Dresden china, when it is not Dresden china. * * * A dry-goods merchant selling an article of linen as Irish Linen could be sued by all the haberdashers of Ireland and all the linen dealers of the United States.

American Washboard Co. v. Saginaw Mfg. Co., 103 F. 281, 285–86 (6th Cir.1900). Why does the Court of Appeals for the Second Circuit decide to permit the plaintiff's cause of action in *Mosler*? As a practical matter, how broad is the *Mosler* exception to the general rule?

On certiorari, the Supreme Court reversed the Second Circuit. Mosler Safe Co. v. Ely–Norris Safe Co., 273 U.S. 132, 47 S.Ct. 314, 71 L.Ed. 578 (1927). The Court explained:

The Circuit Court of Appeals held that if, as it took it to be alleged, the plaintiff had the monopoly of explosion chambers and the defendant falsely represented that its safes had such chambers, the plaintiff had a good case * * *.

At the hearing below all attention seems to have been concentrated on the question passed upon and the forcibly stated reasons that induced this Court of Appeals to differ from that for the Sixth Circuit. But, upon closer scrutiny of the bill than seems to have been invited before, it does not present that broad and interesting issue. The bill alleges that the plaintiff has a patent for an explosion chamber as described and claimed in said Letters Patent; that it has the exclusive right to make and sell safes containing such an explosion chamber * * *. It then is alleged that the defendant is making and selling safes with a metal band around the door at substantially the same location as the explosion chamber of plaintiff's safes, and has represented to the public that the said metal band was employed to cover or close an explosion chamber by reason of which the public has been led to purchase defendant's said safes as and for safes containing an explosion chamber, such as is manufactured and sold by the plaintiff herein. * * *

It is consistent with every allegation in the bill and the defendant in argument asserted it to be a fact, that there are other safes with explosion chambers beside that for which the plaintiff has a patent. The defendant is charged only with representing that its safes had an explosion chamber, which, so far as appears, it had a perfect right to do if the representation was true. If on the other hand the representation was false as it is alleged sometimes to have been, there is nothing to show that customers had they known the facts would have gone to the plaintiff rather than to other competitors in the market, or to lay a foundation for the claim for a loss of sales. The bill is so framed as to seem to invite the decision that was obtained from the Circuit Court of Appeals, but when scrutinized is seen to have so limited its statements as to exclude the right to complain.

Id., 273 U.S. at 133–34. Given the reason for the reversal, the Second Circuit's substantive rule continued to be persuasive and ultimately gained general acceptance.

JOHNSON & JOHNSON v. CARTER–WALLACE, INC.

United States Court of Appeals for the Second Circuit, 1980.
631 F.2d 186.

MANSFIELD, CIRCUIT JUDGE:

Johnson & Johnson ("Johnson"), manufacturer of Johnson's Baby Oil and Johnson's Baby Lotion, appeals from a judgment of the United States District Court for the Southern District of New York * * * dismissing at the end of the plaintiff's case * * * its suit for injunctive relief brought under § 43(a) of the Lanham Act, 15 U.S.C. § 1125(a), against Carter–Wallace ("Carter"), the manufacturer of NAIR, a leading depilatory product. Because we believe Johnson's showing on the required elements of its false advertising claim was sufficient to withstand a motion to dismiss, we reverse and remand for further proceedings.

Johnson's claim arises out of Carter's use of baby oil in NAIR and its advertising campaign regarding that inclusion. In 1977, Carter added baby oil to its NAIR lotion and initiated a successful advertising campaign emphasizing this fact. NAIR is sold in a pink plastic bottle with the word "NAIR" written in large, pink letters. A bright turquoise-blue banner, open at both ends, contains the words "with baby oil." In addition to its packaging of NAIR, Carter's television advertisements emphasize that NAIR contains baby oil.[2]

Alleging that Carter is making false claims for NAIR with baby oil * * *, plaintiff filed the instant suit for injunctive relief under § 43(a) of the Lanham Act, 15 U.S.C. § 1125(a), and under New York's common law of unfair competition. * * * Johnson's false representation claim alleges that Carter's "NAIR with baby oil" campaign falsely represents to consumers that the baby oil in NAIR has [a] moisturizing and softening effect on the skin of the user. While recognizing that Carter's advertising makes no explicit claims for its product, Johnson alleges that this claim is implicit in the manner in which NAIR has been marketed. It contends that these false claims have unfairly dissuaded consumers from using its products in favor of NAIR with baby oil.

        * * *

In dismissing Johnson's false advertising claim, the trial court did not reach either the question of whether Carter advertises or implies in its advertising that baby oil as an ingredient in NAIR has a moisturizing and softening effect, or the issue of whether such a claim is false. Instead, its dismissal was "granted on the ground that [Johnson] failed to carry its burden of proving damage or the likelihood of damage." Just what that burden is and what evidence will satisfy it, are the central issues in this appeal.

DISCUSSION

Prior to the enactment of § 43(a) of the Lanham Act, liability [for false representations in marketing] was generally confined to "palming-

---

2. The court has viewed samples of Carter's television advertisements. Carter's commercials all featured several young women dancing and singing while dressed in clothing that revealed their legs. A typical audio portion of these commercials is as follows:

"Who's got Baby Oil?

Nair's got Baby Oil.

If you're a baby goil, Nair with Baby Oil.

Nair with Baby Oil.

It takes off the hair so your legs feel baby-smooth.

And Nair's baby-soft scent smells terrific, baby.

Who's got Baby Oil?

Nair's got Baby Oil.

Soft-smelling Nair with Baby Oil.

Nair, for baby-smooth legs."

off" cases where the deceit related to the origin of the product. In these cases the offending product was foisted upon an unwary consumer by deceiving him into the belief that he was buying the plaintiff's product (normally an item with a reputation for quality). Other instances of false advertising were safe from actions by competitors due to the difficulty of satisfying the requirement of proof of actual damage caused by the false claims. In an open market it is normally impossible to prove that a customer, who was induced by the defendant through the use of false claims to purchase the product, would have bought from the plaintiff if the defendant had been truthful.

The passage of § 43(a) represented a departure from the common law * * * and from the need to prove actual damages as a prerequisite for injunctive relief. This departure marked the creation of a "new statutory tort" intended to secure a market-place free from deceitful marketing practices. The new tort, as subsequently interpreted by the courts, differs from the common law action * * * in two important respects: (1) it does not require proof of intent to deceive, and (2) it entitles a broad range of commercial parties to relief.

The broadening of the scope of liability results from a provision in § 43(a) allowing suit to be brought "by any person who believes that he is or is likely to be damaged by the use of any false description or representation." 15 U.S.C. § 1125(a). Whether this clause is viewed as a matter of standing to sue, or as an element of the substantive claim for relief, certain bounds are well established. On the one hand, despite the use of the word "believes," something more than a plaintiff's mere subjective belief that he is injured or likely to be damaged is required before he will be entitled even to injunctive relief. On the other hand, as the district court in this case recognized, a plaintiff seeking an injunction, as opposed to money damages, need not quantify the losses actually borne. What showing of damage in between those two extremes will satisfy the statute is the subject of the instant dispute.

Johnson claims, in effect, that once it is shown that the plaintiff's and the defendant's products compete in a relevant market and that the defendant's ads are false, a likelihood of damage sufficient to satisfy the statute should be *presumed* and an injunction should issue "as a matter of course." The district court, in contrast, drew the line as follows: "Of course, J & J (Johnson) need not quantify its injury in order to obtain injunctive relief. But J & J must at least prove the existence of some injury caused by Carter." The court had said that "J & J has failed to prove that its loss of sales was in any way caused by NAIR's allegedly false advertising."

Both the case law and the policy behind § 43(a) indicate that the district court's construction of the statute placed too high a burden on the plaintiff in this case. To require a plaintiff to "prove the existence of some injury caused by" the defendant, is to demand proof of actual loss and specific evidence of causation. Perhaps a competitor in an open market could meet this standard with proof short of quantified sales loss, but it is not required to do so. The statute demands only proof providing a reasonable basis for the belief that the plaintiff is likely to be damaged as a result of the false advertising. The correct standard is whether it is *likely* that Carter's advertising has caused or will cause a loss of Johnson sales, not whether Johnson has come forward with specific evidence that Carter's ads actually resulted in some definite loss of sales. Contrary to Johnson's argument, however, the likelihood of injury and causation will not be presumed, but must be demonstrated. If such a showing is made, the plaintiff will have established a reasonable belief that he is likely to be damaged within the meaning of § 43(a) and will be entitled to injunctive relief, as distinguished from damages, which would require more proof. We believe that the evidence offered by Johnson, though not overwhelming, is sufficient to prove a likelihood of damage from loss of sales.

Initially, we find that Johnson has shown that it and Carter are competitors in a relevant market. Although Johnson's Baby Oil and Lotion do not compete with NAIR in the narrower depilatory market, they do compete in the broader hair removal market. NAIR is used for hair removal by depilation. Johnson's Baby Lotion has been promoted as a substitute for shaving cream and is used for removal of hair by shaving. Also, both of Johnson's products are used as skin moisturizers after shaving or after the use of depilatories. Such indirect competitors may avail themselves of the protection of § 43(a); the competition need not be direct. Moreover, Carter's advertising campaign itself, by its emphasis on baby oil, directly links the depilation and the moisturizer markets. Johnson's stake in the shaving market gives it a "reasonable interest to be protected against the alleged false advertising."

To prove a likelihood of injury Johnson must also show a logical causal connection between the alleged false advertising and its own sales position. This it has done with specific evidence. It has shown that large numbers of consumers in fact use its baby lotion for shaving and its baby oil as an after-shave and after-depilation moisturizer. Carter's "NAIR with baby oil" campaign affects both markets. First, NAIR's share of the hair removal market has increased since its baby oil advertising began. For each new depilatory user, a corresponding decline in the use of shaving products such as oils and lotions appears probable. Second, the use of baby oil after depilation is likely to be reduced if, as Johnson contends, Carter's advertising conveys to consumers the idea that NAIR's baby oil has a moisturizing and softening effect and leads the consumer to believe that use of a second, post-depilation, moisturizer is unnecessary. Of course, if Carter's ads are truthful, then its gains at Johnson's expense are well earned. If false, however, the damage to Johnson is unfair.

Johnson's case is supported by more than just the above logic. First, sales of its baby oil have in fact declined. Second, a consumer witness testified at trial that she switched from use of baby oil by shaving to NAIR because it was advertised as containing baby oil. Third, Johnson introduced surveys indicating that some people, after viewing NAIR ads, thought they would not have to use baby oil if they used NAIR. Together, Johnson's evidence was enough to prove a likelihood of competitive injury resulting from the NAIR advertising.

That much of the decline in Johnson's Baby Oil sales may be due to competition from lower priced baby oils, does not save Carter. * * * Further, the possibility that the total pecuniary harm to Johnson might be relatively slight does not bar injunctive relief.

Finally, Johnson's inability to point to a definite amount of sales lost *to Carter* (a failure which would bar monetary relief) does not preclude injunctive relief. Likelihood of competitive injury sufficient to warrant a § 43(a) injunction has been found in the absence of proof of actual sales diversion in numerous cases. Although the overall likelihood of harm to the plaintiff from the defendant's ads in some of these cases was perhaps greater than here, * * * there was little or even no evidence of any actual sales losses to the defendant. * * *

Sound policy reasons exist for not requiring proof of actual loss as a prerequisite to § 43(a) injunctive relief. Failure to prove actual damages in an injunction suit, as distinguished from an action for damages, poses no likelihood of a windfall for the plaintiff. The complaining competitor gains no more than that to which it is already entitled—a market free of false advertising.

While proof of actual diversion of sales is not required for a § 43(a) injunction to issue, proof that the advertising complained of is in fact false is essential. This issue, though briefed by parties in this case, is not before the court at this time. The district court did not reach the question for purposes of determining whether permanent relief should issue. Since the action was dismissed at the close of the plaintiff's case, Carter was afforded no opportunity to introduce additional evidence answering the plaintiff on this point. Johnson, having shown that it is likely to be damaged by Carter's advertising, must prove that the NAIR advertising was false before being entitled to injunctive relief under the Lanham Act. Should the district court find that the defendant's advertising conveys a false message, irreparable injury for the purpose of injunctive relief would be present for the very reason that in an open market it is impossible to measure the exact amount of Johnson's damages.

Accordingly, this cause is reversed and remanded for further proceedings in conformity with this opinion.[5]

---

5. The record discloses strong evidence, including Carter's internal documents, admissions of its chief executive, independent expert opinion, and consumer surveys, that Carter's advertising of "NAIR with baby oil," some of which we viewed upon argument, is perceived as informing the public that the baby oil in NAIR has moisturizing benefits, leaving the skin smoother and softer than it would be without the oil. Indeed, from our review of the record and viewing of the NAIR advertisements the purpose and effect of the latter clearly appears to have been to lead consumers to believe that if they used NAIR with baby oil they would gain benefits from the product in the form of a moisturizing or softening effect not realized when baby oil is absent. Upon remand, therefore, the essential issue will be whether the presence of baby oil in NAIR does in fact have such a moisturizing or softening effect.

NOTES AND QUESTIONS

1. *Section 43(a) standing.* The statutory language creating the false advertising cause of action, as amended, provides:

> (a)(1) Any person who, on or in connection with any goods or services, or any container for goods, uses in commerce * * * any false or misleading description of fact, or false or misleading representation of fact, which—
>
>   * * *
>
>   (B) in commercial advertising or promotion, misrepresents the nature, characteristics, qualities, or geographic origin of his or her * * * goods, services, or commercial activities,
>
> shall be liable in a civil action by any person who believes that he or she is or is likely to be damaged by such act.

15 U.S.C.A. § 1125(a).

Unlike its common-law predecessor, the § 43(a) false advertising cause of action is intended to benefit consumers, at least indirectly, as well as competitors. As the Sixth Circuit has explained:

> Protecting consumers from false or misleading advertising * * * is an important goal of the statute and a laudable public policy to be served. * * * [C]ompetitors have the greatest interest in stopping misleading advertising, and a private cause of action under section 43(a) allows those parties with the greatest interest in enforcement, and in many situations with the greatest resources to devote to a lawsuit, to enforce the statute rigorously.

Coca–Cola Co. v. Procter & Gamble Co., 822 F.2d 28, 31 (6th Cir.1987). The legal community was slow to recognize and exploit the breadth of the new statutory provision. Though § 43(a) was enacted in 1946, its use did not become prevalent until the 1970's and 80's.

Section 43(a) eliminates the requirement, imposed at common law, that a false advertising plaintiff demonstrate direct, specific loss of customers resulting from the defendant's allegedly false advertisement. On the other hand, the *Johnson* court refuses to *presume* a likelihood of injury and causation from the falsity of the advertising and the fact that the parties compete. The *Johnson* court holds that the plaintiff must demonstrate a "reasonable basis for the belief that the plaintiff is likely to be damaged as a result of the false advertising." Given what the court accepts as an adequate demonstration of likelihood of injury, is the requirement meaningful? Is the standard set forth in *Johnson* too liberal? If so, what should the standard be? On the other hand, if part of the purpose of § 43(a) is to protect consumers from false advertising, why require a plaintiff to demonstrate even a likelihood of injury to itself? Should the plaintiff be required to demonstrate a likelihood of injury to the public?

In McNeilab, Inc. v. American Home Products Corp., 848 F.2d 34 (2d Cir.1988), the defendant, manufacturer of Advil pain reliever, advertised that "like Tylenol, Advil doesn't give me minor [occasional] stomach upset." Plaintiff, the manufacturer of Tylenol, sued, alleging § 43(a) false advertising, and obtained a preliminary injunction. On appeal, the defendant challenged the district court's finding that irreparable harm to the plaintiff could be presumed. In upholding the finding, the Second Circuit distinguished the *Johnson* decision:

> *Johnson & Johnson* involved misleading, non-comparative commercials which touted the benefits of the product advertised but made no direct reference to any competitor's product. The injury in such cases accrues equally to all competitors; none is more likely to suffer from the offending broadcasts than any other. The Lanham Act, however, only authorizes actions by one "who believes that he is or is likely to be damaged." 15 U.S.C. § 1125(a). Thus, we required some indication of actual injury and causation to satisfy Lanham Act standing requirements and to ensure a plaintiff's injury was not speculative.
>
> This case, by contrast, presents a false comparative advertising claim. Thus, the concerns voiced in * * * *Johnson & Johnson* regarding speculative injury do not arise. A misleading comparison to a specific product necessarily diminishes that product's value. By falsely implying that Advil is as safe as Tylenol in all respects, AHP deprived McNeil of a legitimate competitive advantage and reduced consumers' incentive to select Tylenol rather than Advil. This is analogous to a Lanham Act trademark dispute. An infringing mark, by its nature, detracts from the value of the mark with which it is confused.

Id., 848 F.2d at 38.

The plaintiffs in both *Johnson* and *McNeilab* sought injunctive relief, and the court held that they could obtain it without demonstrating actual injury or the extent of their injury. As the *Johnson* court suggests, a plaintiff seeking damages would have a greater burden of proof. If the plaintiff seeks actual damages based on its lost sales, it must demonstrate actual customer reliance on the false advertisement. Damages may be recovered for injuries other than lost sales, however. For example, the plaintiff might seek profits lost on sales at reduced prices necessitated by the false advertising; the costs of completed advertising to respond to the defendant's offending ads; or quantifiable harm to the plaintiff's reputation, to the extent that completed corrective advertising has not repaired that harm. See ALPO Petfoods, Inc. v. Ralston Purina Co., 913 F.2d 958, 969 (D.C.Cir.1990).

While § 43(a) makes no restriction on its face, several Circuit Courts of Appeals have held that defrauded consumers have no standing to sue for false advertising. In the course of drafting and enacting the Trademark Law Revision Act of 1988, the House Judiciary Committee recommended that Congress expressly amend § 43(a) to provide consumers with standing. H.R. Rep. No. 1028, 100th Cong., 2d Sess. 33 (1988). Congress, however, declined to adopt the recommendation. Assuming that their standing were established, is it likely that many consumers would avail themselves of the § 43(a) cause of action?

2. *False or misleading descriptions or representations of fact.* The generally accepted elements of a § 43(a) false advertising claim for injunction

include: 1) a defendant's false or misleading statement of fact in advertising about its own product; 2) the statement actually deceived or had the capacity to deceive a substantial segment of the audience; 3) the deception was material, in that it was likely to influence the purchasing decision; 4) the defendant caused its goods to enter interstate commerce; and 5) the plaintiff has been or is likely to be injured as a result.

A statement may be explicitly false or implicitly false and misleading in this context. A number of cases have focused on the proper method of analyzing the alleged falsity of a statement. The Court of Appeals for the Second Circuit set forth the framework for the analysis in Coca–Cola Co. v. Tropicana Products, Inc., 690 F.2d 312, 317 (2d Cir.1982):

> When a merchandising statement or representation is literally or explicitly false, the court may grant relief without reference to the advertisement's impact on the buying public. When the challenged advertisement is implicitly rather than explicitly false, its tendency to violate the Lanham Act by misleading, confusing or deceiving should be tested by public reaction.

In *Tropicana*, the defendant's television advertisement showed American Olympic athlete Bruce Jenner squeezing an orange while saying "It's pure, pasteurized juice as it comes from the orange." The advertisement then showed Jenner pouring the fresh-squeezed juice into a Tropicana carton while the audio stated "It's the only leading brand not made with concentrate and water." Plaintiff, the maker of Minute Maid orange juice, brought suit for § 43(a) false advertising, and sought a preliminary injunction. The court of appeals found the advertisement literally or explicitly false:

> [T]he squeezing-pouring sequence in the Jenner commercial is false on its face. The visual component of the ad makes an explicit representation that Premium Pack is produced by squeezing oranges and pouring the freshly-squeezed juice directly into the carton. This is not a true representation of how the product is prepared. Premium Pack juice is heated and sometimes frozen prior to packaging. Additionally, the simultaneous audio component of the ad states that Premium Pack is "pasteurized juice as it comes from the orange." This statement is blatantly false— pasteurized juice does not come from oranges. Pasteurization entails heating the juice to approximately 200 degrees Fahrenheit to kill certain natural enzymes and microorganisms which cause spoilage. Moreover, even if the addition of the word "pasteurized" somehow made sense and effectively qualified the visual image, Tropicana's commercial nevertheless represented that the juice is only squeezed, heated and packaged when in fact it may actually also be frozen.

Id., 690 F.2d at 318. Since the ad was false on its face, there was no need to consider how consumers would perceive it. The court of appeals ultimately found that the plaintiff had demonstrated a likelihood of success on the merits.

When a statement is literally true, it may still serve as the basis for § 43(a) false advertising liability if misleading, or implicitly false. Otherwise, "clever use of innuendo, indirect intimations, and ambiguous suggestions could shield the advertisement from scrutiny precisely when protection against such sophisticated deception is most needed." American Home Products Corp. v. Johnson & Johnson, 577 F.2d 160, 165 (2d Cir.1978). Pursuant to the *Tropicana* rule, the truth or falsity of such advertisements must be tested by public reaction. The plaintiff must provide evidence—usually in the form of consumer surveys or other market research—demonstrating that the relevant consumers understood the ad to convey the alleged false message. See Johnson & Johnson * Merck Consumer Pharmaceuticals Co. v. Smithkline Beecham Corp., 960 F.2d 294, 297–98 (2d Cir.1992).

In *Smithkline*, the district court had relied upon consumer survey results to reject the plaintiff's argument that the defendant's advertisement had a misleading impact. On appeal, the plaintiff argued that the district court failed sufficiently to consider factors other than consumer survey evidence, such as "1) the general 'commercial context' or sea of information in which consumers are immersed; 2) the defendant's intent to harness public misperception; 3) the defendant's prior advertising history; and 4) the sophistication of the advertising audience." *Id*. The court of appeals rejected the challenge. It explained:

> Appellant's criticism of the district court's findings misconstrues the proper role of consumer survey evidence in the analysis of implied falsehood claims. Generally, before a court can determine the truth or falsity of an advertisement's message, it must first determine what message was actually conveyed to the viewing audience. Consumer surveys supply such information. "Once the meaning to the target audience has been determined, the court, as the finder of fact, must then judge whether the evidence establishes that they were likely to be misled."

> Three of the factors * * *, commercial context, defendant's prior advertising history, and sophistication of the advertising audience, only come into play, if at all, during the latter part of the court's analysis. In a particular case, these factors may shed some light on whether the challenged advertisement contributed to the meaning that was ultimately gleaned by the target audience. In other words, in determining whether an advertisement is likely to mislead or confuse, the district court may consider these factors after a plaintiff has established "that a not insubstantial number of consumers" hold the false belief allegedly communicated in the ad.

> Absent such a threshold showing, an implied falsehood claim must fail. This follows from the obvious fact that the injuries redressed in false advertising cases are the result of public deception. Thus, where the plaintiff cannot demonstrate that a statistically significant part of the commercial audience holds the false belief allegedly communicated by the challenged advertisement, the plaintiff cannot establish that it suffered any injury as a result of the advertisement's message. Without injury there can be no claim, regardless of commercial context, prior advertising history, or audience sophistication.

> However, we have held that "where a plaintiff adequately demonstrates that a defendant has intentionally set out to deceive the public," and the defendant's "deliberate conduct" in this regard is of an "egregious nature," a presumption arises "that consumers are, in fact, being

deceived." This presumption, which may be engendered by the expenditure "of substantial funds in an effort to deceive consumers and influence their purchasing decisions," relieves a plaintiff of the burden of producing consumer survey evidence that supports its claim. *Id.* In such a case, once a plaintiff establishes deceptive intent, "the burden shifts to the defendant to demonstrate the absence of consumer confusion." * * *

Id., 960 F.2d at 298–99.

A "statistically significant part of the commercial audience" may be considerably less than 50% of the audience. To the extent that advertising conveys useful information to members of the audience who were not deceived, is imposition of liability in such cases in the public interest? See Restatement (Third) of Unfair Competition § 2, cmt d (1995).

3. *Other approaches to regulating false advertising.* The Federal Trade Commission ("FTC") is empowered to prevent "unfair or deceptive acts or practices" in or affecting interstate commerce. 15 U.S.C.A. § 45. Armed with both rulemaking and adjudicatory powers, the FTC has played an important role in policing false advertising. The FTC is strictly concerned with the general public interest, and acts directly, in its own capacity to prevent and remedy fraud on consumers. The Federal Trade Commission Act provides no means for private enforcement of its provisions, and no forum or vehicle to resolve private disputes among competitors.

A number of states have enacted "Little FTC Acts," patterned after the federal act, and after the Unfair Trade Practices and Consumer Protection Act, developed by the Federal Trade Commission and published by the Council of State Governments in 1967. Unlike the federal provision, many of these state statutes authorize not only government agency regulation but also private consumer causes of action to enforce their provisions against errant businesses. Some of the statutes are broad enough to accommodate suits by competitors, as well. For a listing of these state statutes, see Restatement (Third) of Unfair Competition § 1, Statutory Note (1995).

The Uniform Deceptive Trade Practices Act, promulgated by the National Conference of Commissioners on Uniform State Laws in 1964 (revised in 1966), was "designed to bring state law up to date by removing undue restrictions on the common-law action for deceptive trade practices." *Id.*, Prefatory Note. Section 3 of the Act provides that a "person *likely to be damaged* by a deceptive trade practice of another" may obtain injunctive relief. (Emphasis added.) This relief is "in addition to remedies otherwise available against the same conduct under the common law or other statutes." *Id.* "Deceptive trade practices" for purposes of the Act include passing off, false advertising and commercial disparagement. See *Id.*, at § 2. A significant number of states have adopted the Act. They are identified in Restatement (Third) of Unfair Competition § 2, Statutory Note (1995).

PROBLEMS

1. R. Co. and M. Co. are competing makers of diltiazem, a drug for treatment of hypertension and angina. M. Co. developed "M–Heart," a sustained release drug to be taken once per day, which the FDA approved for

hypertension and angina. R. Co. launched its own drug, called "R–Cardio," in one-a-day sustained release tablets, and received FDA approval for the treatment of hypertension, but not angina. (The FDA classified R–Cardio as a "BC" drug, rather than an "AB" drug, meaning that R–Cardio was "not necessarily bioequivalent" to M–Heart. The FDA will classify drugs as "bioequivalent" when their rate and extent of absorption by the body make them interchangeable.) R. Co. sold its drug for a lower price than did M. Co.

M. Co. issued advertisements stating the unsubstantiated claim that R–Cardio might be only 75% as bioavailable as M. Co.'s M–Heart. In a subsequent advertisement, M. Co. stated that the results of a laboratory study (the "6730 Study") showed that R–Cardio delivers only 74 to 81 percent of the relative dose of M–Heart.

R Co. responded by issuing advertisements featuring images such as two similar gasoline pumps or airline tickets with dramatically different prices, accompanied by the slogan, "which one would you choose?"

Each Company has alleged false advertising against the other.

a.   What, precisely, should R. Co. have to demonstrate in order to prove that each of the two M. Co. advertisements is "false?"

b.   In what way might R. Co.'s advertisement be found false or misleading?

2.   Yumm Co. and Delish Co. are both national pizza restaurant chains. Yumm Co. adopts the slogan: "Better Ingredients. Better Pizza." Yumm Co. later runs a series of ads stating that it uses "fresh-pack" tomato sauce and fresher dough than its competitors, and that its dough is produced with "clear filtered water" while the "biggest chain" (which happens to be Delish Co.) uses "whatever comes out of the tap." Yumm Co. follows these claims with its slogan.

Yumm Co.'s claims about its pizza sauce, dough, and the water it uses are not literally false. However, there is no scientific or other support for Yumm Co.'s suggestion that its "fresh-pack" sauce is superior to Delish Co.'s tomato paste. Moreover, while the two companies use different processes in making their pizza doughs, there is no quantifiable difference between pizza dough produced through Yumm Co.'s "cold or slow fermentation method" and Delish Co.'s "frozen dough method."

Delish Co. has sued Yumm Co. for false advertising under Lanham Act § 43(a), claiming that both the slogan and the ads are false and misleading. How would you evaluate the claim?

3.   A Co. manufactures and sells several regional brands of dried pasta, including Mueller's, Golden Grain, Mrs. Grass, Ronco, Luxury, R & F, Global A 1, Pennsylvania Dutch, and Anthony's. It places the phrase "America's Favorite Pasta" on its packaging. On various packages, the phrases "Quality since 1867," "Made from 100% Semolina," or "Made with Semolina" accompany the phrase "America's Favorite Pasta." The packaging also contains a paragraph in which the phrase "America's Favorite Pasta" appears. The paragraph states (1) pasta lovers have enjoyed A Co.'s pasta for 130 years; (2) claims A Co.'s "pasta cooks to perfect tenderness every time," because A Co. uses "100% pure semolina milled from the highest quality durum wheat;" and

(3) encourages consumers to "[t]aste why A Co.'s pasta is America's favorite pasta."

B Co. sent A Co. a letter demanding that it cease and desist using the phrase "America's Favorite Pasta." Consequently, A Co. filed suit for declaratory judgment that its use of the phrase does not constitute false or misleading advertising under the Lanham Act. In a counterclaim, B Co. asserts that A Co.'s use of "America's Favorite Pasta" constitutes false and misleading advertising because the phrase conveys that A Co.'s pasta is a national pasta brand or the nation's number one selling pasta. Both parties agree that C Co. sells the most dried pasta in the U.S. and that A Co.'s brands are regional.

A Co. moves to dismiss the counterclaims. How should the court rule?

III. COMMERCIAL DISPARAGEMENT

U.S. HEALTHCARE, INC. v. BLUE CROSS OF GREATER PHILADELPHIA

United States Court of Appeals for the Third Circuit, 1990.
898 F.2d 914, *cert. denied,* 498 U.S. 816, 111 S.Ct. 58, 112 L.Ed.2d 33 (1990).

SCIRICA, CIRCUIT JUDGE.

[A fierce comparative advertising war has resulted in this litigation, in which the parties accuse one another of disparagement pursuant to Lanham Act § 43(a)(1)(B) and common-law commercial disparagement.]

1. *Section 43(a) of the Lanham Act.*

Section 43(a) of the Lanham Act, 15 U.S.C. § 1125(a) (1988), which was recently amended, creates a cause of action for any false description or representation of a product. This proscription extends to misleading descriptions or representations. "While it has been stated that a failure to disclose facts is not actionable under § 43(a), it is equally true that a statement is actionable under § 43(a) if it is affirmatively misleading, partially incorrect, or untrue as a result of failure to disclose a material fact." 2 J. McCarthy, *Trademarks and Unfair Competition* § 27:7B (2d ed. 1984).

The pre-amendment version * * * applied only to statements made by a defendant about its own products, not to statements about the plaintiff's products. As amended, however, § 43(a) encompasses statements made by a defendant about "his or her *or another person's*" products. 15 U.S.C. § 1125(a) (emphasis added).

When analyzing a challenged advertisement, the court first determines what message is conveyed. Sometimes this determination may be made from the advertisement on its face. Nonetheless, "[c]ontext can often be important in discerning the message conveyed."

After determining the message conveyed, the court must decide whether it is false or misleading. Mere puffing, advertising " 'that is not deceptive for no one would rely on its exaggerated claims,' " is not actionable under § 43(a). If the advertisement is literally true, the plaintiff "must persuade the court that the persons 'to whom the advertisement is addressed' would find that the message received left a false impression about the product." * * *

The plaintiff must also show that defendant's misrepresentation is " 'material, in that it is likely to influence the purchasing decision.' " However, "there is no requirement that the falsification occur willfully and with intent to deceive."

Next, § 43(a) requires that the defendant use the false or misleading description or representation "in commerce." The commerce requirement has been broadly interpreted.

Finally, § 43(a) provides a remedy to one who "is or is likely to be damaged by [the false or misleading description or representation]." 15 U.S.C. § 1125(a). To recover damages, a plaintiff must show that the "falsification [or misrepresentation] actually deceives a portion of the buying public." "This does not place upon the plaintiff a burden of proving detailed individualization of loss of sales. Such proof goes to quantum of damages and not to the very right to recover." * * *

* * *

3. Commercial Disparagement.

A commercially disparaging statement—in contrast to a defamatory statement—is one "which is intended by its publisher to be understood or which is reasonably understood to cast doubt upon the existence or extent of another's property in land, chattels or intangible things, or upon their quality, ... if the matter is so understood by its recipient." *Menefee v. Columbia Broadcasting Sys., Inc.*, 458 Pa. 46, 54, 329 A.2d 216 (1974) (quoting Restatement of Torts § 629 (1938)). In order to maintain an action for disparagement, the plaintiff must prove 1) that the disparaging statement of fact is untrue or that the disparaging statement of opinion is incorrect; 2) that no privilege attaches to the statement; and 3) that the plaintiff suffered a direct pecuniary loss as the result of the disparagement.

The distinction between actions for defamation and disparagement turns on the harm towards which each is directed. An action for commercial disparagement is meant to compensate a vendor for pecuniary loss suffered because statements attacking the quality of his goods have reduced their marketability, while defamation is meant to protect an entity's interest in character and reputation. In *Menefee*, the Pennsylvania Supreme Court made the following observation:

> One of the most important purposes for which liability for the publication of matter derogatory to another's personal reputation is imposed is to enable the person defamed to force his accuser into open court so that the accusation, if untrue, may be branded as false by the verdict of a jury. The action for disparagement has no such purpose

and cannot be used merely to vindicate one's title to or the quality of one's possessions. . . .

Id. (quoting Restatement of Torts introductory note to Chapter 28).

Given the similar elements of the two torts, deciding which cause of action lies in a given situation can be difficult. The Court of Appeals for the Eighth Circuit gave the following time-honored explanation of when impugnation of the quality of goods crosses the line from disparagement of products to defamation of vendors:

> [W]here the publication on its face is directed against the goods or product of a corporate vendor or manufacturer, it will not be held libelous per se as to the corporation, unless by fair construction and without the aid of extrinsic evidence it imputes to the corporation fraud, deceit, dishonesty, or reprehensible conduct in its business in relation to said goods or product.

National Ref. Co. v. Benzo Gas Motor Fuel Co., 20 F.2d 763, 771 (8th Cir.), *cert. denied*, 275 U.S. 570, 48 S.Ct. 157, 72 L.Ed. 431 (1927).

* * *

NOTES AND QUESTIONS

1. *The common-law commercial disparagement claim.* The common-law cause of action for commercial disparagement has many alternative names, including product disparagement, trade libel, slander of title, and injurious falsehood. As the *U.S. Healthcare* opinion suggests, the cause of action is closely related to the law of libel and slander, though the causes of action are directed to different interests: Libel and slander protect the plaintiff's personal interest in reputation, while commercial disparagement protects commercial, economic interests.

The greatest hurdle for common-law commercial disparagement plaintiffs has been the "special damages" requirement. Traditionally, to satisfy the special damages requirement, the commercial disparagement plaintiff had to plead and prove actual, specific economic harm. Some courts held that proof of special damages requires detailed evidence of individual transactions and specific customers lost as a result of the disparaging publication. See, e.g., Testing Systems, Inc. v. Magnaflux Corp., 251 F.Supp. 286, 290 (E.D.Pa. 1966). Some courts were somewhat more liberal. See, e.g., Trenton Mutual Life & Fire Ins. Co. v. Perrine, 23 N.J.L. 402 (Sup. Ct. 1852) (Court accepts evidence of a general loss of business when the plaintiff demonstrates that it is impossible to prove specific losses because of the nature of his business). Some jurisdictions have imposed the pleading and proof of special damages as a prerequisite both for a damages award and for injunctive relief, while others are more lenient with respect to suits for injunctions. See, e.g., Systems Operations, Inc. v. Scientific Games Development Corp., 414 F.Supp. 750 (D.N.J.1976), *rev'd on other grounds*, 555 F.2d 1131 (3d Cir.1977). The special damages requirement might have been met more readily long ago, when many businesses and the communities they served were small and the plaintiff was likely to know his customers personally. In today's large, complex and impersonal marketplace, a strict special damages requirement may prove impossible to satisfy.

The precise elements of the commercial disparagement cause of action may differ from one jurisdiction to the next. The Court of Appeals for the Third Circuit, in *U.S. Healthcare,* finds that under Pennsylvania law, the commercial disparagement plaintiff must prove three elements: 1) that the disparaging statement of fact is untrue or that the disparaging statement of opinion is incorrect; 2) that no privilege attaches to the statement; and 3) that the plaintiff suffered a direct pecuniary loss as the result of the disparagement.

Should a defendant be held liable for stating an "incorrect" *opinion* about the plaintiff's goods or services? How does one determine whether a statement is one of fact or one of opinion? The court notes that statements constituting mere "puffery" are not actionable. What is "puffing," and why should it not support a disparagement claim?

Why must a disparaging statement be false or incorrect? Why not have a cause of action for truthful disparagement? For example, suppose that the defendant told consumers that the plaintiff's product had been designed by an ax murderer. While true, the fact is totally irrelevant to the quality of the product and is highly prejudicial. Should the law condone such competitive behavior? See L. Altman, R. Callmann, The Law of Unfair Competition, Trademarks and Monopolies, §§ 11.04, 11.14 (4th ed. 1981 & supp.)

Consider the Restatement (Second) of Torts definition of the disparagement cause of action, which it calls "injurious falsehood:"

> One who publishes a false statement harmful to the interests of another is subject to liability for pecuniary loss resulting to the other if
>
> (a) he intends for publication of the statement to result in harm to interests of the other having a pecuniary value, or either recognizes or should recognize that it is likely to do so, and
>
> (b) he knows that the statement is false or acts in reckless disregard of its truth of falsity.

Restatement (Second) of Torts § 623A (1976).[2] Note that the Restatement added intent and knowledge requirements that had not been included in the First Restatement's treatment of the subject. See Restatement of Torts §§ 624–629 (1938). These requirements were added partly due to concerns that strict liability or liability based on negligence might prove unconstitutional under the First Amendment, see § 623A, *supra,* cmt c, and partly due to concerns that the earlier approach (deleting requirements of intent and knowledge) had been predicated on a false analogy to cases of personal defamation. See Prosser, *Injurious Falsehood: The Basis of Liability,* 59 Colum. L. Rev. 425 (1959). In your view, were these concerns justified?

2. *Statutory disparagement causes of action.* In 1988, Congress amended Lanham Act § 43(a) to extend to false descriptions and representations of fact concerning "another person's goods, services, or commercial activities."

---

2. ©1976, The American Law Institute. Reprinted with the permission of The American Law Institute

Courts are likely to construe the new federal cause of action for commercial disparagement to dispense with detailed proof of special damages and intent or fault requirements imposed at state law, as they did in the case of false advertising claims. Note, however, that § 43(a)(1)(B) requires that the defendant's misrepresentation be "in commercial advertising or promotion." Why impose this limitation?

The Uniform Deceptive Trade Practices Act has also undertaken to update the common law of commercial disparagement. Like § 43(a), § 2(a)(8) of the Uniform Act rests liability on *false or misleading statements of fact* that disparage the goods, services or business of another. Section 3(a) provides: "A person likely to be damaged by a deceptive trade practice of another may be granted an injunction against it under the principles of equity and on terms that the court considers reasonable. Proof of monetary damage, loss of profits, or intent to deceive is not required."

IV. MISAPPROPRIATION

BOARD OF TRADE OF CITY OF CHICAGO
v. DOW JONES & CO., INC.

Supreme Court of Illinois, 1983.
98 Ill.2d 109, 74 Ill.Dec. 582, 456 N.E.2d 84.

GOLDENHERSH, JUSTICE:

[Plaintiff Board of Trade brought an action for declaratory judgment seeking a declaration that its offering of a commodity futures contract utilizing the Dow Jones Industrial Average as the underlying commodity would not violate defendant's legal or proprietary rights.]

[Defendant publishes the Wall Street Journal and maintains the Dow Jones News Service, through which it distributes financial news to subscribers.] It produces several stock market indexes, the Dow Jones Industrial Average, Transportation Average, and Utilities Average, which are computed on the basis of the current prices of stocks of certain companies selected by defendant's editorial board.

The financial news furnished by defendant is disseminated * * * to brokerage houses, banks, financial institutions, individual investors, and others who are interested in stock market news. * * * Plaintiff has a "Subscription Agreement" under which it pays defendant for its News Service and is allowed to compute and display the Dow Jones Averages on plaintiff's trading floor on a continuous, "real time" basis.

Plaintiff is the oldest and largest commodities exchange market in the United States. * * * All commodities exchanges in the United States are regulated by the Commodities Futures Trading Commission (CFTC), and no exchange may trade a futures contract until the CFTC approves the futures contract and designates the exchange as a contract market for that contract.

A futures contract is a contract traded on a commodities exchange which binds the parties to a particular transaction at a specified future date. A stock index futures contract is a futures contract based upon the value of a particular stock market index. Dr. James H. Lorie, stipulated by the parties to be an expert, called by plaintiff, testified that these contracts have been traded since February 1982. At the time of trial they were traded on the Kansas City Board of Trade based on the Value Line Average, on the Chicago Mercantile Exchange based on the Standard & Poor's 500 Stock Index and on the New York Futures Exchange based on the New York Stock Exchange Composite Index. He stated that their "overriding purpose is the management of risk." Unlike other futures contracts, no underlying commodity exists to be delivered at the future date, but rather the transaction is settled by the delivery of a certified promissory note in lieu of cash. * * *

Plaintiff, desiring to be designated as a contract market for stock index futures contracts, devoted more than two years to developing its own index to be used as the basis for its stock index futures contract. During the greater part of this period, the Securities and Exchange Commission (SEC) and the CFTC were in a dispute concerning which agency had jurisdiction to regulate stock index futures contracts. In December 1981, the two Federal agencies agreed on the scope of their respective jurisdiction and on recommendations to Congress for regulatory legislation. They agreed that the CFTC would regulate trading in stock market index contracts and that such trading would be permitted only if the contracts were based on widely known and well-established stock market indexes. This jurisdictional agreement effectively precluded CFTC approval of a contract based on the index developed by plaintiff.

On February 26, 1982, plaintiff submitted an application to the CFTC asking that it be designated as a contract market for Chicago Board of Trade Portfolio Futures Contracts. The application proposed the use of three indexes, the stock market index, transport index, and the electric index portfolio contracts. * * * No mention of the Dow Jones name appeared in the application, but the stocks used in each of the indexes were identical to those used in the Dow Jones averages. In a draft proposal to the CFTC for trading "CBT indexes," the Dow Jones averages stock lists were cut out of the Wall Street Journal and pasted into the proposals. The CFTC advised plaintiff that the CBT indexes were not just similar to, but were identical to the Dow Jones averages and that this should be explicitly stated in its application. On May 7, 1982, plaintiff amended its application to state that the CBT indexes were identical to Dow Jones averages and that when Dow Jones changed a component stock or revised the divisor, plaintiff would make the same change so that the CBT indexes would remain identical to the Dow Jones averages. Plaintiff also added a disclaimer to the application disclaiming any association with Dow Jones. On May 13, the CFTC approved plaintiff's use of the stock market index portfolio contract, but did not rule concerning the use of the transportation or utility index portfolio contracts.

* * *

Plaintiff argues that the appellate court's holding erroneously expands the tort of misappropriation and that its decision contravenes public policy. Citing * * * *International News Service v. Associated Press* (1918), 248 U.S. 215, 39 S.Ct. 68, 63 L.Ed. 211, plaintiff argues that competitive injury is a fundamental prerequisite essential to a finding of misappropriation. * * * It argues that it has done nothing immoral or unethical but has merely created a "new product" which is "outside the primary market which the producer of the original product originally set out to satisfy * * *." Finally, plaintiff argues that the appellate court's decision is against public policy in that it grants what amounts to a common law patent monopoly to defendant which permits it to exclude others from using its product for any purpose "regardless of whether the producer is being injured or intends to exploit the product itself."

Defendant responds that the tort of misappropriation should be flexible so that, by carefully tailoring their misappropriation to avoid the strict rules of the tort, "enterprising pirates" cannot avoid the application of the doctrine. * * * [D]efendant argues that under the doctrine of misappropriation direct competition is not essential to tort liability. Defendant argues that plaintiff seeks to exploit defendant's reputation for accuracy and impartiality without compensating it for its good will. Finally, in response to plaintiff's argument that the appellate court's opinion is against public policy, defendant argues that the appellate court's opinion is consistent with public policy in that it maintains the incentive for the creation of intellectual property. Defendant argues that if its rights in the averages are not protected, there will be a diminished incentive for it to continue to provide the averages. Defendant points out that it does not seek to monopolize the production of stock indexes and that plaintiff is free to develop its own, but that it desires to protect its rights in the averages which it created and continues to produce.

* * *

The doctrine of misappropriation as a form of unfair competition was first enunciated by the Supreme Court in *International News Service v. Associated Press* (1918), 248 U.S. 215, 39 S.Ct. 68, 63 L.Ed. 211. In that case, INS was copying news stories from bulletin boards of members of AP and transmitting the fresh news contained on those bulletin boards to its own members. Thus, INS could obtain information collected by AP at great expense and transmit this information to its midwestern and west coast members, who could then print the news at the same time as the competing AP members or, in some instances, earlier. In affirming the decree enjoining the practice the majority opinion suggested that without the revenues derived from this exclusive, timely presentation of the news,

AP or other news services would not have sufficient incentive to continue performing their services.

* * *

Competing with the policy that protection should be afforded one who expends labor and money to develop products is the concept that freedom to imitate and duplicate is vital to our free market economy. Indeed, when the doctrine of misappropriation was first enunciated, Justice Brandeis recognized this competing policy:

> "He who follows the pioneer into a new market, or who engages in the manufacture of an article newly introduced by another, seeks profits due largely to the labor and expense of the first adventurer; but the law sanctions, indeed encourages, the pursuit." (*International News Service v. Associated Press* (1918), 248 U.S. 215, 259, 39 S.Ct. 68, 79, 63 L.Ed. 211, 229 (Brandeis, J., dissenting)).

Similarly, Professor Rahl reasons:

> "Substantial similarity of alternatives can come about in only one of two ways—by independent development or by imitation. While there are many instances of simultaneous independent innovation, our economy would still be in the Dark Ages if this were the only circumstance under which competing alternatives could be offered. Imitation is inherent in any system of competition and it is imperative for an economy in which there is rapid technological advance." Rahl, *The Right to "Appropriate" Trade Values*, 23 Ohio St. L.J. 56, 72 (1962).

In balancing the factors that should determine which of the competing concepts should prevail, it appears unlikely that an adverse decision will cause defendant to cease to produce its averages or that the revenue it currently receives for the distribution of those averages will be materially affected. Defendant correctly asserts that it will lose its right to prospective licensing revenues in the event that in the future it elects to have its name associated with stock index futures contracts, but reliance upon the existence of a property right based upon the ability to license the product to prospective markets which were not originally contemplated by the creator of the product is somewhat "circular."

Alternatively, holding that plaintiff's use of defendant's indexes in the manner proposed is a misappropriation may stimulate the creation of new indexes perhaps better suited to the purpose of "hedging" against the "systematic" risk present in the stock market.

Whether protection against appropriation is necessary to foster creativity depends in part upon the expectations of that sector of the business community which deals with the particular intangible. If the creator of an intangible product expects to be able to control the licensing or distribution of the intangible in order to profit from his effort, and similarly those who would purchase the product expect and are willing to pay for the use of the intangible, a better argument can be made in favor of granting protection. The record shows that the plaintiff sought to develop its own index prior to the CFTC's requirement that the contracts be based on well-known, well-established indexes. It then offered defendant 10 cents per transaction, which it estimated would be somewhere between $1 million and $2 million per year, for the use of its name and averages. While there appears to be some dispute as to whether this offer of payment was primarily for the use of defendant's name or for the use of the averages, the offer of money is relevant to the extent that it acknowledges the value of the association of defendant's name and good will with the averages it produces.

To hold that defendant has a proprietary interest in its indexes and averages which vests it with the exclusive right to license their use for trading in stock index futures contracts would not preclude plaintiff and others from marketing stock index futures contracts. The extent of defendant's monopoly would be limited, for as defendant points out, there are an infinite number of stock market indexes which could be devised. As one commentator notes, the effect of granting a "monopoly" at the base of the production pyramid is much less objectionable than granting a monopoly at the top of the pyramid:

> "Social cost assumes more manageable size and so less significance near the base of the pyramid. Exclusive rights in a special kind of typewriter key are far less objectionable than a monopoly in the lever, because far less is swept into the monopolist's control." *Developments In the Law: Competitive Torts*, 77 Harv.L.Rev. 888, 938 (1964).

We conclude that the possibility of any detriment to the public which might result from our holding that defendant's indexes and averages may not be used without its consent in the manner proposed by plaintiff are outweighed by the resultant encouragement to develop new indexes specifically designed for the purpose of hedging against the "systematic" risk present in the stock market.

We have considered plaintiff's contention that defendant has failed to prove that the proposed use of the averages would cause it injury. The publication of the indexes involves valuable assets of defendant, its good will and its reputation for integrity and accuracy. Despite the fact that plaintiff's proposed use is not in competition with the use defendant presently makes of them, defendant is entitled to protection against their misappropriation.

       * * *

SIMON, JUSTICE, dissenting:

The majority opinion fairly identifies the general approach to the common law tort of misappropriation. In order to determine whether that tort will lie we must balance Dow Jones' interest in preventing the use of its average by the Board of Trade against society's interest in the widest use and dissemination of intellectual property. Obviously, both interests are important and require fair consideration in the balancing process. Unless the creators of intellectual property have some protection against the appropriation of their ideas by others they will be discouraged from producing them; on the other hand, unless society can demand that the owners of intellectual property allow it to be appropriated by people who have developed novel and productive uses for it, the pace of innovation will slow.

I would allow the Board of Trade to use the Dow Jones Averages for its stock market futures contracts. The majority errs, in part, because it has failed to place enough emphasis on the unfettered access to ideas in the public domain, a privilege which is essential to our free market economy. * * *

The common law tort of misappropriation has been limited to cases where intellectual property, lawfully obtained, is used in direct competition with the person who created it. * * * The competitive-injury requirement has a sound basis in policy, for it allows the tort of misappropriation to protect the creators of intellectual property against actual injury to their business, but at the same time it allows for suitable reward for people who develop novel uses for information and ideas that are freely obtained from the public domain.

     * * *

* * * The majority is swayed by what it sees as "unjust" enrichment—the Board of Trade's plan to earn a profit by the free use of an idea developed by Dow Jones at considerable cost. I do not regard this use as "unjust" in the least. The Board of Trade proposed to use information that Dow Jones had freely allowed the public to acquire in a business that Dow Jones has not shown the slightest interest in pursuing. If "unjust enrichment" has become the only element for the tort of misappropriation in Illinois, I fear that there will be few commercial ideas and little information left in the public domain. I view the proper elements of the tort of misappropriation to be a combination of unjust enrichment and competitive injury. Although the former feature may be present in this case, neither the majority opinion nor Dow Jones reveals where to find the latter feature.

UNITED STATES GOLF ASSN. v. ST. ANDREWS SYSTEMS, DATA–MAX, INC.

United States Court of Appeals for the Third Circuit, 1984.
749 F.2d 1028.

BECKER, CIRCUIT JUDGE.

This appeal * * * arises from a lawsuit brought by appellant, the United States Golf Association ("U.S.G.A."), the governing body of amateur golf in the United States. The U.S.G.A. has developed a system for deriving the "handicaps" of amateur golfers, the core of which is a mathematical formula. Appellee Data–Max, Inc., d/b/a St. Andrews Systems, markets small computers that are programmed to calculate a golfer's handicap based on the U.S.G.A. formula. The U.S.G.A. brought this suit to enjoin Data–Max from using its formula as the basis for its computerized handicap system.

The U.S.G.A. bases its claim for an injunction on two theories. The first is that the use of the U.S.G.A. formula by Data–Max amounts to a "false designation of origin," and thus violates both section 43(a) of the Lanham Act, 15 U.S.C. § 1125(a), and the New Jersey common law against unfair competition. The second theory is that the use of the formula is a "misappropriation" under the doctrine of *International News Service v. Associated Press*, 248 U.S. 215 (1918), as that doctrine has been adopted by New Jersey. * * *

We conclude that the U.S.G.A. handicap formula is "functional," and thus that the U.S.G.A. cannot enjoin the use of the formula either under section 43(a) of the Lanham Act or under state law on the basis of any association in the public mind between the formula and the U.S.G.A. We also conclude that the U.S.G.A.'s claim does not fall within the "misappropriation" doctrine as it has been adopted by the State of New Jersey, largely because in using the formula Data–Max will not compete directly with the U.S.G.A., and thus will not interfere with the economic incentives of the U.S.G.A. to maintain and update its handicap formula. * * *

I.   FACTS AND PROCEDURAL HISTORY

The U.S.G.A. has been the governing body of amateur golf in the United States since 1894. It seeks to promote the game of golf by numerous means, including the establishment of rules and regulations for play, the promotion of amateur tournaments, and the regulation of its member golf clubs. Among the services that the U.S.G.A. provides to amateur golfers is a "handicap" formula that allows golfers of different skill levels to compete with each other on an equal basis. The U.S.G.A. handicap system takes account of the difficulty of the course on which a round is played and provides "safeguards" against the inflation of handicaps by excluding particularly bad holes and by counting only the best ten of a golfer's last twenty rounds.

[The U.S.G.A. has developed the handicap formula over a period of eighty years, regularly refining and improving it.]

Data–Max was incorporated in 1980 for the purpose of providing golfers, primarily those who do not belong to U.S.G.A.-member clubs, with "instant handicaps." A computer program to calculate a handicap based on the U.S.G.A. formula is central to the products and services that Data–Max offers. Data–Max has sold or leased its computer to U.S.G.A.-member golf clubs, which use the computer in calculating handicaps.[2] Data–Max also markets a subscription telephone handicap service, which enables a

---

2. The U.S.G.A. has no objection to this aspect of Data–Max's business, since the handicap is ultimately provided by a member golf club. The U.S.G.A. objects to an unauthorized organization, such as Data–Max, providing handicaps derived by means of the U.S.G.A. formula directly to golfers.

golfer to call in a new score and immediately receive an updated handicap, and a computer that enables a golfer to directly enter a new score and receive an updated handicap.

* * *

C.   The Misappropriation Claim

The doctrine of "misappropriation," which is a distinct branch of the law of unfair competition, originated with the Supreme Court's decision in *International News Service v. Associated Press*, 248 U.S. 215, 39 S.Ct. 68, 63 L.Ed. 211 (1918) ("*I.N.S.*"). The doctrine has been applied to a variety of situations in which the courts have sensed that one party was dealing "unfairly" with another, but which were not covered by the three established statutory systems protecting intellectual property: copyright, patent, and trademark/deception as to origin. The doctrine has also been the subject of considerable scholarly attention. Application of the misappropriation doctrine requires courts to contend with the basic problem of the law of intellectual property: balancing the rights of the creator of ideas or information to exploit them for commercial gain against the public's right to free access to those ideas. Concomitantly, the dilemma posed by the doctrine can best be viewed as an attempt to provide the necessary incentives to the creators of intellectual property without unnecessarily restricting the public's free access to information.[12] * * *

* * *

After the Supreme Court's decision in *Erie Railroad v. Tompkins*, 304 U.S. 64, 58 S.Ct. 817, 82 L.Ed. 1188 (1939), misappropriation became a question of state, rather than federal law. * * *

A federal aspect to the problem of the scope of the misappropriation doctrine was reintroduced by the Supreme Court's decisions in *Sears, Roebuck & Co. v. Stiffel Co.*, 376 U.S. 225, 84 S.Ct. 784, 11 L.Ed.2d 661 (1964), and *Compco Corp. v. Day–Brite Lighting, Inc.*, 376 U.S. 234, 84 S.Ct. 779, 11 L.Ed.2d 669 (1964). The Court held that the decision by Congress to exclude certain types of intellectual property from protection under the patent and copyright laws was a policy decision that the societal interest in free access to those ideas outweighed the need to provide incentives for their production, and that state law doctrines which protected such intellectual property were preempted by that policy decision. Subsequent decisions of the Supreme Court have made clear, however,

---

12. The dilemma can also be framed in terms of balancing the natural right of a producer in the fruits of his or her labor against the public's access right. The constitutional provision authorizing copyrights and patents, and the statutes implementing it, are based on the "incentive" theory, in contrast to continental systems that are based on a "natural rights" theory. *I.N.S.*, however, explicitly recognized that the creator's interest is rooted in the "labor, skill and money" which has been devoted to the creation. Professor Baird believes there is little practical difference between relying on the "incentive" theory and relying on the "natural rights" theory. Baird, *Common Law Intellectual Property and the Legacy of International News Service v. Associated Press*, 50 U.Chi.L.Rev. 411, 420–21 (1983). In our view, using the incentive theory to define the limits of misappropriation is more appropriate, since it is based on a "social" interest (incentives for creation) which can be balanced against another social interest (free access), while the natural rights theory requires a balancing of incommensurables.

that the misappropriation doctrine has not been completely eviscerated. The Court has not rejected the *Sears-Compco* doctrine, nor has it clearly defined where the power of the states to protect interests in intellectual property ends, and where the realm of federal preemption begins. The problem before us, therefore, is to apply the misappropriation doctrine as we believe the New Jersey courts would apply it, in light of the limitations which we believe federal preemption places on the permissible scope of state-law protection for intellectual property.

[The court notes the decision in *Board of Trade v. Dow Jones, supra,* as well as that in Standard & Poor's Corp. v. Commodity Exchange, Inc., 683 F.2d 704 (2d Cir.1982). In the latter case, the Second Circuit, applying New York law, upheld a preliminary injunction against the Commodities Exchange ("Comex"), which was using the Standard & Poor's 500 ("S & P 500") as the basis of its stock index futures contract without Standard & Poor's authorization. Standard & Poor's had licensed another entity to create a stock market index future based on the S & P 500.]

This case is similar to the stock market index cases in a number of significant respects. As in the stock market index cases, the plaintiff here is seeking to exclude a rival from using a formula it has derived for commercial gain. The formulas in all three cases serve useful functions—in the stock market cases, the index is designed to track the general movement of the stock market; in this case, the formula is designed to indicate a golfer's level of competence. None of these formulas, however, is unique to its function. As a result of their creators' efforts, the respective formulas are generally accepted by the public as reliable means of performing their respective functions. Although the plaintiffs spend some time and effort updating their formulas, and also compute results by means of their formulas, the primary value of the results produced are not their inherent value in performing the underlying functions, but rather in the fact that they enable the public to discuss the underlying matters (*i.e.*, the direction of the stock market or the ability of golfers) by means of a common set of terms.

In determining whether the misappropriation doctrine should be applied in this case, however, we must keep in mind the basic policies that underlie the doctrine and its limits. In *I.N.S.*, the Court based its conclusion in substantial part on the fact that I.N.S. was using information which A.P. had developed in direct competition with A.P. in its primary market, the sale of newspapers. I.N.S.'s activity, if not checked, could have destroyed A.P.'s incentive to create the information involved, and this would not only have harmed A.P. but also would have left the public without the information. If, on the other hand, I.N.S. had used the information in a different manner—for instance, in writing a story on American correspondents covering the war—the use of A.P.'s information would not have affected A.P.'s incentive to gather the information. Although A.P. might have been better off if it had exclusive rights to such derivative uses of its information, providing legal protection might also harm the public, since A.P. might never have produced the story about correspondents covering the war. Indirect competition of this sort—use of information in competition with the creator outside of its primary market—falls outside the scope of the misappropriation doctrine, since the public interest in free access outweighs the public interest in providing an additional incentive to the creator or gatherer of information.

The competition in this case is indirect. The U.S.G.A. is not in the business of selling handicaps to golfers, but is primarily interested in the promotion of the game of golf, and in its own position as the governing body of amateur golf. The handicap formula was developed to further these two goals. A member of a golf club who obtains his handicap through his club does not pay for that service, and the U.S.G.A. is not directly affected by the number of official handicaps the clubs calculate each year or by the number of golfers who obtain handicaps. Data–Max, on the other hand, is in the business of providing "instant handicaps" to golfers, either by selling or leasing its computers to golf clubs, or by providing handicaps directly to golfers who cannot obtain "instant handicaps" through their clubs. The U.S.G.A. does not object to the sale or lease of Data–Max's computers, and does not attempt to provide the direct services which Data–Max provides to golfers. Thus, it is inconceivable that Data–Max's business will interfere with the U.S.G.A.'s incentive to maintain or update the handicap formula.

The absence of direct competition with the producer's primary use of the information was not viewed as dispositive by either the Illinois Supreme Court in *Dow Jones* or the Second Circuit in *Standard & Poor's*. The court in *Dow Jones* concluded that direct competition was unnecessary, and the court in *Standard & Poor's* found "direct competition" between S & P and Comex, even though the competition was outside S & P's primary market. Neither of these cases makes a persuasive argument for dispensing with the "direct competition" requirement. Since direct competition has generally been seen as necessary to a finding of misappropriation, and since it properly balances the competing concerns of providing incentives to producers of information while protecting free access, we believe that New Jersey would require direct competition in a misappropriation case, absent a substantial justification for making an exception.

A possible justification for dispensing with the direct competition requirement in this case, which was also present in *Dow Jones* and *Standard & Poor's*, is the fact that the information involved is so closely associated with the creator and has so little intrinsic value that the use of the information by the competitors is really an attempt to trade on the "good will" of the creator, and thus should be prohibited. The fact that the U.S.G.A. formula, like those involved in the stock market cases, is only one of a potentially large number of possible approaches to the underlying problem (quantifying the ability of golfers to enable them to compete with (and bet with) other golfers on an equitable basis) reduces the cost to the public of recognizing proprietary rights in the formula. The presence of so many alternatives also indicates that the primary value to Data–Max of using the U.S.G.A. formula is the public acceptance that the U.S.G.A. has built up for it over the years. This public acceptance could be characterized as part of the U.S.G.A.'s "good will." We must determine, therefore, whether the New Jersey courts would interpret the misappropriation doctrine in such a way as to dispense with the "direct competition" requirement on the facts of this case.

We conclude that, at least on the facts of this case, New Jersey would not dispense with the requirement of direct competition.[23] The public acceptance of the U.S.G.A.'s handicap formula stems from the golfing public's desire to have a uniform system of quantifying recent performances in a way that will allow equitable competition among golfers of differing abilities. The U.S.G.A., in furtherance of its role as the governing body of amateur golf, has provided such a system and, in the absence of a better system, the public has apparently accepted it. Under this state of affairs, the emergence of a single standard becomes largely a function of the need for uniformity. To require Data–Max to use a different formula would effectively destroy its ability to provide a handicapping service, since the U.S.G.A. formula is widely accepted by the golfing public. The purpose of a handicap is comparison between golfers, and handicaps based on different formulas cannot be readily compared.

Because the U.S.G.A. formula is the equivalent of an "industry standard" for the golfing public, preventing other handicap providers from using it would effectively give the U.S.G.A. a national monopoly on the golf handicapping business. Where such a monopoly is unnecessary to protect the basic incentive for the production of the idea or information involved, we do not believe that the creator's interest in its idea or information justifies such an extensive restraint on competition. This case provides a good example of why such a restraint would harm the golfing public. Data–Max has expended time and creative energy in devising its own products and services. It has not only created the program used to calculate handicaps by computer, but has devised a handicapping service which improves on that provided by the U.S.G.A., at least to the extent that Data–Max provides a golfer with a fresh handicap faster than the U.S.G.A. does. In addition, the U.S.G.A. has not been completely deprived of the opportunity to be compensated for its "good will" in connection with the handicap formula. To the extent that the approval of the U.S.G.A. would enhance the value of "instant handicaps," the U.S.G.A. has an opportunity, if it wishes to exercise it, of offering either Data–Max or other companies the use of the U.S.G.A. name in marketing its products and services.

* * *

---

23. We further note that expanding the misappropriation doctrine in such a way that it might give the creator of a particular idea or piece of information that has been made public a permanent monopoly over its commercial use could raise problems of preemption under the *Sears-Compco* doctrine.

N<small>OTES AND</small> Q<small>UESTIONS</small>

1. *The misappropriation cause of action.* As the opinions in *Board of Trade* and *United States Golf* suggest, the *I.N.S.* case is generally acknowledged to be the source of the misappropriation doctrine. That case is reprinted in Chapter One, *supra.*

The classic elements of the misappropriation cause of action are: 1) the plaintiff has invested time, money, skill or labor to create an intangible trade value; 2) the defendant has appropriated that intangible trade value in a manner that can be characterized as "reaping where it has not sown" or taking a free ride off the plaintiff's effort; and 3) the plaintiff has suffered injury as a result. See 2 J.T. McCarthy, McCarthy on Trademarks and Unfair Competition § 10.5. It seems fairly clear that the first two elements are satisfied in both *Board of Trade* and *United States Golf.* Is the third element satisfied in *Board of Trade*? If so, how? If not, is the court essentially saying that injury is not necessary? Did the court substitute another consideration in place of injury? If so, what was the substituted consideration?

2. *The purpose of the misappropriation doctrine.* In *Board of Trade,* what does the Illinois Supreme Court appear to view as the purpose of the misappropriation doctrine? Is it to enforce basic standards of commercial morality—to prevent parties from "reaping where they have not sown"? Is reaping where one has not sown inherently immoral or unfair? Under the specific circumstances of the *Board of Trade* case, was the Board of Trade's action in using the stock index immoral or unfair?

Is the purpose of the misappropriation doctrine to provide a flexible means of promoting public policy? If so, what is the public policy? How was it promoted by a finding of misappropriation in *Board of Trade*? Do you agree with the Illinois court's balancing of the potentially conflicting policy interests?

Is the purpose of the misappropriation doctrine to protect business good will? Did the court in *United States Golf* find that the defendant was not taking the plaintiff's good will, or that the taking of good will under the circumstances was not sufficient to justify granting relief? If the latter, what were the circumstances the court found influential? Under what, if any, circumstances might the court have found that the appropriation of a plaintiff's good reputation and public acceptance justified misappropriation relief?

In National Football League v. Governor of Delaware, 435 F.Supp. 1372 (D.Del.1977), the court grappled with the implications of a defendant's taking good will in the absence of competition. In that case, the Delaware State Lottery instituted lottery games based on participants' predictions of the scores generated in National Football League ("NFL") games. The lottery tickets listed teams by city names (e.g., Tampa), rather than trade name or mark (Buccaneers). The NFL sued to enjoin the lottery games, alleging a number of legal theories, including misappropriation. In evaluating this claim, the court acknowledged that the plaintiffs had made a great investment in developing public acceptance and popularity, and that the defendant lottery intended to capitalize on the NFL popularity and reputation when it chose NFL games as the subject matter of its lottery. The defendants conceded that in making this election they expected to generate revenue which would not be generated from betting on a less popular pastime. The court observed:

> It is undoubtedly true that defendants seek to profit from the popularity of NFL football. The question, however, is whether this constitutes wrongful misappropriation. I think not.
>
> We live in an age of economic and social interdependence. The NFL undoubtedly would not be in the position it is today if college football and the fan interest that it generated had not preceded the NFL's organization. To that degree it has benefitted from the labor of others. The same, of course, can be said for the mass media networks which the labor of others have developed.
>
> What the Delaware Lottery has done is to offer a service to that portion of plaintiffs' following who wish to bet on NFL games. It is true that Delaware is thus making profits it would not make but for the existence of the NFL, but I find this difficult to distinguish from the multitude of charter bus companies who generate profit from servicing those of plaintiffs' fans who want to go to the stadium or, indeed, the sidewalk popcorn salesman who services the crowd as it surges towards the gate.
>
> While courts have recognized that one has a right to one's own harvest, this proposition has not been construed to preclude others from profiting from demands for collateral services generated by the success of one's business venture. General Motors' cars, for example, enjoy significant popularity and seat cover manufacturers profit from that popularity by making covers to fit General Motors' seats. The same relationship exists between hot dog producers and the bakers of hot dog rolls. But in neither instance, I believe, could it be successfully contended that an actionable misappropriation occurs.
>
> The NFL plaintiffs, however, argue that this case is different because the evidence is said to show "misappropriation" of plaintiffs' "good will" and "reputation" as well as its "popularity." To a large extent, plaintiffs' references to "good will" and "reputation" are simply other ways of stating their complaint that defendants are profiting from a demand plaintiffs' games have generated. To the extent they relate to a claim that defendants' activities have damaged, as opposed to appropriated, plaintiff's good will and reputation, I believe one must look to other lines of authority to determine defendants' culpability. In response to plaintiffs' misappropriation argument, I hold only that defendants' use of the NFL schedules, scores and public popularity in the Delaware Lottery does not constitute a misappropriation of plaintiffs' property.

Id., 435 F.Supp. at 1378.

In light of your evaluation of the purposes of the misappropriation cause of action, should relief be limited to cases in which the parties compete? If so, how strictly would you define competition? For example, would you consider the parties in *United States Golf* to be competitors for this purpose?

3. *The interface between the misappropriation cause of action and other intellectual property doctrines.* In *Board of Trade*, the plaintiff argued that a

finding of misappropriation would essentially grant Dow Jones a common-law patent in its stock index. Is that true? If so, would misappropriation relief undermine Congress' purposes in setting strict standards for patents, and limited terms of protection? In *United States Golf*, the court found that the plaintiff's handicap formula was "functional," and thus could not be protected under the law of passing off. Under those circumstances, would it be appropriate to grant property rights in the formula under the state law of misappropriation, even if the parties were competitors? For that matter, in a classic trademark infringement setting, could a trademark owner simply circumvent the "likelihood of confusion" limitation by pleading that the defendant "misappropriated" its trademark? Taken to its logical extremes, the doctrine of misappropriation is so broad that it could be used to circumvent most of the limitations built into other intellectual property causes of action, undermining the careful balance of competing interests devised by courts and legislative bodies. Putting aside the issues of federal preemption, which we will examine in a later chapter, is this worrisome? When faced with this reality, courts have generally tended to be conservative in applying the misappropriation doctrine.

The new Restatement (Third) of Unfair Competition goes further. It would eliminate the misappropriation cause of action altogether, regardless of whether the parties are competitors. Restatement (Third) of Unfair Competition § 38 (1995). The drafters explain in comment b:

> Protection against the misappropriation of intangible trade values insures an incentive to invest in the creation of intangible assets and prevents the potential unjust enrichment that may result from the appropriation of an investment made by another. However, the recognition of exclusive rights in intangible trade values can impede access to valuable information and restrain competition. Unlike appropriations of physical assets, the appropriation of information or other intangible assets does not ordinarily deprive the originator of simultaneous use. The recognition of exclusive rights may thus deny to the public the full benefits of valuable ideas and innovations by limiting their distribution and exploitation. In addition, the principle of unjust enrichment does not demand restitution of every gain derived from the efforts of others. A small shop, for example, may freely benefit from the customers attracted by a nearby department store, a local manufacturer may benefit from increased demand attributable to the promotional efforts of a national manufacturer of similar goods, and a newspaper may benefit from reporting on the activities of local athletic teams. Similarly, the law has long recognized the right of a competitor to copy the successful products and business methods of others absent protection under patent, copyright, or trademark law.

> Achieving a proper balance between protection and access is often a complicated and difficult undertaking. Because of the complexity and indeterminacy of the competing interests, rights in intangible trade values such as ideas, innovations, and information have been created primarily through legislation. The patent and copyright statutes illustrate the intricacy required to harmonize the competing public and private interests implicated in the recognition of rights in intangible trade values. Both statutes contain elaborate mechanisms intended to balance the

interests in protection and access. Protection under the patent act, for example, is limited to innovations that are new, useful, and non-obvious to persons having ordinary skill in the art. The copyright act grants rights in works of authorship subject to a complex system of exemptions and limitations. Both statutes grant rights only for a limited term, after which the discovery or writing enters the public domain and may be freely appropriated by others.

The common law of unfair competition has generally recognized rights against the appropriation of intangible trade values only when the recognition of such rights is supported by other interests that justify protection, and then only when the scope of the resulting rights can be clearly defined. The protection of trade secrets, for example, reflects the established interests in preserving confidential relationships and promoting physical security. Protection against an appropriation of the commercial value of a person's identity implicates interests in privacy, reputation, and personal autonomy. In the absence of such additional interests, the common law has resisted the recognition of general rights against the appropriation of information and other intangible trade values.[3]

* * *

PROBLEM

1. Plaintiffs, all well-known news gathering and reporting organizations, maintain web sites on which they post current, important news stories. They permit site visitors to read the stories free of charge. Defendant, an entity that engages in no gathering of news itself, creates a web site that provides a series of hyperlinks to various news stories posted on the plaintiffs' sites. Visitors to defendant's site simply click their mouse on a particular news topic, and are able to view a plaintiff's article on that topic (as posted on the plaintiff's web site) through defendant's "frame." The frame divides the visitor's computer screen into sections, one of which features the plaintiff's news story, the rest of which feature banner advertisements. The defendant sells advertising space in the banner sections to various commercial entities. The hyperlinks that permit defendant's site visitors to view materials on the plaintiffs' sites do not themselves reproduce the plaintiffs' news articles.

The plaintiffs sue, alleging misappropriation. How would you evaluate their claim?

---

3. ©1995, The American Law Institute. Reprinted with the permission of the American Law Institute

CHAPTER SEVEN

THE RIGHT OF PUBLICITY

■ ■ ■

I. THE NATURE AND PURPOSE OF THE RIGHT OF PUBLICITY

HAELAN LABORATORIES, INC. v. TOPPS CHEWING GUM, INC.

United States Court of Appeals for the Second Circuit, 1953.
202 F.2d 866, *cert. denied*, 346 U.S. 816, 74 S.Ct. 26, 98 L.Ed. 343 (1953).

FRANK, CIRCUIT JUDGE.

After a trial without a jury, the trial judge dismissed the complaint on the merits. The plaintiff maintains that defendant invaded plaintiff's exclusive right to use the photographs of leading baseball-players. * * *

1. So far as we can now tell, there were instances of the following kind:

(a). The plaintiff, engaged in selling chewing-gum, made a contract with a ball-player providing that plaintiff for a stated term should have the exclusive right to use the ball-player's photograph in connection with the sales of plaintiff's gum; the ball-player agreed not to grant any other gum manufacturer a similar right during such term; the contract gave plaintiff an option to extend the term for a designated period.

(b). Defendant, a rival chewing-gum manufacturer, knowing of plaintiff's contract, deliberately induced the ball-player to authorize defendant, by a contract with defendant, to use the player's photograph in connection with the sales of defendant's gum either during the original or extended term of plaintiff's contract, and defendant did so use the photograph.

Defendant argues that, even if such facts are proved, they show no actionable wrong, for this reason: The contract with plaintiff was no more than a release by the ball-player to plaintiff of the liability which, absent the release, plaintiff would have incurred in using the ball-player's photograph, because such a use, without his consent, would be an invasion of his right of privacy under Section 50 and Section 51 of the New York Civil Rights Law; this statutory right of privacy is personal, not assignable;

therefore, plaintiff's contract vested in plaintiff no "property" right or other legal interest which defendant's conduct invaded.

Both parties agree, and so do we, that, on the facts here, New York "law" governs. And we shall assume, for the moment, that, under the New York decisions, defendant correctly asserts that any such contract between plaintiff and a ball-player, in so far as it merely authorized plaintiff to use the player's photograph, created nothing but a release of liability. On that basis, were there no more to the contract, plaintiff would have no actionable claim against defendant. But defendant's argument neglects the fact that, in the contract, the ball-player also promised not to give similar releases to others. If defendant, knowing of the contract, deliberately induced the ball-player to break that promise, defendant behaved tortiously.

* * *

2. The foregoing covers the situations where defendant, by itself or through its agent, induced breaches. But in those instances where [the defendant did not induce a breach, but nonetheless knowingly] used a photograph of a ball-player without his consent during the term of his contract with plaintiff [we have a different problem].

With regard to such situations, we must consider defendant's contention that none of plaintiff's contracts created more than a release of liability, because a man has no legal interest in the publication of his picture other than his right of privacy, i.e., a personal and non-assignable right not to have his feelings hurt by such a publication.

A majority of this court rejects this contention. We think that, in addition to and independent of that right of privacy (which in New York derives from statute), a man has a right in the publicity value of his photograph, *i.e.*, the right to grant the exclusive privilege of publishing his picture, and that such a grant may validly be made "in gross," *i.e.*, without an accompanying transfer of a business or of anything else. Whether it be labelled a "property" right is immaterial; for here, as often elsewhere, the tag "property" simply symbolizes the fact that courts enforce a claim which has pecuniary worth.

This right might be called a "right of publicity." For it is common knowledge that many prominent persons (especially actors and ball-players), far from having their feelings bruised through public exposure of their likenesses, would feel sorely deprived if they no longer received money for authorizing advertisements, popularizing their countenances, displayed in newspapers, magazines, busses, trains and subways. This right of publicity would usually yield them no money unless it could be made the subject of an exclusive grant which barred any other advertiser from using their pictures.

We think the New York decisions recognize such a right.

* * *

[P]laintiff, in its capacity as exclusive grantee of a player's "right of publicity," has a valid claim against defendant if defendant used that player's photograph during the term of plaintiff's grant and with knowledge of it. * * *

* * *

LUGOSI v. UNIVERSAL PICTURES

Supreme Court of California, 1979.
25 Cal.3d 813, 160 Cal.Rptr. 323, 603 P.2d 425.

* * *

BIRD, CHIEF JUSTICE, with JUSTICES TOBRINER and MANUEL, dissenting.

* * *

Although Bela Lugosi died more than 20 years ago, his name still evokes the vivid image of Count Dracula, a role he played on stage and in motion pictures. So impressed in the public's memory, the image of Lugosi as Dracula was profitably marketed by defendant Universal Pictures, which had employed Lugosi to portray Count Dracula in the motion picture *Dracula*. Specifically, Universal Pictures concluded licensing agreements which authorized the use of Lugosi's likeness in his portrayal of Count Dracula in connection with the sale of numerous commercial merchandising products.

Plaintiffs, beneficiaries under Bela Lugosi's will, commenced this action for damages and an injunction against further licensing of Lugosi's likeness on the ground that such use was unauthorized and infringed on their interest in controlling the commercial use of Lugosi's likeness. This case thus presents the novel question in California of the nature and scope of an individual's interest in controlling the commercial exploitation of his or her likeness. I conclude that Universal Picture's licensing of Lugosi's image was unauthorized and infringed on Lugosi's proprietary interest in his likeness. * * *

II. THE RIGHT OF PUBLICITY

The fundamental issue in this case is the nature of Lugosi's right to control the commercial exploitation of his likeness. The trial court found Universal's licensing agreements constituted a tortious interference with Lugosi's proprietary or property interest in the commercial use of his likeness, an interest which had descended to plaintiffs. Universal asserts that Lugosi's interest is protected only under the rubric of the right of privacy. Since that right is personal and ceased with Lugosi's death, plaintiffs cannot recover damages based on Universal's conduct. Accordingly, the critical question is whether an individual's interest in the commercial use of his likeness is protected solely as an aspect of the right of privacy or whether additional or alternative protection exists.

A. Privacy or Publicity

The common law right of privacy creates a cause of action for "an interference with the right of the plaintiff . . . 'to be let alone.' " (Prosser, *Privacy* (1960) 48 Cal.L.Rev. 383, 389.) "The gist of the cause of action in a privacy case is . . . a direct wrong of a personal character resulting in injury to the feelings. . . . The injury is mental and subjective. It impairs the mental peace and comfort of the person and may cause suffering much more acute than that caused by a bodily injury." (*Fairfield v. American Photocopy Equipment Co.* (1955) 138 Cal.App.2d 82, 86–87, 291 P.2d 194, 197.) Since the right of privacy developed to protect an individual from certain injuries to his feelings and assaults on his peace of mind, he need not suffer any injury to his property, business or economic interests as a prerequisite to initiating a suit for an invasion of privacy.

The appropriation of an individual's likeness for another's commercial advantage often intrudes on interests distinctly different than those protected by the right of privacy. Plaintiffs in this case have not objected to the manner in which Universal used Lugosi's likeness nor claimed any mental distress from such use. Rather, plaintiffs have asserted that Universal reaped an economic windfall from Lugosi's enterprise to which they are rightfully entitled.

Today, it is commonplace for individuals to promote or advertise commercial services and products or, as in the present case, even have their identities infused in the products. Individuals prominent in athletics, business, entertainment and the arts, for example, are frequently involved in such enterprises. When a product's promoter determines that the commercial use of a particular person will be advantageous, the promoter is often willing to pay handsomely for the privilege. As a result, the sale of one's persona in connection with the promotion of commercial products has unquestionably become big business.

Such commercial use of an individual's identity is intended to increase the value or sales of the product by fusing the celebrity's identity with the product and thereby siphoning some of the publicity value or good will in the celebrity's persona into the product. This use is premised, in part, on public recognition and association with that person's name or likeness, or an ability to create such recognition. The commercial value of a particular person's identity thus primarily depends on that person's public visibility and the characteristics for which he or she is known.

Often considerable money, time and energy are needed to develop one's prominence in a particular field. Years of labor may be required before one's skill, reputation, notoriety or virtues are sufficiently developed to permit an economic return through some medium of commercial promotion. For some, the investment may eventually create considerable commercial value in one's identity.

In this context, the marketable product of that labor is the ability of a person's name or likeness to attract the attention and evoke a desired response in a particular consumer audience. That response is a kind of good will or recognition value generated by that person. While this product is concededly intangible, it is not illusory.

An unauthorized commercial appropriation of one's identity converts the potential economic value in that identity to another's advantage. The user is enriched, reaping one of the benefits of the celebrity's investment in himself. The loss may well exceed the mere denial of compensation for the use of the individual's identity. The unauthorized use disrupts the individual's effort to control his public image, and may substantially alter that image. The individual may be precluded from future promotions in that as well as other fields. Further, while a judicious involvement in commercial promotions may have been perceived as an important ingredient in one's career, uncontrolled exposure may be dysfunctional. As a result, the development of his initial vocation—his profession—may be arrested. Finally, if one's identity is exploited without permission to promote products similar to those which the individual has already endorsed, the unauthorized use resembles unfair competition. While the product which first used the celebrity paid for the privilege of trading on his publicity value, the second product has secured a costless endorsement. The simultaneous presence in the market of these competing products may cause the latter to be mistaken for the former and will probably diminish the value of the endorsement.

Accordingly, the gravamen of the harm flowing from an unauthorized commercial use of a prominent individual's likeness in most cases is the loss of potential financial gain, not mental anguish.[11] The fundamental objection is not that the commercial use is offensive, but that the individual has not been compensated. Indeed, the representation of the person will most likely be flattering, since it is in the user's interest to project a positive image. The harm to feelings, if any, is usually minimal.

The individual's interest thus threatened by most unauthorized commercial uses is significantly different than the personal interests protected under the right of privacy. Recognition of this difference has prompted independent judicial protection for this economic interest. The individual's interest in the commercial value of his identity has been regarded as proprietary in nature and sometimes denominated a common law "right of publicity." This right has won increasing judicial recognition, as well as endorsements by legal commentators.

The right of publicity has been regarded as "the right of each person to control and profit from the publicity values which he has created or purchased." (Nimmer, *The Right of Publicity (1954),* 19 Law & Contemp. Prob. 203, 216.) * * *

---

11. This is not to suggest that commercial misappropriations of one's likeness may not inflict noneconomic injuries. Commercial misappropriations may injure a person's feelings in several ways. First, the person may find any commercial exploitation undesirable and offensive. Second, while certain commercial uses may be acceptable or even desirable, a particular use may be distressing. Third, other individuals, unaware that the use is unauthorized, may disparage one who would sell their identity for that purpose, thereby inducing embarrassment, anger or mental distress. Further, any unauthorized use infringes on one's effort to control the public projection of one's identity, including the desire for solitude and anonymity.

Further, there is a broader social objective implicit in according judicial protection to the right of publicity, analogous to the policies underlying copyright and patent law. The Supreme Court recently described the purpose of granting copyright protection as encouraging "people to devote themselves to intellectual and artistic creation ...," and thereby secure the benefits of such labors for the entire society. Similarly, providing legal protection for the economic value in one's identity against unauthorized commercial exploitation creates a powerful incentive for expending time and resources to develop the skills or achievements prerequisite to public recognition and assures that the individual will be able "to reap the reward of his endeavors...." While the immediate beneficiaries are those who establish professions or identities which are commercially valuable, the products of their enterprise are often beneficial to society generally. Their performances, inventions and endeavors enrich our society, while their participation in commercial enterprises may communicate valuable information to consumers.[19]

The reasons for affording independent protection for the economic value in one's identity are substantial and compelling, as attested by the increasing number of jurisdictions which have done so. I am similarly persuaded that an individual's right of publicity is entitled to the law's protection.

The common law can readily accommodate judicial recognition of the right of publicity. " 'The rules of the common law are continually changing and expanding with the progress of the society in which it prevails. It does not lag behind, but adapts itself to the conditions of the present so that the ends of justice may be reached.' " Specifically, this court has long recognized that the concept of "property" is not static but changes to accommodate creative developments and novel legal relationships. * * *

Universal argues that judicial recognition of an independent right of publicity is unnecessary in light of the adequate protection afforded under the common law right of privacy. However, the interest at stake in most commercial appropriation cases is ill-suited to protection under the umbrella of the right of privacy. First, the *raison d'etre* of the common law

19. One commentator has suggested a related benefit which may flow from recognizing an individual's right of publicity:

"The use of celebrities' names and pictures appears to be a characteristic of advertising. Advertisers would probably continue to use celebrities' pictures even if they knew that other advertisers could freely make similar use of the same names and pictures. In other words, if free use of names and pictures developed, they would probably continue to attract the consumer's attention, provoke emulation, and, perhaps, suggest sponsorship. If society chooses to allow uses of names and likenesses in advertising, it might prefer that consumers not be misled about the willingness of a celebrity to associate himself with a product or service. It might give celebrities a cause of action for unconsented uses of names and likenesses in furtherance of that objective. Similarly, society might decide that the 'emulating' behavior of consumers would channel itself more acceptably if the persons emulated had some control over the decision to link their names and likenesses with particular products. Indeed, persons whose personalities attract consumers might find that coercing advertisers to forego some forms of undesirable advertising behavior advances their interests. Allowing individuals to control the advertising use of their personalities could thus provide a private law mechanism for advertising regulation." (Treece, *Commercial Exploitation of Names, Likenesses, and Personal Histories* (1973) 51 Texas L.Rev. 637, 647, fn. omitted.)

right of privacy is protection against assaults on one's feelings; an unauthorized commercial appropriation usually precipitates only economic loss, not mental anguish. Second, since the representation of the individual is often flattering, substantial linguistic acrobatics are required to construct a privacy claim on the ground that the use is offensive to a reasonable person. Third, if information about a person is already in the public domain, there can be no claim for an invasion of privacy; to that extent, the right of privacy has been waived. Yet it is publicity which frequently creates value in the individual's identity. To deny a claim for damages for commercial misappropriation because the claimant is prominent is to deny the right to the very individuals to whom the right is most valuable. Fourth, if treated as an aspect of privacy, the use of one's identity for commercial purposes may not be assigned because privacy is a personal, nonassignable right. Such a limitation precludes transferring this economic interest, thereby substantially diminishing its value. In short, conforming a claim for the misappropriation of the commercial value in one's identity to the requirements of the right of privacy requires a procrustean jurisprudence.

B. The Scope of the Right of Publicity

The parameters of the right of publicity must now be considered. This case presents two questions: (1) whether the right extends to the likeness of an individual in his portrayal of the fictional character; and (2) whether the right dies with the individual or may be passed to one's heirs or beneficiaries.

Because the right protects against the unauthorized commercial use of an individual's identity, the right clearly applies to the person's name and likeness. However, such protection would appear to be insufficient because many people create public recognition not only in their "natural" appearance but in their portrayal of particular characters. Charlie Chaplin's Little Tramp, Carroll O'Connor's Archie Bunker and Flip Wilson's Judge and Geraldine exemplify such creations. Substantial publicity value exists in the likeness of each of these actors in their character roles. The professional and economic interests in controlling the commercial exploitation of their likenesses while portraying these characters are identical to their interests in controlling the use of their own "natural" likenesses. Indeed, to the extent one's professional endeavors have focused on the development of one or more particular character images, protection for one's likeness in the portrayal of those characters may well be considerably more important than protection for the individual's "natural" appearance. Hence, there appears to be no reason why the right of publicity should not extend to one's own likeness while portraying a particular fictional character.[26]

---

26. This protection extends only to the individual's likeness—a representation or image of the person while portraying the particular character. Nothing herein is intended to extend protection to the idea for the character or to the character itself. Nothing in the right of publicity prohibits another person, for example, from developing and playing a sympathetic tramp character similar to the one portrayed by Chaplin.

Lugosi's likeness in his portrayal of Count Dracula is clearly such a case. Many men have portrayed Count Dracula in motion pictures and on stage. However, the trial court found that Universal did not license the use of an undifferentiated Count Dracula character, but the distinctive and readily recognizable portrayal of Lugosi as the notorious Transylvanian count. Universal thereby sought to capitalize on the particular image of Lugosi in his portrayal of Count Dracula and the public recognition generated by his performance. Such use is illustrative of the very interests the right of publicity is intended to protect. Hence, Lugosi had a protectible property interest in controlling unauthorized commercial exploitation of *his* likeness in his portrayal of Count Dracula.

Recognizing Lugosi's legitimate interest in controlling the use of his portrayal of Count Dracula limits neither the author's exploitation of the novel Dracula[27] nor Universal's use of its copyrighted motion picture. Lugosi only agreed to allow Universal to make limited use of his likeness in their 1930 contract. Further, Lugosi's right certainly does not prohibit others from portraying the character Count Dracula. Consequently, nothing established herein suggests that any of the individuals involved in contemporary cinematic or theatrical revivals of Count Dracula's nocturnal adventures have violated Lugosi's right of publicity. The only conduct prohibited is the unauthorized commercial use of *Lugosi's likeness* in his portrayal of Count Dracula. To the extent that Universal or another seeks such use, that right can be secured by contract.

[The dissent then argues that the right of publicity is descendible.]

NOTES AND QUESTIONS

1. *The right of publicity and the right of privacy.* The *Haelan* opinion coined the term "right of publicity," and was the first judicial opinion to recognize the right as a distinct cause of action, separate from the invasion of privacy claim. Professor Melville Nimmer pursued the distinction in his influential article, *The Right of Publicity*, 19 L. & Contemp. Prob. 203 (1954). In 1960, Professor William Prosser published his famous article, *Privacy*, 48 Cal. L. Rev. 383 (1960), which provided the definitive description of the privacy cause of action, but may have diffused recognition of the type of claim asserted in *Haelan* and *Lugosi* as a cause of action distinct from the law of privacy.

In his article, Professor Prosser divided the privacy cause of action into four categories: 1) "intrusion upon the plaintiff's seclusion or solitude, or into his private affairs;" 2) "public disclosure of embarrassing private facts about the plaintiff;" 3) "publicity which places the plaintiff in a false light in the public eye;" and 4) "appropriation, for the defendant's advantage, of the plaintiff's name or likeness." *Id.*, 48 Cal. L. Rev. at 389. The fourth, "appro-

---

27. This case does not present the question of the relative rights of the novel's copyright holder and Lugosi and his heirs in commercial exploitations of Lugosi's likeness in his portrayal of Count Dracula. However, it should be noted that the trial court found that the novel Dracula has always been in the public domain in the United States due to the author's failure to comply with a requirement of the copyright law in existence when the novel was published.

1058 Rights in Consumer Good Will Pt. 4

priation," category encompassed the situation in which a defendant makes an unauthorized use of a plaintiff's name or likeness to advertise or sell a product.

In the "appropriation" category, the nature of the plaintiff's injury may depend on whether she is a private person or a celebrity. The private plaintiff may experience mental distress at seeing her name or likeness on the label of products or plastered on billboards, and wish to assert a "right to be let alone." Her damage consists of injury to a personal interest: her sense of dignity and mental tranquility. As Judge Frank notes in *Haelan*, a celebrity, such as a baseball player or an actress, may suffer a different kind of injury, primarily economic in nature. This sets the celebrity's claim apart from all the other "privacy" claims falling within Professor Prosser's four categories. While Prosser himself appeared to recognize the differing interests, his decision to include the celebrity's claim within his fourth "privacy" category (and the subsequent Restatement (Second) of Torts' adoption of his framework, Restatement (Second) of Torts § 652A (1977)), may have led some litigants and courts to overlook the important distinction between the interests being asserted by the celebrity "appropriation" claimant and other right to privacy claimants.

Overlooking the distinction may lead to findings that are difficult to justify conceptually. For example, by analogy to rights of privacy, some authorities have indicated that the right of publicity cannot be assigned, devised or passed by intestate succession. A much stronger argument can be made for alienability of an economic interest, such as the right of publicity, than of a personal "right to be left alone." The issue of rights transfer will be explored in more depth below.

Today, the relationship between the invasion of privacy and right of publicity causes of action remains unsettled. Some jurisdictions appear to view the celebrity's economic injury claim as encompassed within the "privacy" cause of action, while others recognize it as a separate and distinct cause of action, known as the "right of publicity." Many states have yet to make their position clear. Those jurisdictions that continue to view the celebrity's economic injury claim as a privacy claim may differ in the extent to which they apply rules and reasoning developed in the context of personal privacy claims to vindicate celebrities' economic interests. The uncertainty pervading the right of publicity cause of action has lead one court to liken it to a "haystack in a hurricane." Ettore v. Philco Television Broadcasting Corp., 229 F.2d 481, 485 (3d Cir.), *cert. denied*, 351 U.S. 926, 76 S.Ct. 783, 100 L.Ed. 1456 (1956).

While some jurisdictions draw their "right of publicity" cause of action from the common law, others have enacted statutes that encompass a right of publicity claim. See, e.g., Cal. Civ. Code §§ 3344, 3344.1 (West 2010); Fla. Stat. Ann. § 540.08 (West 2010); Mass. Gen. Laws Ann. ch. 214, § 3A (West 2010); N.Y. Civ. Rights Law §§ 50–51 (McKinney Supp. 2009). The language of these statutes varies greatly, and may place restraints on assertion of the cause of action that would not exist in the more flexible common law. While some states, such as California, recognize a common-law cause of action that coexists with the statutory cause of action, others, such as New York, have held that the statute supersedes any common-law cause of action.

While the U.S. Court of Appeals in *Haelan*, exercising diversity jurisdiction, found that New York would recognize a common-law right of publicity apart from its "privacy" statute, the New York courts had not actually done so. Many years later, in Stephano v. News Group Publications, Inc., 64 N.Y.2d 174, 485 N.Y.S.2d 220, 474 N.E.2d 580 (1984), the New York Court of Appeals held that claims for economic injuries arising from unauthorized commercial use of a person's likeness were subsumed under the state's privacy statute, and that no common-law right of publicity existed in New York.

Sections 50 and 51 of the New York Civil Rights Law provide that any person or business who uses a living person's name, portrait, picture or voice for advertising purposes or for purposes of trade without written consent will be liable to the person so exploited. The *Stephano* court noted that §§ 50 and 51 were enacted to protect privacy interests. Nonetheless, the statutory language literally encompassed the economic injury claim of a celebrity, and would provide the sole avenue for relief. In rejecting *Haelan's* interpretation of New York law, the New York Court of Appeals conceptually reunited the privacy and publicity causes of action that the *Haelan* court had attempted to distinguish. Of course, the *Haelan* decision has been highly influential in other states, and the *Stephano* court's decision, based on the state's unique statutory provision, need not undercut that influence.

For an exhaustive survey of all the relevant state statutes, as well as examples of foreign approaches to the right of publicity, see 1 J.T. McCarthy, The Rights of Publicity and Privacy ch. 6 (4th ed. & Supp.).

2. *The relationship of the right of publicity to other causes of action.* The right of publicity is closely related to several legal doctrines in addition to the law of privacy. To begin, do you see a relationship with the unfair competition cause of action for misappropriation? How would you describe the relationship?

The right of publicity is also closely related to the unfair competition doctrines of passing off, trademark dilution, and false advertising. One or more of these causes of action might be pleaded in the alternative to a right of publicity claim in many fact settings. How would you articulate the relationship? What elements differentiate each of these unfair competition causes of action from the right of publicity claim?

What is the relationship between the right of publicity and copyright? What are the key differences? The similarities are strongest in cases in which the plaintiff claims that the defendant appropriated his identity by taking his artistic creation or performance, which is closely linked with his identity in the public's mind. The most famous case involving such a claim is Zacchini v. Scripps–Howard Broadcasting Co., 433 U.S. 562, 97 S.Ct. 2849, 53 L.Ed.2d 965 (1977).

In *Zacchini*, the plaintiff made his living by performing a human cannon-ball act in which he was shot from a cannon into a net 200 feet away. Each performance took about 15 seconds. While plaintiff was performing at a fair ground, a television reporter filmed his entire act without his permission. Defendant television station broadcast the film over the evening news, along with a favorable commentary. Plaintiff brought suit for damages. The Ohio Supreme Court found the plaintiff's right of publicity would have been violated, except that the defendant was protected from liability by the First Amendment. On certiorari, the United States Supreme Court found that the First Amendment did not in fact shield the defendant from liability. With regard to the right of publicity cause of action, the Supreme Court stated:

> The broadcast of a film of petitioner's entire act poses a substantial threat to the economic value of that performance. As the Ohio court recognized, this act is the product of petitioner's own talents and energy, the end result of much time, effort, and expense. Much of its economic value lies in the "right of exclusive control over the publicity given to his performance"; if the public can see the act free on television, it will be less willing to pay to see it at the fair. The effect of a public broadcast of the performance is similar to preventing petitioner from charging an admission fee. "The rationale for [protecting the right of publicity] is the straightforward one of preventing unjust enrichment by the theft of good will. No social purpose is served by having the defendant get free some aspect of the plaintiff that would have market value and for which he would normally pay." Moreover, the broadcast of petitioner's entire performance, unlike the unauthorized use of another's name for purposes of trade or the incidental use of a name or picture by the press, goes to the heart of petitioner's ability to earn a living as an entertainer. Thus, in this case, Ohio has recognized what may be the strongest case for a "right of publicity" involving, not the appropriation of an entertainer's reputation to enhance the attractiveness of a commercial product, but the appropriation of the very activity by which the entertainer acquired his reputation in the first place.

> Of course, Ohio's decision to protect petitioner's right of publicity here rests on more than a desire to compensate the performer for the time and effort invested in his act; the protection provides an economic incentive for him to make the investment required to produce a performance of interest to the public. This same consideration underlies the patent and copyright laws long enforced by this Court. * * *

Id., 433 U.S. at 575–77.

3. *The underlying justifications for a right of publicity.* The majority opinion in *Lugosi* accepted that Lugosi had a right of publicity during his lifetime (though it did not explore the scope of that right in any depth), but held that the right did not descend to Lugosi's heirs upon his death.

Justice Bird's dissent reviews the numerous justifications that have been given for the right of publicity cause of action. Which do you find most convincing? Do you find the incentive rationale persuasive? What about the concern that unauthorized use of a plaintiff's identity on products similar to products actually endorsed by the plaintiff may cause consumer confusion? Does the possibility that other causes of action may be available to vindicate these interests affect your evaluation of the need for the right of publicity cause of action?

What is your response to the following:

> The rationales underlying the recognition of a right of publicity are generally less compelling than those that justify rights in trademarks or

trade secrets. The commercial value of a person's identity often results from success in endeavors such as entertainment or sports that afford their own substantial rewards. Any additional incentive attributable to the right of publicity may have only marginal significance. In other cases the commercial value associated with a person's identity is largely fortuitous or otherwise unrelated to any investment made by the individual, thus diminishing the weight of the property and unjust enrichment rationales for protection. In addition, the public interest in avoiding false suggestions of endorsement or sponsorship can be pursued through the cause of action for deceptive marketing. Thus, courts may be properly reluctant to adopt a broad construction of the publicity right.

Restatement (Third) of Unfair Competition § 46, cmt c (1995).[1]

Compare the following observation from a leading authority on the right of publicity:

> While several rationales or reasons have been argued to support the right of publicity, the one that appeals the most to me is the simplest and most obvious. It is the natural right of property justification. It is an appeal to first principles of justice. Each and every human being should be given control over the commercial use of his or her identity. Perhaps nothing is so strongly intuited as the notion that my identity is mine—it is my property, to control as I see fit. Put simply, my identity is "me." The existence of a legal right to control identity would seem to be essential to any civilized society.

McCarthy, *Public Personas and Private Property: The Commercialization of Human Identity*, 79 Trademark Rep. 681, 685 (1989).[2]

How would you evaluate the *Lugosi* dissent's argument that Lugosi's right of publicity should extend beyond his "natural" likeness to encompass his likeness in portraying Count Dracula? Should it matter how similar or different the likeness is to the plaintiff's "natural" likeness? What if the portrayal involves use of a face mask or heavy make-up? Should it matter whether the plaintiff or someone else designed the mask or make-up? What if the plaintiff's appearance in portraying the fictitious character matches a description of the fictitious character written into the original novel or screen play? Might it be difficult, in some cases, to prove whether the defendant has identified the actor in his portrayal of the role or the role itself?

Consider Justice Mosk's view of the issue, set forth in his concurring opinion in *Lugosi*:

> We are not troubled by the nature of Lugosi's right to control the commercial exploitation of *his* likeness. That right has long been established. The issue here is the right of Lugosi's successors to control the commercialization of a likeness of a dramatic character—i.e., Count Dracula—created by a novelist and portrayed for compensation by Lugosi in a film version produced by a motion picture company under license from the successor of the novelist. * * *

---

1. © 1995, The American Law Institute. Reprinted with the permission of The American Law Institute.

2. © 1989, J. Thomas McCarthy. Reprinted by permission of the copyright owner.

Bela Lugosi was a talented actor. But he was an actor, a practitioner of the thespian arts; he was not a playwright, an innovator, a creator or an entrepreneur. As an actor he memorized lines and portrayed roles written for him, albeit with consummate skill. * * *

Merely playing a role under the foregoing circumstances creates no inheritable property right in an actor, absent a contract so providing. Indeed, as the record discloses, many other actors have portrayed the same role * * *. Thus neither Lugosi during his lifetime nor his estate thereafter owned the exclusive right to exploit Count Dracula any more than Gregory Peck possesses or his heirs could possess common law exclusivity to General MacArthur, George C. Scott to General Patton, James Whitmore to Will Rogers and Harry Truman, or Charlton Heston to Moses.

I do not suggest that an actor can never retain a proprietary interest in a characterization. An original creation of a fictional figure played exclusively by its creator may well be protectible. Thus, Groucho Marx just being Groucho Marx, with his moustache, cigar, slouch and leer, cannot be exploited by others. Red Skelton's variety of self-devised roles would appear to be protectible, as would the unique personal creations of Abbot and Costello, Laurel and Hardy and others of that genre. * * *

Here it is clear that Bela Lugosi did not portray himself and did not create Dracula, he merely acted out a popular role that had been garnished with the patina of age, as had innumerable other thespians over the decades. His performance gave him no more claim on Dracula than that of countless actors on Hamlet who have portrayed the Dane in a unique manner.

25 Cal.3d at 825–26 (Mosk, J., concurring). Compare McFarland v. Miller, 14 F.3d 912 (3d Cir.1994) (A court should consider whether the public has come to associate the actor with the character he has portrayed. "Where an actor's screen persona becomes so associated with him that it becomes inseparable from the actor's own public image, the actor obtains an interest in the image which gives him standing to prevent mere interlopers from using it without authority.").

II. THE SCOPE OF THE RIGHT OF PUBLICITY

WHITE v. SAMSUNG ELECTRONICS AMERICA, INC.

United States Court of Appeals for the Ninth Circuit, 1992.
971 F.2d 1395, *cert. denied,* 508 U.S. 951, 113 S.Ct. 2443, 124 L.Ed.2d 660 (1993).

GOODWIN, SENIOR CIRCUIT JUDGE:

This case involves a promotional "fame and fortune" dispute. In running a particular advertisement without Vanna White's permission, defendants Samsung Electronics America, Inc. (Samsung) and David Deutsch Associates, Inc. (Deutsch) attempted to capitalize on White's fame to enhance their fortune. * * *

Plaintiff Vanna White is the hostess of "Wheel of Fortune," one of the most popular game shows in television history. An estimated forty million people watch the program daily. Capitalizing on the fame which her participation in the show has bestowed on her, White markets her identity to various advertisers.

The dispute in this case arose out of a series of advertisements prepared for Samsung by Deutsch. The series ran in at least half a dozen publications with widespread, and in some cases national, circulation. Each of the advertisements in the series followed the same theme. Each depicted a current item from popular culture and a Samsung electronic product. Each was set in the twenty-first century and conveyed the message that the Samsung product would still be in use by that time. By hypothesizing outrageous future outcomes for the cultural items, the ads created humorous effects. For example, one lampooned current popular notions of an unhealthy diet by depicting a raw steak with the caption: "Revealed to be health food. 2010 A.D." Another depicted irreverent "news"-show host Morton Downey Jr. in front of an American flag with the caption: "Presidential candidate. 2008 A.D."

The advertisement which prompted the current dispute was for Samsung video-cassette recorders (VCRs). The ad depicted a robot, dressed in a wig, gown, and jewelry which Deutsch consciously selected to resemble White's hair and dress. The robot was posed next to a game board which is instantly recognizable as the Wheel of Fortune game show set, in a stance for which White is famous. The caption of the ad read: "Longest-running game show. 2012 A.D." Defendants referred to the ad as the "Vanna White" ad. Unlike the other celebrities used in the campaign, White neither consented to the ads nor was she paid.

Following the circulation of the robot ad, White sued Samsung and Deutsch in federal district court under: (1) California Civil Code § 3344; (2) the California common law right of publicity; and (3) § 43(a) of the Lanham Act, 15 U.S.C. § 1125(a). The district court granted summary judgment against White on each of her claims. White now appeals.

I. Section 3344

White first argues that the district court erred in rejecting her claim under section 3344. Section 3344(a) provides, in pertinent part, that "[a]ny person who knowingly uses another's name, voice, signature, photograph, or likeness, in any manner, . . . for purposes of advertising or selling, . . . without such person's prior consent . . . shall be liable for any damages sustained by the person or persons injured as a result thereof."

White argues that the Samsung advertisement used her "likeness" in contravention of section 3344. In *Midler v. Ford Motor Co.*, 849 F.2d 460 (9th Cir.1988), this court rejected Bette Midler's section 3344 claim concerning a Ford television commercial in which a Midler "sound-alike" sang a song which Midler had made famous. In rejecting Midler's claim, this court noted that "[t]he defendants did not use Midler's name or anything else whose use is prohibited by the statute. The voice they used was [another person's], not hers. The term 'likeness' refers to a visual image not a vocal imitation.''

In this case, Samsung and Deutsch used a robot with mechanical features, and not, for example, a manikin molded to White's precise features. Without deciding for all purposes when a caricature or impressionistic resemblance might become a "likeness," we agree with the district court that the robot at issue here was not White's "likeness" within the meaning of section 3344. Accordingly, we affirm the court's dismissal of White's section 3344 claim.

II.   Right of Publicity

White next argues that the district court erred in granting summary judgment to defendants on White's common law right of publicity claim. In *Eastwood v. Superior Court,* 149 Cal.App.3d 409, 198 Cal.Rptr. 342 (1983), the California court of appeal stated that the common law right of publicity cause of action "may be pleaded by alleging (1) the defendant's use of the plaintiff's identity; (2) the appropriation of plaintiff's name or likeness to defendant's advantage, commercially or otherwise; (3) lack of consent; and (4) resulting injury." *Id.* at 417, 198 Cal.Rptr. 342. The district court dismissed White's claim for failure to satisfy *Eastwood's* second prong, reasoning that defendants had not appropriated White's "name or likeness" with their robot ad. We agree that the robot ad did not make use of White's name or likeness. However, the common law right of publicity is not so confined.

The *Eastwood* court did not hold that the right of publicity cause of action could be pleaded only by alleging an appropriation of name or likeness. *Eastwood* involved an unauthorized use of photographs of Clint Eastwood and of his name. Accordingly, the *Eastwood* court had no occasion to consider the extent beyond the use of name or likeness to which the right of publicity reaches. That court held only that the right of publicity cause of action "may be" pleaded by alleging, *inter alia,* appropriation of name or likeness, not that the action may be pleaded *only* in those terms.

* * *

[The subsequent case law indicates] that the right of publicity is not limited to the appropriation of name or likeness. In *Motschenbacher v. R.J. Reynolds Tobacco Co.,* 498 F.2d 821 (9th Cir.1974), the defendant had used a photograph of the plaintiff's race car in a television commercial. Although the plaintiff appeared driving the car in the photograph, his features were not visible. Even though the defendant had not appropriated the plaintiff's name or likeness, this court held that plaintiff's California right of publicity claim should reach the jury.

In *Midler*, this court held that, even though the defendants had not used Midler's name or likeness, Midler had stated a claim for violation of her California common law right of publicity because "the defendants . . .

for their own profit in selling their product did appropriate part of her identity" by using a Midler sound-alike.

In *Carson v. Here's Johnny Portable Toilets, Inc.*, 698 F.2d 831 (6th Cir.1983), the defendant had marketed portable toilets under the brand name "Here's Johnny"—Johnny Carson's signature "Tonight Show" introduction—without Carson's permission. The district court had dismissed Carson's Michigan common law right of publicity claim because the defendants had not used Carson's "name or likeness." In reversing the district court, the sixth circuit found "the district court's conception of the right of publicity . . . too narrow" and held that the right was implicated because the defendant had appropriated Carson's identity by using, *inter alia*, the phrase "Here's Johnny."

These cases teach not only that the common law right of publicity reaches means of appropriation other than name or likeness, but that the specific means of appropriation are relevant only for determining whether the defendant has in fact appropriated the plaintiff's identity. The right of publicity does not require that appropriations of identity be accomplished through particular means to be actionable. It is noteworthy that the *Midler* and *Carson* defendants not only avoided using the plaintiff's name or likeness, but they also avoided appropriating the celebrity's voice, signature, and photograph. The photograph in *Motschenbacher* did include the plaintiff, but because the plaintiff was not visible the driver could have been an actor or dummy and the analysis in the case would have been the same.

Although the defendants in these cases avoided the most obvious means of appropriating the plaintiffs' identities, each of their actions directly implicated the commercial interests which the right of publicity is designed to protect. As the *Carson* court explained:

> [t]he right of publicity has developed to protect the commercial interest of celebrities in their identities. The theory of the right is that a celebrity's identity can be valuable in the promotion of products, and the celebrity has an interest that may be protected from the unauthorized commercial exploitation of that identity. . . . If the celebrity's identity is commercially exploited, there has been an invasion of his right whether or not his "name or likeness" is used.

Carson, 698 F.2d at 835. It is not important *how* the defendant has appropriated the plaintiff's identity, but *whether* the defendant has done so. *Motschenbacher, Midler*, and *Carson* teach the impossibility of treating the right of publicity as guarding only against a laundry list of specific means of appropriating identity. A rule which says that the right of publicity can be infringed only through the use of nine different methods of appropriating identity merely challenges the clever advertising strategist to come up with the tenth.

Indeed, if we treated the means of appropriation as dispositive in our analysis of the right of publicity, we would not only weaken the right but effectively eviscerate it. The right would fail to protect those plaintiffs most in need of its protection. Advertisers use celebrities to promote their products. The more popular the celebrity, the greater the number of people who recognize her, and the greater the visibility for the product. The identities of the most popular celebrities are not only the most attractive for advertisers, but also the easiest to evoke without resorting to obvious means such as name, likeness, or voice.

Consider a hypothetical advertisement which depicts a mechanical robot with male features, an African–American complexion, and a bald head. The robot is wearing black hightop Air Jordan basketball sneakers, and a red basketball uniform with black trim, baggy shorts, and the number 23 (though not revealing "Bulls" or "Jordan" lettering). The ad depicts the robot dunking a basketball one-handed, stiff-armed, legs extended like open scissors, and tongue hanging out. Now envision that this ad is run on television during professional basketball games. Considered individually, the robot's physical attributes, its dress, and its stance tell us little. Taken together, they lead to the only conclusion that any sports viewer who has registered a discernible pulse in the past five years would reach: the ad is about Michael Jordan.

Viewed separately, the individual aspects of the advertisement in the present case say little. Viewed together, they leave little doubt about the celebrity the ad is meant to depict. The female-shaped robot is wearing a long gown, blond wig, and large jewelry. Vanna White dresses exactly like this at times, but so do many other women. The robot is in the process of turning a block letter on a game-board. Vanna White dresses like this while turning letters on a game-board but perhaps similarly attired Scrabble-playing women do this as well. The robot is standing on what looks to be the Wheel of Fortune game show set. Vanna White dresses like this, turns letters, and does this on the Wheel of Fortune game show. She is the only one. Indeed, defendants themselves referred to their ad as the "Vanna White" ad. We are not surprised.

Television and other media create marketable celebrity identity value. Considerable energy and ingenuity are expended by those who have achieved celebrity value to exploit it for profit. The law protects the celebrity's sole right to exploit this value whether the celebrity has achieved her fame out of rare ability, dumb luck, or a combination thereof. We decline Samsung and Deutch's invitation to permit the evisceration of the common law right of publicity through means as facile as those in this case. Because White has alleged facts showing that Samsung and Deutsch had appropriated her identity, the district court erred by rejecting, on summary judgment, White's common law right of publicity claim.

[The court also reversed the district court's grant of summary judgement against White's Lanham Act § 43(a) claim.]

IV. THE PARODY DEFENSE

In defense, defendants cite a number of cases for the proposition that their robot ad constituted protected speech. The only cases they cite which are even remotely relevant to this case are *Hustler Magazine v. Falwell*, 485 U.S. 46, 108 S.Ct. 876, 99 L.Ed.2d 41 (1988), and *L.L. Bean, Inc. v. Drake Publishers, Inc.*, 811 F.2d 26 (1st Cir.1987). Those cases involved parodies of advertisements run for the purpose of poking fun at Jerry Falwell and L.L. Bean, respectively. This case involves a true advertisement run for the purpose of selling Samsung VCRs. The ad's spoof of Vanna White and Wheel of Fortune is subservient and only tangentially related to the ad's primary message: "buy Samsung VCRs." Defendants' parody arguments are better addressed to non-commercial parodies.[3] The difference between a "parody" and a "knock-off" is the difference between fun and profit.

V.   CONCLUSION

In remanding this case, we hold only that White has pleaded claims which can go to the jury for its decision.

ALARCON, CIRCUIT JUDGE, concurring in part, dissenting in part:

* * *

In each of the federal cases relied upon by the majority, the advertisement affirmatively represented that the person depicted therein was the plaintiff. In this case, it is clear that a metal robot and not the plaintiff, Vanna White, is depicted in the commercial advertisement. The record does not show an appropriation of Vanna White's identity.

In *Motschenbacher*, a picture of a well-known race driver's car, including its unique markings, was used in an advertisement. Although the driver could be seen in the car, his features were not visible. The distinctive markings on the car were the only information shown in the ad regarding the identity of the driver. These distinctive markings compelled the inference that Motschenbacher was the person sitting in the racing car. We concluded that "California appellate courts would ... afford legal protection to an individual's proprietary interest in his own identity."

---

3. In warning of a first amendment chill to expressive conduct, the dissent reads this decision too broadly. This case concerns only the market which exists in our society for the exploitation of celebrity to sell products, and an attempt to take a free ride on a celebrity's celebrity value. Commercial advertising which relies on celebrity fame is different from other forms of expressive activity in two crucial ways.

First, for celebrity exploitation advertising to be effective, the advertisement must evoke the celebrity's identity. The more effective the evocation, the better the advertisement. If, as Samsung claims, its ad was based on a "generic" game-show hostess and not on Vanna White, the ad would not have violated anyone's right of publicity, but it would also not have been as humorous or as effective.

Second, even if some forms of expressive activity, such as parody, do rely on identity evocation, the first amendment hurdle will bar most right of publicity actions against those activities. In the case of commercial advertising, however, the first amendment hurdle is not so high. *Central Hudson Gas & Electric Corp. v. Public Service Comm'n of New York*, 447 U.S. 557, 566, 100 S.Ct. 2343, 2351, 65 L.Ed.2d 341 (1980). Realizing this, Samsung attempts to elevate its ad above the status of garden-variety commercial speech by pointing to the ad's parody of Vanna White. Samsung's argument is unavailing. Unless the first amendment bars all right of publicity actions—and it does not, *see Zacchini v. Scripps–Howard Broadcasting Co.*, 433 U.S. 562, 97 S.Ct. 2849, 53 L.Ed.2d 965 (1977)—then it does not bar this case.

Because the distinctive markings on the racing car were sufficient to identify Motschenbacher as the driver of the car, we held that an issue of fact had been raised as to whether his identity had been appropriated.

In *Midler v. Ford Motor Co.*, 849 F.2d 460 (9th Cir.1988), a singer who had been instructed to sound as much like Bette Midler as possible, sang a song in a radio commercial made famous by Bette Midler. A number of persons told Bette Midler that they thought that she had made the commercial. Aside from the voice, there was no information in the commercial from which the singer could be identified. We noted that "[t]he human voice is one of the most palpable ways identity is manifested." We held that, "[t]o impersonate her voice is to pirate her identity," and concluded that Midler had raised a question of fact as to the misappropriation of her identity.

In *Carson v. Here's Johnny Portable Toilets, Inc.*, 698 F.2d 831 (6th Cir.1983), the Sixth Circuit was called upon to interpret Michigan's common-law right to publicity. The case involved a manufacturer who used the words, "Here's Johnny," on portable toilets. These same words were used to introduce the star of a popular late-night television program. There was nothing to indicate that this use of the phrase on the portable toilets was not associated with Johnny Carson's television program. The court found that "[h]ere there was an appropriation of Carson's identity," which violated the right to publicity.

The common theme in these federal cases is that identifying characteristics unique to the plaintiffs were used in a context in which they were the only information as to the identity of the individual. The commercial advertisements in each case showed attributes of the plaintiff's identities which made it appear that the plaintiff was the person identified in the commercial. No effort was made to dispel the impression that the plaintiffs were the source of the personal attributes at issue. The commercials affirmatively represented that the plaintiffs were involved. * * * The proper interpretation of *Motschenbacher*, *Midler*, and *Carson* is that where identifying characteristics unique to a plaintiff are the only information as to the identity of the person appearing in an ad, a triable issue of fact has been raised as to whether his or her identity has been appropriated.

The case before this court is distinguishable from the factual showing made in *Motschenbacher*, *Midler*, and *Carson*. It is patently clear to anyone viewing the commercial advertisement that Vanna White was not being depicted. No reasonable juror could confuse a metal robot with Vanna White.

The majority contends that "the individual aspects of the advertisement ... [v]iewed together leave little doubt about the celebrity the ad is meant to depict." It derives this conclusion from the fact that Vanna White is "the only one" who "dresses like this, turns letters, and does this on the Wheel of Fortune game show." In reaching this conclusion, the majority confuses Vanna White, the person, with the role she has assumed as the current hostess on the "Wheel of Fortune" television game show. A recognition of the distinction between a performer and the part he or she plays is essential for a proper analysis of the facts of this case. As is discussed below, those things which Vanna White claims identify her are not unique to her. They are, instead, attributes of the role she plays. The representation of those attributes, therefore, does not constitute a representation of Vanna White.

Vanna White is a one-role celebrity. She is famous solely for appearing as the hostess on the "Wheel of Fortune" television show. There is nothing unique about Vanna White or the attributes which she claims identify her. Although she appears to be an attractive woman, her face and figure are no more distinctive than that of other equally comely women. She performs her role as hostess on "Wheel of Fortune" in a simple and straight-forward manner. Her work does not require her to display whatever artistic talent she may possess.

The majority appears to argue that because Samsung created a robot with the physical proportions of an attractive woman, posed it gracefully, dressed it in a blond wig, an evening gown, and jewelry, and placed it on a set that resembles the Wheel of Fortune layout, it thereby appropriated Vanna White's identity. But an attractive appearance, a graceful pose, blond hair, an evening gown, and jewelry are attributes shared by many women, especially in Southern California. These common attributes are particularly evident among game-show hostesses, models, actresses, singers, and other women in the entertainment field. They are not unique attributes of Vanna White's identity. Accordingly, I cannot join in the majority's conclusion that, even if viewed together, these attributes identify Vanna White and, therefore, raise a triable issue as to the appropriation of her identity.

The only characteristic in the commercial advertisement that is not common to many female performers or celebrities is the imitation of the "Wheel of Fortune" set. This set is the only thing which might possibly lead a viewer to think of Vanna White. The Wheel of Fortune set, however, is not an attribute of Vanna White's identity. It is an identifying characteristic of a television game show, a prop with which Vanna White interacts in her role as the current hostess. To say that Vanna White may bring an action when another blond female performer or robot appears on such a set as a hostess will, I am sure, be a surprise to the owners of the show. * * *

[T]he fact that an actor or actress became famous for playing a particular role has, until now, never been sufficient to give the performer a proprietary interest in it. I cannot agree with the majority that the California courts, which have consistently taken a narrow view of the right to publicity, would extend the law to these unique facts.

   * * *

1. _Identifying the plaintiff._ The _White_ case addresses the issue of _how_ the plaintiff was identified. There seemed little question that she had in fact been identified to the public through the defendant's advertisement, by virtue of the combination of the robot's dress, hair, jewelry and the Wheel of Fortune setting.

Obviously the defendant's use must evoke the plaintiff's identity before a right of publicity cause of action will lie. Thus, for example, if a photograph of the plaintiff has been used, a person viewing the photograph should be able to identify the plaintiff without special visual aids. See, e.g., Cal. Civ. Code § 3344(b) (West 2010). Likewise, if the plaintiff's name has been used, it must appear from the total context that the plaintiff, rather than someone else, is being identified. See, e.g., Hooker v. Columbia Pictures Industries, Inc., 551 F.Supp. 1060 (N.D.Ill.1982) (finding that use of "T.J. Hooker" for a fictitious television policeman did not identify T.J. Hooker the woodcarver). The issue of identifiability ultimately is an issue of fact. While the common law does not appear to impose an intent requirement, evidence that the defendant in fact intended to identify the plaintiff may support a finding that he succeeded in doing so. See Restatement (Third) of Unfair Competition § 46, cmts d and e (1995).

How many people must be able to identify the plaintiff? While most right of publicity plaintiffs are "celebrities," celebrity status is not mandatory. See, e.g., Restatement (Third), _supra,_ § 46, cmt d ("The identity of even an unknown person may possess commercial value. Thus, an evaluation of the relative fame of the plaintiff is more properly relevant to the determination of appropriate relief"). Should a different (lower) standard of identifiability be applied in the case of non-celebrity plaintiffs?

The majority in _White_ holds that the means by which a defendant appropriates or "evokes" the plaintiff's identity is not determinative. Is this broad rule consistent with the purposes of the publicity cause of action identified in Justice Bird's dissent in _Lugosi_? Does the result in the _White_ case efficiently promote those purposes? If your answer is no, how would you alter the rule? Should the cause of action be restricted to appropriation of the plaintiff's name or likeness? If so, would use of a plaintiff's nickname suffice? See Hirsch v. S.C. Johnson & Son, Inc., 90 Wis.2d 379, 280 N.W.2d 129 (1979). How about a cartoon characterization? See Ali v. Playgirl, Inc., 447 F.Supp. 723 (S.D.N.Y.1978). What about a photograph of a look-alike? See Onassis v. Christian Dior–New York, Inc., 122 Misc.2d 603, 472 N.Y.S.2d 254 (1984), _affirmed,_ 110 A.D.2d 1095, 488 N.Y.S.2d 943 (1985). Putting aside the issue of the descendability of rights, what if the defendant used a bad Elvis impersonator in its ad, who very clearly was not Elvis, or even Elvis returned from the dead?

What if the defendant evoked the plaintiff's identity, but included a disclaimer in the advertisement making it clear that the image or sound being projected was not, in fact, the plaintiff, and that plaintiff was not in any way associated with the advertiser? Would this be sufficient to avoid liability under the majority view in *White*? Under Judge Alarcon's view? Should it be?

2. *The doctrine of first sale.* In Allison v. Vintage Sports Plaques, 136 F.3d 1443 (11th Cir.1998), the Court of Appeals for the Eleventh Circuit found that the doctrine of first sale (or doctrine of exhaustion), which has routinely been applied in the law of patents, copyrights, and trademarks, also limits the common-law right of publicity. In *Allison*, the defendant purchased sports trading cards that had been made with the plaintiff sports figures' authorization, placed the cards in frames, some of which incorporated clocks, and resold them. The Eleventh Circuit determined that the "gist" of the defendant's actions was merely to resell the cards, not to use the plaintiffs' names and likenesses to sell frames and clocks. Thus, the doctrine of first sale sheltered the defendant from liability.

3. *Descendability.* As the *Haelan* opinion suggests, the transferability, and particularly the descendability of the right of publicity to a celebrity's beneficiaries or next of kin, has posed some difficulties. The problem stems from the traditional link between the right of publicity and the right of privacy, discussed earlier. Because privacy rights are personal in nature, and protect the holder's interest in dignity, reputation, and peace of mind, they end upon his death. This fact has led some jurisdictions to hold that publicity rights die with the holder, as well.

The majority of jurisdictions to consider this question, however, have reasoned that since the right of publicity primarily protects economic, rather than personal interests, it should be treated like other economic rights, such as copyrights and trademarks, which do descend. Some jurisdictions have reached this result through judicial opinion, while others have enacted statutes to that effect. Does continuation of publicity rights after the holder's death appreciably further the purposes of the cause of action? Are there convincing arguments that could be made against descendability?

Once it is determined that a right of publicity descends, the question arises whether it has any durational limit. For example, if a drawing of Ben Franklin were used in an advertisement today, would his descendants have a cause of action? Should they? Or should some cut-off be devised? The majority in *Lugosi* recognized this problem and cited the difficulty in "judicially selecting an appropriate durational limitation" as a justification for finding that the right is not descendible. *Lugosi*, 25 Cal.3d at 824. In her dissent, Justice Bird agreed that the duration of the right should be limited, but argued that this should pose no barrier to finding that the right descends. She looked to the duration of federal copyright for guidance in specifying the term of post-mortem publicity rights. 25 Cal.3d at 847 (Bird, C.J., dissenting).

Several state legislatures appear to have found Justice Bird's reasoning persuasive, for they have limited statutory post mortem publicity rights to 50 (or now, 70) years. See, e.g., Nev. Rev. Stat. § 597.790 (West 2010). Indeed, after the California Supreme Court's opinion in *Lugosi,* that State's legislature enacted a new descendible statutory right of publicity that would exist for up to fifty (subsequently augmented to seventy) years after the personality's death. Cal. Civ. Code § 3344.1 (2010). A few states, however, have deviated from this approach. Oklahoma, for example, recognizes the post mortem right for 100 years, Okla. Stat. Ann. tit. 12, § 1448 (West 2010), while Tennessee recognizes a right for ten years and however long thereafter the right continues to be commercially exploited. Tenn. Code Ann. § 47–25–1104 (West 2010). This lack of uniformity may make national marketing campaigns more difficult.

PROBLEM

1. "Guzzle" is a highly popular nationally broadcast sit-com which centers on a neighborhood bar and the bar's regular patrons. The sit-com has run with high ratings for a solid decade. Jerry Kane and John Schwartz, both relatively unknown young actors, achieved celebrity status through their portrayal of two of the regular Guzzle barflies, named "Katz" and "Dolittle." Kane and Schwartz have played "Katz" and "Dolittle" for the entire run of the program. Their characters always occupy certain seats at the end of the Guzzle bar. Productions, Inc., which owns the copyright in the Guzzle programs, licenses Airports, Inc. to operate a chain of airport bars designed to look like the bar in the Guzzle series. Airports' "Guzzle" bar decor includes two life-size moving robotic figures seated in the customary Katz and Dolittle seats at the end of the bar. Airports, Inc. calls the figures "Jones" and "Smith." The robotic figures' facial features differ from those of Kane and Schwartz and the characters they played. Kane and Schwartz sue Airports, Inc. for violation of their right of publicity. How should the court resolve the claim?

III. THE RIGHT OF PUBLICITY AND FIRST AMENDMENT RIGHTS

WHITE v. SAMSUNG ELECTRONICS AMERICA, INC.

United States Court of Appeals for the Ninth Circuit, 1993.
989 F.2d 1512.

* * *

The petition for rehearing is DENIED and the suggestion for rehearing en banc is REJECTED.

KOZINSKI, CIRCUIT JUDGE, with whom CIRCUIT JUDGES O'SCANNLAIN and KLEINFELD join, dissenting from the order rejecting the suggestion for rehearing en banc.

I

Saddam Hussein wants to keep advertisers from using his picture in unflattering contexts. Clint Eastwood doesn't want tabloids to write about him. Rudolf Valentino's heirs want to control his film biography. The Girl Scouts don't want their image soiled by association with certain activities. George Lucas wants to keep Strategic Defense Initiative fans from calling it "Star Wars." Pepsico doesn't want singers to use the word "Pepsi" in their songs. Guy Lombardo wants an exclusive property right to ads that show big bands playing on New Year's Eve. Uri Geller thinks he should be paid for ads showing psychics bending metal through telekinesis. Paul Prudhomme, that household name, thinks the same about ads featuring corpulent bearded chefs. And scads of copyright holders see purple when their creations are made fun of.

Something very dangerous is going on here. Private property, including intellectual property, is essential to our way of life. It provides an incentive for investment and innovation; it stimulates the flourishing of our culture; it protects the moral entitlements of people to the fruits of their labors. But reducing too much to private property can be bad medicine. Private land, for instance, is far more useful if separated from other private land by public streets, roads and highways. Public parks, utility rights-of-way and sewers reduce the amount of land in private hands, but vastly enhance the value of the property that remains.

So too it is with intellectual property. Overprotecting intellectual property is as harmful as underprotecting it. Creativity is impossible without a rich public domain. Nothing today, likely nothing since we tamed fire, is genuinely new: Culture, like science and technology, grows by accretion, each new creator building on the works of those who came before. Overprotection stifles the very creative forces it's supposed to nurture.

The panel's opinion is a classic case of overprotection. Concerned about what it sees as a wrong done to Vanna White, the panel majority erects a property right of remarkable and dangerous breadth: Under the majority's opinion, it's now a tort for advertisers to *remind* the public of a celebrity. Not to use a celebrity's name, voice, signature or likeness; not to imply the celebrity endorses a product; but simply to evoke the celebrity's image in the public's mind. This Orwellian notion withdraws far more from the public domain than prudence and common sense allow. It conflicts with the Copyright Act and the Copyright Clause. It raises serious First Amendment problems. It's bad law, and it deserves a long, hard second look.

    * * *

III

* * * Intellectual property rights aren't like some constitutional rights, absolute guarantees protected against all kinds of interference, subtle as well as blatant. They cast no penumbras, emit no emanations: The very point of intellectual property laws is that they protect only against certain specific kinds of appropriation. I can't publish unauthorized copies of, say, *Presumed Innocent*; I can't make a movie out of it. But I'm perfectly free to write a book about an idealistic young prosecutor on trial for a crime he didn't commit. So what if I got the idea from *Presumed Innocent*? So what if it reminds readers of the original? Have I "eviscerated" Scott Turow's intellectual property rights? Certainly not. All creators draw in part on the work of those who came before, referring to it, building on it, poking fun at it; we call this creativity, not piracy.

The majority isn't, in fact, preventing the "evisceration" of Vanna White's existing rights; it's creating a new and much broader property right, a right unknown in California law. It's replacing the existing balance between the interests of the celebrity and those of the public by a different balance, one substantially more favorable to the celebrity. Instead of having an exclusive right in her name, likeness, signature or voice, every famous person now has an exclusive right to *anything that reminds the viewer of her*. After all, that's all Samsung did: It used an inanimate object to remind people of White, to "evoke [her identity]."[17]

Consider how sweeping this new right is. What is it about the ad that makes people think of White? It's not the robot's wig, clothes or jewelry; there must be ten million blond women (many of them quasi-famous) who wear dresses and jewelry like White's. It's that the robot is posed near the "Wheel of Fortune" game board. Remove the game board from the ad, and no one would think of Vanna White. *See* Appendix. But once you include the game board, anybody standing beside it—a brunette woman, a man wearing women's clothes, a monkey in a wig and gown—would evoke White's image, precisely the way the robot did. It's the "Wheel of Fortune" set, not the robot's face or dress or jewelry that evokes White's image. The panel is giving White an exclusive right not in what she looks like or who she is, but in what she does for a living.[18]

This is entirely the wrong place to strike the balance. Intellectual property rights aren't free: They're imposed at the expense of future creators and of the public at large. Where would we be if Charles Lindbergh had an exclusive right in the concept of a heroic solo aviator? If Arthur Conan Doyle had gotten a copyright in the idea of the detective story, or Albert Einstein had patented the theory of relativity? If every author and celebrity had been given the right to keep people from mocking them or their work? Surely this would have made the world poorer, not richer, culturally as well as economically. This is why intellectual property law is full of careful balances between what's set aside for the owner and what's left in the public domain for the rest of us: The relatively short life of patents; the longer, but finite, life of copyrights; copyright's idea-expression dichotomy; the fair use doctrine; the prohibition on copyrighting facts; the compulsory license of television broadcasts and musical compositions; federal preemption of overbroad state intellec-

---

17. Some viewers might have inferred White was endorsing the product, but that's a different story. The right of publicity isn't aimed at or limited to false endorsements; that's what the Lanham Act is for. Note also that the majority's rule applies even to advertisements that unintentionally remind people of someone. California law is crystal clear that the common-law right of publicity may be violated even by unintentional appropriations.

18. Once the right of publicity is extended beyond specific physical characteristics, this will become a recurring problem: Outside name, likeness and voice, the things that most reliably remind the public of celebrities are the actions or roles they're famous for. A commercial with an astronaut setting foot on the moon would evoke the image of Neil Armstrong. Any masked man on horseback would remind people (over a certain age) of Clayton Moore. And any number of songs—"My Way," "Yellow Submarine," "Like a Virgin," "Beat It," "Michael, Row the Boat Ashore," to name only a few—instantly evoke an image of the person or group who made them famous, regardless of who is singing.

* * *

tual property laws; the nominative use doctrine in trademark law; the right to make soundalike recordings. All of these diminish an intellectual property owner's rights. All let the public use something created by someone else. But all are necessary to maintain a free environment in which creative genius can flourish.

The intellectual property right created by the panel here has none of these essential limitations: No fair use exception; no right to parody; no idea-expression dichotomy. It impoverishes the public domain, to the detriment of future creators and the public at large. Instead of well-defined, limited characteristics such as name, likeness or voice, advertisers will now have to cope with vague claims of "appropriation of identity," claims often made by people with a wholly exaggerated sense of their own fame and significance. Future Vanna Whites might not get the chance to create their personae, because their employers may fear some celebrity will claim the persona is too similar to her own. The public will be robbed of parodies of celebrities, and our culture will be deprived of the valuable safety valve that parody and mockery create.

Moreover, consider the moral dimension, about which the panel majority seems to have gotten so exercised. Saying Samsung "appropriated" something of White's begs the question: *Should* White have the exclusive right to something as broad and amorphous as her "identity"? Samsung's ad didn't simply copy White's schtick—like all parody, it created something new. True, Samsung did it to make money, but White does whatever she does to make money, too; the majority talks of "the difference between fun and profit," but in the entertainment industry fun is profit. Why is Vanna White's right to exclusive for-profit use of her persona—a persona that might not even be her own creation, but that of a writer, director or producer—superior to Samsung's right to profit by creating its own inventions? Why should she have such absolute rights to control the conduct of others, unlimited by the idea-expression dichotomy or by the fair use doctrine?

To paraphrase only slightly *Feist Publications, Inc. v. Rural Telephone Service Co.*, 499 U.S. 340, 349, 111 S.Ct. 1282, 1289–90, 113 L.Ed.2d 358 (1991), it may seem unfair that much of the fruit of a creator's labor may be used by others without compensation. But this is not some unforeseen byproduct of our intellectual property system; it is the system's very essence. Intellectual property law assures authors the right to their original expression, but encourages others to build freely on the ideas that underlie it. This result is neither unfair nor unfortunate: It is the means by which intellectual property law advances the progress of science and art. We give authors certain exclusive rights, but in exchange we get a richer public domain. The majority ignores this wise teaching, and all of us are the poorer for it.

* * *

VI

Finally, I can't see how giving White the power to keep others from evoking her image in the public's mind can be squared with the First Amendment. Where does White get this right to control our thoughts? The majority's creation goes way beyond the protection given a trademark or a copyrighted work, or a person's name or likeness. All those things control one particular way of expressing an idea, one way of referring to an object or a person. But not allowing *any* means of reminding people of someone? That's a speech restriction unparalleled in First Amendment law.

What's more, I doubt even a name-and-likeness-only right of publicity can stand without a parody exception. The First Amendment isn't just about religion or politics—it's also about protecting the free development of our national culture. Parody, humor, irreverence are all vital components of the marketplace of ideas. The last thing we need, the last thing the First Amendment will tolerate, is a law that lets public figures keep people from mocking them, or from "evok[ing]" their images in the mind of the public.[29]

The majority dismisses the First Amendment issue out of hand because Samsung's ad was commercial speech. So what? Commercial speech may be less protected by the First Amendment than noncommercial speech, but less protected means protected nonetheless. And there are very good reasons for this. Commercial speech has a profound effect on our culture and our attitudes. Neutral-seeming ads influence people's social and political attitudes, and themselves arouse political controversy. "Where's the Beef?" turned from an advertising catchphrase into the only really memorable thing about the 1984 presidential campaign. Four years later, Michael Dukakis called George Bush "the Joe Isuzu of American politics."

In our pop culture, where salesmanship must be entertaining and entertainment must sell, the line between the commercial and noncommercial has not merely blurred; it has disappeared. Is the Samsung parody any different from a parody on Saturday Night Live or in Spy Magazine? Both are equally profit-motivated. Both use a celebrity's identity to sell things—one to sell VCRs, the other to sell advertising. Both mock their subjects. Both try to make people laugh. Both add something, perhaps something worthwhile and memorable, perhaps not, to our culture. Both are things that the people being portrayed might dearly want to suppress.

Commercial speech is a significant, valuable part of our national discourse. The Supreme Court has recognized as much, and has insisted

---

29. The majority's failure to recognize a parody exception to the right of publicity would apply equally to parodies of politicians as of actresses. Consider the case of Wok Fast, a Los Angeles Chinese food delivery service, which put up a billboard with a picture of then-L.A. Police Chief Daryl Gates and the text "When you can't leave the office. Or won't." (This was an allusion to Chief Gates's refusal to retire despite pressure from Mayor Tom Bradley.) Gates forced the restaurant to take the billboard down by threatening a right of publicity lawsuit.

See also Samsung Has Seen the Future: Brace Yourself, Adweek, Oct. 3, 1988, at 26 (ER 72) (Samsung planned another ad that would show a dollar bill with Richard Nixon's face on it and the caption "Dollar Bill, 2025 A.D. . . . ," but Nixon refused permission to use his likeness).

that lower courts carefully scrutinize commercial speech restrictions, but the panel totally fails to do this. The panel majority doesn't even purport to apply the *Central Hudson* test, which the Supreme Court devised specifically for determining whether a commercial speech restriction is valid. The majority doesn't ask, as *Central Hudson* requires, whether the speech restriction is justified by a substantial state interest. It doesn't ask whether the restriction directly advances the interest. It doesn't ask whether the restriction is narrowly tailored to the interest. These are all things the Supreme Court told us—in no uncertain terms—we must consider; the majority opinion doesn't even mention them.

     * * *

VII

For better or worse, we *are* the Court of Appeals for the Hollywood Circuit. Millions of people toil in the shadow of the law we make, and much of their livelihood is made possible by the existence of intellectual property rights. But much of their livelihood—and much of the vibrancy of our culture—also depends on the existence of other intangible rights: The right to draw ideas from a rich and varied public domain, and the right to mock, for profit as well as fun, the cultural icons of our time. In the name of avoiding the "evisceration" of a celebrity's rights in her image, the majority diminishes the rights of copyright holders and the public at large. In the name of fostering creativity, the majority suppresses it. Vanna White and those like her have been given something they never had before, and they've been given it at our expense. I cannot agree.

APPENDIX

Vanna White   Ms. C3PO?

NOTES AND QUESTIONS

1. *Commercial use and the First Amendment.* The advertisement in *White* undoubtedly was "commercial speech." As Judge Kozinski notes in his dissent, while commercial speech receives a lower level of First Amendment protection than other ("fully protected") varieties of speech, it nonetheless is subject to some protection. Should the First Amendment have protected Samsung's use of White's identity in its ad? If not, is there any case in which the First Amendment should shield a defendant who has used a plaintiff's identity in commercial advertising? How about the case of the Chinese restaurant advertisement invoking Police Chief Gates, described in Judge Kozinski's footnote 29? Should a political figure ever have a right of publicity cause of action?

A right of publicity cause of action arises when the defendant uses the plaintiff's identity for commercial purposes. If the defendant hopes to profit from the use, it is likely to be deemed a "use for commercial purposes." Indeed, unauthorized use of the plaintiff's identity to solicit contributions to nonprofit charitable organizations may qualify. See Restatement (Third) of Unfair Competition § 47, cmt a (1995). It is important to note, however, that the concept of "use for a commercial purpose" is broader than the concept of "commercial speech," as defined for First Amendment purposes. Thus, the right of publicity might be violated by "non-commercial speech," which is entitled to the fullest degree of First Amendment protection. The *Zacchini* case (discussed *supra*) illustrates that in such cases, the First Amendment may or may not prohibit the right of publicity claim, depending on the circumstances.

In *Zacchini*, the Ohio Supreme Court had held that the defendant's broadcast of the plaintiff's human cannonball act on the evening news was privileged under the First Amendment, so that the plaintiff's right of publicity claim must be dismissed. The United States Supreme Court agreed that the First Amendment was applicable in its full force, but reversed the Ohio court's judgment that it immunized the defendant from suit. The Court observed:

> The Ohio Supreme Court held that respondent is constitutionally privileged to include in its newscasts matters of public interest that would otherwise be protected by the right of publicity, absent an intent to injure or to appropriate for some nonprivileged purpose. If under this standard respondent had merely reported that petitioner was performing at the fair and described or commented on his act, with or without showing his picture on television, we would have a very different case. But petitioner is not contending that his appearance at the fair and his performance could not be reported by the press as newsworthy items. His complaint is that respondent filmed his entire act and displayed that film on television for the public to see and enjoy. This, he claimed, was an appropriation of his professional property.

Zacchini, 433 U.S. at 569. In finding that the First Amendment did not prohibit the right of publicity claim, the Court stressed several considerations, in addition to the fact that the defendant had broadcast the plaintiff's entire fifteen–second act. First, the state had an important interest in encouraging its residents to engage in creative activities for the entertainment of others. Second, the defendant's broadcast interfered with the plaintiff's ability to make a living as an entertainer. Moreover, permitting the suit would not deprive the public: The plaintiff did not seek to enjoin the broadcast of his performance, but only to recover damages as payment for the defendant's use of it. The Court explained: "The Constitution no more prevents a State from requiring respondent to compensate petitioner for broadcasting his act on television than it would privilege respondent to film and broadcast a copyrighted dramatic work without liability to the copyright owner." *Id.*, 433 U.S. at 575. The Court thus balanced the First Amendment interests against the interests of the state and of the plaintiff, taking into account the severity of the impact that permitting recovery would have on the public interest.

In cases involving right of publicity claims against uses constituting fully-protected (as opposed to commercial) speech, courts have sometimes engaged in an analysis analogous to the fair use defense analysis used in copyright infringement cases to evaluate the defendant's First Amendment interests. Why should the copyright fair use doctrine be relevant?

In *Comedy III Productions, Inc. v. Gary Saderup, Inc.*, 25 Cal.4th 387, 21 P.3d 797, 106 Cal.Rptr.2d 126 (2001), the California Supreme Court upheld statutory right of publicity claims brought by the heirs of The Three Stooges against an artist who produced and marketed T-shirts bearing a likeness of those comedians reproduced from the artist's charcoal drawing. In addressing the defendant's First Amendment defense, the court found that the portrait was an expressive work entitled to full First Amendment protection, and recognized that the case precedent called for a balancing of First Amendment interests against the interests of the individual and the state in protecting publicity rights.

> [The] inquiry into whether a work is "transformative" appears to us to be necessarily at the heart of any judicial attempt to square the right of publicity with the First Amendment. * * * When artistic expression takes the form of a literal depiction or imitation of a celebrity for commercial gain, directly trespassing on the right of publicity without adding significant expression beyond that trespass, the state interest in protecting the fruits of artistic labor outweighs the expressive interests of the imitative artist.

> On the other hand, when a work contains significant transformative elements, it is not only especially worthy of First Amendment protection, but it is also less likely to interfere with the economic interest protected by the right of publicity. As has been observed, works of parody or other distortions of the celebrity figure are not, from the celebrity fan's viewpoint, good substitutes for conventional depictions of the celebrity and therefore do not generally threaten markets for celebrity memorabilia that the right of publicity is designed to protect. Accordingly, First Amendment protection of such works outweighs whatever interest the state may have in enforcing the right of publicity. The right-of-publicity

holder continues to enforce the right to monopolize the production of conventional, more or less fungible, images of the celebrity.

* * *

Another way of stating the inquiry is whether the celebrity likeness is one of the "raw materials" from which an original work is synthesized, or whether the depiction or imitation of the celebrity is the very sum and substance of the work in question. We ask, in other words, whether a product containing a celebrity's likeness is so transformed that it has become primarily the defendant's own expression rather than the celebrity's likeness. And when we use the word "expression," we mean expression of something other than the likeness of the celebrity.

We further emphasize that in determining whether the work is transformative, courts are not to be concerned with the quality of the artistic contribution—vulgar forms of expression fully qualify for First Amendment protection. On the other hand, a literal depiction of a celebrity, even if accomplished with great skill, may still be subject to a right of publicity challenge. the inquiry is in a sense more quantitative than qualitative, asking whether the literal and imitative or the creative elements predominate in the work.

Furthermore, in determining whether a work is sufficiently transformative, courts may find useful a subsidiary inquiry, particularly in close cases: does the marketability and economic value of the challenged work derive primarily from the fame of the celebrity depicted? If this question is answered in the negative, then there would generally be no actionable right of publicity. When the value of the work comes principally from some source other than the fame of the celebrity—from the creativity, skill, and reputation of the artist—it may be presumed that sufficient transformative elements are present to warrant First Amendment protection. If the question is answered in the affirmative, however, it does not necessarily follow that the work is without First Amendment protection—it may still be a transformative work.

In sum, when an artist is faced with a right of publicity challenge to his or her work, he or she may raise as affirmative defense that the work is protected by the First Amendment inasmuch as it contains significant transformative elements or that the value of the work does not derive primarily from the celebrity's fame.

Comedy III Productions, 25 Cal.4th at 404–407.

In Doe v. TCI Cablevision, 110 S.W.3d 363 (Mo. 2003), the Missouri Supreme Court considered right of publicity claims brought by a former hockey star against the publisher of a comic book that had used the star's name as the name of one of the comic's characters. In evaluating the defendant's First Amendment defense, the court recognized the California Supreme Court's "transformative" standard, described above, and also considered the "relatedness" test employed by the Restatement (Third) of Unfair Competition § 47 cmt. c:

The Restatement * * * employs a "relatedness" test that protects the use of another person's name or identity in a work that is "related to" that

> person. The catalogue of "related" uses includes "the use of a person's name or likeness in news reporting . . . use in entertainment and other creative works, . . . use as part of an article published in a fan magazine or in a feature story broadcast on an entertainment program . . . dissemination of an unauthorized print or broadcast biography, [and use] of another's identity in a novel, play, or motion picture. . . ." Restatement (Third) of Unfair Competition sec. 47 cmt. c at 549. The proviso to that list, however, is that "if the name or likeness is used solely to attract attention to a work that is *not related* to the identified person, the user may be subject to liability for a use of the other's identity in advertising. . . ." *Id.* (Emphasis added.)

Doe, 110 S.W.3d at 373. The court went on to reject both the Restatement and the California approach:

> The weakness of the Restatement's "relatedness" test and California's "transformative" test is that they give too little consideration to the fact that many uses of a person's name and identity have both expressive and commercial components. These tests operate to preclude a cause of action whenever the use of the name and identity is in any way expressive, regardless of its commercial exploitation. Under the relatedness test, use of a person's name and identity is actionable only when the use is solely commercial and is otherwise unrelated to that person. Under the transformative test, the transformation or fictionalized characterization of a person's celebrity status is not actionable even if its sole purpose is the commercial use of that person's name and identity. Though these tests purport to balance the prospective interests involved, there is no balancing at all—once the use is determined to be expressive, it is protected. At least one commentator, however, has advocated the use of a more balanced balancing test—a sort of predominant use test—that better addresses the cases where speech is both expressive and commercial:

>> If a product is being sold that predominantly exploits the commercial value of an individual's identity, that product should be held to violate the right of publicity and not be protected by the First Amendment, even if there is some "expressive" content in it that might qualify as "speech" in other circumstances. If, on the other hand, the predominant purpose of the product is to make an expressive comment on or about a celebrity, the expressive values could be given greater weight.

> Lee, [*Agents of Chaos: Judicial Confusion in Defining the Right of Publicity–Free Speech Interface,* 23 Loy. L.A. Ent. L. Rev. 471, 500 (2003)].

Id., at 373–74. Applying this standard to evaluate the facts before it, the Missouri court found the defendant's use of the plaintiff's name to be unprotected under the First Amendment. The plaintiff demonstrated that the defendant used his name for commercial advantage (to attract hockey fans to buy the comic). The defendant argued that it had used the name as a "metaphorical reference to tough-guy enforcers," that is, to suggest that the comic book character bearing the plaintiff's name was, like the plaintiff, a "tough-guy enforcer." Nonetheless, the defendant conceded that the comic character was not intended to *be* the plaintiff or to constitute a parody or other commentary about the plaintiff. Under these circumstances, the court found that the predominant purpose in using the plaintiff's name was to sell comic books and related products rather than literary expression. Under these circumstances, the interest in protecting publicity rights outweighed First Amendment interests and thus should predominate.

Which approach makes most sense?

2. *Remedies.* Injunctions against further exploitation are standard in right of publicity actions, since damages frequently are inadequate to remedy a plaintiff's interest in controlling or developing her own public image, and may be difficult to measure even when appropriate. Moreover, commercial exploitation of the plaintiff's identity is often a continuing wrong. Preliminary injunctions may also be available, but courts' sensitivity to granting prior restraints on speech may preclude this remedy, especially in cases falling outside of the "commercial speech" context.

Monetary damages generally consist of the fair market value of the use of the plaintiff's identity. This value may be determined through evidence of what "comparable" personalities receive for "comparable" commercial uses of their identities, or through evidence of what plaintiff herself has received for licensing similar uses in the past. If the plaintiff is able to demonstrate that the defendant's use injured her ability to capitalize on her identity in the future (for example, by associating her with shabby products, thus decreasing demand for her future product endorsements), she may be able to recover for this projected loss of income, as well. In some jurisdictions the defendant's profit may be recovered, to the extent that it exceeds the plaintiff's loss, and punitive damages may be permitted in particularly egregious cases. See 2 J.T. McCarthy, The Rights of Publicity and Privacy §§ 11.30–11.36 (4th ed. & Supp.).

PROBLEMS

1. X, a professional artist, specializes in painting sports scenes. He travels to important sports events and creates paintings of the games and the top athletes at play. Recently, X traveled to an international golf tournament and created a painting that featured Y, the famous golfer who won the tournament, in the foreground and other golf greats and Y's caddie in the background. X entitled the print "The Masters of Golf" and sold rights to Publishing, Inc. to reproduce and sell 2,000 limited edition prints of the painting. Shortly thereafter, Y sued Publishing, Inc., alleging infringement of his publicity rights. How should the claim be resolved?

2. Defendant produces "The Big El Show," which is patterned after an actual Elvis Presley stage show, though on a lesser scale. In addition to an Elvis impersonator, who sings songs that Elvis made popular and imitates Elvis' appearance, dress, movements, singing voice and style, the show features a band that uses the same name as the real Elvis' band, and opens in a similar fashion to real Elvis stage show openings. The defendant advertises the show with a photograph of the impersonator, who is indistinguishable

from the real Elvis, and with statements such as "Reflections on a Legend . . . A Tribute to Elvis Presley", and "Looks and Sounds LIKE THE KING."

Assuming that the right of publicity descended to Elvis's estate on his death, and that Elvis's estate brings a right of publicity claim, how should the court rule? Is the production sheltered under the First Amendment?

PART FIVE

CONCLUDING CONSIDERATIONS

■ ■ ■

CHAPTER EIGHT

FEDERAL-STATE RELATIONS

■ ■ ■

I. SUPREMACY CLAUSE PREEMPTION

SEARS, ROEBUCK & CO. v. STIFFEL CO.

United States Supreme Court, 1964.
376 U.S. 225, 84 S.Ct. 784, 11 L.Ed.2d 661.

MR. JUSTICE BLACK delivered the opinion of the Court.

The question in this case is whether a State's unfair competition law can, consistently with the federal patent laws, impose liability for or prohibit the copying of an article which is protected by neither a federal patent nor a copyright. The respondent, Stiffel Company, secured design and mechanical patents on a "pole lamp"—a vertical tube having lamp fixtures along the outside, the tube being made so that it will stand upright between the floor and ceiling of a room. Pole lamps proved a decided commercial success, and soon after Stiffel brought them on the market Sears, Roebuck & Company put on the market a substantially identical lamp, which it sold more cheaply, Sears' retail price being about the same as Stiffel's wholesale price. Stiffel then brought this action against Sears in the United States District Court for the Northern District of Illinois, claiming in its first count that by copying its design Sears had infringed Stiffel's patents and in its second count that by selling copies of Stiffel's lamp Sears had caused confusion in the trade as to the source of the lamps and had thereby engaged in unfair competition under Illinois law. * * *

The District Court, after holding the patents invalid for want of invention, went on to find as a fact that Sears' lamp was "a substantially exact copy" of Stiffel's and that the two lamps were so much alike, both in appearance and in functional details, "that confusion between them is likely, and some confusion has already occurred." On these findings the court held Sears guilty of unfair competition, enjoined Sears "from unfairly competing with (Stiffel) by selling or attempting to sell pole lamps identical to or confusingly similar to" Stiffel's lamp, and ordered an accounting to fix profits and damages resulting from Sears' "unfair competition."

The Court of Appeals affirmed. That court held that, to make out a case of unfair competition under Illinois law, * * * Stiffel had only to prove that there was a "likelihood of confusion as to the source of the products"—that the two articles were sufficiently identical that customers could not tell who had made a particular one. Impressed by the "remarkable sameness of appearance" of the lamps, the Court of Appeals upheld the trial court's findings of likelihood of confusion and some actual confusion, findings which the appellate court construed to mean confusion "as to the source of the lamps." The Court of Appeals thought this enough under Illinois law to sustain the trial court's holding of unfair competition, and thus held Sears liable under Illinois law for doing no more than copying and marketing an unpatented article. * * *

Before the Constitution was adopted, some States had granted patents either by special act or by general statute, but when the Constitution was adopted provision for a federal patent law was made one of the enumerated powers of Congress because, as Madison put it in *The Federalist* No. 43, the States "cannot separately make effectual provision" for either patents or copyrights. That constitutional provision is Art. I, § 8, cl. 8, which empowers Congress "To promote the Progress of Science and useful Arts, by securing for limited Times to Authors and Inventors the exclusive Right to their respective Writings and Discoveries." Pursuant to this constitutional authority, Congress in 1790 enacted the first federal patent and copyright law, and ever since that time has fixed the condition upon which patents and copyrights shall be granted. These laws, like other laws of the United States enacted pursuant to constitutional authority, are the supreme law of the land. When state law touches upon the area of these federal statutes, it is "familiar doctrine" that the federal policy "may not be set at naught, or its benefits denied" by the state law. This is true, of course, even if the state law is enacted in the exercise of otherwise undoubted state power.

The grant of a patent is the grant of a statutory monopoly; indeed, the grant of patents in England was an explicit exception to the statute of James I prohibiting monopolies. Patents are not given as favors, as was the case of monopolies given by the Tudor monarchs, but are meant to encourage invention by rewarding the inventor with the right, limited to a term of years fixed by the patent, to exclude others from the use of his invention. During that period of time no one may make use, or sell the patented product without the patentee's authority. But in rewarding useful invention, the "rights and welfare of the community must be fairly dealt with and effectually guarded." To that end the prerequisites to obtaining a patent are strictly observed, and when the patent has issued the limitations on its exercise are equally strictly enforced. To begin with, a genuine "invention" or "discovery" must be demonstrated "lest in the constant demand for new appliances the heavy hand of tribute be laid on each slight technological advance in an art." Once the patent issues, it is strictly construed. It cannot be used to secure any monopoly beyond that contained in the patent, the patentee's control over the product when it leaves his hands is sharply limited, and the patent monopoly may not be used in disregard of the antitrust laws. Finally, and especially relevant here, when the patent expires the monopoly created by it expires, too, and the right to make the article—including the right to make it in precisely the shape it carried when patented—passes to the public.

Thus the patent system is one in which uniform federal standards are carefully used to promote invention while at the same time preserving free competition. Obviously a State could not, consistently with the Supremacy Clause of the Constitution, extend the life of a patent beyond its expiration date or give a patent on an article which lacked the level of invention required for federal patents. To do either would run counter to the policy of Congress of granting patents only to true inventions, and then only for a limited time. Just as a State cannot encroach upon the federal patent laws directly, it cannot, under some other law, such as that forbidding unfair competition, give protection of a kind that clashes with the objectives of the federal patent laws.

In the present case the "pole lamp" sold by Stiffel has been held not to be entitled to the protection of either a mechanical or a design patent. An unpatentable article, like an article on which the patent has expired, is in the public domain and may be made and sold by whoever chooses to do so. What Sears did was to copy Stiffel's design and to sell lamps almost identical to those sold by Stiffel. This it had every right to do under the federal patent laws. That Stiffel originated the pole lamp and made it popular is immaterial. "Sharing in the goodwill of an article unprotected by patent or trade-mark is the exercise of a right possessed by all—and in the free exercise of which the consuming public is deeply interested." To allow a State by use of its law of unfair competition to prevent the copying of an article which represents too slight an advance to be patented would be to permit the State to block off from the public something which federal law has said belongs to the public. The result would be that while federal law grants only 14 or 17 years' protection to genuine inventions, States could allow perpetual protection to articles too lacking in novelty to merit any patent at all under federal constitutional standards. This would be too great an encroachment on the federal patent system to be tolerated.

Sears has been held liable here for unfair competition because of a finding of likelihood of confusion based only on the fact that Sears' lamp was copied from Stiffel's unpatented lamp and that consequently the two looked exactly alike. Of course there could be "confusion" as to who had manufactured these nearly identical articles. But mere inability of the public to tell two identical articles apart is not enough to support an injunction against copying or an award of damages for copying that which the federal patent laws permit to be copied. Doubtless a State may, in appropriate circumstances, require that goods, whether patented or unpatented, be labeled or that other precautionary steps be taken to prevent customers from being misled as to the source, just as it may protect businesses in the use of their trademarks, labels, or distinctive dress in the packaging of goods so as to prevent others, by imitating such markings, from misleading purchasers as to the source of the goods. But because of the federal patent laws a State may not, when the article is unpatented and uncopyrighted, prohibit the copying of the article itself or award damages for such copying. The judgment below did both and in so doing gave Stiffel the equivalent of a patent monopoly on its unpatented lamp. That was error, and Sears is entitled to a judgment in its favor.

COMPCO CORP. v. DAY–BRITE LIGHTING, INC.

United States Supreme Court, 1964.
376 U.S. 234, 84 S.Ct. 779, 11 L.Ed.2d 669.

Mr. Justice Black delivered the opinion of the Court.

As in *Sears, Roebuck & Co. v. Stiffel Co.*, the question here is whether the use of a state unfair competition law to give relief against the copying of an unpatented industrial design conflicts with the federal patent laws. Both Compco and Day–Brite are manufacturers of fluorescent lighting fixtures of a kind widely used in offices and stores. Day–Brite in 1955 secured from the Patent Office a design patent on a reflector having cross-ribs claimed to give both strength and attractiveness to the fixture. Day–Brite also sought, but was refused, a mechanical patent on the same device. After Day–Brite had begun selling its fixture, Compco's predecessor began making and selling fixtures very similar to Day–Brite's. This action was then brought by Day–Brite. One count alleged that Compco had infringed Day–Brite's design patent; a second count charged that the public and the trade had come to associate this particular design with Day–Brite, that Compco had copied Day–Brite's distinctive design so as to confuse and deceive purchasers into thinking Compco's fixtures were actually Day–Brite's, and that by doing this Compco had unfairly competed with Day–Brite. The complaint prayed for both an accounting and an injunction.

The District Court held the design patent invalid; but as to the second count, while the court did not find that Compco had engaged in any deceptive or fraudulent practices, it did hold that Compco had been guilty of unfair competition under Illinois law. The court found that the overall appearance of Compco's fixture was "the same, to the eye of the ordinary observer, as the overall appearance" of Day–Brite's reflector, which embodied the design of the invalidated patent; that the appearance of Day–Brite's design had "the capacity to identify [Day–Brite] in the trade and does in fact so identify [it] to the trade"; that the concurrent sale of the two products was "likely to cause confusion in the trade"; and that "[a]ctual confusion has occurred." On these findings the court adjudged Compco guilty of unfair competition in the sale of its fixtures, ordered Compco to account to Day–Brite for damages, and enjoined Compco "from unfairly competing with plaintiff by the sale or attempted sale of reflectors identical to, or confusingly similar to" those made by Day–Brite. The Court of Appeals held there was substantial evidence in the record to support the District Court's finding of likely confusion and that this finding was sufficient to support a holding of unfair competition under Illinois law. Although the District Court had not made such a finding, the appellate court observed that "several choices of ribbing were apparently available to meet the functional needs of the product," yet Compco "chose precisely the same design used by the plaintiff and followed it so closely as to make confusion likely." A design which identifies its maker to the trade, the Court of Appeals held, is a "protectible" right under Illinois law, even though the design is unpatentable. * * *

　　* * *

Notwithstanding the thinness of the evidence to support findings of likely and actual confusion among purchasers, we do not find it necessary in this case to determine whether there is "clear error" in these findings. They, like those in *Sears, Roebuck & Co. v. Stiffel Co.*, were based wholly on the fact that selling an article which is an exact copy of another unpatented article is likely to produce and did in this case produce confusion as to the source of the article. Even accepting the findings, we hold that the order for an accounting for damages and the injunction are in conflict with the federal patent laws. Today we have held in *Sears, Roebuck & Co. v. Stiffel Co.* that when an article is unprotected by a patent or a copyright, state law may not forbid others to copy that article. To forbid copying would interfere with the federal policy, found in Art. I, § 8, cl. 8, of the Constitution and in the implementing federal statutes, of allowing free access to copy whatever the federal patent and copyright laws leave in the public domain. Here Day–Brite's fixture has been held not to be entitled to a design or mechanical patent. Under the federal patent laws it is, therefore, in the public domain and can be copied in every detail by whoever pleases. It is true that the trial court found that the configuration of Day–Brite's fixture identified Day–Brite to the trade because the arrangement of the ribbing had, like a trademark, acquired a "secondary meaning" by which that particular design was associated with Day–Brite. But if the design is not entitled to a design patent or other federal statutory protection, then it can be copied at will.

As we have said in *Sears*, while the federal patent laws prevent a State from prohibiting the copying and selling of unpatented articles, they do not stand in the way of state law, statutory or decisional, which requires those who make and sell copies to take precautions to identify their products as their own. A State of course has power to impose liability upon those who, knowing that the public is relying upon an original manufacturer's reputation for quality and integrity, deceive the public by palming off their copies as the original. That an article copied from an unpatented article could be made in some other way, that the design is "nonfunctional" and not essential to the use of either article, that the configuration of the article copied may have a "secondary meaning" which identifies the maker to the trade, or that there may be "confusion" among purchasers as to which article is which or as to who is the maker, may be relevant evidence in applying a State's law requiring such precautions as labeling; however, and regardless of the copier's motives, neither these facts nor any others can furnish a basis for imposing liability for or prohibiting the actual acts of copying and selling. * * *

Since the judgment below forbids the sale of a copy of an unpatented article and orders an accounting for damages for such copying, it cannot stand.

NOTES AND QUESTIONS

1. *The scope and impact of Sears and Compco.* The *Sears* and *Compco* decisions caused a considerable stir, since they could be construed to curtail a well established tradition of state law protection against the copying of distinctive, non-functional product features that create a likelihood of consumer confusion. A number of commentators criticized the decisions and speculated about their scope. Lower courts initially applied the decisions strictly to preempt state product feature trade dress infringement claims. However, subsequent Supreme Court decisions (set forth below), which seemed to retreat from the hard-line view set forth in *Sears* and *Compco*, encouraged some lower courts to find ways to distinguish *Sears* and *Compco* and uphold the state claims. How might one distinguish *Sears* and *Compco* in order to uphold state unfair competition protection of product features?

The Court had to decide in *Sears* and *Compco* whether enforcement of the state law would frustrate accomplishment of Congress' purposes in enacting the patent and copyright laws. What does the Supreme Court view Congress' purposes to be? Did the *Sears* and *Compco* cases involve functional or nonfunctional product features? Does it matter for purposes of the Court's opinions? Did the Court view the defendants' intent as a relevant consideration? Should it be? Is it relevant that the Lanham Act provides a cause of action against copying distinctive, non-functional product features that cause a likelihood of consumer confusion?

Could the language and reasoning of *Sears* and *Compco* be interpreted to preempt other state intellectual property causes of action? For example, what are the apparent implications of *Sears* and *Compco* for state trade secret claims? For state misappropriation causes of action? How about state right of publicity claims, or claims for undeveloped ideas?

KEWANEE OIL CO. v. BICRON CORP.

United States Supreme Court, 1974.
416 U.S. 470, 94 S.Ct. 1879, 40 L.Ed.2d 315.

MR. CHIEF JUSTICE BURGER delivered the opinion of the Court.

We granted certiorari to resolve a question on which there is a conflict in the courts of appeals: whether state trade secret protection is preempted by operation of the federal patent law. * * *

I

Harshaw Chemical Co., an unincorporated division of petitioner, is a leading manufacturer of a type of synthetic crystal which is useful in the detection of ionizing radiation. In 1949 Harshaw commenced research into the growth of this type crystal and was able to produce one less than two inches in diameter. By 1966, as the result of expenditures in excess of $1 million, Harshaw was able to grow a 17–inch crystal, something no one else had done previously. Harshaw had developed many processes, procedures, and manufacturing techniques in the purification of raw materials and the growth and encapsulation of the crystals which enabled it to accomplish this feat. Some of these processes Harshaw considers to be trade secrets.

The individual respondents are former employees of Harshaw who formed or later joined respondent Bicron. While at Harshaw the individual respondents executed, as a condition of employment, at least one agreement each, requiring them not to disclose confidential information or trade secrets obtained as employees of Harshaw. Bicron was formed in August 1969 to compete with Harshaw in the production of the crystals, and by April 1970, had grown a 17–inch crystal.

Petitioner brought this diversity action in United States District Court for the Northern District of Ohio seeking injunctive relief and damages for the misappropriation of trade secrets. The District Court, applying Ohio trade secret law, granted a permanent injunction against the disclosure or use by respondents of 20 of the 40 claimed trade secrets until such time as the trade secrets had been released to the public, had otherwise generally become available to the public, or had been obtained by respondents from sources having the legal right to convey the information.

The Court of Appeals for the Sixth Circuit held that the findings of fact by the District Court were not clearly erroneous, * * * [and that] the District Court properly applied Ohio law relating to trade secrets. Nevertheless, the Court of Appeals reversed the District Court, finding Ohio's trade secret law to be in conflict with the patent laws of the United States. The Court of Appeals reasoned that Ohio could not grant monopoly protection to processes and manufacturing techniques that were appropriate subjects for consideration under 35 U.S.C. § 101 for a federal patent but which had been in commercial use for over one year and so were no longer eligible for patent protection under 35 U.S.C. § 102(b).

We hold that Ohio's law of trade secrets is not preempted by the patent laws of the United States, and, accordingly, we reverse.

II

* * *

The subject of a trade secret must be secret, and must not be of public knowledge or of a general knowledge in the trade or business. This necessary element of secrecy is not lost, however, if the holder of the trade secret reveals the trade secret to another "in confidence, and under an implied obligation not to use or disclose it." These others may include those of the holder's "employees to whom it is necessary to confide it, in order to apply it to the uses for which it is intended." Often the recipient of confidential knowledge of the subject of a trade secret is a licensee of its holder.

The protection accorded the trade secret holder is against the disclosure or unauthorized use of the trade secret by those to whom the secret has been confided under the express or implied restriction of nondisclosure or nonuse. The law also protects the holder of a trade secret against disclosure or use when the knowledge is gained, not by the owner's volition, but by some "improper means," Restatement of Torts § 757(a), which may include theft, wiretapping, or even aerial reconnaissance. A trade secret law, however, does not offer protection against discovery by fair and honest means, such as by independent invention, accidental disclosure, or by so-called reverse engineering, that is by starting with the known product and working backward to divine the process which aided in its development or manufacture.

Novelty, in the patent law sense, is not required for a trade secret. * * * However, some novelty will be required if merely because that which does not possess novelty is usually known; secrecy, in the context of trade secrets, thus implies at least minimal novelty.

The subject matter of a patent is limited to a "process, machine, manufacture, or composition of matter, or ... improvement thereof," 35 U.S.C. § 101, which fulfills the three conditions of novelty and utility as articulated and defined in 35 U.S.C. §§ 101 and 102, and nonobviousness, as set out in 35 U.S.C. § 103. If an invention meets the rigorous statutory tests for the issuance of a patent, the patent is granted, for a period of 17 years * * *. This protection goes not only to copying the subject matter, which is forbidden under the Copyright Act, 17 U.S.C. § 1 et seq., but also to independent creation.

III

The first issue we deal with is whether the States are forbidden to act at all in the area of protection of the kinds of intellectual property which may make up the subject matter of trade secrets.

* * * In the 1972 Term, in *Goldstein v. California*, [412 U.S. 546, 93 S.Ct. 2303, 37 L.Ed.2d 163 (1973)] we held that the cl. 8 grant of power to Congress was not exclusive and that, at least in the case of writings, the States were not prohibited from encouraging and protecting the efforts of those within their borders by appropriate legislation. * * *

Just as the States may exercise regulatory power over writings so may the States regulate with respect to discoveries. States may hold diverse viewpoints in protecting intellectual property relating to invention as they do in protecting the intellectual property relating to the subject matter of copyright. The only limitation on the States is that in regulating the area of patents and copyrights they do not conflict with the operation of the laws in this area passed by Congress, and it is to that more difficult question we now turn.

IV

The question of whether the trade secret law of Ohio is void under the Supremacy Clause involves a consideration of whether that law "stands as an obstacle to the accomplishment and execution of the full purposes and objectives of Congress." *Hines v. Davidowitz*, 312 U.S. 52, 67, 61 S.Ct. 399, 404, 85 L.Ed. 581 (1941). We stated in *Sears, Roebuck & Co. v. Stiffel Co.*, that when state law touches upon the area of federal statutes enacted pursuant to constitutional authority, "it is 'familiar doctrine' that the federal policy 'may not be set at naught, or its benefits denied' by the state law. This is true, of course, even if the state law is enacted in the exercise of otherwise undoubted state power."

The laws which the Court of Appeals in this case held to be in conflict with the Ohio law of trade secrets were the patent laws passed by the Congress in the unchallenged exercise of its clear power under Art. I, § 8, cl. 8, of the Constitution. The patent law does not explicitly endorse or forbid the operation of trade secret law. However, as we have noted, if the scheme of protection developed by Ohio respecting trade secrets "clashes with the objectives of the federal patent laws," *Sears, Roebuck & Co. v. Stiffel Co., supra*, then the state law must fall. To determine whether the Ohio law "clashes" with the federal law it is helpful to examine the objectives of both the patent and trade secret laws.

The stated objective of the Constitution in granting the power to Congress to legislate in the area of intellectual property is to "promote the Progress of Science and useful Arts." The patent laws promote this progress by offering a right of exclusion for a limited period as an incentive to inventors to risk the often enormous costs in terms of time, research, and development. The productive effort thereby fostered will have a positive effect on society through the introduction of new products and processes of manufacture into the economy, and the emanations by way of increased employment and better lives for our citizens. In return for the right of exclusion—this "reward for inventions,"—the patent laws impose upon the inventor a requirement of disclosure. To insure adequate and full disclosure so that upon the expiration of the 17–year period "the knowledge of the invention enures to the people, who are thus enabled without restriction to practice it and profit by its use," the patent laws require that the patent application shall include a full and clear description of the invention and "of the manner and process of making and using it" so that any person skilled in the art may make and use the invention. When a patent is granted and the information contained in it is circulated to the general public and those especially skilled in the trade, such additions to the general store of knowledge are of such importance to the public weal that the Federal Government is willing to pay the high price of 17 years of exclusive use for its disclosure, which disclosure, it is assumed, will stimulate ideas and the eventual development of further significant advances in the art. The Court has also articulated another policy of the patent law: that which is in the public domain cannot be removed therefrom by action of the States.

"[F]ederal law requires that all ideas in general circulation be dedicated to the common good unless they are protected by a valid patent." *Lear, Inc. v. Adkins*, 395 U.S., at 668, 89 S.Ct., at 1910.

The maintenance of standards of commercial ethics and the encouragement of invention are the broadly stated policies behind trade secret law. * * *

Having now in mind the objectives of both the patent and trade secret law, we turn to an examination of the interaction of these systems of protection of intellectual property—one established by the Congress and the other by a State—to determine whether and under what circumstances the latter might constitute "too great an encroachment on the federal patent system to be tolerated." *Sears, Roebuck & Co. v. Stiffel Co.*

As we noted earlier, trade secret law protects items which would not be proper subjects for consideration for patent protection under 35 U.S.C. § 101. As in the case of the recordings in *Goldstein v. California*, Congress, with respect to nonpatentable subject matter, "has drawn no balance; rather, it has left the area unattended, and no reason exists why the State should not be free to act." *Goldstein v. California, supra*, 412 U.S., at 570, 93 S.Ct. at 2316.

Since no patent is available for a discovery, however useful, novel, and nonobvious, unless it falls within one of the express categories of patentable subject matter of 35 U.S.C. § 101, the holder of such a discovery would have no reason to apply for a patent whether trade secret protection existed or not. Abolition of trade secret protection would, therefore, not result in increased disclosure to the public of discoveries in the area of nonpatentable subject matter. Also, it is hard to see how the public would be benefitted by disclosure of customer lists or advertising campaigns; in fact, keeping such items secret encourages businesses to initiate new and individualized plans of operation, and constructive competition results. This, in turn, leads to a greater variety of business methods than would otherwise be the case if privately developed marketing and other data were passed illicitly among firms involved in the same enterprise.

Congress has spoken in the area of those discoveries which fall within one of the categories of patentable subject matter of 35 U.S.C. § 101 and which are, therefore, of a nature that would be subject to consideration for a patent. Processes, machines, manufactures, compositions of matter and improvements thereof, which meet the tests of utility, novelty, and nonobviousness are entitled to be patented, but those which do not, are not. The question remains whether those items which are proper subjects for consideration for a patent may also have available the alternative protection accorded by trade secret law.

Certainly the patent policy of encouraging invention is not disturbed by the existence of another form of incentive to invention. In this respect the two systems are not and never would be in conflict. Similarly, the policy that matter once in the public domain must remain in the public domain is not incompatible with the existence of trade secret protection. By definition a trade secret has not been placed in the public domain.

The more difficult objective of the patent law to reconcile with trade secret law is that of disclosure, the *quid pro quo* of the right to exclude. We are helped in this stage of the analysis by Judge Henry Friendly's opinion in *Painton & Co. v. Bourns, Inc.*, 442 F.2d 216 (2d Cir.1971). There the Court of Appeals thought it useful, in determining whether inventors will refrain because of the existence of trade secret law from applying for patents, thereby depriving the public from learning of the invention, to distinguish between three categories of trade secrets:

> "(1) the trade secret believed by its owner to constitute a validly patentable invention; (2) the trade secret known to its owner not to be so patentable; and (3) the trade secret whose valid patentability is considered dubious." *Id.*, at 224.

* * *

As to the trade secret known not to meet the standards of patentability, very little in the way of disclosure would be accomplished by abolishing trade secret protection. * * *

Even as the extension of trade secret protection to patentable subject matter that the owner knows will not meet the standards of patentability will not conflict with the patent policy of disclosure, it will have a decidedly beneficial effect on society. Trade secret law will encourage invention in areas where patent law does not reach, and will prompt the independent innovator to proceed with the discovery and exploitation of his invention. Competition is fostered and the public is not deprived of the use of valuable, if not quite patentable, invention.

Even if trade secret protection against the faithless employee were abolished, inventive and exploitive effort in the area of patentable subject matter that did not meet the standards of patentability would continue, although at a reduced level. Alternatively with the effort that remained, however, would come an increase in the amount of self-help that innovative companies would employ. * * * Security precautions necessarily would be increased, and salaries and fringe benefits of those few officers or employees who had to know the whole of the secret invention would be fixed in an amount thought sufficient to assure their loyalty. Smaller companies would be placed at a distinct economic disadvantage, since the costs of this kind of self-help could be great, and the cost to the public of the use of this invention would be increased. * * *

Another problem that would arise if state trade secret protection were precluded is in the area of licensing others to exploit secret processes. The holder of a trade secret would not likely share his secret with a manufacturer who cannot be placed under binding legal obligation to pay a license fee or to protect the secret. The result would be to hoard rather than disseminate knowledge. Instead, then, of licensing others to use his invention and making the most efficient use of existing manufacturing and marketing structures within the industry, the trade secret holder would tend either to limit his utilization of the invention, thereby depriving the public of the maximum benefit of its use, or engage in the time-consuming and economically wasteful enterprise of constructing duplicative manufacturing and marketing mechanisms for the exploitation of the invention. The detrimental misallocation of resources and economic waste that would thus take place if trade secret protection were abolished with respect to employees or licensees cannot be justified by reference to any policy that the federal patent law seeks to advance.

Nothing in the patent law requires that States refrain from action to prevent industrial espionage. In addition to the increased costs for protection from burglary, wire-tapping, bribery, and the other means used to misappropriate trade secrets, there is the inevitable cost to the basic decency of society when one firm steals from another. A most fundamental human right, that of privacy, is threatened when industrial espionage is condoned or is made profitable; the state interest in denying profit to such illegal ventures is unchallengeable.

The next category of patentable subject matter to deal with is the invention whose holder has a legitimate doubt as to its patentability. The risk of eventual patent invalidity by the courts and the costs associated with that risk may well impel some with a good-faith doubt as to patentability not to take the trouble to seek to obtain and defend patent protection for their discoveries, regardless of the existence of trade secret protection. Trade secret protection would assist those inventors in the more efficient exploitation of their discoveries and not conflict with the patent law. In most cases of genuine doubt as to patent validity the potential rewards of patent protection are so far superior to those accruing to holders of trade secrets, that the holders of such inventions will seek patent protection, ignoring the trade secret route. For those inventors "on the line" as to whether to seek patent protection, the abolition of trade secret protection might encourage some to apply for a patent who otherwise would not have done so. For some of those so encouraged, no patent will be granted and the result

> "will have been an unnecessary postponement in the divulging of the trade secret to persons willing to pay for it. If (the patent does issue), it may well be invalid, yet many will prefer to pay a modest royalty than to contest it, even though *Lear* allows them to accept a license and pursue the contest without paying royalties while the fight goes on. The result in such a case would be unjustified royalty payments from many who would prefer not to pay them rather than agreed fees from one or a few who are entirely willing to do so." *Painton & Co. v. Bourns, Inc.*, 442 F.2d, at 225.

The point is that those who might be encouraged to file for patents by the absence of trade secret law will include inventors possessing the chaff as well as the wheat. * * * Some of the chaff may not be thrown out. This Court has noted the difference between the standards used by the Patent

Office and the courts to determine patentability. * * * More [invalid] patents would likely issue if trade secret law were abolished. Eliminating trade secret law for the doubtfully patentable invention is thus likely to have deleterious effects on society and patent policy which we cannot say are balanced out by the speculative gain which might result from the encouragement of some inventors with doubtfully patentable inventions which deserve patent protection to come forward and apply for patents. There is no conflict, then, between trade secret law and the patent law policy of disclosure, at least insofar as the first two categories of patentable subject matter are concerned.

The final category of patentable subject matter to deal with is the clearly patentable invention, i.e., that invention which the owner believes to meet the standards of patentability. It is here that the federal interest in disclosure is at its peak; these inventions, novel, useful and nonobvious, are "the things which are worth to the public the embarrassment of an exclusive patent." The interest of the public is that the bargain of 17 years of exclusive use in return for disclosure be accepted. If a State, through a system of protection, were to cause a substantial risk that holders of patentable inventions would not seek patents, but rather would rely on the state protection, we would be compelled to hold that such a system could not constitutionally continue to exist. In the case of trade secret law no reasonable risk of deterrence from patent application by those who can reasonably expect to be granted patents exists.

Trade secret law provides far weaker protection in many respects than the patent law. While trade secret law does not forbid the discovery of the trade secret by fair and honest means, *e.g.*, independent creation or reverse engineering, patent law operates "against the world," forbidding any use of the invention for whatever purpose for a significant length of time. The holder of a trade secret also takes a substantial risk that the secret will be passed on to his competitors, by theft or by breach of a confidential relationship, in a manner not easily susceptible of discovery or proof. Where patent law acts as a barrier, trade secret law functions relatively as a sieve. The possibility that an inventor who believes his invention meets the standards of patentability will sit back, rely on trade secret law, and after one year of use forfeit any right to patent protection, 35 U.S.C. § 102(b), is remote indeed.

Nor does society face much risk that scientific or technological progress will be impeded by the rare inventor with a patentable invention who chooses trade secret protection over patent protection. The ripeness-of-time concept of invention, developed from the study of the many independent multiple discoveries in history, predicts that if a particular individual had not made a particular discovery others would have, and in probably a relatively short period of time. If something is to be discovered at all very likely it will be discovered by more than one person. Even were an inventor to keep his discovery completely to himself, something that neither the patent nor trade secret laws forbid, there is a high probability that it will be soon independently developed. * * *

We conclude that the extension of trade secret protection to clearly patentable inventions does not conflict with the patent policy of disclosure. * * *

Our conclusion that patent law does not pre-empt trade secret law is in accord with prior cases of this Court. Trade secret law and patent law have co-existed in this country for over one hundred years. Each has its particular role to play, and the operation of one does not take away from the need for the other. Trade secret law encourages the development and exploitation of those items of lesser or different invention than might be accorded protection under the patent laws, but which items still have an important part to play in the technological and scientific advancement of the Nation. Trade secret law promotes the sharing of knowledge, and the efficient operation of industry; it permits the individual inventor to reap the rewards of his labor by contracting with a company large enough to develop and exploit it. Congress, by its silence over these many years, has seen the wisdom of allowing the States to enforce trade secret protection. Until Congress takes affirmative action to the contrary, States should be free to grant protection to trade secrets.

　　　　* * *

MR. JUSTICE DOUGLAS, with whom MR. JUSTICE BRENNAN concurs, dissenting.

Today's decision is at war with the philosophy of *Sears, Roebuck & Co. v. Stiffel Co.*, and *Compco Corp. v. Day–Brite Lighting, Inc.* * * * We held that when an article is unprotected by a patent, state law may not forbid others to copy it, because every article not covered by a valid patent is in the public domain. Congress in the patent laws decided that where no patent existed, free competition should prevail; that where a patent is rightfully issued, the right to exclude others should obtain for no longer than 17 years, and that the States may not "under some other law, such as that forbidding unfair competition, give protection of a kind that clashes with the objectives of the federal patent laws."

The product involved in this suit, sodium iodide synthetic crystals, was a product that could be patented but was not. Harshaw the inventor apparently contributed greatly to the technology in that field by developing processes, procedures, and techniques that produced much larger crystals than any competitor. These processes, procedures, and techniques were also patentable; but no patent was sought. * * *

The District Court issued a permanent injunction against respondents, ex-employees, restraining them from using the processes used by Harshaw. By a patent which would require full disclosure Harshaw could have obtained a 17–year monopoly against the world. By the District Court's injunction, which the Court approves and reinstates, Harshaw gets a permanent injunction running into perpetuity against respondents. In *Sears*, as in the present case, an injunction against the unfair competitor issued. We said: "To allow a State by use of its law of unfair competition to prevent the copying of an article which represents too slight an advance to be patented would be to permit the State to block off from the public something which federal law has said belongs to the public. The result would be that while federal law grants only 14 or 17 years' protection to genuine inventions, States could allow perpetual protection to articles too lacking in novelty to merit any patent at all under federal constitutional standards. This would be too great an encroachment on the federal patent system to be tolerated."

The conflict with the patent laws is obvious. The decision of Congress to adopt a patent system was based on the idea that there will be much more innovation if discoveries are disclosed and patented than there will be when everyone works in secret. * * *

  * * *

NOTES AND QUESTIONS

1. *The Kewanee decision.* What general rule can you distill from the *Kewanee* decision? Is the rule consistent with *Sears* and *Compco?*

When the Supreme Court determines that trade secret law does not withdraw matter from the public domain, does it conceive of "the public domain" in the same way that it did in *Sears* and *Compco?*

The *Kewanee* Court identifies three public policies that Congress sought to promote in enacting the patent laws. Are these three policies equivalent to the public policy goal that the Court described in *Sears* and *Compco?* If not, does the *Kewanee* Court take the *Sears* and *Compco* policy concern into account in evaluating the impact of the trade secret laws?

Do you agree with the Court's assumption that, because of its weaker protection, the trade secret cause of action will not deter patent applications for clearly patentable inventions? Do you agree with the Court's assumption that the "ripeness of time concept of invention" will minimize any loss of disclosure caused by the availability of trade secret protection? If you disagree with the Court's assumptions in these matters, were the assumptions crucial to the result? Could the Court still have justified reaching the result that it did?

From a practical standpoint, does the result in *Kewanee* make sense?

2. *The Aronson case: state contract protection for inventive ideas.* Five years after *Kewanee*, the Burger Court again addressed the preemption issue. In Aronson v. Quick Point Pencil Co., 440 U.S. 257, 99 S.Ct. 1096, 59 L.Ed.2d 296 (1979), Aronson applied for a patent for her new form of keyholder, and while the application was pending, she negotiated a contract with Quick Point for the manufacture and sale of the keyholder. Quick Point agreed to pay Aronson a royalty of 5% of the selling price in return for "the exclusive right to make and sell keyholders of the type shown" in the patent application. The agreement further provided that if Aronson's patent application was rejected, the royalties would be reduced to 2½%. Apart from a provision giving Quick Point the right to cancel the agreement whenever the volume of sales failed to meet expectations, the agreement contained no limit on its duration.

Quick Point commenced manufacturing and selling the key holders, which proved to be a considerable success. When the PTO ultimately rejected Aronson's patent application, Quick Point reduced the royalty payments, as provided in the agreement, but continued manufacturing the keyholder and paying Aronson for the next fourteen years. While sales continued to be good, competitors, who were not bound to pay royalties to Aronson, began to sell the keyholder in competition with Quick Point. In 1975, Quick Point filed for a declaratory judgement, asserting that it was not obligated to pay royalties because the royalty agreement was unenforceable. Quick Point asserted that the state law that might otherwise make the contract enforceable was preempted by federal patent law. The Supreme Court rejected the argument.

The Court noted that the parties clearly contracted with full awareness of the possibility that a patent might not issue. The Court continued:

Enforcement of Quick Point's agreement with Mrs. Aronson is not inconsistent with any of [the three purposes of patent law, as described in *Kewanee*]. Permitting inventors to make enforceable agreements licensing the use of their inventions in return for royalties provides an additional incentive to invention. Similarly, encouraging Mrs. Aronson to make arrangements for the manufacture of her keyholder furthers the federal policy of disclosure of inventions; these simple devices display the novel idea which they embody wherever they are seen.

Quick Point argues that enforcement of such contracts conflicts with the federal policy against withdrawing ideas from the public domain and discourages recourse to the federal patent system by allowing states to extend "perpetual protection to articles too lacking in novelty to merit any patent at all under federal constitutional standards," *Sears, Roebuck & Co. v. Stiffel Co.*, 376 U.S. 225, 232, 84 S.Ct. 784, 789, 11 L.Ed.2d 661 (1964).

We find no merit in this contention. Enforcement of the agreement does not withdraw any idea from the public domain. The design for the keyholder was not in the public domain before Quick Point obtained its license to manufacture it. In negotiating the agreement, Mrs. Aronson disclosed the design in confidence. Had Quick Point tried to exploit the design in breach of that confidence, it would have risked legal liability. It is equally clear that the design entered the public domain as a result of the manufacture and sale of the keyholders under the contract.

Requiring Quick Point to bear the burden of royalties for the use of the design is no more inconsistent with federal patent law than any of the other costs involved in being the first to introduce a new product to the market, such as outlays for research and development, and marketing and promotional expenses. For reasons which Quick Point's experience with the Aronson keyholder demonstrate, innovative entrepreneurs have usually found such costs to be well worth paying.

Finally, enforcement of this agreement does not discourage anyone from seeking a patent. Mrs. Aronson attempted to obtain a patent for over five years. It is quite true that had she succeeded, she would have received a 5% royalty only on keyholders sold during the 17-year life of the patent. Offsetting the limited terms of royalty payments, she would have received twice as much per dollar of Quick Point's sales, and both she and Quick Point could have licensed any others who produced the same keyholder. Which course would have produced the greater yield to the contracting parties is a matter of speculation; the parties resolved the uncertainties by their bargain.

No decision of this Court relating to patents justifies relieving Quick Point of its contract obligations. We have held that a state may not forbid the copying of an idea in the public domain which does not meet the requirements for federal patent protection. *Compco Corp. v. Day–Brite Lighting, Inc.*; *Sears, Roebuck & Co. v. Stiffel Co.* Enforcement of Quick Point's agreement, however, does not prevent anyone from copying the keyholder. It merely requires Quick Point to pay the consideration which it promised in return for the use of a novel device which enabled it to pre-empt the market.

* * *

Id., 440 U.S. at 262–65. Is it likely that the Court would reach the same result if Aronson depended on a quasi-contract (contract implied in law) theory or on the "property" theory of idea law to recover for Quick Point's use of her inventive idea, rather than on an express contract? How might the Court's analysis differ? See Barrett, *The "Law of Ideas" Reconsidered*, 71 J. Pat. & Trademark Off. Soc. 691, 726–737 (1989). What if the contract Aronson was seeking to enforce was a "shrink-wrap" license that accompanied all copies of a computer program offered for sale to the public, and prohibited reverse engineering of the program as a means of protecting the program's trade secrets? Would the Court's preemption analysis be likely to differ from that in the *Aronson* case?

Under the rule set forth in Brulotte v. Thys Co., 379 U.S. 29, 85 S.Ct. 176, 13 L.Ed.2d 99 (1964), if Aronson had gotten a patent, her royalties contract with Quick Point would have become unenforceable when the patent expired. *Pitney Bowes v. Mestre*, 701 F.2d 1365 (11th Cir.1983), *cert. denied,* 464 U.S. 893, 104 S.Ct. 239, 78 L.Ed.2d 230 (1983). Moreover, under *Lear, Inc. v. Adkins*, 395 U.S. 653, 89 S.Ct. 1902, 23 L.Ed.2d 610 (1969), if Aronson had gotten a patent and Quick Point, as licensee, had successfully challenged its validity, Quick Point would have been relieved from liability for royalties, notwithstanding the contract. That being so, why should Aronson be entitled to enforce the contract in perpetuity under the facts of that case?

BONITO BOATS, INC. v. THUNDER CRAFT BOATS, INC.

United States Supreme Court, 1989.
489 U.S. 141, 109 S.Ct. 971, 103 L.Ed.2d 118.

JUSTICE O'CONNOR delivered the opinion of the Court.

We must decide today what limits the operation of the federal patent system places on the States' ability to offer substantial protection to utilitarian and design ideas which the patent laws leave otherwise unprotected. * * * In this case, the Florida Supreme Court * * * struck down a Florida statute which prohibits the use of the direct molding process to duplicate unpatented boat hulls, finding that the protection offered by the Florida law conflicted with the balance struck by Congress in the federal patent statute between the encouragement of invention and free competition in unpatented ideas. [W]e now affirm the judgment of the Florida Supreme Court.

I

In September 1976, petitioner Bonito Boats, Inc. (Bonito), a Florida corporation, developed a hull design for a fiberglass recreational boat which it marketed under the trade name Bonito Boat Model 5VBR. Designing the boat hull required substantial effort on the part of Bonito. A set of engineering drawings was prepared, from which a hardwood model was created. The hardwood model was then sprayed with fiberglass to create a mold, which then served to produce the finished fiberglass boats for sale. The 5VBR was placed on the market sometime in September 1976. There is no indication in the record that a patent application was ever filed for protection of the utilitarian or design aspects of the hull, or for the process by which the hull was manufactured. The 5VBR was favorably received by the boating public, and "a broad interstate market" developed for its sale.

In May 1983, after the Bonito 5VBR had been available to the public for over six years, the Florida Legislature enacted Fla.Stat. § 559.94 (1987). The statute makes "[i]t ... unlawful for any person to use the direct molding process to duplicate for the purpose of sale any manufactured vessel hull or component part of a vessel made by another without the written permission of that other person." § 559.94(2). The statute also makes it unlawful for a person to "knowingly sell a vessel hull or component part of a vessel duplicated in violation of subsection (2)." § 559.94(3). Damages, injunctive relief, and attorney's fees are made available to "[a]ny person who suffers injury or damage as the result of a violation" of the statute. § 559.94(4). The statute was made applicable to vessel hulls or component parts duplicated through the use of direct molding after July 1, 1983. § 559.94(5).

On December 21, 1984, Bonito filed this action in the Circuit Court of Orange County, Florida. The complaint alleged that respondent here, Thunder Craft Boats, Inc. (Thunder Craft), a Tennessee corporation, had violated the Florida statute by using the direct molding process to duplicate the Bonito 5VBR fiberglass hull, and had knowingly sold such duplicates in violation of the Florida statute. * * * Respondent filed a motion to dismiss the complaint, arguing that under this Court's decisions in *Sears, Roebuck & Co. v. Stiffel Co.*, and *Compco Corp. v. Day–Brite Lighting, Inc.*, the Florida statute conflicted with federal patent law and was therefore invalid under the Supremacy Clause of the Federal Constitution. The trial court granted respondent's motion, and a divided Court of Appeals affirmed the dismissal of petitioner's complaint.

On appeal, a sharply divided Florida Supreme Court agreed with the lower courts' conclusion that the Florida law impermissibly interfered with the scheme established by the federal patent laws. The majority read our decisions in *Sears* and *Compco* for the proposition that "when an article is introduced into the public domain, only a patent can eliminate the inherent risk of competition and then but for a limited time." * * *

II

* * *

From their inception, the federal patent laws have embodied a careful balance between the need to promote innovation and the recognition that imitation and refinement through imitation are both necessary to invention itself and the very lifeblood of a competitive economy. * * *

* * * To qualify for protection, a design must present an aesthetically pleasing appearance that is not dictated by function alone, and must satisfy the other criteria of patentability. [The Court describes the limitations on patentability posed by the novelty, statutory bar and nonobviousness provisions of 35 U.S.C.A. §§ 102 and 103.]

* * * Taken together, the novelty and nonobviousness requirements express a congressional determination that the purposes behind the Patent Clause are best served by free competition and exploitation of either that which is already available to the public or that which may be readily discerned from publicly available material. See *Aronson v. Quick Point Pencil Co.*, 440 U.S. 257, 262, 99 S.Ct. 1096, 1099, 59 L.Ed.2d 296 (1979) ("[T]he stringent requirements for patent protection seek to ensure that ideas in the public domain remain there for the use of the public").

The applicant whose invention satisfies the requirements of novelty, nonobviousness, and utility, and who is willing to reveal to the public the substance of his discovery and "the best mode ... of carrying out his invention," is granted "the right to exclude others from making, using, or selling the invention throughout the United States," for a period of 17 years. The federal patent system thus embodies a carefully crafted bargain for encouraging the creation and disclosure of new, useful, and nonobvious advances in technology and design in return for the exclusive right to practice the invention for a period of years. * * *

The attractiveness of such a bargain, and its effectiveness in inducing creative effort and disclosure of the results of that effort, depend almost entirely on a backdrop of free competition in the exploitation of unpatented designs and innovations. The novelty and nonobviousness requirements of patentability embody a congressional understanding, implicit in the Patent Clause itself, that free exploitation of ideas will be the rule, to which the protection of a federal patent is the exception. Moreover, the ultimate goal of the patent system is to bring new designs and technologies into the public domain through disclosure. State law protection for techniques and designs whose disclosure has already been induced by market rewards may conflict with the very purpose of the patent laws by decreasing the range of ideas available as the building blocks of further innovation. The offer of federal protection from competitive exploitation of intellectual property would be rendered meaningless in a world where substantially similar state law protections were readily available. To a limited extent, the federal patent laws must determine not only what is protected, but also what is free for all to use. * * *

Thus our past decisions have made clear that state regulation of intellectual property must yield to the extent that it clashes with the balance struck by Congress in our patent laws. * * * We have long held that after the expiration of a federal patent, the subject matter of the patent passes to the free use of the public as a matter of federal law. * * * Where the public has paid the congressionally mandated price for disclosure, the States may not render the exchange fruitless by offering patent-like protection to the subject matter of the expired patent. * * *

In our decisions in *Sears, Roebuck & Co. v. Stiffel Co.*, and *Compco Corp. v. Day–Brite Lighting, Inc.*, we found that publicly known design and utilitarian ideas which were unprotected by patent occupied much the same position as the subject matter of an expired patent. * * *

The preemptive sweep of our decisions in *Sears* and *Compco* has been the subject of heated scholarly and judicial debate. Read at their highest level of generality, the two decisions could be taken to stand for the proposition that the States are completely disabled from offering any form of protection to articles or processes which fall within the broad scope of patentable subject matter. Since the potentially patentable includes "anything under the sun that is made by man," *Diamond v. Chakrabarty*, 447 U.S. 303, 309, 100 S.Ct. 2204, 2207, 65 L.Ed.2d 144 (1980), the broadest reading of *Sears* would prohibit the States from regulating the deceptive simulation of trade dress or the tortious appropriation of private information.

That the extrapolation of such a broad preemptive principle from *Sears* is inappropriate is clear from the balance struck in *Sears* itself. The *Sears* Court made it plain that the States "may protect businesses in the use of their trademarks, labels, or distinctive dress in the packaging of goods so as to prevent others, by imitating such markings, from misleading purchasers as to the source of the goods." Trade dress is, of course, potentially the subject matter of design patents. Yet our decision in *Sears* clearly indicates that the States may place limited regulations on the circumstances in which such designs are used in order to prevent consumer confusion as to source. Thus, while *Sears* speaks in absolutist terms, its conclusion that the States may place some conditions on the use of trade dress indicates an implicit recognition that all state regulation of potentially patentable but unpatented subject matter is not *ipso facto* preempted by the federal patent laws.

What was implicit in our decision in *Sears*, we have made explicit in our subsequent decisions concerning the scope of federal pre-emption of state regulation of the subject matter of patent. Thus, in *Kewanee Oil Co. v. Bicron Corp.*, we held that state protection of trade secrets did not operate to frustrate the achievement of the congressional objectives served by the patent laws. Despite the fact that state law protection was available for ideas which clearly fell within the subject matter of patent, the Court concluded that the nature and degree of state protection did not conflict with the federal policies of encouragement of patentable invention and the prompt disclosure of such innovations.

Several factors were critical to this conclusion. First, because the public awareness of a trade secret is by definition limited, the Court noted that "the policy that matter once in the public domain must remain in the public domain is not incompatible with the existence of trade secret protection." Second, the *Kewanee* Court emphasized that "[t]rade secret law provides far weaker protection in many respects than the patent law." This point was central to the Court's conclusion that trade secret protection did not conflict with either the encouragement or disclosure policies of the federal patent law. The public at large remained free to discover and exploit the trade secret through reverse engineering of products in the public domain or by independent creation. Thus, the possibility that trade secret protection would divert inventors from the creative effort necessary to satisfy the rigorous demands of patent protection was remote indeed. Finally, certain aspects of trade secret law operated to protect non-economic interests outside the sphere of congressional concern in the patent laws. As the Court noted, "[A] most fundamental human right, that of privacy, is threatened when industrial espionage is condoned or is made profitable." There was no indication that Congress had considered this interest in the balance struck by the patent laws, or that state protection for it would interfere with the policies behind the patent system.

* * *

At the heart of *Sears* and *Compco* is the conclusion that the efficient operation of the federal patent system depends upon substantially free trade in publicly known, unpatented design and utilitarian conceptions. In *Sears*, the state law offered "the equivalent of a patent monopoly," in the functional aspects of a product which had been placed in public commerce absent the protection of a valid patent. While, as noted above, our decisions since *Sears* have taken a decidedly less rigid view of the scope of federal pre-emption under the patent laws, we believe that the *Sears* Court correctly concluded that the States may not offer patent-like protection to intellectual creations which would otherwise remain unprotected as a matter of federal law. Both the novelty and the nonobviousness requirements of federal patent law are grounded in the notion that concepts within the public grasp, or those so obvious that they readily could be, are the tools of creation available to all. They provide the baseline of free competition upon which the patent system's incentive to creative effort depends. A state law that substantially interferes with the enjoyment of an unpatented utilitarian or design conception which has been freely disclosed by its author to the public at large impermissibly contravenes the ultimate goal of public disclosure and use which is the centerpiece of federal patent policy. Moreover, through the creation of patent-like rights, the States could essentially redirect inventive efforts away from the careful criteria of patentability developed by Congress over the last 200 years. We understand this to be the reasoning at the core of our decisions in *Sears* and *Compco*, and we reaffirm that reasoning today.

III

We believe that the Florida statute at issue in this case so substantially impedes the public use of the otherwise unprotected design and utilitarian ideas embodied in unpatented boat hulls as to run afoul of the teaching of our decisions in *Sears* and *Compco*. It is readily apparent that the Florida statute does not operate to prohibit "unfair competition" in the usual sense that the term is understood. The law of unfair competition has its roots in the common-law tort of deceit: its general concern is with protecting *consumers* from confusion as to source. While that concern may result in the creation of "quasi-property rights" in communicative symbols, the focus is on the protection of consumers, not the protection of producers as an incentive to product innovation. * * *

With some notable exceptions, including the interpretation of the Illinois law of unfair competition at issue in *Sears* and *Compco*, the common-law tort of unfair competition has been limited to protection against copying of nonfunctional aspects of consumer products which have acquired secondary meaning such that they operate as a designation of source. The "protection" granted a particular design under the law of unfair competition is thus limited to one context where consumer confusion is likely to result; the design "idea" itself may be freely exploited in all other contexts.

In contrast to the operation of unfair competition law, the Florida statute is aimed directly at preventing the exploitation of the design and utilitarian conceptions embodied in the product itself. The sparse legislative history surrounding its enactment indicates that it was intended to create an inducement for the improvement of boat hull designs. * * * To accomplish this goal, the Florida statute endows the original boat hull manufacturer with rights against the world, similar in scope and operation to the rights accorded a federal patentee. Like the patentee, the beneficiary of the Florida statute may prevent a competitor from "making" the product in what is evidently the most efficient manner available and from "selling" the product when it is produced in that fashion. The Florida scheme offers this protection for an unlimited number of years to all boat hulls and their component parts, without regard to their ornamental or technological merit. Protection is available for subject matter for which patent protection has been denied or has expired, as well as for designs which have been freely revealed to the consuming public by their creators.

* * *

That the Florida statute does not remove all means of reproduction and sale does not eliminate the conflict with the federal scheme. In essence, the Florida law prohibits the entire public from engaging in a form of reverse engineering of a product in the public domain. This is clearly one of the rights vested in the federal patent holder, but has never been a part of state protection under the law of unfair competition or trade secrets. * * * The duplication of boat hulls and their component parts may be an essential part of innovation in the field of hydrodynamic design. Variations as to size and combination of various elements may lead to significant advances in the field. Reverse engineering of chemical and mechanical articles in the public domain often leads to significant advances in technology. If Florida may prohibit this particular method of study and recomposition of an unpatented article, we fail to see the principle that would prohibit a State from banning the use of chromatography in the reconstitution of unpatented chemical compounds, or the use of robotics in the duplication of machinery in the public domain.

* * * Given the substantial protection offered by the Florida scheme, we cannot dismiss as hypothetical the possibility that it will become a significant competitor to the federal patent laws, offering investors similar protection without the *quid pro quo* of substantial creative effort required by the federal statute. The prospect of all 50 States establishing similar protections for preferred industries without the rigorous requirements of patentability prescribed by Congress could pose a substantial threat to the patent system's ability to accomplish its mission of promoting progress in the useful arts.

* * *

* * * In [both *Sears* and *Kewanee*], state protection was not aimed exclusively at the promotion of invention itself, and the state restrictions on the use of unpatented ideas were limited to those necessary to promote goals outside the contemplation of the federal patent scheme. Both the law of unfair competition and state trade secret law have coexisted harmoniously with federal patent protection for almost 200 years, and Congress has given no indication that their operation is inconsistent with the operation of the federal patent laws.

Indeed, [by virtue of Congress' passage of Lanham Act § 43(a) and its explicit statutory safeguards for trade secret information provided to federal agencies] there are affirmative indications from Congress that both the law of unfair competition and trade secret protection are consistent with the balance struck by the patent laws. * * * The case for federal preemption is particularly weak where Congress has indicated its awareness of the operation of state law in a field of federal interest, and has nonetheless decided to "stand by both concepts and to tolerate whatever tension there [is] between them." The same cannot be said of the Florida statute at issue here, which offers protection beyond that available under the law of unfair competition or trade secret, without any showing of consumer confusion, or breach of trust or secrecy.

* * *

Congress has considered extending various forms of limited protection to industrial design either through the copyright laws or by relaxing the restrictions on the availability of design patents. Congress explicitly refused to take this step in the copyright laws, and despite sustained criticism for a number of years, it has declined to alter the patent protections presently available for industrial design. It is for Congress to determine if the present system of design and utility patents is ineffectual in promoting the useful arts in the context of industrial design. By offering patent-like protection for ideas deemed unprotected under the present federal scheme, the Florida statute conflicts with the "strong federal policy favoring free competition in ideas which do not merit patent protection." We therefore agree with the majority of the Florida Supreme Court that the Florida statute is preempted by the Supremacy Clause, and the judgment of that court is hereby affirmed.

NOTES AND QUESTIONS

1. *The Bonito Boats decision.* In your opinion, does the Court successfully reconcile *Sears* and *Compco* with the *Kewanee* and *Aronson* decisions? After *Bonito Boats*, what factors appear to be the most important in determining whether state causes of action for intellectual property will be preempted under the Supremacy Clause?

The Florida direct molding statute did not prohibit all copying or use of the protected boat hulls. In *Kewanee* and *Aronson* the Court found the fact that the state laws at issue precluded only some uses to be an important factor. Why not in *Bonito Boats*?

In *Kewanee*, the Court stressed that the trade secret laws operated to protect the interest in privacy, a non-economic interest outside the sphere of Congressional concern in the patent laws. Did the Florida direct molding statute not protect any comparable additional interest? In Interpart Corp. v. Italia, 777 F.2d 678 (Fed.Cir.1985), *overruled*, Midwest Industries v. Karavan Trailers, 175 F.3d 1356 (Fed.Cir.1999), the Court of Appeals for the Federal Circuit, in upholding a California anti-plug molding statute against preemption claims, stressed that the statute prevented "unscrupulous competitors" from using a method of copying that the state considered "unfair." Why did the Supreme Court in *Bonito Boats* not credit the state's interest in preventing marketplace conduct that it deems unfair?

What is the justification for anti-plug molding provisions? Do they benefit the public, or only the manufacturers of boat hulls? Is the *Bonito Boats* Court's evaluation of this issue a factor in its decision? Are you convinced by the Court's arguments that the anti-plug molding statute, by preventing a form of reverse engineering, may impair innovation in the field of aquadynamic design?

After *Bonito Boats*, may the states apply their unfair competition laws to enjoin the copying of distinctive, nonfunctional product features when the copying leads to a likelihood of consumer confusion? See Restatement (Third) of Unfair Competition § 16, cmt c (1995).

2. *Protection for boat hull designs.* In the Digital Millennium Copyright Act, Congress created a *sui generis* federal right to prevent the copying of boat

hulls, replacing the state protection that was found preempted in *Bonito Boats*. See 17 U.S.C.A. §§ 1301–1332.

PROBLEMS

1. Jones conceives of an innovative purchasing concept for cars. Through advertisements he attracts numerous individuals who are interested in buying a particular model of car, and forms a pool. Acting as the agent for the pool, Jones approaches the manufacturer of the designated model of car and negotiates a contract to purchase cars for everyone in the pool at wholesale prices. Through this method, each member of the pool is able to purchase one of the cars at a lower price than would be available from a retail dealer, even after paying Jones a modest commission. (Jones can charge a modest commission and still profit, because he has relatively little overhead cost.)

During the next several years, Jones invests heavily in extensive advertising and promotion of the purchasing method to attract more individual purchasers and to educate the public about the new purchasing method. Through his efforts he develops wide-spread public acceptance and demand for his purchasing method and builds a large and profitable business. Thousands of consumers begin to use his service to purchase cars, lending institutions widely accept and grant loan applications to purchase cars through Jones' method, and car dealers begin to appoint special sales representatives to facilitate Jones' large purchase orders.

At that point, Smith sets up to capitalize on Jones' concept and compete with Jones in soliciting consumers to form automobile purchasing pools. Due to Jones' investment of money and effort to promote the concept and educate the public about its benefits, Smith's business is successful, without the need for the same kind of investment.

Jones sues Smith for misappropriation. Is the claim likely to be preempted?

2. Pharmaceutical Co. (P.C.) asked University Researcher (U.R.) to do a study comparing the rate of iron absorption associated with its multivitamin and that of a competitor. U.R. conducted the study, using general University research funds, and found that neither multivitamin provided for a sufficiently high rate of iron absorption. U.R. then devised and tested a new formulation that would provide a significantly higher rate of iron absorption. U.R. wrote a paper for publication and provided a "confidential" copy of the paper to P.C. Based on the paper, without U.R.'s knowledge, P.C. reformulated its multivitamin to conform with U.R.'s new formulation and filed a patent application for the new formulation, naming one of its own scientists as the inventor. Upon discovering the resulting patent, U.R. and her University filed suit against P.C. alleging, among other things, and unjust enrichment or "quasi-contract" theory of recovery. P.C. moves to dismiss the claim on the ground that it is preempted by patent law. How should the court rule?

3. The State Legislature determined: "The excessive prices of prescription drugs in the State is threatening the health and welfare of the residents of the State as well as the State government's ability to ensure that all

residents receive the health care they need, and these excessive prices directly and indirectly cause economic harm to the State and damage the health and safety of its residents." The Legislature then enacted (and the Governor signed) "The Excessive Pricing Act," which provides:

> It shall be unlawful for any drug manufacturer or licensee thereof, excluding a point of sale retail seller, to sell or supply for sale or impose minimum resale requirements for a patented prescription drug that results in the prescription drug being sold in the State for an excessive price.

While the statutory term "excessive price" is not specifically defined, the statute states that "[a] prima facie case of excessive pricing shall be established where the wholesale price of a patented prescription drug in the State is over 30% higher than the comparable price in any high income country in which the product is protected by patents or other exclusive marketing rights." A "high income country" is defined as one of "the United Kingdom, Germany, Canada, or Australia." If a challenger makes the defined prima facie case, the burden shifts to the defendant to prove that "the prescription drug is not excessively priced given demonstrated costs of invention, development and production of the prescription drug, global sales and profits to date, consideration of any government funded research that supported the development of the drug, and the impact of price on access to the prescription drug by residents and the government of the State." The Act provides for a wide array of remedies.

A pharmaceutical research and manufacturers' association has now brought suit for declaratory judgment that the Act is unenforceable as preempted by the federal patent laws. How should the court rule?

II. STATUTORY PREEMPTION: COPYRIGHT ACT § 301

NATIONAL BASKETBALL ASSN. v. MOTOROLA, INC.

United States Court of Appeals, Second Circuit, 1997.
105 F.3d 841.

WINTER, CIRCUIT JUDGE:

Motorola, Inc. and Sports Team Analysis and Tracking Systems ("STATS") appeal from a permanent injunction entered by Judge Preska. The injunction concerns a handheld pager sold by Motorola and marketed under the name "SportsTrax," which displays updated information of professional basketball games in progress. The injunction prohibits appellants, absent authorization from the National Basketball Association and NBA Properties, Inc. (collectively the "NBA"), from transmitting scores or other data about NBA games in progress via the pagers, STATS's site on America On–Line's computer dial-up service, or "any equivalent means."

The crux of the dispute concerns the extent to which a state law "hot-news" misappropriation claim based on *International News Service v. Associated Press*, 248 U.S. 215, 39 S.Ct. 68, 63 L.Ed. 211 (1918) ("*INS*"), survives preemption by the federal Copyright Act and whether the NBA's claim fits within the surviving *INS*-type claims. We hold that a narrow "hot-news" exception does survive preemption. However, we also hold that appellants' transmission of "real-time" NBA game scores and information tabulated from television and radio broadcasts of games in progress does not constitute a misappropriation of "hot news" that is the property of the NBA.

* * *

I. BACKGROUND

The facts are largely undisputed. Motorola manufactures and markets the SportsTrax paging device while STATS supplies the game information that is transmitted to the pagers. The product became available to the public in January 1996, at a retail price of about $200. SportsTrax's pager has an inch-and-a-half by inch-and-a-half screen and operates in four basic modes: "current," "statistics," "final scores" and "demonstration." It is the "current" mode that gives rise to the present dispute.[1] In that mode, SportsTrax displays the following information on NBA games in progress: (i) the teams playing; (ii) score changes; (iii) the team in possession of the ball; (iv) whether the team is in the free-throw bonus; (v) the quarter of the game; and (vi) time remaining in the quarter. The information is updated every two to three minutes, with more frequent updates near the end of the first half and the end of the game. There is a lag of approximately two or three minutes between events in the game itself and when the information appears on the pager screen.

SportsTrax's operation relies on a "data feed" supplied by STATS reporters who watch the games on television or listen to them on the radio. The reporters key into a personal computer changes in the score and other information such as successful and missed shots, fouls, and clock updates. The information is relayed by modem to STATS's host computer, which compiles, analyzes, and formats the data for retransmission. The information is then sent to a common carrier, which then sends it via satellite to various local FM radio networks that in turn emit the signal received by the individual SportsTrax pagers.

Although the NBA's complaint concerned only the SportsTrax device, the NBA offered evidence at trial concerning STATS's America On–Line ("AOL") site. Starting in January, 1996, users who accessed STATS's AOL site, typically via a modem attached to a home computer, were provided with slightly more comprehensive and detailed real-time game

---

1. The other three SportsTrax modes involve information that is far less contemporaneous than that provided in the "current" mode. In the "statistics" mode, the SportsTrax pager displays a variety of player and team statistics, such as field goal shooting percentages and top scorers. However, these are calculated only at half-time and when the game is over. In the "final scores" mode, the unit displays final scores from the previous day's games. In the "demonstration" mode, the unit merely simulates information shown during a hypothetical NBA game. The core issue in the instant matter is the dissemination of continuously-updated real-time NBA game information in the "current" mode. Because we conclude that the dissemination of such real-time information is lawful, the other modes need no further description or discussion.

information than is displayed on a SportsTrax pager. On the AOL site, game scores are updated every 15 seconds to a minute, and the player and team statistics are updated each minute. The district court's original decision and judgment did not address the AOL site, because "NBA's complaint and the evidence proffered at trial were devoted largely to SportsTrax." Upon motion by the NBA, however, the district court amended its decision and judgment and enjoined use of the real-time game information on STATS's AOL site. Because the record on appeal, the briefs of the parties, and oral argument primarily addressed the SportsTrax device, we similarly focus on that product. However, we regard the legal issues as identical with respect to both products, and our holding applies equally to SportsTrax and STATS's AOL site.

The NBA's complaint asserted six claims for relief [including state law misappropriation and federal copyright infringement].

The district court dismissed all of the NBA's claims except the first—misappropriation under New York law. Finding Motorola and STATS liable for misappropriation, Judge Preska entered the permanent injunction, reserved the calculation of damages for subsequent proceedings, and stayed execution of the injunction pending appeal. Motorola and STATS appeal from the injunction * * *.

II. THE STATE LAW MISAPPROPRIATION CLAIM

A. *Summary of Ruling*

Because our disposition of the state law misappropriation claim rests in large part on preemption by the Copyright Act, our discussion necessarily goes beyond the elements of a misappropriation claim under New York law, and a summary of our ruling here will perhaps render that discussion—or at least the need for it—more understandable.

The issues before us are ones that have arisen in various forms over the course of this century as technology has steadily increased the speed and quantity of information transmission. Today, individuals at home, at work, or elsewhere, can use a computer, pager, or other device to obtain highly selective kinds of information virtually at will. *International News Service v. Associated Press*, 248 U.S. 215, 39 S.Ct. 68, 63 L.Ed. 211 (1918)("*INS*") was one of the first cases to address the issues raised by these technological advances, although the technology involved in that case was primitive by contemporary standards. *INS* involved two wire services, the Associated Press ("AP") and International News Service ("INS"), that transmitted news stories by wire to member newspapers. INS would lift factual stories from AP bulletins and send them by wire to INS papers. INS would also take factual stories from east coast AP papers and wire them to INS papers on the west coast that had yet to publish because of time differentials. The Supreme Court held that INS's conduct was a common-law misappropriation of AP's property.

With the advance of technology, radio stations began "live" broadcasts of events such as baseball games and operas, and various entrepreneurs began to use the transmissions of others in one way or another for their own profit. In response, New York courts created a body of misappropriation law, loosely based on *INS*, that sought to apply ethical standards to the use by one party of another's transmissions of events.

Federal copyright law played little active role in this area until 1976. Before then, it appears to have been the general understanding—there being no case law of consequence—that live events such as baseball games were not copyrightable. Moreover, doubt existed even as to whether a recorded broadcast or videotape of such an event was copyrightable. In 1976, however, Congress passed legislation expressly affording copyright protection to simultaneously-recorded broadcasts of live performances such as sports events. See 17 U.S.C. § 101. Such protection was not extended to the underlying events.

The 1976 amendments also contained provisions preempting state law claims that enforced rights "equivalent" to exclusive copyright protections when the work to which the state claim was being applied fell within the area of copyright protection. See 17 U.S.C. § 301. Based on legislative history of the 1976 amendments, it is generally agreed that a "hot-news" *INS*-like claim survives preemption. H.R. No. 94–1476 at 132 (1976), reprinted in 1976 U.S.C.C.A.N. 5659, 5748. However, much of New York misappropriation law after *INS* goes well beyond "hot-news" claims and is preempted.

We hold that the surviving "hot-news" *INS*-like claim is limited to cases where: (i) a plaintiff generates or gathers information at a cost; (ii) the information is time-sensitive; (iii) a defendant's use of the information constitutes free riding on the plaintiff's efforts; (iv) the defendant is in direct competition with a product or service offered by the plaintiffs; and (v) the ability of other parties to free-ride on the efforts of the plaintiff or others would so reduce the incentive to produce the product or service that its existence or quality would be substantially threatened. We conclude that SportsTrax does not meet that test.

B. *Copyrights in Events or Broadcasts of Events*

The NBA asserted copyright infringement claims with regard both to the underlying games and to their broadcasts. The district court dismissed these claims, and the NBA does not appeal from their dismissal. Nevertheless, discussion of the infringement claims is necessary to provide the framework for analyzing the viability of the NBA's state law misappropriation claim in light of the Copyright Act's preemptive effect.

1. *Infringement of a Copyright in the Underlying Games*

In our view, the underlying basketball games do not fall within the subject matter of federal copyright protection because they do not constitute "original works of authorship" under 17 U.S.C. § 102(a). Section 102(a) lists eight categories of "works of authorship" covered by the act, including such categories as "literary works," "musical works," and "dramatic works." The list does not include athletic events, and, although the list is concededly non-exclusive, such events are neither similar nor analogous to any of the listed categories.

Sports events are not "authored" in any common sense of the word. There is, of course, at least at the professional level, considerable preparation for a game. However, the preparation is as much an expression of hope or faith as a determination of what will actually happen. Unlike movies, plays, television programs, or operas, athletic events are competitive and have no underlying script. * * *

What "authorship" there is in a sports event, moreover, must be open to copying by competitors if fans are to be attracted. If the inventor of the T-formation in football had been able to copyright it, the sport might have come to an end instead of prospering. Even where athletic preparation most resembles authorship—figure skating, gymnastics, and, some would uncharitably say, professional wrestling—a performer who conceives and executes a particularly graceful and difficult—or, in the case of wrestling, seemingly painful—acrobatic feat cannot copyright it without impairing the underlying competition in the future. A claim of being the only athlete to perform a feat doesn't mean much if no one else is allowed to try.

For many of these reasons, Nimmer on Copyright concludes that the "[f]ar more reasonable" position is that athletic events are not copyrightable. 1 M. Nimmer & D. Nimmer, Nimmer on Copyright § 2.09[F] at 2–170.1 (1996). Nimmer notes that, among other problems, the number of joint copyright owners would arguably include the league, the teams, the athletes, umpires, stadium workers and even fans, who all contribute to the "work."

Concededly, case law is scarce on the issue of whether organized events themselves are copyrightable, but what there is indicates that they are not. * * *

* * *

2. *Infringement of a Copyright in the Broadcasts of NBA Games*

As noted, recorded broadcasts of NBA games—as opposed to the games themselves—are now entitled to copyright protection. The Copyright Act was amended in 1976 specifically to insure that simultaneously-recorded transmissions of live performances and sporting events would meet the Act's requirement that the original work of authorship be "fixed in any tangible medium of expression." 17 U.S.C. § 102(a). * * * [The legislative history] makes clear that it is the broadcast, not the underlying game, that is the subject of copyright protection. * * *

* * *

We agree with the district court that the "[d]efendants provide purely factual information which any patron of an NBA game could acquire from the arena without any involvement from the director, cameramen, or others who contribute to the originality of a broadcast." Because the SportsTrax device and AOL site reproduce only factual information culled from the broadcasts and none of the copyrightable expression of the games, appellants did not infringe the copyright of the broadcasts.

C. The State–Law Misappropriation Claim

The district court's injunction was based on its conclusion that, under New York law, defendants had unlawfully misappropriated the NBA's property rights in its games. The district court reached this conclusion by holding: (i) that the NBA's misappropriation claim relating to the underlying games was not preempted by Section 301 of the Copyright Act; and (ii) that, under New York common law, defendants had engaged in unlawful misappropriation. We disagree.

1. Preemption Under the Copyright Act

a) Summary

When Congress amended the Copyright Act in 1976, it provided for the preemption of state law claims that are interrelated with copyright claims in certain ways. Under 17 U.S.C. § 301, a state law claim is preempted when: (i) the state law claim seeks to vindicate "legal or equitable rights that are equivalent" to one of the bundle of exclusive rights already protected by copyright law under 17 U.S.C. § 106—styled the "general scope requirement"; and (ii) the particular work to which the state law claim is being applied falls within the type of works protected by the Copyright Act under Sections 102 and 103—styled the "subject matter requirement."

The district court concluded that the NBA's misappropriation claim was not preempted because, with respect to the underlying games, as opposed to the broadcasts, the subject matter requirement was not met. The court dubbed as "partial preemption" its separate analysis of misappropriation claims relating to the underlying games and misappropriation claims relating to broadcasts of those games. The district court then relied on a series of older New York misappropriation cases involving radio broadcasts that considerably broadened *INS*. We hold that where the challenged copying or misappropriation relates in part to the copyrighted broadcasts of the games, the subject matter requirement is met as to both the broadcasts and the games. We therefore reject the partial preemption doctrine and its anomalous consequence that "it is possible for a plaintiff to assert claims both for infringement of its copyright in a broadcast and misappropriation of its rights in the underlying event." We do find that a properly-narrowed *INS* "hot-news" misappropriation claim survives preemption because it fails the general scope requirement, but that the broader theory of the radio broadcast cases relied upon by the district court were preempted when Congress extended copyright protection to simultaneously-recorded broadcasts.

b) "Partial Preemption" and the Subject Matter Requirement

The subject matter requirement is met when the work of authorship being copied or misappropriated "fall[s] within the ambit of copyright protection." *Harper & Row, Inc. v. Nation Enter.*, 723 F.2d 195, 200 (1983), *rev'd on other grounds,* 471 U.S. 539, 105 S.Ct. 2218, 85 L.Ed.2d 588 (1985). We believe that the subject matter requirement is met in the instant matter and that the concept of "partial preemption" is not consistent with Section 301 of the Copyright Act. Although game broadcasts are copyrightable while the underlying games are not, the Copyright Act should not be read to distinguish between the two when analyzing the preemption of a misappropriation claim based on copying or taking from the copyrightable work. We believe that:

> [O]nce a performance is reduced to tangible form, there is no distinction between the performance and the recording of the performance for the purposes of preemption under § 301(a). Thus, if a baseball game were not broadcast or were telecast without being recorded, the Players' performances similarly would not be fixed in tangible form and their rights of publicity would not be subject to preemption. By virtue of being videotaped, however, the Players' performances are fixed in tangible form, and any rights of publicity in their performances that are equivalent to the rights contained in the copyright of the telecast are preempted.

Baltimore Orioles Inc. v. Major League Baseball Players Assn., 805 F.2d 663, 675 (7th Cir.1986), *cert. denied,* 480 U.S. 941, 107 S.Ct. 1593, 94 L.Ed.2d 782 (1987).

Copyrightable material often contains uncopyrightable elements within it, but Section 301 preemption bars state law misappropriation claims with respect to uncopyrightable as well as copyrightable elements. In *Harper & Row*, for example, we held that state law claims based on the copying of excerpts from President Ford's memoirs were preempted even with respect to information that was purely factual and not copyrightable. We stated:

> [T]he [Copyright] Act clearly embraces "works of authorship," including "literary works," as within its subject matter. The fact that portions of the Ford memoirs may consist of uncopyrightable material ... does not take the work as a whole outside the subject matter protected by the Act. Were this not so, states would be free to expand the perimeters of copyright protection to their own liking, on the theory that preemption would be no bar to state protection of material not meeting federal statutory standards.

723 F.2d at 200. The legislative history supports this understanding of Section 301(a)'s subject matter requirement. The House Report stated:

> As long as a work fits within one of the general subject matter categories of sections 102 and 103, the bill prevents the States from protecting it even if it fails to achieve Federal statutory copyright because it is too minimal or lacking in originality to qualify, or because it has fallen into the public domain.

H.R. No. 94–1476 at 131, reprinted in 1976 U.S.C.C.A.N. at 5747.

Adoption of a partial preemption doctrine—preemption of claims based on misappropriation of broadcasts but no preemption of claims based on misappropriation of underlying facts—would expand significantly the reach of state law claims and render the preemption intended by Congress unworkable. It is often difficult or impossible to separate the fixed copyrightable work from the underlying uncopyrightable events or facts. Moreover, Congress, in extending copyright protection only to the broadcasts and not to the underlying events, intended that the latter be in the public domain. Partial preemption turns that intent on its head by allowing state law to vest exclusive rights in material that Congress intended to be in the public domain and to make unlawful conduct that Congress intended to allow. * * * [We] reject the separate analysis of the underlying games and broadcasts of those games for purposes of preemption.

c) The General Scope Requirement

Under the general scope requirement, Section 301 "preempts only those state law rights that 'may be abridged by an act which, in and of itself, would infringe one of the exclusive rights' provided by federal copyright law." *Computer Assoc. Int'l, Inc. v. Altai, Inc.*, 982 F.2d 693, 716 (2d Cir.1992). However, certain forms of commercial misappropriation otherwise within the general scope requirement will survive preemption if an "extra-element" test is met. As stated in *Altai*:

> But if an "extra element" is "required instead of or in addition to the acts of reproduction, performance, distribution or display, in order to constitute a state-created cause of action, then the right does not lie 'within the general scope of copyright,' and there is no preemption."

Id. (quoting 1 Nimmer on Copyright § 1.01[B] at 1–15).

> * * *

We turn, therefore, to the question of the extent to which a "hot-news" misappropriation claim based on *INS* involves extra elements and is not the equivalent of exclusive rights under a copyright. Courts are generally agreed that some form of such a claim survives preemption. This conclusion is based in part on the legislative history of the 1976 amendments. The House Report stated:

> "Misappropriation" is not necessarily synonymous with copyright infringement, and thus a cause of action labeled as "misappropriation" is not preempted if it is in fact based neither on a right within the general scope of copyright as specified by section 106 nor on a right equivalent thereto. For example, state law should have the flexibility to afford a remedy (under traditional principles of equity) against a consistent pattern of unauthorized appropriation by a competitor of the facts (i.e., not the literary expression) constituting "hot" news, whether in the traditional mold of *International News Service v. Associated Press*, 248 U.S. 215, 39 S.Ct. 68, 63 L.Ed. 211

(1918), or in the newer form of data updates from scientific, business, or financial data bases.

H.R. No. 94–1476 at 132, reprinted in 1976 U.S.C.C.A.N. at 5748 * * *. The crucial question, therefore, is the breadth of the "hot-news" claim that survives preemption.

In *INS*, the plaintiff AP and defendant INS were "wire services" that sold news items to client newspapers. AP brought suit to prevent INS from selling facts and information lifted from AP sources to INS-affiliated newspapers. One method by which INS was able to use AP's news was to lift facts from AP news bulletins. Another method was to sell facts taken from just-published east coast AP newspapers to west coast INS newspapers whose editions had yet to appear. The Supreme Court held (prior to *Erie R. Co. v. Tompkins*, 304 U.S. 64, 58 S.Ct. 817, 82 L.Ed. 1188 (1938)), that INS's use of AP's information was unlawful under federal common law. It characterized INS's conduct as

> amount[ing] to an unauthorized interference with the normal operation of complainant's legitimate business precisely at the point where the profit is to be reaped, in order to divert a material portion of the profit from those who have earned it to those who have not; with special advantage to defendant in the competition because of the fact that it is not burdened with any part of the expense of gathering the news.

INS, 248 U.S. at 240, 39 S.Ct. at 72–73.

The theory of the New York misappropriation cases relied upon by the district court is considerably broader than that of *INS*. For example, the district court quoted at length from *Metropolitan Opera Ass'n v. Wagner–Nichols Recorder Corp.*, 199 Misc. 786, 101 N.Y.S.2d 483 (N.Y.Sup.Ct.1950), *aff'd*, 279 A.D. 632, 107 N.Y.S.2d 795 (1st Dep't 1951). *Metropolitan Opera* described New York misappropriation law as standing for the "broader principle that property rights of commercial value are to be and will be protected from any form of commercial immorality"; that misappropriation law developed "to deal with business malpractices offensive to the ethics of [ ] society"; and that the doctrine is "broad and flexible."

However, we believe that *Metropolitan Opera's* broad misappropriation doctrine based on amorphous concepts such as "commercial immorality" or society's "ethics" is preempted. Such concepts are virtually synonymous for wrongful copying and are in no meaningful fashion distinguishable from infringement of a copyright. The broad misappropriation doctrine relied upon by the district court is, therefore, the equivalent of exclusive rights in copyright law.

* * *

Moreover, *Computer Associates Intern., Inc. v. Altai Inc.* indicated that the "extra element" test should not be applied so as to allow state claims to survive preemption easily. "An action will not be saved from preemption by elements such as awareness or intent, which alter 'the action's scope but not its nature'.... Following this 'extra element' test, we have held that unfair competition and misappropriation claims grounded solely in the copying of a plaintiff's protected expression are preempted by section 301.''

In light of cases such as * * * *Altai* that emphasize the narrowness of state misappropriation claims that survive preemption, most of the broadcast cases relied upon by the NBA are simply not good law. Those cases were decided at a time when simultaneously-recorded broadcasts were not protected under the Copyright Act and when the state law claims they fashioned were not subject to federal preemption. For example, *Metropolitan Opera*, 101 N.Y.S.2d 483, involved the unauthorized copying, marketing, and sale of opera radio broadcasts. As another example, in *Mutual Broadcasting System v. Muzak Corp.*, 177 Misc. 489, 30 N.Y.S.2d 419 (Sup.Ct.1941), the defendant simultaneously retransmitted the plaintiff's baseball radio broadcasts onto telephone lines. As discussed above, the 1976 amendments to the Copyright Act were specifically designed to afford copyright protection to simultaneously-recorded broadcasts, and *Metropolitan Opera* and *Muzak* could today be brought as copyright infringement cases. Moreover, we believe that they would have to be brought as copyright cases because the amendments affording broadcasts copyright protection also preempted the state law misappropriation claims under which they were decided.

Our conclusion, therefore, is that only a narrow "hot-news" misappropriation claim survives preemption for actions concerning material within the realm of copyright.[6] * * *

In our view, the elements central to an *INS* claim are: (i) the plaintiff generates or collects information at some cost or expense; (ii) the value of the information is highly time-sensitive; (iii) the defendant's use of the information constitutes free-riding on the plaintiff's costly efforts to generate or collect it; (iv) the defendant's use of the information is in direct competition with a product or service offered by the plaintiff; (v) the ability of other parties to free-ride on the efforts of the plaintiff would so reduce the incentive to produce the product or service that its existence or quality would be substantially threatened.[8] * * *

INS is not about ethics; it is about the protection of property rights in time-sensitive information so that the information will be made available to the public by profit seeking entrepreneurs. If services like AP were not

---

6. State law claims involving breach of fiduciary duties or trade-secret claims are not involved in this matter and are not addressed by this discussion. These claims are generally not preempted because they pass the "extra elements" test.

8. Some authorities have labeled this element as requiring direct competition between the defendant and the plaintiff in a primary market. "[I]n most of the small number of cases in which the misappropriation doctrine has been determinative, the defendant's appropriation, like that in *INS*, resulted in direct competition in the plaintiffs' primary market ... Appeals to the misappropriation doctrine are almost always rejected when the appropriation does not intrude upon the plaintiff's primary market." Restatement (Third) of unfair Competition, § 38 cmt. c, at 412–13. * * *

assured of property rights in the news they pay to collect, they would cease to collect it. The ability of their competitors to appropriate their product at only nominal cost and thereby to disseminate a competing product at a lower price would destroy the incentive to collect news in the first place. The newspaper-reading public would suffer because no one would have an incentive to collect "hot news."

We therefore find the extra elements—those in addition to the elements of copyright infringement—that allow a "hot-news" claim to survive preemption are: (i) the time-sensitive value of factual information, (ii) the free-riding by a defendant, and (iii) the threat to the very existence of the product or service provided by the plaintiff.

2. *The Legality of SportsTrax*

We conclude that Motorola and STATS have not engaged in unlawful misappropriation under the "hot-news" test set out above. To be sure, some of the elements of a "hot-news" *INS* claim are met. The information transmitted to SportsTrax is not precisely contemporaneous, but it is nevertheless time-sensitive. Also, the NBA does provide, or will shortly do so, information like that available through SportsTrax. It now offers a service called "Gamestats" that provides official play-by-play game sheets and half-time and final box scores within each arena. It also provides such information to the media in each arena. In the future, the NBA plans to enhance Gamestats so that it will be networked between the various arenas and will support a pager product analogous to SportsTrax. SportsTrax will of course directly compete with an enhanced Gamestats.

However, there are critical elements missing in the NBA's attempt to assert a "hot-news" *INS*-type claim. As framed by the NBA, their claim compresses and confuses three different informational products. The first product is generating the information by playing the games; the second product is transmitting live, full descriptions of those games; and the third product is collecting and retransmitting strictly factual information about the games. The first and second products are the NBA's primary business: producing basketball games for live attendance and licensing copyrighted broadcasts of those games. The collection and retransmission of strictly factual material about the games is a different product: e.g., box-scores in newspapers, summaries of statistics on television sports news, and real-time facts to be transmitted to pagers. In our view, the NBA has failed to show any competitive effect whatsoever from SportsTrax on the first and second products and a lack of any free-riding by SportsTrax on the third.

With regard to the NBA's primary products—producing basketball games with live attendance and licensing copyrighted broadcasts of those games—there is no evidence that anyone regards SportsTrax or the AOL site as a substitute for attending NBA games or watching them on television. In fact, Motorola markets SportsTrax as being designed "for those times when you cannot be at the arena, watch the game on TV, or listen to the radio . . .".

The NBA argues that the pager market is also relevant to a "hot-news" *INS*-type claim and that SportsTrax's future competition with Gamestats satisfies any missing element. We agree that there is a separate market for the real-time transmission of factual information to pagers or similar devices, such as STATS's AOL site. However, we disagree that SportsTrax is in any sense free-riding off Gamestats.

An indispensable element of an *INS* "hot-news" claim is free riding by a defendant on a plaintiff's product, enabling the defendant to produce a directly competitive product for less money because it has lower costs. SportsTrax is not such a product. The use of pagers to transmit real-time information about NBA games requires: (i) the collecting of facts about the games; (ii) the transmission of these facts on a network; (iii) the assembling of them by the particular service; and (iv) the transmission of them to pagers or an on-line computer site. Appellants are in no way free-riding on Gamestats. Motorola and STATS expend their own resources to collect purely factual information generated in NBA games to transmit to SportsTrax pagers. They have their own network and assemble and transmit data themselves.

To be sure, if appellants in the future were to collect facts from an enhanced Gamestats pager to retransmit them to SportsTrax pagers, that would constitute free-riding and might well cause Gamestats to be unprofitable because it had to bear costs to collect facts that SportsTrax did not. If the appropriation of facts from one pager to another pager service were allowed, transmission of current information on NBA games to pagers or similar devices would be substantially deterred because any potential transmitter would know that the first entrant would quickly encounter a lower cost competitor free-riding on the originator's transmissions.

However, that is not the case in the instant matter. SportsTrax and Gamestats are each bearing their own costs of collecting factual information on NBA games, and, if one produces a product that is cheaper or otherwise superior to the other, that producer will prevail in the marketplace. This is obviously not the situation against which *INS* was intended to prevent: the potential lack of any such product or service because of the anticipation of free-riding.

For the foregoing reasons, the NBA has not shown any damage to any of its products based on free-riding by Motorola and STATS, and the NBA's misappropriation claim based on New York law is preempted.

* * *

NOTES AND QUESTIONS

1. *Preemption of state law.* Why did Congress wish to preempt state causes of action that emulate copyright? What is the relationship of Copyright Act § 301 preemption to Supremacy Clause preemption, discussed in the prior section? What, if any, effect does § 301 have on *federal* causes of action providing rights equivalent to copyright in copyrightable subject matter? See 17 U.S.C.A. § 301(d).

2. *The subject matter of copyright.* Section 301 only preempts state causes of action to the extent that they protect "works of authorship that are fixed in a tangible medium of expression and come within the subject matter of copyright as specified by sections 102 and 103" of the Copyright Act. 17 U.S.C.A. § 301(a). The "subject matter" issue has posed relatively few difficulties. There is general agreement that § 301 preempts state causes of action protecting works that fall within the general subject matter set forth in §§ 102 and 103 (for example, literary works, musical works, pictorial, graphic or sculptural works) but fail to qualify for copyright due to insufficient originality, a failure to provide proper copyright notice, or expiration of their term of protection.

The language of § 102(b), however, has raised some questions. Section 102(b) provides: "In no case does copyright protection for an original work of authorship extend to any idea, procedure, process, system, method of operation, concept, principle, or discovery, regardless of the form in which it is described, explained, illustrated, or embodied in such work." Suppose that a plaintiff brings a state cause of action to prevent the defendant from reproducing ideas, facts ("discoveries") or principles described or employed in the plaintiff's copyrightable work. If granted, would this state claim provide rights in the "subject matter of copyright" for purposes of § 301? In *National Basketball Ass'n*, the Second Circuit construed §§ 301 and 102(b) to answer this question in the affirmative. The Fourth and Sixth Circuits have reached the same conclusion. See United States v. Board of Trustees of the University of Alabama, 104 F.3d 1453 (4th Cir.1997), *cert. denied*, 522 U.S. 916, 118 S.Ct. 301, 139 L.Ed.2d 232 (1997)(claim that defendants wrongfully converted the ideas and methods in plaintiff's doctoral dissertation is preempted under § 301); Wrench LLC v. Taco Bell Corp., 256 F.3d 446 (6th Cir. 2001), *cert. denied*, 534 U.S. 1114, 122 S.Ct. 921, 151 L.Ed.2d 885 (2002)(advertising ideas and concepts are within the subject matter of copyright for purposes of § 301 evaluation). However, the Eleventh Circuit and several district courts have interpreted the statutory language of § 102(b) to place ideas, facts, methods of operation, etc., outside the scope of copyrightable subject matter, so that the states are free to protect them in such circumstances. See Dunlap v. G&L Holding Group, Inc., 381 F.3d 1285 (11th Cir. 2004)(claim for conversion of idea did not assert rights in subject matter of copyright); Rand McNally & Co. v. Fleet Management Systems, Inc., 591 F.Supp. 726 (N.D.Ill. 1983)(misappropriation claim alleging that defendant copied road map publisher's procedures, processes, and systems for calculating mileage data); Bromhall v. Rorvik, 478 F.Supp. 361 (E.D.Pa.1979) (quasi-contract claim alleging that defendant wrongfully took details of scientist's research techniques and experiment results and published them). Based on the statutory language, how would you construct an argument for this interpretation? If § 301 did not preempt a state cause of action giving rights in facts or ideas employed in the plaintiff's copyrightable work, would the First Amendment prohibit it? Would the state cause of action be likely to withstand a Supremacy Clause preemption challenge, as well?

3. *Legal or equitable rights equivalent to the exclusive rights of copyright.* The second branch of the § 301 preemption test has given the courts greater difficulty than the first. The "extra element" test, discussed in the *National*

Basketball Ass'n opinion, is the most widely adopted approach to determining whether the state right at issue is "equivalent" to one of the exclusive rights of copyright.

Courts applying the "extra element" test have stressed that, to avoid preemption, the "extra element" in the state cause of action must render the state right "qualitatively different" from the copyright cause of action. Only extra elements that alter the "nature" (as opposed to the "scope") of the action will do this. The *National Basketball Ass'n* court mentions awareness and intent as extra elements that would only alter the scope of the action. Do you agree that an extra element of "commercial immorality" falls into the same category? If not, would you find that the alleged extra element of "commercial immorality" differentiates misappropriation sufficiently from copyright to avoid § 301 preemption? How would you enunciate the difference between elements that alter the scope and elements that alter the nature of a cause of action?

Assume that X brings a trade secret action against Y, a former employee who has started a competing business, alleging that Y is incorporating portions of X's trade secret computer program into the program Y's new company is developing for sale. X alleges that Y's actions violate a confidentiality agreement that Y signed when he first entered X's employ and gained access to X's program. Would the trade secret claim be preempted? It seeks redress for the unauthorized reproduction of a computer program, which is copyrightable subject matter. To prevail in his trade secret action, however, X must demonstrate that the program was a trade secret and that Y breached a duty of confidentiality—elements beyond what would be required to demonstrate copyright infringement. Does the imposition of these "extra elements" render the state trade secret claim "qualitatively different" from the copyright infringement claim? Courts have generally found that it does. See, e.g., Brignoli v. Balch Hardy & Scheinman, Inc., 645 F.Supp. 1201 (S.D.N.Y.1986).

How would you evaluate breach of contract claims in which the alleged breach entails defendant's reproduction, adaptation, public distribution, performance or display of copyrightable subject matter, in violation of the terms of the contract? Contract plaintiffs must demonstrate the "extra element" of a bargained-for exchange, which need not be demonstrated in copyright infringement actions. Courts have generally (but not always) found that this extra element renders the claim "qualitatively" different from copyright infringement. *Compare Brignoli, supra,* (no preemption of contact claim) *with* Madison River Management Co. v. Business Management Software Corp., 351 F.Supp.2d 436 (M.D.N.C. 2005)(some contract claims preempted). What if the contract at issue is a general "shrinkwrap" or "mass market" license that undertakes to prohibit all purchasers of mass-produced software from making certain reproductions or adaptations of the software? Should the analysis be the same as in the case of individually bargained contract restrictions? In ProCD, Inc. v. Zeidenberg, 86 F.3d 1447 (7th Cir.1996), the Court of Appeals for the Seventh Circuit equated shrinkwrap licenses with negotiated contracts, and found no § 301 preemption:

> Rights "equivalent to any of the exclusive rights within the general scope of copyright" are rights established by law—rights that restrict the

options of persons who are strangers to the author. Copyright law forbids duplication, public performance, and so on, unless the person wishing to copy or perform the work gets permission; silence means a ban on copying. A copyright is a right against the world. Contracts, by contrast, generally affect only their parties; strangers may do as they please, so contracts do not create "exclusive rights."

Id., 86 F.3d at 1454. While the court recognized "the possibility that some applications of the law of contract could interfere with the attainment of national objectives and therefore come within the domain of § 301(a)," it found that "general enforcement of shrinkwrap licenses" created no such interference. *See also* Bowers v. Baystate Technologies, Inc., 320 F.3d 1317 (Fed. Cir.), *cert. denied*, 539 U.S. 928, 123 S.Ct. 2588, 156 L.Ed.2d 606 (2003). For a different perspective on the issue, see Karjala, *Federal Preemption of Shrinkwrap and On–Line Licenses*, 22 U. Dayton L. Rev. 512 (1997). See also Vault Corp. v. Quaid Software Ltd., 847 F.2d 255 (5th Cir.1988)(finding a state statute authorizing enforcement of specified shrinkwrap provisions preempted under a Supremacy Clause preemption analysis).

State claims for passing off whose facts entail the unauthorized reproduction, adaptation, public distribution, performance or display of copyrightable subject matter also are usually upheld. See, e.g., Donald Frederick Evans and Associates, Inc. v. Continental Homes, Inc., 785 F.2d 897, 914 (11th Cir.1986) (Passing off claims entail the extra elements of deceptive or fraudulent conduct by a competitor and a likelihood of consumer confusion. "Rather than going to the question of copying in the manufacture of a product, unfair competition goes to the question of marketing.")

Of course, each case is determined on its specific facts, the court's evaluation of the essence of the plaintiff's allegations, and the nature of the state cause of action at issue. A plaintiff cannot escape § 301 preemption merely by adopting the label of a different state cause of action, when the substance of his claim is essentially copyright infringement. For example, in Motown Record Corp. v. George A. Hormel & Co., 657 F.Supp. 1236 (C.D.Cal. 1987), the plaintiffs owned the copyright in the hit song "Baby Love," which had been made popular by The Supremes (a recording group consisting of three young African–American women who tended to wear bouffant hairdos and sequined formal gowns when performing), and they also owned trademark rights in "The Supremes." The defendants ran a commercial advertisement for Hormel's "Dinty Moore" beef stew featuring three young African–American women with bouffant hair and sequined formal gowns singing "Dinty Moore, My Dinty Moore," to the tune of "Baby Love." The plaintiffs brought suit, alleging a number of state law claims, including unfair competition and violation of a California right of publicity statute which prohibited use of a person's name, voice, signature, photograph or likeness in advertising or selling without permission. The court found both these claims preempted.

In their unfair competition claim the plaintiffs alleged, among other things, that the defendants' deliberate broadcast of the advertisement falsely implied that the song and the image of The Supremes were utilized with the plaintiffs' permission. The defendants argued that this claim was preempted because its gravamen was "nothing more than the alleged taking of plaintiffs' intellectual property." *Id.*, 657 F.Supp. at 1239. The court agreed that the unfair competition claim was not qualitatively different from copyright infringement, stating that the "essence of plaintiffs' complaint is derived from defendants' alleged unauthorized use of a copyrighted work. The additional allegation that the use falsely implied permission was not sufficient to change the nature of the claim." *Id.*, at 1240.

Likewise the court found the additional element of use in commercial advertising insufficient to save the statutory right of publicity claim. In this particular case, the court noted, the claim revolved around the unauthorized use of the copyrighted song, "Baby Love." There might be no right of publicity claim without the unauthorized use of the song, since the song served to identify The Supremes. The court recognized that the publicity statute might not always be preempted, but given the unique nature of these plaintiffs' complaint, the basic act that constituted the alleged infringement of the right of publicity—the unauthorized use of plaintiffs' composition—was the same as the act of copyright infringement.

4. *Special exceptions to § 301 preemption.* Section 301 expressly leaves state common-law copyright intact for some types of works. First, the statutory language makes it clear that the states are free to provide copyright protection for works that are unfixed. Thus, for example, the states may provide rights for strictly oral compositions, or improvised works of music, choreography or drama that are never preserved in a tangible copy or phonorecord with the author's permission.

Second, § 301(c) specifically preserves state protection of sound recordings fixed prior to February 15, 1972, the date on which federal copyright was first made available for sound recordings. Since the amendment extending federal copyright to sound recordings did not encompass works fixed prior to its effective date, such works would be completely unprotected unless state record piracy laws were preserved. Section 301(c) preserves them for pre-February 15, 1972 sound recordings, as long as the cause of action arises before February 15, 2067. Causes of action arising on or after that date are preempted, to avoid the possibility of perpetual state protection.

5. *The additions of the Visual Artists Rights Act.* Prior to 1990, federal copyright law provided no explicit protection for moral rights. Under § 301, state moral rights laws could only be preempted if they were "equivalent" to the economic rights set forth in Copyright Act § 106. One could argue that state moral rights of integrity, prohibiting certain alterations of copyrightable works, may be equivalent to the § 106(2) exclusive right to adapt a copyrighted work in some cases, and thus preempted. But see Wojnarowicz v. American Family Association, 745 F.Supp. 130, 136 (S.D.N.Y.1990) (New York Artists' Authorship Rights Act claim "requires proof of elements not required to prove copyright infringement, namely (a) the artwork must be altered, defaced, mutilated or modified; (b) the altered, defaced, mutilated or modified artwork must be attributed to the artist, or displayed in such circumstances as to be reasonably understood to be his work; and (c) this attribution must be reasonably likely to damage the artist's reputation.")

In 1990, Congress enacted the Visual Artists Rights Act ("VARA"), which provided, in a new § 106A, rights of attribution and integrity for a limited class of "works of visual art." 17 U.S.C. §§ 101, 106A. VARA also amended § 301 to preempt state rights "that are equivalent to any of the rights conferred by section 106A with respect to works of visual art to which the rights conferred by section 106A apply." 17 U.S.C.A. § 301(f)(1). Congress further provided, however, that state rights or remedies would not be preempted with respect to "activities violating legal or equitable rights which extend beyond the life of the author." 17 U.S.C.A. § 301(f)(2).

PROBLEMS

1. X is a character actor who became famous playing the role of "Ace," a hot-shot space ship engineer in a highly popular, long-running television science fiction drama. Y makes and broadcasts a commercial advertisement for a product that features an actor who is a dead-ringer for X, wearing a coverall somewhat similar to the coverall that "Ace" wears in the television show, in a setting that looks like the engine room of a space ship. X sues Y for infringement of his state right of publicity. Should his claim be preempted under § 301?

2. Acme Co. provides telephone service for a designated geographic area in Nebraska. In connection with its service, it publishes a telephone directory. The directory white pages list each Acme subscriber and the subscriber's town and telephone number. The entries are organized alphabetically by the subscriber's last name. Brown Co. publishes a state-wide telephone directory that lists all telephone service subscribers in Nebraska. After Acme refused to enter into a contract authorizing Brown to reproduce the contents of Acme's white pages in its own directory, Brown simply reproduced the contents without Acme's authorization. Brown's state-wide directory competes with Acme's local directory for advertising. Acme has sued Brown for misappropriation in state court. Should the claim be deemed preempted under § 301?

3. Betsy Boss, a highly popular chanteuse, recorded the song "Ain't you sumpthin," early in her career. It was perhaps her greatest hit, and established her fame. Although Boss did not write the song, and does not own the copyright in it, many people associate the song with her, because she made it famous and her recording of it remains extremely popular. "Ain't you sumpthin" is often mentioned as representing the epitome of Boss's distinctive singing style.

Boss refuses to engage in advertising for products other than her own recordings and concerts. Speed Motorcycles, Inc. tried to convince her to sing in one of its television commercials, but she refused. Speed then hired a Boss "sound alike" to sing "Ain't you sumpthin" in Boss' distinctive style. It played the resulting music as background in a television ad. It did not use Boss's name or likeness in the commercial. Boss nonetheless brought suit, alleging three causes of action, which are described below.

a. A state unfair competition claim alleging that the public associates the song "Ain't you sumpthin" with Boss. Boss alleges by playing the song in its advertisement, Speed falsely represented that Boss endorsed or was affiliated with Speed motorcycles, leading to a likelihood of consumer confusion.

b. A Lanham Act § 43(a) claim to the same effect as the state unfair competition claim.

c. A state right of publicity claim alleging that by using a singer who imitated Boss's voice and distinctive style, Speed made an unauthorized use of Boss' identity for commercial purposes.

Are any of these claims likely to be preempted under Copyright Act § 301?

Appendix

■ ■ ■

US005425497A

United States Patent [19]

Sorensen

[11] Patent Number:	5,425,497
[45] Date of Patent:	Jun. 20, 1995

[54] **CUP HOLDER**

[76] Inventor: **Jay Sorensen,** 3616 NE. Alberta Ct., Portland, Oreg. 97211

[21] Appl. No.: **150,682**

[22] Filed: **Nov. 9, 1993**

[51] Int. Cl.⁶ B65D 3/22
[52] U.S. Cl. 220/738; 220/903; 294/31.2
[58] Field of Search .... 294/27.1, 31.2, 33, 294/149, 152; 220/710.5, 753, 758, 759, 412, 738, 739, 903; 229/1.5 B, 1.5 H, 89, 90

[56] **References Cited**

U.S. PATENT DOCUMENTS

1,632,347	6/1927	Pipkin .
1,771,765	7/1930	Benson .
1,866,805	7/1932	Haywood 294/31.2
2,028,566	1/1936	Seipel et al. .
2,266,828	12/1941	Sykes .
2,591,578	4/1952	McNealy et al. .
2,617,549	11/1952	Egger .
2,661,889	12/1953	Phinney .
2,675,954	4/1954	Vogel .
2,853,222	9/1958	Gallagher .
2,979,301	4/1961	Reveal .... 229/1.5 H X
3,049,277	8/1962	Shappell .
3,123,273	3/1964	Miller .... 229/1.5 B
3,157,335	11/1964	Maier .... 229/1.5 B
3,908,523	9/1975	Shikaya .
4,685,583	8/1987	Noon .... 294/31.2 X
5,092,485	3/1992	Lee .
5,145,107	9/1992	Silver et al. .

Primary Examiner—Johnny D. Cherry
Attorney, Agent, or Firm—Kolisch, Hartwell, Dickinson, McCormack & Heuser

[57] **ABSTRACT**

A cup holder is disclosed in the form of a sheet with distal ends. A web is formed in one of the ends, and a corresponding slot is formed in the other end such that the ends interlock. Thus the cup holder is assembled by rolling the sheet and interlocking the ends. The sheet can be an elongate band of pressed material, preferably pressed paper pulp, and is preferably formed with multiple nubbins and depressions. In one embodiment, the sheet has a top and bottom that are arcuate and concentric, and matching webs and cuts are formed in each end of the sheet, with the cuts being perpendicular to the top of the sheet.

6 Claims, 1 Drawing Sheet

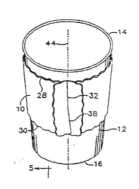

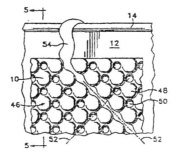

U.S. Patent   June 20, 1995   5,425,497

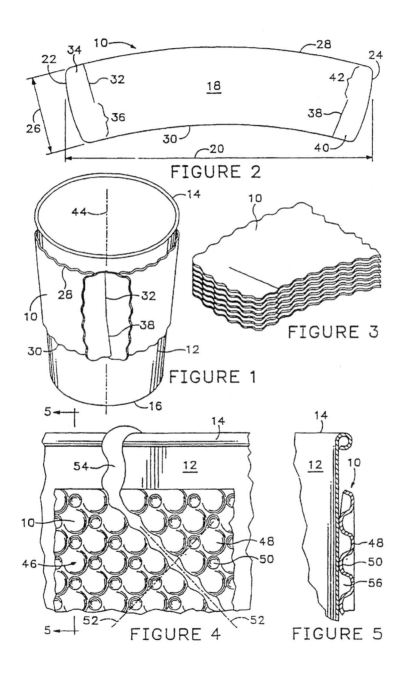

FIGURE 2

FIGURE 1

FIGURE 3

FIGURE 4

FIGURE 5

5,425,497

1

CUP HOLDER

FIELD OF THE INVENTION

The present invention relates generally to holders for cups. More particularly, the invention relates to a disposable cup holder that can be stored flat and then assembled by a user to fit around a cup. The resulting cup and holder combination increases the gripability and insulation value of the cup.

BACKGROUND ART

A cup holder is a removable device that encompasses a cup to provide added features to the cup. These features can include gripability, insulation value, and decoration. By gripability it is meant that the cup and holder combination is easier to hold in a human hand. Insulation value is important if the cup is holding hot or cold liquids, particularly if the cup is a thin disposable paper cup which has little inherent insulation value. Decoration can include features that make the cup more appealing, such as texture or color, or features that communicate to the user of the holder, such as advertising or instructions.

A conventional cup holder includes a three-dimensional body into which the cup is inserted. These bodies can be in the shape of an annular ring, such as that shown in U.S. Pat. No. 2,028,566, or in the shape of a cup that is oversized relative to the cup to be held, such as that shown in U.S. Pat. No. 2,617,549. In order to provide insulation value from a material that is thermally conductive, such as paper, the cup holders are usually provided with annular grooves or vertical flutes so that the holder is only in contact with the cup at the valleys in the grooves or flutes. These grooves or flutes provide a structural integrity to the cup holders such that they must be packaged in substantially the same form as they will be used. Thus a significant volume is required to store a quantity of the cup holders. Therefore it is cumbersome for a retailer selling drinks in cups to use the cup holders because a significant amount of shelf space is required just to have a sufficient quantity of cup holders accessible for immediate use.

It is an object of the invention to reduce the volume required to store cup holders.

Conventional cup holders may also require significant amounts of handling and operations to be assembled. It is a further object of this invention to reduce the number of steps involved in making a cup holder ready for ultimate use by the consumer.

An object of the invention is to produce a cup holder by bending a sheet and interlocking the ends.

It is a further object of the invention to improve the gripability of a cup.

Yet another object of the invention is to thermally insulate the hand of a user from the liquid held in a cup.

Another object of the invention is to form a cup holder from a substantially flat sheet of pressed paper pulp.

SUMMARY OF THE INVENTION

The invented cup holder is designed for use with an upright cup. The cup is in turn designed for holding hot or cold liquids, and has an open rim and closed base.

The invented cup holder is formed from a sheet of flat material, preferably pressed paper pulp. The sheet is formed to have a length defined by a first end and a second end. The sheet has a width defined by a top and

2

a bottom. Two cuts are made in the sheet, the first cut extending partially across the width of the sheet and adjacent one end. The second cut also extends partially across the width of the sheet, but is adjacent the end of the sheet opposite from the first cut. Preferably, one of the cuts severs the top of the sheet and the other of the cuts severs the bottom of the sheet. A holder conforming to a cup can then be made by rolling the sheet into a substantially cylindrical shape and interlocking the first end with the second end by interlocking the first cut with the second cut. Once the cylindrically shaped cup holder is made, a cup can be inserted into the cup holder.

The sheet includes a texture to increase the gripability and insulation value of the cup holder. In one embodiment, the texture includes multiple nubbins and depressions interspersed about the sheet, preferably in a uniform repeating geometrical pattern. The depressions can be aligned in rows forming troughs, so that any liquid that should spill on the cup holder will tend to trickle along the troughs.

If the cup holder is to hold a tapered cup, the holder fits the cup better if the top and bottom of the sheet are arcuate and essentially concentric. Preferably, the first cut is substantially non-parallel to the second cut such that the first cut and the second cut extend along lines that are substantially perpendicular to the arcuate top. When a sheet so formed is made into a cup holder, the resulting holder is tapered with a top and bottom that define planes essentially parallel to the planes defined by the rim and base of the cup to be held. The cuts will also be aligned with the taper of the cup when the holder is assembled, that is, the cuts will extend along a line that is substantially perpendicular to the above planes.

Alternatively, the present invention can be viewed as a combination of a cup and a cup holder. The cup holder is an elongate band having ends that detachably interlock. When the ends are so interlocked, the elongate band extends in a continuous loop. One method of interlocking the ends is by forming interlocking slots in the band. Preferably, the band includes a texture to increase the gripability and insulation value of the combination. The texture can include multiple nubbins and depressions interspersed about the band, preferably in a uniform repeating geometrical pattern. If the cup used as part of the combination is tapered, the tipper and lower surfaces of the band can be concentric arcuate shapes so that the continuous loop formed from the band is approximately conformed with the cup.

BRIEF DESCRIPTION OF THE DRAWINGS

FIG. 1 is a perspective view of an assembled cup holder formed in accordance with one embodiment of the present invention, in combination with a cup.

FIG. 2 is a top plan view of the cup holder of the present invention, shown unassembled.

FIG. 3 is a perspective partial view of a stack of the cup holders shown in FIG. 2.

FIG. 4 is a partial :front elevation of the combination shown in FIG. 1, shown with liquid spilled on the cup holder.

FIG. 5 is a partial front sectional view of the combination shown in FIG. 4, taken along the line 5—5 shown in FIG. 4.

5,425,497

3

DETAILED DESCRIPTION AND BEST MODE OF CARRYING OUT THE INVENTION

Referring to FIG. 1, the cup holder 10 is shown in combination with a cup 12. Cup 12 is usually a tapered paper cup with an open rim 14 and a closed base 16. Cup holder 10 is shown in its assembled state in FIG. 1, and can be described as a continuous loop.

Cup holder 10 is shown unassembled in FIGS. 2 and 3, and is in the form of a sheet 18, also described as an elongate band having distal ends. Sheet 18 has a length 20 defined by a first end 22 and a second end 24. Sheet 18 also has a width 26, defined by a top 28 and a bottom 30. Top 28 and bottom 30 are preferably arcuate in shape. Thus top 28 can be described as an elongate arcuate surface and bottom 30 can also be described as an elongate arcuate surface. Elongate arcuate surface 28 is essentially concentric with elongate arcuate surface 30, such that the radius of surface 28 is longer than the radius of surface 30 by an amount approximately equal to width 26.

A first cut 32 is made in sheet 18 adjacent first end 22. First cut 32 extends partially across width 26, and preferably severs top 28 such that a first tab 34 and first web 36 are formed. A second cut 38 is made in sheet 18 adjacent second end 24. Second cut 38 extends partially across width 26, and preferably severs bottom 30 to form a second tab 40 and second web 42.

When sheet 18 is configured as described above, a cup holder can be assembled as follows. Sheet 18 is rolled into a substantially cylindrical shape, and cuts 32 and 38 are interlocked with webs 42 and 36, respectively, thereby interlocking first end 22 with second end 24. The resulting cup holder forms a continuous loop as shown in FIG. 1, and can hold cup 12 by inserting cup 12 into cup holder 10. Elongate arcuate surface 28 forms an open annular top that is substantially parallel with rim 14 of cup 12. Elongate arcuate surface 30 forms an open annular bottom that is substantially parallel to base 16 of cup 12. Cup 12 extends through the open top and open bottom and, as shown in FIG. 5, encircles cup 12 so that cup holder 10 has an inner surface 58 and an outer surface 60. First cut 32 and second cut 38 extend along a line shown generally at 44. Line 44 is substantially perpendicular to rim 14 of cup 12. Alternatively, line 44 can be described as extending along the taper of cup 12.

As shown in FIGS. 4 and 5, sheet 18 is provided with a texture indicated generally at 46. Texture 46 includes multiple nubbins 48 and oppositely shaped discrete, approximately semi-spherically shaped depressions 50 distributed on substantially the entire inner surface 58 of sheet 18. Nubbins 48 and depressions 50 are arranged in a repeating geometrical pattern. Preferably, depressions 50 are aligned in rows forming troughs indicated generally by line 52 in FIG. 4.

Should liquid spill on cup holder 10, as indicated generally at 54 in FIG. 5, liquid 54 will tend to trickle along troughs 52. When the combination of cup holder 10 and cup 12 is held by a human hand, the hand will tend to be held away from troughs 52 by nubbins 48. Thus the hand will be kept out of contact with liquid 54. Furthermore, as shown in FIG. 4, when cup holder 10 is placed on an upright cup 12, troughs 52 extend along lines that intersect both rim 14 and lines extending along the taper of cup 12 at acute angles. Thus the flow of liquid 54 down cupholder 10 is slowed relative to the flow of liquid down vertically oriented flutes.

4

In addition, texture 46 provides an increased gripability to the cup and cup holder combination. Specifically, nubbins 48 provide a surface texture which is more easily held by a human hand.

Texture 46 also adds an insulation value to the combination because depressions 50 define non-contacting regions 56 of sheet 18, and thus reduce the surface contact between cup holder 10 and the hand of a user and cup 12, respectively. Thus conductive heat transfer is reduced. The insulation value is also increased by air gaps 56 formed by texture 46.

Furthermore, texture 46 is pleasing in appearance, and therefore provides decoration for cup holder 10.

Cup holder 10 as described above and shown in the figures is made from a reversible, two-sided sheet 18. That is, when sheet 18 is rolled to form a continuous loop, either of the textured sides can serve as the outside of cup holder 10. The reversibility of cup holder 10 is particularly evident when, as shown in FIG. 5, inner surface 58 and outer surface 60 are mirrored, that is, when each depression 62 on inner surface 58 defines a nubbin 48 on outer surface 60 and each depression 50 on outer surface 60 defines a nubbin 64 on inner surface 58. Non-reversible cup holders are, however, envisioned within the scope of the present invention.

Alternatively, the present invention can be viewed as a method of making a cup and cup holder combination. The method includes the steps of providing a flat sheet with a texture, forming the flat sheet into an elongate band 18 having a top elongate arcuate surface 28 and a bottom elongate arcuate surface 30. Elongate arcuate surface 28 is severed with a first cut 32 extending partially across elongate band 18. Elongate arcuate surface 30 is severed with a second cut 38 extending partially across elongate band 18. Elongate band 18 is then rolled to form a substantially cylindrical shape, and first cut 32 is interlocked with second cut 38 to form a continuous loop. A cup 12 is then inserted into cup holder 10.

Many materials are envisioned for use in making sheet 10, however pressed paper pulp is preferred. Pressed pulp, similar in properties to that used to make semi-rigid paper products such as egg cartons, is pleasing to the touch, partially absorbent, easily formed and relatively inexpensive.

INDUSTRIAL APPLICABILITY

The invented cup holder and cup and cup holder combination are applicable in any situation where the gripability, insulation value, or decoration of a cup needs to be augmented. It is particularly applicable for a cup holder for holding paper coffee cups.

While a preferred embodiment of the invented cup holder and cup and cup holder combination have been disclosed, changes and modifications can be made without departing from the spirit of the invention.

We claim:

1. A cup and holder combination comprising:

a cup for holding hot or cold liquids; and

a holder defined by a band mounted on and encircling the cup, the band having an open top and an open bottom through which the cup extends and an inner surface immediately adjacent the cup with a plurality of discrete, spaced-apart, approximately semi-spherically shaped depressions distributed on substantially the entire inner surface of the band so that each depression defines a non-contacting region of the band creating an air gap between the

5,425,497

5

band and the cup, thereby reducing the rate of heat transfer through the holder.

2. The cup and holder combination of claim 1, wherein the band also has an outer surface opposite the inner surface, with a plurality of discrete, spaced-apart, approximately semi-spherically shaped depressions distributed on substantially the entire outer surface of the band.

3. The cup and holder combination of claim 2, wherein the inner and outer surfaces of the band are mirrored, with each depression on the inner surface defining a nubbin on the outer surface and each depression on the outer surface defining a nubbin on the inner surface.

4. A holder for encircling a liquid-containing cup to reduce the rate of heat transfer between the liquid contained in the cup and a hand gripping the holder encircling the cup, comprising a band of material formed with an open top and an open bottom through which

6

the cup can extend and an inner surface immediately adjacent the cup, the band including a plurality of discrete, spaced-apart, approximately semi-spherically shaped depressions distributed on substantially the entire inner surface of the band so that each depression defines a non-contacting region of the band creating an air gap between the band and the cup, thereby reducing the rate of heat transfer through the holder.

5. The holder of claim 4, wherein the band also has an outer surface opposite the inner surface, with a plurality of discrete, spaced-apart, approximately semi-spherically shaped depressions distributed on substantially the entire outer surface of the band.

6. The holder of claim 5, wherein the inner and outer surfaces of the band are mirrored, with each depression on the inner surface defining a nubbin on the outer surface and each depression on the outer surface defining a nubbin on the inner surface.

* * * * *

INDEX

References are to Pages

COPYRIGHT—Cont'd
Technological measures, see circumvention and rights management information
Termination of transfers, 687–90
Term of protection, 406–07, 672–90
Thin copyright, see infringement, direct
Total concept and feel, see infringement, direct
Trade–Related Aspects of Intellectual Property Protection, Agreement on, (TRIPs), 408, 566, 577–78
Trademark and unfair competition law, compared, 494, 547, 586
Transfer of rights, see assignment and licenses
Transformative use, see fair use
Universal Copyright Convention, 407
User interfaces, see computer programs
Visual Artists Rights Act, see moral rights
WIPO Copyright Treaty, 408, 629
WIPO Performances and Phonograms Treaty, 408, 629
Words, short phrases, titles, labels and other "minimal" works, 431–32
Works made for hire, see ownership
Works of authorship, see subject matter of copyright and originality requirement
Works of visual art, see moral rights
World Trade Organization (WTO), see Trade–Related Aspects of Intellectual Property

COPYRIGHT OFFICE
Generally, 409, 629–30, 670–72

COVENANTS NOT TO COMPETE
Generally, 63–66

CRIMINAL PENALTIES FOR INFRINGEMENT
See remedies

CUSTOMER LISTS
See trade secrets, customer lists

DAMAGES
See remedies

DESIGN PATENTS
See patents, design patents

DESIGNS OF PRODUCTS
See functional product features

DILUTION OF TRADEMARK
See trademarks, dilution

DISPARAGEMENT, COMMERCIAL
See unfair competition, commercial disparagement

DROIT DE SUITE
See copyrights, *droit de suite*

DROIT MORAL
See copyrights, moral rights

EXHAUSTION
See first sale doctrine

FAIR USE
Copyrights, 410, 608–27

FAIR USE—Cont'd
Trademarks, 702–09, 939–45, 972

FALSE ADVERTISING
See unfair competition, false advertising

FEDERAL CIRCUIT, COURT OF APPEALS
Generally, 124, 130–31, 712, 822

FEDERAL TRADE COMMISSION
Generally, 1029

FIRST AMENDMENT
Copyright, 410, 676–84
Right of publicity, 1060, 1072–82
Trademarks, 703, 853–54, 966, 972, 988–91
Unfair competition, 1034–35

FIRST SALE DOCTRINE
Copyrights, 546–59
Patents, 281–300
Right of publicity, 1071
Trademarks, 916–33

FREE RIDING
Generally, 15–16, 858, 937, 1015, 1035–49

FUNCTIONAL PRODUCT FEATURES
Copyright protection, 481–96
Design patent protection, 377, 396–98
Trademark and unfair competition protection, 787–805, 1086–91

GENERAL AGREEMENT ON TARIFFS AND TRADE (GATT)
See Trade–Related Aspects of Intellectual Property Rights, Agreement on

GRAY MARKET
See parallel imports

IDEAS, COMMON–LAW PROTECTION
Generally, 17, 102–19
Concreteness requirement, 103, 113–14
Confidential relationships, 103, 118
Contract, express, 103, 107–08, 114–16
Contract implied in fact, 103, 108–11, 116–17
Contract implied in law, 103, 111–12, 117–18
Novelty requirement, 103, 112–13
Property theory of recovery, 103, 118
Trade secret law, compared, 118

INDUSTRIAL DESIGN
See functional product features

INJUNCTIVE RELIEF
See remedies

INTERNATIONAL CONVENTION FOR PROTECTION OF NEW VARIETIES OF PLANTS
Generally, 376

INTERNATIONAL INTELLECTUAL PROPERTY PROTECTION
Generally, 20–30

†